REPRESENTATIVE GOVERNMENT
IN EARLY MODERN FRANCE

Studies presented to the
International Commission
for the History of Representative
and Parliamentary Institutions

LXIII

Etudes présentées à la
Commission Internationale
pour l'histoire des
Assemblées d'Etats

REPRESENTATIVE GOVERNMENT IN EARLY MODERN FRANCE

J. RUSSELL MAJOR

NEW HAVEN AND LONDON
YALE UNIVERSITY PRESS

Designed by Thos. Whitridge
and set in Monophoto Baskerville type
by Asco Trade Typesetting Ltd., Hong Kong
Printed in the United States of America by
The Murray Printing Co., Westford, Mass.

Library of Congress Cataloging in Publication Data

Major, James Russell.
    Representative government in early modern France.

    (Studies presented to the International Commission for the history of representative and parliamentary institutions; 63)
    Bibliography: p.
    Includes index.
        1. France. États généraux.   2. Representative government and representation
—France—History.
    I. Title.   II. Series: Études présentées à la Commission internationale pour l'histoire des assemblées d'états; 63.
JN2413.M317   320.9'44'02   79–14711
ISBN 0-300-02300-6

I   2   3   4   5   6   7   8   9   10

To
Joseph R. Strayer

In Memory of
E. H. Harbison
Joseph J. Mathews

CONTENTS

ACKNOWLEDGMENTS

ONE OF THE MOST REWARDING ASPECTS OF COMPLETING A BOOK IS TO BE ABLE to lay it aside and to turn to something new and more refreshing, but equally pleasant is the opportunity it provides to thank those who have assisted in various stages of the enterprise. My first debt of gratitude is to the institutions that generously supported my research. In the chronological order in which I received them, I would like to express my appreciation to the Social Science Research Council, the John Simon Guggenheim Memorial Foundation, the Institute for Advanced Study, and the National Endowment for the Humanities for the fellowships they awarded to me. My thanks also go to Emory University for two sabbatical leaves.

I also owe a heavy debt to many individuals. To the numerous archivists and librarians who assisted me in my sojourns in France, I give special thanks. A similar expression of gratitude is due the librarians at Emory University. At various stages of the project, many departmental secretaries have been called upon to transform my illegible hand into neat pages of typescript. Of their number I would like to express my appreciation especially to Janet Clark, Dabney Pelton, and Jocelyn Shaw.

I have profited greatly from frequent contact with my graduate students over the years. Their ideas, their questions, and their occasional skepticism have done much to stimulate my thinking. My debt is especially great to three of them who assisted me in specific stages of my work. Kenneth Dunkley generously loaned me his microfilm collection on Richelieu and Brittany, Luke Swindler speeded my work by transcribing several documents, and Donna Bohanan assumed the boring chore of proofreading the manuscript and checking the bibliography.

A number of scholars have generously shared their dissertations and unpublished articles with me. Their kindness has enabled me to fill gaps that would otherwise have existed in this work and to avoid errors on several occasions. Among them are Donald A. Bailey, Elizabeth A. R. Brown, David Buisseret, John Bell Henneman, Sarah H. Madden, Marie José Naurois-Destenay, Bernadette Suau-Noulens, Llewain Scott Van Doren, and William A. Weary. To Professors Henneman and John C. Rule I wish to express my appreciation for their willingness to read and criticize part of this book.

Every historian owes a debt of gratitude to his family, and I more than most. In the early stages of my research, my four children were uprooted from their home and school for an extended stay in Europe, an inconvenience that they underwent in good spirit. Still greater is my debt to my wife, who has accompanied me on all my research expeditions to France, lived in small provincial hotels, camped in the Bois-de-Boulogne, found apartments under the most difficult circumstances, and did all else that she could to further my efforts, including copying documents in the archives. Without her cooperation and assistance, this book could not have been written.

Finally, as I complete this book, which in a way is the culmination of all my research to date, research that in a very real sense began thirty years ago while I was a graduate student at Princeton University, I am especially conscious of the great debt that I owe to three historians: Jinks Harbison, an eloquent teacher and inquiring scholar who first attracted me to the age of the Renaissance; Joe Strayer, who taught me to like and appreciate the importance of institutional history and who has continued to assist me in many ways through the years; and Joe Mathews, who, as departmental chairman when I first came to Emory in 1949, provided wise guidance and generous support to my endeavors. To these three scholars I wish to express my deepest appreciation. To them this book is gratefully dedicated.

ABBREVIATIONS

AAE	Archives du Ministère des Affaires Etrangères: Mémoires et documents: France
AC	Archives Communales
Actes François Ier	*Catalogue des actes de François Ier* (Paris, 1887–1908), 10 vols.
Actes Royaux	The printed acts in the BN. In view of their long titles, I have given the number of the act as cited in the *Catalogue général des livres imprimés de la Bibliothèque Nationale: Actes Royaux*, ed. A. Isnard (Paris, 1910–60), 7 vols.
AD	Archives Départementales
AHG	*Archives historiques du département de la Gironde* (Bordeaux, 1859–1932), 58 vols.
AN	Archives Nationales
BEC	*Bibliothèque de l'Ecole des Chartes*
B. Mun.	Bibliothèque Municipale
BN	Bibliothèque Nationale
BN, ms. fr.	Bibliothèque Nationale, manuscrits français
BN, ms. n. a. fr.	Bibliothèque Nationale, manuscrits nouvelles acquisitions françaises
Henri IV, *Lettres*	*Recueil des lettres missives de Henri IV*, ed. Berger de Xivrey (Paris, 1843–76), 9 vols.
HL	Claude de Vic and Jean Vaissete, *Histoire générale de Languedoc* (Toulouse, 1872–92), 15 vols.
IAC	*Inventaire sommaire des archives communales antérieures à 1790*
IAD	*Inventaire sommaire des archives départementales antérieures à 1790*
Isambert	*Recueil général des anciennes lois françaises depuis l'an 420 jusqu'à la Révolution de 1789*, ed. François-A. Isambert et al. (Paris, 1821–33), 29 vols.
Mallet	Jean R. Mallet, *Comptes rendus de l'administration des finances du royaume de France* (London, 1789)
Michaud	*Nouvelle collection des mémoires pour servir à l'histoire de France*, ed. Joseph F. Michaud and Jean-J.-F. Poujoulat (Paris, 1836–39), 32 vols.

Ord.	*Ordonnances des rois de France de la troisième race*, ed. Denis F. Secousse et al. (Paris, 1723–1849), 21 vols.
Ord. François Ier	*Ordonnances des rois de France, règne de François Ier* (Paris, 1902–), 9 vols. to date
PRO	Public Record Office, London
Richelieu, *Lettres*	*Lettres, instructions diplomatiques et papiers d'état du Cardinal de Richelieu*, ed. Denis-L.-M. Avenel (Paris, 1853–78), 8 vols.
Richelieu, *Mém.* SHF	*Mémoires du Cardinal de Richelieu*, ed. Horric de Beaucaire et al. (Paris, 1907–31), 10 vols.
Richelieu, *Mém.* Michaud	*Mémoires de Cardinal de Richelieu*, pub. in *Nouvelle collection des mémoires pour servir à l'histoire de France*, ed. Joseph F. Michaud and Jean-J.-F. Poujoulat (Paris, 1836–39), sér. 2, vols. 7–9
Richelieu, *Papiers*	*Les papiers de Richelieu*, ed. Pierre Grillon (Paris, 1975–), 2 vols. to date
Sully, *Mém.* Michaud	*Mémoires des sages et royales oeconomies d'estat* … , ed. Joseph F. Michaud and Jean-J.-F. Poujoulat (Paris, 1836–39), sér. 2, vols. 2–3
Sully, *Mém.* SHF	*Les oeconomies royales de Sully*, ed. David Buisseret and Bernard Barbiche (Paris, 1970–), 1 vol. to date. Pub. by the Société de l'Histoire de France.
Valois	*Inventaire des arrêts du Conseil d'Etat, règne de Henri IV*, ed. Noël Valois (Paris, 1886–93), 2 vols.

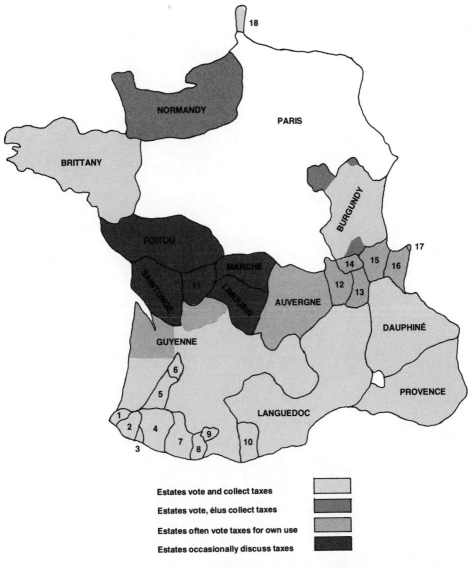

RENAISSANCE FRANCE (Boundaries of 1601)

NORMANDY

PARIS

BRITTANY

BURGUNDY

POITOU

MARCHE

SAINTONGE

LIMOUSIN

AUVERGNE

GUYENNE

DAUPHINÉ

LANGUEDOC

PROVENCE

18

17

14 15 16

12 13

6

5

1

2

4

3

7

9

8

10

11

Estates vote and collect taxes

Estates vote, élus collect taxes

Estates often vote taxes for own use

Estates occasionally discuss taxes

1.	LABOURD	7.	BIGORRE	13.	PLAT PAYS OF LYONNAIS
2.	NAVARRE	8.	QUATRE-VALLÉES	14.	BEAUJOLAIS
3.	SOULE	9.	NÉBOUZAN	15.	BRESSE
4.	BÉARN	10.	FOIX	16.	BUGEY
5.	MARSAN	11.	ANGOUMOIS	17.	GEX
6.	GAVARDAN	12.	FOREZ	18.	BOULONNAIS

INTRODUCTION

THIS IS THE STORY OF A RENAISSANCE STATE. MY IDEAS CONCERNING THE NATURE of this state and the society that it reflected began to germinate when I started to work on my doctoral dissertation in late 1947. Since that time I have published a number of books and articles concerning the French state[1] in which I tried to demonstrate that its consultative aspects persisted between 1484 and 1560, when there were no full meetings of the Estates General; that suffrage expanded during the Renaissance, a fact which supports my contention in this book that there was an increase in popular participation in government;[2] and that the people, through their representative, municipal, village, and other institutions, were responsible for much of the creative energy that characterized the age. These studies also revealed that the aristocracy was the dominant social class, that there was a bitter quarrel between the bourgeoisie and the royal officials in many towns, and that the administrative structure was hopelessly confused.[3]

Here and there my conclusions have been accepted, but to my knowledge the only textbook to adopt my point of view is my own.[4] Some historians have voiced strong disagreement in lengthy reviews and in other writings.

1. These books and articles are cited in relevant sections in the bibliography.

2. Giuliano Procacci has argued that in *The Deputies to the Estates General of Renaissance France* (Madison, 1960) I did not provide enough evidence to prove that the suffrage expanded. He is, of course, correct in saying that the material on the elections in 1484 is scanty, but I think he is incorrect when he refuses to use data on bailiwick assemblies convoked for purposes other than to elect deputies to the Estates General. In their letters of convocation the kings told the bailiwick officials to assemble their jurisdictions "in the accustomed manner." It is difficult to believe that "the accustomed manner" in 1560 was not more likely to be interpreted as referring to recent meetings for which some records survived than to 1484, when the bailiwick last elected deputies to the Estates General. Furthermore, there is ample evidence based on elections to the Estates General alone to prove that there were pressures to extend the suffrage between 1560 and 1614 and that an extension did take place, especially in areas where there were no provincial estates. For the review, see *Rivista Storica Italiano*, LXXIII (1961), pp. 371–76.

3. In his article "La géographie administrative de la France à la fin du Moyen Âge: élections et bailliages," *Le Moyen Âge*, LXII (1961), pp. 293–323, Bernard Guénee has suggested that boundaries and jurisdictions were more stable and precise than Dupont-Ferrier and others have imagined. His evidence is derived almost entirely from the bailiwick of Senlis, but even here there were quarrels concerning the status of Pontoise, Beauvais, and Chaumont-en-Vexin when bailiwick assemblies were held. See my *The Deputies*, pp. 27–29.

4. *The Western World: Renaissance to the Present*, 2d ed. (Philadelphia, 1971), and for the period concerned an almost identical work: *The Age of the Renaissance and Reformation* (Philadelphia, 1970). In a book of readings Gordon Griffiths has concurred. See his contribution to *Transition and Revolution: Problems and Issues of European Renaissance and Reformation History*, ed. Robert M. Kingdon (Minneapolis, 1974), pp. 13–51.

Part of our differences can be attributed to the fact that I did not define my terms with sufficient care. Therefore, before embarking on this study, I would like to correct this grave deficiency. By a *constitutional monarchy*, I mean one in which there are significant institutional, theoretical, and/or practical limitations upon the authority of the king. The institutional limitations might be at the national, multiprovincial, provincial, or local level. They might be Estates Generals, central assemblies of many provinces, provincial estates, or local (bailiwick, etc.) estates. They might be sovereign courts, municipal governments, or village assemblies. The theoretical limitations include placing the monarch under more tangible conceptions than those provided by divine and in most cases natural law, by assigning authority to institutions such as Parlements and Estates or to magistrates not fully under royal control, and by believing that royal charters of privileges were essentially irrevocable although they might be renewed each reign. The practical limitations include having a bureaucracy or an army that was too small or too disobedient to implement royal policy and to enforce the king's desires. A monarchy becomes absolute when these institutional and theoretical limitations are removed and the king has the necessary bureaucracy and army to impose his will.

There are various degrees of absolutism and of constitutionalism. Even Hitler suffered from some limitations, and the best modern constitutions are sometimes subverted. In this and other works I hope to prove that France lay clearly in the constitutional sphere during the sixteenth century, but that it was gradually transformed during the seventeenth century until by the end of the first decade or so of Louis XIV's personal reign, it had become a predominantly absolute monarchy, although there was still resistance to royal authority and a fundamental law determined the succession to the throne.

It would be impossible to study in depth all the institutions and ideas that might have limited royal authority and to relate how they eventually succumbed to the Bourbon kings. I have therefore chosen the provincial estates as my central theme and will treat political ideas and other institutions in a summary fashion.

My description of the Renaissance monarchies as being popular, consultative, and inherently weak has also come under attack. In making these assertions I did not mean that kings were necessarily personally popular or that their authority rested directly upon the consent of the people. Rather I meant that the kings had to have the support of a substantial portion of the leading elements of the population before they could hope to be obeyed. United opposition from nobles, royal officials, or towns could effectively stall their efforts. Even if the opposition was not united, royal acts could be virtually ignored on the local level. In saying that the Renaissance monarchs were inherently weak, I did not mean that they were necessarily actually weak. Some were very strong. Rather I argued that they had neither a large enough nor a loyal enough army or bureaucracy to impose their will. They were strong only to the extent that they could persuade the leaders in society to support them. To secure this support they could grant those who gave faithful service higher titles; ennoblement; offices in the church, army, court, or bureaucracy; and pensions, gifts, monopolies, special privileges, and so forth.

Since there was insufficient largesse to reach more than a small percentage of the vocal elements of the population at intervals frequent enough to secure their support, kings found it necessary to consult influential persons when making important decisions and to justify the course of action determined upon. Even in routine acts kings first pointed out that they had secured the advice of their councils and then explained the reasons for the course of action they adopted. When they asked for well-established taxes at the normal rate, they were at still more pains to explain why it was imperative that they receive no less. When significant changes were desired or in time of crisis, larger consultative bodies, including Assemblies of Notables and Estates Generals, were convoked both to ascertain the desires of the people who counted and to explain royal policy to them, an explanation that those who attended were expected to carry back to their constituents. To be strong a king had to be enough of a politician to persuade his leading subjects to provide support. A king who failed in this and did not dispense patronage fairly was likely to face rebellions, as the last Valois kings found to their discomfiture.

Bernard Guenée has dealt with my concept of Renaissance decentralization in a penetrating critique.[5] To him there are three meanings of centralization: personal centralization, which takes place when a fief reverts to the crown; institutional centralization, which occurs when a monarch creates financial and judicial courts either in the capital or in the provinces; and geographic centralization, which involves centering these institutions in a capital. We agree that personal centralization and geographical decentralization took place during the fifteenth century, but I would argue that institutional, or what I would prefer to call administrative, decentralization also occurred. The medieval state was certainly decentralized administratively, but instead of becoming centralized with the passing of the great feudal dynasties, it remained decentralized because of the creation of provincial sovereign courts and the growing administrative role of the estates in many parts of France.

Guenée and I agree that the officers of the Parisian sovereign courts opposed geographic decentralization and that the inhabitants of the provinces usually wanted it. There is a misunderstanding, however, when it comes to explaining why the Renaissance kings adhered to the wishes of the latter. He assumes that I attribute this decision to their weakness. It would

5. B. Guenée, "Espace et état dans la France du bas Moyen Âge," *Annales* 23 (1968): 744–58.

be more correct to say that I attribute it largely to their inherent weaknesses that made it advisable for them to seek popular support. The kings were not compelled to make this concession. Charles VI, the weakest of kings, did not do so. Rather Charles VII began the process after he was well on the way to reconquering his kingdom. By his acts and those of his successors, provincial particularism became coupled with loyalty to the crown. I suspect that Charles VII acted reluctantly but that Louis XII, who was more anxious to win the affection of his subjects, did so without hesitation. In any case, I concur with Guenée that geographical decentralization took place because the kings recognized it as the most effective way to govern France in view of the size of the country and the wishes of the inhabitants of provinces far removed from Paris.

There is another area of disagreement. To Guenée the people's desire for provincial sovereign courts was greater than their desire for provincial estates.[6] I question this. Wherever provincial courts were created, there were already estates. There was no need to ask for them. Indeed, it was often the estates that sought the courts. There has been a tendency to overemphasize the role of the courts in regard to the estates in part because they have been more frequently studied, but more important, I suspect, has been the tendency of historians to rely too heavily on the writings of the jurists whose legal background obviously drew them toward the Parlements. The primacy of the estates as centers of provincial loyalty is suggested by the fact that the clergy, the nobles, and the deputies of the towns participated while only the lawyers and their clients habitually had direct contacts with the courts. Not until many of the estates ceased to exist in the seventeenth century did the courts become more important in the minds of the provincials. Even then it is doubtful whether the Parlements of Rennes, Toulouse, or Dijon ever supplanted the estates of Brittany, Languedoc, or Burgundy.

Professor Guenée insists that a distinction be made between provincial and local units of government, a position in which I am in complete accord although in the past I have not been sufficiently clear on this point.[7] Provinces such as Dauphiné and Burgundy, for example, had considerable difficulty incorporating local jurisdictions. Hence, unless otherwise clearly stated, I will use the term *central* to refer to assemblies in which many provinces participated, as occurred when the estates of Languedoil were convoked, *provincial* for meetings of the estates of a single province, and *local* for assemblies of bailiwicks, seneschalsies, and the smaller jurisdictions of which they were composed. Although some provincial and even local estates were called Estates Generals by contemporaries, I will use the term only to mean the national assembly unless otherwise clearly indicated.

Salvo Mastellone has disagreed with nearly every aspect of my in-

6. Ibid., p. 755.
7. Ibid., pp. 748–49.

terpretation of the Renaissance monarchy.[8] Some of his objections relate to my characterization of this state as being popular, consultative, and decentralized, but the central thrust of his argument is that, on the practical level, its principal characteristic was the growing importance of royal officials and that on the theoretical level it should be viewed through the eyes of Seyssel and Bodin. To me the emergence of the bureaucracy in terms of numbers, social status, and influence did not take place until the late sixteenth and seventeenth centuries when it proved to be as much a hindrance as a help in creating a more absolute monarchy. As to Seyssel and Bodin, I find much in their writings to support my position, but I also believe that even their views must be balanced against what might be called popular political thought. I hope that this book will provide evidence to support my position.

A word is warranted concerning my methodology. The archives of some of the provincial estates are so vast that it would take a lifetime to exploit just one of them for the Renaissance. In other cases, the archives have been lost or scattered, and it would require many years to find the surviving documents and piece together their history. Therefore I have attempted to show how each of the estates evolved and functioned using published documents and secondary works wherever possible. Only when a drastic change seemed threatening or when the estates came under attack have I gone deeply into the archives. Since the role of the estates was generally accepted by the crown from the late fifteenth to the seventeenth century, I have moved rapidly over their history. Whenever the crown demanded more than the accepted minimum tax, the estates invariably resisted, and usually a compromise figure was reached. Of greater significance was the growing ability of the people to use the estates as instruments of self-government. Hence, I have chosen to stress this theme. When the crown began to attack the estates after the Wars of Religion, I have gone into more detail. This portion of the book may seem to be overlong, but I did not want to limit myself to a few examples because the estates of one province were often threatened while those in other provinces were being treated in the traditional fashion. This fact needed to be demonstrated. Also some detail is necessary to show how the estates functioned, especially since very few of them have been studied during this period. An abridged version of this book will be published for readers who prefer to acquaint themselves with my interpretation without wading through the mass of evidence. I am sure that future historians of the individual estates will find much to add and some statements to correct, but I believe that I have been sufficiently thorough for my general interpretation to stand.

I have generally used Webster's spelling for the names of persons and

8. S. Mastellone, "Osservazioni sulla 'Renaissance monarchy' in Francia," *Fondazione Italiana per la storia amminstrativo* 1 (1964): 421–30.

places although to do so compelled me to add an "s" to Lyon. On the other hand, I have usually retained the French names for institutions and offices except in those instances in which the English equivalent is so like the French that no confusion could result. Among the exceptions to the latter rule are that I have translated *procureur du roi* as king's attorney but have left the *procureur* of the estates in French because he was much more than an attorney. *Avocat* has been rendered as barrister; *greffier*, clerk; and *huissier*, usher. I hope that this policy will enable those who do not read French to understand the text better without causing confusion in the minds of the specialists.

Institutional history is most unstylish in our day. Nevertheless it is of the greatest importance. Institutions are created and evolve in response to the needs of the government and/or the governed. Once established, they direct or at least limit the directions that society can take by any means short of revolution. For this reason an understanding of institutional history is essential for the understanding of a society and how it evolved. In an ideal study, the history of an institution and a society are interwoven as Mousnier has so often done for France and Neale, Namier, and others have done for England. I have been tempted to use such an approach, but if I had done so, I could have dealt with only one of the assemblies of the estates and the society of the province that it served. Social history in depth can be written only about a limited number of people. Since my central theme was the Renaissance state, I thought that it could best be explored by treating all the many and varied representative institutions that then existed in France. The relations between the crown and the notables in the various provinces are stressed, and much is suggested concerning the nature of that society—or rather societies—but there is no time to explore my hypotheses in depth. With regret I must leave to others the task of dealing with the officials of Laplume with its sixteen hearths who proudly summoned the communities of the viscounty of Bruilhois to assemblies, the sturdy alpine villagers of the valley of Queyras who preserved their assembly to the Revolution, and the glorious struggle of the *plat pays* of Dauphiné against the privileged. In like manner, the social aspirations of the proud prelates, nobles, and burghers who participated in the three estates of Languedoc, or of Burgundy, or of Béarn must await other historians. The archives of most of the estates have been lost or widely dispersed, but enough remain to make these institutions splendid sources for the study of the aspirations and needs of the various orders of society. If this study leads these neglected riches to be exploited by others, it will have achieved one of its objectives.[9]

9. For an indication of the research opportunities based on the archives of the estates, see my "French Representative Assemblies: Research Opportunities and Research Published," *Studies in Medieval and Renaissance History* 1 (1964): 181–219.

I

THE GROWTH OF
REPRESENTATIVE GOVERNMENT
IN RENAISSANCE FRANCE

HISTORY IS THE SUCCESSION OF EVENTS, BUT THESE EVENTS ARE MEANINGLESS unless they are organized into a coherent pattern in which occasional aberrations are ignored and only the dominant characteristics are stressed. Out of this process has emerged our concept of periods of history. Academically we are organized on the basis of three periods—the ancient, the medieval, and the modern—but it would be difficult to find an informed person who would defend this division today. The ancient world can claim a number of periods, and the medievalist can justify at least two. It is equally apparent that our modern era has undergone a series of such profound changes since the Renaissance that it also must be divided into several periods.

It has long been my contention that the Renaissance constitutes an autonomous period of history that can be separated from both the Middle Ages that preceded it and what has usually been called the Age of Absolutism or the Age of the Baroque that followed. There is admittedly a certain artificiality in making these distinctions because every period has borrowed heavily from its predecessor, and this artificiality becomes especially apparent when dealing with institutional and social history where changes tend to be evolutionary in character. Several generations are likely to elapse before a new direction becomes apparent. Thus the Black Death, the Hundred Years War, and other factors led to the partial disintegration of the French medieval government and society and forced the crown and the people to seek new solutions to their problems. These solutions fluctuated, however, between constitutional monarchy with widespread popular participation and arbitrary rule in the king's name that was made possible by permitting the magnates to exploit the royal treasury.

About the middle of the fourteenth century, it had seemed probable that representative institutions would achieve a permanent place in the governmental structure of France, but this medieval flowering of the estates that has been so much emphasized by historians withered before it could bear fruit, and it was not until the reign of Charles VII that they again enjoyed an important role in the government. That spineless king would have preferred to suppress the estates once more after he no longer had need of them, but he was only partly successful. During his reign and those of his successors, the provincial estates played an ever increasing role in the government of over half of France. It is their history that will now be considered.

I

THE FAILURE
OF THE MEDIEVAL ESTATES

1. The Origins and the Decline of the Estates

UNTIL RECENTLY IT WAS FASHIONABLE TO FIND THE ORIGINS OF THE ESTATES
General in the curia regis of the Capetians, but in fact the men of that day
used a half-dozen terms to refer to assemblies, and those of a nonjudicial
nature were never called curia. Rather the Capetian assemblies appear to
have been derived from the already time-honored obligation of kings to seek
and subjects to give counsel. Consent was rarely sought because it was
necessary only when the rights of others were specifically involved.[1] The
nature of the problem to be considered was an important factor in determining whom a king summoned, although when important affairs were considered, he found it expedient to seek at least the magnates' opinions because
if they advised him to take a step, they were morally obligated to support his
actions. As society became more complex in the late Middle Ages and
Renaissance, the composition of assemblies varied even more widely, with
members of the sovereign courts, royal officials, and burghers being called
upon to participate when the subject under discussion made their presence
desirable. Thus the medieval and Renaissance monarchies shared consultative characteristics, but the variety of meetings made it difficult for well-
defined institutions to emerge. Not until 1484 did the Estates General take
on a definite composition that clearly separated it from other consultative
assemblies, but by then it had become an occasional instrument to be used
in time of crisis. Furthermore, other forms of consultative assemblies continued to be convoked.[2]

The variety of provincial and local assemblies was even more bewildering.
Feudal magnates and bishops found it advisable to seek the counsel of men
from their fiefs and dioceses just as their kings were doing. Royal officials far

1. G. I. Langmuir, "Counsel and Capetian Assemblies," *Studies Presented to the International
Commission for the History of Representative and Parliamentary Institutions* (Louvain, 1958), 18:19–34.
2. J. R. Major, *Representative Institutions in Renaissance France* (Madison, 1960), and "The
Assembly at Paris in the Summer of 1575," in *Post Scripta: Essays on Medieval Law and the
Emergence of the European State in Honor of Gaines Post*, ed. Joseph R. Strayer and Donald E.
Queller (Rome, 1972), pp. 699–715.

removed from Paris followed suit, and the inhabitants of several areas sometimes joined together for their mutual protection.[3] Nowhere were these developments more in evidence than in southern France where representative elements began to appear in assemblies before the close of the twelfth century. Although taxes might be imposed to provide a force to maintain the peace or to bribe a bishop not to debase the coins he minted, the principal purpose of these meetings was to give counsel, not consent. Townsmen often participated with noble and cleric. In the latter half of the thirteenth century, procurations were sometimes used, although more often consuls attended meetings by virtue of their office. These developments did not lead directly to the formation of provincial and local estates, although they must have provided valuable precedents. By the late thirteenth century, the feudal and diocesan assemblies were in a state of decline. Even the most precocious of these local institutions, the General Court of Agenais, was suffering a similar fate.[4] Not until the fourteenth century did national, provincial, or local estates assume a semi-institutional structure, and even then many of their ad hoc qualities remained.

The assemblies at Paris in 1302 and at Tours in 1308 have been traditionally regarded as the earliest meetings of the Estates General, but there were at least five other kinds of national assemblies during the same period. Some were ceremonial or military in nature; others were enlarged meetings of the council or separate assemblies of the clergy, nobility, or towns that were sometimes concerned with taxation, a role that even the Parlement of Paris seemed on the verge of assuming at one point. With such a wide variety of assemblies to choose from, the occasions requiring the presence of all the more important elements of society were varied and limited. In 1302 it was the quarrel with Boniface VIII and in 1308 the condemnation of the Templars that led to their summons. Such occasions were not likely to repeat themselves often or to lead those who attended to claim special powers. Their role was to learn the reasons for the king's actions and to carry his explanation back home. Yet these assemblies were significant because of the number of persons who were involved, the efforts the crown made to obtain elected and empowered delegates, and the tendency they fostered in noble, townsman, and cleric to think of themselves as belonging to separate estates, a concept that did not develop until the fourteenth century.[5]

3. G. Dupont-Ferrier has correctly argued that there were multiple origins of the provincial estates. See his "De quelques problèmes historiques relatifs aux Etats provinciaux," *Journal des Savants* (August–October 1918): 315–57.

4. See especially Thomas N. Bisson, *Assemblies and Representation in Languedoc in the Thirteenth Century* (Princeton, 1964).

5. T. N. Bisson, "The General Assemblies of Philip the Fair: Their Character Reconsidered," in *Post Scripta*, pp. 537–64. Only the towns sent deputies to the assembly at Paris in 1314. Joseph R. Strayer and Charles H. Taylor, *Studies in Early French Taxation* (Cambridge, Mass., 1939), p. 83.

By the late thirteenth century, the French kings could no longer support themselves from their domain even in time of peace. To supplement their income the last Capetians and early Valois rulers taxed the clergy, sought to extend the feudal aids beyond their immediate vassals to their other subjects, extracted forced loans that often were not repaid, and milked the Jews of all they could. It must have come almost as a relief to the kings when they were at war and could declare that an urgent necessity existed, a situation that in accordance to Romano-canonical principle justified levying a subsidy. In some periods, as between 1315 and 1321, they used large central assemblies of various types to persuade their subjects that a levy was justified, but consent to actual taxes was neither given nor in all probability requested.[6] To obtain the money it was necessary to go to individual magnates, towns, and local assemblies. If the need was obviously great, the king could simply summon the *arrière ban*, in which he sought to include all his subjects on the grounds that there was a universal obligation to military service, and fine those who did not personally enter the army. There was little talk of the right of subjects to consent to taxes, and when they attended large assemblies, it was in theory to give their counsel and in practice to strengthen the king's hand in his local negotiations by endorsing his requests. Even with these preparations, resistance to tax collectors was strong. The kings rarely extracted all they wanted from a locality, and in 1314 there was well-organized and dangerous opposition in many provinces. Under these varying circumstances, representative institutions could not develop in a coherent fashion.[7]

Philip V made elaborate preparations for an assembly in 1321, but he was unable to extract even an admission from the secular estates that several reforms he proposed were worthy of financial support. Whether he asked for actual consent for a tax or merely for counsel has not been determined, but his rebuff was so complete that neither he nor his successors held another large assembly until 1343.[8] As a substitute they reverted to the practice of supplementing their domanial income in time of peace by clerical levies, feudal aids, custom duties, and various extraordinary measures that they

---

6. For these assemblies see Strayer and Taylor, *Studies*, and the articles published by C. H. Taylor in *Speculum* 13 (1938): 295–303; 14 (1939): 275–99; 19 (1954): 433–58; and 43 (1968): 217–44. At Bourges in 1316, Louis X did win a grant from an assembly of towns from the bailiwicks or seneschalsies of Bourges, Auvergne, Mâcon, and perhaps Sens, but it does not seem to me that the area involved is sufficient for the meeting to be called a large central assembly. E. A. R. Brown, "Assemblies of French Towns in 1316: Some New Texts," *Speculum* 46 (1971): 288–92. For the theory behind the doctrine of urgent necessity, see Gaines Post, *Studies in Medieval Legal Thought* (Princeton, 1964).

7. For supporting evidence, see especially Strayer and Taylor, *Studies*.

8. John B. Henneman, *Royal Taxation in Fourteenth Century France: The Development of War Financing, 1322–1356* (Princeton, 1971), pp. 34–36, esp. n.107. E. A. R. Brown, "Subsidy and Reform in 1321: The Accounts of Najac and the Policies of Philip V," *Traditio* 27 (1971): 399–430.

hoped would not provoke widespread opposition. In this they were also disappointed, for Philip VI experienced serious difficulties between 1332 and 1335 when he tried to collect 'aids for the marriage of his eldest daughter and the knighting of his eldest son.[9]

When the Hundred Years War commenced, the Valois kings emphasized their subjects' obligation to render financial assistance to benefit the common good because of the evident necessity that existed. If the military threat was officially terminated by a truce, tax collection was expected to halt. To collect the money, negotiations with leading nobles, town officials, and sometimes local assemblies were undertaken. The degree of opposition to a tax depended more on the proximity of the enemy than on the measures the government undertook to secure approval of the levy. A meeting of the three estates such as the one at Orleans in March 1333 was exceptional, and its activities apparently centered on problems related to coinage and feudal aids.[10]

The advent of the Hundred Years War multiplied the financial needs of the crown. In March 1341 Philip VI introduced the *gabelle*, a sales tax on salt, without seeking consent at the national level. Opposition to this and other revenue measures was so strong that he called a meeting of the Estates General at Paris in 1343. Here the towns from Languedoil agreed to a general sales tax in return for a promise of coinage reform. Those from Languedoc did not acquiesce at the meeting, but later, after individual negotiations with the crown, they made grants.[11]

Philip was soon in financial difficulty again, the people became increasingly restless, and the English were threatening. Faced with this situation, he determined to create an adequate army financed by taxes whose nature would be determined by his subjects in each locality and collected by officials whom they elected. Meetings of the estates of Languedoil in Paris and of Languedoc in Toulouse during the winter of 1345–1346 produced few results other than marking the beginning of the split of the Estates General into two parts, but the disastrous French defeat at Crécy and the loss of Calais awakened most Frenchmen to the seriousness of the situation. When an Estates General met in Paris near the close of 1347, those who attended adopted the program Philip had developed several years before. Meetings of the estates at the bailiwick and seneschalsy level in 1348 were

9. Henneman, *Royal Taxation*, pp. 36–115. On the crown's efforts to collect taxes from 1332 to 1335, see E. A. R. Brown, "Customary Aids and Royal Fiscal Policy under Philip VI of Valois," *Traditio* 30 (1974): 101–258.

10. Henneman, *Royal Taxation*, pp. 116–67. See also his conclusions, pp. 303–305, 320–29. In 1339 an official of the Chamber of Accounts did suggest having a central assembly of the three estates at Paris to raise money, but he clearly thought that the king would opt for separate negotiations with the secular estates in the individual bailiwicks and provinces and with the clergy. P. S. Lewis, *Later Medieval France* (London, 1968), p. 333.

11. Henneman, *Royal Taxation*, pp. 154–77.

still necessary to determine the nature of their respective taxes and to elect the tax collectors, who became known as *élus*. Further concessions sometimes had to be granted on these occasions, but the essential fact remains that a national assembly had granted a sum nearly nine times as large as that received from a war subsidy twenty years before and had set the amount each local area was to pay. Everyone, regardless of his station in life, was to contribute. Local negotiations were completed rapidly, and the king seemed guaranteed a substantial sum to support an army. This tax would not have to be abandoned if there was a truce as had happened so often when the arrìere ban had been summoned. The opportunity for a national representative assembly to develop in France was never better, for the crown's success with such an assembly in 1347 suggested that others would follow at regular intervals. The Black Death, however, struck France before the tax could be collected. Countless taxpayers were decimated, but perhaps more serious, the royal bureaucracy was thrown into chaos because of the deaths of so many bureaucrats. Only a small portion of the tax was ever collected, and the promising experiment came to an end.[12]

The Black Death also forced the English and French to make a truce, a step that reduced the financial requirements of the crown, but not to such an extent that the need for tax revenue was removed. Nevertheless the estates of Languedoc that met in Montpellier in January 1351 and those of Languedoil that assembled in Paris the following month were asked only to endorse the idea of a subsidy. Actual consent was usually given at the local level in 1351 and the years that immediately followed. Normandy and Burgundy were exceptions to this rule because here efforts were made to employ provincial estates for this purpose, an experiment that was unsuccessful in the latter duchy.[13] The use of local and provincial estates to consent to taxes was to have long-range significance, for by 1355, when the crown once again employed a central assembly to vote a tax, they had become so strongly entrenched that they could reject the decision of a central assembly.

In 1355 John II decided to return to the use of central assemblies, and the three estates of Languedoil met in Paris in December. Those who attended promised to raise and support an army of thirty thousand for one year. Instead of permitting each locality to provide its share of the money as it saw fit, as was done in 1347, the estates specified that a general sales tax and the gabelle be levied. Nine officials chosen by the estates were to administer the tax at the national level, and the élus were to be used at the local level. Since taxation had become an annual affair, it was provided that the estates would meet again the following year. The size and unpopular nature of the tax and the absence of an obvious national emergency, coupled with the failure to

12. Ibid., pp. 177–238.
13. Ibid., pp. 239–63.

consider the desires of the various localities, led to widespread resistance. In a meeting of the estates in March 1356, an income tax was substituted for the sales tax, and in May the estates increased the proportion the wealthy were to pay; but the resistance continued. The bailiwick estates, which had been meeting frequently since 1348, were no more willing to submit to taxes levied and administered by a central assembly than they were to those levied and administered by the king. Without local support, little could be collected.[14]

When King John was defeated and captured at Poitiers in September 1356, the situation abruptly changed. The events of the four years that followed had a profound effect on both the estates and taxation. In the absence of the king, his teenage son, Charles, assumed the direction of the state. Meetings of central assemblies became frequent, and there was at least a chance that they could become a permanent part of the institutional structure. The perilous plight of the country left no one in doubt of the necessity to tax. To the time-honored doctrine of evident necessity was added the equally accepted obligation to pay the ransom of a captive lord. Out of this double duty, a permanent system of taxation emerged. Selfish factions won control of the three estates of Languedoil, however, with the result that Charles turned against representative assemblies. When he reestablished the position of the monarchy in the 1360s, there was little room for such institutions in his thinking. The marriage between taxation and representative assemblies did not take place, and in most of France the king taxed without consent.

There is little need to follow in detail the complex events during these years. The estates of Languedoil that met in Paris in October 1356 offered to support an army of 30,000 men if Charles would dismiss some of his leading advisers and appoint a council consisting of members of the estates. After some hesitation, he refused and disbanded the estates.[15] His efforts to raise money through local negotiations failed, however, and a threatening demonstration in Paris compelled him to abandon his plan to profit from currency manipulation. In desperation he once more turned to the three estates of Languedoil, and they met again in Paris in February 1357. This time the demands of the three estates were more modest, and Charles granted their requests. In a long ordonnance it was forbidden to alter the coinage without the consent of the three estates. Some members of the council were replaced by men more acceptable to the estates, but the estates did not attempt to establish a permanent apparatus for determining who the members of the council should be. In return for these reforms the estates

---

14. Ibid., pp. 288–302.

15. John B. Henneman, *Royal Taxation in Fourteenth Century France: The Captivity and Ransom of John II, 1356–1370*, Memoirs of the American Philosophical Society 116 (Philadelphia, 1976), pp. 27–29, 35–36 (hereafter cited as Henneman, *1356–1370*). I am deeply indebted to Professor Henneman for making a copy of this book available to me before it was published.

again promised to support an army of 30,000 men, this time financed by a 15 percent income tax on nobles and a less onerous tax on the wealthy bourgeoisie and other non-nobles. The tax was to be levied in the provinces by élus appointed by the three estates and directed by officials at Paris, whom they also named.[16]

These auspicious developments were largely negated by the king, who concluded a two-year truce with the English, ordered that the tax not be collected because it was no longer necessary, and cancelled a meeting of the estates scheduled for April. Fighting with the English did not cease, however, and a serious threat was posed by rebel troops and brigands. Desperate for want of money, Charles ordered that the tax be collected anyway, but John's action provided an ideal excuse for those who did not wish to contribute, and tax receipts were disappointing. Neither the estates that met in April in spite of John's orders nor those that assembled in July could overcome local resistance. Their failure to produce money removed Charles's need to govern in conjunction with them, and in August he broke with Etienne Marcel, the provost of the merchants of Paris, and with other more extreme reformists. His independence was short-lived, however. In October he held an assembly of the towns in Paris, and in November the three estates of Languedoil met.[17]

Meanwhile, there was growing disenchantment with the three estates in the provinces. Nobles were alienated by the efforts to tax them heavily, reformers were distressed that their plans were going awry, conservatives balked at their radicalism, and many were as angered at their ignoring local susceptibilities as they had been at the crown's. Attendance at the estates fell. Apparently no nobles participated in the meeting in the winter of 1358. Perhaps in an effort to regain lost support, those who attended levied a 15 percent income tax on the clergy and non-nobles but abandoned the tax on the nobles. They also agreed to permit each town to raise an equivalent amount by some other means if it so desired. Nevertheless, fearful of the strong particularistic feelings, they forbade the provincial estates to meet and authorized their financial officials at Paris to appoint élus. Whether these half-measures would have placated the countryside will never be known, because on February 22 Etienne Marcel aroused a Paris mob that attacked the royal palace and slaughtered two prominent nobles in Charles's entourage before his eyes. Now permanently alienated, Charles departed from Paris, won support in several meetings of the local estates, and directed the three estates of Languedoil to assemble in Compiègne in May. This time the nobles attended in sufficient numbers to take the leadership of the estates from the bourgeoisie. They sought to retain the reforms that had been enacted and voted a 5 percent tax on their income to pay their share of the

16. Ibid., pp. 43–49.
17. Ibid., pp. 49–60.

costs of raising an army. It was not necessary, however, for Charles to use this force against the Parisians, because on July 31 Marcel was killed by his opponents in that city. Two days later Charles was able to reenter his capital.[18]

A rare opportunity for a central assembly to become part of the institutional system had been lost. During the three years that preceded, the three estates had voted money in return for concessions but had been unable to collect what they had given. This was due to their failure to consider the forces of particularism that had become stronger because of the growth of the local estates during the preceding fifteen years and to their alienation of a large part of the nobility whose cooperation was necessary if taxes were to be collected efficiently. The inability of the three estates to make good their promises and their effort to control the government permanently alienated Charles and made a lasting impression on Frenchmen. Perhaps it was the events of the late 1350s that caused many sixteenth-century jurists to insist that the estates had no authority independent of the king even while they were asserting that a good and wise king consulted his subjects. Certainly when Charles de Marillac, archbishop of Vienne, sought to persuade the Council of Fontainebleau to revive the Estates General in 1560, he addressed himself specifically to these events and somewhat weakly argued that the situation was not as bad in his day because France was at peace, its king was not a captive, and there were only a few people who robbed and pillaged.[19]

But the opportunity was lost because the time was approaching when the ransom question would have to be considered seriously. Although the Estates General that met in Paris in May–June 1359 advised Charles to reject a disadvantageous agreement that John had negotiated with England, peace was made in May 1360 at Brétigny, near Chartres. By the terms of the treaty, the French were obliged to pay 3,000,000 écus for John's release, of which 600,000 écus were due in four months. Such a sum would be difficult to raise in a peaceful, prosperous, united country and out of the question for France at that time. Poitou, Limousin, Périgord, Quercy, Rouergue, and Guyenne were surrendered to Edward III in full sovereignty with a corresponding loss of taxpayers. Brigands so terrorized what remained of France even after the formal war had ceased that towns and bailiwicks appropriated money raised to pay the English to provide for their own defense. Nevertheless, in spite of the fact that the French were perpetually delinquent in their payments, the ransom marked "a turning point in the history of French taxation."[20]

18. Ibid., pp. 60–81.

19. For the jurists, see William F. Church, *Constitutional Thought in Sixteenth-Century France* (Cambridge, Mass., 1941), pp. 159–78; and for Marillac, see J. R. Major, *The Estates General of 1560* (Princeton, 1951), pp. 31–36.

20. Henneman, *1356–1370*, pp. 94–95 (quote on p. 109).

2. TAXATION WITHOUT CONSENT

The obligation to pay a lord's ransom was a clearly established feudal aid, and John's vassals contributed with unprecedented willingness. His other subjects, however, had in the past resisted efforts to transfer the burden of feudal aids to them, but in this instance "the feudal obligations of royal vassals and the Romano-canonical principle that taxes for the common profit were justified in time of evident necessity" joined to involve all Frenchmen in a joint fiscal endeavor.[21] For a number of years a tax would be necessary to pay the large sum involved and this tax would be levied in time of peace. This in itself was something of an innovation because the French had usually been reluctant to admit that necessity could exist without a war. Furthermore, consent was not theoretically required for taxes involving feudal aids or evident necessity. In some instances in practice, it might be advisable to hold a consultative central assembly for propaganda purposes or to initiate local negotiations, but the acceptance of the tax was so general that even these limitations to the crown's ability to levy the tax were not frequently invoked.

The immediate need to raise 600,000 écus to secure John's release led the crown to seek forced loans, but on December 5, 1360, John, now freed, issued the tax ordonnance necessary to repay these loans and to provide for subsequent payments on his ransom. Without the benefit of a central assembly, he established the gabelle and a sales tax on wine and other products, called the *aides*, that were to be paid by everyone. The élus, who had been officials temporary elected to collect a specific tax, now became permanent royal officials who were to arrange for the farming of these taxes. The diocese was usually chosen as the jurisdiction for an élu, but eventually some of them were subdivided for tax purposes, and all became known as *élections*. Royal treasurers were established at Paris to supervise their work. At the same time the currency was stabilized, a measure that was both popular with the people and necessary to ensure efficient tax collection.[22]

Just as there was no central assembly, there was no need for provincial and local estates to consent to the taxes or even to take the necessary administrative steps for their collection. In some bailiwicks the three estates did meet to provide for their defense against the companies of soldiers who continued to pillage after peace had been made. Especially noteworthy was the activity of the estates of individual parts of Normandy and Auvergne. A few magnates such as the duke of Burgundy made use of the estates for their own purposes, as well as for the needs of the king. The estates of the counties of Artois and Boulonnais met together in May 1361 and offered the king a direct tax to replace the sales taxes. Since their grant was for one year, they

21. Ibid., p. 110.
22. Ibid., pp. 117–18.

had to be reconvoked annually thereafter, a need which gave birth to the estates of the former county and perhaps of the latter. Nevertheless, with some exceptions, the period of the estates' great activity that had begun in 1348 came to an end.[23]

When a central assembly met in Amiens in 1363, those present apparently raised no objection to the sales tax and gabelle that had been levied without their consent. Indeed the problem of brigandage was so severe that they added a direct tax to support an army of 6,000 men without stipulating the time limit of the levy or asking to be assembled again. Like the indirect taxes, the levy was to be supervised by the élus and was usually collected without recourse to the local estates. Another milestone had been passed, and the crown now had at its disposal both direct and indirect taxes that fell on all subjects in Languedoil except in the apanages that already had the former tax.[24]

Meanwhile, somewhat different developments were taking place in Languedoc where the language, law, and traditions of the people differed from those of the north. Their experience with various types of assemblies was longer, and their sufferings from the war came earlier and persisted with an intensity equaled in few other parts of France. During the decade prior to 1356, the towns of Languedoc had usually met alone to provide for their defense, but that October, following the defeat and capture of the king at Poitiers, all three estates were summoned to meet at Toulouse. Here a head and a property tax were voted that fell more heavily on the clergy and third estate than on the nobles, who were considered to be personally exempt from war subsidies. Languedoc's per capita contribution was greater than that of Languedoil, but in return for this sacrifice the three estates extracted important concessions. They were given the right to appoint the four treasurers who were to collect the tax and pay the troops as directed by a committee of twenty-four persons whom they chose. They were authorized to meet when they desired and to appoint a committee of twelve to audit the accounts. Furthermore, not only was their contribution to remain in Languedoc and be devoted to the war effort, but the entire income derived from the royal domain in the region was to be treated in like manner. Languedoc, in effect, wished to become a separate fiscal unit that paid its own expenses but contributed little or nothing to the kingdom as a whole.[25]

The three estates of Languedoc met frequently between 1357 and 1359, and there were also some assemblies of the towns and of the individual seneschalsies. At first the estates insisted that taxes cease when truces were made, but it soon became apparent that brigands and unemployed troops were no respecters of diplomatic niceties. Furthermore, a bloody feud

23. Ibid., pp. 206–25.
24. Ibid., pp. 225–28; Roland Delachenal, *Histoire de Charles V* (Paris, 1902), 2:349–51.
25. Henneman, *1356–1370*, pp. 124–27; *HL*, 9:668.

between the counts of Armagnac and Foix kept the region in turmoil. As a result, Languedoc, like Languedoil, had to resort to peacetime levies. In March 1359 the three estates established the gabelle but were careful to keep control over its imposition. For some unexplained reason, the nobility and clergy ceased to be summoned to the estates in 1360, and the assembly was further truncated by the loss of Quercy, Rouergue, Périgord, and other lands by the terms of the treaty of Brétigny. Hence, it was only the towns of the three seneschalsies of Toulouse, Carcassonne, and Beaucaire that voted the count of Foix 200,000 florins in return for making peace in July 1360. Later that same month they agreed to give a comparable sum to his rival, the count of Armagnac. The province was therefore already overly burdened when King John imposed the heavy sales taxes that December to pay his ransom. Furthermore, English and French freebooters continued to harass the countryside and even seized the important fortress of Pont-Saint-Esprit on the right side of the Rhône River near Avignon.[26]

The approval of the estates was not required before the ransom taxes could be levied. However, sales taxes had always been more unpopular in Languedoc than in the north, and it is not surprising that during 1361 and 1362 the towns reached an agreement with the crown to replace them by a hearth tax designed to yield a slightly smaller sum. The seneschalsy of Beaucaire carried on its own negotiations, but the other two seneschalsies acted together. The gabelle that had been established in 1359 was retained to meet local needs. Depredations by the freebooters made it necessary for the towns of Languedoc to meet frequently during the 1360s, but there were no assemblies of the three estates. There were difficulties in collecting the full amount that had been agreed upon both because of the tumultuous conditions in the province and the return of the plague in 1361. A recount of the number of hearths made in 1364 revealed that they had declined by 58 percent since before the Black Death of 1348. Under such circumstances, a large proportion of the money that was collected had to be diverted to local needs, just as in the north.[27]

The development of a permanent system of taxation that was not dependent on any type of formal consent did not remove the king's need to consult his subjects in order to learn their problems and, if possible, provide suitable remedies. Perhaps to ensure his control over such meetings, Charles seems to have summoned fewer persons to attend central assemblies than he had done in the 1350s. In 1367 he held successful meetings of the deputies from part of Languedoil in Compiègne, Chartres, and Sens that led to two ordonnances in July in which he tried to provide better protection for his subjects and to reduce the sales tax and the gabelle.[28]

26. Henneman, *1356–1370*, pp. 128–60.
27. Ibid., pp. 161–95.
28. Ibid., pp. 242–44.

The approaching break with England in 1369 made it advisable to have the towns of Languedoil send deputies to Paris in May, where in conjunction with Parlement they could be persuaded of the justice of the king's cause and his need for financial assistance. When the war was actually renewed some months later, restricted meetings of the estates of Languedoil were held in Rouen and Paris. Ransom payments, of course, ceased, and taxes once collected for this purpose were diverted to support the war. Additional money was realized by instituting a heavy hearth tax. Meanwhile, an assembly of the towns of the three seneschalsies of Languedoc was success-fully pressed into increasing contributions significantly. Having elevated his revenue to the point that he could carry on a successful war with the English, Charles saw no further need to convoke the three estates to central assem-blies, and no more took place during his reign.[29]

When Charles V died in 1380 at the age of forty-two, he could have taken comfort in his financial position had not his very success troubled his conscience. Not only had he established an adequate system of taxation on a permanent basis, but he had also developed the institutional framework to gather and administer his revenues. There are no trustworthy figures concerning his income from taxes, but it probably came to about 2 million livres per year.[30] What this meant to the French people is suggested by the fact that Montpellier paid about twenty times as much taxes in 1370 as in 1328. The high level of this tax income was essential to the crown; its revenue from the domain had decreased from about 647,000 livres during the reign of Philip VI to less than 50,000 because of losses to the English, grants of apanages to members of the royal family, and the depredations of war. It also had lost the large sums that had been made from the coinage manipulation earlier in the century.[31]

To farm the indirect taxes and to apportion the direct taxes, élus had been established throughout Languedoil, including the apanages of the princes. Formerly the elected agents of the estates, they had been transformed into salaried royal officials. In like manner the treasurers whose counterparts had originally been chosen by the estates to administer taxes at the national level had become servants of the crown. The inhabitants of Languedoc, however, managed to retain a more autonomous position.[32]

In comparison with later rulers, the most favorable aspect of Charles's tax position was that both the clergy and the nobility contributed, although in some levies they were treated separately. The clergy had escaped the war subsidies based on the arrière ban because they were not expected to fight, but until the treaty of Brétigny, they regularly paid the *décime* with papal

29. Ibid., pp. 254–55, 266–70.
30. Maurice Rey, *Le domaine du roi et les finances extraordinaires sous Charles VI, 1388–1413* (Paris, 1965), pp. 260–62.
31. Henneman, *1356–1370*, pp. 261–65, 294–96.
32. Ibid., pp. 291–93.

permission. Even after peace was nominally restored, they occasionally paid this tax. Like others they were subject to the sales tax and gabelle for John's ransom and were usually required to pay municipal taxes on their personal property. The nobles had been subject to heavy income taxes by the estates of Languedoil between 1356 and 1358, but the difficulties of making them actually contribute and the approach of peace brought this levy to an end. They were unquestionably subject to the tax to pay John's ransom, and those who did not actually participate in the war that followed paid the hearth tax. Cleric, noble, royal official, and others might try to escape the tax collector and sometimes enjoy success, but these people who were best able to assume the fiscal burden did make significant contributions during the period. More serious was the tendency for apanage princes and great nobles to appropriate part of the royal taxes collected in their lands for their own use, a practice that Charles may have accepted as much because this was the best way to provide for local defense as because of his affection for his kinsmen.[33]

Evidence indicates that in the 1350s there was a growing belief that subjects should consent to taxes, but its extent should not be exaggerated. Little or no progress was made in this direction after 1369. Taxes were imposed without the benefit of central assemblies and in most instances without consulting the local estates. When brigands presented a grave threat, bailiwicks or seneschalsies might meet together to plan for their mutual protection as in Auvergne, Languedoc, and parts of Normandy, but essentially the estates functioned at the local level only to meet local needs. Where these needs existed, the crown often used these assemblies to further its own tax objectives, but when it was not convenient, the crown was quite capable of taxing without convoking any assembly, as it so often did in Normandy.[34]

Between 1369 and 1374 Charles further increased his revenue by reconquering most of the English possessions in France and incorporating his new subjects into his tax system. By 1380 he must have been in an enviable financial position, a situation that was not shared by his subjects, whose numbers had been decimated by the plague and who suffered from marauding troops and an economic recession. Under these circumstances, it is not surprising that his conscience began to trouble him, and as death approached in September, he revoked the hearth tax, reducing his revenue from Languedoil by one-third. Because the hearth tax bore most heavily on the countryside, his act gave satisfaction to the nobles and peasants, but he created parallel demands from the towns that the sales taxes also be removed. Perhaps a frugal government could have managed without the hearth tax, but the uncles who governed in the name of the twelve-year-old

33. Ibid., pp. 278–83.
34. For a somewhat similar argument, see ibid., pp. 284–88.

Charles VI did not number frugality among their limited virtues. As the new reign began, therefore, the French people were demanding further concessions and the royal princes were pondering means to restore royal revenue. The result was a brief revival of central and local assemblies.[35]

Several sessions of the three estates of Languedoil were held in Paris between November 1380 and January 1381. The efforts of those who attended, aided by unrest in Paris and other towns, led to the crown's issuing ordonnances in November 1380 and January 1381 abolishing the sales taxes and all other levies that had been instituted since the reign of Philip IV. The removal of taxes imposed by the crown, however, did not prevent the provincial and local estates from making gifts. At first they refused to do so, but after the issuance of the second and more far-reaching of the ordonnances, the estates of Normandy, followed by some other local estates and towns in Languedoil, voted the hearth tax for one year. Meanwhile, in January 1381 the three estates of Languedoc met together for the first time since 1359 and refused to offer any assistance. For a moment it looked as though the gains the crown had made during the previous half-century would be lost, and it would once more become financially dependent on the questionable generosity of the provincial and local estates stimulated, perhaps, by the prior admission of a central assembly that some aid was needed.[36]

In March 1381 the crown took further steps to placate the people by authorizing the local estates to elect their own tax collectors and promising that all money raised would be assigned to the war effort. In spite of these concessions, resistance to taxation continued, and when the sales taxes were reimposed by royal fiat in 1382, there were uprisings in Languedoil and in Languedoc. The insurrections were quickly suppressed, and the crown continued to levy the sales taxes in Languedoil without obtaining the consent of a central assembly. For the moment Languedoc was more fortunate, and in the summer of 1383 its three estates were convoked to give their adherence to the sales taxes. From then until 1418, the sales tax remained the basic source of royal income. It was not sufficient, however, to meet all the requirements of the court, and in most years a new direct tax, known as the *taille*, was imposed.[37]

35. H. A. Miskimin, "The Last Act of Charles V: The Background to the Revolts of 1382," *Speculum* 38 (1963): 433–37. E. A. R. Brown, "Taxation and Morality in the Thirteenth and Fourteenth Centuries," *French Historical Studies* 8 (1973): 1–28; Henneman, *1356–1370*, pp. 299–301. For the ordonnance revoking the hearth tax see *Ord.*, 7:710–11.

36. Henneman, *1356–1370*, pp. 301–302. *Ord.*, 6:527–28, 552–54. L. Mirot, "Les Etats généraux et provinciaux et l'abolition des aides au début du règne de Charles VI," *Revue des questions historiques* 74 (1903): 398–446; Paul Dognon, *Les institutions politiques et administratives du pays de Languedoc du XIIIe siècle aux Guerres de Religion* (Toulouse, 1895), pp. 229–30, 606–615.

37. *Archives administratives de la ville de Reims*, ed. Pierre Varin (Paris, 1848), 3:514. Henneman, *1356–1370*, pp. 303–306; Mirot, "Les États généraux," pp. 446–55; Dognon, *Les institutions politiques*, pp. 616–17.

Between 1382 and 1418, the three estates of Languedoil met only in 1413. In addition, there was a little-known assembly in 1411 that might justify being classified as an Estates General, but except during this two-year span there was an absence of central assemblies.[38] The provincial and local estates in the north fared little better. In Normandy, where the crown raised about a fourth of its tax revenue, no meetings of the provincial estates were held between 1382 and their revival under English auspices in December 1420. Even local estates in Normandy were exceptional, and when they met it was usually in response to local defense needs.[39] In other crown lands in the north, the blackout was to be permanent. We hear little more of the estates of Vermandois, Senlis, Chartres, or other bailiwicks except when they were assembled to ratify a treaty, codify their custom, or, after 1483, to elect deputies of the Estates General.[40]

At first the estates in southern France were more fortunate. The three estates of Languedoc met at least four times between 1382 and 1393. In addition, the deputies of the towns met frequently, but between February 1393 and December 1417 both types of provincial assemblies went into an eclipse.[41] The local estates underwent similar experiences. At first they were rather active, and at times several of them formed alliances to provide for their common defense. The Cévennes bailiwicks of Velay, Vivarais, and Gévaudan comprised a natural region for cooperation. For a brief period in the 1380s, the estates of Rouergue, Quercy, and Auvergne joined them to form a cooperative arrangement of the inhabitants of the mountainous region of central and southern France. These activities, however, bore no fruit, for in 1393 the crown substituted royal tax officials for those of the estates and began to impose levies arbitrarily. Between that year and 1419, we can document only three meetings of the estates of Velay, one of the estates of Vivarais, and one of the estates of Gévaudan. In addition, there was one joint meeting. Surviving evidence suggests that the other local estates in Languedoc suffered a similar fate.[42] If further research were done,

---

38. For the assembly of 1411, see Alfred Coville, *Les Cabochiens et l'ordonnance de 1413* (Paris, 1888), p. 142, n.3, and *Correspondance de la mairie de Dijon extraite des archives de cette ville*, ed. Joseph Garnier (Dijon, 1868), 1:9–11.

39. Henri Prentout, *Les Etats provinciaux de Normandie* (Caen, 1925), 1:96–143. See also Charles M. Radding, *The Administration of the Aids in Normandy, 1360–1389* (Ann Arbor, University Microfilms, 1973).

40. Since assemblies of the estates of this region were exceptional, they have not been individually studied, but for their occasional meetings during the Renaissance, see my *The Deputies to the Estates General of Renaissance France* (Madison, 1960).

41. Dognon, *Les institutions politiques*, pp. 230, 239–43, 616–19. The only provincial assembly Dognon found between 1393 and 1417 consisted of the deputies of the towns and took place in July 1403. Ibid., p. 240. Maurice Rey, however, believes that there was an assembly of the estates in 1396. See his *Le domaine*, p. 330, n.1.

42. Etienne Delcambre, *Les Etats du Velay des origines à 1642* (Saint-Etienne, 1938), pp. 71–81, 108–109. Auguste Le Sourd, *Essai sur des Etats de Vivarais depuis leur origines* (Paris, 1926),

and certainly if more documents had survived, this list could probably be extended, but the general lack of meetings of even the local estates in the north after 1382 and in the south after 1393 would nevertheless be striking. Over two centuries ago Secousse was able to provide an impressive list of the meetings of the central, provincial, and local estates during John's reign. It is equally striking how rarely they are mentioned thereafter in the ordonnances he published until they were revived around 1420.[43]

The role of the estates in the lands of the feudal magnates varied during this period. In some areas, as in Brittany, Bourbonnais, and Comminges they cannot yet be said to have been born; in others as Béarn they were only beginning to see the light of day. Where they were well established or proved useful to their lord, they often continued to meet, even when the king took his subjects' money without their consent. In the duchy of Burgundy the number of meetings of the three estates slackened after 1382, but it was only between 1389 and 1412 that two- or three-year intervals between meetings became relatively common. In 1361 the three estates of Artois began to vote the king a direct tax in return from being freed from paying the sales tax, but they rarely made special gifts to their own counts, who were content to expropriate part of the money designated for the crown. This practice continued long after the Valois dukes of Burgundy inherited the territory in 1384, and it was sufficient to ensure at least one annual meeting until the second decade of the fifteenth century when Duke John the Fearless began to convoke the estates frequently to support his own activities; at the same time he overlooked his fiscal obligations to Paris.[44]

A combination of the defense against marauding troops and the needs of their overlord, the duke of Bourbon, led the estates of Forez to meet at least fourteen times between 1381 and 1393. The pace then slackened, there were only three known meetings during the remainder of the century and five between 1400 and 1436. The Bourbon dukes also utilized the estates of Bourbonnais when the occasion warranted.[45] Jean, duke of Berry, was

pp. 40–47, 299; J. Deniau, "Les Etats particuliers du pays de Gévaudan," *Soc. des letters, sciences et arts de la Lozère: Chroniques et Mélanges* 5 (1930): 9–11. Deniau thinks that the estates met regularly during this period but offers no evidence. There probably were more meetings, however, than the two cited. Françoise Lehoux, *Jean de France, duc de Berri* (Paris, 1966), 2:93–94, 206–10. For a general survey of the estates under Charles VI, but one that does not sufficiently stress their decline, see Rey, *Le domaine*, pp. 348–63.

43. For Secousse's account see *Ord.*, 3:xix–ci. The estates met more frequently in exposed regions such as Rouergue, but even there the pace slackened between 1396 and 1420. See J. Rouquette, *Le Rouergue sous les Anglais* (Millau, 1887).

44. Joseph Billioud, *Les Etats de Bourgogne aux XIVᵉ et XVᵉ siècles* (Dijon, 1922), pp. 379–83; Charles Hirschauer, *Les Etats d'Artois de leurs origines à l'occupation française, 1340–1640* (Paris, 1923), 1:193–197, 2:7–17; Rey, *Le domaine*, pp. 365–66.

45. Etienne Fournial, *Les villes et l'économie d'échange en Forez aux XIIIᵉ et XIVᵉ siècles* (Paris, 1967), pp. 119, 231, 331, 333, 335, 364–66, 376–80, 449, 464, 477; A. Vayssière, "Les Etats de Bourbonnais," *Bul. de la soc. d'émulation du département de l'Allier* 18 (1886): 361–414.

reluctant to use the estates of that duchy, but between 1372 and his death in 1416, the three estates of his county of Poitou met at least fifteen times and in nearly every instance voted him an aid. Conspicuously absent were grants for the king, a situation which strongly suggests that royal taxes were collected without consent.[46] Only in troubled Auvergne did the duke make frequent use of the estates. Between his acquisition of the duchy in 1360 and 1387, they met on an average of over once a year, although there were occasional periods of several years when they did not assemble. The most common reason for the meetings was to provide for local defense. After 1387 the frequency of meetings slackened, and during the remaining twenty-nine years of the duke's life, there were only eleven known assemblies.[47]

One other territory, Dauphiné, needs to be considered. Still nominally part of the empire and theoretically ruled by the heir to the French throne, Dauphiné nevertheless was governed by the king and his council. Its special status, however, led it to receive special consideration, and the crown remained content to extract what money it could through its estates. Alone among the Paris-governed lands the three estates of Dauphiné were in a healthy state in the decades around 1400, and they alone developed a bureaucracy that was to enjoy a continuous history from the late fourteenth until the early seventeenth century.[48]

It is not surprising that a wise and victorious king like Charles V should have been able to abandon central assemblies and ignore the local estates in northern France. He and many of his subjects had been alienated by the estates of Languedoil in the 1350s and had little desire to renew the experiment. What does require explanation is why after a brief revival in the early 1380s the estates—central, provincial, and local—sank into oblivion again during the reign of Charles VI except in the lands of some of the magnates. Charles began his reign as an unpromising boy in 1380, and from 1392 until his death in 1422 he enjoyed only brief periods of lucidity. The necessity to defend the kingdom could rarely be convincingly demonstrated to justify taxes until late in his reign because the English kings, Richard II and Henry IV, had domestic problems that prevented them from doing much more than dream of continental adventures. Yet in spite of a mad king and the lack of any compelling reason for relatively heavy taxation, levies were annually made on a larger portion of France without the consent of the estates than at any other time before in its history. Indeed, not until well

46. Lehoux, *Jean de France*, cites meetings of the three estates of Berry only in 1373, 1375, and 1378: 1:303, 357, 424, n.6. Joseph M. Tyrrell, *A History of the Estates of Poitou* (The Hague, 1968), pp. 134–36.

47. My list of meetings is derived from Lehoux, *Jean de France*, 1:65, n.2; 98, nn.4, 6; 99, n.1; 103, n.5; 120–24; 135; 144, n.3; 168; 180, n.8; 181; 186; 234; 262; 346, n.5; 349; 358; 380; 433, nn.1, 3; 434–36; 441–42; 446; 452; 2:38; 133, n.4; 135, nn.5, 6; 137, n.3; 138; 139; 207; 312; and René Lacour, *Le gouvernement de l'apanage de Jean, duc de Berry, 1360–1410* (Paris, 1934), p. 377.

48. Rey, *Le domaine*, pp. 363–65.

into the seventeenth century was the crown again to exercise such unilateral tax powers.

Most striking is the lack of any concerted demand for holding the estates from the 1360s until about 1420, except briefly in the early 1380s.[49] Clearly the estates had become discredited, and the idea of a subject's right to consent to taxation had not yet become a generally accepted principle. "Above all things," it was suggested to Charles VI in 1408, "be sure that no great assemblies of nobles or of communes take place in your ... kingdom, but take all questions and discords which have arisen and will arise into your own hands, and, as king and sovereign, leave them to law and justice."[50] To some, at least, taxation was solely a royal preserve, and in 1412 a king's attorney in the Court of Aids declared "that the king can put tailles and aides on his kingdom, as an emperor, for its defense and permits no lord whatsoever to levy anything without his consent."[51] Other comparable statements have been found.[52] Hence, it is not surprising that when a royalist spokesman raised the question of the financial needs of the crown during the estates of Languedoil that met in Paris in 1413, he did not specifically ask that consent be given to a tax. Those who attended also avoided the question. Instead they directed their attention toward securing administrative reforms, economies, and the appointment of honest officials. Even though the long ordonnance that resulted from their efforts was promulgated at a time when government officials were threatened by the Parisian populace, it contained no proposal for further meetings of the estates of Languedoil or for the revival of the local estates, despite the fact that the many articles in the document dealing with the sales taxes and gabelle prove that those who attended recognized that there would be annual taxes in the years to come. Clearly the aspirations of the men of 1413 were less exalted than those of Étienne Marcel over fifty years before.[53]

The treaty of Troyes of May 1420 in which Charles VI recognized his son-in-law, Henry V of England, as his heir provides evidence concerning the role the two monarchs and their advisers assigned to the estates. The three estates of both kingdoms were to swear to uphold the treaty, and no agreement was to be reached with the so-called Dauphin, the future Charles VII, without the consent of both assemblies (article 29). Henry undertook to defend and preserve the rights and privileges of "all peers, nobles, cities, towns, communities, and individuals" (article 9) and to seek the "advice

---

49. Ibid., p. 325. Rey limits his observation to the period 1381–1413.

50. P. S. Lewis, *Later Medieval France* (London, 1968), p. 372.

51. Gustave Dupont-Ferrier, *Etudes sur les institutions financières de la France à la fin du Moyen Age* (Paris, 1932), 2:42.

52. Rey, *Le domaine*, p. 166, n.4.

53. For the estates and ordonnance of 1413, see Alfred Coville, *Les Cabochiens et l'ordonnance de 1413* (Paris, 1888); H. Moranvillé, "Remonstrances de l'université et de ville de Paris à Charles VI sur le gouvernement du royaume," *BEC* 51 (1890): 420–42.

and consent" of the estates of both kingdoms in his efforts to prevent future discords between the two realms (article 24), but when it came to taxation he engaged himself only not "to impose any impositions or exactions on our [Charles's] subjects without reasonable and necessary cause, nor otherwise than for the public good of the said kingdom of France" (article 23). The consent of the estates was necessary to ensure the acceptance and implementation of the treaty, but on taxation, the monarchs would go no further than to reiterate the old doctrine that the goods of subjects should not be taken except in case of evident necessity and for the public good.[54]

When the three estates met in Paris in December 1420 to ratify the treaty of Troyes, the question of financing the war was also considered. In the tax ordonnance that followed, Charles stated that he sought the "advice and counsel" of the deputies and that it was upon their "good advice and counsel" that he had chosen the least burdensome imposition that was possible. The word *consent* was once more scrupulously avoided.[55]

The reason the crown tried to avoid the use of the word *consent* in regard to taxation is obvious, but why was there so little demand from the vocal elements of the population that the estates meet regularly and give their approval to all the levies that were made?[56] No medieval king could tax unless the nobles permitted the money to be collected from their "subjects," and the upper bourgeoisie used municipal governments to impose levies on townsmen. The cooperation of the small but important body of royal officials was also important. Their united opposition could have easily forced a weak king like Charles VI to come to terms, but they did nothing. Only circumstantial evidence can be offered to explain their inaction, but this evidence is most persuasive.

Already in the reign of Charles V, magnates had often been permitted to take about a third of the royal taxes collected from their lands, but under the mad Charles VI, his kinsmen and other great nobles frequently took all the revenue. Towns were sometimes given permission to retain part of the taxes collected from within their walls. It been estimated that from 700,000 to a million livres of the total royal tax revenue of from 2 million to 2.4 million livres found their way into their hands. Little wonder the princes and other magnates did not present a united front against taxation; their own financial position depended upon the capacity of the crown to extract money from its subjects. Since they had large clienteles both within and without the royal government who depended upon them for their offices or their salaries, the forces favoring heavy taxes were almost irresistible.[57]

54. *Ord.*, 11:86–90.

55. Ibid., 109, 110.

56. The crown was more disposed to use the word *consent* in regard to clerical taxation. In 1398 an ordonnance stated that an assembly of the clergy had agreed "to consent" to a levy for three years. *Ord.*, 8:290.

57. Rey, *Le domaine*, esp. pp. 198–203, 269–76. See also his *Les finances royales sous Charles VI:*

Some influential persons did not profit directly or indirectly from this largesse, but their silence in effect was often bought by the growing practice of exempting them from taxation. Exemption had been rare during the latter half of the fourteenth century. Occasionally the nobility or the clergy might be asked to pay a different sort of tax than other citizens, there were instances when nobles who were actually bearing arms were excused, and with decreasing frequency other less justifiable exceptions were made; but cases can also be cited when even members of the royal family were specifically included. France had seemed well on the way to becoming a country in which the rich as well as the poor, the noble as well as the peasant, contributed. However, the need for additional taxes because of a revival of the English threat after the Lancastrian succession and the grave weakness of the government led this trend to be reversed around the turn of the century. On January 30, 1404, Charles imposed a tax on his entire kingdom that was to be paid by everyone, including his uncles and brother, except nobles frequenting arms, clergymen who were to pay another tax, and paupers. Then in May in a series of ordonnances, he exempted the members of Parlement, the Chamber of Accounts, treasurers, and royal officials at Paris. In 1406 the widows of such officials were added to the exemption, and in 1408 the nobles of Languedoc who did not engage in trade were excused from all tailles and sales taxes. Some towns, university faculties, and others were added to the ever-growing list, and the society of the old regime in which those who could afford to pay did not and those who could not afford to pay did began to take form.[58] With some of the most powerful persons in the kingdom profiting from taxes and others escaping paying their share, it is not surprising that there was no strong opposition to Charles VI's fiscal policies or a concerted demand that the estates give consent to the levies that were made. It was Charles's very weakness in dealing with the powerful forces in his kingdom that enabled him to exercise absolutist tax powers even though the crown had sunk to its lowest depths in centuries.

The decline of the local and provincial estates under Charles V and their demise in most of France under Charles VI meant that their reappearance under Charles VII was essentially a rebirth. The break in their history around the turn of the century marks the dividing line between the medieval and Renaissance assemblies. Fourteenth-century man had shown considerable capacity for self-government. In 1314, long before their estates were

---

Les causes du déficit, 1388–1413 (Paris, 1965), pp. 571–612. C. M. Radding persuasively argues that Rey overestimated Charles VI's tax revenue. See his "Royal Tax Revenues in Later Fourteenth Century France," *Traditio* 32 (1976): 366.

58. *Ord.*, 9:4–8, 141–42, 360–68, 12:218–20. For a general account of the growth of exemptions, see Dupont-Ferrier, *Etudes*, 2:162–90. Some later kings, notably Charles VII, Charles IX, and Louis XIV, did attempt to make the privileged pay, but only the last had much success.

born, nobles, clergymen, and townsmen in the duchy of Burgundy had banded together to resist taxation and other unreasonable actions of the crown. The formal alliance that they signed provided for governors to defend their interests and to call them into session in case of emergency. In addition, there were to be annual meetings. Similar alliances were made in Champagne and other territories in northern and eastern France. These territorial alliances joined together in a formidable confederation. Their authors were not yet mature enough to demand representative assemblies to give consent to taxation, but they did extract promises of reform and charters of privileges from the crown.[59]

By the 1350s provincial and local estates were being formed in many parts of France to defend their constituents from marauding troops and to vote and levy taxes. The three estates of Languedoil even appointed tax collectors and royal councillors, and they arranged for periodic meetings without formal summons by the king. Indeed, it was their very precociousness that turned both the crown and many people against such assemblies and contributed to their decline. Then, too, most Frenchmen clung tenaciously to the belief that in normal times the king should support himself and his government from his own income. Taxation to them was a temporary expedient. So long as they adhered to this opinion, there was an ad hoc quality about the estates that worked against the development of fixed procedures, and those they appointed to collect taxes were regarded as temporary officials. Therefore, as the monarchy grew stronger in the 1360s and 1370s and the English threat lessened, an able king and his officials could bypass the various estates. Many influential persons became accustomed to profiting from the royal treasury, and still more won exemption from taxation. As a result, there was little organized protest against taxation without the consent of the estates, even when an insane king sat upon the throne.[60] The concept that there was a role for representative assemblies did not die, however, and these institutions could be quickly recreated in a more favourable climate when a need for their services became more apparent.

59. André Artonne, *Le mouvement de 1314 et les chartes provinciales de 1315* (Paris, 1912), pp. 21–25; Elizabeth A. R. Brown, "Charters and Leagues in Early Fourteenth Century France: The Movement of 1314 and 1315" (Ph.D. diss., Harvard University, 1960).

60. There were a few, of course, who were probably exempt from taxes who did protest against taxation and call for a meeting of the three estates. For example, Clémengis, a member of the faculty of the University of Paris, took this position. André Lemaire, *Les lois fondamentales de la monarchie française* (Paris, 1907), pp. 49–51.

2

THE RENAISSANCE MONARCHS
AND THEIR POLICIES

IT IS DIFFICULT TO SAY HOW LONG THE SYSTEM OF GOVERNMENT THAT HAD existed in France from the 1360s would have lasted if the members of the royal family had continued to agree on the division of the spoils, for as long as the Valois princes were united, it was difficult for the opposition to be heard. The brothers of Charles V had stood together, but in 1404 Philip the Bold of Burgundy died, and his son, John the Fearless, was soon at odds with his first cousin, Louis, duke of Orleans, brother of the mad king Charles VI, and an insatiable plunderer of the royal treasury. In 1407 John had Louis murdered. The count of Armagnac assumed leadership of the Orleanists, and a bloody feud ensued in which John sought public support by posing as a reformer who desired nothing better than to oust the wrongdoers and create an honest, frugal government. He won considerable popularity in Paris, and in 1413, during one of his periods in power, the estates of Languedoil was held. The reforms proposed by this assembly were stillborn as we have seen. Nevertheless with the Valois family divided and its most vigorous member supporting the popular cause, the old system of government was threatened. All that was needed to impel significant changes was a new and successful invasion from England.

1. THE ENGLISH INVASION AND THE ESTATES IN OCCUPIED FRANCE

Both the Burgundian and the Armagnac factions had sought English assistance, but when Henry V led an army across the channel, he came committed only to achieve his own ends: the acquisition of the royal crown of France and the ducal crown of Normandy, which he regarded as being his by hereditary right. His spectacular victory at Agincourt in 1415 had no immediate military results, but several years later he began to conquer Normandy methodically. Instead of uniting to repel the invader, the Valois princes persisted in their quarrel. John the Fearless seized Paris and "rescued" the mad king from the Armagnacs in May 1418, but the following year he himself was treacherously murdered by the Armagnacs in circumstances which gravely implicated the dauphin, Charles, who had become the nominal leader of that faction. Philip the Good, John's successor, felt compelled to avenge his father and made an alliance with England. Any chance of expelling the English came to an end, and France was doomed to years of civil war.

In their quest for support, the Burgundians had traditionally worn the mantle of reform. To lend credence to their pose, they abolished all taxes except the gabelle in those parts of Auvergne, Languedoc, and Guyenne that recognized their regime. The dauphin, Charles, who styled himself "lieutenant general" and later "regent" of the kingdom, followed suit by suppressing the *aides* or sales taxes in Auvergne and perhaps elsewhere. Both factions were thus left with the choice of trying to govern the lands they controlled with such income as could be derived from the remnants of the domain, the gabelle, and various expedients, or of reviving the estates to consent to new levies. Faced with this dilemma, the contending parties adopted separate courses that were to affect deeply the history of the estates in their respective areas.[1]

Gradually France became divided into at least four parts. By the terms of the treaty of Troyes, the English were to govern Guyenne and Normandy with only token acknowledgment of the suzerainty of the Paris government, and Philip of Burgundy was to have a similar privilege in his hereditary lands. What remained of the territory under their control was administered by officials in Paris who for the most part were Burgundian appointees. South of the Loire River the cause of the dauphin, Charles, was generally favored, but the magnates who controlled so much of the region often went their individual ways when it came to such matters as holding the estates and seeking consent to taxation.

Although Henry V was acknowledged by Charles VI as his heir, he was clever enough to see that it would be necessary to establish a firm base in France to make good his claim, because his English subjects were not likely to be generous in their support for a foreign venture for many years. Therefore he sought to implant his rule firmly in the wealthy province of Normandy where he claimed to be hereditary duke by virtue of his Angevin ancestors. To secure Norman allegiance, he made their institutions autonomous and staffed them almost entirely with natives. He and his successor also recreated the provincial estates and held them frequently to vote financial support for their regimes. It is to the English occupation more than anything else that the Normans owed the existence of their estates during the Renaissance. In return, they gave their suzerain more loyalty than many French historians have cared to admit. The limited evidence that survives suggests that the local estates in Guyenne were equally active, and in 1420

1. *Ord.*, 10:429–31, 455–56; Gaston du Fresne de Beaucourt, *Histoire de Charles VII* (Paris, 1881), 1:389–92. C. M. Radding has shown that Charles VI had less revenue than his father and that this contributed to the quarrel between the Valois princes. See his "Royal Tax Revenues in Later Fourteenth Century France," *Traditio* 32 (1976): 361–68.

an assembly of the three estates of the duchy met. Here Henry was less of an innovator because his father, and perhaps his earlier predecessors, appear to have utilized the estates frequently, but by his actions he gave them further impetus. (See chaps. 4 and 6, sec. 1.)

Philip the Good continued to summon the estates in those of his lands where they had previously existed. Both in the Low Countries and in Burgundy, he eventually tried to consolidate the estates to form Estates Generals or at least assemblies embracing a wider territory. However he created few new estates of importance in his hereditary lands and none in the territories that he administered, such as Champagne. Of the provinces governed by the Paris officials, only Languedoc, which they held briefly, experienced a revival of its estates. Elsewhere the English and Burgundians apparently preferred to tax lightly than to seek larger sums from the hard-pressed people by holding the estates. For this reason the long silence of the estates in the Ile-de-France, Chartres, Vermandois, and Picardy that had begun in the 1360s was continued with barely noticeable interruptions.[2]

2. CHARLES VII, LOUIS XI, AND THE ESTATES

Although over half of France recognized Charles in 1418, he was in no position to impose heavy taxes arbitrarily. Without prestige or experience, he was soon to be declared illegitimate by his mother and barred from the succession to the throne by the treaty of Troyes. He therefore quickly turned to the estates. In May 1418 he held a regional assembly at Limoges that voted 100,000 francs. In attendance were deputies from Poitou, Saintonge, Limousin, Périgord, Angoulême, and La Marche. Perhaps this experiment was unsatisfactory, because in 1419 and 1420 Charles turned to the provincial and local estates. One or more meetings were held in Dauphiné, Auvergne, Limousin, Touraine, La Marche, Poitou, Saintonge, and Languedoc, which he had regained from the Anglo-Burgundians, and no doubt elsewhere.[3] Equally important, the local estates in the south began to regain control over the appointment and collection of taxes, a process that soon led to the disappearance of royally appointed élus in the region.[4]

2. Edouard Perroy, *The Hundred Years War* (London, 1951), pp. 253–58. *HL*, 9:1044–45, 10:1985–90; *Ord.*, 10:449–50. The Anglo-Burgundians did hold a meeting of the Estates General at Paris in October 1424 and of the estates of Champagne and Picardy earlier that year. B. J. W. Rowe, "The Estates of Normandy under the Duke of Bedford, 1422–1435," *English Historical Review* 46 (1931): 554, 567–68.

3. J. R. Major, *Representative Institutions in Renaissance France, 1421–1559* (Madison, 1960), p. 22; A. Thomas, "Nouveaux documents sur les Etats provinciaux de la Haute-Marche," *Annales du Midi* 25 (1913): 430–34. Joseph M., Tyrrell, *A History of the Estates of Poitou* (The Hague, 1968), p. 137; Denys d'Aussy, ed., "Registres de l'échevinage de Saint-Jean d'Angély, 1332–1496," *Archives historiques de la Saintonge et de l'Aunis* 32 (1902): 260.

4. Henri Gilles, *Les Etats de Languedoc au XVe siècle* (Toulouse, 1965), pp. 174–86; Etienne Delcambre, *Les Etats du Velay des origines à 1642* (Saint-Etienne, 1938), pp. 109–10.

In 1421 Charles again altered his tactics and summoned the Estates General to meet at Clermont in Auvergne. By this act he inaugurated a fifteen-year experiement in which there were meetings of the Estates General or of the estates of Languedoil on an average of about once a year. Occasionally, as in 1422, 1429, and 1430, there were no such meetings, but in some other years there were more than one or there were regional assemblies of the estates of eastern and western Languedoil. In these meetings Charles nearly always asked for financial assistance but was generally voted less than he requested. The proportion of this sum to be paid by each jurisdiction in the kingdom or in the area that had participated in the meeting was then established. The final step was to collect the promised money, and it is here that no pattern can be established for all of those parts of France that acknowledged Charles.[5]

Dauphiné was still part of the Empire. Its inhabitants did not participate in the French assemblies, and any contribution they made to Charles was voted by its estates. The powerful counts of Foix and Armagnac kept their lands outside the sphere of royal administration. Périgord and probably Quercy, which lay along the frontier of Guyenne, had enough to do to protect themselves from English raids and were therefore left out of Charles's fiscal plans.[6] Languedoc and Rouergue attended meetings of the Estates General with reluctance when they went at all. Their presence in such an assembly did not constitute acceptance of their share of the tax. Rather they insisted on having meetings of their own estates after these sessions, where they generally appropriated less than their assigned share. Auvergne and the other jurisdictions in central France deputed to these assemblies with more willingness, but they were equally determined to pay only taxes they approved in their local assemblies. They also had no compunction in reducing the amount requested. In these areas central assemblies, at best, served as a forum in which Charles and his advisers could explain their financial needs. Once those who had attended had agreed on a certain sum, it was possible to put moral pressure on the provincial and local estates to vote at least a large portion of their share.[7]

There were, however, other parts of France where the local estates had rarely met, and taxes had nearly always been levied by royal fiat. In the early days of his reign, Charles was in no position to continue this practice, and in 1425 when he attempted to tax unilaterally regions without strong estates, he ran into resistance.[8] However, in these localities it usually sufficed to obtain consent either in a central assembly or in the local estates. The three estates of Poitou had become active only in 1390 when the duke of

5. Major, *Representative Institutions*, pp. 25–31, 151.

6. A. Thomas, "Le Midi et les Etats Généraux sous Charles VII," *Annales du Midi* 1 (1889): 291–92.

7. Major, *Representative Institutions*, pp. 25–31, 35.

8. Beaucourt, *Histoire*, 2:584–85.

Berry, their count, began to convoke them every few years to vote him an aide. The revival of the English threat led to more frequent meetings in the 1410s, but when Charles himself became their count in 1416, the estates were still not so entrenched but that he could impose a tax voted by a central assembly. Only once between 1421 and 1438 is there evidence that the estates approved a tax that had already been voted by a central assembly. On other occasions, such taxes were collected without consultation except at the municipal level. The estates of Poitou did meet fourteen times during this period, but the purpose of these meetings was to vote taxes for the crown in years when there were no central assemblies, to alter the nature of a royal levy, or to vote money for local purposes.[9]

The generally dormant estates of Touraine sprang to life. In 1420 and 1422, when there were no central assemblies, they voted the dauphin financial assistance. In August 1423 the estates of Languedoil met at Selles and was prevailed upon to revive the aides. Since sales taxes were generally unpopular, a number of local estates, including Touraine, met late that year to substitute a direct tax. During the next five years central assemblies voted taxes that were collected in Touraine without any known action on the part of the local estates. Then in 1429 and 1430, there was another lull in the use of central assemblies, and once more Charles turned to the local estates. The estates of Touraine met with those of Anjou at Angers in September 1429, alone at Tours in November of that year, and again in September 1430. Then in the spring of 1431 Charles once more turned to central assemblies, and the estates of Touraine became less active.[10]

A similar situation seems to have existed in Saintonge. As a frontier province, its estates had not completely disappeared in the preceding period. There had been meetings in 1412, 1413, and again in 1417 when problems of defense were considered, but royal taxes were frequently imposed without consent. From 1418 the town of Saint-Jean d'Angély, which provides a principal source of information, participated regularly in the central assemblies Charles convoked. In 1419 and 1420 when there were no central assemblies, the three estates of Saintonge met, and they occasionally did so in other years. However, it is clear that taxes agreed upon in the central assemblies were frequently, and perhaps always, levied on Saintonge without consulting the local estates.[11]

In Lyonnais the situation was somewhat different. There were no towns of secondary importance to compete with Lyons, while in Poitou, Touraine, and Saintonge there had been smaller centers of sufficient size to warrant consideration. As a result, even in the most opportune times, meetings of the

9. Tyrrell, *History of the Estates,* pp. 35–38, 134–40.

10. Beaucourt, *Histoire,* 359 and n.3, 405, 2:581. A. Thomas, "Les Etats Généraux sous Charles VII," *Revue historique* 40 (1889): 68–71.

11. D'Aussy, "Registres de Saint-Jean d'Angély," pp. 8, 18, 61–63, 203–05, 239, 260, 297, 304–05, 328, 330, 350, 354, 357, 366–67, 373, 374–76, 377, 378, 414, 415, 417–18, 420.

estates in Lyonnais were exceptional. The first recorded meeting of the three estates of Lyonnais did not take place until January 1422 when an effort was made to unite the resources of the region to halt pillaging. Charles also asked for troops but was voted fewer than he desired. Undeterred, he ordered the estates to meet later that year and obtained 6,000 of the 8,000 écus requested.[12] In August 1423 the estates of Languedoil met at Selles and voted to revive the aides. The inhabitants of Lyonnais, like those in most other parts of France, were strongly opposed to these sales taxes, and in December the three estates assembled to substitute a direct levy. The crown set a figure of 16,000 livres per year for three years as being their share, but they could be persuaded to vote only 5,000. The only other recorded meeting of the estates during Charles's reign was in 1447.[13]

Louis Caillet, a historian of Lyons, has attributed the failure of the estates of Lyonnais to be more active to a quarrel between the clergy and burghers of that city and to the weakness of the nobility in the seneschalsy. To these possible explanations must be added the failure of the town and the plat pays to cooperate. The latter had an organization of its own whose activities are frequently alluded to in the rich documentation that survives in Lyons. But neither the villages that participated in the assemblies of the plat pays nor the deputies they elected left specific records of their activities. The town and the plat pays cooperated in the early 1420s both in the estates of Lyonnais and in delegations they elected in separate meetings to go to court. On several occasions, however, inhabitants of the plat pays deserted the town and went their own way. It was the municipal officials of Lyons, on the other hand, who refused to negotiate jointly with the crown in 1427. The idea that they would be stronger if they acted with the plat pays was voiced, but the majority believed that they could win greater concessions if they negotiated alone, a practice that they followed thereafter.[14]

In 1436 Charles held his last central assembly for essentially financial purposes. In that year the three estates of Languedoil had met in Poitiers and voted a taille of 200,000 livres and revived the aides to run for three years, but after that period had elapsed, Charles continued to collect the aides in Languedoil without the consent of central, provincial, or local assemblies on the pretext that they had been granted in perpetuity. He also began determining the amount of the taille in Languedoil without consult-

---

12. There is a detailed treatment of the role of Lyons in the central assemblies in Louis Caillet, *Etude sur les relations de la commune de Lyon avec Charles VII et Louis XI, 1417–1483* (Lyon, 1909), pp. 22–84. Jean Déniau, *La commune de Lyon et la guerre Bourguignonne, 1417–1435* (Lyon, 1934), pp. 407, 426–27, 430–32. Beaucourt, *Histoire*, 1:364 nn. 1, 3; 440, 465–66, 469. For documents, see *Registres consulaires de la ville de Lyon ou recueil des déliberations du conseil de la commune*, ed M.-C. and G. Guigue (Lyon, 1882–1926).

13. Déniau, *La commune*, pp. 444–47; Caillet, *Etude sur les relations*, pp. 35–38, 137, 484–85.

14. Caillet, *Etude sur les relations*, pp. 44–49, 62, 283, 358–61, 382–85; Déniau, *La commune*, pp. 458–59.

ing the central assembly in 1437, but where it was customary, he continued to summon the local estates to vote their share.[15]

In 1439 and again in 1440, Charles convoked the Estates General to advise on whether he should make peace. In the first meeting they voted a taille of 100,000 livres in addition to the levy of 300,000 Charles had imposed on his own authority earlier in the year. A feudal uprising led Charles to cancel the meeting scheduled for 1440. Thereafter he held no central assemblies of the three estates during his reign, but he continued to convoke meetings of a single order, such as the clergy, and to hold various types of consultative assemblies, which were devoid of representative elements.[16]

Charles's abandonment of central assemblies did not mean that he levied the taille at will. The provincial and local estates continued to meet in most parts of France where they had been summoned to approve their share of taxes voted in central assemblies. Instead the new policy meant that rather than haggling over whether they should contribute their full share of a tax set in a central assembly, these assemblies now asked whether they should pay their share of a tax set by the king and council alone. Languedoc and Rouergue had always opposed central assemblies, and some other regions, such as Dauphiné, had never participated in them. Small wonder they made little or no protest over their abandonment.

The apparent losers were the inhabitants of areas where the local estates had not habitually been assembled to approve taxes voted in central assemblies, for they now lost whatever right they had had to determine how much they would contribute. Included were the inhabitants of Maine, Anjou, Berry, Orléanais, Touraine, Poitou, Saintonge, and Lyonnais who had long recognized Charles and also those in the newly conquered provinces of the Ile-de-France, Champagne, and southern Picardy. At first there seemed to be at least a chance that Charles would use the estates in these provinces. The towns of Champagne were assembled after their recapture in 1431, and hardly had Paris been reoccupied in 1436 than the nearby towns gathered together to hear a request that the aides be established. In January the following year the towns of Champagne met at Reims. However the abandonment of the estates of Languedoil after the reestablishment of the aides in 1436 was paralleled by the disappearance of these assemblies.[17]

---

15. Unless otherwise indicated, this and the following seven paragraphs are taken from Major, *Representative Institutions*, pp. 31–39 except insofar as I have modified my position because of the findings of Tyrrell, *History of the Estates*, pp. 46–54. See also P. S. Lewis, ed., *The Recovery of France in the Fifteenth Century* (New York, 1972), pp. 294–311.

16. Charles was apparently planning to hold another meeting of the estates just before his death in 1461. Malcolm G. A. Vale, *Charles VII* (Berkeley, 1974), pp. 181–82.

17. Beaucourt, *Histoire*, 3:435–36; E. Cosneau, *Le Connétable de Richemont* (Paris, 1886), pp. 257, 265 n.6. An assembly of the towns was also held in 1445–46. Major, *Representative Institutions*, p. 43.

They had been ignored by the English and neglected by their French sovereigns since the 1360s. As a result, they had not become deeply embedded in tradition, and to our knowledge no tears were shed at their passing.

The abandonment of central assemblies led to few protests in areas without active local estates. During the period in which Charles had summoned them, the municipal leaders of Lyons had once pleaded to be excused from paying a tax until after the estates had met. In 1426 those of Tours had warned against the three estates of one locality taking action without the others, and in 1435 they had told the king that if he needed money, he should assemble the estates "of all his obedience." So far as we know, however, neither Lyons nor Tours protested when Charles abandoned central assemblies.[18] Equally silent were those jurisdictions like Poitou where the estates were fairly active but where levies voted in central assemblies had usually been collected without their formal approval. Here taxes decreed by Charles without the consent of a central assembly were accepted just as if such a meeting had been held. The most marked difference was that the élus assumed full responsibility for collecting the tax; earlier they had shared it with the royal commissioners and the estates.

The people in these regions quietly accepted this change in policy because their estates had not become sufficiently established to be regarded as essential to the preservation of their privileges and to the maintenance of low taxes. Indeed, the généralités of Normandy and Languedoc, where the provincial estates were strong, were more heavily taxed than the généralités of Languedoil and Outre-Seine, where active estates were rare. During the reign of Charles VIII, Normandy and Languedoc sought to have an investigation that would lead to the various parts of France being taxed more equitably, but their efforts were thwarted by undertaxed Champagne and other provinces where there were no estates.[19]

Those who were in the best position to protest—that is, the nobles, clergy, royal officials, and bourgeois oligarchies of the large towns—had escaped most taxes by the end of the reign of Charles VI and usually had no strong, personal interest in the matter. Philippe de Commynes said that the nobility permitted Charles VII to tax without the consent of the estates because of the pensions he gave them, and in 1429 the count of Foix admitted that the crown granted the large towns in Languedoc remission to taxes so that they would be more willing to vote for taxes when the estates met, taxes that would fall heavily on the smaller towns and communities that were less able to defend themselves.[20] Indeed towns such as Lyons and Poitiers believed

18. *Registres de Lyon*, 2 : 12; Lewis, *Recovery of France*, p. 301.

19. A. Spont, "Une recherche générale des feux à la fin du XVᵉ siècle," *Ann-bulletin de la soc. de l'histoire de France* 29 (1892): 222–36.

20. Philippe de Commynes, *Mémoires*, ed. J. Calmette (Paris, 1925), 2 : 289; P. S. Lewis, *Later Medieval France* (London, 1968), p. 367.

that they could fare as well or better in direct negotiations with the crown as when they acted through the local estates. The principal losers were the inhabitants of the small towns and villages, and they rarely participated in the estates. Thus those who lost by the implementation of the new policy were those who were not in a position to offer effective protests even if they had had the wisdom to do so.

It is not difficult to explain why Charles embarked on this new course. He had revived the estates in the desperate days of his youth, but now that he was well on the way to reconquering his kingdom, he was anxious to revert to the policies of Charles VI. The central assemblies had served him well. He had sought to have the electorate give those who attended full powers. In the meetings they had always voted him a substantial portion of the money that he requested, and in parts of France this sufficed for him to collect the tax without further negotiations with provincial estates. Even where the provincial estates also had to be convoked, the fact that his needs had been established by a central assembly must have had some propaganda value when negotiations began. Charles had no reason to fear central assemblies. At no time had they sought to take control of the government as those in the 1350s had done. On the other hand, they were time-consuming and costly to hold, and their complaints were often irritating. Some of his subjects were outspoken in their opposition to their use. Hence after 1436 when central assemblies were no longer necessary to him, he ceased to convoke them regularly, but he and his Valois successors continued to turn to them occasionally when it appeared to their advantage to do so. Provincial estates were even more time-consuming and expensive because there were so many of them. Where local sentiment in their favor was not strong, Charles ceased to employ them in tax matters, though if the occasion arose when one of them could be of use, Renaissance monarchs had no hesitation in calling a meeting.

By the early 1440s, Charles felt that he was in a position to turn on some of the best established local and provincial estates. In 1443 he told the three estates of Languedoc that he had enough of such assemblies after they had refused to vote him all that he had asked, but a few generous, well-placed bribes were enough for the estates to win friends at court who persuaded the weak-willed king to relent. (See chap. 3, sec. 1.)

The estates in central France were less fortunate. From 1445 they had been asked to consent to two direct taxes. One, the *taille des gens de guerre*, was designated for the support of permanent garrisons established in each province that year. The other taille was assigned to support the general war effort and other governmental activities. By 1452 the garrisons could be reduced and the second taille abandoned altogether because the reconquest of Normandy and Guyenne during the preceding two years appeared to terminate the war with the English and brought additional lands to the crown that were assigned part of the burden of supporting the government.

Seeing his opportunity, Charles directed the élus in Haute- and Basse-Auvergne to collect the taille without convoking the estates. In Haut- and Bas-Limousin, La Marche, and Périgord where there had hitherto been no élus, they were established to assume the duties of apportioning the taxes that had formerly been performed by the royal commissioners sent to hold the estates and by officials that these assemblies elected. Once more the annual consent to taxes by the estates was dispensed with. There was little or no protest because the people were more pleased by a 30 percent reduction in taxes than they were angered by the loss of the right to consent to those that remained.[21]

Although seriously weakened, the estates in central France did not die suddenly. The feudal lords of Auvergne, Bourbonnais, Forez, and La Marche continued to summon their respective estates to grant them financial assistance. These estates and those of Limousin also assembled to look after their own needs and upon occasion to perform some service for the crown. However, since the élus had become essential elements in the tax-collecting process, it was necessary to obtain royal approval for any tax to benefit the feudal overlord or the estates themselves before it could be assessed. The duke of Bourbon continued to convoke the estates of Bourbonnais frequently until around the close of the fifteenth century, and when in session those present often seized the opportunity to send deputations to the king to protest against royal taxes. The estates of Auvergne, Forez, and Périgord remained active during the sixteenth century, and the king himself occasionally made use of the estates of Haut- and Bas-Limousin and Haute- and Basse-Marche for tax purposes.[22]

The estates of Normandy refused to vote all the money Charles requested to support the army in 1450–51. In retaliation he took advantage of the existence of élus in the province and ordered them to collect taxes without convoking the estates. Then for some reason he reversed himself in 1458 and

---

21. Major, *Representative Institutions*, pp. 41–43; Antoine Thomas, *Les Etats provinciaux de la France centrale sous Charles VII* (Paris, 1879), esp. 1:88–100, 164–69. For the somewhat similar experience of Tours, see B. Chevalier, "Pouvoir royal et pouvoir urbain à Tours pendant la Guerre de Cent Ans," *Annales de Bretagne* 81 (1974): 703–05.

22. Thomas, *Les Etats provinciaux*, 1:169–74. For Bourbonnais see A. Vayssière, "Les Etats du Bourbonnais," *Bul. de la soc. d'émulation du département de l'Allier* 18 (1886–91): 361–414. Vayssière does not say that Charles VII ceased to ask the estates for consent around 1451, but the documents he publishes and Charles's treatment of the other estates in central France suggest that he did. For documents, see pp. 379–83. My belief that the Bourbon dukes ceased to convoke the estates regularly around 1500 is based on Vayssière's failure to cite any meetings thereafter, although the accounts of Moulins upon which he based his study are available for 1502–03 and 1513–21 after a long gap between 1471 and 1502. Also, when the three estates of Bourbonnais met in 1521 to redact their custom, procedural errors were made such as convoking Saint-Pourçain, one of the thirteen good towns of Basse-Auvergne, that are best explained by the assumption that the estates had not met for some years. Vayssière, "Les Etats," pp. 385–88. In the ordonnance of 1439, Charles VII forbade nobles and other persons to appropriate royal taxes and to levy taxes. *Ord.*, 13:312–13.

specifically promised not to levy taxes without the consent of the three estates, thereby ensuring that they enjoyed a healthy existence during the Renaissance. (See chap. 6, sec. 1.)

The situation is more obscure in Guyenne, where the estates of the seneschalsy of Bordeaux had been active under the English and there had been occasional meetings of those of the whole duchy. Both assemblies had negotiated with Charles VII in 1451, and in return for the submission of the entire duchy, Charles granted terms that seemed to ensure a prominent role for the estates and the autonomy of the province. In the accord Charles swore that the inhabitants would not be compelled to pay any taxes (article 18), that a sovereign court would be created at Bordeaux (article 20), and that money would be minted in that city "with the advice and deliberation of the officers and people of the three estates of the said province" (article 23).[23] Apparently the pledge concerning taxation was soon violated, and the Bordelais invited the English to return in 1452. Once more Charles VII drove the English from France, and this time he was in a position to impose his terms on the Bordelais. He abolished their right to have a sovereign court and placed the province in the jurisdiction of the Parlement of Paris (article 4). In addition, he established the aides and levied them by royal decree (article 2), but conspicuous by their absence was his failure to mention of the estates or the taille.[24]

Can we assume, as has nearly always been done, that the estates ceased to exist and that the taille was henceforth levied by royal fiat. If this was Charles's intention, why did he not include the taille with the aides as a tax that he would directly control? These are troublesome questions and before one makes the traditional assumption that the estates were abandoned and that henceforth Charles VII levied the taille at will, one must explain how the taille was apportioned and collected. As far as is known, Charles appointed élus only in Lannes and Périgord, but the estates continued to function in both seneschalsies in spite of the presence of royal tax officials.[25] Elsewhere in Guyenne, including Bordelais, we must assume that the estates or their officers apportioned and supervised the collection of taxes. There is proof that they did in some seneschalsies during Charles's reign and in all of those without élections during the reign of Francis I.[26] In Dauphiné, also,

23. *Ord.*, 14:139–45.

24. Ibid., pp. 270–75.

25. See chap. 4, sec. 2. Charles also created élections in Haut- and Bas-Limousin, but these seneschalsies were detached from Guyenne in 1542.

26. Gilbert Jacqueton specifically attributes the apportionment of the taille in Guyenne to the commissioners and the estates. See his *Documents relatifs à l'administration financière en France de Charles VII à François Ier* (Paris, 1891), p. 280 n.13. Alfred Spont was aware of the absence of élus in Guyenne and the existence of estates, but he underestimated the latter's importance. See his *Semblançay* (Paris, 1895), p. 53 n.2, p. 65 n.5. In Bordelais, the center of the uprising in 1452, there was a meeting of the three estates in 1461, and there may have been one in 1459 and in

(*Continued next page*)

the estates continued to be active in the years following the Hundred Years War. (See chap. 3, sec. 2.)

It is apparent that Charles VII, unlike Charles V, did not establish a relatively uniform tax administration after defeating the English, although his victory was far more complete. Part of the reason for his failure to do so must be attributed to his personal weakness. It was easy to rid himself of the central assemblies because there was little demand for them, but where the provincial or local estates had responded strongly to his occasional efforts to curtail their activities, he had ultimately acquiesced to their desires. Perhaps by this time the estates in southern France and Normandy had become so important in the people's mind that he would have had difficulty in destroying them even if he had had the energy to try. Certainly with each passing year, it became more difficult to alter the characteristics that the Renaissance monarchy had assumed. Perhaps Louis XI (1461–83) had the last real chance to do so until after the Wars of Religion.

On the surface Louis XI seemed an ideal candidate to change the direction that the monarchy was taking. He was a man of tremendous energy, he was one of the few Valois kings who had a truly original mind, he was both able and willing to grasp new ideas, and he was determined to be obeyed. One is entranced by hearing him suggest that a system of uniform weights and measures and a common law be established, that internal tolls be removed, and that the nobility be permitted to engage in trade as in Italy.[27] But he never consistently pursued these policies and on his death left the existing order as entrenched, or perhaps more entrenched, than before. Except perhaps during the first couple of years of his reign, he was relatively consistent in his desire to break the power of those overmighty subjects whom he did not trust, but to do so he had to seek the support of other nobles, who by his death were stronger than before. In 1464 he told the Milanese ambassador that he wanted peace with England so that "he could keep himself from being put into subjection by the barons of his realm."[28] Seven years later he suggested to another Milanese envoy that France and Milan reduce Savoy to the mode and form of the French monarchy so that its duke could impose taxes and military service in the French fashion.[29]

---

other years. *IAD, Gironde, sér. E*, ed. Gaston Ducaunnès-Duval (Bordeaux, 1898), 1:79, 3:234. Although Charles initially abandoned his idea of creating a Parlement at Bordeaux, he partially mollified local opinion by having Grand Jours there so that the inhabitants would not have to appeal their cases to Paris. These facts suggest that Charles was less severe on Bordelais than has sometimes been argued and that the estates continued to be active. A careful examination of the few surviving communal registers and account books might provide the necessary proof.

27. Major, *Representative Institutions*, p. 53. The best general treatments of the government of Louis XI remain R. Doucet, "Le gouvernement de Louis XI," *Revue des cours et conférences* 14–15 (1922–24), and Charles Petit-Dutaillis, *Histoire de France*, ed. E. Lavisse (Paris, 1911) 4: pt. 2, 399–419.

28. Paul M. Kendall, *Louis XI* (New York, 1971), p. 128.

29. Helmut G. Koenigsberger, *Estates and Revolutions* (Ithaca, 1971), pp. 51–52.

Louis's efforts to achieve his objectives were marred by a lack of intellectual stability. At times he was impetuous and acted without considering the implications and dangers of a move. On other occasions he was unduly cautious. More serious were his defects in character. He was cunning, deceitful, and cruel, and he surrounded himself by people of like caliber. His chancellor was a man whom Charles VII had removed from Parlement because of his corruption. Once in office the new chancellor utilized his position to sell justice. Louis's most famous adviser, Philippe de Commynes, had deserted his Burgundian master in search of more lucrative rewards. Louis even included in his entourage a cleric who had forged a papal bull permitting the count of Armagnac to marry his sister. To retain the loyalty of this motley crew, Louis showered land, offices, and money on them to a degree hitherto unknown in French history. To some extent he was successful, but neither he nor his servants were of a sort to inspire respect or confidence.

At first Louis reversed his father's policies and sought popularity by instituting tax reforms and giving the estates a greater role in tax administration. He offered to permit the provincial estates to choose any tax they desired to replace the aides and taille. The élus were to be abolished, and the estates were to appoint the necessary officials to levy and collect taxes. Where there were no provincial estates, Louis directed his officials to determine the least objectionable form of tax; but instead of waiting for them to reach a decision, he abolished the aides in the countryside and compensated himself for his loss by increasing the taille.[30] Many towns were exempted from the taille, and some of them were relieved from part of the aides as well. Indeed Louis seemingly shared the popular dislike of the latter tax to such a degree he abolished the Court of Aids as well. Bordeaux was forgiven its rebellion in 1452 and granted exemption from all aides, tailles, and other subsidies. "At the request of the people of the three estates of our *pays* and duchy of Guyenne, and especially of our town of Bordeaux and the *pays* of Bordelais," Louis established a Parlement in that city.[31] When it became necessary in 1463 to impose an additional tax to repay the mortgage the duke of Burgundy held on some towns in the Somme region, he turned to the estates. There were regional assemblies at Montferrand for eastern Languedoil, at Tours for western Languedoil, and at Troyes for Champagne and the surrounding region. In addition, the local estates met in Périgord, Lannes, and the Somme region itself.[32]

Unexplainedly Louis soon abandoned most of these reforms except those dealing with Guyenne. Perhaps he had come to realize that the suppression

---

30. Major, *Representative Institutions*, pp. 50–51.

31. *Ord.*, 15:502. For other decrees on topics in this paragraph, see especially ibid., pp. 377–81, 536–37, 627–30. For the Court of Aids, see Gustave Dupont-Ferrier, *Nouvelles études sur les institutions financières de la France à la fin du Moyen Age* (Paris, 1933), pp. 23–24. See also Henri Sée, *Louis XI et les villes* (Paris, 1891), pp. 224–29.

32. Major, *Representative Institutions*, p. 51.

of the élus and the Court of Aids would seriously weaken the monarchy, perhaps he tired of haggling with the estates over how large the new, single tax should be, or perhaps the estates themselves became disillusioned. Whatever the reasons, the tax machinery that his ancestors had so laboriously constructed was operating in full force again by 1464. Louis convoked only one meeting of the Estates General during his reign, a step he took for propaganda rather than financial purposes, but he held frequent assemblies of the deputies of the towns and of other groups. The avowed purpose of these meetings was to give advice, but the loquacious king often used them as a forum to test his own ideas, and he frequently failed to heed the counsel that was given.[33]

Louis suppressed the estates of Artois when he seized the county following the death of Charles the Bold, but in general he was willing to employ such institutions.[34] No other king, however, was more insistent that he be given all that he demanded. At first the size of his levies were not unreasonable. As late as 1469 the taille was set at 1.2 million livres, only 150,000 more than it had been at the beginning of his reign. But then the amount skyrocketed. By 1471 it reached 1.9 million livres; it peaked in 1481 at 4.6 million livres and then declined somewhat.

Since the size of the aides and gabelle fluctuated very little, Louis's tax revenue grew from about 1.75 million livres to over 4.6 million at the end of his reign, an increase of over two and one-half fold. It is easy to see where all this money went. Louis nearly doubled the size of his army and employed several thousand Swiss mercenaries. He lavished gifts and pensions on those whose services he wanted whether they were his own officials, great nobles, or foreign potentates. Even the cost of his court was half again as large as that of his father who had not himself been noted for his frugality when in his later years he had the wherewithal to spend. It might seem that with so many great fiefs reverting to the crown, the revenue from the domain would have grown enough to alleviate the burden of the people, but at the close of Louis's reign it brought only 100,000 livres because he gave away nearly all the lands that came into his possession, keeping only the titles of duke of Burgundy or count of Provence for himself.[35]

Too often Louis XI has been seen as the creator of an absolute national monarchy, but to accomplish such a feat, it was not enough to impose his will in an arbitrary fashion and extract vast sums from his poorer subjects. It was necessary to create an effective administrative machine and to win support for the new system from substantial segments of the population so that it could be perpetuated after his death. Louis did none of these things.

33. Ibid., pp. 54–58.

34. Charles Hirschauer, *Les Etats d'Artois de leurs origines à l'occupation française, 1340–1640* (Paris, 1923), 2:214–17.

35. A. Spont, "La taille en Languedoc de 1450 à 1515," *Annales du Midi* 2 (1890): 367–70, 498; Petit-Dutaillis, *Histoire* 4:404–06.

His permanent administrative innovations were few. As one recent authority has observed, "Although Louis XI is famous for his high-handed use of the fiscal system, he changed it hardly at all."[36] Certainly he won few genuine supporters for his method of government. Even the townsmen whom he had favored in his tax policies at the expense of the peasant and to whom he had made numerous concessions were not sorry at his passing because he had also handled them roughly upon occasion.[37] When the Estates General met at Tours in January 1484, those who attended devoted most of their efforts to undoing his work and returning to the policies of his father. Louis XI had made Charles VII a popular king, a feat that the poor dauphin of Joan of Arc could never have accomplished for himself.[38]

Two matters were discussed at this meeting of the Estates General that would have profoundly influenced the history of representative assemblies in France if they had been implemented. First, the deputies voted a taille for two years and asked for authority to name officers to participate in its division among the various jurisdictions. At the end of the two-year period, they wanted to meet again to consider the tax question. The chancellor accepted these conditions, but when the period elapsed, the crown proceeded to set the amount of the taille and to apportion it without consulting the Estates General. Second, a suggestion was made that the élus be abolished and that provincial estates be established in all of France to consent to taxes. Some royal councillors succeeded in persuading the deputies from areas where there were estates not to support this proposal since they themselves already had this privilege. As a result of this selfish particularism, no article was included in the cahier to this effect, and the nature of the Renaissance monarchy was not significantly altered by this momentary revival of the Estates General.[39]

3. THE DECENTRALIZED MONARCHY

Thus the monarchy that Charles VII had established gradually hardened as the years went by. Its fiscal and judicial structure was becoming so set that even the Wars of Religion left it intact. One thing was abundantly clear: there was to be no national or central assembly to give consent to taxation although consultative assemblies of various types were to be frequently held

36. Martin Wolfe, *The Fiscal System of Renaissance France* (New Haven, 1972), p. 52.

37. For a recent interpretation of Louis's relations with the towns, see B. Chevalier, "The Policy of Louis XI towards the *Bonnes Villes*: The Case of Tours," in *The Recovery of France in the Fifteenth Century*, ed. P. S. Lewis (New York, 1971), pp. 265–93.

38. Major, *Representative Institutions*, pp. 77–80; Jehan Masselin, *Journal des Etats généraux de France tenus à Tours en 1484 sous le règne de Charles VIII*, ed. A. Bernier (Paris, 1835), pp. 661–703.

39. Masselin, *Journal*, pp. 446–53, 486–89; Major, *Representative Institutions*, pp. 102–05, 112–16.

and royal ordonnances were to stipulate that they were issued upon the advice of many prominent persons. Some parts of France were to have representative assemblies that regularly voted taxes for the crown's and for their own use. Other areas were to have estates that voted taxes for local needs and protested against exactions that the crown imposed by fiat. Still other areas were to have estates that occasionally dealt with tax matters. And finally in parts of France the estates met only on rare occasions when there was need to ratify a treaty, to redact the custom, or to elect deputies to the Estates General.

With the role of the estates in taxation varying so much from one part of France to another, it is not surprising that no clearly defined, generally accepted theory of consent developed. After the decline of the idea of consent to taxation during the reigns of Charles V and Charles VI, it was revived in the 1420s because of the weak position in which Charles VII found himself. In his letters of convocation, he asked that deputies be given full power "to consent" to what would be decided, although his chancellery never developed a rigid formula for making this request.[40] In seeking to impose a tax voted by the estates of Languedoil, he did not hesitate to point out that those who had attended had "consented" to the levy. Even after a central assembly had given its approval, he was careful to tell the commissioners whom he sent to hold the provincial estates to ask those assembled "to consent" to their share.[41] A form of the verb *octroyer*, however, was the one most frequently used in referring to a grant by a central, provincial, or local assembly.[42] Charles also began to give formal recognition of the right of provinces to consent to taxation. Languedoc won this distinction in 1428 and Normandy in 1458,[43] while in 1438 he referred to Haut-Limousin as though its inhabitants had long had this privilege.[44]

40. For example, the deputies to the 1421 Estates General at Clermont were to have "bon et souffisant pouvoir de par vous pour consentir, accorder et conclure tout ce qui en ladicte assemblée sera advisié, conseillié et determiné." Beaucourt, *Histoire*, 1:360. Those who attended the estates of Languedoil in January 1423 were to have "puissance de par vous de consentir et accorder tout ce qui ... sera pour le bien dessus dit advisié, appoinctié et conclut." Ibid., 2:578. Those who attended the estates of Languedoil in August 1423 were to have "tout povoir d'accorder et consentir de vostre part tout ce qui sera advisé et conclud en la dite assemblée." *Bul. de la soc. arch. de Touraine* 4 (1877–1879): 152. Those who attended the estates of eastern Languedoil in April 1435 were to have "puissance d'accorder, consentir et octroyer ce que requerrons." Caillet, *Etude*, pp. 436–37. A. Thomas has published a number of letters of convocation in "Les Etats Généraux sous Charles VII," *Le cabinet historique* 24 (1878): 212–21.

41. See for example, *Bul. de la soc. arch. de Touraine* 4 (1877–79): 152–53, and Thomas, *Les Etats provinciaux*, 2:48, 49.

42. See for example Thomas, "Nouveaux documents," pp. 435–37, 443, 447, 448.

43. Feudal magnates had often recognized the right of the estates to consent to taxes at an earlier date; for example, this privilege was recognized in Aquitaine in 1368 and again in 1395, in Foix in 1391, and in Béarn in 1398. Lewis, *Later Medieval France*, p. 363. For recognition of the right of consent, especially by Charles VII, see Gustave Dupont-Ferrier, *Etudes sur les institutions financières de la France à la fin du Moyen Age* (Paris, 1932), 2:32–33, n.38.

44. Thomas, *Les Etats provinciaux*, 2:94.

Further evidence of the growth of the idea of consent to taxation may be found in the argument that a royal official made before the Court of Aids that "no *aides* or subsidies would be imposed in the future without summoning the three estates."[45] In 1442 some feudal magnates thought it worthwhile to complain about taxes being levied without calling "the princes, prelates, barons and people of the three estates of the kingdom."[46] A few historians and memoir writers picked up the theme, especially after the close of the Hundred Years War had apparently removed the necessity for a standing army and the attendant taxation. One official reported seeing a book predicting that the three estates would eventually be driven to take over the administration of taxes. Thomas Basin argued that the need for an army had ended with the coming of peace and the troops should be disbanded because they oppressed the people.[47] Philippe de Commynes repeatedly stated that neither the king of France nor any other monarch had the right to tax without consent, and he was sharply critical of Louis XI's tax policy.[48]

Others who were less vocal but no less influential held the contrary view. Commynes reported that around 1484 there were some people "of low estate and little virtue who had said then and several times since that it is the crime of lese majesty to speak of assembling the estates because it would diminish the authority of the king."[49] Perhaps some kings felt less strongly on the subject, but Charles VII dispensed with the practice of convoking the Estates General after 1440 and rejected a proposal by some magnates that it be revived.[50] He sought the consent of only the well-established provincial and local estates, some of which specifically had the right to agree to taxation. In making financial requests to the estates, Charles and his successors invariably offered justification for their needs, but what if the estates failed to vote the desired amount, or if unforeseen needs made it advisable to increase taxes after the estates met? Such circumstances rarely occured in Charles's reign after the close of the Hundred Years War, because he was able to reduce taxes at that time and to avoid significant increases thereafter. Louis XI was somewhat less fortunate and much more extravagant. When he was fearful that the estates of Dauphiné would not vote the desired amount in 1465, he instructed his commissioners to use force. When additional funds were needed immediately from Languedoc, he ordered that the tax be collected without waiting to call the estates. Louis justified these acts on the ground of necessity, which he, like so many of his predecessors,

45. Lewis, *Later Medieval France*, p. 343; Thomas, "Les Etats Généraux," p. 203.

46. *Chronique de Mathieu d'Escouchy*, ed. G. du Fresne de Beaucourt (Paris, 1864), 3:75. See also 4:28–29, 58, 62.

47. Lewis, *Later Medieval France*, p. 362; Thomas Basin, *Histoire de Charles VII*, ed. Charles Samaran (Paris, 1944), 2:25–33.

48. Commynes, *Mémoires*, esp. 2:217–22, 289–90.

49. Ibid., p. 219.

50. Enguerran de Monstrelet, *La chronique*, ed. L. Douët-d'Arcq (Paris, 1862), 6:49–50.

believed took precedence over privilege.[51] The concept of privilege itself he never attacked. Indeed at the beginning of his reign he confirmed the privileges of towns, provinces, and other groups without hesitation, and during his regime he was generous in granting new privileges, especially to the towns. When Lorenzo de Medici asked permission to send a galley to Languedoc, Louis regretfully refused to give permission until he had "informed the three estates of my province of Languedoc in order to obtain their consent, because through the privileges that I have granted them no foreign galleys can land in the said *pays*."[52]

The doctrine of evident necessity was invoked by some members of the council during the Estates General of 1484. Strong reaction against the heavy fiscal exactions of Louis XI had led to an insistence on the part of the deputies that they determine the amount of the taille. When they refused to agree to as much as the council thought necessary, some councillors and other royal officials accused the Norman deputies of protecting subjects "from paying to the prince as much as the needs of the state require ... which is contrary to the laws of nations.... We believe that you have the pretension of writing the constitution of an imaginary monarchy and of suppressing our ancient laws." And then they added, "We do not doubt that the king has the right to take the goods of his subjects in order to provide for the dangers and the needs of the state. Otherwise, of what good is it to have a king if one deprives him of the power to bring opponents and disaffected persons to their senses?"[53]

The doctrine of evident necessity was thus opposed to the right of consent. The deputies in 1484 succeeded in winning a reduction of the taille to a third its former amount, eloquent testimony of the extravagance of Louis XI. It is not surprising, however, that the crown did not see fit to convoke the Estates General again, and consent to taxes at the national level ceased. Locally the issue remained, and the question was whether future monarchs would invoke the doctrine of evident necessity so frequently that it would reduce the privilege of consenting to taxes to a farce or whether they would use it only in grave emergencies when there was no time to call a special session of the estates and no way to find money from other sources. The answer was soon given. In May 1485 when the government found that it needed an additional 463,500 livres, it called special sessions of the various provincial estates to ask them to consent to their shares.[54] This became the normal practice of the Renaissance monarchs until well into the reign of Henry III.

51. A. de Reilhac, *Jean de Reilhac, secrétaire, maître des comptes, général des finances et ambassadeur des rois Charles VII, Louis XI, et Charles VIII* (Paris 1886), 1:210–15; Jules Tardif, *Monuments historiques* (Paris, 1866), nos. 2489, 2529. For other examples, see Dupont-Ferrier, *Etudes,* 2:41–42.

52. *Lettres de Louis XI, roi de France,* ed. Joseph Vaësen (Paris, 1895), 5:136;

53. Masselin, *Journal,* pp. 419–21.

54. Major, *Representative Institutions,* 115–16.

Thus when the Renaissance monarchs sought consent to taxation, they did so at the provincial level. In a similar fashion they decentralized their judicial institutions. The medieval monarchs had tried to maintain the essential unity of their justice and administration. As their territory expanded, they had sought to placate the people by establishing *Grand Jours*, or temporary sovereign courts composed partially or entirely of members of the Parlement of Paris. Thus unity had been kept, and the people had been spared the burden of carrying their appeals to Paris. Even Languedoc, with its separate law, language, and culture, had always been kept in theory and generally in practice under the jurisdiction of the Parlement of Paris. It was therefore a marked reversal of medieval policy when Charles issued an ordinance creating a Parlement at Toulouse in March 1420. He professed to take this step because of the great distance and the perils of travel between Languedoc and Poitiers, where he had established his own Parlement during the Anglo-Burgundian occupation of Paris. He could have added with greater truth that he did so because he wanted to ensure the loyalty of the south whose inhabitants had been seemingly on the verge of throwing their lot with the Burgundians some months before. By 1428 this threat had been removed, and over the protests of the estates of Languedoc he merged the Parlement at Toulouse with that of Poitiers, although the distance and probably the dangers of travel were no less.[55]

With the return of Parlement to Paris in 1436, the estates of Languedoc once more pressed for a separate Parlement. Charles initially gave way but then sought a compromise when the Parlement of Paris argued that there should be only one Parlement for the kingdom. Continued solicitations by the estates eventually had their effect, however, and in 1444 a Parlement once more opened its doors at Toulouse to those who sought sovereign justice.[56]

It is clear that Languedoc wanted its own sovereign court and that members of the Parlement of Paris were opposed to reducing their jurisdiction by creating what some called a two-headed monster. But what of Charles? Why did he break with medieval tradition and create a second Parlement that was to survive until the Revolution? His initial step in 1420 may have been an act of desperation necessitated by his precarious position, but by 1444 he could have ignored the estates of Languedoc had he so desired. He and his more immediate advisers were less interested than the Parisian sovereign courts in creating a centralized state. They also had a better idea of what was necessary to establish a stable regime. In an age of relatively small and questionably loyal armies and bureaucracies, the key to

55. Ferdinand Lot and Robert Fawtier, *Histoire des institutions françaises au Moyen Age* (Paris, 1958), 2:469–75; André Viala, *Le Parlement de Toulouse et l'administration royale laïque, 1420–1525 environ* (Albi, 1953), 1:48–58. *Ord.*, 11:59–60.

56. Viala, *Le Parlement de Toulouse*, 1:65–72; Lot and Fawtier, *Histoire*, 2:475–76; *Ord.*, vol. 13, lxx–lxxiv, 231.

monarchical authority lay not in geographic and administrative centralization but in winning the acquiescence of vocal elements of the population to
the regime. By creating a Parlement at Toulouse, Charles bound the
inhabitants of Languedoc more closely to the crown.[57]

In 1437, even before he definitely committed himself to creating a second
Parlement, Charles had ordered that a Court of Aids be established at
Montpellier for Languedoc and part of Guyenne because of the distance of
this region from Paris and the dangers of travel. After the reconquest of
Normandy in 1450, he preserved the Exchequer, from which evolved the
Norman judicial and financial sovereign courts. Neither distance nor danger
can explain the failure to incorporate Normandy fully into the Parisian
administrative system. Charles acted as he did solely because of his desire to
placate the Normans, who had enjoyed considerable autonomy under the
English. Guyenne had also been semiautonomous, and at the request of its
estates, Charles was prepared to establish a Parlement at Bordeaux in 1451.
Even the decision of the Bordelais to invite the English to return the
following year did not sour him so much on the idea of local autonomy as to
prevent him from instituting a Grand Jours there. Finally, in 1453 the
dauphin, Louis, transformed the *Conseil Delphinal*, which was already a
sovereign court, into a Parlement, and three years later Charles gave his
approval to this act. The monarchy had therefore taken a firm course in the
direction of decentralization when Charles died in 1461.[58]

Charles, who was caught between the desires of the provincial estates and
the advice of his sovereign courts and probably plagued by divided opinion
among his councillors, had hesitated before destroying the unity of his
courts. A weak, indecisive man, he had moved cautiously. Louis, on the
other hand, was more given to precipitous actions than to lingering doubts.
Soon after becoming king, he gave Guyenne its Parlement, and at some
point during his reign established in Normandy a second Court of Aids, this
time seated in Caen.[59] The death of Charles the Bold offered him his biggest
opportunity to put his institutional concepts into practice because both the
duchy and county of Burgundy came into his hands. He recognized the
right of the estates of the duchy to consent to taxation and transformed the
ducal judicial and administrative organs of government into a Parlement
and a Chamber of Accounts. He also promised to give the county of
Burgundy a Parlement in response to the request of the estates.[60]

The process of decentralization was furthered in other ways. Charles

---

57. For a discussion of the meaning of "centralization" and the strength of the French
monarchy, see B. Guenée, "Espace et état dans la France de bas Moyen Age," *Annales*
23 (1968): 744–58. As noted in the introduction, I do not fully accept his definitions.

58. Gustave Dupont-Ferrier, *Les origines et le premier siècle de la Chambre ou Cour des Aides de Paris*
(Paris, 1933), pp. 64–67. Lot and Fawtier, *Histoire*, 2:283–84, 482–83, 490–93, 498.

59. Dupont-Ferrier, *Les origines*, pp. 66–67; Lot and Fawtier, *Histoire*, 2:483–84.

60. Sée, *Louis XI*, p. 279.

divided the older part of the royal domain into four sections, each with a treasurer, but he retained a central Chamber of the Treasury at Paris. As time passed these sections, called *généralités*, were subdivided. New généralités were created when feudal dependencies escheated to the crown. In 1454 Charles decided to hold local assemblies of the estates to codify the customs in the various provinces and bailiwicks. Once these customs were definitely established and put into writing, it became virtually impossible for a common law to develop for the entire country by any means short of revolution. Charles even turned over to the diocesan clergy the responsibility of electing bishops, but these positions were too valuable to let escape, and bishoprics became among the most valuable gifts at the disposal of his successors.[61]

4. THE VALOIS KINGS, 1483–1562

The form that the monarchy had begun to take during the reign of Charles VII became cemented during that of Charles VIII and especially Louis XII. Charles VIII was a sickly, slightly deformed child of mediocre intelligence when he came to the throne, and for nearly a decade the government was in the hands of his able older sister, Anne de Beaujeu, and her husband. When he did take over the government, Charles made concessions to the English, Spanish, and the Habsburgs to ensure peace on France's borders and then, in 1494, embarked on the Italian wars. The effort to conquer Naples has generally been regarded as utter folly by modern historians, but on the domestic scene Charles was relatively successful. The taille had to be increased, but in only one year did it exceed 3 million livres, a figure below what his father had assessed during the last seven years he had ruled.[62]

In 1498 the kindly, popular Charles died suddenly, and his cousin Louis, duke of Orleans, came to the throne. A combination of hardship and self-indulgence had aged the new monarch more than his thirty-five years warranted. In spite of his poor health, he managed to carry on the war in Italy with initial success and to provide France with the most efficient

---

61. Major, *Representative Institutions*, p. 6.

62. Historians have been so preoccupied with the Italian wars that the government of France under Charles VIII and Louis XII has never been adequately studied, but see Yvonne Labande-Mailfert, *Charles VIII et son milieu, 1470–1498* (Paris, 1975); Henry Lemonnier, *Histoire de France*, ed. E. Lavisse (Paris, 1911), 5, pt. 1:133–48; Wolfe, *Fiscal System*, pp. 59–61; and Major, *Representative Institutions*, pp. 117–20. To the assemblies cited here should be added the meeting of the three estates at Moulins in June–July 1495. Louis Caillet, *Les ducs de Bourbonnais et la ville de Lyon* (Moulins, 1912), pp. 61–72. Figures on the taille cited here and in the following paragraph are from A. Spont, "La taille en Languedoc de 1450 à 1515," *Annales du Midi* 2 (1890): 505, 509. It is probable that Burgundy, Picardy, Dauphiné, Brittany, and Provence were not included in these figures. See P. Dognon, "La taille en Languedoc de Charles VII à Francois Ier," *Annales du Midi* 3 (1891): 347–49.

government that it enjoyed during the Renaissance. Louis made every effort to keep taxes low. The taille fluctuated around the two million mark until 1512 when military reverses compelled him to increase it. He is supposed to have forgone the customary gift for his joyous accession to the throne and to have halted the collection of a special tax to suppress a revolt in Genoa when the uprising petered out, an honest act that had no precedent for over a century and a half. Although Louis made no move to revive the Estates General to consider tax matters, both he and Charles VIII held frequent consultative assemblies, and both respected the right of provincial estates to consent to taxes where this right existed. Other privileges were also honored, laws were enforced, and the kingdom enjoyed unparalleled tranquility and prosperity.[63]

The idea of provincial sovereign courts was so imbedded in their minds and those of their advisers that when the estates of Burgundy wanted to suppress their new Parlement as an economy measure in 1484, Charles VIII assumed the burden of paying its judges. As governor of Normandy Louis had become aware that the practice of holding meetings of the Exchequer for a month or six weeks at irregular intervals every year or two was inadequate to provide justice. On becoming king, he therefore summoned some Normans to Paris where he offered to give them a Parlement.[64] "The king is your debtor, he owes you justice,"[65] Louis's chancellor declared several times in his presence. Love of tradition and the realization by some barons and prelates who participated in the Exchequer that the plan would deprive them of their role caused those present to hesitate to endorse Louis's proposal. They asked that the estates be convoked, and when this was done the deputies endorsed the idea of a permanent sovereign court but asked that it retain the traditional name of Exchequer.[66] After giving Normandy the court in 1499, Louis made a similar present to Provence two years later.

Had Charles VIII and Louis XII created provincial sovereign courts because of their weakness? Obviously not. They had often taken the initiative in establishing and preserving these institutions. Nevertheless, by accepting, nay even encouraging, provincial autonomy and by respecting the privileges of their subjects, Charles VIII and Louis XII strengthened the monarchy. People with as little historical association with the crown as those of Dauphiné and Provence and those who had been devoted to their dukes as the Burgundians learned to become loyal subjects. In an age when the crown had neither an adequate army nor a bureaucracy to compel obedience, this accomplishment was of the highest importance. Louis XII, especially, came to be considered an ideal monarch. Named "the father of

63. Major, *Representative Institutions*, pp. 117–25; Wolfe, *Fiscal System*, pp. 61–66.

64. Guenée, *Espace et état*, pp. 756–57; Amable Floquet, *Historie du Parlement de Normandie* (Rouen, 1840), 1:317–25.

65. Floquet, *Histoire*, 1:325–26.

66. Ibid., pp. 326–33.

his people" around the middle of his reign, he was rightfully famous for his efforts to spare his subjects from taxes, to render them justice, and to provide them with security. Small wonder his praises were sung throughout the sixteenth century. Even after Henry IV had made his great contribution, there were still cries to return to the days of Louis XII. His role, like that of Louis IX, was more to make the monarchy beloved than to change its character. Louis XII was never a candidate for sainthood—a man who divorced a saintly wife and called a schismatic council to suspend the pope could hardly hope for such an honor—but his contribution to the monarchy, like that of his godly predecessor, nonetheless exceeded that of the currently much-admired activists whose harsh measures brought reactions from their people.

Louis XII died early in 1515 worrying, it is said, that "this big boy," his son-in-law and successor, Francis I, "will spoil everything."[67] His concern was at least partly justified. Expenses mounted. Francis continued his predecessors' costly wars in Italy and spent far more on his châteaux and his court. Pensions multiplied; Swiss, Germans, and England's Henry VIII shared the royal largesse. To meet these demands the taille was gradually increased from about 2.4 million to 5.3 million livres during the course of the reign, and the gabelle was tripled in northern and central France.[68] Still this was not enough, and Francis sought to tap those who usually escaped fiscal exactions. Sometimes he won papal permission to levy décimes on the clergy, but most often he turned to assemblies of the individual dioceses to obtain consent.[69] When these sources proved inadequate, he sought the assistance of the closed towns. In 1538 he asked them for money to support 20,000 infantry, and in 1543 he increased his request to 50,000 for six months. Thereafter, there were years when the closed towns were asked for nothing and years when the tax was less heavy, but the figure set in 1543 came near to being a norm.[70]

Francis's capture at Pavia and the need to pay his ransom provided an opportunity to seek financial assistance from the nobility. When John II had fallen into the hands of the English in 1356, nobles, like others, had been assessed without consent, but so firmly entrenched had their privileges become by the 1520s that Francis held local or provincial assemblies to seek their consent, although ransoming a lord was among the most accepted obligations of a vassal. In one such meeting he told the nobility of the Ile-de-France that he did not want them to pay the taille; he explained, "I am a gentleman; it is the principal title I bear and the one I esteem the most. As a

67. Jean-J. Clamageran, *Histoire de l'impôt en France* (Paris, 1868), 2 : 101.

68. Ibid., 102–06, 110–12, 117–21; Wolfe, *Fiscal System*, pp. 99–100.

69. Roger Doucet, *Les institutions de la France au XVIᵉ siècle* (Paris, 1948), 2 :835; *Ord. François Iᵉʳ*, 8 :310–13, 446–50. Countless references to dioceses giving consent can be found in *Actes François Iᵉʳ*. See for example, 4: nos. 11,580, 12,536, 12,707, 12,708, 13,161–63, 13,688.

70. Clamageran, *Histoire*, 2 : 113; Wolfe, *Fiscal System*, 116.

gentleman and your king, I speak to you as gentlemen. I pray you ... to offer me such gifts and presents that will enable me to know the love and affection you bear me."[71] In response the nobles of the Ile-de-France offered a tenth of the revenue from their fiefs.

In spite of these efforts Francis was faced with constant deficits. To meet his needs he turned to expedients. He sold part of the domain, the crown's jewels, and those of the church. More serious for the future, he began to create needless offices to sell, and established the *Parties Casuelles* to handle the transactions. When borrowing was necessary, the king could either turn to foreign bankers who charged exorbitant rates, or he could demand that his officials, wealthy burghers, or some other group loan him the required sum. If the latter method was used, Francis usually paid no interest, for usury was a sin and it was the duty of his subjects to provide money in emergencies. It was therefore advantageous to king and subjects alike to have the city of Paris borrow the needed money on its credit and pay a relatively modest interest of $8\frac{1}{3}$ percent that was guaranteed by taxes designated for this purpose. The merchant received interest, and the king paid lower rates than he would have to foreigners. In this fashion the *rentes sur l'hôtel de ville* were born, and a class of persons partly supported by monetary investments came into being.[72]

The immediate importance of these revenue-raising innovations should not be exaggerated. The number of offices Francis created was limited, and his borrowing was surprisingly restricted. During his thirty-two-year reign, his revenue merely doubled, growing at an average annual rate of less than 2.2 percent. A slow rise in prices justified this increase, and a generally prosperous economy would have enabled the nation to carry the burden easily if the well-to-do had paid their share of the taxes.[73]

Francis's other innovations were also less striking than they have sometimes been depicted. In 1523 he created a special treasury at Paris to which royal revenue not needed for authorized local expenses was sent. Previously each financial jurisdiction had retained the money it collected until it was moved on royal order to a place where it was needed or turned over to creditors who presented the proper papers. This experiment with a centralized treasury was abandoned because it was not successful, and in 1542 Francis divided the country into seventeen généralités that became "the main unit for fiscal administration." The treasurers were told to reside in their respective généralités rather than in Paris, and the financial system became more decentralized than before.[74]

Francis's experiment with a more centralized fiscal administration was motivated by the desire to develop a war chest reserve, not by any impulse

71. Major, *Representative Institutions*, p. 138.
72. Lemonnier, *Histoire de France*, 5, pt. 1:239–42; Wolfe, *Fiscal System*, pp. 80–81, 91–93, 101–03.
73. Wolfe, *Fiscal System*, p. 99.
74. Ibid., pp. 77–97.

toward centralization for its own sake. Indeed he continued the practice of creating sovereign courts in the new territories that he added to the crown. When he confiscated the principality of Dombes from the duke of Bourbon in 1523, he gave the inhabitants a Parlement. Brittany and Savoy also received Parlements, and Chambers of Accounts were established at Montpellier and Rouen.[75]

Francis saw as little need for the Estates General as he did for centralized courts, and no meetings were convoked during his reign. After 1517 he did not assemble the deputies of the towns, and there was a decline in the use of other types of consultative assemblies. Nevertheless Francis's dislike for central assemblies should not be exaggerated. He apparently looked upon them as being time-consuming and useless under most circumstances, but he was not doctrinally opposed to them. In 1515 and again in 1523, he specifically gave his mother the authority to convoke the Estates General when he appointed her regent.[76] In addition, he accepted the existence of the provincial and local estates, recognized their right to give consent to taxation, and generally respected their privileges. When he took the principality of Dombes from the duke of Bourbon, he promised the inhabitants that they would have to pay only those taxes that they consented to in their estates, and he made a similar guarantee to the Bretons when their duchy was finally reunited with the crown.[77] His decision to tax the clergy regularly led to frequent assemblies of the first estate to give consent, especially at the diocesan level. The nature of the monarchy that had been inaugurated by Charles VII and had become firmly established under Charles VIII and Louis XII was not significantly altered. Glamorous and powerful as Francis seemed to his contemporaries, one can only agree with Roger Doucet, the most careful student of his reign, that he had "neither the strength of mind nor the steadfast will to apply himself to a systematic transformation of society and institutions."[78]

Henry II (1547–59) was even more unlikely to make fundamental changes than his father. Less intelligent and less self-confident, any new policies he inaugurated were adopted more by necessity than by design. He continued the costly wars in Italy and made little effort to curb the expense of the court or the size of the pensions. Prices in the 1550s rose more sharply than in the earlier period and explain much of the increased costs of government. Under such circumstances Henry began to borrow heavily in Lyons and Italy and to issue new rentes on the hôtel-de-ville of Paris. He also increased the taille and sought new sources of revenue.[79]

75. *Ord. François Ier*, 3:241–44, 311–14, 7:177–79; *Actes François Ier*, 4: no. 13,424: Doucet, *Les institutions*, 1:210–25.

76. Major, *Representative Institutions*, pp. 126–40.

77. *Ord. François Ier*, 3:312; 6:275–79.

78. Roger Doucet, *Etude sur le gouvernement de François Ier* (Paris, 1921), 1:349.

79. Wolfe, *Fiscal System*, pp. 104–13.

One potential source of taxes was to raise the gabelle in southwestern France to the same level as in the north. Francis I had begun to move in this direction in 1537 but had initially desisted when he had met strong protests. When he and his son renewed the effort in the 1540s, there were revolts, the last of which was brutally suppressed. The government then sought an accommodation, and in return for substantial sums it first reduced and finally in 1554 abolished the gabelle in southwestern France. Negotiations leading to these agreements caused increased activity of the estates in Guyenne and a revival of those along its northern border. Regional assemblies of Poitou, Saintonge, Angoumois, Haut- and Bas-Limousin, Haute- and Basse-Marche, and La Rochelle, where the estates had not been active in tax matters for generations, were frequently held. Périgord and, less often, other parts of Guyenne participated.[80]

In 1549 Henry created one important new tax, the *taillon*, in response to complaints that the underpaid troops had lived off the countryside. The taillon, which was collected after the fashion of the taille, was designated to augment substantially the military's pay; in return the soldiers were forbidden to require food, lodging, and other services from the inhabitants.[81]

In spite of new and higher taxes, increased borrowing, and expedients, Henry's financial situation steadily deteriorated. The crisis came in August 1557 when the French army was defeated by the Spanish at Saint-Quentin. Paris itself was threatened, and there was a desperate need for an enlarged army. Henry sought contributions from the closed towns, but they proved uncooperative. He then turned to a central assembly to explain to his subjects his desperate needs. The composition of the assembly in Paris in January 1558 was somewhat similar to those of Charles VII: members of the first two orders were generally individually summoned and the towns rather than the bailiwicks deputed for the third estate. Here the crown asked for a loan of 6 million livres, one-third of which was to come from the clergy and the remainder from the closed towns. At first there was resistance, but the news of the capture of Calais created sufficient enthusiasm to persuade those present to acquiesce to the royal desires. There remained the slow and sometimes painful task of negotiating the details of the loan with the individual towns.[82]

The peace that followed did no more than slow the decline in the fiscal position of the crown, and the accidental death of Henry II in 1559 led in turn to the reigns of his three sons, none of whom combined the intelligence, the energy, and the will to rule effectively. In desperation the government turned again to a central assembly in 1560. This time those who attended were elected in bailiwick assemblies as for the estates of 1484. It soon became

80. Tyrrell, *History of the Estates*, pp. 58–64, 144–45.
81. Doucet, *Les institutions*, 2:575–76.
82. Major, *Representative Institutions*, pp. 144–47.

evident that the three estates would make no financial concessions on the grounds that their constituents had not authorized them to do so. In the closing meeting the chancellor, Michel de L'Hôpital, expressed the hope that the taille could be eventually reduced to the same level as under Louis XII. To accomplish this it would be necessary to redeem the domain, recover alienated taxes, and pay the crown debts, feats that could be achieved only if the people made new fiscal sacrifices. L'Hôpital therefore asked each estate for a special six-year contribution and offered to permit them to name a committee to oversee its collection.[83] In short, he proposed to return to the days of the captivity of John II when the privileged paid taxes and the estates participated in their collection.

The Estates General of 1560 was followed by a meeting at Pontoise the following year in which the deputies were to be empowered to respond to the crown's financial proposals. Nevertheless the third estate was willing to offer only its goodwill, and the nobility proved no more generous. Both estates, however, expressed their willingness to see the crown solve its financial problems at the expense of the church. Thoroughly alarmed, the clergy signed the contract of Poissy, which provided the king with a substantial sum for a period of years. In return, they were given the right to assess and collect the tax and to have syndics to defend their interests. Furthermore their willingness to made financial concessions led to regular meetings of their order from that time until the Revolution. If the secular orders had proved equally generous, might they not have obtained similar privileges? Might not the Estates General, even at this late date, have become an integral part of the government just as the assemblies of the clergy? One can never know, but it is certain that the secular estates gained little by their refusal to cooperate, because in September 1561 the crown imposed a wine tax on them anyway. This tax was submitted to the provincial and local estates for consideration and marks the last new levy that was imposed before the outbreak of the Wars of Religion the following year. But before considering that costly series of conflicts it is necessary to demonstrate how the provincial estates became increasingly important during the Renaissance.[84]

83. J. R. Major, *The Estates General of 1560* (Princeton, 1951), pp. 101–04.

84. J. R. Major, "The Third Estate in the Estates General of Pontoise, 1561," *Speculum* 29 (1954): 474–76. The crown tried to associate the Estates General with the wine tax in the decree that established it but made no specific claim that the deputies had given their consent. Isambert, 14: 118–19. The procès-verbal of the third estate, Bibl. du Sénat, ms. 379, reveals clearly that they had not done so.

3

THE GREAT PAYS D'ETATS

THE DISTINCTION SO OFTEN MADE BETWEEN THE PAYS D'ÉTATS AND THE PAYS d'élections is inadequate to describe the situation in Renaissance France, for in many provinces the estates and the élections existed side by side. Yet the distinction is not altogether meaningless. In the pays d'états committees and officials appointed by the estates apportioned and collected the taxes that they voted, but in provinces with both estates and élections, royal officials generally performed this duty. This meant that if the estates repeatedly refused to vote the desired amount in a province in which the estates were responsible for collecting taxes, the king had no choice but to do without or to direct the officials of the estates to collect the desired sum anyway. It is very unlikely that these officials would refuse to obey a strong monarch who gave such an order, but it is equally probable that they would proceed in such a halfhearted fashion that little additional money would be collected. Where royal officials gathered the taxes, on the other hand, it was much easier to obtain revenue that had not been voted by the estates.

In addition to sums designated for the crown, the provincial estates voted taxes to pay per diem allowances to those who attended their sessions, the salaries of their officials, the costs of their deputations to the king and council, and the expenses of pleading before the sovereign courts. They also appropriated money to protect their province during times of trouble, repair roads and bridges, make rivers navigable, support educational institutions, finance the publication of books, give presents to royal officials who defended their interests before the crown, and a host of other things. Some kings tried to curb these expenditures so as not to overburden the people, and it was obviously easier for them to do so in regions in which their officials, and not those of the estates, collected taxes. Hence in provinces in which there were no élections, the estates were in a better position both to withstand royal pressure and to follow their own inclinations than they were elsewhere. They will therefore be treated separately.

This chapter and the three that follow show how the estates were born or reborn during the Renaissance; how their composition and procedures assumed clearly defined forms; how they came to appoint syndics to protect their interests and committees to act in their name when they were not in session; how they developed their own bureaucracies, established archives, and apportioned and collected taxes; and how they provided increasing services to the people of their districts. In short, we will consider how the estates flowered in over half of France during the Renaissance.

1. THE ESTATES OF LANGUEDOC

Representative assemblies first appeared in France in the south, but it was not until Philip VI decided to hold separate meetings of the three estates of his northern and southern provinces during the winter of 1345–46 that the estates of Languedoc were born. At first seven seneschalsies were included, but by the terms of the treaty of Brétigny (1360), France lost part of these lands, and the boundaries of Languedoc were restricted to the three large seneschalsies of Toulouse, Carcassonne, and Beaucaire (later Nîmes). Unfortunately from the standpoint of the development of a stable institutional structure, the crown did not henceforth rely solely on the three estates of the province. Instead it often convoked assemblies of the towns, of the estates of the individual seneschalsies, and of other groups as the situation dictated. As a result, none of these types of assemblies acquired definite compositions or procedures, nor did they develop permanent bureaucracies, although in October 1356 the deputies to the provincial estates were precocious enough to elect tax collectors, auditors for their financial accounts, and a standing committee to act for them between sessions. (See chap. 1, sec. 1.)

The ad hoc quality of these assemblies persisted until 1393. During these years they continued to nominate tax officials who had to be approved by the royal governor, but it is probable that these appointments were made for each new tax, a procedure that continued to delay the development of a full-blown bureaucracy although the same person might be chosen year after year. The idea of having a standing committee to act for the estates between their sessions also appears to have been forgotten. Then, between February 1393 and December 1417, all types of assemblies in Languedoc went into an eclipse. Taxes were collected without consent, and tax officials were appointed by the crown without consultation. Any type of assembly was exceptional, and if one took place, it was more likely to be designed for local defense than to raise money for the king. Meanwhile another type of royal official, the élus, had been established in Languedoc in 1360, as in other parts of France, to collect the indirect taxes that were imposed to pay the ransom of King John. Subsequent developments are not altogether clear, but eventually the diocese that served as the jurisdiction of the élus emerged as the basic territorial unit for taxes in Languedoc above the towns and communities.[1]

---

1. Paul Dognon, *Les institutions politiques et administratives du pays de Languedoc du XIIIe siècle aux Guerres de Religion* (Toulouse, 1895), pp. 275–83, 364–71; Henri Gilles, *Les Etats de Languedoc au XVe siècle* (Toulouse, 1965), pp. 27–28.

When the dauphin, Charles, decided in 1420 to revive the earlier royal practice of using the estates to win public support for his policies, he persisted in appointing the tax receivers for the seneschalsies but negotiated with the three estates over the amount that they should pay and permitted them to determine the nature of the levy. Representatives of the estates participated once more in the division of direct taxes among the seneschalsies. The seneschalsies then chose deputies to divide taxes among the dioceses, where in turn they were divided among the towns and communities. Not until around 1454 did the estates take the obvious step of bypassing the seneschalsies and apportioning taxes among the dioceses. Thus it was only in the latter half of the fifteenth century that the familiar structure of representative assemblies in Languedoc took form, and the estates of the seneschalsies that once had been so important began to wither away, although they never altogether disappeared. When there was urgent need for speed, the crown occasionally turned to them as late as the seventeenth century to vote a tax, and when the provincial estates were in session, the deputies from this or that seneschalsy sometimes assembled to deal with local problems. Nevertheless during the course of the fifteenth century, the provincial estates were gradually able to assert their claim to be the sole tax-consenting agency under normal circumstances and to limit the diocesan assemblies to the role of tax apportioning institutions.[2]

The provincial estates were also faced with the problem of obtaining and retaining the crown's recognition of their right to consent to taxes. Whatever progress toward this goal that they had made during the 1350s had been lost by the close of the century. When Charles VII turned to the estates in 1420, he probably saw in their approval of a tax more a temporary propaganda device to ease the problem of the tax collectors than the first step toward the establishment of the right to give consent. Not until 1428 when the three estates complained about a tax that their governor levied without their approval did Charles forbid anyone to make impositions without his consent and that of the estates.[3]

When his position became much stronger following his reconciliation with Burgundy, his coronation, and the recapture of Paris, he and his advisers were in a position to dream of returning to the days of Charles VI when taxes had been levied without consulting the estates. After 1436 he did not summon the estates of Languedoil primarily to deal with his financial problems, and by 1443 he had become so irritated at the persistent refusal of the three estates of Languedoc to vote the sum he asked that he rejected unofficially most of the articles in their cahier and indicated that he had had enough of such assemblies because they were very expensive and damaging to him and to the province. The three estates caught the hint and offered to

2. Dognon, *Les institutions politiques*, pp. 281–92; Gilles, *Les Etats*, pp. 29–40.
3. Gilles, *Les Etats*, pp. 44–47. *HL*, 10, 2079–83.

substitute a tax called the *équivalent* for the aides the king wanted. Equally important, they voted their governor 16,000 livres and other royal officials a total of 5,000 livres in the hope that they would persuade the weak-willed king to change his mind. They did, and most of the requests of the estates were now granted, including the creation of a Parlement at Toulouse, the abolition of the élus, which gave the estates almost exclusive control over the apportioning of taxes, and a promise to retain the estates with all their liberties and privileges. After a period of some fluctuation, the équivalent became a tax on the sale of meat, fish, and wine that was farmed under the direction of the estates and designed to yield 73,000 livres per year for the king. If the farm exceeded this figure, the three estates used the surplus to reduce the taille. If it fell short, they had to make good the deficit, usually by increasing the taille.[4]

Although the concept of consenting to the équivalent was retained, it became in reality a fixed tax that could not be altered by the estates, but the estates could and did refuse to vote the additional taxes that were requested. Louis XI succeeded in establishing a minimum of 187,975 livres for the équivalent and the taille together, but as his needs quickly surpassed this figure, he asked for additional sums which he insisted that the estates vote. His demands reached 534,000 livres in 1483, but following his death that same year, taxes were reduced. Only 295,867 livres were voted in 1491 at the eve of the Italian wars. Louis's successors did succeed in adding to the basic minimum that the estates must vote and these taxes had become fixed at 304,000 livres by the close of the reign of Henry II.[5]

This situation has caused historians to see the late fifteenth and early sixteenth centuries as an era of the decadence of the estates, but the reverse was more nearly true. It was during these years that the estates lost their medieval ad hoc character and became a true institution with reasonably well-defined membership, duties, and procedures. The representation of the clergy in the estates during the sixteenth century consisted of the archbishops and bishops of the twenty-two dioceses, but it was not until 1469 that the archbishop of Auch and the bishop of Lombez were excluded and the bishop of Pamiers was permitted to participate as late as 1506. At one time abbots adorned the assembly, and it was only in 1481 that the last of their number attended. Also, some cathedral chapters once sent deputies, but this practice ceased at about the same time. If a bishop could not attend, he usually deputed his vicar general, but sometimes laymen were given procurations until the practice was forbidden in 1502. Thus it was only around the turn of the century that the first estate assumed its familiar and unique form.[6]

A rather large number of barons were summoned during the Middle

4. Gilles, *Les Etats*, pp. 54–56 n.71, 196–210, 309–18. *HL*, 9:1148–52.

5. Gilles, *Les Etats*, pp. 63–70; *HL*, 11:108–09, 146, 323; P. Dognon, "La taille en Languedoc de Charles VII à François Ier," *Annales du Midi*, 3 (1891): 343.

6. Gilles, *Les Etats*, pp. 81–83.

Ages, but their record of attendance was so poor that some of them were dropped from the rolls. In the more distant regions, they adopted the practice of taking turns participating. As a result, by the sixteenth century attendance by the barons or their proctors rarely exceeded that of the clergy, although as late as 1612 the estates had to decree that the number of nobles who participated must be reduced to twenty-two.[7] The third estate, with the inevitable exceptions, came to be represented by delegations from the episcopal cities and the towns whose turn it was to stand for the other localities in their respective dioceses. It was probably during the reign of Louis XI that the custom of the third estate's having the same number of votes as the other orders combined was adopted, although deputations to court had assumed this form sometime before.[8]

The unique composition of the estates was of profound significance. The exclusion of all the clergy except the prelates and all but a small fraction of the leading nobles made them highly aristocratic. The presence of the towns did little to alter this situation because they were dominated by bourgeois patricians who nearly always sent their *consuls*. On the other hand, the fact that the deputies of the third estate had as many votes as the other two orders combined gave them an enviable position that was enhanced because their attendance record was nearly perfect, while the nobles and clergy did so poorly that frequent legislation was necessary requiring them to attend or to send proctors. Since the estates adopted and retained the practice of deliberating and voting in a single chamber, the third estate theoretically enjoyed a preponderance of power, although its potential strength was mitigated by the influence the prelates could wield among its members.

When the estates met, the crown was represented by commissioners especially appointed for the purpose. Included among their number was the governor or lieutenant general and several high officials in the provincial financial administration. Their principal role was to explain the king's financial needs and to do their best to see that the estates quickly gave him all he wanted. This necessitated an appearance at the opening of the session, but thereafter they usually dealt with deputations the estates sent to them. As a result, the deputies were left free to have their own president and to function as they desired. It was not until the early sixteenth century that the archbishop of Narbonne was recognized as the president of the estates by virtue of his office. In his absence the archbishop of Toulouse presided if he were present. If not, the senior bishop from the standpoint of the date of his coronation was given the honor.[9]

The deputies took measures to protect their deliberations from outside interference. Royal officials were eventually forbidden to serve as proctors of

7. Ibid., pp. 85–94; *Loix municipales et économiques de Languedoc*, ed. Jean Albisson (Montpellier, 1780), 1:350.

8. Gilles, *Les Etats*, pp. 94–111.

9. Ibid., pp. 112–13, 128–35.

the nobles, as deputies of the towns, and as officers of the estates. In 1555 the king himself forbade Parlement to interfere in their affairs. The deputies voted to take an oath to keep their deliberations secret, and from 1522 they decreed that none of their members should reside in taverns for fear that too much wine would loosen their tongues in the presence of strangers. The following year Francis I granted the deputies the privilege of being free from arrest while they were in session. In 1559 they adopted the secret ballot to replace a show of hands. Thus, as the sixteenth century progressed, their autonomy became more and more assured.[10]

The three estates were slow to develop a bureaucracy. At first the duties of clerk were performed in part by a dependent of the presiding prelate and in part by the secretary of the royal commissioners. Not until 1455 is there a reference to an official clerk of the estates, and only in the 1480s did he assume the duties that had been performed by the secretary of the royal commissioners. In 1480 the three estates began to have a syndic to defend their interests before the king's council and the sovereign courts and to perform various administrative duties when they were not in session. Soon additional syndics and lawyers had to be appointed to assist him in his growing duties, and the seneschalsies named syndics of their own. Treasurers were appointed in the early sixteenth century to administer the money allocated for the estates, and the bureaucracy continued to expand thereafter as the estates became increasingly active. In 1486 the deputies took the important step of establishing an archive in Montpellier so that records would be available to enable them to defend their privileges, to support their constant litigation, and to assist in the administration of the province.[11] It is a striking fact that so many of these developments took place during the reign of Louis XI, who treated the estates in a more arbitrary fashion than any of his successors did. Little did he realize that by permitting the three estates to develop clearly defined privileges and to play an essential administrative role, he was ensuring them a permanent place in the Renaissance monarchy and placing them in a position to check the authority of the crown.

Since the estates of Languedoc consented to taxation and held the primary responsibility of dealing with the crown, there is no need to trace the history of the diocesan estates or tell how they came to appoint syndics and develop small bureaucracies. Some general idea of their compositions, however, is in order. The local bishop, or in practice more often his vicar-general, was usually the presiding officer in each of the diocesan estates and the only representative of the clergy. Some nobles had had a right to attend the estates during the Middle Ages, but they soon lost interest in an institution that served primarily to divide the diocesan tax, which had been

10. James E. Brink, *The Estates of Languedoc, 1515–1560* (Ann Arbor, University Microfilms, 1974), pp. 111–37; *Ord. François Ier*, 3:254–55.
11. Gilles, *Les Etats*, pp. 114–27, 136–37, 162–64.

set by the estates of Languedoc, among the parishes. Lack of interest led to the failure to attend, and this negligence in turn led to the loss of the right to participate in many instances. Here and there a few nobles still took part in the estates, or claimed the right to do so, but with several exceptions, they did not play an appreciable role. The third estate was dominated by the *consuls* of the principal towns. In the civil diocese of Toulouse, for example, there were about two hundred communities, but only ten master towns were represented in the diocesan estates. These towns took turns providing one of the deputies of the diocese in the estates of Languedoc. The syndic served as the other. The town of Toulouse did not participate in the diocesan estates but enjoyed separate representation in the provincial assembly. In Lavour the bourgeois-patricians of the larger towns asserted their control in a somewhat different fashion. Five master towns sent two deputies each to the diocesan assembly, three sent one each, and twenty-four smaller localities took turns being represented, two enjoying this privilege each year. The delegation to the estates of Languedoc consisted of the first *consul* of Lavour, the syndic of the diocese, and a deputy named by one of the five principal towns who took turns exercising this right.[12]

Although most of the diocesan assemblies followed the pattern of either Toulouse or Lavour, four retained the characteristics of assemblies of the three estates. The bishop, two other ecclesiastics, and the deputies of two chapters had the right to attend the estates of Albi for the clergy. Seven nobles held seats and 11 master towns and 111 other communities were invited to participate, a surprisingly large number, but the *consuls* of the master towns predominated the activities of the third estate. The remaining three—Vivarais, Velay, and Gévaudan—were bailiwicks dependent in the seneschalsy of Beaucaire and Nîmes, but they nevertheless enjoyed a slightly more independent status than the typical diocesan estates. No clergyman as such had a seat in the estates of Vivarais, but the bishop of Viviers was one of the ten *barons de tour* who took turns going to the estates of Languedoc. Thirteen towns alternated in providing the deputy of the third estate. The estates of Gévaudan consisted of eight ecclesiastics, twenty nobles, eight of whom took turns representing their order in the provincial estates, and the *consuls* or deputies of eighteen towns. Velay was unique in the minimal participation of the third estate. Only the *consuls* of Le Puy joined with ten ecclesiastics and eighteen barons in the meetings of the estates. Excluded elements sought admission to the diocesan estates especially during the Wars of Religion and the Fronde, but in the long run they had very little success. Once the essential structure of the estates took form during the late fifteenth and early sixteenth centuries, there were few permanent changes. As in the estates of Languedoc, the diocesan estates usually deliberated together and voted by head.

12. For the composition of the diocesan estates, see J. R. Major, *The Deputies to the Estates General of Renaissance France* (Madison, 1960), pp. 89–95.

Thus by the early sixteenth century, representative institutions in Languedoc had assumed or nearly assumed their final form. The three estates were in a strong position to defend their interests against encroachments from within the province and from the crown. Oddly enough one of the most serious challenges to the estates came from the magistrates in the Parlement of Toulouse, although Parlement had been created by the crown at their request. The cause of this dispute grew out of the fact that Roman or written law provided the basis for the legal and property laws of the province as in most of southern France. The feudal regime had never fully penetrated into the region, and land, except for benefices, was considered to be allodial unless it could be proven to be seigneurial. As a result, only benefices and seigneurial lands escaped the taille; the remaining holdings, constituting perhaps as much as 90 percent of the province, paid this tax regardless of the status of the owner. Tax digests or cadastres were prepared in each diocese that indicated the relative earning power of every piece of taxable land, and it was upon the basis of this information that the taille was apportioned.[13]

In Languedoc and elsewhere where the taille was *réelle* rather than *personnelle* (that is, where the status of the land rather than the status of the owner determined whether it was taxed), the privileged orders sought to obtain the exemptions accorded to those of their status in northern France. To their credit the nobility made little effort in this direction, although they acquired a large amount of common land on which they were taxed. In one region near Toulouse they owned 51.1 percent of the taxable land in 1786 and paid 55.9 percent of the taxes while the peasants held only 11.9 percent of the land and paid 7.7 percent of the taxes. The university communities and royal officials were more selfish, and the estates fought their pretensions because to permit them to withdraw their holdings from the cadastres would increase the tax burden upon those who remained. The medical faculty and students of the University of Montpellier who were in residence finally obtained exemption from Francis I after years of litigation, but to mitigate the effect of this concession on other taxpayers, he reduced the taille on Languedoc by a modest 300 livres. The magistrates in the Parlement of Toulouse were even more persistent, and when the estates tried to block their design, they threatened to refuse to register decrees supporting provincial privileges. Nevertheless the magistrates were able to win exemption for only one of their houses. The result of the episode, which reveals the weak and vacillating nature of the Renaissance monarchy, was that the three estates maintained their position in the matter of the taille.[14]

The principal disputes between the estates and the crown during the first

13. Brink, *Estates*, pp. 17–28.

14. Ibid., pp. 28–54, 59 n.26. Brink has published some of his findings concerning the quarrel between the estates and Parlement in "Les Etats de Languedoc de 1515 à 1560: Une autonomie en question," *Annales du Midi*, 88 (1976): 287–305.

sixty years of the sixteenth century centered on the questions of taxation and the creation of new offices. The taille and the équivalent had become fixed by 1474 at a total of 187,975 livres, but this figure was so low that the crown always had to ask for an additional sum, the *octroi*, collected after the manner of the taille. Eventually it became virtually mandatory for the three estates to vote most of the octroi, but they always retained and exercised the right to reject part of the crown's requests. In addition, the *taillon*, still another tax levied on the same basis as the taille, was established in 1549 to support the army; it became fixed at 71,743 livres. Finally Languedoc was subject to the gabelle, a tax on the sale of salt. As this revenue was assigned to pay the magistrates in the province, it too became fixed at a basic minimum, but the estates did exercise a voice in any increases that might be sought. Thus as the sixteenth century progressed, the amount that the deputies were forced to vote continued to increase, but they nevertheless held the financial demands of the crown in check. In 1491, before the Italian wars had begun, they voted 295,867 livres exclusive of the gabelle and in 1558, the final year of the conflict, 463,059. Although this was an increase of about 60 percent, it was insufficient to compensate for inflation and was less than Louis XI had extracted in 1483.[15] Le Roy Ladurie has calculated that at Montpellier taxes little more than doubled between 1480 and 1560, while wheat prices nearly tripled, and Montpellier was a larger and more prosperous town at the latter date.[16]

The kings turned to expedients because of their inability or unwillingness to extract all the money they needed from the estates. One of the most common was the creation and sale of offices. Francis I was by no means the first French monarch to indulge in this questionable practice, but he systemized the abuse. In May 1519 he issued a decree creating élus and other royal tax officials in the dioceses of Languedoc and in parts of Guyenne.[17] One might be tempted to see his action as an important step in the direction of creating an absolute monarchy, for with royal tax officials it would be easier to bypass the estates. It seems clear, however, that he had no such intention. In the instructions that he gave his commissioners to the estates, he declared: "Neither we, nor our successors, will levy any taxes on the said *pays* without assembling the Estates to seek their consent, as has been the custom in the past, including the acceptance of lists of grievances, requests and remonstrances which the said Estates care to offer towards remedies and provisions which are reasonably needed."[18] When the estates met and protested the creation of the élus, Francis quickly agreed to suppress them in return for 71,800 livres.[19]

---

15. Dognon, *Les institutions politiques*, pp. 498–513, 518–20, 534–37; *HL*, 11:108–09, 145, 323.
16. Emmanuel Le Roy Ladurie, *Les paysans de Languedoc* (Paris, 1966), 1:295–96.
17. Brink, *Estates*, pp. 65–75; *HL*, 11:203–205.
18. Brink, *Estates*, p. 76.
19. Ibid., pp. 76–80.

The three estates were well aware that if the king created offices for sale and then expected the people to pay their salaries, the whole question of consent to taxation was placed in jeopardy. They therefore strongly asserted that their privileges prohibited the creation of new offices without their consent, and in the "Great Charter" of 1522, they won a promise from Francis I that neither he nor his successors would erect or impose new offices on the province without "the consent of the people of the estates."[20] But Francis soon forgot his promise, and in the early 1540s he was once more at odds with the estates over the creation of offices, including the élus. The estates asked that all positions erected since 1520 be suppressed. Francis conceded that he had promised not to create new offices without consent but pleaded that his financial needs compelled him to do so. In return for 100,000 livres, he agreed in 1544 to suppress a number of positions, including the élus, and promised once more to respect the privileges of the province.[21]

Neither Francis I nor his son, Henry II, who came to the throne three years after the contract of 1544, adhered to the promises that had been made. In 1555, in response to the complaints of the estates, the crown offered to suppress offices created during the preceding decade in return for another 100,000 livres. The estates complied. Included among the positions the crown once more abandoned were the élus.[22]

Part of the reason that taxes did not keep pace with inflation between about 1480 and 1560 is to be found in the attitude of the kings. They were hesitant to apply force to increase taxes year after year in a climate of opinion in which taxes, like all else, were thought to be static, and any upward movement was attributed to greed. Part of the explanation, however, must lie in the growing maturity of the estates whose composition, procedures, and privileges were being clearly defined. Not the least explanation for the strong position of the three estates was their capacity to tax not only to support their own activities but also to bribe influential royal officials to defend their interests. As early as 1443, the deputies had distributed lavish gifts to their governor and others to persuade Charles VII to abolish the élus and to preserve their privileges.

The obvious way to check the expanding administrative role of the three estates and to prevent them from bribing officials was to limit their taxing powers, but monarchs were slow to recognize this fact. Louis XI seemingly had no objection to seeing the estates spend more and more until 1481, when the costs of their activities soared to the point where he believed his own share of the taxes might be jeopardized. He then placed a 2,000-livres ceiling on their expenses, less than a third of what they had spent the year before.

20. Ibid., pp. 82–85. For the Great Charter, see *Ord. François Ier*, 3:134–64 (quote on p. 159).
21. Brink, *Estates*, pp. 89–92.
22. *HL*, 11:315–17. Brink, *Estates*, pp. 92–95.

These restrictions were quickly forgotten, however, and the three estates strengthened their position during the regency that followed Louis's death in 1483. Among the concessions they won were the right to vote on those royal taxes that had been approved by the Estates General of France and to levy whatever sums they wanted for their own activities. The value of the gifts the estates gave leaped to 21,120 livres in 1484, but this did include the compensation of their deputation to the Estates General some months before.[23]

To ensure a favorable reception to their cahiers, the deputies voted gifts for their governor, the king's commissioners, and important personages at court. In 1526 Anne de Montmorency, the future constable, became governor and began the long connection of his family with the province which was to last with only brief interruptions for over a century. To secure his goodwill, the estates voted him 12,000 livres the year of his appointment and lesser sums thereafter except when he was in the province and served as the principal royal commissioner. In this capacity he was granted a princely 20,000 livres in 1533. In return, Montmorency performed many services for the province. He was careful to inform the estates of what he had done and saw to it that others extolled his services. When he fell from favor in 1541, Francis forbade governors to accept money from the estates and the estates from voting them presents. At the same time Francis sought to curb the independence of the communities by forbidding them to tax without his authorization and to reduce the costs of holding the estates by limiting the number of *consuls* each town could send. Such reforms, however, were short-lived, and soon everything was progressing as before.[24]

In spite of their successes, the three estates were becoming restive even before Henry II was accidentally killed in a tournament in 1559; but once his relatively strong, if none too intelligent, hand was removed, they became bolder. In the meeting that took place at Nîmes that October, the estates refused to consent to a 50,000 livres tax; but they did vote Montmorency 18,000 livres for that year, 10,000 for the preceding year, and 8,000 for two commissioners. The following year the deputies once more rejected a royal tax but distributed 26,000 livres between their governor and two commissioners, with the request that they obtain the crown's concurrence for this act. In 1561 when the king sought to pay his debts by establishing a tax on wine brought into the closed towns, the deputies asked to substitute a less objectionable levy. The commissioners agreed and suggested that a million livres would do. The deputies offered half that amount and elected a deputation to take their proposal to court. Here a figure of 600,000 was agreed upon in return for the crown's making a number of other concessions. This arrangement was approved in a special meeting of the estates in April

23. Gilles, *Les Etats*, pp. 71–74, 170–72; Dognon, *Les institutions politiques*, pp. 545–73.
24. *HL*, 11:223, 244, 264–65, 274, 310; Dognon, *Les institutions politiques*, pp. 549–51, 570–71.

1562, and it was decided to raise the money over a six-year period by placing a tax on salt. The estates' tax-consenting role, which had never been lost in theory, was thus fully implemented whenever the king sought to increase an old tax or to create a new one, although they always showed him proper deference. They asked the king to accept less rather than bluntly refuse his requests.[25]

2. THE ESTATES OF DAUPHINÉ

Humbert II (1333–49), the last of the dauphins of the house of La Tour-du-Pin, expanded the territory of his principality and provided it with two sovereign courts, the *Conseil Delphinal* and the Chamber of Accounts, and the University of Grenoble, but his extravagant ways forced him to sell Dauphiné to the French ruling house in 1349. This transaction was facilitated by the fact that Humbert had no sons. By the terms of the agreement, known as the *Transport*, Dauphiné was not united with France because it was a fief of the emperor; instead it was awarded to the eleven-year-old grandson of the reigning king, the future Charles V. The young dauphin swore to respect the rights and privileges of his new subjects, and his vassals in turn rendered him homage.[26]

From the standpoint of the inhabitants of Dauphiné, the most obvious difference the transfer of sovereignty made was the substitution of a governor for a resident dauphin, for neither Charles nor any future dauphin except Louis XI actually assumed the direction of the government. Less apparent but nevertheless significant was the increased use of assemblies of the three estates. Humbert had often summoned the nobility, the clergy, and the towns, but he had normally asked only one or two estates to meet at a given locality at the same time. At first Charles sought no subsidies from his new subjects, but following the disastrous defeat at Poitiers in 1356, he was no longer in a position to avoid the risk of offending them. After first strengthening his position by rendering homage to the emperor and receiving the title of imperial vicar, he summoned the three estates to meet together in 1357 to provide financial assistance.[27]

Assemblies of the estates were irregular during the next two decades, but between 1377 and 1407 they met at least twenty-nine times. At first the composition of the assemblies varied greatly, but by 1391 most of the allodial territories had been drawn into the political system, and the various

25. *HL*, 11:323, 327–29, 368.

26. Roland Delachenal, *Histoire de Charles V* (Paris, 1909), 1:27–55; Gaston Letonnelier, *Histoire du Dauphiné* (Paris, 1958), pp. 42–43, 59–62; *Histoire du Dauphiné*, ed. Bernard Bligny (Paris, 1973), pp. 124–27, 134–36.

27. A. Dussert, "Les Etats du Dauphiné aux XIVᵉ et XVᵉ siècles," *Bul. de l'Académie Delphinale*, sér. 5, 8 (1914): 36–48; Letonnelier, *Histoire*, pp. 63–64.

categories of clergymen, nobles, and towns had each merged together to form their respective estates. The first two estates had established their right to be partially exempt from taxes, and a rudimentary tax administrative structure had been developed.[28] The three estates were entering the half-century period that has been interpreted as their golden age.

During these fifty years the three estates met nearly every year, and sometimes more often, to vote subsidies for the king and to provide for their own defense. At first they engaged in a bitter quarrel with their governor, but following his recall in 1407, a more normal relationship with the chief royal representative was established. The slow transition of the estates from being an extraordinary gathering to being a regular institution with a defined role in the affairs of the province was reflected by the beginning of a rudimentary archives in 1413.[29]

During this period the eldest son of the king was given the title of dauphin at birth, but he did not theoretically assume responsibility for governing the territory until he became of age. Even then the king's advisers exercised considerable influence, although the fiction of autonomy from France was preserved. In 1440 the dauphin, Louis II (afterward Louis XI of France), was entrusted with partial responsibility for the government of his principality, but for the next seven years there was no appreciable change because he remained in France. It was there that he took the oath to respect the privileges of his subjects and received deputations from the estates bearing their grievances and offering considerably less money than he required.[30]

In January 1447 Louis, then twenty-three, set out for Dauphiné to receive the homage of his subjects after having obtained permission from his father, Charles VII, to be absent from court for four months. Once out of Charles's reach, he began to govern Dauphiné as an independent prince, even going to the extent of undermining his father's foreign policy and marrying without permission. With his accustomed energy he extended his territory, transformed the old Conseil Delphinal into a Parlement, created a chancellery, reorganized the administration, and brought previously semiautonomous towns, bishops, nobles, and owners of allodial property more fully within the body politic. Louis also displayed a willingness to convoke the three estates and a capacity to obtain from them most of what he wanted when he was in attendance. They customarily met early each winter to vote more generous sums than when he was absent at his father's court. In return, he granted a number of their requests. The one known exception to this procedure took place in 1452 when the plague prevented the estates from

28. Dussert, "Les Etats du Dauphiné," 8:48–120, 300–01, 331–32; *IAD, Isère, sér. B*, ed. J. -J. -A. Pilot-Dethorey (Grenoble, 1884), 2:238–39. Allodial property was more common in Dauphiné than in most of France. See Gérard Chianéa, *La condition jurdique des terres en Dauphiné au 18ᵉ siècle* (Paris, 1969), pp. 285–320.

29. Dussert, "Les Etats du Dauphiné," 8:121–215, 164; *IAD, Isère, sér. B*, 2:239–42.

30. Dussert, "Les Etats du Dauphiné," pp. 216–30; *IAD, Isère, sér. B*, 2:242.

meeting, but Louis ordered that the same tax that had been voted the preceding year be collected.[31]

The three estates profited in some respects from Louis's efforts to consolidate his position, because the special status that had been enjoyed by some bishops, nobles, towns, and allodial property owners had made it as difficult for them to function efficiently, as it had for the dauphin. Unfortunately Louis granted several towns exemptions from the taille, thereby weakening the partial unity that he had achieved and imposing a further burden on the peasants. Angered by his arbitrary acts, dissidents in the three estates appealed to Charles VII. Charles descended on Dauphiné in 1456 with an army, leaving Louis little choice but to submit or to flee to his cousin of Burgundy, the course that he ultimately chose.[32]

The flight of Louis and the arrival of Charles left the three estates in a predicament. They had taken an oath of homage to Louis who would have ample opportunity to avenge himself on those who betrayed him when he replaced his aging father on the throne of France. Furthermore, they recognized, in some instances belatedly perhaps, that their own autonomous status vis-à-vis France was related to the preservation of Louis's active role as dauphin. On the other hand, Charles himself had once been their dauphin, and they had become Louis's subjects only when Charles had turned the principality over to his son after he had become of age. To return to their former master was less unappealing than if there had been no previous ties. Furthermore, Charles had an army, and they were powerless to offer prolonged resistance. After considerable hesitation, the three estates and nearly all the dauphinal officials swore obedience to Charles; he in return promised to respect their privileges. Thereafter the eldest sons of the kings of France continued to bear the title of dauphin, but they were never again entrusted with the government of their principality. Dauphiné became distinguishable from other French provinces with estates and sovereign courts primarily because its governor had more authority and acted as a sort of viceroy in a theoretically independent state.[33]

The historian of the estates of Dauphiné has seen this period as marking the beginning of the decadence of the estates, but he offered little evidence to support this conclusion. The three estates continued to meet at least once a

---

31. Dussert, "Les Etats du Dauphiné," 8:231–58; Paul M. Kendall, *Louis XI* (1971), pp. 68–72; *Histoire du Dauphiné*, ed. Bligny, pp. 175–79.

32. Dussert, "Les Etats du Dauphiné," 8:260–64; Kendall, *Louis XI*, pp. 397–98.

33. Dussert, "Les Etats du Dauphiné," 8:264–89. For more details see also his "Fin de l'indépendance politique du Dauphiné," *Bul. de l'académie delphinale*, sér. 5, 1 (1907): 5–55. *Dispatches of Milanese Ambassadors, 1450–1483*, ed. Paul M. Kendall and Vincent Ilardi (Athens, 1970), 1:234–44. *IAD, Isère, sér. B*, 2:242–43. For the powers of the governor and lieutenant governor, see Llewain Scott Van Doren, *War, Taxes, and Social Protest: The Challenge to Authority in Sixteenth Century Dauphiné* (Ph. D. diss., Harvard University, 1970), pp. 5–23. I am indebted to Professor Van Doren for permitting me to see this work and also several articles before they were published.

year during the century that followed, and the increased royal fiscal demands were paralleled by the increased administrative role of the three estates. Dauphiné was gradually transformed from a principality into a province, but its estates grew in importance while the change was taking place.[34] This is not to say that Dauphiné did not suffer from the fiscal demands of her kings. Louis XI repeatedly sought additional revenue when he came to the throne, although he treated the province with more consideration than the rest of France. When the three estates complained that some taxes were levied without their consent, he promised to halt the practice but then violated his pledge the next time he felt in need. The important point, however, is that Louis continued to use the three estates and left their duties and privileges intact so that they were prepared to assume a more important role when he died in 1483.[35]

Dauphiné profited in several respects from the death of the unpopular king. In 1462 Louis had ceded the important counties of Valentinois and Diois to the pope in order to further his Italian aspirations, an act which suggests that he had no more concept of a national state or a national foreign policy than had his immediate successors. Both the estates and the Parlement of Dauphiné had protested at the time, and they were now able to obtain the revocation of the gift. The decision of the Estates General of Tours in 1484 to cut the taille to about a third of what it had been led to a reduction of Dauphiné's share to a mere 20,000 livres, little more than 1 percent of the total amount that fell on the kingdom. Occasionally Charles VIII and Louis XII sought further assistance, and the inhabitants suffered frequently from the passage of troops after the opening of the Italian Wars in 1494, but except in 1513, the crown's additional requests were modest and, on the whole, Dauphiné prospered during the two reigns. Taxes were low and privileges were scrupulously respected. More than a century later, Nicolas Chorier, the Dauphinois historian, stated that Louis XII wanted every royal judicial and financial official to take an oath from the president of the estates to respect the privileges of the province. Even though this report is legendary, it is certainly true that in 1508 the first edition of the *Statuta delphinalia* appeared containing numerous official acts to serve as a basis for the legal defense of provincial rights should they come under attack.[36]

34. Dussert, "Les Etats du Dauphiné," 8:216; A. Dussert, "Les Etats du Dauphiné de la Guerre de Cent Ans aux Guerres de Religion," *Bul. de l'Académie Delphinale*, sér. 5, 13 (1922); xii, xv.

35. Dussert, "Les Etats du Dauphiné," 13:esp. 39–40, 59–61, 70 n.4.

36. Scott Van Doren, "War Taxation, Institutional Change and Social Conflict in Provincial France—The Royal *Taille* in Dauphiné, 1494–1559," *Proceedings of the American Philosophical Society* 121 (1977): 70–74; Dussert, "Les Etats du Dauphiné," 13:esp. pp. 24–25, 90, 93, 120, 125–26, 137–38, 140–44, 147–48, 162 n.1. For an example of how determined Charles VIII was to respect the privileges of his subjects even at the cost of criticizing his predecessors, see *Lettres de Charles VIII*, ed. P. Pélicier (Paris, 1900), 2:340–42.

Shortly after coming to the throne, Francis I received the homage of the ambassadors from Dauphiné and then swore to respect their privileges just as his predecessors had done. He was equally careful to retain the taille at the ridiculously low figure of 20,000 livres that had been established by the Estates General of 1484. His financial requirements were nevertheless heavy, primarily because of the Italian war. To meet his expenses he mortgaged his domain in Dauphiné, to the profit of the nobles and bourgeoisie, and created offices for sale, although it was specifically contrary to the privileges of the province to do so without the consent of the estates. There were also levies on the clergy and the closed towns. Once in November 1529, the estates met in a special session and voted a tax to pay the ransom of the dauphin, who was a hostage of the emperor. The nobles, in another meeting the following month, also agreed to contribute.[37]

Dauphiné would have fared well had it not been for its unfortunate location along the routes to Italy. Whenever a French army was dispatched to Italy during the wars, the three estates were expected to provide food and forage for the transit. If they failed to do so, the troops took what they wanted, and the inhabitants suffered even more grievously. As a frontier province, Dauphiné had a greater need for garrisons to defend its borders and to carry the war to the enemy. Royal requests for funds for these purposes began to leap forward rapidly in 1536, thereby increasing the burdens on the inhabitants. In 1537 they paid 275,549 livres and the following year 382,000 livres. The crown was neither unaware of nor unsympathetic with their problems. In 1536 Francis contributed 15,000 livres to meet their needs, in 1537 and in 1538 he returned the don gratuit of 20,000 livres, and in 1539 he exempted Dauphiné from the levy on the closed towns. His demands, however, increased more rapidly than his willingness or ability to make compensatory concessions. The peasants suffered while the bourgeoisie, who paid less than their share of taxes, prospered from the increased traffic through their towns.[38]

At times the crown attempted to control the activities of the estates and to draw Dauphiné more within the kingdom. An edict of 1523 prescribed that taxes not needed to pay officials and troops in Dauphiné be turned over to the royal treasurers in Paris. Military expenses and the increased activities of the estates soon negated such infringements on Dauphinois' liberties, because such a high percentage of the taxes they voted were assigned to local needs. Francis attempted to reduce the expenses of the three estates and forbade them to meet without his consent unless there was an emergency. When the estates did assemble, his appointee was to preside, and only matters mentioned in the letters of convocation were to be discussed. Some

37. Dussert, "Les Etats du Dauphiné," 13: pp. 164, 171–73, 190, 197, 211.

38. Ibid., pp. 174–76, 213. *Histoire du Dauphiné*, ed. Bligny, p. 204; Van Doren, "War Taxation," pp. 74–83.

of these provisions, such as the insistence on royal permission to meet, had long been the practice; others, such as who was to preside, were ignored. Furthermore, during the last decade of the reign, the estates won back some of the tax-collecting powers they had lost, and their own activities continued to expand.[39]

Henry II took the traditional oath to respect the privileges of Dauphiné and did little to alter its government during his reign, but his pressing financial needs led him to seek additional revenue from every possible source. His most important innovation was an attempt to relieve the local inhabitants of the burden of supporting his troops by providing them a substantial increase in pay. With great reluctance the estates voted 24,000 livres in 1550 to carry out this policy. By 1557 the don gratuit of 20,000 livres that had been established in 1484 had been augmented by 63,000 livres in various taxes to support the military. In addition, royal officials and merchants were subject to forced loans, and the clergy was expected to contribute. Nevertheless Henry II's taxes were substantially lower than those of his father during the last decade of his reign, and on occasion Louis XI had extracted nearly as much at a time when prices were lower and the people were less prosperous. Furthermore, the estates had been preserved, and their capacity to participate in the government of the province had increased.[40]

The general principles that determined who was summoned to the estates had become fairly well established by the beginning of the fifteenth century. Included were nobles and ecclesiastics with rights of justice and the consuls or deputies of the towns and communities. A roll of 1488 lists 36 clergymen and 270 nobles who were invited to attend and 115 towns and communities that were asked to send representatives. By 1608 the number of nobles and clergy summoned had increased somewhat, but the number of towns and communities had decreased to 85. Since the three estates usually deliberated and voted together at this time, the nobility enjoyed a predominant role, even though towns often sent two representatives.[41]

Between 1367 and 1400 the three estates took important steps toward developing an administrative arm to help them in their work. They sometimes elected committees that functioned during their sessions and employed secretaries to record what was done. They also chose *commis* to divide the tax that they voted among the various jurisdictions and to ensure that it was collected by those who were responsible. They named receivers to administer the taxes that were collected and auditors to verify the accounts of their financial officials. In 1391 they created the position of *procureur* in order to have someone to look after their interests between their meetings,

39. Dussert, "Les Etats du Dauphiné," 13: pp. 177–78, 201–07, 213–14, 229–33.

40. Ibid., pp. 44–45, 246, 253–55, 268; Van Doren, "War Taxation," pp. 90–95.

41. Dussert, "Les Etats du Dauphiné," 8:292–99, 311–13, 13:xiv–xv, xvii, 250 n.6, 328–31. The roll for 1608 is in AD, Isère, Fonds Chaper, J 524².

and in 1413 they took the initial steps to establish an archives by assuring that basic documents concerning the privileges of the provinces were available.[42]

Between 1400 and 1550 the administrative structure of the estates became more sophisticated, and the size of the bureaucracy expanded. The procureur was given one or two assistants, and receivers were appointed in each bailiwick. The number of secretaries and clerks increased, and an usher was named and given an assistant. Ambassadors were sent to court with increasing frequency, and a true archives was established in the *Maison du Pays* whose location was marked on a map of Grenoble prepared in 1575.[43]

By far the most important development during this period was the emergence of the *Assemblées des Commis des États*, which served as a sort of executive arm of the estates. Commis were appointed in the late fourteenth century, but initially their duties were largely limited to problems related to tax collection. As the activities of the estates increased after the close of the Hundred Years War, the commis met more frequently. The composition of these meetings varied, but by the mid-sixteenth century it was becoming customary for the *consuls* of eight (later ten) leading towns to be invited to participate, along with a smaller representation from the other orders.[44]

During the Hundred Years War the administrative duties of the three estates and their agents did not extend far beyond apportioning and supervising the collection of taxes, although through their cahiers they were able to influence a wide variety of other activities. After the war the three estates continued their role in the tax field, expanded their administrative contributions by providing logistical support for troops passing through their province to Italy, and engaged in a broad variety of other activities.[45] To add weight to their appeals, they voted salaries and presents for their governors and other royal officials. Early in the sixteenth century, governors usually received 6,000 livres and their lieutenants 2,000, substantial amounts at a time when the don gratuit for the king was only 20,000 livres. By 1550 the amount had increased to 8,000 and 4,000, respectively, and additional sums were added on special occasions. Sometimes the gifts of the estates were for more altruistic purposes; once 1,000 livres was voted for the universities of Grenoble and Valence so that they could afford "good rectors."[46]

The estates and the commis did not exhaust the representative institutions

42. Dussert, "Les Etats du Dauphiné," 8:59–68, 119–20, 164, 314–22.

43. Ibid., 13:xvii–xviii, 38; Alexandre Fauché-Prunelle, *Essai sur les anciennes institutions autonomes ou populaires des Alpes Cottiennes-Briançonnaises* (Grenoble, 1857), 2:510–24.

44. Dussert, "Les Etats du Dauphiné," 8:xvii–xviii, 63–65, 157, 204 n.4, 250, 255, 262 n.4. Fauché-Prunelle, *Essai*, 2:613–26. Among the other names given to this institution were *Assemblées des commis du pays*, *Assemblées des dix villes*, later *Assemblées des commis du pays, des consuls des villes et commis des villages*, and finally *Assemblées du pays*.

45. Dussert, "Les Etats du Dauphiné," 8:322–24; 13:xix–xxv.

46. Ibid., 13:63–65, 170–71, 203 n.3, 233, 247 nn.2, 3, 252 nn.1, 2, 256. Van Doren, *War, Taxes*, pp. 9–10, 20–21.

in Dauphiné that met regularly before the Wars of Religion, for the Alpine region boasted a complex system of assemblies, some of them as old as the estates of Dauphiné. At the bottom of a hierarchy of institutions were the assemblies of the *escartons*. The typical escarton assembly was composed of the deputies of the communities of a valley; neither the nobility nor the clergy was represented by right. These escartons included from four to twenty-one communities and assembled on orders of the *consuls* of the leading town whenever the need for a meeting arose. The bailiwick of Briançon had five escartons prior to the treaty of Utrecht in 1713 when the three that were on the Italian side of the Alps were ceded to Piedmont-Savoy. The bailiwick of Embrun had three escartons, but the bailiwick of Gap does not appear to have had any. Each of these bailiwicks had a representative assembly to which the communities sent deputies. Finally there was the assembly of the three mountain bailiwicks which embraced most of the mountainous region of the province.[47]

The escartons met quite frequently, and the individual bailiwicks appear to have assembled about twice yearly on order of the first *consul* of the capital town. The assemblies of the three mountain bailiwicks probably came into existence somewhat later and met less often. In addition to the usual problems that representative institutions devoted their energies to during this period, those of the mountainous region of Dauphiné also had to provide supplies for the troops who passed through their valleys to Italy. Possessed with a generous suffrage, capable of meeting legally on the call of the *consuls* of the leading towns, and freed from the dominating influence of the nobility and clergy, the assemblies provide fine examples of how popular initiative could function during the Renaissance. Unlike the estates of Dauphiné, the escartons continued to meet until the Revolution.

Dauphiné's well-entrenched privileges coupled with its active representative institutions should have placed it in a strong position to combat any absolutist tendencies the monarchy might display, but an unusually bitter clash between the third estates and the other two orders known as the *procès des tailles* so poisoned the atmosphere that cooperation between the estates became impossible, and in the end they all fell before the crown.[48]

The taille was réelle in the mountain bailiwicks; that is, the nobles, clergymen, and other privileged persons had to pay this tax on any nonnoble

---

47. For discussions of these assemblées see Fauché-Prunelle, *Essai*, 2:311–39, and Dr. Chabrand, "Les escartons dans l'ancien Briançonnais," *Bul. de la soc. d'études des Hautes-Alpes* 2 (1883): 241–49. See also *IAC, Guillestre*, ed. Paul Guillaume (Gap, 1906), pp. lxxxviii–xci, 417–24; *IAD, Hautes-Alpes, sér. E*, ed. Paul Guillaume (Gap, 1913), 2:72–124; and P. Vaillant, "Les origines d'une libre confédération de vallées: les habitants des communautés briançonnaises au XIIIᵉ siècle," *BEC* 125 (1967): 301–48.

48. For the procès des tailles, see Dussert, "Les Etats du Dauphiné," 13:273–86; Van Doren, *War, Taxes*, pp. 194–281, and "War Taxation," pp. 79–93; A. Lacroix, "Claude Brosse et les tailles," *Bul. de la soc. d'archéologie et de statistique de la Drôme* 31–33 (1897–99); and *Histoire du Dauphiné*, ed. Bligny, pp. 204–209.

land they owned. The taille was usually considered personnelle in the remainder of the province, and here the privileged were free from royal impositions on their land whether it was noble—that is, subject to the ban and arrière ban—or not. Because of the ever-growing number of persons with a privileged status and their continual purchase of peasant holdings, the amount of land subject to the taille steadily diminished in areas where the taille was personnelle. At the same time royal fiscal demands increased, thereby placing the nonprivileged in a very difficult position. Friction was inevitable.

A similar situation existed in other parts of France, but in Dauphiné several factors caused the quarrel between the privileged and nonprivileged to be far more bitter. In the first place a reasonable argument could be offered that all the inhabitants in Dauphiné were privileged because of the provision in the *Transport* of 1349 that the territory as a whole was exempt from taxation. The inhabitants, of course, could vote the king a don gratuit if they so desired, but if they did so, all should be required to contribute because in accordance with the *Transport*, everyone enjoyed equal status vis-à-vis the king. To support this contention, evidence could be cited proving that the nobility had occasionally made contributions until well into the reign of Francis I.

Even if it was conceded that the privileged did not have to contribute to the don gratuit, it could be argued that they should pay their share of the expenses undertaken for the common good of the province. As a frontier province through which troops passed, most of the taxes that were collected were spent in Dauphiné to pay for the provisioning of these forces and for the support of the garrisons. It was to everyone's advantage that this be done; well-paid, well-fed troops plundered less than those who were not. Nearly all of the remaining taxes were assigned to pay royal officials, to repair roads and bridges, and for other local purposes. Between 1600 and 1610, the first decade for which accurate information exists, the actual revenue the crown drew from Dauphiné fluctuated from 720 to 42,161 livres, far less than that contributed by any other part of France of comparable size.[49]

A final circumstance that made the dispute more serious in Dauphiné than elsewhere was the fact that the taille was neither universally réelle nor personnelle. It was only natural that the nonprivileged in the lowlands should try to get the concept that the taille was réelle extended to their region, while the few privileged who inhabited the mountain bailiwicks wanted to remove their nonnoble lands from the tax roles both because of the social stigma attached to paying the taille and for obvious financial reasons.

In addition to the problem of what the privileged should pay, there was the question of who the privileged were. The status of the new nobles, the

49. Mallet, pp. 186–87.

nonnoble clergymen who owned private property, the faculties of the two universities, the less important royal officials, and the advocates who pleaded cases before Parlement was bitterly disputed. Furthermore, such towns as Gap, Montélimar, Crest, and Embrun claimed to be tax exempt, and the towns in general attempted to transfer as much of the tax burden to the countryside as possible. Finally, the burghers claimed that they should not be assessed in the villages for the rural land they owned because they were expected to disclose these holdings to the municipal tax assessors. If their claim was recognized, it would decrease the amount of taxable land, thereby increasing the amount each peasant would have to pay to meet his village's quota. It would also enable the urban farm owners to evade part of their tax obligations because there was no way the city tax assessors could discover whether they had declared all their holdings. As long as the crown was content to draw only 20,000 livres a year from the province, these explosive issues remained dormant, but in the early 1520s Francis I began to demand additional sums for his war with the emperor. The commis of the estates continued to divide the ordinary tax among the nonexempt localities, but arguing that all should contribute to the common defense, they required the exempt towns to pay their share of the extraordinary levies. The inevitable quarrel ensued. In 1537 Francis ruled in favor of the estates, but it was not until 1558 that the last of the exempt towns, Gap, surrendered to the inevitable.[50]

Meanwhile the villagers were becoming increasingly exasperated. The towns were using their influence in the estates to transfer to them a large part of the expense of supplying troops moving through the province and other taxes that the crown intended the urban dwellers to pay. In August 1547 representatives of the villages appealed to Parlement for justice, but the first president of that body thought it best to turn the matter over to the estates that were about to meet in Grenoble. Here the villages won some support, but in the end their request for more representation in the estates and a voice in the meetings of the commis was denied, and they were given only minor concessions in tax matters. When Henry II passed through Grenoble the following year, he was persuaded to issue an edict ordering that the tax digest be revised to secure a more equitable distribution of the fiscal burden. In the meantime, the inhabitants of the towns were to pay the taille on their rural land that they had acquired since 1518. At first the towns refused to accept this decision, but after further negotiations, an agreement was made in 1552–53 which called upon burghers to pay taxes on their rural land in the village where it lay.[51]

Quarreling did not immediately cease, but town and village came to realize that it was to their mutual advantage to cooperate to make the

50. Van Doren, "War Taxation," pp. 78–83; Dussert, "Les Etats du Dauphiné," 13:213–15.
51. Dussert, "Les Etats du Dauphiné," 13:286–92; Van Doren, *War, Taxes*, pp. 194–201.

privileged pay more of the ever-increasing tax burden. At first they hoped to have the taille declared to be réelle throughout the province, but the Parlement of Grenoble, whose members had a heavy vested interest in retaining the status quo, ruled against them. They then appealed to Paris but made the mistake of offering their governor such a small gift that he did not feel obligated to press their case. Defeated in their efforts to have the principle of the taille réelle adopted, the third estate then directed its efforts toward taxing the nonnoble property of new and false nobles, nonnoble clergymen, lesser royal officials, university faculties, and other whose claim to legal exemptions could be challenged with some hope of success.[52]

Instead of attempting to divide and rule, the royal government directed its efforts toward having the contestants reach a compromise. In the estates held in Grenoble in February 1554, an accord was finally reached in which the privileged won every important point. In this meeting the third estate was outnumbered nearly three to one, and there were charges that its deputies were intimidated. The third estate therefore appealed to king and council after the meeting. In a decree given in June 1556, the privileged were again upheld on almost every point. Nonnoble clergymen were to pay taxes on their common land to support certain designated military expenses, and everyone was to contribute to the costs of repairing roads, bridges, fountains, and walls, but there was little else in the edict to provide consolation for the third estate.[53]

The estates of February 1554 did make two rulings on procedures that placed the third estate in a slightly better position in the future. Previously voting had been by head, and as the number of nobles alone who attended exceeded the representation of the towns, the third estate had been in a disadvantageous position. Henceforth even if two estates were unanimously in favor of a measure, it would not pass unless at least one member of the remaining estate concurred. With unanimity the towns could block actions by the other two estates, although the latter outnumbered them more than two to one in the assembly. That unanimity proved difficult to achieve, however, because of the jealousy among the towns and the tendency of some of them to choose deputies from the privileged class. The second ruling was that when important matters were to be considered by the commis, where a simply majority continued to suffice to pass a measure, the third estate was to have a representation drawn from the *consuls* of the eight principal towns equal to that of the other two orders combined. Judging by later developments this ruling was not always followed.[54]

The decree of 1556 did not settle the debate over who should pay the taille in Dauphiné, but for the next two decades, the dispute only simmered while

52. Ibid., pp. 217–24.

53. Dussert, "Les Etats du Dauphiné," 13:292–312, 340–49; Van Doren, *War, Taxes,* pp. 225–36, and "War Taxation," pp. 92–93.

54. Dussert, "Les Etats du Dauphiné," 13:343–44. Fauché-Prunelle, *Essai,* 2:594–96.

the towns awaited an opportunity to renew the attack on the clergy and nobility, and the villages the means to present their case against priest, noble, official, and burgher. On the surface, at least, Dauphiné had fared badly during the century before the Wars of Religion. The ordinary taxes which the estates were expected to vote automatically had grown from 20,000 livres in 1484 to 83,514 livres, an increase of from 25,000 to 30,000 livres more than could be justified by inflation. The buying power of this sum was still far less than the revenue that Louis XI had collected from the province, but to it must be added the extraordinary levies which would bring the real value of the total taxes collected in the 1550s about to the point that the Spider King had exacted in his most demanding years.

Dauphiné also suffered from the growing division between the social classes. In contrast to the statesmanlike decision of the nobility and clergy of Languedoc to join the third estate in trying to prevent anyone from becoming exempt from the taille, the privileged classes in Dauphiné banded together to block concessions being made to the inhabitants of the countryside. During the course of the century they purchased more and more nonnoble land, thereby reducing the amount of taxable property. With rising taxes this placed a heavy burden on the peasants, who began to organize to defend their rights. Soon they were to have their own syndic, and eventually, after nearly a century of struggle, they were to achieve their objective of having the taille declared réelle in Dauphiné. The three estates, too, had greatly improved their organization and procedures. Their bureaucracy had grown significantly, and the crown was actually extending their administrative role in the province.

3. The Estates of Burgundy

The origins of the estates of Burgundy are still shrouded in mystery despite a good history of the institution and a splendid, more recent study of the medieval duchy.[55] As so often happened elsewhere, the first appearance of the clergy, nobility, and bourgeoisie in assemblies apparently took place in connection with a judicial institution, the ducal Parlement. The duties of Parlement were less narrowly conceived than at a later date, for in 1282 those present at one of its meetings agreed to a tax to fall on all the inhabitants of the duchy. Meetings of a nonjudicial nature involving the three orders took place in 1314 as part of the reaction against the fiscal exactions of Philip the Fair, but no clear connection has been established

---

55. Joseph Billioud, *Les Etats de Bourgogne aux XIVe et XVe siècles* (Dijon, 1922). Jean Richard, *Les Ducs de Bourgogne et la formation du duché du XIe du XIVe siècle* (Paris, 1954). See also Richard's excellent article, "Les Etats de Bourgogne," *Schweizer Beiträge zur Allgemeinen Geschichte* 20 (1962–63): 230–48, also published in *Anciens Pays et Assemblées d'Etats* 35 (1966): 299–324.

between these assemblies and those of the estates that apparently came into being around the middle of the fourteenth century.[56]

The first assemblies that were indisputably meetings of the estates owed much to royal influence. In 1349 Duke Eudes IV died , leaving his young grandson, Philippe de Rouvres, as his heir and his daughter-in-law, Jeanne de Boulogne, as regent during the minority. The following year Jeanne married John, then duke of Normandy and soon to be king of France. John immediately assumed responsibility for the government and in 1352, following what was becoming a more frequent practice in France, summoned the three estates to consent to a tax. Only five clergymen, four nobles, and the representatives of thirteen towns attended, but this small group mustered the courage to reject his demands. On several occasions the three estates were equally recalcitrant in 1356, but the following year when the duchy was threatened with invasion, they proved more cooperative. The premature death of Philippe de Rouvres in 1361 permitted John to take possession of the duchy, and three years later his son, Philip the Bold, was established there as the first of the Valois dukes.[57]

The Valois dukes of Burgundy were favorably disposed toward the provincial estates. Philip the Bold convoked the estates of Burgundy two or three times a year until 1382, just before he began to gather together his wife's rich inheritance in the Low Countries. The pace then slackened until 1440 when the three estates again began to be held on an average of more than once a year. By 1459 their activities had become so great that they had to establish their own archives. During this period and the succeeding centuries, the number of those summoned increased dramatically from the meager group who had attended in 1352. By the reign of Louis XIV, the bishops, abbots, deans, and priors were summoned for the clergy; nobles with fiefs for the second estate; and deputies from twenty-five towns, plus some additional representation from adjacent counties, for the third estate. In all, hundreds were invited to attend, but as late as the closing decades of the sixteenth century, it was rare that even a hundred chose to do so. The three estates normally deliberated apart to determine their respective positions. When they had finished, a plenary session was held to determine the position of the assembly. Here each order was given one vote.[58]

In 1384 Philip the Bold inherited the counties of Burgundy, Nevers,

---

56. Richard, *Les Ducs*, pp. 373–74, 438; Elizabeth A. R. Brown, *Charters and Leagues in Early Fourteenth Century France: The Movement of 1314 and 1315* (Ph.D. diss., Harvard University, 1960).

57. Richard, "Les Etats," pp. 230–34; Billioud, *Les Etats*, pp. 13–17.

58. For a catalogue of the sessions of the medieval estates, see Billioud, *Les Etats*, pp. 369–416. For the changing compositions of the estates, see ibid., pp. 25–52; Richard, "Les Etats," pp. 233–37; Richard Vaughan, *Philip the Good* (London, 1970), p. 198; Henri Drouot, *Mayenne et la Bourgogne* (Paris, 1937), 1:95–96; and Alexandre Thomas, *Une province sous Louis XIV* (Paris, 1844), pp. 9–13.

Rethel, Artois, and Flanders through his wife. In the years that followed he and his successors added to their already extensive domains. To govern his lands, Philip the Bold established a council at Dijon to supervise the activities of his judicial, administrative, and financial officials in the duchy of Burgundy, the counties of Burgundy and Nevers, and less important adjacent territories, and a council at Lille to perform similar duties for Flanders, Artois, and Rethel. Out of these councils a Chamber of Accounts emerged first at Lille and later at Dijon. Philip himself usually resided in Paris where he and a few officials provided meager central direction for his scattered lands. The ducal territories centering on the two Burgundies and in what is now the Low Countries continued to be treated separately under his successors.[59]

Philip the Bold and his son, John the Fearless, thought of themselves as French princes, but Philip the Good assumed a more independent position because of his estrangement from Charles VII following the murder of his father and the invasion of Henry V of England. It would be foolish to ascribe to him the desire to build anything that could be called a modern state or to foster a Netherlandish nationalism. Nevertheless he not only continued his predecessor's policy of developing similar institutions in each of the territories he acquired and in strengthening his control over them, but he also made a more concerted effort to create one set of central institutions over the local ones in the Low Countries and to a lesser extent to create another over those in the Burgundies. Among those established in the Low Countries was an Estates General, which slowly evolved during his reign as an increasing number of provinces were directed to participate. The Estates General enabled Philip and his principal officials to explain their policies in a single meeting and the provinces themselves to deal with matters of common interest. Particularism remained very strong, but nevertheless the Estates General had become enough of a unifying force to serve as the instrument that held the Netherlandish provinces together following the death of Charles the Bold in 1477.[60] Less well known but more pertinent to this study were Philip's efforts to create a Burgundian Estates General.

Under the last Valois dukes, participants in the Burgundian Estates General included representatives from the duchy and county of Burgundy

59. Richard Vaughan, *Philip the Bold* (London, 1962), pp. 113–50; and *John the Fearless* (London, 1966), pp. 9–19.

60. I find Vaughan's argument that Philip the Bold created the Burgundian state and that Philip the Good was largely ineffectual unconvincing. See his books cited in note 59 and his *Philip the Good*, pp. 164–204. Though obviously dated, Pirenne's "The Formation and Constitution of the Burgundian State," *American Historical Review* 14 (1909): 477–502, is brilliant. For more balanced and up-to-date accounts, see Helmut G. Koenigsberger, *Estates and Revolutions* (Ithaca, 1971), pp. 125–43; J. Richard, "Les institutions ducales dans le duché de Bourgogne," in *Histoire des institutions françaises au Moyen Age*, ed. Ferdinand Lot and Robert Fawtier (Paris, 1957), 1:209–47; and Robert Wellens, *Les Etats Généraux des Pays-Bas, des origines à la fin du règne de Philippe le Beau* (Heule, 1974). Wellens argues persuasively that the meeting in Bruges in January 1464 should be considered the first Estates General.

and from the so-called *pays adjacents* of the duchy. These pays adjacents consisted of the county of Auxonne, which the dukes acquired in 1280, the county of Charolais, which they purchased from a vassal in 1390, and the counties of Auxerre and Mâcon and the castellany of Bar-sur-Seine, which they formally acquired by the treaty of Arras in 1435, although they had seized them a decade or two before. The last three, having been royal possessions, had élus at the time they were annexed and remained under the jurisdiction of the Parlement of Paris until the Revolution; Auxonne and Charolais escaped the élus and were assigned to the Parlement of Dijon when it was created some years later. In addition, there were royal enclaves in the medieval duchy whose fiscal administration was charged to élus seated at Autun, Chalon, and Langres, but the revenue from these élections was assigned to the dukes by the terms of the treaty of Arras. [61]

The early Valois dukes had displayed no interest in creating an Estates General, although they could have done so more easily than their successors. The county of Auxonne had had no estates in the fourteenth century, and the dukes had levied taxes on it that were based on a percentage of what the estates of the duchy had voted. The absence of an assembly in Auxonne ought to have made it easy for the dukes to summon its leading clergymen, nobles, and the deputies of the towns to participate in the estates of the duchy thereby creating a single institution, but they failed to do so. Early in the fifteenth century, however, John the Fearless began to summon the three estates of Auxonne to meet alone, strong evidence that he was more interested in extracting as much money as he could from his domains than in developing a consolidated administration for his widespread lands.[62]

The county of Charolais was a feudal dependency of the Burgundian duchy, and as such some of its inhabitants participated in the Burgundian estates after their creation in the second half of the fourteenth century. Charolais also had a count, who convoked the estates of the county in 1383 to vote an aide. In 1390 the count sold his rights to John the Fearless, who, instead of continuing to summon representatives from Charolais to the estates of the duchy, convoked the three estates of the county time and again although, so far as can be ascertained, they had met only once prior to the purchase. In doing so John again missed an easy opportunity to let a nascent institution die through lack of use, thus creating another barrier to the unification of his Burgundian lands.[63]

61. Billioud, *Les Etats*, pp. 345–46; Richard, "Les Etats," p. 235; and "L'élection financière d'Autun du XIVe au XVIe siècle," *Mém. de la soc. Eduenne*, n.s. 50 (1947): 1–14. The three small élections of Autun, Châlon, and Langres were suppressed by an edict of August 1561. *Recueil des édits, déclarations, lettres-patentes, arrêts du Conseil, ordonnances, et autres réglements, émanés du roi et son Conseil, concernant l'administration des Etats de Bourgogne* (Dijon, 1787), 2:219–22.

62. F. Moreau, "La suppression des Etats du comté d'Auxonne et leur réunion aux Etats du duché de Bourgogne," *Mém. de la soc. pour l'hist. du droit et des institutions des anciens pays bourguignons, comtois et romands* 2 (1935): 189–90.

63. L. Laroche, "Les Etats particuliers du Charolais," *Mém. de la soc. pour l'hist. du droit et des institutions des anciens pays bourguignons, comtois et romands* 6 (1939): 145–49.

Even Philip the Good initially failed to integrate the lands he acquired early in his reign with those of the duchy. In 1433 (and perhaps earlier) he summoned the three estates of Mâconnais, and in 1436 he convoked those of the élection of Autun, although neither institution had probably become so well established that it could not have been safely abandoned in favor of a larger assembly. Clearly institutional consolidation had not yet become a ducal policy.[64]

Soon, however, Philip the Good began to try to create an Estates General of his Burgundian territories just as he was doing in his lands in the Low Countries. His son, Charles the Bold, continued the effort. The estates of Auxerre, Bar-sur-Seine, Autun, and the other former royal enclaves were allowed to die, and representatives from these localities were incorporated into the estates of the duchy. By 1477, when Charles the Bold died, Auxonne, Charolais, and Mâconnais were the only pays adjacents that continued to have periodically convoked estates. At first irregularly and then habitually, the dukes summoned representatives from these counties to meet with those of the duchy; a true Estates General came into being. The estates of the pays adjacents apparently sought this development because the size of the grant the duke requested from them was largely determined by the size of the grant made in the ducal estates. To have an effective voice in taxation, they therefore had no choice. The marriage was not an easy one, however, because their representation in the Estates General, their administrative role, and especially the proportion of the total grant they were to pay were in constant dispute.[65]

Philip the Good and, more determinately, Charles the Bold also sought to combine the estates of the county of Burgundy with those of the duchy, although they held the former as a fief of the emperor. Some joint assemblies were held, thereby bringing into being an Estates General fully comparable to the one they were creating in the Low Countries. The county, however, resisted this effort; only once did it send representatives to sit with those of the duchy after Charles's death in 1477.[66]

After the composition of the estates of the pays adjacents had become established, an abbot, eight priors, and a dean were invited to participate for the clergy in Auxonne. Charolais permitted a few important curés to join the upper clergy, but Mâcon was more restrained, participation being limited to the bishop, the deputies of two chapters, and three important abbots. Nobles with fiefs were summoned in all three counties. Twelve towns or bourgs deputed to the estates of Auxonne, five to the estates of Charolais, but only four to the estates of the relatively large county of Mâcon. Curés

64. Jean Roussot, *Un comté adjacent à la Bourgogne aux XVIIe et XVIIIe siècles: Le Mâconnais, pays d'Etats et d'élection* (Mâcon, 1937), pp. 28–37; Richard, "Les Etats," p. 235.

65. Billioud, *Les Etats*, pp. 349–64; Richard, "Les Etats," pp. 236–37; Roussot, *Un comté*, pp. 40, 169–71.

66. Billioud, *Les Etats*, pp. 365–67.

and the villagers were generally excluded as they were in the estates of the duchy.[67]

For a long time the representation of the pays adjacents in the Burgundian Estates General fluctuated, but during the sixteenth century, it became customary for five towns in Auxonne and four in Auxerre to take turns sending deputies. Mâcon and Charolais deputed one voting member from each order, and the little county of Bar-sur-Seine, in memory of its past importance, was assigned three seats in the third estate. This arrangement gave the pays adjacents smaller representation in the Estates General than their size and population warranted, but it did not prevent the officials of the estates from dividing the royal taxes voted by the Estates General between the duchy and the pays adjacents in accordance to a fixed ratio, which was frequently challenged and occasionally altered.[68]

At first the three estates of the duchy permitted ducal officials to apportion and collect the few taxes they voted, but soon they sought to appoint those who performed this task. By 1384 a permanent tax-collecting bureau had come into being, but until 1438 its members, known as élus, were as likely to be appointed by the duke as by the estates. Thereafter the ducal voice was reduced, and the composition of the Chambre des Élus was slowly stabilized. By 1515 it had become customary for the clergy to choose an élu alternately from the bishops, the abbots, and the deans who had seats in the estates. The nobility elected an élu, but the mayor of Dijon served automatically as one of the two élus of the third estate, the other being taken by turn from one of nine other leading towns. These élus served for three years. The dukes, who were opposed to having the financial administration slip entirely from their grasp, adopted the practice of appointing one élu to serve with those of the estates. The sixteenth-century kings continued this custom and also had two members of the Chamber of Accounts at Dijon participate. Because these last two officials and the two élus of the third estate were assigned only one vote each, the élus of the estates cast three ballots to the two held by the royal officials.[69]

The principal role of the élus was to apportion and collect taxes, but they soon expanded their activities to engage in nearly every aspect of administration. In addition, they served as the spokesmen of the three estates when they were not in session. From their inception, they had a clerk to assist them in their duties, but until 1476 this important official was named by the dukes. In that year when there was some confusion over whom Charles the Bold had appointed to the post, the élus seized the opportunity to induct the candidate who was most acceptable to them. The duke accepted their

67. *IAD, Côte-d'Or, sér. C, introduction aux tomes III et IV*, ed. Joseph Garnier (Dijon, 1959), pp. l–li; Roussot, *Un comté*, p. 58.

68. Billioud, *Les Etats*, pp. 349–62; Drouot, *Mayenne*, 1:96–97; Laroche, *Les Etats*, pp. 161–63; Roussot, *Un comté*, p. 61 n.3.

69. Billioud, *Les Etats*, pp. 159–72; *IAD, Côte-d'Or*, ed. Garnier, pp. xiii–xv.

decision, and after the reunion with France the following year, Louis XI permitted them to retain this ducal prerogative. Other officials of the élus and the estates were gradually added. In the sixteenth century, a clerk with one assistant sufficed for the estates, but a century later there were three assistants. There were also two syndics, three barristers in Parlement, a treasurer for the province and for each of the bailiwicks, and a growing number of other officials, especially in those parts of the duchy where there were no élections. Where élections did exist, the élus worked with local royal tax officials. The three estates were well aware that the élus were capable of abusing their authority. Beginning in 1584 they appointed a commission (later called the *alcades*) that consisted of one, and later two, members of each estate to investigate the élus' activities near the end of their term of office and to report its findings to them.[70]

The estates in the pays adjacents also developed bureaucracies. In Mâconnais meetings of the estates did not become periodic until near the close of the fifteenth century, and it was only then that the composition of the estates became fixed. The estates then moved quickly to increase their administrative role. As a pays d'élection, the élus had apportioned and collected taxes at the time of Valois dukes and Louis XI, but during the reign of Charles VIII, the estates began to claim that it was the privilege of their officials, also called élus, to do so. In 1506, Louis XII issued a decree saying that they could. The royal élus were to be permitted to be present when the élus of the estates divided the taxes, but they were denied their usual fees. At the same time the estates appointed a receiver to look after the tax revenues. In 1515 they created the post of syndic. Soon they gave the syndic an assistant, and around 1550 they began to appoint a secretary. Throughout this period the élus of the estates not only played the dominant role in tax matters but also served as a committee to look after the interests of the province between the sessions of the estates.[71] The estates of Charolais also had élus, a syndic, a receiver, and other officials to collect taxes and administer the county.[72]

Although the administrative organs of the estates of Burgundy continued to develop during the sixteenth century, they were sufficiently formed by 1477, when the province was reunited with the crown, for Louis XI to have no choice but to continue to use them or face the well-organized opposition of the leading inhabitants, many of whom looked back nostalgically to the days of the Valois dukes. There is no reason to believe that Louis ever considered repressing the estates. Early in his reign, he had actually revived or created some provincial estates in France and had offered to substitute tax officials appointed by the estates for those of the crown. Although he soon

70. Billioud, *Les Etats*, pp. 172–79; Drouot, *Mayenne*, 1:97–99; *IAD, Côte-d'Or*, ed. Garnier, pp. xxi–xxiii, xxx–xxxiii.

71. Roussot, *Un comté*, pp. 43, 55–62, 89, 122, 130–31.

72. Laroche, *Les Etats*, pp. 158–90.

abandoned this position, he at no time launched a concerted attack against the provincial estates. In spite of his occasional arbitrary acts and excessive fiscal demands, there seem to have been more representative institutions in France at the close of his reign than in the beginning. It is therefore not surprising that Louis issued letters confirming the privileges of the Burgundians in a more detailed and explicit fashion than before and that he made no attempt to subordinate their institutions to comparable ones in Paris. Their Chamber of Accounts was recognized as a sovereign court, and a Parlement was created at Dijon, although there was ample precedent for placing the entire duchy under the jurisdiction of the Parlement of Paris.[73]

Louis XI did not neglect the estates when he established himself in Burgundy. In March 1477 he issued a letter guaranteeing that those who attended would be free from arrest during their travels and deliberations. More important, he made a promise, which was repeated by his successors, that he would levy no taxes without their consent. Nevertheless Louis did not hesitate to find excuses for imposing a hearth tax to build some châteaux and for increasing the gabelle to pay the officers of the newly created Parlement without receiving the concurrence of the estates. These arbitrary acts should not necessarily be construed as being part of an effort to destroy the estates. Between January 1477 and December 1482, Louis held five meetings of that body, although none was concerned with taxation.[74]

The Burgundian deputies to the Estates General of France that met in Tours in 1484 following Louis's death were loud in their complaints about the way their province had been treated, and they displayed great intransigence when it came to accepting their share of the taille of 1.5 million livres that the assembled deputies agreed should be imposed on the kingdom. Before they departed from Tours, the Burgundians obtained a letter from the new king, Charles VIII, stating that they had not consented to any tax and that all levies had to be approved by the three estates of the province. Then in June 1484, the estates met and refused to vote any of the 45,000 livres that had been assigned as their share at Tours. The crown assembled the estates again in August, only to meet with refusal once more. Finally, in a third meeting in September, the estates voted 30,000 livres. During the remainder of the century, the crown sought to persuade the three estates to accept an annual taille of 45,000 livres, but as late as 1500 they were agreeing to only 40,000.[75]

73. J. R. Major, *Representative Institutions in Renaissance France, 1421–1559* (Madison, 1960), pp. 50–51. J. -L. Gay, "Fiscalité royale et Etats généraux de Bourgogne, 1477–1589," in *Etudes sur l'histoire des assemblées d'états*, ed. François Dumont (Paris, 1966), pp. 180–82; *Recueil des Etats de Bourgogne*, 1 : 178–211; R. de Chevanne, "Les Etats de Bourgogne et la réunion du duché à la France, en 1477," *Mém. de la soc. d'archéologie de Beaune* 43 (1929–30): 196–245.

74. Billioud, *Les Etats*, pp. 120, 137–38, 411–12; Gay, "Fiscalité royale," pp. 182–85; *Recueil des Etats de Bourgogne*, 1 : 186, arts. 17, 18.

75. Major, *Representative Institutions*, pp. 115–16. Billioud, *Les Etats*, pp. 412–13, 460–65; Gay, "Fiscalité royale," p. 185.

Between the start of the sixteenth century and the Wars of Religion, the crown continued its efforts to persuade the Burgundians to assume their share of the fiscal burden, but not until 1524 did they consent to pay a taille of 50,000 livres. There it remained, although from the beginning the king was requesting 120,000 livres. The niggardly attitude of the three estates toward the crown was not repeated when it came to dealing with their governor, to whom they looked for support at court. In 1524 they voted him 10,000 livres, a fifth of the sum they offered the king, and then added 2,000 for his wife. Nor were the three estates unmindful of their own safety. Beginning in 1539 they contributed 10,000 livres annually to pay a constabulary whose job it was to exterminate thieves and other evildoers.[76]

During this period the crown and the estates quarreled continually over whether or to what degree Burgundy should pay the various forms of indirect taxes and contribute to the military effort. In 1548 the king requested that the estates approve a new tax, the taillon, to support 250 lances. After some deliberation, the estates offered to provide for 50 or 60 lances in return for specified concessions. In the end a compromise figure of 150 lances was reached. In 1561 when the government tried to impose a tax on wine brought into towns, the three estates countered with an offer of 120,000 livres to be paid over a period of six years, a proposition that the crown accepted only when they increased the sum to 150,000. In 1557 the king asked for 25,000 or 30,000 livres to repair the defenses of the Burgundian towns but was granted only 20,000 livres, although the measure was obviously designed to protect the inhabitants. A requested loan of 30,000 livres was reduced to 20,000 through the efforts of the élus.[77]

So it went. The three estates consistently resisted royal machinations to increase old taxes and to introduce new ones. The fact that they adopted the custom early in the sixteenth century of assembling every third year reduced the crown's opportunity to put pressure on them.[78] Generally disputes were settled by a compromise which left the Burgundians paying more than before but still less than their share of the costs of the government. Considering the rise in prices and the improved economic conditions during the three-quarters of a century following their reunion with France, the Burgundians fared very well indeed. As a result, the crown was driven to the creation of offices and other expedients in order to procure the necessary funds.

In January 1555 Henry II created six élections in the duchy of Burgundy and the county of Auxonne, each of which was to have seven officers. It is most unlikely that this step was designed to undermine the estates because Henry confirmed their privileges several months later. Rather it was a

76. Gay, "Fiscalité royale," pp. 186–87; *IAD, Côte-d'Or, sér. C,* ed. Joseph Garnier (Dijon, 1886), 3:54.

77. Gay, "Fiscalité royale," pp. 188–200, 206–07.

78. Ibid., p. 181.

monetary expedient, for these and other offices that were created at the same time were promptly put on sale. With equal promptness the élus of the estates secured Henry's permission to hold a special meeting of the estates in July where they were authorized to offer 20,000 livres in return for suppressing the élections and all the new offices. That August Henry accepted the offer on the condition that the estates also compensate those who had already purchased positions. He had found a way to extract more money from the estates, but the Burgundians had freed themselves from an institution that would have eventually threatened their liberties if and when the crown embarked on an absolutist course.[79]

4. The Estates of Provence

Provence, unlike Burgundy, did not escheat to the crown of France as a feudal dependency; rather it was a county with nominal ties to the Holy Roman Empire that was inherited in 1481 through the provisions of the will of one of the last reigning counts. These provisions, which Louis XI accepted, stipulated that the union between France and Provence was to be only in the person of their common king and count. The terms of the union were defined in greater detail by the three estates in January 1482 and August 1486. The king swore to respect these terms, and the agreement was formally ratified in a special meeting of the estates in April 1487. In addition to requiring that the king rule in his capacity of count of Provence, the terms of this agreement stipulated that only those acts registered by a council seated in Provence would be executed, that the grand seneschal and other great officers would be resident, that all other offices and important benefices would be given to natives, that there would be no superior courts outside the province to which the inhabitants would have to appeal, and that no tax would be levied without the consent of the three estates. Provence was to be to France what Aragon was to Castile, a co-equal but weaker partner in one of those dynastic conglomerations so typical of the Renaissance monarchies.[80]

The three estates of Provence were born in the thirteenth century; by the time of the union with France, their composition, organization, and procedures were fairly well established. Two archbishops, twelve bishops, and ten abbots and other dignitaries sat for the first estate. Nobles with fiefs were admitted for the second estate, and from one to five deputies from each of the *vigueries* and bailiwicks into which Provence was divided represented the third estate. Marseilles and Arles, as terres adjacentes, did not ordinarily

---

79. *Recueil des Etats de Bourgogne*, 2:59–62, 68–79, 97–98.

80. *Les Bouches-du-Rhône: Encyclopédie départementale*, ed. Paul Masson (Marseilles, 1920), 3:275–83. The chapters on institutions were written by Raoul Busquet and published separately as *Histoire des institutions de la Provence de 1482 à 1790* (Marseilles, 1920).

contribute to the expenses of the province. As a result, their voting privileges were removed around the middle of the sixteenth century, but they were permitted to continue to depute two observers each to safeguard their interests. Royal officials were excluded from the estates in 1538. Absenteeism on the part of the first two estates was common. Rolls of those who attended in 1480 and 1487 reveal that twelve were present on each occasion for the clergy, an average of fifty-eight attended for the nobility, and forty-three came for the third estate on one occasion and forty-six on the other. Since the three estates deliberated together and voted by head, the voting power of the nobility was approximately equal to that of the other two orders combined. In 1544 and again in 1626, the third estate sought to limit the combined representation of the clergy and nobility to the number it enjoyed, but this attempt to imitate the estates of Languedoc was stillborn.[81]

By the middle of the sixteenth century, it had become customary for the chief town in each of the twenty-three vigueries into which Provence was then divided and a few other important communities to send a deputy to the provincial estates. If the viguerie was important enough to be assigned more than one deputy, at least one was elected in an assembly of the viguerie. During the fourteenth century, the clergy and nobility had attended these meetings, but by the sixteenth century only the communities sent someone, usually a *consul*, to participate. The *consuls* of the chief town could convoke the viguerie. They did so not only to elect deputies to the estates and to hear their reports after the meeting but also to deal with various administrative matters, including tax collection and road building. The vigueries had treasurers, clerks, and other officials. In general, they served Provence in a manner comparable to the way the diocesan assemblies served Languedoc.[82]

During the latter part of the fourteenth century, the estates of Provence had elected tax officials and clerks, but a permanent bureaucracy had not developed because these appointees served a single assembly and collected a single tax. After 1400, officials of the count assumed the tax-collecting duties, as had happened in France a few decades before, and the role of the three estates declined. Another blow fell in 1420 when the count refused to permit them to appoint a permanent committee to look after their interests between meetings. In spite of these setbacks, the three estates began to make slow but steady progress a decade or two later. After 1434 they played a very important legislative role, and in 1437 their right to consent to taxation was recognized in a formal written document. Finally, in 1480 they won the right to have a long-sought permanent committee, the *procureurs du pays*, to act for them between sessions.[83]

81. *Les Bouches-du-Rhône*, 3:448–50, 466–69. For the estates before the reunion with France see ibid., 2:639–56, 680–88; Gaspard H. de Coriolis, *Dissertation sur les Etats de Provence* (Aix, 1867), pp. 11–101 passim.

82. *Les Bouches-du-Rhône*, 3:462–67, 532–39; M. -J. Bry, *Les vigueries de Provence* (Paris, 1910).

83. *Les Bouches-du-Rhône*, 2:647–48, 680–88.

For a century, membership in the procureurs du pays varied, but by 1578 it had come to consist of the Archbishop of Aix, or in his absence his vicar general, the three *consuls* of Aix, and the assesseur of that town, who were known as the procureurs du pays nés because they owed their membership to the position they held. In addition, the three estates elected two members from the clergy and two from the nobility to serve as procureurs du pays joints. To this last group, the towns took turns sending two deputies. The procureurs du pays, who served as the executive arm of the estates, were charged with defending the interests of the province before the sovereign courts and the king's council and enforcing the ordonnances of the estates on a wide variety of matters, including highway building, the lodging of troops, public health during epidemics, and tax administration. Ordinarily the procureurs nés, with their seats in Aix where the sovereign courts, the Bureau of Finances, and the great officers of the crown were located, acted alone under the presidency of the archbishop, but when serious problems arose, the procureurs joints were also summoned. Other officials who served the three estates when they were not in session included a treasurer, whom they secured the right to name in 1544, a provincial agent, who was first appointed in 1538 to handle legal cases, and upon occasion from 1582, an agent at Paris. Several other lawyers and clerks were also employed.[84]

There was some friction between the crown and the estates prior to the Wars of Religion, but on the whole there were fewer quarrels than might have been expected. French institutions such as a Parlement, a Court of Accounts that combined the functions of the Chamber of Accounts and the Court of Aids elsewhere, and a Bureau of Finances were established in Aix to perform the duties formerly assigned to organs of government created by the counts. These innovations were in keeping with the pledge Louis XI had made to the Provençals that they would not have to appeal cases outside their county. Indeed by putting sovereign courts in Provence, the Valois kings assured that as long as the monarchy lasted, the province would enjoy a wide degree of autonomy.[85]

Francis I concluded that the estates were spending too much money on their own activities. In 1529 he forbade them to levy taxes without his authorization. Six years later he made a far-reaching effort to control their activities by forbidding anyone to issue letters of convocation without his permission unless there was an emergency. Once in session, the estates were not to make any statutes or ordonnances unilaterally. To reduce transportation and per diem expenses, he directed that the estates be held only once a year and that all the procureurs du pays nés come from Aix, a practice

---

84. Ibid., 3:450–61, 488–510; Bernard Hildesheimer, *Les assemblées générales des communautés de Provence* (Paris, 1935), pp. 85–96, 115–32.

85. *Les Bouches-du-Rhône*, 3:329–39, 424–29, 439–43. It is difficult to evaluate the relations between the crown and the estates during this period because prior to 1568 the procès-verbaux of the estates survives only for the years 1536 to 1545.

that had not yet become customary. To prevent graft he ordered the seneschal and other officials to verify the books concerning the money the estates levied for their own expenses. The estates countered by refusing to vote 8,000 livres that was requested in 1536, but changed their decision because of the approach of the emperor's army. Francis, in turn, soon abandoned his effort to have all the procureurs come from Aix, and much of the remainder of his legislation on the estates remained dormant. The estates generally voted Francis and his successor what they asked. This cooperative spirit was in part achieved because the demands of the crown were relatively modest. The basic tax, the *fouage*, became fixed at a mere 25,000 livres during the sixteenth century, the taillon was created in 1549 with the consent of the estates, and a subsidy of 20,000 livres was established in 1561 in lieu of the wine tax imposed after the Estates General of Pontoise.[86]

During the Wars of Religion a new institution, the assembly of the communities, was spawned in Provence. The reason for its creation may be found in the governor's need during the intervals between the annual meetings of the three estates to raise additional revenue to pay the troops required to pacify the province. The procureurs alone lacked the authority to tax or to borrow the necessary sums. It was time-consuming and expensive to call special meetings of the three estates—time-consuming because of the need first to hold assemblies of the vigueries to elect deputies, and expensive because of the large number of persons who had to be given stipends for attending. What was needed was an assembly that could be brought together quickly and that was sufficiently representative for its financial acts to be accepted by the communities. The solution was to add deputies from the towns with direct representation to the estates to the meetings of the procureurs nés et joints. Their role was to act as leaders in getting the other communities in their vigueries to pay their share of any taxes that were voted. Excluded from the new assembly were the clergy and nobility, except for their procureurs, and the deputies of the vigueries.

There had been several assemblies of the towns during the fourteenth century, and a few more meetings had been held during the 1520s, but the assembly of the communities was essentially a creation of the 1570s and 1580s. In summoning the communities during these years, the governor was not trying to create an institution to supplant the estates or even to create a new institution at all; his goal was to take the necessary measures to get a job done. Only gradually as the assembly of the communities proved its usefulness did it take on a fixed form. Not until the close of the sixteenth century was it given a definite name or did it become customary for all the towns with the right to participate in the estates to send deputies. During the reigns of Henry III and Henry IV, the three estates generally met during the winter to vote the routine taxes for the coming year. They retained the

86. Ibid., pp. 340–51, 421–24, 459–62, 551; *Ord. François Ier*, 7:282–83.

exclusive right to elect the procureurs joints for the three estates, to appoint the treasurer and clerks, and to admit new towns to the estates. The assembly of the communities elected the syndic of the communities and voted additional sums required between the regular meetings of the estates. Both could send deputations to the king and deal with the countless matters that might be called to their attention.[87]

The towns must have welcomed the creation of the assembly of the communities because it gave them an organization in which they were decidedly the predominant element. This was especially true because the nobility, not being content to be the most numerous element in the three estates, had organized a separate assembly of their own in 1548. The occasion for this meeting was the convocation of the arrière-ban and the need to take legal action in a quarrel with the communities over tax matters. Other meetings followed in quick succession during the 1550s, several often taking place during the same year. Thereafter their frequency varied greatly depending on the problems confronting the order. The nobles elected two or more syndics to look after their interests when they were not in session. As their activities became more numerous, they added a clerk, a barrister, and a treasurer. To pay the salaries of these officials and the costs of their litigation and deputations to court, they levied a tax based on the income from their fiefs.[88]

The clergymen also instituted a general assembly, but it was less active than that of the nobility, perhaps because they already had their provincial and diocesan assemblies and from 1561 were part of a national system of representation. They too had their syndics, their lawyers, and their clerks to look after their affairs during the long periods when they were not in session.[89]

By the close of the Renaissance, Provence had provincial estates and an assembly for each estate, complete with permanent officials to do its bidding. More unique was the presence of the procureurs from the other estates in the assembly of the communities which gave that institution some claim to act for the province as a whole.

5. The Estates of Brittany

Although the dukes had begun to summon the leading Breton barons and clergymen to assemblies that became known as Parlements by the beginning of the thirteenth century, the provincial estates of Brittany developed more slowly than those in many other parts of France. Not until 1352 can it be

87. Hildesheimer, *Les assemblées générales*, pp. 9–63, 115–34; *Les Bouches-du-Rhône*, 3:475–80.

88. *Les Bouches-du-Rhône*, 3:508–21; *IAD, Bouches-du-Rhône*, sér. C., ed. Louis Blancard (Marseilles, 1884), 1:154–61.

89. *Les Bouches-du-Rhône*, 3:521–24.

proven that the towns named deputies to these Parlements. The duties of the early parlements were essentially judicial and political. Only rarely were they asked to agree to a tax, but taxes were sometimes levied on ducal orders without consent. The term *estates* began to be used in 1408, but only at the close of the ducal period did the Parlement and estates become clearly distinct institutions.[90]

When Duke Francis II died in 1488, he left his daughter, Anne, as his heir. Two French kings, Charles VIII and Louis XII, had to marry her and one, Francis I, had to marry her daughter before Brittany was united with the French crown. Far from threatening the existence of the three estates, the successive steps between 1491 and 1532 that led to the reunion of Brittany assured them a permanent place in the government of the province. Charles VIII, and much more specifically Louis XII and Francis I, promised not to levy taxes without their consent and designated them as custodians of the privileges of the province.[91] Under the Valois and early Bourbon kings, the estates met at least once a year, their composition became more clearly defined, and they began to elect permanent officials. For the clergy the nine bishops, the forty abbots, and the deputies of the nine cathedral chapters were gradually accepted as composing the first estate, although only the chapters habitually availed themselves of the privilege of participating through their deputies. Initially only the barons and other leading nobles were convoked, but by the early seventeenth century gentlemen without fiefs were permitted to attend. The number of towns that were directed to elect deputies also increased until 1614, when a peak of forty-four was reached. During the fifteenth century those who attended voted by head, but in the course of the sixteenth century, it became customary to vote by order, although deliberations continued to be in common under most circumstances, and three estates nearly always presented a common front when they dealt with the crown in taxation, petitions of grievances, and other matters.[92]

The earliest mention of a syndic, a treasurer, and a clerk of the estates is to be found in the meetings of 1522–26, but these positions had already been in existence for several years at least. In 1530 the three estates established a modest fund of 800 livres to pay their expenses; by 1575 it had grown to 8,000 livres. This increased activity is also reflected by efforts that were begun in 1534 to maintain an archives. In the course of the sixteenth century, an usher and an assistant syndic were added to the officers of the estates.[93] The three estates were slow to develop a permanent committee to

90. Armand Rebillon, *Les Etats de Bretagne de 1661 à 1789* (Paris, 1932), pp. 15–22; Marcel Planiol, *Histoire des institutions de la Bretagne* (Rennes, 1955), 3:173–216; Arthur Le Moyne de la Borderie and Barthélemy-A. Pocquet, *Histoire de Bretagne* (Paris, 1906), 4:255–61, 608–12.

91. Rebillon, *Les Etats*, pp. 22–23, 197–201.

92. Ibid., pp. 80–85, 104–15; Planiol, *Histoire*, 3:178–86, 209–10; Henri Sée, *Les Etats de Bretagne au XVIᵉ siècle* (Paris, 1895), pp. 12–17.

93. Sée, *Les Etats*, pp. 28–33; Rebillon, *Les Etats*, 26–27.

act for them during the intervals between sessions because of their suspicion that the crown might attempt to use such a body to impose taxes. During the Wars of Religion, Henry III frequently convoked special meetings of the estates in the spring to vote additional sums, especially when the entire amount requested had not been granted in the regular meeting the previous fall. These special meetings, which were generally poorly attended, were called *petits états* by the Bretons, who suspected that they were less able to resist the importunities of the crown. The three estates asked that they be assembled only once a year and in 1588 went to the length of annulling the gifts that had been made in the previous special session. In spite of their dislike of giving authority to any group, the three estates had to appoint standing committees in the early 1580s to treat with royal officials between sessions, and near the close of the decade, they began to name others to do all in their power to prevent the crown from levying taxes to which they had not given their consent.[94]

The Valois kings retained the same tax structure as the dukes did. More surprisingly, the amount they tried to extract from the province did not increase significantly until 1542 in spite of growing prosperity and inflation. The general pattern was for the kings to direct their commissioners to ask for the same amount that was granted during the preceding year. When their needs were greater, they sometimes told the commissioners to get all they could, but the estates normally voted the usual amount anyway. In several years, the total taxes fell below that reached under the dukes, and in a few instances the estates granted a little extra, but in general the basic tax, known as the *fouage*, remained at six or seven livres per hearth for a half-century following the marriage of Charles VIII and Anne of Brittany.[95] Only in 1539 is there evidence that a king acted in an arbitrary manner during this period. In that year the estates had thrown obstacles in the way of collecting a routine fouage and had refused to vote 18,000 livres to make a Breton river navigable. Angrily, Francis I ordered that both taxes be collected anyway.[96]

By 1542 Francis's financial needs had become so great that he sought to increase his Breton revenue significantly by raising the fouage from the usual six or seven livres to eight livres per hearth. Since this would establish a precedent, the sympathetic commissioners asked for a fouage of seven livres and an additional sum equal to the amount that the king would receive if the fouage was increased to eight livres. After considerable debate and strong protests, the estates consented to the commissioners' proposal. The ruse, however, was only partially successful. Although the basic fouage

94. Rebillon, *Les Etats*, pp. 461–62; Sée, *Les Etats*, pp. 37–40; C. de La Lande de Calan, "Documents inédits relatifs aux Etats de Bretagne de 1491 à 1589," *Archives de Bretagne* 15 (1909); pt. 2, 288.

95. Sée, *Les Etats*, pp. 59–61; La Lande de Calan, "Documents," pt. 1, 1–113; *Ord. François Ier*, 1:268–75, 2:139–43, 515–21, 6:28–34, 275–79.

96. La Lande de Calan, "Documents," pt. 1, 91–93.

remained at seven livres per hearth, additional sums collected after the manner of the fouage were demanded by the crown in 1543 and frequently thereafter.[97]

The estates also had the privilege of voting taxes on goods sold in towns that were exempt from the fouage. At first these levies were exceptional, but beginning in 1543, Francis succeeded in winning consent for such a tax designated to pay the province's share of the costs of an army of 50,000 infantry, and it too became a permanent fixture. On the other hand, between 1555 and 1557 the three estates managed to escape from a tariff, the obligation to pay for convoys for their merchant vessels, and the erection of some additional judicial offices, albeit at the price of voting large extraordinary levies.[98]

The Bretons' success was due primarily to the powerful position their estates enjoyed. Among the privileges they claimed were the right to consent to the creation of new offices and the installation of garrisons, as well as the more common privilege of consenting to taxation. The hard-pressed kings sometimes violated these privileges in an effort to increase their revenue, but they were usually quick to reach a compromise with the estates.[99] The estates did not scorn to give presents to their governors and other important officials who doubtless reciprocated by urging the kings to be lenient. As a result, the real income the crown received from Brittany declined until near the close of Francis I's reign and probably did not recover before the commencement of the Wars of Religion. A side effect of the fortunate position of the Bretons was that it led them to develop the offices and institutions necessary to carry out their will in a more leisurely fashion than the inhabitants of other, more threatened provinces.

All the estates that have thus far been treated defined their composition and procedures, increased their functions, and developed bureaucracies during the Renaissance. Only in Dauphiné had the three estates begun to make significant progress in any of these directions prior to the second quarter of the fifteenth century. They all managed to moderate royal fiscal demands, and if due weight is given to inflation, only Dauphiné was paying more taxes at the outbreak of the Wars of Religion than it had under Louis XI. At times the kings had violated their privileges by taxing without consent, creating offices for revenue purposes, and instituting other measures designed to improve their financial position, but at no point did any of them seek to weaken or destroy the estates, which emerged in 1560 in a stronger position than ever before.

97. Ibid., pp. 105–119. Sée, *Les Etats*, pp. 61–62.

98. Sée, *Les Etats*, pp. 62, 67, 70–71, 81–82; La Lande de Calan, "Documents," pt. 1, 134–41.

99. Sée, *Les Etats*, pp. 53–59.

4

THE ESTATES IN GUYENNE

THERE WAS A LARGE VARIETY OF ESTATES IN GUYENNE. AT THE TOP OF THE hierarchy stood the provincial assemblies, which were referred to as the three estates of the duchy of Aquitaine (or Guyenne) during the Middle Ages. The term *duchy* continued to be used to describe these meetings long after Guyenne had reverted to the crown, but the term *government* was also employed during the sixteenth century to denote the same type of assembly. Finally, negotiations concerning a wine tax established in 1561 caused the généralité to become the territorial unit that defined the provincial estates in this area. Beneath the regional assemblies were those of the three estates or of the individual estates of the seneschalsies and of financial jurisdictions, called *recettes*. Still smaller were a wide variety of assemblies of counties and similar jurisdictions.

1. The Estates of the Duchy,
Government, and Généralité

Assemblies of the secular estates appeared in Agenais in the late twelfth century and in the seneschalsy of Guyenne, or Bordeaux (as it will hereafter be called to avoid confusion with the duchy), by the middle of the thirteenth century, but the estates of the duchy were probably not utilized until a much later date. Perhaps their real beginning did not occur until after Edward III had won full sovereignty over a greatly extended duchy by the terms of the treaty of Brétigny (1360) and had turned it over to his eldest son, the Black Prince, to govern as an autonomous apanage. That doughty warrior was in constant need of money. Mindful of the convenience of the English system of winning consent to taxation in one large assembly rather than numerous small ones, he convoked the three estates of his duchy annually between 1364 and 1368. In 1368, he succeeded in winning a five-year grant in return for numerous concessions, including a promise not to levy taxes without consent. This act, coupled with a similar pledge made by the duke of Lancaster in 1395, suggests that representative assemblies were frequent during the period of English rule, although neither the prince nor the duke specified that consent would be obtained from the estates of the duchy rather than local assemblies. Furthermore the constant fluctuation in the boundaries of the duchy must have mitigated against the formation of a well-established institution commanding the loyalty of the people.[1]

Representatives of the estates negotiated the transfer of Guyenne to the French in 1451 and received from Charles VII a confirmation of their privileges in return. Discontent with French rule grew rapidly, however, and many of the inhabitants supported the English when they returned the following year. As a result, the privileges of Guyenne were not reconfirmed after the French reconquest in 1453, thereby giving Charles, who had soured on the use of large assemblies, a justification for abandoning the estates of the duchy. Louis XI was more sympathetic to representative assemblies than his father had been during his later years, and it was at the request of the three estates of the duchy that he created a Parlement in Bordeaux in 1462. There may have been no further meetings of the estates of the duchy until he named his brother, Charles of France, duke of Guyenne in 1469. Charles was a kindly if somewhat indolent prince, who was anxious to win the affection of his subjects. He appears to have been on the verge of increasing the role of the estates of Normandy when he was transferred from that duchy to Guyenne. Once in Guyenne, he lost little time in summoning the three estates of his newly acquired apanage to meet before him in Cahors in February 1470. Here a well-attended assembly voted him 120,000 livres to pay his debts, which his officials were to collect over a three-year period. The three estates apparently had no bureaucracy of their own at this time. Charles died prematurely in 1472 before he had occasion to renew the experiment that had proved so successful.[2]

With the death of Charles, the duchy escheated to the crown, and soon governors were acting in the king's name in southwestern France. It is possible that the three estates of the duchy were not summoned during the next two generations, although the smaller seneschalsy and recette assemblies continued to be active. A revival of the ducal assembly did take place during the reign of Francis I. In July 1528 he authorized the renewal of trade with Spain in response to a request from "the people of the three estates of our pays and duchy of Guyenne."[3] The following month Francis

---

1. Thomas N. Bisson, *Assemblies and Representation in Languedoc in the Thirteenth Century* (Princeton, 1964), pp. 73–101; Désiré Brissaud, *Les Anglais en Guyenne* (Paris, 1875), pp. 272–86; Eleanor C. Lodge, *Gascony under English Rule* (London, 1926), pp. 100–01, 146–47; *Archives municipales de Bordeaux* (Bordeaux, 1867), 1:172–77, 259–67; Léon Cadier, *La sénéchaussée des Lannes sous Charles VII* (Paris, 1885), pp. 12–13; Roland Delachenal, *Historie de Charles V* (Paris, 1928), 4:55–60.

2. Lodge, *Gascony*, pp. 127–34; *Archives municipales de Bordeaux*, 2:41–51; J. R. Major, *Representative Institutions in Renaissance France, 1421–1559* (Madison, 1960), pp. 44–45, 51; *Ord.*, 15:502; Henri Stein, *Charles de France* (Paris, 1919), pp. 262–63, 317–22, 380–81, 714–19, 755, 778–80. Henri Prentout, *Les Etats provinciaux de Normandie* (Caen, 1925–27), 1:190–92, 2:111–12.

3. *Ord. François Ier*, 5:168. I have not made a thorough search in the archives for assemblies of the duchy during this period but have not stumbled on any meetings between 1470 and 1528 in my limited investigation.

named as governor Henri d'Albret, king of Navarre and grandfather of the future Henry IV. The estates of some (if not all) of the individual seneschalsies or recettes soon responded by voting Albret a special gift in honor of his appointment and no doubt to secure his good will, but no ducal assembly was apparently held.[4]

The opportunity for the estates of the duchy to play a more active role came when Francis I decided to extend the gabelle and the greniers à sel to southwestern France. Because of its long period under English rule, the region had been subject to only a 25 percent sales tax on salt, known as the *quart du sel*, when Francis came to the throne. In 1537 he took the first step toward putting Guyenne on an equal basis with most of the remainder of France by increasing the sales tax to 37.5 percent. The reaction was immediate. Complaints flowed into court, and in August Francis dispatched the bishop of Bazas to the south with a commission to assemble the three estates of the duchy of Guyenne to hear their complaints. Bazas instructed the estates of the seneschalsies to send deputies to several meetings that were held in Bordeaux between November 1537 and January 1538, but a mutually satisfactory solution was not achieved. In April 1542 Francis issued a decree once more raising the gabelle. Rebellions broke out in La Rochelle, Saintonge, and parts of Guyenne that caused him to retract, but only for a moment, for in July 1544 he took the final step of creating greniers à sel in Guyenne and other parts of France where they had not formerly existed.[5]

Several months before he created the greniers à sel, Francis had erected six élections in Guyenne with the usual officials to assume the tax-collecting duties that had previously been performed by the estates of the recettes.[6] He had also appointed a clerk of the estates of the duchy of Guyenne "for the good of our service" and to secure "more prompt and accurate information concerning the affairs of the estates."[7]

One might be tempted to see these steps as an effort to supplant the tax officials of the estates by those of the king in order to be in a position to suppress these representative institutions. Such a program would have been furthered by having a royally appointed clerk of the estates of the duchy who would be in a position to keep the council informed. It is possible that some of Francis's advisers considered such a plan, but it is more likely that these offices were created and sold as a means to increase royal revenue, for during this period Francis was seeking additional funds by a number of other

4. BN ms. Languedoc (Doat), 234, fols. 95–96v. AD, Gironde, E suppl. 2345. L. de Cardenal, "Catalogue des assemblées des Etats de Périgord de 1378 à 1651," *Bul. phil. et hist. (jusqu'à 1715) du comité des travaux historiques et scientifiques* (1938–39): 253.

5. Roger Doucet, *Les institutions de la France au XVIe siècle* (Paris, 1948), 2:584–86; AN, J 972, no. 5; AC, Agen, CC 49, assemblies of October–December 1537; *Les jurades de la ville de Bergerac*, ed. G. Charrier (Bergerac, 1894), 3:85, 87–88; Jean J. Clamageran, *Historie de l'impôt en France* (Paris, 1868), 2:119–24.

6. *IAD, Gironde, sér. 1 B*, ed. Jean-A. Brutails (Bordeaux, 1925), p. 16.

7. Francis to Pierre Secondat, July 13, 1544, AD, Haute-Garonne, C 3796. See also *Actes Francois Ier*, 4: nos. 13,907, 14,090.

extraordinary means. In August 1543 he alienated 600,000 livres worth of his domain and created five additional councillors in the Parlement of Bordeaux. In the next year he raised a loan of 300,000 livres in Guyenne and comparable sums in other parts of France. He also added an additional president and a chamber to Parlement, created a new seneschalsy at La Réole with the accompanying officers, and appointed four new councillors in the seneschalsy of Bazas, all measures that brought money into the royal coffers but did little to further an absolutist course. Additional evidence that the élections were created because of the need for money is provided by the fact that they were suppressed in May 1545 at the behest of the estates who paid a high price for this favor. Most of the other offices that had been created suffered similar fates because of the protests and, no doubt, the willingness of those concerned to pay.[8] What happened to the clerk of the estates of the duchy is not known beyond that we hear no more of the position, a fact suggesting that this post was also soon suppressed. Opposition to the creation of the clerkship had come largely from the officers of Henri d'Albret, king of Navarre, who was governor of Guyenne. This indicates that estates had not yet developed a bureaucracy of their own and were relying on the officials of their governor to perform these duties just as they had relied on those of their duke to apportion taxes before the duchy had escheated to the crown for the final time in 1472.[9]

Francis also abandoned his effort to raise the gabelle to the same level as in most other parts of France. The events are obscure, but it is evident that the three estates of Guyenne met and offered the king 400,000 livres to abolish the gabelle.[10] Perhaps because the sum was too small, this proposal came to naught. Another revolt followed that was brutally repressed in 1548, but not without making both the crown and estates more willing to reach an agreement. The estates of Guyenne once more swung into action. Deputies from jurisdictions in southwestern France met on eight occasions between April 1549 and October 1553. Their deliberations led first to the abolition of the greniers à sel and a reduction in the salt tax in return for a grant of 450,000 livres to the crown and later to the total abolition of the salt tax in return for 1,195,000 more. Two thirds of this sum was provided by the third estate, but the remaining third was taken from the nobility and clergy. Henri d'Albret himself presided over most of these meetings and seemingly

8. *IAD, Gironde, sér. 1 B*, pp. 13–16. *IAD, Gironde, sér. E. suppl.*, ed. Jean-A. Brutails (Bordeaux, 1901), 2:193; L. Bourrachot, "L'emprunt forcé de 1544 en Bazadais," *Cahiers de Bazadais* 8 (1968): 11–12. For the offer the estates of Comminges made to Francis I for the suppression of the élections, see AD, Haute-Garonne, C 3416.

9. *IAD, Gironde, sér. 1 B*, p. 15; Stein, *Charles de France*, pp. 778–80.

10. The estates of Guyenne probably assembled during the summer of 1544 to make Francis I the offer. See the letter of convocation dated July 4, AD, Haute-Garonne, C 3416. The three estates of Périgord met during the spring of 1546 to apportion their share of the 400,000 livres. *Les jurades de Bergerac*, 3:160–62, 183–84.

utilized the opportunity they afforded to summon the deputies of every possible province, perhaps to extend the boundaries of his vaguely defined government and more certainly to enhance his prestige. Included were not only the seneschalsies that were undisputedly in the duchy of Guyenne but also Poitou, Haut- and Bas-Limousin, Saintonge, Angoumois, Haute- and Basse-Marche, and the town and government of La Rochelle. The Aquitaine of the Black Prince was thus recreated and, with it, the largest regional representative assembly in France.[11]

Once the problem of the gabelle was solved, there may have been a three-year lull before there was another regional assembly. Henri d'Albret died in 1555, perhaps without having the opportunity to indulge himself again in such a meeting, and he was replaced as governor by his son-in-law, Antoine de Bourbon, king of Navarre. Navarre assembled the estates of Guyenne in Bordeaux in September 1556. Hardly had the meeting terminated than the syndics of local estates petitioned Henry II to continue to convoke the regional assembly. The dioceses and provinces of Guyenne had their individual estates to levy the taille and to regulate their respective affairs, they pointed out, but a regional assembly was needed to deal with matters concerning the entire duchy. Henry II acquiesced and on October 24, 1556, ordered Antoine to have each subordinate jurisdiction in his government elect one deputy from each estate to attend an assembly in a convenient locality of his own choosing.[12] In Bordeaux in September of the following year, Antoine presided over the deputies of the estates elected from the jurisdictions clearly within his government, as well as from Haut-Limousin and La Rochelle. Whatever the original intent of the inhabitants of Guyenne in asking for the meeting, the crown turned it into an appeal for money to support the army in Picardy, which had just suffered a severe defeat at Saint-Quentin, and to a charge to the individual towns that were in exposed positions to look to their defenses at their own expense.[13]

The three estates of the government of Guyenne met in Bordeaux in March and May 1561 to elect deputies to attend the Estates General of Pontoise and again in Périgueux in July 1566 to protest a tax on wine that

11. The estates were held in Tarbes in April 1549, in Poitiers in July and twice in November 1549, in Pau in January 1550, in Poitiers in 1550, in St.-Jean-d'Angély in July 1552, and in Poitiers in October 1553. *Registres consulaires de la ville de Limoges*, ed. Emile Ruben (Limoges, 1867–69), 1:427–32, 472–74, 477–80, 2:23–44; *Les jurades de Bergerac*, 3:188–89; Cardenal, "Catalogue," pp. 255–58; Joseph M. Tyrrell, *A History of the Estates of Poitou* (The Hague, 1968), pp. 57–64; *AHG*, 28 (1893): 48–49; AC, La Réole, BB 3, fols. 72–73, 78–81v, 90v; AC, Agen, BB 27, fols. 99–100; *Archives historiques de Poitou* 12 (1882): 39–40.

12. AD, Haute-Garonne, C 3796, *Cahiers des remonstrances des Etats de Comminges aux rois de France ou à leurs lieutenants généraux en Guyenne, 1537–1627*, ed. Jean Lestrade (Saint-Gaudens, 1943), pp. 11–13.

13. *Registres de Limoges*, 2:135–57; *Archives historiques de la Saintonge et de l'Aunis* 17 (1889): 126–28; AC, Auch, BB 5, fols. 8, 12v–15v; AD, Haute-Garonne, C 3467, C 3796; AC, Gourdon (Lot), AA 4; *Cahiers de Comminges*, pp. 13–36.

had hitherto been dealt with by the third estates of the généralité of Guyenne and the other jurisdictions separately. Haut-Limousin participated in all of these assemblies, and Bas-Limousin and Auvergne were represented in the last. The future of provincial assemblies, however, lay not with the government or duchy but rather with the généralité.[14]

The généralité of Guyenne was created by Francis I in 1523 out of the oversized financial jurisdiction of Languedoil. Initially it consisted of Haut- and Bas-Limousin, and Périgord, where there were both élections and estates, although the estates of the two Limousins rarely met, and Rouergue, Quercy, Agenais, Condomois, Bazadais, Armagnac, Lannes, Comminges, and Rivière-Verdun, where there were only estates. An élection consisting of Bordeaux and the surrounding communities was created at some point prior to 1530. In 1542 Haut- and Bas-Limousin were detached from the géné- ralité, and in 1558 they were united with other provinces to form a new généralité with its seat in Limoges. Thus by 1542 the two Limousins, the two Marches, Poitou, Saintonge, Angoumois, and La Rochelle, which had once been a part of the duchy of Guyenne, had become excluded from the généralité.[15] Some of these excluded seneschalsies occasionally participated in the assemblies of the duchy until 1566, but in none of them were the estates regularly convoked after the close of the Hundred Years War. Charles VII had removed the most important reason for their existence when he appointed élus within their jurisdictions to levy and collect taxes. Thus although the estates of these provinces continued to meet occasionally during the sixteenth century, they were not convoked thereafter except to elect deputies to the Estates General.[16]

The généralité was chosen as the jurisdiction for the estates in the southwest in the fall of 1561 when the crown decided to impose a tax on wine brought into the towns and their suburbs in order to pay its debts. The king's council attempted to associate the levy with the actions of the Estates General that had met in Pontoise in August, although both the nobility and the third estate had refused to contribute anything and had suggested that the king obtain the necessary money from the clergy. The wine tax was to be collected for six years and was to be paid by everyone, including the princes

14. *Registres de Limoges*, 2:220–22, 315–18; AC, Auch, BB 5, fols. 22v–23; AD, Haute-Garonne, C 3490; *AHG*, 33 (1900); 192–208; L. de Cardenal, "Note sur les archives des Etats de Périgord," *Bul. de la soc. hist. et arch. du Périgord* 39 (1912): 150–52; AD, Gironde, G 40, no. 2.

15. L. Desgraves, "La formation territoriale de la généralité de Guyenne," *Annales du Midi* 62 (1950): 239–48; *Actes Francois I*^{er}, 4: no. 14,469. Desgraves, "La formation," p. 242, states that the élection of Bordeaux was established between 1523 and 1571, but an act of 1530 proves that it existed at that time. *Actes Francois I*^{er}, 6: no. 20,105. He also said that there was an élection in Lannes, p. 241, but as noted on p. 116 below, the élection was suppressed after the death of Charles VII.

16. Antoine Thomas, *Les Etats provinciaux de la France centrale sous Charles VII* (Paris, 1879). Of these estates, only those of Poitous have been systematically studied. See Tyrrell, *Estates of Poitou*.

of the blood.[17] To an important wine-producing region such as Guyenne, this tax posed a serious threat. Deputies at the Estates General learned of the levy before they departed from Pontoise and made their inevitable protest. As a result of their efforts, they secured royal letters dated October 4 convoking the estates of the seneschalsies to consider an alternate tax and to name deputies to attend a meeting of the third estate of the généralité in Agen in November. It was logical for the généralité rather than the government to be selected as the jurisdiction to be summoned because the meeting was concerned solely with taxation, but the Renaissance monarchy was not noted for its logic, and the estates of the government had been used to deal with tax matters on previous occasions. Hence other unknown factors may have been involved. Undue significance should not be attached to the shift, however, because the claims of the governor of Guyenne over the jurisdictions to the north of the généralité had always been vague. In March and May 1561 when the government served as the electoral unit for the Estates General at Pontoise, only Haut- and Bas-Limousin had participated from outside the généralité. The shift to convoking the généralité alone in November 1561 simply meant that the three estates of the two Limousins carried on one set of negotiations to alter the nature of the wine tax and the third estates of the généralité of Guyenne carried on another. Of greater interest and even less explainable was the decision to consult only the third estate in Guyenne; the other orders were theoretically subject to the wine tax and had participated in the assemblies of the government on previous occasions when financial matters had been debated.[18]

So little advanced notice was given of the meeting that there was insufficient time to summon the estates of Rouergue, Armagnac, and Quercy to select deputies, so these provinces were represented by their uninstructed syndics. The first item of business was the election of the officers. A clerk of the town council of Agen was chosen as clerk of the estates without opposition, but a dispute broke out over the choice of a presiding officer. The two deputies from the town and seneschalsy of Bordeaux claimed that the position belonged to one of them as a right because their city was the capital of Guyenne and its representatives had customarily presided over the third estate in the assemblies of the government. The other delegates denied this pretension but proceeded to elect Guillaume Le Blanc, a barrister in the Parlement of Bordeaux who had represented Guyenne in the Estates General at Pontoise, because of his experience and personal qualities. This

---

17. J. R. Major, *The Estates General of 1560* (Princeton, 1951), pp. 103–04, and "The Third Estate in the Estates General of Pontoise, 1561," *Speculum* 29 (1954): 460–76, esp. 474; Isambert, 14:117–22. It was specifically stated in the meeting of the estates of the généralité of Guyenne that the wine tax had not been voted in the Estates General. *AHG* 28:58.

18. G. Zeller, "Gouverneurs de provinces au XVIe siècle," *Revue historique* 185 (1939): 239–40; *AHG* 35:197–98; *Registres de Limoges*, 2:220–22, 229–33, 235, 251–55.

compromise solution, however, failed to satisfy the other representative from Bordeaux.[19]

Having created these difficulties, the deputies from Bordeaux caused further discord by presenting procurations prepared by the meetings of the seneschalsy and of the town of Bordeaux instructing them to accept the wine tax rather than make the king a counteroffer to secure its removal. This decision was caused by their fear that the other jurisdictions would make them pay a disproportionately large share of any sum offered the king in lieu of the revenue from the wine tax. The other deputies argued that decisions in the assembly should be made by *"la pluralité des voix et par la majoure et plus saine partye,"* but Le Blanc persisted in his insistence on following his instructions and departed from the meeting.[20] Those who remained elected a deputy from Agen as presiding officer and voted to send a delegation to court with two procurations, one offering the king 500,000 livres to be collected over a six-year period from the entire généralité, including Bordeaux and the seneschalsy of Lannes, which claimed to be exempt because it was a frontier province. If the king refused to accept, the second procuration, which included an offer of 600,000 livres, was to be submitted. Both stipulated that the tax would be levied by the municipal officials or their deputies and used to redeem the royal domain and to pay the crown debts in the généralité rather than be turned over to royal tax officials.[21]

A second assembly of the estates of the généralité was held at Gourdon in January 1562 to permit the deputies from Quercy, Rouergue, and Armagnac to approve the arrangements made at Agen, a step that they could not take at that meeting because they had received no instructions from their respective estates. At Gourdon the amount to be paid to the crown by each of the seneschalsies in return for revoking the wine tax was set. Apparently several of the seneschalsies felt that they had been asked to contribute too much, because in April when the king accepted the estates' offer of 600,000 livres to be collected over a period of six years, he reapportioned the amount each jurisdiction was to pay. Since neither the town nor the seneschalsy of Bordeaux had sent deputies to the meeting at Gourdon and had persisted in their refusal to accept a substitute for the wine tax, the king at this time reduced the annual levy to 74,000 livres, leaving the remaining 26,000 to be paid by the recalcitrant city and seneschalsy, which was permitted to keep the wine tax. The king also ordered that new meetings of the estates be held to decide how the tax should be levied. They were to elect a receiver to accept the money that was collected and to use it to redeem the mortgaged domain and to pay the crown's debts in the

19. *AHG*, 2°:44–50, 63.
20. Ibid., p ,3.
21. Ibid.   ,. 50–61.

généralité. The deputies were also authorized to levy an additional sum to pay their expenses.[22]

In April 1562 the king convoked a meeting of the estates of the individual seneschalsies to learn the amount that he had set as their share of the new tax and to consider how the money should be raised. They were also instructed to elect deputies to a meeting of the third estate of the généralité which would be held at Condom in July to deal collectively with the tax. At Condom, Jean de Maliac was elected receiver of the estates and instructed to levy, take, and receive the money due the king and to employ it to redeem his domain and to pay his debts. If the king or anyone else instructed Maliac to divert this revenue, he was to notify the deputies of the estates rather than obey. The estates in return promised to pay for all damages he might suffer for his disobedience. The estates also approved the amount that the king had set for each seneschalsy to pay in return for the removal of the wine tax. To this figure were added sums to reimburse Maliac for his services and to pay the costs of deputations and other activities. Finally the king was asked to postpone the initiation of the tax until January 1563.[23]

The nobility and the clergy of Guyenne had not participated in these meetings, but they must have watched the developments with interest because they were subject to the wine tax in accordance to the original royal decree. In their pronouncements, the third estate had voiced the opinion that the privileged and nonprivileged alike should pay any tax offered as a substitute. In April 1562 deputies of the nobility and clergy met in Moissac. Almost nothing is known of their deliberations, but it is probable that they protested against being subject to taxation because in October of that year the king confirmed their traditional exemption at the same time that he gave final approval to the proposals the third estate had made at Condom.[24]

One might suppose that at this point the activities of the third estate of the généralité would decline, but this was not the case. There were arguments over whether the tax was fairly distributed among the seneschalsies, and efforts were made to get the levy removed altogether before the six-year period had ended. These considerations led to new meetings, six taking place between the July 1562 assembly in Condom and the summer of 1565. Then came the inevitable attempt of the crown to extend the tax beyond the

22. Ibid., pp. 67–69. There were protests over the division of the tax in January 1563. AD, Haute-Garonne, C 3796.

23. *AHG* 28:70–84. In view of the general distrust of royal tax officials, it is interesting to note that Maliac was accused of fiscal dishonesty in 1570 and later found guilty. *Commentaires de Blaise de Monluc*, ed. Paul Courteault (Paris, 1964), p. 1185 n.4. In January 1617 the estates of the généralité took another step toward expanding the bureaucracy by appointing one general agent to look after regional interests at court and another to do so at home. AC, Agen, BB 42, fols. 315v–17.

24. AD, Haute-Garonne, C 3480; *AHG* 28:84–88.

initial six years and with it five more sessions between December 1567 and May 1569. In all there were at least forty-six meetings of the third estate of the généralité between November 1561 and the succession of Henry IV to the throne in August 1589.[25]

The peculiar circumstances leading to the formation of the estates of the généralité strongly influenced its organizations and procedures. The nobility and clergy had not been summoned to deliberate on the wine tax, and they rarely sent deputies to the meetings in later years. The town and seneschalsy of Bordeaux had refused to accept the alternate tax and were therefore not involved in the negotiations and renegotiations on this subject. They often failed to send deputies to the meetings, and leadership in the third estate was seized by the municipal officials of Agen. In this objective the Agen officials were aided by the fact that the regional Bureau of Finances was established in their midst between 1542 and 1566, thereby making their city the financial capital of the généralité. The Bureau of Finances was transferred back to Bordeaux in 1566, but by this time the position of Agen was ensured. The central location of Agen in the généralité also contributed to its rise to a position of leadership.[26]

Of interest is the attitude of the crown toward these developments. It had permitted, indeed perhaps encouraged, the series of assemblies of the three estates of the government following the revolt against the gabelle in 1548, and it had encouraged the development of the estates of the généralité in the post-1561 period. The goal of the crown was to extract money from the region, a feat that it believed could be better accomplished by working in conjunction with representative assemblies than in opposition to them. To secure cooperation and to enable the deputies to function effectively, the crown had been willing for them to choose the form of the tax, to have a clerk, to vote sums to support their activities, to elect the official who would receive the taxes, and to provide guarantees that the money raised would be used to redeem the royal domain and to pay the king's debts, not diverted to other purposes.[27]

There was nothing unusual in this attitude of the crown. Near the close of the Estates General of Orléans, Chancellor L'Hôpital had told the deputies of the third estate that they could appoint a committee consisting of échevins of the towns and other responsible persons to collect any additional taxes

25. The principal sources for a history of the estates of Guyenne are the archives of the estates of Comminges, now located in AD, Haute-Garonne, C 3401–807, and the archives of the estates of Agenais in AC Agen, which are located in AD, Lot-en-Garonne. Additional information may be found in the archives in Auch, Lecture, Bordeaux, Périgueux, and other towns in the region.

26. Desgraves, "La formation territoriale," p. 243.

27. In 1564 the estates also won the crown's approval to replace the receivers to whom the collected tailles were given by an appointee of the estates, but this substitution was blocked by the intransigence of the royal tax officials. *AHG,* 28:91–93.

they would agree to pay, and the Estates General of Pontoise was designed to give the vocal elements of the population an opportunity to express their opinion as to the best means to raise money for the crown. The government, in short, was anxious to rule in conjunction with the estates in return for additional revenue. The deputies of the secular orders at the two national assemblies, however, were unwilling to pay this price. It is significant that in Guyenne the third estate was willing, and a large provincial assembly emerged as a result of the desires of both the crown and the inhabitants themselves.[28]

Finally the slow development of the provincial estates prevented that institution from being able to assert its authority over the estates of the seneschalsies. The shifting between convoking the duchy, government, and généralité and the changing boundaries of these jurisdictions delayed the appearance of a permanent bureaucracy until 1562 and of a definite territorial base until a few years later. By that time the estates of the seneschalsies were already over a century old. They had matured much more rapidly and were firmly entrenched in their right to consent to taxes and to apportion them with the assistance of the royal commissioners who convoked them. As a result, when the third estate of the généralité finally emerged, it was in no position to assert its authority over the more advanced estates of the seneschalsies as the three estates of Languedoc had done over the assemblies of the seneschalsies and dioceses within their jurisdiction. The estates of Provence, Dauphiné, and Burgundy had also established control over their respective provinces by subordinating or destroying local assemblies and smaller jurisdictions claiming special privileges, except for the autonomous status enjoyed by the cities of Marseilles and Arles. In Guyenne, on the other hand, the estates of the généralité provided only an opportunity for the deputies to discuss their mutual problems and to seek additional strength in dealing with the crown by arriving at a common approach. Any tax that these deputies agreed upon had to be consented to by the estates of their respective seneschalsies. It will therefore be necessary to consider the estates in each of these smaller jurisdictions.

2. The Estates of the Seneschalsies and Recettes

A formulary prepared by the royal chancellery around 1530 reveals much concerning the way in which the estates of the receptes were to be convoked. In Rouergue and Quercy where the tax receivers were appointed by the estates, the letters of convocation were to be addressed to the seneschals. In Agenais, Comminges, Armagnac, Condomois, Rivière-Verdun, and Lannes where the receivers were royal officials, the letters were to be addressed to

28. Major, *Estates General of 1560*, pp. 103–04.

them. Nothing was said about where letters should be sent convoking the three estates of Périgord and Bordelais but presumably they were addressed to the élus for there were élections in both jurisdictions. Those who attended the assemblies of the estates in Guyenne were to be furnished with "sufficient powers to conclude and accord that which will be required there by us."[29] Then, in a later formulary prepared in 1558, we learn that the deputies who attended were "to grant and accord to us [the king] freely the sums of money that they [the commissioners] will require."[30] These documents strongly suggest that there was a fully developed system of representative assemblies in Guyenne that regularly gave consent to taxation, and an investigation of what actually took place confirms this suspicion, although to some extent the seneschalsy of Bordeaux was a special case.

Bordeaux was one of the two seneschalsies in which there was an élection throughout most of the sixteenth century, but it had a multitude of representative institutions. In addition to meetings of the three estates, there were separate assemblies of the clergy, the nobility, and the third estate of the seneschalsy and the *filleules*, a group of smaller towns whose representatives took a written oath to respect the privileges of Bordeaux, to aid it against enemies, to renounce foreign alliances, and to march under its banner in time of war against anyone save the king. The mayor and *jurats* swore in return to respect the privileges of the daughter towns and to defend them against attack. These contracts, which date back at least to 1379, thus took the form of an indenture that was beginning to supplant the older lord and vassal relationship as the governing tie among the nobility. The military aspect of the contracts between Bordeaux and the daughter towns presumably declined after the close of the Hundred Years War, but its mayor and jurats continued to enjoy a leadership role that included summoning the representatives of these localities to assemblies. Since these towns were located in the seneschalsy, it is often difficult to distinguish between their meetings and those of the third estate.[31]

An archivist found only twenty-one meetings of the three estates of the seneschalsy between 1320 to 1653, but there were undoubtedly many more, especially during the period of the English rule.[32] The deliberations of the municipal officials of Bordeaux survive for only seven years in the period prior to the revolt of 1548, all of them falling between 1406 and 1422. They reveal that the three estates of the seneschalsy were then meeting on an

---

29. BN ms. fr. 14,368, fol. 35. For dating the manuscript, see Hélène Michaud, *Les formulaires de grande chancellerie 1500–1800* (Paris, 1972), pp. 74–82.

30. BN ms. n.a. fr. 20,526, fol. 18v.

31. *Historie de Bordeaux*, ed. Charles Higounet (Bordeaux, 1965–66), 3:455, 4: 284, 297; *Archives municipales de Bordeaux*, 1:440–45. Thirty-seven towns were summoned by the jurats of Bordeaux to the metting of the filleules in June 1588. AC, Bordeaux, AA 26, no. 1.

32. A. Leroux, "Chronique," *Revue historique de Bordeaux* 11 (1918): 57.

average of one or more times a year. In addition, there was one meeting of the three estates of the duchy of Guyenne in Dax during the spring of 1420.[33]

The three estates of the seneschalsy may have continued to be active between the reannexation by France and the establishment of the élus, but once the crown organized its own tax-collecting machinery, meetings became rarer, although the estates appear to have retained a voice in the apportionment of the taille. The jurats preserved the right to summon representatives from the filleules when they thought it expedient, and this they did on at least five occasions between 1573 and 1585. However, the fiscal role of the assemblies in the seneschalsies had changed; instead of the three estates voting taxes, the third estate protested against levies and observed the division of taxes by the élus. Assemblies of the clergy of the diocese of Bordeaux were frequent after 1561 because of the need to choose delegates to the national meetings of their order and to deal with the levies that they agreed to pay. The nobility, on the other hand, rarely met except to elect deputies to the Estates General.[34]

The history of the assemblies in Périgord differs from those in Bordelais. Prior to the treaty of Brétigny in 1360, Périgord had been part of Languedoc, and its leading citizens had participated in the meetings of the three estates of that province. During the brief period of English rule that followed, they presumably attended the assemblies of the duchy of Guyenne. At what point they developed their own assemblies is not known, but the first recorded meeting of the three estates was in 1378. Judging by the scant surviving records, meetings were rather frequent thereafter. Even the advent of the élus at the close of the Hundred Years War brought no reduction of activity as it had in many other provinces. Indeed by 1522 the three estates had a syndic, and by 1554 they elected representatives, called *définiteurs*, who acted for them when they were not in session. The estates normally

33. *Archives municipales de Bordeaux*, 3:i, 95, 99, 117, 138, 170, 177, 288–93, 297, 298, 4:2, 4–5, 28–33, 270–71, 294, 326, 369–84, 578. For references to the estates under the English, see Malcolm G. A. Vale, *English Gascony, 1399–1453* (Oxford, 1970), pp. 28 n.5, 35, 44, 63, 69, 81, 86, 198.

34. Scant material survives on the first century of French rule, but references to meetings of the three estates are found in AN, KK 648, no. 119; *IAD, Gironde, sér. G*, ed. Alexandre Gouget et al. (Bordeaux, 1892), 1:166–95 passim; *Registre du clerc de Ville*, ed. Pierre Harlé (Bordeaux, 1912), pp. 282, 299, 304; *Recueil des privilèges accordés à la ville de Bordeaux par Charles VII et Louis XI*, ed. Marcel Gouron (Bordeaux, 1937), pp. 135, 163–64, 167; *Archives municipales de Bordeaux*, 11, *Registres de la jurade*, 6:314; BN, ms. fr. 18,153, fol. 404v; *AHG*, 10:409, 21:303–06, 32:108–09. The best sources for the assemblies of the filleules during the Wars of Regligion are the archives of Bourg-sur-Gironde and Saint-Emilion. See esp. AD, Gironde, E suppl. 590, 2345–47, 4403, 4406–17, 4463. My belief that the estates participated in the apportionment of the taille is based on the report of a jurat who had been deputed to take part in the "estates and the apportionment" of the taille of 1585 by the municipal council of Saint-Emilion. BB 9, p. 251. For references to assemblies of the clergy see AD, Gironde, G 26, G 35, G 40, G 45, G 47, G 287–90, G 479, G 585–87.

functioned as a single house and chose together their syndic and définiteurs, who numbered six from each estate by the close of the century.[35]

The vigor of the estates can be partly attributed to the continued presence of the nobility and clergy. In Normandy, Auvergne, and Bordelais, these two orders lost interest after the élus assumed the principal tax-collecting role. Furthermore the three estates in Périgord generally presented a united front to the crown by electing and instructing their delegations together. This cooperative spirit may have been facilitated by the controlling position the bourgeois patricians of Périgueux, seconded by those of Bergerac and Sarlat, enjoyed in the third estate. As possessors of offices, owners of rentes and landed estates, and citizens of towns having extensive privileges, they had more in common with the nobility than with the petit bourgeoisie and peasants of the small towns and villages, whose interests they sometimes ignored. It is true that by 1553 the officials of twenty-four smaller towns had the right to be summoned to the estates, but their voice was rarely decisive. With the coming of the Wars of Religion, higher taxes and marauding troops increased the suffering of the countryside. Finally in 1583 eight of the smaller towns with seats in the estates charged that the urban patricians were permitting them to suffer while they profited from their connections with tax officials and gave presents to the syndic of the estates in return for his support. They asked that a special syndic be named to represent the plat pays, a request that the spokesman for Périgueux rejected, although several other concessions were granted.[36]

The estates of Bordeaux and Périgord, like those of the généralité, were subject to one potential threat. It was not necessary for them to meet each winter to vote and apportion the taille, and several years often elapsed between their meetings. The jurats of Bordeaux and the syndics and définiteurs of Périgord, however, were permanent officials who kept watchful eyes on the privileges and welfare of their respective seneschalsies. As long as the monarchy accepted the existence of representative institutions, they could arrange for meetings whenever there was need.

There were no élections in the remaining seneschalsies in Guyenne, but the good fortune of their inhabitants resulted from their constant vigilance and willingness to pay rather than from royal favor. In September 1519 and again in April 1544, Francis I created élections in the généralité, but on each

35. Cardenal, "Catalogue;" 243–55. *IAC, Périgueux*, ed. Michel Hardy (Périgueux, 1894), pp. 15, 254. AD, Dordogne, 5C 11, 5C 21, fol. 59–59v.

36. A 1553 list of "those accustomed to be called" consisted of the bishops, abbots, priors, and syndics of the chapters (but not the curés) for the clergy, the nobles with fiefs, and the officials of twenty-seven towns. Jean-J. Escande, *Histoire du Périgord*, 2d ed. (Paris, 1957), pp. 380–81; L. de Cardenal, "Les Etats de Périgord sous Henri IV," in *L'organisation corporative du Moyen Age à la fin de l'Ancien Régime. Etudes présentées à la commission internationale pour l'historie des assemblée d'états* (Louvain, 1939), 3:165–71.

occasion he suppressed them the following year. Henry II and Henry III renewed the effort, but always the estates succeeded in obtaining the cancellation of the objectionable edict in return for compensating those who had purchased the newly created offices. So readily did the kings give in that it is evident that their aim had been to provide offices to sell. Once this transaction had taken place, they were happy enough to see the estate reimburse the new magistrates in return for abandoning their positions. The crown not only escaped having to pay salaries to these people but also could look forward to creating the same offices again in a few decades, thereby making another profit.[37]

That part of Guyenne in which there were no élections was divided into recettes to provide royal officials with an administrative framework in which to apportion the taxes desired from the region as a whole. The boundaries of these recettes did not necessarily conform to those of the seneschalsies. Where they did not, the recette was assembled when routine taxation was involved, but the seneschalsy was sometimes convoked to deal with other matters, including taxation, in special circumstances. Since the boundaries of the recettes were more frequently changed than those of the seneschalsies, there was an inordinate amount of confusion. Gascogne, for example, was a single recette until 1475 when Louis XI subdivided it into the recettes of Agenais, Condomois (including Bazadais, Albret, and Astarac), Armagnac, and Comminges. At this time Bazadais was a seneschalsy, but Condomois was joined with Agenais. Both had estates, as did Astarac. In addition, there were nine counties, viscounties, and baronies, known as the aides du pays d'Agenais, which were for the most part located in the seneschalsy of Armagnac but contributed about half of the taille levied on Agenais. These jurisdictions normally deputed to the estates of Agenais, but they also sent deputies to the estates of the seneschalsy of Armagnac when the occasion warranted.[38]

Assemblies of the secular estates of Agenais can be traced back to the late twelfth century, but meetings of the three estates do not appear to have

37. L. Desgraves, "Aux origines de l'élections d'Agen, 1519–1622," *Recueil de travaux offert à M. Clovis Brunel* (Paris, 1955), pt. 1, pp. 357–65. Numerous earlier revocations of edicts establishing the élus were cited in the register of the *Conseil d'Etat* of February 12, 1611, when the élus were once more removed from Agenais and other jurisdictions in Guyenne. See *Edict du roy, contenant révocation et supression des huit bureaux d'élections, establis en la généralité de Guyenne par édict du mois de janvier 1603* (Agen, 1612), pp. 15–19. A copy is located in BN, F 46,923 (3). AD, Haute-Garonne, C 3804.

38. G. Tholin, *Des tailles et des impositions au pays d'Agenais durant le XVIe siècle jusqu'aux réformes de Sully* (Agen, 1874), pp. 11–12, extract from *Recueil des travaux de la soc. d'agriculture, sciences et arts d'Agen*. The complex situation of the aides du pays d'Agenais can be best viewed by studying the viscounty of Bruilhois because of the rich archives of Laplume. See E. d'Antin, "Une commune gasconne pendant les Guerres de Religion, d'après les archives de Laplume," *Revue de l'Agenais* 21 (1894): 237–67.

become common before 1436.[39] By 1486 they were so well established that Charles VIII gave them permission to meet when they desired, to elect syndics, and to levy a taille of 300 livres per year to pay the expenses incurred by their activities. By the time of the Wars of Religion, the nobility and clergy had ceased to attend unless specifically summoned by the governor or seneschal, and the consuls of Agen had assumed the duties of syndic of the third estate by virtue of their position as magistrates in the principal town of the jurisdiction. They summoned the consuls of the smaller towns and communities to meetings without obtaining royal permission but failed to observe the 300 livres limit that had been set for their expenses. In normal times the deputies to the estates devoted much of their efforts to seeking reductions of long-standing taxes and to trying to block new impositions. They carried on litigation with the local nobility over whether they should pay the taille on their nonnoble lands and with other jurisdictions in Guyenne over what proportion of this tax they each should contribute. In short, they did all that was in their power to defend the privileges of the seneschalsy and to protect their citizens from outside exploitation.[40]

The leaders of the third estate were less altruistic in their dealings with the mass of the population. They paid themselves good salaries for the work they did for the estates and for their respective communities and added the sums necessary to meet these expenses to the taxes levied for the crown. The agents who collected these taxes were their appointees, and there is reason to believe that they often found means to be exempted. Rarely were their financial records properly audited by royal officials. During the Wars of Religion, the Catholics turned the estates into a political and military instrument to aid their cause. So frequently did the estates assemble that in 1569 the deputies decided that the consuls of the twelve principal towns would be sufficient to act in the name of the third estate if circumstances so warranted.[41] When Henry IV came to the throne in 1589, he was confronted by a well-organized and active third estate, but one that was vulnerable because of the absence of the nobility and the jealousy of several towns that dreamed of becoming seats of separate seneschalsies or other jurisdictions.

One of these towns, Condom, had succeeded in its ambition before the

39. Bisson, *Assemblies*, pp. 73–101, 234–46, 287–88; *AHG*, 31:116, 119, 121, 32:16–27, 39–40, 47, 50–51, 53, 59–60, 63–67. The three estates of Agenais did meet in 1363, but no further meeting has been found until 1436. G. Tholin, "Requête des trois états du pays d'Agenais au roi Edouard III," *Bul. hist. et phil. du comité des travaux historiques et scientifiques* 17 (1899): 426–30. See also *AHG*, 29:284, and P. S. Lewis, *Later Medieval France* (London, 1968), 369–70.

40. G. Tholin, *Des tailles*, pp. 9–25, 40. There is no history of the estates of Agenais, but Tholin has described the events that took place during the Wars of Religion, including the activities of the estates, in "La ville d'Agen pendant les Guerres de Religion du XVIᵉ siècle," *Revue de l'Agenais* 14–20 (1887–93).

41. Tholin, "La ville d'Agen," *Revue* 15 (1898): 338.

Wars of Religion began. Here a presidial seat was established in 1551, but its survival was by no means assured. "Those of Agen," a clerk noted in the municipal register, "have a great many friends in the privy council."[42] As was so clearly predicted, the officials of Agen immediately sought to obtain the suppression of the new seat. The battle that ensued was not finally resolved until the reign of Louis XVI over two centuries later. The episode provides an excellent example of the difficulty, indeed the impossibility, of the crown's permanently resolving any dispute between two determined antagonists. It also provides additional evidence of how the citizens of Renaissance France sought to obtain their ends. To counter Agen, the municipal officials of Condom offered the king of Navarre 1,000 livres, and later still more, in return for his support. Larger sums were provided their deputy to court to win sympathetic ears. In 1554 when they learned that Agen had promised Henry II 15,000 livres in return for suppressing the new seat, they once more countered by naming a deputy to court. The capacity of the little town to pay the costs of the battle by taxing its citizens had long since been exhausted, and the local officials borrowed whatever was needed to compete with Agen's offer. Although they won, their victory achieved at the cost of fleecing the poorer inhabitants and contracting a substantial debt. Furthermore the struggle was renewed later. The fruits of the judicial offices that were created fell to those who could afford to purchase them. The opportunity of being elected to the Estates General of France now that Condomois was an independent seat went to the same sort of people. Municipal pride was served, but it was most appreciated by the well-to-do. The whole affair was even more profitable to the nobles, courtiers, royal councillors, and the king himself upon whom Condom and its rival showered presents. Ironically Condom was immediately confronted by the attempts of towns assigned to its jurisdiction to escape dependence just as Condom had escaped from Agen. Furthermore the king of Navarre obtained letters in 1556 erecting his lands of Albret into a duchy and freeing them from judicial appeals to the presidial jurisdictions, including Condomois, in which they were located. As late as 1639 Bazadais and Condomois joined in offering Louis XIII 45,000 livres in return for suppressing the presidial seat that had been established in Albret so that appeals would once more flow into their courts.[43]

Louis XI placed Condomois in the same recette as Bazadais and the county of Astarac when he subdivided Gascogne in 1475. This act probably explains the creation of a new representative institution that in 1601 was referred to as "the Estates General of the province of Condomois, Astarac, and Bazadais," to which the towns of Condomois deputed directly.[44]

42. Joseph Gardère, *Historie de la seigneurie de Condom et de l'organisation de la justice dans cette ville* (Condom, 1902), p. 172.

43. Ibid., pp. 159–210.

44. AC, Mézin, BB 2, fol. 65.

Astarac, which was then a fief of the duke of Epernon, sent its syndic, and the parishes of Bazadais first met and chose a deputation. The principal duty of this assembly was to consider the royal tax proposals and to divide the amount agreed upon among the smaller jurisdictions. In 1582, one of the few years for which much information is available, the king failed to get all he requested. After the tax was divided between the jurisdictions, the estates of Astarac and Bazadais met separately to apportion their share among their respective parishes.[45]

Except for apportioning royal taxes, the key representative institutions were the individual estates of Condomois and Bazadais. Sessions to elect deputies to the assemblies of the généralité and to deal with local affairs were frequent. Apparently the *consuls* of Condom and Bazas could convoke the third estate of their respective jurisdictions when they so chose. The nobility of Condomois and Bazadais rarely participated except when deputies were chosen to attend the Estates General, but those of the county of Astarac did. As in Agenais the assemblies were vulnerable to determined royal opposition because of the failure of the nobility and clergy to play active roles, but during the Wars of Religion they appear to have been at the peak of their influence.[46]

Representative assemblies in Armagnac were already two centuries old in 1473 when Jean V's murder enabled Louis XI to assert royal authority in the region. Louis did not hesitate to assign the count's property to his supporters, but he was careful to retain the regalian rights that this great feudal lord had exercised in his own hands. He made the royal presence felt that same year by transferring the seat of the seneschalsy from Auch to Lectoure, a step that caused a bitter quarrel between the two towns that was not resolved until 1639 when the seneschalsy was divided and a new one created with its seat at Auch. Vic-Fezensac, which had similar aspirations, added a third dimension to the dispute. The seneschalsy included the aides

45. J. Duffour, "Les Etats d'Astarac de 1582," *Revue de Gascogne*, sér. 2, 6 (1906): 19–30; Jean-J. Monlezun, *Historie de la Gascogne* (Auch, 1850), 5:460–62.

46. For the estates of Bazadais prior to 1589, see L. Bourrachot, "L'emprunt forcé de 1544 en Bazadais," *Cahiers du Bazadais* 8 (1968): 21–22; AC La Réole, AA 5, and scattered references in BB 1–4; and AC, Monségur, BB 1. See also *AHG*, 13:394–97, 15:43–47. For clergy see *AHG*, 28:351–52, 377–78. For the estates of Condomois see scattered references in AC, Astaffort, BB 1; AC, Francescas, BB 1–5; and AC, Mézin, BB 1, located in AD, Lot-en-Garonne, and in AC, Condom, BB 1–8 located in AD Gers. See also *AHG*, 25: 43–47, and BN ms. fr. 21,425, fol. 10. For an account of how the third estate of Condomois met many times in 1522 to consider a request from Francis I to pay, clothe, and arm 300 infantry and how it ended by refusing to do so, see Abbé Barrère, "Extrait et analyse d'un registre de l'hôtel de ville de Condom," *Revue de Gascogne* 13 (1872): 473–74. The estates did finally agree to furnish some francs-archers for three months. The duchy of Albert sent deputies to the Estates General of 1560, 1576, and 1614. During the early seventeenth century, the estates sometimes met for other purposes. On other occasions the individual towns, depending on their location, sent deputies to the estates of either Bazadais or Condomois. There is insufficient documentation to determine the procedures followed during the sixteenth century.

du pays d'Agenais, which were normally taxed with the recette of Agenais but sometimes sent deputies to the estates of Armagnac and contributed to certain taxes that fell on that jurisdiction. By the late sixteenth century some of the confusion had been removed, and for tax purposes Armagnac consisted of seven collectes, each with its own representative assembly. At this time individual clergymen, nobles, and communities had ceased to receive direct summons to the estates of Armagnac, and the collecte meetings had become instruments for electing deputies to these assemblies and for dividing any taxes that might be agreed upon there among the parishes. The syndic of the nobility, occasionally joined by a few other members of his order, participated with the deputies of the third estate in some of the collecte assemblies and in the estates of Armagnac, but the clergy usually preferred to act through their diocesan and provincial assemblies.[47]

The three estates of Lannes were active during the period of English rule, and when the seneschalsy was temporarily reconquered by the French in 1443, it was to this assembly that Charles VII turned to receive an oath of obedience in the name of the inhabitants. They readily complied, for unlike Bordeaux they had not enjoyed close economic ties with England, and several of their leading nobles had long since declared for the French. Mindful of their loyalty, Charles freed the inhabitants of Lannes from the subordinate status they had held under the seneschal of Guyenne and confirmed their privileges when their permanent annexation took place in 1451. Although these privileges included exemption from taxation, they did not preclude the possibility that the king might ask them to consent freely to a levy. Thus Charles requested the three estates to vote a tax to repair the fortifications of Bayonne, Saint-Sever, and Dax in 1455, 1457, 1459, and perhaps other occasions. In voting these extraordinary impositions, the three estates were careful to stipulate that their action should not be construed as prejudicing their tax-exempt status, and the sire d'Albret obtained a special

47. Charles Samaran, *La maison d'Armagnac au XVe siècle* (Paris, 1907), pp. 223–34; *IAD, Gers.* ed. P. Tierny and R. Pagel (Auch, 1909), sér. B, i–ii. Paul Parfouru and J. de Carsalade-du-Pont, "Comptes consulaires de la ville de Riscle de 1441 à 1507," *Archives historiques de la Gascogne* 12 (1886): v–vi, xvii–xxvii; Ferdinand Lot and Robert Fawtier, eds., *Histoire des institutions françaises au Moyen Age* (Paris, 1957), 1:202–03; A. Degret, "Les assemblées provinciales du clergé gascon," *Revue de Gascogne* 55–62. (1914–26). For the estates in the fifteenth century, see Samaran, *La maison d'Armagnac*, pp. 32–34, 61, 96, 109, 146–47, 229, 231, 240, 259, 262–64, 266, 268, 272–73, 280, 284–88, 291–92, 299, 302, 321–22, 324–25, 342, 344, 346, 396–97, 452–55, 458–59. For the sixteenth century, see AC, Auch, BB 5, and the valuable documents concerning the collecte of Vic-Fezensac in AD, Gers, E. suppl. 23,985 and 23,936. The viscounty of Bruilhois with its hilltop capital of Laplume, a metropolis of sixteen hearths, served as a collecte. The *consuls* of Laplume summoned the deputies from the surrounding villages to elect deputies to the estates of Armagnac and Agenais and to deal with local affairs. See D'Antin and AC, Laplume, BB 4–5. For the procedures of the collectes and estates in the seventeenth century, see A. Branet, "Les Etats d'Armagnac en 1631–1632," *Bul. de la soc. archéologique du Gers* 14 (1913): 168–83, 214–29.

letter to this effect when he permitted the tax to be levied on "his subjects" in the seneschalsy.[48]

There was some friction between Charles VII and the estates, and during his reign an élection was created in Lannes. Relations with Louis XI were even worse. In 1463 Louis told his commissioner to take action against members of the estates who refused to consent to the 15,000 livres tax for the fortifications. By these acts the two kings dealt severe blows to the three estates, but their activities did not altogether cease as their historian, Cadier, has suggested.[49] Louis XI probably suppressed the élection at the beginning of his reign, for neither he in 1463 nor Francis I in 1518 addressed letters concerning tax levies to the élus and a formulary prepared around 1530 specifically states that there were no élus in Lannes at that time.[50] Meetings of the third estate were frequent during the early 1480s, and all three estates met in April 1490. On three occasions Francis I and Henry II confirmed the privileges of the inhabitants, including their tax-exempt status, at the request of the three estates, and in 1545 Francis suppressed an élection after he had reestablished it the year before. Since there were rarely élus in the seneschalsy, it was necessary for the government to convoke the three estates and persuade them to vote and collect any money that was extracted as formularies prepared around 1530 and 1558 clearly show. In 1569 when Charles IX sent directives to the commissioners to hold the estates, he ordered that the salary of "the clerk of the estates" be included in the levy and that the three estates "accord and grant" the sum desired. The chance survival of the procès-verbal of a meeting of the third estate at Saint-Sever in December 1575 to vote and divide the taille suggests that this is exactly what took place. The absence of the other estates, as in so many seneschalsies in Guyenne, should also be noted. Unfortunately there was a heated rivalry between Dax, Saint-Sever, and Bayonne that must have weakened the third estate and sometimes caused Bayonne to refuse to attend.[51]

The birth of representative institutions occurred later in the county of Comminges than elsewhere in southern France. The first known assembly of the three estates did not take place until 1412, and only a half-dozen more meetings have been documented prior to the complete and final reunion of

48. Léon Cadier, *La sénéschaussée des Lannes sous Charles VII* (Paris, 1885), pp. 39–46. For references to the estates of Lannes during the period of English rule, see Brissaud, *Les Anglais en Guyenne*, pp. 272–86; *AHG*, 37:453–69; *Archives municipales de Bordeaux, registres de la jurade, 1414–1416, 1420–1422*, 4:1–2, 4, 31–32, 54, 381–82; and Vale, *English Gascony*, pp. 43–44, 69, 81, 184, 212.

49. Cadier, *La Sénéschausée des Lannes*, pp. 46–48, 57–59, 87–90.

50. Ibid., pp. 87–90; AN K 81, no. 29; BN ms. fr. 14,368, fols. 13, 35–37.

51. *Archives municipales de Bayonne: Délibérations du corps de ville: Registres Gascons* (Bayonne, 1896), 1:7, 188, 204, 219, 282–88, 504, 2:193. AC, Dax, AA 5. ms. BN. fr. 14,368, fols. 35–37, ms. n.a. fr. 20,526, fol. 18v; ms. n.a. fr. 3643, no. 962; and ms. mélanges de Colbert, 366, no. 318; *AHG*, 25:500–01; AC, Saint-Sever, 2:1 (1519–1789). Major, *The Deputies*, pp. 99–100; *Actes François Ier*, 4: no 14,469, 8: no. 32,575.

the county with the crown in 1502.[52] Probably the estates did not become periodic until after Charles VIII spelled out the privileges of the county in June 1496 in more detail than was customary and included among them "the right to assemble the three estates on condition that they be convoked by us or by our officers and that they meet within the boundaries of the county."[53] Even the villages in the upper valleys of the Pyrenees were slow to organize assemblies in this area. Only during the Renaissance and after the assertion of royal authority did the estates of Comminges became a vigorous institution that met several times a year and dominated local administration.[54]

During the Middle Ages the county had been more closely associated with nearby Toulouse than with Guyenne, and it was royal officials from that city who assumed control upon the death of the last count in the direct line in 1454. Louis XI, however, assigned Comminges to Guyenne for administrative purposes, where it remained after its final reunion to the crown. Thus Comminges was included in the généralité of Guyenne when it was created in 1523 and participated in the meetings of its estates. The county remained in the jurisdiction of the Parlement of Toulouse, and the seneschal seated in that city countinued to claim, though without much success, the right to summon the deputies of Comminges to the infrequent meetings of the three estates of his jurisdiction throughout the sixteenth century.[55]

Perhaps this proximity to Languedoc caused the estates to be even less democratic than some of the other seneschalsies in Guyenne. Only the bishops of Lombez and Couserans and four abbots were usually convoked for the first estate, but in the 1520s their number was increased by the abbess of Fabar. The list of nobles convoked grew from thirty-five in 1502 to forty-six in 1544, but during the Wars of Religion, especially, only a handful usually attended. The *consuls* from the chief towns of the eight royal castellanies dominated the third estate. To their number was added several smaller towns, and after the massacre of Saint Bartholomew, the aides or territories attached to Comminges were normally represented. In theory the chief towns of the castellanies looked after the interests of the villages in their jurisdictions, but in practice they often shoved an unfair portion of the tax burden onto them. As a result, there were strong protests from the rural populace, which led to the inclusion of their procureurs in the estates between 1552 and 1572. By 1520 the estates had syndics to look after their interests when they were not in session, and soon thereafter there is evidence

52. Charles Higounet, *Le comté de Comminges* (Toulouse, 1949), pp. 576, 593, 599–601, 621, 634–36, 660.

53. S. Mondon, "Privilèges de la comté de Comenge comprenant le traité des lies et passeries de 1513," *Revue de Comminges* 30 (1915): 13–16.

54. Higounet, *Le comté de Comminges*, pp. 392–94.

55. Ibid., pp. 609–15, 627–28; J. R. Major, *The Deputies to the Estates General of Renaissance France* (Madison, 1960), pp. 105–106.

that they employed a treasurer, a clerk who also served as a secretary, and an archivist. The three estates deliberated together and voted by head rather than by order, a procedure that would have led to the predominance of the nobility if they had attended in larger numbers. Actually the *consuls* of the leading towns were the most influential persons in the estates during the sixteenth century.[56]

The judge of Comminges, whose seat was at Muret, and the king's attorney also participated in the estates, but their presence did not curtail the activities of these assemblies. Indeed both royal officials were on the payroll of the estates, and both were among the most stalwart defenders of the privileges of the county. Because the judge could authorize emergency meetings of the estates, there were often sessions between the annual assemblies that were attended by royal commissioners in which taxes were voted and divided among the subordinate jurisdictions. Two or three meetings per year usually sufficed prior to the Wars of Religion, but during the critical years between 1567 and 1590, the estates met between four and eleven times annually, except in 1572 when there were only two meetings. Royal pressure forced taxes higher and higher during the sixteenth century, but the estates were by no means powerless to mitigate this trend. Often they rejected new taxes, won reductions in old ones, and altered the nature of unpopular levies.[57]

The *jugeries* of Rivière and Verdun were detached from nearby Toulouse and assigned to Guyenne for administrative purposes at the same time as Comminges. Too few documents survive to permit the reconstruction of the history of the estates or the development of its bureaucracy and procedures. The absence of royal tax officials indicates that meetings of the estates were periodic. All three orders participated in the early sixteenth century, but by 1601 the nobility and clergy had ceased to do so, and the third estate was represented by the *consuls* of twelve towns. Meetings of the third estate appear to have been regular, and deputations were sent to the estates of Guyenne when the occasion demanded. Each of the three estates had a syndic.[58]

56. M. J. de Naurois-Destenay, *Les Etats de Comminges aux XVIᵉ et XVIIᵉ siècles* (thesis, Ecole Nationale des Chartes, 1953–54), pp. 27–60, 140–44. A copy of this thesis is deposited at the AN. I am indebted to the author for permission to consult her work. See also Bertrand de Gorsse, "Les Etats de Comminges," *Revue de Comminges*, 46 (1932): 13–21.

57. Naurois-Destenay, pp. 60–71, 87–88, 100, 103–28; V. Fons, "Les Etats de Comminges," *Mém. de la soc. impériale archéologique du midi de la France* 8 (1861–65): 186–87, 192–93.

58. AN, K 73, no 42, *Ord. François Iᵉʳ*, 1 : 279–83; BN ms. fr. 21,424, fols. 165–204; BN ms. fr. 21,428, fols. 16–21. In some of these tax documents, the royal commissioners were told to assemble the estates; in others they were not, but this does not prove that they did not do so, for they were expected to proceed in the accustomed manner. Thus, although Francis I directed that a tax be levied on Rouergue in 1537 without mentioning the estates, the estates met and voted the tax. *Ord. François Iᵉʳ*, 8 : 440–46 and n.1. For Antoine Thomas's discussion of this problem, see *Les Etats provinciaux de la France centrale sous Charles VII* (Paris, 1879), 1 : 181–82. For

The clergy and barons of Rouergue were summoned to meetings by the late twelfth century, and within a hundred years there was an assembly, which deputies from the seigneurial villages may have attended. The vicissitudes of the Hundred Years War led to the real formation of the assemblies of the three estates. Soon after 1360, Rouergue passed to the English; the change of masters led to more frequent meetings, and the pace did not slacken at first when the French resumed control. Soon after the turn of the century, however, a bitter quarrel ensued between the three estates and the count of Armagnac, who was the feudal lord over much of the province. The count sought a gift of 12,000 écus, but the estates were unwilling to vote more than half that amount in spite of the pressure he applied in meeting after meeting. At length the count began to negotiate with the individual towns, but was again repulsed. The towns in return appealed to the king. Instead of lending a sympathetic ear, that distant monarch asked money to redeem nearby centers still held by the English. When the estates refused, the royal commissioners arrested the deputies of the communes, and the count seized the goods of merchants being transported on the highways. After some further resistance, the towns gave in, but with relations thus poisoned, the three estates were rarely convoked for more than a decade. Charles VII found it necessary to revive them, however, and they remained active during the two centuries that followed.[59]

Rouergue had been affiliated with Languedoc during the fourteenth century, but during the fifteenth century the province had become associated with the duchy of Guyenne. When the généralité was created in 1523, the province was divided into three recettes: the Haute-Marche of Rouergue, with its seat at Millau, the Basse-Marche with its seat at Villefranche, and the county of Rodez with four castellanies. In dividing the province in this fashion, the crown was adhering to long-established procedures. By the middle of the fifteenth century, it had become customary for the three estates of Rouergue to vote a tax and then to divide it among these three subordinate jurisdictions, each of which had its estates.[60] Unlike

the estates in the late sixteenth and seventeenth centuries, see Abbé Jean Contrasty, *Histoire de Sainte-Foy-de-Peyrolières* (Toulouse, 1917), pp. 198–210, and Abbé Galabert, "Note sur les Etats de Rivière-Verdun," *Bul. de la soc. archéologique du midi de la France* 10 (1879): 105–10.

59. For the medieval estates, see esp. Bisson, *Assemblies and Representation*, pp. 105–11, 275–76; Jean B. Rouquette, *Le Rouergue sous les Anglais* (Millau, 1887), pp. 24–25, 30–31, 53–54, 78, 94–95, 116, 125–28, 132–35, 205 260, 267–70, 274, 280, 286, 303, 315, 323, 337, 345–55, 369–81, 385–86, 395, 398–412, 425–32; Bernadette Suau-Noulens, *La ville de Rodez au milieu du XVᵉ siècle* (thesis, Ecole Nationale de Chartes, 1971), pp. 132–46 (a copy is deposited at the AN; I am indebted to the author for permission to consult her work); Samaran, *La maison d'Armagnac*, pp. 33–34, 61, 63, 67, 70, 96, 107, 163, 173, 203, 279, 342, 348; J. Artières, "Documents sur la ville de Millau," *Archives historiques du Rouergue* 7 (1930): 219, 312, 317, 356–58, 361–67, 428–29, 430–31; AN, KK 648, nos. 106–119; and the numerous documents in AD, Averyron, sér. C.

60. See for example Artières, *Documents de Millau*, 339–40, for 1459.

Armagnac the subordinate jurisdictions did not elect deputies to the estates of Rouergue; rather, the upper clergy, the leading nobles, and the consuls of the more important towns were invited to attend. At these meetings the three estates deliberated and voted together. The friction that developed was more often within each estate than between the estates. The bishop of Rodez's right to preside was occasionally challenged by the bishop of Vabres. Rodez and Villefranche vied for the honor of being the host town, a dispute that was partially resolved by holding the estates alternately in each. Millau, dissatisfied at being excluded, sought—though unsuccessfully—to obtain a three-way split in 1553.[61]

By 1478 (and very likely earlier) the three estates of Rouergue had a syndic.[62] The estates of the Haute- and Basse-Marche and of the county of Rodez had similar officials. The four institutions also had tax receivers and other servants to do their bidding. In 1537 when their right to appoint receivers came under attack, the provincial estates declared that Rouergue was a pays d'états, not a pays d'élection. As such, they and the three subordinate assemblies had enjoyed the privilege of appointing receivers to collect the taxes imposed on them for such a long time that no one remembered when they had not done so. Confronted by the forces of tradition, Francis I ordered that this privilege be preserved.[63]

The composition and procedures of the three estates of Quercy closely resembled those of Rouergue. The bishop-count of Cahors was the virtually undisputed president of the estates, although some of his other pretensions were challenged. The upper clergy, the leading nobles, and the *consuls* of the towns made up the remainder of the assembly. During the course of the sixteenth century, the number of those summoned for the clergy increased from ten to twelve, for the nobility from twenty-five to twenty-nine, and for the third estate from the *consuls* of twenty-one towns and castellanies to the *consuls* of twenty-seven. Changes so minor suggest the stability of the institution. In their annual session the three estates usually deliberated together and made their pronouncements in the name of the province as a whole. When important matters arose between sessions, a committee of twelve consisting of two clergymen, two nobles, and the *consuls* of eight important towns, were authorized to act. For routine administration the estates employed three syndics, a clerk, an assistant clerk, and four tax

---

61. A history of the three estates of Rouergue is needed. For some inadequate comments, see H. Affre, *Dictionnaire des institutions, moeurs et coutumes de Rouergue* (Rodez, 1903), 161–66, and Marc-A. de Gaujal, *Etudes historiques sur le Rouergue* (Paris, 1858), 1:385–406. For an account of the procedures of the estates written around 1623, see "Mémoire sur la tenue des Etats de Rouergue, écrit vers 1623 par Durieux, député de Rouergue," *Bul. hist. et philologique du comté des travaux historiques et scientifiques* (1885): 23–27.

62. *Ord.*, 18:428.

63. *Ord. François Ier*, 8:402–06.

assessors.[64] It is impossible to ascertain when these offices were created, but as early as 1447 the three estates had a clerk and by 1551 they had a syndic.[65]

The three estates of Quercy, active throughout most of the fifteenth and all of the sixteenth century, turned their efforts primarily to trying to avoid taxes and to collecting those they could not escape. In 1491, for example, they succeeded in persuading Charles VIII to accept fewer than the five hundred foot soldiers that his governor requested.[66] When it came to their own appropriations, they were more generous. As early as 1520 they began to give Galiot de Genouillac, a leading local noble high in royal favor, 2,000 livres per year "because of the good services that he rendered them."[67] How often Galiot performed services for the province is not known, but in 1539 he persuaded Francis I not to establish the gabelle there, an act in itself worth far more than his annual gratification. His son, who was seneschal of Quercy, received a similar reward. The three estates displayed more interest in education than most of their sister institutions. In 1555 they attempted to entice Cujas, the eminent law professor, to the University of Cahors; in 1570 they participated in the establishment of a college in that same town; and by 1579 they were contributing 6,300 livres annually to the support of the university, the colleges in Cahors and Montauban, and elementary schools in six other towns.[68]

The estates in the seneschalsies and recettes of Guyenne are the least known in France. Even local historians rarely recognize the fact that they met regularly during the sixteenth century to consent to taxes to support the royal government and their own activities. In conjunction with the royal commissioners, they apportioned these taxes among the subordinate jurisdictions. They all had syndics and other officials, and most of them either had standing committees to act for them or had arrangements with the municipal officials of the capital town to do so when they were not in session. In the fifteenth century, the clergy and nobility had usually attended, but during the course of the sixteenth century, they ceased to do so regularly in Bordelais, Lannes, Agenais, Condomois, Bazadais, and Rivière-Verdun and nearly ceased to do so in Armagnac. This is surprising because except in Bordelais the taille was réelle and the privileged were expected to pay taxes

64. For medieval assemblies in Quercy, see Bisson, *Assemblies and Representation*, pp. 124–32, 147–60, 285–88. M.-J. Baudel, *Notes pour servir à l'histoire des Etats provinciaux du Quercy* (Cahors, 1881). Major, *The Deputies*, p. 103. BN ms. fr. 18,678, fols. 165–68.

65. Baudel, *Notes*, pp. 23, 29.

66. *Lettres de Charles VIII*, ed. P. Pélicier (Paris, 1902), 3:169–70.

67. Guillaume Lacoste, *Histoire générale de la province de Quercy*, 2d ed. (Cahors, 1968), 4:46.

68. Ibid., 69–70, 92, 101–03; Eugène Sol, *La vie économique et sociale en Quercy aux XVI et XVII siècles* (Cahors, 1950), pp. 258–59; Edmond Cabié, *Guerres de Religion dans le sud-ouest de la France* (Paris, 1906), pp. 541–44. For the educational appropriation of 6,300 livres in 1600, see BN ms. Clairambault 360, fols. 12–14v.

on the common land they held. In Périgord, on the other hand, the taille was personnelle, and the nobles and clergy enjoyed the same tax privileges as in northern France, yet they continued to participate in the meetings of the estates. So great was the vitality of these institutions that when the third estate of the généralité began to be frequently convoked after 1561, it was never able to assert control over the tax-consenting process as its counterparts had in other regions of France. Nevertheless the fact that the crown encouraged the creation of such a large institution with its own bureaucracy is a strong indication that the Renaissance monarchs were quite content to govern in cooperation with representative assemblies.

5

THE ESTATES
OF THE HOUSE OF FOIX-NAVARRE

THE KINGS OF FRANCE HAD ACQUIRED DAUPHINÉ, BURGUNDY, PROVENCE, AND Brittany during the late Middle Ages and the early stages of the Renaissance, and in the same general period they had gradually reasserted control over Guyenne. It was only when the Renaissance was well past its peak, however, that they were able to join the lands of the house of Foix-Navarre to the crown. This house ruled Béarn and Navarre as independent states and the county of Foix and the viscounties of Bigorre, Nébouzan, and Soule as vassals of the kings of France. All of these territories contained thriving estates that were summoned on the orders of the head of the family.

The house of Foix-Navarre had acquired other lands as well, such as the extensive duchy of Albret, in which there were no regularly convoked estates, and Andorra, Armagnac, Rodez, Périgord, and Quercy. The county of Andorra was never assimilated into France, and in the other territories, the family's feudal position had eroded to such an extent that the estates were summoned on royal authority and turned their taxes over to the royal treasurers at Bordeaux. I have therefore treated them with the estates in Guyenne.

1. THE GATHERING OF THE LANDS

The gathering of the lands of the house of Foix-Navarre began in 1252 when the heir of the count of Foix married the heiress of the viscount of Béarn. During the century that followed, the descendants of this union profited by the Hundred Years War to play the English against the French, and the French against the English so as to obtain recognition of Béarn as an independent state free of all feudal ties. Not content with the territorial gap between Béarn and Foix, they bent every effort to acquire the intervening feudal dependencies. They obtained Bigorre, Nébouzan, and several smaller territories, leaving only the county of Comminges separating them from their objective. A well-timed marriage added Navarre to this conglomeration of independent and dependent states in 1479. When the thirteen-year-old Catherine fell heir to these far-flung estates in 1483, both France and Spain were determined to influence her choice of husband. After some hesitation, Catherine and most of her subjects, who had a voice in such affairs, opted for the seven-year-old Jean II d'Albret, heir to vast estates that lay to the north and west of Béarn.

The choice of a French noble to be Catherine's husband was by no means obvious because the ruling family had close blood ties with the royal house of Aragon. As count of Castelbon, its head was the vassal of that king, and as co-seigneur of Andorra and king of Navarre, he held extensive lands to the south of the Pyrenees. Furthermore Spanish influence had penetrated to the north of the mountains where the inhabitants of Béarn and Bigorre had *fors,* or charters of privileges, like Aragon itself that were so explicit that they approached being written constitutions. Finally the estates of Navarre, Catherine's largest territory, preferred a Spanish marriage. The French alliance did not prevent Louis XII and the more rapacious judges of the Parlement of Toulouse from trying to reassert Valois sovereignty over Béarn. Only by entering into an alliance against Spain in 1512 could Béarnese independence be preserved. This act, however, provided what little excuse was needed for Ferdinand to seize the larger part of Navarre, to which he had a flimsy dynastic claim. When Catherine died in 1517, she bequeathed to her son, Henry II d'Albret, extensive lands to the north of the Pyrenees and an overwhelming desire to regain the lost portions of the kingdom of Navarre, a desire that was a major determinant of his and his successor's policy for a half-century.[1]

Unlike the Valois dukes of Burgundy, the medieval counts of Foix made little attempt to develop centralized administrative and judicial organs over the various territories they acquired. The union of these lands was essentially a personal one in which the counts and their council served as the only common links between them. One exception to this generalization is that a single assembly of the estates was held for Béarn, Marsan, and Gabardan as early as 1391, and this arrangement became habitual before the middle of the fifteenth century. Those summoned apparently made no protests about being invited to a single assembly probably because their local estates were in such a nascent state of development that those concerned felt no deep-rooted loyalty to them. If this interpretation is correct, it provides one more example of how adjacent territories could be joined together if no significant institutional development had taken place. Taxes voted by the estates of Béarn, Marsan, and Gabardan, as the institution was called, were appor-

---

1. For the early history of the house of Foix-Navarre, see especially Pierre Tucoo-Chala, *Gaston Fébus et la vicomté de Béarn, 1343–1391* (Bordeaux, 1959), and *La vicomté de Béarn et le problème de la souveraineté des origines à 1620* (Bordeaux, 1961). For the critical period between 1472 and 1494, see Eva Stone Duncan, *The Government of Béarn, 1472–1494* ((Ph.D. diss., Emory University, 1968).

tioned among the jurisdictions, with Béarn, the largest, paying the greatest amount.[2]

As the Middle Ages drew to a close, the rulers of the house of Foix-Navarre began to show more interest in achieving greater unity in their lands north of the Pyrenees. In 1484, 1491, 1513, and 1519 the estates of Foix, Bigorre, and Nébouzan were instructed to send deputies to assemblies with the estates of Béarn, Marsan, and Gabardan, which were called "Estates Generals" as early as 1513. Initially these meetings dealt only with matters of direct interest to all the hereditary lands, such as the choice of a husband for a female heir or the taking of an oath of allegiance, but later monetary problems and the support of the ruling house were considered. However, the estates of these territories were too well developed for there to be any hope that they would surrender their tax·voting and administrative responsibilities to an Estates General as Marsan and Gabardan had done at an earlier date when they had been successfully united with Béarn.[3]

Henri d'Albret (1517–55) did not pursue his ancestors' half-hearted efforts to create an Estates General of his lands to the north of the Pyrenees. Perhaps he realized that his combined Albret-Foix-Navarre inheritance was more than he could ever hope to bring together in an effective assembly, or perhaps the particularism of his subjects was so great that they were unwilling to participate in an Estates General. Certainly the young prince had no objection to large assemblies, for he did much to further the development of the estates of his government of Guyenne. (See Chap. 4, sec. 1.) He did, however, take steps to draw his lands together administratively in ways that would bring him into less direct conflict with the people. In 1520 he established a Chamber of Accounts at Pau, which had jurisdiction over all of his French lands, including Navarre. Seven years later he created a second Chamber at Nérac, to which he assigned the lands that came from his Albret inheritance, Foix, and Nébouzan. These two chambers brought

2. Léon Cadier did not deal with Marsan and Gabardan in his study of the estates of Béarn. However, documents he and others have published leave no doubt of their presence. For a list of towns in Marsan and Gabardan that participated in the estates of 1517, see his *Les Etats de Béarn depuis leurs origines jusqu'au commencement du XVIe siècle* (Paris, 1888), p. 451. For documents concerning the joint activities of the estates of the three jurisdictions, see his "Le livre des syndics des Etats de Béarn," *Archives historiques de la Gascogne* 18 (1889); and Henri Courteault's continuation in vol. 10 of the second series of the same journal published in 1906. The nobility and the jurats of the communities in the viscounties of Marsan and Gabardan participated in assemblies by the second half of the thirteenth century, but these assemblies do not seem to have had an administrative function. Cadier, *Les Etats*, pp. 60–61. For the 1391 meeting, see ibid., pp. 404–14.

3. Cadier, *Les Etats*, pp. 186–87, 351, 381, 385, 393, 431–32; Cadier, "Le livre des syndics," pp. xxvi, 83–87; Courteault, "Le livre de Syndics," pp. 73–78, 169–70.

increased efficiency to the administration of his domains; the income he received from Béarn nearly doubled between 1531 and 1550.[4]

Henri d'Albret married Marguerite d'Angoulême, sister of Francis I and sympathizer with the Protestant movement. Under her protection Protestantism took root in Béarn and, to a lesser extent, in the fiefs that were held from the crown of France. His successor, Jeanne d'Albret (1555-72), openly embraced the Protestant faith and made Calvinism the established church in Béarn and Navarre, although her husband, Antoine de Bourbon, finally opted for the old religion. Jeanne's decision opened her lands to renewed threats from the French crown, but her efforts, coupled with those of her subjects, preserved her territories intact for her son, Henry of Navarre (1572-1610).

Most of the lands of the house of Foix-Navarre had extensive privileges, including exemption from royal taxation. Nevertheless the possibility existed that the king or their count might ask the estates for special funds. As a result, the same give and take between lord and estates existed here as elsewhere, except that the Pyrenean people were even more determined to defend their special status. Our survey of these estates will begin with Foix, the oldest of the hereditary lands, and proceed westward toward the Atlantic to Navarre and Soule.

2, THE ESTATES
OF FOIX, NÉBOUZAN, AND BIGORRE

The assembly of the estates of the county of Foix was apparently born during the final decade of the fourteenth century, but only occasional glimpses of its activity may be had prior to the closing years of Henry IV's reign. The inhabitants enjoyed the privilege of being exempt from royal taxes, but they had to engage in a constant battle to prevent royal officials in Toulouse from subjecting them to the customs, levies on closed towns, and other assessments imposed on that seneschalsy. Fortunately, the French kings sided with them, but these same rulers were prone to pressure them to pay the taxes due their count.[5]

In the early sixteenth century the bishop of Pamiers, five abbots in commendam, thirty-seven nobles, and the deputies from twenty-eight towns and communities were invited to attend the estates. The number of nobles and towns who could take part increased thereafter, especially between 1612 and 1615, although only those who owned designated noble land were supposed to attend for the second estate. When in session the three estates

4. *IAD, Basses-Pyrénées, sér. B*, ed. P. Raymond (Paris, 1863), p. 10; Charles Dartigue-Peyrou, *La vicomté de Béarn sous le règne de Henri d'Albret 1517-1555* (Paris, 1934), p. 250.

5. Germain Arnaud, *Mémoire sur les Etats de Foix, 1608-1789* (Toulouse, 1904), pp. x-xii; H. Castillon, *Histoire du comté de Foix* (Toulouse, 1852), 2:75, 83, 128, 156, 185, 201, 225-26, 288, 298-99, 305; *Actes François Ier*, 4: nos. 13,159, 13,855, 14,035, 5: nos. 15,320, 17,728, 17,794, 7: no. 25,872; BN ms. Languedoc (Doat), 234, fols. 157-58v, 269-71v.

normally deliberated and voted as a single house. They had a number of officers, including two syndics, a treasurer, one or two secretaries, auditors, and tax collectors. Eventually they also employed an engineer, an inspector of the mines, a master of the ports, an advocate at the king's council, and an agent at Paris. During the course of the seventeenth century, it became customary for various commissions or committees to be appointed to look into complex matters more carefully than the estates as a whole could during their sessions. One of these was designated to act if an emergency arose when the estates were not in session.[6]

The history of the three estates of the viscounty of Nébouzan is even less well documented. This fief came into the possession of the house of Foix-Navarre in the early fourteenth century. Like so many of the other territories in the vicinity of the Spanish frontier, it possessed many privileges, including exemption from the customs, gabelle, and taille. Royal officials in Toulouse occasionally attempted to incorporate the viscounty into the tax system of Languedoc, but by successful appeals to the king, the inhabitants were able to preserve their position.[7] Royal recognition of these privileges did not prevent the king from asking the estates for "donations," however. In 1610 Henry IV fixed the viscounty's minimum contribution at 2,000 livres. Whether the king received more than that thereafter was a matter for negotiation with the estates. This sum could not have seemed very large, for in 1596, the estates had voted 3,300 livres and in 1599, 4,050. All three orders participated in the meetings. They usually sat in the same chamber but voted apart.[8]

The county of Bigorre was formed in the early ninth century. By 1109 the counts had created a feudal court out of which the assemblies of the three estates were born by 1283. Little is known of the early history of the three estates, of how they fared as their county was transferred from one lord to another until, in 1425, Charles VII bestowed it upon Jean de Gailly, count of Foix. From that time until the reunion with the crown in July 1607, Bigorre numbered among the feudal dependencies held by the house of Foix.[9]

By the close of the Wars of Religion, the composition of the estates had become relatively stable. Of the clergy, only the bishop of Tarbes and eight other ecclesiastics, all abbots, priors, or commanders in the Order of Malta, were invited to participate; the chapters and parish clergy were excluded. The second estate in Bigorre was divided into two groups: the barons and the simple gentlemen. Traditionally there had been only eight barons, but in 1596 Henry IV created a ninth, and Louis XIV brought the total number to eleven, where it remained until the Revolution. Other nobles were

6. Arnaud, *Mémoire*, pp. 1–68.

7. *Actes François Ier*, 4: nos. 13,350, 13,855, 14,035, 14,548; 5: nos. 15,320, 17,728.

8. Valois, 2: no. 15,602; Ad, Basses-Pyrénées, B 1393.

9. Gilbert Pène, *Les attributions financières des Etats du pays et comté de Bigorre aux XVIIe et XVIIIe siècles* (Bordeaux, 1962), pp. 17–29.

summoned only if they owned fiefs, a qualification that only eighty met in 1602. Nobles without fiefs unsuccessfully sought admission in 1599, and titled royal officials were similarly rebuffed in 1607. Seven towns, two lesser localities, and five valleys elected deputies to represent the third estate. These valleys had their own representative assemblies to deal with local matters as well as to name deputies to the county assembly. Thus, small as it was, Bigorre boasted a half-dozen representative institutions, and the county assembly assumed the proud title of the Estates General of Bigorre.[10]

It is impossible to trace the history of the three estates of Bigorre prior to the late sixteenth century. By that time it had become customary for the seneschal to issue writs of summons when instructed to do so by the count and to preside over the assembly when it met. In 1611 the king's council ordered that he be replaced as president of the estates by the bishop of Tarbes. Decisions were usually made in the name of the three estates, but they were arrived at in a unique and complex manner. Routine royal taxes were voted by the three estates together, but if an extraordinary levy or other important matters were involved, the clergy, the barons and lesser nobles, and the deputies of the third estate separated to deliberate. When they reassembled each order cast one vote with the majority ruling in all matters except taxation. Here the order that voted the least carried the day, an arrangement that favored the third estate, upon which most of the burden fell.[11]

The three estates elected syndics for the nobility and for the third estate, the bishop of Tarbes serving in effect in this capacity for the clergy. In addition, they chose a clerk or secretary and a treasurer. When the estates were not in session, a committee consisting of the two ecclesiastics, four nobles, and four members of the third estate acted in their name. The archives of the estates were kept in the town hall of Tarbes.[12]

As a frontier province, Bigorre was exempt from the taille and other direct taxes, but this did not prevent the king or the count from asking for free gifts called "donations." For example, Francis I extracted 1,674 livres from the inhabitants of Bigorre to help pay his ransom following his capture in the battle of Pavia and then proceeded to turn the money over to the king of Navarre, their count. Privileged or not, Francis included Bigorre in his requests for financial assistance in 1536, 1538, and doubtless on other occasions. Even when he acknowledged the county's exemption from custom duties in 1544, he at the same time authorized its lord, the king of Navarre, to tax its exports to Spain.[13]

---

10. My list of those summoned is based on the roll prepared in 1602. See AD, Hautes-Pyrénées, 1:11. Pène's data reflect the increased participation of the gentlemen and the towns during the seventeenth and eighteenth centuries, pp. 30–57. For the use of the term *Estates General,* see the letters of convocation in AD, Hautes-Pyrénées, C 128.

11. Pène, *Les attributions financières,* pp. 57–60, 316–19; *Lettres Henri IV,* 1:510–11.

12. Pène, *Les attributions financières,* pp. 62–70, 87, 318.

13. *Actes François I,* 1: no. 3056, 3: nos. 8654, 10,249, 4: nos. 13,855, 14,035, 14,548.

3. The Estates of Béarn

Nearly every province and town in France had its privileges, but none were more far reaching or jealously guarded than those of Béarn. These privileges were embodied in six charters known as the fors. One of the fors, which was drawn up about 1188, applied to the whole viscounty, and the remaining five were initially applicable to three mountain valleys and two towns, but gradually the for of one of these towns was granted to other communities. The preamble to the Fors de Béarn claimed that the laws and rights of the people preceded the creation of the seigneur and that the people could remove that seigneur and select another if he violated their privileges. Each new seigneur was called upon to swear to uphold the fors. First a series of feudal courts and later the three estates did their best to see that he did so.[14]

During the eleventh century the viscount was advised, assisted, and to a considerable degree controlled by a feudal court to which all the nobles were summoned. Such an assembly proved unwieldy from the standpoint of the viscount and burdensome to many of those obligated to attend. As a result, an assembly consisting of the two bishops and the leading barons, known as the *Cour des jurats-barons*, was eventually created to act in routine legislative and judicial matters. Only when issues of exceptional importance were to be considered were all the nobles summoned to a meeting known as the *Cour Majour*. Finally, the growing importance of the towns led to the formation of the *Cour des Communautés* during the thirteenth century. With its creation Béarn possessed an assembly of the leading nobles and bishops, an assembly of all the nobles, and an assembly of the representatives of the towns and communities. There is no positive evidence, however, that these bodies began to function together as estates prior to 1391. Indeed, during the long reign of the powerful and autocratic Gaston Fébus (1343–91), the cours were rarely convoked, and their judicial duties were assumed by the seneschal's court.[15]

Gaston Fébus so hated Mathieu de Castelbon, his nephew and legal heir, that he signed a treaty permitting Charles VI of France to succeed him as sovereign of Béarn. This threat to Béarnais independence led the Cour Majour and the Cour des Communautés to meet on their own initiative shortly after Gaston Fébus's death in 1391 to form a union to protect their privileges. They rejected the treaty with Charles and elected Mathieu as their seigneur on the condition that he took an oath to respect the fors and secure Charles's recognition of their independence. A well-placed bribe at court enabled Mathieu to meet the latter condition, and he reluctantly took

---

14. Duncan, *Government of Béarn*, pp. 123–32; P. Tucoo-Chala, "Les institutions de la vicomté de Béarn," in *Histoire des institutions françaises au Moyen Age*, ed. Ferdinand Lot and Robert Fawtier (Paris, 1957), 1:323–25.

15. Duncan, *Government of Béarn*, pp. 132–39; Tucoo-Chala, "Les institutions," pp. 325–34.

the oath before the estates several years later. By these acts the estates of Béarn became a definitely constituted body that was henceforth in a position to participate in the government.[16]

Mathieu quickly displayed dictatorial tendencies, but his death without direct heirs in 1398 provided the estates with an opportunity to impose an additional twenty-nine articles on his successors, which included a proviso that the seigneurs must "take nothing from their subjects and consent to nothing without their will."[17] The succession of a minor in 1436 enabled the estates to make more demands before recognizing a new seigneur. Once additional articles were accepted by one seigneur, they were included among those that his successor was required to swear to uphold. The result was that the balance between the seigneur and the estates shifted during the late fourteenth and fifteenth centuries from favoring the former to favoring the latter. Thus "between 1470 and 1517 the internal history of Béarn merges with that of the estates."[18]

During the late Middle Ages the composition of the estates and their administrative organs became permanently established. The fact that the estates grew out of the decision of the Cour Majour and the Cour des Communautés to cooperate in 1391 led to the emergence of a two-house rather than the more common three-house assembly. The upper house, or *Grand Corps*, consisted of two bishops, three abbots, twelve barons, and about four hundred nobles who were vassals of the viscount, although only about a tenth of the nobles usually attended. The *Second Corps* consisted of the deputies of the four leading towns, three valleys, and about thirty-five smaller towns and localities situated in Marsan and Gabardan, as well as in Béarn. The concurrence of both houses was necessary. If they did not immediately agree, a committee was appointed to seek a compromise. If it failed, the measure was void, an arrangement that gave the commoners a veto over all legislation.[19]

The estates participated in political, financial, administrative, and legislative affairs. They provided for regencies during minorities, helped to select the husbands of viscountesses, authorized the viscount to raise troops except for the relatively unimportant feudal host, and, of course, voted taxes. To perform these varied and important tasks, the estates were electing syndics as early as 1468 and appointing secretaries at a somewhat later date. Around 1479 they began to choose auditors to watch over the viscount's fiscal administration and to prevent him from levying more than the authorized amount. The right to appoint the treasurer of Béarn passed from the

16. Tucoo-Chala, "Les institutions," p. 335. Cadier, *Les Etats*, pp. 135–49, 404–14. Tucoo-Chala disagrees with Cadier on some aspects of the formation of the estates. Neither explains the presence of Marsan and Gabardan at the estates of 1391.

17. Duncan, *Government of Béarn*, p. 269.

18. Cadier, *Les Etats*, p. 174.

19. Tucoo-Chala, "Les institutions," pp. 336–37; Cadier, *Les Etats*, pp. 225–33.

viscount into their hands, and in 1482 an *abrégé des Etats* was organized that could be quickly summoned in case of need during the intervals between the sessions of the estates. It consisted of three clergymen, four nobles, and fourteen representatives of the towns and valleys. In 1493 the estates began to delegate two persons to sit in the viscount's Privy Council to ensure that their privileges were observed. This group gradually evolved into the Sovereign Council, which was to play an important judicial and administrative role during the sixteenth century.[20]

The fifteen-year-old Henri d'Albret inherited this truncated sovereignty in 1517. One might think that when this able and gallant prince reached manhood he would attempt to break the power of the estates. Instead he treated the deputies with unfailing courtesy, respected their privileges, and replied favorably to their cahiers whenever it was possible. They responded with a deep and sincere affection that became especially strong during the last years of his life when Pau became his principal residence.[21] His daughter, Jeanne d'Albret, continued his policies with equal success until her attempt to turn her state into a Protestant stronghold raised the ire of the estates.

4. THE ESTATES OF NAVARRE AND SOULE

The Basque-speaking kingdom of Navarre, like the viscounty of Béarn, had its fors and its estates. The latter grew out of *Cort Mayor* to which prelates, nobles, and townsmen were summoned during the twelfth and thirteenth centuries. By 1355 the *Cortes*, or estates, had emerged as a tax-consenting institution that was summoned by the monarch every few years. Ferdinand, king of Aragon and de facto ruler of Castile, seized the entire kingdom in 1512 and received the oath of fidelity of the Cortes some months later. Henri d'Albret recovered the one province that was north of the Pyrenees in 1521 and gradually consolidated his position. By 1530 the two Navarres had become permanently separated with the heights of the Pyrenees as their boundary, and Henri d'Albret had made significant progress in fashioning the institutions to govern his truncated kingdom of about a hundred parishes. Among the most important of these was a chancellery created in 1524 to serve as the highest court in the land and an Estates General that had been convoked for the first time one year before. At first Henri followed the traditional practice of holding the three estates every two or three years, but from 1535 he assembled them annually. The fact that he created and regularly used a representative assembly to which he presented his requests

20. Tucoo-Chala, "Les institutions," pp. 337–39; Cadier, *Les Etats*, pp. 277–368; Duncan, *Government of Béarn*, pp. 273–93.

21. Charles Dartigue-Peyrou, *La vicomté de Béarn sous le règne de Henri d'Albret* (Paris, 1934), pp. 259–61.

for financial assistance rather than imposing the taxes he desired provides further evidence that the rulers of his day accepted the role of such institutions, inconvenient though they might be on some occasions.[22]

Only the bishops or vicar-generals of Bayonne and Dax, in whose dioceses Navarre lay, three priors, and an important priest were summoned to the estates to represent the clergy. Since the episcopal seats were outside the kingdom, the bishops and vicar-generals rarely attended. Because the other clergymen were also occasionally absent, the first estate was small indeed. Nevertheless the clergy did not unite with the nobility to form a single house as in Béarn but rather constituted a separate chamber. Feudalism had never penetrated into Navarre and the other Basque regions, so oaths of fealty were not taken, and all land was considered to be allodial. Admission to the second estate was limited to those who were proprietors of noble houses. Nevertheless the second estate was numerous because over a hundred houses were so designated. The system of basing attendance on the ownership of designated properties made it difficult for new nobles created by the king to win admission. Hence the size of this estate remained more static than in many other localities. Five towns and seven valleys or *pays* sent twenty-six deputies to stand for the third estate. These valleys and pays had their own assemblies, which not only designated the deputies to the Estates General but also dealt with local affairs. Small though it was, Navarre was indeed richly endowed with representative assemblies.[23]

The three estates normally presented a united front before the king, but to decide what position to take, the members of each order were polled separately. Concurrence by a majority in two estates was sufficient to approve a measure, except that the position taken by the third estate was the determining factor in financial questions because it was upon this order that the burden fell.[24] To assist in their deliberations and to look after their interests when they were not in session, the three estates appointed permanent officials and held special, hastily called sessions. These officials included at an early date a syndic who was drawn from the nobility but was trained in law, a treasurer, a secretary, and an usher. During the eighteenth century an additional secretary was appointed, and an agent was established in Paris to look after their interests. The kingdom was so small that instead of electing a committee to act in emergencies, those who attended the estates by right and those who had been elected to participate in the previous

22. J. B. Daranatz, "Les Etats de Basse-Navarre," *Gure-Herria* 3 (1923): 723–32, 4 (1924): 80–85, 210–12; Alain Destrée, *La Basse-Navarre et ses institutions de 1620 à la Révolution* (Saragossa, 1955), pp. 20–22, 40–42, 127–32, 153–55; Maria Puy Huici Goñi, *Las Cortes de Navarra durante la edad moderna* (Madrid, 1963), pp. 13–30, 440; Gustave Bascle de Lagrèze, *La Navarre française* (Paris, 1881–1882), 1:9, 2:1–21.

23. Destrée, *La Basse-Navarre*, pp. 158–77, 289–314. Because all property in Navarre was allodial, the difference between a noble and nonnoble house depended on whether the king had renounced his right to tax it. Daranatz, "Les Etats," 4:85–95, 276–83.

24. Destrée, *La Basse-Navarre*, pp. 216–20. Daranatz, "Les Etats," 4:216.

session were summoned. This procedure removed the necessity for special elections, thereby saving time. But many could not attend on short notice, so these sessions, known as *les Jointes de Navarre*, were denied the right to tax and were permitted to make only provisional recommendations that were binding until the next meeting of the estates.[25]

In developing their procedures and in determining what permanent positions to establish, the estates undoubtedly drew heavily on the precedents of the once united kingdom. At first it was possible to rely on the memory of those who had participated in meetings south of the Pyrenees before the kingdom was dismembered, but later the estates had to appeal to the Cortes of Spanish Navarre where the medieval archives of the assembly were kept for information concerning precedents.[26] It is not surprising that the estates continued the tradition of sending deputies to each new king to request that he appear before them and take an oath to preserve their fors, customs, and privileges. Henri d'Albret instructed his commissioner to make this pledge in his name, but as far as can be ascertained none of his successors took the oath before the estates or had someone do so for them. Louis XIV made the pledge in a nearby town in 1660, but other kings or their ministers were content to promise to respect the Navarrese privileges just as they did for the various French provinces.[27]

The little viscounty of Soule with its sixty-nine parishes lay pressed up against the Pyrenees between Béarn and Navarre. The inhabitants, like those of Navarre, spoke Basque and like those of both their larger neighbors they had estates. Almost nothing is known of the early history of the three estates, but in the eighteenth century they consisted of an upper house to which the clergy and nobility were admitted and a lower house consisting of the representatives of the parishes. When a decision had to be made, the jurats of the parishes were summoned to hear about the problem. They then returned to their parishes and assembled all heads of households to decide what position to take on the proposals that had been made. After they had been instructed in this fashion, they reconvened for the vote. In 1730 the upper house began to meet in the same chamber as the third estate. This led to the abandoning of the refer-back system, and thereafter the parishes gave their deputies authority to act in their names.[28]

25. Destrée, *La Basse-Navarre*, pp. 177–96, 276–84; Daranatz, "Les Etats," 3:274–75, 367–68, 538–39.

26. Destrée, *La Basse-Navarre*, p. 220 n.97.

27. Ibid., pp. 35–40; Daranatz, "Les Etats," 4:219–23.

28. H. Jolly and H. Courteault, "Essai sur le régime financier des petits pays d'états du midi de la France au XVIIIe siècle," *Bul. de la soc. des sciences, lettres et arts de Pau*, sér. 2, 54 (1931): 165–66; M. Etcheverry, "A travers l'histoire anecdotique de Bayonne et des pays voisins," *Bul. de la soc. des sciences, lettres et arts de Bayonne* 59 (1937): 107–18; M. Nussy-Saint-Saëns, "Contribution à un essai sur la coutume de Soule," *Bul. de la soc. des sciences, lettres et arts de Bayonne* 62 (1940): 85–97; Etienne Dravasa, *Les privilèges des Basques du Labourd dans l'ancien régime* (Saint-Sabastien, 1952), p. 191.

5. OTHER ESTATES IN THE SOUTHWEST AND NORTHWEST

In addition to the estates that responded to the call of the head of the house of Foix-Navarre-Albret and those that regularly deputed to the estates of Guyenne, there were three other jurisdictions in the southwest with representative assemblies. Two, Quatre-Vallées and Labourd, were directly under the king; the third, Turenne, was convoked by a viscount.

Quatre-Vallées had belonged to the counts of Armagnac until 1497, when it passed to the crown. Little survives concerning the functioning of the assembly prior to the late seventeenth century. Well before that time, each of the four valleys had its syndic and its assembly that met when necessary to look after local affairs and to elect deputies to the general assembly of all four valleys. Nobles sometimes sought to participate, but they were usually excluded by the sturdy Pyrenean villagers.[29]

The Basque bailiwick of Labourd in the southwest corner of France also had a representative assembly that yielded to none in its democratic composition and procedures. The origins of this institution, called the *Bilçar*, are shrouded in mystery. As early as 1125 the viscount summoned the nobility to assemblies, but soon thereafter Labourd passed to the English, where it remained for three centuries. Upon its reunion with France, Labourd was given a tax-exempt status, presumably because of its frontier position, but this did not prevent the French kings from asking for contributions or the inhabitants from assessing themselves to meet local needs. Now and then rulers confirmed Labourd's favorable tax position, though sometimes for only a limited number of years, but by 1513 (and probably earlier) there were enough fiscal demands to require a syndic to supervise the collection of taxes and to defend the interests of the bailiwick when the Bilçar was not in session.[30]

The oldest surving journal of the Bilçar is for 1595. By then the nobility had ceased to attend, and only the third estate was represented. Assemblies could be convoked by the syndic with the permission of a royal official. When he did so, the council of each parish chose one of its number to attend a meeting at the seat of the bailiwick at Ustaritz. Here the syndic explained the reasons for the assembly. When he had done so, the deputies returned to their parishes where they assembled the inhabitants to determine what action to take concerning the proposals. When the Bilçar met a second time, the deputies voted as instructed by their constitutents, and the majority of the parishes ruled. Since every head of a household, including women,

29. Armand Sarramon, *Les Quatre-Vallées: Aure, Barousse, Neste, Magnoac* (Albi, 1954), pp. 279–86.

30. Dravasa, *Les privilèges*, pp. 69–83, 196–202; P. Yturbide, "Les syndics généraux du pays de Labourd," *Bul. de la soc. des sciences, lettres et arts de Bayonne* 32 (1910): 169–80; *Actes François Ier*, 4: no. 12,814, 7: nos. 26,613, 26,880. Henry IV issued letters confirming Labourd's exemption to the taille, taillon, and other subsidies during the latter stages of the religious wars. *IAD, Gironde, sér. C*, ed. Alexandre Gouget and Jean-A. Brutails (Bordeaux, 1893), 2:187.

participated in the election of the community officials and since each official who attended the Bilçar had to refer back to the inhabitants for instructions before he could vote, there was an exceptional degree of popular control in Labourd. Twenty-seven communities were represented in the Bilçar of 1595, and this number had increased to forty by the eighteenth century.[31]

The viscounty of Turenne was one of the few territories with a representative assembly that was still being regularly summoned in the seventeenth century by a great noble. The special status of the little viscounty of fewer than a hundred parishes was recognized during the thirteenth century. Time and again the kings from Philip III through Francis I, Henry IV, and Louis XIV issued declarations affirming that the inhabitants should not be subject to royal taxes. The viscounts, who rendered only simple homage to the French kings, exercised many of the rights usually allocated only to sovereigns, including summoning the estates when it pleased them. The origin of this assembly is lost in the past, but it had clearly been functioning for some time in 1467, when, at the viscount's request, Louis XI recognized his right to convoke it.[32]

Initially the viscounts summoned the three estates of all the viscounty to meet together, but for an unknown reason they divided the assembly near the close of the fifteenth century. From then until 1703, the customary practice was to hold one meeting for the part of the viscounty that lay in Quercy and a second meeting for that part that was in Limousin. Around the middle of the sixteenth century, the clergy ceased to attend, and the nobility came to be represented only by its syndics. The resulting assemblies were small indeed. Representatives from four towns and the syndic of the nobility composed the estates of Limousin, and deputies from three towns and the syndic of the nobility made up the estates of Quercy. A clerk, a receiver, and a sergeant were appointed by the viscount for both assemblies, but these officials were required to take an oath before both representative bodies to serve them faithfully and to reveal none of their secrets. The nobility in each section of the viscounty elected its syndic, who served for life, but the two syndics took an oath to the viscount. A system of mutual obligations and responsibilities was thereby established.[33]

Early in the seventeenth century, the nobility of Quercy failed to replace its syndic, and the post remained vacant for many years. When the viscount attempted to revive the office in 1623, the three towns regarded it as an innovation and protested strongly. The viscount abandoned the attempt. He tried again in 1640, and again there was a quarrel, but at length—in 1666—he suppressed the office. Nevertheless, by the close of the century the nobles once more had a syndic who sat with the estates.[34]

31. Dravasa, *Les privilèges*, pp. 84–139.
32. René Fagé, *Les Etats de la vicomté de Turenne* (Paris, 1894), 1:22–43, 2:50–52.
33. Ibid., 1:49–127.
34. Ibid., pp. 93, 96–100.

The viscounts were unable to support themselves and to pay the costs of governing the viscounty with the income from their domain, they therefore had to appeal to the estates for financial aid. At first their requests for assistance were not annual, but they gradually became so. By 1575 it had become customary to give the viscount a fixed amount each year, but his expenses continued to mount, and he frequently found it necessary to ask for additional support. At no time was the right of the estates to consent to taxation questioned. Occasionally the estates voluntarily voted the viscount a special present. Members of his family and his servants were often remembered. In return, the viscount defended the privileges of the viscounty when the crown attempted to impose royal taxes. The estates also voted taxes to pay their deputies and their own officials, to meet the costs of their assemblies, and to build and repair roads, bridges, and buildings, including the château of Turenne because of the protection it provided. They helped to support the château's garrison, financed a system of public instruction, carried on suits in the royal courts, and supervised the apportionment and collection of taxes. In the eighteenth century the fiscal demands of the viscount became so great that he was frequently at odds with the estates. Finally in 1738, he sought a solution to his financial difficulties by surrendering his rights to the crown. By this act the last of the estates of a feudal lord came to an end.[35]

The northwest provinces also had estates during the Renaissance, but except for limited periods, they dealt with the Valois dukes of Burgundy or their Habsburg successors and not with the kings of France in spite of their nominal suzerainty until 1526. These estates do not, therefore, properly form a part of a study of the growth of representative government in France. The one exception is the county of Boulogne, a subordinate fief to the county of Artois. Little can be ascertained concerning the early history of the three estates of the county beyond that they probably began to meet regularly in the 1360s to vote sums to the crown as a substitute for the aid to pay King John's ransom. For a time at least they assembled in conjuction with the three estates of the county of Artois, but following the death of Charles the Bold in 1477, the ties between the two counties were severed. Boulonnais became part of the royal domain, and Artois soon passed into the hands of the Habsburgs.[36]

As inhabitants of a frontier province, the Boulonnais claimed to be exempt from taxes. Their contribution, they insisted, was to defend the borders of the kingdom against foreign attack. They would, of course, contribute to the general expenses of the kingdom if they so desired but only with the consent of the three estates. They persisted in calling their

35. Ibid., pp. 139–311. The duke of Montpensier did not suppress the estates of Dombes until 1739, but Dombes was not technically a part of France. See chap. 6, sec. 3.

36. John B. Henneman, *Royal Taxation in Fourteenth Century France: The Captivity and Ransom of John II, 1356–1370* (Philadelphia, 1976), pp. 210, 272.

contribution an *octroi* until the Revolution. Elus may have been established in their midst by Francis I, but these intruders were definitely suppressed, and the three estates met together or separately as the occasion warranted until the close of the Old Regime. When they were not in session, they had permanent officials to look after their interests and to play key roles in administering the province.[37]

37. On the élus, see G. Dupont-Ferrier, "Essai sur la géographie administrative des élections financières en France de 1356 à 1790," *Ann. -bul. de la soc. de l'histoire de France* (1928), 244. On the other hand when Henry III recognized the privileges of Boulonnais in 1575, he specifically stated that the county had never had élus. P. Héliot, "La guerre dite de Lustucru et les privilèges du Boulonnais," *Revue du Nord* 21 (1935): 272 n.12. For references to the estates, see L. Bénard, "Analyse sommaire des principaux documents contenus dans les registres du roy de la sénéchaussée du Boulonnais," *Mém. de la soc. académique de l'arrondissement de Boulogne-sur-Mer* 20 (1900): 5, 9, 10, 25–28, 30, 33, 39–41, 49, 59, 61–65, 268–79, 326, 329–31, 351–52; *IAD, Pas-de-Calais, sér. C*, ed. Jules-Aime Cottel (Arras, 1882), 1:1–45 passim, and below chap. 17, sec. 2.

6

THE ESTATES
IN THE PAYS D'ELECTIONS

IN THE REMAINING PARTS OF FRANCE THE PRINCIPAL RESPONSIBILITY FOR apportioning and collecting taxes belonged to royal officials. In all these jurisdictions the three estates were occasionally assembled during the Renaissance to elect deputies to the Estates General, ratify treaties, and codify customs.[1] In some provinces such as Poitou, Saintonge, Haut- and Bas-Limousin, Haute- and Basse-Marche, and Angoumois the estates were also sometimes consulted on tax matters, but because meetings were held irregularly, they did not appoint syndics and other officials or play permanent roles in local government. In still other provinces where there were élections, the estates met regularly to deal with tax and other matters during the Renaissance. Although their position was inherently weak when they negotiated with the crown, they were nevertheless able to exert varying amounts of influence in their respective areas. The most important of these institutions was the estates of Normandy, for the Normans provided from 20 to 25 percent of the taille that was turned into the royal treasury.

1. THE ESTATES OF NORMANDY

Historians of the estates of Normandy and the Renaissance Normans themselves have generally looked back to the charter they obtained from Louis X in 1315 as providing the bulwark of their liberties. This document was indeed significant, but on the question of taxation, Louis did no more than to promise not to make any impositions except in cases of "evident utility or urgent necessity."[2] Since he reserved for himself the right to determine when such a situation existed, his pledge in this regard had little importance. It was not until 1339 that there is conclusive evidence that the three estates of the duchy met, although there had been earlier assemblies of the individual estates and various parts of the province. In that year Philip

---

1. For these estates see my *The Deputies to the Estates General of Renaissance France* (Madison, 1960).

2. *Ord.*, 1:587–94.

VI granted a charter detailing the privileges of the province in a more specific manner than the earlier one of 1315. In return the estates voted him a substantial sum to be used for an invasion of England.[3]

Meetings of the estates of the duchy or of smaller jurisdictions within it were common from then until 1362, but thereafter the crown ignored the former and often levied taxes without consulting even the local estates. As he approached death in 1380, Charles V became conscience-stricken and cancelled the hearth tax. Acting under pressure, the regents for his youthful son removed the aides as well. The strong fiscal position that Charles had achieved was thus temporarily terminated, and it once more became necessary to negotiate with the three estates for funds. The estates of the duchy met in December 1380 and again in February 1381, when they were given the right to designate the officials who were to levy the hearth tax they voted and to appoint the commander of the troops they were to support. It appeared as though the Normans were going to free themselves from the élus, but the following year the crown sought to increase the hearth tax and restore the aides without consulting the estates. The resistance was widespread, especially among the lower classes in the towns. Charles severely punished Rouen for its misdeeds but convoked the estates to meet in the spring of 1382 to approve both the increase in the hearth tax and the aides. In June the three estates met again to vote further taxes, but by the close of the summer the crown felt strong enough to impose additional levies without consulting them.[4]

The most probable explanation why the crown was able to tax without consent both before 1381 and after 1382 is that it employed Norman nobles and rich burghers to impose the levies, and it often gave a third of the sum that they collected from the peasants to their lords and from the urban inhabitants to their municipal governments. Under such circumstances the nobility and urban elite profited almost as much from taxes as the king did, and they did not insist that consent to taxation be obtained from the estates. The estates that met in 1381 and 1382 made no such provisions for the nobles and the towns. As a result, the upper classes failed to cooperate, and the lower classes, unchecked by their natural leaders, rioted. Thus through the simple expedient of sharing royal tax revenue with the local elite after the fall of 1382, the government of Charles VI managed to collect taxes once more without the consent of the estates of the duchy and without experiencing further difficulty from the peasants and urban poor. Revenue sharing

---

3. For the estates of 1339 and a critique of the evidence of whether the estates met in 1337, see John B. Henneman, *Royal Taxation in Fourteenth Century France* (Princeton, 1971), pp. 122–23, 139–40.

4. Alfred Coville, *Les Etats de Normandie, leur origines et leur dévelopement au XIVe siecle* (Paris, 1894), pp. 106–42, 257–63. Henri Prentout, *Les Etats provinciaux de Normandie* (Caen, 1925), 1:96–143; C. M. Radding, "The Estates of Normandy and the Revolts of the Towns at the Beginning of the Reign of Charles VI," *Speculum* 47 (1972): 79–83.

had proved to be a better method of obtaining taxes than the consent of the estates and was employed henceforth until the English domination.[5]

Henry V of England invaded Normandy in 1415, and by 1419 the entire province was in his hands. Instead of continuing the arbitrary rule of the French, he and the duke of Bedford, who became the regent for his infant son after his death, sought to win the loyalty of the Normans by respecting their privileges and giving them nearly all the administrative positions in the province. The provincial estates were revived and were used as instruments to secure the cooperation of the people, as well as to vote taxes. Meetings were held on an average of over once a year. To reduce Norman dependency on Paris, the English even created a university at Caen to train a clergy and a bureaucracy that they hoped would be loyal to them. When the French reconquered the province in 1450, Charles VII was faced with the problem of whether to govern in the English fashion or return to the policy of his father and uncles.[6]

Charles's initial impulse was to permit the Normans to retain the institutions that had served them under the English. In 1449 and again in 1450, he promised that he would confirm their charter, but after the three estates of 1450–51 had refused to vote the entire sum he requested for the support of the army, he adopted the policy of ordering that taxes be collected without their consent. For five years the estates did not meet. Then, in the spring of 1458, Charles once more underwent a change of heart and finally confirmed the Norman charter. He made one important change in the wording of the new document: instead of following the earlier charters and promising not to levy taxes except in case of "urgent necessity," a phrase that left open the possibility that the king alone would determine the severity of his needs, Charles specifically promised to levy only taxes agreed to by the three estates.[7] Prior to this time, meetings of the estates had been irregular and fragmentary, except during the period of English rule; now they became "regular and periodic."[8]

The usual practice was for the three estates to meet in November or December to vote taxes for the following year. Until the reign of Henry IV, the only break in this pattern was occasioned by Louis XI's failure to hold meetings in 1467 and 1468 because he was engaged in a struggle with his brother and other great nobles for the control of the duchy. Earlier Louis had shown that he had no fear of the three estates by offering them the

---

5. Radding," Estates of Normandy," pp. 83–90.

6. Prentout, *Les Etats de Normandie*, 1 : 144–55; Charles Robillard de Beaurepaire, *Les Etats de Normandie sous la domination anglaise* (Evreux, 1859). B. J. H. Rowe, "The Estates of Normandy under the Duke of Bedford, 1422–1435," *English Historical Review*, 47 (1931): 551–78, shows conclusively that contrary to Prentout's opinion, Bedford used the estates for purposes other than to vote taxes.

7. Prentout, *Les Etats de Normandie*, 1 : 156–72.

8. Ibid., p. 171.

privilege of raising the 400,000 livres that his father had collected from the province in any manner they desired. More significant, he was also willing to give them the right to appoint officials to supervise the apportionment and collection of the taxes, a step that was to be accompanied by the suppression of the élus. The experiment, however, was short-lived. The Normans were disappointed to discover that the use of their own officials did not lead to a reduction in taxes; earlier they had attributed their burden largely to dishonest and incompetent royal appointees. Furthermore, Louis finally realized that the substitution of the tax officials of the estates for his own weakened his authority.[9]

The willingness of Louis XI to use the three estates should not be construed as meaning that he was incapable of treating them harshly. From his reign indirect taxes appear to have been collected without their consent. Furthermore, in 1466 he arbitarily ordered that 40,000 more écus be levied than they had voted, and by 1477 the taxes on the province reached 500,000 livres. The Normans won a reduction of the taille to 250,000 livres following Louis's death, and when Charles VIII tried to repeat his predecessor's act of levying a larger taille than the three estates had voted, he was forced to reconvene them to consider the matter. Instrumental in winning this victory was the duke of Orleans, governor of the duchy and the future Louis XII of France. In return for his services the estates voted him a handsome present of 14,000 livres.[10]

The Italian wars made it necessary for the well-intentioned Louis XII to increase taxes, and under his less conscientious successor, Francis I, they grew more rapidly. By 1537 the taille reached 994,750 livres, a level at which it apparently remained until the end of the reign. In addition, écus were sometimes requested to pay for the war, and in 1549 the taillon was inaugurated to provide further support for the garrison. In all, the Normans contributed about a fifth of all the direct taxes the crown received. Surviving documentation does not permit one to judge the degree of their resistance to these increases or the number of times they won reductions, but there is no doubt that the right to consent to direct taxes was retained. A formulary used by the royal chancellery that was addressed to the commissioners to the estates directed them to see that the estates were willing to grant (*octroier*) the desired sum. Extraordinary sessions of the estates were called to vote taxes in excess of those granted in the regular meetings in order to avoid the necessity of imposing them by royal fiat, and, finally, the estates displayed their independence by refusing to ratify the treaty of Moore with England in 1525 because a financial obligation was involved.[11] Indirect taxes were another matter; here the consent of the estates ceased to be sought in the

9. Ibid., pp. 173–92, 2:229–34.
10. Ibid., 1:203, 225–27, 231, 2:162–63, 3:28–29.
11. Ibid., 1:244–84, 2:148–50, 163–67, 3:138.

latter half of the fifteenth century. Protests against these levies by the estates, were, however, strong and frequent.[12]

During the fourteenth century the provincial estates consisted of individually summoned ecclesiastics and nobles and the deputies of the chapters and towns. Gradually the mode of convocation changed, and by the early sixteenth century seven archbishops and bishops and six dukes and counts retained the right of receiving writs of summons. These magnates rarely exercised their privilege of attending the estates. Instead one deputy for the clergy and one for the nobility were elected in each of the seven bailiwicks of the province, and one deputy was chosen from the third estate in each of the thirty-one viscounties. In addition, the towns of Rouen and Caen won the right to have separate representation prior to Henry IV's succession to the throne. The electoral procedure became increasingly democratic during the Renaissance. Nobles without fiefs, curés, and peasants were usually allowed to participate, although here and there a cathedral chapter or town managed to retain a favored position. In most of the viscounties members of the three estates voted together for the representatives, and in the provincial estates they sat as a single chamber and voted by bailiwick rather than by order or as individuals.[13]

The three estates were slow to develop their own bureaucracy and administrative machinery. The procureur of Rouen acted as the syndic for the estates after the reunion of the duchy with the crown, and it was not until 1569 that the two offices were separated. Among the syndic's duties was to keep the archives of the estates. The estates also had a clerk, but he was appointed by the crown and also served the royal commissioners. During most of the sixteenth century, the holder of this post also occupied the office of treasurer of the estates. It was probably not until 1578 that the estates had a treasurer and not until 1609 a clerk who did not double as a royal official.[14]

The three estates of Normandy were among the first to have their agents apportion and collect the taxes they voted, but in 1382 this role was assumed by royal officials. Under Francis I representatives of the estates appear to have assisted the royal commissioners in dividing the tax among the subordinate jurisdictions, but they soon ceased to do so. As a result of a determined effort in 1579, the three estates won the right to have representatives of the third estate present when the élus divided the sum to be levied among the parishes in the individual élections, but on the whole their role in fiscal administration was modest during the Renaissance.[15]

The three estates appropriated funds to pay the salaries of their officials,

12. Ibid., 2:216–40.

13. Major, *Deputies to the Estates General*, pp. 46–52. BN ms. fr. 14,368, fols. 28–30; Prentout, *Les Etats de Normandie*, 2:296.

14. Prentout, *Les Etats de Normandie*, 1:11–12, 2:376–89, 400–12.

15. Ibid., 2:172–85; Henneman, *Royal Taxation*, pp. 231, 286; BN ms. fr. 14,368, fol. 29.

the expenses of their deputations to court, the costs of holding their meetings, and for their other activities. In 1527 the amount allocated for these purposes stood at 2,000 livres, but it was steadily increased to 12,337 livres by 1582. In addition, the estates voted handsome presents for their governors and other royal officials in anticipation of or in return for their services.[16] Through their cahiers the estates sought to influence nearly every aspect of provincial life.[17] At times they were successful; at times they failed. Their strength lay in the relatively cooperative attitude of the various social classes and in the generous suffrage that prevailed. Their weakness was derived from the failure of prelates and nobles to participate in these proceedings in large numbers and from the crown's control of the tax-collecting machinery. Since the Normans furnished about a fifth of the direct taxes in the kingdom, royal officials kept a watchful eye on the province and were ready to exploit every opportunity that arose.

2. THE ESTATES IN AUVERGNE

Assemblies of the three estates of Auvergne date back to the dawn of the Hundred Years War, and during that struggle their meetings became frequent. Even the creations of élus in 1355 and the formal establishments of élections in Clermont and St. Flour somewhat later had no immediate effect on their vitality. In Basse-Auvergne this was largely because the duties of these officials were limited to assessing indirect taxes and judging disputes that arose concerning the taille. The taille itself was apportioned among the towns by their deputies to the estates and in the countryside by commissioners named by the nobility and clergy but authorized to act by the king. In Haute-Auvergne the élus cooperated with appointees of the estates in apportioning the taille. In 1452, as the Hundred Years War was drawing to a close, Charles VII suddenly altered this procedure. Instead of appointing commissioners to hold the meeting of the three estates to secure their consent to taxation, as was customary, he simply sent letters to the élus in Clermont and St. Flour directing them to apportion the taxes. At this point, according to Antoine Thomas, the existence of the élus in Auvergne became decisive; their presence enabled the king to bypass the estates, even though a nobleman and a clergyman continued to assist them in the countryside in Basse-Auvergne. There was no public outcry because the termination of the war enabled the king to reduce the total tax burden on the province by over one-third. From that time Thomas believed that the three estates were rarely convoked. When they did meet to vote a tax for the duke of Auvergne or for their own affairs, the levy itself was made by the élus only after royal

16. Prentout, *Les Etats de Normandie*, 1:278–80, 2:168–72, 417–21.
17. Ibid., 2:284–375.

permission had been granted. There were occasional meetings to redact the customs or for other purposes, but to Thomas the estates were clearly in a state of decline after 1452.[18]

There is some truth in Thomas's analysis, but he greatly underestimated the activity of the estates after 1452. During the remainder of the century the three estates or the deputies of the good towns of Basse-Auvergne usually met from one to six times a year, except in the 1470s when on at least one occasion Louis XI ordered that taxes be levied without convoking the estates.[19] Two tendencies can be noted during this period. First, from about 1490 the nobility and clergy of Basse-Auvergne ceased to attend except on rare occasions, and at some point the two orders took a similar course in Haute-Auvergne. There is no information to explain why they did so. We can only assume that they believed that their interests were adequately protected by the hierarchies within their respective orders and that they were tired of attending the frequent meetings desired by the towns. The second tendency was for the good towns of Haute- and Basse-Auvergne to meet separately. The representatives of the two parts of the province had often met in their respective jurisdictions during the Hundred Years War, and even when they had assembled together, the two urban groups had not acted as a single house. Furthermore the taxes that they had voted had been divided among the towns of Basse-Auvergne, the plat pays of Basse-Auvergne, and Haute-Auvergne in accordance with a fixed ratio. With this tradition of separatism, they went their separate ways after the nobility and clergy had left them to their own devices. (They will therefore be treated separately during the postmedieval period.)[20]

By 1506, when detailed archival material becomes available, the muni-

18. Antoine Thomas, *Les Etates provinciaux de la France centrale sous Charles VII* (Paris, 1879), 1:73–77, 88–97, 164–74. For references to the estates between 1356 and 1413 see Françoise Lehoux, *Jean de France, duc de Berri* (Paris, 1966), 1:65 n.2, 98 nn.4–5, 99 n.1, 113 n.5, 120–24, 135, 144 n.3, 168, 180 n.8, 181, 186, 234, 262, 346 n.5, 349, 358, 380, 433 nn.1, 3, 434–36, 441–42, 446, 452; 2:38, 133 n.4, 134, 135 nn.5, 6, 137 n.3, 138–39, 207, 312, and Réné Lacour, *Le gouvernement de l'apanage de Jean, duc de Berry, 1360–1418* (Paris, 1934), pp. 77–81, 250–59, 330–32, 374–85. The élus were initially regarded as temporary officials. Only when they became permanent were élections established. Gustave Dupont-Ferrier, *Etudes sur les institutions financières de la France à la fin du Moyen Age* (Paris, 1930), 1:22–39.

19. No meetings have been found for 1460, 1470–73, 1475–78, and 1481. AD, Puy-de-Dôme, 4F 147–49. The purpose of Louis's order in 1473 was to provide funds for the conquest of Roussillon. For other references to meetings of the estates between 1452 and 1500, a few of which were not included in G. Rouchon manuscripts located at AD, Puy-de-Dôme, 4F 140–53, see *IAC, Clermont-Ferrand, fonds de Montferrand*, ed. Teilhard de Chardin (Clermont-Ferrand, 1902), 1:18, 75, 79, 80, 475, 478, 481–82; Thomas, *Les Etats provinciaux*, 273–75; AC, Clermont-Ferrand, fonds de Clermont, Aa 4, Aa 6; AN, KK 648, nos. 98–100; and *IAC, St. Flour*, ch. V, art. 2, no. 9. This inventory is unpublished, and the documents have been lost. *Lettres de Louis XI*, ed. Joseph Vaësen and Etienne Charavoy (Paris, 1885), 2:284 n.1. BN ms. fr. 22,296, fol. 14, BN ms. fr. 21,426, fols. 1–8.

20. Thomas, *Les Etats provinciaux*, 1:56–58, 73–77.

cipal officials of Clermont had come to dominate the administration of Basse-Auvergne. In 1402 the three estates had voted to establish an archives, but if they actually attempted to carry the plan out, they soon abandoned the effort, and by the start of the sixteenth century the municipal officials of Clermont were performing this duty for the third estate. The nobility and clergy apparently made no provisions for their records; they used the archives preserved by the municipality when they had need of data, despite the fact that they both had syndics who could have preserved important documents. By this time the officials of Clermont had already established themselves as syndics of the third estate with the right to convoke the good towns when they desired. They did so frequently, and from 1513 it was customary to summon only four or five towns to send deputies when minor matters were to be considered. Even so all thirteen good towns generally met three or four times a year. No permanent clerk was appointed, and the official pronouncements of the assemblies were recorded by a local notary employed for the occasion.[21]

At first Clermont had little difficulty in preserving its dominant position within the third estate because of its size, comparative wealth, and great antiquity. As seat of the bishop, Clermont was the undisputed ecclesiastical capital of the province, and the presence of some royal officials in adjoining Montferrand where the seat of the bailiwick was located caused little difficulty. However, the judicial capital of Basse-Auvergne was at Riom. Here the judges won control over the municipal government and used their position to attack Clermont in the assemblies. As early as 1528 they sought to have a syndic elected by all the good towns, and during the Wars of Religion they became increasingly aggressive. What galled them most was to see mere *échevins* in a rival city summon the third estate, an act they regarded as a regalian right that could only be exercised in the king's name by royal officials, namely themselves. Their jealousy was to become involved in a more legitimate dispute between the good towns and the plat pays.[22]

How the thirteen good towns that stood for the third estate were initially chosen is a mystery. Several did not erect walls separating themselves from the plat pays until after they had seats in the provincial assembly, and others, including Clermont, were numbered in this select group several centuries before they were given jurisdiction and other privileges freeing

21. Ibid., pp. 10–11. G. Rouchon, "Le tiers état aux Etats provinciaux de Basse-Auvergne aux XVIᵉ et XVIIᵉ siècles," *Bul. philologique et historique (jusqu'à 1715) du comité des travaux historiques et scientifiques* (1930–31): 167–68; AD, Puy-de-Dôme, 4F 140.

22. Major, *Deputies to the Estates General*, pp. 82–83; Rouchon, "Le tiers état," pp. 172, 174–75. At this time Riom was nearly as large as Clermont, being taxed on the basis of 390 hearths as opposed to the latter's 400. R. Sève, "Une carte de Basse Auvergne de 1544–1545 et la demande d'agrégation aux bonnes villes présentée par Ambert," *Mélanges géographiques offerts à Philippe Arbos* (Clermont-Ferrand, 1953), p. 168. For Riom's effort to elect a syndic, see AD, Puy-de-Dôme, 4F 140, pp. 276–77, 281. The attempt was repeated in 1573. See AD, Puy-de-Dôme, 4F 143.

them from direct interference from their feudal lords. Under such circumstances it is not surprising that during the 1540s four of the more important excluded communities began to press for admission to the meetings of the third estates. Their efforts failed, but when the king imposed a tax on the closed towns of the kingdom in 1554, the good towns held a separate meeting of forty-seven excluded communities to ask them to assume part of the burden. As an enticement they offered to obtain a decree from the king's council requiring the clergy and nobles to pay taxes on the common land they purchased, that is, in effect, to declare that the taille was réelle in Basse-Auvergne. Either beguiled by this promise or still submissive to the authority of the good towns, the deputies of the excluded localities accepted the additional burden.[23]

Nothing came of the proposal to make the nobility and clergy pay the taille on the common land they acquired, but the patience of the inhabitants of the plat pays was becoming exhausted. In 1560, when the échevins of Clermont summoned their representatives to submit suggestions that might be included in the cahier of the third estate that was to be taken to the Estates General, they not only prepared a cahier of their own but also elected a deputy to take it to that assembly. Shocked at this presumption, the échevins refrained from convoking the plat pays to assist in preparing the cahier for the Estates General that met in 1561. In 1576 the problem of representation in the third estate came to the fore once more when, through an error in the chancellery, a letter ordering that deputies be elected to the Estates General was sent to the royal officials in Riom. These officials saw their opportunity and convoked the three estates of the province. To ensure their predominance in the assembly, they summoned not only the other good towns but also the excluded communities. The échevins of Clermont protested, and the king's council hastily corrected the mistake and directed that the estates be summoned in the accustomed manner. Twelve of the good towns responded to Clermont's call, but Riom, the thirteenth, became the location of a meeting of the deputies of three hundred or four hundred excluded towns and villages. Both assemblies elected deputies, and although the king's council once more sided with Clermont, the deputies chosen at Riom were also seated.[24]

The inhabitants of the plat pays were too aroused to accept defeat. They elected a syndic in 1578 to defend them from the exploitive tendencies of the thirteen good towns and to agitate for expanding the representation in the third estate. In their efforts the plat pays were supported by the nobility as well as by Riom. The good towns tried to settle the matter by giving the syndic a seat in their assembly with full voting privileges, but he insisted that

---

23. Rouchon, "Le tiers état," pp. 170–74, 177–79; Séve, "Une carte de Basse Auvergne," pp. 165–71.

24. Major, *Deputies to the Estates General*, pp. 82–83; Rouchon, "Le tiers état," pp. 179–80.

twelve places be provided for the excluded communities. The governor sought a solution based on this proposal, but the matter was still unresolved when the Estates General of 1588 was convoked. Once more the chancellery inadvertently directed the royal officials at Riom to assemble the estates. Once more rival assemblies were held at Riom and Clermont, and two deputations were dispatched to Blois. At this point the council decided to act decisively and decreed that the plat pays should set up a system so that six additional localities would have seats in the assembly of the good towns on a rotating basis. A procureur, a secretary, and a receiver were to be elected who were to reside in Clermont, a directive that would have reduced the role of the échevins of that town if it had been enforced, and the office of syndic of the plat pays was to be suppressed. The thirteen good towns became nineteen and the plat pays caused little trouble henceforth, but Clermont retained its position of dominance, to the dissatisfaction of the royal officials in Riom.[25]

Clermont and the other good towns also began to have trouble with the nobility and clergy. Only a small fraction of their number who were eligible to attend meetings of the three estates during the fifteenth century did so and from the 1490s they were rarely convoked. When all three estates were summoned in November 1551 to try to circumvent Henry II's effort to establish the gabelle in Auvergne, the clergy could muster only four of its number at the opening session. No nobles at all were present at the time. Ultimately about twenty came, a small proportion of the thousand or more noble houses in the province. Other meetings of the three estates followed during the decade, and eventually the magazines for the storage and sale of salt were abolished in return for a surprisingly modest sum, but not without friction developing among the three estates because the nobility and clergy did not wish to contribute. Hardly had this matter been settled than the crown imposed a tax on wine that everyone was supposed to pay. There was general agreement that a sum should be offered in return for suppressing the tax, but the nobility and clergy resisted efforts to make them accept part of the burden. Instead they took the offensive against the good towns, charging that they overburdened the inhabitants of the plat pays with levies that they voted for their own purposes. On this last dispute, at least, a compromise was reached in 1568, when it was agreed that the syndics of the clergy and nobility would attend the assemblies of the good towns on those occasions that it was necessary to levy over 6,000 livres to support their activities.[26]

The position of the three estates and the good towns of Basse-Auvergne after Charles VII had begun to order the élus to collect royal taxes without their consent was obviously weaker than that enjoyed by the estates of

---

25. Rouchon, "Le tiers état," pp. 180–83; Major, *Deputies to the Estates General*, p. 83.

26. AD, Puy-de-Dôme, 4F 141, esp. pp. 5–20, 4F 142; Antoine Bergier and Verdier-Latour, *Recherches historiques sur les Etats généraux et plus particulièrement sur l'origine, l'organisation et la durée des anciens États provinciaux d'Auvergne* (Clermont-Ferrand, 1788), pièces justificatives, no. 67.

Normandy where there were also élus. Nevertheless their role in royal taxation should not be discounted. If the king ordered that a tax be imposed, the magistrates of Clermont could protest in the name of the third estate by virtue of their status as perpetual syndics, or they could summon a meeting of the good towns to elect a delegation to go to court to plead their cause. In exceptional cases they obtained permission for the three estates to meet in order to present a stronger front as they did in the 1540s and 1550s to obtain the suppression of the gabelle. By these acts they sometimes won reductions in taxes or altered the tax to a less objectionable form as in the case of the levy on the sale of wine. Either the three estates or the good towns had to consent to taxes desired by their duke and either assembly could levy taxes to support local activities. These activities included making rivers navigable, trying to insure better behavior on the part of the troops, and dealing with vagabonds. During the Wars of Religion these representative assemblies played a major role in trying to provide for the defense of the province.[27]

The king reserved the right to approve the taxes voted by the estates and the good towns and sometimes encouraged them to make appropriations. For example, in 1508 Louis XII authorized the three estates of the two Auvergnes to vote their duke 30,000 livres, but they were willing to give him only 20,000. In 1516 Francis I gave the duke approval for a 50,000 livres tax but stipulated that the three estates must consent to the levy.[28] The three estates and the good towns were supposed to secure the king's permission for their taxes. In 1470 they obtained authorization to levy 2,000 livres to pay for the services a number of individuals had rendered. In 1514 they sought permission to borrow money so that they would not have to tax so heavily that year. In 1528 the magistrates of Clermont urged their fellow deputies to vote their governor 10,000 livres, but when they had done so, royal approval had to be sought. On the other hand, when Saint-André, their governor, persuaded the king to give him letters authorizing a levy of 6,000 livres in 1551, the estates refused to concur because they had already voted him 10,000 livres to be collected over a two-year period.[29]

The position of the three estates and good towns of Auvergne was not so different from provinces in which there were no élections. So long as the consultative traditions of the Renaissance monarchy were preserved, there was considerable give and take between them and the crown. But there was a danger. If the nature of the monarchy changed, the presence of the élus made it easier for the king to impose taxes without considering their wishes and to stifle their activities by not permitting the élus to collect the taxes that they voted for their own purposes.

27. *IAC, Clermont-Ferrand*, 1:20–21; AD, Puy-de-Dôme, 4F 141–44.

28. *IAC, Clermont-Ferrand*, 1:318–19; AN, P 1372[B], no. 2085.

29. BN ms. fr. 22,296, fol. 14; AD, Puy-de-Dôme, 4F 140, pp. 55–56, 270–80; *IAC, Clermont-Ferrand*, 1:42.

Enough evidence survives to indicate that the three estates of Haute-Auvergne underwent a somewhat similar transition. Initially there were probably only four towns—St. Flour, Aurillac, Maurs, and perhaps Mauriac—that sent delegates to the assemblies; but in 1510 Salers and Chaudesaigues joined the original four, and in 1569 ten towns participated in a joint assembly of the three estates of both Auvergnes at Clermont. By 1576 this procedure had changed; it had become customary for each of the four original good towns to hold local assemblies of the communities in the provostship of which they were the seat and to depute to the assemblies of the third estate. This arrangement was challenged by Salers in 1592 and again in 1595 in conjunction with three other towns, but unsuccessfully; there was no expansion of the number of good towns as had occurred in Basse-Auvergne. The lesser towns had to content themselves with being represented in the provostship assemblies where they appear to have been relegated to inferior positions by the principal town.[30]

St. Flour, like Clermont, claimed the right to convoke the third estate, but unlike Clermont it could exercise this privilege only after receiving permission from the governor or bailiff, a restriction that made it easier for the representatives of the crown to curtail its activities during the seventeenth century. Both the bishop and the élus had their headquarters in St. Flour, but the presidial seat was located in Aurillac, a situation that led to a rivalry between the two towns comparable to that between Clermont and Riom.[31]

3. The Estates in the Government of Lyons

The fifteenth-century dukes of Bourbon made no effort to create an Estates General that drew participants from their fiefs of Auvergne, Forez, Beaujolais, Bourbonnais, and La Marche as their cousins of Burgundy had done. When their various lands cooperated, it was likely to be on the initiative of the local estates. In 1423 the three estates of Auvergne negotiated a defensive alliance with Bourbonnais, Forez, Beaujolais, and Combraille that lasted for some years. They did not, however, feel obligated to limit their negotiations to other Bourbon fiefs, and in 1437 they made an alliance with some nobles in Velay and Gévaudan. Bourbonnais and Forez appear to have shared the same deputation to the Estates General of France in 1484, but instances of cooperation between the various estates in the Bourbon apanage were too few to provide a base for the creation of a large assembly.[32]

30. Major, *Deputies to the Estates General*, pp. 83–84; Thomas, *Les Etats provinciaux*, 1:35; AC, Aurillac, AA 2 bis. AC, St. Flour, ch. V, art. 3, no. 8; Bergier and Verdier-Latour, *Recherches*, pp. 23–24, pièces justificatives, no. 68.

31. Major, *Deputies to the Estates General*, p. 84.

32. E. Perroy, "L'état Bourbonnais," in *Histoire des institutions françaises au Moyen Age*, ed. (*Continued on next page*)

For some years following the reunion of the Bourbon apanage with the crown, the Valois kings did no better, but in 1547 Henry II combined these lands with Lyonnais and the bailiwick of Saint-Pierre-le-Moutier to form a large new government. A few years later, in 1556, a meeting of the estates of the government at Moulins lent its support to breaking a truce with the Habsburgs and to edicts against clandestine marriages and infanticide. Further meetings of the estates at Moulins followed in March and June 1561 to elect deputies to attend the Estates General of Pontoise.[33] Soon thereafter this large, unwieldy government was subdivided. A new, smaller government whose boundaries approximately coincided with those of the généralité of Lyons became the base of the new estates during the latter half of the sixteenth century.

The estates of the government and généralité drew their participants from Forez, Lyonnais, and Beaujolais. Sometimes only the syndics of the third estate of the first two provinces and a deputy from the town of Villefranche attended. On other occasions, the nobility and clergy also participated. The composition and the procedures of the meetings never became institutionalized, and often when we read that Villefranche was told to send someone to Lyons, we are left in doubt as to whether he was to attend an actual meeting of the estates. Or again, when we find the syndics of Forez, the plat pays of Lyonnais, and a spokesman for Beaujolais appearing before the king's council, we cannot always ascertain whether they had been directed to do so in a common meeting or whether they had merely decided to act together to strengthen their position. Since Mâconnais and Vivarais were in the same farm for the salt tax as the government of Lyonnais, their representatives were often asked to attend when issues related to this tax were discussed. To all of these problems occasioned by the nascent state of the estates, we must add the absence of adequate source material, especially for the period prior to 1567. As a result, one can do little more than demonstrate their activity.[34]

In November 1568 Villefranche was told to elect an échevin to attend an assembly at Lyons on the fifteenth that was to deal with the farm of the salt tax. In February 1570 there was another meeting on the same subject, and that November the deputies of the town of Lyons, the plat pays of Lyonnais,

---

Ferdinand Lot and Robert Fawtier (Paris, 1957), 1:315–16; Antoine Thomas, *Les Etats provinciaux de la France centrale sous Charles VII* (Paris, 1879) 1:81–82, 2:21–23, 39–42, 86–88; Jehan Masselin, *Journal des Etats Généraux de France tenus à Tours en 1484 sous le règne de Charles VIII*, ed. A. Bernier (Paris, 1835), p. 726. André Leguai argues that the Bourbon dukes developed a state, but he offers little evidence to support his conclusions. See his *De la seigneurie à l'état: le Bourbonnais pendant la Guerre de Cent Ans* (Moulins, 1969).

33. Lucien Romier, *La carrière d'un favori: Jacques d'Albon de Saint-André* (Paris, 1909), pp. 245–46; AC, Lyon, AA 147, BB 82, fols. 19v–24v, 27v–28v.

34. The most valuable printed source is *Registres consulaires de la ville de Villefranche*, ed. Abel Besançon and Emile Longin (Villefranche-sur-Saône, 1905–19). Unhappily there is a gap between 1489 and 1567. A thorough exploitation of the rich archives of Lyons would undoubtedly yield further material.

Forez, Beaujolais, and Vivarais filed a joint plea concerning this unpopular farm. They won some relief. That December there was a meeting at Lyons to which the échevins of Villefranche were to take their complaints concerning justice, taxes, and troops. Further meetings were held in March 1572 and June 1573.[35] There may have been only one or two more assemblies during the 1570s, but in the 1580s and 1590s there were not more than four years in which the government did not assemble, and in some years there were two or more meetings. Although royal taxes were set by the crown, these estates protested with occasional success against heavy exactions and the creation of useless offices. They raised and borrowed money to support their own activities, including waging war for the League, and they appointed auditors to verify the accounts of their officials. In short, the assembly of the government of Lyonnais performed much the same functions as the estates of other provinces where there were élections except that it in no way supplanted the estates of the component jurisdictions.[36]

Within the government of Lyonnais, meetings of the third estate of Forez, the plat pays of Lyonnais, Franc-Lyonnais, and Dombes were apparently commonplace throughout the Renaissance. Meetings of the third estate of Beaujolais may have ceased near the close of the fifteenth century, but they were renewed to some extent under the leadership of Villefranche before or during the early stages of the Wars of Religion. The diocese at Lyons included so much of the government that the archbishop and its assembly served to defend the interests of the clergy. The nobles, on the other hand, made little use of assemblies. Only those of Forez retained an organization throughout the Renaissance.

As far as can be ascertained, there were no meetings of the three estates of Forez before 1360, but they assembled frequently during the 1380s and 1390s. Those who participated quickly learned the art of seeking the aid of their feudal overlord in their negotiations with the king and in bribing his officials to ensure that their petitions received favorable responses. Local economic interests were not ignored, and in 1393 the estates voted a tax to repair a bridge over the Loire.[37]

The three estates met together less frequently during the fifteenth and sixteenth centuries; the more common practice was for the nobility and the thirteen towns that made up the third estate to hold separate assemblies. Eighty-five percent of the county lay in the diocese of Lyons, so it is not

---

35. *Registres de Villefranche*, 2:68–69, 99, 127–29, 132, 135, 160–61, 191–92.

36. Ibid., pp. 234–35, 270, 281–82, 327–30, 334–37, 339–40, 354–55, 374–75, 379, 453–54, 541, 565, 569–70, 577, 588–89, 3:2, 22–24, 38–39, 41, 67, 79–80, 290, 332–33, 407, 429; *IAC, Lyon*, ed., F. Rolle (Paris, 1865), 1: BB 123, BB 124. AD, Loire, C 32, nos. 1, 25; AD, Rhône, C 408, fols. 15v, 35v–36v, 106v–07.

37. For the medieval estates see Etienne Fournial, *Les villes et l'économie d'échange en Forez aux XIIIe et XIVe siècles* (Paris, 1967), pp. 119, 231, 331, 333, 335, 364–66, 376, 377–80, 449, 464, 477.

surprising that the clergy met under the auspices of the archbishop when its interests were concerned. Between 1560 and 1614 the clergy always united with Lyonnais to send joint delegations to the Estates General. By 1563 the towns had a syndic, and they soon added two procureurs to their staff to look after their interests when they were not in session. For a period of uncertain duration during the Wars of Religion, they also had a council, which they authorized to act in their name provided that matters of major importance were referred to them before any decisions were made. The nobles had a syndic and four councillors and the clergy their ecclesiastical hierarchy to serve as their spokesmen during the intervals between meetings.[38]

At some point prior to 1406 Charles VI created an élection in Forez with its seat in Montbrison. There is insufficient documentation to ascertain what immediate effect this had on the right of the estates to consent to taxation, but in the long run it reduced them to a position comparable to that held by the estates in Auvergne; that is, they continued to vote sums of money for their count and for their own needs but could do no more than protest against royal levies with vehemence. Assemblies of the three estates or of the towns made a grant to their countess in 1528, appropriated funds to make the Loire River navigable in 1572, offered to support an army of 300 foot and 50 horse in 1577, and protested strongly against an increase in the taille in 1578. On the last occasion they sought the assistance of their governor and pointedly settled a 2,250 livres account with the queen to pave the way for their negotiations with the crown.[39]

There was little chance that assemblies of the three estates would develop in the seneschalsy of Lyonnais. A bitter quarrel between the clergy and burghers of Lyons over their respective rights and privileges during the fifteenth century precluded close cooperation. Furthermore the affluent church owned so many fiefs in the countryside that the nobility was in a far weaker position than in most of the rest of France. Hence except for a brief period of moderate activity early in the reign of Charles VII, meetings of the three estates were exceptional. The clergy with its archbishop and powerful cathedral chapter felt it could act alone, and the nobility, perhaps because of its weakness, never developed any form of corporate organization. The real question, therefore, was whether the large and wealthy town of Lyons would assume leadership over the smaller towns and villages of the plat pays or whether it would follow an independent course.

For a brief time it seemed possible that Lyons would accept a role in

38. Jean-B. Galley, *Les Etats de Forez et les treize villes* (Saint-Étienne, 1914), pp. 27–41, 75–78; Auguste Bernard, *Histoire du Forez* (Montbrison, 1835), 2 : 143, 266.

39. G. Dupont-Ferrier, "Essai sur la géographie administrative des élections financières en France de 1350 à 1790," *Ann.-bul. de la soc. de l'hist. de France* (1928): 307; Galley, *Les Etats de Forez*, pp. 39, 41, 42, 56–68; AD, Loire, C 32, no. 24; Bernard, *Histoire du Forez*, 2 : 166–79, 202. For examples of the role of the estates and the crown in taxation see AD, Rhône, C 408, fols, 19–20, 56–59v, 68–71v, 79v–85, 92–93, 105v–06, 114–18, 132.

regard to the smaller neighboring localities similar to that exercised by Clermont, Agen, and Bordeaux. As early as July 1418 the municipal officials of Lyons decided that they and the plat pays should each send a deputy to the dauphin, Charles, to ask him to abolish the gabelle. This and other entries in the municipal registers during the decade 1416–26 reveal that there were frequent contacts between the two. Clearly, the plat pays was already regarded as a separate entity both by the municipal officials of Lyons and the crown. On the other hand, there is no evidence that the communities of the plat pays had become a formal corporation with a syndic to defend their collective interests. When the *consuls* of Lyons wanted to contact the plat pays, they wrote to the *consuls* or other officials of the individual localities and not to an elected officer of the plat pays as they probably would have if there had been one. Even during this period of frequent joint action, the town apparently tried to place more of the tax burden on the plat pays, and the plat pays was at times inclined to follow a separate course.[40] The matter came to a head in October 1427. The town council decided to elect its own deputation to a central assembly to meet at Poitiers because all but one person present at the meeting felt that Lyons was more likely to obtain a tax reduction if it acted alone. The only dissenter argued that combined action by the town and plat pays would strengthen their plea for concessions, but on this occasion and thereafter until the Fronde, Lyons always elected its own delegation to meetings of the Estates General and other central assemblies. The plat pays did likewise in those instances that it was represented at all.[41]

Contacts between the town and the plat pays did not totally cease after 1427. Meetings of the three estates of the seneschalsy took place in 1447, 1481, 1482, and 1483 to treat with military reforms, the repopulation of Arras, and the marriage of the dauphin (later Charles VIII), and to elect deputies to the Estates General. In rare instances the town and plat pays undertook a joint endeavor, but essentially the third estate became, or rather remained, divided into two separate entities.[42]

Once the ties between the town and the plat pays were broken, evidence that there were assemblies of the latter is scant indeed (although this does not prove that they ceased to exist). Lyons' selfish treatment of the smaller towns and villages probably contributed to their retaining a separate identity. Tax documents always distinguished between the two, and when

40. *Registres consulaires de la ville de Lyon*, ed. M.-C. Guigue (Lyon, 1882), 1 : 14, 28, 53, 62, 118, 123, 135, 182, 194, 209, 211–12, 217, 312–13, 349–52, 2 : 22, 29, 80–81, 117, 163–66, 178–79, 193.

41. Ibid., 2 : 247–49.

42. Ibid., p. 427; Louis Caillet, *Etude sur les relations de la commune de Lyon avec Charles VII et Louis XI, 1417–1483* (Lyons, 1909), pp. 137, 245–46, 283, 484–85, 543, 622–23; *IAC, Lyon*, 1 : BB 17, CC 91; P. Viollet, "Election des députés aux Etats généraux réunis à Tours en 1468 et en 1484," *BEC*, sér. 6, 2 (1866): 38.

the representatives of the plat pays attended the meeting of the three estates of the seneschalsy to elect deputies to the Estates General of 1484, they submitted memoirs that were "to the prejudice of the town of Lyons," or at least so the *consulat* of that powerful city thought.[43]

During the fifteenth century the individual towns and parishes sent deputies to the meetings of the seneschalsy. If one of them had an important matter to take to Lyons, its officials handled the matter themselves. The syndics of Anse, for example, appealed to the *consulat* of Lyons to send deputies to court to secure the revocation of the taille of 1417 and offered to pay their share of the expenses if this were done, for they could not afford to undertake such an expensive mission on their own. The deputies of thirty-seven parishes participated in an assembly in January 1426 and ten in a meeting in December 1481, but in the latter instance they said that they acted for the other towns and parishes of Lyonnais, a statement that suggests that there had been a larger meeting of the plat pays to name them as their spokesmen. Conspicuously absent in these and other surviving documents is any mention of a syndic to act in the name of, or at the expense of, the plat pays when an individual town as Anse or the countryside as a whole needed a spokesman at Lyons or at court.[44]

At some point between 1481 and 1525, the inhabitants of the plat pays became formally organized as a corporation with duly empowered pro-cureurs or syndics to act in their name. Probably it was at the procureurs' request that in June 1522 Francis I ordered the élus to make the clergy pay the taille on the common lands they had acquired in Lyonnais during the preceding thirty years. Certainly it was they who pleaded with the same king three years later to free the plat pays from the obligation to help repair the walls of Lyons.[45] In the years that followed the inhabitants of the plat pays and their spokesmen dealt with problems concerning the passage of troops through the region, the heavy royal fiscal demands, and above all the need for a more equitable distribution of the taille. This last involved them in a long and bitter fight with the town of Lyons.[46]

In 1462 Louis XI had granted the inhabitants of Lyons the privilege of being exempt from the taille on the goods they possessed in Lyonnais. Soon there were quarrels between the parishes and the citizens of Lyons who demanded that their rural property be removed from the tax rolls, a step that would increase the amount the local inhabitants would have to pay to meet their quota. At some point the plat pays began to act collectively in

43. Viollet, "Election," p. 56. Caillet has published many documents proving that the distinction between the town and plat pays was retained. See his *Etude*, esp. pp. 542–44.

44. Guigue, *Registres consulaires*, 1:53, 2:164; Caillet, *Etude*, p. 46–48, 245–46, 358–61, 622–23.

45. BN ms. fr. 2702, fols. 64v–66v, 121–22.

46. Ibid., fols. 124–24v, 131v, 147–47v, 159–59v. *IAC, Lyon*, AA 138, BB 44, BB 63, 2: CC 316; *Ord. Francois Ier*, 4:309–11.

this matter as well as in its quarrel with the clergy. Quickly the town government of Lyons sprang to the aid of its citizens. As late as 1522 clerical ownership of once taxable lands may still have offered the greater threat to the plat pays, but by mid-century higher prices for agricultural produce led the burghers to turn ever increasing sums to rural investments. As more and more land was removed from the tax roles, the burden on the peasants increased. The result was frequent litigation in the courts and before the king's council.[47] Although they were only partially successful, the syndics of the plat pays kept up the battle well into the following century.[48] When not engaged in litigation, the syndics defended the interests of the plat pays in other matters. In the spring of 1583, for example, they won from the king a 25 percent reduction in taxes and the removal of export duties on wheat that passed through Lyons.[49]

In the early fifteenth century all the parishes of the plat pays sent their officials or deputies to attend the assemblies of Lyonnais, but by 1568 a system of indirect suffrage had been introduced. The parishes in each of five subordinate jurisdictions met and elected deputations to attend the assembly of the plat pays where a new syndic was chosen and auditors were named to examine the accounts of his predecessor. In such meetings, we can assume that taxes were voted to support the various activities of the plat pays and other matters were discussed.[50] In spite of a paucity of documents and the presence of élus in Lyonnais, one can therefore confidently state that during the Renaissance the parishes of the plat pays constituted a formal corporation with elected officials to defend their interests.

A narrow strip of territory that extended northward along the east bank of the Saône River from the gates of Lyons did not participate in the assemblies of the plat pays of Lyonnais because its four thousand inhabitants had long enjoyed a special status. This territory, known as Franc-Lyonnais, was an integral part of the seneschalsy of Lyons but was not included in the élection of that name. Its inhabitants claimed the privilege of not paying taxes, but they had to be constantly on the alert to protect this precious right. In 1525 they won a decree from the Parlement of Paris forbidding the élus of Lyons to include them on the tax rolls, and in 1551 they were excused from a

47. Maurice Pallasse, *La sénéchaussée et siège présidial de Lyon pendant les Guerres de Religion* (Lyons, 1943), pp. 202–13; *IAC, Lyon*, 1: AA 153, BB 97, 100, 105, 109, 114, 118, 130; Richard Gascon, *Grand commerce et vie urbaine au XVIe siècle: Lyon et ses marchands* (Paris, 1971), 2:862–70. For the merchants' exploitation of the plat pays, see ibid, 2:811–62.

48. The plat pays won favorable decrees in October 1561, March 1570, and February 1578, but in August 1581, the king's council ruled that the inhabitants of Lyons did not have to pay the taille on their nonnoble property in Lyonnais. In this last decree, the syndics of the plat pays did obtain a reduction in the taille of four thousand livres. *Les édicts et ordonnances des rois de France*, ed. A. Fontanon (Paris, 1611), 4:1148.

49. AD, Rhône, C 408, fols. 118–19, 138–39. Many more examples could undoubtedly be given for the late sixteenth century and thereafter if AD, Rhône were fully exploited.

50. Caillet, *Etude*, pp. 44–48, 358–59; Pallasse, *La sénéchaussée*, pp. 202–204.

recently established levy to support the royal army. By 1554 the *consuls* of the communes had adopted the practice of meeting to elect a procureur and a syndic to defend their interests. There was, of course, nothing to prevent the inhabitants from voting their king a don gratuit, and by the mid-sixteenth century, it had become customary for the third estate to assemble every eight years and vote 3,000 livres to defray a small part of their sovereign lord's expenses. It is impossible to reconstitute the history of this assembly during the Renaissance, but it survived intact until the Revolution.[51]

Medieval Beaujolais also straddled the Saône River, the western part being known as Beaujolais du Royaume and the eastern part, which lay in the Empire, as Dombes. As far as can be ascertained, the estates of this region were formed only after the dukes of Bourbon acquired the seigneury in 1400.[52] Prior to that time the Valois kings had imposed taxes on Beaujolais du Royaume by fiat, and the seigneurs appear to have been content with their feudal revenues and a portion of the royal taxes. The capture of the duke of Bourbon at Agincourt in 1415 and the need to provide for their own defense ushered in a period of activity on the part of the estates. In 1418 they sought the aid of Lyons to repel a Burgundian invasion. In 1420 Beaujolais refused to grant an aide to the duchess, but Dombes proved more generous. In 1421 the estates of Beaujolais and Dombes asked the duchess not to sell the latter to pay her husband's ransom and offered financial assistance to make such a move unnecessary. Other gifts to the ducal family followed, but it is impossible to ascertain how frequently the estates met.[53]

Although originally Beaujolais was a single seigneury and the estates of Beaujolais du Royaume and Dombes assembled together, they became completely separate institutions at an early date. The latter, being in the Empire, enjoyed a preferred position. Even after Dombes was given to Louise of Savoy following the treason of the constable and later reverted to the crown, its right to be exempt from the taille, except for the don gratuit voted by the estates, was respected. So careful were the Valois kings to preserve its special status that the tiny sovereignty was even provided with a Parlement. In 1561 Charles IX gave Dombes to the duke of Montpensier. Under their new lords the estates continued to meet at regular, though at long, intervals to vote relatively modest sums. But in 1739 they were suppressed by an angry and heavily indebted duke after they had failed to

---

51. G. Debombourg, *Histoire du Franc-Lyonnais* (Trévoux, 1857), pp. 156–68; Pallasse, *La sénéchaussée*, p. 227; AD, Rhône, C 417, fol. 367v–68. For a map of Franc-Lyonnais and Dombes, see André Steyert, *Nouvelle histoire de Lyon et des provinces de Lyonnais, Forez, Beaujolais, Franc-Lyonnais et Dombes* (Lyons, 1899), 3:334*–35*.

52. E. Perroy, "La fiscalité royale en Beaujolais aux XIVe et XVe siècles," *Le Moyen Age*, sér. 2, 29 (1928): 31 n.3.

53. Ibid., pp. 5–47; Louis Aubret, *Mémoires pour servir à l'histoire de Dombes*, ed. M.-C. Guigue (Trévoux, 1868), 2:490, 494, 495–96, 500; *Registres de Villefranche*, 1:127, 141, 202, 228–29, 246.

grant as large a don gratuit as he desired. Henceforth, 50,000 livres was to be imposed annually without convoking the estates in spite of the protests of the local Parlement. In 1762 Dombes reverted once more to the crown, and nine years later Louis XV suppressed its Parlement. It is significant, however, that the Renaissance monarchs had accepted the special status of Dombes and its estates and that it remained for a duke and a king of the eighteenth century to destroy its most cherished privileges.[54]

Beaujolais du Royaume, as an integral part of France, was less fortunate. During the first half of the reign of Charles VII, it was subject to levies voted by the estates of Languedoil and to occasional direct negotiations for gifts, but from 1446 there does not appear to have been any form of approval for royal taxes.[55] The estates of Beaujolais, therefore, were the creation of the dukes who, unlike the kings, were not in a position to tax without consent. The earliest known meeting of the three estates took place in 1420, and by 1450 it is possible that they were being held annually to vote financial aid to their duke. It has been assumed that they followed this practice until they were discontinued by Francis I following the reunion with the crown.[56] In fact, there is little concrete information to suggest that the three estates were held regularly after around 1485, and it may be that Francis I inherited a seriously weakened institution. Certainly it was one that was not needed by the crown; for three-quarters of a century, royal taxes had been collected there without any form of consent.[57] Yet the third estate did not altogether cease to have a spokesman during the sixteenth century; or if it did, it had found one again by the early stages of the Wars of Religion.

The voice that emerged to speak for Beaujolais was that of the échevins of Villefranche. Pierre Louvet, an early exploiter of the archives, student of the estates of Languedoc and Provence, and resident of Villefranche, declared around 1670, "As Beaujolais has no syndic the *échevins* of Villefranche assemble in their *hôtel de ville* the officers and *échevins* of the castellanies ... under the authority and presidency of the bailiff or his lieutenant general."[58] Louvet had access to the now-lost registers of the deliberations of

54. On Dombes see the scattered references in Aubret, vols. 2–4, and *Bibliotheca Dumbensis, ou recueil des chartes, titres et documents relatifs à l'histoire de Dombes*, ed. Joannès-E. Valentin-Smith and M.-C. Guigue (Trévoux, 1854–85). Perroy, "La fiscalité royale," pp. 31–38; Pierre Lenail, *Notice historique sur le Parlement de Dombes, 1523–1771* (Lyon, 1900).

55. Perroy, "La fiscalité royale," pp. 19–22. *Registres de Villefranche*, 1:146, 239, 257.

56. Perroy, "La fiscalité royale," pp. 34, 38. By 1450 the dukes were receiving annual gifts, but whether the estates of Beaujolais met annually to vote them or whether they met less frequently and voted them for several years at a time cannot be ascertained.

57. The registers of Villefranche, the principal source for the history of the estates, are missing for the years 1489–1567. Other sources have only occasional references to meetings under the last dukes. See for example, Aubret, *Mémoires*, 3:177, 180, 205.

58. Pierre Louvet, *Histoire de Villefranche* (Lyons, 1671), p. 66. For Louvet's life, see Léon Galle and Georges Guigue's introduction to their edition of his *Histoire du Beaujolais* (Lyons, 1903).

Villefranche for the 1489–1567 period, but he may have based his statement on more recent history. One can only say that by 1567 when documentation once more becomes available, the échevins, guided by assemblies of the inhabitants, were acting for Beaujolais as a whole and with a confidence that suggests that they had been doing so for some time. For example, in November 1567 when the duke of Nevers demanded food for his army, the échevins obtained it from various individuals and promised that they would be repaid by a tax that would be levied on the *"pays* de Beaujolais."[59] In July 1568 when the governor of Lyonnais, Forez, and Beaujolais informed them that five companies were to be stationed in one of the smaller towns of Beaujolais and the province was to supply food for them, the échevins borrowed money in Lyons to pay a past debt and to meet this new requirement, but at the same time they asked the governor for letters authorizing a tax to repay the loan. In August they negotiated another loan in Lyons to support the troops, which was to be repaid by the inhabitants of Beaujolais as well as Villefranche. In November they dispatched an échevin to Lyons to attend a meeting concerning the farm of the gabelle. Judging by later, better documented meetings on the same subject, their deputy acted as the syndic of Beaujolais along with the syndics of Forez and the plat pays of Lyonnais and perhaps deputies from the estates of Mâconnais and Vivarais who were in the same salt farm. Two weeks later an assembly of the town decided that it would be wise for Beaujolais to give their governor and his lieutenant 3,000 livres to ensure their favor. This time they did not feel justified in acting alone and the chief town in each castellany was invited to send deputies to Villefranche where the gifts were voted and the problem of supporting the troops was discussed.[60]

So it went year after year. The échevins of Villefranche, directed by assemblies of the inhabitants of the town, found money and supplies for troops in the region, thereby reducing the probability that the defenseless inhabitants would be plundered. They acted for Beaujolais in assemblies of the government in Lyons, sought to have taxes levied to meet their obligations, and appealed to the king's council and to the sovereign courts to defend the interests of the province. They tried to obtain reductions in taxes, the abolition of unnecessary offices, and the inclusion of the common lands owned by the nobles and clergy in the tax rolls. To further these objectives they saw to it that their governor received an annual present. Sometimes

59. *Registres de Villefranche*, 2 : 19–23. Since Villefranche replaced Beaujeu as the capital of Beaujolais only when the seat of a royal bailiwick was established there in 1530 following the death of Louise of Savoy, it is probable that the échevins of that town assumed their leadership role after that date but some years before 1567.

60. *Registres de Villefranche*, 2 : 54–57, 62–63, 68–73. There may have been a second meeting of the third estate of Beaujolais, for on December 12 there is a reference to the fact that the échevins were to hear "those of the pays" the following day. Ibid., p. 75.

they arranged for meetings of the échevins of the chief towns of the castellanies; sometimes they acted alone in the name of the province.[61]

Villefranche's relations with the smaller towns appear to have been surprisingly good, perhaps because when controversial decisions needed to be made, someone was ready to point to the need to obtain the consent of the pays. On the other hand, when it was to the advantage of Beaujolais for an échevin of Villefranche to deny that he had any authority to speak for the province, he did not hesitate to take that position. In the summer of 1589 the duke of Nemours, their governor, sought to obtain money from Beaujolais through an échevin who had been deputed to Lyons. When accosted, the échevin responded that he represented only the men and inhabitants of Villefranche and was not charged to speak for those of Beaujolais. Nemours, perhaps angry, directed that the pays of Beaujolais elect a syndic of its own, but nothing came of his suggestion. Hence, though the third estate of Beaujolais did not become a legal corporation with specifically elected spokesmen like the plat pays of Lyonnais, it came very close to doing so. By not going all the way, the inhabitants escaped some of the disadvantages that came with having a syndic who was capable of binding them and thereby subjecting them to the importunities of the king and his officials.[62]

Thus in Normandy, Auvergne, and the government of Lyonnais, as well as in such scattered provinces as Bordelais, Périgord, and Mâconnais where there were élections, the estates continued to meet frequently during the Renaissance. In Normandy no direct taxes were supposed to be collected without consent. Elsewhere the people were less fortunate in this regard, but they continued to participate in assemblies of the three estates or of the towns and plat pays and to have either syndics or officials of capital towns defend their interests. Their assemblies voted taxes for their feudal lords, if they had any, and to pay the costs of their activities. In these provinces as in those that had no élections, the estates played important administrative roles during the Renaissance.

---

61. For other examples of the échevins of Villefranche acting for Beaujolais as a whole prior to the succession of Henry IV, see ibid., pp. 84–86, 93, 99, 117–24, 127–32, 135, 138–39, 157–61, 191–92, 234–35, 237, 267, 269–70, 272–73, 281–82, 287–88, 319–23, 327–30, 339–40, 354–55, 358–59, 368, 374–76, 379, 386, 400, 448, 453–54, 473–75, 486–90, 500–02, 515–18. See also AD, Rhône, C 408, fols. 10v–12, 49–49v, 85v–86, 97–98. It is impossible to tell how often the third estate of Beaujolais met or what it did because its activities were rarely included in the register of Villefranche and sometimes there is no allusion to a meeting. Thus the appeal of "the men and inhabitants of the pays of Beaujolais" before the king's council in March and April 1582 (AD, Rhône, C 408, fols. 49–49v, 97–98) is not reflected in the registers. On April 11, 1585, Villefranche decided to summon the castellanies to meet the following Monday, but the register gives no indication of what happened at the meeting, or indeed if it was actually held. *Registres de Villefranche*, 2:400.

62. *Registres de Villefranche*, 2:139, 160, 541.

7

THE NATURE OF THE
RENAISSANCE STATE AND SOCIETY

1. The Growth of Representative Government: A Summary

THE RENAISSANCE WITNESSED THE GROWTH OF REPRESENTATIVE GOVERNMENT IN France. It was not at the national level—here the central assemblies lost one opportunity in the mid-fourteenth century and another during the early part of the reign of Charles VII—but at the local and provincial level. Here the estates had also shown promise in the early stages of the Hundred Years War, only to be stifled by Charles V in the 1360s or soon thereafter. Of the lands directly under the crown, Dauphiné alone continued to enjoy its estates, a good fortune that must be attributed to its unique position. Some of the great feudal dependencies of the crown preserved their assemblies because of the financial needs of their dukes, but even here there was generally a decline in activity. Thus after a precocious beginning in the fourteenth century, the provincial estates had to be born again during the Renaissance.

The medieval assemblies had an ad hoc quality both as to the jurisdictions that were convoked and to those who were summoned. It was only after the revival of the estates during the reign of Charles VII that the meetings of the seneschalsies of Languedoc were virtually terminated and those of the dioceses were subordinated to the provincial estates. Then the semiautonomous towns, bishops, nobles, and owners of allodial property were brought more fully within the body politic in Dauphiné. Not until around the middle of the fifteenth century did the Valois dukes of Burgundy abandon the smaller estates in the lands adjacent to their duchy and begin to try to consolidate their territories. The estates of Auxerre, Bar-sur-Seine, Autun, and the other former royal enclaves were allowed to die, and representatives from these localities were incorporated into the estates of the duchy. Even then the process was incomplete; not until 1668 was the county of Auxonne absorbed and in 1751 Charolais suffered a similar fate, while Mâconnais retained its estates until the Revolution. In Provence the assemblies of the vigueries had to be subordinated to the provincial estates, but the powerful towns of Marseilles and Arles were able to maintain their autonomous position. The Parlement of Brittany, like that of England, performed political and administrative, as well as judicial, functions, and it was only near the close of the ducal period that the assembly of the estates emerged as a separate institution.

The English monarchs were more favorably disposed toward representative assemblies than were Charles V and Charles VI. Henry V revived the estates of the duchy of Normandy in 1420 and insofar as local assemblies were allowed to exist thereafter, they were kept in a strictly subordinate capacity. In Guyenne the English influence was less permanent. The three estates of the duchy were probably their creation, and one of the earliest promises in France to seek consent for taxation was made by the Black Prince in 1368. The fluctuating boundaries of the duchy, followed by Charles VII's suppression of its privileges after the rebellion in 1452, prevented the estates from establishing their position. Hence the estates of the seneschalsies and recettes, not those of the region, became the tax-consenting bodies. Some of these institutions can be traced well back into the fourteenth century, but others appeared relatively late. Only one meeting of the three estates of Agenais has been found before 1436, and the estates of Périgord may not have assembled before 1378. The three estates of Comminges first met in 1412, but they were rarely convoked until the county passed into royal hands at the close of the century. The estates of Béarn, the best known and most important of those near the Pyrenees belonging to the feudality, emerged only in 1391. The earliest known meeting of the estates of the seneschalsy of Lyons was in 1418 and of Beaujolais in 1420.

The fifteenth century did not see an end to the creation of representative institutions. The estates of Guyenne, revived by Louis XI and occasionally utilized by Francis I, began to meet frequently and became a permanent part of the institutional structure of the region just before the Wars of Religion. The conquest of most of Navarre by the Spanish gave the French claimant an opportunity to dispense with the estates in what remained, but he chose to create a new assembly in 1523. The first known meeting of the government of Lyonnais was in 1556. The estates of Poitou, Saintonge, Angoumois, Haut- and Bas-Limousin, Haute- and Basse-Marche, and the town and government of La Rochelle were revived around the middle of the century to deal with the gabelle, although they soon became moribund again. When the duchy of Savoy fell to Francis I, he preserved the estates, as did Henry IV when he conquered Bugey, Bresse, and Gex.

In the meetings of the Estates General in 1560 and 1561, Chancellor L'Hôpital asked the three orders to assist in paying the crown's debts and in redeeming the domain. In return he was willing to permit them to name a committee to oversee the collection of the tax. If his proposal had been accepted, the Estates General would almost certainly have been reborn. Instead only the clergy responded favorably, and from that time until the end of the Old Regime, the members of this order met regularly to vote don gratuits for the king. They elected syndics to defend their privileges, developed a bureaucracy, and created a system of diocesan and arch-diocesan assemblies that had their own officials. At about the same time the Protestants established a system of national and provincial synods and political assemblies to govern their church and to defend their interests. The Catholic League also formed councils of the Holy Union at Paris and in most of the provincial capitals of France in the late 1580s that included members of the three estates and royal officials.[1] The desire to unite and form corporations with syndics to act in its name spread to the bureaucracy. In 1586 the treasurers in the various Bureaux of Finances obtained the right to elect deputies. These deputies eventually formed an assembly that met in Paris where policies were adopted and syndics were elected. At first the privilege was rarely used, but in the 1640s the assembly of the treasurers was of considerable importance. At this time the élus also formed a repre-sentative assembly and elected syndics. Both corporate groups of financial officials were to play important roles in the Fronde, at which time the sovereign courts also sought strength in greater unity. Not to be outdone, the nobility of a substantial part of France took advantage of the Fronde to form a union, adopt a system of electing deputies by bailiwicks to an assembly that prepared a cahier to present to the king, and sought to meet periodi-cally as the clergy had been doing for a century.[2]

The growing demand for representative institutions awakened by Charles VII gathered momentum in the century and a half that followed. During the Estates General of 1484, some deputies proposed that provincial estates be established in the parts of France where they did not yet exist and that no taxes be levied without the consent of these assemblies. They also urged that the élus be suppressed because they were almost as injurious to the people as the taille, but there was not enough support for these proposals to include them in the cahier. At least part of the explanation for the failure of these measures to obtain more backing lay in the belief of the Norman deputies that there was no need for them to take an affirmative stand because they themselves already enjoyed favorable rights and privileges.[3]

By the time the Estates General met in 1561, this selfish attitude had passed, and the nobility urged that the estates of the bailiwicks be convoked each year on October 15 without further directives from the crown to impose taxes and to administer their jurisdictions. In the Estates General of 1576

1. Henri Drouot, *Mayenne et la Bourgogne* (Paris, 1937), 1:135–36, 2:41–58; Ferdinand Pouy, *La chambre du conseil des Etats de Picardie pendant la Ligue* (Amiens, 1882).

2. Jean-Paul Charmeil, *Les trésoriers de France à l'époque de la Fronde* (Paris, 1964), pp. 247–52; R. Mousnier, "Recherches sur les syndicats d'officiers pendant la Fronde," *XVII siècle* 42–43 (1959): 76–117; Jean-Dominique Lassaigne, *Les assemblées de la noblesse de France aux XVIIe et XVIIIe siècles* (Paris, 1965), pp. 66–84, 206–15.

3. Jean Masselin, *Journal des Etats généraux de France tenus à Tours en 1484*, ed. A. Bernier (Paris, 1835), pp. 486–89.

both the nobility and third estate sought to have the élus abolished. The nobles recommended that in regions lacking estates, the bailiwicks be convoked every three years to elect one syndic from each order to assume the tax functions of the élus. In Languedoc and Guyenne where the nobility and clergy (except for the bishops in the former) had little or no voice in apportioning taxes in the dioceses, they also sought to have syndics elected. The third estate opted for assemblies of the towns to replace the élus. Both recommendations involved extending the system of estates to all of France.[4] In 1588 when the Estates General again met, the clergy and nobility asked that provincial estates be created throughout the country, while the third estate preferred to place its trust in consent to taxes by the Estates General. By the time the king convoked the Estates General in 1614, the desire for provincial estates had either waned or the deputies were much more pliant, for the demand for more estates that had peaked in 1588 was scarcely voiced at all.[5]

There was an ad hoc quality about who was summoned to the medieval assemblies. In some instances large numbers attended, but only five clergymen, four nobles, and the representatives of thirteen towns took part in the first known assembly of the duchy of Burgundy in 1352. With the advent of frequent meetings during the last three-quarters of the fifteenth century, a degree of order began to be introduced concerning who was summoned to the various provincial estates. But even then the composition of the estates continued to change. By the 1480s there was a near consensus that the number of voting members of the third estate in Languedoc should equal that of the other two orders combined, but another generation elapsed before the composition of the clergy became fixed, and as late as 1612 it was necessary to redefine the membership of the nobility. Yet the composition of the three estates of Languedoc was the most specifically regulated of all. Probably around 1500 the nobility and clergy ceased to participate regularly in the estates of Haute- and Basse-Auvergne, Agenais, and Condomois, and the assemblies of the towns replaced those of the three estates. In Provence it was not until the 1580s that the assemblies of the communities came to be convoked more frequently than those of the three estates. By the time this happened, the nobility in some other provinces were displaying more interest in participating, and there were pressures to increase the suffrage.[6]

The members of the third estate, who paid most of the taxes, nearly always displayed the greatest interest in representative assemblies. As a

4. Georges Picot, *Histoire des Etats généraux*, 2d ed. (Paris, 1888), 2:224–25, 3:286–87; *Recueil des cahiers généraux des trois ordres aux Etats-Généraux*, ed. Lalourcé and Duval (Paris, 1789), 2:163–64, 175–77, 231–32, 310–12.

5. Picot, *Histoire*, 4:48–49, 5:142–44; *Recueil des cahiers*, 3:80–81, 140–41, 231–32.

6. In addition to my discussion of the estates in the preceding chapters, see my *Deputies to the Estates General of Renaissance France* (Madison, 1960), for material on the composition of the estates and how the suffrage was increased.

result, the smaller towns and villages that were excluded exerted pressure during the Renaissance to participate. In Normandy and Haute-Auvergne, they were accommodated by the creation of electoral assemblies of the viscounties and provostships, which they could attend without much expense. In Languedoc diocesan assemblies to which some of them sent deputies were formed to apportion taxes. In Guyenne some of the smaller communities were included in most of the estates of the seneschalsies. Where they were not, there were sometimes subordinate assemblies of collectes, valleys, counties, and viscounties in which they took part. But their voices in these localities were heard only weakly. More fortunate were the inhabitants of the valleys of the Alpes in Dauphiné and in the Pyrenees who had their own representative institutions through which they might participate in larger assemblies.

These modest efforts to give a role to the mass of the country people were not duplicated in all of France. In some regions the leading towns were determined to dominate the third estate completely. Here the smaller towns and villages often banded together to prevent the urban centers from tranferring part of the taxes intended for them onto the countryside and to make the burghers pay taxes on the rural lands they held. First perhaps in Lyonnais, then in Dauphiné, Basse-Auvergne, Velay, and Périgord they formed their own assemblies and elected syndics to defend their rights.[7] Thus, if by 1500 the estates were beginning to take form, demands that their composition be changed continued to be made throughout the sixteenth century.

While the estates were being created or revived and were taking form during the Renaissance, they were also receiving recognition for their privileges and developing procedures that enabled them to function more independently of the crown. After threatening the very existence of the estates of Languedoc, Charles VII relented in 1443. He suppressed the élus and promised to retain the institution with all its privileges. Francis I, that supposedly absolute monarch, pledged that neither he nor his successors would levy taxes or create offices in Languedoc without the consent of the estates. He also granted the deputies the privilege of being free from arrest while traveling to and from the estates and while they were in session. They in turn sought to safeguard their position by refusing to permit royal officials to serve as deputies or officers of the estates and by taking oaths to keep their deliberations secret. In 1555 Henry II forbade Parlement to interfere in their affairs, and in 1559 they adopted the secret ballot.

Charles VII also considered terminating the three estates of Normandy and actually collected taxes there for five years without consulting them, but in 1458 he reversed his position and included in his confirmation of the

---

7. Etienne Delcambre, *Les Etats de Velay des origines à 1642* (Saint-Etienne, 1938), pp. 159–65, 477–82.

Norman charter a promise not to tax without the consent of the three estates. His grandson, Charles VIII, gave the three estates of Agenais permission to meet whenever they desired. Dauphiné, Burgundy, Provence, and Brittany already had estates when they were acquired by the French crown. In each instance the reigning monarch promised to respect their privileges at the time of the reunion. Louis XI detailed the Burgundian privileges in a more specific fashion than ever before when he took possession of the duchy in 1477. He even promised the deputies to the estates that they would be free from arrest during their travels and deliberations. The three estates of Provence had won the right to consent to taxation from their count in 1437, but not until 1538 were royal officials forbidden to serve as deputies. The dukes of Brittany had often levied taxes without consulting their Parlement, which doubled as their estates, but after the reunion with France, first Charles VIII and later, Louis XII and Francis I, promised not to levy taxes without the consent of the three estates and designated them as custodians of the privileges of the province. Among these privileges that the three estates claimed were the right to consent to the creation of offices and the installation of garrisons. Louis XII even promised that new laws would not be applied to Brittany without their consent.[8]

During the Renaissance the estates also began to appoint syndics and to develop permanent bureaucracies, acts that leave no doubt that they had become legal corporations.[9] The medievel estates had appointed officials to collect a single specified tax after which their offices lapsed. Only when it became generally accepted that taxation would be an annual affair—during the reign of Charles VII—did the estates feel the need to develop a permanent bureaucracy. Furthermore, whatever temporary steps that were taken in the mid-fourteenth century were terminated when Charles V discontinued the practice of convoking the estates. Thus the three estates of Languedoc did not appoint a permanent clerk until 1455, a syndic until 1480, and a treasurer to administer the money allocated for their use until 1522. As their administrative role increased, they felt the need to expand the bureaucracy and to create an archives to preserve their records, which they did in 1486. The seneschalsies also had syndics, and the dioceses developed their own bureaucracies. In the 1380s the crown had asserted its authority to appoint diocesan receivers, and it was not until 1419 that the three estates of Velay regained a voice in naming this official. Only in the middle third of the century did they, and apparently the estates of the other dioceses, assume full control over the appointment of these officers. A little earlier, in the 1420s, they began to name syndics.[10]

8. Roger Doucet, *Les institutions de la France au XVIe siècle* (Paris, 1948), 1:351.

9. On the relationship between the appointment of syndics and the enjoyment of corporate status, see Gaines Post, *Studies in Medieval Legal Thought* (Princeton, 1964), pp. 39–50.

10. Henri Gilles, *Les Etats de Languedoc au XVe siècle* (Toulouse, 1965), pp. 114–27;
(*Continued on next page*)

Because the provincial estates in Guyenne did not become a permanent institution until the eve of the Wars of Religion, and even then did not supplant the estates of the seneschalsies, the deputies never developed a full-fledged bureaucracy. They apparently had a clerk for a brief period in 1544, and in 1562 they appointed a receiver on orders of the king. On the seneschalsy level, however, considerable growth took place. Nearly all of these estates had syndics: Rouergue by 1478, Agenais by 1486, Comminges by 1520, Quercy by 1551, and Périgord by 1552. Quercy boasted a clerk by 1447 and eventually added an assistant clerk, two more syndics, and four tax assessors. Comminges had a treasurer, a clerk, and an archivist, and the three estates of Périgord were electing a committee to act for them between sessions by 1544. The bishops of Cahors and Rodez played important roles in looking after the interests of the estates between meetings in Quercy and Rouergue, respectively, and the municipal officials of Bordeaux, Agen, and Condom performed similar services for Bordelais, Agenais, and Condomois.

The Normans were much slower in developing a bureaucracy. The attorney of Rouen appears to have acted as syndic and archivist of the estates after the duchy was reconquered from the English until 1569 when a full-time syndic was appointed. Probably not until 1578 did the estates have a treasurer and 1609 a clerk who did not double as a royal official. The Burgundians moved more rapidly. In 1438 they increased their influence over the appointment of the members of the Chambre des Elus at the expense of their duke, and in 1476 they obtained from him the right to appoint the clerk. Thereafter the bureaucracy continued to grow, and in 1584 the estates began to appoint a committee known as the alcades to investigate the activities of the élus near the close of their term of office.

During the first quarter of the fifteenth century, the counts of Provence replaced the tax collectors appointed by the estates with their own officials and refused to permit the estates to appoint a committee to look after their interests between meetings. However, this trend was reversed, and in 1437 the right of the three estates to consent to taxation was recognized in a written document. In 1480 they obtained the long-sought permanent committee, and after the reunion with France in 1481, they continued to strengthen their position. In 1538 they began to appoint an agent to handle legal cases, in 1544 they secured the right to name a treasurer, and in 1582 they began to have an agent in Paris. The three estates of Brittany were relatively new and underdeveloped at the time of the reunion with France,

---

Delcambre, *Les Etats de Velay*, pp. 108–10, 137–40; Auguste Le Sourd, *Essai sur les Etats du Vivarais depuis leur origines* (Paris, 1926), pp. 49, 87–106. Le Sourd, p. 100, points out that Louis XI confirmed the right of the estates of Vivarais to appoint a receiver in 1481. However, Delcambre, p.109 n. 163, shows that the estates of Velay, Gévaudan, and Vivarais shared a receiver in 1418. J. Deniau reports that the estates of Gévaudan had a syndic as early as 1403, but I am doubtful whether this was a permanent appointment. See his "Les Etats particuliers du pays de Gévaudan," *Bul. de la soc. des lettres, sciences et arts de la Lozère* 5 (1930): 11.

but their administrative role increased rapidly under the Valois kings. By 1526 they had a syndic, a treasurer, and a clerk, and by 1534 they were taking steps to establish an archives. The three estates of Béarn enjoyed a strong position during the last third of the fifteenth century, when they also began to have a syndic, secretaries, auditors to watch over the viscount's fiscal administration, a treasurer, and an abbreviated assembly that could be quickly summoned in an emergency.

Only in Dauphiné did the estates violate the general chronology developed above. Because of their relatively precarious position in this newly acquired fief of the Empire, the Valois kings continued to use the estates to obtain consent for taxation between the 1360s and 1420 when they did not convoke them in France. As a result, the three estates matured more rapidly. Before this period closed, they had an attorney, tax collectors, a treasurer, and a rudimentary archives. Their bureaucracy continued to grow, and by the mid-sixteenth century they had formed the Assembleés des Commis des Etats to serve as a sort of executive arm.

The Valois kings were not always pleased with the rapidly growing administrative role of the estates, although it was the estates' resistance to taxes that bothered them the most. Charles VII created élections in Lannes and in parts of central France. Louis XI sometimes violated the very privileges he had just granted by taxing without consent, and he also attempted to limit the amount that the estates of Languedoc could levy for their own use. Thereafter the kings seem to have been more receptive to the growing role of the estates. Francis I was probably motivated by a desire to profit from the sale of offices when he created élus in Guyenne and Languedoc in 1519 and in Guyenne again in 1544. In any case, he quickly abandoned the scheme when offered suitable compensation by the estates, as did his son, Henry II, after he had created élus in Burgundy in 1555. Occasionally the initiative for creating élections did not come from the crown, but the results were the same. In 1552 some villages in Comminges pleaded with the king to establish an élection there in the hope that it would enable them to escape the financial exactions of the estates. Led by their syndic, a nobleman, they were successful, but a few years later, after he had profited from the sale of the new offices, Henry II suppressed them on the request of the three estates. For a price the estates had once more triumphed.[11] Francis I attempted to reduce the expenses of the estates of Dauphiné and Provence and to curb their activities to some extent, but his efforts failed. He lacked the persistence to do battle with the estates even if he had the desire.

While they were developing their procedures and creating their bureaucracies, the estates in Normandy, Mâconnais, and the provinces in which there were no élus continued to exercise their right to consent to taxes,

11. AD, Haute-Garonne, C 3804.

although they gave the king what he wanted more often than not. In terms of areas, these estates controlled about 52.4 percent of France and paid over half the taxes during the sixteenth century.[12] In the remainder of France the estates did not normally give consent to taxes before they were collected, but this does not necessarily mean that they were moribund. In about 8.2 percent of the country, the estates met regularly, had permanent officials, voted taxes for their own purposes, and prepared remonstrances to the king when they thought that they were taxed too heavily or had other complaints.[13] In another 12.6 percent the estates occasionally met to deal with tax matters.[14] Only in the remaining 26.9 percent of France was the role of the estates largely limited to electing deputies to the Estates General, redacting customs, and ratifying treaties during the sixteenth century. These duties alone, however, led to about a dozen meetings in each jurisdiction between 1483 and 1651, and occasionally there were assemblies for other purposes as in Touraine in 1464, 1466, and 1486.[15]

The argument that representative government increased in France at the provincial level during the Renaissance is hardly revolutionary. Henri Prentout, one of the few historians to undertake a serious study of one of the important provincial estates during this period, stoutly maintained that not only the Norman estates but also those of the other provinces held their own. He based his argument primarily on the fact that they continued to consent to taxation. Henri Gilles saw the estates of Languedoc's control over taxation weakening under Louis XI, but recognized that this diminution was paralleled by their growing administrative role. Barthélemy Pocquet declared that the assembly of the estates was "the great institution which gave

12. I obtained this figure by adding the areas of current departments or estimated fractions of departments that were then controlled by the estates. These departments were Côte-d'Or, Saône-et-Loire, Yonne ($\frac{2}{3}$), Isère, Hautes-Alpes, Drôme, Bouches-su-Rhône, Var, Basses-Alpes, Alpes-Maritimes ($\frac{1}{3}$), Seine-Maritime, Eure, Calvados, Orne, Manche, Ille-et-Vilaine, Côtes-du-Nord, Finistère, Morbihan, Loire-Atlantique, Lot, Aveyron, Gironde ($\frac{1}{3}$), Lot-et-Garonne, Tarn-et-Garonne, Landes, Gers, Hautes-Pyrénées, Basses-Pyrénées, Ariège, Haute-Loire, Lozère, Ardèche, Gard, Hérault Aude, Tarn, Haute-Garonne, Pyrénées-Orientales ($\frac{1}{4}$), and Pas-de-Calais ($\frac{1}{4}$). If Artois, Flanders, and Walloon Flanders (Lille), whose counts were vassals of the kings of France until 1526, or if Savoy, which was held by France between 1536 and 1559, were included, the proportion of France with estates would be higher.

13. Cantal, Puy-de-Dôme, Loire, Rhône, Dordogne, and Gironde ($\frac{2}{3}$). With the acquisition of Bresse, Bugey, and Gex at the turn of the century, the percentage of France in this category increased to 9 percent.

14. Charante, Creuse, Haute-Vienne, Corrèze, Vendée, Deux-Sèvres, Vienne, Charente-Maritime.

15. Ardennes ($\frac{3}{4}$), Maine-et-Loire, Sarthe, Mayenne, Somme, Seine, Seine-et-Oise (as formerly constituted), Seine-et-Marne, Oise, Aisne, Loiret, Eure-et-Loir, Loir-et-Cher, Cher, Indre, Indre-et-Loire, Marne, Aube, Haute-Marne, Yonne ($\frac{1}{3}$), Allier, and Nièvre. I have included the last two departments although the estates of Bourbonnais in the former and the estates of Nevers in the latter may have had some additional activity. For the estates of Touraine, see Bernard Chevalier, *Tours, ville royale, 1356–1520* (Louvain, 1975), pp. 518, 523.

Brittany a real vitality and unique character."[16] Charles Higounet went further: "In the course of the sixteenth century, it was the estates of Comminges which really administered the province."[17] The same phenomenon took place in one of the few surviving feudal principalities. "The beginning of the sixteenth century," Oppetit-Perné recently declared, "marked the shift from the viscount's direct administration of the viscounty [of Turenne] to that of the estates."[18] Henri Drouot insisted that as that century drew to a close, the Burgundian estates "still enjoyed a more extended prestige than Parlement."[19] To their activities in the defense of the province, he largely attributed the development of a Burgundian consciousness. "To these estates," he insisted, "the Burgundy of the sixteenth century owed in great part its existence."[20]

With local historians often insisting that the estates did not fare too badly during the sixteenth century, we are faced with the problem of why those who have generalized from their works have nearly always insisted that the estates were a medieval phenomenon and that their role declined sharply during the Renaissance. Roger Doucet, the most widely read of these authors, recognized that the estates became "one of the essential elements of provincial life in the middle of the fifteenth century because by that time royal taxes had become permanent and it was necessary to convoke assemblies annually to consent to them."[21] He then demonstrated that only after this had happened did the estates attain "their full development and regular activity."[22] At this point, while admitting the growing administrative role of the estates, he insisted on their decadence: "The sixteenth century saw the provincial estates flower with respect to their administrative organs, but with respect to their political activities, they were only ghosts without vitality."[23]

In his critique of the provincial estates, Doucet distinguished too sharply between administrative and political activity, and he compounded this error by assuming that the latter was much more important. Actually, it was through their administrative role that the estates made themselves necessary to the crown and to the inhabitants of their respective provinces. Furthermore, their petitions, which the kings generally granted unless they would cause financial loss, exercised a profound influence on legislation. What seemed to trouble Doucet and others was that the crown raised taxes higher

16. Henri Prentout, *Les Etats provinciaux de Normandie* (Caen, 1925), 2:513; Gilles, *Les Etats de Languedoc*, pp. 279–80; Barthélémy Pocquet, *Histoire de Bretagne* (Rennes, 1913), 5:75.

17. *Dictionnaire d'histoire et de géographie ecclésiastique* 13 (1956): 381.

18. D. Oppetit-Perné, "La vicomté de Turenne à la fin du XVe siècle essai d'histoire économique," *Positions des thèses de l'Ecole Nationale des Chartes* (1971): 141.

19. Drouot, *Mayenne*, 1:94.

20. Ibid., p.100.

21. Doucet, *Les institutions*, 1:339.

22. Ibid., p.350.

23. Ibid., p.357.

and higher during the Renaissance, and a large proportion of these levies were automatically voted by the estates. Hence those historians who have insisted that the Renaissance estates were decadent have based their position very heavily on what they conceived to have been the estates' role in taxation.

It is unquestionably true that taxes rose during the Renaissance and that the estates nearly always voted traditional levies without serious debate, but if these facts alone are considered, erroneous conclusions will be made. Population growth, territorial expansion, the rise in national income, and inflation must be given their due weight. Unhappily there are no precise data for all of France for any of these factors. Even surviving statistics on royal taxes are nearly always based on what the king asked for, not on what he received. Towns, provincial estates, the clergy, and others sometimes prevailed upon the king to take less than he desired. After a tax had been set, a village might obtain a reduction or even the cancellation of a tax if its crops were destroyed, and entire provinces sometimes won clemency when they were preyed upon by marauding troops. On the other hand, if the king found that he had underestimated his needs, he often imposed increments on the inhabitants of this or that province or on his kingdom as a whole. Dauphiné especially suffered on this score because it lay in the path of the armies sent to Italy.

When Louis XI ascended the throne in 1461, the taille stood at 1.055 million livres and the total tax revenue at 1.75 million livres. By the time he died in 1483, he had increased the taille to 3.9 million livres and his total tax revenue to 4.6 million livres. This achievement was accomplished at a time when prices, the economy, and the population were relatively stable.[24] Several new provinces were acquired during these years, but essentially Louis's success must be attributed to his browbeating his subjects in both the regions with estates and in those without. At about the time of his death, the picture changed. Prices, which had begun to inch forward several decades earlier, more than doubled by 1560, and the population may have come close to doing the same if we generalize from a tripling of the number of houses in Provence and a doubling of the number of the heads of family in Languedoc. More important the economy improved rapidly. As a result, the buying power of the tax revenue declined from Louis XI's death until the Wars of Religion, although the real gross national income was rising. The taille that Montpellier paid slightly more than doubled between 1480 and 1560, and the levy on the sale of wine and meat grew even more slowly, but prices nearly tripled and the population and wealth of the town increased. As late as 1580–90 taxes consumed only 6.2 percent of the gross agricultural product in Languedoc. It has been estimated that even if we take the beginning of the reign of Francis I when taxes were quite low as a base, the

24. A. Spont, "La taille en Languedoc de 1450 à 1515," *Annales du Midi* 2 (1890): 367–70.

crown's revenue grew no faster than the income of the people during the remainder of the century. In 1581 a contemporary observed that the real income of the crown had fallen. Renaissance France, indeed, must have been a taxpayers' paradise.[25]

The continual demands that Francis I and other monarchs made on their subjects must be interpreted as efforts to maintain their purchasing power, not as callous exploitation of the people. Their failure to achieve greater success drove them to such expedients as creating offices to sell and borrowing heavily. Also, the willingness of the estates to vote increasingly higher taxes must be related to the fact that they were in reality paying less. This is not to say that royal taxation caused no suffering, for all Frenchmen did not share in the general prosperity, and the tax burden was not equitably distributed. The burghers and especially the nobles paid less than their share of the rising taxes, although certainly the former and very likely the latter were becoming more prosperous. The real wages of urban workers fell, but as the population of the towns grew, the taxes that each laborer had to pay probably declined after an adjustment is made for inflation. It was the peasants who suffered. There were also increasing numbers of them to pay taxes, but the amount of land they held was at best constant, and probably diminishing, because of purchases by nobles and burghers who did not have to pay taxes on their rural holdings in many parts of France. More serious, the desire of peasants to provide for their numerous offspring caused them to divide their holdings among their children. As a result, with each passing generation, peasant farms became smaller. Land that was more than adequate to support one family in 1480 was incapable of supporting three families in 1560. Hence, although taxes did not increase in real terms, they had become burdensome on the peasants by the latter date. For this reason the peasants organized in many parts of France to combat rising taxes and to make the privileged classes pay them on the nonnoble land they had purchased.[26]

The crown was aware of the peasants' problems and tried to obtain additional resources by tapping the increased wealth of the towns, but more often than not the towns succeeded in shifting at least part of the tax onto the plat pays. Furthermore, respect for the privileged classes, or perhaps fear

25. Emmanuel Le Roy Ladurie, *Les paysans de Languedoc* (Paris, 1966), 1:191, 222, 294–96, 2:1026–27; Frank C. Spooner, *The International Economy and Monetary Movements in France, 1493–1725* (Cambridge, Mass., 1972), pp. 305–15; Martin Wolfe, *The Fiscal System of Renaissance France* (New Haven, 1972), pp. 99–106; John H. M. Salmon, *Society in Crisis: France in the Sixteenth Century* (London, 1975), pp. 31–32, 37–38, 47–49.

26. Le Roy Ladurie, *Les paysans*, 1:237–313; Salmon, *Society in Crisis*, pp. 27–56. My belief that the nobility as a whole improved its economic status is derived largely from James B. Wood, *Social Structure and Social Change among the Nobility of the Election of Bayeux, 1463–1666* (Ann Arbor, University Microfilms, 1973), and William A. Weary, *Royal Policy and Patronage in Renaissance France: The Monarchy and the House of La Trémoille* (Ann Arbor, University Microfilms, 1972).

of arousing their anger, made the government reluctant to make them pay taxes on the peasant holdings they purchased in the provinces where the taille was personnelle. Thus the reluctance of the crown to put pressure on nobles, burghers, and priests to contribute more of their increased wealth to its support left to the peasants, those who suffered most from the demographic rise, the burden of supporting most governmental activities.

It seems undeniable that the estates greatly increased their role in the government during the Renaissane and that Catholic clergymen and Protestants alike organized assemblies and created bureaucracies to look after their interests. Even in parts of France that lacked estates, the people had increased their activity. During the late Middle Ages, councils were formed in the bailiwicks and seneschalsies and gradually assumed many of the duties of the bailiffs and seneschals. These councils consisted of the royal officials of both the local capital and the secondary seats, nobles, burghers, lawyers, and, initially at least, members of the clergy. Little is known about this institution that was common to nearly all of France and was probably of especial importance in regions in which there were no estates.[27] Its significance, however, was attested by Dupont-Ferrier, the leading authority on local institutions, when he declared that with the decline of bailiff and seneschal, "the true governor of the bailiwick and seneschalsy was the council. It is due to it, in great part, that the bailiwicks and seneschalsies were to remain the administrative nucleus of the kingdom."[28]

The towns also enjoyed an enviable role during the Renaissance. Charles VII showered privileges upon them in return for their support during the Hundred Years War. Automatic ennoblement of their officials and exemption from taxes were among the rewards that he granted. Furthermore, he gave municipal charters to some towns that had not previously enjoyed them and generally refrained from excessive interference in their internal affairs.[29] In many repects Louis XI went further, for he sought to strengthen the towns so that they could play a more significant role in the administration and defense of the kingdom. He readily gave them permission to tax their citizens and increased their privileges, powers, and duties. At a time when he was heavily increasing the fiscal burden on the population as a whole, he actually reduced the taxes on their inhabitants because he wanted "to see his *bonnes villes* autonomous, assured of steady resources, capable of maintaining

27. Gustave Dupont-Ferrier, *Les officers royaux des bailliages et sénéschaussées et les institutions monarchiques locales en France à la fin du Moyen Age* (Paris, 1902), pp. 245–67; Doucet, *Les institutions,* 1:256–58. For our ignorance of these councils see B. Guénée, "L'histoire de l'état en France à la fin du Moyen Age," *Revue Historique* 232 (1964): 354.

28. Dupont-Ferrier, *Les officiers royaux,* p. 267.

29. Charles Petit-Dutaillis, *Les communes françaises caractères et évolution des origines au XVIIIe siècle* (Paris, 1947), pp. 222–31.

public order within their confines, and pretty free in their behaviour vis-à-vis his officers if not vis-à-vis himself."[30] The towns often shirked the additional responsibilities that he sought to impose on them, such as providing for their own security and supplying his armies with food. To see that they did not do so, Louis frequently interfered in their internal affairs and tampered with their elections. Upon his death, the meddling largely ceased, but the privileges he had granted were confirmed by his successors.[31]

Far from witnessing the decadence of towns, the sixteenth century was a time of growth. Not since the thirteenth century had they enjoyed such a rapid increase in wealth and population. Important urban centers like Rennes, Nantes, Clermont, Bellac, and Saumur that had failed to obtain constitutions at an earlier date now received them, as did a host of lesser localities. The repeated efforts of the crown to extract more revenue from within their walls and its partial success in doing so should not be interpreted as an indication of weakness. In terms of real money, they paid less as time went on, and this is doubly true if their increased wealth and population is considered. Francis I and Henry II might audit municipal accounts and interfere in municipal elections when the occasion warranted, but the real measure of the towns' status was that Henry forbad his officials to hold municipal offices for fear that they would become more enamoured with their new constituents' devotion to local autonomy than with his service. Probably the limited inroads that the kings did make into municipal autonomy during the first half of the sixteenth century were more than compensated for by the number of new towns that were given charters. In the Wars of Religion, the privileged towns, now more numerous than ever before, were able to regain whatever independence that they had lost to the crown, but a few of them did fall under the influence of local magnates. The échevins of Rouen actually began to refer to their city as a "republic," and in 1564 they suggested that they keep a permanent agent at court as the clergy had begun to do.[32]

The enviable position of the towns during these wars and their ability to transfer their responsibilities to others was not lost on contemporaries. La Noue wrote that "the great cities extracted all the profits that they could, chattered about their privileges, and threw all the charges and burdens on the poor country people." Another observer charged that "following the example of Paris every town is a republic that furnishes no more than it pleases, contributes to public expenses as it wishes, and receives neither

30. B. Chevalier, "The Policy of Louis XI towards the *Bonnes Villes*: The Case of Tours," in *The Recovery of France in the Fifteenth Century*, ed. P. S. Lewis (New York, 1971), p. 276.

31. Ibid., pp. 276–93; Petit-Dutaillis, *Les communes françaises*, pp. 230–40.

32. Philip J. Benedict, *Rouen during the Wars of Religion: Popular Disorder, Public Order, and the Confessional Struggle* (Ann Arbor, University Microfilms, 1975), p. 56. There is an essay on the sixteenth-century towns in Doucet, *Les institutions*, 1:360–95.

garrisons nor governors except on such conditions as it desires,"[33] Modern historians have often agreed. Georges Tholin declared that "the Agenaise republic was still half independent." More recently François Lebrun entitled a chapter in a history of Angers, "L'Autonomie Municipale 1475–1657."[34]

The varied and essential activities of the municipal governments need hardly be stressed. They levied and collected taxes for their own needs and those of the king. When he requested too much, they usually sent deputies to court to negotiate reductions. Town governments were active in regulating economic matters, enforcing law and order, and rendering justice. They built fortifications, purchased artillery and munitions, and raised troops for their defense and occasionally to take the offensive. In the fields of health, education, and welfare, they were much more active than were the provincial estates. They frequently financed and controlled primary and secondary schools and occasionally assisted universities. In short, in many respects the role of municipal governments was larger during the Renaissance than today, for their military and fiscal duties were then much greater, and they performed most of the functions of their modern counterparts.

Spectacular as the growth of towns was during the Renaissance, the vast majority of the population continued to reside in villages, but here too people displayed a growing capacity for self-government. During the late Middle Ages the seigneur gradually ceased to play a direct role in the administration of the village. For himself, or more correctly for his agents, he reserved only the administration of justice, the imposition of the feudal obligations, and the management of his own lands. In his place emerged the assembly of the community that was attended by the heads of households, including women in some instances. With the advent of a permanent system of taxation, it fell to this assembly to elect officials to apportion and collect the impositions. Since by the close of the fourteenth century villages were recognized as being corps or corporations having legal personalities, their assemblies elected syndics to represent them in disputes. Gradually the syndic was transformed from a temporary official designated to perform a single task into a permanent official charged with administering the village. During this same period the parish priest ceased to manage the property of the church, and the laity began to elect *marguilliers*, or churchwardens, to perform this duty.[35]

33. Doucet, *Les institutions*, 1:362.

34. G. Tholin, "La ville d'Agen pendant les Guerres de Religion du XVIe siècle," *Revue de L'Agenais* 20 (1893): 199; François Lebrun, *Histoire d'Angers* (Toulouse, 1975), pp. 39–81.

35. For village and parish administration, see Doucet, *Les institutions*, 1:396–402, 2:754–55; Albert Babeau, *Le village sous l'ancien régime*, 5th ed. (Paris, 1915); Lucien Merlet, *Des assemblées de communautés d'habitants dans l'ancien comté de Dunois* (Châteaudun, 1887); and Peter S. Lewis, *Later Medieval France* (London, 1968), pp. 275–81. The rise of village self-government appears to have been a Western European phenomenon and may have been the deciding factor in preventing the peasantry from sinking back into serfdom as their Eastern European brethren did. See R. Brenner, "Agrarian Class Structure and Economic Development in Pre-Industrial Europe," *Past and Present* 70 (1976): esp. pp. 56–60.

These village and parish officials managed the common lands, repaired the church and other public buildings, and performed a host of other duties in addition to collecting taxes and defending local interests against king, seigneur, curé, town, and other villages. Some villages even sought to provide primary education and rudimentary care of the sick. As their local role increased, they began to play a larger part in national and provincial affairs. In 1483 the deputies of the villages were rarely asked to participate in the bailiwick assemblies to elect deputies to the Estates General, but during the sixteenth century they were increasingly summoned to such meetings, as well as to assemblies to redact the customs and for other purposes. By the time that elections to the Estates General were held during the Fronde, they were called upon to participate almost everywhere except in provinces in which there were strong provincial estates that sought to retain the traditionally limited suffrage. In such regions the villages had often organized their own assemblies and elected syndics to serve as their spokesmen. Thus towns and villages came to play greater roles in the government during the Renaissance, although within the towns themselves the suffrage often became more restricted.[36]

The rise of village self-government seems to point to the nobles' reduced role at that level. Their relative lack of interest in the estates as evidenced by their poor attendance record, especially in Auvergne and parts of the southwest where they actually ceased to be summoned, suggests that their political role in the provinces may also have deteriorated. Nothing could have been further from the case, however. The towns regularly deputed to the estates and villages demanded admission because they felt threatened and sought the security provided by collective action. The nobility, on the other hand, attended the estates in smaller numbers than permitted because they occupied a position of strength. It is true that the old lord-vassal relation was in a state of decline, but to replace it, the nobles developed a new feudalism based on a patron-client relationship through which the great nobles largely controlled the provinces and the lesser nobles sought employment and advancement by entering their service. At first the establishment of a patron-client relationship was formalized by a special oath or indenture in which the client swore to serve his lord faithfully and the patron promised to protect the client from any harm that might befall him, but during the course of the sixteenth century, the written oath was gradually abandoned although one indenture for as late as 1620 has been found. Nevertheless the idea of fidelity remained strong well into the seventeenth century.[37]

36. Major, *Deputies to the Estates General*, esp. pp. 124–28. Others have recognized the important role the people played in the government. See F. Dumont, "Gouvernants et gouvernés en France au Moyen Age et au XVIᵉ siècle," and R. Mousnier, "La participation des gouvernés à l'activité des gouvernants dans la France du XVIIᵉ et du XVIIIᵉ siècles," *Schweizer Beiträge zur Allgemeinen Geschichte* 20 (1962–63): 188–99, 200–29.

37. For the patron-client relationship see J. R. Major, "The Crown and the Aristocracy in

(*Continued on next page*)

The patrons provided their clients and their clients' relatives with employment in their service or used their influence to obtain positions for them in the bureaucracy, the army, and the church. They found places for them in the king's household, in the courts (including the Parlement of Paris itself), and in nearly every branch of the administration. One might suppose that when Charles VII created the permanent army in 1445, he would have filled it with mercenaries and members of the third estate so that it would have been a more reliable instrument to use against the magnates; but, in fact, the nobility obtained a stronger position in the new companies than they had enjoyed in the royal forces a generation or two before. The episcopacy also became an aristocratic preserve. Of the 144 Frenchmen Francis I nominated to be bishops between 1516 and 1547, 123 were nobles and 6 were nonnobles (the social origins of the remainder are unknown).[38] This situation posed a serious threat to royal authority because the first loyalty of the clients was to their patron; more than once they followed him into revolt against the king. Thus the patron-client relationship provided the magnates with followers to do them service and the clients with positions. It functioned throughout France and made the provincial estates less essential than they were for the third estate, but where these assemblies did exist, patron and client alike made use of them just as they did other institutions.

It has often been suggested that the economic position of the nobility deteriorated during the Renaissance because of rising prices, extravagance, poor business methods, wars, and a host of other things. Such statements are generally based on literary evidence, however, and the limited amount of concrete information that has been found suggests that the opposite was true. Rarely had the nobility prospered so much as in the seventy-five years preceding the Wars of Religion. Between 1488 and 1541, the La Trémoilles were able to increase their seigneurial revenue, exclusive of any income from the crown, by 220 percent. Even after an adjustment is made to compensate for inflation, the growth of their purchasing power was 135 percent. In addition, they received large sums from the crown. Their expenditures rarely exceeded their income by a significant amount. Between 1488 and 1566 their worst record was for 1554–66 when their average annual expenditure exceeded their average income, but only by thirteen hundred livres. The kings of France did not manage their affairs so well. Henry II was virtually bankrupt in 1559. Henri d'Albret, however, may have competed in

Renaissance France," *American Historical Review* 69 (1964): 631–45, and Roland Mousnier, *Les institutions de la France sous la monarchie absolue* (Paris, 1974), pp. 85–93. Robert R. Harding, *Anatomy of a Power Elite: The Provincial Governors of Early Modern France (New Haven, 1978)*, pp. 21–37. W. A. Weary, "The Administration of Patronage in Fifteenth and Sixteenth Century France: Assumptions, Practices, and Institutions" (unpublished manuscript, 1974).

38. Marilyn M. Edelstein, *The Recruitment of the French Episcopacy under the Concordat of Bologna in the Reign of Frances I* (Ann Arbor, University Microfilms, 1972), p. 102. For the army, see Philippe Contamine, *Guerre, état et société à la fin du Moyen Age* (Paris, 1972).

efficiency. He nearly doubled his revenue from Béarn between 1531 and 1550. Of course it could be argued that the La Trémoille and the Albret were exceptional cases because of their great wealth and influence, but a study of the nobility of the élection of Bayeux shows that 161 of the 259 nobles received less than fifty livres per year from their fiefs in 1552. We do not know their financial situation at an earlier date, but in that year the seigneurial income of the typical old noble was as large as that of the new one. This same relative situation held true in 1640, by which time the mean income of the class had increased enormously.[39] In parts of France where the taille was personnelle or in dispute, the nobles' economic activity is attested by frequent peasant complaints that they were purchasing nonnoble land, thereby removing it from the tax roles and leaving the unprivileged with a greater burden. Thus the nobility had a system that enabled them to play a politically influential and economically profitable role during the Renaissance. (See especially pp. 76–80, 326–31.)

2. THE RENAISSANCE MONARCHY IN POLITICAL THOUGHT

The people, then, increased their role in the government of France during the Renaissance. The provincial estates that had emerged around 1350 had been laid to rest in the last third of the century, only to be reborn again during the reign of Charles VII. In the intervening period Charles V and Charles VI came nearer to enjoying "absolutist" tax power than any other kings in French history.[40] Are we then to say that the monarchy reached its peak in the reign of the mad Charles VI and then slowly declined during the Renaissance before the rising tide of popular government? Are we to argue that Francis I was but a pale image of that rarely lucid monarch? Of course not! There can be no doubt that Charles was a weak king and that Francis was a strong one. Our seeming paradox will be resolved only if we accept the proposition that the growth of self-government paralleled the growth of monarchical government. Liberals in the nineteenth century assumed that the two must be in conflict with each other, that the one could not wax unless the other waned, but this was not the assumption of the Renaissance man. In practice and in theory, he saw the strength of the state as dependent on cooperation between the king and the people.

Even Machiavelli, that disillusioned cynic who so often counseled cruelty and deceit, was careful to add that "it is well to seem merciful, faithful, humane, sincere, religious, and also to be so." "The prince," in short, "must

39. Weary, *Royal Policy*, pp. 82, 204–16; Charles Dartigue-Peyrou, *La vicomté de Béarn sous le règne de Henri d'Albret, 1517–1555* (Paris, 1934), p. 250; Wood, *Social Structure*, pp. 65–80.

40. The term *absolutist* tax power is used by Martin Wolfe in *The Fiscal System of Renaissance France* (New Haven, 1972), pp. 25–66, but he assumes that these powers were seized by Charles VII.

... avoid those things which will make him hated or despised." Only then could he be truly strong. "Therefore, the best fortress is to be found in the love of the people, for although you may have fortresses they will not save you if you are hated by the people."[41] Erasmus, so different in nearly every respect, was equally certain that a king's strength depended less on his army than on whether he had gained the love of his subjects. "He does not lose his prerogatives, who rules as a Christian should," he informed the future emperor, Charles V. "The following arguments will make this clear. First, those are not really yours whom you oppress in slavery.... But they are really yours who yield obedience to you willingly and of their own accord. Secondly, when you hold people bound to you through fear, you do not possess them even half. You have their physical bodies, but their spirits are estranged from you. But when Christian love unites the people and their prince, then everything is yours that your position demands, for a good prince does not demand anything for which service to his country does not call."[42]

Claude de Seyssel, Thomas More, and many others shared similar views.[43] So commonplace was the belief during the Renaissance that the strength of a state was dependent upon the support of the people that it survived the early stages of seventeenth century absolutism and sometimes assumed strange forms. Cardinal Mazarin, who did so little to please the French people during the many years he governed them and who came within an ace of losing his post because of this oversight, informed his ambassador to England in 1646 that it would be less damaging to France if "the king of Great Britain was reestablished in his traditional authority, although we were certain that [his state] would be our enemy, than if it became a republic ... in the uncertainty whether it would be a friend or a foe of this crown."[44] His justification for preferring a definite to a possible enemy across the English Channel was based on the premise that there a king could not tax enough to support a war without provoking the resistance of his subjects, but that "in a free state, as a republic," the people would pay as much as was necessary to obtain their objective because taxes would be voluntary and the objective would be set with the unanimous consent of all.[45]

No Valois king was so patriotic as to establish a republic in order to make

41. Machiavelli, *The Prince*, trans. L. Ricci and rev. E. R. P. Vincent (New York, 1950), chaps. 18, 20, 21.

42. Erasmus, *The Education of a Christian Prince*, trans. Lester K. Born (New York, 1936), pp. 179–80.

43. J. R. Major, "The Renaissance Monarchy as seen by Erasmus, More, Seyssel, and Machiavelli," in *Action and Conviction in Early Modern Europe: Essays in Memory of E. H. Harbison*, ed. T. K. Rabb and J. E. Seigel (Princeton, 1969), pp. 17–31.

44. *Recueil des instructions données aux ambassadeurs et ministres de France depuis les traités de Westphalie jusqu'à la Révolution française*, ed. J. J. Jusserand (Paris, 1929), 24:35.

45. Ibid., p. 35.

France stronger, but they were surprisingly willing to permit provincial estates and other popular institutions to increase their roles and occasionally to encourage them to do so. When he ascended the throne, Louis XI attempted to reform the tax structure. Where there were provincial estates, he planned to replace the taille and aides by a single tax designed to yield an equal amount but levied as the estates desired and collected by their officials. Where royal tax officials had been established, they were to be discharged. In Normandy, Languedoc, Dauphiné, and perhaps elsewhere, steps were actually taken to implement his plan, but they were soon halted, in the case of Normandy, at least, at the request of the three estates themselves. Again, in 1561 the crown offered to permit the deputies at the Estates General to appoint a committee to supervise the collection of taxes as part of an unsuccessful effort to win their support for additional levies. Some months later the clergy proved more cooperative, and in return for a substantial sum, they were allowed to establish their own tax-collecting machinery and to assemble periodically thereafter.[46] Between the close of the Hundred Years War and the outbreak of the Wars of Religion, the crown rarely sought to check the ever-expanding bureaucracies and functions of the provincial estates. When it did move, it achieved only temporary success.

We must therefore abandon the liberal assumption that the kings and the estates were natural adversaries. Rather their roles can be more aptly compared with those of the president and Congress of the United States. Disagreements between the two are frequent and at times one tries to dominate, but each accepts the existence of the other and makes no effort to destroy it. The concept of representative government was not invented until the creation of the Dutch republic near the close of the Renaissance; until then, kings rarely saw reason to fear representative institutions. Since their bureaucracies were small by modern standards and sometimes disobedient, they found it useful to utilize the officials of the estates and other popular institutions. Furthermore, the modest size of their armies made it advisable for them to rule by persuasion rather than by force.

This is not the place to explore the role of the estates in the political thought of the Renaissance, but it might be suggested that an investigation of this subject should be divided into two parts. The first part should consist of a study of the opinions of jurists, royal officials, and other persons trained in law or finance, a traditional approach that has already produced several excellent books. The second and equally important part should treat what might be termed popular political thought, the thinking of the leaders of society, including the officials and members of the provincial estates. Because these people did not write elaborate theses explaining their views in a coherent, detailed fashion, it is necessary to obtain an understanding of

---

46. J. R. Major, *Representative Institutions in Renaissance France* (Madison, 1960), p. 50, and *The Estates General of 1560* (Princeton, 1951), pp. 103–04.

their beliefs from a speech to one of the assemblies, an article in a cahier, or a single sentence in a book.

The jurists and royal officials can be classified into two categories. First there were those who wrote under the influence of Roman law and declared that their kings were "absolute." In the early sixteenth century their adulation for their ruler reached its height. They called him "the vicar of Christ in his kingdom," "the king of kings," and "a second sun on earth." He was, one of them declared, "like a corporeal God."[47] Yet in spite of such extravagant phrases, these jurists remained constitutionalists. Most of them were connected with the Parlement of Paris or lived within its jurisdiction where there were few provincial estates to trouble their concepts concerning monarchical power. It served their interests as well as their convictions to exalt their sovereign over the feudal magnate and the vast array of semi-autonomous corporative institutions, but when the crown began to intervene too much, it was another matter. As early as 1481 Cosme Guymier was likening Parlement to the Roman senate, and the claims of the parlementarians grew in the century that followed. Even those who eulogized the king to excess, like Barthélemy de Chasseneuz, declared, or came very close to declaring, that the king could not set aside the custom. He and his successors came equally near to denying that the king could compel Parlement to register a decree by a *lettre de jussion*. Indeed, in the early seventeenth century Bernard de la Roche-Flavin specifically made such a claim.[48] It was largely in reaction to growing pretensions of Parlement that the kings had to turn the *lit de justice* into an instrument to enforce their will.[49]

The second category of scholarly theorists consisted of those who derived their inspiration more from practical experience in government or from history and French customary law. They believed that all power originated with the king or that it had been granted to him in perpetuity by the people, but that in either case there were definite checks on his power. To Claude de Seyssel these checks consisted of the obligation to obey the fundamental laws of the state, to submit to the religious obligation to be just and to the legal obligation to respect the privileges of provinces, towns, and social classes, and to give heed to the Parlements, the guardians of the law. Seyssel's successors retained his emphasis on the sovereign courts and frequently stressed the role of the Estates General as well. Indeed, there was a notable

47. Julian H. Franklin, *Jean Bodin and the Rise of Absolutist Theory* (Cambridge, 1973), p. 7.

48. Ibid., pp. 7–19. See also the excellent treatment of these jurists by William F. Church, *Constitutional Thought in Sixteenth-Century France* (Cambridge, Mass., 1941), pp. 43–73.

49. Sarah Hanley Madden has shown that there were only two authenticated uses of the phrase *lit de justice* in the registers of Parlement prior to 1527 and that considerably more time elapsed before this ceremonial assembly was used largely to overcome parlementary opposition. See *The Lit de Justice of the Kings of France: Historical Myth and Constitutional Event in Late Medieval and Early Modern Times* (Ann Arbor, University Microfilms, 1975).

increase in the discussion of the duties of the Estates during the latter part of the sixteenth century.[50] Thus the growth of self-government in Renaissance France was paralleled by a growing emphasis of theorists on institutional checks on the crown. "Hence," a recent authority has declared, "looking back at the entire period from the end of the fifteenth century to 1572, we may conclude that the dominant trend of political ideas was favourable to constitutionalism."[51]

In the 1570s critics of royal authority became more numerous and theories of resistance became more fully developed. In reaction, its defenders became more extreme. Nevertheless some royalist spokesmen continued to adhere to the older concept of a mixed or limited monarchy in which the king and his subjects cooperated in governing in accordance to the law. In what was probably the assembly of the estates of Clermont-en-Beauvaisis to elect deputies to the Estates General of 1588, the lieutenant of the bailiwick and a famous jurist, Louis Le Caron, reiterated the Renaissance concepts of cooperation and the supremacy of the law: "The difference between a prince and a tyrant is that the prince governs with advice, in accordance to the law, a people who voluntarily obey him, and the tyrant rules, in accordance to his pleasure, a people who are compelled to obey him."[52] He then informed his listeners: "I believe that the opinion of Polybius is correct, that of the three kinds of government ..., to wit monarchy, aristocracy, and democracy, one cannot exist alone. Rather the three together, organized and limited, form a true republic. Still, one of them dominates and surpasses the others who are only its aids or members. So it is in France where there is a king who has sovereign power, yet he governs with the advice of the peers of France who are the ancient and natural councillors of the kingdom, through whom is represented aristocracy; and the people ... who are summoned by the king to be heard concerning the most important affairs of the kingdom ..., through whom is revealed a form of democracy."[53]

Most fiscal officials who wrote about taxation worked within the jurisdiction of the Chamber of Accounts of Paris where assemblies of the estates were rare, just as the jurists lived under the sway of the Parlement in that city. Those who were exposed to the estates, however, usually discussed the problem of consent to taxation. Jean Combes, who was born in Riom in 1512 and served first as lieutenant particular of Auvergne and then as president of the Court of Aids in Clermont, published a treatise on the taille

---

50. Church, *Constitutional Thought*, pp. 22–42, 74–178. For the rise of historical consciousness, see Donald R. Kelley's excellent *Foundations of Modern Historical Scholarship: Language, Law, and History in the French Renaissance* (New York, 1970).

51. Franklin, *Jean Bodin*, p. 21.

52. *Louis Le Caron, Responses et decisions du droict françois* (Paris, 1612), unpaginated frontmatter.

53. Ibid. For Le Caron's thought see D. R. Kelley, "Louis Le Caron Philosophe," in *Philosophy and Humanism: Renaissance Essays in Honor of Paul Oskar Kristeller*, ed. Edward P. Mahoney (New York, 1976), pp. 30–49.

in 1576. As the son of an official and later an official himself at Riom, he was probably jealous of the échevins of Clermont and disapproved of their right to convoke assemblies of the good towns. It is not surprising, therefore, that he ignored this institution or that he called the king absolute and thought that everyone should aid him in case of urgent necessity. Nevertheless, he believed that the king should obtain the consent of the estates for taxation under normal circumstances, and he stressed the mutual friendship between the king and his subjects.[54]

Jean Hennequin came from Champagne where there were no assemblies, but he became acquainted with Norman fiscal practices. After insisting that the early Valois kings had promised not to levy taxes without the consent of the estates except in cases of necessity, he confessed that this practice was no longer followed except in a few provinces such as Normandy where the three estates were held every year. They had, however, only traces of their former liberties because they were expected to vote what the king wanted whether the country was at peace or at war.[55] Years later René-Laurent La Barre, the president of a Norman élection, declared that "the fundamental laws of the kingdom neither permit nor authorize anyone, not even the kings, to raise armies or to levy taxes without the deliberation of the public and the consent of the Estates, the three orders of the kingdom being for this gathered together and assembled," He recognized, of course, that this situation no longer existed for France as a whole, but he called attention to the continued activities of the estates in Burgundy, Normandy, and Auvergne.[56]

The second part of an investigation of political thought concerning the estates should concentrate on the ideas of the leaders of society who were not employed by the crown and whose power and prestige were not dependent on royal authority. Here we are blessed with few studies except for the periods of the Religious Wars and the Fronde, but the evidence that is available suggests a widespread belief that ultimate authority still rested with the people. For those who accepted this premise, it logically followed that kingship was originally elective, that kings who violated the rights and privileges of their subjects could be deposed, and that a new king could be elected. If an individual expressed one of these three principles, he would very likely adhere to the other two if he were compelled to carry his thought to its logical conclusion. Closely related to these concepts is the principle that a king could not take the property of his subjects without their consent.

The idea that the people preceded the monarchy and elected their kings can be found in the Old Testament and was widely accepted during the

---

54. Jean Combes, *Traité des tailles et autres charges* (Paris, 1584), esp. fols. 6–16.

55. Jean Hennequin, *Le guidon général des finances* (Paris, 1585), fols. 78–78v.

56. René-Laurent La Barre, *Formulaire des esleuz* (Rouen, 1622), pp. 76–77. Pertinent extracts have been reprinted in *Cahiers des Etats de Normandie sous les régnes de Louis XIII et de Louis XIV*, ed. Charles de Robillard de Beaurepaire (Rouen, 1878), 3:429–35.

Middle Ages. A. J. Carlyle, who based his study of political thought far more on administrative documents than most other scholars, found that as late as the fourteenth century the leading theorists, except for Wyclif, "seem clearly to agree with each other, and with the normal character of mediaeval political thought, in holding that the authority of the prince was derived from the community, that it was limited by law, and that, in the last resort, the community could resume the authority which it had given, and depose the prince who was incompetent or who wilfully and persistently disregarded the law." [57]

Around 1418 Jean de Terre Rouge, a royal official, reiterated these ideas by asserting that the kingdom really belongs to the "Three Estates and the whole civil and mystical body of the realm," and that kings were only the administrators. [58] It is true that he soon strayed from the logic of his position, but not so Philippe Pot, seigneur de La Roche, who insisted during the meeting of the Estates General of 1484 that those present had the right to elect the king's council when there was a minority:

> Kingship is a dignity and not an heredity, and as such it does not pass to the nearest relatives in the way in which a patrimony passes to its natural guardians. If, then, the commonwealth is not to be bereft of government, the care of it must devolve upon the Estates General of the realm, whose duty it is, not to administer it themselves, but to entrust its administration to worthy hands.
>
> History and tradition tells us the kings were originally created by the votes of the sovereign people, and the prince is placed where he is, not that he may pursue his own advantage, but that he may strive unselfishly for the welfare of the nation. The ruler who falls short of this ideal is a tyrant and a wolf, and is no true shepherd of his flock. Have you not often read that the commonwealth is the people's common concern? Now if it be their concern, how should they neglect it and not care for it? Or how should flatterers attribute sovereign power to the prince, seeing that he exists merely by the people's will? And so I come to the question under discussion, namely, to the problem which arises when a king by infancy or otherwise is incapable of personal rule. Now we are agreed that the commonwealth is the people's; that our king cannot himself govern it; and that it must be entrusted to the care and ministry of others. If then, as I maintain, this care devolves neither upon any one prince, nor upon several princes, nor upon all of them together, it must of necessity return to the people from whom it came, and the people must resume a power which is their own, the more so since it is they alone who suffer from the evils of a

57. Alexander J. Carlyle and Robert W. Carlyle, *A History of Medieval Political Theory in the West* (Edinburgh, 1962), 6:62–63.

58. Ralph E. Giesey, *The Juristic Basis of Dynastic Right to the French Throne* (Philadelphia, 1961), p. 13.

long interregnum or a bad regency. I do not suggest that the right of government is taken from the sovereign. I argue only that government and guardianship, not rights and property, are for the time being transferred by law to the people and their representatives; and by the people I mean all subjects of the crown, of what rank soever they be. If, then, you will regard yourselves as the deputies of all the estates of the realm and the depositaries of the aspirations of them all, you cannot avoid the conclusion that the main object of your convocation is to direct the government by your counsels in the vacancy which has arisen through the minority of our sovereign. To this were you bidden by the letters which convened the estates and by the speech which the chancellor delivered in the presence, and with approval, of kings and princes. Nothing could more clearly refute the opinions of those who hold that we have been summoned here merely to vote taxation, and are not concerned with other objects—opinions contradicted by the traditions of the constitution as well as by the course of events.[59]

At the dawn of the sixteenth century James Almain, a member of the faculty of the Univeristy of Paris, insisted that the power of the king was derived from the people and that they could depose him if they desired. John Major, a Scotsman who served on the faculty of the same institution, held similar views. In the 1550s it is likely that the concept of elective kingship was debated at the university,[60] and in January 1577, Claude de Bauffremont, the speaker of the nobility, informed Henry III in the meeting of the Estates General that the nobility "placed the crown on the head of the first king."[61] Thus the historian and jurist, François Hotman, was not as out of touch with the thinking of many Frenchmen as some have thought when he published *Francogallia* in 1573.[62] In this book he argued that some regions of ancient Gaul were ruled by councils of the nobility and others were kingdoms. These "kingdoms were not hereditary but conferred by the people on someone who had a reputation for justice; and, in the second place, the kings did not possess an unlimited, free and uncontrolled authority, but were so circumscribed by specific laws that they were no less

59. Jean Masselin, *Journal des Etats généraux de France tenus à Tours en 1484*, ed. A. Bernier (Paris, 1835), pp. 146–51. I have used the excellent but abridged translation of John S. C. Bridge with minor changes. See his *History of France from the Death of Louis XI* (Oxford, 1921), 1:77–79. For Pot's role in the estates, see Major, *Representative Institutions*, esp. pp. 69–70, 82, 87–89;, 93, 95, 111, 166 n.37, 168 n.83.

60. Carlyle and Carlyle, *History*, 6:241–49, 488–89. R. A. Jackson, "Elective Kingship and *Consensus Populi* in Sixteenth-Century France," *Journal of Modern History* 44 (1972): 156.

61. Gerard F. Denault, *The Legitimation of the Parlement of Paris and the Estates General, 1560–1614* (Ann Arbor, University Microfilms, 1975), p. 500.

62. For pamphlets published just before 1573 in which views similar to Hotman's were voiced, see François Hotman, *Francogallia*, ed. R. E. Giesey and J. H. M. Salmon (Cambridge, 1972), pp. 38–49.

under the authority and power of the people than the people were under theirs."[63] In addition to these regional states, Hotman supposed that there was a council for all of Gaul. The Romans conquered Gaul, but during the third century the Franks, assisted by the Gauls, began the long, slow process of driving them from the land. Together they elected Childeric the first king of Francogallia. During the centuries that followed, kings were elected and, when necessary, deposed by the council. Hotman conceded that the council, which he associated with the Estates General, had usually elected the king from the same family and that from the time of the Capetians, there had been a gradual erosion of the ancient constitution, but he held that it had not been fully subverted until the reign of Louis XI.

Bèza, Du Plessis Mornay, and other Huguenot writers accepted the concept of an ancient constitution and the right to elect and depose kings when the need arose, although the central thrust of their arguments often differed from that of Hotman. The pamphleteers of the Catholic League adhered to somewhat similar views and almost put their theory into practice by electing a king in 1592–93. They had no need to borrow their ideas from their Huguenot rivals, however, for there was an ample base in the popular political thought of the times on which they could build.[64] Statements concerning the constitutional importance of the Estates General persisted until the Fronde, when they were reiterated by Claude Joly and a number of pamphleteers before becoming less commonplace during the personal reign of Louis XIV.[65]

The writers thus far discussed dealt primarily with the Estates General and the central government. It has rarely been recognized that somewhat similar theories evolved concerning the role of the provincial estates. Pierre de Saint-Julien, for example, traced the estates of Burgundy back to the ancient Gauls. Born of a noble Burgundian family, his love of history caused him to enter the clergy, although he was the eldest of sixteen children. The deanship of Chalon-sur-Saône was given to him, along with other rich benefices, but his greatest pleasures were derived from his controversial historical investigations and his election to the office of élu of the estates of Burgundy in 1566.[66]

63. Ibid., p. 155. For a summary of Hotman's argument, see ibid., pp. 62–72.

64. For League political thought, see Frederic J. Baumgartner, *Radical Reactionaries: The Political Thought of the French Catholic League* (Geneva, 1976). The survival of Hotman's argument well into the seventeenth century is attested by Michel de Marillac's complaint that it still found some adherents in a few towns formerly held by the Huguenots, including Lyons. Denault, *Legitimation*, p. 344.

65. For a recent study of political thought during the Fronde, see Elizabeth C. Adams, *Seventeenth-Century Attitudes toward the French Estates General* (Ann Arbor, University Microfilms, 1976).

66. For Saint-Julien's life, see *Bibliographie universelle*, ed. Joseph François Michaud (Graz, 1969), 37:339–40. For his election as élu, see *IAD, Côte-d'Or sér. C*, ed. Joseph Garnier (Dijon, 1886), 3:111.

Saint-Julien argued that the Burgundians were Gauls, whose society consisted of druids, soldiers, and plebians from whom emerged the three estates. The various regions of Gaul had local assemblies, and there was also an Estates General that elected a sovereign magistrate for a one-year term. Saint-Julien recognized that the French monarchy had long ago become hereditary and that the Burgundian estates had lost some of their ancient authority, but he nevertheless insisted that these estates were the envy of their less fortunate neighbors and that their élus enjoyed a position comparable to that of the tribunes of Rome.[67] "It would be better," he wrote, "for Burgundy to have lost the title of first peerage of France than the Estates." The estates of such provinces as Burgundy, Languedoc, Dauphiné, and Brittany "are the foundation of their liberties and the true tie which holds the men who are in the same government in society and friendship."[68]

In no place did Saint-Julien cite Hotman nor did he list him in his bibliography. His inspiration appears to have come from his own study of history, his practical experience as an official of the Burgundian estates, and the general climate of opinion of his day. Indeed the crown granted permission to publish his book in May 1567, which suggests that he had established his basic argument prior to that time; that is, at least six years before Hotman published the *Francogallia*. Saint-Julien did refer to events subsequent to 1567, such as the massacre of Saint Bartholemew, but it is probable that he owed little or nothing to Hotman and other Protestants whose religious beliefs he strongly opposed. In the end he joined the Catholic League and is the probable author of a pamphlet in which he argued that France was an elective rather than a hereditary monarchy.[69]

That there was a widespread belief in the antiquity of the estates is suggested by a Catholic League manifesto published in 1576 advocating that "the ancient rights, pre-eminences, franchises, and liberties of the provinces and estates of this kingdom be restored as they were at the time of king Clovis, the first Christian king."[70] Not to be outdone, the syndic of the Haute-Marche of Rouergue traced the history of the estates of Rouergue from the time of Julius Caesar until the reign of Henry IV.[71] Jean Savaron, a noted jurist and future deputy to the Estates General of 1614, insisted that the estates of Auvergne dated back to the time of the druids and Romans.[72] Nor were such legends to die quietly with the advent of royal absolutism. During the reign of Louis XIV, the first president of the Parlement of Dijon

67. Pierre de Sainct-Julien, *D'l'origine des Bourgongnons et antiquité des Estats de Bourgongne* (Paris, 1581), pp. 15–23, 31–80.

68. Ibid., p. 64.

69. Ibid., p. 59. *Bibliographie universelle*, 37:339.

70. *Histoire de la Normandie*, ed. Michel de Boüard (Toulouse, 1970), p. 271.

71. AD, Aveyron, C 1902.

72. Jean Savaron, *Les origines de Clermont, ville capitale d'Auvergne* (Clermont, 1607), pp. 254–55.

could still speak of the provincial estates at the time of the Gauls and of the very great antiquity of the Burgundian assembly.[73] The three estates of Navarre laid claim to less age but were more accurate when they informed Louis XIV in their cahier in 1672 that their first king "was the creation and the creature of his subjects; they drew him from their midst and put him at their head in order to fight the Moors; they submitted to his domination in order to conserve their goods and their liberty."[74] A century later Jean Albisson, a lawyer and official of the estates of Languedoc who was eventually to serve the first republic, found the origins of that institution in the municipal regime established by the Romans.[75] Thus, from the Middle Ages until the Revolution, some Frenchmen believed that the provincial estates were older than the monarchy itself, and they occasionally drew the logical implications from this premise.

3. THE PRINCE AND THE ESTATES IN EUROPE

If the capacity of the people to govern themselves increased in France, which has long been considered the prime example of an absolute monarchy, it scarcely needs to be asserted that a similar phenomenon occurred elsewhere in Europe. German historians have long interposed an age of the *Ständestaat*, or Estates-State, between the feudal state and the absolute state.[76] During the thirteenth century, they argue, power passed from the emperor to the princes, but during the fourteenth century, leagues of nobles, towns, and other groups interposed themselves between the princes and their subjects. By 1400 these groups or estates had organized themselves into fairly stable assemblies with permanent committees to serve their needs. Their power usually equaled and sometimes surpassed that of the prince, with the result that ordered political life was difficult. Around 1450, however, these historians assert, the princes were able to revive their authority and provide a counterbalance to the power and divergent interests of the estates. They sought to persuade their subjects to abandon their narrow provincialism by creating single representative institutions for all their lands to be used as instruments "for welding together the haphazard conglomerations of

73. Alexandre Thomas, *Une province sous Louis XIV: situation politique et administrative de la Bourgogne, de 1661 à 1715* (Paris, 1844), p. 39.

74. Alain Destrée, *La Basse Navarre et ses institutions de 1620 à la Révolution* (Saragossa, 1955), p. 410.

75. *Loix municipales et économiques de Languedoc*, ed. Jean Albisson (Montpellier, 1780), 1:316, 322.

76. For an admirable synthesis of their work prior to World War II, see Geoffrey Barraclough, *The Origins of Modern Germany* (Oxford, 1947). In a study that has not received the attention it deserves in the English-speaking world, Emile Lousse has applied the corporative theory to late medieval Europe. See his *La société d'ancien régime: organisation et représentation corporatives* (Louvain, 1943). He includes a bibliographical essay.

domains, fiefs, counties and lordships, which were the legacy of the Middle Ages, and for restoring political unity; by forcing the separate estates to accept their position as members of one body politic, the princes created in Germany the unity of the territorial state."[77]

Recent scholarship suggests that these older historians have exaggerated the role of the princes in creating the territorial states, for in spite of a growing acceptance of primogeniture, some rulers persisted in the practice of dividing their lands among their sons, sometimes over the protests of the estates. More serious, the older historians have professed to see a growth of princely authority and a corresponding decline of the estates beginning with the Reformation, although they have conceded that only in Bavaria did the estates lose much ground before the seventeenth century. In fact, the ability of Germans to govern themselves continued to develop throughout the sixteenth century. If princely power grew, so did that of the estates. Clashes were frequent, but there was no deep-rooted antagonism between the two, and each accepted the existence of the other. Indeed, as in France, it appears that the growth of the princes' power depended on the support given them by their subjects and expressed largely through assemblies of the estates that assumed much of the burden of government.

During the late fifteenth and sixteenth centuries, the estates in the German principalities lost what remained of their ad hoc quality. Their rights and privileges were defined. They developed procedures, created committees, appointed officials who levied and collected taxes, and controlled a treasury separate from that of the prince. Few aspects of government, including dynastic policy and foreign affairs, escaped their attention. To protect their interests when they were not in session, they appointed permanent committees and in general played an increasingly important role in affairs of state. Their administration was more efficient than that provided by any but the ablest of the princes, and their credit was so good that they could borrow money at lower rates of interest than their sovereigns could. In short, "With the exception of Catholic Bavaria, their position everywhere became stronger in the course of the sixteenth century."[78]

The growth of representative institutions in Germany during the Renaissance was not limited to the principalities. Estates also developed in many of the ecclesiastical states, but more striking was the attempt at imperial reform, the development of strong estates in some of the circles into which Germany was divided, and the formation of cantonal and regional assemblies of the imperial knights in some regions. Under the leadership of Berthold von Henneberg, archbishop of Mainz and chancellor of the Empire, a determined effort was launched in 1485 to reform the government under the auspices of the Reichstag. Partial success was achieved. An

77. Barraclough, *Origins of Modern Germany*, p. 347.

78. Francis L. Carsten, *Princes and Parliaments in Germany* (Oxford, 1959), p. 431. My description of the German estates is based primarily on this book and the same author's *The Origins of Prussia* (Oxford, 1954).

Imperial Cameral Court was created and charged with maintaining the public peace. The bulk of its members were appointed by the estates, and it functoned outside of imperial control. A national tax was established that was to be administered by seven treasurers, six of whom were to be named by the estates. Efforts to create a permanent committee to act for the Reichstag when it was not in session failed at this time, but it was agreed that the Reichstag should meet annually, a provision that was not always adhered to. Nevertheless, by 1497–98 the Reichstag had become "an institution of central importance to the public life of the German Nation."[79] In 1519 it further entrenched its position by inaugurating the practice of having a newly elected emperor sign a capitulation or contract setting limitations on his authority and guaranteeing it a voice when important decisions were made.[80]

The Reichstag was not content to strip the emperor of much of his judicial authority, to prevent him from controlling the new national tax, and to impose other limitations on his actions; it also denied him the right to enforce the decisions of the Imperial Cameral Court and to maintain the public peace. These tasks were assigned to the ten circles into which the Empire had been divided in 1500 and 1512. These circles were given an executive arm consisting of a captain and four councillors and an assembly of the estates. Their role was rapidly expanded, and by 1560 they were responsible for such tasks as collecting taxes, mobilizing units of the imperial army, keeping the peace, and managing the currency. In circles where there was no great prince and authority was fragmented, as in Swabia, Franconia, and the Rhineland, the circle assemblies displayed their greatest vitality. "The preservation of the imperial system," Friedrich Carl Moser asserted in 1747, "depends largely upon ... the western imperial circles." About two decades later another observer declared, "Without the circles our German empire would not be able to exist; it would be impossible to carry on any government, it would be impossible to raise any imperial army."[81]

The free imperial knights had found organizations to protect themselves

---

79. S. W. Rowan, "A Reichstag in the Reform Era: Freiburg im Breisgau, 1497–98," in *The Old Reich: Essays on German Political Institutions, 1495–1806*, ed. James A. Vann and S. W. Rowan (Brussels, 1974), p. 56.

80. I have based this and the following paragraph primarily on the collection of essays published in Vann and Rowan's *Old Reich*; G. Benecke, *Society and Politics in Germany, 1500–1750* (London, 1974); studies on imperial reform by F. Hartung and K. S. Bader reprinted in *Pre-Reformation Germany*, ed. Gerald Strauss (New York, 1972), pp. 73–161; James A. Vann, *The Swabian Kreis: Institutional Growth in the Holy Roman Empire* (Brussels, 1975); and R. Wines, "The Imperial Circles, Princely Diplomacy and Imperial Reform 1681–1714," *Journal of Modern History* 39 (1967): 1–29. For an explanation of why an assembly of the estates did not develop in the ecclesiastical principality of Speyer, see Lawrence G. Duggan, *Bishop and Chapter: The Governance of the Bishopric of Speyer to 1552* (New Brunswick, 1978). On the role of peasants in assemblies in southern Germany, see Peter Blickle, *Landschaften in Alten Reich: Die staatliche Funktion des gemeinen Mannes in Oberdeutschland* (Munich, 1973).

81. Wines, "Imperial Circles," pp. 3, 27.

from the princes during the fourteenth century in many parts of Germany, but not until 1529 when the knights in Swabia, Franconia, and the Rhineland made a voluntary contribution to Emperor Charles V and in return received a guarantee of their imperial status did their political and administrative role become assured. During the following generation they formed cantonal assemblies whose officers met frequently in a regional diet. The usual bureaucracy developed. There was a canton treasury before 1539, and a regional one was recommended in 1560.[82] Thus sixteenth-century Germany witnessed a growth in the importance of the estates in the various principalities, the emergence of a stronger, better-organized Reichstag with its own organs of government, and the creation of representative institutions in the newly created circles and among the imperial knights.

The role of the estates also increased in the Low Countries during the Renaissance. Some of the provincial estates in what is now Belgium could boast of medieval origins, but others such as those of Namur, Tournay-Tournaisis, and Stavelot-Malmédy were fifteenth- and even sixteenth-century creations. As in Germany it was only after 1500 that the composition and procedures of the various assemblies became established. Thereafter, there were modifications but no more transformations. The estates of Hainaut won the right to collect and administer taxes in 1448, and those of Liège did so at about the same time. The estates of Flanders exercised similar functions from 1543 and those of Luxembourg from 1594. The development of permanent committees to act for the estates when they were not in session came more slowly, but they existed almost everywhere by 1600. The estates intervened in or were consulted about nearly every aspect of government, although only in the realms of finance and public works did they enjoy almost total control.[83]

The Estates General in the Low Countries was even more clearly a product of the Renaissance. The first meeting deserving that title took place in Bruges in January 1464. To it came deputies from ten of the provinces owing allegiance to the Burgundian dukes, but there had been occasions when representatives of two or more provinces had met together before that time. On the other hand, the ad hoc quality of the localities and estates summoned to attend persisted well into the sixteenth century. In 1477, long before the Estates General became a stable institution, its members took advantage of the death of Charles the Bold to obtain extensive privileges, but these privileges were not uniformly respected, and a balance between the dukes and the estates was achieved. The Estates General provided the dukes with an opportunity to explain their policies to the representatives of the

---

82. M. J. LeGates, "The Knights and the Problems of Political Organizing in Sixteenth-Century Germany," *Central European History* 7 (1974): 99–136.

83. J. Dhondt, "Les assemblées d'Etats en Belgique avant 1795," *Anciens pays et assemblées d'Etats* 33 (1965): 230–32, 244, 248–52. The individual articles on the various estates in what is now Belgium upon which Dhondt's account is based are published in the same volume.

large assortment of duchies and counties over which they ruled and to negotiate with them for financial assistance. In 1513 the ducal representatives suggested that the deputies appoint an official to administer a proposed tax, but they refused. Not until 1558 did the three estates name their first permanent officer, a treasurer, and only after they broke with Philip II in 1576 did they begin to develop a permanent bureaucracy comparable to that found in most of the French provincial estates.[84]

One factor that delayed the Estates General in achieving maturity was the provincialism constantly displayed by the counties and duchies that persistently refused to give their deputies full powers. This limited the use of the institution to the dukes because it was always necessary for the deputies to refer to their constituents for instructions before any action could be taken. In spite of this handicap, Henri Pirenne has asserted that the Estates General "not only gave the prince an opportunity to deliberate with his subjects as a whole; but it also provided the most potent of the means of unification which had brought together the seventeen Burgundian provinces."[85]

To the east in Bohemia and still more so in Hungary and Poland where the kings were elective, the national and provincial diets were the dominant elements in the government. Before the onslaught of these noble-dominated institutions, the position of the crown, especially in Poland, waned. One would have to travel farther east to Russia to find an independent Slavic state in which there was no assembly equal or superior to the king. Even here, outside or at least on the very limits of Western civilization, there were signs that representative assemblies might emerge. In the meeting of the Zemski Sobor in 1598, delegates of the common people participated in the election of a czar, but before a century had elapsed, the institution, after a rather uneventful existence, passed from the scene.[86]

To the north in Scandinavia, there was a long tradition of direct participation by freemen in assemblies, especially at the local and provincial level, but these bodies were not truly representative in character. The questions were whether a national assembly would be established, what form it would take, and what its relationship to the monarch would be. In Iceland where there was no effective royal authority and contact with Europe was very limited, the people were able to organize their own form of government

84. J. Gilissen, "Les Etats Généraux des pays par deçà, 1464–1632," *Anciens pays et assemblées d'Etats* 33 (1965): 261–321; Helmut G. Koenigsberger, *Estates and Revolutions: Essays in Early Modern European History* (Ithaca, 1971), pp. 125–43; Robert Wellens, *Les Etats Généraux des Pays-Bas des origines à la fin du règne de Philippe le Beau, 1464–1506* (Heule, 1974).

85. H. Pirenne, "The Formation and Constitution of the Burgundian State," *American Historical Review* 14 (1909): 500.

86. For very brief accounts of these assemblies and a bibliography, see Alec R. Myers, *Parliaments and Estates in Europe to 1789* (London, 1975), pp. 39–47, 82–88, 111–12, 122–27. See also Karol Górski, *Communitas princeps corona regni* (Warsaw, 1976).

free from outside interference. As early as 930 they established the Althing, a national assembly to which cases from the provincial assemblies could be appealed. The Althing was more a law court than a legislative body, and it lacked the executive authority to enforce its decisions. Chieftains were obligated to attend with some liegemen, but any freeman could do so if he desired. Not until 1799 did it cease to meet on the picturesque hillside at Thingvellir and begin to assemble indoors in Reykjavik, and not until 1845 was its composition altered to give it a more truly representative character.[87]

Changes took place more rapidly on the continent, where Denmark and Sweden soon emerged as elective kingships, and Norway, after a period of independence, became attached to the Danish crown. National assemblies of nobles and prelates were held in Denmark at an early date to elect kings and deal with other matters, and in 1468 the townsmen and free peasants were called upon to elect deputies to a national assembly. Soon the new assembly was claiming to nominate officials and approve wars as well as to vote taxes. It played an important role during the Reformation and declined only as the Renaissance drew to a close.[88]

The Swedish Riksdag began to emerge during the last third of the fifteenth century, but its composition and procedures retained an ad hoc quality well into the seventeenth century. As late as 1587 it met in the open air, and provincial assemblies had to approve the taxes and laws it voted. It did not even meet between 1529 and 1544.[89] Nevertheless the Riksdag proved to be a valuable tool of the crown. It was used "by the nationalist kings and regents of the fifteenth century in their struggle against the union with Denmark. After that struggle had ended in the emancipation of Sweden and the election of Gustav Vasa to the throne in 1523, the Riksdag was co-opted by the monarchy to give weight to attacks upon its enemies. It assisted Gustav Vasa to carry through the Reformation; it strengthened his position by making his throne hereditary; and it countenanced Erik XIV's savage persecution of his opponents among the nobility."[90] To obtain the support of the Riksdag, however, the kings had to pay some attention to the desires of its members, and slowly the Riksdag developed the procedures necessary for it to become effective in its own right, although this did not occur until near the close of the Renaissance.

In the south of Europe, representative assemblies germinated and reached maturity earlier. Urban elements began to attend the Cortes in the Spanish kingdoms in the late twelfth century, and from the second quarter of the

87. Knut Gjerset, *History of Iceland* (New York, 1924), pp. 33–48, 346, 377; Jón Jóhannesson, *A History of the Old Icelandic Commonwealth*, trans. H. Bessason (Winnipeg, 1974), pp. 35–93.

88. Myers, *Parliaments and Estates*, p. 88.

89. Michael Roberts, *The Early Vasas* (Cambridge, 1968), pp. 42–43, 111, 190–94. See also his *Gustavus Adolphus* (London, 1953), 1:283–315.

90. M. Roberts, "The Constitutional Development of Sweden in the Reign of Gustav Adolf," *History* 24 (1940): 329.

thirteenth century the towns sent proctors empowered and instructed in accordance with the procedures of Roman law.[91] Nevertheless there was an ad hoc quality about the composition and procedures of the early Spanish assemblies that paralleled that of the French estates. This fluid situation undoubtedly contributed to the ability of the crown to merge the Cortes of Leon and Castile into a single assembly soon after the final union of the two kingdoms under Ferdinand the Saint in 1230. Again as in France, the Castilian Cortes had high aspirations during the fourteenth century. Beginning in 1302 the deputies won a promise that they would not be arrested and that their property would not be seized during sessions, but the fact that they asked repeatedly that this promise be renewed suggests that it was not enforced. They were more successful in their efforts to exercise freedom of speech during their meetings and to consent to taxation. It even appeared likely between 1371 and 1384 that the king's council would be based on representation from the Cortes.[92] Again as in France, the Castilian Cortes suffered a decline in the late fourteenth and early fifteenth centuries. During this period of royal weakness, the council became dominated by magnates and lawyers, legislation and taxation largely escaped the Cortes' control, the nobility and clergy gradually ceased to participate, and the number of towns that sent deputies dropped from forty-nine in 1391 to seventeen before stabilizing at eighteen with the admission of Granada after its conquest.[93]

Ferdinand and Isabella won the cooperation of the Cortes in their efforts to restore order when they came to the throne. Once they were firmly in power, they allowed the institution to become dormant, not as a result of any fear that it inspired, but rather because they were no longer confronted by a crisis and had sufficient funds to govern without having to seek consent for extraordinary taxation. Then the death of their only son, their eldest daughter, and a grandson between 1497 and 1500 made it advisable to convoke the Cortes four times in quick succession to ensure a peaceful succession to the throne. Their daughter, Joanna, and her husband even undertook the long voyage from Flanders to Castile to be present when the Cortes recognized their right to the throne. Thereafter Ferdinand's active foreign policy assured the Cortes a continued role. In return for voting taxes,

91. See Gaines Post, *Studies in Medieval Legal Thought* (Princeton, 1964), pp. 70–79, and J. F. O'Callaghan, "The Beginnings of the Cortes of Léon-Castile," *American Historical Review* 74 (1969): 1503–37.

92. Roger B. Merriman, *The Rise of the Spanish Monarchy* (New York, 1918), 1:217–28; Myers, *Parliaments and Estates*, pp. 59–62; Luis Suárez Fernández, "The Kingdom of Castile in the Fifteenth Century," in *Spain in the Fifteenth Century, 1369–1516*, ed. Roger Highfield (New York, 1972), p. 92.

93. Fernandez, "Kingdom of Castile," pp. 91–95; Merriman, *Rise of the Monarchy*, 1:221, 246–55. For the representation of the towns in the Cortes in the early sixteenth century, see Charles D. Hendricks, *Charles V and the Cortes of Castile: Politics in Renaissance Spain* (Ann Arbor, University Microfilms, 1976), pp. 48–64.

the deputies won a number of important concessions, including the right of the towns to collect the sales tax upon which the crown was heavily dependent. Thus by the time Ferdinand died in 1516, the position the Cortes had enjoyed in the high Middle Ages had been largely restored.[94]

At first Charles V and his foreign entourage were not disposed to cater to Castilian susceptibilities. They appointed foreigners to key positions, levied a tax of questionable legality, and substituted tax farmers for the town officials as collectors for the sales tax. Their departure from Spain in 1520 was followed by a revolt of the towns that was soon suppressed by the nobility, but a nobility that was in sympathy with many of the objectives of the rebels. Most historians have believed that the triumphant Charles V was able to govern with scant regard to the Cortes thereafter, but this view has recently been forcibly challenged. Instead the revolt convinced Charles that he would have to make major concessions in order to win the loyalty of his new subjects.[95] He "initiated a consistent policy of nominating only Castilians to the kingdom's bishoprics and archbishoprics. He gave sinecures in his court to a substantial number of Castilians. He removed the unpopular president of Castile's Royal Council. And he personally attended to Castile's defense against French attacks."[96] Also pleasing to Castilians, he married an Iberian princess and raised his children in their land.

Charles also decided to use the Cortes as a forum to effect a reconciliation with towns. He summoned it periodically during the remainder of his reign and permitted it to establish a permanent committee to represent its interest between sessions. This committee, in turn, quickly developed its own bureaucracy. Charles gave careful attention to the petitions of the Cortes and granted many of its requests, especially in economic, social, and judicial matters. He abandoned his plan to use tax farmers to collect the sales tax and assigned this duty once more to the towns. The amount to be levied was fixed at a relatively low figure, and he came to rely more and more on the flexible *servicio* for which he always sought the Cortes' consent. So effective did the Cortes' control over taxation become that after allowances are made for inflation, the total of the three principal taxes that Charles collected in Castile actually declined during the course of his reign. Thus, while the Castilians prospered and paid less and less, Charles drifted toward bankruptcy even more rapidly than did his French rivals.[97]

In 1538–39 Charles tried to get the nobles and clergy to participate in the Cortes once more, but he soon abandoned the effort when he found that the former were strongly opposed to higher taxes and were seeking to form a common policy with the deputies of the towns. As a result of their recalcitrance, the nobles were not henceforth summoned, but they continued

94. Hendricks, *Charles V and the Cortes*, pp. 65–88.
95. Ibid., pp. 5–12, 89–172.
96. Ibid., p. 355.
97. Ibid., pp. 173–357 passim.

to enjoy a powerful position in the towns and in many regions managed to shift part of the tax burden on to the commoners by using their influence at the local level.[98] Philip II, like his father, recognized the potential usefulness of the Cortes and went to considerable trouble to get deputies elected with full powers. When they met, he kept them in session for long periods of time. Nevertheless the Cortes continued to be able to reject his requests although its attitude was generally cooperative.[99]

Indeed a recent student of Philip's reign has declared that "all tax grants resulted from arduous bargaining in which the Cortes was far from being a junior partner, or victim of a 'fait accompli.'"[100]

The Cortes in Aragon, Catalonia, and Valencia early assumed much stronger positions in regard to their common king than the Cortes of Castile was able to do. Taxation and legislation were much more fully under their control, and at an early date they had permanent committees to look after their interests when they were not in session and to perform administrative tasks. In addition to the Cortes of the individual kingdoms, there was also a General Cortes in which the Cortes of the three kingdoms and representatives from Majorca participated.[101]

Neither Ferdinand II nor his grandson, Emperor Charles V, made a serious effort to curtail the privileges of the three kingdoms. If they convoked the Cortes infrequently, it was because it was difficult to get them to vote significant sums. Doubtless the inhabitants were content to pay such a small price to escape taxes, especially as they retained their committees to look after their interests during the long intervals between sessions. Philip II continued the policy of his ancestors until after the Aragonese revolt of 1592, when he limited the control of the Cortes' permanent committee over taxation. Otherwise he made only minor changes involving the role of the Cortes. Furthermore, because the other kingdoms had not participated in the uprising, he saw no need to curtail their privileges.[102]

The Aragonese kings extended their decentralized system of government with its extensive use of representative institutions to Italy as they acquired

98. Ibid., pp. 231–40, 260–67.

99. Merriman, *Rise of the Monarchy*, 4:422–33; J. Beneyto, "Les Cortès d'Espagne du XVIe au XIX siècles," *Anciens pays et assemblées d'Etats*, 35 (1966): 465–68; Gordon Griffiths, *Representative Government in Western Europe in the Sixteenth Century* (Oxford, 1968). On p. 11 he lists the meetings of the Cortes between 1505 and 1601 and on pp. 1–9 and 30–75, he provides ample evidence of the survival of an independent spirit on the part of the deputies.

100. A. W. Lovett, *Philip II and Mateo Vázquez de Leca: The Government of Spain, 1572–1592* (Geneva, 1977), p. 104.

101. Merriman, *Rise of the Monarchy*, 1:433–40, 460–71, 481–84; Myers, *Parliaments and Estates*, pp. 62–65. Antonio Marongiu, *Medieval Parliaments*, trans. S. J. Woolf (London, 1968), pp. 65–76.

102. John H. Elliott, *Imperial Spain, 1469–1716* (London, 1963), pp. 70–71, 276–77; John Lynch, *Spain under the Habsburgs* (Oxford, 1964), 1:42–43, 343–44; Myers, *Parliament and Estates*, pp. 98–100.

kingdoms there. The Angevin rulers of Sicily and Naples had experimented with large assemblies, but even in Sicily these meetings did not begin to assume an institutional form until the reign of the Aragonese Martin I (1392–1409). Under Alfonso the Magnanimous (1416–58) the power of the Sicilian Parliament achieved an equilibrium with that of the crown. Financial contributions became dependent on redress of grievance, and laws were as much a product of the will of the deputies as that of the sovereign. This independence seemed too extensive to Ferdinand II, although he was favorably inclined toward representative institutions. The formal contractual nature of the relationship between crown and Parliament ceased, and the direct connection between the vote of a subsidy and the redress of grievances was abandoned. On the other hand, Ferdinand increased the power of the barons and abolished a number of taxes. He and his successors were careful to respect Parliament's privileges and made only modest demands for financial assistance. Under these circumstances the estates continued to mature. It was not until 1567–70 that the committee that acted for Parliament between sessions assumed its final form. Thus Sicily provides one of the finest examples of cooperation between the sovereign and a representative institution in governing a realm during the Renaissance.[103]

Emperor Frederick II created a parliament in Naples, but his Angevin successors permitted it to fall into disuse. However, it was revived by Alfonso the Magnanimous near the middle of the fifteenth century and utilized to good effect by Ferdinand of Aragon. "Paradoxically," Marongiu writes, "it was under Ferdinand the Catholic, when the kingdom of Naples became a Spanish province, that parliamentary activity developed and the representative institution became an important instrument of government."[104] The Parliament of Sardina owed an equally great debt to Ferdinand, although antecedents of the institution date back to 1421 and earlier, for it was during his reign that the institution's role in voting taxes and in participating in legislative and administrative matters became ensured.[105]

Assemblies were held in the Papal States at an early date; the popes may well have been the first to summon empowered deputies from corporate communities. During the fourteenth century, it appeared possible that a parliament would evolve for the entire territory and provincial estates for the various regions, but both types of institutions sank into oblivion during the fourteenth century for reasons that are not altogether clear. Only in the March of Ancona did a representative assembly survive and to it came only the deputies of the towns. As elsewhere, however, the Renaissance saw this assembly mature into a full-fledged institution.[106] "Because of the frequency

103. Marongiu, *Medieval Parliaments*, pp. 109–17, 157–70; Koenigsberger, *Estates and Revolutions*, pp. 80–93; Griffiths, *Representative Government*, pp. 81–117.

104. Marongiu, *Medieval Parliaments*, pp. 154–55. On Alfonso see Alan Ryder, *The Kingdom of Naples under Alfonso the Magnanimous* (Oxford, 1976), pp. 8–9, 124–35.

105. Marongiu, *Medieval Parliaments*, pp. 131–48.

106. Ibid., pp. 117–19, 170–77; Post, *Studies*, pp. 80–90.

of convocations, by the last quarter of the sixteenth century the activities of the congregation [Parliament] developed rapidly, its sphere of competence grew more extensive and its rules of procedure became more explicit."[107]

The Parliament of the county of Friuli in the partriarchate of Aquileia achieved a position of considerable importance in nearly every aspect of government during the fourteenth century. Venice curtailed its political and administrative independence when it annexed the county in 1420. Nevertheless, the Parliament continued to display its capacity to develop administrative organs. In 1475 it created a permanent official, called a *chancellor*, and in 1484 it established a committee of ten "to take over responsibilities for the convocation and composition of the assemblies."[108] Increased taxation led the peasants to organize their own representative assembly during the early years of the sixteenth century, a step that weakened the Parliament but provides another example of how even the lowest elements of society could govern themselves during the Renaissance.[109]

The dukes of Savoy began to convoke the Parliament of Piedmont in the early fourteenth century, although there were precedents for such assemblies. However, not until around the middle of the fifteenth century did the Piedmont Parliament become a powerful force in the government, and during the next hundred years it constantly strengthened its position. Even when the French occupied most of Piedmont in 1536, the situation did not change, for they were anxious to win the loyalty of their new subjects. The French summoned Parliament regularly, and during their rule the deputies began to elect a committee to act in their name when they were not in session. The small portion of Piedmont that remained in the hands of the hereditary dukes also continued to enjoy their assemblies until 1554, when Emmanuel Philibert abandoned the practice because of the difficulty in obtaining funds from his poverty-stricken subjects. In addition to Piedmont the dukes of Savoy dealt with Parliaments in Savoy, Nice, Bugey, Bresse, and the Pays de Vaud. The last two institutions were especially strong. They also convoked assemblies of the third estate in the valley of Aosta and the Marquisate of Saluzzo. The former began to elect a permanent committee to act in its name in 1536 and the latter in 1559 during the period of the French occupation.[110]

In northeastern Italy a parliament was created in the county of Gorizia in the fifteenth century and another one in the county of Gradisca at an undetermined date.[111] In most of northern Italy, however, they were not established, for here the city state was the most common form of government. These cities, which expanded into the countryside during the fourteenth and fifteenth centuries, made no attempt to win the loyalty of their

107. Marongiu, *Medieval Parliaments*, p. 174.
108. Ibid., p. 188.
109. Ibid., pp. 119–23, 177–92.
110. Ibid., pp. 123–27, 196–209; Koenigsberger, *Estates and Revolutions*, pp. 19–79.
111. Marongiu, *Medieval Parliaments*, pp. 210–11.

new subjects by giving them a voice in the government through the use of representative institutions. Rather, the oligarchy that controlled the municipal government tried to hold all power in its hands and govern through traditional local institutions. Even where the "tyrant" supplanted the oligarchy, the treatment of the countryside remained much the same. In the art of governing a territory, most Italian rulers displayed less imagination than the monarchs to the north and the contados were notoriously disloyal to the capital city. When Mantua annexed the marquisate of Montferrat in 1533, it snuffed out the weak Parliament that existed there rather than using it to win the loyalty of the inhabitants as the French did in the lands of the duke of Savoy they occupied three years later.[112]

To the west of France across the English Channel another Parliament slowly emerged. It was only during the reign of Henry VIII that the membership of the House of Lords became determined by hereditary right rather than by royal selection. At the same time the counties and towns in Wales and the palatine of Chester began to send deputies to the Commons; the palatine of Durham did not do so until a century later. In terms of administration and privileges, the English Parliament lagged far behind the national diets in most continental counties and the provincial estates of France. The chancellor presided over the Lords, and the speaker of the Commons was nominated and paid by the crown. Each house had a clerk and a sergeant-at-arms who were also royal appointees and salaried officials, although most of their income was derived from fees for services rendered. These officials appointed clerks and others to assist them and paid them from their own funds. Except for these essentially royal officials, there was no parliamentary bureaucracy. Since no taxes were levied to support parliamentary activities, there was no need for a treasurer. Royal tax collection was handled by others. Parliament had no permanent committee to look after its interests when it was not in session and no lawyer or syndic to plead its cause. The clerk of the Lords was provided with a place to store his records, but the clerk of the Commons had to keep his in his home. Not until the last quarter of the seventeenth century was he assigned a room, hardly an archives, for this purpose. As a result, many documents have been lost; but even if everything had been preserved, the quantity of records prepared would have fallen far below that of one of the great provincial estates of France. By the start of the sixteenth century, it required twenty to forty large folios to inscribe the journal of the estates of Languedoc and by mid-century it sometimes took a hundred. Only at the latter date was the Commons journal born, and for a long period the entries were brief.[113]

112. Ibid., pp. 193–96.
113. Rosslyn K. Gilkes, *The Tudor Parliament* (London, 1969), esp. pp. 34, 67–79, 119–20; John E. Neale, *The Elizabethan House of Commons* (London, 1949), pp. 332–48, 366–67.

The Tudor sovereigns kept a tighter reign on their Parliament than their continental counterparts did. They and their ministers interfered in elections, prepared legislation to be considered before the session opened, placed privy councillors in both houses who played important roles in the debates and committee work, used patronage and intimidation to influence deputies, curtailed freedom of speech, and forbade some subjects to be considered. With the membership of the House of Lords consisting of ecclesiastics they appointed and some nobles they had created, they had one chamber that was steadfastly loyal. Thus the legislation and the taxes they requested were usually voted, and measures they opposed rarely passed both houses. The concept of redress of grievances in return for a financial grant had not become accepted. Elizabeth pocketed the money that was voted and vetoed bills as she wished. Furthermore Parliament voted each new king tunnage and poundage for life. Taken with their large domain and other income, this made the Tudors more independent of parliamentary taxation than any other monarchs in Europe. A frugal king who lived in peace could forgo parliamentary assistance. As a result, summons were less frequent than in most continental countries. Even Elizabeth held only thirteen sessions of Parliament, less than one for every three years of her reign. In France kings had to summon most of the provincial estates at least once a year to provide for their needs.[114]

From the above description Parliament would appear to have been a most unlikely institution to succeed, but there were circumstances that in the long run more than compensated for these shortcomings. In spite of a large number of special rights and liberties, the Norman conquest had made England the most centralized country in Europe. There were no strong provincial loyalties or provincial estates to thwart the will of Parliament as there were in France, the Low Countries, and most other states. The concept of a community of the realm developed early. Although local ties remained strong, when the great struggle with the king took place during the seventeenth century, Parliament did not have to contend with representative assemblies in the various counties that went their separate ways. In England the nobility and gentry paid taxes, a fact that made them more anxious to resist royal exactions than their continental counterparts who generally contributed very little. Hence, although Parliament met infrequently, it did evolve procedures, however slowly. Its members learned to work together, and their committee structure improved. In 1606, almost by accident, they invented the Committee of the Whole House, a device that enabled them to escape the guidance of their royalist speaker. At the same time, the inept Stuart kings paid less attention to parliamentary elections and were less

114. Gilkes, *Tudor Parliament*, pp. 28–33, 53–61, 141–46; Neale, *Elizabethan House of Commons*, pp. 212–60, 282–300, 381.

careful to place able councillors in the Lords and Commons. Under these circumstances the Commons gradually took the initiative and successfully challenged the crown as the mid-seventeenth century approached.[115]

In England then, as on the continent, the Renaissance witnessed the growing role of the people in the government that paralleled the growth of monarchical power. The social classes who participated in this growth varied from one place to another, with even the peasants participating in many localities. Probably only the lower classes in the towns lost ground as a whole, not so much because of the growth of royal authority as because of bourgeois efforts to control municipal governments. German historians have often depicted the age as a dualism in which king and Parliament struggled for predominance. Such a struggle did take place in some states for limited periods of time, but it would be more accurate to describe the Renaissance as a period in which the crown and the estates cooperated. This cooperation enabled strong rulers to emerge in most parts of Europe who did not owe their power to their armies or their bureaucracies. It also gave the representative assemblies time to win established places in the hearts of the people, to develop their procedures, their permanent committees, and their bureaucracies so that they became parallel organs of government. The oft-quoted statement of Henry VIII expressing the unity between the crown and the assemblies could have been made as accurately by Ferdinand of Aragon or for that matter Francis I of France in regard to the estates of their respective kingdoms or provinces: "We at no time stand so highly in our estate royal," Henry told the Commons in 1543, "as in time of Parliament wherein we as head and you as members are conjoined and knit together in one body politic."[116]

---

115. Gilkes, *Tudor Parliament*, pp. 156–76; W. Notestein, "The Winning of the Initiative in the House of Commons," *Proceedings of the British Academy* 11 (1924): 125–75.

116. Alfred F. Pollard, *Henry VIII* (London, 1905), p. 258. For similar statements by Frenchmen, see J. R. Major, *The Estates General of 1560* (Princeton, 1951), pp. 31–37.

II

THE ORIGINS OF ROYAL ABSOLUTISM

THE RENAISSANCE SYSTEM OF GOVERNMENT WORKED ADMIRABLY SO LONG AS the aspirations of the kings and the parliaments were essentially the same. Monarchs such as Henry VIII of England, Ferdinand of Aragon, Francis I of France, and Charles V of the Empire, and for that matter of the better part of Europe, appeared to their contemporaries as being far more powerful than their predecessors, as indeed they were, but during their reigns the parliaments continued to expand their roles in government. Indeed, it was the ability of the rulers to utilize these assemblies that constituted one of the principal sources of their strength. However, during the late sixteenth and seventeenth centuries, the situation changed. The overwhelming desire of the people for order that had contributed so heavily to their willingness to cooperate with their monarchs waned as their memory of the troubles of the late Middle Ages faded. At the same time, two new elements of great importance emerged to disrupt the body politic.

The first of these was the religious revival that began in the fifteenth century, especially in the Low Countries, and slowly spread through Europe. Unhappily for the prospect of continued cooperation between monarch and subject, it led to a revolt against the Catholic church, and numerous Protestant churches emerged. As long as the ruler and the people remained of the same religion, as in Spain, the religious revival caused little difficulty. Furthermore, monarchs on the periphery of Europe, where the religious revival arrived last, found that they could change their religion and that of their subjects with surprising ease. Ultimately, however, all of Europe became more devout. If at this point a significant number of people belonged to one church and their king to another, trouble was likely to occur. Thus before the religious revival became firmly planted in England, the Tudors had little difficulty in changing the state religion, but once the people had become deeply religious, they met strong opposition. Even Elizabeth had trouble restraining the Puritans, and her less competent successors failed miserably in their efforts to do so.

The second new element that disrupted the body politic was a constitutional crisis. The rapid inflation of the late sixteenth century placed a severe strain on the kings. If their Parliaments refused to vote additional taxes, they either had to order that levies be made without consent or to economize. The situation worsened during the seventeenth century when most monarchs became involved in the Thirty Years War and those of Louis XIV. Armies became much larger, and the costs of equipping soldiers multiplied with the advent of uniforms, barracks, and more expensive weapons. As the inflationary spiral ceased, the economy of most of Europe became stagnant or actually declined. Under such circumstances, a monarch who could not extract more money from his Parliament was left with a choice of breaking its power and levying taxes without consent or of abandoning his aggressive policies, thereby leaving his kingdom at the mercy of wealthier foes.

In determining the outcome of the struggle that ensued, the human element was very important. An able king might postpone the constitutional crisis and ultimately contribute much toward resolving it in favor of the monarchy when it came. In the same manner, a great opposition leader, a Cromwell, might enhance the chances that the king would be defeated. Actually able rulers in two states, Savoy and Bavaria, solved their constitutional problems before they reached crisis proportion. Duke Emmanuel Philibert seized upon the fact that the three estates of Piedmont had cooperated with the French when they had occupied his lands during the Italian wars to justify discontinuing their assemblies in 1560. He did permit the nobles to keep their syndics and the towns and communities to assemble in many of his domains, but henceforth he set the amount of taxes that were to be paid without seeking consent.[1] In Bavaria the three estates had slowly lost ground during the sixteenth century, but it remained for the ambitious Maximilian I to reduce them to a semidormant state a little before the Thirty Years War.[2] But France had no gifted rulers, and what might have been a manageable situation if a Ferdinand of Aragon or an Elizabeth of England had sat upon the throne became a revolutionary one under the last of the Valois.

---

1. Helmut G. Koenigsberger, *Estates and Revolutions: Essays in Early Modern European History* (Ithaca, 1971), pp. 72–79. F. Hildesheimer, "Nice au XVIIe siècle: institutions locales et vie urbaine," *BEC* 133 (1975): 43–44.

2. Francis L. Carsten, *Princes and Parliaments in Germany* (Oxford, 1959), pp. 357–406.

8

THE PROVINCIAL ESTATES DURING THE WARS OF RELIGION

IN JULY 1559 HENRY II WAS ACCIDENTALLY KILLED IN A TOURNAMENT HELD IN honor of his daughter's marriage to Philip II of Spain. His successor, the fifteen-year-old Francis II, was a weak, unhealthy lad who was heavily influenced by his beautiful wife, the ill-fated Mary, queen of Scots, who in turn was guided by her Guise uncles. When Francis died in December 1560, the throne passed to Charles IX, a minor. His mother, Catherine de Medici, became regent and continued to be the principal directing force in the government after the weak-willed Charles became of age. Charles in turn died in May 1574 while still in his twenties and was succeeded by his brother, Henry III. Henry was more intelligent than his immediate predecessors, but he had an unstable character that prevented him from taking concerted action for long periods of time and from attracting support to the monarchy. After a trouble-filled reign of fifteen years, he was assassinated in July 1589, and the Valois dynasty came to an end.

With such monarchs as heads of state, it is scarcely surprising that France soon found itself in chaos. Calvin had begun to send missionaries to France in 1555, and by 1559 they had won so many converts that they secretly held a national synod in Paris. The following year Admiral Coligny publicly proclaimed that there were 2,150 Protestant churches and communities in the country. To many it appeared likely that within a year or two France would become predominantly Calvinist. What made the Calvinists so dangerous was not only their splendid organization at the local, provincial, and national level and their dedicated missionary spirit but also their close ties to the nobility. From the late 1550s increasingly large numbers of nobles joined the new church. Threatened as the early Protestant churches were, they put themselves under the protection of sympathetic local magnates. Soon Louis, prince of Condé, became the leader and protector of the movement at the national level. Although a man of relatively limited means in spite of his exalted birth, he was able to attract a large number of adherents. Thus part of the warrior class of the nation became allied with a dynamic religious movement.

Some of the nobles who joined Condé were sincere converts to the new faith, but many, like the young prince himself, were motivated more by ambition, greed, the desire for fame, and the love of adventure than by religious zeal. Unhappily, the crown was unable to satisfy the demands of these restless spirits. Henry II and Philip II had terminated the Italian wars in 1559 as much because they both were bankrupt as because they desired to exterminate heresy in their domains. As a result, there were numerous unemployed soldiers in France and a limited amount of patronage to dispense. A wise monarch would have divided his favors evenly among the magnates to keep them and their clients content, but after the death of Henry II, the Guise used their influence with their niece, Queen Mary, to take control of royal patronage and distribute what posts there were to their followers. From April through June 1560 no positions were awarded at the behest of the rival Bourbon and Montmorency families. When Francis II died that December, the control of the patronage passed to Catherine de Medici. Catherine tried to keep various factions at court by distributing the limited number of royal favors more equitably.[1] At the same time she sought to resolve the religious problem by holding a colloquy at Poissy in which she hoped that Catholic and Protestant would agree on a definition of faith. She also held meetings of the Estates General at Orléans and Pontoise that were intended to reduce popular discontent by introducing reforms and to solve the crown's financial problems by approving a new tax. Her plan failed except that the thoroughly frightened Catholic clergy agreed to contribute a considerable sum to pay the crown's debts.

Meanwhile the rapid growth of Calvinism drove the Catholic branch of the powerful Montmorency family into the arms of the equally devout Guise. Condé, the other disaffected nobles, and the Protestants also grew closer together. In March 1562 the duke of Guise massacred some Protestants who were illegally holding church services at Vassy and took the royal family into "protective custody." Condé in turn raised an army to "rescue" the king. Those who answered his call were rarely his vassals, but they took an oath not only to obey him but also "to hold ourselves in readiness as far as we are able in money, arms, and horses, and other required things, ... to accompany him wherever he commands, and to render him faithful service."[2] This document, which might be called a collective indenture, tied Protestant and other disaffected nobles to Condé in a sort of patron-client relationship and ushered in the Wars of Religion.

The first war lasted for less than a year, and the peace that followed was preserved until the latter half of 1567. Three years of almost continual warfare followed, but a peace was made in August 1570 that was to be sealed two years later by the marriage of Henry of Navarre and Marguerite of Valois, the king's sister. It was during this festive occasion when the

1. Robert C. Harding, *Anatomy of a Power Elite: The Provincial Governors of Early Modern France* (New Haven, 1978), pp. 34–35, 383.

2. J. R. Major, "The Crown and the Aristocracy in Renaissance France," *American Historical Review* 69 (1964): 637.

Huguenot chieftains were gathered in Paris that the massacre of Saint Bartholomew occurred. Catherine probably hoped that by exterminating their leaders she would destroy the capacity of the Huguenots to resist, but she only made the members of the rival religion more irreconcilable. There was a brief war followed by a precarious peace. Then in 1576 the situation worsened; Henry of Navarre fled from the court and resumed leadership of the Huguenots. The Catholics formed the League to defend their church. Again, a truce was called after another brief war, but the situation became still more serious in 1584 when the last son of Catherine died, leaving Henry of Navarre heir to the throne. The Guise signed a treaty with Philip II of Spain in January 1585 to obtain financial assistance for the defense of the Catholic religion. The war now deepened into a long bloody conflict. Henry III had the duke of Guise assassinated in December 1588 during the meeting of the Estates General of Blois. He hoped that this desperate act would enable him to reassert control over the Catholics, but the reverse happened. Guise's brother, the duke of Mayenne, became the new League leader, and the ultra-Catholic reaction was so strong that Henry was driven into an alliance with Navarre. Then, in July 1589 he himself was murdered, leaving Navarre king by hereditary right but with only the Protestants and some politically minded Catholics to assist him in making good his claim to the throne. For four years Navarre tried to do so without success. Finally in July 1593 he took the perilous leap and once more became a convert to Catholicism. Slowly the League leaders began to rally to his cause, but the war was not terminated until 1598 when the last of their number recognized him as king and peace was made with Spain.

From this brief account it can be seen that although France was a troubled country throughout the eight wars that were fought between 1562 and 1598, it was not until after the 1567–70 conflicts and still more after the massacre of 1572 that the situation became critical and not until after 1588 that the country sank into anarchy. With this rough chronology in mind, it is now necessary to see how the estates fared during the long struggle.

1. The Estates of Burgundy

The early stages of the Wars of Religion brought no significant changes in the relations between the crown and the estates in Burgundy, but beginning in 1569, the king's expectation that the inhabitants would pay the expenses of troops passing through the province began to cause trouble. The élus had little recourse but to furnish some money on such occasions, or the soldiers would take what they needed. They sought, however, to reimburse the province by deducting the amount assigned to the troops from the sum the estates had already voted the king for that year. If they failed, they had to increase the levy beyond that granted by the estates to make good the amount given the military, an act that in effect circumvented the right to give consent. Added to this difficulty was the expense of maintaining a garrison, which the Burgundians argued that they did not need in spite of their frontier position.[3]

By 1576 the Burgundians were losing their complacency. The king had made what seemed to them an unnecessarily generous peace with the Protestants, an act that they thoroughly disapproved both because they were overwhelmingly Catholic and because they were asked to pay part of the costs of the concessions that had been made. In this frame of mind the élus steadfastly refused to make any advances to pay the unwanted garrison, and the three estates backed their decision when they met. This done, the Burgundians deputed to court where they won a conspicuous victory by securing a 50 percent reduction in the taillon for that year.[4]

The crown and the estates once more clashed in 1577. Henry III had determined on a war to crush the Protestants and had put himself at the head of the newly formed Catholic League largely because he hoped to use it as an instrument to persuade people to accept higher taxes and to provide troops. The Burgundian towns were asked for a special contribution and the province as a whole for 3,000 infantry and 800 horse, a burden the inhabitants had little inclination to bear, especially because their deputies to the Estates General at Blois the previous year had counseled conversion by persuasion rather than by war. Neither the individual towns nor the bailiwick assemblies of the third estate were willing to contribute anything or to join the League as the king had directed. In a special meeting of the three estates at Dijon in June, the nobility joined the representatives of the towns in their refusal to take the oath to the League or to contribute to a general war against the Protestants. All the three estates would do was to raise the salt tax enough for one year to provide 40,000 livres to support 400 arquebusiers who were to remain in the province for its defense. These troops were to be commanded by captains the estates named, and the money to pay them was to be kept in the hands of their officials. As an additional check, the estates forbad the élus to make any advances on future taxes. Again they had clearly won a victory, and Henry III, seeing that the League could not be turned into an instrument to further his designs, abandoned it and made peace with the Protestants.[5]

Blocked once more by the three estates, Henry placed increased reliance on measures that escaped their direct control, such as duties on exports, alienating the royal domain in spite of the opposition expressed by the Estates General at Blois, and creating new offices to sell. Included among the last was a Bureau of Finances, which was authorized by an edict in July

---

3. J.-L. Gay, "Fiscalité, royale et Etats généraux de Bourgogne 1477–1589," in *Etudes sur l'histoire des assemblées d'états*, ed. François Dumont (Paris, 1966), pp. 201–03.

4. Henri Drouot, *Notes sur la Bourgogne et son esprit public au début du règne de Henri III, 1574–1579* (Dijon, 1937), pp. 80–82.

5. Ibid., pp. 98–118; Gay, "Fiscalité," pp. 203–04.

1577. The bureau posed a threat to the autonomy of the financial officials of the estates, as well as to the pocketbook of the people who were expected to pay the salaries of the treasurers. It was these measures, and not the intrigues of the Guise, as has been suggested, that led to the recalcitrant attitude of the estates in their regular triannual meeting, which was held at Dijon in May 1578.[6]

When the assembly opened, the royal commissioner asked for a large contribution, but after three days of deliberations behind closed doors, the estates dispatched a deputation to the king to protest the extraordinary taxes and the failure to implement the decisions reached at the Estates General at Blois. They then prorogued the meeting until their deputies returned without voting the customary taille for three years. On August 1 the three estates reassembled to hear the deputies' report, but the king had not given specific replies to all of their proposals so they disbanded without voting any taxes. On October 31 the estates met for the third time that year. On this occasion the king's commissioner brought satisfactory replies to most of their requests, and the estates voted the traditional 50,000 livres per year for three years on the condition that all extraordinary taxes would cease and that the newly created offices would be abolished. As the Parlement of Dijon had already verified an edict on the salt tax, the matter was still not settled, and deputies were once more sent to court. This time the Burgundians were probably joined by the equally irate deputies from Normandy and Brittany. The combined pressure from the provincial estates, plus his mother's advice that more could be gained by conciliation than by obstinacy, finally led Henry to give in. The estates once more emerged victorious.[7]

It is perhaps unfortunate that the three estates were too distrustful of the king to meet him halfway when they again assembled in March 1579. His commissioner pleaded with them to contribute toward paying his debts, but amid expressions of good intentions, they insisted that his debts be verified and that the other provincial estates join with them in a plan for common action.[8] In 1580 the desperate king sought to impose a tax on the sale of wine and to persuade the closed towns to contribute to the support of an army of 50,000 men. The three estates offered to increase the tax on salt in return for being perpetually freed from the wine tax, but they balked at paying their alloted share for the troops. When the king asked for 1,000 military engineers, the nobility and clergy offered 300, but the third estate flatly refused to give anything.[9]

The three estates met again in the spring of 1581 to vote the taille for three

6. Drouot, *Notes sur la Bourgogne*, pp. 120–35.

7. Ibid., pp. 135–49; *Journal de Gabriel Breunot*, ed. Joseph Garnier (Dijon, 1864), 1:243–44; *IAD, Côte-d'Or, sér. C*, ed. Joseph Garnier (Dijon, 1886), 3:117–18; G. Weill, "Les Etats de Bourgogne sous Henri III," *Mém. de la soc. bourguignonne de géographie et d'histoire* 9 (1893): 124–27.

8. AD, Côte-d'Or, C 3016, fols. 4–9; Weill, "Les Etats de Bourgogne," pp. 128–29.

9. AD, Côte-d'Or, C 3016, fols. 29v–38; Weill, "Les Etats de Bourgogne," pp. 129–30.

years. The king asked for 120,000 livres per year, but they were willing to give only the traditional 50,000. They also complained of the cost of supporting troops in the province and asked that newly created offices be suppressed. They were not so parsimonious, however, as to fail to vote their governor 16,000 livres, their lieutenant general 8,000 livres, and their respective secretaries 150 livres each. Also not forgotten were the first president of the Parlement of Dijon and the king's secretary of state, who was responsible for Burgundy.[10]

The extraordinary sessions of the estates had netted so little that Henry abandoned the practice of calling them, and the next meeting of the estates was held in 1584 at the expiration of the three-year grant made in 1581. This time the third estate protested against giving even the usual 50,000 livres. After some debate the slightly more generous sentiments of the nobility and clergy prevailed. The usual amount was voted, but the king was asked to be content with less because of the poverty of the province. Other taxes were protested, as was the creation of new offices. Efforts were made to control the treasurers in the Bureau of Finances and to prevent the royal representatives in the Chambres des Elus from taking action on important matters without summoning the élus of the estates.[11] Denied access to additional taxes in spite of war and inflation, the hard-pressed monarch increased his reliance on the creation of offices, the ennoblement of wealthy citizens who were willing to pay for the honor, and taxes (such as the customs) that escaped the direct control of the estates. The three estates protested all these measures when they met in May 1587 for the final time during the reign and even carried the attack by asking that the Bureau of Finances be abolished and that merchants not be permitted to become royal officials because it diverted them from trade. Once more they voted the traditional 50,000 livres for three years.[12]

Contrary to one authority's statement, the three estates did not steadily lose ground during Henry III's reign.[13] It is true that the king continued to create new offices in spite of their protests, that they were vulnerable during the three-year intervals between their sessions, and that they occasionally disagreed among themselves, especially over the question of whether the consent of all three orders was necessary for the approval of a tax. To counter these weaknesses the three estates branded those who invented new offices as "the sworn enemies of all the province."[14] They repeatedly instructed the élus to levy no taxes without their consent and sought to obtain permission for the élus to convoke all or at least some of their number when emergencies arose. In this last they were not successful, but by remaining on good terms

10. AD, Côte-d'Or, C 3016, esp. fols. 47–54, 57–61v.
11. Ibid., esp. fols. 94v–97v, 101–03, 117, 127–29.
12. Ibid., esp. fols. 135–42v, 168v–70.
13. Weill, "Les Etats de Bourgogne," p. 132.
14. Ibid., p. 133.

with the royal officials responsible for Burgundian affairs and with the relevant sovereign courts through generous presents and other considerations, they were able to hold their own.[15]

It was inevitable that most Burgundians would opt for the League. The trend in this direction was accelerated when news of the assassination of the duke of Guise arrived during the last few days of December 1588, and the Protestant Henry IV's ascension to the throne some months later drove them further into its arms. The province was overwhelmingly Catholic. Its governors since 1543 had been members of the house of Guise. The current incumbent, the duke of Mayenne, had held the post since 1573. Although a colorless figure who had only recently begun to establish close ties with the Burgundians, he quickly won substantial support, especially in the towns. Nevertheless most of the higher clergy had a lukewarm attitude toward him, and a large part of the nobility retained their royalist sentiment.

The bulk of the members of the sovereign courts sided with the Catholic League, but a small minority abandoned Dijon and established royalist tribunals. The provincial estates also became divided. The first to be convoked were those of the League. Here the initiative was taken by the Council of the Holy Union at Dijon, a pro-League organization consisting primarily of members of the sovereign courts, municipal officials of that town, and a few ecclesiastics and captains. The members of this council attempted to direct the League movement in Burgundy, and in August 1589 they convoked an extraordinary meeting of the estates without first obtaining the consent of the cardinal of Bourbon, whom they acknowledged as their king although he was a captive of the Protestants, or of Mayenne, who doubled as lieutenant general of the kingdom and their governor. The meeting, which opened in Dijon on August 21, was obviously designed in part to rally waverers to the League by summoning them to recognize the cardinal of Bourbon as their king and Mayenne as his lieutenant general. A second purpose of the meeting was to raise troops, a project toward which the fourteen nobles and fourteen clergymen who attended agreed that their order should contribute.[16]

The League also sponsored the regular triannual meetings of the estates in 1590 and 1593 and another extraordinary session in 1592. On the first occasion those assembled voted to grant the traditional taille of 50,000 livres per year for three years and to continue to support the military effort. The customary gifts were also made. In 1592 the estates were less generous and voted only 75,000 livres of the 180,000 requested by the League leaders for the war. The following year the estates again sought to limit their contributions to the war by setting a maximum of 135,000 livres that could be levied for that purpose. They also refused to vote the customary taille

15. AD, Côte-d'Or, C 3016 passim.
16. Henri Drouot, *Mayenne et la Bourgogne* (Paris, 1937), 1:367–72, 2:41–58.

because of the poverty of the province. Mayenne was asked to revoke any gifts he had made that were charged to the province, but he himself and the other officials were given their usual presents.[17]

The royalists held the regular triannual meeting of the estates at Semur in May 1590 where they too voted a taille of 50,000 livres per year for three years, a levy to support the garrisons in the towns, and the customary gifts to their governors and other influential persons. There was no meeting of the royalist estates in 1593. Henry IV authorized their convocation early that year, and meetings were actually called at least three times prior to the restoration of peace in Burgundy, but the assembly was postponed on each occasion. There were, however, some assemblies of the élus with other notable persons. Under these circumstances the élus appointed in 1590 continued to function although their commission from the estates expired at the end of three years as they pointedly reminded the king in October 1594. During this period, taxes continued to be collected to support the military, but the élus were not merely rubber stamps. They frequently reduced the size of the taxes and loans the crown requested, fought against the creation of new offices, and refused to support a company in July 1594 in spite of the direct orders of the king. They were equally adamant against surrendering the tax rolls to the royalist lieutenant general because to do so would imperil their control over the tax-collecting machinery. Finally they rejected numerous proposals that they pay for garrisons in private châteaux.[18]

In spite of the efforts of both the League and the royalist estates, the need to prosecute the war and, more important, to provide for their own defense often made it necessary to levy extraordinary taxes or to borrow. Faced with an emergency situation, the League chiefs proved even less merciful than the king, and that part of Burgundy they controlled contributed about four times as much in 1590–92 as the entire province had in 1584–86 when Henry III was their master. Furthermore many towns had to go deeply into debt in order to provide for their defense. Hence all but the most adamant Leaguers must have been relieved to see peace restored to the province by the close of the summer of 1595. Here as elsewhere Henry recognized the privileges of the towns as well as of the province as a whole in return for being accepted as king. By January 8, 1596, calm had been sufficiently restored for the three estates, now reunited, to meet once more.[19]

---

17. AD, Côte-d'Or, C 3016, esp. fols. 212–13, 230v–31, 266–70, 276–77v; Drouot, *Mayenne,* 2:59–61, 269–72; *Journal de Breunot,* 1:84–85; Hippolyte Abord, *Histoire de la Réforme et la Ligue dans la ville d'Autun* (Autun, 1881), 2:147–51, 287–88, 369–71.

18. M. Wilkinson, "A Provincial Assembly during the League," *Transactions of the Royal Historical Society,* 3d series, 9 (1915): 71–74; *Recherches sur la Ligue en Bourgogne,* ed. H. Drouot and L. Gros (Dijon, 1914), pp. 49–69, 85, 89–92, 96, 155, 163–64, 178–80; Abord, *Histoire de la Réforme,* 2:108–11, 258–61.

19. Drouot, *Mayenne,* 2:104–13, 443–62.

2. THE ESTATES OF NORMANDY

The wealthy but overtaxed province of Normandy embraced Protestantism to a greater degree than any other region north of the Loire River. Lower Normandy and its capital, Caen, and the lesser nobility were especially susceptible to the new religion. As a result, the Religious Wars were at times bitter here. Rouen itself was sacked in 1562, and numerous lesser places suffered.[20]

Despite the turbulence in the province, the estates met annually in the fall during the reigns of Francis II and Charles IX. Protestants were soon excluded from the deliberations, and petitions to the king asked for more severe measures against them, but little of significance took place concerning the three estates. Not until the reign of Henry III did they have major confrontations with the crown.[21]

On June 17, 1574, shortly after the death of Charles IX and before Henry III had returned from Poland, Catherine de Medici ordered that an additional 100,000 livres be levied on the province without consulting the estates, an act she justified by the need to pay the troops. The reaction of the officials of the estates and of the estates themselves when they met in November is not known, but perhaps this act contributed to the decision of the estates that met in October 1576 to respond unfavorably to a royal request for a total of 1,391,140 livres. Following his mother's example, Henry countered by ordering the élus to collect the tax anyway.[22]

Little is known of what took place when the Norman estates met in 1577 beyond that Henry asked for the same sum as before. There may have been considerable friction because of his attempts to raise additional funds by the sale of offices and patents of nobility. Such acts angered the Normans almost as much as an attempt to increase taxes would have done. This was especially true because the need for large sums was not apparent at that moment, for the country was in a state of relative peace and the crown had done little to implement the reforms suggested by the Estates General that had met at Blois in 1576–77.[23]

In 1578 some Burgundians invited the Normans to cooperate in an effort to compel the crown to reduce taxes and introduce reforms. Perhaps it was for this reason that the crown anticipated difficulty when the Norman estates

---

20. Michel de Boüard, ed., *Histoire de la Normandie* (Toulouse, 1970), pp. 362–68.

21. Henri Prentout, *Les Etats provinciaux de Normandie* (Caen, 1925), 1:284–99. For documents see *Cahiers des Etats de Normandie sous le règne de Charles IX*, ed. Charles de Robillard de Beaurepaire (Rouen, 1891).

22. *Letters de Catherine de Médicis*, ed. Hector de la Ferrière (Paris, 1895), 5:21; *Cahiers des Etats de Normandie sous le règne de Henri III*, ed. Charles de Robillard de Beaurepaire (Rouen, 1887), 1:238, 247–48; Prentout, *Les Etats provinciaux*, 1:301–02.

23. Prentout, *Les Etats provinciaux*, 1:303–304; *Cahiers sous Henri III*, 1:222–28, 240–45, 287–95.

met in November 1578. Pomponne de Bellièvre, a trusted councillor and president in the Parlement of Paris, was dispatched to Normandy to add his persuasive talents to those of the regular commissioners. His speech before the estates on November 19 was conciliatory, although he did warn the deputies not to follow the example of those in some other provinces who had failed to render the obedience they owed the king. It was reported that when Bellièvre departed, he was satisfied, but if this was so he must soon have altered his opinion. In a brief but strongly worded cahier, the estates asked that taxes be reduced to the amount levied during the reign of Louis XII, that useless offices be abolished, that the recommendations of the Estates General of Blois be implemented, and that their privileges be respected.[24]

Catherine de Medici expressed disappointment at the actions of the estates but recommended to her son that concessions be made. Henry followed her advice when he gave his reply to the deputation the Normans sent to court. He could not limit taxes to the amount collected during the reign of Louis XII, he explained, because of his pressing needs, but he canceled a levy that was to fall on the clergy and held out the hope that there would be some reduction in the taille. He also promised to respect their privileges, reduce the garrison, and suppress some offices provided the estates would reimburse the occupants. Finally, at the request of the deputies, he directed the estates to meet again in March 1579.[25]

Henry ordered his officials to begin to collect the taille before the estates met, but he and Catherine did everything else they could to placate the Normans. They dispatched an agent to explain the fiscal needs of the crown to municipal officials, reduced the amount of the taille, promised further cuts to regions that had suffered most from troops, speeded work on an ordonnance based on the cahiers of the Estates General of 1576, and sent the duke of Montmorency and Bellièvre to attend the estates in the the expectation that the prestige of the former would add weight to the royal proposals.[26]

Bellièvre advised the king that it would be necessary to reduce taxes in order to avoid trouble, and his advice was heeded. When he appeared before the estates in March, he was able to report that the king would be satisfied with 100,000 fewer livres than originally demanded. Cajoled by Bellièvre and Montmorency, the estates proceeded to vote substantially more than Louis XII had ever exacted from them, though still less than the king desired. When the deputies brought the cahier to court, Henry reduced his demands by another 20,000 livres and gave favorable replies to most of their

24. *Cahiers sous Henri III*, 1:5–8, 307–308, 315–17; Prentout, *Les Etats provinciaux*, 1:304–16; BN, ms. fr. 3389, fols. 77–79, 91–96.

25. *Lettres de Catherine de Médicis*, 6:153, 155, 159, 177–78, 199, 201–02, 273–74; *Cahiers sous Henri III*, 1:8–13; Prentout, *Les Etats provinciaux*, 1:316–19; 3:189–90.

26. Prentout, *Les Etats provinciaux*, 1:319–20, 3:189–90; *Lettres de Catherine de Médicis*, 6:266–67, 297 n.; *Cahiers sous Henri III*, 1:327–28, 2:341–43; BN ms. fr. 15,905, fols. 4–6, 10–14v.

other requests. Included was a promise not to levy any taxes without assembling the estates.[27]

The offensive of the three estates did fall short of its goal in one important respect. In article 27 of their cahier, they had asked that they and other elected representatives of the people be permitted to apportion and collect taxes. All royal tax officials were to be suppressed. Henry sidestepped this revolutionary suggestion by stating that "for the present he could not undertake such a change and new order." Then, pretending to believe that the estates had been motivated only by the inequality of the present assessments, he promised to dispatch "some men of honor and great authority" to Normandy to establish good order in the collection of taxes. In spite of this rebuff, the confrontation of 1578–79 had ended in a victory for the estates.[28]

On September 1, 1579, Catherine de Medici advised Henry to attend the estates of Normandy that fall because his presence would be of infinite value, but he failed to heed her advice and substituted arbitrary will for persuasion. When his commissioners were unable to cajole the estates into voting more than the usual sum, they ordered the tax officials to begin to levy the requested amount in six weeks anyway, unless in the intervening time the estates could persuade the king to take less. Thus the right to consent to taxes was transformed into the right to ask for a reduction in taxes, although Henry III had confirmed the Norman privileges that very year.[29] Important as it was, the immediate significance of this development should not be exaggerated. In the past when the three estates and the commissioners had not reached an agreement on the size of the tax, it had been customary for the former to dispatch deputies to the king to plead their cause. The new procedure limited the amount of time that the deputies had to present their case, a stipulation that did not seem to cause concern because in the following year the estates made no protest. Indeed Henry's primary motive may have been to limit the time that negotiations could delay the initial steps being taken to apportion taxes.[30]

The critical question posed by the new procedure was whether the king would order that a larger tax be levied than the deputies could be persuaded to accept without calling a special meeting of the estates. The estates that

27. Edmund H. Dickerman, *Bellièvre and Villeroy* (Providence, 1971), p. 48; Prentout, *Les Etats provinciaux*, 1:319–22; *Cahiers sous Henri III*, 1:19–21, 55, 329–33, 344–49. The estates also persuaded Henry to stay a commission to reform the eaux et forêts that had been given to a Jean Bodin of Paris. Ibid., 2:34–35, 346–47. Bodin persisted in his efforts to execute his commission in spite of the protests of the estates. Ibid., 1:65; 2:50–51, 85–86, 133–34, 154.

28. *Cahiers sous Henri III*, 1:39–40.

29. *Letters de Catherine de Médicis*, 7:115, 201–202. *Cahiers sous Henri III*, 1: esp. 71–78, 126–29, 359–72.

30. It should be remembered that Normandy contributed about a fifth of the royal taxes. It was therefore very desirable to avoid delays in implementing the tax collection.

met in November 1580 recognized this fact and pointedly asked the king to levy only taxes that they voted. If an emergency arose, they requested that those who had participated in the previous meeting be assembled, a procedure that would avoid the delay of holding new elections, or as a minimum that the deputies to court and the syndic be summoned. The king promised to adhere to their request except in case of "urgent necessity."[31] In 1583 and again in 1584 the estates asked that meetings be held by the middle of October in order to have ample time to present their petition to the king before the first of the year when the apportionment of the taille had to take place.[32]

The trouble with this arrangement was that Henry was always confronted with "urgent necessity" in the 1580s. The commissioners and the estates could not reach an agreement on the size of the tax in any of the meetings between 1580 and 1587, and probably not in 1588, the final meeting during the reign, although there are insufficient data to be certain. In each of these years the three estates sent deputies to court to plead their cause. Invariably Henry expressed his sympathy, but except in 1584 when he granted a rebate of 152,445 livres, he ordered that the entire sum be collected without their consent. The only other financial concession that he granted was in 1585 when he agreed to allocate a portion of the tax to reimburse officials who had purchased offices that the estates wanted abolished.[33]

A dangerous precedent had been established, yet it is improbable that Henry III intended to undermine the estates. He continued to summon them annually and was willing to confirm the Norman charter when requested. The difficulty was that in his mind the doctrine of urgent necessity took precedence over the privileges of the province and any promise that he might make. He used this and comparable phrases constantly when he rejected the requests of the estates for tax relief. In other respects many of the efforts of the estates bore fruit. They reformed the custom, provided more adequate support for the University of Caen, and discharged their syndic over the opposition of the royal commissioners. As an institution they were still very much alive when Henry III fell before an assassin in 1589.[34]

The assassination of the duke of Guise, followed by that of Henry III some months later, left Normandy in turmoil. Quickly the province became a battleground between the principal armies of the leading protagonists. Both Henry IV and the League attempted to hold meetings of the estates near the close of 1589. The latter may never have taken place, and the former had to

31. *Cahiers sous Henri III*, 1:104.

32. Ibid., 2:64, 94–95.

33. Ibid., 1:170, 183–93, 2:23, 30–31, 69–73, 101–05, 143–47, 192–202, 231–35, 298, 302. Prentout, *Les Etats provinciaux*, 1:332–33, 2:153–54, fails to mention all these concessions.

34. Prentout, *Les Etats provinciaux*, 1:322–31, 334–35, 2:383–86.

be postponed until April of the following year because of the military situation. This assembly was marred by the usual quarrels over precedence, but no information survives concerning what Henry requested or how much money the estates granted. For the next two and one-half years, the war precluded the possibility of holding a meeting. As a result, during 1591, 1592, and 1593 taxes were levied by whoever happened to control this or that locality without the consent of the estates and perhaps even without the orders of the king or the League chief.[35]

3. THE ESTATES OF BRITTANY

Because the Protestants found few adherents in Brittany, the province was relatively peaceful until the assassination of the duke of Guise in December 1588 pitted Leaguer against royalist and both Spain and England sent troops to intervene. The absence of armed conflict until the last decade of the wars did not mean that the Bretons escaped altogether, for they were confronted with ever-increasing demands from the crown to provide financial assistance to support the royal cause in other provinces.

In 1562 during the first of the Wars of Religion, Catherine de Medici tried to extract a forced loan and a tax on the closed towns from the Bretons without waiting for the estates to meet. The governor protested but did manage to collect some money.[36] When the emergency passed, the government returned to more orthodox practices. It readily consulted the three estates when it sought the necessary money to redeem the mortgaged royal domain. After long negotiations it was agreed that the estates would contribute 500,000 livres for this purpose over a five-year period provided that the king would limit the other charges on the province to the amount levied under Louis XII. The arrangement proved unsatisfactory to both sides. The king demanded that the three estates, which met in September 1567, pay the remaining 140,000 livres that they owed the following year and that they cease levying taxes for their own purposes without permission. The estates countered by charging that the crown had not kept its part of the bargain and had violated the privileges of the province. The situation was undoubtedly aggravated by the fact that the syndic and the treasurer of the estates had been arrested the preceding year on false charges that they had misappropriated some of the funds to redeem the domain. The estates secured their release, but only after their archives had been taken to Paris so that the records of the case could be verified. The most lamentable result of

---

35. *Cahiers des Etats de Normandie sous le règne de Henry IV*, ed. Charles de Robillard de Beaurepaire (Rouen, 1880), 1:201–10; Prentout, *Les Etats provinciaux*, 1:335–37.

36. *Documents pour servir à l'histoire des guerres civiles en France, 1561–1563*, ed. A. Lublinskaya (Moscow, 1962), pp. 101, 110–15, 125–27, 135–37; Harding, *Anatomy*, p. 101.

the episode was that the archives were never returned, and today we have a continuous series of journals of the estates only from 1567.[37]

The estates that met in November 1568 were again faced with the demand that the remaining 140,000 livres be paid. After pointedly reminding the king that taxes had not been reduced as promised and that actually only 40,000 livres was needed to redeem the rest of the domain, they voted that the entire amount the king requested be paid over a period of two years provided that other taxes were reduced to the amount levied at the time of Louis XII.[38]

The estates that met in 1569 and 1570 were relatively uneventful. The king complained about his financial needs, but requested only the traditional sums. The three estates, on the other hand, voiced concern that taxes had not been rolled back to the amount levied by Louis XII, but met the royal demands and gave generous presents for their governor and other royal officials who were in a position to provide them assistance. Also noteworthy was the decision to seek permission to increase the costs of holding the estates from 800 to 3,000 livres.[39]

In April 1571 Charles IX bypassed the estates and directed the judges and other royal officials to apportion a tax of 300,000 livres on the Breton towns and bourgades to pay their share of the sum owed to the foreign troops who had been employed in the late war. It was certainly to the advantage of the Frenchmen as a whole to rid the kingdom of these troublemakers, but the royal directive was in direct violation of the privileges of the estates. Furthermore few (if any) of the offending troops were in the province. In consequence, there was a loud outcry, and the king had to convoke a special meeting of the estates in May. After some debate the estates awarded only 120,000 livres to the hard-pressed king and resumed the offensive during the regular meeting of the estates that September by asking that the garrison in the province be disbanded.[40]

Charles refused to accept this situation and convoked another special session of the estates to meet in March 1572 to vote the remainder of the 300,000 livres he had previously requested, as well as an additional sum to redeem the domain. As an enticement, he offered to permit the estates to raise the money as they saw fit and suggested that it could be done without increasing the amount the towns would pay by a combination of borrowing, placing an export tax on wheat, creating offices to sell, and other measures. As a further inducement Charles offered to permit the estates to levy 5,000

37. C. de La Lande de Calan, "Documents inédits relatifs aux Etats de Bretagne de 1491 à 1589," *Archives de Bretagne* 15 (1908): pt. 1, 146, 156–58, 169–72, 179–81; Henri Sée, *Les Etats de Bretagne au XVIe siècle* (Paris, 1895), pp. 72–73; Armand Rebillon, *Les sources de l'histoire des Etats de Bretagne* (Paris, 1932), pp. 15–17.

38. La Lande de Calan, "Documents inédits relatifs;" pt. 1, 195–96.

39. Ibid., pp. 197–219.

40. Ibid., pp. 219–28, 233, 235.

livres per year for their own expenses, 2,000 more than they had thought necessary several years before. The nobility and clergy accepted the entire proposal, but the deputies of the third estate refused to make further contributions toward redeeming the domain, although their urban constituents would now escape most of the burden.[41]

The debate concerning the redemption of the domain was renewed during the regular session of the estates in October 1572. This time the privileged orders supported the third estate in its refusal to make further contributions for this purpose. When the royal commissioner expressed dissatisfaction, some of the nobles and all the third estate publicly stated that the mortgage would be paid only if the king replied favorably to their requests. Again, an extraordinary session of the estates was necessary, and this time the king directed the commissioners to levy the tax to redeem the domain even though the three estates refused to give their consent. Faced with this threat the nobility and clergy weakened, but the deputies of the third estate stood firm, although the privileged orders placed the blame on them for any dire consequences that might befall the province.[42]

In spite of these threats the third estate refused to abandon its position, and the meeting disbanded without the commissioners taking any steps to make good their threats. The crown renewed the attempt to get the estates to pay the mortgage on the domain in the regular meeting of the estates in October 1573, but the deputies of the third would go no further than to agree that a committee could be appointed to look into the matter. By the following spring, Charles IX had become more concerned with his desire to raise a large army to crush the Protestants. He called a special session of the estates to ask for a grant of 90,000 livres but was met with the refusal of the now united estates to offer anything. Charles immediately convoked a second extraordinary meeting and this time was able to obtain a grant of 60,000 livres to be raised from the towns and bourgades. With this matter out of the way, the regular meeting of the estates, which was held in Nantes in October 1574, was relatively uneventful.[43]

In the period 1571–74 Charles IX had mixed threats with concessions in his effort to obtain more revenue from Brittany. Ultimately, after nine sessions of the estates had been held in a space of less than four years, he had obtained part, but only part, of what he had demanded. Hard-pressed though the three estates were, they had maintained their privileges and had succeeded in reducing the tax burden that would have fallen on the inhabitants had they not existed. Perhaps it was their very success, coupled with the fiscal problem created by war and inflation, that caused the crown to alter its tactics. Instead of holding special meetings of the estates between

41. Ibid., pt. 2, 1–11.
42. Ibid., pp. 11–25. Sée, *Les Etats de Bretagne*, pp. 42–43.
43. La Lande de Calan, "Documents inédits relatifs," pt. 2, 25–60.

the annual fall sessions, Henry III began to order that taxes be levied and forced loans extracted without consent after he came to the throne. The syndic reported to the estates of September 1575 that over 300,000 livres had been raised in this fashion since their previous meeting. Faced with these arbitrary acts, the three estates refused to grant 50,000 livres for the payment of the infantry and directed their officials and those of the towns to resist royal attempts to tax without consent in the future.[44]

In 1576 Henry sought to meet his financial needs by creating new offices in Brittany, ennobling forty persons, and asking for 30,000 livres to recast some cannon. To counter this attack the three estates protested against the new creations and ennoblements and refused to grant the money. In an effort to block any royal effort to levy the the sum anyway, they repeatedly directed provincial officials to resist illegal levies and the creation of new offices they had not authorized. This done, the estates took the offensive by asking the king to relieve them from paying four companies of gendarmes. To muster support for their cause at court, they voted 4,000 livres for the duke of Montpensier, their governor, 4,000 for his wife, and 2,000 for their gentlemen, ladies, secretaries, and servants.[45]

The estates of 1577 continued its predecessors' vigorous protests against royal fiscal policies. Those who attended refused to vote all the funds that the king requested and asked that the gendarmes in the province be removed because they cost over 240,000 livres a year.[46] Under these circumstances the situation was very tense in the fall of 1578 when it was time for the estates to meet. Unfortunately Montpensier's illness led to the postponement of the meeting. About 800 nobles and some other persons gathered at Fougères on October 15 at the time the assembly was to have been held. A rumor was widespread that the crown intended to discontinue the estates and dispatch troops to the province to enforce the collection of taxes. A commissioner sent to Brittany to hold the estates warned the crown that the Bretons were strongly opposed to the troops and had reached an understanding with the other provinces in the kingdom. In order to prevent serious trouble, he recommended that a conciliatory policy be adopted and that if the governor attended the estates, he bring only a small retinue in order not to cause alarm. When the three estates finally met in December, a representative of the crown went to considerable length to dispel the rumor that the government intended to violate their privileges. He was partly successful. Henry III was able to report to his mother that the meeting had gone rather quietly. Nevertheless the three estates voted less than was requested, and the crown sought to placate them further by holding a special meeting the

44. Ibid., pp. 2, 67, 71.
45. Ibid., pp. 79, 81, 86–88, 94–95.
46. Ibid., pp. 96–110.

following March in order to give its responses to their cahier, responses that were more favorable than usual.[47]

The concessions that Henry had granted the estates of Normandy in 1578 had been followed by a crackdown in 1579, but a better fate was in store for the Bretons because they were stronger and less tax revenue was at stake. Catherine de Medici urged Henry to attend the regular meeting of the estates in the fall of 1579 in the belief that his presence would make the deputies more generous. He failed to heed her advice, but in spite of poor health the duke of Montpensier was sent to assure those who assembled of the king's goodwill. To placate the estates still more, Henry requested only 10,000 écus in addition to the traditional levies. The estates, in turn, were more restrained, and although they refused to give the additional money, they did suggest that they would once more contribute to redeem the mortgaged royal domain. The era of limited cooperation continued until 1587 in spite of rumors of unrest and repeated charges by the estates that taxes to support troops in the province were being levied without consent.[48]

The history of Brittany, though not immediately of the estates, entered a new phase in 1582 with the appointment of the duke of Mercoeur as governor. Cousin of the duke of Guise, brother-in-law of Henry III, and, equally important, husband of a claimant of the ducal throne, Mercoeur was in a strong position to chart Brittany on an independent course. The session of the estates he presided over in the fall of 1582 was, however, more favorably disposed toward the crown than most of its predecessors. A special annual grant of 210,000 livres for five years was voted. The king had asked for 258,000, but he could hardly have been dissatisfied with this comparatively generous showing. In addition, the estates offered a large sum in return for the abolition of certain offices and other concessions.[49]

During the next five years there was a relative degree of harmony. The estates made annual complaints about taxes being levied without their consent and offices being created in spite of promises not to do so. Nevertheless the king kept his demands within bounds, and the estates usually gave him most of what he asked. Mercoeur received gifts of from 12,000 to 18,000 livres per year in addition to comparable sums to support his guard, and others profited from less handsome sums voted by the estate.[50] By 1587, however, royal needs had become so great that Henry

---

47. Ibid., pp. 110–36; *Lettres de Catherine de Médicis*, 6:102–04, 125, 155, 233–34, 403–04. The estates of 1580 voted the commissioner 6,000 livres in recognition of his efforts that had reacted so much to their advantage. La Lande de Calan, "Documents inédits relatifs," pt. 2, 162.

48. La Lande de Calan, "Documents inédits relatifs," pt. 2, 137–84; *Lettres de Catherine de Médicis*, 7:115, 361.

49. La Lande de Calan, "Documents inédits relatifs," pt. 2, 184–202.

50. Ibid., pp. 202–55 passim.

once more began to press the estates for additional money. To a special session of the estates that met in March, he addressed a request for 120,000 livres to be levied on the towns and large bourgs. The estates refused, but the desperate king ordered that the tax be collected anyway. By the time the regular session opened in September, 66,000 livres had been raised. In his request for funds for the following year, Henry had the temerity to ask that the estates approve the remaining 54,000 livres. After many protests they finally agreed on the condition that the letters sent ordering that the tax be collected specifically state that they had given their consent. Thus they sought to maintain the concept that they had a right to approve taxes. To remove any doubt they refused a request that they support a garrison at Dinon. Funds were available, however, to give the Jesuits 9,000 livres to establish a college at Rennes.[51]

Henry's financial situation made it imperative to hold another extraordinary session of the estates in March 1588. The 210,000 livres that had been voted in 1582 for five years had expired, and he sought to have it renewed for three more years. The estates, however, would offer only 120,000 livres. When their regular meeting was held in August, Henry renewed his demands for the full 210,000 livres, but once more the estates refused to accede to his desires.[52] They took the precaution of including in their remonstrances a clause asking that all of their privileges be respected, to which the king replied that hereafter he would make no extraordinary levies "without the advice and consent of the said estates,"[53] a promise he came nearer keeping than anyone probably imagined because less than a year later he was struck down by an assassin.[54]

During his early years as governor Mercoeur had been careful to remain on good terms with both the League and royalist factions. Not until several months after the assassination of his cousin, the duke of Guise, did he finally determine to throw his lot with the former. Most clergymen and towns followed his lead, but a significant portion of the nobility and several important towns, including Rennes, opted for the royalist cause. Spain sent troops to support the Catholics, and England countered by dispatching several thousand men to aid the Protestants. As a result, Brittany, which had thus far been spared the soldier though not the tax collector, became an important battleground of the civil war. In place of one parlement and one representative assembly, the province soon boasted two, one for each contending faction. Tax collectors for the rivals vied with each other in extracting money from the impoverished people.

51. Ibid., pp. 255–72.

52. Ibid., pp. 272–300.

53. Ibid., 291.

54. Henry probably intended to keep his promise. He planned to hold an extraordinary session of the estates in the spring of 1589, presumably in lieu of taking arbitrary steps to raise money. Pierre-Hyacinthe Morice, *Mémoires pour servir de preuves à l'histoire ecclésiastique et civile de Bretagne* (Paris, 1746), 3: 1498–99 (hereafter cited as *Preuves*).

Mercoeur did not hold a meeting of the estates until March 1591. To explain his failure to take this step during the two preceding years, he cited the war. This probably was not the real reason, but whatever his motives, the behavior of the deputies proved that he had no cause to doubt their willingness to cooperate. Indeed the large turnout of the clergy and the towns ought to have strengthened his hand by revealing broad support for the League cause. Heartened, Mercoeur held further meetings of the estates in the springs of 1592, 1593, and 1594, after which he abandoned the practice and returned to collecting what taxes he could without obtaining consent. The estates had done nothing to merit such neglect. They had complained about the behavior of the troops, especially those of Spain, and about the impoverishment of the people, but they had voted substantial sums to support the League cause. Probably Mercoeur failed to convoke the estates in 1595 and thereafter because he anticipated a small attendance that would reveal his declining fortunes.[55]

Henry was also slow to turn to the estates. The first meeting in his reign was held in December 1590, and the second did not take place until two years later. Thereafter the estates met annually except that the meeting that would normally have been held in the fall of 1594 did not take place until January 1595. Problems created by the war, coupled with the fear that a limited attendance would reveal his weakness, no doubt account for the failure to hold meetings in 1589 and 1591. Indeed, Henry actually issued letters of convocation in October 1589, only to have to postpone the meeting. The turnout of the first and third estates for the assembly that was finally held in December 1590 was hardly gratifying. Exclusive of some refugees, only five clergymen and eight towns participated with thirty-eight nobles. Little wonder Henry decided to wait until 1592 before trying again.[56]

On the whole, these early estates were cooperative. In addition to the customary taxes, they voted 193,500 of the 300,000 livres requested in 1590 to support the military effort,[57] and in December 1592 they again provided funds beyond the normal levy in spite of complaints that their governor had ordered that a tax be collected without their consent. The Parlement at

55. Documents on the estates of the League are located at AD, Ille-et-Vilaine, C 3187–C 3206. *Choix de documents inédits sur l'histoire de la Ligue en Bretagne*, ed. Anatole de Barthélemy (Nantes, 1880), pp. 86–89, 119–25, 131–33, 142–43, 154–55; Gaston de Carné, "Correspondance du duc de Mercoeur et des ligueurs Bretons avec l'Espagne," *Archives de Bretagne* 11 (1899): 120–22, 139. For an account of the estates of the League, see Arthur Le Moyne de la Borderie and Barthélémy Pocquet, *Histoire de Bretagne* (Rennes, 1913), 5:187–89, 279. For Mercoeur's objectives, see F. Joüon des Longrais, "Le duc de Mercoeur," *Bul. archéologique de l'association bretonne* 13 (1894): 212–93.

56. AD, Ille-et-Vilaine, C 2643, pp. 65–68; Henri IV, *Lettres*, 8:363–64; Pierre Hyacinthe Morice, *Histoire ecclésiastique et civile de Bretagne* (Guingamp, 1836), 12:425–28; Louis Grégoire, *La Ligue en Bretagne* (Paris, 1856), p. 51.

57. AD, Ille-et-Vilaine, C 2643, p. 114; La Borderie and Pocquet, *Histoire*, 5:185–87; Morice, *Histoire*, 12:425–38; Morice, *Preuves*, 3:1529–31.

Rennes protested against this practice, and Henry's council was quick to forbid anyone to levy taxes without his permission. Yet a month later in March 1593, that same council ordered that a tax be imposed in spite of the protests of the representatives of the estates. The extraordinary nature of this last order is revealed by the proviso that it be done for one year only and that it not establish a precedent prejudicial to the privileges of the province. Clearly Henry's goal was to obtain money to carry on the war, not to establish an absolutist regime.[58]

During this period Henry's position was too desperate for him to offer the Breton royalists any aid. Left to their own devices, the royalist estates continued the practice that had begun in the 1580s of appointing a committee to act for them when they were not in session. They were fearful that the king or his governor would prevail upon their appointees to levy taxes that they had not authorized, so they carefully instructed them in October 1593 and on other occasions "to prevent everything contrary to the liberty, rights, and laws of the province and to what will be resolved and concluded in the general assembly of the estates."[59] Included in their resolutions was a proposal to borrow money from the English and Dutch and to seek additional troops from the former state, although they complained bitterly about the behavior of those who were already in Brittany. Henry even supported these negotiations of his subjects with foreign powers. Furthermore the government of the loyalist portion of the province rested largely in their hands.[60]

The estates that were scheduled to meet in the fall of 1594 had to be postponed to January 1595. When the deputies finally assembled, they were confronted with a demand for 138,948 livres per month to support the military. The estates offered less, and the royal commissioners suggested a compromise figure of 100,000 livres per month. The deputies countered by pointing out that for years they had contributed money for the war in other provinces and that now it was time for the king to send an army to aid them. They further charged that those involved in the disbursement of the funds for the army had been guilty of embezzlement and that many of the garrisons in the province were unnecessary.[61] The same theme was renewed when the three estates met in November. This time they refused to consider the crown's request for funds for the army until a detailed account of military expenditures was provided. The royal commissioners were reluctant to make this concession, but in the end they acceded to the request of the estates and also agreed to permit three deputies to participate in the Council

58. AD, Ille-et-Vilaine, C 2643, pp. 129–242 passim; BN ms. Clairambault 654, pp. 55–56, 496–70.

59. AD, Ille-et-Vilaine, C 2643, p. 357.

60. Ibid., pp. 372–77, 403–404, 500–516; Louis Joseph de Carné, *Les Etats de Bretagne* (Paris, 1875), 1:232–39; *Choix de documents*, pp. 152–53; Morice, *Preuves*, 3:1557–58, 1571–97, 1603–05.

61. AD, Ille-et-Vilaine, C 2644, pp. 1–170 passim; Morice, *Histoire*, 13:134–40.

of Finances that handled the fiscal affairs of the province. In return the estates voted most of the funds that the king required.[62] Unhappily for the Bretons, the royal commander levied what taxes he needed to support his troops, whether they had been granted by the estates or not.[63]

The three estates that met in December 1596 proved much more cooperative because Henry himself promised to come to the province if Mercoeur did not quickly make peace. Not only did they give him what he asked, but they also promised an additional 450,000 livres when he arrived. Henry's representatives had carefully coached the estates to make this offer, and they responded affirmatively because they believed that his presence at the head of an army would lead to the restoration of order. Henry, however, opted to remain in Rouen where the Assembly of Notables was meeting.[64] When the estates assembled a year later, Henry's commissioners were still promising that he would soon come to restore peace in Brittany, in return for a substantial grant. In addition to the customary taxes, the estates offered Henry 600,000 livres but stipulated that it was not to be paid until he actually appeared in Brittany. The commissioners sought more money, but the estates refused. To raise even the smaller amount, it was necessary to borrow a substantial sum. Henry continued to delay. Not until after he had begun peace negotiations with Spain and accepted the submission of Mercoeur did he make good his promise to visit his Breton subjects.[65] In April 1598 he issued the edict of Nantes, and in May he personally attended a meeting of the estates at Rennes. The Wars of Religion had finally come to an end.

During the final years of the struggle, the crown had levied taxes without consent in Brittany as elsewhere. There was always a danger that such arbitrary acts would establish dangerous precedents, but Henry obviously preferred persuasion to force. To increase the chances that he could win consent to taxes, he ordered those devoted to his service to attend the estates.[66] There were also signs that the three estates had strengthened their institutional structure. During the 1580s and 1590s they often appointed a committee to act in their interest when they were not in session, and in 1595 three of their number had been temporarily taken into the Breton Council of

62. AD, Ille-et-Vilaine, C 2644, esp. pp. 199–219, 226–42, 394. Carné, *Les Etats*, 1:242–44; Morice, *Histoire*, 13:172–81.

63. AN, E 1b, fol. 123; Valois, 1:3105.

64. AD, Ille-et-Vilaine, C 2644, pp. 552–53, 688; Morice, *Histoire*, 13:220–25; Carné, *Les Etats*, 1:240–47. *Mémoires et correspondance du Duplessis-Mornay*, ed. A. D. de La Fontenelle de Vaudoré and P.-R. Arguis (Paris, 1824–25), 7:36–40, 66–71.

65. AD, Ille-et-Vilaine, C 2655, pp. 1–2, 36–38, 131–34; Morice, *Histoire*, 13:300–06; Henry IV, *Lettres*, 8:683–84, 687–88; La Borderie and Pocquet, *Histoire*, 5:327–29.

66. For several letters requesting supporters to attend the estates, see Henry IV, *Lettres*, 8:669–70, 684. A number of Breton nobles received pensions, but the estates regarded them as their servants, not those of the crown, and often asked that pensioners who did not attend their meetings lose their stipends. Sée, *Les Etats de Bretagne*, pp. 17, 102–03.

Finances. Thus by the time the civil war closed, the estates had made some gains as well as absorbed some losses. It remained to be seen whether Henry would continue his arbitrary acts once peace was restored and whether the estates would continue to appoint a committee to act in its name between meetings.

4. THE ESTATES OF LANGUEDOC

The Wars of Religion were fought more bitterly in Languedoc than in many other provinces because the Protestants were more nearly equal to the Catholics in strength. Eight of the episcopal seats were in their hands during the first war, and throughout the conflict they maintained a strong position in the east based on such towns as Nîmes, Montpellier, and Privas. Western Languedoc remained predominantly Catholic, and Toulouse became the capitol of the adherents of the old religion. In the estates that opened in Béziers in November 1561, the Protestants urged that some Catholic churches be given to them, but by a vote of thirty-seven to twenty-one, the assembly refused to recommend this step to the king. Seeing that they were outnumbered, the Protestant organized their own estates a year later after the Wars of Religion had begun. For the remainder of the century, the estates of Languedoc functioned with many of its seats vacant because of frequent Protestant defections and the preoccupation of many Catholics with the war.[67]

On May 13, 1563 Henri de Montmorency, seigneur de Damville, a younger son of Constable Anne de Montmorency, was appointed to replace his father as governor. A gallant soldier, an able diplomat, and a farsighted statesman, the younger Montmorency was to serve in this capacity for over half a century. At first he adopted a militant Catholic position and cruelly used Protestants upon occasion, but by 1566 he had begun to veer toward a more moderate position. The increasing coldness of his relations with the Guise, followed by the murder of his cousin, Coligny, and numerous Protestants in the massacre of St. Bartholomew in 1572, completed his transition from an ultra-Catholic to a *politique* leader determined to base his power in the south on an alliance between liberal Catholic and Protestant forces. Though Toulouse and some other Catholic centers refused to adhere to this policy and eventually became strongholds of the League, he was able to impose his authority on most of the province. During this period he won the respect and affection of the bulk of the inhabitants and firmly entrenched the position of this family in the province.[68]

67. *HL*, 11:367, 424-25, 12:633-47. On the Protestant assemblies, see Gordon Griffiths, *Representative Government in Western Europe in the Sixteenth Century* (Oxford, 1968), pp. 254-71.

68. On Montmorency, or Montmorency-Damville as he was often called, see Franklin C. Palm, *Politics and Religion in Sixteenth-Century France* (Boston, 1927).

The early years of Montmorency's governorship saw few significant changes taking place in the estates. In 1567 the crown granted the three estates' request to increase from 8,000 to 10,000 livres the amount they could levy to support their activities without obtaining the permission of the council. The young governor's rapport with the estates was such that he was voted gratifications totaling 72,000 livres between 1567 and 1569. His lieutenant general, Joyeuse, received 20,000 during the same period. Such large grants were subject to the approval of the crown, but kings rarely thought it advisable to risk offending such powerful persons by refusing to sanction these levies.[69]

The king himself fared less well. In 1570, 1571, and 1572 his commissioners made unsuccessful efforts to obtain an additional 80,000 livres from the estates. By 1574 he was willing to abandon the effort, ostensibly because of the poverty of the people, but in 1576 he was more successful in realizing a 30,000 livre increase. By 1580 the three estates were again rejecting the royal demands, although they found the funds to offer Villeroy, the secretary of state charged with their affairs, a gratification of 300 livres and his assistant 90. The following year the king was again repulsed in spite of the presence of Montmorency, Joyeuse, and Bellièvre (who was then superintendent of finances) as commissioners. The trio was sufficiently persuasive to win presents for themselves. In 1582 the crown cut its request by 100,000 livres and was thereby more successful in its negotiations. That same year Montmorency and Joyeuse received 33,120 livres to support their companies. Direct royal taxes on the province for 1583 did not differ significantly from those of 1563 in spite of the civil war and inflation. The estates had been more than successful in protecting the inhabitants from the royal fiscal requirements.[70]

The estates that met in October 1582 voted taxes for 1583, but no assembly was held to vote taxes for 1584. It has been suggested that a meeting of the syndics of the dioceses of the généralité of Toulouse was intended to take its place, but the purpose of this assembly was to provide some data for the commissioners that Henry III had sent out to gather information preparatory to a meeting of the Assembly of Notables in 1583. The official explanation given to the estates in July 1585 when they next met was that the king had intended to hold a meeting in July 1584 to vote the taxes for that same year but had not done so because of the troubles and tumults in the province. Instead he had gone to each of the dioceses and asked for the same amount that had been levied the year before. It is unlikely that the failure to ask the three estates to vote taxes in 1584 was intended as an attack on their privileges. Rather, the real cause seems to

69. *HL*, 11:491, 514, 526, 12:849–50.

70. *IAD, Haute-Garonne, sér. C*, ed. Adolphe Baudouin (Toulouse, 1903), 2:75–95 passim; *HL*, 11:539, 542, 691, 698.

have been the bitter enmity that existed between Montmorency and his lieutenant, Joyeuse, which precluded any possibility that they and their followers could have worked peaceably together in the estates. The quarrel between the two nobles was patched up in December 1584, and the three estates were once more assembled in July 1585. On this occasion the king asked those present to consent to a tax for that year and also for 1586 so that it would not be necessary to bear the expense of another meeting, but the deputies refused because they had been empowered to act only for the current year.[71]

The relations between Montmorency and Joyeuse soon worsened. Henry III chose to back his favorite, Joyeuse, and the ultra-Catholic party in Languedoc. Montmorency made an alliance with Henry of Navarre, who had become heir apparent to the throne upon the death of the duke of Anjou in 1584, and placed his hopes on the liberal Catholic-Protestant coalition that he had been building for some years. Both men governed the portions of Languedoc which they held and summoned the three estates when the occasion demanded. At first those of Joyeuse had royal approval, and it was Montmorency who acted on his own authority. Then, with the assassination of the duke of Guise in December 1588, the situation was reversed. Joyeuse chose the League and acted on the authority of the self-appointed lieutenant general of the kingdom, Mayenne, while Henry III once more recognized Montmorency as governor. Between August 1585 and March 1596 Joyeuse held the estates twenty-two times, and Montmorency was hardly less busy with fifteen sessions. Both men found it necessary to extract everything they could from the territory they held in order to pay for the war and to support their troops during the periods of armed truces. Dioceses and towns that could not pay their quotas were forced to borrow unless they were fortunate enough to escape paying what they owned. In such confusion and with the estates divided, little of permanent significance in their history took place.[72]

Montmorency immediately recognized Henry IV as king upon his predecessor's assassination, but he was not without expectations of reward. In 1590 he pointed out to Henry the losses that he had suffered in the royalist cause and suggested that he be given Joyeuse's property in compensation. The desperate king could only acquiesce. As 1593 drew to a close, Henry bestowed on Montmorency the office of constable, the most coveted honor in France. There may have been more subtle reasons for the appointment than mere gratitude because it provided an excuse to summon the powerful governor to court. With Henry's conversion it had become possible to buy the submission of the League chieftains, a less expensive and less bloody method than conquering them. Far from giving Montmorency

---

71. *HL*, 11:709–28; *IAD, Haute-Garonne, sér. C*, 2:95–96; Germain de la Faille, *Annales de la ville de Toulouse* (Toulouse, 1701), 2:375–78.

72. *IAD, Haute-Garonne, sér. C*, 2:95–147, 724–29 passim; *HL*, 11:729–866 passim.

Joyeuse's property, it would be necessary to recognize the League leader as governor of that part of Languedoc which he held in return for laying down his arms. Such a step could be best taken with Montmorency out of the way and reasonably content with his new office. Henry also knew that there were distinct advantages to having Montmorency more directly involved in his government because of the special position he held of being trusted by the pope, with whom Henry was then negotiating for absolution and at the same time trusted by the Protestants who were uneasy now that he had announced his conversion to Catholicism.[73]

The rumor was already spreading that Languedoc was to be divided when the royalist estates opened in February 1595. Shocked at the very thought of partition, the deputies pleaded that the unity of the province be preserved and that Montmorency be retained as their governor. Henry as usual sought a compromise. By the terms of the treaty he made with Joyeuse in January 1596, Montmorency was to remain as governor of the entire province, but in his absence Joyeuse was to act as the lieutenant in the areas he controlled, and the duke of Ventadour, who doubled as Montmorency's nephew and son-in-law, was to serve as the lieutenant in the remainder of the government. Thus when peace was restored to Languedoc, the theoretical unity of the province was maintained, but in effect Montmorency was to remain at court and Ventadour and Joyeuse were each to govern the region in which they held sway.[74]

5. THE ESTATES OF DAUPHINÉ

Dauphiné, like Languedoc, was troubled by the problems caused by a large Protestant minority. Heresy had been deeply rooted in parts of the province during the Middle Ages. This fact, coupled with its proximity to Geneva, made it almost inevitable that a strong Protestant movement would develop. William Farel, that fiery Dauphiné preacher who had enticed Calvin to Geneva, joined with others to spread the new religion in the mountains and on the plains. Converts among the nobility and burghers were especially numerous. In addition several leading ecclesiastics, including the bishop of Gap, abandoned the Catholic faith, and the bishop of Valence seemed on the point of following their example. Under such favorable circumstances, the baron Des Adrets, an able but cruel Protestant leader, made himself master of most of the province during the spring and summer of 1562.

The prince of Condé, who professed to be fighting to free the king from his Guise captors, named Des Adrets lieutenant general in Dauphiné. In this capacity he held Protestant assemblies at Montélimar in December 1562 and

73. Palm, *Politics and Religion*, pp. 196–210.
74. *HL*, 11:847–48, 860–68, 12:1533–63.

at Valence in January-February 1563 that aped the estates in nearly every respect except that the clergy was not convoked. Des Adrets hoped to persuade those who attended to make peace, but they proved to be very militant. They not only voted taxes to support an army but also established two councils. One council composed entirely of nobles was to direct the military effort and the other council consisting of three persons designated by the nobility, seven by the leading towns in Protestant hands, and, somewhat surprisingly, two by the villages, was to handle political, administrative, and fiscal affairs. To the second council a general syndic and two secretaries were also appointed. In addition, the assemblies at Montélimar and Valence made provision for religious reform, the administration of justice, and the increased security of their church through alliances with their co-religionists in Languedoc, Lyons, and Provence.[75]

The two assemblies were obviously modeled after the estates and were frequently referred to as estates by contemporaries. Furthermore, the political council was somewhat similar to the *commis*, or abridged arm of the estates, although its composition was more democratic and its duties more inclusive. Aided by this obvious borrowing from existing practices, the Dauphinois Protestants came close to preparing a written constitution that enabled them to govern that part of the province they controlled without reliance on the crown. The councils and estates apparently functioned throughout the period of the wars, although the proportion of the province the Protestants controlled was never again as large as it had been during the winter of 1563. At first, the Protestant estates dominated the government, and it was they who elected a new leader following the arrest of Des Adrets early in 1563, because he was about to join the Catholics. As the wars continued, however, the difficulty of holding meetings increased, and the need to obtain funds became more urgent. Protestant military leaders began to impose taxes on their own authority. What had begun as a somewhat more democratic form of government ended by being an arbitrary one.[76]

Meanwhile the crown had continued to hold the estates annually or more often when the occasion demanded. Some Protestants attended in periods of peace, and there was time to indulge in economic and social disputes. In the estates of 1564, the villages renewed their old complaint that the towns did

---

75. A. Dussert, "Le Baron des Adrets et les Etats du Dauphiné," *Bul. de l'Académie Delphinale*, sér. 5, 20 (1929): 93–136; Eugène Arnaud, *Histoire des Protestants du Dauphiné aux XVIᵉ, XVIIᵉ et XVIIIᵉ siècles* (Paris, 1875–76), 1:226–27, 481–88, 515–18, 2:46–54; A. Lacroix, *L'arrondissement de Montélimar* (Valence, 1882), 6:114–28.

76. *IAD, Drôme*, ed. A. Lacroix (Valence, 1879–98), 3:422, 5:256; 6:149. Some documents on the Protestant assemblies have been published by J. Roman in *Actes et correspondance du connétable de Lesdiguières* (Grenoble, 1878), 3 vols., and in "Documents sur la Réforme et les Guerres de Religion en Dauphiné," *Bul. de la soc. de statistiques des sciences naturales et des arts industriels du département de l'Isère*, sér. 3, 15 (1890). Llewain Scott Van Doren, *War, Taxes, and Social Protest: The Challenge to Authority in Sixteenth Century Dauphiné* (Ph.D. diss., Harvard University, 1970), pp. 189–93.

not pay their share of taxes, and royalist Vienne tried to get the estates to assume the 26,000 livre debt it had incurred to support the Catholic cause. Charles IX ordered the commis to levy a tax for this purpose after the three estates had met, but they failed to do so. When he persisted, the commis agreed that 5,200 livres would be levied annually for four consecutive years on two conditions: first, the sum must be deducted from the don gratuit and, second, the next estates must approve the transaction. Clearly, the three estates, or more accurately, their administrative organ, could still function semiautonomously.[77]

The estates were held regularly in the years that followed, but with the renewal of the civil wars, two ominous notes appeared. First, beginning in 1573 the lieutenant general, and in several instances the king, began to order that taxes be levied without the consent of the estates in case of emergency. Sometimes the lieutenant general consulted the sovereign courts or the commis who were in Grenoble, and they only acted in time of crisis, but nevertheless a dangerous precedent was established in the name of the need for haste.[78] Second, there was a growing tendency for the third estate to act alone. In 1566 the ten leading towns met to discuss the transportation of salt, and an edict may have been issued governing the procedures in these assemblies. If it was, the edict can be taken as a sign of the growing importance of meetings of individual estates that led to the eventual loss of unity among the three estates.[79]

In 1568 the crown asked for 30,000 livres per month to support 200 horse and 3,000 foot soldiers. Although the deputies of the third estates must have been pleased that the nobility was requested to contributed 5,000 livres, they balked because of the proverty of the province. Four years later Genoble took the initiative in asking that an assembly of the towns be held, and by 1574 the split among the estates was becoming serious. With the amount of land in the hands of those who claimed to be tax exempt increasing rapidly, the costs of war remaining high, and the province already deeply in debt, the third estate began to attempt once more to make the privileged pay the taille on their nonnoble property.[80]

Henry III himself presided over the estates that met at Romans in January 1575. His presence was dictated by his desperate need for money to

77. AD, Isère, IC 3 n.15; Pierre Cavard, *La Réforme et les Guerres de Religion à Vienne* (Vienne 1950), p. 127.

78. L. S. Van Doren, "Civil War Taxation and the Foundations of Fiscal Absolutism: The Royal Taille in Dauphiné, 1560–1610," *Transactions of the Western Society for French History* 3 (1976) 1:35–53. Charles IX levied a tax without consent in July 1572. The crisis years were 1573, 1576–78, 1580–83, and 1587–89.

79. *IAD, Drôme*, 6:304–21. The edict is cited in the catalog of the B. Mun., Grenoble in ms. 1357 under the title of *Edit réglementant les assemblées générales des villes, 1566*, but it could not be located when I was there.

80. *IAD, Drôme*, 6:304, 323–24, 326–27; *IAC, Grenoble*, ed. A. Prudhomme (Grenoble, 1880), BB 24, BB 26. AD, Isère, IC 3 n.16. Van Doren, *War, Taxes*, pp. 238–43.

support the war, and it was enough to persuade the deputies of the third estate to provide for a force of 2,000 infantry. Their generosity was doubtless stimulated by the nobility's willingness to maintain 20 horse and the clergy's offer of a large contribution. Henry did not, however, make any decisions concerning the taille in spite of appeals from the third estate because he was fearful of alienating the privileged, and the quarrel over who should pay was renewed the following year when the elections to the Estates General of Blois were held.[81]

There were conflicting opinions over whether the various bailiwicks should elect the deputies or whether the provincial estates should assume the chore. The resulting confusion provided the third estate with an opportunity to prepare a separate cahier rather than participate in the preparation of a common one for the province as a whole. In this document, the third lodged complaints against the commis of the estates and the behavior of its officers. They charged that although the consuls of the ten principal towns were members of the commis along with only two ecclesiastics, six nobles, and the general syndic of the estates, it was actually the tool of the privileged orders, most of whom resided in Grenoble where they could be quickly summoned, while many of the towns were too far away to participate in hurriedly called meetings. The general syndic, who was usually a noble, was an instrument of the majority of the commis who were present and therefore acted in the interests of the privileged orders. Under these circumstances, the members of the third estate had difficulty presenting their grievances to the king and defending their interests. To help correct these evils, they asked to elect their own syndic, and to alleviate their burdens they requested that new nobles be subject to the taille and that old nobles pay the tax on the common land they held. Unhappily for the towns, the villages around Grenoble also seized the opportunity to express their grievances. In the end neither element in the third estate won satisfaction at Blois because Henry III refused to make any decision for fear of alienating some of the contestants.[82]

The deputies of the estates that met in March 1577 devoted part of their energies to quarrels over procedure. There was a debate over whether the bishop of Grenoble or the archbishop of Embrun or of Vienne should preside and whether the estates should always meet in Grenoble where the archives were kept or rotate the honor of being host among the leading towns. The

---

81. J. R. Major, "The Assembly at Paris in the Summer of 1575," in *Post Scripta*, ed. Joseph R. Strayer and Donald E. Queller (Rome, 1972), p. 704; A. Dussert, "Catherine de Médicis et les Etats du Dauphiné," *Bul. de l'Académie Delphinale*, sér. 6, 2 (1931): 131–32; AD, Isère, Fonds Chaper, J 524¹; *IAC*, Grenoble, BB 27; Alexandre Fauché-Prunelle, *Essai sur les anciennes institutions autonomes ou populaires des Alpes Cottiennes-Briançonnaises* (Grenoble, 1857), 2 : 457; Van Doren, *War, Taxes*, pp. 243–45.

82. Cavard, *La Réforme*, pp. 198–202. Dussert, "Catherine," pp. 132–33; J. R. Major, *The Deputies to the Estates General of Renaissance France* (Madison, 1960), p. 110. Van Doren, *War, Taxes*, pp. 248–57.

clergy offered a décime, and the nobility promised to support 300 horse, but the third estate balked. It was only with some difficulty that they were finally persuaded to give 36,000 livres to pay 1,200 infantry for three months. When this sum proved insufficient, the crown ordered the commis to meet in November to vote an additional 36,000 livres. As usual, not enough *consuls* of the leading towns could attend to outvote the commis of the clergy and nobility, but those who did go refused to commit the third estate to so large a sum.[83]

During these years the *consuls* of the ten leading towns had acted as spokesmen for the third estate. When their interests had clashed with those of the crown or the privileged, they had been energetic, though not too successful, defenders of their order. Once a tax had been decided upon, however, they had always shoved as much as possible upon villages. It is not surprising, therefore, that the villages wanted their own spokesman. In 1578 they succeeded in winning from the three estates the right to elect a commis who would participate in all the meetings of the commis. The most likely explanation for this concession is that it was anticipated that the new commis would be only that, just another voice in the assemblies of the commis. Had it been suspected that he would become a true syndic of the villages who would take the lead in the struggle over who should pay the taille for two generations to come, the privileged would have refused just as they had refused to permit the third estate as a whole to have its own syndic several years before.[84]

In late 1578 and in 1579 matters came to a head. There was a general desire in the province for more self-government, peace, and lower taxes, but the need was especially urgent in the villages whose inhabitants bore the brunt of the fiscal burden and at the same time suffered most from the depredations of war. The inhabitants of the smaller towns joined the peasants to defend themselves against the soldiers and the tax collectors. At Romans the bourgeois oligarchy was ousted from the municipal government by the common people. Larger towns took advantage of the confusion to demand that royal garrisons be withdrawn. At the same time they organized bourgeois militias to defend themselves against the growing radicalism of urban worker and peasant alike. It was under such trying circumstances that an exceptionally long meeting of the estates took place in Grenoble in April and May 1579.[85]

In spite of the growing animosity between the upper bourgeoisie of the leading towns and the urban workers and peasants, the third estate managed to retain a united front at Grenoble. Here a cahier was prepared that was addressed as much to the other orders as to the king. The argument that

83. Dussert, "Catherine," p. 134; Van Doren, *War, Taxes*, pp. 257–59.

84. Van Doren, *War, Taxes*, pp. 260–61.

85. Dussert, "Catherine," pp. 135–40; L. S. Van Doren, "Revolt and Reaction in the City of Romans, Dauphiné, 1579–1580," *The Sixteenth Century Journal* 5 (1974): 71–100.

Dauphiné numbered among its privileges exemption from all taxes was clearly stated. If the estates chose to vote a don gratuit, it should fall on everyone, regardless of what personal exemptions they might claim. That certain land should be considered as exempt was conceded. Therefore the old nobility, clergy, and members of the sovereign courts were asked to pay the taille only on the common land they had acquired during the past twenty years or would acquire in the future. On the other hand, the third requested that the privileged contribute on the basis of their noble and nonnoble land alike to pay garrisons, governors, deputations to court, and other expenses undertaken in the common interests of the province. They also asked that assemblies be held alternately in each of the ten leading towns, that they have as many representatives in the meetings of the commis as the other two orders combined, and that they have a syndic who would reside in Grenoble during his term of office to look after their interests. After some debate the estates disbanded without reaching any decision.[86]

Meanwhile Catherine de Medici had been making a tour of the southern provinces in an attempt to restore order. She arrived in Dauphiné in July 1579 and immediately set about trying to settle the disputes among the various social classes and between the two religions. The estates were summoned to meet again in Grenoble in August. The third repeated the proposals it had made in the spring, but the privileged orders were unwilling to pay the taille on the common lands they held, and they once more refused to permit the third to have its own syndic. The clergy did consent to pay one or two décimes in case of war, and the nobles expressed willingness to put 100 *lances* in the field for six months at their own expense, but they would not go further. Catherine accepted their decision, and Henry III concurred in what she had done. The estates ended with Catherine believing that she had resolved the dispute, but in reality she had accomplished nothing.[87]

One reason Catherine showed little sympathy for the third estate was that she associated its program with the village leagues and the urban uprisings that were then taking place. The leagues were suppressed in 1580, but not before the demands of the third estate that the number of those who paid the taille be increased had become linked with sedition and rebellion in the minds of the crown and the privileged, this despite the fact that the leaders of the third disavowed the leagues on several occasions.[88]

When the estates met in May 1580, the nobles, true to the pledge they had made in 1579 and thoroughly frightened by the peasants, offered 30,000 livres to help pay for the costs of the war and submitted to the salt tax. The clergy gave two décimes valued at a total of 23,900 livres, but the hard-

86. Dussert, "Catherine," pp. 139–45, 166–75; Cavard, *La Réforme*, pp. 216–22; Van Doren, *War, Taxes*, pp. 262–66.

87. Dussert, "Catherine," pp. 145–55, 175–89; Cavard, *La Réforme*, pp. 222–24; Van Doren, *War, Taxes*, pp. 266–74.

88. Van Doren, *War, Taxes*, pp. 282–365; Cavard, *La Réforme*, pp. 210–39.

pressed members of the third estate had to contribute 120,000 livres. With their movement discredited, they had no recourse but to bide their time until a favorable opportunity arose to resume the procès des tailles.[89]

The three estates as a whole continued to resent the extraordinary exactions of the crown. In 1583 they refused to grant the 78,000 livres the king requested to redeem his mortgaged domain, but in 1584 they voted a total of 180,000 livres for more routine purposes, including a 6,000 livres gift to their lieutenant general. In 1585 the estates again refrained from making any extraordinary concessions, but the suffering of the poor became so intense because of poor harvests that the general syndic appealed to Parlement to halt the export of grain.[90]

Unfortunately for the people, the refusal of the three estates to vote a tax did not prevent the lieutenant general from later increasing the levy they authorized on the grounds of military necessity. He might consult the Parlement or the commis to give his act the air of legality, but this did not alter the fact that in time of war he took what he needed. It also became customary to levy taxes voted by the estates without waiting for the approval of the king's council, a procedure that actually gave the estates greater autonomy because it enabled them to raise money for their own purposes without outside check. Thus as the war progressed, the estates became more independent of the crown, and the lieutenant general became more independent of the estates.[91]

Nevertheless it continued to be advantageous for the government to obtain from the estates as large a grant as possible because there was less local resistance to taxes that had been voted than to levies made by fiat. Therefore, the government continued to insist that its demands be met. In January 1586 the estates were requested to grant 30,000 livres per month in addition to the customary don gratuit and taillon, to support the troops. The third estate appealed to the clergy and nobility for assistance, but the former refused on the grounds that they had already made substantial contributions and the latter with the excuse that they offered their lives to the king's service. The third estate in the end assumed the entire burden, although it was necessary to borrow 100,000 livres to make the initial payments. Grenoble managed to get its resident nobility and clergy to pay a portion of its debts and to transfer the burden of supporting its garrison to the countryside, but the smaller towns and villages were less able to defend themselves. They made pitiful pleas to the king for assistance, and when they could pay no more, they shifted to borrowing. In 1588 the commis committed the province to an additional debt of 200,000 livres.[92] And this

---

89. Dussert, "Catherine," p. 163 n. 108.

90. *IAC, Grenoble*, BB 35, BB 37; *IAD, Drôme*, 3:232, 6:4. AD, Drôme, C 1024; *Bul. de l'Académie Delphinale* 2 (1847): 308–15.

91. Van Doren, *War, Taxes*, pp. 156–58.

92. *IAC, Grenoble*, BB 38–40; *IAD, Drôme*, 6:304.

was only the beginning! Between 1589 and 1593 the assessment per hearth that the government sought averaged from about five to seven times as much as before. Some of these taxes were voted by the estates, but more often the lieutenant general turned to the commis or simply registered the tax decree in the sovereign court. How much he collected is another matter, but there is no doubt that he extracted all that he could from the pockets and the credit of the people.[93]

Meanwhile a new Protestant leader, François de Bonne, seigneur de Lesdiguières, had emerged in Dauphiné. Although a member of only the minor nobility, his ability as both a soldier and a statesman led to his election as head of the Protestant party in 1577 when he was only thirty-four. During the years that followed, he conquered the more mountainous part of the province. Soon after the ascension of Henry IV, he made a treaty with Alphonse d'Ornano, the Catholic lieutenant general in Dauphiné, and together they began to reconquer the province. Grenoble fell in December 1590, and that same month the estates recognized Henry IV as king.[94] Other league strongholds remained to be taken, and several campaigns were necessary to terminate the duke of Savoy's intrigues in the province, but slowly a degree of order returned.

6. THE ESTATES OF PROVENCE

At first the activities of the three estates of Provence during the Wars of Religion did not differ greatly from their counterparts in other parts of France. To the crown's inevitable requests for money they responded favorably, except when more than the traditional sums were requested. On such occasions they gave at least something grudgingly so that by 1583 they were able to claim that they were paying six times as much as formerly. To make themselves heard in the council at Paris, they sent deputations armed with cahiers and gave presents to their governor and other influential persons. Thus the estates of November 1569 voted their governor 5,000 livres and their lieutenant general 3,000. In 1573 a newly appointed governor was granted 12,000 livres and two mules, and a similar amount was accorded another governor in 1578. Officials at Paris were not forgotten; in 1582 Villeroy, the secretary of state in charge of Provence, was given 1,500 livres.[95]

The crown seems to have made fewer additional demands on Provence than on the other provinces, but on the other hand, it left the three estates greater responsibility for raising troops for their own defense. Hardly a

93. Van Doren, "Civil War Taxation," pp. 36–38, 51–53.

94. *Actes de Lesdiguières*, 1:146–47; *Histoire du Dauphiné*, ed. Bernard Bligny (Toulouse, 1973), pp. 234–37.

95. Gustave Lambert, *Histoire des Guerres de Religion en Provence, 1530–1598* (Toulon, 1870; reprint ed., Nyons, 1972), 1:368–70; *IAD, Bouches-du-Rhône, sér. C*, ed. Louis Blancard (Marseilles, 1884), 1:2–6.

meeting of the estates passed without the governor's asking them to levy taxes or to borrow for this purpose. The nobility and clergy, with considerable prodding from the third estate, occasionally contributed to these expenses, but they were angered in 1569 when the procureurs nés unilaterally asked the king to make them pay part of the subsidy levied in lieu of a tax on wine.[96]

During the most serious periods of the civil wars, the needs of the government were often so imperative that there was no time to convoke the estates to vote a tax or to authorize a loan. Beginning in December 1578 the practice was inaugurated of summoning only the procureurs nés et joints and the deputies of nineteen towns to perform these duties that had once been the sole prerogative of the three estates. The governor or, in his absence, Parlement convoked these meetings, and the number of those who attended was often smaller than that suggested by the list of those summoned. It was an ad hoc arrangement made necessary by the repeated emergencies that occurred, but it did serve to lend an element of legality, or at least of popular approval, for the taxes that were levied and the loans that were negotiated. These assemblies were held every few months in the 1580s, but in several years the three estates did not meet at all. Not until the close of the century did these meetings become institutionalized under the name of the assembly of the communities.[97]

Events began to take an unusual turn in 1586 when the count of Angoulême, governor of Provence and bastard brother of the king, was killed in a brawl while waiting for a meeting of the assembly of the communities to open. Freed from Angoulême's influence, the Catholic League was able to assert control over the assemblies that met during the two succeeding years. Discouraged by their inability to control these meetings, the royalists broke with the pro-League towns and assembled in Pertius in October 1588. The League-controlled Parlement of Aix countered by directing the communities to send deputies the following month to Marseilles. For the next six years, there were two provincial estates and two assemblies of the communities in Provence. During this period the royalists held seven meetings of the estates and eight of the communities, and the Leaguers five of the estates and four of the communities. The procureurs du pays and most of the bishops sided with the League, as did about half the vigueries and half the towns, including Aix and Marseilles. A larger percentage of the nobility preferred the royalist assemblies, and perhaps it was their assistance, coupled with the Gascon army brought by the duke of Epernon, the new governor, that initially turned the tide in favor of the king.[98]

96. Gaspard H. de Coriolis, *Dissertation sur les Etats de Provence* (Aix, 1867), pp. 282–91.

97. See above pp. 92–93. *Les Bouches-du-Rhône. Encyclopédie départementale*, ed. Paul Masson (Marseilles, 1920), 3:475–77; *IAD, Bouches-du-Rhône, sér. C*, 1:4–8.

98. *IAD, Bouches-du-Rhône, sér. C*, 1:7–13; *Les Bouches-du-Rhône*, 3:38–44, 469–73; Maurice Wilkinson, *The Last Phase of the League in Provence, 1588–1598* (London, 1909), pp. 4–45.

Threatened with defeat, the League leaders did not hesitate to summon an assembly of the communities to ask the duke of Savoy to intervene. The duke entered Provence in October 1590 with a small army and was warmly welcomed by a number of towns, including Arles, Marseilles, and Aix, where he held the estates in January 1591. A few hailed him as their count, and the Parlement of Aix, more informed of legal niceties, conferred on him the military and administrative responsibilities of governing the province. Fortunately for the royalist cause, the duke soon became discouraged and withdrew his troop, but he continued to plot with his Provençal supporters. Even after Henry had been recognized by Aix and most other towns in 1594 and had replaced Epernon as governor by the more popular duke of Guise, the unity of the estates was not immediately restored. Three times between November 1594 and June 1595, Epernon held meetings of the estates or of the communities of the area he still held in obedience in defiance of the king. Not until November 1595 did the estates again meet united as before the war.[99]

During this period, nothing of permanent constitutional significance took place except the creation of the assembly of the communities. The defection of Aix made it necessary to replace the procureurs nés from that town by elected officials from royalist communities, but Aix resumed its privileged status upon recognizing Henry as king. Royalist and League estates alike were faced with continual financial demands to pay the army. If the troops were undisputedly there for their own protection, the estates or the assembly of the communities on either side generally provided the money by voting higher taxes or by borrowing, but if the troops were to be assigned elsewhere, they were apt to balk. In December 1593 Henry complained bitterly at the shortsighted refusal of the royalist estates to contribute to the war against the duke of Savoy in Piedmont, since it was this campaign that prevented that ambitious neighbor from invading Provence. When peace was restored, he had little reason to remember the estates with affection.[100]

7. The Estates in Auvergne and Lyonnais

In Auvergne and Forez where there were élus, the king set the amount of the tax that was to be collected to meet his needs, and the estates could only plead with him to reduce the size of the levy. However, the estates could also vote taxes to provide for their own needs, including the defense of their respective provinces. Under these circumstances it is not surprising that the crises provoked by the Wars of Religion ensured the continued activity of the estates. Nowhere was this more true than in Basse-Auvergne.

99. *Les Bouches-du-Rhône*, 3:44–63; Lambert, *Histoire des Guerres de Religion*, 2:1–436; L. B. Simpson, "The Struggle for Provence, 1593–1596: A Sidelight on the Internal Policy of Henry IV," *University of California Publications in History* 17 (1942): 1–23.

100. *Henri IV, Lettres*, 4:65–66.

The échevins of Clermont were proud of their privilege of convoking the thirteen good towns of Basse-Auvergne, and the necessities provoked by the wars caused them to do so every few months. Occasionally the good towns acted to obtain a reduction in royal taxes, and at times they were successful; in 1580, for example, they were freed from contributing to the costs of the siege of Mende and were given a reduction in their contribution to support an army of 50,000 men.[101] More often the good towns devoted their energies to defending their province. Sometimes they raised troops for this purpose or to conduct a siege, sometimes they supplied armies that passed through their territory in order to reduce the likelihood of pillaging, and sometimes they paid army commanders to stay away. In 1570 the prince of Condé and the duke of Alençon extracted no less than 150.000 livres from them in return for keeping their troops out of the region.[102] When the good towns dared, they fought back against these exactions. With debts mounting to 300,000 or 400,000 livres in 1580, they granted only 6,000 of the 12,200 livres their governor requested to pay for additional troops, and they kept his salary at 482 livres per month. In 1585 they voted him 3,000 livres because of the special services they hoped he would render them at court, but they rejected his repeated requests for 5,000 livres to repair the fortifications at Issoire. A later plea for the same amount to get some troops out of the province brought forth only 3,000 livres.[103]

The good towns borrowed heavily, but most of their expenses had to be met by taxation. Under these circumstances, the nobility and clergy were soon reminded of their duty toward the peasantry, or at least the need to prevent others from milking them dry before manorial dues were paid. In 1565 their representatives sought entrance into the archives of the good towns to learn how taxes were levied in former times. Their request, which the towns were most reluctant to grant, was not only a sad commentary on their record keeping but also on their memory. As late as 1535–36 they had had to give their consent through individual procurations before the good towns could impose a tax of over 6,000 livres on "their subjects" in order to provide presents for their governor. The matter was soon settled amicably, and from 1568 permission of the syndics of the two orders had to be sought before over 6,000 livres could be levied to defray local expenses.[104] The king made less difficulty in granting permission to tax, and in 1570 he gave the governor and good towns virtual carte blanche to levy whatever they needed

101. *IAC, Clermont-Ferrand, Fonds de Montferrand*, ed. E. Teilhard de Chardin (Clermont-Ferrand, 1902), 1:23.

102. Antoine Bergier and Verdier-Latour, *Recherches historiques sur les Etats généraux et plus particulièrement sur l'origine, l'organisation et la durée des anciens Etats provinciaux d'Auvergne* (Clermont-Ferrand, 1788), pièces justificatives, no. 70.

103. *IAC, Clermont-Ferrand*, 1:25, 47–57 passim; AD, Puy-de-Dôme, 4F 142–44 passim.

104. AD, Puy-de-Dôme, 4F 142 *IAC, Clermont-Ferrand*, 1:21, 44, 46–47; Bergier and Verdier-Latour, *Recherches*, pièces justificatives, nos. 60–62; André Imberdis, *Histoire des guerres religieuses en Auvergne* (Moulins, 1840), 1:155–59.

for defense. The smaller towns and villages were less easily satisfied, but in 1588 after a long struggle, they won the right to choose six of their number on a rotating basis to send deputies to meet with those of the original thirteen. The arrangement proved satisfactory and it was the schism between Catholic, politique, and Huguenot that plagued the province when the assassination of the duke of Guise brought new woes to the troubled land. (See chap. 6, sec. 2.)

François de La Rochefoucauld, count of Randon and governor of Basse-Auvergne, quickly opted for the League. With equal conviction the town of Clermont, although Catholic, chose the royalist side. This was enough to place its rival, Riom, in the League camp. Both protagonists sought the allegiance of the nobility, clergy, and other towns by summoning frequent meetings of the three estates and the deputies of the towns (there were no fewer than sixteen assemblies of one type or the other sponsored by the League during the last five years the war lasted in the province). The schism permitted Riom to assume its long-desired role of leader of the third estate, while the Clermontoise capitalized on their loyalty by persuading Henry III to transfer the Bureau of Finances and presidial seat from Riom to their city. A majority of the towns opted for the League, and three hundred of the four hundred nobles who took sides made the same choice. Eight hundred nobles, however, preferred to remain neutral until the probable victor could be more clearly ascertained. Randon's death in battle in March 1590 was followed by a stalemate in which there was more pillaging than fighting. The estates on both sides devoted most of their efforts to negotiations and to raising money through borrowing and taxation to pay for their defense. Finally, in 1594 the municipal leaders of Riom made peace because they feared that Henry IV would eventually triumph and reward Clermont for its fidelity by permitting it to keep the financial and judicial institutions permanently. Other towns and individuals quickly followed Riom's example, and royal authority was slowly restored.[105]

The towns and provostships of Haute-Auvergne seem to have assembled from one to four times a year during the Wars of Religion. Occasionally the other two orders participated. In December 1569 the three estates met at St. Flour to elect deputies to a joint meeting with the three estates of Basse-Auvergne at Clermont to discuss means to defend the two provinces. Earlier that year there had been a joint meeting of the deputies of the third estate in the same city to provide supplies for the army of the duke of Anjou. In January 1577 the towns of Haute-Auvergne met alone to vote taxes for their defense and to ask the king to divert royal taxes to this purpose. Later that

105. AD, Puy-de-Dôme, 4F 145. AC, St. Flour, ch. 5, art. 2, nos. 11–15; F. Leclercq, "Les Etats provinciaux de la Ligue en Basse-Auvergne de 1589 à 1594," *Bul. phil. et hist. (jusqu'à 1610) du comité des travaux historiques et scientifiques* (1963): 913–29; Imberdis, *Histoire des guerres religieuses*, 2: 86–483.

year they assembled again to take measures concerning the audit of the military accounts.[106]

The pace quickened in 1585, and the war entered its worst phase in 1589 when Aurillac opted for the king and St. Flour chose the Catholic League. In March of that year the deputies of the League towns met in St. Flour and resolved to try to capture the royalist town of Salers, but a truce was soon agreed upon between the opposing forces in that part of the province. In January 1591 several royalist towns met at Aurillac and elected deputies to an assembly of the three estates of Haute- and Basse-Auvergne that had been convoked by the count of Auvergne who was responsible for both provinces. In the late spring the royalists met again in Aurillac and granted 36,000 livres to their governor and his troops and 900 to his lieutenant. In 1593 the royalists voted 16,500 livres for the commander of the powerful château of Carlat in return for his services and expenses. The levy was approved by the king's council in January of the following year. In March and again in July 1594, the royalists sent delegations to the king to ask for lower taxes on the grounds that the province had suffered heavily from the war and that the nobility had purchased nearly half the land from the poor farmers, thereby reducing the tax base. The first appeal led to a 30,000 livre reduction in the taille designated for the garrison in the province, but this concession was revoked a few months later because of the necessity to pay the troops. Finally, St. Flour made peace with the king, and in January 1595 the deputies of the four towns and provostships assembled together once more at St. Flour.[107]

In the government of Lyonnais, there were assemblies of the three estates of Forez, of the plat pays of Lyonnais, of the third estate of Beaujolais, as well as of the government as a whole during the Wars of Religion. These assemblies, like those in other parts of France, dealt with many matters, but taxation and the military were their biggest preoccupations.

8. The Estates in Guyenne

The three estates of the généralité of Guyenne flourished during the latter part of the sixteenth century. First there was the problem of finding a substitute for the wine tax that was imposed in 1561 for six years, and then it was necessary to deal with the renewal of the tax in 1567. Finally in the

106. AC, St. Flour, ch. 5, art. 2, no. 10; *IAC, Aurillac*, ed. Gabriel Esquer (Aurillac, 1906), AA 21, BB 11.

107. AC, Aurillac, AA 21, AA 21bis. Portions of these documents are published in *IAC*, Aurillac. See also BB 9–12. AC, St. Flour, ch. 5, arts. 3, 4. *Dictionnaire statistique ou histoire, description et statistique du département du Cantal*, ed. Déribier-du-Châtelet (Aurillac, 1857), 5:224–28. AN, KK 648, fol. 117. BN ms. fr. 18,159, fols. 25, 332v–333. Valois, 1:nos. 1023, 1415.

1570s and 1580s the Wars of Religion led to many meetings to deal with the defense of the region and the support of troops. In all, between November 1561 and the succession of Henry IV to the throne in August 1589, the estates of the généralité met at least forty-six times. Although these assemblies undoubtedly contributed much toward the establishment of a common approach in dealing with the problems the region confronted and in combating the fiscal exploitation of the crown, they were essentially advisory in nature. Taxes were voted and, except in Bordelais and Périgord where there were élus, collected by the estates of seneschalsies or recettes. It is therefore hardly worthwhile to explore the confused history of the estates of the généralité in detail, but it is advisable to provide an indication of the activities of the assemblies in the ten smaller jurisdictions.

Because there was a large Protestant minority in Guyenne, the Wars of Religion were unusually bitter, and the third estate especially was very active. In Agenais meetings of the three estates were rare, but the consuls of Agen convoked the third estate so often that in 1569 it was agreed that the twelve principal towns could act for the order if circumstances so warranted. In their meetings, the third estate protested against taxes and tried to transfer the burden to others when it became obvious that someone must pay. They found the attempt of the nobility and royal officials to escape paying taxes on the common land they owned, in spite of the fact that the taille was réelle in Agenais, especially irritating. Many taxes were imposed on the order of the lieutenant general in Guyenne or the local military commanders. At times the suffering in the region became so acute that the estates or the individual communities found it necessary to borrow. By the end of the war Agen itself owed 24,000 livres. The estates advocated many reforms during this period and in 1583 pushed for a meeting of the Estates General to reform the administration of the kingdom. In spite of repeated and excessive demands on the part of the crown and local officials, however, the concept of consent was not lost. On October 22, 1588, for example, Henry III told the estates that they were "to grant and accord us freely the sums which they [the commissioners] will require of you on our behalf."[108]

The three estates of Comminges underwent similar experiences. The demands of war and the need for self-defense led to frequent meetings. Between 1567 and 1590 the estates assembled from four to eleven times annually except in 1572 when there were only two meetings. The normal taille and related taxes still stood at a figure under 20,000 livres during the Wars of Religion, but in addition the estates had to raise 190,000 livres from 1568 to 1570 for food, munitions, and pay for the military. In spite of heavy taxes, a debt of 35,000 livres had accrued by 1570. The three estates protested vigorously against these levies, but in the end they generally had to

---

108. AC, Agen, AA 17. On the estates of Agenais see esp. ibid., CC 61–84. *AHG* 29 (1894): 1–281, contains many documents concerning the estates and taxation. On the wars, see G. Tholin, "La ville d'Agen pendant les Guerres de Religion du XVIe siècle," *Revue de l'Agenais* 14–20 (1887–98).

pay. In nonmilitary affairs they were better able to assert themselves. In 1581, for example, they refused to pay part of the costs of repairing the harbor at Bayonne and of supporting the garrisons in the Protestant security towns. Only the thought of what unpaid, hungry troops might do opened their purses. That the crown had no intention of undermining the estates is suggested by the fact that between 1490 and 1594 their privileges were confirmed ten times.[109]

The three estates of Armagnac appear to have met about twice a year. At times there must have considerable confusion in the seneschalsy, for part of it was controlled by Henry of Navarre and part by the king. Thus in 1585 Navarre summoned the three estates to Lectoure where they appropriated 1,200 livres for him and 4,000 livres per month for their protection, but when he sought additional funds in the winter of 1587–88 Henry III's lieutenant in Guyenne forbad the viscounty of Bruilhois to send deputies under pain of being treated as rebels.[110]

Rouergue was plagued by the dissatisfaction of the smaller towns and villages, which believed that they were exploited by those who controlled the estates. There was also a rivalry between the principal towns, a disagreement among the three estates, and a conflict between Protestants and Catholics. In February 1579 several small towns won a decree from the Parlement of Toulouse forbidding the estates to make gifts to anyone and limiting the size of the deputations to court. Parlement further ruled that the third estate would deliberate alone when taxes were being considered that only it would pay, but that the three orders would continue to deliberate together when taxes to fall on everyone were to be voted upon.[111] Either to prevent financial abuses, perhaps in response to complaints from the smaller towns and villages, or to have more offices to sell, Henry III created élections throughout Guyenne in July 1581, but he revoked the edict in August 1582.[112] That September he sought to correct the abuses that the estates in Guyenne were accused of permitting by forbidding them to assemble or to levy taxes without his permission or that of the governor if it were a matter

109. M. J. de Naurois-Destenay, *Les Etats de Comminges aux XVIᵉ et XVIIᵉ siècles* (thesis, Ecole Nationale des Chartes, 1953–54), pp. 100, 103–05, 109, 112–13, 134. AD, Haute-Garonne, C 3486–662. Jean Lestrade has published some documents from this collection in *Cahiers des remonstrances des Etats de Comminges aux rois de France ou à leurs lieutenants généraux en Guyenne, 1537–1627* (Saint-Gaudens, 1943), and "Les Huguenots en Comminges," *Archives historiques de la Gascogne*, sér. 2, 5 (1900): 1–498. See also P.-E. Ousset, "Les députés d'Aspet aux Etats du Comminges," *Revue de Comminges* 87 (1974): 15–29.

110. AC, Lecture, BB 4; Henri IV, *Lettres*, 8:294–96; AC, Laplume, BB 4, p. 79. For numerous references to the estates between 1556 and 1581, see AC, Auch, BB 5 passim.

111. Camille Couderc, *Note sur les fastes consulaires de Bernard Arribat et documents sur l'histoire de Villefranche et du Rouergue à la fin du XVIᵉ siècle* (Rodez, 1893), pp. 18–20.

112. AC, Agen, AA 17. Henry was then creating a number of offices to sell in the region. For example, he created a new seneschalsy out of Agenais with its seat at Villeneuve-sur-Lot and considered creating another one at Sainte-Foy, but having profited from his endeavor, he suppressed the new seneschalsy a few months before he did the élections. Tholin "La ville d'Agen," *Revue* 17 (1890): 494, 496.

of paying troops to defend the province. He also directed that the syndics be elected from among the retiring *consuls* of the principal towns and serve for one year only. This decree also remained a dead letter in Rouergue at least, for in spite of further directives by the council and Parlement, it was necessary for Villefranche to ask that it be enforced in 1594.[113]

Millau opted for Protestantism at an early date and soon became the center for the estates of the members of that religion. The Catholic estates continued to function and proved their strength by winning a reduction in taxes in 1585 and on other occasions. During the troubled years that followed, Rodez opted for the League, but its rival, Villefranche, recognized Henry IV. In hope of a reward for its loyalty, Villefranche petitioned Henry for an exemption from paying its share of a tax of 660,000 livres that the League estates had voted Mayenne for 1594 and to free it from all tailles for the next ten years. Henry readily forbad the League assessment but refused to permit Villefranche to escape other taxes. Soon after this episode Rodez recognized Henry, and the estates, though still quarreling, became united once more.[114]

The three estates of Quercy, like those in other parts of Guyenne, were a major factor during the Wars of Religion. Henry III, for example, wrote them in 1585 to obtain their assistance for his army. Three years later Marshal Biron complained that they had taken no note of his military exploits which had been accomplished at his own expense. All he professed to want was an expression of their gratitude, and this is all the estates specifically gave when they met the following month. They did not, however, take Biron's altruism at its face value, for they pointed out that the king had forbidden them to tax without permission, a rule they were not so anxious to observe when it was not to their advantage. Fearful of offending the powerful marshal, they did vaguely hold out hope for a grant when the taille was next collected.[115]

Limited surviving evidence suggests that the third estate was active in Lannes,[116] Condomois,[117] and Rivière-Verdun[118] during the Wars of

113. Couderc, *Note sur les fastes consulaires*, pp. 20–28.

114. Ibid., pp. 72–74, 169–78. For the Protestant estates, see AD, Aveyron, 2E 157.4, and J.-L. Rigal, "Mémoires d'un Calviniste de Millau," *Archives historiques du Rouergue* 2 (1911): 259–60, 282–88, 310, 313–15, 320, 335–37, 343–44, 360–61, 439, 447–48.

115. Edmond Cabié, *Guerres de Religion dans le sud-ouest de la France et principalement dans le Quercy* (Paris, 1906), pp. 744–45, 797–98, 810–11. There are numerous documents concerning the estates in this work. See also De Villaret, "A Montcuq en 1587: Affaires consulaires se rattachant à la lutte contre les Protestants d'après des documents inédits," *Bul. de la soc. des études littéraires, scientifiques et artistiques du Lot* 48 (1927): 1–40, and 49 (1928): 90–103.

116. BN ms. fr. 21,425, fol. 11; AC, Saint-Sever, II, 1 (1519–1789); *Archives municipales de Bayonne: Délibérations du corps de ville. Registres Français* (Bayonne, 1906), 2:387–88, 392, 400.

117. AC, La Réole, BB 4, fol. 198; AC, Monségur, BB 1, p. 405; J. Duffour, "Les Etats d'Astarac de 1582," *Revue de Gascogne* 47 (1906): 19–30; BN ms. fr. 21,425, fol. 10.

118. Jean Contrasty, *Histoire de Sainte-Foy-de-Peyrolières* (Toulouse, 1917), pp. 198–210; BN ms. fr. 21,428, fols. 20–21.

Religion. The same generalization can be made about the three estates of Périgord and the third estate of Bordelais, although the élus served as tax collectors in these seneschalsies. The three estates of Périgord or their permanent executive arm, the définiteurs, opposed the creation of new offices for sale and the constant increase in the taille with occasional success. In 1584, for example, some offices were suppressed without compensation, and the taille was reduced as a result of their syndics' visit to court. The estates became divided because Bergerac was Protestant, while Périgueux and Sarlat remained loyal to the Catholic cause. The three estates were also troubled by the demand of the smaller towns and plat pays for a syndic and a larger voice in their deliberations. One of their demands was that the élus be suppressed, while in seneschalsies where officials of the estates collected the taille, such as Comminges, the plat pays had asked that an élection be established in 1552. Whether employed by the crown or the estates, tax officials were likely to be unpopular.[119]

A group of nobles met in Bordeaux in May 1563 and asked the king to establish an assembly of the estates in the seneschalsy of Guyenne similar to those that functioned in all the other jurisdictions in the government of Guyenne, but the council refused to countenance this innovation. The three estates did meet in Bordeaux in November 1582 and possibly at other times, but the more common practice was for the town officials of Bordeaux to assemble the *filleules*, or daughter towns. In 1573, 1580, 1585, and doubtless many other occasions, the principal subject of the meeting was taxation.[120]

When Henry IV came to the throne in 1589, he found most of eastern Guyenne in the hands of the Catholic League. The ultra-Catholic Parlement of Toulouse had rallied the important towns and provincial estates within and bordering on its jurisdiction to the League cause. Agen became the administrative capital with a Parlement and a Bureau of Finances to serve the League-controlled portions of the généralité. Even more rapidly the League leaders organized the representative assemblies in the area under their control. The estates of the généralité met in Aurignac in June 1589 and again in Toulouse that August to raise an army and to provide money for its support. Further meetings were held at Gimont in May and at Auch in July 1590, at Agen and at Saint-Julien in 1591, at Agen again in 1592, and at Moissac in 1594. At these assemblies the League chiefs asked for funds to

---

119. BN ms. fr. 22,382, fols. 33–36; L. de Cardenal, "Catalogue des assemblées des Etats de Périgord de 1378 à 1651," *Bul. phil. et hist. (jusqu'à 1715) du comité des travaux historiques et scientifiques* (1938–39): 261–65; and de Cardenal, "Les Etats de Périgord sous Henri IV," *L'organisation corporative du Moyen Age à la fin de l'ancien régime* (Louvain, 1939), 3: 165–81.

120. References to assemblies in Bordelais are found in AC, St. Émilion, AA 5, BB 9, BB 11; AC, Bourg-sur-Gironde, BB 1. For the petition to form an assembly of the estates, see *Documents des guerres civiles*, p. 228.

carry on their activities. Smaller amounts were generally voted, and these totals were divided among the recettes whose estates were asked to give their consent to their assigned burden. The tax was then levied under the supervision of the officials of the estates and the *consuls* of the towns and communities. Thus the royal financial administrative system was duplicated and with it the friction between what today would be called the executive and legislative branches of the government. For example, the League governor wanted the estates of 1592 to vote a huge sum for his army, Agenais' share alone coming to 240,000 livres, but the municipal officials of Agen did not think that the recette could pay over 54,000 livres since the nobility and clergy would not contribute.[121]

On the royalist side Marshal Matignon persuaded the town and Parlement of Bordeaux to side with the king in spite of their Catholic sentiments. This city became his capital and principal source of strength. He also drew considerable support from the countryside where many nobles were vassals or clients of the Bourbons or hopeful of royal favor. From the outset he was beset by financial problems, but he appears to have made less use of the estates than the League did. The estates of Condomois and Bazadais functioned normally in 1589; there was the usual protest against certain taxes coupled with a gift of wine to Matignon, but the taille was apportioned and collected. In the fall the royalist deputies of the généralité met at Marmande and voted 90,000 livres. The following January the Parlement of Bordeaux asked Henry to convoke the estates of the seneschalsy of Bordeaux, a petition that was granted but perhaps not acted upon. Thereafter there was silence on the royalist front as far as the estates were concerned. In January 1590 Matignon reported that financial officials had begun to collect taxes without waiting for the king to hear remonstrances of the people. When this revenue did not suffice, he resorted to forced loans and increased levies on river commerce.[122]

This apparent abandoning of the estates should not be interpreted as a deliberate attack on representative institutions. Royalist strength lay in the

121. François Gébelin, *Le gouvernement du Maréchal de Matignon en Guyenne* (Bordeaux, 1912), pp. 26–29. For the estates of 1589 see AC, Agen, BB 37, fols. 29–31v; AD, Haute-Garonne, C 3643, C 3796. For the estates of 1590 see AD, Haute-Garonne, C 3648, C 3649; AC, Agen, BB 37, fols. 50–51; AD, Gers., I 1628. For the estates of 1591, see AC, Agen, BB 35, fol. 107, BB 37, fols. 85–86v; AD, Haute-Garonne, C 3652, C 3653. For the estates of 1592 see AC, Agen, BB 35, fol. 125, BB 37, fols. 150v–54v; AD, Haute-Garonne, C 3657. For the estates of 1594, see AC, Haute-Garonne, C 3662; AC, Agen, CC 150, fol. 39–39v. I have found no meeting for 1593. For an account of the League in Agenais, see G. Tholin, "La ville d'Agen pendant les Guerres de Religion du XVIᵉ siècle," *Revue de l'Agenais* 19 (1892): 22–39, 118–33, and 20 (1893): 52–67, 177–200. See also Naurois-Destenay, *Les Etats de Comminges*, pp. 149–50; Jean Lestrade, "Les Huguenots en Comminges," *Archives historiques de la Gascogne*, sér. 2, 5 (1900): 156–57, 180–81, 185–86, 246–51; and *Cahiers des Etats de Comminges*, pp. 90–94.

122. Gébelin, *Le gouvernement du Maréchal*, pp. 105–21, 140–46. AC, La Reóle, BB 4, pp. 198–99. *AHG*, 4:221–24, 229; Henri IV, *Lettres*, 3:860.

recettes of Bordeaux, Lannes, and Condomois-Bazadais. Only the last two had estates that met regularly prior to Henry's reign. Outside these three jurisdictions and the Haute-Marche of Rouergue, the royalists controlled insufficient contiguous territory to make holding the estates feasible. Furthermore, most of the towns, the backbone of the provincial estates in Guyenne, had sided with the Catholic League.[123] Matignon himself does not seem to have been opposed to representative assemblies. He or his subordinates dealt with the deputies of the various League estates constantly from 1592 trying to arrange truces, and the final settlements made in May 1594 in part resulted from the efforts of a large royalist assembly that met at Lectoure. By the terms of the peace, Henry confirmed the privileges of the League provinces and towns and exonerated them from paying the arrears in royal taxes prior to 1594.[124]

9. The Estates of Béarn and Navarre

Béarn and Navarre are of special interest during the Wars of Religion. Here the sovereign became a Protestant, but initially most of the people were Catholics, a situation that led to considerable friction and raised important constitutional questions. Henri d'Albret and his wife, Marguerite d'Angoulême, had been Catholics, but the latter's willingness to shelter the religiously unorthodox had permitted Protestants to gain an early foothold in Béarn and other territories of the house of Foix-Navarre. The Protestants were still in a minority, however, when their daughter, Jeanne d'Albret, publicly announced her conversion in December 1560. At first Jeanne proceeded cautiously. Both France and Spain were anxious to gobble up her tiny state, and a charge that she was turning it into a Protestant bastion to serve as a base from which to propagate heresy in the surrounding territory was as good an excuse as any that could be found to justify such an act. Furthermore, her husband, Antoine de Bourbon, opposed giving the Protestants encouragement because he had joined the Catholic camp in the vain hope that this would lead Philip II to return Spanish Navarre to him. The estrangement of the couple and Antoine's death in November 1562 freed Jeanne from his restraining influence. During the spring and summer of 1563, she forbade Corpus Christi processions, ordered that images be removed from the churches of Pau and Lescar, and appealed to Calvin for ministers to aid in the conversion of her subjects. The estates that met in June of that year protested vigorously against the prohibition of religious

123. A three-year gap in the municipal register of La Réole, the best source for the estates of the recette of Condomois-Bazadais, prevents a reconstruction of the activities of the estates here in the early 1590s.

124. Gébelin, *Le gouvernement du Maréchal*, pp. 147–69; letters from Comminges to Henry IV, BN ms. fr. 23,194, fols. 308–09, 316, 330.

processions, but Jeanne sheltered herself behind a technicality in the *fors* to refuse to countermand her order. It is interesting to note that the Grand Corps voted only thirty-six to twenty-nine to make remonstrances on this issue, thereby demonstrating the deep inroads that Calvinism had already made into the nobility, but that only a handful of the towns failed to take a pro-Catholic position.[125]

The opposition of the estates coupled with the growing possibility that Spain would intervene caused Jeanne to slow her pace, much to the discomfiture of the Protestant ministers. In spite of her growing moderation, a head-on collision took place when the estates met in January–February 1564. Both houses threatened to depart before any taxes were voted if Jeanne did not satisfy their religious complaints. At first she did nothing, but finding the estates intransigent, she promised on February 2 to permit Catholic and Protestant alike to worship as they pleased. Nine days later the victorious estates voted her the ordinary donation of 10,000 Béarnese écus plus an additional grant of 8,000. By her act she had prevented a possible rebellion, and perhaps more important, had retained the protection of Catherine de Medici, then regent of France and the only possible counterbalance to the power of Spain.[126]

Jeanne was not in Béarn when the estates met in 1565 and 1566. The Catholics, who were still in a majority, presented some complaints against the special favors granted to the Calvinists, but on the whole the two sessions were relatively uneventful. Hardly had the estates disbanded in 1566, however, than the still-absent Jeanne issued an ordinance in which she frankly avowed her intention to suppress the Catholic religion. Its articles prohibited gambling, drunkenness, dancing, and the like, outlawed religious processions throughout the viscounty, strengthened the Protestant hold over the educational system, and assigned the revenue of vacated benefices to the poor of the reformed church unless Protestants were named as the new incumbents. The syndics of the estates and the upper clergy, who had boycotted the previous meeting of the estates, protested to the Sovereign Council that the ordinance was contrary to both their privileges and the principle of freedom of conscience established two years before. Agitation became widespread and Jeanne's lieutenant general suspended the application of the ordinance, but not before some leading Catholics began to conspire to overthrow her regime.[127]

Jeanne was present when the estates met in Pau during the summer of

125. Charles Dartigue-Peyrou, *Jeanne d'Albret et le Béarn d'après les délibérations des Etats et les registrès du Conseil Souverain, 1555–1572* (Mont-de-Marsan, 1934), pp. 50–54; Nancy L. Roelker, *Queen of Navarre, Jeanne d'Albret, 1528–1572* (Cambridge, Mass., 1968), pp. 135–224; Marc Forissier, *Histoire de la réforme en Béarn* (Tarbes, 1951), 1:49–142.

126. Dartigue-Peyrou, *Jeanne d'Albret*, pp. 61–66; Roelker, *Queen of Navarre*, pp. 224–26, 267–68.

127. Dartigue-Peyrou, *Jeanne d'Albret*, 71–81. Roelker, *Queen of Navarre*, pp. 239–40, 268–69.

1567, but this did not deter the Catholics from protesting vigorously against the various provisions of the ordinance of the preceding year which Jeanne had begun to enforce upon her return to Béarn. In the upper house the voting was again close—the Catholics won by the narrow margin of forty-nine to forty-two—but in the third estate, only Pau and three other localities fully supported the Protestant cause. Faced with a deadlock, Jeanne had to choose between fulfilling what she regarded as her Christian duty or responding favorably to the wishes of her subjects. She initially adopted the former course, but as far as can be ascertained the estates countered by voting her no money that year. Furthermore, shortly after they disbanded, a serious Catholic rebellion broke out in Navarre which soon led Jeanne to see the need to pacify her Catholic subjects in Béarn. Reluctantly she restored their religious rights and freedom of conscience. The estates that met in April 1568 were much calmer, and the chastened Jeanne was voted 18,000 Béarnais écus.[128]

One of the reasons Jeanne desisted momentarily in her effort to turn Béarn and Navarre into Calvinist strongholds was the threat of Catholic intervention from France. To remove the possibility in the future, she needed to strengthen the Protestant position in that country, and especially in Guyenne. Perhaps for this reason Jeanne decided to abandon the neutrality she had previously adopted in the French religious wars and to take her young son, Henry, to La Rochelle to join the other Protestant leaders. In October 1568, less than a month after her arrival in the Protestant stronghold, Charles IX's council ordered the baron de Terride to conquer Béarn. Aware of the threat to their independence, the estates met soon after in a special session and voted 15,000 Béarnais écus to put the viscounty in a state of defense. Catholic joined Protestant in this endeavor. Indeed it was the bishop of Oloron who proposed the heavy levy, and in a special meeting in December the nobles, Catholic and Protestant alike, swore to defend the little viscounty.[129]

The unity before the French, however, was short-lived, for once Terride had overrun most of the viscounty during the spring of 1569, the cause of Béarnais independence seemed lost. Under such circumstances many Catholics could not resist the temptation to join the conquerors. Terride reconstituted the Sovereign Council and held a rump meeting of the estates in July. Steps were taken to restore Catholicism and to confiscate the goods of those who continued to resist. Meanwhile Jeanne had directed the count of Montgomery to lead an army in relief. He struck in August, and in a brilliant two-week campaign drove Terride's forces from the viscounty. At

128. Dartigue-Peyrou, *Jeanne d'Albret*, pp. lxx–lxxv, 83–98; Roelker, *Queen of Navarre*, pp. 269–70.

129. Dartigue-Peyrou, *Jeanne d'Albret*, 103–109; Pierre Tucco-Chala, *La vicomté de Béarn et le problème de la souveraineté* (Bordeaux, 1961), pp. 124, 193; Roelker, *Queen of Navarre*, pp. 291–301.

last Jeanne was in the position she had always desired. Many of her Catholic subjects had been proven traitors, thereby forfeiting all claim to her goodwill, and she had the military capacity to enforce the changes she wished. Furthermore, the restoration of peace in France in the summer of 1570 and Philip II's growing preoccupation with the revolt in the Netherlands removed the likelihood of intervention by either of her powerful neighbors.[130]

Immediately after his victory Montgomery reconstituted the Sovereign Council with loyal Protestants. With this now-subservient instrument, Jeanne was able to issue ordinances in September 1569 removing from office Catholics who did not adjure and forbidding priests to perform the sacraments. The estates, now thoroughly Protestant, met in a special session in September of the following year to remove from office one of their syndics who had joined the rebels and to renew their oath of fidelity to their viscountess. In March 1571 the estates elected new syndics and sent a deputation to Jeanne to request that they be consulted in the impending religious settlement. When Jeanne returned to Béarn, she summoned the estates to meet in the fall. It was in response to their request, a request that she doubtless inspired, that she issued the ordinance giving the Béarnaise reformation its final form. In doctrine and ecclesiastical organization, the Geneva model was followed, except that secular authority was more clearly spelled out as being supreme. The wealth of the Catholic church was assigned to support the Protestant ministry and a system of free public education. Loyal Catholics were not banished nor was their property confiscated, but Catholic rites were outlawed and Catholics were compelled to attend Protestant services.[131]

Jeanne's decision to impose the reformation through the estates ensured their survival just as the English Henry VIII's decision to act through Parliament had given that institution renewed life some years before. In 1567 Jeanne and the estates had been deadlocked over the religious issue. The delicate balance that must exist between the monarch and the estates if the extremes of absolutism or republicanism were to be avoided was threatened. Only after military victory had turned the estates into a Protestant stronghold could cooperation between the devout monarch and the representative assembly be restored. This is not to say that there were no longer disputes. The estates that met in February 1572, the last that were to take place in Jeanne's reign, elected a deputation to follow her to the French court to complain that the religious ordinances of the preceding few weeks were contrary to the fors.[132]

Jeanne died in June 1572. Her eighteen-year-old son, Henry III of

---

130. Dartigue-Peyrou, *Jeanne d'Albret*, pp. lxxix–lxxxvii, 109–11.
131. Ibid., pp. lxxxviii–ic, 111–29, 141–64; Roelker, *Queen of Navarre*, pp. 271–78.
132. Dartigue-Peyrou, *Jeanne d'Albret*, p. 131.

Navarre, afterward Henry IV of France, became the sovereign of the little viscounty. At the age of four, Henry had nominally acted as his mother's representative during a meeting of the estates, and he had often been voted handsome gifts by that body. It was he who represented his mother when the estates met in February 1572 for the last time in her reign. Young as he was, he had already obtained some experience in dealing with representative assemblies when he inherited the scattered lands of the house of Foix-Navarre-Albret.[133]

Some years elapsed before Henry had an opportunity to exercise these talents, for by June he was on his way to Paris, there to marry and to suffer confinement after the massacre of St. Bartholomew. Indeed, only by abjuring and issuing an edict that October reestablishing Catholicism in Béarn could he assure that his life would be spared. Led by the baron d'Arros, the lieutenant general Jeanne had appointed and Henry had confirmed upon her death, the Béarnaise refused to abandon Calvinism. When the French dispatched an army with Henry's outward consent to compel obedience, the Béarnais forces put it to flight and captured its commander. From then until his retirement in 1575, D'Arros, the Sovereign Council, and the estates proved quite capable of governing the viscounty without the aid of a sovereign prince.[134]

In spite of the defeat of the Catholic army, Henry continued his efforts to restore Catholicism as long as he was a captive. In May 1575 he appointed a Catholic governor who quickly found himself at odds with the Sovereign Council and the estates. He summoned the clergy to the latter and did what he could to further the Catholic cause in Béarn. The estates resisted, but before the outcome could be clearly seen, Henry escaped, reaffirmed his membership in the Calvinist church, and in January 1577 named his eighteen-year-old sister, Catherine, regent of Béarn, Navarre, and Foix. Catherine was as staunch a Calvinist as her mother and furthered the interests of that church as much as she could. Her dedication to the Protestant cause enabled harmony with the estates to be restored. There were occasional threats from French Catholics that led to the transfer of the archives of the estates to the powerful fortress of Navarrenx, but after the campaigns of 1568–73 Béarn suffered little from the civil war. Not until Henry ascended the throne in 1589 and abjured in 1593, shortly after recalling his sister from Pau, was the enviable position of the viscounty once more threatened.[135]

Jeanne d'Albret was less successful in her efforts to impose Calvinism on Navarre. Indeed, she managed to drive her little Basque kingdom into revolt in 1569. Even when she restored her authority, she was unable to

---

133. Ibid., pp. 23, 25, 32, 41, 74, 77, 98, 128, 131.
134. Forissier, *Histoire de la réforme*, 2:9–16.
135. Ibid., pp. 17–43. Forissier's treatment of the estates is inadequate. After 1569 Béarn was invaded only once, in 1592.

suppress Catholicism as she had done in Béarn. Neither the translation of the New Testament into Basque nor the efforts of Basque-speaking preachers was sufficient to persuade a significant number of the inhabitants to accept the new faith. In the spring of 1571 the estates stated that there were not a dozen Protestants in the kingdom and pleaded for the right to practice their religion. Faced with such overwhelming opposition, Jeanne dared not impose Calvinism as firmly as she had done in Béarn. Her death the following year and Henry's recantation after the massacre of St. Bartholomew removed the threat of further inroads, but until 1601 the estates felt it necessary to make annual pleas for liberty of conscience and the restoration of the confiscated goods of the church.[136]

Little can be ascertained concerning the actual functioning of the estates in the other lands of the house of Foix-Navarre during the Wars of Religion, but something can be learned of Henry of Navarre's attitude toward these institutions from his correspondence with his governors, the *consuls* of the towns, and other officials in Foix. In 1576 he asked his governor and the *consuls* of Carlat to speed the collection of the taxes voted by the estates. In January 1577 he told the governor to do all in his power to persuade the estates to agree voluntarily to support 500 foot soldiers for four months, and in the following months he praised him for the manner in which he had handled the assembly. In June 1581 Henry instructed his governor to cajole the estates into increasing their customary donation, and in July he thanked him for the careful way in which he had conducted the meeting. As tangible evidence of his gratitude Henry gave him the income from two benefices. In 1584 Henry announced his intention of going to Foix near the close of the estates in order to hear the petitions of his subjects. In 1596 he promised the estates that he would try to satisfy their desires and in return asked them to grant more than their customary donation because of his pressing needs. In 1598 he repeated the same formula. Always Henry associated the redress of grievances with the voting of a tax. Never did he question the existence of the estates or their role.[137]

The care Henry devoted to winning the cooperation of the estates of his hereditary lands did not always produce the desired results, however. When the seneschal requested the three estates of Bigorre for a grant for him in 1576, they refused to take any action until their lord had arrived to hear their grievances personally, this despite the fact that they had voted him nothing during the preceding year or two. In 1585 and in 1586 they were

136. Alan Destrée, *La Basse-Navarre et ses institutions de 1620 à la Révolution* (Saragossa, 1955), pp. 24–26; Forissier, *Histoire de la réforme*, 1 : 197–202, 209, 277–81, 289–92.

137. T. Desbarreaux-Bernard, *Quatre lettres inédites de Henry IV* (Toulouse, 1866), p. 6; C. de La Hitte, "Lettres inédites de Henri IV à M. De Pailhès," *Archives historiques de la Gascogne* 10 (1886): 14–17, 37–38, 64, 78–84. For other letters concerning the estates see La Hitte, pp. 36, 58–59, 63, 66, 69, and Desbarreaux-Bernard, p. 5

content to grant the modest sum of 1,000 livres. In 1587 they were more generous and gave Henry 4,000 livres and his sister, Catherine, who was his heir apparent, 2,000. In 1589, the year Henry became their king as well as their count, they extended themselves by granting him 9,000 livres and his sister a third that amount. From then through 1598, they voted Henry from 3,000 to 6,000 livres annually and his sister half that sum. On the whole, Henry's deportment in his dealing with the estates in his hereditary lands provided an admirable model for a constitutional king.[138]

10. THE ESTATES, THE WARS OF RELIGION, AND BODIN'S CONCEPT OF SOVEREIGNTY

The Wars of Religion presented a serious threat to the provincial estates, but the timing and the severity of the threat varied from one province to another. From the beginning there were strong Protestant minorities in Languedoc and Dauphiné who quickly developed their own system of self-government at the expense of the authority of the estates as well as of the king. For the most part, however, the estates survived the 1560s and much of the 1570s without excessive strains being placed on their positions. In Burgundy, Brittany, Languedoc, and even in Normandy and Dauphiné, the king convoked special sessions of the estates on one or more occasions when it became necessary to levy additional taxes or when some other matter was in dispute. In Auvergne and Guyenne where the échevins of the capital town frequently had the right to convoke the third estate, meetings were especially numerous.

The difficulty arose when an unfriendly army threatened a province and there was no time to indulge in the slow and cumbersome process of convoking the estates and holding the necessary elections. To meet this situation, smaller meetings were developed that could be assembled with relative rapidity. The three estates of Brittany and those of some other provinces were reluctant to see their authority fragmented, but the need for speed was so great that they had no alternative. During this period the assembly of the communities was created in Provence, and meetings of the twelve principal towns in Agenais began to be substituted occasionally for full assemblies of the third estate. Sometimes permanent committees of the estates, such as the commis of Dauphiné, or the officers of the estates, such as the élus of Burgundy, were called upon to act. At times the initiative to hold a meeting was taken by the king or an officer of the estates, but most often it was the

138. *IAC, Vic-Bigorre,* ed. Jean Pambrun (Tarbes, 1924), p. 3; Gilbert Pène *Les attributions financières des Etats du pays et comté de Bigorre aux XVIIe et XVIIIe siècles* (Bordeaux, 1962), pp. 95–96, 491.

royal governor who wanted some sort of an authorization to levy a tax to defend his government. Legal levies were easier to collect than those imposed by fiat, and this was especially true where the tax-collecting machinery was in the hands of the estates. The three estates often protested when they were bypassed, and the committees and officers grumbled, but they had little choice but to cooperate. An invading army or even an unpaid friendly garrison posed more of a threat to them than the collection of a few thousand livres without the consent of the full estates.

There were instances even in the early days of the wars when taxes were levied without a pretense of obtaining some form of consent. The forced loans the crown sought for the most part from its own officials and well-to-do burghers should not be considered taxes because they were generally repaid without interest from future levies. Such taxes as those the government of Charles IX attempted to impose on the Breton towns in 1562 and 1571 and the levy that Catherine de Medici placed on Normandy in 1574 without the consent of their respective estates were, however, clear infractions of their privileges, unless one is willing to accept the crown's argument that "urgent necessity" took precedence over the rights of subjects. Henry III found it necessary to act arbitrarily more often. In 1584 he bypassed the estates of Languedoc and went directly to the dioceses for a tax, and in 1587 he ordered that 120,000 livres be imposed on the towns and bourgs of Brittany in spite of the fact that the estates had refused to authorize the levy. Henry, however, was a desperate man who was soon to risk everything by having the duke of Guise assassinated, but even he generally preferred to raise money by forced loans, the sale of offices and patents of nobility, and taxes imposed in the routine fashion.

Actually the estates' control over taxation was threatened more often by the governor, the Huguenots, and the League than by the crown. A governor was responsible for the defense of his government. When it was threatened, he often failed to wait for the next meeting of the estates or to obtain the king's permission to tax. Rather he turned to a quickly assembled abbreviated form of the estates or to their officers or permanent committee and demanded the needed funds. If consent was not granted, he sometimes acted unilaterally, but on the whole the need was so obvious that those consulted generally granted at least part of what was asked. In divided Dauphiné, he sometimes sought a semblance of legality by turning to Parlement. From the first the Huguenots appropriated royal taxes in the regions they controlled. Their commanders negotiated for funds with towns held by members of their faith and took what they wanted from the Catholic localities they seized. When the Catholic League completely broke with Henry III after the assassination of the duke of Guise, its leaders behaved in a similar fashion.

It will never be possible to write an accurate history of taxation during this confused period or to determine how much the crown and other groups received.[139] Certainly the people, and none more so than the inhabitants of the unprotected plat pays, suffered greatly. During the last decade of the conflict, it is improbable that more than a small portion of the taxes levied in the king's name ever reached his coffers. Some military commanders, as Lesdiguières, profited from the collapse of royal tax authority to amass fortunes. Governors became accustomed to having troops supported at the taxpayers' expense and to ruling in their governments with little concern for directives from the crown. Their clients occupied key positions in the local royal administration and courts of law, all of which boded ill for the future of royal authority.

In one sense, the role of the estates increased as France sank into civil war and finally into anarchy. Like their governors, the estates largely escaped from royal control. They levied what taxes they chose with very little limitations from Paris. They expanded their duties to include raising armies and negotiating with foreign powers. They met more frequently and improved their procedures in order to cope with emergencies. Indeed, the three estates of Burgundy, Brittany, and Normandy massed a counterattack against the crown in 1578 designed to curb royal taxation and to secure the enactment of the reforms proposed by the Estates General of Blois. The Normans sought to rid themselves of the élections, but none of the estates won more than temporary success. Individually they were no match for their desperate monarchs, and collective action was very difficult because they met at different times and communication was so slow that they could not hope to coordinate their efforts. To secure unity of action, the Normans proposed in 1579 that another meeting of the Estates General be held, and Agenais made a similar suggestion in 1583.

Nevertheless the provincial estates lost heavily during the wars in some respects. Areas that were controlled by the Huguenots escaped their jurisdiction, and in 1589 many of them became divided into royalist and League assemblies. Furthermore they frequently found that their governor was a more severe taskmaster than their far-away king had been. Their near monopoly over taxation was broken both because Huguenot- and League-controlled regions escaped their authority, and taxes were often levied arbitrarily. Finally, they fell deeply into debt and sometimes lost the goodwill of the inhabitants of the plat pays because they taxed them so heavily.

Yet the Wars of Religion did not in themselves damage the estates permanently. The crown made no institutional changes that significantly affected their role in government. In Guyenne élections were created in 1581, but they were abandoned the following year. As peace was restored,

139. For useful attempts to explain taxation during the Wars of Religion, see Martin Wolfe, *The Fiscal System of Renaissance France* (New Haven, 1972), pp. 104–213. See also H. Michaud, "L'ordonnancement des dépenses et le budget de la monarchie, 1587–1589," *Ann.-bul. de la société de l'histoire de France* (1970–71): 87–150.

the estates were reunited once more and the king forbad everyone, including
the governors and the estates, to levy taxes without his permission. Of course
Henry IV, like his Valois predecessors, had sometimes taxed without
consent, and this could be a dangerous precedent, but he had justified his
action on the basis of the widely accepted doctrine of urgent necessity. With
the return of peace and necessity removed, was there any reason to believe
that the Renaissance system of the crown and the estates playing dual roles
in the government could not be restored? Certainly Henry's treatment of the
estates in his hereditary lands gave justification for such a hope.

There was one cloud on the horizon. Most people were tired of civil war
and wanted peace at any price. If it became a choice of fighting to protect
their privileges or permitting them to be eroded by crown, they would very
likely choose the latter course. This attitude was reflected in the works of the
political theorists. When Jean Bodin published the *Methodus* in 1566, he
believed that "the civilized and proper form of sovereignty was supremacy
within the law."[140] He was still confident of France's future as late as 1572,
but the worsening situation soon led him to embark on a long political
treatise designed to strengthen the position of the king and to crush the
emerging Huguenot theory of mixed sovereignty.[141] "Sovereignty," Bodin
now declared, "is the absolute and perpetual power of a commonwealth ...
that is to say, the greatest power to command."[142] Sovereignty could be
exercised by a king, an aristocracy, or the people through the estates, but
Bodin much preferred the first solution. All institutions were subordinate to
the sovereign, and none of them had any independent authority. "But
someone will say," he postulated, "that there could be a commonwealth in
which the people appointed officials, controlled expenditures, and granted
pardons, which are three marks of sovereignty; and the nobility made laws,
determined on peace and war, and decided on taxes which are also marks of
sovereignty; and in addition in which there was a royal magistrate above
them all to whom all the people in general and individually rendered faith
and liege homage and who judged in the last resort and from whose
judgment there was no appeal." Such a state, Bodin admitted, would have
elements of democracy, aristocracy, and monarchy because sovereignty
would be divided, but he insisted that "no such state has ever been found or
could even be imagined since the attributes of sovereignty are indivisible."[143] Then, having rejected the possibility of a mixed state, Bodin

---

140. Julian H. Franklin, *Jean Bodin and the Rise of Absolutist Theory* (Cambridge, 1973), p. 38.
On Bodin's political thought, see also William F. Church, *Constitutional Thought in Sixteenth-
Century France* (Cambridge, Mass., 1941), pp. 194–242; and *Jean Bodin: Proceedings of the
International Conference on Bodin in Munich*, ed. Horst Denzer (Munich, 1973), pp. 151–397.
141. Franklin, *Jean Bodin*, p. 49.
142. Jean Bodin, *Les six livres de la république* (Paris, 1583), bk. 1, ch. 8, p. 122.
143. Ibid., bk. 2, ch. 1, p. 266.

admitted that sovereignty was divided between the king and the nobility in Denmark and Sweden, but these were corrupted commonwealths in which there were intrigues and civil wars. Hence sovereignty was indivisible in the well-ordered state, and where the nobility had seized some of the attributes of sovereignty, there was chaos.

Although Bodin insisted that France was a pure monarchy and that neither the estates nor any other institution had independent authority, he thought that representative assemblies and other popular institutions served a useful purpose. Like most other royalist theorists of his day, he saw the Estates General as an institution that increased the authority of the king. "We conclude therefore," he wrote, "that the sovereignty of the monarch is neither altered nor diminished by the presence of the estates. On the contrary, his majesty is much greater and more illustrious seeing all his people acknowledge him as their sovereign."[144] Corporations, communities, and provincial estates were equally valuable to the sovereign, Bodin thought, although he admitted that tyrants feared assemblies of their subjects and sought to destroy them: "Nevertheless, the just monarchy has no more assured foundation than the estates of the people and corporate groups because if it is necessary to levy taxes, assemble troops, or defend the state against enemies, it cannot be better done than by the estates of the people of every province, town, and community."[145] Bodin, who had studied law in Toulouse, then enumerated many of the advantages of holding the provincial estates and gave some specific examples of the activities of those of Languedoc.[146]

To enable the king to cope with the growing disorders in France, Bodin had assigned him the sole power to make human law and denied that the magnates, sovereign courts, and estates had any independent authority. Nevertheless he was not an absolutist. The king, he asserted, was under divine and natural law. These intangible concepts would not in themselves have provided much protection had he not insisted that property was a natural right and that therefore "there is no prince in the world who has the power to levy taxes on the people at his pleasure any more than he can take their goods." At this point, however, Bodin weakened his position by accepting the medieval doctrine that "if the necessity is urgent, the prince should not wait for the estates to assemble or the people to consent since their safety depends on his foresight and diligence."[147] Bodin also placed the king under fundamental law and argued that he was bound by the contracts that he had made, a proviso that offered some protection for provincial privileges.

In spite of Bodin's reservations, he was attacked by a Genevan for having

144. Ibid., bk. 1, ch. 8, p. 141.
145. Ibid., bk. 3, ch. 7, p. 500.
146. Ibid., bk. 3, ch. 7, pp. 501–502.
147. Ibid., bk. 1, ch. 8, p. 140.

given the king too much power. Angrily he responded in the preface to the
1578 edition of the *République* that he had been

> the very first, even in the most perilous times, to refute unhesitatingly the
> opinions of those who write of enlarging the rights of the treasury and of
> the royal prerogative, on the grounds that these men grant to kings an
> unlimited power, superior to divine and natural law. But what could be
> more in the interest of the people than what I have had the courage to
> write: that not even to kings is it lawful to levy taxes without the fullest
> consent of the citizens? Or of what importance is my other statement: that
> princes are more stringently bound by divine and natural law than those
> subject to their rule? Or that princes are bound by their covenants exactly
> as other citizens are? Yet nearly all the masters of legal science have taught
> the contrary. But when I perceived on every side that subjects were
> arming themselves against their princes; that books were being brought
> out openly, like firebrands to set Commonweals ablaze, in which we are
> taught that the princes sent by providence to the human race must be
> thrust out of their kingdoms under a pretense of tyranny, and that kings
> must be chosen not by their lineage, but by the will of the people; and
> finally that these doctrines were weakening the foundations not of this
> realm only but of all states; then I denied that it was the function of a
> good man or of a good citizen to offer violence to his prince for any
> reason.[148]

Bodin had indeed tried to provide a theoretical framework to increase the
king's power so that he could cope with the civil disorders of the day and at
the same time preserve the right of the estates to consent to taxation and to
participate in the government. However, his acceptance of evident necessity
left a loophole that permitted the king to bypass the estates to obtain
additional funds whenever the need arose, and his insistence on the omnipotent and indivisible nature of sovereignty imperiled their administrative
role. Later theorists were to remove the safeguards that Bodin had erected.
Property, in the minds of many, ceased to be a natural right and therefore
could be appropriated by the king at his good pleasure. The administrative
role of the estates that Bodin had praised became abhorrent. Since the estates
had no independent authority to perform these functions, their work could
be terminated by royal command. But as theory and practice do not always
march arm and arm, it is now necessary to investigate the relationship
between Henry IV and the estates after peace was restored.

---

148. I have used the translation of Kenneth D. McRae in his edition of Knolles's translation
of Jean Bodin, *The Six Bookes of a Commonweale* (Cambridge, Mass., 1962), pp. A 71–72.

9

HENRY IV, SULLY, AND THE
ESTATES IN GUYENNE AND BRESSE

WHEN JACQUES CLEMENT STRUCK DOWN HENRY III ON AUGUST 1, 1589, THE allied royalist and Huguenot armies appeared on the verge of capturing Paris. Mayenne, the chief of the Catholic League, was talking of seeking death in a sortie from the beleaguered city. His demise, coupled with the fall of the capital, might have started a chain reaction leading to the collapse of the League and the end of the civil wars that had plagued France since 1562. But Henry's death completely altered these prospects. His successor by hereditary right, Henry of Navarre, was unacceptable to many Catholics because of his Protestant faith. To retain his Catholic troops, Henry issued a declaration on August 4 in which he promised to maintain the Catholic religion and to receive instruction from a church council which he would summon within six months. Only Catholicism was to be practiced in towns held by Catholics, and only Catholics were to be appointed as governors of newly conquered places. In spite of these concessions, many great Catholic nobles returned to their governments with their followers where they sought to create semi-independent hereditary principalities. Protestants were disgruntled at seeing so much promised to the Catholics and sometimes deserted to improve their fortunes in the provinces. Soon the once-powerful army of 40,000 men had dwindled to a mere 22,000.[1]

The attitude of the towns was even more discouraging. Most of them gave their loyalty to the Catholic League, and those did not only halfheartedly offered Henry their allegiance in return for recognition of all their privileges. Barely a sixth of France remained under his control. The League was unable to unite what was left, and much of France lapsed into neutrality.

At first, Henry dared not receive the promised instruction from a church council; to do so would further alienate his Protestant supporters without guaranteeing the allegiance of a significant number of Catholics. He also abandoned a promise he had made to hold the Estates General within six months, for few would be impressed by an assembly attended by deputies from such a small part of France.

---

1. This and the following paragraphs are derived from my *Bellièvre, Sully, and the Assembly of Notables of 1596*, Transactions of the American Philosophical Society 64, pt. 2 (Philadelphia, 1974), pp. 4–10.

Under these circumstances the war continued. At first Henry's position improved, but the League, aided by Spain, was soon able to block further advances. Finally, in May 1593, he decided to gamble that a change in religion would win enough Catholics to his cause to compensate for any possible defection among the Protestants. It would also mitigate the threat that a League-convoked Estates General would elect a Catholic king. His abjuration, which took place in July, brought him more Catholic support than he had dared hope, and the grant of papal absolution in September 1595 removed the last religious excuse denying him recognition as king. By the summer of 1596 only Mercoeur, among the great League chiefs, had failed to make his peace, and he was obviously more interested in receiving a good price for his submission than in making a final stand to preserve his position in Brittany. Spain remained a stubborn and dangerous foe, but so much of France was now in Henry's hands that the time had clearly come to restore financial and administrative order to his kingdom.

1. The Financial Problems

Henry's position was critical. His debts stood at about 200 million livres, but his unalienated annual income was only in the vicinity of 6.9 million livres, less than 30 percent of his annual expenses. His income was low for a number of reasons. The domain, aides, and a large portion of other royal revenues had been alienated. The religious wars had caused considerable suffering among the people. The inhabitants of the plat pays were in an especially difficult situation, and peasant uprisings in the 1590's were frequent. Laborers in the towns found their wages lagging behind the rapid rise in prices. Neither peasant nor artisan could pay more taxes. Indeed, the royal council had to spend a considerable portion of its time listening to requests for tax reductions. Even some tax farmers had to plea for relief because the taxes they were to collect did not yield the anticipated amount.

It was not that the French paid so few taxes but rather that much of what was paid did not reach the hands of the king. Governors, provincial estates, and towns levied taxes without the consent of the king, and part of what was legally collected found its way into the hands of the great nobles and municipal officers, as well as royal officials, who were notoriously corrupt. To obtain the money to carry on the war, Henry had to turn to expedients. He borrowed from whomever he could, alienated what remained of the royal domain, created unneeded offices, and was ready to issue patents of nobility in return for remuneration. These measures brought him into frequent conflicts with the sovereign courts who sought to prevent these acts by refusing to register his decrees. When they did so, he usually overrode their opposition, but not without incurring their anger. In January 1596 the first president of the Parlement of Dijon boldly informed Henry that the officers of his sovereign courts were "a barrier between the crown and the people designed to defend the latter from taxes and extraordinary burdens."[2]

Henry was also often thwarted by the great nobles who controlled much of his army and had clients within the royal bureaucracy as well as among the gentry of the countryside. Not content with their already powerful position, they sought additional lands, offices, and revenues for themselves and their followers. Biron asked for the county of Périgord in full sovereignty and, prodded by a group of magnates, the youthful duke of Montpensier approached Henry with the proposition that the governments should become hereditary property for which the holders would render the king simple liege homage. In return they would furnish a well-equipped army to carry on the war. Henry tactfully but firmly rejected this amazing offer which, if accepted, would have returned the monarchy to the days before Philip Augustus.

Nevertheless, Henry had to make some concessions to his followers in order to retain their loyalty and to win the allegiance of the League chiefs: he had to promise governorships, offices, and large sums of money. He usually gave them less than they wanted, but the fact remains that he regained his kingdom more through bribes than by force of arms. Towns and provincial estates had become accustomed to pursuing semi-independent courses, and Henry usually found it expedient to recognize their privileges. By the summer of 1596 when nearly all of France save Brittany recognized him as king, he was on the verge of bankruptcy, and he was in a weaker position in regard to the magnates, provincial estates, sovereign courts, and towns than any of his predecessors since the fifteenth century, with the possible exception of Henry III during the last years of his reign.

The big problem that faced Henry IV was what form the restored monarchy should take. Should he try to reconstitute the Renaissance monarchy with its privileged estates and towns and its magnates whose numerous clients were scattered throughout the bureaucracy and the countryside? Or should he embark on a new course and slowly undermine the position of the magnates and corporate groups so that a new, more centralized, more absolute monarchy could emerge? It is not certain that Henry ever thought specifically in these terms. His approach to government was pragmatic rather than theoretical. He wanted to establish his dynasty firmly on the throne, and he wanted to be obeyed. To secure these objectives and to provide for his pleasures, he knew that he had to improve his financial position. Beyond this he may not have gone very far, but he found at least two ministers who were capable of visualizing all aspects of his government and projecting coherent plans for the restoration of the

2. R. Charlier-Meniolle, *L'Assemblée des Notables tenue à Rouen en 1596* (Paris, 1911), p. 19.

monarchy. The first of these ministers was Pomponne de Bellièvre (1529–1607), and the second was a Protestant noble, Maximilian de Béthune, baron of Rosny and later duke of Sully (1560–1641).[3]

The elderly Bellièvre could call upon vast experience to formulate his plan. He had been a bailiwick lieutenant general, a member of Parlement, a diplomat, a royal councillor, a superintendent of finances, and an intendant in Lyons. He saw the need for a strong monarchy and concurred with those who believed that kingship was a divinely ordained institution and that the estates, sovereign courts, municipal governments, and other constituted bodies derived their authority from the crown. On the other hand, he was equally firm in his belief that the king was under the law, that the rights and privileges of the various constituted bodies and social classes should be respected, and that through consultation the vocal elements of the population could be persuaded to support needed reforms, even at some costs to themselves.

As a member of the Council of Finances in the winter of 1595–96, Bellièvre was constantly called upon to provide Henry IV with money to support the war. The difficulties he encountered pointed to the need for a new approach to royal finances. He prepared a plan that offered some chance for fiscal solvency and persuaded Henry to summon an Assembly of Notables to consider his proposals. To balance the budget, Bellièvre recommended that the king's personal and household expenses be reduced and that the amount spent on pensions, the military, and the bureaucracy be cut substantially. He also urged that the interest on the rentes be lowered. The total savings from these measures would come to 11,580,000 livres, but a deficit of 6,420,000 livres would still remain. Additional revenue was clearly mandatory, and this was especially true because Bellièvre felt that it was necessary to reduce the taille by 3 million livres in order to relieve the hard-pressed plat pays. It could be secured, he thought, by more efficient tax collection and a levy on goods brought into the towns.[4]

Bellièvre's proposals were bold indeed. A reduction of the household expenses, pensions, and the military establishment would hurt the nobility. A cut in the number and salary of royal officials would antagonize that vocal class. Lower interest rates on the rentes and the transferral of part of the incidence of taxation from the country to the town would antagonize the urban communities. As if this were not enough, Bellièvre also struck a blow at the court aristocracy and, through it, at the patron-client relationship by recommending that taxes yielding nearly half the royal revenue be placed under a specially created Conseil du Bon Ordre and devoted exclusively to

3. Major, *Bellièvre*, pp. 3–4. On Bellièvre's life, see Edmund H. Dickerman, *Bellièvre and Villeroy* (Providence, 1971), and Raymond F. Kierstead, *Pomponne de Bellièvre* (Evanston, 1968). On Sully see David Buisseret, *Sully* (London, 1968).

4. Major, *Bellièvre*, pp. 10–11. For Bellièvre's financial plan, see ibid., pp. 14–16. His proposal is located at BN ms. fr. 15,893, fols. 390–93.

paying salaries, rentes, and other contractual obligations. The remaining revenues were to continue to be administered by the Council of Finances and used for the royal household, the military, and related expenses. Thus Bellièvre hoped to reduce the courtiers' influence in financial affairs by removing nearly half of the royal revenue from their grasp and at the same time establish the credit of the monarchy by ensuring that salaries and debts were paid. The council accepted Bellièvre's proposals with several minor changes, but Henry objected to assigning nearly half of his income to the Conseil du Bon Ordre and evidently refused to permit Bellièvre to submit that part of his program to the Assembly of Notables.[5]

It was one thing to prepare a plan that would lead to financial solvency and another to win the backing necessary for its implementation, especially when its provisions would injure the most influential classes in the kingdom. It was for this reason that Bellièvre thought it necessary to hold an Assembly of Notables to prepare public opinion to accept his suggestions. The meeting opened in Rouen on November 4. For several months those who attended went over the financial accounts of the royal tax officials seeking some way in which solvency could be achieved without new taxes. In the process many of the abuses of the regime were revealed. The count of Saint-Paul and the duke of Epernon were accused of imposing taxes for their own profit. The provincial and diocesan estates of Languedoc were charged with levying large sums to gratify influential persons and with ignoring royal decrees or obtaining their reversal in the sovereign courts. The future duke of Sully, who had but lately entered the Council of Finances, may well have had his eyes opened to the need to make more fundamental changes than Bellièvre proposed.[6]

The notables refused to recommend a reduction of the interest on the rentes, but in the end they were persuaded to accept a 5 percent sales tax on merchandise sold in the towns. This tax, known as the *sol pour livre* or the *pancarte*, was not expected to yield enough revenue to enable the crown to reduce the taille, but the notables sought to relieve the peasantry by recommending that the exemptions to the taille that had been granted to lesser royal officials, to towns during the past thirty years, and to those who had purchased patents of nobility since 1577 be revoked. They also asked Brittany, Provence, Dauphiné, and Burgundy to pay an additional 658,518 livres annually because they were less heavily taxed than the rest of France. Like Bellièvre, the notables wanted revenues divided into two parts, one of which was to be assigned to meet the contractual obligations of the crown, but they did not suggest that a Conseil du Bon Ordre be created as a semi-

5. Bellièvre's proposal as modified by the council has been published by Albert Chamberland under the title of *Un plan de restauration financière en 1596* (Paris, 1904). For my reasons for attributing this document to Bellièvre rather than to Forget de Fresne, see Major, *Bellièvre*, n. 90.

6. Major, *Bellièvre*, pp. 18–22.

independent agency to administer it. Nevertheless Henry told the notables before they disbanded that he would not accept such a rigorous division of his revenue because he needed more flexibility to meet his obligations. Finally the notables stressed economy, efficiency, and honesty in government. They asked that the sale of offices cease, that salaries be cut 10 percent, and that the size of the bureaucracy, the royal household, and the military establishment be reduced. As a further economy they recommended that the provincial and diocesan estates in Languedoc be held every third year rather than annually. To ensure honesty they urged that the accounts of royal tax officials and those of the estates, towns, and communities be audited.[7]

Thus Bellièvre was successful in persuading the notables to adopt most of a program that involved essentially a restoration of the Renaissance monarchy, albeit a more honest, frugal, and efficient one. Henry's objectives are more difficult to define. He took a direct hand only in persuading the notables to accept the pancarte and in pressing Achille de Harlay, the first president of the Parlement of Paris, to obtain a declaration from them that royal officials should not become involved in the affairs of the princes and other seigneurs. This declaration, if enforced, would have greatly reduced the influence of the nobility on the government and seriously curtailed their ability to extract money from the royal treasury, to tax illegally, and to escape punishment for their misdeeds. Are we to conclude that Henry's principal concerns at this time were to obtain more money and to remove the influence of the high nobility from the bureaucracy? Later developments suggest that this may have been the case.[8]

The key to the future of France lay less in how fully the notables accepted Bellièvre's proposals than in how well the king and his council implemented them. For about six months, the progress that was made must have exceeded Bellièvre's expectations. Steps were taken to weaken the venal system of officeholding and to reduce the size of the bureaucracy. The patron-client system was attacked, and royal officials were forbidden to accept positions in the houses of the princes. The burden of taxation was shifted somewhat from the country to the towns by the establishment of the pancarte over considerable opposition and the reduction of the taille by 10 percent. Most surprising of all, pressure from the town and Parlement of Paris finally led Henry to divide his revenue into two parts and to create a Conseil du Bon Ordre, or a Conseil Particulier as he called it, to administer the portion assigned to meet the contractual obligations of the crown. Finally a Chamber of Justice was established to investigate and punish those guilty of financial malpractices.[9]

When the Spanish captured Amiens on March 11, 1597, and threatened the remainder of Picardy and Paris itself, it soon became apparent that

7. Ibid., pp. 22–23.
8. Ibid., pp. 19, 21.
9. Ibid., pp. 23–26. This Chamber of Justice was called a *Chambre Royale*. On the institution, see J. F. Bosher, "Chambres de Justice in the French Monarchy," in *French Government and Society*

Bellièvre's reform program was not compatible with the increased financial needs of the crown. New offices had to be created to sell, the Conseil Particulier had to be abandoned because Henry could not afford such a rigorous division of his income, and the Chamber of Justice was abolished in return for a substantial gift from the financial officials. The greatest casualty was Bellièvre himself. His fall was not sudden, but his belief that "one must act gently and after due thought" produced less money than Sully's harsh, brusque approach.[10] Gradually Henry came to rely more on the younger man in monetary matters. By June 1598, following the end of the war with Spain, Sully was the acknowledged leader of the financial administration, and several years later the office of superintendent of finances was revived for his benefit. Bellièvre, however, did not immediately lose the confidence of his sovereign. He was elevated to the chancellorship in 1599 and continued to influence the government until Henry took the seals from him in the early winter of 1604–05.[11]

Sully gave Bellièvre the compliment of borrowing some aspects of his program. He sought to make the fiscal administration honest and efficient. He dispatched commissioners to the provinces to audit accounts, and on several occasions the Chamber of Justice was reconstituted. He tried to make the towns bear more of the costs of government by increasing the gabelles and other sales taxes and by slashing the taille that fell so heavily on the countryside. He even managed to reduce the interest rate of the rentes in spite of considerable opposition. By 1600 the budget was once more balanced, and by the time of Henry's assassination in 1610, a substantial portion of the crown's debts had been repaid, most of the domain had been redeemed, and a large treasure had been stored in the Bastille for emergency. To accomplish this miracle Sully had acted ruthlessly. He showed little regard for the duly constituted bodies and often ignored the protests of the sovereign courts. Although he eventually succumbed to pressure and abandoned the pancarte, he insisted that the estates pay the king's debts and redeem his domain. Beginning in 1605 he also made demands, in his capacity of *grand voyer*, for considerable sums for building and repairing roads and bridges. Between 1600 and 1604 from 4,000 to 46,600 livres were spent annually for this purpose, but between 1605 and 1610 from 595,469 to 1,224,153 livres were expended each year.[12]

Neither ruthlessness nor heavy fiscal demands inevitably lead to absolutism, however. For France to become absolute it was necessary to under-

---

1500–1850: Essays in Memory of Alfred Cobban, ed. J. F. Bosher, (London, 1973), pp. 19–40, and Françoise Bayard, "Les Chambres de Justice de la première moitié du XVIIe siècle," *Cahiers d'histoire* 19 (1974): 121–40.

10. Buisseret, *Sully*, p. 46.

11. Major, *Bellièvre*, pp. 26–28.

12. Mallet, pp. 192–93.

mine the estates and other duly constituted bodies. Did Henry and Sully try to move in this direction? Did they attempt to curb the independence and limit the activities of the estates? Did they try to undermine their position by reducing their expenses and replacing their officials by those of the crown? It is such questions as these that we must investigate as we turn to the history of the individual provincial estates. We begin with those in the généralité of Guyenne and the lands France took from Savoy in 1600, for it is in these two regions that Henry and Sully most clearly revealed their policies.

2. THE ESTATES IN GUYENNE

The royalist estates were not active in Guyenne during the early years of Henry IV's reign because of the strength of the Catholic League, especially in the towns. As a result, only after peace was restored in the généralité in May 1594 did relations between the crown and the estates once more become important. At first Henry's hold on the upper classes in most of the region was too precarious for him to seek more than a restoration of the status quo. This was especially true because a movement of the peasants, known as the *croquants*, had reached serious proportions by the close of 1593, especially in the mountainous parts of the généralité, whether in the north in Périgord and Quercy or in the south in Comminges. The cause of the movement was misery provoked primarily by marauding troops, brigands, and heavy taxation, much of which was illegally imposed by the military. The failure of some nobles to pay the taille on the nonnoble lands they held was decried, and the bourgeoisie of the larger towns, who themselves constituted a privileged class and often doubled as tax collectors, came under attack. For the most part the croquants sought the restoration of order and social justice by petitioning the king and electing syndics to represent their interests, but there were a few armed clashes. The very fact that contemporaries believed that as many as 30,000 peasants attended a single meeting must have given those in authority a sense of insecurity.[13]

Henry had had considerable experience with provincial estates. His ancestral lands of Bigorre, Nébouzan, Foix, Soule, Béarn, and Navarre had active estates with whom he had negotiated since his mother's death in 1572. As governor of Guyenne during his predecessor's reign, he had witnessed the activities of the very assemblies whose fate he was soon to determine. The outgoing consuls of Agen in 1594 confidently reported to their successors that the king was going to convoke the estates of Guyenne in the near future,

---

13. Yves-Marie Bercé, *Histoire des Croquants* (Geneva, 1974), pp. 257–93. Emmanuel Le Roy Ladurie, *Les paysans de Languedoc* (Paris, 1966), 1:399–404; L. de Cardenal, "Les Etats de Périgord sous Henri IV," in *L'organisation corporative du Moyen Age à la fin de l'Ancien Régime* (Louvain, 1939), 3:165–81.

but as far as is known no such meeting was held in 1595.[14] Indeed Henry's correspondence with his lieutenant general, Marshal Matignon, at this time reveals a desire to please his subjects but considerable reluctance to hold any meetings that were not absolutely necessary. In April 1595 he wrote to Matignon that he had granted as many of the requests he had received from the town of Bordeaux as possible but that "it seemed best neither to give nor to refuse them permission to hold the estates of my province of Guyenne (Bordeaux), as they had requested, until I had your opinion.... The time is not right to hold such assemblies which ordinarily do more to free my subjects from expenses than to assist and aid me in my affairs, because no one now looks further than his individual welfare. Therefore, I want you to skip this assembly if it is possible and postpone it to a more opportune time."[15] Because there were élus in the seneschalsy of Bordeaux, the failure to convoke the estates caused few problems, and Matignon managed to stave off holding them until January 1596 when his master's position was more secure. There were a few meetings thereafter during the reign.[16]

Périgord, the other jurisdiction in which the élus had already been established, presented a more serious problem. Here the Catholic League was very strong, and the crown confronted all three estates with their syndic and their définiteurs to look after their affairs when they were not in session. Hardly had the viscount of Bourdeille, the newly appointed governor, arrived in Périgord at the close of 1593, than he was pressed by the syndic to hold a meeting of the estates.[17] Obviously reluctant since many of the leading towns had not yet returned to obedience, Bourdeille asked Henry for instructions. Henry's reply has been lost, but after the submission of Périgueux a few months later, Bourdeille once more wrote to him concerning the estates in response to the pleas of the syndic. The syndic, he pointed out, argued that a meeting of the estates was necessary to elect his successor (his term of office had expired) and to deliberate on the affairs of the province. This time Bourdeille favored the proposal, but he took the precaution of recommending that the clergy be freed from paying the décimes and the peasants from paying the tailles that they owed, and that lettres de faveur be sent to selected nobles to insure "the good will of the three orders."[18]

The three estates met a few weeks after Bourdeille made his recom-

---

14. AC, Agen, BB 35, fol. 145v.

15. Henri IV, *Lettres*, 4:343. At about the same time Henry reacted in a similar fashion to a request that the estates of Agenais meet. *IAC, Agen*, ed. Auguste Bosvieux and Georges Tholin (Paris, 1884), AA 26.

16. AD, Gironde, C 3888, fol. 5. The three estates were convoked in October 1596 (Henry IV, *Lettres*, 4:1054); and the third estate met in 1609. AC, *Bourg-sur-Gironde*, BB 3. There may have been a few other meetings.

17. Bourdeille to Henry, January 4, 1594, BN ms. fr. 23,194, fols. 174–75.

18. Ibid., April 17, 1594, fol. 189.

mendation, prepared a cahier with twenty articles, and elected a deputation to take it to the king. The contents of this cahier reveal a strongly Catholic, bourgeois-patrician bias. Included were requests that only Catholic church services be permitted in Périgord and that only Catholics be allowed to hold offices. Frightened by the croquants, they asked that the king suppress those who rose up against his authority and that of "the officers of justice." Absent from the list of signatures on the cahier was any representative from Bergerac and the other Protestant towns or from the smaller communities with seats in the estates. The Catholics and the bourgeois-patricians were determined to impose their will on the remainder of the province. They even asked that garrisons be established in Périgueux and Sarlat that would be paid by the crown but commanded by the mayors and *consuls* of the two towns rather than by a royal governor.[19] This proposal and perhaps others alienated Bourdeille, who believed that his own position was threatened. On two occasions Henry had to assure him that he would make no concessions that would undermine his authority.[20]

Henry could not see the Périgord delegation because he was with his army in Picardy, but he instructed his council to make as favorable replies as possible. He also dispatched a councillor to Périgord to try to conciliate the croquants, who in turn sent a delegation to Paris. Henry made some concessions, but there were several clashes between the peasants and some nobles led by Bourdeille during the summer of 1594. The situation was still tense that October when Henry authorized another meeting of the estates, which was held the following February.[21] By this time, Protestant Bergerac had resumed its privileged position beside Périgueux and Sarlat, but the split between these three towns and the smaller localities had become wider than ever. The latter insisted on having their own syndic to represent their interests and on preparing separate cahiers to present to the king; in short, they wanted to become a sort of fourth estate. Representatives of the three leading towns resisted, but in the end a compromise was achieved. The seneschalsy would continue to have only one syndic, but he would be elected by the three estates, not by the three principal towns alone. In addition, three of the six définiteurs of the third estate were assigned to the smaller towns. There is evidence that several inhabitants of the small towns had provided part of the leadership for the croquants and that the rural unrest which resulted contributed to the willingness of the government and the

19. *IAC, Périgueux*, ed. Michel Hardy (Périgueux, 1894), AA 36; Cardenal, "Les Etats de Périgord," p. 173.

20. Henri IV, *Lettres*, 4: 143, 154–55. In November 1594 Henry tried to mollify Bourdeille by permitting him to nominate someone for the bishopric of Périgueux and giving him command of a company, but to no avail. By January 1595, Bourdeille was trying to get him to maintain a garrison in two of his castles, and by March he was complaining about his salary. Ibid., pp. 299, 320, 1036.

21. Ibid., 111–12, 154–56, 167–68, 184–85.

more privileged classes to make concessions. Once the smaller towns were given a more influential position within the estates, they became less interested in the croquants. The latter returned to their villages where they soon became satisfied because with the restoration of peace had come the removal of the disorderly troops from the countryside.[22]

Meanwhile Matignon had been devoting much of his energy to restoring order in the seneschalsies without élus. Here the cooperation of the estates was more essential because they controlled the tax-collecting machinery. Assemblies were held under royal auspices in Agenais, Armagnac, Quercy, Rivière-Verdun, and perhaps elsewhere during the spring and summer of 1594, but the primary purpose of these meetings was for the estates to renew allegiance to the crown and to receive confirmation of their privileges. The estates of Comminges did not assemble until November because of continued unrest. In spite of this delay, there is evidence that factionalism was present at the meeting. Under these circumstances what taxes the government collected for that year had been voted by League or rump royalist assemblies and were extracted with considerable difficulty.[23]

Apparently conditions were still too unsettled for the estates to meet in January 1595 to vote the taxes for that year, and not until late winter or early spring were the estates of Agenais, Quercy, Armaganc, Rouergue, and Comminges assembled. This delay made it necessary to levy the January and April quarters of the taille simultaneously, a burden that most of the war-torn region could not bear. The little town of Laplume had to borrow 600 livres in Agen, and many other communities were doubtless forced deeper into debt. More serious from the crown's point of view, the estates of Comminges, Quercy, and Rouergue refused to vote the necessary funds to support the troops in the area. The hard-pressed Matignon lectured the king on the ease with which these seneschalsies obtained reductions in taxes and claimed that such concessions only made them more insolent and less amenable to voting taxes in the future. To improve the situation he visited Comminges that summer, and he sought to intimidate the three estates of Quercy and Rouergue by holding them in his presence the following winter.[24]

There were limits, however, to what even the tactful and popular marshal could do. In February 1596 when he asked the estates of Rouergue for

22. Cardenal, "Les Etats de Périgord," pp. 174–81; Bercé, *Histoire*, pp. 272–93. The smaller towns and plat pays unsuccessfully requested that the élus be suppressed. Ibid., p. 276.

23. AC, Agen, AA 50; E. d'Antin, "Une commune Gasconne pendant les Guerres de Religion," *Revue de l'Agenais* 21 (1894): 177–78; *AHG*, 14:325–26; E. Albe, "Inventaire raisonné et analytique des archives municipales de Cahors," *Bul. de la soc. des études . . . du Lot* 47 (1926): 148. For Comminges, see BN ms. fr. 23,194, fols. 308–09, 316, 330.

24. D'Antin, "Une commune Gasconne," pp. 179, 258–59; AC, Rodez (bourg), BB 10, fols. 229–30; AC, Millau, AA 17; AD, Haute-Garonne, C 3664; *AHG*, 14:341–42, 345; AN, E l[b] fols. 59–60.

396,000 livres for the uncollected taxes in 1595 and for 1596, the estates countered by requesting to be freed from all arrears and by offering a mere 75,000 livres for 1596 because of the poverty of the people. Matignon suggested a compromise figure of 240,000 livres for both years, but the estates would do no more than ask the king to be content with 180,000 livres. This done, the three estates asked for permission to levy 120,000 livres to pay the debts of the province and the expenses of the estates. A committee of three clergymen, three nobles, and the *consuls* of six towns was chosen to look after the interests of the province when the estates were not in session, and the meeting came to an end.[25] Quercy proved no more amenable, and the marshal emerged with only 100,000 livres of the 400,000 requested for the arrears due and for 1596. Obviously sympathetic to the plight of the people, he simply sent copies of the minutes of the two assemblies to Montmorency, who was then an influential member of the Council of Finances, with the request that action be taken to ensure the welfare of the poor inhabitants.[26]

The third estate of Agenais, or the twelve principal towns, met on four occasions during 1596 to seek a reduction in taxation and the cancellation of the arrears they owed. In addition to the usual petitions and deputations, those who assembled sought permission to hold a meeting of the provincial estates of Guyenne to deal with the common problems faced by the seneschalsies. High on this list was the heavy duty charged for commerce on the Garonne River and its tributaries.[27] Comminges continued its protests against taxation with some success.[28] In spite of numerous concessions by the crown, the syndics of Rouergue predicted that they would have difficulty collecting taxes because of the opposition of the nobility, the Parlement of Toulouse, and the officers of the presidial seat at Villefranche. Reports of trouble came from Périgord also.[29]

On October 31 letters were issued calling upon Guyenne to contribute 654,000 livres toward the cost of the government in 1597, and less than a month later the généralité was assessed an additional 600,000 livres to defray the costs of the war.[30] At the same time Henry sent a letter directing the three estates of Agenais to meet to hear his commissioners explain his needs and "to grant and accord us freely the sums of money they will require of you."[31] In the meeting, which took place late in January the following year, the members of the third estate, acting alone, agreed to pay their share of

25. AC, Millau, AA 12; AD, Gironde, C 3804, fols. 202–13.
26. *IAD, Gironde, sér. C*, ed. Alexandre Gouget and Jean-A. Brutails (Bordeaux, 1893), 2 : C 3805; *AHG*, 14:347.
27. AC, Agen, CC 95, fols. 1–21v.; AD, Gironde, C 3804, fols. 37–45.
28. AD, Haute-Garonne, C 3666.
29. *IAD, Gironde*, C 3888.
30. Ibid.
31. AC, Agen, CC 95, fol. 25.

the initial tax but dispatched a deputy to court to ask that their portion of the extraordinary levy to pay for the war be cut in half and that other grievances be satisfied.[32] The syndic of Périgord won tax concessions for his province, as no doubt did many others, but in spite of continued concessions, Guyenne was slow to return to normalcy. In March Henry found it necessary to direct the estates of Rouergue to meet in Rodez rather than Villefranche, where a murder had recently taken place, in order to compel recognition of his authority. Undaunted the syndic of the Haute-Marche of Rouergue prepared a history of the three estates at about this time in which he traced their origins back to the time of Julius Caesar. In August the Parlement of Bordeaux reported considerable unrest in the various provinces in Guyenne. Members of the third estate, aided by some nobles, were holding large assemblies and defying the authority of the king. It was essential that Matignon, who had gone to Rouen some months before to attend the Assembly of Notables, return to Guyenne to content the people and to suppress uprisings. But it was too late. Matignon had died a short time before.[33]

During the years that followed, a slow but discernible change took place in the relations between the crown and the provincial estates and towns of Guyenne. This change was not caused by Matignon's death. His successor, Alfonso d'Ornano, was even more sympathetic to the needs and aspirations of the inhabitants and constantly sought to further their interests at court. A native of Corsica, he had come to France in 1569 to seek his fortune. A gallant soldier and faithful servant of the king, he slowly rose to the rank of marshal of France. Two facts depict his character. When the plague broke out in Bordeaux in 1604, he went there to offer what help he could in spite of orders from the king to leave the city rather than expose his life, this at a time when it was customary for those in authority to flee from epidemics, leaving the people to their own devices. Second, he lived unostentatiously and died with relatively modest means, proof that he was honest, although he did accept presents from those for whom he did favors, a practice of the times.[34] Rather, the change in relations must be attributed to the growing influence of Sully coupled with the declining influence of Bellièvre, especially in matters of finance.

From 1594 until near the close of 1597, the existence of the provincial estates had never been called into question. Every effort of the government had been directed toward returning to the practices that had been followed prior to the Wars of Religion. Where there were no élections, the estates had been asked to vote taxes for the use of the crown and had added to them

---

32. Ibid., fols. 25v–43; D'Antin, "Une commune Gasconne," p. 230.

33. *IAD, Gironde,* C 3806; Henri IV, *Lettres,* 4:713; AD, Aveyron, C 1902; *AHG,* 14:348–49.

34. There is no satisfactory biography of Ornano, but see Luigi Filippi, *Pour les Corses: Essai sur le Maréchal de France Alfonso d'Ornano, 1548–1610* (Algiers, 1915).

levies to support local activities. These taxes had been divided and collected under their auspices and those of the *consuls* of the towns and communities. Where there were élections, the élus had performed these services, and meetings of the estates had been less frequent, but the jurats of Bordeaux had provided a powerful protective umbrella over the smaller towns in the seneschalsy, and the syndic and définiteurs had been staunch defenders of the privileges of Périgord. It is true that Henry IV was less dedicated than Bellièvre to a return to the old order, but he had only opposed holding assemblies at inopportune times. He had postponed a meeting of the estates of the seneschalsy of Bordeaux in 1595 and was very likely responsible for the failure to assemble the estates of Guyenne during the immediate postwar years, but there is no evidence that he wanted to alter the basic structure of the government.

Henry placed the blame for his financial difficulties more on the dishonesty and inefficiency of royal officials than on those of the estates and towns, and it was upon them that his anger fell. In March 1596 an edict was issued reducing the number of treasurers in each généralité to two, and near the close of the year, Gilles de Maupeou, who was to become one of Sully's most trusted financial officials and a staunch enemy of the provincial estates, attempted to put this measure into effect by entering the office of the Bureau of Finance at Bordeaux with royal letters forbidding anyone but the two senior officials to exercise their offices. In March 1597 a clerk was created in each élection to verify the rolls of the élus, and in May the first Chamber of Justice was established to investigate financial officials. Nearly all the recommendations of the Assembly of Notables had been directed against royal financial officers; except in Languedoc, those of the provincial estates and towns escaped almost without censure.[35]

Between the waning months of 1597 and 1600, the officials of the estates came under the council's attack as much as those of the crown. Thereafter in Guyenne they bore the brunt of Sully's and his master's displeasure. The first serious blow at the position of the provincial estates and towns was dealt in November 1597. In response to various complaints, the Council of Finance forbade the *consuls* in Guyenne to levy taxes without royal permission and directed that their records be verified by the seneschal of their respective jurisdications.[36] In July 1598 the council struck out at the related problem of the failure of the estates to levy all the taxes ordered by the crown. The "people of the estates, syndics, and deputies of the provinces and

35. Jean-Paul Charmeil, *Les trésoriers de France à l'époque de la Fronde* (Paris, 1964), p. 263 n. 148. Charmeil attributes the 1596 edict to Sully (p. 10), but Sully had not yet even become a member of the Council of Finances. *IAD, Gironde*, C 3888. *Actes Royaux*, 1: nos. 4786, 4815. Maupeou was also in Guyenne in May and June 1597. BN ms. fr. 18,161, fol. 161.

36. BN ms. fr. 18,161, fol. 69. There was, of course, nothing new about forbidding taxation without royal permission, and on January 29, 1598, Henry wrote the treasurers throughout France to see to it that neither the élus nor anyone else did so. *Actes Royaux*, 1: no. 4908.

recettes of Quercy, Rouergue, Comminges, and Rivière-Verdun" were specifically singled out for not imposing the special levies to support the war in 1596 and 1597 and were directed to do so at once. Furthermore in anticipation that the estates would appeal to the sovereign courts to intercede, the Parlements of Toulouse and Bordeaux were forbidden to take any action that would cause a delay.[37]

On August 23, 1598, Henry directed that commissioners be sent to most of the généralités in France to ensure that the taille was apportioned and collected in a fair, honest, and efficient manner. This precaution was not unusual. Councillors or *maîtres des requêtes* had often been dispatched to the country on administrative and investigative missions. Raymond de Viçose, intendant and general controller of finances, for example, had served as Matignon's financial adviser from 1594 until near his death and after a break of several years had acted in the same capacity for Ornano. Although a true ancestor of the intendants in many respects, he occupied a position distinctly inferior to that of the lieutenant generals and acted more as a defender of provincial liberties at court than as a representative of royal authority in the provinces.[38]

Henry's decision to appoint commissioners in 1598, however, may have had special significance for Guyenne. Guyenne was, as far as is known, the only généralité where the estates rather than the élus were primarily responsible for tax collection to which commissioners were sent, a circumstance suggesting that Henry was especially dissatisfied with the representative assemblies in this region.[39] Furthermore the man chosen to head the commission was Michel de Marillac, then a maître des requêtes and later, as keeper of the seals, the most implacable and dangerous foe the provincial estates ever had. Whether his experience in Guyenne contributed to the formulation of his low opinion of representative assemblies cannot be said. All we know is that his friend and biographer, Nicolas Lefèvre, reported that Chancellor Cheverny had dispatched him to the généralités of Limoges and Guyenne where he had been given virtual carte blanche to do what was necessary. Included in his orders were commissions to convoke the estates of Agenais, Rouergue, Quercy, Comminges, and Rivière-Verdun.[40] During its January meeting in 1599 the third estate of Agenais asked its syndic to appeal to Marillac for a reduction of the taille, and in a March meeting his assistance was sought in persuading the king to permit them to levy a tax of over 10,000 livres to meet the expenses of several legal cases

37. AN, E l^c, fol. 5–5v.

38. B. Barbiche, "Les commissaires députés pour le 'régalement' des tailles en 1598–1599," *BEC* 118 (1960): 58–96. On Viçose see D. Buisseret, "A Stage in the Development of the French *Intendants*: The Reign of Henry IV," *The Historical Journal* 9 (1966): 28–30.

39. Barbiche, "Les commissaires," p. 62, knew that commissioners were sent to Guyenne but apparently was not aware that there were no élections there except in Bordelais and Périgord.

40. BN ms. fr. 14,027, ch. 2; or Bibl. Sainte-Geneviève, ms. 826, fols. 37–37v.

before the sovereign courts and other obligations. In the latter request, at least, they were successful.[41]

Marillac had intended to attend the estates of Comminges in April, but the distance to Aurignac where the meeting was held was greater than he had anticipated. When he found that he could not arrive in time, he arranged for a delegation from the estates to meet him in Toulouse. What took place there is not known, but in October, after Marillac had returned to Paris, the deputy Comminges had sent to court wrote that attempts were being made to destroy their privileges. Marillac had made a partial report to the council, and it had been decidedly unfavorable. To put him in a more friendly mood before the council consulted him again, the deputy reported that he had promised that the estates would pay him 3,000 livres to which he had some claim. The three estates that met in December concurred and sent their deputy 4,500 livres to settle their debt with Marillac and to interest other persons in their cause. In that same meeting an attempt was made to reduce expenses by agreeing to hold fewer meetings and by limiting the number of those who attended. Also a committee appointed to investigate charges brought by several communities that the fiscal administration of the estates was dishonest made its report. It found, as most groups that investigate themselves do, that nothing reprehensible had been done. One wonders if Marillac had known of these charges and what effect they may have had in formulating his opinion of the estates.[42]

The report of the commissioners who had been sent to the pays d'élections led to an edict of March 1600 designed to correct the abuses committed by the royal tax collectors, but Marillac's mission was not followed by a comparable directive for the pays d'états.[43] He was, however, very likely in part responsible for the assignments given to Etienne de Pontac and Jean de Martin, treasurers at Bordeaux, in September 1599 and the spring of 1600 respectively. Pontac's mission was to investigate charges that the estates of the Haut-Marche of Rouergue, the Bas-Marche of Rouergue, Quercy, Rivière-Verdun, and Comminges had levied taxes without the king's permission. He was to verify all tax levies and to have money collected without authority turned over to royal tax officials. In addition, he was to install *receveurs particuliers triennaux* in Rouergue and Quercy to apportion the taxes

41. AC, Agen, CC 95, fols. 88v, 100v–01, 106v–08v.

42. AD, Haute-Garonne, C 3674, C 3676; Jean Lestrade, *Cahiers des remonstrances des Etats de Comminges aux rois de France ou à leurs lieutenants généraux en Guyenne, 1537–1627* (Saint-Gaudens, 1943), pp. 101–03, a publication of the *Soc. des études du Comminges*, vol. 2. For other references of Marillac's activities in Guyenne, see Valois, 1: nos. 4859, 5255. M.-J. de Naurois-Destenay, *Les Etats de Comminges aux XVIᵉ et XVIIᵉ siècles* (thesis, Ecole Nationale des Chartes, 1953–54), pp. 98–102, 166–68.

43. Isambert, 15:226–38. Earlier, on February 10, the council had responded to a complaint that the élus in Orléanais were levying unauthorized taxes. BN ms. fr. 10,842, fols. 134v–35.

in spite of the protests of the estates, who quite properly interpreted this measure as an attack on their prerogatives.[44]

Martin's assignment was to hold the estates of the various provinces in Guyenne and to study their procedures. He found that they were needlessly burdening the people by the costs of their frequent meetings, which they often held on their own initiative, and by the sums they levied to support their own activities. He issued directives that struck severe blows at the independent position the estates had enjoyed. The length of their sessions, the number who could attend, and their daily remuneration were strictly limited. Meetings were to be called only with the express permission of the king, and a limit was set on the amount that could be voted to support their legitimate activities.[45]

The estates of Rivière-Verdun, for example, were to meet only with the king's permission. Attendance was to be limited to one deputy from each of the twelve principal towns and to the syndic to whom any excluded community was to give its remonstrances. A maximum of six livres per day for a period of no more than eight days was to be paid to those who attended, including time to travel to and from the meeting. The costs of deputations to court were to be levied upon the people only if prior approval was received from the treasurers in Bordeaux in tax questions and the lieutenant general when other matters were concerned. Royal officials were to attend the estates to see that these regulations were obeyed, and not more than 3,000 livres per year were to be levied to support all of these activities.[46]

Where the estates engaged in activities which Martin believed truly benefited the people, he was a little more lenient. After reducing the costs of holding the three estates of Quercy from 5,760 to 3,600 livres and the costs of legal suits and deputations to court from 6,700 to 3,000 livres, he permitted appropriations of 6,300 livres to support the University of Cahors and four secondary schools and 100 livres to assist the printer of the university. In addition, a maximum of 60 livres could be allocated to six convents to provide alms, 9.6 more could be given to the poor of the town in which the estates were held, and an equal sum could be allocated to the hospital in that locality. The total came to nearly 13,500 livres, but omitted from this figure was the 3,600 livres customarily given to the seigneur de Thémines, the governor, in recognition of the favors and assistance he rendered the

44. AN, E 2ᵃ, fols. 72, 84, 247. See also Valois, 1: no. 5081.

45. On March 24, 1600, the king instructed Martin to investigate the tailles in Comminges, Rivière-Verdun, and Quercy, and on May 6 commissions were issued for him to hold the estates. He held the estates of Comminges in September 1600. AD, Haute-Garonne, C 3680; of Condomois, Astarac, and Bazadais in January 1601 (AC, Mézin, BB 2, fols. 63–65; AC, Condom, BB 18), of Armagnac later that month (AD, Gers, E Suppl. 23,936, fols. 191v–94), and of Agenais on February 5 (AC, Agen, CC 95, fols. 140v–57v.).

46. AD, Gironde, C 3873 bis, fols. 26v–27v.

seneschalsy. Martin did not specifically disapprove; there were limits to how far he dared offend that influential noble. He merely stipulated that this sum could be levied only with the permission of his majesty, an old proviso but one that was more honored in the breach than in its observance. If followed, the governor would be as beholden to the king as to the estates and as much a representative of his majesty in Quercy as he was of the three estates at court.[47]

On August 10, 1600, one day after Martin had issued his directive concerning the estates of Quercy, Sully wrote him expressing his pleasure at his earlier accomplishments.[48] On November 15, 1601, after he had completed his long and difficult mission, the king's council issued a series of decrees based upon his recommendations. Included were directives that the debts of the estates be verified. After this was done, the estates were to be permitted to levy taxes to meet the heavy obligations that they had assumed during the Wars of Religion. Meanwhile creditors were forbidden to take legal action against the officials of the estates. The tax collectors of the estates were told to account for the levies they had made during the past decade.[49] This last measure, coupled with the revival of the Chamber of Justice in August, posed a new threat, for under Sully's direction a determined effort was made to examine the account books of the officials of the estates and the towns, as well as those of the crown. A few months later, those who supplied information leading to the recovery of money illegally taken were promised one-tenth of the amount collected.[50]

These measures led to increased activity on the part of the estates. Martin's directives hampered their actions, limited their ability to bribe royal officials to support their cause, and reduced the profits of attending the meetings, but they were only designed to prevent the abuses committed by the estates and to reduce the tax burden upon the people. The capacity of the estates to act, and to act vigorously, remained. Their principal concern and that of the towns was the newly created Chamber of Justice, which soon dispatched commissioners to examine their books. The very strength of their opposition suggests their guilt, although even an honest administrator might be fearful of being caught in some mistake. The *consuls* of Agen, for example, warned their counterparts in the other towns in Guyenne sometime in 1602 that the commissioners had no respect for their traditional methods of

47. BN ms. Clairambault 360, fols. 12–14v.

48. AD, Haute-Garonne, C 3710.

49. Valois, 2: nos. 6630, 6639, 6641, 6643–50. Numerous decrees were issued during the remainder of Henry's reign dealing with the verification of the debts of the estates and towns and giving authorization for taxes to be levied to satisfy creditors. See, for example, Valois, 2: nos. 7765, 7943, 8547, 9281, 9536, 9817, 9998, 11,088, 11,264, 11,739, 12,039, 12,628, 12,633, 12,911, 13,570, 14,020, 14,109.

50. *Ordonnances ... concernant l'autorité et la jurisdiction de la Chambre des Comptes de Paris* (Paris, 1728), 1: 432–40; *Actes Royaux*, 1: nos. 5164, 5179.

bookkeeping and would arbitrarily condemn them to pay large fines. Indeed, some of Sully's emissaries were as brutal in their methods as their master was. Also cause for concern was the crown's attempt to derive more income from the traffic on the Garonne, Dordogne, and other rivers in the généralité upon which so much commerce depended.[51]

Since the actions of the crown affected the entire region, there were advantages in the seneschalsies working together. Acting under the leadership of the consuls of Agen, they sought and obtained permission from Ornano on five occasions between November 1602 and November 1603 for the estates of Guyenne to meet. The seneschalsy estates were also active both in their usual tax duties and in assisting the efforts of the larger institution. Initially the estates were partly successful. Their November 1602 meeting led to the preparation of a cahier and the election of Viçose, the king's intendant, and another deputy to go to court. As a result of their endeavors, the order sending out commissioners was temporarily revoked in December, but the Chamber of Justice was allowed to continue to exist. In February 1603 the estates again met in Agen to send a deputation to the king to obtain a final revocation of the edict on the commissioners.[52]

The estates attributed their success in part to the good offices of Marshal Ornano. For a reward the councillors of Agen voted to give him a fine horse as Condom and Bayonne had already done, but mindful of the new restrictions on their activities, they added the stipulation that it be done under the good pleasure of the king.[53] The victory of the estates, however, was short-lived, for Sully and his master had determined to deliver a far more serious blow to their liberties. In January 1603 they issued an edict creating eight new élections in Guyenne.[54] By this act royal officials were to replace those of the provincial estates as tax collectors. Henceforth the money the king wanted was to be levied, and the estates were to lose the capacity to collect taxes they might vote for their own purposes. They were to be placed at the mercy of the élus whose actions were directed by royal officials in Bordeaux and in Paris. They were not to be destroyed by a royal edict; they were to be allowed to wither slowly because the principal reason for their existence was removed.

The estates, however, did not despair. The crown had created élections in all or part of Guyenne four of five times before, and on each occasion they

51. AC, Agen, CC 116.

52. Ibid., AA 33, BB 40, fols. 132v–38, 143–47, CC 116; AD, Dordogne, 5C 29, fol. 23–23v; AC, Mézin, BB 2, 153v–54; Valois, 2: no. 7387; Georges Tholin, *Des tailles et des impositions au pays d'Agenais durant le XVIe siècle jusqu'aux réformes de Sully* (Agen, 1874), pp. 28–30. The *consuls* of Agen wrote to the *consuls* and syndics in the other seneschalsies to explain why they feared the commissioners and to notify them that they has asked Ornano to hold the estates in Agen on November 20, 1602. AC, Agen, CC 116.

53. AC, Agen, BB 40, fols. 148v–49.

54. *Actes Royaux*, 1: no. 5252.

had succeeded in having the offending edict revoked by providing the king with a special gift or by reimbursing those who had purchased the offices.[55] They had to repeat the process once more. First, the sympathetic Ornano was to be persuaded to use his influence at court on their behalf and to arrange for the estates of Guyenne to meet. Here deputies could be elected to try to persuade the sovereign courts to delay implementation of the king's edicts in order to provide time for other deputies who were sent to Paris to get these edicts revoked.

Ornano was ready enough to play the role assigned to him. On January 25, 1603, he wrote both Henry and Bellièvre expressing the satisfaction of the urban aristocracy at the decision to suspend the edict creating the commissioners. In a subtle fashion he related the current calm in the généralité to this decision. It could have been otherwise, he hinted, because Marshal Biron who had recently been executed for treason had had many clients in the region. There were reports of large assemblies of his vassals and clients, and his confederate, the duke of Bouillon, was in Guyenne at that moment trying to make trouble. Thus Ornano took the position he was to maintain throughout the coming struggle: peace in Guyenne was dependent on retaining the status quo. Changes affecting the privileges of the inhabitants were likely to lead to unrest.[56] One suspects that his letter to Bellièvre provoked a sympathetic response, but events proved that Sully was determined to push forward. A struggle between the two men ensued in the council.

The estates met in Agen in May 1603. Viçose and another delegate were elected to seek the permanent revocation of the edict sending commissioners to Guyenne and the removal of Martin's regulations, which hampered their activities. A few weeks after his arrival at court, Viçose informed Ornano that the king had turned their petition over to Bellièvre to be answered. No doubt heartened that the aging chancellor rather than Sully had been assigned this task, Ornano wrote him on July 19 asking that he look favorably upon the petition of the towns and communities of the généralité.[57]

Once more Guyenne was victorious; on August 2, 1603, the edict on the commissioners was permanently revoked. Joyfully the estates of Guyenne met in Agen in October to express the gratitude of the généralité in a tangible way. Taxes were voted to raise 6,000 livres for Ornano, 1,500 for his son, and 600 for his secretary. In addition, each of the successful deputies was voted 4,500 livres, a handsome sum well in excess of the expenses they

---

55. Tholin, *Des tailles*, pp. 26–27.

56. *AHG*, 14:387–89; BN ms. fr. 15,897, fol. 351. For other letters concerning Biron and Bouillon, see *AHG*, 14:367–68, 377, 380–83.

57. AC, Agen, AA 33, CC 116, CC 118; BN ms. fr. 15,897, fol. 339.

had incurred. The total levy came to 21,700 livres which was divided among the ten seneschalsies, although several of them had not been represented.[58]

The estates were now at the high-water mark of their success. In November, for the fourth time that year, the deputies of the towns and seneschalsies assembled in Agen, this time with the hope of completing their victory by securing the revocation of the edict creating the élections. They sought the support of the sovereign courts and the treasurers at Bordeaux and sent a new deputation to the king.[59] When the deputies arrived at court, they found that there had been a shift in the balance of power in the council where nonjudicial matters were decided by the vote of the majority of those attending unless the king chose to override their decision. During most of 1603, Bellièvre had managed to hold his own because Sully's constant quarreling with the great nobles had caused him to lose favor temporarily with the king. On October 20 the papal nuncio reported that Henry had taken away the management of the affairs of the princes of the blood from Sully and that it was rumored that he would be relieved from the direction of finances or that at least a colleague would be named to work with him. A minister believed to be on the verge of losing favor had difficulty winning the backing of a majority of the council. It was presumably for this reason that the deputies from Guyenne had been able to get the edict on the commissioners revoked, and Bellièvre had succeeded in preventing the implementation of the paulette, a device for making offices hereditary in return for an annual payment, which Sully had pushed through the council by an eight to six vote in November 1602 before the momentary shadow was cast over his career. By the end of 1603, however, Sully was once more in favor, and the nuncio was reporting that the king wanted to take the seal away from Bellièvre because his great age prevented him from exercising his office. The shift in the council in Sully's favor must have been very slight because he was unable to farm the paulette until December 1604. Indeed, he feared that the deputies from Guyenne would persuade a majority in the council or the king to revoke the edict creating the élections, but he was strong enough to block the effort of the delegation elected in November 1603.[60]

The battle between Sully and the estates was also joined in Guyenne, with the minister once more winning most of the victories. The treasurers at Bordeaux refused to permit the tax to be levied to reward Ornano and the others because the king had not given his authorization, and in April 1604 the Parlement of Bordeaux verified the edict creating the élections over the

---

58. AC, Agen, BB 40, fols. 162–68, CC 116; BN ms. fr. 18,168, fols. 17–18v.

59. AC, Agen, AA 33, BB 40, fols. 168v–169v, CC 116.

60. Bernard Barbiche, *Correspondance du nonce en France, Innocenzo del Bufalo, 1601–1604* (Rome and Paris, 1964), pp. 584, 632; R. Mousnier, "Sully et le Conseil d'Etat et des Finances," *Revue Historique* 192 (1941): 71, 73. For the paulette, see chap. 11, sec. 3.

opposition of the estates.[61] In spite of the council's decision to recall the commissioners from Guyenne, Sully sought other means to halt illegal taxation and to investigate fiscal records in search of fraud and illegal exemptions from taxation, which numerous reports from the généralité had undoubtedly led him to believe existed. Indeed in January 1602 before his recall, a commissioner had written Bellièvre that there was not a town or village consulate which had not imposed taxes without permission. The towns, he had further commented, were ruled by closed castes whose selfish actions would cause the common people to welcome the commissioners.[62]

Rouergue and Quercy were the first to feel Sully's authority. In December 1602, the month the edict on the commissioners was temporarily revoked, the council issued a decree creating a *receveur alternatif des tailles* in each of the recettes in the two seneschalsies to keep a better eye on what taxes were collected. These posts existed in all the other élections and recettes in the kingdom, the edict stated, but they had not been established in Rouergue and Quercy because of the opposition of the estates. Freed of these royal overseers, the estates had imposed excessive taxes on the people.[63] Many months, however, lay between the creation of a new position and its effective use by a new appointee. In October 1605 two receivers in Quercy had to be told to reside in their jurisdiction during the year in which they exercised their office. Three months more elapsed before two of the receivers designated for Rouergue were appointed. Meanwhile local opposition continued. The treasurers in Bordeaux reported to Sully in August 1603 that Quercy and Rouergue were resisting new taxes, and the following year the president of the Parlement of Toulouse wrote to the king that the estates were stirring up trouble and preventing their decrees from being executed.[64] In February 1605 the council was compelled to order that the entire tax imposed on Rouergue be levied immediately.[65]

In spite of the revocation of the edict on the commissioners, Sully remained determined to have the tax records of the towns verified and turned to royal officials located in the province. In March 1603 the Parlement of Bordeaux was persuaded to order the *consuls* of Agen to turn over their accounts for the past three years to the clerk of the seneschal, but by one means or another they avoided doing so. When two new tax positions were created in Agenais, the assistant syndic of the estates purchased one for 9,000 livres to keep it from falling into unfriendly hands, and the citizens of Agen so frightened the appointee to the other that he abandoned his

61. AD, Gironde, C 3874 bis, fol. 135–35v. The deputy who represented the estates before the treasurers was the intendant of finance, Viçose.

62. BN ms. fr. 15,899, fols. 275–76.

63. *Actes Royaux*, 1: no. 5247.

64. Valois, 2: nos. 9714, 9954; AD, Gironde, C 3874, fols. 36, 39–40v; BN ms fr. 23,198, fols. 288–95.

65. Valois, 2: no. 8972.

position. Frequent attempts were made by the estates and towns to obtain rulings from the sovereign courts, first to block the implementation of Martin's decrees and later to prevent the inspection of their account books, but the king's council took some cases under its own jurisdiction and forbade the sovereign court to take cognizance of the others.[66]

When the three estates of Comminges met in March 1604, they made a virtue of necessity by unanimously adopting regulations limiting the costs of holding their meetings. Their reason was that these expenses had served as a pretext for several evil-intentioned inhabitants of the province to create a disturbance in order to injure "the honor and dignity of the said estates." They then proceeded to oppose some royal taxes and to plan to work in conjunction with other seneschalsies to prevent the establishment of the élections. Nevertheless, the following year it was once more necessary for the council to issue a decree forbidding them and the estates of Rivière-Verdun to levy more than 3,000 livres per year without the king's authorization.[67]

Sully could not prevent the estates of the seneschalsies from meeting because until the élus actually assumed the duties of their office, the estates and their agents were needed to collect taxes. He could and did, however, prevent the estates of the généralité from assembling. They had met five times between November 1602 and November 1603 when Bellièvre was still influential, but there is no evidence that they assembled again with royal permission until May 1609. As 1604 wore on and no concrete united action was taken to block the actual establishment of the élections, the towns became restive. Finally in September, Agen took the initiative and invited deputies from other towns to come to an unauthorized meeting of the généralité early in October. Three times the *consuls* of Nerac wrote Agen to ask if Ornano had authorized the meeting. Upon not receiving an affirmative reply, they sent no deputies. Others were less law-abiding; during the meeting, it was decided that a number of towns would send deputies to Ornano to ask him to summon the estates of Guyenne so that united action could be taken against the installation of the élus and other royal innovations. Apparently Sully had arranged for Ornano to be instructed not to permit such an assembly, but the lieutenant general did give the *consuls* of Condom permission to convoke the recette of Condomois, Astarac, and Bazadais to decide what action to take against the élus. Other jurisdictions may have received similar permission. Where they did not, the capital town elected a deputy or the syndic acted on his own initiative. During the winter of 1604–05, representatives appeared at Paris from all the seneschalsies in Guyenne, including Bordeaux and Périgord where élections had long been established, but where there were complaints about the heavy tax on river commerce, a concern of the pays d'états as well. Instead of the normal two

66. Tholin, *Des tailles*, p. 32; Valois, 2: nos. 6639, 6643, 7025, 7107.
67. AD, Haute-Garonne, C 3686; Valois, 2: no. 9305; AD, Gironde, C 3975.

deputies representing the entire généralité, Sully was besieged by a number of men because he had refused to permit the estates of Guyenne to assemble.[68]

The estates of Agenais did not meet, but the municipal officials of Agen chose their first *consul*, Julien de Camberfore, sieur de Selves, to represent the seneschalsy as well as their town. Selves arrived in Paris around the middle of December 1604 and quickly contacted the king, who referred him to Sully and his council.[69] There followed a ten-month battle between the powerful minister and the resourceful, outspoken defender of municipal liberties. Their frequent engagements are clearly revealed by Selves's numerous letters to the *consuls* of Agen, letters which also provide specific information concerning Sully's intentions regarding the provincial estates, not just in Guyenne but in all of France. Neither Sully nor Selves were intellectuals. Sully made no learned explanations of royal prerogative such as James I was then regaling the elected representatives of the English people, and Selves made no comments on the concept of popular sovereignty that had lately found some defenders in France. Sully justified his acts in terms of the corruption of the estates and the welfare of the people; Selves in terms of tradition and privilege.[70]

The contest between the two men was not as uneven as it may initially seem. Selves was not important nationally, though he was locally. He had had the forethought to obtain favorable letters from Ornano to the king and to other influential persons before coming to Paris.[71] A spokesman of traditional privileges and procedures, he found supporters in the council itself where Bellièvre had not been alone in advocating making the old system of government work rather than embarking on a course leading to royal absolutism. To achieve his objectives, on the other hand, Sully had to retain the support of the king and a majority of the council, some of whom were susceptible to being influenced by the gratifications the deputies from Guyenne were sure to offer. His proud demeanor and fiery temper had won him many enemies whose numbers were augmented by his firm opposition to graft and corruption that had lined the pockets of courtiers and officials for so long a time. During the early months of 1605, he once more thought that he was on the verge of disgrace. Under such circumstances he called upon all his resources to meet the threat from Guyenne.[72]

68. AC, Agen, AA 33, CC 120; Bazas to Agen, July 24, 1604; La Croix to Agen September 10, 1604. AC, Condom, BB 18. The list of provinces with deputies at Paris was prepared from Selves's correspondence at AC, Agen, CC 111, CC 120, CC 123.

69. Selves's December letters to Agen are in AC, Agen, CC 111, CC 120.

70. My account of Selves is drawn heavily from my article, "Henry IV and Guyenne: A Study Concerning the Origins of Royal Absolutism," *French Historical Studies* 4 (1966): 363–83. I am indebted to this publication for permission to reproduce portions of the article here. Tholin, *Des tailles*, pp. 32–50, deals with Selves's mission and publishes excerpts from some of his letters.

71. Selves to Agen, December 21, 1604, AC, Agen, CC 111.

72. Sully, *Mém.* Michaud, 3:20–25, 34–40. Sully reported that his enemies accused him of disbursing royal funds in such a manner as to win the support of certain great nobles.

Sully's first line of defense was to try to discourage or frighten the deputies so that they would not present their petitions to the council. He gave Selves several audiences a week during the early months of his mission and used the occasions to reveal all he had learned from investigations that had been held in Guyenne by Martin and other financial officials, from reports from the Parlement of Bordeaux, and from disgruntled local inhabitants. In their first meeting in December 1604, Sully told Selves that the current financial administration in Agenais made the establishment of élections necessary and that most of the inhabitants of the seneschalsy favored this step. Later he commented upon the small revenue the king received from Agen and the heavy burden borne by the people, comments accompanied by a question of whether money was levied for gifts and local purposes, a question to which Selves could give only an affirmative answer. Nobles, churchmen, and judges had told Sully that the *consuls* had turned the towns into petty tyrannies. Most damaging of all was a report submitted by D'Arnal, the king's attorney in Agenais, charging that the *consuls* and syndics imposed taxes without permission, spent large sums on deputations, made excessive profits, exempted themselves from taxes, and divided the taille unfairly. The establishment of the élection, he argued, was necessary, and those who opposed this act were guilty of peculation.[73]

When Selves persisted in his mission in spite of being informed of the mass of evidence that had been collected to persuade the councillors to remain firm, Sully adopted more discreditable tactics. On one occasion he threatened to throw Selves in the Bastille on the grounds that he had a faulty procuration, and if Selves's charges are correct, he even tampered with the deputies' mail. As a precaution Selves often entrusted his dispatches to friends going to Guyenne rather than to the post. He sometimes repeated information given in an earlier letter and in several instances wrote twice the same day to ensure that one letter would arrive safely. When it became necessary to send very secret information to Guyenne, around the first of April 1605, the deputies from the généralité decided that one of their number should go in person.[74]

Sully tried to discourage deputies from remaining long at court by refusing to authorize payment for their services. One of Selves's tasks was to try to persuade the council to approve the tax voted by the estates of Guyenne in 1603 to reward those who had participated in the negotiations for securing the revocation of the edict on the commissioners. On January 22, 1605 the council decided to permit Ornano and his son to keep the 7,500 livres that had been voted them but then pointedly refused to compensate the deputies for their expenses. Little wonder as his mission extended month after month, Selves raised the question of his own payment, but he doggedly

73. See especially Selves to Agen, AC, Agen, CC 123, nos. 3, 5, 10, 11, 12, 15, 17. D'Arnal's report is in CC 122.

74. Ibid., CC 123, nos. 3, 12, 13, 17, 19, 24.

remained at court even after he had been recalled by the estates of Agenais.[75]

During the course of his conversations with Selves, Sully revealed some of the plans for the reorganization of France. Guyenne was not to be the only pays d'états in which élections were to be established. The king, he declared, "wants the taille to be levied in all of France in the same fashion."[76] Languedoc, Dauphiné, and Provence, he stated, were earmarked for élections. A week or so before this audience, Selves had written that he had learned from an unnamed source it had been decided to establish the élus in these same provinces. Later, in April, he urged the *consuls* of Agen to put a high priority on winning Ornano's support because when the crown wanted to treat the inhabitants of Brittany like those of Guyenne, Marshal Brissac, their lieutenant general, had backed them so strongly that they had obtained part of what they wanted.[77]

Henry IV and Sully, then, intended to substitute royal officials for those of the estates wherever they existed in France and to supervise the towns and villages carefully when they performed the tax-collection duties that remained to them. Henceforth the king could levy whatever tax he pleased, and the estates would be allowed to die because the funds they voted for their own use would be levied by the élus only if they were authorized to do so. Gone would be the money to offer handsome presents to important persons in return for their assistance in winning concessions at court and blocking undesired actions. As small a matter as sending a deputation to Paris could be undertaken only with the crown's concurrence. This would not be often, Selves early concluded, for "those who come here for the welfare of the people are hardly welcome." "There is nothing so odious here," he wrote, "as syndics and deputies."[78]

From the first, Selves clearly realized the threat that the establishment of the élus posed for the towns and estates. In moments when he despaired of success, he punctuated his letters with such phrases as "[they want] to abolish the privileges of the towns in order to be able to do as they please, and remove the means of complaining." Or, "Adieu liberties! privileges! *Consular* offices will not longer have their luster or power." Or again, "They have created *élus* in order to reduce the authority of the *consulat*.... If we do not take care, we will be *consuls* only to have the streets cleaned."[79]

Selves was not a man to accept defeat without a struggle. Upon his arrival

75. Ibid., nos. 3, 11–13, 32, 38; BN ms. fr. 18,186, fols. 17–18v. On March 29, Viçose, the intendant of finance turned deputy, was finally permitted to keep 1,800 of the 4,500 livres that had been voted him. Ibid., fols. 219v–20. I have found no evidence that the other deputy was compensated.

76. Selves to Agen, AC, Agen, CC 123, no. 13. There is a similar statement in no. 2.

77. Ibid., nos. 3, 11.

78. Ibid., nos. 12, 20. For similar statements see nos. 18, 19, 25, 26.

79. Ibid., nos. 10, 19, 20.

in Paris, he had sought interviews with the leading members of the council. Unfortunately, one potential ally, Bellièvre, was of little use because the king had decided to take the seals from him and give them to Brulart de Sillery, who took the oath as keeper of the seals on January 5, 1605. The aging Bellièvre was left the title of chancellor but ceased to be influential in the government.[80] Denied this potential source of support, Selves quickly found others. On December 21, he reported that Sillery himself, Forget de Fresnes, the secretary of state for Guyenne, Villeroy, the influential secretary for foreign affairs, Antoine de Loménie, who became secretary of state in 1606, and Guillaume de L'Aubespine, baron de Châteauneuf, a councillor, did not believe that it was obligatory to establish élections in Guyenne, but they added that it would be necessary to fight Sully. Gilles de Maupeou, on the other hand, handled him as roughly as did Sully.[81]

Selves quickly recognized the advisability of joining forces with the deputies from the other provinces in Guyenne in order to have "a stronger battery against the canons of M. de Rosny [Sully]."[82] Cooperation, however, proved difficult. Some representatives had not been adequately instructed, presumably because the estates had not been permitted to meet, and they were present only as syndics or deputies of a town. Others, like those of Rouergue and Quercy, preferred to try to persuade the sovereign courts in Toulouse and Montpellier to refuse to verify the edicts creating the new élections, a type of resistance not as promising for Agen because the courts in Bordeaux (in whose jurisdiction it lay) were less friendly. As a result, Selves cooperated closely only with the deputy from Bazadais, who was in a similar position.[83]

Selves's instructions had been to secure the revocation of the edict creating the élus on the grounds that Agenais and other seneschalsies in Guyenne had paid a substantial sum in 1582 in return for the crown's abolishing the élections forever. This position was just, but Selves was not so naive as to believe that justice alone would prevail at the court of Henry IV. It was necessary to offer the king a sufficient sum to reimburse him for the loss of the revenue he anticipated from the sale of offices in the new élections. Unfortunately the estates of Guyenne had not been allowed to meet to authorize such an offer. Indeed Selves could not even make a proposal in the name of Agenais alone because he had no assurance that the other towns in the seneschalsy would be willing to pay the price necessary to be rid of the élection, since in fact he had been deputed by the town council of Agen alone. Soon after his arrival in Paris, he had reported that no one except Sully and Maupeou thought that it was necessary to have élus in Guyenne. He repeated this observation on March 3, just five days before the letters

80. Ibid., no. 8; Kierstead, *Pomponne de Bellièvre*, pp. 134–36.
81. Selves to Agen, AC, Agen, CC 111, CC 120.
82. Ibid., CC 123, no. 6.
83. Ibid., CC 120, CC 123, nos. 6, 12, 13, 17, 19.

Ornano had sent to the king and the councillors had won him and several other deputies a hearing. Sully, who had wanted to send them away without replying to their petition, had left the room in anger when it was decided to admit them in deference to the marshal. With Sully gone, the audience went well, but Selves clearly anticipated the unfavorable reply that was handed down on March 10. On that day he reported that the majority of the councillors were favorable to their position but that Sully "is so absolute that no one resists him."[84]

Selves knew that Sully would now want to proceed to establish the élections, but he still did not despair. In a meeting in which Viçose played the role of experienced adviser rather than intendant of finance, Selves and several other deputies from Guyenne adopted a plan which was so secret that it was decided that one of their number should go in person to Guyenne to win the support of their constituents. They dared not write about it because of "the perfidity of the world and the interception of letters."[85] Part of this plan was to obtain permission for the estates of Guyenne to meet and offer the king a substantial sum of money in return for abandoning the élections. But there had to be something more involved because there was no reason to keep this a secret. Indeed the possibility of a financial offer must have been suggested informally to the council, because on March 22 Selves reported that it had been discussed on three occasions but Sully had been opposed. Certainly the secret was important to Selves because he constantly urged the *consulat* at Agen to adopt the plan.[86] The key to the secret can almost certainly be found in his letter of April 22 in which he told of a deputy who had been sent by Ornano and the Parlement of Bordeaux to protest to the king and council against the tyrannies of the new tax farmers of the river commerce. Sully had received him "as lovingly as he did us" and wanted to send him away without being heard. The king, however, fearing some disturbance, had given reasonable satisfaction. "Use this information," Selves hinted.[87] The *consuls* in Guyenne, then, were to see to it that there was enough unrest to cause Henry to intervene personally rather than leave the decision to his brutal and inflexible minister.

First they needed permission to hold the estates. At one point Sully persuaded Henry to tell Ornano to forbid the meeting. A few days later Henry reversed himself, but the estates of Guyenne did not meet. The

---

84. Ibid., nos. 17–21. One of the arguments the deputies from Guyenne offered in their petition was that the élus would burden the people because they charged for their services, while the *consuls* of the towns levied taxes for nothing. They admitted that the estates and towns sometimes taxed them for their own purposes, but this was done only for such necessary work as repairing roads, bridges, walls, and town gates. The petition also dealt with the tax on commerce on the Garonne and Dordogne rivers and the prerequisites of the receivers of the tailles. AN, E 8b, fols. 47–50.

85. Selves to Agen, AC, Agen, CC 123, no. 1.

86. Ibid., nos. 3, 23–26, 29, 30, 32.

87. Ibid., no. 32.

second step was to win Ornano's support, and early in July Agen dispatched a deputy to Bordeaux for this purpose.[88] The third was to ensure that there were enough disturbances in Guyenne to cause the king to hesitate to defy the wishes of the inhabitants. Here there was no necessity for the *consuls* to act, for the nobility and Protestants were then causing grave concern. Finally, there was the need to win as much support at Paris and elsewhere as possible and when all was ready, to find means to bypass Sully and go directly to the king. Among those enlisted were Ornano, the seneschal of Guyenne, Forget de Fresne, the secretary of state for Guyenne, and the relatively obscure Nicolas de Netz, a councillor in the Court of Aids. Probably all of them expected some sort of reward, but no one was as blunt as Netz. "Send a well-filled purse," Selves wrote on September 12, "... to pay M. de Netz because he has frankly told us that he will do nothing without money," a request that he repeated on October 17.[89]

By the middle of June Selves believed he was in a position to act. He had apparently received authority to make the king a concrete offer, though probably only in the name of Agenais, whose estates had met in April. Sully had gone to Châtellerault to attend a Protestant assembly, and Henry's latest mistress, the countess of Moret, had agreed to act as a go-between the deputy and her lover, for which service, Selves pointed out, it was necessary to give her a "fine present."[90] About three weeks later he reported that he was awaiting the king's decision concerning the élus through the intercession "of one of his friends. If this fails there is no hope." However, Henry was unwilling to make a decision in Sully's absence, and when the minister returned near the end of August, he was as intransigent as before. By that time the estates of Agenais, discouraged, had voted to recall Selves, but the intrepid deputy followed the court in its wanderings until late October, hoping somehow to alter the decision of the crown.[91]

Why had Selves failed? He himself had attributed his difficulties to the inability of the seneschalsies in Guyenne to cooperate more closely.[92] He may have been partially correct because the estates of Guyenne had never been able to relegate the smaller estates to a secondary status as the estates of Languedoc had its diocesan and seneschalsy assemblies. However, other rivalries lessened Guyenne's capacity to resist. The failure of the nobility and clergy to participate in many of the seneschalsy estates must have weakened them. It is noteworthy that the most effective resistance was offered by the estates of Comminges, Rouergue, and Quercy, where the three estates acted as a unit. To make matters worse the third estate in Condomois and Agenais was quarreling with the nobility over whether the taille was réelle or

88. Ibid., nos. 28–30, 34, 36; Verduc to Agen, July 14, 1605, AC, Agen, CC 124.
89. Ibid., CC 123, nos. 28, 30, 34, 38, 40.
90. Ibid., no. 34, BB 40, fols. 250v–52, CC 124; Agen to the twelve towns, April 6, 1605.
91. Ibid., CC 123, nos. 4, 35, 37–40, CC 124, Agen to Selves, August 23, 1605.
92. Selves to Agen, AC, Agen, CC 123, nos. 2, 19.

personnelle, that is, over whether nobles should pay this tax on the nonnoble land they owed. Part of Selves's missions was to support this suit at court.[93] Even the towns in Agenais were quarreling among themselves, and Selves devoted much of his time trying to thwart Villeneuve-sur-Lot's special deputy to court who was seeking a general levy on the region to repair a bridge.[94] But these factors provide only half the answer; the other half lies in Sully's dogged determination and Henry's decision to give him his support.

Henry IV had had a choice. He could make a handsome profit by accepting Selves's offer and abandoning the idea of creating élections, or he could persist in his original determination and make an immediate profit by selling the new offices. If he chose the latter, he would incur the burden of paying the élus' salaries indefinitely and the risk of provoking an uprising in an already troubled region. Acting on Sully's advice, and apparently against that of the majority of his council, he chose the less profitable and more dangerous course. Surely his goal and that of his minister must have been to undermine the estates and towns so that their own authority could be more fully implemented. In doing so, they took a step toward creating an absolute state, a step that Sully had declared would be followed by others as the provincial estates fell one by one before the élus.

The defeat of Selves did not bring the battle at court to an end, but during the several years that followed it subsided somewhat.[95] The most interesting events took place in the seneschalsies where every effort was made to delay the installation of the élus or to prevent them from functioning as desired. The three estates of Rouergue proved very successful in practicing the former art. Taking advantage of the sympathetic attitude of the councillors in their presidial seat and at the Parlement of Toulouse, they fought the case in the courts. But legalities never bothered Sully. When the estates, which met late in 1605 to vote the taxes for the following year, adjourned to February 1606 without doing so, Sully instructed a treasurer of Bordeaux to proceed immediately with levying the tax anyway.[96] Since the élus were not yet prepared to function because of the legal disabilities placed in their way, the three estates continued to perform their fiscal administrative duties. In November 1606 Sully obstinately addressed the letters for the tax for 1607 to the élus. The estates, in a well-attended meeting the following January, complained bitterly about this attack on their liberties. Someone suggested that they send a deputation to court to secure the

93. During this period the council declared several times that the tailles were réelle, but the nobles persisted in their suit. Valois, 2:6646, 8188, 9800. To pay the costs of the suit, the third estate of Agenais had to levy a tax of 18,092 livres. Ibid., no. 10,229. For Selves's comments on this question, see AC, Agen, CC 123, nos. 15, 17, 20, 24.

94. AC, Agen, CC 123, nos. 4, 31, 32, 35, 36, 38; Valois, 2: nos. 6212, 8721, 12,011, 14,686.

95. Verduc, who replaced Selves as Agen's deputy at court, devoted most of his attention to other matters. His correspondence is in AC, Agen, CC 120, CC 124.

96. Valois, 2: no. 9869.

suppression of the élus as Quercy had just done, but it was decided not to do so for the time being. Instead they voted their governor 6,000 livres "in consideration of the good offices which he has rendered until now and renders every day to the province ... to obtain the suppression of the edict on the *élus*."[97] They then elected a committee of eighteen to oversee the levying of the tax and to watch out after the affairs of the province during the year. They did limit the expenses of holding the estates to the prescribed amount, and the money they voted their governor was "under the good pleasure of the king." Otherwise Sully had little to show for his efforts.[98]

The year 1608 passed uneventfully; by December the élus were not yet installed. Sully's limited patience was nearing an end. The estates met as usual in late January 1609 and elected the bishop of Rodez to go to court to obtain the suppression of the élections. At this point Sully intended to permit the estates to levy the tax as usual because he merely told the syndics to act in conformity with earlier guidelines established by the council, but by March he could contain himself no longer. He directed the élus to levy the sums stated in their commissions in spite of the opposition of the three estates and the officers of the presidial seat. An appeal these officials made to the Parlement of Toulouse against the élus was removed and taken to the council to be resolved, and the syndics, *consuls*, and receivers were forbidden to tax in the future without specific instructions from the king. Furthermore, they were to account for 340,000 livres they had levied between 1606 and 1608 in excess of the sums required by the king. Later, the years to be included were extended from 1604 to 1609. With the installation of the élus, there was no longer any need for the estates from Sully's point of view, and no evidence has been found that the customary meeting was held in January 1610.[99]

To combat the élus the three estates of Comminges combined deputations to court with appeals to the Parlement of Toulouse. As insurance against the failure of both these methods, their resourceful deputy to Paris in 1606 borrowed a substantial sum in the name of the estates to provide the down payment for the purchase of these offices for 25,250 livres. If élus there must be, they would be friendly. An executive committee of the estates approved this bold act, but it came under attack when the three estates met in Muret in February 1607. This meeting was opened with an impassioned speech by

---

97. AD, Aveyron, C 1903, fols. 23v–24. This gift and a comparable one voted the following year were disallowed, presumably by Sully, but the governor evidently persuaded Henry to reverse this decision because a tax was levied for this purpose in 1609. *IAD, Gironde*, C 3814.

98. The committee of eighteen, under the presidency of the bishop of Rodez and in the company of the syndics and receivers of the three marches, met six times in 1607 and once in January 1608. AD, Aveyron, C 1903, fols. 76–132.

99. *IAD, Aveyron, sér. G*, ed. Charles Estienne and L. Lempereur (Rodez, 1934), 1: G 86, G 89; AD, Aveyron, C 1904; AC, Rodez (bourg), BB 11, fols. 122–23; *IAD, Gironde*, C 3891; Valois, 2: nos. 13,511, 14,508, 14,737, 15,177, 15,619; Marc-A.-F. de Gaujal, *Etudes historiques sur le Rouergue* (Paris, 1858–59), 2:487.

the syndic of the third estate, in which he alluded to the presence in Muret of a treasurer from Bordeaux who had come to establish the élection and spoke strongly to the effect that this action posed a threat to their liberties. The estates then voted unanimously to oppose the installation of the élus by every means at their disposal and instructed the syndic to make an appeal to the Parlement of Toulouse. This he had already begun to do, and several weeks before the Parlement had instructed the newly appointed élus not to assume their duties before submitting the edict creating their positions for verification. That afternoon, however, there were several complaints about the estates' excessive levies, their inefficient administration, and their unfair apportionment of taxes, but it was nevertheless decided to complete the purchase of the offices in the élection. By this act the estates incurred an additional debt over half as large as the annual taille they paid to the king.[100]

Such actions as these made it necessary for the three estates of Comminges to levy more taxes than authorized by the king to meet their creditors, thereby incurring the wrath of both the government and some of the people. Although the estates had repeatedly been told not to tax without permission, it was necessary for the council to repeat this order in November 1606. In May 1607 the executive committee of the estates met to verify the accounts of one of their former officials who had borrowed money on the credit of the seneschalsy to meet its expenses. He claimed 63,964 livres, but it was found that he had inflated this fugure by 5,000 livres. A further investigation was ordered that was almost certainly supplemented by one conducted by one of Sully's officials before the decree was issued in December 1608 to levy 44,135 livres, the equivalent of the taille for one year, to pay the debts of the province. Rigorous accounting by the estates and the crown had reduced the alleged debt by about 30 percent.[101]

The year 1608 witnessed a struggle between two towns over which should be chosen as the seat of the élection at the same time that the three estates were continuing their opposition to the installation of the élus. By the close of the year all possibility of legal obstruction had come to an end, and taxes for 1609 were presumably levied and collected under the direction of élus indebted for their position to the estates. The three estates evidently hoped that this unusual arrangment would enable them to continue much as they had done before, but under the watchful eye of Sully and his subordinates, this was not to be the case. In July 1610 the treasurers of Bordeaux ordered the élus of Comminges not to levy any taxes imposed by the estates for the affairs of the seneschalsy, including the money necessary to defray the costs of their meeting earlier that year.[102]

100. AD, Haute-Garonne, C 3692, C 3693, C 3805; V. Fons, "Les Etats de Comminges," *Mém. de la soc. imperiale archéologique du midi de la France* 8 (1861–65): 203.

101. Valois, 2: nos. 10,600, 11,914, 12,825; AD, Haute-Garonne, C 3695.

102. *IAD, Gironde,* C 3813; AD, Gironde, C 3875, fol. 49–49v.

Agen was less successful in staving off the installation of the élus, an event which probably took place in January 1607.[103] Unfortunate as this was in itself for the consulat, it was made worse by the fact that the senior élu was none other than D'Arnal, the king's one-time attorney who had compiled the evidence of the *consuls'* corruption and submitted it to Sully several years before, to the detriment of Selves's mission. The arrangement was not likely to be harmonious. The four meetings of the estates held between January 1607 and February 1609 were largely devoted to efforts to secure the abolition of the élections, tariffs, and river tolls, or at least a reduction of the charges that could be imposed.[104] An interesting episode took place in one of the aides of Agenais which indicates the resourcefulness of the estates and Ornano's sympathy for their cause. The *consuls* of Laplume had received permission to assemble the estates of the viscounty of Bruilhois for one purpose and then proceeded to deal with other matters, at least so the king's attorney in Agenais charged. A bitter quarrel ensued between the deputies from Bruilhois and the attorney on this subject in Ornano's presence in Bordeaux. The marshal firmly defended the estates, saying that he had authorized their meeting which could deal with the entire political order and that they had acted for the general good.[105]

One by one the other seneschalsies succumbed to Sully's insistence that the élus be installed and permitted to perform their duties. The struggle appears to have been particularly bitter in Quercy. In May 1609 the council peremptorily forbade the three estates to meet and declared that taxes would be levied by the élus. It also assumed jurisdiction over a case the syndic had instituted against these officials. Taxes to support the activities of the estates that Martin had approved were permitted to continue, but the three estates as a body that assembled frequently and had a permanent staff to collect taxes and to look after local interests was to come to an end.[106]

The fate of Périgord reflects the changing attitude of the crown toward the provincial estates during the first few years of the seventeenth century as Bellièvre's role declined and Sully became Henry's most trusted minister. The three estates met in February 1595 and arranged a compromise between the three large towns in the province and the numerous smaller ones. Henry himself wrote the governor expressing his satisfaction with their work. Clearly he had no intention of destroying the estates at this time, but

---

103. The syndic of Comminges told the estates in February 1607 that treasurer Prugnes had just installed the élus in Agenais. However, Prugnes's commission to do so was revoked by the council on January 9. Fons, "Les Etats de Comminges," p. 203. Valois, 2: no. 10,725.

104. AC, Agen, CC 130, CC 131; AC, Laplume, BB 6, fols. 28–29v, 34v–35v. D'Arnal's purchase of the office of élu gives credence to Selves's charge that he and others were motivated by the desire for office when they supplied Sully with information suggesting the need for élections. AC, Agen, CC 123, no. 19.

105. AC, Laplume, BB 6, fols. 35v–38v.

106. Valois, 2: nos. 13,641, 13,642, 14,952; *IAD, Gironde*, C 3815.

they did not meet again during his reign. Henry's final decision to terminate the estates may not have been taken until 1606, but it was probably made a few years earlier. Following their usual practice the three estates of 1595 had elected définiteurs and syndics to look after the interests of the seneschalsy when they were not in session. These définiteurs, of whom there were six from each estate, were to serve for nine years. In addition, three syndics were appointed to serve three-year terms in succession. Thus nine years were to elapse before there was any compelling need to assemble the estates again. Lapses of several years between sessions had been routine in the past. The estates had met only once between 1579 and 1588. There was no cause for surprise when they did not assemble after 1595 during the remainder of the century, but it was a veritable revolution when they did not meet by 1605 because the mandate of the définiteurs and syndics expired. Hélie de Jehan, attorney of the king, mayor of Périgueux, and one-time syndic, presented Henry with a stirring appeal in 1606 to permit the three estates to be held to elect new officials, but by this time Sully had his master's ear, and no meeting took place.[107]

During the trying years following the failure of Selves's mission, each province had concentrated on defending itself, but the need for united action continued to be recognized. The syndic of the nobility of Armagnac visited the estates of Comminges in December 1605 and suggested that the seneschalsies of Guyenne unite in an effort to block the establishment of the élus. Comminges sent a deputation to Ornano to seek his advice and assistance. The marshal responded by writing the king to tell him that the establishment of the élections was causing strong resentment in Guyenne because there was a tradition passed on from father to son that the élus would subvert their privileges, franchises, and liberties which had been preserved for so many years under the crown. The bourgeoisie and the inhabitants of the plat pays were especially fearful that they would be overtaxed because the nobles might escape paying the taille on their nonnoble land. He expressed concern that the edict would lead to unrest and, in conjunction with the seneschal of Quercy, urged that it be revoked.[108] This letter was probably intended to secure a more favorable reception for a number of petitions from the estates that flowed into Paris in 1606 and thereafter, but it had no effect. Sully moved relentlessly forward, installing the élus as rapidly as he could overcome local resistance.[109]

107. Henri IV, *Lettres*, 4:319; *IAC, Périgueux*, AA 37. For a list of the meetings of the estates, see L. de Cardenal, "Catalogue des assemblées des Etats de Périgord de 1378 à 1651," *Bul. phil. et hist. (jusqu'à 1715) du comité des travaux historiques et scientifiques* (1938–39): 264–66.

108. AD, Haute-Garonne, C 3690; Ornano to Henry, January 7, 1607, BN ms. fr. 23,198, fols. 321–22.

109. There was some sort of petition against the élus signed by the deputies of Guyenne in 1606. *IAD, Aveyron*, G 89. The estates of Quercy protested against the élus in December 1606 or January 1607, but Rouergue decided not to do so. AD, Aveyron, C 1903, fols. 33v–34. The

Sully's efforts to extract more money from river tolls also caused concern. In November 1607 the *consuls* of Agen, Cahors, and Montauban complained to the treasurers at Bordeaux that they were being overcharged by the tax farmers and were otherwise mistreated by them. The estates of Agenais which met in February 1609 determined to seek joint action with the *consuls* and syndics of the other provinces. Especially irritating was a proposal to establish a new toll at the confluence of the Garonne and Dordogne rivers. Perhaps as a matter of tactics, the élus, although discussed, were shoved back into a secondary position.[110]

Agenais's appeal to Ornano to permit a meeting of the estates of Guyenne, the first since November 1603, was successful.[111] Ornano himself had always been sympathetic with the aspirations of the estates, but he would hardly have given permission without the king's consent or at least the belief that he would not object. What caused Henry to be willing to have the estates assemble is a matter for conjecture. Probably the tolls were cited as the reason for the assembly, and it is likely that Henry thought that the people had legitimate cause for complaint on this subject. Indeed, a treasurer from Bordeaux had just investigated the tax farmers.[112] Perhaps the estates would offer a substantial sum in return for being rid of the tolls altogether. In any case, little harm could be done by permitting an assembly on this subject. If the estates also requested to be free of the élus, and Henry was not so naive as to believe that they would not, he could always say no.

The estates were scheduled to open on May 1, but there was a one-day delay because the deputies from Rouergue and Armagnac had not yet arrived. No representatives from Périgord, where the estates had been suppressed, or from Bordeaux were apparently anticipated. On May 2 a petition was prepared, and a delegation was elected to take it to court. That same month Bordeaux summoned its filleules to prepare a cahier and choose deputies to present it to the king.[113] The two delegations must have arrived at Paris at about the same time, and there they remained until the council considered their grievances on November 21. The activities of the deputies

---

estates of Agenais protested against the élus in January 1607, January 1608, and October 1608. AC, Agen, CC 130, CC 131. AC, Laplume, BB 6, fols. 28–29v. The estates of Bazadais protested in March 1606. AC, Casteljaloux, BB 3.

110. AC, Agen, CC 130, CC 131.

111. In the spring of 1607, deputies from the communities of Agenais, Condomois, Bazadais, and Rivière-Verdun asked for an interpretation of the edict of May 10, 1607, forbidding the towns to levy taxes without permission, but I have found no evidence that the estates met to elect the deputies. It is more likely that the towns or estates sent deputies individually, although probably there was some correspondence to ensure proper coordination. AC, Agen, CC 128; *IAD, Aveyron,* G 95.

112. AC, Agen, CC 130.

113. Ibid., BB 40, fols. 368v–69v; AC, Laplume, BB 6, fols. 58–61v; *IAD, Gironde, sér. E suppl.,* ed. Gaston Ducaunnès-Duval (Bordeaux, 1901), 2:67.

and the reasons for the long delay are unknown, but perhaps it was occasioned by Sully's desire to keep them away from the council and their determination to be heard. The cahier of Guyenne consisted of twenty-nine articles of which the élus, tolls, tariffs, heavy taxation, investigating commissions, and the recent failure to hold the estates periodically came under attack. That of Bordeaux was even longer. Both had many points in common, and both suffered the same fate in the council where Sully was usually victorious; but if his triumph resulted from the long delay he imposed upon the deputies, he had one bitter pill to swallow.[114] He had to order a levy of 9,848 livres to pay the costs of holding the estates of Guyenne and the expenses of their deputies to court, some of the latter drawing allowances for as many as 211 days.[115]

The deputies' most immediate satisfaction was the issuance of ordonnances designed to correct the abuses of the farmers responsible for the river tolls and limiting the circumstances under which they had to be paid. Of greater long-range significance was the council's decision to order the treasurers at Bordeaux to investigate the activities of the élus and the fees they charged. The estates must have been prepared for this eventuality because enough material was made available for the treasurers to act with unaccustomed speed. In February they accused the élus of levying three times the authorized amount to pay their salaries and fees. In March this figure was upped for the élus in Agenais, Condomois and Lannes, and they were required to send their records to Bordeaux. The élus of Agenais, the treasurers declared, were causing universal complaints, and they suspended the salaries of those in Lannes until they explained what they were doing. In a letter to Sully the treasurers blamed the delay in collecting taxes in 1610 on the élus' inexperience and negligence.[116]

The treasurers of Bordeaux may not have been free from provincial loyalties, but during Henry's reign they served the crown more faithfully than most. Their condemnation of the élus should not be attributed too largely to a desire to save the estates. Rather it resulted from their belief that the élus were dishonest, inefficient, and arrogant to the local inhabitants. Whatever the faults of the syndics and other officials of the estates, and there were many, those of the élus were worse. This fact was probably not lost on the royal councillors, few of whom shared Sully's view that the élus should be used as a means to break the power of the provincial estates and towns. It was to have profound significance after Sully's dismissal from office early in the following reign.

114. Valois, 2: nos. 14,688, 14,689.
115. AD, Gironde, C 3977; Valois, 2: no. 14,891.
116. AD, Gironde, C 3875, fols. 1–12, 274–75; AC, Agen, CC 133; Valois, 2: nos. 14,750, 14,830, 14,911, 14,912.

3. THE ESTATES OF BRESSE, BUGEY, AND GEX

The only other territories in which Sully was able to establish the élus were Bresse, Bugey, and Gex. France conquered these lands in a brief campaign during the summer of 1600. They had belonged to the house of Savoy for centuries except for a brief interlude between 1536 and 1559 when they, along with the duchy of Savoy itself and part of the principality of Piedmont, had been incorporated into the French monarchy. During the Wars of Religion, the house of Savoy seemed on the verge of securing its revenge as Dauphiné and Provence were almost within its grasp. The recognition of Henry IV by the Catholic League chiefs and the signing of the peace of Vervins with Spain in 1598 terminated the duke's annexationist policy on the French side of the Alps, but he continued to hold the marquisate of Saluzzo, a French enclave in his Italian lands which he had taken in 1588. The diplomats at Vervins were unable to resolve the troublesome question of disposing of this small territory and asked the pope to arbitrate. In February 1600 it was finally agreed that the duke would have three months to decide whether he would surrender Saluzzo or cede Bresse and several Alpine valleys as compensation. The duke did not give up hope of keeping both territories, because he anticipated support from Spain and hoped to profit from intrigues he was carrying on with the duke of Biron and other French nobles. Exasperated at the duke of Savoy's refusal to carry out the provisions of the February treaty, Henry launched an attack on his territories. He was aided by Sully's efficient use of artillery, and the Savoyan strongholds on the French side of the Alps fell in quick succession. Bourg, the capital of Bresse, was taken on August 12, and Chambéry, the capital of the duchy of Savoy, fell on August 23. Negotiations were resumed, and by the terms of the treaty of Lyons, January 1601, Savoy surrendered the French-speaking provinces of Bresse, Bugey, and Gex to France but kept Saluzzo. France had won a narrow salient extending to the environs of Geneva that cut one of the main Spanish routes from Italy through Franche-Comté to the Rhineland and Low Countries, but had seemingly abandoned its century-old goal of controlling part of Italy.[117]

The Savoyard dukes had had an elaborate system of representative institutions in their lands. There had been assemblies in which participants came from all parts of their domain, but their more common practice had been to hold separate meetings for those who dwelt on the Italian and French sides of the Alps. In addition, the three estates of Bresse and Bugey sometimes deliberated together and sometimes apart. Meetings of the individual estates were frequently held in both provinces, the syndics of

117. Jules Baux, *Histoire de la réunion à la France des provinces de Bresse, Bugey et Gex* (Bourg-en-Bresse, 1852).

Bourg having the right to convoke the third estate of Bresse if they obtained permission from the local ducal official. The very wealth of alternative forms of representation was probably detrimental to the survival of these assemblies because the loyalty of the inhabitants was not centered in any one institution. The French preserved the system between 1536 and 1559 when they first controlled the region, but the able, autocratic duke, Emmanuel Philibert, began to reduce the power of the estates when he resumed control over the area in 1559. After 1563, meetings of the three estates of Bresse and Bugey became rare, and the size of the tax was set by the duke. Nevertheless the nobles and ecclesiastics continued to elect syndics to represent their respective orders, and the municipal officials of Bourg continued to summon the communities to protest the size of the tax and other matters, to vote and levy additional sums for local use, and to divide the assessments among the various localities. Assemblies of the three estates and of the individual estates of Gex also continued to function. In the three territories the taille was actually collected by the officials of the individual communities. Hence Henry IV inherited a system in which he determined the size of the taille but was dependent on local officials to collect it, a situation which made delays and protests commonplace. This was especially true because additional taxes could be added by the third estate for such local purposes as bribing the governors and other royal officials to support their cause and paying deputations to carry their appeals to court.[118]

The situation was not likely to please Henry. Hardly had the success of the Savoyan campaign become apparent than he began to consider how to administer his anticipated territorial gains. In a letter dated August 19, 1600, he indicated his willingness to rely heavily on Bellièvre's advice in matters of justice and on Sully's advice in matters of finance.[119] Subsequent events suggest that the influence exercised by each minister was paramount in his designated field. In September, when it seemed likely that France would annex the duchy of Savoy as well as other ducal territories west of the Alps, Bellièvre sent Henry a comprehensive plan for the establishment of justice. "The province of Savoy conquered by your majesty's armies," he began, "cannot be preserved without the justice which gives to each person what belongs to him and holds the people in their duty." To secure this objective, he recommended that a Parlement be established in Chambéry to serve as the final court of appeal from inferior courts in Bresse, Bugey, and other occupied Savoyard territories west of the Alps. He buttressed his argument by pointing out that Francis I and Henry II had permitted

118. A. Tallone, "Les Etats de Bresse," *Annales de la soc. d'émulation et d'agriculture de l'Ain* 55 (1927): 272–344; Helmut G. Koenigsberger, *Estates and Revolutions* (Ithaca, 1971), pp. 19–79; AD, Ain, C 886, G 307; Louis Ricard, *Les institutions judiciaires et administratives de l'ancienne France et spécialement du bailliage de Gex* (Paris, 1886), pp. 165–83, 190–91.

119. *Lettres inédites de Roi Henri IV au Chancelier de Bellièvre du 8 février 1581 au 23 septembre 1601*, ed. Eugène Halphen (Paris, 1872), pp. 256–57.

Chambéry to have a Parlement when they owned these lands between 1536 and 1559 and that the dukes of Savoy had operated a somewhat similar sovereign senate there. Indeed the terms of the capitulation of Chambéry provided that a sovereign court be established. Bellièvre countered claims of the Parlement of Grenoble to extend its jurisdiction over the duchy of Savoy by saying that "it would be very difficult to persuade the Savoyians to recognize the justice of those of Dauphiné because of the old jealousy and hate which exists between the two nations." In regard to the aspiration of the Parlement of Dijon to extend its jurisdiction over Bresse and Bugey, an aspiration supported by Biron, who apparently hoped that success in this regard would further his ambition to add these lands to his government of Burgundy, Bellièvre pointed out that the territory of governments did not necessarily coincide with those of Parlements. In short, his recommendations, which he stated had the support of the members of the council who were with him, marked an effort to continue the traditions of the Renaissance monarchy, traditions which involved a recognition of the rights and privileges of the inhabitants of conquered territories and a willingness to allow them a considerable degree of self-government even at the cost of perpetuating a decentralized judicial system.[120]

In the terms of the treaty of Lyons, Henry promised to respect the rights, privileges, and immunities of his new subjects and in response to their petitions, he issued one general and numerous specific decrees. Since the duchy of Savoy was not annexed, there was no need to create a new Parlement, but a presidial seat was authorized for Bourg in July 1601 to which appeals were to be made from bailiwick courts in Belley and Gex. Important cases could be appealed from the presidial court to the Parlement of Dijon. This provision raised no immediate opposition for the inhabitants of the annexed territories were accustomed to appealing to the sovereign senate in Chambéry.[121]

Sully's approach was diametrically opposed to Bellièvre's. Long before the treaty of Lyons had been signed, Jean Maillard, a treasurer at Dijon, and his brother, Pierre, had been dispatched to the newly conquered regions to collect the quarterly payment of the taille that was due in September. Protests by the two syndics of Bourg that the town was too impoverished because of the pillaging of Biron's troops made a scant impression, and on December 15 they reported to the municipal council that Pierre Maillard had threatened to imprison them if they did not collect the taille for the September and December quarters, a sum coming to over 900 livres, and a

120. Bellièvre to Henry IV, September 1600, BN ms. fr. 15,894, fols. 370–72v.

121. The treaty of Lyons, petitions from the towns of Bourg and Saint-Trivier, the nobility of Bugey and Valromey, and the town and bailiwick of Gex, and a decree confirming the privileges of Bresse are published in Baux, *Histoire de la réunion*, pp. lxvii–cxl. *Mémoires historiques de la ville de Bourg, extraits des registres municipaux de l'hôtel-de-ville de 1536 à 1789*, ed. Jules Baux (Bourg-en-Bresse, 1870), 3 : 101–09.

tax on wheat. The councillors recognized that the king would not give the town relief unless Biron and his lieutenant, the baron de Lux, could be persuaded to testify that they were too poor to pay. Unfortunately, they were in no condition to offer the two nobles suitable presents for their anticipated services, so they voted to give 48 livres obtained by selling the metal in a large clock belonging to the town to the secretaries of the nobles in return for preparing a statement testifying to their poverty and persuading their masters to sign it. But Biron insisted on consulting a financial official in Mâcon before taking any action. This delay enabled the councillors to question officials in the small neighboring town of Montluel on how they had won an exemption from the taille, but in other respects it was most unfortunate. On January 8, 1601, Pierre Maillard, exasperated at the delay, threatened to seize the goods of the bourgeoisie and to imprison the syndics if immediate action was not taken. The town officials stepped up their efforts, but not enough to satisfy the impatient Maillard who imprisoned a syndic and confiscated the goods of several burghers on January 18. An appeal to the baron de Lux to release the syndic was successful, but the deputations to Biron and to the king's councillors in Lyons produced no immediate relief.[122]

Meanwhile other towns in Bresse that were suffering from similar exactions suggested that the third estate of the province be assembled to send a joint protest to the king. By the time the meeting was held in Bourg on March 29, new problems had arisen to trouble the plagued citizens. Instead of reducing the taille for 1601, Jean Maillard was attempting to divide 60,000 livres among the communities of the province, nearly 12,000 more than was customary. To make matters worse, he insisted that the taille was personnelle in Bresse, a ruling which freed nobles and ecclesiastics from paying the tax on their nonnoble land, thereby increasing the burden that fell on the third estate. Those present protested these actions and asked that a delay be granted in collecting the tax until they had had time to appeal again to the king.[123]

Other problems beset the municipal officials. To provide for two crippled soldiers, Henry IV entrusted them with the administration of the property of the hospital. Creditors demanded payment, and the sieur de Boisse, the newly appointed governor of the town, wanted the fortifications repaired. There was not even enough money to send the long anticipated deputation to Paris to defend their privileges or to start legal proceedings against the nobility and clergy to make them pay the taille on their common lands, much less to pay creditors or to repair walls. Boisse befriended the municipal officials either through sympathy or because he anticipated a reward. He persuaded the baron de Lux to free the town from the expense of repairing

122. *Mémoires de Bourg*, 3:117–31.
123. Ibid., pp. 127, 131–35.

the walls. The syndic responded with a modest present that was approved by the town council. Boisse assisted in obtaining a reduction of the municipal taille and even offered to lend 150 livres to enable the town to send the deputation to Paris. The councillors did not feel that they could borrow such a sum until they had some means of repayment and sought his assistance in obtaining permission from Lux to levy a tax for this purpose. Thus a relationship was established in the newly acquired territory that was already common elsewhere in France in which governors permitted towns to tax in order to be able to give them presents and to carry on their own activities.[124]

The resistance of the municipal officials removed any doubt that may have existed in the minds of Henry IV and Sully concerning whether the old fiscal and municipal structure should be allowed to continue. On February 20, 1601, Sully presented a decree to the Council of Finances creating élections in Bresse, Bugey, and Gex. Several years elapsed before the élus actually began to perform their duties, but the crown's intention of substituting royal tax officials for those of the towns and communities was clearly evident.[125] This step was not regarded as sufficient to control the municipal officials of Bourg who had proved especially difficult. In the fall of 1601 when it became time to hold elections, Boisse directed, in accordance with orders from the king, that the inhabitants nominate an enlarged slate of syndics and councillors from which he would choose those who would actually serve. With élus and more cooperative municipal officials, Sully and his master apparently hoped to impose their will on the newly acquired territories.[126]

Meanwhile other French taxes were being established. In March 1601 the initial steps were taken to introduce a grenier à sel with the accompanying requirement that the inhabitants purchase a large amount of salt at inflated prices. An announcement in January 1602 that the pancarte was about to be established was enough to cause the town to give Boisse six barrels of wine costing 114 livres in the hope that he would once more come to their assistance. One can easily imagine how Sully enjoyed these prospects of additional revenue, but perhaps the greatest immediate reward the crown received from the conquered provinces was derived from the sale of the newly created financial and judicial offices at prices so exorbitant that there was some difficulty in disposing of them.[127]

In the midst of these events the deputies of Bourg finally set forth to plead

124. Ibid., pp. 135–52.

125. AN, E 3ª, fols. 6ov–61. The élection of Gex was never established, and the tiny jurisdiction was incorporated into the élection of Bugey seated at Belley. The new élections were placed in the généralité of Burgundy. That Henri IV and Sully cooperated closely on the financial arrangements for the new territory is indicated by a letter the former wrote on March 20, 1601. See Henri IV, *Lettres*, 5:396–98.

126. *Mémoires de Bourg*, 3:154–57.

127. Ibid., pp. 130–35, 163–65; Valois, 2: nos. 6471, 6574, 7189, 6750, 6765, 6768, 6858.

their cause before king and council in Paris. When delegations had traveled to Chambéry, Lyons, and Mâcon during the fall and winter of 1600–01, they had had to go on foot, so great was the poverty of the town, but this time, armed with a loan, they went by carriage. Nothing is known of their negotiations, but their petition with the royal reply dated November 29, 1601, testifies to the failure of the fiscal part of their mission. To their pleas that the grenier à sel, the pancarte, and the élection not be established, the crown turned a deaf ear. To their request that the taille be reduced, they won only a promise that their welfare would be considered in the future insofar as the affairs of his majesty permitted. Also disconcerting to the town magistrates, though perhaps not to the citizenry, was the abrupt refusal to permit the syndics and communities of the bailiwick to levy taxes to support their activities even though they had received permission from local royal officials. Without the power to tax, the activities of the local institutions of self-government would be stifled, a prospect not too disconcerting to the crown.[128] Less direct was the response to a request that the three estates be assembled "as in the other provinces of France in order to deliberate on what would be in the service of His Majesty and the public good."[129] Here the council simply stated that the king would receive petitions from individuals and groups as the occasion arose.

The delegation did win a decree confirming the rights and privileges of the inhabitants of the province insofar as they did not contravene the laws of France. To leave no doubt, the new method of tax collection, including the use of élus, was carefully spelled out, and once more taxation without the king's consent was specifically forbidden. One senses Bellièvre's hand here as elsewhere when the legal rights of baronies, counties, and the various social classes were preserved and Sully's hand when an exception was made in the area of fiscal administration.[130]

On January 13, 1602, representatives of the towns and communities of Bresse assembled in Bourg in the presence of several Burgundian financial officials to apportion the taille in the province for that year. The crown had set a total of 108,000 livres to be imposed on the newly acquired territories, but what troubled the assembly more than the size of the levy was the decision that had been made to collect only 6,000 livres from Gex and 34,000 from Bugey, the remaining 68,000 livres to be taken from Bresse. This uneven division was attributed "to those of Bugey," and the deputies decided to protest. They also agreed that Bourg and the smaller localities would cooperate closely in an effort to make the clergy and nobility pay the taille on their nonnoble land and to stay the publication of the decree establishing the pancarte until an appeal could be made to the king.[131]

128. *Mémoires de Bourg*, 3: 162–63; Baux, *Histoire de la réunion*, pp. lxxxi–xciv.
129. Baux, *Histoire de la réunion*, p. xciii.
130. Ibid., pp. xcv–civ.
131. *Mémoires de Bourg*, 3: 165–74.

There is no need to continue a chronological account of the woes that fell on Bourg and the other communities in Bresse following their annexation to the crown. The pancarte was eventually removed, only to be replaced by another tax.[132] An intended increase in the taille was countermanded by the crown in 1604, and a substantial sum was allocated to the town to repair its fortifications and pay part of its debts. Once more the triumph was short-lived. In 1605 the taille on Bresse was raised to 106,145 livres, the town of Bourg being asked to contribute 300 livres more than the year before. Efforts to shift part of the tax burden to Bugey and Gex and to make the clergy and nobility pay the taille on their nonnoble land failed.[133]

Bourg was also in difficulty because of the debts it had contracted, debts that were reported in November 1602 to exceed 80,000 livres. Henry had permitted the municipal magistrates to levy a small tax on wine brought into the town, but the yield proved inadequate to satisfy the creditors, who proceeded to attach the goods of one of the syndics. More local taxation was necessary, but Henry was reluctant to grant permission either because he wanted to protect his poor subjects from the magistrates or desired to ensure that the limited amount that they could pay went into his own treasury. Whatever his reasons, the relief he granted was barely sufficient to keep the municipal government functioning, and he carefully checked to see how money levied for local purposes was spent. In 1604, for example, he surrendered 18,000 livres derived from the salt tax, but by the time this sum was divided with the other communities in Bresse, Bugey, and Gex, the amount that went to Bourg was adequate to provide only a partial solution, and borrowing in emergencies continued to be necessary.[134]

The presence of royal officials in Bourg caused increasing problems. In 1602 they attempted to gain access to the tax records with the apparent intention of seeing that the town magistrates paid their share, this in spite of the fact that the syndics and secretaries claimed to be exempt from the taille. In addition, the élus interfered with the assessment of other taxes that had traditionally been the responsibility of the municipal officials. The inhabitants went to some length in 1602 to block Belley's efforts to have the presidial seat moved there, but they must have wondered at the wisdom of their endeavor when the president of the seat began to interfere in the municipal jurisdiction and to claim precedence over the town magistrates. It must have been especially galling when the Maillard brothers made their periodic visit to Bourg in January 1603 and announced that taille on Bresse was being increased 1,500 livres to pay the royal officials. When the syndics

132. Valois, 2: no. 7467; *Mémoires de Bourg*, 3:234, 259–60, 268, 279–80, 301–02.

133. *Mémoires de Bourg*, 3:261–62, 274, 276, 281, 307; *IAD, Côte d'Or, sér. C*, ed. Joseph Garnier (Dijon, 1883), 2:86; Valois, 2: nos. 11,804, 11,806.

134. *Mémoires de Bourg*, 3:173–74, 181, 186, 205–06, 215, 232–33, 261–62, 281–83; Valois, 2: no. 13,874.

protested, the Maillards, as usual, threatened to throw them into jail.[135]

On this occasion, as on many others, the town sought the assistance of their governor, the sieur de Boisse, and sent deputations to court. Boisse invariably lent them a favorable ear, and they in turn gave him presents to retain his favor. That same November an entry in the town registry states that it was customary to give Boisse a present "in order to keep ourselves always in his good favor." This time it was six barrels of good wine.[136] A later entry dated January 3, 1605, noted that "it is a good and laudable custom in this town to give our governor, M. de Boisse, a present." And later, "The council has decided that in consideration of the numerous favors that the town daily receives from M. de Boisse, the syndics would give him in its name a present that he would like costing from 135 to 150 livres, and enter this expense in the municipal accounts."[137] The fact that Boisse was a Huguenot and the townsmen Catholic did not alter this friendly relationship based on mutual self-interest. Boisse exploited a local abbey and saw to it that a Protestant church and cemetery were established in their midst, but these actions counted less to the burghers than that he had long been a trusted servant of the king who referred to him as his "creature."[138]

Assemblies of the third estate of Bresse were held occasionally during the remaining years of Henry's reign. It met in December 1604 when a quarrel occurred between a syndic and Boisse's lieutenant who acted for him in his absence. In 1607 there was either another meeting of the third estate of Bresse, a joint one with the deputies from Bugey and Gex, or both. The following year the deputies of Bresse assembled once more. The usual purpose of these assemblies was to discuss the division of the taille, but the third estate of the newly acquired provinces presented a joint petition in December 1607 dealing with such matters as tolls, the creation of offices, the recall of investigating commissioners, and the reduction of the taille, a tax which they claimed was 30,000 livres higher than under the Savoyard dukes. The dukes have been called absolute monarchs, but their activities paled before those of Henry IV and Sully, who created new taxes, raised old ones, appointed tax officials to see that the money was collected, and interfered with the electoral procedures to ensure the choice of friendly magistrates. To reduce the activities of local magistrates and the sums they had available to bribe royal officials, they also limited the amount the town could tax for its own purposes. Little wonder the historian of Bourg does not share the general admiration for the first Bourbon king and his efficient minister.[139]

135. *Mémoires de Bourg*, 3:172–73, 178–79, 199, 211–13, 265, 283–84, 295–300, 306–07, 4:14–15; *IAC, Bourg*, ed. Joseph Brossard (Bourg, 1872), p. 62.

136. *Mémoires de Bourg*, 3:211, 249.

137. Ibid., pp. 303–04.

138. Ibid., pp. 183–84, 289–93, 298. For Henry's reference to Boisse as his "creature," see Henri IV, *Lettres*, 5:488.

139. *IAC, Bourg*, pp. 62, 63; Valois, 2: nos. 11,762; 11,806; 12,956; *Mémoires de Bourg*, 3:307–08. The local inhabitants were freed from paying the tolls in 1609. Valois, 2: nos. 13,653, 14,625.

Little is known concerning the activities of the nobility of Bresse after the annexation of the province by Henry IV, but we are better informed about the clergy. Although Bresse, Bugey, and Gex were divided among the dioceses of Lyons, Belley, and Geneva, the local clergy not only participated in their respective diocesan assemblies but also joined together to form an assembly of the newly acquired provinces. In addition, the clergy of each province sometimes met alone. The type and frequency of these assemblies varied with the circumstances, but the clergy appears to have been more active under the Savoyard dukes during the sixteenth century than the towns were and continued to meet as the occasion demanded after the annexation to France. The extension of the diocese of Lyons into the new provinces caused considerable litigation dating back to the regime of the dukes over whether the Lyonese clergy was subject to clerical taxation on the benefices they held there. In 1608 the Council of Finances ruled in their favor, but undaunted, the clergy of Bresse and Bugey continued litigation on this subject until the Revolution. Like the third estate the clergy was forced to borrow to meet its obligations, but in 1608 the bishops of the three dioceses were permitted to levy a tax of 14,000 livres to liquidate debts. That same year the benefice holders in the annexed provinces won exemption from the décime and other royal impositions on the clergy in return for a mere 6,000 livres to be paid at each new accession to the throne. Under Henry IV the clergy clearly enjoyed a preferred position when compared with the burghers of the hard-pressed towns.[140]

Our knowledge of events in Bugey is derived largely from the joint actions its inhabitants took with those of Bresse, for in these cases the relevant documents are often preserved in Bourg. Evidence derived from this source, taken with other scattered material, points to similar experiences following annexation. In November 1601 Henry answered a petition that had been presented to him and his council by the nobility in much the same way that he had replied to the third estate of Bresse at the same time. Once more social privileges were preserved, but a deaf ear was turned to pleas that the élection and the pancarte not be established and that the estates be restored to the strong position they had occupied during the previous French administration before Emmanuel Philibert had embarked on his absolutist policies. Even the problem of a deeply indebted third estate appears the same. In addition to the assistance Henry gave Bugey in conjunction with Bresse, he ordered in 1610 that 2,000 livres collected from fines be applied to the acquittal of its debts and those of Gex.[141]

The situation in Gex was somewhat different because the Alps barred it

---

140. *IAD, Ain, sér. G.*, ed. Joseph Brossard (Bourg, 1891), pp. 68–70, 77, 81. Valois, 2: nos. 10,921, 12,444. Henry did not fail, however, to collect the entire gift the clergy had voted him at the time of the annexation. Ibid., no. 13,027.

141. Baux, *Histoire de la réunion*, pp. cv–cxxi; Valois, 2: nos. 10,442, 11,252, 15,161. Contemporary documents usually refer to Bugey as "Bugey and Valromey."

from the rest of France, making it a geographic and economic satellite of Geneva located only ten miles away. The little bailiwick, which consisted of only twenty-six parishes, had become almost completely Calvinist, and many of its acres were owned by citizens of Geneva. Included was land that had formerly belonged to the Catholic church. This situation caused the Genevans to bend every effort to persuade Henry IV to surrender Gex to them. Henry refused, but he was sufficiently anxious to retain the friendship of that town to grant its citizens other concessions. Pressure from the papacy caused him to reestablish Catholicism there, but to avoid offending the Genevans and the French Protestants, he gave the Catholics only three churches and those church lands which had not been alienated. To balance this small concession, Henry paid pensions to the Protestant clergy. Not until 1612 could the saintly François de Sales, exiled bishop of Geneva, persuade the crown to return the remaining Catholic churches, and with them the part of the former church property which had not come into the possession of Genevans. Even with this assistance, the Catholics could not prevent most of the inhabitants of Gex from remaining stubbornly Protestant.[142]

Henry adopted the same conciliatory tactics in financial matters, one suspects to the disappointment of Sully. Treasurer Maillard arrived in Gex soon after the French occupation and immediately set about imposing 24,000 livres in taxes, no doubt as directed by Sully. Certainly Sully was far less sympathetic than his master was when dealing with the ambassadors from Geneva. In October 1601 Henry granted the Genevans temporary reprieve from paying the taille and tolls in Gex, a reprieve that soon became permanent. Gradually these and other differences were straightened out, to the advantage of the Genevans. Tax levies on Gex had to be substantially reduced because so many property owners were granted exemptions. This in turn led to charges from Bresse that Gex was not paying its share, and petitions to the council from Bresse replaced those of the Genevans.[143]

The bailiwick of Gex had its provincial estates, but we have only scattered knowledge of its activities in the early seventeenth century. Led by the town the third estate submitted a petition that was answered by the king and council in March 1604. It reveals something of the local situation. The Savoyard dukes had levied only 3,549 livres on the bailiwick, but in 1601 the taille alone had been set at 6,000 livres. Reductions accorded by the council

---

142. Francis Decrue de Stoutz, *Henri IV et les députés de Genève* (Geneva and Paris, 1901), pp. 213–366 passim, extract from *Mém. de la soc. d'hist. et d'arch. de Genève* 25. Etienne-Jean Lajeunie, *Saint François de Sales* (Paris, 1966), 1:423–26, 454–75. Ruth Kleinman, *Saint François de Sales and the Protestants* (Geneva, 1962), pp. 94–135 passim. Valois, 2: nos. 10,704, 12,168. Henri IV, *Lettres*, 5:486–90, 531–32, 539–40, 8:810–11. Barbiche, *Correspondance ... Innocenzo del Bufalo* pp. 77–79, 177, 182, 187, 202, 210, 216, 221–22 227–28, 237–38, 245. Henry was careful to consult Bellièvre concerning the religious settlement in Gex. See BN ms. fr. 15,896, fols. 355, 372.

143. Decrue de Stoutz, *Henri IV*, pp. 241–42, 251–52, 258–59, 270–74; Valois, 2: nos. 6581, 6872, 7247, 10,067, 11,804, 11,806, 12,366.

to compensate for the exemptions granted to the Genevans had not been fully implemented by local tax officials, and complaints were lodged against the salt tax tolls and other levies. In spite of the stress they placed on the poverty of the people, the bailiwick was so deeply in debt that the petitioners sought permission to levy 3,000 livres a year until the debt was liquidated (this was in addition to some revenue from the salt tax the king had assigned for this purpose). No specific request was made that assemblies of the estates be held regularly, as Bresse and Bugey had done in 1601. Perhaps those who drafted the petition did not feel threatened. Certainly Gex participated with Bresse and Bugey in preparing a joint petition to the crown in 1607. On the whole, Gex seems to have suffered less than the other two bailiwicks as a result of the annexation because of its ties with Geneva, but even here the transition was not a happy one. With the new regime came new and higher taxes that were more rigorously collected, and a number of arrogant tax officials led by the Maillard brothers ran roughshod over the local magistrates. The estates of Gex, like those of Bresse and Bugey, were allowed to continue to exist, but the removal of their power to tax without special royal permission limited their activities. There is no evidence that Henry interfered in municipal elections in Gex as he did in Bourg, but certainly his actions following the annexation reduced the ability of the inhabitants to govern themselves as fully as before.[144]

144. Little that remains in the archives of the estates of Gex dates back before 1675. AD, Ain, C 999–1025; Baux, *Histoire de la Réunion*, pp. cxxiii–clx; Ricard, *Les institutions judiciaires*, pp. 204–08, 264–79; Valois 2: no. 11,762.

IO

HENRY IV, SULLY, AND THE OTHER ESTATES

HENRY IV AND SULLY HAD ATTACKED THE ESTATES IN GUYENNE IN PART BECAUSE they received more reports of tax abuses being committed by them than by their counterparts in other parts of France. There were unfavorable statements from such royal officials as Michel de Marillac and Jean de Martin, but there were also complaints of abuses from some of the people. In 1552 a nobleman who served as syndic of the villages of Comminges had gone so far as to try to have an élection created there.[1] Equally significant, the estates in Guyenne were weaker than those in most other parts of France. The provincial assembly never established its supremacy over those of the seneschalsies, and the nobility and clergy were relatively inactive in most jurisdictions. Similarly the estates in Bresse, Bugey, and Gex were weak when they were incorporated into France because of the absolutist tendencies of the Savoyard dukes and the failure of the first two orders to participate fully. Hence Henry IV and Sully were able to impose élections on both regions in spite of numerous protests and delaying tactics on the part of the estates. But what of the great pays d'états? We have seen that Sully told Selves, the intrepid deputy from Agen, that he intended to establish élections in them as well, but their stronger position made it more dangerous for him to take this step. It is now necessary to investigate how and to what extent he and his master moved in this direction.

1. THE ESTATES OF LANGUEDOC

Several years elapsed after the restoration of peace in Languedoc before the estates were reunited. This unusual situation resulted from an agreement reached between Henry IV and the duke of Joyeuse, the local Catholic League chief, in January 1596. By its terms Montmorency was to remain governor of the entire province, but Joyeuse was to serve as his lieutenant in

---

1. AD, Haute-Garonne, C 3804, nos. 11, 13; M. J. Naurois-Destenay, *Les Etats de Comminges aux XVIe et XVIIe siècles* (thesis, Ecole Nationale des Chartes, 1953–54), p. 130. In Périgord where there were élus, on the other hand, the plat pays asked that they be suppressed and that taxes be apportioned and collected by the officers of the estates. See chap. 9, n.22.

Toulouse and other areas he controlled. The duke of Ventadour, who was also Montmorency's son-in-law and nephew, was to be the lieutenant of the remainder of the province. It was presumed that Montmorency, as constable and valued royal adviser, would normally reside at court. Both of his lieutenants were to hold the estates of their respective jurisdiction during the two years that followed, after which the estates were to be reunited under conditions that were not defined.[2]

The three estates in Joyeuse's territory had actively engaged in the negotiations with Henry, and in March 1596 they formally recognized him as their ruler after he had given a favorable reply to their cahier. When they next met in December, Joyeuse delivered an eulogy concerning their valiant and generous king and then proceeded to ask for the same sum for 1597 as had been granted for the current year. The estates protested against the tolls on the Garonne and Tarn rivers, but the only real controversy took place over how much money to appropriate to buy wheat and munitions for the towns along the Spanish border. In spite of several attempts, Joyeuse could persuade the estates to vote only half the sum he thought necessary.[3]

Henry wrote Joyeuse a series of letters before the estates met in October 1597 stating that he had recognized Montmorency's infant son as his eventual successor in the governorship and instructing him to see that the edict was registered by the Parlement of Toulouse and presented to the estates. He also said that he wanted the estates to vote the usual tax plus money to support the garrison in the province and from 1,000 to 1,200 infantrymen because of the Spanish threat. The three estates accepted the first two taxes without much difficulty, but they would do no more than name a committee with the authority to borrow the money necessary to support the infantry should a Spanish invasion become imminent. They also protested against the investigatory commissions that were in the province and the increases in the salt tax. Finally they took steps to liquidate their own debts that they had incurred in the late wars.[4]

The estates that Ventadour opened in November 1596 and December 1597 followed a somewhat similar pattern. In both meetings the usual basic

2. *HL*, 12:1533–34. My account of the meetings of the estates of Languedoc is based largely on the procès-verbaux. Copies are located in the archives of Hérault, Haute-Garonne, and in many other departments in Languedoc. I have used the collection in AD, Hérault, which are uninventoried and unnumbered. Folio numbers are therefore not useful to those using other manuscripts, but readers who do so can readily find the location of the source by consulting the detailed inventory of the collection in AD, Haute-Garonne, sér. C that was prepared by Adolphe Baudouin and published in Toulouse in 1903. I have also cited the inadequate summaries of the estates in *HL* because this work is available in every research library, although tax appropriations are occasionally inaccurately given.

3. AD, Hérault, procès-verbal of the estates of Joyeuse, December 1596; *HL*, 11:844–47, 852, 857–58, 864–66, 872.

4. Henri IV, *Lettres*, 8:654, 661, 664; AD, Hérault, procès-verbal of Joyeuse's estates, October–November 1597; *HL*, 11:874–75.

taxes were accorded without difficulty, but those present balked at assessments for the military, including a plea that they grant 150,000 livres to support some Mediterranean galleys. They also rejected a royal proposal to create a regiment commanded by one of Montmorency's bastard sons; but mindful of their debt to that house and their need for its continued assistance, the estates voted the aspiring young man 1,500 livres on the condition that he not raise these troops. Ventadour's company and guards fared better; 42,000 livres was voted for their support.[5]

In addition to the usual gratifications, the estates of 1597 voted to give 300 livres to Jean de Serres, historiographer to the king, to enable him to prepare and publish a description of Languedoc, including an account of the privileges of the province. More was promised when the work was done, but Serres proved to be but another of a long line of scholars who failed to make full use of their fellowship, the book was never completed. A member of the medical faculty of Montpellier was voted 180 livres to enable him to search for herbs with medicinal value to be planted in a garden of the town for the use of doctors and apothecaries.[6]

These estates also sought to take care of their debts by allocating the revenue derived from the farm of the salt tax to this purpose, and like their counterparts in upper Languedoc, they protested to the king about investigating commissioners and river tolls, this time on the Rhône. Ventadour summoned a large assembly in April to hear the report of the deputies who carried these and other petitions to court. Montmorency, they said, had received them graciously and had done all in his power to further their cause, but the king had not been able to accede to their requests. Oblivious of the fact that they had refused to vote most of the funds requested to support the war because of the poverty of the people, they then offered the king 300,000 livres in return for revoking all commissions and suppressing newly created offices. Henry rejected the offer, probably because he hoped to get more from the frightened financial officials and the sale of the offices. Those present then decided to oppose the verification of the new edicts in the sovereign courts.[7] Henry, who was beginning to follow Sully's advice in financial matters, appropriated some tax revenue to support the military that had previously been left at the disposal of the estates, transferred a case

5. AD, Hérault, procès-verbaux of Ventadour's estates of November–December 1596 and December–January 1597–98; *HL*, 11:870–71, 875–78. The discouragement of a commissioner (Rochemaure) who was trying to extract money from the estates is reflected in a letter he wrote to Bellièvre. BN ms. fr. 15,911, fol. 53.

6. AD, Hérault, procès-verbal of the estates of December–January 1597–98, fols. 23–23v; *HL*, 11:877.

7. AD, Hérault, procès-verbal of the estates of December–January 1597–98; *HL*, 11:877–78. For letters of one of the commissioners to establish the grenier à sel, see Des Barreaux to Bellièvre, BN ms. fr., 15,911, fols. 183, 210.

from the Parlement of Toulouse, overruled an edict of the Court of Aids of Montpellier, and persisted in his determination to derive more income from the salt tax.[8]

Ventadour and Joyeuse quarreled over who should hold the estates during the winter of 1598–99 when that institution was scheduled to be reunited. Henry decided on the former, but the difficulty was resolved in a most unusual manner. Joyeuse, who had abandoned the cowl with papal permission in order to fight for the Catholic League, decided to reenter the Capuchin order, a step that freed Henry to name Ventadour lieutenant general of the entire province. The three estates were once more united when they finally met during the spring of 1599. Part of the deliberations that took place during this meeting was devoted to an effort to complete the return to their normal state. The king was asked to assemble the estates in September or October so that the taxes voted for the following year could be apportioned in time for the people to pay them in four quarterly installments as had been the earlier practice. Nobles and prelates were requested to attend in person in order to return the estates to their former splendor, and the king was asked to deprive those members of the second estate of their seats if they did not do so at least once every three years. Support was promised to the University of Toulouse provided the faculty would attend more assiduously to its duties and students would cut out their debauchery so that the institution could resume its former splendor. Henry asked the three estates for a special appropriation of 300,000 livres per year for five or six years to enable him to pay his debts, but only after considerable persuasion by Ventadour did they decide to offer 150,000 livres per year for four years on the condition that newly created offices be abolished, the river tolls be suppressed, and other concessions be made. Henry accepted these conditions although he did place upon the estates the burden of reimbursing those who had purchased the offices.[9]

No noteworthy events took place during the estates that met in Carcassonne near the close of 1599 to vote the taxes for the following year, but the estates of 1600 were more important. Montmorency attended for the first time in some years after being prompted by the king to ask those present to vote the customary present due him because of his marriage to Marie de Medici. Henry was too tactful to suggest the amount that should be offered but not too tactful to point out the size of the gifts of Paris, Rouen, and the clergy, or to enlist the services of a bishop with a seat in the estates to work on his behalf. Montmorency did his best, but the estates, after consulting their archives and finding that it was not customary to provide wedding

8. Valois, 1: nos. 4805, 5000, 5003, 5178; Henri IV, *Lettres*, 5:47, 49.

9. AD, Hérault, procès-verbal of the estates of April–May 1599; *HL*, 11:880–84, 12:1608–17.

presents, refused to give him anything. They regarded the war with Savoy as more worthy of support and granted 90,000 livres for this purpose.[10]

During this period the three estates were becoming increasingly restive over supporting the garrison stationed in Languedoc. In 1601 when Henry asked for 59,660 livres for this purpose, the estates voted only 31,430. Montmorency, who was again present, said that this was insufficient, and the estates finally agreed to pay what he thought necessary. He put the figure at 48,000 livres, and the estates voted this amount.[11]

Following the exposure of Biron's treasonable negotiations with Spain, Ventadour became so worried about the state of the defenses of his government that in July 1602 he asked the Parlement of Toulouse for authorization to spend 90,000 livres in the royal coffers of Béziers to repair the fortifications of that town as well as those of Narbonne and Carcassonne. Parlement decided to write the king before taking action. Not optimistic about the outcome, Ventadour contacted him to ask for permission to convoke the estates earlier than usual that year in order to provide funds, but Henry was evidently less concerned about the Spanish because they did not meet until October.[12] During this meeting Ventadour informed those present that Montmorency had persuaded the king to accept 53,700 livres for the garrisons, a scant reduction from the initial request for 59,660 livres made the previous year. The estates, ignoring the Spanish threat, asked that the king suppress the garrisons or at least reduce the cost to 36,000 livres. Ventadour refused to accept this amount, but finally a compromise figure of 39,000 livres was agreed upon. The estates even delayed payment on the 150,000 livres that had been voted in 1599 for four years until Ventadour assured them that the king would fulfill his side of the agreement.[13]

This round had gone to the estates, but the meeting that opened in December 1603 ended in a draw. Henry sought a four-year extension of the 150,000 livres tax to pay his debts. The estates offered only 100,000, which the commissioners rejected. Finally, after considerable haggling, the estates accepted the 150,000 figure, provided that the agreement that had been reached in 1599 was fully executed, the province continued to have part of

---

10. AD, Hérault, procès-verbal of the estates of October–November 1600; *HL*, 11:884–88; Henri IV, *Lettres*, 5:317. On November 25, Henry wrote Montmorency expressing satisfaction at hearing the report that the estates had voted 90,000 livres for his marriage, but he evidently confused this sum with that voted for the war with Savoy. Ibid., p. 356. The following year Henry told Montmorency to inform the estates of his displeasure that they had not levied the 30,000 livres they had voted for his marriage. Could he have again been misinformed? Ibid., p. 438.

11. AD, Hérault, procès-verbal of the estates August–September 1601; *HL*, 11:890–91; Henri IV, *Lettres*, 5:331.

12. BN ms. fr. 15,577, fols. 221–22, 227, 237–38.

13. AD, Hérault, procès-verbal of the estates of October–November 1602; *HL*, 11:892.

the revenue from the salt tax, the rentes were paid in full, and other concessions made.[14]

Until this point, the three estates had held their own against the crown; both sides had made concessions, and more often than not the government had accepted less than it had asked. The estates owed their success both to the influence of their friends and the preference of most of the king's councillors for compromise rather than confrontation. Gratifications were regularly voted to Montmorency and Ventadour. Members of their families and their servants were given gifts when the occasion warranted. The constable's infant son was voted 6,000 livres in 1599 in recognition of Henry's promise that he would succeed his father as governor and Ventadour's secretary benefited from the largesse of the estates in 1604. The king's secretary of state for Languedoc was voted 1,500 livres in 1603, and 600 more was given to his two assistants to make them more favorably disposed to the objectives of the deputation to court.[15] By 1604, however, Sully, who had earlier curried the constable's favor, had won a paramount position in the Council of Finances and was in a position to join battle with the powerful Montmorency family over whether Languedoc should remain a semi-self-governing province in return for making an annual contribution to the royal treasury, or whether its provincial and diocesan estates and its towns should be weakened by a series of measures culminating in the establishment of the élus.[16]

The dangers of the new situation that confronted the three estates became apparent when their deputies to court the previous year made their reports during their meeting in the fall of 1604 just before Selves began his ill-fated mission to defend Agenais. On November 18 a syndic who had been a member of the delegation informed the estates that Sully and the council had refused to accept the concessions that the king's commissioners had made in return for the renewal of the 150,000 livres tax for four years. In doing so they had technically voided the tax, but on the twenty-third, Ventadour told the estates that they would have to continue the levy.[17]

14. AD, Hérault, procès-verbal of the estates of December–January 1603–04; *HL*, 11:894.

15. *HL*, 11:884; AD, Hérault, procès-verbal of the estates of November–December 1604, fol. 33v. The king, of course, had to agree to these gratifications, but approval was normally so routine that Henry wrote the estates in October 1603 before they actually met, giving permission to provide Ventadour with a don gratuit of an unspecified amount. Ibid., AA 44.

16. In 1604 Sully prepared a list of ways in which money could be raised to present to the king at Fontainebleau. Included was the creation of élus in Languedoc. BN ms. fr. 18,510, fol. 99. On December 8, 1602, Villeroy informed Bellièvre that Sully "has great care to preserve the friendship of those here, especially that of the Constable of France." Edmund H. Dickerman, *The King's Men: The Ministers of Henry III and Henry IV, 1574–1610* (Ann Arbor, University Microfilms, 1965), 3:97.

17. AD, Hérault, procès-verbal of the estates of November–December 1604, fols. 7v–8, 23–25.

Persuasion, not resistance, appeared to him to be the safer policy, especially as he may have had reason to be optimistic about the chances of success. It is true that after the previous meeting he had written Bellièvre saying that the estates had voted the tax only because of his assurances that the agreement would be honored, and that the waning influence of the chancellor had not been sufficient to halt Sully.[18] Ventadour almost certainly knew, however, that after the syndic had been rebuffed by the council, he had gone to Montmorency to plead for his assistance. Probably Montmorency in turn had presented the case to the king, for when the bishop of Carcassonne spoke to him about the subject, Henry expressed his regret that the province had not been given satisfaction and instructed him to see Sully. When he did so, he found the minister much more accommodating for causes one may easily guess. For some reason, it was not until December 1, after the estates had twice refused to vote the money, that the bishop gave this information to those present. Although heartened by this news, the three estates would do no more than ask Ventadour and the bishop to get the council to make the promised concessions when they were at court. Only after this was done would they authorize a special assembly consisting of a bishop, a baron, and a delegate from the chief town in each diocese to borrow or to impose a tax to obtain the 150,000 livres.[19]

It is impossible to reconstruct Ventadour's negotiations with the king and council, but the results suggest that there were advantages to being a duke and having the constable as both uncle and father-in-law. In one issue after another Sully must have given way, for Ventadour was able to report that the rentes which the minister had been trying to reduce would be paid in full, river tolls would be reduced, and dioceses and communities would be freed from having their books examined by the Chamber of Accounts. So successful was Ventadour that the special assembly provided for by the estates was held, and arrangements were made to raise the 150,000 livres for the king. With such recent victories the estates that opened in October 1605 witnessed no confrontations with the crown or its representatives. The salt tax was reduced at the request of the estates after they had promised to raise the lost revenue by another tax, the perennial desire to have new offices suppressed was expressed, and the king was asked to remove the garrisons from the province except along the frontiers.[20]

The aging Montmorency chose 1606 as the year to present his twelve-year-old son to the people of Languedoc as their future governor. His progress through the province was little short of royal, and his reception by the estates was cordial. A highlight of the occasion must have occurred when

18. Ventadour to Bellièvre, January 26, 1604, BN ms. fr. 15,897, fol. 515. On January 21, the estates also wrote Bellièvre on the same subject. BN ms. fr. 15,899, fol. 537.

19. AD, Hérault, procès-verbal of the estates of November–December 1604, fols. 39v–42.

20. Valois, 2: no. 9798. Ventadour's report on the results of his negotiations was placed in the procès-verbal of the estates of October–November 1605.

the attractive but ill-fated boy swore that he would devote his life to the service of the king and the maintenance of their privileges. Under such circumstances even the tactless Sully knew that the moment was not ripe for a new attack on the province. The three estates complained that their cahier of the previous year had not been answered as favorably as they had hoped, but it was they who carried the attack by not appropriating as much to pay the garrison as the year before. If this displeased the constable, he must have been gratified by the gifts of the estates, which included 6,000 livres for his son.[21]

The two-year calm should not be interpreted as an indication that Sully had lost interest in Languedoc. He was merely waiting for a more opportune moment to strike. There is no reason to doubt that his ultimate objective was to establish the élus as he had told Selves several years before. To do so, two preliminary steps were necessary. First, the power of the three estates to tax would have to be limited so that they could not afford large delegations that spent months at court intriguing with and sometimes bribing influential persons. Second, royal officials would have to receive the money collected by the estates in order to be sure that it was not improperly spent and inspect their account books and those of the dioceses and towns to gather evidence of corruption. Only when the capacity of the estates to resist had been weakened and evidence of dishonest administration uncovered could he hope to persuade the king to adopt his plan over the objections of Montmorency and Ventadour. Sully undoubtedly believed that far more tax money found its way into the hands of the three estates than the small proportion of the total levy that was assigned to them would suggest. Selves reported that advocates of the élus at court had told him that of the 3.6 million livres imposed on Velay during the preceding fifteen years, only 600,000 had been for the king. A similar situation, they believed, existed in the other dioceses in Languedoc as well as in Guyenne.[22] With élus established, this drain could be halted, and the king could impose what taxes he liked without waiting for the consent of the estates as he did in Normandy. If the estates proved troublesome, he could cease to convoke them altogether as he had done in Périgord.

So unsuccessful had Sully's efforts been that in reopening the battle with the estates during the spring of 1607, his first move was to try to recover a loss, for the reduced appropriation the estates had voted for the garrisons in 1606 had made necessary a reduction in artillery, a branch of the service of which he was grand master. He protested to the constable the first of May 1607, and Henry, at his behest, followed his example a few weeks later. By September there were plans to create new offices in the dioceses, and Henry was soon telling Montmorency that protests were expected on this score from

21. AD, Hérault, procès-verbal of the estates of October 1606. *HL*, 11:897–900.
22. AC, Agen, CC 123, no. 2.

the estates when they met. Montmorency was to take a firm hand and permit nothing to happen prejudicial to royal authority.[23]

When the estates opened in November 1607, one of the syndics reported that the Chamber of Accounts was once more insisting on examining the diocesan and municipal tax records and had imprisoned a *consul* from Narbonne and a diocesan official from Nîmes. Other violations of the promises the crown had made in 1599 and 1604 in return for the special 150,000 livres each year were soon revealed. The rentes were being cut in half, and the salt tax was being arbitrarily increased once more. In addition, the clergymen in part of the province were being made to pay the franc fief although the king had agreed that they would not have to do so. A large delegation was elected to go to court, and Ventadour sent a hurried messenger asking for a delay in the execution of the decrees of the Chamber of Accounts. The three estates decided to remain in session until they learned the outcome of their mission. For a time they dealt with minor affairs, carefully refraining from acting on the crown's financial requests. Only after Ventadour announced that the Chamber of Accounts had been ordered to delay executing the edicts for four months did the estates recess until it was nearly time to hear the outcome of the struggle that was taking place at court.[24]

Ventadour proceeded to Paris where he and Montmorency gave the deputation all the assistance they could and were credited by it for the few successes that were won. By the terms of the decrees of March 6, 1608, the diocesan and communal records concerning money collected for local use were to be audited by the Chamber of Accounts. Unless special permission was obtained, capitals of dioceses were to levy a maximum of 900 livres per year for their own use, chief places of vigueries 600, and other communities 300. The provincial estates were limited to 10,000 livres per year for their activities. Disgruntled, the three estates suggested that the king forgo his special 150,000 livres but voted Montmorency and Ventadour 18,000 each and the former's son 6,000. Perhaps most galling of all, they had so far exceeded their own 10,000 livre limit that they had to request permission to levy 24,000 to pay the costs of their session of nearly five months and their large deputation to court.[25]

Sully was almost certainly behind these moves, and his hand can be seen even more clearly in an edict of March 15, 1608, harshly forbidding the estates to levy any money for their own support unless at the same time they

23. Henri IV, *Lettres*, 7:255–57, 366–67, 374–75.

24. AD, Hérault, procès-verbal of the estates of November–March 1607–08; *HL*, 11:900–01.

25. BN ms. fr. 18,173, fol. 121v, printed in *Lois municipales et économiques de Languedoc*, ed. Jean Albisson (Montpellier, 1780–87), 6:41–44. For discussions of the March edict, see Paul Gachon, *Les Etats de Languedoc et l'édit de Béziers, 1632* (Paris, 1887), pp. 185, 196–97, and Etienne Delcambre, *Les Etats du Velay des origines à 1642* (St. Etienne, 1938), pp. 238–41, 281–82, 291–99.

collected 18,000 livres to construct a bridge at Toulouse, a project in which he was very interested, having added the office of grand voyer to his many responsibilities a few years before. On September 30 the council completed its work by issuing a series of decrees setting the amount the diocesan estates could levy for their own purposes without receiving special permission, granting them permission to levy specific sums to pay their debts, and increasing the amount that the provincial estates could tax for its activities without the crown's approval from 10,000 livres to 20,000.[26]

When the estates opened in Beaucaire in November 1608, Ventadour told those assembled that the king wanted the same amount that was accorded the previous year. If the three estates would reduce their own expenses, it would lighten the burden on the people and minimize the effect of those who were complaining to the council about the large sums that they were spending. The council was about to appoint one of the maîtres des requêtes to verify the accounts of the taxes collected for the king when Ventadour had intervened on the grounds that this would violate the privileges of the province. As a result, he and the other commissioners had been assigned the task.[27]

No one seems to have been too concerned about the sympathetic duke investigating their records, but the royal decree of March 6, 1608, that charged the Chamber of Accounts with the task of verifying the diocesan and municipal extraordinary levies, that is, those in part assigned for their own use, was still in effect. During their previous meeting the estates had accused officers of the chamber of stealing documents from their archives, and on this occasion the deputy from Toulouse charged that the chamber had calumniously informed the king that they were misappropriating public funds. This accusation had led the council to direct them to examine their books. It was altogether impractical, the deputy argued, for any court to verify the records of 5,000 communities annually, especially as a majority of the *consuls* could not read or write and did not keep records in account books. Indeed in some areas, any records that existed were made by notching sticks. The chamber had arrested municipal officials, broken down the doors of the houses of the *consuls*, seized records from the communal archives, and in general treated those in the dioceses and towns with provincial responsibilities in a violent manner. Thoroughly aroused, the three estates sent a deputation headed by the bishop of Carcassonne to court and determined to remain in session until they had learned the outcome of the mission.

Ventadour was more conscious than the deputies of how determined Sully was to have short sessions of the estates in order to reduce their costs. He therefore urged that after other business had been transacted, those present

26. Valois, 2: nos. 12,573–624 passim.

27. For this and the two following paragraphs, see AD, Hérault, procès-verbal of the estates of November–January 1608–09; and *HL*, 11:902–03.

give full powers to a committee if they had not heard from their delegation by that time. On the question of the quarrel with the Chamber of Accounts, he reported that he had written to the king and Sully on their behalf. Although he assured the estates that they would receive justice from the council, he probably revealed his true assessment of the situation when he advised them to open direct negotiations with the chamber. The estates complied, but they asked Ventadour and the other commissioners to verify the expenses of the towns and dioceses. When the bishop of Carcassonne returned, he assured the estates of the king's good intentions but also advised that a friendly settlement be made with the chamber. After voting gifts for the two Montmorencies, Ventadour, and the wives of both dukes and electing a new deputation to court to plead their cause against the Chamber, the estates adjourned after having been in session for two months.

During the interval between this meeting of the three estates and the one that opened in January 1610, Sully continued his efforts to curtail their expenses and those of the towns and dioceses. In May 1609 the estates were again forbidden to send deputations to the king without his permission, except that after each session, one syndic could bring their cahier to court. As the time for the estates drew nearer, Sully became more active. Decrees in September required the commissioners to the estates of Languedoc to see that the diocesan estates limited their expenses to those set by the council in 1608 and renewed the order forbidding the provincial and diocesan estates and the towns to levy any tax or to borrow money at interest without permission. In November the council created three receivers for the extraordinary revenue in each diocese in Languedoc, a measure that aroused the opposition of the three estates because it meant that taxes levied for their own use as well as royal taxes would be turned over to royal officials rather than their own. The council also directed the treasurers of the Bureau of Finance to verify the accounts of the farmer of the gabelle in spite of the opposition of the syndics of the estates.[28]

The quarrel with the Chamber of Accounts preoccupied the three estates when they assembled in January 1610. By this time they had worked out a compromise with the chamber, only to have had it set aside by the council. The estates were heartened, however, by a letter Henry wrote Ventadour early in February 1610 saying that in spite the decree of his council, he was anxious for them to reach an accord with the chamber. The negotiations were renewed under Ventadour's auspices. At one point the duke complained that he had already devoted twenty-three days to conferences on the subject, but in the end a new agreement was reached. Once more the support of Montmorency and Ventadour had enabled the estates to win a

---

28. Valois, 2: nos. 13,638, 14,335, 14,337, 14,636, 14,637; Gachon, *Les Etats de Languedoc*, pp. 137–39; Delcambre, *Les Etats du Velay*, pp. 281–86.

victory over Sully, but they were less successful in halting the exploitive efforts of the king. In December 1608, Henry had assigned to his wife the income in most of Languedoc from the *franc fiefs*, that is, the fee nonnobles paid their feudal overlords when they obtained possession of a fief. But now, persuaded by the estates, he abandoned this right in return for 120,000 livres. Another royal privilege was to create new offices, and it cost the estates 45,000 livres to free themselves from the lieutenants of the provosts and the diocesan clerks Henry had authorized in 1607.[29] It is interesting to note that Montmorency had advised him to create these offices. On one hand, he was a defender of the privileges of Languedoc because his own position of governor was enhanced by any independence the inhabitants obtained and retained. On the other hand, he appears to have joined his sovereign in fleecing them in this matter, presumably to their mutual profit.[30]

This was the last meeting of the estates during Henry's reign. Those present must have been reasonably well satisfied because in addition to the princely sums they voted members of the Montmorency and Ventadour families, they gave the secretary of state in charge of their province 1,500 livres "because of the favors he ordinarily renders" and added 300 more for his assistants.[31] They had lost a little ground during the previous years, but once the quarrel with the Chamber of Accounts was settled partially to their satisfaction, their grievances consisted primarily of the substitution of royal receivers for their own tax collectors and the limitation placed on their daily stipends for attending the estates, both matters which were set aright during the months that followed.[32]

Sully had made a determined effort to break the power of the provincial and diocesan estates of Languedoc, but on critical issues he and the Council of Finances had often been overruled by the king. The cause of Henry's leniency is not difficult to find, for when he had acted, it had been at Montmorency's behest. The relations between the two men have never been fully explored. Henry undoubtedly owed his throne to the constable more than to any other man, but he was ever more generous in buying the submission of his enemies than in rewarding his friends. More important was the bond of friendship and mutual respect that existed between the two men. Both had been born into great noble families and had demonstrated their abilities as soldiers, diplomats, statesmen, and leaders of factions. Both had engaging personal characteristics that won the loyalty of those who served them, and both shared the faults of their class. Henry is reported to have

29. AD, Hérault, procès-verbal of the estates of January–March 1610; *HL*, 11:904–06.

30. Henri IV, *Lettres*, 7:366.

31. AD, Hérault, procès-verbal of January–March 1610, fol. 76v.

32. AD, Hérault, A 46, fol. 184–84v; Gachon, *Les Etats de Languedoc*, pp. 138–39; Delcambre, *Les Etats du Velay*, pp. 282–83.

said that if ever the Bourbons died out, no family in Europe was more worthy of the crown of France than the Montmorency.[33]

Henry probably trusted Montmorency more than he did any other great noble capable of causing serious trouble. When Joyeuse withdrew to a monastery, he had made Ventadour, Montmorency's son-in-law, lieutenant general in all of Languedoc instead of keeping the province divided by appointing a member of the rival house to the vacant post. He had designated Montmorency's son to succeed his father as governor, although by doing so he turned Languedoc into a virtual hereditary possession of that house. Nevertheless Henry knew that there were limits to any man's loyalty. To interfere in Languedoc too much against Montmorency's wishes could lead to a serious revolt, for the constable had the wealth, ability, and prestige to bring together a more formidable coalition of nobles than anyone else in France, and he could count on the support of the bulk of the clergy and burghers in his government. Cardinal Richelieu, who had one or more frank conversations with Sully, reported that Henry was well aware of the financial abuses of the estates and the powerful position of the governor but that he had not dared to establish the élus there as he would have liked to have done.[34]

In addition to Henry's relations with Montmorency, events in France and in Europe probably influenced his treatment of Languedoc. Unrest in Guyenne in 1604 occasioned largely by the edict on the élus, coupled with continued intrigues at home and with Spain, may have caused the assault against Languedoc in that year to be terminated, while the approaching war with Spain in 1610 probably contributed to Henry's reversal of Sully's policy at that time. Also, a possible factor was Condé's flight to Flanders with his wife to remove her from Henry's attentions. The teenage princess was Montmorency's daughter, and the amorous, aging king needed her father's assistance in persuading her to return.

Although the three estates of Languedoc owed their good fortune primarily to the influence of their governor and to events that took place elsewhere in France and in Europe, they themselves were not without credit. There was little friction between the three orders, and they joined together in defending their provincial privileges. Complaints against the nobility and clergy centered on their failure to attend the sessions. Those who did so functioned effectively with the deputies of the towns and dioceses. Bishops who undertook missions to court refused payment for their services more often than not, a rare virtue at this time. It was to the unity of prelate, noble, and townsmen, the well-organized procedures of the provincial assembly, and the clearly subordinate position of the diocesan estates that the people of Languedoc owed their strong position against outside interference.

33. *Lettres intimes de Henri IV*, ed. L. Dussieux (Paris 1876), p. 224 n.2.
34. Richelieu, *Mém.* SHF, 9:302–03.

2. THE ESTATES OF PROVENCE

Peace was not restored to Provence until 1595, and it was only near the close of that year that the estates again met united as before the war. On the surface the conflict between the crown and the estates was terminated. Raoul Busquet, the archivist and historian of Provence's institutions, is content to limit himself to a short paragraph on the remainder of the reign. "Beginning in 1599," he tells us, "the Estates are devoted and submissive auxiliaries of the royal government."[35] Certainly there were fewer conflicts between the crown and the estates than in most other provinces, but whether the estates should be described as submissive or the crown as cautious is another matter. Henry's fiscal demands were relatively moderate, as Busquet himself notes. The crown's receipts from Provence stood at 175,803 livres in 1600, but instead of rising in 1601 to meet the costs of the war with Savoy, they were actually reduced, perhaps to ensure the loyalty of a frontier province that had welcomed the Savoyard army a few years before. Levies on Provence were increased thereafter, but only three times during the last decade of Henry's reign did the Provençal contribution to the treasury exceed that of Brittany, and at no point did it approach that of the two généralités into which Languedoc was divided.[36]

Most of the estates' initial efforts were directed toward reducing military expenses. In December 1595 they permitted the duke of Guise, their governor, to determine the size of his army provided it did not exceed 2,000 horse and 4,000 infantry, but thereafter they were less cooperative. In October 1597 they refused to provide the 2,000 men the duke said the king wanted for a siege. In 1600 they opposed an increase in the taillon, in 1602 a new salt tax and a levy of 600 troops, and in 1604 a tax to repair some fortifications. In 1601 Henry wrote Sully complaining that 6,000 livres that the Provençals had appropriated to support the military had been diverted to other purposes against his will. He admitted that it would be difficult to get this sum out of them but was disposed to try anyway. When it came to asserting his rights as feudal overlord, he was more successful. The towns made a contribution to defray his marriage expenses and in 1608 offered to pay him a large sum in return for the redemption of the right of franc-fief. Henry made less effort to raise money in Provence by selling offices than he did elsewhere, but when he did move in this direction, as in March 1606 when he created two hussiers in each royal seat, he insisted that his decree be implemented in spite of the opposition of the estates.[37]

35. *Les Bouches-du-Rhône: Encyclopédie départementale*, ed. Paul Masson (Marseilles, 1920), 3:473.
36. Mallet, pp. 188–89.
37. *IAD, Bouches-du-Rhône, sér. C*, ed. Louis Blancard (Marseilles, 1884–92), 1:13–17 passim; 2:470–71; Valois, 2: nos. 6118, 11,857, 12,822; Henri IV, *Lettres*, 5:412. The difficulty in extracting money from the Provençals is revealed by a letter from a thoroughly discouraged *(Continued on next page)*

Provence was also less plagued by investigators from Paris than most other regions, but they were not altogether absent. A commission to reform the salt tax and the tolls in Provence, Languedoc, and Dauphiné did operate in the late 1590s, to the discomforture of the estates. The sieur de Châteauvieux, an appointee of Sully acting in his capacity of grand voyer, incurred their wrath in 1605 and 1609, but his actions were not a threat to the privileges of the province. More dangerous were the efforts of the Court of Accounts and some specially created auditors to look into the accounts of the communes and the estates, in spite of vigorous protests. It has been suggested that Guillaume Du Vair, a councillor of state who was sent to Provence in 1596 and named first president of the Parlement of Aix three years later, served as an intendant. If this is so, he was one of those royal officials so prevalent at this time who managed to win the trust of the independent-minded provincials and at the same time retain the confidence of the crown. If Henry gave him generous rewards, it is equally worthy of note that upon learning that he was being appointed bishop of Marseilles, the estates of 1603 asked that he be retained in his judicial post. That Du Vair could satisfy both parties is suggestive that his mission was more to observe and report than to upset the status quo.[38]

The estates themselves were left to operate as they pleased. The crown made no attempt to limit the length of their sessions, the number of deputies who attended, the amount of their salary, or the size and pay of the deputations to court. The letters convoking the estates in February 1598 did assign the duty of electing the procureurs du pays to the commissioners holding the estates. There was an immediate protest, and a deputation was sent to the duke of Guise to discover his intentions. Guise attributed the directive to an inexperienced person in the chancellery and assured the deputies that there had been no intention to infringe on the liberties of the estates. The procureurs continued to be chosen as before.[39]

Left largely to their own devices, the estates initially devoted most of their attention to the restoration of order and the payment of their debts. In October 1597 the assembly of the communities asked that only native gentlemen be named governors of fortified places. They also petitioned that all citadels and new fortifications be occupied or demolished. The three estates that met in February–March 1598 came out firmly for raising such structures because the costs of garrisoning them imposed a burden on the

---

royal official whom Henry IV had assigned this task in the assembly of October 1597. BN ms. fr. 23,195, fol. 333.

38. Valois, 1: nos. 3066, 3899, 4030; D. Buisseret, "A Stage in the Development of the French *Intendants*: The Reign of Henry IV," *The Historical Journal* 9 (1966): 35, 37; *Les Bouches-du-Rhône*, 3: 303; *IAD, Bouches-du-Rhône, sér. C*, 1 : 14, 16–18 passim; 2 : 470; AD, Bouches-du-Rhône, C 10, fols. 74v–75, 90–91v.

39. AD, Bouches-du-Rhône, C 8, fol. 79v.

people. To leave them empty was to invite unruly elements to occupy and use them as bases from which to prey upon the inhabitants with relative impunity. The estates faced a dilemma, however, for they lacked the money to pay for the necessary labor. No member of the second estate is recorded as opposing these measures. The one registered complaint was from a noble who claimed that when some royal engineers destroyed a fort, they also tore down some nearby buildings, which belonged to him. In 1600 the estates expressed a desire to establish an arsenal in Aix, and an order was issued to transport the artillery scattered around the province there. This move both kept cannon from falling into the hands of dissident groups and assured that there would be adequate weapons in a central location that could be used in case Savoy invaded during the war that was then taking place.[40]

Debts plagued the Provençals as they did the other inhabitants of France. In addition to the ordinary obligations incurred by the war, they had to give Epernon, their former governor, 150,000 livres to depart after Henry had relieved him of his post. Lesdiguières, the Protestant commander in neighboring Dauphiné, also had to be compensated for the efforts he had made to restore order in Provence. The royal council mitigated the situation by issuing decrees to protect the officials of the estates and of the towns from prosecution for nonpayment in order to give them time to verify their obligations and to raise the necessary funds without imposing unbearable hardships on the people. Heavy taxes ordered by the estates of December 1607 finally provided sufficient funds to satisfy Lesdiguières and some of their remaining creditors. To reduce the burden upon the people by broadening the tax base, the three estates instigated civil suits to make towns with special privileges, such as Arles and Toulon, and the members of the sovereign courts contribute. They also successfully resisted efforts by the nobility to escape paying taxes on the nonnoble land they held.[41]

In spite of these problems, the three estates found the time and money to attend to the educational, cultural, and economic welfare of the province. As early as 1569 they were allocating funds to support a college in Aix. In October 1603 the institution received a formal charter from Henry IV that authorized the teaching of theology, jurisprudence, medicine, and belles lettres. An increment in the salt tax was ordered to provide support for the faculty. In 1602 the estates voted 600 livres to pay for the publication of a map and a book on the antiquities of Provence, and the following year they promised 3,000 livres to César Nostradamus to assist in the preparation and

40. Ibid., fols. 64v, 68v, 83–83v, 151–53, 159–59v, 188v–89v; *IAD, Bouches-du-Rhône, sér. C,* 1:14–15.

41. *IAD, Bouches-du-Rhône, sér. C,* 1:14–17, 159–60 passim; 2:502–03; *IAD, Bouches-du-Rhône, sér. B.* ed. Raoul Busquet (Marseilles, 1919), 3:147–49, 153–54, 159, 162 passim; Valois, 2:8890, 9249; Henri IV, *Lettres,* 6:404–05; *Lettres inédites du roi Henri IV au chancelier de Bellièvre, 1603,* ed. Eugène Halphen (Paris, 1883), p. 50. For data concerning the almost unbelievable size of Provence's debt to certain individuals, see *IAD, Bouches-du-Rhône, sér. C,* 2:471.

publication of his monumental *Histoire de Provence*. Only half the sum had been paid when the estates met in 1606, and steps were taken to correct this situation. When the work was completed, the estates of 1609 charged the bishop of Riez with the task of reading and evaluating the manuscript before it was sent to press. These estates also contributed 700 livres to the discoverer of a remedy for rabies. To promote economic recovery and to encourage trade, the estates sought a uniform system of weights and measures and invited Arles and Marseilles to conform. Bridge and road repairs also came to their attention.[42]

Provence was able to escape so largely from the none too delicate attentions of Henry IV and Sully in part because of influence at court. The estates did not fail to give substantial sums to the young duke of Guise. His routine annual appropriation was 15,000 livres for his salary and 60,000 livres for his guards, but occasionally there were other gifts; in 1,600, for example, the nobility decided to contribute 3,000 livres toward the construction of a governor's mansion in Aix. By 1609 the relations between the estates and Guise were more strained. Only a personal appeal by the duke in which he pointed out that he had assisted the province on every possible occasion prevented a substantial cut from being imposed on the appropriation for his troops. The duke's two secretaries customarily received 600 and 300 livres, respectively, for their services. Nor was Forget de Fresne, the king's secretary of state who was charged with the affairs of Provence, neglected. By 1606 the assesseur of Aix had only to point out that it was customary to vote him 1,200 livres and his assistant 300 for the estates to approve the appropriation unanimously. The one unusual aspect of the grant to Forget de Fresne was that it was to purchase a gift, usually a rug.[43]

Influence alone, however, is not enough to explain why Guise's Provence escaped more lightly than Montmorency's Languedoc. For a time Henry courted the young duke in view of the fact that he enjoyed an undeserved popularity with ex-Leaguers because of his murdered father. As late as 1604 Henry found it advisable to insist that the chancellor seal some letters to enable Guise to enjoy the fruits of a gift he had made him on his appointment to the governorship. But this is hardly enough to suggest that Guise had more credit in Paris than Montmorency. Rather, the gentle treatment accorded Provence must be attributed to Henry's insecure position there. The estates had invited Savoy to intervene during the civil wars, and the duke had been well received in many quarters. Hardly had order

42. *IAD, Bouches-du-Rhône, sér. C*, 1:3, 6, 14–18 passim, 160, 374. The clergy was to contribute 900, the nobles 1,200, and the third estate 900 livres to Nostradamus. AD, Bouches-du-Rhône, C 10, fols. 27v–28, 170–70v. For Peiresc's opinion of the salt tax to support the university, the new faculty appointments, and the cure for rabies, see *Lettres de Peiresc*, ed. Philippe Tamizey de Larroque (Paris, 1888–98), 6:14–25, 7:510.

43. AD, Bouches-du-Rhône, C 9, fol. 20–20v, C 10, fols. 24v–25, 31–33v, 39, 86v–87, 91v–92, 159–62, 174v–77.

been restored than war had broken out with Savoy in 1600. Once more it became advisable not to test the loyalty of the Provençals too strongly. Disturbing reports continued to flow in to Paris even after the Savoyard problem had been settled. Some nobles met secretly at night during estates in January 1606, one informer wrote, and in 1609 he added the disturbing news that President Coriolis of the Parlement of Aix, a man who had done much to persuade the Provençals to invite the duke of Savoy to intervene during the Religious Wars, was openly leading the opposition in the estates.[44]

It is possible that in 1607–08 Sully was beginning to act against the estates. By this time Guise had lost most of his credit at court, the foreign situation was relatively calm, and the duke of Savoy had learned better than to tackle France alone.[45] The evidence that such a move was considered, however, is limited to Sully's comments to Selves. It is true that there were no meetings of the three estates between January 1606 and December 1607 and again between December 1607 and September 1609. These widely spaced assemblies contrast sharply with the practice during the first decade after the Wars of Religion when the three estates met every year, and there were occasional assemblies of the nobility or of the communities between these annual sessions. The explanation for the wide gaps between meetings seems to lie in the absence of the duke of Guise rather than in a reluctance of Henry and Sully to convoke the estates. Royal letters convoking the estates were issued in April 1607, but the estates could not be held until Guise returned from court early in November. In March 1609 the king again authorized the estates, but the meeting did not take place until September when Guise could be present.[46]

These gaps immediately raise the question of whether royal taxes were collected for 1607 prior to the December meeting of the estates and in 1609 prior to the September assembly. The answer appears to be that the ordinary basic taxes that the estates had come to vote automatically were collected by the tax officials of the estates and communities, presumably upon the authorization of the procureurs of the estates, but that there were no increments in royal taxation or levies for other purposes. Thus in December 1607 the estates had to appropriate double the usual amount in order to give Guise's company of ordonnance its back pay and to provide for it the coming year. Double the usual gift was also appropriated for Guise's secretaries and for Forget de Fresne. Extraordinary levies also had to wait until the estates met in September 1609 to provide the necessary authorization. Thus delays in holding the estates caused by Guise's dallying at court did not prevent the basic royal taxes from being collected each quarter, but

44. Henri IV, *Lettres*, 6:240; AAE, ms. 1700, fols. 80–80v, 140–41, 153–55.

45. For Henry's low opinion of Guise in 1608, see Henri IV, *Lettres*, 7:567. Guise was even so tactless as to have an affair with Henriette d'Entragues, Henry's mistress.

46. AD, Bouches-du-Rhône, C 10, fols. 65v–66v, 69, 146.

they did remove any immediate hope that the crown may have had of obtaining additional sums. Henry asked for an extra 36,000 livres for 1607 but had to wait until December for the estates to consider the matter, which they then refused.[47]

There is no reason to doubt that Sully ultimately intended to establish élus in Provence, but he evidently preferred to attack the liberties of one province at a time. Guyenne had fallen before he began to undermine the estates of Languedoc, and Languedoc was no doubt to fall before Provence had its turn. However, by 1609 the approaching war with Spain made it inadvisable to tamper with the privileges of a frontier province of such questionable loyalty, and the death of Henry IV the following year removed any chance that a concerted effort would be made to undermine the estates.

The three estates of Provence also deserve some credit for their success. There had been indications during the later stages of the Wars of Religion that their meetings might be superseded by those of the communities which could gather on shorter notice, but after 1600, when a state of relative calm had been restored, the three estates reassumed their traditional role, and the assembly of the communities was rarely convoked during the remainder of the reign. In spite of bickering about what contributions the clergy and nobility should make, there was sincere cooperation between the orders. The three estates deliberated together, and many of their decisions were recorded as being unanimous. The procureurs du pays nés provided permanent executives for the estates and there were a number of salaried officials to do their bidding. Perhaps their greatest weakness came from their failure to integrate fully the important towns of Arles and Marseilles into the province.

3. THE ESTATES OF DAUPHINÉ

The decision of Alphonse d'Ornano, the Catholic lieutenant general in Dauphiné, to support Henry IV rather than the Catholic League and his willingness to cooperate with François de Bonne, seigneur of Lesdiguières, the Protestant leader, led to the reassertion of royal authority in the province at an earlier date than in most of France. Grenoble was taken in December 1590, and that same month the estates recognized Henry IV as king. Other League strongholds remained to be taken, and several campaigns were necessary to terminate the duke of Savoy's intrigues in the province, but by 1595 a reasonable degree of order had been restored. With order came the impetus to return to normal conditions. The taille for 1596 was substantially reduced, and it continued to drop until it reached the level of a generation or so before in terms of buying power. With order it became possible to abandon the practice of seeking the consent of the commis, the officers of the

47. Ibid., fols. 70, 85v–86v, 90v–92.

estates, or ad hoc groups that could be assembled quickly, just as it had become possible to terminate the assemblies of the communities in Provence. Thereafter the question was whether the three estates would always be requested to give their consent to taxes or whether levies would often be imposed arbitrarily by the king or his lieutenant general.[48]

Each of the estates was strongly opposed to taxes, but whether they were more interested in giving consent or making another estate pay a larger share is another matter. In a meeting that had been held in Grenoble in March 1589, the estates had resolved that "all extraordinary contributions, subsidies, and impositions, for whatever cause, are cancelled and revoked without communities being held in any way responsible for paying them."[49] Such verbiage, however, had little effect during a period of warfare, and the taille the government sought soared to 2.85 million livres in 1592. A large portion of these taxes were never collected, and ultimately Henry cancelled the arrears, but enough pressure was placed on the people for them to resume the procès des tailles when the three orders assembled in the spring of 1591 and in January 1592. Ornano, the royalist lieutenant general, may have been disconcerted by the action of the third estate because he summoned the *consuls* of the towns to meet at Saint-Marcellin in May 1592. Grenoble specifically instructed its deputies not to retract any of the decisions that had been made, and in September it requested that Ornano hold another assembly of the towns, this time to elect deputies to go to the king to complain about the heavy charges that fell on the third estate. Ornano consented, and there were meetings of the ten towns in October and again in November. The nobility also met alone in October 1592 and offered to pay the taille on the nonnoble land they acquired in the future, but in further meetings that were held in 1593, the third estate did not express satisfaction with this proposal and the nobility rescinded its offer.[50]

In March 1594 the third estate protested against taxes being levied without consent and in a later meeting refused to approve a heavy royal demand. Henry cut the tax in half and then ordered that it be levied anyway. That August when the estates met in Grenoble, the third sought and obtained permission to deliberate apart, but it joined with the other orders in electing a deputation to the king to protest the continued heavy tax

48. L. S. Van Doren, "Civil War Taxation and the Foundations of Fiscal Absolutism: The Royal *Taille* in Dauphiné, 1560–1610," *Proceedings of the Western Society for French History* 3 (1975): 35–53. The taille was momentarily increased in 1600 to meet the expenses incurred by the war with Savoy.

49. Llewain Scott Van Doren, *War, Taxes, and Social Protest: The Challenge to Authority in Sixteenth Century Dauphiné* (Ph.D. diss., Harvard University, 1970), p. 160.

50. Ibid., pp. 160–67; Alexandre Fauché-Prunelle, *Essai sur les anciennes institutions autonomes ou populaires des Alpes Cottiennes-Briançonnaises* (Grenoble, 1857), 2:468–69; *IAC, Grenoble,* ed. Auguste Prudhomme (Grenoble, 1886), 1: BB 44–45; Pierre Cavard, *La Réforme et les Guerres de Religion à Vienne* (Vienne, 1950), p. 348; *Recueil des édits et declarations du roy, lettres patentes et ordonnances . . . ,* ed. Alexandre Giroud (Grenoble, 1720), 1:168.

burden. Several nobles offered to assist the third estate in winning the
support of Ornano and Lesdiguières for lowering taxes and halting illegal
exactions, but their efforts did not prevent the quarrel between the estates
from deepening the following year.[51]

When the estates met in Grenoble in January–February 1595, the quarrel
among the orders was renewed. The town of Grenoble instructed its deputy
not to consent to any tax unless the nobility and the clergy voted an
equivalent amount. Another meeting, this time of the third estate alone, was
held in August, but the efforts of Ornano and Lesdiguières to obtain
additional funds met with a blunt refusal. The commis and the deputies of
the leading towns and many villages then went to Lyons to plead their cause
before Henry IV, who was then in that city. The spokesman of the third
estate gave a pitiful description of the suffering of the people because of
heavy taxation and the cruel treatment they received from the nobility. The
orator for the nobility responded by linking the third estate's demand that
the privileged orders pay more taxes with the uprisings of 1579–80. Henry
granted the third estate a delay in paying its taxes and the principal on its
debts and ordered that no further levies be made without his permission. He
did nothing, however, to make the nobles contribute more, and a few weeks
later he proceeded to impose a heavy tax without consent.[52]

Constable Montmorency took advantage of the Lyons meeting to try to
get the nobility to seek a solution to the quarrel over the taille. As a result of
his efforts, the nobles suggested that the dispute be arbitrated when the three
estates met in Saint-Marcellin in January 1596. Suspicious, the third estate
asked them to make an offer, but none was forthcoming. The third once
more sent deputies to court, who charged that the decrees enacted on their
behalf at Lyons were not being enforced and that Lesdiguières was levying
taxes without Henry's permission or the consent of the estates. Evidently the
deputation was less successful than desired, because by summer there was
talk of holding an assembly of the ten principal towns to elect syndics to
prosecute the case against the privileged orders and to levy from 30,000 to
36,000 livres to pay their expenses.[53]

The third estate sought the advice of some leading lawyers and began a
systematic campaign to gather data at the local level concerning false nobles,
officials illegally claiming exemptions, families that had been ennobled since
1518, and land that any of these groups had acquired since that date. The

---

51 Cavard, *La Réforme*, p. 362; AD, Isère, Fonds Chaper, J 524[1]; *IAD, Drôme*, 3:213, 6:332;
IAC, Grenoble, BB 47; Van Doren, *War, Taxes*, p. 167 n.39.

52. *IAC, Grenoble*, BB 49; AD, Drôme, C 1024; Cavard, *La Réforme*, pp. 385–86, 392; Valois,
1: nos. 2523, 2698; Van Doren, *War, Taxes*, p. 169; *Mémoires de Eustache Piémond*, ed. J. Brun-
Durand (Geneva, 1885), pp. 470–74.

53. Cavard, *La Réforme*, pp. 393–94; *IAC, Grenoble*, BB 51; Henri IV, *Lettres*, 4:488–89; *Actes
et correspondance du connétable de Lesdiguières*, ed. L.-A. Douglas and J. Roman (Grenoble, 1878),
1:270–74.

results were startling. If these data can be trusted, from half to two-thirds of the tallageable land had come into the hands of those who claimed exemptions, thereby placing an impossible burden on the unprivileged in view of the high taxes that the war had necessitated and the heavy debts that the estates, towns, and villages had incurred. To provide legal arguments to support this statistical evidence that a broader tax base was necessary, a series of pamphlets were written, generally taking the familiar position that the don gratuit was freely granted by all three estates and therefore should be paid by everyone. There was no reason for the third estate to pay all the taxes. Nobles were not always serving in the army and the feudal levy was of little military value. During these years assemblies of the towns were frequent, and the third estate often deliberated separately when all three estates were assembled. Some towns such as Grenoble had been represented in these meetings by nobles, but to ensure the purity of their order, this practice was stopped. Few meetings ended without new deputations being sent to court. There, as in spring 1597, the deputies argued that the first two estates had always paid taxes until 1554, but since that time they and the royal officials had shifted the burden to the people. Gone was any sign of being content if the privileged paid the taille on recently acquired nonnoble land, a compromise that would have been acceptable in 1579 before the tax burden had become so intolerable.[54]

The nobles and royal officials were also active. The former were careful to congratulate Bellièvre on his elevation to the chancellorship and sent him a steady stream of flattering letters stressing his reputation for justice. At times the sovereign courts went out of their way to injure the third estate. They even refused to honor some of the concessions Henry IV had made at Lyons in 1595. Delays in paying taxes and in repaying loans that he had granted were set aside, and his edict revoking ennoblements that had taken place during the preceding twenty years was largely ignored. The members of the Chamber of Accounts refused to permit a representative of the third estate to enter their court with the commis, although the estates had ruled that a member of the third would be present whenever the commis assembled.[55] To defend their cause before the council, the privileged retained Claude Expilly, a well-educated lawyer who had already served in both the

54. Cavard, *La Réforme*, pp. 394–403; A. Lacroix, "Claude Brosse et les tailles," *Bul. de la soc. d'archéologie et de statistique de la Drôme* 32 (1878): 54–68, 149–60. For pamphlets for the most part located in BN, LK², 661–65, see Claude de La Grange, *La juste plaincte et remonstrance faicte au Roy et à nosseigneurs de son Conseil d'Estat par le pauvre peuple de Daulphiné* ... (Lyon, 1597), and *Responses et salvations des pièces produictes par les gentz du tiers estat du Daulphiné* (Paris, 1599); Jean Vincent, *Les prières du tiers estat de Daulphine* ... (Lyons, 1598), and *Réplique pour le tiers estat de Daulphiné, aux défences des deux premiers ordres* ... (Paris, 1600); and Antoine Rambaud, *Plaidoyez pour le tiers-estat du Daulphiné* ... (Paris, 1600). For the petition of the third estate in 1597, see AD, Isère, 1C 4, n.18.

55. For letters of nobles to Bellièvre, see BN ms. fr. 15,898, fols. 401, 427–28, 431, ms. fr. 15,899, fols. 539, 543, 549, 551, 553; Cavard, *La Réforme*, pp. 401–02; *IAD, Grenoble*, BB 57.

Parlement and the Chamber of Accounts and who soon became one of the leading literary figures in the province. In an eloquent defense of his clients, Expilly again associated the activities of the third estate with the seditious movement of 1579–80 and decried the egalitarian aspects of their proposals. He answered their arguments one by one and justified the exemptions accorded the privileged. The poor people, he charged, were oppressed not by the nobility but by their creditors, who were merchants, and other wealthy members of the third estate. Nobles, both of the long and short robe, had rendered conspicuous services to the crown during the late wars and had suffered heavy financial losses.[56]

Henry and his council were anxious to have the contestants resolve their own difficulties. Montmorency had tried to arrange a compromise in 1595. Representatives of the nobility and third estate were specifically summoned to the council in October 1596, but when agreement could not be reached, the council refrained from imposing a solution. Lesdiguières, who had replaced Ornano as lieutenant general on February 3, 1597, and several other officials once more attempted to find a mutually satisfactory solution in 1599 by recommending that the clergy contribute several décimes and the nobility several arrière bans. The members of the third estate flatly rejected this proposal and refused to accept any compromise. They voted the traditional don gratuit but refused to grant 180,000 livres for the military unless the other orders gave their share. Lesdiguières, who shared the prejudices of his class, discouragingly reported to Bellièvre that the concessions the privileged had offered to make did not move "these people," and that once more they were deputing to Paris. Here Henry made a few minor concessions but imposed 150,000 livres on the province without obtaining consent.[57]

Neither this deputation nor those that immediately followed could persuade the council to decide on the fundamental issues at stake. Decrees continued to be issued protecting the officials of the estate from their creditors, verifying the debts of the province, and assigning part of the gabelle to repay those that were legitimate and part to redeem the royal domain by 1613. Taxes, however, had to be collected even though one of the three estates—the one that was actually to pay them—refused to give its adherence. In February 1600 letters were prepared ordering that 27,514 livres be levied to support the garrison. The syndic and the receiver of the estates immediately protested, and the king had to repeat his directive on August 1. The syndic of the estates sought a further delay until the estates

56. Claude Expilly, *Plaidoyez* (Paris, 1621), pp. 362–406.
57. Valois, 1: no. 2948; *IAC, Valence*, ed. A. Lacroix, (Valence, 1914), BB 13; *Actes de Lesdiguières*, 1:344; Cavard, *La Réforme*, pp. 404–05; Van Doren, *War, Taxes*, pp. 172–73; *Mém. de Piémond*, pp. 468–70.

could meet, and it was not until May 1601 that the letter was actually registered by the Chamber of Accounts.[58]

During the summer of 1600 Henry was in Lyons where he received deputies from the estates and Bellièvre spent some time in Grenoble itself. Both king and chancellor must have been informed of the situation through these direct contacts, as well as through letters and new deputations. In a meeting at Grenoble in the winter of 1601, the third estate decided neither to vote nor to levy any more taxes until the question of who was to pay the taille was settled. This forced Henry and his advisers to conclude that the three estates would never reach a compromise and that it was necessary for them to impose a solution, although such a step was certain to alienate a large portion of the population. Convinced of the power of the third estate to force a decision, the deputy from Gap to the estates of 1601 reported to his constituents in April that the council would soon announce its position. The indecision or procrastination, however, continued, and on March 2, 1602, Henry had to order Bellièvre to have the council give the dispute its undivided attention for fifteen days, a directive which led to the decree's being issued on April 15, 1602.[59]

When the council was finally forced to act, it sided with the nobles and royal officials. They were members of these classes as were their friends in Dauphiné. Lesdiguières pleaded for the cause of the nobility as did the members of the sovereign courts in Grenoble. To have done other than it did, the council would have had to reverse the agreement of 1554 and the settlement made by Catherine de Medici in 1579. In an age in which officials rarely consciously altered the status quo in matters of privilege and social status, only exceptional circumstances would have led them to do so in this case. Yet Henry and his councillors had tried to effect a compromise and had avoided making a decision as long as they could. Before his death, Cheverny had apparently favored turning the case over to the Parlement of Paris since the Parlement of Grenoble was obviously biased, but Henry had directed that the council retain jurisdiction over the case. No doubt he recognized that political and social considerations rather than judicial ones should be used to resolve the dispute. If a compromise could not be reached, it was a question of whether the nobility and bureaucracy or the towns and villages could be more safely alienated. With such a choice the council

58. Valois, 2: nos. 6098, 6397, 6544; AD, Isère, B 3263, nos. 1–4; *IAD, Isère, sér. B*, ed. A. Prudhomme (Grenoble, 1919), 4:336–39. In July 1602 Lesdiguières complained that some of his troops had not been paid for two years. *Actes de Lesdiguières*, 1:424.

59. *IAC, Gap*, ed. Paul Guillaume (Gap, 1908), 1:66, 67, 70; *Lettres inédites du roi Henry IV au chancelier de Bellièvre, 1581–1601*, ed. Eugène Halphen, p. 268; *IAC, Valence*, BB 13; *Actes de Lesdiguières*, 1:355, 378, 392–93, 396–97; *Lettres inédites du roi Henry IV à Monsieur de Bellièvre, 1602*, ed. E. Halphen (Paris, 1881), pp. 3–4; *IAD, Drôme*, ed. A. Lacroix (Valence, 1898), 6:333–34.

naturally favored the former, but its members did so reluctantly. In August 1597 Sillery had written Bellièvre a letter in which he said that the third estate was "truly worthy of compassion," but he had also pointed out that a decision favorable to them would have dire consequences.[60]

By the terms of the decree, nobles and important royal officials were to continue to be exempted from paying the taille on the nonnoble land they owned. Their leaseholders and sharecroppers were to pay, and they themselves were to contribute to a few local expenses, such as the repair of roads and bridges, but that was all. The council did revoke ennoblements during the past twenty years and order that a search for false nobles be made, but the crown's right to create new nobles was affirmed. What is surprising is that the third estate had persisted so long and had refused several possible compromises when its leaders should have been aware of the odds that were against them. Still more surprising was its decision to continue to resist for another generation until victory finally came.[61]

The reactions to the decree varied. Lesdiguières immediately flooded Bellièvre with letters asking that certain of his henchmen be declared nobles in order to remove any doubt concerning their status.[62] The third estate, disappointed at the decision of the council, could gain little by appealing to the sovereign courts to prevent the implementation of the decree because their members were among the privileged who benefited from its provisions. Nevertheless the leaders of the third estate did not desist in their efforts to improve the lot of the people. In their cahiers they continued to complain about the injustices perpetrated by the decree of 1602. However, because it was useless to devote much effort to trying to get the council to reverse its decision so soon after it had been made, they attacked the vague aspects of the ruling, such as the definition of which officials were exempt from the taille. They sought to have the taille divided more equitably within their order, to expose false nobles, and to prevent new ennoblements. They also tried, without success, to institute a tax on the sale of wine that would fall on the privileged and exclude them from participating in the fiscal administration. Differences among the towns continued to exist, and the relations between the towns and the villages were often tense. One factor that contributed to the latter development was the emergence of Claude Brosse as the syndic of the villages.[63]

Brosse was the chatelain of an important noble family and styled himself as the seigneur of Serizin when he served as a deputy in the Estates General

---

60. BN ms. fr. 15,911, fol. 84.

61. The decree of April 15, 1602, has been published in Giroud, *Recueil des édits*, 1:167–72.

62. *Actes des Lesdiguières*, 1:415–16, 423–24, 426–28, 443–44.

63. Lacroix, "Claude Brosse, 32:233–38; *IAC, Grenoble*, BB 63, BB 65, BB 67, BB 76; *IAC, Gap*, 1:75, 82, 85, 86, 88, 89; Valois, 2: nos. 10,880, 13,493, 13,814. *Lettres inédites du roi Henri IV au chancelier de Bellièvre (1604)*, ed. E. Halphen (Paris, 1883), pp. 46–47; BN ms. fr. 15,899, fols. 557, 559; *Actes de Lesdiguières*, 1:483.

of 1614, but he was probably born into the third estate and early in his career espoused the peasants' cause. Around 1599 he was elected syndic of the villages and in that capacity participated in the efforts of the third estate to make the nobles contribute that had led to the decree of 1602. A man of exceptional energy, courage, and devotion to his adopted cause, he was to persist in his attempt to have the taille declared réelle in Dauphiné until he finally achieved success in the 1630s. As a result of his efforts, he incurred the enmity of the nobility of the robe and of the sword. To protect him from the Parlement of Grenoble, the king's council had to assume jurisdiction over cases concerning him, and in 1608 it authorized him to carry a pistol to defend himself.[64]

When the interests of the towns and the third estate coincided, Brosse worked with the influential burghers, but when they failed to do so, he did not hesitate to attack them just as he did the nobles. One of the most serious problems that confronted the villages was that they were deeply in debt. Many of Brosse's appearances before the council were directed toward verifying these debts and securing delays in their repayment. He even persuaded the three estates that met in Valence in 1604 that the towns should contribute toward the liquidation of village indebtedness. His success in this move must be attributed to support received from the privileged orders because after the meeting some towns repudiated the agreement. Victory eventually came in another form, however, in December 1609 when the council issued a decree reducing the debts of the villages. Another of Brosse's objectives was to obtain a greater voice for the villages in the deliberations of the province. In 1606 he complained to the king that in the meetings of the commis, the villages had only one vote to the ten for the leading towns, although only a tenth of the units of taxation lay behind their walls. He asked that the villages and the towns each have five votes and complained about the underrepresentation of the former in the estates as well. Here the council sidestepped the request by referring the matter to an investigatory commission then in Dauphiné.[65]

Faced by a continual threat, royal officials used their control over the courts to advantage, and they and the nobility kept up their contacts with the king's council.[66] The nobility had occasionally held separate assemblies in the sixteenth century, but the quarrel with the third estate made so many

---

64. Lacroix, "Claude Brosse," 32:238–42; Valois, 2: nos. 10,422, 12,362.

65. Lacroix, "Claude Brosse," 32:243–48; *IAC, Grenoble*, BB 67, BB 69; *IAC, Romans*, BB 22; BN ms. fr. 15,898, fol. 484, ms. fr. 15,900, fol. 679; Valois, 2: nos. 9656, 9670, 10,426, 10,436, 10,477, 10,971, 11,410, 12,378, 12,380, 12,381, 12,396, 12,397, 12,439, 12,453, 14,744, 14,793; *Cayers presentez au roy par le syndic des communautez villageoises ... 5 aoust 1606*, a copy at BN, LK², 669.

66. For letters to Bellièvre, for the most part from the nobility, see BN ms. fr. 15,898, fols. 375, 381, 401, 427–28, 431, 466, 484, 489, 493, ms. fr. 15,899, fols. 12, 14, 18, 545–72, ms. fr. 15,900, fols. 496, 613–14, 679.

meetings necessary that by May 1602 they were keeping an account of their proceedings in a large register. They had a council that met frequently and, with the permission of a favorably disposed governor or Parlement, convoked provincial assemblies to which the nobles of each bailiwick and seneschalsy elected deputies. To strengthen its position, the second estate welcomed new nobles, and from 1609 members of the clergy often participated. The position of the new nobles was so precarious that they taxed themselves to pay for their defense against the third estate, and one of their number wrote a pamphlet to prove that more nobles were needed.[67]

As Dauphiné had become socially divided, the provincial estates had also split asunder. Until the later stages of the Wars of Religion, the three orders had deliberated together, voted by head, and taken extreme care to present a united front before the crown. By the turn of the century, however, nobles, towns, and villages were frequently holding separate meetings and had developed instruments to look after their interests when they were not in session. The provincial estates continued to meet at least once a year, but the three orders usually deliberated apart. The crown had not sought to divide and rule but rather had tried to heal the differences among the three estates throughout the period. Henry had always assigned a high priority to settling the disputes in Dauphiné, and in June 1604 he once more directed Bellièvre to provide the disputants with as much contentment as possible immediately.[68]

During the Wars of Religion taxes had often been levied without the consent of the estates just as in other parts of France. What was nearly unique about Dauphiné was that the government continued this practice after peace had been restored. This undoubtedly threatened the position of the three estates, but its motivation was to obtain the necessary revenue to govern the province and not, for the moment at least, to destroy the representative assembly. The quarrel between the orders had been so bitter that the third estate had often refused to approve any levy unless the other estates contributed, or at best it had voted inadequate amounts. The government was therefore virtually compelled to order that the needed sums be collected anyway and justified its action in terms of the widely accepted doctrine of urgent necessity. Its goal through 1602 and probably thereafter was not to destroy the estates but to reconcile the differences among the orders so that they could agree on what each should pay. Dauphiné was on Sully's list of provinces to receive élections, but he took no steps to implement his design. Indeed he interfered less in Dauphiné than in most other provinces.[69]

67. AD, Isère, 1J 175, fols. 1–341v; Valois, 2: no. 13,932. AD, Isère, 1C 4, nos. 22–26; Pierre de Boissat, *Remerciement au roi par les anoblis du Dauphiné* (Paris, 1603).

68. *Lettres du Henri IV au Bellièvre (1604)*, p. 32.

69. Van Doren, "Civil War Taxation." In this article Van Doren shows clearly that from 1595, numerous taxes were levied in Dauphiné without any form of consent. From a modern

Henry received very little revenue from Dauphiné. In the decade that began in January 1600, there were three years in which the Dauphinois paid only 720 livres into his treasury, and the maximum amount was a mere 37,888 livres.[70] Dauphiné's taxes were spent in Dauphiné. Thus when an order was issued in Henry's name to levy a tax without the consent of the estates, it was to meet local needs and not to line his own pockets. This raises the question of who was responsible for most of the illegal taxes. The answer appears to be Lesdiguières. From the time he had become the leader of the Protestant movement in Dauphiné, he had often taxed his co-religionists and everyone else in his control without consent. He was named lieutenant governor shortly after order was restored, and it was only from that time that it was difficult to justify taxes in terms of "urgent necessity," but the practice of ordering that levies be made without the consent of the estates became commonplace at about this time. Sometimes Lesdiguières sought the king's permission or turned to a sympathetic sovereign court before imposing a tax, but he was widely believed to have acted unilaterally on many occasions. He used this money to support his clients and his small private army and to establish an arsenal large enough to equip a major force. He also embarked on an ambitious building program in Grenoble and elsewhere. In the process he acquired a considerable fortune.[71]

Lesdiguières was not an unmitigated misfortune for Dauphiné, in spite of his financial exploitation of the people and his decision to throw his weight behind the nobility in the quarrel concerning the taille. A man of great determination and exceptional administrative ability, he obtained such a firm hold over the province that neither Henry nor Sully thought it prudent to interfere more than necessary. Catholic and Protestant were made to live together in peace. When provincial deputations were sent to Paris, Lesdiguières dispatched letters supporting their cause except in those rare instances when he himself was at court and could further their interests in person. When Henry IV was assassinated in 1610, Dauphiné was still semiautonomous although its privileges were sometimes violated, especially in fiscal matters. However, its divided body politic was no longer capable of defending itself once its powerful protector and exploiter departed from the scene.

---

point of view, this is certainly absolutist, but in the period under consideration, many believed that in cases of urgent necessity, it was legitimate to tax without consent. Henry made no attempt to create élections or otherwise alter provincial institutions, steps necessary before a truly absolutist regime could be established. Finally, insofar as there was an absolutist regime, it was imposed by Lesdiguières.

70. Mallet, pp. 186–87.

71. Charles Dufayard, *Le connétable de Lesdiguières* (Paris, 1892), pp. 267–75, 278–326. For examples of Lesdiguières activities and those of the crown, see *IAC, Grenoble*, BB 71; AD, Isère, B 3263, 1C 4 no. 21; *Actes de Lesdiguières*, 1:487–88, 492–96, 503, 539.

4. THE ESTATES OF BURGUNDY

Organized resistance ceased in Burgundy around the close of the summer of 1595, and the reunited estates met in Dijon in January of the following year. Here they devoted most of their energies to trying to obtain a reduction in taxes. First, they attacked the high costs of the garrisons in the province and asked the king to suppress those that were not necessary for the defense of the frontier. To facilitate this move they advocated tearing down the fortified châteaux that were in the interior. They protested a new subsidy on wheat, wine, and other merchandise on the grounds that it was imposed in defiance of their privileges, and they asked that the salt tax be reduced. The creation of new offices they decried, and they petitioned the king to broaden the tax base by revoking exemptions to the taille that had been granted to bailiwick officials. So strongly were the estates opposed to such innovations that they decreed that a red page would be inserted in the register containing the names of those who suggested new taxes or offices so that posterity would recognize them as being the enemies of the king, the province, and the people. Then, after asking for a three-year moratorium on the payment of debts, the estates voted the usual taille of 50,000 livres per year for three years, agreed to support their governor's horseguards, elected new officers, and named deputies to go to the king to present their case. Clearly, neither the long wars, internal dissension, nor a six-year lapse since the last royalist estates had weakened their capacity to resist. Indeed the duke of Biron, their governor, became so angered that he accused the bishop of Autun of being a better Spaniard than royal servant. Opponents of the wine tax, he declared, were serving their own interests rather than the public good and should be shut up in a cage for two or three years.[72]

The élus devoted the long intervals between the meetings of the estates to partially successful negotiations with the crown for a reduction in taxes and to trying to restore order in Burgundy. Their efforts were countered by new demands from the hard-pressed king, and in 1597 they were forced to agree to a heavy tax to support the army in Picardy although the three estates had repeatedly told them to permit no levies that had not been accorded in full assembly. The necessity to defend the realm provided theoretical justification for this act. When the élus were confronted with the problem of bribing an Italian condottierre called La Fortune to abandon his stronghold of Seurre and stop ravaging the countryside, they followed a similar path and imposed a tax which fell in part on the clergy. The clergy protested because their élu had not been present when the levy had been decreed. Necessity, whether because of the war in Picardy or ravaging troops at home, had in both instances taken precedence over legality. The question to

72. AD, Côte-d'Or, C 3016, esp. fols. 296–307v, 313, 320v, 324–27v; Hippolyte Abord, *Histoire de la Réforme et la Ligue dans la ville d'Autun* (Autun, 1881), 2:545–46.

be decided was whether a return to traditional procedures would take place after peace and order had been restored.[73]

On the whole, the situation seemed propitious when the estates again convened in Dijon in January 1599. Extraordinary taxation was no longer necessary because the war with Spain had ended and order had been newly restored in Burgundy. Henry, who had not hesitated to interfere in municipal elections in former Catholic League towns immediately after their submission, was now prepared to permit the elections to proceed more freely.[74] The same more relaxed attitude was reflected in the deliberations of the three estates. The estates had little success when they joined with Parliament in trying to prevent the implementation of the Edict of Nantes, but they could take considerable pleasure in the reduction of the costs of the garrisons from a peak of 354,000 livres in 1597 to 84,000 in 1599 and 64,000 in 1600. Biron, their governor, was voted 21,000 livres, and others were reimbursed for their services. Protests were made against the remaining taxes, and the traditional taille of 50,000 livres per year for three years was voted.[75]

Biron promised to assist the Burgundian deputies when they were at court, and through his aid they achieved at least partial success. Furthermore Dijon won a 50 percent reduction in its contribution to Henry's sister that had been imposed on the occasion of her marriage. Through Biron's intercession the town escaped altogether a much heavier levy to help the king pay his own marital expenses.[76]

The crown's willingness to meet the Burgundians more than halfway now that the exigencies of war had ended was reflected in other ways. On January 24, 1600, Henry addressed a letter both to the treasurers in the Bureau of Finances at Dijon and to the élus concerning the tax for the garrisons, but on March 21 he apologized to the latter and promised in the future to respect their privileges by issuing tax instructions through them alone.[77] More tangible evidence of the province's special status was soon forthcoming. At a time when officials in other parts of France were being subjected to a rigid audit of their accounts, President Jeannin was dispatched for this purpose to Dijon. Jeannin, a loyal Burgundian, one-time Leaguer, and valued royal adviser, promised to use his influence in the council on the province's behalf and informed the élus that he had such confidence in them that it would suffice if they sent a statement of their

73. *IAD, Côte-d'Or, sér. C,* ed. Joseph Garnier (Dijon, 1886), 3:130–32; AD, Côte-d'Or, C 3016, fols. 365v–66v; *Journal de Gabriel Breunot,* ed. J. Garnier (Dijon, 1864), 3:60–61, 78–80, 103; *Correspondance de la mairie de Dijon,* ed. J. Garnier (Dijon, 1870), 3:14–21; BN ms. fr. 18,169, fols. 26–26v; Valois, 1: nos. 3757, 4869, 5079, 5182, 2:7529, 7750.

74. *Correspondance de Dijon,* 3:7–8, 23–26; Abord, *Histoire de la Réforme,* 2:527–32.

75. AD, Côte-d'Or, C 3016, esp. fols. 363, 366v–68v, 401v–02v, C 5382. AN E 2ª, fol. 189.

76. *Correspondance de Dijon,* 3:22–23, 32–33, 52–53.

77. AD, Côte-d'Or, C 5382.

receipts, expenses, and debts to Paris. To deal with the last problem, the provincial debts, an extraordinary meeting of the estates was held in Dijon in February 1601.[78]

The special assembly performed its work with dispatch. It asked the king to permit a tax to be levied to pay the provincial debts that would fall on everyone except nobles living nobly and officers of the Parlement, the Chamber of Accounts, and the Bureau of Finances. The élus were directed to seek a reduction in the salt tax, and the king was begged to incorporate the newly conquered territories of Bresse, Bugey, and Gex into the government of Burgundy where they would assume a position comparable to that of the pays adjacents. Following the session satisfactory arrangements were made with the king's council concerning a tax to pay the debts, and Bresse, Bugey, and Gex were placed under the jurisdiction of the Parlement and Bureau of Finance at Dijon, but deputies from their estates never took seats in the Burgundian assembly although the issue was raised again in 1602.[79]

On the surface at least there was little friction between the crown and the estates in their triennial meeting, which was held in May 1602. Those who attended wanted to reduce the salt tax and the levy to support the garrison, but they voted the regular taille of 50,000 livres without protest. Biron, who was arrested for treason the following month, was evidently in high favor with the estates. In addition to his usual 16,000 livres, he was voted a special gift of 30,000 livres in recognition of his "favors and good offices." His secretaries were not forgotten nor were others who had served the estates.[80]

The friendly relations with the crown did not prevent the Burgundians from quarreling among themselves. The estates attacked the treasurers of the Bureau of Finances for imposing a tax without their consent to reimburse some officers of the Chamber of Accounts whose positions had been suppressed. They refused to permit the number of élus to be increased by admitting more members of the Chamber of Accounts and forbade the élus to deal with important matters unless those appointed by the estates were present. They protested against a decree of the Parlement of Dijon which declared that the descendants of the presidents and councillors of Parlement were noble, and they directed their syndic to seek registration of a royal edict revoking recent letters of ennoblement and exemption from the taille. To the discomfiture of Dijon, they ruled that in the future they would meet in different towns rather than remaining sedentary there.[81]

The most bitter reproaches of all were reserved for the élus. Near the beginning of the meeting, Jean de Souvert, a lawyer employed by the estates, attacked the élus' administration of the affairs of the province. He was especially bitter in his denunciations of Bénigne Fremiot, president of

78. *IAD, Côte-d'Or, sér. C,* 3:133; Valois, 2: no. 6076; *Journal de Breunot,* 3:213.
79. AD, Côte-d'Or, C 3016, esp. fols. 421v–25, 437; Valois, 2: nos. 6522, 6538.
80. AD, Côte-d'Or, C 3016, esp. fols. 437, 441v, 444–49v, 464–66v.
81. Ibid., esp. fols. 435, 437–38, 449, 457–57v, 462–62v.

the Parlement of Dijon, staunch supporter of Henry IV, and one-time mayor of Dijon, who was involved in many provincial activities including, according to Souvert, some dealings in the salt trade that cost the general public a huge sum. To prevent disclosure, Souvert charged, Fremiot was trying to obtain for his son, André, abbot of Saint-Étienne of Dijon, the post of élu of the clergy. Fremiot countered by appealing to Parlement and to the estates, where he was accompanied by the élus who sought to defend their administration. Victory in the end lay with him, for his son was elected élu in spite of Souvert's charges.[82]

Between 1602 and 1605 the relations between the crown and the estates changed. Three factors probably explain the new royal attitude: the accumulation of evidence that the élus were corrupt or inefficient, the growing influence of Sully, and the crown's belief that following Biron's conspiracy Burgundy was so firmly in royal hands that its well-entrenched privileges could be safely attacked.

Jeannin had been in Dijon when Souvert made his charges in the estates, but he was probably too good a Burgundian to return to Paris with such reports. This hypothesis is supported by the fact that Fremiot continued in Henry's good graces as evidenced by the appointment of his son, who had so recently been elected élu of the clergy, as archbishop of Bourges in 1603. There were many other potential sources of information, however, for not all Burgundians were as loyal as Jeannin, nor can one imagine that Sully would leave the financial accounts of an important province like Burgundy unaudited. At least one deputy to court wrote frantically home for financial records to satisfy the zealous minister.[83]

Circumstantial evidence indicates that just before Biron's arrest, opinion in the royal council was about evenly divided concerning the Burgundian question and, for that matter, on whether to retain the traditions of the Renaissance monarchy or to embark on a new, more absolutist course. The issue that arose which suggests the situation in council, concerned the county of Auxerre, a pays adjacent in which there was an élection. For several years the county had spearheaded an effort on the part of the pays adjacents to secure the right of their inhabitants to be elected to the Chambre des Elus of the estates. The clergy and nobility of the duchy made no difficulty in admitting their candidacy as they could count on outvoting the representatives of the outlying counties, but the third estate balked because the right to name their élu rotated from one leading town to another. To give towns in the pays adjacents turns would delay their enjoyment of the honor. Hence they saw to it that conditions were established that were so severe

---

82. *Journal de Breunot*, 3:234–37; AD, Côte-d'Or, C 3016, fols. 435, 460, 475; Jean de Souvert, *Articles présentez à Messieurs des trois Estats du pays de Bourgogne, par M. Jean de Souvert, leur conseil, pour y estre par eux délibéré en leur assemblée* (n.p., n.d.). In this printed version Souvert did not attack Fremiot.

83. *Journal de Breunot*, 3:236. *Correspondance de Dijon*, 3:84–85.

that only Auxerre retained an interest. In 1602 the estates voted to admit Auxerre provided that the élection of Auxerre was abolished and the fiscal administration was incorporated into that of the duchy. The difficulty was that the élus of the élection, as venal royal officials, would have to be reimbursed for the loss of their positions. The estates thought that Auxerre alone should shoulder this burden. Auxerre, on the other hand, insisted that everyone contribute and appealed to the king's council to resolve the dispute. In August 1602 that body ruled that Auxerre should have its turn in furnishing the élu for the third estate but said nothing about whether the élection should be abolished or who should compensate the dispossessed officials, the real reasons for the appeal in the first place. Conceivably the explanation for this strange oversight should be attributed to an administrative error, but it is more logical to assume that the divided council simply sidestepped the issue. If this is true, it suggests that Sully had already come to see the élection as the key to replacing the Burgundian estates in their tax-collection function and was loathe to abandon one that already existed. By preventing the council from acting, Sully really won because the case died in the law courts. There is no concrete evidence that this is the proper explanation, but in the preceding year élections had been created in Bresse, Bugey, and Gex, and in the following year they were created in the généralité of Guyenne. Furthermore in 1604 Sully was preparing to move against Burgundy itself.[84]

It is impossible to trace the steps that led to the formulation of Sully's Burgundian policy following the estates of May 1602. In June Biron was arrested, and there was concern at court that parts of Burgundy might rise in his defense, but the royal fears proved so unfounded that the very absence of trouble may have emboldened Sully to be more aggressive and led other councillors to take his point of view. A deputy from Dijon was in Paris at the time of the arrest. Far from trying to start a revolt, his reaction was to advise the magistrates to petition Henry for permission to demolish the château in the town. The king and Sully would treat the proposal favorably, for they had approved a similar request by Semur six or seven weeks before. The inhabitants of Autun partially demolished the château in their town without first receiving royal persmission. The governor of the château pleaded with the king to punish the burghers for their unauthorized act. The burghers deputed to court, where Henry threatened to make them repair the walls at their own expense, but in the end Jeannin, who was a native of Autun, arranged a compromise whereby the town paid a 3,000 livre compensation to the governor and 1,000 to the commander of the château.[85]

84. A. Guillois, "La fin d'un 'pays adjacent': l'union du comté d'Auxerre aux Etats de Bourgogne, 1668," *Annales de Bourgogne*, 33 (1961): 11–17.

85. *Correspondance de Dijon*, 3:61–62, 65–74; Abord, *Histoire de la Réforme*, 2:556–68, 3:369–76.

The élus were also bent on destroying châteaux, not on fomenting rebellion. They received Henry's authorization to tear them down in ten more towns and to raze all other fortifications constructed during the late wars. Thus Henry graciously gave the Burgundians permission to dismantle the province at their own expense and in the process deprived Biron's clients of the posts he had assigned them as château commanders. To the Burgundians, however, a garrisoned fort was an expense and an ungarrisoned one a threat because dissidents or robbers could seize it and overawe the local inhabitants. Except for the few nobles who had a personal interest in saving a particular château, there was no protest from the second estate.[86]

The élus stopped payment on the gifts of 46,000 livres that the estates had so recently voted Biron. What good could come from treating a disgraced man so generously? A small part of this sum was assigned to the troop commanders Henry rushed to the province, but the duke of Bellegarde, the new lieutenant general, refused to accept the 12,000 livres proffered him in return for his good services. He was less squeamish, however, when presented with silver plate by the town of Dijon.[87]

Burgundy was quiet and secure when a deputy from Dijon reported from Paris in January 1604 that nothing could be done in financial matters without Sully. To satisfy that taskmaster he requested that detailed financial records be sent to him immediately. Whether there was any relationship between the discussion that followed and a proposal to establish élections in Burgundy that Sully presented to the king at Fontainebleau that spring or summer cannot be determined. This proposal was combined with a number of others dedicated to the problem of how money could be raised rapidly. After the item concerning the Burgundian élections, Sully had noted that 250,000 livres could be realized through the sale of the offices created as a result. Conceivably he was thinking of the élections only as financial expedients, but this seems unlikely; during the preceding year, the crown had ordered that they be established in Guyenne for what to Sully was certainly an administrative purpose. Probably he was planning a move against the Burgundian estates and was emphasizing the financial blessings that would follow such a step in order to win his master's support and perhaps that of some councillors.[88]

Whatever Sully's purpose, it is certain that some Burgundians became alarmed. Shortly before the triennial meeting of the estates opened in June 1605, Jean de Souvert published a long pamphlet in which he stressed that the most important privilege of the province was the right to have assemblies of the estates, but he hinted that this privilege was threatened. Taxes too

86. *IAD, Côte d'Or, sér. C,* 3:134–35; Henri IV, *Lettres,* 8:827–60 passim.

87. *IAD, Côte-d'Or, sér. C,* 3:134; *IAC, Dijon, sér. B,* ed. Louis de Gouvenain (Paris, 1867), 1:120.

88. *Correspondance de Dijon,* 3:84–85; BN ms. fr. 18,150, fol. 99.

often escaped the direct control of the estates, he charged, and those collected were unwisely spent.[89]

It is likely that the difficulty experienced in installing élus in Guyenne caused Sully to delay his attack on Burgundy. President Fremiot, one of the principal royal spokesmen in the estates, was seemingly answering his old antagonist, Souvert, when he stressed that the king would maintain their privileges, including the right to assemble once every three years. He then proceeded to lend credence to one of Souvert's charges by asking the estates to consent to a heavy tax of an undesignated amount. The estates complained about the numerous instances in which cases were evoked from the provincial courts to Paris and protested the crown's growing practice of sending letters on impositions to the Bureau of Finances rather than to the élus of the estates. To ensure their control over the bureau, they insisted, as they had so often done in the past, that the Chamber of Accounts could send only two of its members to sit with the élus and that these two members could not be used on deputations to court or on provincial business. No important transactions were to take place without at least two élus' representing the estates being present. Having done all they could to ensure the position of the élus, the estates voted the king his usual 50,000 livres, Bellegarde 16,000, and lesser amounts to others.[90]

Sully had abandoned for the moment the idea of a full-scale assault on the estates, but he did not give up all of his aggressive designs. Soon after the estates had ended, he had a directive sent in his capacity of grand-voyer to the élus telling them to levy a tax to repair some roads. Later, presumably at his instigation, the Chamber of Accounts at Dijon sought to examine the tax records of the estates since 1596, but the élus refused to surrender the necessary documents. The worst blow fell in March 1608. The three-year grants made in the preceding assembly of the estates had expired, and the meeting for that year had not yet been held. Faced with this situation the council directed the élus to impose the tax for the garrisons anyway or the money would be taken from the province by the military financial officials.[91]

When the estates finally opened in September 1608, those who attended were more in a mood to curtail taxes than to submit to further royal interference. They asked to be relieved of all obligation to support the garrison, protested the creation of some new offices as being contrary to their privileges, and refused to establish a fund to repair roads and bridges. Others were treated more kindly than the king. The Jesuits were given 3,000 livres to pay for the construction of a classroom building in Dijon, Bellegarde was granted 16,000 livres, and others received gifts. Henry was voted the

---

89. Jean de Souvert, *Advis pour Messieurs les gens des trois Estats du païs et duché de Bourgogne, sur le subject de leur assemblée du mois de may prochain, 1605* (n.p., n.d.). For a summary see William F. Church, *Constitutional Thought in Sixteenth Century France* (Cambridge, Mass., 1941), pp. 313–14.

90. AD, Côte-d'Or, C 3017, esp. fols. 1–10, 14–14v, 17, 27v–28, 35–35v.

91. *IAD, Côte-d'Or, sér. C*, 3: 135–36; Valois, 2: nos. 12,042; 12,277.

usual 50,000 livres and with it came the obligation to hear the deputies of the estates dispatched to him with their complaints.[92]

Henry received the deputies courteously, but he became angry because of their constant references to their privileges and their efforts to escape the expense of redeeming the royal domain and demolishing several fortified châteaux. Provinces with estates, he charged, had always deceived him. They never kept their promises. As for their privileges, "The finest privilege that the people could have was to be in the good graces of their king." This last thought pleased him so much that he repeated it, and the deputies departed after being told that they were like little children who asked for sugar after reciting a verse.[93]

Sully more than echoed his master's attitude. There is little doubt that he was primarily responsible for a decree of the council in June 1609 forbidding the élus to levy taxes without permission and for an order directing them to impose 20,000 livres to repair highways in the province, although the estates had refused to appropriate money for this purpose.[94] He was probably also responsible for creating a royal receiver in Mâconnais to replace the receiver of the estates, but at the cost of 10,000 livres the estates thwarted his design.[95]

Henry's relations with Dijon also changed during the last years of his reign. After interfering in municipal elections immediately after the town's return to obedience in 1595 to ensure the choice of a loyal mayor, he had defended the town against the efforts of Parlement to intervene. Sully and the municipal officials had found a common interest in canal building and making rivers navigable, and it was through royal favor that Dijon was able to block an effort of the estates to hold their meetings in other towns as well. In 1608, however, Henry began to interfere in municipal elections once more, and in May 1609 his council decreed that henceforth the king would choose the mayor from a list of three candidates presented him by the town. This act posed a serious threat to the estates as well because the mayor had a seat in the Chambre des Elus. If he became a royal appointee, the king would control half the voting strength in that important committee.[96]

There can be no doubt that the Burgundian estates were seriously threatened during the last years of Henry's reign. Sully as superintendent of finances frequently addressed letters to the Bureau of Finances rather than to

92. AD, Côte-d'Or, C 3017, esp. fols. 56, 60, 63, 77–85v.

93. P. Beaune, "Henri IV aux députés des Estats de Bourgogne, 1608," *Le Cabinet Historique* 6 (1860): pt. 1, 122–25.

94. Valois, 2:13,929. In a separate decree the élus were forbidden even to impose taxes without permission to demolish several châteaux. See no. 13,925. *IAD, Côte-d'Or, sér. C*, 3:136.

95. Jean Roussot, *Un comté adjacent à la Bourgogne aux XVIIᵉ et XVIIIᵉ siècles: Le Mâconnais, pays d'états et d'élection* (Mâcon, 1937), pp. 89, 131–32.

96. *Correspondance de Dijon*, 3:viii–xiv, xxxiv–xxxvi, 23–26, 32–33, 36–39, 56–57, 86–92, 94–110; Valois, 2: nos. 13,226, 13,350, 13,351, 13,693.

the Chambre des Elus, and as grand voyer he directed the latter to levy taxes for road construction that had not been consented to by the estates. In spite of repeated efforts, the estates were unable to win significant reductions in taxes except immediately following the wars. Henry was obviously impatient at talk of their privileges and inclined to give Sully an increasingly free hand. Nevertheless Sully had never carried out the threat that he had made to Selves that he would create élections in Burgundy. The estates and their officers remained intact. The institutional structure was not changed. Only the arbitrary hand from Paris had to be removed for the estates, still so vigorous, to spring back to their former position.

5. The Estates of Brittany

Brittany was the last province in France to be pacified. In 1596 and again in 1597, the three estates had offered substantial sums to Henry if he came to Brittany at the head of an army to defeat the Catholic League chief, Mercoeur, and to drive the Spanish from a toehold they held in the province. In spite of repeated promises, Henry waited until he had begun peace negotiations with Spain in February 1598 and had reached an agreement with Mercoeur. When he finally entered Brittany, he was at the head of his court, not his troops, but he nevertheless wanted the first installment of the 600,000 livres he had been promised for coming. It had been his intention to hold the estates in Nantes where in April he issued the famous edict that gave his Protestant subjects a degree of religious freedom, but on the last day of that month, he transferred the meeting to Rennes where it opened on May 18, just two days after the restless king had departed for Picardy to attend to the final details of the peace treaty with Spain.[97]

The instructions Henry gave his commissioners before he left contained some valuable concessions. The levy of 120,000 livres per month to support his troops and all but one of the taxes instigated by Mercoeur were terminated, and the arrears in the *fouage* through 1596 were cancelled. On the other hand, in addition to the usual taxes, Henry wanted the estates to assume his Brittany-related debts, including the substantial sums he had promised Mercoeur and other League chiefs for making peace. Finally he demanded the remainder of the 600,000 livres that had been offered him in return for coming to Brittany. After some negotiations the estates voted, in addition to the customary taxes, 2.4 million livres to be raised by a tax on wine and salt to fulfill their obligations to the king and the king's Breton-

97. Henri IV, *Lettres*, 4:960, 1068, 1069; *Lettres inédites de Henri IV*, ed. Augustin Galitzin (Paris, 1860), pp. 264–68; Valois, 1: no. 4726; Dom Pierre Hyacinthe Morice, *Histoire ecclésiastique et civile de Bretagne* (Guingamp, 1836), 13:352–53; Arthur Le Moyne La Borderie and Barthélemy Pocquet, *Histoire de Bretagne* (Rennes, 1913), 5:339–49.

related debts. In return they asked that the size of the garrison be reduced, new offices suppressed, fortified châteaux demolished, and the 10,000 livres assigned annually for pensions be given only to Breton nobles who attended the estates. With these decisions the estates came to an end. The initial encounter between Henry and his reunited duchy had been reasonably satisfactory to the crown and the estates alike.[98]

Before departing Henry took other steps to restore order and to provide for the administration of Brittany. To the post of governor he named his four-year-old bastard son, César, duke of Vendôme. Since Vendôme was far too young to perform the duties of his office, Henry appointed Hercule de Rohan, duke of Montbazon, to serve as lieutenant general in the diocese of Nantes and Charles de Cossé, count and later duke of Brissac, to serve as lieutenant general in the other eight dioceses. He also directed Gilles de Maupeou to straighten out the entangled financial affairs of the province, a task to which that energetic royal servant devoted his considerable skill for a year and a half.[99]

Despite the efforts of Maupeou and other royal officials, Henry was unable to realize the entire amount that had been voted in 1597 and 1598. When the three estates met in December 1599, he confronted them with demands that they pay what was still due on the 600,000 livres he had been promised for coming to Brittany and the 2.4 million that had been voted the preceding year. In addition Henry wanted 66,000 livres which he claimed had been part of the special grant in 1598 but whose collection Parlement had blocked. The estates refused to vote this last grant but offered 300,000 livres if the king would abolish certain designated offices. In addition to whittling down Henry's financial demands, the three estates could also take satisfaction from the fact that they successfully opposed a royal demand that they elect a new syndic on the grounds that the one that they had chosen the preceding year was not a noble.[100]

By October 1600 when the estates again met, Henry was in a position to ask for only the usual taxes and what was still owed to him. As a result, the session was quieter than most. Part of the explanation for Henry's restraint was that he was trying to obtain large sums from individual closed towns to help defray the expenses of his marriage to Marie de Medici. Those present took a stand opposing the gifts.[101] The estates of 1601 was equally unevent-

98. AD, Ille-et-Vilaine, C 2645, esp. pp. 155–64, 201, 231–37; La Borderie and Pocquet, *Histoire de Bretagne,* 5:349–50; Robert S. Trullinger, *The Royal Administration of Bretagne under Henri IV, 1598–1610* (Ann Arbor, University Microfilms, 1972), p. 50 n.63. Louis Joseph de Carné, *Les Etats de Bretagne* (Paris, 1875), 1:249–54. Morice, *Histoire,* 13:353–62.

99. Trullinger, *Royal Administration;* pp. 130–61, 321–23.

100. Ibid., pp. 93–96, 426; AD, Ille-et-Vilaine, C 2645, pp. 393–400, 406–08, 435, 456–58, 463–65, 474–77; Henri IV, *Lettres,* 5:40, 8:751. For decrees on financial affairs in Brittany, see Valois, 1: nos. 4813, 4870, 4883, 4899, 4962, 5151, 5326, 5436, 5439, 5497.

101. AD, Ille-et-Vilaine, C 2645, esp. pp. 564, 640–41, 677.

ful, but by the fall of 1602 Henry thought that Brittany had recovered enough from the war to be able to make a new commitment.[102] As a result, he directed his commissioners to ask the estates to redeem the royal demain and other crown property that had been mortgaged in Brittany. To increase the chances that his request would be treated favorably, he directed the constable of Montmorency to attend, a privilege the aging duke had by virtue of his ownership of the barony of Châteaubriand. Probably others who were favorable to the royal cause were also asked to appear because attendance for the clergy jumped from eleven to seventeen over the previous year and for the nobility from twenty-two to seventy-seven. During the session some nobles attempted without success to get the three estates to obtain a delay in paying the debts they had contracted during the Wars of Religion. The three estates were equally recalcitrant when it came to the question of redeeming the domain. They did vote funds to continue payments on the 2.4 million livres they had granted in 1598. The king in return suppressed some offices that he had created the year before but refused to reduce the size of the garrison.[103]

In 1603 Henry again asked the estates to repay the mortgage on the royal domain, but they once more refused.[104] When he persisted the following year, the estates expressed a willingness to redeem part of the domain if he would cease to charge them for the garrison in Brittany and make other concessions. The commissioners were unable to promise to do so, and another year passed with nothing being done about the domain. From the standpoint of the estates, however, a landmark was reached. The grant of 2.4 million livres they had voted in 1598 was so nearly paid that they could reduce the sales tax on wine and direct that whatever was left over from the sum that was collected be applied to their own debts.[105]

The Bretons' ability to block Henry's repeated efforts to have them redeem the domain must be attributed in part to the fact that unlike other provinces, they controlled the farming of indirect taxes on wine, salt, and other products which were the source for nearly all special grants. Furthermore the money collected by the farmer of these taxes was turned over to the treasurer of the estates, not to an official of the crown, a procedure which circumvented royal efforts to misuse the funds that were collected. Indeed royal fiscal officials were almost nonexistent in Brittany. The province had neither élus nor a Bureau of Finances. Sully was evidently tempted to correct this last deficiency, for included among a number of fiscal proposals he considered presenting to Henry in 1604 was one establishing a Bureau of

102. Ibid., C 2646, pp. 1–95 passim.

103. Ibid., esp. pp. 121–27, 141–45 175, 214–16. Montmorency sent a procureur instead of attending in person. Ibid., pp. 255–61. Henri IV, *Lettres*, 5:646–47, 8:867–70. Trullinger, *Royal Administration*, pp. 389–90; Valois, 2: nos. 6886, 7448, 7556.

104. AD, Ille-et-Vilaine, C 2646, pp. 271–75, 293, 346–49.

105. Ibid., esp. pp. 401–03, 432, 488–91.

Finances in Brittany. Whether Sully considered this the first step in putting a royal fiscal administration in Brittany to replace that of the estates or whether it should be considered merely an excuse to create more offices to sell cannot be determined, but other actions by Sully during this period suggest the former.[106] In any case, Henry did not act on the suggestion, perhaps because the estates of 1604 did offer "to negotiate" with his representatives on the subject of the domain when they met in 1605.[107]

Henry bent every effort to ensure that the estates took the initial steps to redeem the domain in 1605. He dispatched a special negotiator to Saint-Brieuc where the meeting was held in October and wrote letters to each of the three estates in which he stressed the fact that Dauphiné and other provinces had already begun to do so. The necessary funds, he indicated, could be found by continuing the tax on wine that had been used to pay the huge grant the estates had voted him in 1598. After considerable negotiations, the estates offered to impose a tax for two years on wine sold in detail that was estimated to yield 400,000 livres annually. In return they asked for a number of concessions, including administrative control over the tax and the suppression of many offices. Henry accepted these proposals with a few modifications, and a start was made in the redemption of the domain, whose value was set at 4,722,094 livres.[108]

The estates of 1606 and 1607 passed without significant developments, except for quarrels over the respective roles of the officials of the crown and the provincial estates in the redemption of the domain.[109] In 1608, however, Henry pressed for a new and significant departure from the usual procedures. The estates, he urged, should approve leasing the farm of the wine tax for nine years for a total of 3.6 million livres, enough to redeem what was still owed on the domain. If this step were taken, the estates would lose control over the tax for a long period and with it the opportunity to win annual concessions from the crown in return for its renewal. Furthermore a nine-year tax was likely to come to be considered permanent. Henry must have been well aware of the advantages that would accrue to the crown if the estates would agree because he dispatched Vendôme, his teenage bastard son and the longtime absentee governor of Brittany, to attend the estates. One suspects that an effort was also made to persuade clients of the royal family to attend, for 18 clergymen and a record-breaking 152 nobles appeared at Rennes on the appointed day.[110]

106. BN, ms. fr. 18,510, fols. 97–98. In 1609 Sully raised the possibility of creating élections in Brittany and other provinces in which they did not exist, but he did so in the context of an anticipated war with the Habsburgs. Sully, *Mém.* Michaud, 3:366.

107. AD, Ille-et-Vilaine, C 2646, pp. 491–92.

108. Ibid., esp. pp. 528–29, 537–64, 611–17; Trullinger, *Royal Administration*, pp. 391–95.

109. AD, Ille-et-Vilaine, C 2647, pp. 1–201 passim. Trullinger, *Royal Administration*, pp. 395–99.

110. AD, Ille-et-Vilaine, C 2647, esp. pp. 207–28; Henri IV, *Lettres*, 7:573, 590–91, 600, 8:961–63.

The assembly opened on September 27, and soon representatives of the estates and the crown were engaged in negotiations concerning Henry's proposal. In spite of the pressures that were brought to bear, the three estates refused to surrender control over indirect taxation for so long a period. They did, however, propose that they themselves retain responsibility for the wine tax and redeem the domain over a period of nine years. In short, the issue ceased to be whether the domain should be redeemed. To many of those who attended the estates, the redemption of the domain was desirable because if it yielded the crown income, royal demands should be proportionally less. The question had become one of whether the crown would control the farming of indirect taxes in Brittany as elsewhere in France or whether the three estates would retain this unusual privilege. On December 18, the king's council chose the path toward absolutism by ordering that a tax farmer who had already been given a contract to collect the tax exercise his privilege in spite of the opposition of the Breton estates and the sovereign courts. Then, on February 19, 1609, the council reversed itself and accepted the proposition of the estates. Henry had succeeded in winning a long-term commitment to redeem the domain, but the estates had retained control over indirect taxation.[111]

Sully in his capacity of grand voyer had written the estates of 1608 conveying an offer from the king to pay half the costs of repairing the roads and bridges in Brittany if the estates would pay the other half. His agents had made a similar proposal to the estates the year before, but on both occasions his overtures had been repulsed. The estates preferred to leave the responsibility for road repairs to the local seigneurs, a system that was obviously inadequate. In his usual arbitrary fashion Sully ordered his agents to make the necessary repairs anyway and to pay for them by assessing the neighboring parishes, this despite the fact that the estates had not given their consent and Parlement had tried to prevent such activity. Perhaps driven to take action in self-defense, the estates did vote 6,000 livres for road repairs near Redon in 1609 on the condition that the king contribute an equal sum, but this was not enough to satisfy the dynamic grand voyer. He continued his illegal exactions but failed to provide the promised 6,000 livres in matching funds.[112]

The estates also failed to maintain control over the size of the tax to support the garrison. Each year they asked the king to abolish or at least reduce the number of troops in Brittany. On several occasions they won

---

111. AD, Ille-et-Vilaine, C 2647, esp. pp. 265–73, 280–95; Trullinger, *Royal Administration*, pp. 108–12, 400–08.

112. AD, Ille-et-Vilaine, C 2647, pp. 240–41, C 2648, pp. 46–47; Carné, *Les Etats de Bretagne*, 1:260–61; Trullinger, *Royal Administration*, pp. 365–71. Sully also used his office of grand voyer to supervise the financial affairs of the Breton towns. See Trullinger, "The *Grand Voyer* as an Instrument of Royal Centralization in Brittany under Henry IV," *Proceedings of the Western Society for French History* 3 (1975): 26–34.

reductions, but it was Henry who determined the amount that was needed. Since this tax fell on those who paid the fouage, it became in effect an increment to the fouage that had automatically been voted during the past century. The size of the new tax fluctuated at around 75,000 livres during Henry's reign.[113]

In spite of several setbacks, the three estates emerged at the close of the reign in good condition. They persuaded the council to restore the privilege of farming the wine tax to them in February 1609, and in September they succeeded in abolishing a number of offices in return for financial compensation.[114] Two reasons why the Bretons were successful in withstanding Sully's obvious desire to move toward absolutism were their well-defined privileges that took the form of a written contract with the crown and their strong feeling of provincial loyalty (though not separatism as has sometimes been argued). Furthermore the estates and the sovereign courts usually cooperated in the effort to maintain their respective privileges and those of the province as a whole. Within the estates the three orders generally cooperated. Their leadership was good. From 1602 Henri de Rohan, the future adversary of Richelieu, frequently attended the meetings and presided over his order. Finally they were willing to spend generously to win influential friends. As the time drew near for adjournment, the estates always voted a number of persons gratifications. In 1607, for example, they gave Brissac 9,000 livres for "the continual favors that he does for the said lords of the estates," and the king's secretary of state for Breton affairs, 3,000 livres "in consideration for the good offices that the said sieur de Gesvres does daily ... in His Majesty's council for the said lords of the estates."[115] Brissac's secretaries and Gesvres's commis were nearly always remembered, as were other persons with more prestigious positions. In 1608 when the young duke of Vendôme attended the estates, he was voted 8,000 livres, his governor, 2,000, his preceptor, 1,000, and his two secretaries together 1,000, all of this in addition to the customary grants.[116]

Thus the great provincial estates retained their position in the peaceful years of Henry's reign. Sully dreamed of curbing their power and establishing élections throughout France, but even if he convinced Henry that this should be the ultimate goal, the decision was made to move cautiously. Languedoc, and to a lesser extent Burgundy, were threatened in 1604 and in 1607–09, but Henry was careful to see that his subjects were not pushed too far. In the last year of his reign the pressure was relaxed because of the

---

113. Trullinger, *Royal Administration*, pp. 116–23.

114. Ibid., p. 429.

115. AD, Ille-et-Vilaine, C 2647, p. 179. Royal permission to levy taxes to pay gratifications was necessary, but kings rarely (if ever) offended important persons by refusing. Occasionally grantees encountered administrative difficulties in collecting. See, for example, Brissac to Bellièvre, August 3, 1603, BN ms. fr. 15,897, fol. 546.

116. AD, Ille-et-Vilaine, C 2647, pp. 316–17.

approaching war with the Habsburgs. Perhaps to take advantage of the need for additional money at this time, Sully suggested that élus be established in all the pays d'états, but there is no evidence that his proposal was seriously considered.[117] All the provincial estates complained about taxes being levied without their consent, but only in Dauphiné where the orders were too divided to agree on the necessary taxes to support the provincial government did the practice become commonplace. Here Lesdiguières defended the autonomy of the region, but at the same time he was the principal exploiter of the people.

6. THE ESTATES IN THE HEREDITARY LANDS

When Henry became king, a problem arose concerning the relationship between Béarn and Navarre, which he had ruled as a sovereign prince, and France. There was also need to reconsider the position of Foix, Bigorre, and the other fiefs with the estates that he had governed as a vassal of the Valois sovereigns.

Henry first had to define the relation between Béarn and France when he became the sovereign of both states. The practice had been for new kings of France to unite their personal domain with that of the crown, but in spite of considerable criticism, Henry resisted this move. The desires of the inhabitants of his ancestral domain to retain their special status and the pledges he had made to his creditors when he mortgaged his lands were unquestionably factors in determining his decision. He was also motivated by the fact that until 1596 he was by no means assured that he could assert his claim to the crown of France, and until Catherine's death in 1604, he had a sister who could inherit the Bourbon lands provided that they were not annexed to the royal domain. Indeed it was the possibility that the independent frontier states of Béarn and Navarre would pass to the sister or daughter of a king who had no sons while the French crown passed to a male of a collateral line that led to much of the criticism of Henry's policy. In 1596 he stated his intention to keep the Bourbon and French royal domains separate, perhaps in the hope of settling the matter, but his critics were not silenced. Finally in 1607 he incorporated the fiefs that he had held from the Valois kings with those of the royal domain but reaffirmed the independent status of Béarn and Navarre. The union of the strategically located little states with France continued to be a personal one, and the possibility that they might pass to a woman who would make a Spanish marriage remained.[118] Two years later Henry went a step further and recognized as

117. Sully, *Mém.* Michaud, 3:366.
118. Pierre Tucoo-Chala, *La vicomté de Béarn et le problème de sa souveraineté des origines à 1620* (Bordeaux, 1961), pp. 126–28, 194–96.

being sovereign the neighboring territory of Bidache which belonged to the son of one of his cast-off mistresses. He had, it seems, little concept of nationality and little regard for the jeopardy in which his acts might place the French people.[119]

The Béarnais had retained the independence they so much desired because Henry's interests coincided with their own, but on the religious issue he proved more difficult because he needed the support of the French Catholics and the pope. His decision to rejoin the Catholic church in 1593 raised the question of whether as a Catholic monarch he could long permit laws against his faith to remain in force in a land in which he ruled. Indeed under the terms of the pope's absolution two years later, he promised to restore Catholicism to Béarn. Once Henry had received the papal blessing and French Catholics began to swarm to his banner, he was slow to carry out his promises. However, constant pressure from the French Catholic clergy, coupled with his desire to have the pope annul his marriage to Queen Marguerite, led him to alter his course. In 1599, one year after he had granted similar concessions to French Protestants in the Edict of Nantes, he ordered that part of the confiscated possessions of the Catholic church be restored in Béarn and that Catholics be permitted to worship in twelve parishes. Led by their two bishops, the Béarnais Catholics sought further concessions, and Henry, sometimes reluctantly, granted them part of what they asked. Included were the admission of Catholics to public offices, the restoration of the Cathedral chapters, and the return of the Jesuits near the close of his reign.[120]

The survival of the correspondence and memoirs of the duke de La Force who served as governor of Béarn and Navarre from 1593 to 1621 enables historians to explore the relations among the king, the governor, and the estates during this trying period. They reveal that Henry had a genuine sympathy for the religious and particularistic sentiments of his Pyrenean subjects, but that he would brook no disobedience when their actions threatened his basic policies. In 1583, six years before he became king of France, he interceded with the royal government in an effort to secure an exemption from taxes on Béarnais goods which were transported through France on the Garonne River.[121] Some months after La Force took over the governorship, Henry instructed him to maintain Béarnais customs and assured him that he had the well-being and repose of his subjects at heart. On the other hand, in 1595 when he suspected that the Conseil Souverain might be supporting the efforts of his sister and the count of Soissons to marry, he wrote a two-sentence letter to a member of that body saying that his head would answer for any disobedience. The aggrieved councillor could

119. Ibid., p. 128.
120. Marc Forissier, *Histoire de la réforme en Béarn* (Tarbes, 1951), 2:44–68.
121. *Lettres inédites du roi Henri IV au chancelier de Bellièvre du 8 février 1581 au 23 septembre 1601*, ed E. Halphen (Paris, 1872), pp. 30–31.

only write to La Force, who was then at court, asking him to explain this situation to the popular Catherine and at the same time to speculate about a king who threatened the life of his officials. A year later Henry won the plaudits of the Béarnais by refusing to incorporate them into France. Then in 1598 he expressed his disapproval of the deputies the estates had elected to represent them at court. It was the religious issue, however, that provided the greatest source of disagreement.[122]

La Force was at court in 1599 when Henry decided to remove most of the restrictions on Béarnais Catholics. The clever monarch made sure that his Protestant governor saw the necessity of making this concession in view of the need to get the strongly Catholic French Parlements to accept the Edict of Nantes. Indeed Henry even persuaded La Force that he would go to the length of importing foreign mercenaries to compel the Parlements' obedience if it were necessary. Therefore when La Force returned to Pau, he was prepared to push the edict on the mass through the estates and Conseil Souverain, which served as the Béarnais Parlement. The estates caused him little trouble because the newly appointed bishops and the Catholics persuaded their fellow deputies that if the edict reestablishing Catholicism were accepted, they would make no further demands. The Conseil Souverain, however, proved more difficult; only after making remonstrances to the king did it register the decree in August 1599 with reservations. Henry had brought continual pressure to bear on La Force to win the approval of the Conseil Souverain and the estates. In doing so he had not hesitated to say that he insisted on being obeyed. However, Protestant historians who complain that he violated the privileges of the viscounty are in error. He did not bypass either the Conseil or the estates, and the pressure he imposed was no greater than that he had asserted on the French Parlements to secure the registration of the Edict of Nantes. In a letter dated November 24, 1599, he went to special length to assure La Force and the estates that he would not only respect the fors but also gratify their desire in all matters except in regard to the restoration of Catholicism. La Force, though a staunch Protestant, had recognized the necessity of making concessions to the Catholics and had loyally abetted his efforts. For once a governor had been more the representative of his king in his jurisdiction than of his government at court.[123]

In spite of their promise to the estates to request no concessions beyond those embodied in the edict of 1599, the bishops went to court in 1601 to petition the king to return all the former property of the church and to permit the celebration of Catholic rites throughout the viscounty. The Protestant-controlled estates dispatched a deputation to counter this request.

122. *Mémoires authentiques de Jacques Nompar de Caumont, duc de La Force*, ed. Marquis de La Grange (Paris, 1843), 1:243–44, 254–56, 291.

123. Ibid., pp. 115–16, 127–28, 298, 303–04, 309–10, 313–17; Forissier, *Histoire de la réforme*, 2:52–56.

They succeeded, but Henry granted the bishops several other concessions. Quarreling between Catholics and Protestants continued, however, and in 1603 Henry Sought to shift the burden to La Force by telling him not to permit either faction to send him deputies but to settle the matter himself. It must have come as a welcome change when the estates of 1604 shifted from the religious issue long enough to back the syndic in a successful effort to prevent the registration of an edict against dueling, which they regarded as contrary to the fors. The following year Henry issued an order increasing the number of places in which mass could be celebrated. The Béarnais Protestants protested, and in a renewed effort to resolve the religious issue, Henry summoned the bishops and the Protestant deputies to plead their cause before his council. Its decision, which was favorable to the Catholics, provoked the most serious quarrel between Henry and the estates that took place during his reign.[124]

The edict of 1599 permitting Catholics to hold office had led some members of that faith to be elected to municipal posts and from there to the estates, and even during the height of the Protestant ascendancy Catholic nobles could attend by right. Nevertheless when the estates met in the summer of 1606, the Protestants were still numerically superior in both houses. When they sought to use their power to include anti-Catholic provisions in the cahier, the Catholics withdrew. Following instructions from the king, La Force sought to prevent the deputies from dealing with religious affairs but to no avail. Not only did the Protestant majority protest against the concessions that had been granted the Catholics, but they also refused to vote Henry the customary donation until he had satisfied their grievances. Henry was furious and told La Force in no uncertain terms that withholding taxes was no way to win concessions from him. The Catholics were instructed to name deputies to court to present their case alongside the Protestant delegation the majority in the estates had elected. La Force himself was also summoned.[125]

La Force delayed going to court as long as he could in order to give the king's anger time to cool. When he finally arrived, he assumed the role of the defender of his government by mollifying the anger of the king before the deputies were heard and doing his best to expedite their affairs. This time the Protestant majority won a significant concession, a grant of 6,000 livres annually from the royal purse to support their educational establishment. Nevertheless when the estates next met, they voted to pay the Protestant deputies to court but not the Catholic bishops who had represented the minority religion. One bishop was charged by a member of that body of having insisted that all the curés in his diocese contribute toward his

124. Forissier, *Histoire de la réfoune*, 2:61–64; *Mémoires de La Force*, 1:133–35, 171, 173–74, 323–24, 349, 368–69, 389, 396–97, 399, 401, 407–09.
125. *Mémoires de La Force*, 1:186–89, 432–33.

expenses and jailing those who refused to do so. The Catholics appealed to
Henry, and he ruled that since the estates had paid the Protestant deputies,
they should also pay the Catholic ones. The Protestants protested to him
against plans to admit the two bishops to the Conseil Souverain and to
introduce Jesuits into the viscounty. The exasperated monarch again forbade the estates to deal with religious matters and bluntly told the bishops
that it would be better if they devoted their energies to the people of their
diocese, rather than to traveling to and from court with their protests. The
Catholic offensive subsided, and the last two years of Henry's reign passed
relatively quietly in Béarn. Henry had certainly used pressure to restore
Catholicism, but the essential privileges of his subjects remained intact when
he fell before the assassin in 1610.[126]

Marsan and presumably Gabardan were separated from Béarn at their
own request in 1607 because the inhabitants believed that they were
excessively taxed under the union. Estates were probably organized in the
two viscounties immediately, but there is insufficient documentation to
recount their history. When an effort was made to establish an élection there
in 1632, the estates were clearly functioning, and they continued to exist
until the Revolution. By the eighteenth century, the territory was organized
into the estates of Mont-de-Marsan, which consisted of the mayor and jurats
of that town and the syndic of the surrounding parishes, and the estates of
the Bastilles, to which the remaining parishes of Marsan and those of
Gabardan sent deputies. The clergy and the nobility did not participate in
either assembly. How long this arrangement had existed cannot be ascertained, but it certainly provides another instance of the postmedieval
creation of a representative assembly, this time in the early seventeenth
century.[127]

The situation in Navarre was quite different in one respect, for here the
majority of the people had continued to adhere to the Catholic faith in spite
of the efforts of Jeanne d'Albret to convert them. Henry IV was far less
doctrinaire than his mother and did not pursue her efforts in this respect
prior to his return to Rome. In his youth his principal concern was to extract
all he could from his Catholic Navarrese subjects to help support the
Protestant cause or, more accurately, his own aspirations in France. His
decision to have his sister, Catherine, and then La Force, both Protestants,

126. Ibid., pp. 188–90, 194–96, 210–12, 442–47, 451–53, 455, 462–64, 466–70; *IAD, Basses-Pyrénées, sér. C*, ed. P. Raymond (Pau, 1865), C 703, C 704.

127. *IAD, Landes, sér. A à F*, ed. Henri Tartière (Paris, 1868), introduction, pp. 3–4, 15; *Edict du Roy pour la convocation et assemblée des Estats du Royaume de Navarre et pays de Béarn, Foix et Bigorre, Nébousan, Aure, Morsan ...* (Paris, 1634). A copy is at BN, Actes Royaux, F 46,977 (13). For a brief description of the estates during the eighteenth century, see Maurice Bordes, *D'Etigny et l'administration de l'intendance d'Auch, 1751–1767* (Auch, 1957), 1:297–98, and H. Jolly and H. Courteault, "Essai sur le régime financier des petits pays d'Etats du Midi de la France, au XVIIIᵉ siècle," *Bul. de la soc. des sciences, lettres et arts de Pau*, 2d sér., 54–56 (1931–33).

act as his viceroys in Navarre as well as his governors in Béarn may have caused some concern, but after his conversion to Catholicism in 1593, the Navarrese must have rested more securely. The one important issue that arose during the remainder of the reign was the relation between Navarre and France. In 1596 and again in 1607 Henry refused to incorporate the smaller kingdom into the larger one. When the chancellor of Navarre died near the close of 1606, however, he appointed Sillery, who had recently replaced Bellièvre in the French chancellery, to the position. Sully immediately sought to become superintendent of finances. In fact, if not in theory, Navarre seemed about to be incorporated into France. La Force immediately jumped to the defense of the Navarrese and succeeded in blocking Sully's aspirations. Navarre like Béarn was spared the careful but often brutal fiscal supervision of Henry's great minister.[128]

Henry held the county of Foix and the viscounties of Bigorre, Nébouzan, and Soule as vassal of the Valois kings. Their situation in regard to France was therefore different from that of Béarn and Navarre. Henry would have been happy to have kept them out of the crown's domain and free from routine interference from the royal bureaucracy. Nevertheless these estates had to expend considerable energy in defending their privileges from overly zealous officials. In October 1597 the three estates of Foix won a general confirmation of their status, but this did not prevent the farmer of the gabelle of Languedoc from trying to include Foix in his territory in May 1602. The Council of Finances sought to resolve the resulting dispute that November by establishing a chambre à sel there. With their treasured privilege of being exempt from the gabelle threatened both by the farmer of the gabelle and the council, the estates appealed to Henry, who ruled in their favor in 1604. When Henry succumbed to the pressure of numerous advisers in July 1607 and incorporated those fiefs, which he had held from the French crown, into the royal domain, the sovereign courts of Languedoc immediately sought to extend their jurisdiction over Foix. Once more the estates went into action, and in February 1608 Henry confirmed the administrative autonomy of the province, including the right to have estates, by preventing it from being incorporated into Languedoc.[129]

Henry's treatment of his fiefs of the French crown in tax matters can be investigated only for the viscounty of Bigorre. As a frontier province Bigorre claimed to be exempt from the taille and other direct taxes, but its estates graciously bestowed a donation upon their sovereign each year. In 1589, the year Henry became king, they extended themselves by giving him 9,000

128. Henri IV, *Lettres*, 2:239. *Mémoires de La Force*, 1:189–90, 243–44, 438–39, 441, 466–67, 2:222; Tucoo-Chala, *La Vicomté de Béarn*, pp. 194–96.

129. AN, H¹ 716, nos. 1–2; Valois, 2: nos. 7326, 8246; Germain Arnaud, *Mémoire sur les Etats de Foix, 1608–1789* (Toulouse, 1904), pp. 98–99, 104–105; H. Castillon, *Histoire du comté de Foix* (Toulouse, 1852), 2:318–19; *IAD, Haute-Garonne, sér. B*, ed. J. Moudenc (Toulouse, 1915), 4:144.

livres and his sister and heir 3,000. From then until 1598, they voted Henry from 3,000 to 6,000 livres per year and his sister half that sum. Her marriage in 1599 freed the estates from responsibility toward her, and no further gifts were granted. In 1601 the estates gave Henry an additional 3,000 livres because of his marriage, but their contribution fell drastically the following year when they granted only 1,500 livres. Thereafter Henry IV and his agents were more successful, and except for 1604 when there were heavy snows, the estates were persuaded to vote 4,800 livres or more each year. The fluctuation in the size of the gifts during this period leaves little doubt that despite persuasion and possible threats, the three estates were the final determinant of the amount they gave.[130]

By the close of 1608, however, Henry had incorporated Bigorre into the domain of the crown and farmed its revenue and that of his other former fiefs to his valet de chambre, Antoine Billard. Included were the taxes voted by the estates. Billard naturally sought a more predictable income than could be based on the whim of the deputies, and the latter in turn appealed their case to the Parlement of Toulouse. With his accustomed firmness, Henry removed jurisdiction from these judges and ordered that the dispute be heard before the Grand Conseil. Then, on Billard's request, the Council of Finances decreed in April 1610 that henceforth Bigorre would pay an annual taille of 7,000 livres. From that year until the Revolution, this modest sum was invariably voted by the estates with the stipulation that 300 livres be set aside to pay their expenses.[131]

In return for being exempt from the taille, the inhabitants of Bigorre had been required to support 10 *lances* at an annual cost of about 4,500 livres during the late Middle Ages, but at some point prior to the reign of Francis I, this assessment had been reduced to 1,674 livres to support $4\frac{1}{2}$ lances. Francis I and his successors confirmed this privilege, as did Henry IV in 1596, but doubtless on the instigation of Sully, discontented at receiving such a small sum, an annual taillon of 751 livres was added in 1606. The estates protested, and the council agreed to collect the tax for only two years. In 1608 the council sought to continue the levy anyway, but strong protests from the estates led Henry to reverse its decision. His pledged word was worth this paltry sum, although one can imagine how disgruntled Sully was at losing the opportunity to collect a few additional livres.[132]

The "donation" and the levy for the lances were normally the only direct taxes levied in Bigorre to support the royal government during this period. Additional sums were occasionally required, such as to assist in the construction of a bridge at Toulouse. The inhabitants were also subject to

---

130. Gilbert Pène, *Les attributions financières des Etats du pays et comté de Bigorre aux XVIIe et XVIIIe siècles* (Bordeaux, 1962), pp. 95–97, 491–92.

131. Ibid., pp. 96–97, 102–03; Valois, 2: nos. 12,894, 13,337, 13,947, 14,878, 15,216, 15,406, 15,602; *IAD, Haute-Garonne, sér. B*, ed. J. Judicis (Toulouse, 1903), 2: 76, 81.

132. Pène, *Les attributions financières*, pp. 105–11.

certain indirect taxes such as the customs, but on the whole they were more fortunate than most of the French people.[133]

The estates retained 300 livres of the 7,000 livre "donation" given to their king and count to be used to pay the salaries of those who participated in the meetings, the amount per day due to the seneschal, barons, gentlemen, and deputies of the third estate being set by regulations drawn up in 1608. Presumably the estates also voted gratifications to win the favor of those in power and made appropriations to further the welfare of the province, but specific information supporting this assumption is largely for the post-+ Henry IV era.[134]

It is difficult to escape to conclusion that Henry IV favored the inhabitants of these hereditary lands. They were relatively lightly taxed. Béarn and Navarre were permitted to retain their independent status, and royal officials in Languedoc were prevented from interfering in the affairs of those fiefs that were adjacent. Even the ubiquitous Sully left them to their own devices, and they were spared the horde of investigators from Paris that so troubled the officials of the estates and towns elsewhere in France. Henry's moderation must be attributed primarily to a sentimental devotion to the land of his birth and to the people who had supported him during the Wars of Religion, although gratitude generally was not his strongest trait. He also may have believed that he could not extract enough additional money from these relatively poor lands to make it financially expedient to risk having to suppress a rebellion, a rebellion that would almost certainly take place if he applied too much pressure on the estates or trampled on their privileges. Only the religious issue led to serious conflicts with the estates in the hereditary lands, and this issue appeared well on the way to being settled when he was assassinated in 1610, leaving the position of the estates intact.

7. The Estates of Normandy

When Henry IV inherited the throne, Normandy became divided into two camps. Rouen opted for the Catholic League. Its rival, Caen, chose Henry and dispatched a deputy to him to ask that the provincial estates be held alternately in their city, that the sovereign courts be permanently established there, and that their municipal officials be ennobled. Those who proffered their friendship to the hard-pressed king were nearly as costly as those who chose to be his enemies. Henry held a meeting of the three estates at Caen in April 1590, but the war, which was especially severe in Normandy, prevented him from assembling them again until November 1593. In the intervening period he collected what taxes he could without consent. Those

---

133. Valois, 2: nos. 6973, 12,525.
134. Pène, *Les attributions financières*, pp. 271–88.

deputies who did come to Caen in that year submitted a cahier with 118 articles to the king. Except where money was concerned, Henry's response was generally favorable. To the request that there be no extraordinary levies after the estates had met, he could only reply that he would respect this privilege except in case of urgent necessity. To the plea that he reduce by one-half the stipulated tax for the following year, he once more stressed his financial plight and ordered that the full amount be levied.[135]

In 1594 the League leaders in Normandy accepted Henry as their king, but the three estates were not convoked. Then in November 1595 they were once more assembled, this time at Rouen, where they heard the king request 1,731,000 livres, 309,000 less than he had levied the previous year without consent. Nevertheless the estates pleaded poverty and approved a total of only 1,113,180 livres. Henry IV, like his predecessor, responded by ordering that the full amount be levied anyway.[136] The three estates did not meet in 1596, perhaps because the normal time to assemble coincided with the Assembly of Notables in Rouen, but beginning in 1597 they met in October, November, or December in every year of the reign.

The question immediately arises as to whether there were individuals in the royal administration in the early 1590s who were seeking to destroy the provincial estates. Clearly the échevins of Rouen thought so. When October arrived in 1595 and no letters of convocation had been received, they persuaded the syndic of the estates to visit Caen and perhaps other towns to point out to the municipal officials that failure to hold a meeting that year as well as the preceding year suggested that there was a desire to abolish them. The fact that Henry quickly responded to their request and convoked the estates indicates that factors other than a dislike of assemblies may have been involved.[137]

The only other known contemporary opinion of why the three estates were not assembled is that of Claude Groulart, first president of the Parlement of Rouen. As a loyal though independent-minded supporter of the king who made frequent visits to court, he was probably better informed than the échevins of Rouen and Caen. He attributed the failure to hold the estates in the early 1590s to the fact that "these assemblies are dangerous during civil wars because of the evil proposals which are sometimes made by the deputies."[138] Normandy had been "reduced to obedience" by 1594, but the estates could not be held that year anyway, he reported, because of the ill

135. Henri Prentout, *Les Etats provinciaux de Normandie* (Caen, 1925), 1:335–38; *Cahiers des Etats de Normandie sous le règne de Henri IV*, ed. Charles de Robillard de Beaurepaire (Rouen, 1880), 1:1–64, 201–20; Pierre Carel, *Histoire de la ville de Caen sous Charles IX, Henri III et Henri IV* (Caen, 1886), 218–76 passim.

136. *Cahiers sous Henri IV*, 1:97–102, 240.

137. Ibid., 2:377–80; Prentout, *Les Etats provinciaux*, 3:205–06; Henri IV, *Lettres*, 4:1043, 1044.

138. *Cahiers sous Henri IV*, 1:210–11.

will between Admiral Villars, an ex-Leaguer who held sway in Rouen, and the duke of Montpensier, the newly appointed governor of Normandy. That it was Henry's original intention to assemble the estates in 1594 is indicated by the appointment of Montpensier and Groulart in February to serve as commissioners to hold the meeting. To a request from Caen that the estates be held alternately there and in Rouen, the king's council replied in May that the deputies would be assembled each year in the most convenient town.[139]

This evidence suggests that although Henry and his advisers had no desire to assemble the provincial estates during a civil war when the deputies might adopt an all-too-independent course, or when the meeting was likely to serve as the occasion for a serious quarrel between two powerful nobles, they nevertheless were not doctrinairily opposed to holding these meetings when there was little likelihood of trouble. Indeed it is difficult to see why the crown would strongly object to so impotent an institution. If the deputies did not approve all the money that was requested, the full amount of the proposed tax was levied anyway. Furthermore large sums were extracted from the province through indirect taxes, forced loans, and feudal dues that traditionally were not presented to the estates for consideration. In 1594 a tax was established on the sale of animals and drinks in the towns and large bourgs. A special levy was placed on the closed towns, and sixty patents of nobility were offered for sale in 1595. Two years later the clergy made a special contribution, and a forced loan was extracted from financial officials. The ban and arrière-ban was invoked in 1594 and again in 1597. Those nobles not desiring to serve paid in order to escape their feudal obligations.[140]

It is true that the expenses of holding the estates added to the burden already weighing on the people and, that once assembled, the Normans were in a better position to organize protests against these exactions.[141] However individual towns were quite capable of complaining on their own account, the Parlement and the Court of Aids did their best to block new impositions

---

139. Ibid. p. 228. AN, E Iᵃ, fol. 44; BN ms. fr. 18,159, fols. 128v–30.

140. Prentout, *Les Etats provinciaux*, 3:235–40; *Cahiers sous Henri IV*, 1:214–15, 323–36; Valois, 1: nos. 1915, 2515, 2546, 2550, 2826, 2987, 4102.

141. In 1595, for example, the estates allotted 3,500 livres for the commissioners, 2,838 for the deputies, and 9,000 for "the common affairs of the said province." *Cahiers sous Henri IV*, 1:98–99. Prentout, *Les Etats provinciaux*, 2:135, n.4, accepts 15,000 livres as being the average cost of holding the estates between 1578 and 1607. This figure is certainly too low because the Normans did not vote as much for the commissioners who held the estates as the crown levied to pay them. In 1598 the king levied 9,900 livres, but the estates never voted more than 3,500 livres during this period. *Cahiers sous Henry IV*, 1:254. A more likely estimate of the costs of holding the estates would therefore be 21,000 livres. For taxes levied and payments made to the syndic, see *Cahiers sous Henri IV*, 1:239, and Valois 1: nos. 2251 and 3017. In addition, when the estates were held in Rouen, the town provided the deputies with wine and food. Prentout, *Les Etats provinciaux*, 3:203.

by refusing to register edicts until compelled to do so, and the three estates themselves had a syndic charged with watching over their interests when they were not in session. This official appeared before the king's council to present their case with occasional success. Local financial officials were known to show him letters ordering levies that were not submitted to the estates so that he could protest if he so desired. He acted so determinedly before the Parlement of Rouen that its first president, the royalist Groulart, noted that the syndic was "neither an ephor nor a tribune" of the people, and left no doubt that he thought that he should stop trying to act like one.[142] It was an expense and a nuisance to hold a meeting of the three estates of Normandy, but their existence was probably not yet regarded as detrimental enough to warrant their destruction. They were to remain active well into the reign of Louis XIII.

The thirteen annual meetings of the estates between December 1597 and the end of Henry's reign produced little of interest. What went on in the assemblies is not known. Those who attended were sworn to secrecy, and few thought that their activities were important enough to record. The actions taken by the estates are better known, however (only two of the thirteen cahiers presented to the king have been lost). They reveal that during the first couple of years, some progress was made toward reducing taxes and achieving desired reforms, a fact that must be attributed more to the restoration of peace than to the effectiveness of the Normans. After about 1600, no further progress was made, although in each meeting the deputies pleaded for lower taxes until 1607, when they abandoned the effort and threw themselves on the mercy of the king, with no better results than before.

The king lowered the taille, taillon, and crues for 1598 to 1,246,942 livres before the estates met, but he requested 1,344,776 for 1599 and 1,770,752 for 1600. When the estates voted only 900,000 livres for each of the last two years, the commissioners ordered that the entire sum be imposed anyway but did allow time for deputies to be sent to the king to ask him to reconsider. They were unsuccessful for 1599, but for 1600 they won a reduction of 450,000 livres. In addition, the king canceled the unpaid taille prior to 1597 and granted a delay in paying the tax for that year for those who could not then meet the obligation.[143] Bellièvre reported to the king that the Norman deputies had presented their case with "a great deal of passion," but they owed their partial success to the fact that the reduction lowered the taille only to the approximate figure of the preceding year and

142. Prentout, *Les Etats provinciaux* 2:389–400; Amable Floquet, *Histoire du Parlement de Normandie* (Rouen, 1841), 4:169–91; Valois, 1: nos. 1559, 2713, 3130, 4086, 4175; AN El^b, fols. 53v, 130v; BN ms. Clairambault 652, p. 371.

143. *Cahiers sous Henri IV*, 1:254–55, 121–23, 151–55, 146, 289; *Lettres et chevauchées du Bureau des Finances de Caen sous Henri IV*, ed. Lucien Romier (Rouen, 1910), pp. 115–17.

that the cancellation of the unpaid taille was part of the general policy of the crown.[144]

In the remainder of his reign Henry clearly revealed that he had no intention of making special concessions to the Normans. He demanded 1,794,773 livres for 1601. The estates met in October 1600, voted a total of 900,000 livres, and dispatched their deputation to court with pitiful pleas. Perhaps they attributed their success the preceding year to the king and to Montmorency, who had heard their case with Bellièvre. Bellièvre met them by chance leaving Montmorency's house and asked if they would like to appear before the council. They refused, explaining that they had been charged to speak directly to the king. Bellièvre, evidently fearful that they might prevail upon his kindly, if selfish monarch, especially if they had succeeded in obtaining Montmorency's support, tactfully pointed out to Henry in a long letter that the 450,000 livre reduction previously granted was actually to be applied over a two-year period and that if a new reduction was accorded, other provinces were certain to make similar demands. His logic prevailed.[145]

The years that immediately followed saw the same process repeated time and again; only the estates which met in November 1606 managed to win a reduction in a direct tax. In response to several pleas from the estates that bridges and roads be repaired, Henry included a levy of 33,000 livres for this purpose in his demands for 1607. The deputies, however, had hoped to shove this expense onto someone else's shoulders and did not vote the sum. Instead of ordering that it be imposed provisionally with the other taxes, as was their custom, the commissioners stayed execution until the deputies had consulted the king. Henry's immediate reaction was to order the tax levied anyway, but in the end he relented, and the Normans escaped. The following year Henry repeated his proposal and this time overrode the objections of the estates. By December 1609 the 33,000 livre levy had become an annual affair, and the oft-defeated estates could only complain that the most necessary repairs were not being made. Indeed the year before they had adopted the practice of voting all the king asked, since it had done them no good to do otherwise.[146]

The Norman estates had lost the right to consent to indirect taxes long before Henry came to the throne. They could and did, however, plead that this or that levy be abandoned, reduced, or altered, and several articles in every cahier were devoted to this purpose. Surprisingly enough they were more successful in this area than in the field of direct taxation. The levy on the sale of animals and drinks in the towns and large bourgs, which was

144. Bellièvre to Henry, October 28, 1599, BN ms. fr. 15,894, fols. 327–28.

145. *Cahiers sous Henri IV*, 1:173–76; Bellièvre to Henry, BN ms. fr. 15,894, fols. 455–56v.

146. *Cahiers sous Henri IV*, 2:38, 62, 107, 133, 137–39, 157, 188; Valois, 2: no. 10,660. Prentout, *Les Etats provinciaux*, 1:342–43, 2:333–34.

inaugurated in 1594, was finally revoked in December 1602, although Henry imposed another tax instead. This good fortune was probably due less to the Normans than to Henry's decision to abandon at about the same time the somewhat similar pancarte which had been imposed on most of the country with the approval of the Assembly of Notables. Certainly neither the protests of the Norman estates nor of sovereign courts prevented the king from increasing the salt tax when he so desired.[147]

Taxation was the most disliked manifestation of royal power, but officials sent out by the king's council to investigate various problems were almost equally unpopular. From the arrival of two officials in 1598 to ensure that the taille was equitably levied on all those subject to the tax, one finds the three estates, sometimes assisted by the sovereign courts, doing everything in their power to defeat the investigator's efforts and to ensure their recall. Sometimes they were successful, although their victory should be attributed in part to protests from other provinces or by the willingness of those most threatened to purchase edicts of revocation from a greedy government.[148] The number of royal officials in Normandy came under frequent attack, and there were requests that offices created for revenue purpose be suppressed.[149] At times the desires of the estates coincided with those of the crown as when they petitioned that fortified châteaux be demolished; at times their desires did not conflict with the goals of the central government.[150] In either case, their requests were granted, but one cannot escape the feeling that the deputies who met in Rouen in 1598 were the last ones in the reign to try to increase their authority. They not only sought the revocation of extraordinary commissions and a reduction in taxes, but they also asked that the Estates General of France be convoked and that no taxes be levied in Normandy without their consent.[151] As Sully tightened his control over the council in the years that followed, the deputies were rarely successful in their defensive actions. By 1609 their ineffectiveness was revealed by their complaint that the crown's replies to their cahiers of 1608 were "a pure extract from [their replies to] the *cahiers* of the preceding year."[152]

The presence of élus and the failure of the prelates and great nobles to participate actively in the estates made it difficult for the Normans to check the growth of royal power. Additional factors, however, must also have

---

147. *Cahiers sous Henri IV*, 1:323–36, 2:336–56; Prentout, *Les Etats provinciaux*, 2:235–40, 271–75.

148. B. Barbiche, "Les commissaires députés pour le 'régallement' des tailles en 1598–99," *BEC* 118 (1960): 58–96, esp. 79–81; *Cahiers sous Henri IV*, 1:110–12, 138–39, 150–51, 172–73, 181–82, 197, 2:16–17, 34–35, 98–99, 111, 184–85, 210–11, 224; Prentout, *Les Etats provinciaux*, 3:213–19.

149. *Cahiers sous Henri IV*, 1:17–18, 94–95, 110–11, 120, 137–38, 166–67, 188–89, 2:15, 26–27, 58, 95–96, 127, 151, 172.

150. Ibid., 1:141–42, 215–17, 2:14.

151. Ibid., 1:106–08, 111, 118, 121–23.

152. Ibid., 2:160.

contributed to the weakness of the estates because they were less able to protect the people from Henry's fiscal exactions than were provinces with no estates at all. For example, the general receipts from Normandy amounted to 1,890,263 livres in 1600 out of a total of 9,949,999 livres raised in généralités that had elections, but rarely provincial estates. By 1610 the Norman contribution had increased to 2,088,122 livres, but the total from these généralités had decreased to 9,169,759 livres. It is of interest to compare the sums the king received from Rouen with those of the généralités of Tours and Poitiers where there were no provincial estates (table 1).[153]

TABLE 1

	1600	*1605*	*1610*
Tours	1,048,936	998,609	739,069
Poitiers	1,074,811	964,244	953,901
Rouen	1,144,988	1,426,512	1,288,915

Perhaps these figures merely reflect a belief on the part of officials in Paris that Normandy became relatively more prosperous during the decade, but a gnawing suspicion remains that the other généralités found better means to protect their interest.

Even the town of Rouen appears to have been in a better position to negotiate than the province as a whole. During the spring of 1600 when Henry was trying to raise money to cement his alliance with the Swiss in view of the approaching war with Savoy, Bellièvre wrote him that Paris had granted 150,000 livres and that "we hope to have from 60,000 to 90,000 from Rouen." The amount that Rouen contributed, then, was subject to negotiation, but taxes levied on the province as a whole were in effect established by the crown before the estates met. Paris, it might be added, had been asked to provide as large a sum as possible and had voted a don gratuit of at first 120,000, and later with some persuasion, of 150,000 livres as Bellièvre had reported. The two cities, of course, had their own tax-collecting machinery, but it is surprising that they should have been in a stronger position to negotiate than a province with estates.[154]

Groulart attributed the weakness of the estates to the weakness and

153. Mallet, pp. 186–87. Dauphiné, where there were no élections at this time, is included in these figures.

154. Bellièvre to Henry IV, May 26, 1600, BN ms. fr. 15,894, fols. 365–66v; *Cahiers sous Henri IV*, 2:301–04; *Registres des délibérations du bureau de la ville de Paris*, ed. Paul Guérin (Paris, 1909), 12:290–98.

selfishness of the deputies who attended.[155] For once his judgment seems to have missed the mark. The cahiers the estates prepared were forceful, and their delegations who carried them to Paris were courageous. Even Bellièvre, who constantly dealt with deputies from towns and provincial estates, felt compelled to write on one occasion that those from Normandy presented their case "with a great deal of passion."[156] In 1607 the syndic of the estates and their principal negotiator with the government was dismissed from his office by the king's council because he had been disobedient and insolent to the duke of Montpensier, a prince of the blood and governor of the province. This event reveals one of the causes of the weakness of the Norman estates during Henry's reign: they did not know how to win influential friends at court who would use their position to further their interests.[157]

Most governors were as much representatives of their provinces at court as the representatives of the king in their jurisdictions. In return for their services, provincial estates not only voted their salaries, paid their guards, and provided gifts for their relatives and servants but also gave them special presents when the occasion warranted. The Norman estates do not seem to have made a concerted effort to obtain Montpensier's support by lining his pockets. Indeed the king's commission for holding the estates in 1597 and presumably on other occasions included a provision for levying 19,200 livres to pay the governor and his lieutenant. The estates, however, never appropriated any money specifically to pay their salaries. The levy for this purpose was made anyway by royal command just like other taxes not consented to by the estates. Under these circumstances, Montpensier was indebted to the king for his pay, not the estates, and there is no evidence that he interceded on their behalf at court. In previous reigns the estates had voted the salaries of the governors, and they had occasionally given them special presents as well. Perhaps the Normans had lost the art of bribery; more likely they regarded Montpensier as too stupid and inept to do them much good. Surely, however, their syndic displayed a lack of foresight when he behaved insolently to a relative of the king.[158]

155. *Cahiers sous Henri IV*, 1:202, 229.
156. Bellièvre to Henry IV, October 28, 1599, BN ms. fr. 15,894, fols. 327–28.
157. Valois, 2: no. 11,788.
158. *Cahiers sous Henri IV*, 1:254–55. For gifts and salaries accorded to governors in other reigns, see Prentout, *Les Etats provinciaux*, 1:231, 2:103, 112 n.2, 163, 419–21, and *Cahiers des Etats de Normandie sous le règne de Henri III*, ed. Charles de Robillard de Beaurepaire (Rouen, 1887–88), 1:21, 119, 167–68, 2:26, 67, 102, 144, 194, 232. The documents ordering that the tax be levied usually indicated that the estates had given their consent, but the estates never listed this item in their appropriations, which they usually placed at the end of their cahier each year. *Lettres et chevauchées*, pp. 108, 225. *Cahiers sous Henri IV*, 2:210. BN ms. n.a. fr. 1095, fol. 4. Groulart did report that he had persuaded the estates of 1600 to pay Montpensier, although the previous year they had not wanted to do so. Even if he was correct, and the cahier had omitted this item, the ill feeling between Montpensier and the estates is demonstrated. *Cahiers sous Henri IV*, 1:294.

The commissioners named by the king to hold the estates were treated with almost equal disregard. In 1597 the king specified that they be paid 15,300 livres for their services, but the estates voted only 3,500 livres for this purpose each year until 1608, when they abandoned the effort to limit the amount of taxation by making specific appropriations. Once again, the king imposed the full amount anyway, and the commissioners were beholden to him, not the estates, for their pay. In other provinces the commissioners often interceded with the king to obtain modifications of the size of the tax and received special presents from the grateful estates. Even the fact that many of the commissioners were Normans did not cause them to intercede forcibly on behalf of the province. Indeed their relations with the estates were generally poor. The deputies sometimes pleaded in their cahiers that the number of commissioners be reduced as an economy measure. On the other hand, Montpensier and the commissioners arbitrarily tried to cut the deputies' expense allowance on one occasion.[159] Under these circumstances it is not surprising that Normandy paid an increasing proportion of the nation's taxes, and the protests of its syndic and other deputies were continually overruled by the king's council.[160]

8. THE ESTATES IN AUVERGNE AND FOREZ

The return of peace to Basse-Auvergne in 1594 brought no end to the activities of the towns. In that year the assembly of the nineteen good towns was convoked no fewer than seven times, and on two occasions the deputies of four towns met. The year 1595 was hardly less active. Included in the agenda was one meeting of the three estates. By 1596 the expense of having so many meetings was becoming intolerable, and it was decided to hold assemblies of the nineteen towns only twice a year. In case of emergency the seven towns nearest to Clermont were to be consulted. Admirable as this resolution was, it was adhered to more in the breach than in the observance. A year during the remainder of the Henry's reign in which there were not three or four full assemblies of the towns was exceptional.[161]

The frequency of these meetings was undoubtedly due in part to the right of the échevins of Clermont to convoke the towns, a right they exercised whenever they saw fit. At first it may seem surprising that Henry did not find means to take away this privilege, but his own position was too precarious to attack the liberty of his subjects unless they provided him with

---

159. *Cahiers sous Henri IV*, 1:254–55, 2:201; Prentout, *Les Etats provinciaux*, 3:209. For complaints on the number of commissioners, see *Cahiers sous Henri IV*, 1:72, 228, 2:67; Prentout, Les Etats provinciaux, 2:112–16.

160. Valois, 1: nos. 1559, 2515, 3130, 2: nos. 8539, 9323, 11,541, 13,885, 15,525, 15,639.

161. *IAC, Clermont-Ferrand, fonds de Montferrand*, ed. E. Teilhard de Chardin (Clermont-Ferrand, 1902), 1:33–34, 61, 161–63, 165.

some excuse. Clermont had been loyal during the perilous years; he now had no reason to curtail its privileges. But he did keep a careful eye on the activities of the assemblies. Basse-Auvergne, like other provinces, was visited by numerous commissioners to verify accounts and to report on what they saw. Local inhabitants were also called into service. In 1590 Henry wrote Pierre Durcot, seigneur de la Roussière, a Protestant gentleman who had been in his service prior to his ascension to the throne, to tell him to give his support to the newly appointed governor. Then he added, "And especially you are to attend the assembly of the estates of the province ... in order to propose on my behalf and to put in deliberation what it seems to me to be necessary."[162] Manipulation more than force appears to have been the weapon designated for Basse-Auvergne.

The numerous assemblies between 1594 and 1610 were devoted primarily to trying to reduce royal taxes, to direct crown revenue to local purposes, to prevent the establishment of the gabelle, and to obtain permission to levy taxes to pay the debts the province had incurred. The king continued to set the amount of the annual levy. For example, in 1594 he asked the élection of Basse-Auvergne for 291,000 livres, but the assembly of the towns sought to use from 21,000 to 24,000 livres to redeem several strongholds held by the rebels. Initially they appear to have been unsuccessful, but before the year was out, Henry had allocated an even larger sum to carry on the war in Auvergne. Another victory was achieved when the estates persuaded the king to cancel the arrears of the taille, but the inhabitants of the province must have wished that Clermont had been less loyal to the crown when he imposed a special levy of 120,000 livres on them in order to reimburse the town for advances it had made.[163]

Perhaps the most critical year was 1596. The provincial debt stood at 948,870 livres and the people were poverty stricken, but at first the crown appeared unsympathetic. In August the king's council responded to a lengthy petition from the good towns by forbidding them to tax to pay their debts without the king's permission and limiting the costs of holding the estates. More serious was the refusal to reduce direct taxation on the province beyond an amount that had already been granted. Undaunted the estates pressed their case and in December won a decree halting a levy of 380,243 livres because of the poverty of the people.[164] This victory, coupled with a greater reduction in the taille during the last decade of the reign than was accorded most pays d'élections, suggests that the assembly of the towns was an effective representative of the province. In 1600 Haute- and Basse-Auvergne paid 710,517 livres into the royal treasury in direct taxes. Basse-

162. Henri IV, *Lettres*, 3:206–207. For Roussière see also ibid., 2:393–94, 3:234, 425, 8:335.

163. *IAC, Clermont-Ferrand*, 1:161–63; Valois, 1: nos. 1038, 1052, 1293, 1531, 3003; BN ms. fr. 18,159, fol. 214–14v.

164. AD, Puy-de-Dôme, 4F 145; André Imberdis, *Histoire des guerres religieuses en Auvergne* (Moulins, 1840), 2:474–77. AN, E 1b, fol. 155; *IAC, Clermont-Ferrand*, 1:58–59.

Auvergne won a sharp reduction for 1601, and in 1604 the two provinces contributed a mere 574,708 livres. Only once thereafter in the reign did they turn over more than 600,000 livres to the treasury.[165]

Sully's reduction of the taille, however, was accompanied by an effort to recoup royal losses by instituting the gabelle. The province had purchased exemption from this tax prior to the Wars of Religion, but the eager minister was undeterred by the solemn promises that had been made on this occasion. In 1596 the towns learned of the pending establishment of a grenier à sel in their province. Thoroughly aroused they dispatched one delegation after another to court, but in 1603 Sully emerged victorious, and the gabelle in Basse-Auvergne was turned over to a tax farmer. To soften the blow, Sully allocated part of the anticipated revenue from the salt tax to the province to pay its debts. This enticement ought to have been sufficient to silence opposition because for years the deputies of the third estate had unsuccessfully sought permission to levy a tax in order to meet their obligations. All that they had been able to obtain were decrees protecting the property of their officers from seizure by their creditors until the debts of the province had been verified, a process which took several years. Nevertheless, the good towns knew that the gabelle would fall to a considerable degree on them, while the burden of the taille was overwhelmingly borne by the countryside. Hence they embarked on an extensive program to get rid of the gabelle and to pay their debts by increasing the taille.[166] The first step was to offer something to the king to compensate for the loss of the gabelle, and the second was to find influential persons at court to support their cause. In May 1604 the deputies of the towns assembled and voted to offer the king 120,000 livres in return for being relieved from the gabelle. This action was taken against the advice of the deputy from Montferrand and over the opposition of the plat pays. The deputies then sought the assistance of the count of Auvergne, their governor, and Pierre Fougeux, sieur d'Escures.[167]

The count of Auvergne was the bastard son of Charles IX and Marie Touchet, the mother of Henry's current mistress, Henriette d'Entragues. Auvergne had been intended for the church and had been made grand prior of the Order of Malta and abbot of the important monastery of Chaise-Dieu in Auvergne. However, he was so obviously unsuited for the clerical calling that the pope released him from his vows in 1589 to permit him to embark on a military career. Henry III sought to provide for his future by giving him the counties of Auvergne and Clermont upon Catherine de Medici's death and promised him the governorship of the province. Auvergne immediately sided with Henry IV after his predecessor's assassination, and though only sixteen, he succeeded in saving Sully from possible death or

165. *IAC, Clermont-Ferrand,* 1:36. Mallet, pp. 186–87.

166. *IAC, Clermont-Ferrand,* 1:33–37, 58–66 passim; Valois, 2: nos. 7038, 7147, 7634. AD, Puy-de-Dôme, 4F 145, for 1602 and 1603.

167. AD, Puy-de-Dôme, 4F 145, for 1603 and 1604; *IAC, Clermont-Ferrand,* 1:173.

capture in the battle of Arques by his reckless bravery. Courage, however, was his only virtue. Always short of money, always convinced that he had been inadequately rewarded for his services, he began to plot with Biron as early as 1593 and was later involved in the conspiracies with Savoy and Spain. In 1602 and again in 1604 when he was arrested, he betrayed his accomplices in the hope of winning more lenient treatment. On the first occasion Henry pardoned him and on the second commuted his death sentence to life imprisonment. Auvergne, was, however, freed in 1616, made duke of Angoulême in 1619, and died in 1650, still a contemptible man but a more loyal subject. He had been intelligent enough to learn from his long imprisonment that treason no longer paid.

Henry's letters to Auvergne and to others reveal that he never trusted him, but as the son of a king and the son-in-law of Constable Montmorency, Auvergne was potentially too dangerous to be ignored. During the 1590s Henry sought to keep him loyal through generous presents and hints of greater future rewards. Auvergne's annual pension was a princely 100,000 livres. In 1598 Henry actually told Sully to pay Auvergne before the Swiss mercenaries in order to keep him from stirring up trouble. Such a man was in a position to help the estates if he so desired because prior to his first arrest for treason, Henry was willing to grant him many concessions in the hope of bringing his intrigues to an end. It cannot be proved that the favorable treatment the estates received was due to his efforts, but it can be shown that they sought his services and that he wrangled all he could from them in return.[168]

In 1594 the estates thanked Auvergne and his father-in-law, Constable Montmorency, for their good will. The following January they voted Auvergne 30,000 livres to pay for the costs of the war and to keep his troops out of the province. There was also talk of giving him an additional present. In the spring of 1596 the deputies reminded him of his promise to get rid of the troops and voted him 30,000 livres, but that December they refused to grant a similar sum again on the grounds that they did not have sufficient powers. Probably the countess of Auvergne had acted for her husband on this occasion because it was to her that the deputies conveyed their excuses, but in April 1597 they confronted the governor's lieutenant, who bluntly stated that his master wanted 30,000 livres and had told him to levy the tax. Furthermore Auvergne asked for the right to collect a debt of 72,000 livres that Gévaudan owed the province. This last request was refused, and when the estates met again in June, the governor was somewhat more conciliatory. Finally, in a September meeting the deputies voted Auvergne the 30,000 livres but then agreed to give him the Gévaudan debt which they themselves had been unable to collect instead. In 1603 Auvergne spoke to the king on

168. Henri IV, *Lettres*, 3:586–87, 599–600, 4:437, 767–68, 5:40, 8:806; Valois, 1: nos. 4374, 5469.

behalf of the estates in regard to the salt tax, but his recent treason and his continued flirtation with enemies of the state mitigated any influence he might have had, for Henry had now realized that no amount of concessions would ensure his loyalty. Nevertheless Auvergne, in accordance with a promise he had made, continued to try to further the interests of the estates, no doubt with an eye on a fitting reward, until his second arrest in July 1604.[169]

The sieur d'Escures was a different sort of a man in that he obviously held the confidence of both Henry and Sully. Often he was employed to carry confidential messages between the two, and he was assigned key roles in the arrest of Biron in 1602 and Auvergne in 1604. Perhaps it was during the course of the latter mission that he learned of the problems of the province, or perhaps he became aware of the opportunity that was offered as a result of his travels through the region or from the contact he kept with his native, neighboring Bourbonnais. Whatever the source of his idea, he offered to assist the deputies of the estates in the matter of the gabelle. With their governor in the Bastille, they had no recourse. Escures was promised 6,000 livres on condition that he secure the abolition of the salt tax and an increase in the taille to enable the estates to pay their debts.[170]

During 1604 and 1605, the deputies of the towns won a series of decrees protecting themselves and their agents from their creditors. In one instance the council cancelled a debt that they had incurred in 1589 when they had promised to pay a nobleman to stop plundering the province.[171] An annual increase in the taille of 90,000 livres was also won to provide revenue to pay part of the debts of the province, but the crown persisted in its efforts to establish the salt tax. If all else failed, an assembly of 1605 instructed its deputies to court to have the tax farmed to a native of the province, a petition that was not likely to be received favorably because Sully had already refused to accept the person they had named to administer that part of the salt tax that was to be turned over to them to pay their debts. There was no slackening of the activities of the estates in 1606, for the time had come to reward those who had aided them and the need to continue the battle remained. Nicolas Fayet, a secretary of the Conseil D'Etat, and his nephew were voted presents of 900 livres each for verifying their debts, to which were added three dozen cheeses in return for having performed a similar service for Montferrand. Well might the inhabitants of Auvergne feel that special compensation was in order, for Nicolas Fayet, as an heir of Michel Sublet, sieur d'Heudicourt and intendant of finances, had been in a position to do them untold harm. What favors, if any, he granted we do not

169. AD, Puy-de-Dôme, 4F 145, for 1596, 1597, and 1603; *IAC, Clermont-Ferrand*, 1:33, 37, 59–61, 64–65, 163, 167.

170. Henri IV, *Lettres*, 5:587–89, 593–94, 602, 6:253–55, 278; *IAC, Clermont-Ferrand*, 1:66–67.

171. Valois, 2: nos. 8337, 8338, 8504, 8673, 9651, 9653.

know. Also remembered was one of the king's secretaries and a procureur to the Grand Conseil. The sieur d'Escures asked for the 6,000 livres that had been promised him, but the estates were hesitant, for although an increase in the taille to help pay the debts had been won, the extinction of the salt tax was far from assured. Indeed shortly before he had presented his request, the council had given the creditors of the third estate the right to prosecute in two months if the salt tax was not accepted.[172]

Defeat seemingly came in February 1607 when the crown finally ordered that six greniers à sel be established in Basse-Auvergne and awarded the right to provide the salt for six years to Etienne Blancheteau, an enterprising merchant from Orléans who was one of the largest creditors of the estates. The idea of having a creditor connected with the sale of salt, part of whose proceeds was assigned to acquitting the debt, suggested unusual opportunities for oppression and corruption. Disturbed but undaunted, the third estate invited the nobility and clergy to join them in sending a series of delegations to arrange a settlement of the debt and the revocation of the edict creating the greniers à sel. When the latter effort failed, they tried to prevent the verification of the edict by the Chamber of Accounts. In spite of these efforts the council issued decrees in November 1607, August 1608, and February 1609 ordering that the six greniers à sel be established notwithstanding the opposition of the three estates, and in June 1609 it directed that the Chamber of Accounts immediately verify the edict creating them.[173]

The third estate, aided by the nobility and clergy, was as persistent in its deputations as the council was in its decrees. In 1608 it sought the assistance of Queen Marguerite, Henry's first wife, who had won a suit with the imprisoned count of Auvergne several years before in which she was awarded the counties of Auvergne and Clermont, thereby making her a wealthy property owner in the province. Also contacted was the duke of Bouillon, a notorious troublemaker, but as viscount of Turenne, a large landowner in the region with numerous vassals and clients. Neither magnate was close to the king but both numbered high among those Henry desired to avoid offending unnecessarily. Perhaps it was as a result of their influence that he suddenly reversed himself. On October 24, 1609, the council issued a decree abolishing the greniers à sel and revoking the gabelle on the condition that the province compensate Blancheteau for the losses he would suffer. After a thirteen-year battle the good towns, aided by the nobility and

172. AD, Puy-de-Dôme, 4F 145, for 1606; *IAC, Clermont-Ferrand*, 1:37, 65–67, 72, 175–76, 178; Valois, 2: nos. 10,108, 12,998.

173. Valois, 2: nos. 10,894, 10,927, 11,700–02; 11,708, 11,820, 11,833, 11,835, 11,839, 11,873, 12,357, 13,258, 13,784. *IAC, Clermont-Ferrand*, 1:67–69, 180–81, 183–84. Teilhard de Chardin believed that Blancheteau was the assumed name of the sieur de Flagheac, a long-time creditor of the estates. Ibid.; 1:180. Two decrees of the council, however, prove that they were two different persons and that Blancheteau had acquired the notes against the estates that Flagheac held. Valois, 2: nos. 10, 927, 11,708.

clergy, had finally emerged victorious, and most of the costs of repaying the debt and compensating the crown for the loss of the salt tax had been thrust off on to the plat pays. During the course of the long struggle, they had also won the right to increase the tax levied to support their activities from 6,000 to 12,000 livres.[174]

Basse-Auvergne had been more successful than Normandy in warding off Henry IV and Sully's absolutist policies. Both were provinces in which the élus had already been established, but Basse-Auvergne's third estate, which could be called into session at the whim of the échevins of Clermont, was more active. Another reason for its success was the close cooperation between the estates. Normandy was more democratic than Basse-Auvergne, and the three orders sat together in the meetings, but the nobility and clergy were not sufficiently active to add much strength to delegations sent to court. A third reason was that the good towns of Basse-Auvergne were adept at winning influential friends, while the Normans did not even obtain assistance from their governor. Finally, and perhaps most important, Basse-Auvergne was a poor and troublesome province. The amount of additional money that could be extracted from it was not sufficient to compensate for the cost that would be incurred if it became necessary to suppress a revolt there.

The opposing forces in Haute-Auvergne also patched up their differences in the latter part of 1594, and in January 1595 the deputies from the four towns and provostships assembled in St. Flour in the traditional manner. Further meetings were held in February, May, September, October, and December. So great was the expense of these numerous assemblies that in the last of this series it was decreed that no more than two deputies would be paid from each of the four towns and provostships. Some economy indeed seemed in order. Compensation for the deputies and other expenses for the February meeting in Aurillac came to 829 livres, a significant sum when it is considered that there were five other meetings that same year. Even the nobility who assembled less frequently managed to hold a separate meeting in late October for only 600 livres. In addition, a deputation of the third estate to court cost 14,060 livres. The meetings of the third estate were devoted to such matters as finding ways to suppress the numerous thieves and vagabonds who beset the highways, voting taxes to pay local troops and to support their own activities, and protesting levies designed to benefit the count of Auvergne or the king. Well might they devote their energies to reducing taxes, for they were so high that some nobles were protecting their hard-pressed peasants from tax collectors. A March assembly of the towns and provostship of St. Flour especially signaled out "the subjects" of the viscount d'Estaing for refusing to contribute, and in two undated letters of

174. AD, Puy-de-Dôme, 4F 145, for 1609; *IAC Clermont-Ferrand*, 1:62, 181; Valois, 2: no. 14,538.

about this same period, Henry IV charged that local gentlemen were encouraging peasants not to pay. One wonders if the Marquis de Canillac, the king's own lieutenant in Haute-Auvergne, was not one of the guilty parties as his "subjects" in three parishes were specifically cited for their disobedience.[175]

An assembly of the third estate in May 1596 was followed by ones in December 1596 and in January 1597 in which it was decided to send another deputation to court to plea for lower taxes because of the suffering from the war and the poverty of the people, many of whom were abandoning their homes. They also requested permission to levy 9,000 livres to meet their obligations. To increase their chances of success, the towns voted their newly appointed governor and lieutenant general, Antoine de Roquelaire, 6,000 livres. Roquelaire's efforts on their behalf were assured success on March 19, 1597, when Henry instructed Montmorency to give as favorable a reply to their cahiers as possible because he wanted to give his new governor the means to make himself popular in order to be better obeyed. Eight days after Henry wrote his letter, his council remitted part of the taille. Still not content, the towns dispatched a new deputation to court in April 1598 to plead for lower taxes. Additional meetings were held in that year and in 1599, 1602, and perhaps on other occasions that were also dedicated to persuading the king to tax less and to permit the provincial estates to tax more. A comprehensive decree was issued by the council in March 1602 on these and other matters, but a new round of assemblies was provoked by the issuance of a decree that November creating greniers à sel in Haute-Auvergne.[176]

It was not the creation of the greniers à sel alone that inhabitants objected to but the assigning of the farm provisionally to the gabelles de Languedoc rather than to those of Guyenne which provided dark-colored salt that was considerably cheaper. Several meetings of the third estate of the province were held on this matter in 1603 and at least one in the provostship of St. Flour. Victory was not won by the third estate until the greniers à sel were suppressed in March 1608, and the inhabitants of all but a few parishes were permitted to purchase salt from wherever they pleased. Litigation and appeals continued on behalf of those excluded well into the next reign. During this period there were the usual assemblies, deputations, and requests to highly placed persons for their support. Among those solicited was Henri de Noailles, the recently appointed lieutenant general, who was given an annual stipend of 6,000 livres. An unsuccessful effort was also made

175. AC, St. Flour, ch. 5, art. 3, nos. 6–12, ch. 5, art. 4, nos. 3, 4 (lost); AC, Aurillac, AA 21; BN ms. fr. 10,841, fol. 70v; Henri IV, *Lettres*, 9:128–29, 221. One unnamed town also refused to pay. Ibid., 9:177.

176. AC, St. Flour, ch. 5, art. 3, nos. 13–21; Henri IV, *Lettres*, 4:713–14; BN ms. fr. 18,160, fols. 167v–168; Valois, 2: nos. 7019, 7326.

to get the Court of Aids of Montferrand to intervene on behalf of the parishes excluded in the 1608 edict.[177]

Two other events in Haute-Auvergne might be noted. After the exposure of Biron's conspiracy, Henry ordered Noailles to take possession of the powerful royal château of Carlat because he mistrusted its commander. When Noailles succeeded after employing a complicated stratagem, Henry decided to demolish the structure although it belonged to the crown. To pay for this task he levied a tax of 45,000 livres on Haute-Auvergne. Separate pleas were made to the king to reduce his demands by St. Flour and the other three good towns, but to no avail. Noailles himself was amply reimbursed for his efforts. Unhappy as the third estate must have been at having to pay so large a sum, the alternative to destroying these fortified châteaux was to pay a garrison to keep them from falling into the hands of lawless persons. In 1608 Noailles had to dispatch men to these unguarded châteaux to prevent them from serving as a place of refuge for a band charged with the rape of a local nobleman's daughter.[178]

Almost nothing has survived concerning the activities of the second estates in Haute-Auvergne. We know that the nobility met at Allanche in October 1595 and that some of their number were thought to be discouraging their peasants, or as even Henry's letters said, "their subjects," from paying the taille, but the only known issue that brought them as a class into conflict with the crown was over the question of the ban and arrière-ban.[179] In April 1594, following a precedent set by his predecessor in 1587, Henry in effect imposed a tax on the French nobility in lieu of rendering the military service that was owed him under feudal law. Resistance to this act was especially strong in Auvergne, and the imposition of the levy with an accompanying investigation was delayed by the council in May 1602, probably because of the discovery of Biron's conspiracy, for that restless nobleman and his allies had many clients in the province. The levying of the tax was renewed in March 1604 after Biron's execution and the destruction of Carlat, although the proceeds had been assigned to the count of Auvergne, who had been seriously implicated in the plot. Dissatisfaction on the part of the nobility was also renewed. In June 1605 Noailles wrote Bellièvre saying that he had assembled the nobility at their request and that they had elected a deputy to go to court to ask that the edict be revoked. It was necessary for the good service of the king, he added, that this request be granted because of the serious discontent it was creating among the nobility. His advice does not

177. *Dictionnaire statistique, ou histoire, description et statistique du département du Cantal*, ed. Déribier-du-Châtelet (Aurillac, 1853), 2:101–08; AC Aurillac, AA 21, AA 21bis; AC, St. Flour, ch. 5 art. 4, no. 5 (lost); Valois, 2: nos. 7326, 12,122, 12,260, 13,461, 14,771.

178. *Dictionnaire du Cantal*, 3:39–41; AC, Aurillac, AA 21bis; Valois, 2: nos. 7091, 7834, 9255, 12,276.

179. AC, St. Flour, ch. 5, art. 3, no. 12; Henri IV, *Lettres*, 9:128–29, 221.

seem to have been taken, but even more than in the case of Basse-Auvergne, the emergence of the estates unscathed at the end of Henry's reign may be attributed to the troublesome, rebellious nature of the inhabitants of the region.[180]

The royalists in Forez were so outnumbered that they do not appear to have held assemblies during the peak of the Catholic League. However, after the conversion of Henry IV, they became stronger, and early in 1595 the bailiff was able to summon the three estates to advise on measures to reestablish order. Thereafter separate meetings were held for each of the estates; there were at least nine assemblies of the towns during the remaining fifteen years of Henry's reign.[181] In these meetings the deputies devoted much of their effort to the problems of arrears in taxes, the payment of debts, especially those incurred in reducing the League garrison that had been located in Montbrison, and the dismantling of fortifications. There were the usual protests against new taxes, the usual deputations to court, and the usual willingness, though perhaps somewhat reluctantly given, to contribute toward the governor's company of horse. From the council, on the other hand, came the usual decrees ordering that financial records be made available to and verified by designated royal officials.[182] Exceptional difficulty was encountered controlling the activities of the receivers of the tailles and the élus who quarreled among themselves and exploited the people. Several were imprisoned, but as the reign drew to a close, troubles on this score declined, only to be replaced by others. In June 1609 it was necessary to order that a double lock be placed on the archives at Montbrison with the key to each lock held by a different royal official to prevent the theft of documents needed to resolve a dispute.[183]

The difficulties in administering the unusually large élection of Forez led the crown to issue an edict in November 1597 creating a new élection with its seat at Saint-Étienne. To this élection were assigned 200 of the 406 parishes in Forez. It was to have a complement of twenty-one officers, so

180. *Actes Royaux*, 1: nos. 3955, 4428; Valois, 2: nos. 7024, 8286, 11,984; Noailles to Bellièvre, June 7, 1605, BN ms. fr. 15,900, fol. 636.

181. In addition to the seven meetings cited in Jean-B. Galley, *Les Etats de Forez et les treize villes* (Saint-Etienne, 1914), p. 44, there were assemblies in 1603, 1607, and possibly in other years. Jacques Permezel, *La politique financière de Sully dans la généralité de Lyon* (Lyon, 1935), p. 49; Auguste Bernard, *Histoire de Forez* (Montbrison, 1835), 2:266.

182. AD, Loire, C 32, nos. 26, 27, 29; Permezel, *La politique financière*, p. 19. For decrees on Montbrison see Valois, 1: nos, 2936, 3786, 4906, 2: nos. 6921, 8586, 9444, 12,635; on the verification of accounts, see 1: nos. 3126, 5334, 2: nos. 6429, 6921, 8586, 8699, 9436, 12,028; and on the payment of Forez's debts see 2: nos. 7037, 11,166, 12,635. Montbrison made an unsuccessful effort in 1609 to persuade the other towns to pay part of the debt it had incurred. Galley, *Les Etats de Forez*, pp. 63–64.

183. Valois, 2: nos. 5937, 6417, 8761, 8780, 8792, 8821, 9339, 9602, 9868, 10,011, 10,701, 11,995, 12,132, 12,288, 12,797, 13,172, 13,391, 13,430, 13,921, 14,776, 15,592.

large a number as to suggest that at least one of the crown's motives was to raise money through the sale of offices. The syndic of the third estate quickly obtained the governor's permission to assemble the deputies of the towns. They met at Montbrison on January 19, 1598, in the presence of the bailiff. Included was a representative of the officers of the élection of Forez who were disgruntled at seeing their jurisdiction cut in half. After the syndic had explained the situation, the deputies withdrew from the presence of the royal officials to deliberate. Quickly they reached the conclusion that the syndic should oppose the establishment of the new élection by every means possible because, they charged, the wages, privileges, and exemptions accorded to the new officials would cost annually more than 45,000 livres.[184]

On January 20, the day after the estates met at Montbrison, the Chamber of Accounts in Paris registered the king's edict creating the new élection, but at the same time it took the precaution of asking the treasurers in the Bureau of Finances at Lyons for their opinion. These officials concurred with those at Paris that the vast extent of the élection of Forez made it desirable to divide it in two. In spite of this endorsement, the representatives of the third estate managed to get the offending edict revoked.[185]

The third estate was less fortunate when it assaulted the status of the more privileged inhabitants of the county. Plagued by heavy debts and continual royal demands for funds, the towns met in April 1605 and elected two deputies to go to court to plead that the tax base be expanded to include several categories of persons who, they asserted, were illegally escaping the taille. In spite of the edict of January 1598 revoking ennoblements during the previous twenty years, the names of those thus stripped of their rank had not been returned to the tax rolls. Nobles and clergy, they pleaded, should pay the taille on the nonnoble land they had acquired and children should be taxed when they became fourteen or fifteen years of age rather than when they reached adulthood. When their requests met with little response, the towns renewed their petitions in 1607, this time in conjunction with the third estate of Beaujolais and the plat pays of Lyonnais. This additional pressure brought by the united action of the three provinces led the king's council to seek the advice of royal officials in the généralité. In compliance with their recommendations, the council ruled that the nobles were not obligated to pay the taille on the nonnoble land they held if they exploited it themselves. If they leased the land, the tax was to be paid by the lessee. The decision in regard to the clergy was more favorable to the third estate. Only the patrimony of the church was declared to be tax exempt, and nonnoble ecclesiastics were ruled to be subject to the taille on the land they personally owned. However, the clergy of Forez, Beaujolais, and Lyonnais succeeded in

184. Permezel, *La politique financière*, p. 7; AD, Loire, C 32, no. 27.
185. Permezel, *La politique financière*, pp. 7–8.

blocking the implementation of the ruling. Minors were to be added to the tax rolls when they became eighteen.[186]

Undaunted by their failure to achieve all the goals they had set for themselves in 1605–07, the deputies of the towns turned their attention to the gabelle. Forez was included in the high price tax farm centering on that part of the Rhône valley, but this fact caused no overwhelming concern during the sixteenth century because the enterprising inhabitants found excuses to purchase their salt in neighboring Auvergne, where the price was lower. Sully's reforms, however, led to a tightening of controls, and the inhabitants of Forez were compelled to purchase salt at the appointed places. Between 1601 and 1605 revenue from the farm doubled. In 1608 the syndic of Forez joined with the provost of the merchants of Lyons in an unsuccessful effort to prevent an increase in the tax. The complaints of the good towns against the officers' collecting the gabelle did lead the council to order an investigation.[187] Furthermore they succeeded in obtaining the suppression of some offices in 1606 and in winning permission to levy taxes to support their own activities.[188] If the reign saw the towns make no progress at the expense of the privileged orders or of Sully's reforms, neither did it see them lose any of their privileges.

186. Ibid., pp. 19, 48–53; Galley, *Les Etats de Forez*, pp. 44, 65–67; Valois, 2: nos. 11,232, 11,746, 13,285, 14,519.

187. Permezel, *La politique financière*, pp. 61–64; Valois, 2: nos. 12,815, 13,934.

188. Valois, 2: nos. 10,555, 13,437, 15,270; Galley, *Les Etats de Forez*, pp. 68–69.

II

HENRY IV
AND THE ORIGINS OF ABSOLUTISM

1. HENRY IV AND THE PROVINCIAL ESTATES: A SUMMARY

HENRY IV'S RELATIONS WITH THE PROVINCIAL ESTATES CHANGED DURING THE course of his career, as one might expect. They also varied from one province to another. From the death of his mother in 1572, he had dealt with the estates in his hereditary lands. Here he ever preferred persuasion to force. Whenever possible, he attended the estates because he knew that more money would be forthcoming if he appeared in person. In 1576 the estates of Bigorre refused to take any action until he came to hear their grievances. His far-flung possessions and numerous responsibilities, however, usually made it necessary for him to rely on a governor or other commissioners to treat with the estates. He suggested to these officials how to manage the deputies, praised them if they were successful, and sometimes gave them more tangible rewards (as when he assigned the revenue from two benefices to the governor of Foix who had successfully manipulated the estates in 1581). In the hope of securing a generous subsidy, he unhesitatingly promised to give the estates as favorable replies to their petitions as possible. Even after he was well established on the throne of France, Henry restrained his own demands and protected his earliest subjects from his own officials. He unblushingly permitted Sully to exploit nearly all of France to his profit, but he refused to permit him to become superintendent of finances in Navarre in order to save the inhabitants from his overzealous minister. The one concession he did insist upon was that Catholics be given limited civil and religious rights in Béarn, but this should be considered as a necessary concession to the pope and to Catholics in France and not an attack on Béarnais liberties.

During his first decade as king, Henry's attitude toward the estates in France varied depending on his local strength. When his position was precarious, as it was at first in most of France, he tried to avoid convoking the estates and contented himself with collecting what taxes he could without consent. In 1595 he told Matignon to try to avoid holding the estates of Bordelais, and he let Normandy go as long as three consecutive years without an assembly, but where his position was relatively secure, as in

Dauphiné, his commissioners held the estates regularly from the beginning of his reign. If many taxes were collected there without consent, Lesdiguières was primarily responsible, and the money was spent to satisfy his aspirations or to defray the costs of governing the province, and not to fill the royal treasury in Paris. By 1596 the situation was returning to normal, and the estates resumed their prewar activities. For the next few years there was relative calm. The crown did try to reduce the costs of holding the estates of Basse-Auvergne in August 1596, and there as elsewhere efforts were made to prevent taxation without royal consent, but on the whole the estates seemed well on their way to resuming their prewar status when Sully replaced Bellièvre as Henry's principal adviser in financial matters.

Sully's assault on the provincial estates should probably be dated from Michel de Marillac's unfavorable report on the estates in Guyenne in 1599 and the edict recommended by Jean de Martin in which limitations were placed on their length and the remuneration of those who attended. The estates were forbidden to meet without the king's permission, and ceilings were placed on the amount that they could vote to support their activities. Thus strapped financially the various provincial estates in Guyenne would have difficulty bribing royal officials to support their activities, sending large deputations to court, pursuing the legal cases in which they were often engaged, and carrying on their normal activities. Furthermore they were not allowed to tax to pay the debts they had incurred during the Wars of Religion until their accounts had been verified by royal officials. Even after this was done, Sully only grudgingly permitted the estates to meet their obligations. His motive was probably to ensure that the debts were legitimate and to make certain that the crown had a prior claim on the limited amount that subjects could pay, but by making moneylenders wait for years before they were reimbursed, he must have weakened the credit of the estates.

Sully first revealed that his ultimate goal was to establish élections when he asked the council to install them in the newly conquered and relatively defenseless provinces of Bresse, Bugey, and Gex in February 1601. In January 1603 eight élections were created in Guyenne, and the following year Sully suggested that they be installed in Burgundy. Nothing came of this last proposal, but he did try to increase the representation of the Chamber of Accounts in the Chambre des Elus, the administrative organ of the estates that acted for the parent body during the three-year intervals between its sessions.

The estates of Languedoc, and to a lesser extent those of Burgundy, were threatened in 1604, but the efforts of the crown to spread the system of élections slowed, although there is no reason to doubt that this was Sully's ultimate goal. Several times he frankly said as much to that intrepid deputy from Agen, Julien de Camberfore, sieur de Selves. That he did not complete his design must be attributed largely to the strong resistance his measures encountered in Guyenne. Not until 1609, six years after the élections were created, did the élus function as tax officials throughout the généralité. Nevertheless by the fall of 1607, Sully was prepared to renew his assault on the powerful estates of Languedoc. He began by insisting that the Chamber of Accounts of Montpellier examine the diocesan and municipal tax records and then proceeded the following year to limit the amount that the provincial estates, dioceses, towns, and communities could tax to support their own activities. In November 1608 he created royal receivers for the extraordinary revenue collected in each diocese, and in May 1609 he forbade the estates to send deputations to court without permission. The next step, judging by the pattern that had been followed in Guyenne, would have been the creation of élections, but for the intervention of Montmorency and Ventadour and the approach of war.

Why did Sully seek to create élections? The only time that he mentioned this objective in his memoirs was in a memorandum he prepared for Henry as war approached late in 1609. There, near the end of a list of some sixteen ways in which money could be raised rapidly, was the suggestion that élections be erected in Guyenne, Languedoc, Brittany, and Burgundy. The sale of the resulting offices would undoubtedly yield a tidy sum, but the salaries, perquisites, and privileges of the appointees would cost the crown dearly in the long run. Henry, however, lacked enthusiasm for the idea because of the "great cries" that would be raised from the four provinces.[1]

In emergencies, then Sully might be willing to create élus, like other offices, for the financial return that they would bring, but this was not the reason he insisted on erecting élections in Guyenne. If money had been his motive, he would have permitted the estates of Guyenne to meet and offer to reimburse the élus in return for the abolition of their offices. The crown could retain the proceeds from the sale of the new offices but at the same time escape paying the appointees' salaries after the abolition had taken place. In Sully's mind the stakes were greater. By creating élus he could obtain control of the tax-collecting machinery. Unauthorized taxation by the estates, towns, and communities could be more easily prevented. Repeated edicts against taxation without royal permission had not been enforceable, as is evidenced by the fact that on October 22, 1609, the council had to make still another attempt. Some provincial estates, its members had been informed, had levied taxes without permission and had used the revenue "to make gifts and gratifications without his majesty's knowledge to such persons as it seemed good to them." Such practices were again forbidden, and participants in the estates were told that they would have to

1. Sully, *Mém.*, Michaud, 3:366. Sully included Guyenne on his list although élections had already been created there, an error that is difficult to explain.

pay from their own pockets the amount they gave in unauthorized gratifications. But Sully must have known, as did Gilles de Maupeou, the rapporter
for the decree, that abuses would soon be as prevalent as before.[2]

Furthermore by establishing élections, not only could unauthorized
taxation be reduced but also the crown could impose its will with greater
ease. In Normandy, Auvergne, Forez, Bresse, Bugey, and Gex where there
were élections, the crown decided the amount the élus would collect before
the estates met. The estates might go through the motions of giving consent,
and they could oppose the size of the proposed levy, but these protests were
often ignored, and the taxes were collected anyway. If the estates made too
many difficulties, they could be dispensed with altogether. Such was the fate
of Périgord where the crown refused to permit the estates to meet to elect
new définiteurs after the mandate of the old ones expired at the close of
1604. At this point Périgord ceased to have a duly constituted corporate
body to speak in its name and to act in its interests. There were apparently
no meetings of the estates of the généralité of Guyenne between November
1603 and 1609. In May 1609 the king's council peremptorily told the estates
of Quercy not to meet and declared that the taxes could be levied by the
élus. Elsewhere in Guyenne, the estates continued to function, but, severely
weakened by their loss of the tax-collecting machinery, they seemed destined
to wither away.

If it is clear to us that Sully was determined to reduce the estates to
impotency or destroy them, it was no less apparent to the sieur de Selves of
Agenais, Jean de Souvert of Burgundy, and other representatives of the
estates who had dealings with the powerful minister or his agents. Their
statements that their privileges were threatened were eloquent indeed.

It is more difficult to ascertain Henry IV's role. He wanted money and
was irritated when the estates prevented him from obtaining all he desired.
Like any other strong man, he wished to be obeyed. He was tired of hearing
his subjects prattle about their privileges and told a Burgundian delegation
as much in no uncertain terms. Furthermore Sully could not have established élections in Guyenne over so much opposition without his support.
Yet it is significant that Sully tried to keep the deputations from that
généralité from seeing Henry as though he feared that his greedy, genial
master would succumb to the temptation of accepting a financial offer in
return for abolishing the élus. Then too, one suspects that Henry restrained
Sully from establishing élections in Languedoc, Burgundy, and elsewhere
not because he was opposed to absolutism, but because he saw more clearly
than his arbitrary minister that such an act might lead to a revolt. He
rejected the idea of creating élus in four provinces in 1609 because he knew
that it would cause an outcry. Indeed as war with Spain approached, the

---

2. BN ms. fr. 18,176, fol. 58–58v. There is a copy of the decree in Sully's papers. AN 120,
AP 1, fol. 66v.

estates of Guyenne were permitted to meet once more, and pressure was relaxed on those of Languedoc. Domestic reform was abandoned to facilitate a foreign venture, a choice that was to be made again in the same manner in the following reign, to the detriment of the monarchy.

Henry then was sympathetic with Sully's design, but he restrained him because he saw more clearly the dangers of moving too rapidly. For this reason the estates of Dauphiné, Provence, and Brittany were left unscathed. Sully wanted these and other pays d'états to contribute a larger portion of the taxes, and they were expected to pay the debts their royal master had incurred in regaining their respective provinces and to redeem his domain therein. But other than this, they were permitted to return to the happy situation that they had enjoyed in regard to the monarchy before the Wars of Religion.[3]

In one area Sully did infringe on the privileges of even these estates. In 1599 he was appointed to the newly created post of grand voyer with the responsibility of building and maintaining roads, bridges, and canals throughout the kingdom. Slowly his authority was extended, and by 1605 he was in a position to act effectively. That year the amount spent on transportation facilities jumped from a few thousand livres to over a half million, and from 1607 through 1610 an average of about a million livres was spent annually. Prior to Sully's time, the money that had been devoted to construction and repairs had been furnished by those who used the facilities or by nearby landowners or towns, but under his direction an attempt was made to draw on the resources of the entire kingdom to support the construction of a transportation system based on the needs of the nation as a whole. The result was a major move toward a more centralized administration that brought the crown into conflict with the provincial estates and other local authorities.[4]

Where the provincial estates were weak, as in Normandy, Sully simply ordered that taxes be levied for some specific purpose, such as the construction of a bridge at Rouen, and then spent the money where he pleased despite complaints from the Norman estates. Where the estates were strong, however, serious clashes sometimes occurred because in general such assemblies were much less willing to appropriate money for improved transportation than they were for education or even historical and medical projects. In 1608 Sully forbade the estates of Languedoc to levy any taxes for their own support unless they at the same time collected 18,000 livres to construct a bridge at Toulouse. When the estates of Brittany refused to act on an offer that the crown would pay half the costs for improved transportation if the province would assume responsibility for the remainder, he angrily ordered his agents to make the necessary repairs anyway and pay for

3. David Buisseret, *Sully* (London, 1968), pp. 75–77.
4. Ibid., pp. 81, 105–19.

them by assessing the neighboring parishes, this despite the fact that the estates had not approved the levy. On the whole, however, the strong provincial estates successfully resisted the overzealous minister, and Sully's role as grand voyer is significant because it provides additional examples of his willingness to override the privileges of duly constituted bodies when they prevented him from obtaining his objectives.[5] Well might he tell the English ambassador that "his master had placed him in office to encrease his revenue, and not to deliver justice."[6]

2. Henry IV and the Other Constituted Bodies

Just as Henry IV and Sully launched a limited but nevertheless clearly conceived attack on the estates, they proceeded in like manner against the towns and some of the other duly constituted corporate bodies, although their assult was limited to select localities and institutions in order to avoid serious unrest. During the sixteenth century, the crown continued to grant charters to communities that defined their privileges, and some older towns won increased liberties. It is true that the crown tried to tap the towns' growing wealth and sometimes interfered with their internal activities, but on the whole they held their own until the latter stages of the Wars of Religion when many of them transformed themselves into veritable city-states. To regain their allegiance Henry IV had to recognize their privileges. As a result, by the time he was in a position to consider reorganizing his kingdom, the towns were probably in a stronger position in regard to the crown than at any other period since the close of the Hundred Years War, and they were certainly far more populous and wealthier than they had been then.

The efforts that Henry IV and Sully made to limit the expenditures and audit the accounts of the estates were paralleled by similar attempts in regard to the towns. Municipal officials were not necessarily opposed to having debts audited because the result might be a reduction in the obligations to creditors, but they invariably fought investigations of income and expenditures which were regarded as violations of municipal liberties. However, Sully's motive in tightening his control over municipal finances may have been only to prevent graft and illegal taxation and to ensure greater revenue for the central government. It is more clear that Henry IV's attempts to influence municipal elections were premeditated steps toward absolutism.[7]

5. Ibid., pp. 108, 112–14.

6. *An Historical View of the Negotiations between the Courts of England, France, and Brussels from the Year 1592 to 1617*, ed. Thomas Birch (London, 1749), p. 487.

7. Buisseret, *Sully*, pp. 101–02.

Earlier kings had sometimes interfered in the elections in Paris and a few other strategic localities such as Bordeaux, where the king's lieutenant in Guyenne usually served as mayor, and Bayonne, where the post was often held by the counts of Gramont, but as one authority has said, "The freedom of municipal elections does not appear to have been seriously curtailed before the time of Henry IV."[8] Whenever Henry found an excuse, he reduced the size of the municipal governing body so that he could influence elections more easily and put more pressure on those who were appointed to do his will. Thus in 1595 he replaced the twelve *consuls* of the former Catholic League stronghold of Lyons by a provost of the merchants and four échevins, and in 1597 he used the carelessness of the governing hierarchy of Amiens who had let the Spanish surprise their city to justify reducing the number of échevins from twenty-four to seven. From these seven échevins he himself chose the senior magistrate. A mob in 1602 provided him with the excuse to cut the number of consuls in Limoges from twelve to six and to curtail the suffrage sharply. Another of Henry's practices was to have an urban electorate choose three candidates for mayor, from whose number he appointed one. Nantes, Rennes, and Dijon were subjected to this system. Finally Henry had little hesitation in interfering in the elections in those towns where he made no formal changes in electoral procedure. Poitiers, Marseilles, Paris, Bordeaux, Troyes, and Bayonne all felt his hand.[9]

When a town dispatched deputies to plead its cause before the king's council, they were likely to be subjected to Sully's brutal treatment. On March 29, 1601, a deputy from Lyons reported to his municipal government that any hope for the success of his mission rested upon the kindness of the king because Sully "has either conceived a special hatred against this town or else he treats all the others in a similar fashion. He has dealt us a blow so astonishing that it is unbelievable. The Chancellor [Bellièvre] who listens to us, dares not say a word in the council because Sully has assumed so much authority." When a question concerning custom duties arose, Sully "lost his temper and said that the town of Lyons is worthless to the king. . . . It costs him a hundred thousand *écus* a year. Its inhabitants are mutinous and seditious and do not want to receive the *pancarte*. . . . They have torn it down where it has been posted. . . . The king is no longer obligated to adhere to what he has granted." When an effort was made to answer Sully's charges before the council, he would not listen and shouted that most of the taxes

8. Gaston Zeller, *Les institutions de la France au XVIe siècle* (Paris, 1948), p. 43. Roger Doucet arrived at the same opinion independently. See his *Les institutions de la France au XVIe siècle* (Paris, 1948), 1:362.

9. Jean-H. Mariéjol, *Histoire de France*, ed. Ernest Lavisse (Paris, 1911), 6: pt. 2, 33–35; Robert S. Trullinger, *The Royal Administration of Bretagne under Henri IV, 1598–1610* (Ann Arbor, University Microfilms, 1972), pp. 288–98; Henri IV, *Lettres*, 4:227–28; *Correspondance de la Mairie de Dijon*, ed. Joseph Garnier (Dijon, 1870), 3:101–02.

that had been collected there had been appropriated by those who were in charge of them.[10]

Yet one must not exaggerate the progress that Henry made in obtaining control over the towns. As a whole they remained quite capable of thwarting the royal will by their delaying tactics and in some instances of putting up stout defenses against the royal army, as the following reign was to prove. The pancarte, a 5 percent tax on goods brought into towns, was, for example, a source of constant complaint. It never yielded more than a small fraction of the anticipated revenue, a fact that in itself suggests non-cooperation, and in November 1602 it was abolished. To recover part of his losses Henry increased the taille by 400,000 livres. Once more the towns had succeeded in shifting more of the burden of taxation on to the countryside.[11]

Henry's reconciliation with the Catholic church was too subject to suspicion for him to dare to undermine the position of the Assembly of the Clergy. He did, however, need the financial support of the church. When he assembled the ecclesiastical deputies in Paris early in November 1595, less than a month after he had become reconciled with the pope, he had Bellièvre try to persuade them to renew a contract to furnish financial assistance to the crown for the next ten years and to do something about the arrears that were due from the previous contract. The money the clergy voted for the previous decade had been assigned to pay part of the rentes (the interest the municipal government of Paris owed on money that it had borrowed on its own credit and turned over to the king). Parisian officials were therefore deeply involved in the transaction. For some time the clergy refused to renew the contract until all their grievances had been satisfactorily answered, but in the end a compromise was reached in which they agreed to pay 1.3 million livres per year for ten years in return for favorable responses to many of their demands and the hope that they could make further progress during the forthcoming Assembly of Notables.[12]

In 1600 Henry attempted to extract a special grant of 600,000 livres from the clergy because of his forthcoming marriage and other expenses, but in the end he had to be content with one décime, that is, about half of the amount he requested. Bellièvre and Sully had anticipated that the clergy would give something and had urged Henry to take an active part in the negotiations. By his presence he could obtain more than his servants could

10. *Notes et documents pour servir à l'histoire de Lyon sous le règne d'Henri IV, 1594–1610*, ed. Antoine Péricaud (Lyon, 1845), pp. 174–75.

11. J.-J. Clamageran, *Histoire de l'impôt en France* (Paris, 1868), 2:363–68.

12. *Collection des procès-verbaux des assemblées-générales du clergé de France* (Paris, 1767), 1:555–62, 579–581, 585; A. Chamberland, "Lettre confidentielle de Bellièvre sur le cahier de l'assembleé du clergé de 1595 et réponse inédite du roi au cahier," *Revue Henri IV* 3 (1909–12); 257–74; Louis Serbat, *Les assemblées du clergé de France, 1561–1615* (Paris, 1906), pp. 136–39.

hope to by their own efforts. Nevertheless Henry did not appear before the assembly and contented himself with receiving a deputation.[13]

In 1605 Henry asked the clergy to renew their contract to pay 1.3 million livres per year for another ten years and to give him and his wife special gifts. The town of Paris pointed out to the assembled clergy that they owed 15,075,000 livres in arrears on the rentes. Its spokesmen offered to settle for 5.3 million and later a mere 2.6 million livres, but in the end the king and the clergy joined forces against its pretensions. The clergy renewed the contract and voted Henry 300,000 livres and his wife 100,000 because she had given France a dauphin. In return, the amount they had to pay for the arrears was reduced to 1.2 million livres, or about 8 percent of the sum that the town said that they owed. Perhaps as a salve for their consciences, the clergy then gave 9,000 livres to help complete the construction of the new hôtel de ville in Paris. Only the rentiers could be unhappy at this arrangement. In 1608 Henry again asked the clergy for a special grant of 400,000 livres, and they accorded it to him. Thus, as Henry felt himself more securely seated upon the throne, his aspirations grew from a simple renewal of the ten-year grant to pay part of the rentes of the hôtel de ville at Paris in 1595 to occasional requests for relatively small additional sums, but at no time did he risk offending the clergy in the manner he did many of his other subjects.[14]

One incident reflects the consideration with which Henry and Sully treated the clergy, by whom they were suspect, as opposed to the way they dealt with the provincial estates and the towns. In the course of the Assembly of the Clergy in 1605, a deputation headed by the archbishop of Tours was appointed to visit Sully. Sully received them with "all the kindness and courtesy that they could desire," and when they took their leave he thanked them "with words so courteous that one could imagine nothing more gracious."[15] Perhaps it is suggestive of Sully's reputation for bellicose rudeness that the clerk thought it worthwhile to include these remarks in his journal of the assembly, but it does point to the determination of Henry and even Sully to give no offense to the clergy, although they might try to milk them a little now and then.

If the Catholic church was a source of income to Henry, the Protestants were an expense. Although they made up only 7 or 8 percent of the population, Henry knew that he would have difficulty in mustering sufficient

13. *Collection des procès-verbaux*, 1:669–75; BN ms. fr. 15,894, fols. 365–66v.

14. *Collection des procès-verbaux*, 1:733–49, 792–97; Mariéjol, *Histoire de France*, pp. 56–57; Serbat, *Les assemblées*, pp. 140–43.

15. *Collection des procès-verbaux*, 1:740, 741. Sully could be polite as he demonstrated in his early years in office when he showed deference to his senior colleagues. D. Buisseret and B. Barbiche, "Lettres inédites de Sully à Henri IV et à Villeroy," *Ann.-bul. de la soc. de l'histoire de France, années 1974–1975*, p. 87.

forces to compel their obedience. Therefore when the loyalty of the Protestants became suspect following his conversion to Catholicism, he granted them many concessions in the Edict of Nantes. During the remainder of his reign, however, he attempted to weaken their political organization and to convert their leaders to Catholicism so that they would become less of a threat.

Prior to Henry's conversion to Catholicism, it had seemed as though the elaborate Protestant political organization would cause him little trouble. With their protector as king, they had no need to retain a state within a state, and the Protestant organization at the national level especially withered away through neglect. Henry's reconciliation with the Catholic church, however, completely changed the picture. A few Protestants hoped that he would return to the fold after he had regained his kingdom or dreamed of a union with French Catholics in a trully Gallican church independent of Rome, but the vast majority felt that it was necessary to reconstruct their political organization. In a meeting at Sainte-Foy that began in May 1594, they turned a deaf ear to suggestions that they elect a new protector in the person of the elector of the Palatinate, but they then proceeded to divide France into ten provinces. Each province was to have a council composed of the local dukes and lieutenant generals and from five to seven members elected by the provincial assembly. Among its duties were to provide for the defense of the provinces and to determine the tax that was to be paid by each church. The provincial assemblies were to consist of a noble, a pastor, and a magistrate elected by each colloquy in the jurisdiction. At the summit of this edifice there was to be a general or national assembly consisting of one deputy chosen from each of the provincial assemblies and the Protestant dukes and lieutenant generals. It was thought that the general assembly would meet once or twice a year, but from the spring of 1596 until May 1601 it was in almost continuous session.[16]

The general assembly negotiated the Edict of Nantes by whose terms Protestants were given freedom of conscience, the privilege of worshipping in designated places, the right to hold public office, and other concessions that were to be perpetual. It is the secret provisions related to the edict, however, that were guaranteed for only eight years that concern us most. In them Protestants were permitted to have about a hundred places of security, some of them very strongly fortified. To provide garrisons for these places, Henry promised an annual subsidy not to exceed 540,000 livres. The need to keep such articles secret to avoid arousing the ire of the Catholics is readily understandable, but the eight-year limitation Henry placed upon his prom-

---

16. Emile G. Léonard, *A History of Protestantism*, trans. R. M. Bethell (London, 1967), 2 : 159–67; Léonce Anquez, *Histoire des assemblées politiques des réformés de France, 1573–1622* (Paris, 1859), pp. 60–68.

ise suggests that he intended to do away with that part of the bargain which guaranteed the Protestants an independent political and military existence as soon as possible. Indeed Henry quickly reduced the promised support for the garrisons and displayed considerable reluctance in permitting Protestants to hold political assemblies, but the fact remains that he created, or rather legalized, the existence of a state within a state in France.[17]

In article 83 of the edict, Henry forbade the political assemblies in the provinces to meet, but to persuade the general assembly that had opened in 1596 to disband in 1601, he relaxed this rule and also permitted the Protestants to elect one or two deputies to represent their church at court.[18] There were some precedents for the latter concession, but at this point the practice became standardized. Henry had to permit a general assembly to meet at Sainte-Foy in October 1601 to elect and instruct these deputies, but thereafter he felt strong enough to place additional restraints on the political activities of the Protestants. Only reluctantly did he permit a general assembly to meet at Châtellerault in 1605 to choose new deputies. The conditions he established for this meeting included a limitation on the size of the assembly, the presence of a royal commissioner to ensure that the assembly did nothing except elect the deputies, and the approval of a new procedure for choosing the deputies so that no further political assemblies would be necessary. The destruction of the political assemblies was to coincide with that of the provincial estates of Guyenne, but Henry was too cautious to alarm the Protestants so much that they rebelled. To give them a sense of security while he destroyed their political organization, Henry extended until 1610 the time that they hold the places of security he had granted them in the secret articles related to the Edict of Nantes.[19]

Henry wanted the Protestants to shift the duty of electing their permanent representatives to court to the nonpolitical and less representative synods so as to avoid the necessity of summoning political assemblies for this purpose in the future, but they resisted his efforts. After considerable agitation, they obtained permission to hold another political assembly at Jargeau in October 1608. Here they insisted on empowering their deputies for only two years and on hearing Henry's replies to their cahier before they disbanded. Sully, who informally represented Henry at the meeting, advised that some concessions be made—he was more sympathetic to the desires of the

17. Anquez, *Histoire*, 156–68, 204–05, 498–500. According to Buisseret, *Sully*, p. 84, Henry gave the Protestants about 360,000 livres per year, but this figure presumably included 135,000 livres he contributed for the support of their church.

18. It is listed as article 82 in Isambert, 15:196. Isambert omits article 37 as published in Anquez. Hence there is a discrepancy.

19. Anquez, *Histoire*, pp. 186–87, 207–20, 482; Sully, *Mém.*, Michaud, 3:41–71 passim; Raoul Patry, *Philippe du Plessis-Mornay* (Paris, 1933), pp. 414–16.

Protestants than he was to those of the provincial estates—and in the end they obtained part of what they wanted.[20]

In spite of his efforts, Henry made little or no progress toward weakening the Protestant political organization through these direct attacks, but he also considered two more subtle programs. One was to unite his subjects into a single Gallican church probably through the means of a national church council, but few Protestants had any sympathy for this approach. A second method was to offer rewards to Protestant leaders in return for their conversion. So obsessed was he by the need for religious uniformity that he overlooked the fact that Sully was more useful to him as a loyal Protestant who could check his radical co-religionists, and he sought to win him to Catholicism by a promise of the constableship of France, the governorship of Normandy, and the hand of one of his bastard daughters for his son. Sully, a man of inordinate ambition, must have been tempted, but though tolerant of the beliefs of others, his personal religious convictions proved too strong. The same was true of most other Protestants at this time, and their number actually increased during the first quarter of the seventeenth century. Nevertheless Henry's idea of distributing favors to converts was to become one of the principal means used in the following reign to deprive the Protestant masses of their natural leaders. For lesser converts the assembly of the Catholic clergy in 1605–06 announced its willingness to provide pensions and other gifts.[21]

During the first decade of his reign Henry often clashed with the parlements over their delays in registering his edicts on taxation, the creation of offices, alienations of the royal domain, and other matters, nearly all of which were designed to produce money to carry on the war. Once the need for financial expedients lessened, he had to insist on such controversial measures as the registration of the Edict of Nantes and a decree permitting the Jesuits to return to France. Henry often employed lettres de jussion and occasionally lits de justice to enforce his will, but at no time does he appear to have attempted to undermine the position of his courts. This does not mean that he did not lecture their deputies in as harsh a manner as he and Sully did those of the provincial estates and the towns. In 1597 when the Parlement of Paris balked at his decisions to create a president and ten new councillors in each presidial seat to obtain money to pay his troops, he lost

20. Anquez, *Histoire*, pp. 220–25; Sully, *Mém.*, Michaud, 3:249–50, 253–54. Patry, *Philippe du Plessis-Mornay*, p. 453.

21. Léonard, *History of Protestantism*, 2:360–61, 373–75; D. Buisseret and B. Barbiche, "Les convictions religieuses de Sully," *BEC* 121 (1963): 223–30. A third method of securing conversions was urged upon Henry by the papal see. It consisted of refusing to give offices, honors, and other awards to Protestants, but Henry does not appear to have considered these suggestions seriously. *Correspondance du nonce en France, Innocenzo del Bufalo, 1601–1604*, ed. Bernard Barbiche (Rome, 1964), pp. 139–44, 599, 659.

his temper and repeatedly shouted, "I am the king! I will be obeyed!"[22] Nevertheless it required a lit de justice to get the edict registered. When a dozen lettres de jussion did not suffice to make the Parlement of Bordeaux register a tax edict, he snapped at their deputy: "You say that my people are oppressed; well! It is you and your company that oppresses them! O! wicked company! Well! Who wins his case at Bordeaux? It is he who has the biggest purse! None of my parlements are worth anything, but you are the worst of all.... Oh! wicked company! I know all of you. I am a Gascon like you.... It is only necessary to be a councillor to be rich immediately."[23]

Sully did not trust the officials of his financial courts any more than he did other persons who handled the king's finances, and he was careful to see that their records were examined. He and Henry dreamed of subordinating all the provincial Chambers of Accounts to the one at Paris and of centralizing the fiscal administration by treating the provincial Bureau of Finances in a similar manner. However, although Henry once publicly voiced these intentions, no serious effort was made to put them into effect.[24]

Thus Henry and Sully undermined, or sought to undermine, selected estates and towns. They also tried to destroy the Protestant political assembly, but they were content to extract a little more money from its Catholic counterpart. They regarded the parlements as nuisances that sometimes obstructed legislation, but they took no steps to alter their institutional status, probably because they believed that an occasional tongue-lashing was enough to remind them of their duty. Financial officials were mostly thieves, but careful supervision could prevent their worse abuses. Only the instruments of self-government felt their heavy hand, for they alone appeared able to offer physical resistance to their authority.

3. HENRY IV, THE SWORD, AND THE ROBE

Henry and Sully realized that it would not be enough to weaken the peoples' instruments of self-government to secure a more absolutist regime. It was also necessary to break the independent power of the class they most feared: the nobility of the sword. During the sixteenth century the position of the nobility had steadily improved. The demographic expansion plus new creations had increased their numbers. Rising food prices, the purchase of peasant and church lands, and the development of the sharecropping system had strengthened their economic position, and the emergence of the patron-client relationship had enabled them to replace the decaying feudal system

22. Albert Chamberland, *Le conflict de 1597 entre Henri IV et le Parlement de Paris* (Paris, 1904), p. 35.

23. Mariéjol, *Histoire de France*, 6: pt. 2, 30.

24. Buisseret, *Sully*, pp. 92–95.

with a new, more flexible means to dominate society and government. Magnates had come to control the king's council, and their clients were placed in the sovereign courts, bureaucracy, army, and church. As governors the magnates had become the most important single factor in the provinces where they maintained their position through the aid they received from their clients who served in the estates, the local courts, the bureaucracy, and their guards.[25] Henry could not have won his throne without their assistance, but they made him pay handsomely for their services. Once in power he was constantly troubled by noble conspiracies. To sit securely and peaceably on his throne, he saw that it was necessary to alter the social as well as the institutional structure of his kingdom.

As in his dealings with institutions Henry proceeded cautiously, but his plan was obvious: he would place more reliance on the men of the robe and less on those of the sword. The senior magistrates had generally been uncomfortable with the Catholic League and had flocked to his standard once he had become a Catholic without waiting for the generous bribes the nobility had insisted upon. Furthermore they had no power base of their own from which to launch an assault upon the crown. Hence Henry named them in greater numbers to his council than he did the nobility. Sully, of course, became his principal adviser, and he was careful to solicit the opinions of Montmorency and a few other magnates; nevertheless his appointments reveal a marked shift toward the robe, toward men like Villeroy and Jeannin.[26] Especially noteworthy was the appointment of eighty-eight members of the Parlement of Paris to high administrative positions between 1596 and 1622.[27]

Henry also broke the monopoly the nobility had held on the high positions in the church. Of the 144 Frenchmen Francis I had nominated to be bishops between 1516 and 1547, 123 had been nobles and 6 had been nonnobles (the social origins of the remainder is unknown). On the other hand, of the 92 Frenchmen Henry nominated, 35 came from the third estate and at least 17 of the 57 who were nobles were from families that had not long held the honor.[28]

Henry's actions are significant in themselves and also suggestive of his desire to alter the social balance in his kingdom, but the basis of the power of the nobility lay less in their personal presence in the council and in high

---

25. That the governors increased their authority during the last half of the sixteenth century is the thesis of Robert R. Harding, *Anatomy of a Power Elite: The Provincial Governors of Early Modern France* (New Haven, 1978).

26. Roland Mousnier, *Le conseil du roi de Louis XII à la Révolution* (Paris, 1970), p. 10.

27. Mark L. Cummings, *The Long Robe and the Scepter: A Quantitative Study of the Parlement of Paris and the French Monarchy in the Early Seventeenth Century* (Ann Arbor, University Microfilms, 1974), p. 166.

28. J. M. Hayden, "The Social Origins of the French Episcopacy at the Beginning of the Seventeenth Century," *French Historical Studies* 10 (1977): 27–40.

ecclesiastical preferments than in the patron-client relationship around which their order was organized. Therefore he and Sully took steps that undermined this form of social alignment. In December 1604, after over two years of debate within his council, Henry issued an edict known as the *paulette*, or *droit annuel*, which provided that nearly all royal officials could resign or bequeath their positions to whomever they pleased in return for an annual payment of a sixtieth part of the value of their office. Henry thus made his already venal, semihereditary bureaucracy hereditary. Bellièvre had put forth persuasive arguments against this move. By making offices hereditary, he insisted, deserving people would be denied positions, the quality of the bureaucracy would be lowered, hope for reducing its size would cease, and royal control would be reduced because its members would no longer be subject to dismissal or hopeful for advancement. His well-reasoned predictions should have carried the day if Henry and Sully had looked on the paulette only as a money-raising measure as they pretended. In addition, they almost certainly anticipated that it would weaken the influence of the high nobility in the bureaucracy.[29]

Henry IV, like his predecessors, had long been concerned about the number of royal officials who either owed their position to great nobles or had entered their service after their appointment to public office. In 1596 he had tried to persuade the first president of the Parlement of Paris to support an effort to obtain a declaration from the Assembly of Notables that royal officials should not become involved in the affairs of the princes, and in the following year he had issued a decree forbidding royal officials to accept positions in their houses.[30] Later, in 1599, Gilles de Maupeou, a close associate of Sully, was dispatched to Brittany to reform the Chamber of Accounts. In the edict that resulted, Henry forbade officers of the chamber "to take any office, salary, pension, or gift from princes, seigneurs, and other persons, or to undertake any mission or solicitation in their behalf on pain of being deprived of their offices and arbitrarily fined." Furthermore, when they accepted their positions, they were to "take an oath to observe the contents of the above."[31]

Both Henry and Sully must have known, however, that royal orders could not halt long-standing and profitable practices; they could only make the practitioners less blatant. After considerable hesitation, therefore, Henry

---

29. In his *La vénalité des offices sous Henri IV et Louis XIII*, 2d ed. (Paris, 1971), pp. 594–605, Roland Mousnier argues that Henry and Sully instituted the paulette for financial reasons only. For the reasons why I believe that the patron-client system was also involved, see my *Bellièvre, Sully, and the Assembly of Notables of 1596*, *Transactions of the American Philosophical Society* 64 (Philadelphia, 1974), pp. 28–30, and "Henry IV and Guyenne: A Study Concerning the Origins of Royal Absolutism" *French Historical Studies* 4 (1966): 365–67.

30. Major, *Bellièvre*, pp. 9, 19, 24.

31. Hyacynthe de Fourmont, *Histoire de la Chambre des Comptes de Bretagne* (Paris, 1854), p. 148.

disregarded Bellièvre's objections and approved the paulette. What he anticipated gaining by his decision was probably a lessening of the influence of the magnates because in the future his officers would no longer be indebted to them for their current positions or look to them for future promotions. Existing ties might die slowly, but in the long run the bureaucracy would be his, or at least it would not be the magnates'.

Henry was probably concerned over whether he could control the new hereditary bureaucracy. Bellièvre had warned him that he could not, and a Parisian diarist shared the same fears, a fact that suggests that many ordinary citizens were of this opinion.[32] Perhaps it was for this reason that Henry limited his concession to a period of nine years. Officers would thus know that if they failed to cooperate, the paulette might not be renewed. Furthermore Henry, and more certainly Sully, had a contempt for the men of the robe, and they may have blamed part of the sovereign courts' resistance to their measures to the backing they received from the magnates and the estates. Remove the magnates' influence from the bureaucracy and undermine the estates. Then the spineless lawyers and bureaucrats would become more amenable to the royal will, whether their positions were hereditary or not.

My conclusion is mere conjecture. We have no contemporary evidence of why Henry and Sully acted as they did. We only know that Henry was concerned about the patron-client relationship and that only an overriding consideration would have caused Sully to advocate a measure that would undermine his goal to include more efficient, loyal nobles like himself in the government.[33] The avowed purpose of the paulette was to increase revenue and this was certainly a factor, but it is improbable that it was enough of one because by the time Henry issued the edict in 1604, the budget was more than balanced, and a surplus was being stored in the Bastille. The above hypothesis can be supported by the fact that at some later date Sully told Richelieu that the purpose of the paulette was to reduce the magnates' influence in the bureaucracy, and the usually well-informed Jacques-Auguste de Thou believed that this was a factor.[34] Whatever their motives, by establishing the paulette, Henry and Sully contributed to a momentous change whose antecedents stretched far back into the past and whose culmination was not to be reached until long after their deaths; it was the substitution of a nobility of the robe and of public functions for the nobility of the sword as the class that governed the nation. The new nobility was hereditary, but it was less of a closed caste than most historians have thought. Both before the paulette and between 1604 and 1622, about three-

32. Pierre de l'Estoile, *Mémoires-journaux*, ed. Brunet et al. (Paris, 1889), 8 : 199.
33. Buisseret, *Sully*, pp. 175–77.
34. Major, *Bellièvre*, pp. 29–30.

fourths of the officers in the Parlement of Paris who died or resigned were replaced by nonrelatives. And the turnover became more rapid. Before 1604 only 17.2 percent of the judges served for fewer than nine years, but between 1604 and 1622 51.4 percent did so.[35]

The infiltration of the magnates' clients into the officer corps constituted but one aspect of the threat that overpowerful subjects posed to Henry IV. One danger was that Mayenne, as chief of the Catholic League, would succeed in negotiating a settlement in the name of all his supporters. Peace could be restored more rapidly and at less expense in this fashion, but Mayenne would enjoy in the restored kingdom the position of patron or factional chief of a substantial part of the French nobility. As such he would constitute an intolerable threat to the monarchy. Hence Henry sought to detach the lesser League leaders one by one until the point was reached in which Mayenne could speak only for his immediate family and clients. In March 1594 Henry criticized Sully for not quickly concluding arrangements for the submission of the seigneur de Villars who held a large part of Normandy. In doing so he pointed out that Sully had always advised him to follow the practice Louis XI used in the War of the Public Good of separating his opponents by appealing to their self-interest. This was what he, Henry, was trying to do now because he preferred to spend twice as much dealing separately with each individual than to achieve the same results "in a general treaty with a single chief."[36] In July the following year when Mayenne's price for his submission seemed exorbitant, Henry complained that "such demands are very suspicious and make me believe that the duke of Mayenne wishes to remain a chief of party in order to have the means to agitate again when he wishes. I do not want this in my kingdom and I hope with God's help to prevent it."[37] Finally Henry was successful and peace was restored under conditions which left Mayenne less of a threat than some more dynamic but less prominent former leaders of the League.

The return of peace did not remove the necessity to have officials to maintain order and administer the provinces. Henry continued to use governors or lieutenant generals for this purpose, and he chose them from the ranks of the high nobility or from men like Lesdiguières and Ornano who had rendered distinguished service during the late wars and who, as in the case of the former, had built up such strong positions in their provinces that they could not be easily ousted. Perhaps more than any of his predecessors, however, Henry used special officials to implement his will. Some were maître des requêtes or royal councillors; others were councillors in Parlement or treasurers in the Bureau of Finances in various généralités.

35. Cummings, *Long Robe*, pp. 145, 252.
36. Henri IV, *Lettres*, 4:110.
37. Ibid., 385.

To them should be added the lieutenants Sully sent out in his capacity of grand voyer and grand master of the artillery who were more active than even the agents of the king. Some of these men were given commissions with wide powers and remained in one region for several years. Others were given specific tasks, such as to audit accounts, reform the estates, construct or repair transportation facilities, or supervise the farming of the salt tax in a given region. They were clearly the ancestors of the future intendants, but no one considered them rivals of the governors at this time. Their presence might arouse protests, especially if their task was to examine accounts, but much less attention was paid to them than to the local governor. The low position they were assumed to occupy is suggested by the fact that they rarely shared significantly in the largesse of the estates.[38]

Henry did try to curb the worst offenses of his governors and military commanders. Through his council he issued repeated edicts during the Wars of Religion forbidding them to seize his revenue and to levy taxes without his permission, but as late as 1598 Sully had to persuade a timorous council to halt a tax of some 180,000 livres which the powerful, ill-tempered duke of Epernon had imposed on his government on his own authority. With the restoration of peace and under Sully's vigorous administration, the number of such abuses was reduced and the magnates were denied one source of income. Henry was not guilty, however, of leaving them to their own resources. During the quieter years of his reign, he devoted about 15 percent of his budget to pensions, and there were other forms of largesse as well.[39]

It apparently never occurred to Henry to increase the size of his army so that he could impose his will on his people. Indeed as soon as his war with the League and Spain had ended, he drastically reduced the number of men who were under arms. In Brittany, for example, there were a dozen garrisons in 1599 whose combined strength totaled only 400 men, this despite the fact that the Bretons were among the most provincially minded people in France, and the bulk of them had recognized Henry as king only the year before. By 1608 even this paltry figure had been reduced to 300 men. To strengthen his control over the few troops he did have, Henry reduced the appointive powers of the colonel general of the infantry. It is

38. D. Buisseret, "A Stage in the Development of the French *Intendants*: The Reign of Henri IV," *Historical Journal* 9 (1966): 27–38; Buisseret, *Sully*, p. 101; Doucet, *Les institutions de la France*, 1:422–36. The often-cited letter in which Henry IV assigned Bellièvre, his commissioner to Lyons, responsibility for justice, police, and finance and limited Ornano to military matters was exceptional. Lyons had just returned to its allegiance, Bellièvre was an unusually trusted adviser with special knowledge of the situation there, and Ornano's primary post was that of lieutenant general in Dauphiné. Furthermore as a Corsican adventurer without a large French following, he was in no position to challenge Henry's authority. Henri IV, *Lettres*, 9:398–400; Raymond F. Kierstead, *Pomponne de Bellièvre* (Evanston, 1968), pp. 78–80. For a general treatment that illustrates the superior position the governors enjoyed in regard to the intendants, see Harding, *Anatomy*, pp. 191–99.

39. Major, *Bellièvre*, p. 8; Mallet, pp. 192–93.

probable that he intended to let this position and that of constable remain vacant when the current occupants died.[40]

The one important area in which military changes were actually made that may have contributed to the rise of absolutism was in artillery. In 1599 Sully was appointed grand master of this important arm, and he was soon making full use of his new post. Most of his plans were directed toward being prepared for foreign wars, and it was largely due to his efforts that campaigns against Savoy and Sedan were terminated so quickly. He also had a political motive: to keep artillery out of the hands of potential rebels. In 1605 Henry declared that "to us alone belongs the right to possess artillery," but Sully had long since begun to implement this policy.[41] Supplies of balls and powder were kept in arsenals near the frontier, but the bulk of the cannon was retained in Paris under Sully's watchful eye. From here they could be dispatched to the nearby northeast frontier in case of need. To further this plan Sully did his best to make his guns more mobile. One reason that Biron's conspiracy failed so miserably was that Sully had withdrawn the artillery from his government of Burgundy and had horses and men ready in Paris and Lyons to bring the royal guns into action if the situation so required. In 1603 Ornano assured Henry that cannon could be quietly withdrawn from Catholic towns and châteaux in Guyenne, and he noted, perhaps disapprovingly, that those in Protestant strongholds were not to be touched. On other occasions, the local authorities made difficulties, but usually to no avail. It was not by the expensive process of creating a large army that Henry planned to impose his will but rather by removing the capacity of his subjects to offer effective resistance against his limited forces.[42]

Too much significance has been attached to the destruction of the châteaux-forts after the Wars of Religion. Very few of them had the thick, low, wide-angle bastions necessary to withstand artillery fire and to mount guns to keep the enemy at bay. They were no threat to an army equipped with artillery and therefore no danger to the monarchy itself. However a château-fort that fell into the hands of malcontents or brigands could serve as a base for murder, rape, and pillage, especially because local officials who were without artillery had difficulty mounting effective sieges. In 1599, for example, brigands occupied the fort of Sanson in Vivarais and used it as a base to exact ransoms from the countryside, and a more romantic episode took place in Haute-Auvergne.[43]

40. Trullinger, *Royal Administration*, pp. 323–25; Mariejol, *Histoire de France*, 6: pt. 2, 28–29; Richelieu, *Mém.*, SHF, 1:47–48.

41. Buisseret, *Sully*, p. 153.

42. Ibid., pp. 149–61; *AHG*, 14:403; Buisseret, "Stage in the Development of the French *Intendants*," pp. 35–36; M. Baudot, "L'enquête de Sully sur l'artillerie en 1604," *Bul. philologique et historique (jusqu'à 1610) du comité des travaux historiques et scientifiques* (1963): 930–38.

43. *IAD Haute-Garonne, sér. C*, ed. Ad. Baudouin (Toulouse, 1903), 2:153; Valois, 2: no. 12,276.

Here the sieur de la Volpilière asked the sieur de Fontanges for his young daughter and heir's hand in marriage. When Fontanges refused, the deeply enamored noble raised a small force. Then, in connivance with Madame de Fontanges, he abducted the girl in July 1607 and took both mother and daughter to the château of Pierrefort, which he had previously seized. Fontanges rallied his friends and relatives and laid siege to Pierrefort. The governor of Haute-Auvergne took the precaution of garrisoning three other châteaux which he thought that Volpilière might occupy. Unfortunately for the irate father, Pierrefort was too well fortified to succumb to his efforts. Henry sent artillery, but when Fontanges appealed for financial assistance because his funds were exhausted, Henry turned the matter over to Sully and Sillery to determine whether he should contribute. Evidently the answer was affirmative, for soon 300 royal troops were participating in the action. However, when word came that friends of Volpilière were assembling to try to raise the siege, most of this little army went to disperse them. Seizing this opportunity, Volpilière and his men cut their way through the thinly stretched lines and escaped, leaving several dead and one of their number a prisoner. The latter was hanged in person, and Volpilière and his more fortunate companions were hanged in absentia. Madame de Fontanges was confined to a convent for two years, and her dowry was given to her husband to compensate him for his losses. In 1614 or 1615 Volpilière made another attempt to carry off the heiress, but this time he was unsuccessful. In 1616 she married Louis de Scorailles, with whose aid she became the great-great-grandmother of a mistress of Louis XIV.[44]

The moral of this tale is that there were too many poorly guarded châteaux in Auvergne, and for that matter in all of France. Either adequate garrisons had to be maintained in them to protect them from the likes of the sieur de Volpilière, or they had to be dismantled. The French populace did not have to wait until 1607 to be taught this fact; they learned it early in the Wars of Religion. In the Estates General of 1588 the nobility asked that owners of fortified places guard them more carefully, and the other estates petitioned for their demolition. In 1590 the royalist estates of Burgundy told one noble lady to drive the thieves from her châteaux who were plundering the countryside and asked that some fortresses be dismantled. In 1593 the League estates of Burgundy forbade anyone to construct fortifications or make cannon, and they renewed an earlier injunction that proprietors of châteaux must guard them at their own cost or dismantle them. Thus whether royalist or Leaguer, whether clergyman, noble, burgher, or peasant, Frenchmen wanted the châteaux guarded or dismantled. The provincial

---

44. *Dictionnaire statistique, ou histoire, description et statistique du département du Cantal*, ed. Déribier-du-Châtelet (Aurillac, 1857), 5:26–27; Valois, 2: no. 12,276; Henri IV, *Lettres*, 7:339–40.

estates frequently moved more rapidly in this direction than the crown did and the only debate was over who should pay the costs of demolition and of compensating the owners.[45]

The efforts of the crown to halt the practice of dueling should not be regarded as an attempt to weaken the nobility; rather they were designed to preserve members of that class from self-destruction. During the Estates General of 1588 the nobles themselves asked that the death penalty be imposed on duelists. In April 1602 Henry IV published an edict forbidding anyone to issue a challenge, accept a challenge, or serve as a second in a duel. Soldier that he was, however, he found one excuse or another to pardon those who disobeyed his decree. Little wonder he had to issue another edict on the same subject in June 1609 in which he admitted that his earlier attempt to curb this form of violence had failed. This time he attempted to find a judicial means to settle affairs of honor, and among the possible punishments for infraction of his rule were loss of office, pension, and revenue. A nobleman, it seems, could more properly fear such penalties than the loss of his life. The diarist, L'Estoile, estimated with considerable exaggeration that between 1588 and 1608 7,000 or 8,000 gentlemen lost their lives in duels, but as if to compensate, he could report in 1610 that two gentlemen of the king's guard were executed for this offense. At last Henry had caught up with what one suspects was the view of a majority of the noblemen of France.[46]

One of Sully's activities that certainly contributed to the strengthening of the monarchy was his successful effort to make it financially solvent. In 1596 expenses were three times as large as income. By 1600 the budget was balanced, and by 1610 a surplus of 15 million livres had been amassed, a third of which was safely locked in the Bastille. Furthermore the foreign and domestic debts had been largely liquidated, and steps had been taken to redeem the domain by 1625. The last was being accomplished by letting financiers exploit it for up to sixteen years in return for paying what was due to the mortgagees or by appropriations made by the provincial estates. The interest rate on the rentes had been reduced, and the principal was slowly being repaid. The taille, which fell so heavily on the peasantry, had been cut substantially between 1598 and 1600 and was reduced another half-million livres during the first decade of the seventeenth century. To compensate Sully shifted more of the burden to the towns by increasing indirect taxes by

45. *Recueil des cahiers généraux des trois ordres aux États-généraux*, ed. Lalourcé and Duval (Paris, 1789), 3:55, 143, 148, 228; *IAD, Côte-d'Or, sér. C*, ed. Joseph Garnier (Dijon, 1886), 3:60, 123.

46. *Recueil des cahiers*, 3:143; Isambert, 15:266, 351–58; *Lettres inédites du roi Henri IV au chancelier de Bellièvre, 1603*, ed. Eugène Halphen (Paris, 1883), pp. 53–54, 58; *Lettres inédites du roi Henri IV au chancelier de Bellièvre, 1605*, ed. Eugène Halphen (Paris, 1880), p. 19; Henri IV, *Lettres*, 7:713, 727, 733–34, 737–38, 9:17–18, 98–99. L'Estoile, *Mémoires-Journaux*, 9:277, 10:214–15.

about 3.5 million livres during this decade leaving the crown with a net increase in annual revenue of about 2 million livres. While making these improvements in the crown's financial situation, Sully had been able to give substantial sums to Dutch and lesser amounts to other Protestant continental allies to ensure their continued independence, and he had embarked on an unusually ambitious effort to improve the French transportation system. Furthermore, the restoration of peace, and perhaps to some extent the economic policies of the crown, had led to growing prosperity. These accomplishments lend some justification to Henry's being entitled "le grand" during this period and require that Sully be ranked as one of the greatest ministers who served the Bourbon kings.[47]

More controversial are the steps that Henry and Sully took to establish an absolute state. The provincial estates, towns, Protestant political assemblies, and to a lesser extent the sovereign courts had come under attack. But except for destroying the estates of Périgord, establishing the élus in Guyenne, Bresse, Bugey, and Gex, and interfering in some municipal elections, they made little headway toward undermining the duly constituted corporate bodies that stood in the way of an unimpeded exercise of royal authority, but they did enough to make their goals apparent and to alienate many influential groups. The establishment of a hereditary bureaucracy weakened the influence of the magnates, but it strengthened the capacity of royal officials to resist the crown. Contemporaries clearly recognized the evils of the system, and it was unpopular in many circles. Thus in spite of Henry's great accomplishments, there was intense dissatisfaction in many circles when he was assassinated. With his death the question became one of what direction the inevitable reaction would take and how far it would go.[48]

47. Buisseret, *Sully*, pp. 74–86, 89–91. See also Roland Mousnier's less flattering description in *The Assassination of Henry IV*, trans. J. Spencer (New York, 1973), pp. 187–99. For the domain, see Jeanne Petit, *L'Assemblée des Notables de 1626–1627* (Paris, 1936), pp. 95–96.

48. Mousnier, *Assassination*, has brilliantly underlined the widespread dissatisfaction with Henry IV's rule. However, his study should not be permitted to cause one to lose sight of Henry's positive accomplishments, which were also recognized in his day.

12

THE REPRIEVE, 1610–1620

WHEN HENRY IV WAS ASSASSINATED ON MAY 14, 1610, HE LEFT AS HIS HEIR A child who had not yet celebrated his ninth birthday. A regency was clearly necessary. Tradition assigned this post to the queen mother, Marie de Medici, and her supporters acted quickly to install her in this office before Condé and Soissons, the two most important princes of the blood, who were then absent from Paris, could take any action to share in her authority. Maria was then about thirty-six years old. The daughter of a grand duke of Tuscany and an Austrian Habsburg, she inherited her physical traits from her mother. Tall blonde, and handsome until she added the countless pounds that Rubens was to paint, she had proved a satisfactory wife to Henry in one key respect. In less than ten years of marriage she had borne him six children, including two sons who were to survive to manhood. On the other hand, she was jealous, quarrelsome, and stupid. She loved power because it placed her in the center of things and provided the money to support her extravagances, but she had little concept of how to govern and had to follow the directions of her advisers.

The magnates flocked to court with their numerous clients to render homage to their new king and to see what profit they could win in the new state of affairs. Marie admitted them to an enlarged council but retained Henry's four principal advisers—Sully, Brûlart de Sillery, Jeannin, and Villeroy—in an inner council which continued to exercise the primary role in the governance of the kingdom. She had little love for Sully, but she recognized his financial ability and anticipated that his presence in the inner council would give assurance to the Huguenots. It was necessary to have a good fiscal administration to keep the money flowing from the provinces to Paris so the court rather than officials in the country could profit from royal taxes. However, Sully made the mistake of trying to curtail the exploitation of the treasury in his usual overbearing manner. In one instance when Maria insisted on spending 400,000 livres without telling him why, he could only write in his ledger beside the sum, "I don't know what this entry is all about."[1]

Sully also quarreled with Villeroy over foreign affairs. He recognized the

1. David Buisseret, *Sully* (London, 1968), p. 54.

wisdom of not pursuing Henry's aggressive anti-Habsburg policy during a minority, but he vigorously opposed Villeroy's efforts to make a Spanish alliance cemented by a double marriage, one between Louis XIII and a Spanish princess and the other between the heir to the Spanish throne and one of Louis's sisters. Villeroy had no difficulty drawing Soissons and Bouillon, long numbered among Sully's enemies, into a plan to remove him from the court. Condé and Concini, an Italian high in Maria's favor, lent their adherence. Finally, on January 26, 1611, Sully resigned from his post of superintendent of finances rather than exercise that important office in accordance with the desires of the dominant clique at court. Probably he considered himself so essential that he would be recalled on his own terms, but although the young king expressed regret at his departure, he never employed his father's most valued servant after he had reached his majority.[2]

Sully's departure left Villeroy the undisputed leader of the inner council. He was united with Brûlart de Sillery by ties of marriage, and Jeannin, who became the principal fiscal official, was cooperative. For over fifty years Villeroy had served the crown, for the most part as secretary for foreign affairs, but now at sixty-seven he was to have the dominant voice in domestic matters as well. He had been a close friend of Bellièvre and shared many of his views, but when the now-deceased chancellor had obstinately refused to seal edicts in response to Henry's orders, he had used his influence to have the seals given to Brûlart de Sillery, who was now his close ally. Like Bellièvre he believed that the provincial estates, municipal governments, and other duly constituted bodies derived their authority from the king and should serve as instruments of his policy. For this reason he had no objection to using them when the situation warranted. This emphasis on royal authority should not be interpreted as meaning that Villeroy was an advocate of absolutism. He believed that kings were bound by their own laws in theory and forced to take into consideration the aspirations of their more powerful subjects in practice. When he learned that the emperor had seized some church property in Strasbourg, he wrote: "Our kings are not accustomed to using such means. They confine their authority and power *within the limits of the customary laws which they themselves made and established* for the conservation and protection of their peoples, from which they deviate unwillingly. And we have seen that every time that they have freed themselves from them, they have suffered for it."[3]

In 1611 Villeroy prepared a memorandum for Marie de Medici in which he faced the realities of governing during a minority. In his view France was still a personal rather than a bureaucratic monarchy in which nearly

2. Berthold Zeller, *La minorité de Louis XIII: Marie de Médicis et Sully* (Paris, 1892), pp. 173–78, 210–26.

3. Edmund H. Dickerman, *Bellièvre and Villeroy* (Providence, 1971), p. 49. Dickerman added the italics. This book contains a useful summary of Villeroy's ideas until the death of Henry IV.

everything depended upon the king's ability to isolate and to placate the magnates, whom he regarded as the most important forces in the kingdom. Villeroy began by saying that those who formed leagues against the sovereign should be punished, but then he quickly added that "in as much as it is difficult and dangerous to chastise the magnates, the queen must use the following means to weaken them."[4] First, he urged that Condé be prevented from assuming a position of authority in the council and from making alliances with the other magnates. The magnates should be kept divided by playing on their mutual jealousies, and the nobility should be placated by pensions. Ties should be established with the princes' ministers and favorites and with others who could prevent them from executing their evil designs. In direct opposition to the tactics later used by Louis XIV, Villeroy suggested that the magnates (except Condé) be sent to their individual governments so that they would have more difficulty in forming alliances than if they remained at court. In the provinces their activities could be watched by the Parlements, their lieutenants, and others whom the king could depend on. Negotiations should be commenced with the Huguenots to ascertain their designs, and care should be taken to prevent them from joining Condé. Pensions should be given to influential seigneurs in the province, and they should be forbidden to follow the princes. Requests that princes made for their clients should be refused, and these clients should be directed to address themselves directly to the queen mother so that she would receive credit for any favors that were granted. Agents should be placed in the princes' entourages to report on their activities, and the governors of citadels and towns should be won to her cause in provinces whose governors were united against her service. A check should be made to ascertain whether the commanders of the Swiss guards and the various cavalry units were loyal. The royal guards and cavalry companies should be enlarged—not to discourage revolts but to provide employment for the nobility. Thus Villeroy sought to keep the magnates divided and to isolate the prince of Condé who as first prince of the blood had some claims to being named lieutenant general of the kingdom. Every effort was to be made to use the crown's patronage to build up a large clientele and to make the clients of the princes beholden directly to the queen mother for any favors they received.

Absent from Villeroy's reasoning was any fear of the other elements of the population. "The disease is not, thank God, with the people of the country or of the towns, or with the Parlements, the ecclesiastics, or all the nobility."[5] Such persons, he implied, could be counted on remaining loyal

---

4. Salvo Mastellone, *La Reggenza di Maria de' Medici* (Florence, 1962), p. 229. He prints the entire avis on pp. 229–34; Joseph Nouaillac, *Villeroy, secrétaire d'Etat et ministre de Charles XI, Henry III et Henry IV* (Paris 1909), pp. 521–29.

5. Mastellone, *La Reggenza*, p. 233; Nouillac, *Villeroy*, p. 527

provided that they were left to enjoy their traditional privileges without undue royal interference and without increases in taxation.

Marie de Medici did not wait to receive Villeroy's memorandum before implementing some of his ideas. Henry IV had distributed an average of 3 million livres a year in gifts and pensions, about an eighth of his entire revenue, but Marie increased the amount to 4.7 million livres in 1610 and to between 6.74 million and 7.31 million livres annually from 1611 to 1614. She also increased her household expenses substantially after 1611, and it took about 100,000 livres more per year to support the household of the child king than it had done his father in spite of his wenching and gambling. Much of these increases should be attributed to Marie's extravagances, but part of this money must have found its way into the hands of the court aristocracy. Mindful of the need to avoid causing unrest among the populace, Marie left taxes as they were and even made a few concessions, such as cancelling the arrears in the taille for the years prior to 1603.[6] The inevitable result was an annual deficit that was probably larger than the official figures suggest because all the dispensations of cash in hand may not have been recorded. The difference between the receipts and expenses was met from the treasure that Henry and Sully had accumulated. By the close of 1614 little was left of a sum that has been estimated as large as 20 million livres.[7]

Villeroy had been fearful that the Protestants might become involved in the magnates' plots and was therefore anxious to preserve Henry's religious settlement, staunch Catholic though he was. The Protestants nevertheless became alarmed at seeing France draw closer to Spain. With Sully's departure from court, they no longer had a member of their faith in the inner council of the government. It was with growing alarm that their deputies assembled at Saumur in the spring and summer of 1611 to elect new agents to represent them at court. Amid the intrigues of the Protestant magnates who attended, the deputies sought further concessions from the crown, but Marie de Medici would do no more than extend the time they could hold the places of security for another five years and to promise to continue to provide financial support. Dissatisfied with so short a guarantee and fearful of the future, the Protestants tightened their political organization. They decided to interpose a new organization between the national political assembly and the provincial ones. Under the new arrangement, a provincial council that felt that the local Protestants were endangered could call upon the councils of neighboring provinces to send deputies to a meeting known as the assembly of the circle to determine what course of action to

6. J. Michael Hayden, *France and the Estates General of 1614* (Cambridge, 1974), pp. 220–21. See also Mallet, pp. 193, 218–19, 226; J.-J. Clamageran, *Histoire de l'impôt en France* (Paris, 1868), 2: 405.

7. R. Doucet, "Les finances de la France en 1614," *Revue d'histoire économique et sociale* 18 (1930): 143. Hayden's figure of 15 million is more likely. See p. 21.

take. This step proved important because in most parts of France, the Protestants were so outnumbered that they were anxious to avoid military confrontation with the government. Under these circumstances, the circle assembly provided an opportunity for the Protestants of a region in which they were strong to organize their defense without directly involving their co-religionists elsewhere.[8]

The assembly of Saumur underlined the bitter jealousy that existed between the Protestant magnates, a jealousy that Marie de Medici did her best to exploit in order to lessen the threat from that quarter. In April 1612 she went to the length of forbidding any more political assemblies. The Protestants responded by turning a synod that met at Privas into a political meeting and sought to reconcile the Protestant magnates. Meanwhile the duke of Rohan, who was rapidly emerging as the ablest and most sincere of the younger Protestant chiefs, took steps to strengthen his control over Saint-Jean-d'Angély, an important place of security in the southeast. Marie threatened to use force, but the Protestants countered by holding a meeting of the circle of the western provinces at La Rochelle. After some hesitation Marie chose to negotiate. In return for various concessions, including the right to hold political meetings, Rohan and his fellow Protestants submitted. When Condé revolted in 1614, they refused to participate as if to show that they would remain faithful subjects so long as they were permitted to retain their religious freedom guaranteed by their status of being a state within a state. Thus Marie de Medici's regency ended in a stalemate on the Protestant question.[9]

The Catholic clergy proved much less troublesome but not very generous. Their deputies, who assembled in Paris in August 1610 to audit the accounts of their financial officials, seized the opportunity to ask the regency to cancel the 400,000 livres they had voted Henry IV in 1608. Marie reduced the amount to 300,000 livres but had to appeal to the clergy when they met again in 1612 actually to pay this sum.[10]

In general, Marie sought to retain the status quo in dealing with the towns. In May 1610 Dijon was told to elect three candidates for mayor from whom the king would choose one, just as Henry had directed in June 1608, although Parlement had not registered the decree. Pleas from the deputies of the town, however, led the crown to restore the practice of having the inhabitants choose their own mayor the following year. Bordeaux, where the kings had long appointed the mayor, was less fortunate, and Marie, using

8. Zeller, *La minorité*, pp. 279–93; Jack A. Clarke, *Huguenot Warrior: The Life and Times of Henri de Rohan* (The Hague, 1966), pp. 31–39; Léonce Anquez, *Histoire des assemblées politiques des réformés de France, 1573–1622* (Paris, 1859), pp. 229–50; John Viénot, *Histoire de la Réforme française de l'Édit de Nantes à sa révocation* (Paris, 1934), pp. 139–47.

9. Anquez, *Histoire*, p. 250–64; Clarke, *Huguenot Warrior*, pp. 39–54.

10. *Collection des procès-verbaux des assemblées-générales du clergé de France* (Paris, 1768), 2:5–6, 34–35.

the excuse that conspiracies were being hatched in the town, began to interfere in the election of the jurats as well.[11]

The royal officials proved to be a more difficult problem. At first the government made a modest step in a direction which Bellièvre would have approved. Some offices were suppressed, and an attempt was made to reform the paulette. As a result, there was a decline in the revenue from the sale of offices and growing discontent in the bureaucracy and sovereign courts. This led the government to restore the paulette as it had existed under Henry IV, but lesser nobles who had hoped to obtain offices under the new system were angered and turned more toward the magnates. Thus the very thing that Villeroy had sought to prevent began to take place. By January 1614 Condé was ready to turn from conspiracy to open revolt. To his side came the dukes of Nevers, Bouillon, Longueville, and Mayenne, the son of the League chief, and many of their clients.[12]

Villeroy's advice had not prevented an insurrection, but he had not altogether failed. Some of the magnates remained loyal, and the Protestants, towns, bureaucracy, and the mass of the nobility lent Condé little or no assistance. To rally and retain support, Marie de Medici addressed a letter to all the Parlements, governors, and towns in the kingdom on February 13, 1614, in which she justified the conduct of her government and announced her intention to convoke "some leaders of all the orders and estates in each province in this kingdom in order to have a notable assembly...."[13] Condé countered with a manifesto on February 19 in which he cited all the unpopular acts of the government, including the immense gifts granted to unworthy persons, the proposed Spanish marriages, and the high cost of offices which denied many deserving persons access to them. As a remedy he urged that the Estates General be convoked within three months.[14]

Villeroy may have at first advised that the government quell the revolt before Condé had time to muster his forces, but by March he had returned to his customary caution. On the tenth of that month he addressed another memorandum to the queen mother in which he admitted that the government was momentarily in a strong position because most of the magnates, governors, sovereign courts, royal officials, and towns were loyal, but he argued that the outcome of a trial of strength was so uncertain that it was advisable to make handsome gifts to Condé and his supporters. To minimize the danger that they would win additional support, he recommended that the government renew the promises that it had made to the Protestants and summon the Estates General to undertake a general reformation of the

11. *Correspondance de la mairie de Dijon*, ed. Joseph Garnier (Dijon, 1870), 3:113–14, 118–22; *AHG*, 14:462–65, 484–85.

12. Roland Mousnier, *La vénalité des offices sous Henri IV et Louis XIII*, 2d ed. (Paris, 1971), pp. 253–54, 258–59, 607–08.

13. *Mercure François* (Paris 1617), 3 (1614): 311.

14. Ibid., pp. 317–27.

kingdom in which such matters as the retrenchment of venality of offices and the abolition of the paulette would be considered.[15]

In his memorandum of 1611 Villeroy had revealed his fear of the magnates with their numerous clients, especially if they won the support of the Protestants. In that of 1614 he exposed the weakness of the crown during a minority. He was probably overly cautious, but it is not surprising that he should have been. The royal army was small and the crown still had little control over the magnates, Protestants, and duly constituted bodies. It was still possible that Condé might win further support from these groups. Henry IV had only pointed the way toward absolutism; much more needed to be done. In a minority those close to the crown could only hope to balance the various factions against each other and dispense favors in an open-handed fashion until the young king could personally assume the reins of government.

Marie followed Villeroy's advice, and by the terms of the Treaty of Sainte-Menehould, May 1614, she gave Amboise to Condé along with 450,000 livres. His allies also received generous rewards. On February 22, Marie had had to withdraw half of the 5 million livres Henry and Sully had stored in the Bastille, and by August it was all gone. Furthermore, she had borrowed 600,000 livres and had been unable to pay the rentes in full. The hoard that her son had inherited had been dissipated, but bloody civil wars had been avoided.[16]

2. THE ESTATES GENERAL AND THE ASSEMBLY OF NOTABLES

As part of the agreement with Condé, Marie convoked the Estates General. She probably had no objection to doing so. In December 1610 when Condé had agitated for a meeting, she had offered no opposition because she thought that she could turn it to her advantage. Condé had raised the issue again in April 1613, but it was Marie herself who first suggested holding the Estates General in 1614 in letters written from February 12 to 14. Finally, on February 27, in answer to Condé's belated demand that the Estates General be held, she declared that it had always been her intention to have such a meeting at the end of her regency. This should come as no surprise, for Villeroy and most other Renaissance statesmen approved of assemblies provided that they were held under circumstances favorable to the crown. To make certain that this would be the case, Marie embarked on a tour of the western provinces with her son to quell discontent and to make certain

---

15. J. Nouaillac, "Avis de Villeroy à la reine Marie de Médicis, 10 mars 1614, *"Revue Henri IV* 2 (1907–08): 79–89.

16. L. Batiffol, "Le trésor de la Bastille de 1605 à 1611,"*Revue Henri IV 3 (1909): 209;* Clamageran, *Histoire de l'impôt,* 2:410.

that deputies were elected who were favorable to her cause.[17] Rohan warned
Condé that the queen mother would control the estates because "those on
whom you count will abandon your cause." "Fear and hope are the two
great factors which influence the members of these assemblies; you are
neither in a position to promise them much or to frighten them."[18] Condé
appears to have arrived at the same conclusion, for he declared that it would
be unnecessary to hold the Estates General, but Marie, confident, persisted
in her plan. She held a lit de justice in which Louis, now in his fourteenth
year, was declared to have reached his majority. He in turn named her his
chief of council, and together they participated in the opening of the estates
in Paris on October 27.[19]

Marie's confidence proved justified. Condé soon found that he had very
little influence in the estates, but Marie herself had to watch the deliberations carefully to be certain that the deputies did not unite behind a
common program that would carry such moral force that it would be
difficult for her to reject it. Early in the session the clergy proposed to the
other two orders that when they were in agreement on a matter of general
interest, they should immediately submit a joint petition to the king so that
he could respond before their departure. If this were done, the lengthy
cahiers each estate had submitted in previous meetings just before returning
to their homes would be transformed into individual "bills" approved by the
three "houses" and submitted to the king in council for immediate action.
Marie and her advisers saw the danger and summoned deputies from each
of the estates to inform them that the traditional procedures would be
followed. Opposition to the clergy's proposal had already appeared in the
third estate where numerous Gallicans thought that it was a trick to win
their cooperation for securing the publication of the decrees of the Council of
Trent and the establishment of the inquisition in France. Under these
circumstances they readily accepted Marie's decision. Another possible
danger the Estates General posed for the crown passed, and thereafter when
the three estates dealt with controversial problems, they often had difficulty
reaching agreement.[20]

The first important clash occurred over the related questions of venality of
offices and the paulette. Since the institution of the latter, the price of offices

17. Zeller, *La minorité*, pp. 157, 161–67; Berthold Zeller, *La minorité de Louis XIII; Marie de Médicis et Villeroy* (Paris, 1897), pp. 116–17, 180, 185, 194–202, 237–55. *Mercure François* 3 (1614): 311, 330–31; Hayden, *France and the Estates General*, pp. 62–63.

18. Clarke, *Huguenot Warrior*, p. 52.

19. Georges Picot, *Histoire des Etats généraux*, 2d ed. (Paris, 1888), 4:177–81; Zeller, *Marie de Médicis et Villeroy*, pp. 256–58, esp. 281–82.

20. *Recueil de pièces originales et authentiques, concernant la tenue des Etats-Généraux*, ed. Lalourcé and Duval (Paris, 1789), 6:89–98, 7:64–66, 8:32–35; *Des Etats Généraux et autres assemblées nationales*, ed. Charles J. Mayer (Paris, 1789), 16: pt. 1, 133–36, 141–45; Hayden, *France and the Estates General*, pp. 112–13; Roland Mousnier, *The Assassination of Henry IV*, trans, J.Spencer (New York, 1973), pp. 268–69.

had skyrocketed because by making them hereditary, the danger that premature death would lead to the loss of the investment had been removed. The cost of a councilorship in the Parlement of Paris, for example, increased sixfold between 1606 and 1617. The nobility regarded offices as their due and saw no reason to pay inflated prices for them even when they could afford to do so. Hence they asked that many positions be reserved wholly or in part for their order and that steps be taken to abolish the paulette. The clergy concurred, thereby putting the deputies of the third estate in a difficult position. Most of them had been elected in bailiwick assemblies in which the burgher and the deputy of the village were the most numerous elements. Both opposed venality and had often instructed their deputations to the Estates General to have the practice abolished. In many instances, however, they had chosen royal officials to represent them because they were usually the best-known local notables and were more willing to attend than busy merchants and farmers who had their own affairs to look after. As a result, many deputies of the third estate were caught in a position in which their mandates made it necessary for them to assist the nobility and clergy in their effort to abolish venality, but to do so would transform their offices from a form of property into salaried positions.[21]

To escape from this dilemma, the deputies of the third estate coupled their request for the abolition of venality with a plea that the taille be reduced by 4 million livres. Since the acceptance of the two proposals would cost the crown 5.6 million livres annually, they recommended that pensions be cut by a comparable amount. As this figure was about the size of the budget for pensions, acceptance of the proposal would mean the virtual abolition of this valuable addition to the nobles' income. The nobles, therefore, insisted that the proposals be treated separately, although they were willing to accept a reduction in the amount spent on pensions. A bitter quarrel ensued that was carried on in pamphlets as well as in the debates of the estates. As we have seen, Villeroy had recommended that the nobles be placated on the matter of the offices before the estates met. It is not surprising, therefore, that on March 24, after the formal closing of the estates, the chancellor informed those deputies who were still in Paris that the king would reduce pensions and suppress the paulette and venality of offices.

Preliminary moves against the paulette had already led to strong remonstrances from the sovereign courts. The reaction of the members of the Parlement of Paris to this blow that confirmed their worse suspicions was rapid. On March 28 they invited the princes, dukes, and officers of the crown to meet with them to discuss affairs of state. The king forbade the meeting, but agitation in the sovereign courts continued. Condé, instead of

---

21. For the Estates General of 1614, see Hayden, *France and the Estates General*, pp. 98–173; Mousnier, *The Assassination*, pp. 261–80; and Pierre Blet, *Le clergé de France et la monarchie* (Rome, 1959), 1:3–125.

expressing satisfaction at the abolition of venality, fraternized with the judges, for he saw in them an instrument to assist his drive to control the government. Since no reasonable concessions would appease Condé, the king's advisers decided to counter this threat by satisfying the bureaucracy. On May 13 they postponed the abolition of venality until January 1, 1618, on the grounds that on several previous occasions the crown had promised to continue the paulette through December 1617. In making their decision, the king's advisers were also motivated by the fact that it would be difficult to replace the income from the sale of offices that would be lost, especially as the third estate had balked at the idea of replacing it by an increase in the salt tax.[22]

The second quarrel was between the deputies of the clergy and those of the third estate. The latter attributed the assassination of Henry IV largely to Jesuit and other ultramontane theorists who stressed the ultimate authority of the pope and justified tyrannicide. To counter this position the third proposed as the first article of its cahier that the king promulgate in the estates a fundamental law stating that since he "holds his crown from God alone, there is no power whatever on earth, whether spiritual or temporal, which has any rights over his kingdom, or which is able to take it away from the sacred person of its kings, or to release or absolve their subjects from the allegiance and obedience they owe the monarch, for whatever cause or pretext.... The contrary view, namely that it is permissible to kill or depose our kings, to rise up against them, to shake off the yoke of obedience to them for any reason whatsoever, is impious, detestable, opposed to the truth and to the established state of France which depends directly on God alone."[23]

In response to this proposal, Cardinal Perron made a famous speech in the chamber of the third estate in which he accepted the proposition that kings were not vassals of the pope and were responsible only to God for their administration of temporal affairs. He also condemned the doctrine of tyrannicide, but he refused to concur in the belief that subjects were not justified in rebelling if a king violated his oath to live and die as a Catholic or sought to introduce an alien doctrine into his kingdom. If such a situation arose, the church could absolve subjects from their oath of allegiance. Perron chided the deputies of the third estate for interfering in matters of faith, and the clergy, aided by the nobility, begged the king to forbid them to do so.

Mousnier has argued that the three estates "relinquished all power into the King's hands. They had recourse to royal absolutism and unanimously affirmed the King's undisputed authority." It was they "who ensured the triumph of royal absolutism in France."[24] Such statements are misleading. Undoubtedly the three estates had had enough of tyrannicide and rebellion,

22. Mousnier, *La vénalité*, pp. 608–27.
23. Mousnier, *The Assassination*, p. 382.
24. Ibid., p. 280.

but only the third had been willing to reject religion as a possible justification for revolt. It is perhaps significant that within the third estate the
strongest opposition to the article came from Guyenne, the government that
had felt Henry's hand most heavily.[25] More important, one should not take
statements such as that of the third estate too literally. Men who took up
arms in that day rarely thought of themselves as rebels. They nearly always
proclaimed that they acted to save the king from evil advisers who were
upsetting the established order. The Parlement of Paris endorsed the article
of the third estate, but its members resisted the king whenever they saw fit
and provided the leadership in the early stages of the Fronde. Earlier some
of the provincial Parlements were stirring up discontent. When the king's
council considered what to do about the offending article, it was Condé who
gave it his support.[26] His motive was no doubt to ingratiate himself with the
Parlement of Paris, but he evidently did not think that approval of the
article would serve as a condemnation of his rebellion just before the estates
had met or would stand in the way of his taking up arms again in the near
future. He could always claim that he acted for the good of king and country
and probably longed for a statement from Parlement justifying his right to
do so by virtue of his being the first prince of the blood.

The attitude of the king's council is also of interest. Instead of endorsing
the article of the third estate, it did everything in its power to squelch it. If it
is true that the third estate was asking for an absolute regime, then one must
say that the crown rejected its proposal. What happened was that the
deputies at the Estates General missed another opportunity to establish an
assembly that could influence the conduct of the government at the national
level, but in failing, they did not create absolutism. Rather they left the
relationship unchanged. The struggle between the apostles of absolutism and
the proponents of self-government was to take place at the provincial and
local level where it had raged during the reign of Henry IV.

The cahiers of the estates leave no doubt of the deputies' position. The
nobility requested that their order and the clergy be permitted to meet in
each province once every three years to elect syndics to look after their
respective affairs. They apparently thought that the third estate already had
this privilege. If this article had been implemented, each estate would have
been organized on a corporate basis in every province in the kingdom with a
permanent elected official to defend its interests. The élus, the nobles argued,
should be suppressed throughout France. Presumably at the request of the
deputies from Guyenne, they asked that the three estates in each seneschalsy
in that government be permitted to meet just as they did in Rouergue,
Comminges, and Quercy. Henry had extinguished the estates of Périgord,
and elsewhere in Guyenne only the third estate participated regularly in

25. *Recueil de pièces originales*, 8:86–87.
26. Mousnier, *The Assassination*, pp. 277–78.

assemblies. This situation, which was also true in Auvergne and some other parts of France, evidently caused concern because the nobles urged that the third estate not be permitted to levy any taxes except those for the king without their consent and that of the local clergy. To ensure the independence of the provincial and local estates, the nobles also requested that judicial officers not be permitted to attend unless the bailiff or seneschal could not be present. If this situation arose, the role of the lieutenant of the bailiwick was to be limited to reading the royal letter and making known the king's intentions.[27]

The deputies of the third estate asked that the Estates General be convoked every ten years, but clearly they were more concerned with the local level. They urged that municipal officials be freely elected, a reference no doubt to Henry and his governors' interference in such matters. They were also anxious that local institutions be granted authority to levy taxes to support their activities without having to go to the trouble and expense of obtaining letters from the crown.[28] "Each seneschalsy and diocese," they argued, should be permitted "to impose upon itself for its affairs by the general consent and deliberation of the deputies an amount up to 3000 *livres* and that episcopal and presidial towns be permitted to impose for their affairs with the advice and consent of their inhabitants 1500 *livres*, other royal towns 600 *livres*, small towns 300 *livres*, and parishes 50 *livres*."[29] The clergy, already so well organized at the diocesan and national level, made no such requests.

One of the most interesting facets of the cahiers is the attitude the nobility displayed concerning the patron-client relationship. Instead of defending or at least ignoring the system, they made proposals that would have undermined it had they been implemented. For example, to prevent magnates from using royal patronage to enlarge their number of clients, they requested "that no pensions, offices, or other gifts be given in the future through the intercession of the princes and seigneurs of your kingdom so that those who have them will be bound entirely to your majesty."[30] To prevent magnates from using their own resources to expand their influence into the bureaucracy, they asked that royal officials be forbidden to receive pensions and other presents from them. Judicial officers ought to be specially forbidden to become involved in the magnates' affairs because it would divert them from rendering justice.[31]

It seems clear that most of the deputies of the nobility preferred to be

27. *Recueil des cahiers généraux des trois ordres aux Etats-Généraux*, ed. Lalourcé and Duval (Paris, 1789), 4: 172, 223, 226–27, 268. For a general treatment of the cahiers of the three estates see Hayden, *France and the Estates General*, pp. 174–97.

28. *Recueil des cahiers*, 4:273, 429–34, 454–55.

29. Ibid., pp. 432–33.

30. Ibid., p. 192.

31. Ibid., pp. 213, 228.

beholden directly to the king for any favors they might receive. To have to bind themselves to a prince to receive a royal office or a pension might lead to their being required to follow their patron along the dangerous road toward rebellion. It should be borne in mind that the great magnates themselves did not sit in the estates. Those who served belonged to the leading local families. Many were bailiffs, officers in the army, gentlemen of the king's chamber or members of his household, councillors in the Conseil d'Etat, and the like. They were not, then, potential dispensers of patronage on a large scale, but they were either already beneficiaries of the royal largesse or they were sufficiently prominent that they could reasonably hope to become so. Their cahiers reveal that it lay within the power of the king to assume direct control over royal patronage, bypass the magnates, and dispense his favors directly to them. They in turn would become his majesty's loyal clients and hold the countryside in his obedience. It is strange that so many years were to elapse before this was done on a large scale.[32]

In general, then, the deputies of 1614 were tired of civil wars and violence and of the patron-client relationship that had contributed to the unrest. If these attitudes played into the hands of the absolutists, the deputies' general dissatisfaction with the royal government and their desire for more provincial and local self-government pointed in the opposite direction. The question now became one of to what extent the crown would implement their desires in these and other matters, including the demands for lower taxes, reduced expenses, and general administrative reforms.

Marie did nothing. It would have been difficult to reduce taxes, but many of the requests of the estates would have cost the crown nothing to implement. Probably she and her advisers were too busy with court intrigues and the forthcoming Spanish marriages to devote their energies to such matters. Their failure to act proved costly. The Parlement of Paris was not placated by the decree of May 13, 1615, postponing the abolition of the paulette until January 1618. On May 22 it boldly assumed a political role by demanding that many of the reforms advocated by the estates be enacted. Condé profited by the failure of the crown to act on the proposals of the estates to issue a manifesto in August, and a month later he once more raised the banner of revolt. This time the Protestants in Languedoc, Guyenne, and Poitou lent their assistance. Once more Villeroy counseled negotiations and once more, this time in May 1616, Condé made peace in return for huge gifts for himself and his fellow nobles, but little enough for his Protestant allies who were fast learning the wisdom of not tying their fortunes to the magnates.[33]

That spring and summer Villeroy and the other leading advisers of Henry

32. For the composition of the second estate, see J. R. Major, *The Deputies to the Estates General of Renaissance France* (Madison, 1960), pp. 137–38.

33. Jean-H. Mariéjol, *Histoire de France*, ed. E. Lavisse (Paris, 1911), 6: pt. 2, 179–85.

IV were dismissed. They were all in their seventies, but the main reason for their downfall was not their age but the desire of Concini, Marie's Italian favorite, to have men in the ministry who were more devoted to his service. Claude Barbin, the intendant of Marie's household, assumed responsibility for finances in May. Able and determined, he became the principal figure in the new government and during his short ministry gave finances the firm management that it had lacked since Sully's day. Claude Mangot, the first president of the Parlement of Bordeaux, became first a secretary and then in November, keeper of the seals. At the same time Armand du Plessis, bishop of Luçon, and future cardinal of Richelieu, was made secretary for foreign affairs and war.

The new ministers did not have to wait for the appointment of Richelieu to embark on a bolder course than their predecessors. On September 1 they had Condé arrested, perhaps in response to information brought by Sully. The dukes of Nevers, Mayenne, Bouillon, and other allies of Condé raised the standard of revolt, but this time instead of negotiating, the government dispatched three armies in their direction. Unfortunately the new ministers neglected to note the growing animosity of the neglected young king, now in his sixteenth year, and the influence that Charles d'Albret, seigneur de Luynes, his falconer, exercised over him. Encouraged by Luynes and others, Louis had Concini murdered on April 24, 1617. Barbin and his ministers were dismissed, and Marie de Medici lost her leading role in the government. Luynes became the new favorite, and Villeroy was recalled with the other aging ministers of Henry IV. The magnates, who had professed to be fighting to rid France of the foreign favorite, seized the opportunity to make peace, though without such generous gifts as before.[34]

The problems that confronted Villeroy and his colleagues when they returned to office were identical to those they faced before they were ousted except that the time that had elapsed made their solution more imperative. The cahiers of the deputies to the Estates General of 1614 still had not been acted upon. Failure to do so gave the magnates the excuse to rebel in the name of reform. This was especially true because in May 1616 Condé had been promised that an edict based on the cahiers would be published within three months. Then there was the paulette which was scheduled to expire at the end of the year to the chagrin of the royal officials. If this were permitted to happen, revenue from the sale of offices would decline at a time when expenditures were already exceeding ordinary revenue by from 5 million to 7 million livres per year.[35]

Villeroy left no memorandums advising Luynes what to do, but we can assume with reasonable confidence that he wanted to placate the nobility

34. Ibid., pp. 185–94. Gabriel Hanotaux, *Histoire du Cardinal de Richelieu* (Paris, 1899), 2:129–99; Berthold Zeller, *Louis XIII, Marie de Médicis, Richelieu ministre* (Paris, 1899).

35. Picot, *Histoire des Etats généraux*, 4:254; Mallet, p. 226.

and at the same time satisfy one of the principal requests of all three estates by abolishing the paulette, especially since the king had promised to do so after closing the Estates General. He may have also recalled the prediction that Bellièvre had made in 1602 that if the paulette were established, it would weaken the king's authority. The recent effort of the Parlement of Paris to expand its role from making remonstrances concerning royal edicts to summoning the magnates to a meeting to instigate a general political reformation suggested that his former colleague had been an all-too-successful prognosticator. The financial situation made economies, including a reduction in pensions, necessary. If the venal official was likely to oppose the abolition of the paulette, the magnate was likely to try to block financial reform that affected him adversely. There was also confusion over the duties and personnel in the various councils of the king, which had worsened during the minority. Changes that excluded a magnate or his clients would probably arouse their opposition. Faced with this situation Villeroy and his colleagues adopted a typical Renaissance solution: they would hold an Assembly of Notables in which the sovereign courts and nobles would be persuaded of the necessity for reform. As good and loyal subjects they would accept the required personal sacrifices, or at least enough public pressure could be brought to bear to make them do so.[36]

Since it was the nobility and the bureaucracy who were selected to make the sacrifices, there was no need to summon representatives from the towns or a large number of financial officials as had been done in 1596. Villeroy evidently wanted a smaller, more manageable assembly. To it were called the first president and the attorney general of each of the provincial Parlements, plus one archbishop or bishop and one noble from each of these judicial jurisdictions. The meeting was held in Rouen, so the first president and the attorney general of both the Chamber of Accounts and the Court of Aids of that city were included. The representation from the far larger jurisdiction of the Parlement of Paris was more numerous; three bishops,

---

36. My explanation of the reasons for holding the assembly is supported by that of Fontenay-Mareuil in his memoirs except that he seemingly assigns the initiative to Luynes. Luynes was hardly experienced enough to have planned so complex a meeting and must have acted upon the advice of Villeroy and his colleagues. Pontchartrain specifically attributes the plans to them. *Mémoires de Fontenay-Mareuil*, Michaud, sér. 2, 5:126–27; *Mémoires de P. Phelypeaux de Pontchartrain*, Michaued, sér. 2, 5:396. A. D. Lublinskaya concurs in the belief that one of the purposes of the assembly was to place the Parlement in such a position that they could not block the implementation of the recommendations that would be made, but apparently she does not believe that it was also directed against the magnates. See her "Les assemblées d'états en France au XVIIe siècle. Les assemblées des notables de 1617 et de 1626," *Studies Presented to the International Commission for the History of Representative and Parliamentary Institutions* (Louvain, 1966), 31:169. On learning that the assembly had been convoked, a president of the Parlement of Toulouse predicted that the meeting would see "great efforts against this *droit annuel* and the excessive pensions." P. Tamizey de Larroque, "Trois letters inédites du Président de Sevin à Peyresc," *Revue de l'Agenais 11 (1884): 54.*

four nobles, the first presidents and attorney generals of all the sovereign courts, and the provost of the merchants and the lieutenant civil of Paris were present. In addition, the court, the council, and a number of magnates including Sully came, but they were not formal participants.[37]

To guide the deliberations of the assembly, Villeroy and his colleagues prepared a list of twenty propositions they wanted to have answered. The opening meeting on December 4 was marred by quarrels over the seating arrangement. The members of the sovereign courts claimed precedence over the nobility, and it was not until December 8 that the matter was settled.[38] Those present began to work in earnest the following day, and by December 27 they were ready to submit their decisions to the king. No events of particular interest took place during the sessions. More time was devoted to the paulette and finance than any other matters, but perhaps the most noteworthy occurrence that took place in Rouen was the death of Villeroy on December 12 at the age of seventy-four.[39]

Although Villeroy did not live to manipulate the assembly, his surviving colleagues must have congratulated themselves on the initial results of their work. By limiting the number of participants to a manageable size—fifty-one—and by drawing the nobles from those of middle rank rather than the magnates, they avoided many potential conflicts. Assuredly, however, their greatest stroke of genius was to frame twenty propositions for the notables to respond to and not to let them stray to other matters.

The first proposition pointed out that the need to conduct affairs of state in secret conflicted with the king's professed desire to consult the magnates. Their number was so great that if they participated in his inner council, secrecy could not be preserved. There would be irreconcilable quarrels over precedence, and in any case many could not attend because their duties made it necessary for them to be elsewhere. To solve this dilemma, the notables suggested that the king continue his current practice of using a few intimate advisers such as those he had inherited from his father. In this

37. For a list of deputies and their seating arrangement, see *Des Etats Généraux*, 18:11–16, 119–21, and *Journal inédit d'Arnauld d'Andilly, 1614–1620*, ed. Achille Halphen (Paris, 1857), pp. 327–36. The list published by Charles de Robillard de Beaurepaire in *Louis XIII et l'Assemblée des Notables à Rouen, en 1617* (Rouen, 1883), pp. 98–104, is incomplete, but on pp. 121–29, the author indicates some of the other persons who followed the court to Rouen. It is of interest that Duplessis-Mornay, a participant, had opposed calling a large assembly and had advocated using a committee of not more than eight persons to prepare an edict based on the cahiers of the Estates General of 1614. Raoul Patry, *Philippe du Plessis-Mornay* (Paris, 1933), p. 552

38. *Mémoires de Mathieu Molé*, ed. Aimé Champollion-Figeac (Paris, 1855) 1:156–61; *Des Etats Généraux*, 18:53–113, 121–34. BN ms. fr. 20,631, fols. 167–69.

39. The best accounts of the assembly are located in BN ms. fr. 20,631, fols 167–75v; and ms. Dupuy 631, fols 65–71v. For Villeroy's last days, see De Bouis, *Assemblée des Notables tenue à Rouen en 1617*, pp. 19–22, extract from the *Revue de la Normandie*, September and October 1866. The account printed in *Des Etats Généraux*, 8:119–40, is incomplete, and Molé's, a participant, is very brief. See his *Mémoires*, 1:154–64.

manner the notables were led to support the exclusion of the magnates from the inner council, a practice that Henry IV had followed, but not his predecessor who had drawn the bulk of his councillors from the ranks of the old nobility.[40]

The second proposition dealt with the organization, compensation, procedures, and duties of the various councils. The next three stressed reducing expenses by curtailing the costs of the royal household and the military and by cutting pensions by 3 million livres. The sixth dealt with the need to increase the tax base by reducing the number of persons who were exempt from paying the taille. The seventh recommended that positions in the royal household and the army not be sold. Five dealt with ecclesiastical matters. On the problem of the frequent rebellions that had taken place, the notables urged that the crown assert a near monopoly on the possession of artillery and other weapons and forbid anyone to arm vessels or to negotiate with foreign ambassadors without permission.

Thus far the notables had given the king nearly everything he wanted, although many of the propositions interfered with the position of the magnates. It now became time to turn to the administration of justice, and here the presence of so many members of the sovereign courts led to more resistance. The notables rejected a proposal to create a special itinerate court to hear and judge complaints against the various Parlements and their members. To correct the injustices committed by the presidial courts and subordinate jurisdictions, the council wanted to establish a maître des requêtes in each government. This official was to be changed from time to time to prevent him from developing local ties, but apparently it was the intention of the council that there would always·be someone occupying the office. Had this suggestion been implemented, an official nearly comparable to the intendant of a later date would have been borne. Once more, however, the notables recoiled from the suggestion.

The most troublesome question that came before the notables concerned the paulette. In the nineteenth proposition, the king clearly indicated that he would not renew it for the following year in accordance with the promise he had made to the deputies to the Estates General of 1614. During the fall the sovereign courts had begun to exert pressure to obtain the continuation of the paulette. By December 18 the issue was causing heated discussion among those notables who held venal offices, although it was not until December 23 that formal discussion commenced on the matter. In spite of the protests of the officers of the sovereign courts, Louis XIII remained adamant, and on January 15 he formally abolished the paulette. On the other hand, by a reported vote of thirty-four to seventeen, the notables accepted his proposals that venality cease and that the number of officers be

---

40. For the king's questions and the notables' responses, see *Mémoires de Molé, 1 : 164–212.* For the king's council see Roland Mousnier, *La plume, la faucille et le marteau* (Paris, 1970), pp. 141–78.

reduced. This adherence to the royal wishes cost the officers little. They were probably not fearful that the king would ever be in a financial position to abolish venality, and to assure that he was not, they refused to recommend how he should make good the income that he would lose if he did so. As far as reducing the number of offices was concerned, if this actually happened, it would force up the price of the ones they already possessed.[41]

The assembly had been instructive. By summoning twenty-five members of the sovereign courts and two officials from Paris, but only thirteen nobles and eleven prelates, the king's advisers had ensured that the officers would dominate the voting in the meeting, especially as they were likely to receive some support from the clergy. As a result, the proposed measures that were harmful to the magnates received the solid backing of the assembly, probably as anticipated. The officers themselves had refused to make any sacrifices for the common good, but the king's advisers still regarded them as less of a threat than the magnates were. The important question was whether the magnates would accept the decisions of a meeting in which only a handful of nobles of the middle rank had attended. The king was obviously hopeful that they would, and when he told the notables to return to their homes on January 29, he promised that he would soon send an edict to the Parlements based on the cahiers presented by the Estates General and their own recommendations.[42]

As could have been anticipated, the magnates refused to make any sacrifices, and Louis was not yet in a position to compel their obedience. Their pensions actually cost the crown nearly 200,000 livres more in 1618 than in 1617. By avoiding civil war, military expenses were cut by about 5 million livres, but the gap between ordinary revenue and the expenses in 1618 was still a substantial 4 million livres. Work did proceed on the edict, and on July 24 it was ready to be turned over to the Parlements to be registered.[43] Following the wishes of the Estates General and the Assembly of Notables, its contents reflected a desire to reduce expenses, with the king's household, the garrisons, the army, and pensions being among the areas where savings were to be made. Some articles were designed to reduce the danger of revolts. No subject was to have a guard in time of peace or to make alliances with foreign princes òr treat with their ambassadors. Artillery was to be turned over to the king except where it was needed to defend frontiers, and royal officials were forbidden to enter the service of the magnates. In other articles Louis halted the sale of posts in the army and in

41. BN ms. Dupuy 631, fols. 69v–71v; *Journal d'Arnauld d'Andilly*, p. 339. Mousnier, *La vénalité* pp. 632–36. *Des Etats Généraux*, 18:137–38.

42. *Des Etats Généraux*, 18:138–40.

43. *Mémoires de Ponchartrain*, Michaud, 2d sér., 5:397-98; Mallet, pp. 219-20, 226. *Journal d'Arnauld d'Andilly*, p. 376. On October 7, 1618, Louis wrote the estates of Brittany saying that the edict had been sent to the provincial Parlements. AD, Ille-et-Vilaine, C 2649, pp. 331–35.

the households of members of the royal family. He also expressed a desire to abolish venality and to reduce the number of offices in other areas when he was financially able to do so. Nothing in the edict attacked a subject's legitimate privileges. Indeed it would have been surprising if some articles had. The deputies of 1614 and 1617 had advised to the contrary, and the principal author of the edict was Guillaume du Vair, now keeper of the seals and formerly the first president of the Parlement of Aix where he had won the affection of the Provençals.[44]

For some reason the edict was never promulgated. Probably the Parlements were angry at the king's refusal to renew the paulette and showed their pique by doing nothing, although there was much in the edict that they favored and little that adversely affected them. The king does not appear to have pressed the matter. Still only seventeen and in the hands of weak advisers, he may not have felt strong enough to enforce the provisions that injured the magnates. Once more reform was postponed. There were no significant economies, military expenses increased in 1619 and 1620 because of revolts that involved Marie de Medici, and there were substantial annual deficits.[45]

To find money Louis turned to expedients. In March 1619 he abandoned all pretense of trying to redeem the domain and alienated what remained of the part that Sully had repossessed. That same year he also alienated 300,000 livres from the aides, and in 1620 he reinstated the paulette—in part to insure the loyalty of the sovereign courts during this time of troubles and in part to increase the revenue he received from the Parties Casuelles. The terms under which he renewed the paulette were so unfavorable to the bureaucracy, however, that the Parlement of Paris refused to participate. Nevertheless a combination of the renewal and the new offices he created for revenue purposes increased the yield from the Parties Casuelles to over 13 million livres in 1620, nearly four times what it had been the year before. In 1615 the general assembly of the clergy had voted a ten-year grant of 1.3 million livres per year and in that year, and again in 1619 it gave an additional sum for one year only.[46]

In 1620, then, the situation was far less favorable for the crown than it had been in 1610 when Henry IV and Sully were still at the helm. But what of the provincial estates? Did they, like the magnates, profit from the departure of that remarkable pair to assume a more independent role, or did Villeroy and his colleagues adhere to the policies of their former master in this regard?

44. BN ms. Dupuy 35, fols. 1–54.
45. Mallet, pp. 220, 226.
46. Clamageran, *Histoire de l'impôt,* 2:458. Mousnier, *La vénalité,* pp. 280–86, 635–38; Mallet, p. 209. Blet, Le clergé 1:180, 183; *Collection des procès-verbaux du clergé,* 2:329–37.

3. THE ESTATES IN GUYENNE

The provincial estates in Guyenne had done all in their power to prevent the implementation of the decree of January 1603 establishing eight new élections in the généralité. They had turned to the sovereign courts to secure delays; they had threatened local royal officials and others favorable to the decree; they had sought the support of their sympathetic governor, Ornano, the king's mistress, and other influential persons; they had offered to reimburse the élus if their offices were suppressed, but all to no avail. By 1609 the élus were established everywhere in the généralité, and on November 21 of that year the king's council once more rejected a financial offer in return for the suppression of the élections. So determined, however, were the provincial leaders to defend their liberties that neither this rejection nor the death of their beloved governor in January 1610 terminated their efforts. Perhaps taking their cue from the council's statement that the élus had been created to prevent taxes from being levied without the king's consent and to curb other disorders, the estates now set about to discredit the élus by showing that their fiscal administration was more reprehensible than their own.[47]

Hardly had their petitions been rejected in November 1609 than the deputies from the various provincial estates in Guyenne charged that the élus were imposing unauthorized taxes to increase their own income. The council referred the matter to the treasurers of the Bureau of Finances at Bordeaux, who thereupon launched an investigation. Their findings, as the estates, had anticipated, were that the élus were at least as inefficient and dishonest as the officials of the estates. By February 1610 the treasurers had begun to issue ordonnances against the élus in some seneschalsies for levying many times the amount authorized for their fees. They went to the length of suspending the salary of the élus in Lannes until they presented their books for inspection, and in a letter to Sully they attributed the delays in collecting taxes in Guyenne to the élus' negligence. At last the tide was turning. The élus could no longer appear to the unbiased members of the king's council as the obvious answer to the need for good fiscal administration.[48]

The stage was thus set to launch a new attack on the élus. The assassination of Henry IV provided an excellent excuse for the estates of the seneschalsies to meet in order to send deputies to court to offer their submission to the new king, to obtain a confirmation of their privileges, and at the same time to seek once more to have the élections suppressed.[49]

47. For the decree of November 29, 1609, see BN ms. fr. 18,176, fols. 200–08.

48. BN ms. fr. 18,176, fol. 306; AD, Gironde, C 3875, fols. 1–12, *IAD*, Gironde, sér. C, ed. Alexandre Gouget and Jean-A. Brutails (Bordeaux, 1893), pp. 274–75. AC, Agen, CC 133.

49. AC, Agen, BB 40, fols. 422–25; AC, Laplume, BB 6, fols. 99v, 102–05v; AC, Mézin, BB 3, fols 7v–12. AD, Haute-Garonne, C 3697; *IAD*, *Aveyron, sér. G*, ed. Ch. Estienne and L. Empereur (Rodez, 1934), 1 : G 97.

Whether there was a formal meeting of the estates of the généralité is not known, but deputies from Quercy, Condomois, Lannes, Agenais, Rouergue, Armagnac, Comminges, and Rivière-Verdun joined together on November 20 to sign a petition in which they promised to reimburse the élus for the loss of their offices if the council would suppress them. The élus were useless, they argued, because the taille could be easily divided in accordance with old cadastres. They were costly because of their salaries and special privileges, and their activities were the source of numerous complaints and lawsuits. Pointedly the deputies remarked that in his coronation oath, a king swore to maintain and conserve the privileges of his people. Languedoc, Provence, Dauphiné, Burgundy, Brittany, and several other provinces had continued to have their privileges and estates; only Guyenne, whose fidelity was exceeded by none, had lost hers.[50]

The deputies must have approached the king's council at a time when the struggle between Sully, the apostle of absolutism, and Villeroy, the apostle of appeasement, was reaching its peak. Whether their demands entered directly into this dispute, we do not know. Contemporary observers saw the conflict more in terms of personalities than in policies and have left no clues. But this much is certain: it was not until February 12, 1611, just after Sully fell from power, that the council finally suppressed the eight élections in Guyenne. By the terms of this edict the king "perpetually and irrevocably" suppressed the élections and promised never to reestablish the élus. In return, the eight estates were to reimburse the élus for the costs of purchasing their offices and related expenses, the total figure coming to 252,080 livres. Mindful of the abuses commited by the estates that had ostensibly led to the establishment of the élus in 1603, the council then made a series of regulations designed to prevent their reoccurrence. The estates of the seneschalsies and of the subordinate jurisdictions were to be held annually to impose and apportion taxes designated for the king and for the authorized expenses of the estates. If this provision guaranteed the continued existence of representative assemblies, those that followed seemingly denied them effective roles. Taxes required by the king were to be levied without any "reduction, retrenchment, or delay," and no taxes were to be levied by the estates without the king's express permission. Procedures designed to ensure that the estates obeyed this last injunction were carefully spelled out. To reduce the costs of holding the estates, the number of those who were permitted to attend was limited, some smaller towns being allowed to send deputies in alternate years only. The pay of those who attended was specified, and they were to receive this allowance for a maximum of six days, including travel to and from the meeting. Syndics were to be elected for

---

50. AC, Agen, CC 136. This petition has been printed in *Edict du roy contenant révocation et suppression des huict bureaux d'élections establis en la généralité de Guyenne par édict du mois de janvier 1603* (Agen, 1612), pp. 53–81. A copy is in AC, Agen, CC 143.

terms of one or two years only and were to have no assistants. Furthermore they were forbidden to institute any suit without the permission of the estates.[51]

The publication of an edict and its enforcement, however, are two different things. The estates of the généralité, which were not specifically mentioned in the edict, met several times in some years but failed to assemble in others. The estates of Rouergue,[52] Quercy,[53] Comminges,[54] Armagnac,[55] Condomois,[56] Lannes,[57] Rivière-Verdun,[58] and Agenais[59] held their authorized annual meetings, but in spite of the express provision in the

51. AC, Agen, CC 143, pp. 3–14, 29–52.

52. AC, Rodez (bourg), BB 11, fols. 169v–71v, 202, 221–23v, 242–43, 259v–61, 263v, 283–84, 309, 332v–33, 350v, BB 12 (bourg), fols. 16, 21; AC, Millau, AA 17, nos. 10, 11, 17, 18, 20–23, CC 252; AD, Aveyron, 2E, 677 (AC, Conques), nos. 19, 22, 23; *IAD, Aveyron*, G 77, G 88, G 89, G 97; *IAD, Gironde*, C 3816.

53. The absence of good archives makes it impossible to determine the frequency of meetings of the estates of Quercy, but at least seven and probably ten or more were held from 1611 through 1620. AD, Gironde C 3817, C 3979 (procès-verbal of the estates of 1620); *IAD, Gironde*, C 3897; *IAC, Moissac*, ed. Charles Dumas de Rauly (Montauban, 1906–07), BB 3, CC 46; *IAC, Figeac*, ed. L. Combarieu, BB 5 (printed in *Annuaire du Lot*, 1869); M. J. Baudel, *Notes pour servir à l'histoire des Etats provinciaux du Quercy* (Cahors, 1881), pp. 40–42.

54. The archives for the estates of Comminges, so rich for the sixteenth century, contain little after the reign of Henry IV, probably because many documents were borrowed and not returned. AD, Haute-Garonne, C 3797. For the estates see C 3698–702, C 3804, nos. 107–09; and M. J. de Naurois-Destenay, *Les Etats de Comminges aux XVIe et XVIIe siècles* (thesis, Ecole Nationale des Chartes, 1953–54), pp. 183–90. A copy is at the AN.

55. For the collecte of Vic-Fezensac and frequent references to the estates of Armagnac, see AD, Gers, E suppl. 23,936. See also AC, Lectoure, BB 5, and AC, Auch, BB 6, fols. 53v–54. A majority of those who attended the estates of Armagnac on July 25, 1611, were opposed to voting a tax to suppress the élus. A second meeting had to be convoked, and the élection was abolished. J. Carsalade-du-Pont, "Le journal de maître Jean de Solle," *Revue de Gascogne* 18 (1877): 470–71.

56. The estates of the recette of Condomois, Bazadais, and Astarac consisted of the deputy or syndic of Bazadais and Astarac and the deputies of the towns of Condomois. Frequent meetings of the subordinate estates of Bazadais can be documented. See *IAD, Gironde, sér. E suppl.*, ed. Gaston Ducaunnès-Duval (Bordeaux, 1901), 2:202–06, 409–10; AC, Meilhan (in AD, Lot-et-Garonne), BB 1, fols. 17–17v, 38; *AHG* 19 (1879): 433. The estates of the recette of Condomois must also have met, but little documentation survives. For references see AC, Francescas (in AD, Lot-et-Garonne), BB 10, fols. 57v–59v; AC, Mézin (in AD, Lot-et-Garonne), BB 3, fols. 7–12, 176–81v; *IAD, Lot-et-Garonne, sér. A. B. C. D. E. E suppl. G. et H.*, ed. E. Crozet et al. (Agen, 1863–78), E suppl., pp. 13–14, 68–69; *IAC, Condom*, ed. G. Niel (n.p., n.d.), AA 16, BB 25, BB 26, BB 27.

57. AC, Bayonne, BB 18, pp. 93, 253, 473–75, 478, 481, BB 20, pp. 35, 37, 267–69, 364; AC, Saint-Sever, BB 2, BB 3 passim.

58. Jean Contrasty, *Histoire de Sainte-Foy-de-Peyrolières* (Toulouse, 1917), pp. 200–02, 210.

59. For Agenais, see esp. AC, Agen, BB 40, BB 42, BB 44, BB 45, CC 131–56. The long cahier of the third estate of Agenais that was prepared for the Estates General of 1614 has been published by G. Tholin in "Les cahiers du pays d'Agenais aux Etats-Généraux," *Revue de l'Agenais* 10 (1883): 5–16, 145–60, 244–59, 321–39, 408–16. For the estates of the viscounty of Bruilhois with references to the estates of Agenais and Armagnac, see AC, Laplume, BB 6, and AC, Layrac, BB 1.

edict that they hold no additional assemblies, those of Agenais habitually met several times, and special sessions of the estates of Rouergue, Rivière-Verdun, and probably other seneschalsies sometimes took place. More important is the question of whether the estates actually lost all control or influence over royal taxation. Let us examine this question by considering the estates of the généralité and of Agenais concerning whom we have the most information.

The estates of the généralité met in the summer of 1612 to deal with its affairs, and the deputies who attended the Estates General at Paris during the winter of 1614–15 prepared a cahier for each estate of the généralité to submit to the king.[60] The cahier of the nobility included a request that the three estates (not just the third) be convoked regularly in all the seneschalsies as they were in Rouergue, Comminges, and Quercy. No action was taken by the council on this request, but in 1616 the estates of Guyenne became active once more. During this same period, the third estate of Agenais met from one to three times a year to apportion taxes, to handle matters related to the suppression of the élus, to elect deputies to the Estates General of 1614, and to quarrel about how the taille should be divided within the recette and among all the recettes in Guyenne.[61]

A new era for the deputies of the généralité commenced in 1616 when they decided to offer the king 900,000 livres to be collected over a two-year period in return for suppressing some tolls on wine and several other products transported on the Garonne and Dordogne rivers. The council accepted, but in the shift in the nature of the tax, Bordeaux managed to push a higher portion on the other seneschalsies than they thought justified. In November 1616 the syndics or deputies of seven of them appealed to the council to correct this injustice. The council referred the matter to the Parlement of Bordeaux, but the Parlement, probably sympathetic with the town, failed to take any action.[62] To press the case, deputies from seven seneschalsies gathered in Agen in January 1617 without the permission of the king. The Parlement of Bordeaux questioned the motive of those present, and the Parlement of Toulouse, whose jurisdiction extended into Guyenne, forbade any meetings to take place. The deputies, almost certainly in response to the undercover leadership of the *consuls* of Agen, adopted the pretense that they were merely holding informal discussions, not estates. They were careful not to meet in the town hall of Agen in order to underline the unofficial character of their discussions. At the same time, they kept in close contact with the royal officials then in Agen in order to avoid the charge that they were assembling secretly.

Whether the meeting in January 1617 should be considered as an estates

60. AC, Agen, BB 42, fol. 50–51.
61. *Recueil des cahiers*, 4:268; AC, Agen, BB 42, fols. 159–60, CC 140–50 passim.
62. AC, Agen, CC 151.

may be debated, but certainly those present took as decisive actions as if they had been legally constituted. A deputy was sent to Parlement to defend their interests against the municipal officials of Bordeaux and the tax officials of the généralité. Others were named to try to block extraordinary taxation by appeals to the king's council and sovereign courts. Indeed they even asked that the king assign them part of his ordinary revenue so that they could raise troops to suppress brigandage around Lectoure and Isle-Jourdain. Finally those present decided to appoint two agents to look after their interests on a more permanent basis. One was to remain at court, and the other was to act in généralité. The seneschalsies were to take turns furnishing these officials. Funds to support their activities were to be advanced by their respective seneschalsies, but at the end of their one-year terms, their accounts were to be examined and a taille imposed on the entire généralité to pay their expenses.

The departure of the deputies of the seneschalsies was followed immediately by a meeting of the estates of Agenais to divide royal taxes for 1617 among the various subordinate jurisdictions. Those who attended were angered to discover that the king wanted taxes in excess of those ordinarily levied in Agenais. While they were in session, the news arrived that a decree from the Parlement of Bordeaux had been won that forbade the levying of the extraordinary taxes requested by the king. The royal commissioner sought to have the deputies apportion the extraordinary levy along with the usual taxes anyway, but without success.[63] Similar royal efforts to obtain additional revenue from the other seneschalsies probably also failed because in spite of his request for additional revenue, the king drew slightly less funds from Guyenne in 1617 than in the two preceding years.[64]

There is an amazing unsigned letter to the king that purports to be from the estates of Guyenne meeting in Agen in 1617. Its contents are so far removed from the carefully worded, discreet, unquestionably genuine documents that emerged from the estates that it is difficult to believe that it is authentic. On the other hand, the views it expressed probably reflected those of many persons in Guyenne. The authors began by stating that they had been reduced to a condition that differed little from slavery. They attacked the venality of offices, stressed their own loyalty, and asserted that selfish motives had not led to their resolutions in the estates. For a long time, they informed the king, they had suffered quietly in the hope that when you, the king, were older, you would save us from foreign domination of Concini. Pointedly they reminded Louis that "a mayor of the palace" had once seized possession of the state, and they called upon the young king to take the reins of government from Concini. Until he did so, Catholic and Protestant towns

63. For the meetings of the deputies of Guyenne and the estates of Agenais in 1617, see *AHG*, 28:95–108; AC, Agen, BB 42, fols. 306–08v, 315–21v, 328–29v, CC 152–54.
64. Mallet, pp. 200–01.

alike were resolved to halt the flow of money from the province, not to enrich themselves or to deprive your majesty, but to prevent Concini and the foreigners who served him from pillaging and impoverishing the kingdom. Within two months, Louis XIII was to act as the authors of the letter desired, but one wonders if the call for such blatant use of the power of the purse to dictate royal policy might not have contributed to the dislike that he was soon to reveal for the estates in Guyenne. Unofficial though the letter probably was, the estates during the next few years provided the money to pay local officials and garrisons but did their best to stop the flow of money to Paris just as the authors had recommended.[65]

Faced with so much resistance to taxes, the crown turned to the sale of offices and in September 1617 created commissioners of the tailles and other positions in the parishes and larger jurisdictions. Because these useless officials were to be supported by a 5 percent surcharge on the taille and taillon known as the *sol pour livre*, there were strong protests. Agents of the estates succeeded in preventing the implementation of the decree by blocking its registration by the Parlements of Bordeaux and Toulouse and the Court of Aids at Montpellier.[66] The crown countered by taking measures to override the opposition of the sovereign courts and accused the three estates of Rouergue of violating the rule of 1611. Royal officials were given a larger role in the sessions of the estates and the imposition of taxes, the estates were forbidden to give presents to anyone under any pretext, and the syndics who had violated the rule of 1611 were to be relieved.[67] Still more ominous, a syndic reported from court that an influential person was pressing for the reestablishment of the élus.[68]

The *consuls* of Agen who completed their term of office in 1618 recognized the seriousness of the situation and informed their successors that with considerable difficulty they had secured permission to hold a meeting of the estates of Guyenne early the following year. They hoped that those who attended could be persuaded to offer the king a substantial sum in return for abolishing the commissioners for the taille and the sol pour livre, but they were by no means certain that this could be done because those deputies who did not hold office had little understanding of the threat that the tax was to them. Perhaps their pessimism resulted from a disagreement that broke out among the deputies of the seneschalsies in a little-known meeting of the estates of the généralité in 1618, but events were to prove that their concern was unwarranted.[69]

On February 26, 1619, the estates of the généralité opened in Agen. An

---

65. BN ms. n.a. fr. 22,776, fols. 14–16.

66. AD, Gironde, C 3977; AC, Agen, BB 46, fols. 10–10v.

67. AD, Gironde, C 3808, fols. 100–02v.

68. Loubatèry to Agen, October 12, 1618, AC, Agen, CC 153.

69. AC, Agen, BB 46, fols. 10–11. The estates of 1618 is referred to in the letter of Loubatèry to Agen, October 12, 1618. Ibid., CC 153.

intendant who was temporarily in Guyenne frankly confessed to those present that the commissioners of the tailles had been created to meet the financial needs of the state and suggested that they vote the king some money in return for suppressing the offices and the sol pour livre. A deputy from Armagnac reported that he had learned that some in the généralité were seeking to have the élus reestablished. The deputies voted to continue their efforts to block the registration of the decree creating the commissioners of the tailles in the sovereign courts and disavowed anyone who sought to have the élus reestablished. Perhaps fearful that deputies would limit themselves to these negative actions, the intendant again appeared before the estates on March 2 and asked for money in return for suppressing the offending offices and tax. The following day the estates voted to petition the king to confirm the decree suppressing the élus, abolish the commissioners of the tailles and the sol pour livre, and maintain the privileges and liberties of the provinces. In view of the crown's pressing financial needs, they offered in return 150,000 livres to be paid over two years. To further the chances that their offer would be accepted, they voted the duke of Mayenne, who had recently been named governor of Guyenne, the handsome sum of 20,000 livres in return for his services.[70] The king's council accepted these terms and on March 27 issued the necessary orders to put them into effect. The matter thus ended, to the chagrin of the newly appointed commissioners who offered some resistance.[71]

Hardly had these problems been resolved than a new one arose. In 1616 the estates of Guyenne had offered the king a two-year subsidy that was to yield a total of 900,000 livres in return for abolishing some tolls on wine and other products transported on the Garonne and Dordogne rivers. Tax farmers had responded by offering the crown 900,000 livres for the right of collecting the substitute tax but had encountered so much resistance that they had been unable to recover all this sum. They appealed to the Parlement at Bordeaux, which awarded them 100,000 livres in damages and ordered that the remaining amount that was owed be paid. This situation led to a meeting of the estates of the généralité in Bordeaux on July 23, 1619. Here the deputies expressed their anger at Parlement for taking this action without consulting them, and they fell to quarreling over whether Bordelais was being required to pay its share. The inevitable appeals followed, and Bordelais' proportion was increased.[72]

When the syndic of Agenais made his annual report to the third estate of

70. Bordelais and Périgord did not participate in the estates because élus had long been established there. Lannes and the duchy of Albret were also absent, but the deputies specifically stated they acted in their name. AD, Aveyron, C 1906; AC, Agen, BB 42, fols. 405–13, BB 44, fols. 198–204; AC, Auch, BB 6, fols. 53v–54; AC, Laplume, BB 6, fols. 242v, 245v.

71. AD, Gironde, C 3977; *IAD, Gironde,* C 3820.

72. AC, Agen, CC 153; *Archives municipales de Bordeaux,* vol. 13: *Inventaire des registres de la jurade de 1520 à 1789* (Bordeaux, 1947), 8:9–11.

Agenais in January 1620, he could point with satisfaction to the abolition of the commissioners of the tailles and the sol pour livre, but these accomplishments had been costly.[73] Neither he nor the deputies could have viewed the Paris government with any degree of satisfaction. The three estates of Quercy that met the following month in Figeac displayed far greater discontent. They refused to vote part of the money that was requested by the king, and their syndics added to this injury by failing to collect all of the stipulated taxes. Exasperated, the treasurers at Bordeaux ordered that all public funds in Quercy be seized except those earmarked to support the University of Cahors and to pay the debts of the province.[74]

In the decade following the death of Henry IV, the precarious balance of power between the crown and the estates had been restored. The estates had succeeded in getting the élections abolished and in blocking increases in taxation so effectively that it had become necessary for the crown to find additional revenue by creating offices, establishing new tolls, and employing other expedients in areas that lay outside the direct jurisdiction of the estates. The estates had then made financial concessions in return for the suppression of the tolls and offices, but there had been difficulties in raising the promised sums. Some of the estates such as those of Rouergue and Quercy were clearly disillusioned by the repeated efforts of the crown to extort money by whatever means that were available and had no intention of cooperating. The leaders of Agenais were more subtle in their opposition, but they were perhaps more dangerous because of that very fact.

The dissatisfaction of the crown with the estates must have been intensified when it considered the relative ease with which the two seneschalsies with élections could be taxed. Far from showing a more permissive attitude toward Bordeaux, the crown violated its autonomy by appointing its jurats as well as its mayor. The change was accompanied by a sharp decline in the frequency that the jurats summoned the smaller towns and communities of Bordelais to assemblies during this decade.[75] Périgord also gained nothing from the new regime. About a month after the fall of Sully, the bishop and mayor of Périgueux and a representative of the nobility petitioned the crown to revive the estates, but Marie de Medici refused their request in September 1611 on the ground that such assemblies "make only bad resolutions that are prejudicial to the service of the king and to the good and repose of his subjects."[76] With such a contrasting situation in the same généralité, the

73. AC, Agen, CC 156.

74. AD, Gironde, C 3979; *IAD, Gironde*, C 3897.

75. *Histoire de Bordeaux*, ed. Charles Higounet (Bordeaux, 1966), 4:319–20. The estates of Bordelais and Périgord did, of course, meet to elect deputies to the Estates General of 1614.

76. H. de Montégut, "Les Etats de Périgord," *Bul. de la soc. hist. et arch. du Périgord* 4 (1877): 90. The nobility of Périgord and probably the other estates asked that their provincial estates be revived when they met in 1614 to elect deputies to the Estates General. *IAC, Périgueux*, ed. Michel Hardy (Périgueux, 1894), p. 18.

question was becoming one of how long the rapidly maturing Louis XIII would accept the limitations the estates placed on his power when an alternate form of fiscal administration was so readily available.

4. THE ESTATES OF LANGUEDOC

Henry IV had checked Sully's attempt to weaken the provincial estates of Languedoc shortly before his assassination so that there was relative calm when his son came to the throne. For six years the crown avoided offending the estates by asking for only the usual taxes, although it did hint that more would be welcome. The estates that met in October–November 1610 were informed that they should demonstrate their pleasure at the succession of Louis XIII to the throne, and the deputies who assembled three years later were told that Languedoc was very rich, but Normandy paid more taxes. These subtle approaches produced no additional revenue. In 1610 the deputies eased their consciences, if indeed they were troubled at all, by pointing out that since 1599 they had given the king 1.2 million livres to help him pay his debts, but in 1613 they made no similar comments.[77]

The deputies were more open-handed when they dealt with prominent persons who were in a position to render them services. Members of the Montmorency and Ventadour families were always given handsome presents. The former received 30,000 livres in 1613 and the latter 21,000. In addition, the three estates supported the old constable's and, after his death, his son's company of gendarmes and the royal garrisons in Languedoc, which they controlled. Here there was sometimes a little friction because the estates sought to reduce the costs of both, but in the winter of 1615–16 they gave the younger Montmorency 40,000 livres because of his extraordinary expenses. The year before they had voted him a special grant of 6,000 livres in recognition of his happy succession to the governorship after his father's death. Their young king had not been so fortunate. Secretaries and others who might influence the great or who performed services were not forgotten. The practicality of their approach is reflected by their decision to take the 1,500 livres they had appropriated for Forget de Fresne, the king's secretary of state for Languedoc, and give it to his successor following his death in 1610. Why reward the heirs of a dead man for his past services when only the living could show their gratitude in tangible ways?

The deputies were also careful not to forget themselves. In 1608 Sully had tried to reduce the costs of holding the three estates and thereby lessen their activities by placing a ceiling on their daily allowances and by limiting the

---

77. My account of the estates that met between October 1610 and February 1616 is based on the procès-verbaux of the estates, AD, Hérault. For a detailed summary see *IAD, Haute-Garonne, sér. C*, ed. Ad. Baudouin (Toulouse, 1903), 2:180–201. *HL*, 11:908–23 passim.

duration of the payments to one month regardless of how long they were in session. The deputies that met in the fall of 1610 tried to increase the daily rate and remove the one-month provision. To make these and other changes possible, they also asked that the ceiling of 20,000 livres that they could levy to support their own activities be raised. The crown provided a double victory for the taxpayers by reducing the salt tax as the estates requested but at the same time refusing to abandon the economy rules that Sully had imposed upon them. The deputies renewed their efforts the following year and voted to borrow money so that they could be paid for more than one month. In 1612 they managed to hold their session to the prescribed length but agreed to borrow 32,235 livres to meet their obligations until such time as they could persuade the crown to permit them to levy the necessary taxes. Instead the crown expanded its efforts to impose economies in September 1613 by forbidding dioceses, towns, and communities to borrow. The deputies who met in the fall protested this decree and continued their generous practices by voting to raise the gift to the prelate who presided over their sessions from 300 to 600 livres because of his great expenses.

The three estates provided more money for public works than those in most other parts of France. They contributed toward the construction of an expensive bridge over the Garonne River at Toulouse and provided funds for major repairs on the bridge over the Tarn River at Albi. Perhaps most surprising of all, in view of their usual reluctance to vote money for the military, was their decision during the winter of 1615–16 to spend 200,000 livres to buy munitions to be placed in magazines thoughout the province. The purpose of the purchase was to have the means available to ensure domestic tranquility, not to defend the province against a foreign threat.

The deputies were also careful to preserve their privileges. In January 1612 the duke of Ventadour asked them to take their oath of fidelity to their new king in his presence, but the president of the estates refused because to do so would be contrary to their privileges. Ventadour and the other commissioners were asked to leave the assembly. When they had gone, the clergy, with their hands on their chests, and the secular estates, with their arms raised to God, swore to be faithful and obedient to the king and queen regent. This episode and the far more important negotiations with the crown suggest that the three estates maintained their position and perhaps enhanced their prestige during the six years following the death of Henry IV. Perhaps it was their important role and their growing prestige that led nobles who had not traditionally held seats to seek admittance. Twice the estates had to take action to limit their number to twenty-two.

There must have been an air of tension when the estates opened at Béziers on December 29, 1616. News had arrived a few months before that Condé, who had a number of supporters in Languedoc especially among the Huguenots, had been imprisoned. Equally important, he was the brother-in-law of the young duke of Montmorency who was likely to show his resentment by making little effort to hold the deputies to their duty toward the king. The estates' session began well enough. The intendant announced that the king asked for only the usual taxes, although he had had heavy expenses in restoring order and Brittany had offered an additional 500,000 livres. Quickly it was revealed, however, that the officials of the Chamber of Accounts and the Court of Aids of Montpellier were successfully seeking royal permission to unite into a single court. The deputies determined to oppose this action because unity would make the courts stronger. Since they had had to fight to prevent the Chamber of Accounts from auditing their accounts a short time before, they were very aware of the danger that the union would bring. More serious, the crown had arbitrarily raised the tax on salt without the consent of the estates. The deputies decided not to disband until they heard the report of a deputation they sent to court to rectify the situation. Meanwhile they refused to consider voting the usual taxes. Because some time was likely to elapse before the deputation returned, they decided to establish a permanent commission consisting of several clergymen and nobles and one deputy from each diocese that would remain in session. The other deputies went back to their homes to reduce expenses but were to be recalled when the deputation returned from court.[78]

During the period of custodianship, the commission was kept busier than it had anticipated. Some royal officials sought to increase the salt tax, and others asked for the commission's consent to an extraordinary levy of 180,000 livres. Montmorency, who had done nothing to dissuade the deputies from their obstinate course, agreed that the salt tax would not be increased until the king had heard the deputation that had been sent to court. The commission refused to consider the 180,000 livre request until the estates reassembled, but when Montmorency needed 30,000 livres to suppress an uprising in the Cevennes, they proved more generous.

Meanwhile the deputation to court won a promise that the Chamber of Accounts and Court of Aids would not be united, but on April 6, less than three weeks before Concini's murder, the council refused to revoke the increase in the salt tax. When the deputies reconvened late in May, they voted the usual taxes but refused to grant the additional 180,000 livres and continued their efforts to prevent the increase in the salt tax.

With Montmorency's assistance, the syndic of the estates managed to prevent the execution of the edict increasing the salt tax until the estates again met in January 1618. On this occasion the king's spokesmen again stressed his great needs and pointed out that Guyenne had voluntarily contributed 900,000 livres and Brittany 600,000. From Languedoc they asked only that the salt tax be increased for five or six years and that the 180,000 livres requested the year before be granted. The deputies remained

---

obdurate in spite of some pressure from Montmorency, who had been mollified by Condé's release following Concini's murder. Once more they deputed to the king to prevent the increased tax on salt, but in the end they were unsuccessful.[79]

In November 1618 the three estates were greeted with requests that they contribute 16,000 livres for the expenses of the Languedocians who had attended the Assembly of Notables the year before. They were also asked to provide 200,000 livres to support the troops sent against the sieur de Broteil, governor of Brescou, and to pay the gratification he was given for resigning his post. The three estates voted the former after pointing out that they did not customarily pay the costs of deputations they did not name, but they refused to contribute to the latter unless the fortifications at Brescou were razed. Broteil had used his position to prey upon commerce in Languedoc, and therefore his departure should have been welcome. The estates, however, may have thought that it was a double expense to raise an army to compel obedience and then to buy compliance, especially if the fort were left standing to serve its next occupant in a similar fashion.[80]

The estates that were to meet in the fall of 1619 had to be postponed until May the following year because of a Huguenot uprising in Vivarais. When the deputies assembled, they refused to vote the king a special grant of 400,000 livres, but promised that in their next meeting they would do all they possibly could to give him contentment, provided that he had razed the fort at Brescou. They were far more generous in meeting the expenses incurred by Montmorency in suppressing the uprising, but were obviously disgruntled because he had gone to the syndic and the dioceses for funds to meet the emergency. In the future the dioceses were told not to furnish money to anyone without the approval of the estates, and the syndic of Languedoc who had borrowed 25,000 livres for Montmorency in the name of the estates was threatened with the loss of his office if he did so again. If an emergency arose in the future, the estates asked that Montmorency immediately assemble them to deliberate on what additional funds would be made available.[81]

The first decade of Louis XIII's reign ended with the position of the estates intact. Except for the increase in the salt tax that was to terminate on January 1, 1623, the crown had won little from the province beyond the traditional taxes. The cooperation among the three orders, the relatively efficient procedures of the estates, and the officials they employed contributed heavily to their success. Also important was a strong feeling of

---

79. AD, Hérault, procès-verbal of the estates of January–February 1618; *IAD, Haute-Garonne,* sér. C, 2:206–09; *HL,* 11:929–30.

80. AD, Hérault, procès-verbal of the estates of November–December 1618; *IAD, Haute-Garonne, sér. C,* 2:209–13; *HL,* 11:930–31.

81. AD, Hérault, procès-verbal of the estates of May–June 1620; *IAD, Haute-Garonne, sér. C,* 2:214–17; *HL,* 11:933–36.

provincial loyalty and a willingness to make generous gifts to those who served their interests. Especially noteworthy were the large sums that were voted the Montmorency family, but when we learn that a special grant of 18,000 livres was given the duke in 1618 because of a trip he had made to court to aid the deputies of the province, we begin to suspect that he earned at least part of these sums and that the money was well spent.[82]

5. The Estates of Burgundy

Burgundy remained calm when the news of Henry IV's assassination arrived in May 1610, although initially there were no signs that the new reign would be less heavy-handed than the old. Indeed on May 31, a letter was issued in the name of the youthful Louis XIII directing that the procedure his father had recently established in which he chose the mayor of Dijon from the three candidates who received the most votes would be followed, this despite the fact that Parlement still had not registered the decree. Since the mayor by right was one of the élus who looked after the affairs of the three estates when they were not in session, this procedure not only assured a strong royal presence in the town but also in the Chambre des Elus, the principal administrative organ in the province. By the time elections were held in 1611, however, Sully had been removed from the government and in Louis's name the council abandoned his claim to choose the mayor, another step marking the retreat from absolutism.[83]

In the weeks before the triennial meeting of the Burgundian estates in August 1611, a slightly more relaxed air was therefore apparent. Jean de Souvert, the legal counsel for the estates, castigated the majority of the élus for putting themselves above the three estates by ignoring their directives during the three years since their last meeting. He specifically exempted the élus of the nobility and of the clergy from his charges, however, a fact which strongly suggests that the mayor of Dijon, who had been a royal appointee during this period, had joined with the other élu of the third estate and those of the crown to obtain a voting majority in the Chambre des Elus. In spite of his anger at this situation and his attacks on his enemies, however, Souvert seemed less bitter toward the central government and less fearful that the three estates were endangered than in the statement he had prepared for the estates in 1605.[84]

The meeting of the estates of 1611 was relatively uneventful. The crown asked only for the usual taxes. The deputies countered by requesting that the

82. *HL*, 11:931.

83. *Correspondance de la mairie de Dijon*, ed. Joseph Garnier (Dijon, 1870), 3:113–16, 118–22; *IAC, Dijon*, ed. Louis Gouvenain (Dijon, 1867), 1: BB 248.

84. Jean de Souvert, *Remonstrances à Messieurs des trois Estats du pays et duché de Bourgogne au subject de leur assemblée du huictiesme d'aoust prochain 1611* (n.p., n.d.).

gabelle, garrisons, and taillon be reduced and that several offices be suppressed. They protested against a unilateral royal decree levying a tax to repair the conciergerie of the palace but then voted 8,000 livres for this purpose. In spite of these complaints about royal exactions, the three estates requested that towns continue to have the right to levy taxes for local purposes. Mindful of the need to defend these liberties, they directed that those élus who were members of the Chamber of Accounts not be used as deputies to the king. They voted the traditional don gratuit and gifts for their governor, the royal secretary of state for Burgundy, and other influential persons but they were unsuccessful in obtaining the desired tax reductions.[85]

The élus' administration of the province in the three years that intervened between this meeting of the estates and that of September 1614 passed without serious incident. When the estates opened in 1614, those present were confronted with a royal request for a third of the 180,000 livres they had promised to Henry IV for joining Bresse, Bugey, and Gex to the généralité. The estates responded by saying that they had made no such offer and then forbade the élus to impose it. On the other hand, the estates again failed to obtain a reduction in the traditional taxes.[86]

The relative calm that had characterized the relations between the crown and the estates since the death of Henry IV was broken by the rebellion of the prince of Condé in the fall and winter of 1615–16. The hard-pressed government felt compelled to order that an additional 103,421 livres be imposed during the first three months of the new year and to direct that the 60,000 livres it claimed the estates had promised for the acquisition of Bresse, Bugey, and Gex be given to Bellegarde, their governor, in return for his faithful service (or perhaps more accurately, for not joining the rebels). The total came to about 70 percent of the revenue the crown normally received from the province. Faced with these demands, the élus took the unusual step of summoning a special assembly consisting of only the third estate to meet at Dijon on January 10, 1616. Here the royal demands were rejected because they were prejudicial to the privileges of the province and would impose hardship on the poor people. The only concessions that those who attended would make were to authorize the borrowing of 60,000 livres to pay troops to protect the province and to suggest that the three estates be convoked in a special session if the war were greatly prolonged.[87]

In September the king urged that 30,000 livres be raised to support the 2,900 men judged necessary to secure the province and authorized each bailiwick to elect one clergyman, one noble, and one person from each of the principal towns to meet with the élus at Dijon in October to discuss the

85. AD, Côte-d'Or, C 3017, fols. 101v–02, 105–09v, 113v–15, 118, 119v–20v. For the taillon see C 5220 and for the garrisons C 5383.

86. Ibid., C 3017, fols. 142–47.

87. Ibid., C 3077, fols. 93–100; Mallet, p. 207.

matter. Again, the Burgundians rejected the king's demands, but this time they did vote Bellegarde the 60,000 livres because of the great services he had rendered in maintaining order and supporting their interests at court. By not voting the money when originally requested by the crown and by now freely offering it as their gift, the three estates made Bellegarde beholden to them rather than to the crown, where the proposal had apparently originated.[88]

In the spring of 1617 the élus, with Bellegarde's assistance, again forced the government to withdraw its demands for a special military tax, this time for 125,149 livres, and that November they prevented the levying of the don gratuit because the regular triennial meeting of the estates had not been held that summer. Perhaps the confusion following Concini's assassination had led to the crown's failure to issue the letters of convocation, but whatever the explanation, the élus were so dissatisfied that they persisted in their efforts to prevent the levying of the don gratuit during 1618. To pay the salaries of local royal officials, they would only suggest that the receveur général borrow money on his own credit. At length the council had enough of this obstruction, and letters were issued ordering the estates to meet in the fall of 1618.[89]

When the royal commissioners opened the estates in Dijon on November 18, they were greeted with strong protests over the failure to hold the triennial meeting in 1617. Those present asked that the garrison be cut to the level of 1611 and repeated the usual plea that newly created offices be suppressed. The governor was asked to proceed with the demolition of fortified châteaux that were useless for the defense of the province. When it came time to vote the don gratuit, the deputies protested against the fact that the élus had received commissions from the king in 1617 and 1618 to impose the tax before the three estates had met to give their consent. They then granted the paltry traditional don gratuit of 16,667 livres per year for 1617 and 1618, as well as for the three years that followed. Bellegarde and other royal officials received their usual presents, and the estates came to an end.[90]

During the decade following the death of Henry IV, the three estates had succeeded in restoring and maintaining their former position. With the return to the earlier electoral practices in Dijon, they once more held a precarious majority in the Chambre des Elus, and except for the efforts of the crown to collect taxes in 1617 and 1618 before they had been voted, their privileges had been respected. Their success was largely the result of the

---

88. AD, Côte-d'Or, C 3077, fols. 128–35.

89. Ibid., fols. 156v–62v, 170–76v, 181v, 195–99, 208–210v.

90. Ibid., C 3017, fols. 201v–04, 213v–14, 221v–23. In 1611, 65,951 livres were levied in Burgundy to support the garrisons. In 1616 the total reached 103,421 but by 1619 it had sunk to 71,590 livres. Ibid., C 5383. General receipts from Burgundy decreased from 232,768 livres in 1616 to 177,779 in 1619 and 145,215 in 1620. Mallet, p. 207.

reluctance of the government to upset the status quo, especially during the minority and youth of the king, but the Burgundians' determined defense of their liberties and their willingness to spread their largesse to their governor, the king's secretary of state for Burgundy, and other influential persons were certainly important factors.

The town of Bourg also profited by the death of Henry IV and the removal of Sully to free itself from the obligation to hold meetings of its council in the presence of the president, lieutenant general, or a councillor of the presidial seat. Little is known of the activity of the estates of the newly conquered lands of Bresse, Bugey, and Gex, but there is no reason to believe that they and their syndics did not continue to function during the decade following Henry's death.[91]

6. The Estates of Provence

The remaining estates in provinces in which there were no élections had been left relatively unscathed by Henry IV and Sully. As a result, the new regime marked less of a change in the treatment they received, although a threat that had been hanging over their heads was removed. In Provence either the three estates or the assembly of the communities met every year during the decade after the death of Henry VI except in 1613 and 1619. Neither of these gaps appears to have provoked concern for, as in 1607 and 1609, they were probably caused by the absence of the governor, Guise, rather than by an inclination on the part of the king's council to abandon the practice of holding the estates.[92] More important in stilling the Provençals' concern, perhaps, was the continued activity of the procureurs du pays nés during these long intervals between sessions. Between the estates of December 1612 and the assembly of the communities in August 1614, the procureurs met no fewer than seventeen times to perform tasks as varied as buying fruit and olives for the chancellor, inspecting the construction of a bridge, and arranging for the passage of two thousand troops through the province. The Parlement at Aix became concerned about the procureurs' activities and in 1619 forbade them to summon the procureurs du pays joints, consisting of two members from each estate, to meet with them. The procureurs replied that there were three kinds of assemblies in Provence—those of the estates, those of the communities, and those of the procureurs du pays nés et joint—and that they had the right to convoke the last whenever

91. *Mémoires historiques de la ville de Bourg, extraits des registres municipaux de l'hôtel-de-ville*, ed. Joseph Brossard (Bourg-en-Bresse, 1887), 4:24–25. For reference to the activities of the syndics of Bresse and Bugey, see *IAD, Ain, sér. C*, ed. J. Brossard (Bourg, 1884). C 960, C 994.

92. On September 16, 1619, Louis XIII actually issued letters convoking the estates, but the meeting was postponed. *IAD, Bouches-du-Rhône, sér. C*, ed. Louis Blancard (Marseilles, 1892), 2:1.

it was necessary. Taxation, of course, did not cease in the years in which neither the estates nor the communities met, but the crown was careful to make no new demands on these occasions, and the procureurs permitted the long-established routine taxes to be collected without argument. The assembly of the communities in 1614 and of the estates in 1620 that followed the breaks in the pattern of annual meetings also displayed no rancor.[93]

During this decade the crown made little effort to increase its income from Provence and thereby avoided serious conflicts with the estates. To ensure the continued goodwill of those in Paris, the three estates did not fail to give the king's secretary of state for Provence and his assistant generous presents, nor did they forget their governor and his secretaries. They showed deep concern about their debts and those of the individual communities. They also complained about the price of salt, but the demolition of a château, the construction of a bridge, the suppression of a few offices, and a contribution toward the publication of a manuscript by King René on tournaments rank among their principal activities during this period of calm.[94]

The Provençals took advantage of this relative lull to modify their procedures. In 1611 the practice of electing deputies in the viguerie assemblies to accompany the deputations from the chief towns to the estates was abandoned, and henceforth the lesser towns in each viguerie took turns being represented. The confusion within the second estate caused by the presence of children, servants, and other unauthorized persons, including nobles without fiefs, was corrected, and the use of procureurs in lieu of personal attendance was forbidden. These measures gave the third estate satisfaction; as the swelling attendance in the second estate had caused it concern, for voting was generally by head rather than by order. A final procedural change which took place at the close of this period saw the syndic of the communities join the procureurs du pays in its meetings.[95]

Since the three estates met only in 1611, 1612, 1618, and 1620 during this decade and only the procureurs joints of the clergy and nobility attended the assemblies of the communities, a question arises concerning the degree of activity of the first two estates. The answer to this problem lies in the fact that both the clergy and the nobility had officers to look after their interests. When there was need to consider an important matter or to elect new officials, separate meetings were held. Thus assemblies of the clergy took

93. AD, Bouches-du-Rhône, esp. C 10, fols. 348–75, C 12, fols. 179–85v.

94. Ibid., C 10, fols. 263–67, 270, 336v, 347–47v, C 12, fols. 17, 45, 51, 110v–11, 113v–14, 125v–27, 236v–37, 240–40v. For a summary of the cahiers of the estates, see *IAD, Bouches du Rhône, sér. C*, 2:472–75. For King René's manuscript see *Lettres de Peiresc*, ed. Philippe Tamizey de Larroque (Paris, 1898), 7:779.

95. AD, Bouches-du-Rhône, C 10, fols. 247–47v, 323, C 12, fols. 92v–93, 232v–33, 271v; Gaspard H. de Coriolis, *Dissertation sur les Etats de Provence* (Aix, 1867), pp. 135–36, ix–xii, liii–liv; *Les Bouches-du-Rhône: Encyclopédie départementale*, ed. Paul Masson (Marseilles, 1920), 3:464–65, 491, 511–12.

place in May 1616, September 1617, and on other occasions. The clergy also had an ecclesiastical hierarchy and a diocesan organization to act in its name when the occasion arose.[96] Assemblies of the nobility were more frequent, perhaps because the order lacked an institutionalized hierarchy like the clergy. In only three years did it fail to meet, but these lacunae were compensated for by two meetings each in 1610, 1614, and 1620.[97]

7. THE ESTATES OF DAUPHINÉ

The first meeting of the three estates of Dauphiné that took place in the new reign was held in Valence in February 1611. Since the king asked for only the same taxes that had been voted the year before, the relations between the deputies and the crown were friendly, although the former made their usual effort to escape responsibility for paying the garrisons. As had happened so often before, the third estate and the more privileged orders were the antagonists. The principal difficulty arose over the salt tax. In 1601 the estates and the crown had agreed to establish the salt tax at a rate that it could be farmed for 278,400 livres per year for ten years beginning on January 1, 1602. Of this sum, 150,000 livres was to be applied to redeeming the royal domain, and the remainder was assigned to paying the provincial debts. By 1611 the term of the contract was drawing to a close, and the third estate was anxious to reduce the salt tax sharply and use all that was levied to support its other activities. The nobles and clergy, on the other hand, wanted part of the salt tax to pay their expenses. Lesdiguières, the king's lieutenant general, worked diligently to secure a compromise and was finally successful. Some of the salt revenue was designated for road repairs and the University of Valence. The third estate kept the bulk of the remainder, but its spokesmen finally agreed that a twentieth should be assigned to the nobility and clergy to pay the costs of holding their assemblies, their deputations to court, and the salaries of their officials.[98]

The accord that was reached in 1611 became known as the "union of the three orders" and was frequently referred to thereafter. It did not remove the basic cause of the friction between the estates because the problem centered on the question of whether nobles should pay the taille on the nonnoble land they owned. It did, however, offer a chance for a degree of cooperation so long as the powerful and statesmanlike Lesdiguières was present to reconcile differences and the crown did not revive the issue by raising the taille. The calm that prevailed was enough to enable the estates that met at Grenoble in January 1613 to agree on twenty-seven articles

---

96. *Les Bouches-du-Rhône,* 3:508–24; AD, Bouches-du-Rhône, G 515.

97. AD, Bouches-du-Rhône, C 107, fols. 520v–617.

98. AD, Isère, IC 4, no. 34, IJ 175, fols. 345–88, J 524², procès-verbal of the estates of 1611; *IAD, Isère, sér. B,* ed. Auguste Prudhomme (Grenoble, 1919), 4:336–39.

defining their procedures. Among them were provisions that the estates would meet "every year as has always been observed" and that in view of the union of the three orders there would be no separate assemblies, proposals, deliberations, or delegations.[99]

Full unity, however, was difficult to achieve, and in the years that followed, the clergy and nobility availed themselves of the assemblies of the three estates to discuss their mutual problems. Separate cahiers and deputations were not uncommon. Nevertheless in January 1614 the three estates managed to hold a meeting in Grenoble without encountering very serious problems, although the first two orders complained that the third estate was trying to deprive them of their share of the salt tax. Claude Expilly, a defender of the privileged orders and a leading Dauphinois intellectual, was able to report to the royal commissioners following the meeting that all of the proposals of the three estates were designed to benefit the king and his subjects, not private interests. Formerly, he admitted, the annual meetings of the estates, the frequent assemblies of the commis and the ten towns, and the unnecessarily prolonged deputations to court had done little for the public good in spite of the heavy expenses that they had incurred. He decried the development of a perpetual "corps d'estats" through the use of the commis and the assemblies of the ten towns, and he looked back nostalgically to an earlier day when the estates had no bureaucracy and met only three days each year to prepare their cahiers to present to the king dauphin.[100] Then, in an obvious reference to the accord that had been reached in 1611, he declared that salt was "the symbol of the concord among the three orders: because it is the hieroglyphic of the firm friendship and durable concord that renders the body solider and of very long duration. This is why formerly when friends visited, the first thing their hosts put on the table was salt."[101]

An assembly of the ten towns in Grenoble met late in May 1614,[102] but the first important test of whether the three orders could cooperate came in August at a special session of the estates to elect deputies and prepare cahiers for the Estates General. After some discussion concerning what procedures to follow, those assembled agreed at the suggestion of the third estate that each order would deliberate separately to determine what articles it wanted to include in its cahiers. This separation in itself did not mark an abandonment of a desire for unity, because when the orders had completed their work, joint meetings were held in an effort to prepare a single petition to present to

99. B. Mun., Grenoble, ms. 2312, fols. 69–93v; AD, Isère, IJ 669. Alexandre Fauché-Prunelle, *Essai sur les anciennes institutions autonomes ou populaires des Alpes Cottiennes-Brançonnaises* (Grenoble, 1857), 2:608–12.

100. AD, Isère, IC 7, fols. 259–61, IJ 175, fols. 400v–06; B. Mun., Grenoble, ms. 2312, fols. 94–118; Claude Expilly, *Plaidoyez* (Paris, 1621), pp. 464–74.

101. Expilly, *Plaidoyez*, p. 469.

102. B. Mun., Grenoble, ms. 2312, fols. 125–30v.

the king. When a Protestant proposed an article asking that the Edict of Nantes be maintained, those present unanimously agreed. In religiously divided Dauphiné, the wisdom of toleration had become accepted. On several issues, the deputies of the third estate and those of the more privileged orders were unable to arrive at a common position, for in money matters compromise was more difficult. At length the latter reluctantly agreed that the third estate could submit a separate petition on these points. With this exception, the estates maintained a united front before the crown by submitting a single cahier for the province and electing their deputies together.[103]

By the early months of 1615, the relations among the three orders were becoming frayed. Three times the council of the nobility met to deal with efforts by the third estates to make them pay taxes. Feeling the need for allies, one noble suggested that they strengthen their position by making overtures to "the gentlemen of the long robe," among whom were persons of merit and experience. Thus there were already signs that the quarrel among the orders would lead to a close union between robe and sword that was almost unique during the early seventeenth century.[104] The third estate countered by holding meetings of the ten towns in May and November.[105]

By the time the estates met in late January and early February 1616, a new problem had arisen. The salt tax that had been agreed upon in 1611 was scheduled to be reduced that May. Lesdiguières, however, asked that it be continued at the same level. The privileged orders protested strongly and talked once more of a union with the long robe. The third estate was more amenable, and in the end the tax was extended for another year with part of the proceeds assigned to support troops in the province. Further extensions of the salt tax were to take place only with the consent of the three estates, which was to be given by the clergy in assemblies of the dioceses, by the nobility in assemblies of the bailiwicks and seneschalsies, and by the third estate in "town halls and assemblies of the deputies of the villages." The mutual distrust, however, continued, and soon the council of the first two orders was meeting to make certain that under the terms of the renewal of the tax, they would continue to receive their share.[106]

In May 1617 the three estates mustered enough unity to reject a royal proposal that they increase taxes in order to support the expanded military forces in the province, but they once more fell to quarreling about the distribution of the salt tax, a controversy that was still raging when the estates met in Grenoble in 1619. Here deputies from the dioceses and bailiwicks joined in the deliberations of the first two orders, and they drew

103. AC, Grenoble, AA 39, no. 8.
104. AD, Isère, IJ 175, fols. 400v–17 (quote on fol. 412). The council of the nobility was an ill-defined body that usually included several ecclesiastics and about a dozen nobles.
105. *IAC, Grenoble*, ed. Auguste Prudhomme (Grenoble, 1886), BB 82; AD, Drôme, C 1025.
106. AC, Grenoble, AA 54; AD, Drôme, C 1025; AD, Isère, IJ 175, fols. 417–35v.

closer to the "gentlemen of the long robe" who now had their own council of five to speak for them. In the end the salt tax was continued, and the privileged orders obtained their modest portion.[107]

The bitter quarrel between the nobility and third estate did not abate. Soon after the deputies to the estates of 1619 had departed, the council of the nobility learned that the lieutenant particulier of Vienne had submitted an "insolent" petition to the Parlement of Grenoble and that that body had rendered a favorable decree. The secretary of the nobility never specifically stated the nature of the petition, but it was enough to touch off talk of sending a large delegation to the king. The deputies of the nobility of the bailiwicks were assembled in July, and they were soon deputing to Lesdiguières and Parlement. Before they disbanded, they elected six gentlemen to remain in Grenoble to conserve the dignity of their order. This committee was instructed to consult the council of the long robe and the bailiwicks before taking any important action. To secure the revocation of the offending decree, a deputy was sent to the king, where he spent much of 1620 trying to have the case evoked to Paris where it would be resolved by the king's council. Relations between the privileged orders and the third estate could hardly have been worse when that same year Claude Brosse, the syndic of the villages, reopened the whole question of the settlement concerning the taille that had been imposed by Henry IV. By the close of the first decade of Louis XIII's reign, the three estates of Dauphiné, at times it seemed almost premeditatedly, were moving toward their destruction.[108]

8. The Estates of Brittany

With the assassination of Henry IV, Brittany entered into a new phase. The governor, the duke of Vendôme, now in his teens and free from the restraining hand of his natural father, began to take a direct interest in the province. He presided over the estates that met in September–October 1610 and on occasions thereafter when his presence would further his intrigues. The three estates promptly obtained the confirmation of their privileges and the suppression of a number of offices that Henry had created. They were asked to vote only the usual taxes during the first three years of Louis's reign. The nine-year tax on the sale of wine in detail that the estates had established in 1609 to redeem the royal domain at a rate of 400,000 livres per year was retained, and they continued to give Vendôme, the two

107. AD, Isère, IJ 175, fols. 435v–81. AD, Isère, J 524²; AC, Grenoble, BB 86, fols. 43–43v, 55–56, 58–59.

108. AD, Isère, IJ 175, fols. 481–541; A. Lacroix, "Claude Brosse et les tailles," *Bul. de la soc. d'archéologie et de statistique de la Drôme* 32 (1898): 366–67.

lieutenant generals, the king's secretary of state for Brittany, and other influential persons gratifications to keep them on favorable terms.[109]

In November 1613 Vendôme again appeared before the estates, no doubt to support a request that one of his gentlemen made in his name that the province pay "the guards which he held near his person."[110] The three estates agreed, at an annual cost of 12,000 livres, and in addition they gave him a gratification of 6,000 livres. The estates also appropriated 6,000 livres for the construction of the portal and tower of the cathedral at Rennes, and a like sum was promised to the son of the late Bertrand d'Argentré for the latter's *Histoire de Bretagne*. These gifts suggest that the estates no longer felt that the province was impoverished, but the king requested and received only his usual taxes.[111]

By voting Vendôme money to support his personal guard of a hundred men, the estates put him in a better position to lead a rebellion in Brittany. Early in 1614, he fled from Paris and attempted to do so in conjunction with uprisings by the prince of Condé and other nobles. At this time the royal Breton garrison, about which the estates annually complained, consisted of only three hundred men scattered about in seventeen places. If Vendôme had been a popular and competent leader, he could easily have seized most of the province, but he was not, and few Bretons appear to have assisted him. The regency nevertheless preferred to treat with the rebels, and the principal result of Condé's revolt was the convocation the Estates General of France.[112]

Before the Estates General met, Marie de Medici sought to restore order and to ensure the election of favorably disposed deputies by taking the twelve-year-old Louis XIII on a tour of the western provinces. Her party arrived at Nantes in August, where the estates of Brittany opened on the eighteenth. Fewer Breton nobles than one might think were present on this colorful occasion, possibly because those who had proved disloyal remained away, but both Rohan and Montbazon were there. Representing the crown were the young king and his mother, a host of great nobles, the chancellor, aged counselors (including Villeroy and Jeannin), and rising stars like Michel de Marillac who was one day to be entrusted with the king's seals. The Bretons were in an awkward position. They had unwittingly helped to finance a revolt, and although Vendôme had been pardoned and restored to his government, their own role, however innocent, was not such that it gave them confidence in facing their sovereign king. Furthermore they were angered at having been duped by Vendôme. Therefore they decided to

---

109. AD, Ille-et-Vilaine, C 2648, esp. pp. 10, 15, 72–76, 92–93, 129–30, 141–55, 223–38, 291, 300, 376–80, 398–99.

110. Ibid., pp. 444–45.

111. Ibid., pp. 419–20, 427–28, 444–45, 477–81, 528.

112. Barthélemy Pocquet, *Histoire de Bretagne* (Rennes, 1913), 5:366–69.

demonstrate their loyalty to the crown and at the same time give vent to their spleen by lashing out against him.[113]

These circumstances led the three estates to devote most of their cahier to requests that a number of specified fortifications be raised. They revoked the agreement they had made the previous year to support Vendôme's guards, saying that it had been obtained "by surprise," and they asked the king to deny Vendôme the privilege of having any guards in the province in the future. They forbade anyone to propose to the estates that guards be established, under pain of being declared "enemies of the king and of the province." As further insurance against any future weakness on their part or on that of the crown, they declared that they would discharge any treasurer of the estates who paid any guards that were established. Never, perhaps, was such a high percentage of the estates' requests accorded by the crown.[114]

More difficult was the question of how the cost of suppressing the rebellion would be met. The king wanted a special don gratuit for this purpose, but the three estates responded by suggesting that he take the 400,000 livres raised by the sales tax on wine that was assigned to redeeming the domain. At the same time they extended the tax for one additional year. In this manner, the three estates avoided levying an additional tax, but the idea began to take hold that they should vote the king a don gratuit in addition to the fouage they had given their dukes and the support that they provided for the garrisons. They also voted Marie de Medici a special gift of 50,000 livres and elected deputies favorably disposed toward the crown to the Estates General.[115]

The estates of Brittany were not convoked in 1615, and the usual taxes were collected in 1616 without consent. The atmosphere was therefore tense when the estates once again assembled in Rennes on October 23, 1616, to consider levies for the following year. In his letter to his commissioners, Louis insisted that he had intended to hold a meeting in 1615 but had not done so because a new rebellion by Condé would have made the assembly an "occasion and pretext of various designs prejudicial to our authority and to the repose of the province." Therefore he had postponed the estates and had ordered that only those taxes customarily "consented to" by the estates be collected, although he had had need of "great succor" to suppress the uprising.[116] By not having the estates, Louis thus suggested, the Bretons had been asked to pay less than if they had been held. But no such forbearance was necessary now because the estates were once more in session. Louis's commissioners thus asked for from 900,000 to 1.2 million livres in addition to

---

113. AD, Ille-et-Vilaine, C 2648, pp. 547–65; Pocquet, *Histoire de Bretagne*, 5:369–72; *Mercure François*, 3 (1614): 430–31, 472–75.

114. *Mercure François*, 3 (1614): 475–85; AD, Ille-et-Vilaine, C 2648, pp. 581–87.

115. AD, Ille-et-Vilaine, C 2648, esp. pp. 588–91, 614–15.

116. Ibid., C 2649, pp. 10–11.

the tax to redeem the domain and the usual levies. The estates cut this mammoth demand to 400,000 livres to be raised by a tax on wine but agreed to continue to make payments on the domain.[117]

Although the three estates had cooperated to the extent of offering the king part of what he had requested, they were not disposed to pass over the events of the past year in silence. In the first article of their cahier, they pointed out that annual meetings of the estates and the right to consent to taxes were two of the conditions accepted by earlier kings that formed the basis of the union between Brittany and the crown. "The *fouages* and other monies," they declared, "have been divided and levied on the orders of your officials in the present year without the consent of the estates ... which is directly contrary to the rights, privileges, and liberties of Brittany." The estates then asked the king "to declare and order that henceforth no similar commissions will be expedited nor levies of the *fouage* and other taxes made without the consent of the estates," which would be assembled every year without fail on September 25.[118] Almost meekly the king replied, "The will of the king is to hold the estates of his province of Brittany annually and to conserve and maintain their privileges in that and in all other things."[119]

There is no reason to believe that the failure to issue letters of convocation in 1615 was intended as an attack on the estates. The excuse the crown offered for its inaction was almost certainly sincere. During the fall of 1615 when the estates would normally have been held, Vendôme was busy raising troops in Brittany. On January 5, 1616, the Venetian ambassador reported that Vendôme had offered 800 horse and 3,000 infantry to assist the king, but the royal advisers must have suspected his motives, and, indeed, shortly thereafter he joined Condé.[120]

In 1617 the estates met for three weeks. Their long deliberations were due in part to some confusion in the directions the crown had given its commissioners. Vendôme and Brissac said that the king wanted only the usual taxes in spite of his very great needs. Later another commissioner insisted that the king requested additional assistance, but nearly two weeks elapsed before he set the king's demands at 600,000 livres. As an alternative the estates could surrender the income from the royal domain which they enjoyed while they were redeeming it. Under such circumstances it is not surprising that the three estates procrastinated. Finally they made some concessions concerning the domainal revenue in order to avoid an additional tax.[121]

117. Ibid., esp. pp. 12–14, 44, 84–85.
118. Ibid., pp. 137–38.
119. Ibid., p. 138.
120. Berthold Zeller, *Louis XIII, Marie de Médicis, chef du conseil* (Paris, 1898), p. 216.
121. AD, Ille-et-Vilaine, C 2649, esp. pp. 169–70, 185–86, 191–92, 230–31, 245–46, 258–59, 268–69, 270, 312–13.

By the time the estates opened on October 22, 1618, the original contract to redeem the domain in nine years was about to expire, and the king asked only for the usual taxes plus 200,000 livres to complete this task. After some debate the estates reduced the wine tax but left it high enough to yield 300,000 livres; the extra 100,000 livres was assigned to pay their own debts.[122] With the domain finally redeemed, the crown began to ask for a don gratuit each year in addition to the old ducal taxes and money to support the garrison. The three estates continued to raise it by a levy on the sale of wine, which they usually set at a high enough rate to yield some additional funds to pay their own debts. In 1619 the estates voted a don gratuit of 400,000 livres to be collected over a two-year period "under conditions which will be specifically decreed by the said deputies."[123]

The following year the king sought to increase the don gratuit, and the estates gave him part of what he asked, again being careful to set aside some of the proceeds of the wine tax to pay their debt of 303,935 livres. The most noteworthy event at this session was that the duke of Vendôme asked the estates to support his guard once more. The estates of most other provinces provided their governor with guards, he argued, and it had been customary to do so in Brittany until the practice was discontinued in his early youth. The custom had been reestablished by the estates of 1613 but was revoked the following year during his absence amid charges that he had obtained the original grant "by surprise," a charge which did little credit to his honor. One wishes that there was some way to ascertain the true feelings of the deputies. We know only that they voted this irresponsible bastard son of their former king the necessary 12,000 livres and added 2,000 more for the captain of his guards, perhaps to bind his loyalty to them as well as to his patron.[124]

During the decade the crown had succeeded in adding a don gratuit to the taxes originally accorded the dukes. But this tax essentially replaced the one that had been used to redeem the royal domain, which in turn had been levied only when the estates had finished paying the other Breton-related debts of the crown. Considering the sixty years that elapsed between 1560 and 1620, with their bloody wars and heavy inflation, one is surprised that the crown was able to add only the don gratuit to its list of lucrative Breton taxes, especially as the amount of the don gratuit was still very much a subject for negotiation. Again, one must attribute the success of the Bretons to their important and well-defined privileges, the strength of their provincial loyalty, the cooperation of the three estates, the ability of their leaders, and their willingness to give large gratifications to those in influential positions.

---

122. Ibid., esp. pp. 333–34, 388.
123. Ibid., p. 554. See also pp. 521, 553–54, 563.
124. Ibid., esp. pp. 624, 630, 656, 664, 683–84, 686.

9. The Estates of Normandy

The first decade of Louis XIII's reign did not see a growth in the authority of the three estates of Normandy, but neither did it witness a further decline of their privileges. Henry III had invoked the doctrine of evident necessity to justify ordering that taxes be collected in Normandy without waiting for the consent of the estates. The deputies could protest against the size of the levy, but they were fortunate when they won a reduction. Henry IV had continued this practice, with the result that beginning in 1608, the three estates temporarily ceased to make specific grants to the king and contented themselves with giving a general authorization to levy the taxes he requested in his commission.

The Normans hoped to profit from the minority to improve their position because they once more began to specify the amount of taxes they were willing to pay. In December 1610 and November 1611 the three estates voted only two-thirds of the taille that the crown requested, but the commissioners ordered that the entire amount be collected. In 1612 and 1613 they voted all the taille on the condition that the king exempt them from the grand crue. Once more they failed in their objective, and the government ordered that both taxes be levied. By the time the estates met in September 1614, it was evident that the council was unwilling to bargain. The three estates again voted the entire taille, and this time, probably disheartened, they were content merely to plead with the king to abolish the grand crue.[125]

There are other indications that the estates hoped for a new era following the death of Henry IV, only to be disappointed. The deputies who assembled in Rouen in December 1610 asked permission to levy an additional sum to support their activities. They sought the revocations of extraordinary commissions. They protested against money appropriated to reimburse officers whose positions were to be suppressed being diverted to other purposes. They asked for an accounting of the 33,000 livres Normandy had been contributing annually for the repair of roads and bridges, and they complained about the activities of the lieutenants that Sully had sent to the province in his capacity of grand voyer. Perhaps in a conscious effort to win influence, a matter the importance of which they had not always recognized in the past, they voted to give their new governor, the count of Soissons, 18,000 livres.[126] The following year the estates, emboldened by Sully's loss of favor, asked that his post of grand voyer be abolished. They renewed their assault on useless offices and asked that a wine tax be removed.[127] The

125. *Cahiers des Etats de Normandie sous les règnes de Louis XIII et de Louis XIV*, ed. Charles de Robillard de Beaurepaire (Rouen, 1876), 1:18–19, 47–48, 68–69, 90, 117–18; Henri Prentout, *Les Etats provinciaux de Normandie* (Caen, 1925), 1:347–48.

126. *Cahiers de Louis XIII et de Louis XIV*, 1:12–13, 17, 217, 220, 223–24.

127. Ibid., pp. 25–27, 29, 32, 38–39.

council rejected or sidestepped most of their petitions. The estates nevertheless renewed their list of grievances annually, but one detects a note of
discouragement as they dropped some rejected items, such as the suppression
of the office of grand voyer, and repeated others year after year without
success.[128]

The estates were not convoked in the fall of 1615 to vote taxes for 1616.
The explanation for this oversight lies in the disorders that attended a revolt
led by the prince of Condé and the ease with which the crown could bypass
the estates and order the élus to levy the desired sum. The syndic of the
estates kept informed on developments, but there is no evidence that he
protested against levying taxes without consent. Indeed the crown silenced
some possible opposition by ordering that those who usually served as
commissioners to the estates be paid just as though the estates had been held.
Since the usual commissioners were Norman notables, the king's generosity
was in effect a bribe designed to encourage them to leave matters as they
were.[129]

What is surprising is that when the three estates met in Rouen in
December 1616, they offered no protest against taxes being levied that year
without consent. They complained bitterly about the suffering that marauding troops had occasioned, repeated earlier complaints against the actions of
the provincial officials responsible for roads and bridges, and made charges
that it cost far too much to collect the taille. Nevertheless they voted the
usual 1,803,160 livres that the king required. They did accompany this
grant with the request that other taxes be abolished, but the crown's
response was not favorable although they had taken the precaution of voting
Marie de Medici, their new governor, 18,000 livres.[130]

The duke of Luynes attended the estates of November 1617 in his capacity
of the king's lieutenant general in Normandy, but his presence was not
enough to prevent the deputies from requesting that the various indirect
taxes be reduced or abolished or, surprisingly, to lead them to offer him a
generous gift. They did vote the usual amounts for the king and his mother,
who remained their governor in spite of her disgrace the previous spring, but
on the whole they acted with considerable independence.[131] Indeed during
this session the deputies won their most notable victory of the decade. When
the Chamber of Accounts arrested a deputy, they brought pressure to secure

128. The cahiers of the estates of 1612, 1613, and 1614 are in ibid., pp. 49–121. Yves Durand
has published the cahier that the deputies of the Norman nobility prepared during the Estates
General of 1614 in *Enquêtes et documents* 1 (1971): 86–117.

129. *Cahiers de Louis XIII et de Louis XIV*, 1:287–92, 3:432.

130. Ibid., 1:124–26, 135, 141–44, 299.

131. Ibid., pp. 149–50, 160, 164, 170, 318, 333; J. Fauchon, "Le député de la vicomté
d'Avranches aux Etats de Normandie de 1617," *Revue de l'Avranchin et du pays de Granville*
46 (1969): 181–96; *Journal d'Arnauld d'Andilly, 1614–1620*, pp. 323–26.

his release by refusing to listen to the reading of the king's letters until this had been done.[132]

In November 1618 and January 1620, the estates adopted a different tactic and voted only 1,503,100 livres, 300,000 less than the king had requested in his directives to his commissioners. Both grants were coupled with the plea that the province be relieved of the various indirect taxes. Faced with this situation, the commissioners gave a provisional order that the full amount be collected anyway, and the deputies that the estates sent to court were unable to persuade the king to take less. Yet even in these circumstances, the commissioners still used the word "consent" in regard to the appropriation.[133]

The three estates thus ended the decade where they had begun. Their rights to meet annually and to petition were still unchallenged, but even if they did not vote all the money requested, the king ordered that the entire sum be collected. The existence of the élus made this possible without too much danger of revolt, but the estates themselves may not have made the most of their opportunities. In 1610, 1614, 1616, 1617, and 1620, they voted their governor or lieutenant general 18,000 livres, and there is evidence that the practice was becoming customary, but they did not shower lavish gifts on influential royal officials to the degree that other less wealthy provinces did.[134] Indeed they sometimes sought to have the number of commissioners the king sent to their meetings reduced as a further economy rather than try to win these influential persons to their cause.[135]

10. THE OTHER ESTATES IN FRANCE

The history of the remaining estates in France was relatively uneventful during the first decade of Louis XIII's reign. For one reason or another none of them had felt the heavy hand of Henry IV or Sully. After their departure, therefore, these estates had no lost privileges to recover, and they continued to function as before.

As in the past, the échevins of Clermont convoked the nineteen good towns of Basse-Auvergne when the occasion seemed to warrant. From 1610 through 1620, there were twenty-two meetings, at least one in each year. In addition, there were five meetings of the six nearest towns to Clermont and one meeting of the three estates to elect deputies to the Estates General of 1614. On several occasions the inhabitants of Basse-Auvergne were called

132. *Cahiers de Louis XIII et de Louis XIV*, 1 : 312–13, 329–31. Prentout, *Les Etats provinciaux*, 1 : 349–50.

133. *Cahiers de Louis XIII et de Louis XIV*, 1 : 174, 177–78, 182, 194–95, 207–208, 338.

134. Ibid., pp. 217, 278, 299, 318, 333, 348.

135. Ibid., pp. 45, 168–69, 320.

upon to pay increased taxes to support the troops required to maintain order during Condé's rebellions, but probably the most impressive development was the steady progress toward paying the provincial debt. In 1605 Basse-Auvergne had begun to liquidate it at a rate of 90,000 livres per year. By 1614, 900,000 livres had been repaid, and in December 1621 the deputies of the nineteen good towns received the happy news that they owed only 29,122 livres. Clearly the estates handled their financial affairs far better than the crown did during these years.[136]

Historians have assumed that the assembly of the four towns and pro-vostships of Haute-Auvergne was suppressed during this period. This pre-sumption has been based on a report that intendant Mesgrigny made in 1637 concerning a decree that the late Henri de Noailles, lieutenant of the Haute-Pays, obtained from the king's council at some point prior to 1620. Actually all that Mesgrigny said was that the decree forbade the third estate to assemble without permission, hardly enough to prove its demise, and there is ample evidence that they continued to meet after 1620.[137]

The third estate of Haute-Auvergne did not necessarily assemble every year. The king told the élus what taxes to collect. Only if he asked for too much or there was some other matter that concerned the province did the third estate take action. This action was not difficult to instigate because prior to the decree, the capital of each provostship could assemble the lesser communities, and St. Flour could convoke the four provostships. Since taxes remained about the same and there were no important innovations during the early years of Louis's reign, there appears to have been little activity on the part of the third estate. Beginning in 1616, however, there were one or more meetings of the third estate each year for some time. The crown's desire to create an additional élection in the province, a dispute over the size of its debts, and the king's request for higher taxes were among the most important items discussed. It was probably during this period that Noailles obtained the decree requiring that the king give his permission before the estates could be held. On June 18, 1621, and again on May 11, 1622, when the municipal officials of St. Flour were considering convoking the estates, someone reminded those present that it was first necessary to obtain the king's consent, and deputations were dispatched for this purpose.[138]

136. AD, Puy-de-Dôme, 4F 145, 4F 146; *IAC, Clermont-Ferrand, Fonds de Montferrand*, ed. E. Teilhard de Chardin (Clermont-Ferrand, 1902), 1:66–72, 185–205 passim; Antoine Bergier and Verdier-Latour, *Recherches historiques sur les Etats généraux et plus particulièrement sur l'origine, l'organisation et la durée des anciens Etats provinciaux d'Auvergne* (Clermont-Ferrand, 1788), pièces justificatives, no. 75.

137. *Lettres et mémoires adressés au Chancelier Séguier*, ed. Roland Mousnier (Paris, 1964), 2:1136. My dating of the decree is based on the fact that Noailles resigned his post in favor of his son in 1620.

138. AC, Saint-Flour, ch. 5, art. 6, nos. 51–53, 140; *IAC, Aurillac*, ed. Gabriel Esquer (Aurillac, 1906), BB 14.

The reason for Noailles' action against the third estate probably dated back to a quarrel he had had with St. Flour during the elections to the Estates General of 1614. In that year he directed the three estates to meet at Aurillac where he lay ill with the gout. St. Flour immediately sent deputies to ask him to change the location of the meeting to their city as the letters of convocation had directed. At first Noailles refused to see them, and when he finally did, they fell to quarreling. The deputies wanted Noailles to postpone the elections until he was well enough to go to St. Flour, but he refused. They then laid plans to summon the estates to meet in St. Flour on their own authority, but fled to their homes when they learned that Noailles was planning to have them arrested. In the end, deputies were elected in both St. Flour and Aurillac. The king's council was left to decide who to seat, and Noailles, we may suspect, was infuriated.[139]

The nobles of Haute-Auvergne remained organized. In February 1614 they sought permission to elect a syndic to support the third estate in a quarrel with the farmers of the salt tax and some months later they elected deputies to the Estates General.[140]

The syndics of the third estates of the plat pays of Lyonnais and Forez continued to cooperate with a deputy from the town of Villefranche in representing the interests of the three provinces in the government of Lyonnais. In 1611 and again in 1612, problems concerning the salt tax brought them together.[141] In 1619, at the close of the decade, the desire to provide their governor with twenty men to maintain order led to a meeting. Louis agreed, and Lyonnais was taxed 3,334 livres, Forez 5,000, and Beaujolais 1,666 for their support. Early in 1622 they once more acted together in this regard.[142] The continued activities of the syndics of the third estate of Forez[143] and the plat pays of Lyonnais in meetings of the

---

139. AC, Saint-Flour, ch. 5, art. 1, nos. 14–25.

140. *Dictionnaire statistique, ou histoire, description et statistique du département du Cantal*, ed. Déribier-du-Châtelet (Aurillac, 1853), 2 : 107. A copy of the cahier of the nobles who assembled at St. Flour to elect deputies to the Estates General of 1611 is in B. Mun., Poitiers, Collection Fonteneau, 28, fols. 279–82v.

141. AD, Loire, C 32, no. 4; *IAC, Lyon*, ed. Fortuné Rolle (Paris, 1865), 1: BB 147; *Registres consulaires de la ville de Villefranche*, ed. Abel Besançon and Emile Longin (Villefranche-sur-Saône, 1919), 4:249–53, 271, 305–308.

142. AD, Rhône, C 431, fols. 27v–28, 321–21v. I did not examine C 423–30, which consist of the edicts, declarations, and letter patents of the Bureau of Finances at Lyons for the years 1610–1619. Had I done so, additional meetings of the government and of the individual provinces would almost certainly have been uncovered.

143. The third estate of Forez met on October 25, 1611, the nobility and third estate met in August 1614, and the third estate met in December 1617 to elect a new syndic. AD, Loire, C 32, nos. 4–6. On January 18, 1620, the king's council issued a decree at the request of the syndic of Forez levying 4,324 livres on those who paid the taille in order to support the common affairs of the province. AD, Rhône, C 431, fols. 22v–23.

government prove that their respective estates continued to exist,[144] and Villefranche frequently assembled the other towns in Beaujolais.[145]

It is impossible to reconstruct the history of any of the Pyrenean estates that lay within the confines of France, but as far as can be ascertained, the estates of Bigorre, Foix, Labourd, Nébouzan, Quatre-Vallées, and Soule functioned normally during the first decade of Louis XIII's reign.

Indeed this period can be characterized as a return to normal conditions throughout France. The march toward absolutism commenced by Henry IV and Sully ceased, and following Villeroy's advice the crown returned to the consultative traditions of the Renaissance monarchy. The élections were abolished in Guyenne, and the estates of that region resumed their traditional tax-collecting duties. Threats to the estates of Languedoc, Burgundy, and elsewhere ceased. The government did show a disconcerting tendency not to hold the estates during rebellions or when it was otherwise inconvenient, which necessitated collecting taxes without consent for a year. Even such strong estates as those of Burgundy, Brittany, and Provence joined Normandy in suffering on this score. However there is no reason to believe that the government had any intention of doing away with the estates. They were always summoned again the following year amid profuse explanations from the crown. If there were any ominous signs, they were in Béarn and Navarre, the two little states that were not yet incorporated into the crown of France, but even here it was religion rather than absolutism that motivated the government to take action.

11. The Estates of Béarn and Navarre

Henry IV had respected the privileges of Béarn and Navarre, and he had preserved their status as independent states, but he had insisted that Catholics be permitted to hold office and to practice their religion in a limited number of designated places. The Protestants who controlled the estates and other institutions in Béarn had protested unsuccessfully against these concessions, but they could take satisfaction in the fact that there were definite limits as to how far Henry would go to please his new co-religionists. His death, followed by the growing Catholic strength at court, led the two Béarnais bishops and other Catholics to seek further concessions. Included were demands that the Catholic rite be celebrated in some one hundred

144. The appearance of the former syndics and the two current syndics before the king's council in March 1620 proves that there must have been periodic assemblies of the plat pays to elect them for specified terms. AD Rhône, C 431, fols. 28v–29.

145. The échevins of Villefranche summoned the chief towns of the châtellenies of Beaujolais to meetings in October 1611, February 1612, September 1612, June 1614, and September 1614. *Registres de Villefranche*, 4:249–53, 254–56, 305–08, 312–16. The *Registres* have been published only to 1615.

localities where it was currently illegal, that the church property that Jeanne had confiscated and used largely to support the Protestant clergy be restored, and that a Catholic be appointed to the vacant post of first president at Pau, although Henry IV had promised to name a Protestant. In addition, the Béarnais bishops wanted to be given precedence in the estates and the Conseil Souverain.[146]

These demands and Sully's removal from office in January 1611 further increased the Protestants' fears, and when the three estates of Béarn met that April, they took the unusual step of naming deputies to the general assembly of the French Protestants at Saumur in order to obtain its support. Marie de Medici quickly countered by saying that if the Béarnais wanted to unite with the French churches, she would unite their country with France. Their sovereign court would become a presidial seat, and they would be placed in the jurisdiction of the Parlement of Toulouse. The Béarnais did not take this hint that their quest for French Protestant support would likely cost them their independence and persisted in their course. Marie de Medici failed to implement her threat, but to weaken the Béarnais position, she insisted that they negotiate separately with her council rather than in conjunction with the French Huguenots.[147]

In the years that followed, both Béarnais Catholics and Protestants sought the support of their French co-religionists. The former won the backing of the clergy in the Estates General of 1614, and the latter continued to attend French Protestant assemblies in spite of the crown's disapproval. The Protestant governor of Béarn and Navarre, the marquis of La Force, staunchly defended the privileges of the two states and the rights of his church. As a reward he received generous grants from the estates but was compelled to follow a dangerous and somewhat devious course of protesting his loyalty to the crown at the same time that he raised troops to defend his position and that of his adherents. In the fall of 1615 the crown was prepared to relieve him from his post because of the qualified support he had given to an uprising of some Protestants in conjunction with a rebellion led by the prince of Condé. He survived this threat, but the crown remained suspicious of his motives. As a result, when the determined Mangot and Barbin came to power during the ministerial revolution in the summer of 1616, they began to take steps to strengthen the crown's position.[148]

146. *Mémoires authentiques de Jacques Nompar de Caumont, duc de La Force*, ed. Marquis de la Grange (Paris, 1843), 2 : 13–14; Blet, *Le clergé* 1 : 234–35.

147. *Mémoires de La Force*, 2 : 18–21, 325–26, 330–31, 334, 339, 342; *Mercure François* (Paris, 1615), 2 (1611): fols. 88, 101; AD, Basses-Pyrénées, C 705; Marc Forissier, *Histoire de la réforme en Béarn* (Tarbes, 1951), 2 : 71–73.

148. *Mémoires de La Force*, 2 : 35–39, 89–100, 397, 410–12, 422–48; AD, Basses-Pyrénées, C 706, C 841; Pierre Tucoo-Chala, *La vicomté de Béarn et le problème de sa souveraineté* (Bordeaux, 1961), pp. 128–30; J.-B. Laborde, *Précis d'histoire du Béarn* (Pau, 1943), pp. 270–77; Blet, *Le clergé*, 1 : 235–37; Forissier, *Histoire de la réforme*, 2 : 74–78.

On December 31, 1616, the new leaders of the king's council issued a decree incorporating Béarn and Navarre into the realm of France. The change to some extent was the logical outcome of the constant pleas the Béarnais Catholics and Protestants had made to their co-religionists in France, but it nevertheless led to considerable agitation. The estates of Béarn met in a special session in February 1617 where they argued that the decree was illegal because it contradicted their fors. The state, many thought, was the product of a double contract, one between the viscount and his people and the other between the people and the estates that represented them. Anyone, the estates unanimously declared, who accepted the edict of union was a traitor to his country. They sought La Force's assistance and instructed their syndics to oppose the union by all the proper means at their disposal. Predominantly Catholic Navarre, an innocent victim of the religious quarrel, also protested.[149]

The estates of Béarn and Navarre managed to prevent the implementation of the edict of union until after the assassination of Concini in April 1617. The assembly of the French Catholic clergy that met in Paris shortly thereafter, however, renewed its effort to improve the situation of the Béarnais Catholics. This time their requests were delivered to the favorably disposed and determined young Louis XIII, now acting in his own right. On June 25 his council issued a decree reestablishing the Catholic rite throughout Béarn and returning to the church all the lands and revenue that Jeanne d'Albret had confiscated. The Béarnais were to retain their separate state, but soon their resistance was to put this privilege in jeopardy.[150]

La Force was summoned to court to receive instructions to enforce the decree. Here he vigorously defended the Béarnais position, while in Pau the Conseil Souverain refused to register it. The resulting delay led the Béarnais Catholics to submit a long petition to the king's council in August 1617, but the three estates of Béarn that met in November countered by voting unanimously against union with France and by fifty-seven to fourteen along strictly religious lines against returning the former church property. La Force counseled moderation, but Rohan and other French Protestants offered their support. A deputation was dispatched to the king, and a committee of the estates met frequently in the months that followed.[151] Meanwhile Rohan and others were trying to persuade the estates of neighboring Navarre to take a strong stand.[152]

149. Tucoo-Chala, *La vicomté de Béarn*, pp. 130–31, 196–98; AD, Basses-Pyrénées, C 707, fols. 61–84; *Mercure François* 5 (1617): 68–70, 318–20; Forissier, *Histoire de la réforme*, 2:80–81; Alain Destrée, *La Basse-Navarre et ses institutions de 1620 à la Révolution* (Saragossa, 1955), pp. 29–30.

150. Blet, *Le clergé*, 1:237–39; *Mercure François* 5 (1617): 70–73; Forissier, *Histoire de la réforme*, 2:82–86.

151. *Mémoires de La Force*, 2:100–04, 453–54; AN, E 1685, no. 3; AD, Basses-Pyrénées, C 707, fols. 84–258 passim; Forissier, *Histoire de la réforme*, 2:87–88; *Mercure-François* 5 (1617): 329–30.

152. AN, K 1233, nos. 45–48.

The opposition to the edict returning the church property was so strong that La Force claimed that he could not enforce it, but the crown suspected that he was at the bottom of the resistance. Protestant deputies from Languedoc and Guyenne met with those of Béarn in spite of royal orders not to do so, but soon more cautious French Huguenots were advising their Béarnais brethren to compromise. Nevertheless the Conseil Souverain steadfastly refused to register the king's decree. Royal anger at La Force grew, and his sons lost their court positions. Slowly the one-time favorite was driven from a position of at least outward compliance to the acceptance of rebellion as a desperate means to maintain his position and that of his coreligionists. The youthful Louis XIII also despaired of implementing his will through letters and commissioners. In the summer of 1620 he set out for Guyenne and Béarn with an army after having easily suppressed a rebellion led by his mother. His initial move was probably directed only at the intransigent Protestants, but in the end his march to the south was to inaugurate a new effort to establish royal absolutism in France.[153]

153. *Mémoires de La Force*, 2:104–11, 459–75; Forissier, *Histoire de la réforme*, 2:88–89.

13

FRANCE FINDS A KING,
1620–1624

1. Louis XIII and His Epoch

WHEN LOUIS XIII BEGAN TO MARCH HIS ARMY TOWARD BÉARN AND NAVARRE during the summer of 1620, he was not yet nineteen years old. Of average height, he had inherited his father's restless energy and capacity to endure fatigue. When he accompanied his troops into battle, it was to share their dangers and hardships. He was to be the last of France's soldier kings. Hunting followed war as his favorite pursuit. Then came the mechanical arts and, somewhat surprisingly, architecture, music, sculpture, and painting. For history and literature, he had little interest. His tastes were simple, and frugality was as much a part of his character as it was absent from that of both of his parents. There is no reason to doubt that he was a sincere Catholic, but he never permitted the interest of the church to subordinate those of the crown. Almost as a reaction to his father's conduct, he practiced a strict sexual morality, at least as far as women were concerned. Between 1619 and 1622, he appears to have sincerely loved his wife, Anne of Austria, but a quarrel following a miscarriage and her flirtation with the duke of Buckingham raised an irremovable barrier between the two, for he was too proud to forgive or to forget.[1]

Louis stammered. To avoid embarrassment, he said little when it was not necessary. If he had to take a position, he spoke slowly to cloak his handicap. At times he was morose or bad tempered, and he had a sadistic streak that sometimes caused him to turn a conquered town over to his troops to be sacked and made him immune to the pleas of wives and kinsmen that he spare the lives of rebellious, disobedient, or suspected nobles. He inherited his mother's mediocre mind, and this probably accounted for a certain timidity and lack of confidence that he hid under a cloak of aloofness and largely overcame by his determination to have a glorious reign. To be a great king, as he saw it, he had to win glory upon the battlefield, but even

---

1. On the question of whether Louis was a homosexual, see the somewhat conflicting views of Louis Vaunois, *Vie de Louis XIII* (Paris, 1944), pp. 563–67, and Louis Batiffol, *Le roi Louis XIII à vingt ans* (Paris, 1910), pp. 483–88.

more important, perhaps, he had to mete out a stern justice and to be obeyed. His more intelligent and self-confident father knew when to be flexible, and he was often too forgiving. To Louis such traits were signs of weakness. He dared not let his mediocre mind make such difficult choices. He sought to overcome his handicaps by an unyielding determination and an inflexible will.[2]

These traits appeared early in his career and ought to have given warning of what to expect when he reached manhood. In August 1614, shortly before his thirteenth birthday, Vendôme, his older bastard half-brother who had just led a rebellion, had come to him to protest that he had no other desire than "to be his very humble and obedient servant." With a trembling voice and white with anger, Louis had replied: "Serve me better in the future than you have in the past, and know that the greatest honor that you have in the world is to be my brother."[3] When the baron de Guémadeuc killed another noble and shut himself up in the Château of Fougères rather than surrender to the authorities, Louis, now nearly sixteen, was prepared to march at the head of an army to compel his obedience. Alarmed, Guémadeuc surrendered. He had powerful friends at court, including the marshal of Vitry, who had just rendered the young king a great service by executing Concini. With their aid he no doubt expected to escape with little or no punishment. Instead he was sentenced to death. When his wife threw herself on her knees before Louis and pleaded for mercy, Louis dryly replied: "I owe justice to my subjects and in this instance I prefer justice to mercy."[4] Guémadeuc was beheaded.

Obedience and justice! When Louis was only sixteen, one of his secretaries of state noted these traits when he wrote a prominent noble that Louis "wants to be obeyed and is offended by those who fail him in this duty, unless it is through ignorance. If it is, he pardons freely and listens to reason very easily."[5] A year or two later, Louis wrote to his oft-estranged mother trying to explain his actions and sometimes to reproach her for her deeds. He spoke of his determination to use force "to maintain my authority and the public tranquility of my kingdom and to prevent all movements which could trouble it, to the devastation and ruin of my people."[6] Repeatedly he used such phrases as "to reestablish royal authority," "to conserve the

---

2. On Louis's character, see Vaunois, *Vie de Louis XIII*, and Batiffol, *Le roi Louis XIII*. For somewhat questionable attempts to apply psychoanalytic methods to achieve an understanding of Louis's character, see E. W. Marvik, "The Character of Louis XIII: The Role of His Physician," *Journal of Interdisciplinary History* 4 (1974): 347–74, and "Childhood History and Decisions of State: The Case of Louis XIII," *History of Childhood Quarterly* 2 (1974): 135–99.

3. *Journal de Jean Héroard sur l'enfance et la jeunesse de Louis XIII, 1602–1628*, ed. Eudore Soulié and Ed. de Barthélemy (Paris, 1868), 2:153.

4. Batiffol, *Le roi Louis XIII*, p. 177.

5. *Journal de ma vie: Mémoires du maréchal de Bassompierre*, ed. Audoin de La Crapte de Chantérac (Paris, 1873), 2:417.

6. E. Griselle, "Louis XIII et sa mère," *Revue historique* 105 (1910): 308.

authority," "against my authority," "to the prejudice of my authority," and "to make my authority recognized." He also talked of "the good of my state and the glory of my reign,"[7] but he saw it as being achieved by stamping out factions, suppressing disorder, and reestablishing "public tranquility."[8] "From concord is born the repose of the mind and the tranquility of the soul; from discord comes the ruin of towns, the desolation of the countryside, and all the miseries of life."[9]

Here we see the young Louis. He longs for glory that could be best achieved by restoring order to his kingdom for the the benefit of his people. It is not surprising that he should have such a goal. Was not his father, whom he revered already being called "the great" because he had done this very thing? Louis gave no thought to winning glory by humbling the Habsburgs. The evil genius of Richelieu had not yet directed his attention away from domestic reform. Rather he resumed the policies of the great Henry as he vaguely understood them. Less experienced than his father, yes; less intelligent, yes; but perhaps for these very reasons he was more determined and less willing to compromise.

The France that Louis XIII began to take a personal hand in ruling around 1620 was quite different from what it had been sixty years before. Then the Protestants had been a rapidly expanding, dynamic minority that many thought would soon become the dominant religion in the country. The Wars of Religion checked their growth, but when Henry IV issued the Edict of Nantes in 1598 their numbers stood at 1.25 million, about 7 percent of the total population. With the restoration of peace, they began to win new converts once more, and around 1620 their church peaked, with about 1.6 million members. The Protestant growth then halted and soon began to decline. Henry had adopted the practice of offering handsome rewards to great nobles to defect, and it was during his reign that the Catholic church had begun to give money to pastors and to the laity who did so. Neither policy bore much fruit in the first two decades of the century, but thereafter they both took their toll. More important, there was a decline in religious zeal and a growth of internal conflicts within the Protestant camp. This situation, coupled with less effective leadership and a growing realization that the overwhelming majority of Frenchmen would always be Catholic, led the more lukewarm adherents of the new faith to return to the ancient church. But the most important of all the reasons for the reversal of Protestant fortunes was the rising tide of the Catholic reform movement.[10]

If the history of the last half of the sixteenth century must be thought of largely in terms of the Protestant challenge, that of the seventeenth century

7. Ibid., pp. 310, 312, 315, 321, 322; ibid. 106 (1911): 299, 303.

8. Ibid. 105:308, 320; ibid. 106:299, 303.

9. Ibid. 106:299.

10. For a recent summary of the changing Protestant situation, see Emile G. Léonard, *A History of Protestantism*, trans. R. M. Bethell (London, 1967), 2:359–75.

must be conceived largely in terms of the Catholic revival. This was true not only in France where the devout Catholic party was an important factor in policy decisions but also in most of the rest of the European continent as well. This situation not only propelled the French crown toward a confrontation with its powerful Protestant minority but also became a factor in foreign policy. In the Empire, the resurgent forces of Catholicism were at length ready to assert themselves, while Spain, though weakened, prepared to renew the attempt to bring its rebellious Dutch provinces to obedience. In 1618 and 1619 while the Protestants of Béarn were resisting Louis's efforts to reestablish Catholicism in their little state, their coreligionists in Bohemia reacted even more strongly against Habsburg and Catholic pressures by seizing control of the kingdom and electing as king the Calvinist elector Frederick of the Palatinate. The Austrian Habsburgs counterattacked with the aid of Spain and the German Catholic princes. Soon this conflict became involved with the Spanish effort to reconquer their former Dutch provinces, and a bloody war ensued that was to last until 1648.

Louis's first reaction was to offer to assist the emperor in bringing his rebellious Protestant subjects to obedience, but quickly French dynastic and national interests led him to change his course. In January 1620, he withdrew his promise to help and instead sent an embassy to the Empire to try to restore peace. By refraining from taking an active military role in the conflict, Louis was able to devote his energies to strengthening his position within his own kingdom. He made great strides in this direction, especially between 1620 and 1622. Not until 1624 did he and his advisers succumb to the temptation of trying to prevent the Habsburgs from reaping the full rewards from their initial victories and at the same time of securing some profits for France. They did this by making alliances with the Protestant states and attempting to cut the Spanish supply lines through the Alps to the Empire by intervening in northern Italy and Switzerland. From then until November 1630, there was a tug of war in France between those who favored domestic reform and those who opted for active participation in the European conflict. The ultimate victory of the latter was to have a profound effect on the nature of French government and society.

The growing temptation to intervene in the Thirty Years War paralleled a change in the direction of the economy. The Italian wars of the sixteenth century had been supported by an expanding economy, but now when the French were about to challenge the Habsburgs once more, the economic upturn that had begun in the late fifteenth century came to an end. If a date must be chosen for its termination, the year 1620 would do as well as any, but the French economy was as decentralized as the government and some regions continued to prosper long after that date. For the remainder of the seventeenth century, there was not permanent stagnation but rather limited periods of stagnation that were terminated by several years of bad harvest in which grain prices and the death rate soared. A modest recovery would follow, only to have the process repeated once more. Rarely were there a half-dozen years or more of relative prosperity. It is quite possible that the French population reached a peak on the eve of the bad harvests of 1628–30 that was not surpassed until well into the reign of Louis XV. Under these circumstances the French people were in no condition to engage in a major foreign war in which the size of their armies and the costs of supplying each individual soldier was far greater than it had been when they had first invaded Italy in 1494.[11]

2. Béarn and the Protestant Revolt

The possibility that he might soon be supporting the Protestants in the Empire against their Habsburg lords probably never entered young Louis's mind in 1618, 1619, or 1620. What angered him most then was that his own Protestant subjects were as disobedient and potentially rebellious as those of his Habsburg rivals. Month after month, indeed year after year passed in which the Conseil Souverain refused to register his edict reestablishing the Catholic rite throughout Béarn and returning to the church all the land and revenue that Jeanne d'Albert had confiscated to the benefit of the Protestants. It must have been doubly aggravating because he suspected that instead of trying to implement his will, his governor, La Force, was actually encouraging the Béarnais to defy his commands. At first, he hoped that Béarn would comply. Then in February 1619 Marie de Medici escaped from Blois, where she had been confined since the overthrow of Concini, and joined forces with the duke of Epernon. Peace followed a few months later because Luynes decided that it would be more expedient to make concessions than to fight, but many of the magnates were restive, and it was not unlikely that there would be a general Protestant uprising if Louis enforced his edict against Béarn. Still young and inexperienced, he continued to follow the policy of his cautious advisers. He did not withdraw his edict, but he was not ready to enforce his will through arms.

The political assembly of the Protestants opened at Loudun on September

11. There is a vast literature on the seventeenth-century crisis and numerous detailed works on aspects of the French economy, but see especially the classic statement by E. J. Hobsbawm that has been reprinted with other articles on the subject in *Crisis in Europe, 1560–1660*, ed. Trevor Aston (New York, 1967). For an attempted synthesis of the research on the French economy, see D. Richet, "Croissance et blocages en France du XVᵉ au XVIIIᵉ siècle," *Annales: économies, sociétés, civilisations* 23 (1968): 759–87. For monetary considerations and evidence of regional differences in the French economy, see Frank C. Spooner, *The International Economy and Monetary Movements in France, 1493–1725* (Cambridge, Mass., 1972). J. Michael Hayden has demonstrated that prices were stable between 1603 and 1617. See his *France and the Estates General of 1614* (Cambridge, 1974), pp. 24–27, 224–33. Alexandra D. Lublinskaya has challenged the concept of a seventeenth-century economic crisis. For her arguments, see *French Absolutism: The Crucial Phase, 1620–1629*, trans. Brian Pearce (Cambridge, 1968).

25, 1619, to elect new deputies to represent their interests at court. Those who attended took up the Béarnais cause and dispatched a deputation to the king to treat on this and other matters. Louis refused to negotiate with his subjects in a piecemeal fashion but was willing to reply to their cahier when it was completed and after the assembly had disbanded. This the deputies would not do because once they returned to their homes, they would lose much of their power to secure concessions. Thus an impasse was reached in which deputies went back and forth between the assembly and the king. Not until April 1620 did the Protestants disband after receiving a few minor concessions but no promise that the edict against Béarn would not be executed.[12]

The assembly of Loudun was followed by another uprising led by Marie de Medici and a number of magnates. This time Louis put himself at the head of a small army and moved with such dispatch that the rebels quickly lost heart. Peace was restored in August 1620 with more modest rewards than usual being given the grandees in return for ceasing their bad behavior. Louis now found himself at the head of an army but with no avowed enemies in northern France. It was at this point that Pierre de Bérulle, a leader of the Catholic reformation and future cardinal, urged that he enforce his edict. Early in September, Louis marched at the head of his army to Bordeaux to restore order in Guyenne and to await the arrival of La Force with news from Béarn. When he learned that the Béarnais continued to delay enforcing his edict, he set out for Pau, where he arrived on October 15. So rapid and determined were the government's actions in comparison with the indecision of the past that it is difficult to believe that a new force was not asserting itself. Luynes usually counseled caution, for he feared the hazards of war, and there were others who thought it wiser to proceed slowly with Béarn for fear of provoking a general Protestant revolt. Under such circumstances we can only conclude that Louis himself was taking more direct control over his government.[13]

Louis's stay in Béarn was brief. Within a week he compelled the Conseil Souverain to register the edict restoring the property of the Catholic church, held the estates in which the bishops of Lescar and Oloron resumed their seats and were given the precedence they had once enjoyed, issued an edict uniting Béarn and Navarre to the crown of France, and created a Parlement at Pau to serve Béarn, Navarre, and Soule. To further the Catholic cause, Louis created a Jesuit college, and to ensure his control over the region, he replaced the Protestant governor and garrison of the powerful fortress of Navarrenx by Catholics. By November 7 Louis was back at Paris. A week

12. Léonce Anquez, *Histoire des assemblées politiques des réformés de France, 1573–1622* (Paris, 1859), pp. 316–26.

13. Michel Houssaye, *Le Père de Bérulle et l'Oratoire de Jésus, 1611–1625* (Paris, 1874), pp. 338–44; *Mémoires de Bassompierre*, 2 : 208–13; *Mémoires de Messire François Duval, Marquis de Fontenay-Mareuil*, Michaud, sér. 2, 5 : 153–55. *Mercure François* (Paris, 1621), 6 (1620): 338–46.

later the estates of Navarre met to protest both the reunion of Navarre with France and the loss of their own court and being placed under the jurisdiction of the Parlement at Pau. Louis let them keep their court for four more years, but he made no further concessions. In a few decisive months he had suppressed an uprising in northern France and restored his authority in the south, but the real test was yet to come.[14]

Louis was received as a hero by the Parisian Catholics, but the Protestants, were thoroughly alarmed. A political assembly met in La Rochelle in late December to determine what action to take. When the king ordered it to disband, it refused. Both Luynes and the more moderate Protestants wanted a peaceful solution, but the majority at the assembly at La Rochelle insisted that their co-religionists in Béarn be returned to their former position and that Louis withdraw the troops he had left in the south the preceding year. These conditions were unacceptable. Louis began to arm, and the assembly countered by taking measures to defend the Protestant faith. Unfortunately for its cause, most of the Huguenot magnates refused to participate. As Louis began to move south in the spring of 1621, the Huguenot towns in Saintonge and Guyenne, with few exceptions, opened their gates to him. Saint-Jean d'Angély resisted but was taken after nearly a month's resistance. By July the royal army had reached the powerfully fortified town of Montauban. Here the Protestants defended themselves with such determination that Louis abandoned the siege in November. The following month, Luynes died of the fever, and the campaign of 1621 came to an end.[15]

At the peace negotiations, neither side would make the necessary compromises. In the spring of 1622 Louis resumed the war, and by July he was besieging Montpellier. Once again the royal army was unsuccessful, and peace was made in October. By its terms Louis reconfirmed the Edict of Nantes, thereby assuring the Protestants the continuation of their religious and civil liberties. In the course of the conflict, however, many of their places of security had been taken, and as a condition of peace Louis insisted that all or part of the new fortifications that had been constructed at Montpellier, Nîmes, Castres, and Millau be destroyed and that no more political assemblies be held without his permission. Of the great Protestant strongholds, only La Rochelle and Montauban remained. Equally important was

14. *Mercure François* 6:346–68; *Mémoires authentiques de Jacques Nompar de Caumont, duc de La Force*, ed. Marquis de La Grange (Paris, 1843), 2:115–21; Marc Forissier, *Histoire de la réforme en Béarn* (Tarbes, 1951), 2:99–108; AD, Basses-Pyrénées, C 708, fols. 93–102v; AN, K 1233, nos. 50–52; Pierre Tucoo-Chala, *La vicomté de Béarn et le problème de sa souveraineté* (Bordeaux, 1961), pp. 132–33, 198–99; Alain Destrée, *La Basse-Navarre et ses institutions de 1620 à la Révolution* (Saragossa, 1955), pp. 30–32.

15. Anquez, *Histoire des assemblées politiques*, pp. 331–63; Jack A. Clarke, *Huguenot Warrior: The Life and Times of Henri de Rohan, 1579–1638* (The Hague, 1966), pp. 73–93; Berthold Zeller, *Le connétable de Luynes* (Paris, 1879); Lublinskaya, *French Absolutism*, pp. 183–95.

the changing attitude of the Protestant magnates. Some like Sully had remained neutral throughout the war, and Lesdiguières had actually led a royal army, although he always worked for a peace settlement. During the course of the conflict, other leading Protestant lords, including La Force, had made peace with the king in return for rich rewards. Only Rohan, the greatest and most unselfish of the Protestant leaders, had fought to the end. In less than a year and a half, Louis had gone far toward dismantling the state within a state.[16]

It would be difficult to overestimate the significance of Louis's accomplishment. Although only about 8 percent of the French were Protestants, they were remarkably well organized in areas where they constituted a large portion of the population. Through their assemblies, they commissioned officers, raised armies, voted taxes, and floated loans. Quarrels within their ranks could be bitter, but the government they gave the areas they controlled was at least as effective as that provided by the king in other parts of France. Their armies were not feudal levies but well-organized regiments and companies commanded by officers irrespective of their status in the feudal hierarchy. To support their troops, they not only seized royal taxes but also increased the levies severalfold. The town of Alès, for example, paid between 4,052 and 4,874 livres annually in taxes during the peaceful years 1618–20 but raised 14,116 livres in 1622 when it threw its lot in with the Huguenots.[17] Louis did not destroy this edifice. In the peace of October 1622, he even promised to continue to pay the remaining Protestant garrisons and to authorize the general political assembly to meet every three years to elect the agents to represent their interests at court. What he had done was to dismantle many of their fortifications and, above all, to weaken their will to resist.[18]

Louis accomplished the latter by slowly convincing most of his Protestant subjects that they should put their trust in him rather than in their armies and fortified towns. He had shown that resistance at best brought higher taxes and at the worse suffering and death. Saint-Jean d'Angely had been stripped of its privileges, Clairac had seen its pastor and several prominent citizens hanged, Saint-Antonin and Nègrepelisse had been sacked. Decisive victory could never be theirs because they lacked the strength to mount an offensive. They could only hope to stave off defeat at a terrible cost. As an alternative to war, Louis offered religious freedom, civil rights, and the

16. Clarke, *Huguenot Warrior*, pp. 94–108; Léonce Anquez, *Un nouveau chapitre de l'histoire politique des réformés de France, 1621–1626* (Paris, 1865), pp. 1–23; Berthold Zeller, *Richelieu et les ministres de Louis XIII de 1621 à 1624* (Paris, 1880), pp. 1–140; Lublinskaya, *French Absolutism*, pp. 201–211.

17. For a good detailed study of Protestant organization and government, see Steven M. Lowenstein, *Resistance to Absolutism: Huguenot Organization in Languedoc, 1621–1622* (Ann Arbor, University Microfilms, 1972). For taxation in Alès, see p. 200.

18. Anquez, *Un nouveau chapitre*, p. 21.

possibility of generous rewards in return for loyal service. To Lesdiguières in January 1622 he wrote:

> I want to reward you as a king who wishes to reign in kindness and equity; I leave you your liberty, knowing that nothing should be more free than consciences which God knows how to move when it pleases him. It is also to his holy providence that I place the secret of your calling and that of each of my Protestant subjects. I will not suffer that they be oppressed or violated for their faith. It is indeed true that if, under the cloak of religion, any of them want to undertake illicit things that are contrary to my edicts, I will know how to separate truth from pretext, punish the latter, and protect those who remain in their duty.... I am assured that you will not only contribute your good counsel, but also that you will employ your blood and your life to the achievement of justice so necessary for the repose of the state.[19]

To implement his policy Louis never hesitated to reconfirm the public articles of the Edict of Nantes. When he had insisted in returning the property of the Catholic church in Béarn, he had promised to compensate the Protestants by assigning them revenue from the royal domain to support their religion. The Béarnais resistance to his edict must have taxed his patience, but even after he had imposed his will at the head of an army, he had renewed this pledge, although his chronic financial difficulties prevented him from giving all that was due.[20] Under these circumstances Lesdiguières became a Catholic in return for being made constable, and other nobles followed his example in return for lesser rewards. Even nobles who remained faithful to the reformed church often believed that not only their personal interests but those of their religion could be best served by putting their trust in their king's goodwill. Often municipal leaders also came to believe that their privileges could be best preserved through loyalty to the crown. Only the boldest favored rebellion after 1622.[21]

Professor Lublinskaya has performed a significant service in pointing out that the defeat of the Huguenots was an essential step that had to be taken before the magnates could be subordinated to the will of the crown.[22] During the first decade of Louis's reign, his government had thought it necessary to buy their submission because of its fear that they could draw on the support of the Huguenots. Now that danger was reduced, and by the close of 1629 it was largely removed. The relationship between the Huguenot state within a state and the magnates was clearly recognized by contemporaries. In July 1621 the Venetian ambassador reported, "By taking their fortresses from the Huguenots, the king will thereby put an end to their

19. *Lettres de la main de Louis XIII*, ed. Eugène Griselle (Paris, 1914), 1:98–99.
20. *Mercure François* 5 (1618): 238; Forissier, *Histoire de la réforme*, 2:123.
21. Lublinskaya, *French Absolutism*, pp. 214–15.
22. Ibid., see pp. 159, 175, 212.

military power, and without this all the troublemakers ... will find themselves deprived of a solid support that they could have relied on."[23] Condé
saw matters in the same light and became the most determined foe of the
Huguenots. Either he believed that the destruction of their power would
weaken the other magnates, leaving him the dominant influence over Louis,
as the Venetian ambassador reported in 1622, or as he himself told someone,
he anticipated that he would one day be king and wished to seize every
opportunity to ensure that he would have a peaceful reign.[24]

Lublinskaya, however, is incorrect when she insists that the bourgeoisie
supported the crown's steps toward absolutism.[25] With few exceptions what
the burghers desired was not favors from the court and certainly not an
absolute, centralized government. They wanted above all else to be left
alone, to be permitted to govern their towns, to regulate their local
economy, and to tax for their own needs but not those of the crown—in
short, to live secure in their privileges while enjoying their municipal
autonomy. Protestant burghers had often opened their gates to Louis's army
because they saw that it would be useless to fight, and they hoped through
submission to preserve their religious freedom and their rights of self-
government. Where resistance was practical, and sometimes where it was
not, they had generally fought. Their defeat in southern France was not just
a defeat of the Protestants; it was also a defeat of a portion of the bourgeoisie
who saw their proud walls destroyed, royal garrisons placed in their midst,
and in some instances their elections tampered with.

3. New Elections for Guyenne

Louis was not content to subvert the privileges of his Protestant subjects in
the south. He took advantage of the presence of his armies to renew the
assault on the provincial estates and the assemblies of the towns that his
father had begun nearly two decades before. In September 1621, while he
was besieging Montauban, he issued an edict reestablishing the eight
élections in the généralité of Guyenne that he had suppressed in 1611. At
that time, he had promised never to reestablish them, but in addition to
having the estates compensate the élus for the loss of their offices, he had
made conditions that included a provision that royal taxes would be levied
without "any reduction, retrenchment, or delay" and that the costs incurred
by the estates would be reduced. However, the estates had continued to do
all in their power to prevent increases in taxation and had conducted their

23. Ibid., p. 169.
24. Zeller, *Richelieu*, p. 61; *Mémoires de Fontenay-Mareuil*, pp. 167, 171.
25. Lublinskaya, *French Absolutism*, pp. 2, 153, 167, 330–33. For an unfavorable critique of
her analysis, see D. Parker, "The Social Foundation of French Absolutism 1610–1630." *Past and
Present* 53 (1971): 67–89.

affairs much as they had before the élections had been created in 1603. It was this failure of the estates to adhere to his conditions that Louis used to justify breaking his pledge. He did not, of course, specifically cite the estates' efforts to prevent higher royal taxes; rather he accused them of oppressing his people with their own levies and with failing to follow the prescribed safeguards to prevent fiscal dishonesty.[26]

In June 1622 Louis created two more élections in Guyenne. The aides or territories attached to Agenais, Condomois, and Comminges lay within the jurisdiction of the Court of Aids at Montpellier, and all but the last of these receptes were subject to the courts at Bordeaux. Using this administrative confusion as his principal excuse, Louis stripped Agenais of its aides and created the élection and recepte Lomagne with its seat at Lectoure. The aides of Comminges and Condomois were combined to form the élection and recepte of Astarac with its seat at Mirande.[27] There had long been quarrels between the aides and the parent jurisdictions over what portion of the taille they should pay, and this conflict contributed to Louis's decision to create the two new élections.[28]

Instead of two élections and eight receptes, Guyenne was to have twelve élections, There are several possible reasons for this change: to assert absolute control over taxation and break the power of the estates, to raise money by the sale of the new offices, or as Louis preferred to stress, to prevent the estates from oppressing the people by their spendthrift and dishonest fiscal administration. It is significant that Louis chose to announce the creation of the élections in September 1621 just after his armies had overrun nearly all of Guyenne and he had begun to besiege the town of Montauban. Perhaps his edict was issued after September 15 when the duke of Mayenne, the governor of Guyenne, was killed in action, thereby leaving the généralité without its natural protector. The estates of the généralité had taken the precaution of voting Mayenne 20,000 livres in 1619 shortly after his appointment.[29] Now it was to be of no avail. Possibly even the delay in appointing the duke of Épernon as his successor until the close of August 1622 was intended to leave Guyenne in a more helpless condition. Epernon often ran roughshod over well-established privileges, but he could become a

26. *Recueil des édicts, déclarations, arrests, et règlemens faits en faveur et pour le restablissement des esleus en la province et généralité de Guiéne* (Paris, 1626), p. 14. A copy is located at BN, Actes Royaux, F46,945, no. 2. This *Recueil* does not include the edict of September 1621, but Louis cited his reasons for creating the élections on p. 4 and in his letters appointing the élus that are located in AD, Gironde, C 3823, fols. 3–10, 107–09, 131–33v, 200–05.

27. *Recueil de Guiéne*, pp. 3–9.

28. Georges Tholin, *Des tailles et des impositions au pays d'Agenais durant le XVIᵉ siècle jusqu'aux réformes de Sully* (Agen, 1874), pp. 11–12; extract from the *Recueil des travaux de la soc. d'agriculture, sciences et arts d'Agen*, sér. 2, 4 (1875). Agenais and its aides continued to quarrel several years after their separation. AC, Agen, CC 168.

29. AD, Aveyron, C 1906.

stalwart defender of the estates at court if he thought that it was in his interest to do so.

The evidence that Louis had embarked on the road to absolutism is found in his reaction to the efforts the estates made to prevent the implementation of the decree creating the élections. As was customary under such circumstances, the estates tried to persuade the sovereign courts not to register the decree and the king and council to revoke it. On January 18, 1622, the syndic of Agenais reported to the *consulat* of Agen that the Parlement of Bordeaux had refused to register the decree and would continue to do so unless all the money that the estates had paid for the suppression of the élections in 1611 was returned. Given the financial position of the crown, there was no likelihood of this happening. Nevertheless as an added precaution, the syndic said that he would try to get the offending edict suppressed on the grounds that élections were pernicious institutions.[30]

In spite of its brave words the king compelled the Parlement of Bordeaux to verify the edict on the élections and ignored the deputations to Paris. In June, some or all the provincial estates in Guyenne met and elected deputies to go to the king who was at Toulouse. This time they were empowered to offer 250,000 livres, the same sum that they had given to have the élections suppressed in 1611. Again Louis refused to budge from his position and a suggestion of 300,000 livres did not move him. On June 12, 1622, he issued an edict forbidding the various estates in Guyenne to send deputies to him or to his council under any pretext whatsoever to seek to have the élections suppressed, and on August 25 and 26 he appointed a number of officers to staff them. Still the activity of the estates did not cease. Deputations were sent to Epernon to seek his support and to the sovereign courts and the Bureau of Finances to invite their intervention. The size of the offer to Louis was greatly increased, but even 900,000 livres was not sufficient to shake his determination to have élections in Guyenne. In February and May 1623, he repeated his order that the estates were neither to meet nor to send deputies to him on the subject, but the turmoil continued.[31]

The intendant of justice in Guyenne was kept busy trying to see that the king's orders were obeyed. Many local royal officials sided with the estates. In Condom they were accused of joining the town *consuls* in an effort to prevent the installation of the élus by force. The treasurers in the Bureau of Finances at Bordeaux sought to levy the taille in the traditional manner in 1624, and on January 31 Louis had to threaten to deprive them of their offices if they did not send the royal commissions to the élus to levy the tax

30. Loubatéy to Agen, January 18, 1622, AC, Agen, CC 159.

31. *IAD, Hérault, sér. B*, ed. De Dainville (Montpellier, 1931), pt. 1, 298–308, 312; *IAD, Gironde, sér. B*, ed. Jean-A. Brutails (Bordeaux, 1925), pp. 93–94; AC, Agen, CC 161, CC 166; V. Fons, "Les Etats de Comminges," *Mém. de la soc. imperiale archéologique du midi de la France* 8 (1861–65): 204; B. de Gorsse, "Cahier documental concernant le pais et les Etats de Comminges," *Revue de Comminges* 46 (1932): 11–12; *AHG* 35 (1900): 72–75.

and cease to interfere with their activities. At the same time he once more forbade syndics, *consuls*, and other persons to assemble, to send deputations to him to obtain the suppression of the élections, or to try to prevent the élus from performing their duties. To make certain that no one was unaware of his order, Louis directed that it be published and registered in all local judicial seats and that curés publish it in their parishes.[32]

The extraordinary efforts of the crown enabled the élus to begin to perform their duties early in 1624, but their difficulties were by no means ended. Although the estates were not supposed to take further action in their regard, there was nothing to prevent their syndics, who usually doubled as *consuls* in the leading towns, from appealing to the sovereign courts to secure justice. The syndics of Agenais, Condomois, and Bazadais carried their case to the Parlement of Bordeaux, and the syndic of the newly formed élection of Astarac turned to the Court of Aids at Montpellier. Their attack was on legal grounds, and they soon won decrees from both courts saying that the élus were not to verify the tax roles of the parishes or to be paid for performing this duty; rather they were authorized only to audit the accounts of the higher jurisdictions. The Parlement of Bordeaux even directed that the towns and communities be convoked at the beginning of each year to give them an opportunity to voice objections about the way the élus divided the tax. The élus appealed to the king's council to overturn these rulings that so limited their authority and income, and they won a decision in their favor.[33]

The estates spared no effort to discredit the élus. They persuaded the Parlement of Bordeaux to appoint a commission to conduct a detailed investigation into their activities in Agenais.[34] On their own account they compiled an imposing list of the abuses the élus had committed in Rouergue, Agenais, the Aides of Agenais, Quercy, and Condomois. These newly appointed officials were accused of illegally insisting on examining the tax roles and of levying exorbitant amounts to pay for this activity. They were ignorant, incompetent, and extravagant. They even imposed taxes on one jurisdiction that were supposed to be levied on another. The deputies prepared a cahier to submit to the king in which they asked that the estates continue to be convoked to hear the royal letters read concerning what taxes they were expected to pay, and they sought to have restrictions placed on the activities of the élus.[35] Exasperated, the élus placed a placard on the church doors of Agen accusing the *consuls* of arbitrarily raising obstacles to prevent them from performing their duties and of trying to turn the people against them. In a formal statement they charged that since the *consuls* had not been able to get their offices suppressed, they had tried to render them useless by

32. AC, Agen, CC 166, esp. the printed edict of January 31, 1624.
33. Ibid., CC 167, CC 171.
34. Ibid., CC 172.
35. Ibid., CC 162.

appeals to the courts. The *consuls* had also sought to make them odious in the eyes of the people by saying that taxes would become higher. In other parts of France, they insisted, the élus verified the tax roles of the parishes and were paid for their services. In Guyenne they should have the same privileges.[36]

In 1624 a rumor spread among the peasantry of Quercy that the upper classes would assist them if they rebelled against the élus and high taxes. They responded, but little help came from their social superiors, and their movement was soon brutally suppressed by the local governor.[37]

Throughout the controversy, Louis never wavered. By 1625 there was a notable slackening in the resistance. The élus did complain that the *consuls* of Agen had not permitted them to attend a meeting of the three orders of the town, and the town in turn won a decree from Parlement forbidding the élus to transfer the taille assigned to one parish to another because the former had suffered damage from hail. Perhaps the true situation was best reflected by the need the treasurers at Bordeaux felt to forbid both the élus and the *consuls* of Agen to levy any taxes without the king's permission.[38] Abuses continued to be perpetrated by both sides. Nevertheless Louis's achievement had been remarkable. Two and one-half years after he had issued his edict creating the élections, the élus were collecting taxes, and after another year the controversy had slackened. It had taken his father and Sully twice as long to accomplish as much.

The evidence cited above proves that Louis was determined to have élections in Guyenne at any cost. Why else would he refuse to consider an offer of 900,000 livres to abolish them? Clearly the profit that would come from the sale of new offices was not his principal motive. How then is his insistence on élections to be explained? Louis could hardly have deluded himself into believing that the élections would be a less expensive instrument of tax collection than the estates, for by comparison the estates were amazingly efficient. In some seneschalsies, they appointed a committee to divide the amount that they had voted among the towns, parishes, and other subordinate jurisdictions. In others this task was performed in the presence of the estates by treasurers dispatched by the Bureau of Finances at Bordeaux. The town or parish then added to the sum assigned as its share the amount necessary to meet its own needs plus an additional 5 percent of the total tax which was given to a collector chosen by the *consuls* or his fellow taxpayers. It was this collector who divided and collected the total tax from all of those who paid the taille. When the collector completed his task, which he performed quarterly, he retained the amount designated for the town or

---

36. Ibid., CC 164, CC 167.

37. *Mercure François* 10 (1624): 473–78. For a somewhat slanted account, see Boris Porchnev, *Les soulèvements populaires en France de 1623 à 1648* (Paris, 1963), pp. 49–52.

38. AC, Agen, CC 173.

TABLE 2

Costs of the Estates Collecting Taxes in Rouergue (c. 1620)

Number	Office	Pay	Rights and Expenses	Total (in livres)
3	Syndics	300	60	1,080
3	Greffiers	150	50	600
3	Clerks			30
To those of the estates who apportioned the taxes and audited the accounts				300
Ushers of the estates				10
Writs, messengers, etc.				34
			Total	2,054

parish and turned over the remainder to the receiver of the tailles in the seneschalsy.[39]

The costs of operating this system varied from jurisdiction to jurisdiction and from year to year. It is nevertheless instructive to investigate the expenses incurred by the estates of Rouergue just as the élus replaced their officials. Because Rouergue was the largest seneschalsy in Guyenne and was divided into three marches each with its syndic, greffier, and clerk, the costs of its estates and tax collection were considerably larger than in most jurisdictions.[40] (See table 2.) In addition, collecters of the taille in the parishes were paid fees. On the other hand, since only a small part of the syndics' duties were directly involved in tax collection, most of their salaries should not be charged against this function.

Having estates did lead to other expenses. In the year noted above the three estates of Rouergue also spent 200 livres on deputations. In addition, they appropriated 5,950 livres for a variety of projects, including making road and church repairs, dispatching three Catholic missionaries to

39. For the regulation of February 12, 1611, telling how the estates were supposed to handle tax affairs in Guyenne, see *Edict du roy contenant révocation et suppression des huict bureaux d'élections, establis en la généralité de Guyenne par édict du mois de janvier 1603* (Agen, 1612), pp. 29–51. A copy is at AC, Agen, CC 143. For a description of earlier tax procedures in Agenais, see Tholin, *Des tailles*, pp. 15–24.

40. H. Affre, *Dictionnaire des institutions, moeurs et coutumes du Rouergue* (Rodez, 1903), p. 163. For a contemporary account of the procedures used in Rouergue, see A. Brutails, "Mémoire sur la tenue des Etats de Rouergue, écrit vers 1623, par Durieux, député du pays de Rouergue," *Bul. hist. et phil. du comité des travaux historiques et scientifiques* (1885): 23–27.

Protestant areas, and aiding a Jesuit college at Rodez, a school at Villefranche, and those in need because of attacks of the plague. The total amount expended came to 8,204 livres, without counting the fees paid to the parish collectors.[41]

The edict of 1621 creating the élections in Guyenne provided that they should each have the same number of officers who would receive the same salary, expenses, and fees as elsewhere in France. The number and stipends of the officers in each élection at this time are shown in table 3.[42]

TABLE 3

Costs of the Elus Collecting Taxes in Rouergue

Number	Office	Pay	Expenses	Total (in livres)
1	President	450	75	525
5	Elus	400	75	2,375
1	Comptroller	400	75	475
1	Procureur	100		100
1	Greffier	100		100
2	Ushers	50		100
2	Sergeants	25		50
3	Receivers of the tailles	900		2,700
3	Receivers of the taillon	200		600
19				7,025

Unhappily for Rouergue the salaries of the new officials were only part of the money that they received, for some of them were given substantial fees for verifying the tax roles and other duties. Furthermore, in spite of this vast horde of officials, it was still necessary to retain the collectors in the individual parishes who received a percentage of the total levy just as before. Thus, even if the substantial fees of the royal tax officials are excluded, it cost three and one half times as much to have them collect taxes as it did the officers of the estates who also performed other duties. Indeed if the fees of the royal officials were added to the 7,025 livres they were paid in salaries, the total would be well in excess of the 8,204 livres that the estates of

41. Affre, *Dictionnaire*, p. 163.
42. *Recueil de Guiéne*, pp. 7–8.

Rouergue expended for all of their activities, most of which were devoted to education, public works, and social welfare.[43]

Louis was not content to leave this already unfortunate situation as it was. In June 1622 he created two additional élections, which added 14,050 livres in salaries plus the fees that had to be borne by Agenais, Condomois, Comminges, and their former aides. Nor could the hard-pressed monarch resist creating additional offices. In November 1625 he added five more officers to each of the new élections in Guyenne whose salaries and expenses came to 2,240 livres per year. This brought the total for each élection to 9,265 livres per year. He also created three master clerks and a keeper of the little seal in each élection, who were to be paid by fees. Louis frankly admitted that there was no need for these new offices and that he had created them to obtain money to support his army in southern France. Indeed the new officers were to take turns performing their duties. Finally, in March 1627 he broke up Rouergue and Quercy into three élections each. At this point the people of Rouergue began to support a fiscal administration that cost 27,795 livres annually, without counting the fees, a far cry from the 8,204 livres that had been expended by the estates for all their activities a few years before. This oversized and expensive bureaucracy imposed a heavy burden on Guyenne and removed some of the wealthiest citizens of the region from the tax roles because the officers in the élections down through the greffiers were exempt from the taille and similar taxes.[44]

It is evident that by creating the élections, Louis substantially increased the tax burden that fell on the people, at least as far as it can be ascertained from official records. Why then did he take this step? He undoubtedly realized a large profit from the sale of the offices, and this accounts for the fact that the new jurisdictions were so overstaffed. It would have been financially to his advantage, however, to have accepted the 900,000 livres the estates had offered to get the élections suppressed. It can therefore be concluded that what Louis wanted above all else was to establish control over the tax-collecting machinery. As long as it was in the hands of the estates, he would be faced with resistance and delays in levying royal taxes. He would also have no way to prevent the estates, towns, and communities from levying taxes without permission, thereby reducing his subjects' capacity to contribute to his own treasury. One of the weaknesses of the estates from his point of view was that there was no audit of the accounts at the parish level and above by an outside agency. The committees appointed by the estates and the incoming town and community officials who were usually charged with examining the books of their predecessors were apt to wink at taxes for local purposes that the king had not authorized. When the

43. I have excluded the fees of the collectors of the tailles in the parishes from my comparison because they were common to both systems.

44. *Recueil de Guiéne*, pp. 9–35. *Actes Royaux*, 2: no. 7128.

élections replaced the estates, the élus assumed the role of auditors down to the parish level. Illegal taxes and corruption would hopefully cease, and royal taxes could be more easily collected.

In 1623, the last year before the élus took over the tax-collection machinery, the towns and communities of Agenais were accused of levying 19,680 livres without permission, and the king's council ordered that the receiver of the tailles retain this money until all the facts could be ascertained.[45] Even if the charge were correct, it does not prove that the officials were dishonest. Much or all of the money may have gone to pay the debts that still weighed heavily on many communities or to finance local projects such as those engaged in by the estates of Rouergue. What angered Louis and his advisers was that local elected officials were levying taxes to meet local needs that they themselves determined when in their minds the money would be better spent meeting the king's needs.

Louis also suspected the local elected officials of graft. Perhaps he even thought that they were more dishonest than his own officials, although he certainly knew that they were not above reproach. In 1624 he created a Chamber of Justice to uncover and punish fraud committed by his financial officials and incidentally to encourage them to offer a large sum to call off the investigation. He also thought it necessary to order the Bureau of Finances at Bordeaux to launch an investigation to determine what taxes had been levied without permission in 1625. The élus of Bordelais were especially suspect.[46] Thus Louis ought to have seen corruption as a secondary issue when he compared tax collection by the estates with tax collection by the élus. His primary motive for issuing the edict of September 1621 must have been to control the tax-collecting machinery so that more money would flow into his coffers and less into those of the estates and towns. If these duly constituted bodies withered and died as a result, it was of little concern to him.

To insist that Louis had embarked on a deliberate policy of increasing his authority in Guyenne and decreasing that of rival governing bodies is not to say that he made any direct effort to destroy the estates. An edict forbidding them to meet again under any circumstances would have created further unrest. This is not to say that the local leaders did not feel threatened. On December 28, 1622, the outgoing *consuls* of Agen urged their successors to make every effort to prevent the abolition of the office of syndic of Agenais because as long as this post was filled, there would be someone who could act to protect the interests of the seneschalsy before the king's council and the sovereign courts without having to be empowered by the estates, permission to hold which they apparently thought was in jeopardy. In April 1628 the

45. BN ms. fr. 18,201, fols. 192v–93.

46. *Ordonnances, édits, declarations, arrests et lettres patentes, concernant l'autorité et la jurisdiction de la Chambre des Comptes de Paris* (Paris, 1728), 1 : 476–93; *IAD, Gironde, sér. C*, ed. Alexandre Gouget and Jean-A. Brutails (Bordeaux, 1893), 2: C 3903.

consuls of Agen persuaded the estates to empower them to act as syndics of Agenais and to borrow money in the name of the province. Since the continued existence of a municipal government in Agen appeared certain, this meant that Agenais would have a constituted body with the necessary funds to act in its interests.[47]

At Rodez the gloom was greater. There was talk among the *consuls* of the city during the summer of 1625 that the estates had been suppressed, an exaggeration no doubt, but one that had some substance. Only the *consulats* of Rouergue had been convoked to a recent meeting, and, more serious in their eyes, it had been held in Villefranche.[48]

The estates felt threatened, then, but Louis did not directly question their right to exist. It was enough to break their powers in taxation. If they continued to function for a few more years, it would do little harm. Gradually the people would come to consider their meetings a needless expense, and they would slowly die without causing the outburst that would certainly take place if he acted hastily to achieve this end. We cannot prove that these were the thoughts that went on in Louis's and his advisers' minds, but this is what was to happen.

The quarrel with the élus and with its former aides was enough, with the usual matters, to keep the third estate of Agenais busy until 1630. During this period there were one or more meetings per year. Even the nobles took an interest, and in October 1624 a deputation from them appeared before the king's council to ask that the treasurers at Bordeaux divide the taille fairly and equitably in Agenais rather than "in the accustomed form" as urged by the syndic of the third estate.[49] Try as they would, however, the leaders of Agenais could not find a way to ensure a permanent role for the estates under the new regime. They sought, with only temporary success, to have Parlement require that the élus read the king's commission to levy a tax before the estates and justify their division of the imposition among the subordinate jurisdictions. When this failed, they joined with the other seneschalsies in another effort to have the élections suppressed. Again they ran into insurmountable opposition. In 1627 the king's council imposed a tax to pay a local debt in spite of the opposition of their syndic. A feeling of disillusionment and despair seems to have come over the once proud burghers. After 1630 they assembled irregularly with occasional gaps of four or five years between meetings, although the total extinction of the estates was not to come until several generations later.[50] The three estates of Rouergue were equally active during the first few years, and, as far as can be ascertained, the estates in the other seneschalsies had a similar experience

47. AC, Agen, BB 46, fol. 53, CC 182.

48. AC Rodez (cité), BB 8, fols. 34v–40.

49. BN ms. fr. 18,202, fols. 53v–54.

50. For the estates of Agenais, 1621–29, see esp. AC Agen, BB 44–46, BB 49, BB 51, CC 158–74, CC 176–83.

except that they probably met somewhat less frequently in the early 1620s and sank to a status of only occasional activity several years earlier.[51]

Louis's willingness to permit matters to take their natural course once he had established control over the tax-collecting machinery is illustrated by the formation of a representative institution in at least one of the new élections created in 1622. There had long been local assemblies of the county of Isle-Jourdain, the viscounty of Bruilhois, and perhaps other jurisdictions in the aides of Agenais. When they were taken from Agenais and combined to form the élection of Lomagne, it was natural that they would take steps to form an assembly of the entire jurisdiction to settle their differences with Agenais and to deal with the officers of the élection and other higher authorities. In January 1622, shortly before the élection was established, deputies from the third estate of the viscounty of Bruilhois had appeared before the king's council to argue that they should not have to contribute toward the support of the garrison at Lectoure because they were in the aides of Agenais, not the recepte of Armagnac.[52] Soon thereafter they became part of the new élection and participated with the nobility in assemblies to settle their differences with Agenais over what proportion of the tax that had fallen on the once united élection each jurisdiction should pay. In August 1628 their syndic made an appeal to the king's council, but the assembly of Lomagne was born at a time when the other representative institutions in the region were beginning to die. The tide was too strong to resist, and it soon disappeared, leaving few traces of its brief existence.[53]

51. There are numerous documents concerning the efforts of the various estates to prevent the establishment of the élus, to have the élections suppressed, and to restrict the role of the élus in AD, Gironde. See esp. C 3822–24, C 3877, C 3901, C 3988. For Armagnac and its collectes, see also BN ms. fr. 18,200, fols. 58v–59v, ms. fr. 18,204, fols. 290–92v; AD, Gers, E suppl. 23,936; AC, Auch, BB 6, fol. 256; A. Branet, "Les Etats d'Armagnac en 1631–1632," *Bul. de la soc. archéologique de Gers* 14 (1913): 168–83, 214–29. There is a reference to the "president of the estates of Armagnac" in 1628. See J. Adher, "La 'préparation' des séances des Etats de Languedoc d'après des documents inédits," *Annales du Midi* 25 (1913): 460. For Comminges see also AD, Haute-Garonne, C 3703, C 3703 bis; and M. J. Naurois-Destenay, *Les Etats de Comminges aux XVIᵉ et XVIIᵉ siècles* (thesis, Ecole Nationale des Chartes, 1953–54), pp. 189–97. For Condomois and Bazadais, see also BN ms. fr. 18,202, fols. 84v–85v. *IAC, Condom*, ed. G. Niel (n.p., n.d.), BB 27, BB 32; AC, La Réole, BB 9, fols. 17v, 20v–22v, 30v–31, 53v–54v, 99v–102. For Landes and its provostships, see also AN, E 70ᵃ, fol. 420, E 96b, fols. 231–32; AC, Bayonne, BB 20; AC Dax, BB 1, fol. 71. For Quercy see also BN ms. fr. 18,203, fol. 44–45; AN, E 97ᵃ, fol. 66; M. J. Baudel, *Notes pour servir à l'histoire des Etats provinciaux du Quercy* (Cahors, 1881), pp. 41–42. For Rivière-Verdun see also Jean Contrasty, *Histoire de Sainte-Foy-de-Peyrolières* (Toulouse, 1917), pp. 200–01. For Rouergue see also AD, Aveyron, C 1906, 2E 677; AC Rodez (cité), BB 8, fols, 8v, 18, 18v, 31v–40, 79–83v, 86–91, 105–09, 131v–35v, and (bourg), BB 12, fols. 38, 40v–42, 87–87v, 97, 119v; AN, E 97ᵇ, fol. 376, E 102, fol. 74.

52. AN, E 70ᵃ, fol. 15.

53. AC, Isle-Jourdain, BB 3, fols. 49v–52, 107v–09; AC, Lectoure, BB 5; AC, Laplume, BB 7; AC, Agen, CC 162, CC 168, CC 176. *IAD, Gironde, sér. C*, 2: C 3900, C 3902. AN, E 97ᵃ, fols. 52–53.

It is not known whether the élection of Astarac, the other new jurisdiction established in 1622, ever developed its own assembly, but the estates of the county of Astarac continued to function. In December 1625 deputies of the nobility and third estates appeared before the king's council to obtain permission to have the recently appointed élus levy a tax on the county to pay a debt to two bourgeoisie of Toulouse.[54]

Additional evidence that Louis and his council were willing to permit matters to take their natural course once they had established control over taxation is to be found in their treatment of Lannes. In the fall of 1621, deputies from Tartas asked that their town be permitted to serve as host to the estates, as well as Dax, Saint-Sever, and Bayonne whose privileges were no greater. The council complied and ordered that the estates meet in Tartas in 1622. Thereafter the estates were to assemble alternately in the four towns. Implied in this decree issued so soon after the edict creating the élections was that the estates were to continue to meet indefinitely.[55]

The estates of the généralité were even less fortunate than those of the seneschalsies. Further removed from the people, they enjoyed less popular support. They were also vulnerable because there was no town whose *consuls* had the right to initiate a meeting either by convoking one or, at times when the crown was opposed to such practice, by seeking permission from the governor. There were probably several meetings of the estates, or at least informal gatherings of the deputies of the seneschalsies between 1622 and 1624 to try to get the élections suppressed both by making a financial offer to the king and by discrediting the élus. Another attempt was made in January 1626.[56] Thereafter, as far as can be ascertained, the estates of the généralité met only one time, in February 1635.[57] The largest representative institution in France had ceased to exist.

4. The Threat to the Estates of Languedoc

Just as Louis took advantage of his campaign in Guyenne in 1621 to impose his will on the estates, so also did he plan a similar fate for Languedoc when he led his army there in 1622, this despite the fact that in the two preceding

54. BN ms. fr. 18,203, fols. 160–61.

55. AD, Gironde, C 3822,, fols. 274–76.

56. AC, Agen, CC 161, CC 162, CC 166, CC 178; AC, Rodez (cité), BB 8, fols. 86–88v.

57. AC, Agen, AA 34, BB 55, fols. 19v–24, CC 191. Some towns in Agenais and Bazadais sent deputies to a meeting at Villeneuve in July 1629, but too limited an area was represented for it to be considered a meeting of the estates of the généralité. AC, Agen, BB 51, fols. 111v–16. AC, La Réole, BB 9, fols. 99v–102. The assembly that the prince of Condé held at Bordeaux in December 1638 that has been referred to as a meeting of the estates of Guyenne consisted only of the lieutenant generals of the seneschalsies. BN ms. Dupuy 869, fols. 87–91. *Archives municipales de Bordeaux*, 6. *Inventaire sommaire des registres de la jurade, de 1520 à 1783*, ed. Dast le Vacher de Boisville (Bordeaux, 1896), 1:504–05.

years the estates had been more generous than was their wont. The estates that opened in Pézenas in November 1620 were greeted with a letter from the first president of the Parlement of Toulouse saying that he and his colleagues had refused to verify several edicts that would impose a perpetual burden on the province, but that the king would compel them to do so unless the deputies voted him a notable sum. Thus forewarned, the royal letters asking for a special grant of 600,000 livres to meet the expenses occasioned by the subjection of Béarn could have come as no surprise. In this cause, the commissioner declared, the king had spent 9 million livres in addition to the 40 million that he had expended suppressing uprisings during the past six years. Brittany, which was poorer than Languedoc, had voted 400,000 livres, and Guyenne had given 600,000 despite the disorders that had occured there because of troop movements. Thus primed, the deputies voted the king 400,000 livres to be paid over a two-year period.[58]

When it came to their own affairs, the estates were more generous. They asked that the pay of those who attended the diocesan estates be doubled. Montmorency was given 10,800 livres because of the expenses he had incurred maintaining peace in the province, and provisions were made to summon the estates of the seneschalsies to authorize borrowing money for raising an army should the rebellion spread to Languedoc before the next meeting of the estates. This precaution proved to be wise because in February 1621 the Protestants seized Privas, and the revolt quickly spread to other parts of the province. In March Montmorency assembled the estates of the seneschalsy of Beaucaure and Nîmes where he was accorded 60,000 livres for his army, which he claimed was costing 300,000 livres a month. The estates of the seneschalsies Carcassonne and Toulouse proved more difficult. Both asked that the provincial estates be summoned because such large sums were involved.[59]

The need for money caused the estates to be assembled several months earlier than usual in 1622. From September 11 to January 1, they remained in session. The principal topics of debate were how to repay the 704,300 livres Montmorency and Ventadour said that they had advanced to pay troops to prosecute the war and what contributions to make to them and to the king to support the future conflict. The estates voted to give the two dukes 200,000 livres in 1622 and to extend the salt tax that was scheduled to expire on January 1, 1623, at the same level for three years to provide funds to repay the remainder of the debt. More difficult to satisfy was Montmorency's request for funds to support 4,000 foot and 400 horse to carry on the war, for the estates would do no more than borrow 100,000 livres to pay less than a third of this force. The king had to be content with

58. AD, Hérault, procès-verbal of the estates of November–December 1620; *IAD, Haute-Garonne, sér. C*, ed. Adolphe Baudouin (Toulouse, 1903), 2:217–20; *HL*, 11:938.
59. *HL*, 11:939–43; *IAD, Haute-Garonne, sér. C*, 2:220–21.

the remaining 200,000 livres of the 400,000 that had been promised the year before.[60]

During that first decade of Louis's reign, the three estates had rarely voted more than the traditional taxes, but in 1620 and 1621 they had made substantial contributions, albeit all but 400,000 livres of the additional funds had been assigned to provide for their own protection. Still Louis was not satisfied. Perhaps he was irritated when the three estates that met in the fall of 1621 sought to have an ordonnance revoked which they claimed violated their privilege of consenting to taxes.[61] Perhaps he was upset at their refusal to meet all of his demands. More certainly he was angry because he believed that the estates, the diocesan assemblies, and the towns were levying unauthorized taxes for their own purposes. It is not surprising, therefore, that when he brought his army to the south in 1622 to campaign in Languedoc, he sought to repeat the success he had enjoyed in Guyenne the year before.

In June 1622 Louis issued an edict creating fifteen élections to assume the tax-collecting role of the diocesan estates. At this point the duke of Ventadour, and perhaps his cousin of Montmorency, intervened, and Louis was persuaded to abandon the élections. Either he was encouraged to hope that the estates would mend their ways, or else he realized that he had acted prematurely. His campaign in Languedoc was only beginning, and it was no time to alienate his Catholic subjects there, especially when they had the support of their powerful dukes. But Louis did not abandon his desire to curb the independence of the estates, and in July he issued an edict creating a greffier of the tailles in each diocese, town, and community in the jurisdiction of the Court of Aids of Languedoc. The greffiers of the dioceses were to convoke the diocesan estates, take minutes of their deliberations and the apportionment of the taxes, and participate in auditing the accounts. The greffiers of the towns and communities were to keep an equally watchful eye on the financial activities of the urban officials. They were also assigned one of the two keys necessary to gain access to the local archives so that the municipal officials could not examine their own records without their knowledge. Even if the time had not yet come to establish the élections, the diocesan estates and municipal officials were to be carefully watched. It was they, and not the estates of Languedoc, that actually levied the taxes.[62]

Peace with the Huguenots had been made by the time the estates assembled at Beaucaire in November 1622. Ventadour was the senior royal official who was present at the opening meeting and he prepared his address with more than usual care. "The king," he declared,

60. *IAD, Haute-Garonne, sér. C,* 2:221–24; AD, Hérault, procès-verbal of the estates of September 1621–January 1622; *HL,* 11:948–51, 956–57, 959–60.

61. *IAD, Haute-Garonne, sér. C,* 2:224.

62. Jean Albisson, *Loix municipales et économiques de Languedoc* (Montpellier, 1786), 4:254–57; *IAD, Hérault, sér. B,* ed. De Dainville (Montpellier, 1935), pt. 2, 310; Actes Royaux, 2: no. 6727.

would soon visit the estates. For a year he has had four armies and a navy under arms at a cost of 700,000 *livres* a month, but with this force our twenty-one year old monarch has won many victories. Caesar said "I came, I saw, I conquered;" but our king can say even more; "I came, I saw, I conquered, I pardoned." You must offer him everything that is within your power. Every passion and individual interest must be eradicated and public good placed foremost. I cannot pass over in silence the great complaints that have been made to the king and to his court of Parlement at Toulouse concerning the abuses and frauds that have been committed in the meetings of the twenty-two dioceses of this province where they have used great gifts, gratifications, rewards, travel allowances, and other excessive expenses to crush and oppress the king's subjects. Of 100 *écus* that are imposed, not 10 reach his majesty's purse. This disorder, gentlemen, gave grounds for the edict on the *élus* which was on the point of being verified and registered in the Court of Parlement when I made remonstrances on your behalf as you would have desired. I reiterated these remonstrances in the presence of the king, attended by the princes of his blood, cardinals, dukes, and other leading lords of his council. I gave them assurances of your good behavior and that you would correct the abuses. If judicial officers are guilty of peculation, it is not necessary to abolish Parlement but to punish the guilty. Turning to the king, I said, Sire, you, who are above all other earthly kings, reign by justice, in justice, and with justice. These were my very words. I spoke with such zeal that his majesty granted my request. Cato on beginning and ending his orations before the Roman Senate always said, "Carthage must be destroyed." In like manner I will never cease to say to you that it is necessary to extirpate these abuses if you wish to lighten the burden on the people and establish the public good.[63]

Ventadour's speech was generally applauded, but both his appeal for reform and the king's personal appeal for financial assistance the following week fell on nearly deaf ears. Toward straightening out their own affairs, the three estates would do no more than rule that henceforth those who arrived three or more days late would not be seated. They did ask the barons and prelates to attend in person at least every third year, but they coupled this plea with one that the allowances of those who came be increased. Far more serious was their refusal to vote Louis more than 200,000 livres to be collected over a period of two years, although one of his commissioners had warned them that "they would regret not giving the king satisfaction."[64] Instead those present argued that taxes ought to be reduced because of the sufferings Languedoc had undergone during the rebellion. Their own

63. Ventadour's speech was printed as a pamphlet; it has been republished in *Mercure François* 8 (1622): 874–81. I have omitted some portions of his speech and condensed others.
64. *IAD, Haute-Garonne, sér. C,* 2:226.

unwillingness to cooperate more fully did not prevent them from asking the king to revoke the edict creating the greffiers in the dioceses and towns. Ventadour, who had served Languedoc well as lieutenant general since the days of the Catholic League, fell ill near the close of the estates and died knowing that the deputies had failed to heed his warning that they must correct abuses if they were to preserve their privileges.[65]

The estates that were scheduled to meet the fall of the following year had to be postponed until March 1624. When the deputies assembled, it quickly became apparent that their principal objective would be to obtain the suppression of the edict creating the greffiers in the dioceses and towns. They dispatched a deputation to the king on this matter and agreed not to disband until they had received its report. Montmorency consented to halt the sale of these offices until after the deputation had returned. Louis replied on April 18 that great sums of money had been advanced in anticipation of the execution of the edict but that he had authorized Montmorency to make proposals to the estates on the subject. Montmorency sought to soothe them by explaining that the king had not created the greffiers to infringe on their privileges; rather he needed money and would suppress the edict in return for 1.39 million livres. The estates rejected this proposal and after some debate reached a compromise figure of 720,000 livres. Because the hard-pressed king insisted that 320,000 livres be paid within three months, they agreed to borrow this sum.[66] The episode reveals once more that the king's authority to create offices could infringe on the estates' right to consent to taxation. Of more immediate interest is the problem of explaining why Louis, after abandoning the élections, also gave up his goal of supervising the diocesan and communal fiscal operations. The answer probably lies in his desperate financial situation and the appointment of La Vieuville as superintendant of finances on January 21, 1623.

In December 1620 a royal commissioner had told the estates of Languedoc that it had cost the king 9 million livres to subject Béarn and that he had spent 40 million during the preceding six years because of the revolts of the magnates. Surviving records of military expenditures for the years 1614 through 1620 suggest that the amount spent on the military exceeded the normal rate by about that sum. Then too, there were the gratifications that were given the magnates in return for making peace. This was only the beginning, however, for expenses skyrocketed during the war with the Protestants. The costs of the army (exclusive of the king's household troops), the artillery, fortifications, and the navy reached 18,842,672 livres in 1621 and 22,433,466 in 1622. Between 1612 and 1620, ordinary expenses had exceeded ordinary revenue by between 1.5 and 9 million livres per year.

65. Ibid., pp. 224–26; AD, Hérault, procès-verbal of the estates of November–December 1622; *HL*, 11:980–83.

66. AD, Hérault, AA 44, Louis XIII to the three estates April 18, 1624; procès-verbal of the estates of March–May 1624; *IAD, Haute-Garonne, sér. C*, 2:226–31.

In 1621 the deficit jumped to 15.7 million and it remained at about that level the following year.[67]

Where did the money come from to meet these heavy expenses? The sums Henry IV and Sully had set aside were exhausted by 1615. Thereafter, it had been necessary to alienate the domain, aides, and other anticipated revenues, to borrow, and above all to sell offices. Louis XIII reluctantly reestablished the paulette in July 1620, and he improved the terms under which it operated early the following year in order to increase his funds from this source as well as to placate the bureaucracy. To achieve the maximum profit, he created a multitude of new positions between 1620 and 1622, few (if any) of which were needed. Revenue from the Parties Casuelles, which had averaged around 2 million livres per year under Henry IV, reached 13.3 million in 1620, 14.3 million in 1621, and peaked at 20.1 million in 1622. But the sale of an office was only a disguised loan because it was necessary to pay the appointee a salary, and in many instances fees that bore heavily on the people. With each new creation, as with each new borrowing, the long-run position of the crown worsened. By the close of 1622, the almost insatiable French appetite for offices was nearing satisfaction, the domain and aides were alienated, money had been borrowed in anticipation of the following year's revenue, and the financiers were refusing to give further credit. It was at this point, in January 1623, that Louis named La Vieuville superintendant of finances.[68]

La Vieuville's program was similar to that of Bellièvre and other reformers. He believed that it was necessary to reduce expenses and to abandon the use of expedients that proved costly in the long run. France must avoid foreign wars and make efforts to prevent costly domestic conflicts by not pressing subjects to the point that they might revolt. Louis, who was by nature economical, accepted La Vieuville's proposals. Costs of the households of the members of the royal family were reduced, ordinary pensions were slashed by about 40 percent, and military expenses were cut from 22,433,466 livres in 1622 to 11,891,393 in 1623. In 1623 ordinary expenses totaled only 21,072,944 livres, the lowest figure since 1613 and below the level achieved by any other French government after that date. La Vieuville virtually ceased to create offices, and revenue for the Parties Casuelles fell to 17.4 million livres in 1623 and to 10.3 million in 1624.[69]

During this period the question arose of whether to permit Languedoc to pay a substantial sum in return for suppressing the greffiers. There is no

---

67. *HL*, 11:938; Mallet, pp. 218–21, 226.

68. Roland Mousnier, *La vénalité des offices sous Henri IV et Louis XIII*, 2d ed. (Paris, 1971), pp. 283–89, 636–38; Mallet, pp. 191, 209; Lublinskaya, *French Absolutism*, pp. 225–46. For some offices created between January 1620 and February 1623, see Actes Royaux, 2: cols. 115–66 passim, and F. Véron de Forbonnais, *Recherches et considérations sur les finances de France* (Liège, 1758), 1:327–31.

69. Mallet, pp. 209, 221, 226; Lublinskaya, *French Absolutism*, pp. 249–60.

direct evidence, but La Vieuville probably leaped at the opportunity. In addition to receiving some much-needed money, he could get rid of these officials whose fees would impose a heavy burden on the people, thereby leaving less to pay royal taxes. At the same time he would alleviate discontent in that troubled province.

Other than to economize, the most obvious way to meet the financial crisis was to raise taxes, but the various financial regimes during the early part of Louis's reign apparently did not believe that the provinces without estates could pay any more than they already were. They made an effort to increase custom duties both between some of the provinces and at the expense of foreign merchandise,[70] but the most important drive for additional revenue from 1620 to 1624 was made at the expense of the provincial estates and the clergy. We have already seen how pressure was placed on the estates of Languedoc to pay more. Other estates were subjected to a similar experience, although only in Guyenne and Languedoc where the army was present was an attempt made to establish élections.

5. THE OTHER PROVINCIAL ESTATES AND ASSEMBLIES

There had long been élus in Normandy, and for some years the king had been directing them to collect the desired taxes, whether the estates voted them or not. It is therefore surprising that when the duke of Longueville, the governor, joined Marie de Medici's revolt in the summer of 1620, he could not persuade the mass of the inhabitants to support his cause. Some people in Rouen, Caen, Alençon, and Dieppe were sympathetic, and he won some support from the gentry. Nevertheless Louis XIII struck so rapidly and vigorously that he quickly restored his authority. He soon forgave Longueville, but the deputies who gathered at Rouen in December 1620 represented a defeated province. Under these trying circumstances they offered only 1,503,160 livres, 300,000 less than had been customary in recent years, and asked that they be exempted from all other levies. The commissioners responded by ordering provisionally that all the sums included in the king's letters be imposed, and the deputies the estates dispatched to court were unable to get this decision reversed.[71]

The estates were not convoked in the fall of 1621 to vote taxes for 1622. This failure should not be attributed to a desire on the part of the crown to avoid a confrontation with the representatives of the Norman people. It is true that the syndic of the estates had complained about a number of edicts

70. Forbonnais, *Recherches*, 1:311–13.

71. Arsène Legrelle, *La Normandie sous la monarchie absolue* (Rouen, 1903), pp. 16–27; Amable Floquet, *Histoire du Parlement de Normandie* (Rouen, 1841), 4:331–74; *Cahiers des Etats de Normandie sous les règnes de Louis XIII et de Louis XIV*, ed. Charles de Robillard de Beaurepaire (Rouen, 1877), 2:19–20.

alienating the domain and creating additional offices and patents of nobility to sell, but Louis's advisers had not paid much attention to such protests in recent years. Nor did they avoid summoning the estates in order to raise taxes without incurring the opposition of the assembled deputies, for royal taxes in 1622 were probably less than in 1621.[72] Rather it is more likely that Louis intended to hold the estates but then reversed his plans because of a Protestant uprising in Normandy in October 1621, for on November 19 he directed the Chamber of Accounts at Rouen to pay his commissioners to the estates just as though the meeting had been held because they had been inconvenienced by having to hold themselves in readiness to attend.[73]

Louis ordered the estates to meet in November 1622, but the assembly had to be postponed until January of the following year. When the deputies gathered, they failed to raise any protest in their cahier or in any surviving document against the failure to hold the estates the preceding year. Their only allusion to the matter came in an article in the cahier referring to Louis's directive that the commissioners for 1621 be paid although the estates had not been held. "In the years that your Majesty does not judge it à propos to assemble the estates," they urged, no gifts should be made from the funds set aside for their affairs.[74] The Normans reserved their anger for the new offices that had been created and the lucrative fees and wages that had been assigned to those who purchased them. Louis promised not to give away the money collected for the estates when they failed to meet, but he gave little satisfaction in the matter of the offices because of the state of his affairs. The estates voted 1,503,160 livres, but the king again rejected their plea that all additional taxes be abolished.[75]

The estates that met in December 1623 continued their complaints against the excessive number of royal officials and high taxes. This time they consented to a direct tax of only 1,303,160 livres but repeated their request that all other levies be canceled. Unperturbed the commissioners ordered provisionally that the full amount the king desired be levied anyway, and the Norman deputies to court were unable to persuade him to take less.[76] As far as Normandy was concerned, the four-year period ended just as it had begun. The province continued to be overtaxed, although the size of the levy had been reduced somewhat because of insurrections, plagues, and bad harvests. The three estates remain ineffectual, but too much emphasis should not be placed on the failure to assemble them in the fall of 1621. The crown did not seem to consider this omission as an attack on their privileges nor did they themselves appear to have been concerned.

---

72. *Cahiers*, 2:233–42. In 1620 the crown drew 2,274,004 livres from the two Norman généralités; in 1621, 1,722,697; and in 1622, 1,498,062. Mallet, p. 201.

73. Floquet, *Histoire*, 4:388–401; Legrelle, *La Normandie*, pp. 28–33; *Cahiers*, 2:232–33.

74. *Cahiers*, 2:46. See also p. 251.

75. Ibid., pp. 29–35, 42, 47–48, 248.

76. Ibid., pp. 69–70, 259–80.

During these four years, the relations of the crown with the three estates of Brittany were much worse than with those of Normandy. In spite of its straitened financial circumstances, the government had not pressed the Normans for additional funds because they were already so heavily taxed that further exactions might produce a revolt. The situation was different in Brittany, whose well-organized and determined estates had protected the people in the past. The Bretons could afford to pay more now. Hence clashes between the crown and the estates were almost inevitable. They began in 1621 during the Protestant revolt.

Louis revealed his desperate financial position by having the estates assemble at Rennes on July 5 of that year rather than in the fall as was customary. Vendôme and Brissac headed the list of commissioners, but his principal spokesman was Etienne d'Aligre, a royal councillor who was to become keeper of the seals in January 1624 and chancellor two years later. D'Aligre commenced the offensive by saying that the king wanted 600,000 livres to crush the rebellion. On July 10, after considerable debate, the estates offered 350,000 provided certain conditions were met. The commissioners refused. The estates upped their offer to 400,000 on July 12, but again it was rejected. On July 13, they repeated their proposition. Again a refusal. On July 14, they increased the amount to 450,000 livres but at the same time declared that it was their "last and final resolution." The following morning d'Aligre once more came to the estates to reiterate that the king wanted 600,000 livres, but those present held firm. It was reported that one of the deputies of the towns had said that they ought to give 500,000 livres and that the commissioners "could go to the Devil." This rumor was vigorously denied, and Vendôme was moved to express regrets at the rough methods he had used to raise troops and arm some ships. Nevertheless the deadlock continued. Finally on July 17, the commissioners offered to take 450,000 livres provided that the estates would arm six vessels to rid the coast of pirates. The deputies refused, but that afternoon they relented to the point of offering 475,000 livres provided all their conditions were met. Vendôme was reported to be on the point of accepting the offer. On July 21, the estates sought to settle the matter by raising the figure to 500,000 livres but revealed that they intended to levy the tax over a two-year period. The commissioners apparently thought that they had been negotiating for a one-year grant at that amount because they called the offer "ridiculous." The king needed money immediately. However, they would concur provided that 200,000 livres were provided at once. Again the estates balked. On July 22, the commissioners seemingly surrendered, but it was soon revealed that they had not met all the conditions of the estates. Finally on July 26, the contract between the commissioners and the estates was agreed upon, and the estates disbanded three days later. Never before had the commissioners pushed the estates with so much vigor. Their efforts had brought an additional 150,000 livres, but the offer of the estates still fell far short of the desired one-year grant of 600,000 livres.[77]

Louis renewed his attempt to obtain a special grant of 600,000 livres when the estates opened on December 7, 1622. He had borrowed large sums, one of his commissioners declared, and he had already engaged half of next year's revenue. The deputies nevertheless turned their attention to other matters. Finally on December 15, the commissioners asked them to stop deliberating on the destruction of châteaux and to consider instead the affairs of the king. Two days later the estates made a conditional offer, and the haggling began. On the twenty-sixth, the estates were still offering only 300,000 livres, but an eloquent appeal by the procureur général of the Parlement of Rennes led them to up it to 400,000. The commissioners refused this offer because the money would not be available in 1623 and there were other conditions attached, but a week later they came to terms. The estates farmed the wine tax for a period of two years for 450,000 livres. On December 25, 1623, and again on December 25, 1624, the king was to receive 200,000 livres. The remaining 50,000 was to be used by the estates.[78]

By the time the estates met in November 1623, the Bretons had become accustomed to requests for a don gratuit. In part for this reason and in part because they had more important concerns, they did not express shock when a royal official set the king's needs at 500,000 or 600,000 livres. The new challenge to their privileges came from an edict issued in June creating a Bureau of Finances in Brittany to be staffed by the usual horde of officials. Whether Louis issued the edict to tighten his hold over the financial administration and perhaps as the first step toward establishing élections, or whether his goal was merely to extract more money from Brittany cannot be ascertained. Whatever his motive, the estates were reluctant. When a deputation they sent to court to obtain the revocation of the edict made an unauthorized offer of 500,000 livres, they refused to approve it. After some negotiations, it was decided to farm the tax on the sale of wine for five years for 600,000 livres to be paid in two months. Of this sum 450,000 was to go to the king and the remainder to the estates. Louis, in return, revoked the offending edict. Whatever his original purpose. the threat to create the Bureau of Finances had served to open the pockets of the estates both wider and faster than usual.[79]

77. AD, Ille-et-Vilaine, C 2650, pp. 28–29, 33–35, 40–43, 49–50, 54, 61–62, 65, 73–83, 102–03, 107–10. The contract is on pp. 111–15. It provided for a troop withdrawal. The cahier, pp. 128–34, reveals that 200,000 livres the estates had raised to redeem the domain had been used for other purposes. Louis Joseph de Carné, *Les Etats de Bretagne*, 2d ed. (Paris, 1875), 1:272–75, contains an account of this meeting.

78. AD, Ille-et-Vilaine, C 2650, pp. 202, 246–47, 252, 258, 264–65, 269–70, 276–80, 297, 319, 333, 340–44.

79. Ibid., pp. 373, 405–08, 459–60, 483–85, 511–14, 536–37.

During these years, as before, the estates distributed generous presents to a large number of royal officials, and those excluded sought means to participate in this largesse. Louis learned that several officials were using various pretexts to get the estates to vote them money. To halt this practice he forbade the estates to give any presents to his officials other than their salaries. Nevertheless in addition to the usual gratifications, the estates voted four members of the sovereign courts from 1,000 to 4,000 livres each on the ground that they owed them arrears in their pensions, and they gave 6,000 livres to members of the Chamber of Accounts who had helped suppress the Bureau of Finances. Apparently the collusion that had always existed between the estates and the members of the local sovereign courts was extended during this crisis.[80] One other event of interest was the request the estates made to the duke of La Trémoille to demolish two of his châteaux. La Trémoille, who was one of the barons of Brittany, agreed and left it to his colleagues in the eatates to determine what his compensation should be. They voted him 30,000 livres. It was easier for Louis to pressure the three estates into voting him more than it was for him to limit their gifts to their friends and political supporters.[81]

The deputies of the three estates of Provence who met at Aix in August 1621 were greeted with demands for 300,000 livres beyond the usual taxes because of the expenses of the army. Although the sum was not excessive, a deputation was sent to court to secure a reduction. An agreement to give 240,000 was reached and the estates borrowed this sum in order to pay the king more rapidly.[82] No further demands for extraordinary contributions were made when the estates met in the spring of 1622 and in January 1624.

The échevins of Clermont continued to keep the good towns of Basse-Auvergne active. In 1621 the nineteen towns sent deputies to three meetings and the six nearest towns to two more. In 1622 the count was four and two, in 1623 three and zero, and in 1624 one and zero. The government does not appear to have made any direct demands for additional taxes during these years, but the good towns had to devote much of their time to raising money to support troops in the province and to provide supplies for armies moving to the war zone in the south. They liquidated their old debts but had to borrow upon occasion to obtain the money for the troops rapidly enough.[83] In spite of the requirement that they obtain permission to meet, the towns of Haute-Auvergne were active during this period. They dealt with many of

80. Ibid., pp. 438–39, 514–22, 536–37.

81. Ibid., pp. 401–03.

82. AD, Bouches-du Rhône, C 12, fols. 240–40v, 267–68, 325v–27.

83. AD, Puy-de-Dôme, 4F 146; *IAC, Clermont-Ferrand, Fonds de Montferrand*, ed. Alexandre-V.-Emmanuel Teilhard de Chardin (Clermont-Ferrand, 1902), 72–74, 203–07; AN, E 70[b] fol. 450.

the same problems as their brethren to the north.[84] The syndics of the plat pays of Lyonnais, Forez, and Beaujolais also devoted much of their energy to the support of troops and troop movements.[85]

The three estates of Dauphiné that met at Grenoble in late January and early February 1621 spent most of their time quarreling with each other. Claude Brosse, the syndic of the village, had reopened the old question of the nature of the taille in Dauphiné and the settlement that had been imposed by Henry IV. In spite of the "union of the three orders" that had been achieved in Valence in 1611 and had supposedly brought an end to separate meetings of the individual estates, the nobility, including some members of the long robe, assembled apart from the third estate every few days to draft an article-by-article reply to Brosse's cahier. The clergy often assisted them. The privileged order also quarreled with the third estate about the twentieth of the revenue from an increase in the salt tax that they claimed. The estates did find time to appropriate 166,431 livres for the year, of which 20,144 livres was for the don gratuit to the king, hardly more than the 18,000 they gave Lesdiguières, their governor. Lesdiguières' son-in-law and lieutenant received 6,000 livres, and various other sums were set aside for the military, the bureaucracy, and the affairs of the estates.[86]

The three estates that met at Valence in February and March 1622 were confronted with a royal demand that the province furnish 550,000 livres for the war effort. This sum was to be raised through the sale of some newly created offices, an increase in the salt tax, and new custom duties known as the *douane de Valence*. The three orders voted the usual subsidies but refused to accept the increase in the salt tax or the custom duties. To emphasize their poverty, they asked that the villages be granted a delay in the payment of their debts and that the king limit himself to three commissioners to open the estates. In an unusual move they decided to give Lesdiguières 36,000 livres if he would get the new taxes suppressed. A deputation was also sent directly to court on the matter.[87]

The estates were successful in obtaining a delay for the villages in the payment of their debts, but the increased taxes and other matters led to a meeting of the commis and *consuls* of the towns in April in Grenoble and of the council of the first two orders in that month and again in July. The tax on salt was raised, and Lesdiguières sought a tax on wine as well.[88] The

84. AC, St. Flour, ch. 5, art. 6, nos. 58–65; *IAC, Aurillac*, ed. Gabriel Esquer (Aurillac, 1906), 1: BB 14.

85. AD, Rhône, C 431, fols. 27v–28; AN E 70ᵇ, fols. 321–21v; BN ms. fr. 18,202, fols. 268v–69v.

86. AD, Isère, 1J 175, fols. 542–65v, 1C 4, no. 45.

87. AC, Grenoble, AA 40, BB 88; AD, Isère, 1J 175, fols. 566–82.

88. *Actes et correspondance du connétable de Lesdiguières*, ed. Louis-A. Douglas and Joseph Roman (Grenoble, 1878–84), 2:357–59; AD, Isère, 1J 175, fols. 582v–88; AC, Grenoble, AA 42.

three estates that met in Grenoble in the fall of 1623 continued to discuss the salt tax and the douane de Valence.[89] Since the douane also affected Provence and Languedoc, they dispatched a deputy to attend the next meetings of the estates of these provinces to seek their cooperation in getting it suppressed.[90] Between September 1621 and April 1624 there were also at least five meetings of the three mountain bailiwicks, as well as assemblies of the individual mountain bailiwicks where the salt tax was among the items considered.[91] The various assemblies appear to have been at least partially successful, for the maximum annual revenue the crown drew from Dauphiné in the years 1621–24 was 28,731 livres.[92] The rest of the taxes the inhabitants paid went to support their own government or to supply their own governor with an army to engage in the conflict with the Protestants.

The Burgundian practice of holding the estates every third year put the king at a disadvantage when the need arose for additional funds. He could convoke a special session of the estates, try to persuade the élus to levy an additional sum that had not been consented to, or simply do without. By the close of September 1621 Louis's finances were no longer in a position to permit him to continue to opt for the last solution, and he ordered the Burgundian deputies to assemble at Dijon in November. Because the previous meeting had been held in the fall of 1618 and those who had attended had only voted taxes through 1621, this assembly was not significantly premature. Nevertheless Louis preferred to consider it an extraordinary session and used this as an excuse to convoke only one clergyman and one nobleman from each bailiwick and one deputy from each of the principal towns as he had done in October 1616. Presumably he hoped that a smaller assembly could be more easily persuaded than the full estates to do his bidding. At the meeting, the governor, Bellegarde, and the other commissioners explained royal policy and stressed the need for money to suppress the revolt. They praised the Burgundians and pointed out that the estates of Normandy, Brittany, Languedoc, and Provence had already made substantial contributions. Finally they indulged in flattery: the king wanted only 400,000 livres, "a very mediocre sum for a very great province and the first peerage of the crown." Cajoled but not totally forgetful of their own interests, those present voted 300,000 livres.[93]

89. *Recueil des harangues faites par messire Pierre Scarron, evesque et prince de Grenoble ... et président perpétuel des estats du Dauphiné ...* (Paris, 1634), pp. 39–66; AD, Isère, B 3263; AC, Gap, BB 25, fols. 9, 12, 19v, 39–39v, 45v–48, 54v–55, 63, 64.

90. *IAD, Bouches-du-Rhône,* ed. Louis Blancard (Marseilles, 1884), 1:21; *IAD, Haute-Garonne,* 2:227. The estates of Burgundy did not meet again until 1626, but the élus joined in the effort to get the douane suppressed. *IAD, Côte-d'Or, sér. C,* ed. Joseph Garnier (Dijon, 1886), 3:139.

91. *IAD, Hautes-Alpes, sér. E,* ed. Paul Guillaume (Gap, 1913), 2:80–82; *IAC, Gap,* ed. Paul Guillaume (Gap, 1908–13), 1:119, 2:9–10, 13–14.

92. Mallet, pp. 201–02.

93. AD, Côte-d'Or, C 3017, fols. 254–66.

The regular meeting of the estates was not held until June 1622. Once more Louis asked for a special grant of 400,000 livres, but this time he was met with a blunt refusal. The three estates protested the composition of the previous assembly. Taxes, they declared, could be voted only in a full assembly of the estates. Assuming the offensive, they then asked that the king abandon an 18,000 livre tax on the towns, an increase in the salt tax to provide raises for members of the sovereign courts, and some newly established officies. They even refused to vote one of their lieutenant generals a special gratification that the king had offered him from their treasury. Finally, soothed somewhat by their uncooperative display in the above matters, they did give Louis the traditional don gratuit of 50,000 livres and their governor 16,000 before they disbanded.[94]

Their grants were totally unacceptable to Louis, and he directed Bellegarde to assemble either the bailiwick deputies or the full estates to vote the 400,000 livres. Bellegarde summoned the élus to see which type of meeting was preferable. Not surprisingly, they chose the larger assembly but urged that it be postponed until they had had time to present the remonstrances to the king that the last estates had prepared.[95] But Bellegarde refused, and in August 1622 he assembled the three estates once more in Dijon. Here they learned of their king's indignation at their refusal to provide support for his just war. Somewhat chastened they offered him 150,000 livres.[96]

Three years were to elapse before there was need to convoke the estates again, but the difficulties did not cease. The élus missed no opportunity to complain about the creation of new offices and other fund-raising measures, and Louis found that it was even more difficult to get the Burgundians to collect a tax than to vote one. In September 1623 his chancellor informed a deputy of the élus that he was going to leave two regiments in the province because the money had not been paid. There were still no results. On May 1, 1625, the élus discussed what to do about royal letters dated August 31, 1624, ordering that the remaining 50,000 livres of the promised 200,000 be levied. They refused to act on the ground that the three estates of August 1622 had only raised the initial offer that they had made in June of that year from 50,000 to 150,000 livres. They had not voted two separate grants totaling 200,000 livres. Under such circumstances Burgundy's contribution to the royal treasury reached only 247,293 livres in 1624 and fell to less than 200,000 during the six years that followed.[97]

The element of French society that approved most strongly of Louis's decision to restore the church lands in Béarn and Navarre and of the war with the Protestants that followed was the Catholic clergy. There was never

94. Ibid., fols. 267–310v.
95. Ibid., C 3078, fols. 38–39.
96. Ibid., C 3017, fols. 311–18.
97. Ibid., C 3078, fols. 87–87v, 96–96v, 167–68; Mallet, p. 207.

any doubt that Louis would seek extraordinary aid from them or that they would give generously. The only questions were how much they would offer and how the money could be raised. After some bargaining, the assembly of the clergy that met in 1621 offered 3 million livres, far more than they wanted to pay from their annual income. To obtain the money by alienating church property as they had been done during the Wars of Religion was equally unacceptable. In the end they followed the example of their king and created useless offices to sell. In return they asked that Louis destroy La Rochelle and the other Protestant strongholds, but they did not suggest that Protestants be denied liberty of conscience. Persuasion, not force, was to be used to return them to the Catholic fold. Thus the Catholic clergy's Protestant policy in 1921 was essentially the same as that adopted by Louis XIII in 1622 and as Richelieu is often credited with establishing at a later date.[98]

6. CONCLUSIONS

The difference in the way the crown treated the various provincial estates between 1621 and 1623 is striking. Those in Guyenne received their death blow. Others were treated roughly, yet some were handled with as much consideration as before. If the former had been the weaker estates and the latter those that were strong, the historian's task in explaining the crown's divergent policy would be simple, but the reverse was more nearly the case. The estates of Languedoc, Brittany, and Burgundy were subjected to exceptional pressure to produce more funds, while few additional demands were placed on those of Normandy and Basse-Auvergne.

There is only one hypothesis to explain the crown's lack of consistency. Louis was largely responsible for the policy of firmness that characterized the government from about 1620 when he became old enough to assume a more direct role. At that time, however, he could have had little understanding of the complex fiscal structure of late Renaissance France, and there is no reason to believe that Luynes was much better informed. Schomberg, the superintendent of finances during these years, was an honest, unimaginative official whose previous experience was in the military and diplomacy. It is not unlikely, therefore, that the Council of Finances was left with a freer hand than usual. In August 1619 it was decided to divide this council into four groups composed of an intendant of finances and four other councillors, each charged with dealing with a certain number of provinces.[99] Since an informed higher authority was lacking, it is not unlikely that one group of the

98. Pierre Blet, *Le clergé de France et la monarchie* (Rome, 1959), 1 : 242–64.

99. Roland Mousnier, "Les règlements du conseil du roi sous Louis XIII," *Ann bul, de la soc. de l'histoire de France, 1946–1947* (Paris, 1948): 156–58.

council dealt with the provincial estates under its jurisdiction more severely or with greater gentleness than another.

The group of the council that administered Guyenne was headed by the intendant, Gilles de Maupeou, a Protestant convert who had been one of Sully's most trusted lieutenants. Maupeou had served in the généralité of Guyenne from 1595 to 1597 as a financial investigator and administrator.[100] His reaction to what he saw is not known, but the sieur de Selves, who was sent to court by Agenais in December 1604 to secure the revocation of the edict creating the élus in Guyenne the year before, frequently reported to his constituents that Maupeou was the only member of the council who supported Sully in his insistence that the élections were necessary. On one occasion he wrote that Maupeou had rebuffed him as much as or more than that notoriously rude statesman.[101] It would be logical to suppose that Maupeou seized the opportunity presented by the presence of the royal army in Guyenne in 1621 to renew the attempt that he and his former master had made to establish élections permanently in Guyenne eighteen years before.

The treatment given Brittany and Normandy, the two other provinces with estates that Maupeou's group administered, lends support to the hypothesis. The crown pressed the estates of Brittany more vigorously than ever before to give substantial funds, and in June 1623 it issued an edict creating a Bureau of Finances there to tighten control over fiscal administration and perhaps to pave the way for the establishment of élections in the province. Taxes in Normandy were cut by 300,000 livres, but this happened because the government asked for less in view of the heavy burden that fell on the province and not because the estates voted less. Sully, and presumably Maupeou, wanted to equalize taxes, and this move was designed to do so. The three Norman estates were ignored or rebuffed when it was desirable. Taxes in 1622 were collected without convoking them to give their consent, and on occasions when they refused to vote the full amount requested, the crown ordered that the entire sum be collected anyway.

Another group of the council was responsible for Languedoc, Provence, Auvergne, and Lyonnais. Nothing is known of the position of the intendant, Duret, and at least two of the councillors, Vic and Caumartin, were moderates, but a fourth was Michel de Marillac. Marillac had been dispatched to Guyenne in 1598–99 to ensure that the taille was apportioned and collected in a fair, honest, and efficient manner. It may have been his unfavorable report that led Sully to decide to establish élections there. Soon he was to become the most determined foe the estates ever had. It is probable, therefore, that he was responsible for the decision to take advantage of the presence of a royal army in Languedoc in 1622 to issue an edict

100. *AHG*, 28:219; *Histoire de Bordeaux*, ed. Robert Boutruche (Bordeaux, 1966), 4:352; Valois, 1: no. 4304.

101. AC, Agen, letters of Selves to Agen in CC 111, CC 120, and esp. those of February 11 and March 3 in CC 123.

creating élections. It is also probable that his support among his fellow councillors was so lukewarm that Ventadour and other friends of the estates had little difficulty in securing its suppression. The edict establishing the greffiers in the dioceses, towns, and communities to supervise the entire process of tax apportioning, collecting, and auditing probably had Marillac's backing. This time it was La Vieuville's desire for a balanced budget that led to these offices being suppressed in return for a substantial grant. In view of the predominantly mild attitude of this group of the council, it is not surprising that the estates and assemblies in Provence, Auvergne, and Lyonnais where there were no royal armies escaped unscathed.

Not enough is known of the attitude of the councillors toward the estates in either of the other two groups to offer a persuasive hypothesis as to why the one that dealt with Burgundy was more severe than the one responsible for Dauphiné. Whatever the explanation of the events of these four eventful years, one fact cannot be disputed: Louis XIII had ensured that Béarn and Navarre would always be united with France in the person of the king, he had seriously weakened the power of the Protestant nobles and towns, and he had taken steps to lead to the decline of the estates of the largest généralité in France. Even if he had died in 1624, he would have had claim to be one of the principal architects of the absolute monarchy in France.

14

RICHELIEU AND MARILLAC,
1624–1629

1. THE TWO MEN

CARDINAL RICHELIEU ENTERED THE KING'S COUNCIL ON APRIL 29, 1624, AND assumed the primary responsibility for the conduct of foreign affairs. He owed his appointment to Marie de Medici, Bérulle, and others who had used their influence to persuade Louis to take this step despite his dislike for him that stemmed back to the time when he had briefly served in the government during the Concini era. Once admitted to the council, Richelieu set about to replace La Vieuville as Louis's principal adviser. Because· La Vieuville was an advocate of alliances with the English and the Dutch, Richelieu could not find fault with the general direction of foreign policy. Instead he relied on intrigue and public opinion, which he sought to manipulate through pamphlets to turn the tide in his direction. La Vieuville's diplomatic mistakes in matters of detail did the rest. On August 13 he was dismissed and imprisoned. Richelieu became the most influential member of the council, and Michel de Marillac was named co-superintendent of finances.[1]

Too often the Richelieus have been depicted as members of the minor nobility. In fact the family was an old one. On the paternal side, the cardinal's grandmother was a Rochechouart, and on the maternal side she was the lord of three fiefs and connected with the ancient house of Feuquières. The latter lady had married a La Porte, a lawyer, member of the Parlement of Paris, and himself the lord of two seigneuries. Through him the cardinal had useful connections in the sovereign courts and legal profession. The Richelieus had been clients of the dukes of Montpensier for several generations. The sponsorship of this family, coupled with their own ability, had enabled them to obtain an enviable position. At the time of his premature death in 1590 at the age of forty-two, the cardinal's father was already grand provost of France, knight of the Order of the Holy Ghost,

---

1. Alexandra D. Lublinskaya, *French Absolutism: The Crucial Phase, 1620–1629*, trans. Brian Pearce (Cambridge, 1968), pp. 260–71. Berthold Zeller, *Richelieu et les ministres de Louis XIII de 1621 à 1624* (Paris, 1880), pp. 268–99. Gabriel Hanotaux, *Histoire du Cardinal de Richelieu* (Paris, 1903), 2:547–56.

captain of the royal guards, and friend and companion of the king. Had he lived several more decades, he might have advanced into the front ranks of the nobility.

Too much has also been written concerning the poverty of the family. It is true that the failure of the crown to pay its debts and the difficulty in collecting seigneurial dues during the Religious Wars, coupled with the expenses the cardinal's father incurred because of his court offices, brought the family into difficult straits. Nevertheless the size of some of the transactions in which he was involved reveal his enviable financial status. In 1583 he purchased four ships, in 1585 Henry III gave him a princely 354,000 livres, and in 1590 Henry IV granted him 60,000 more. The family was permitted to have one of its members occupy the episcopal seat at Luçon, one of the hundred-odd in France, albeit not a very lucrative one. In short, when the future cardinal's father died in 1590, the Richelieus were a rising family with a large income and heavy commitments. They still fell far short of the magnate class, but they must have numbered within the top five hundred families in France. One of the greatest ambitions of the cardinal was to advance the Richelieus into the foremost ranks of the nobility, a goal that he achieved although the male line became extinct in his generation.[2]

Volumes have been written about Richelieu's early career depicting how he rose to be the king's first minister through intrigue, flattery, and dissimulation. At times he found himself in the camp of the rebels, but he also sought to avoid becoming too closely attached to any faction and to remain on good terms with everyone with influence. When the king reluctantly admitted him to his council in 1624, both the "good Frenchmen" and the "devouts" welcomed his appointment. Once in power he displayed no gratitude toward Marie de Medici, Barbin, and others who had aided him unless it was clear that they would be his servants. He packed the government with his creatures and insisted on their unquestioned loyalty. In spite of his conduct, in his written pronouncements he always adopted the position of the divine right, absolute monarchist, and of the strictly orthodox Catholic. His Catholicism, however, was of the sort that made salvation easy to achieve, and he was willing to make moral compromises when it was to his advantage or that of the state to do so. Although a product of the Catholic reformation in that he wanted to eradicate abuses and bring Protestants back into the fold, he was almost untouched by the spirituality of that great movement.[3]

2. Maximin Deloche, *Les Richelieu: Le père du Cardinal* (Paris, 1923), pp. 1–14, 191–92, 230, 281–82, 337–44. Luçon was not a wealthy bishopric, but in 1690 its net revenue was at the median of those in France. Georges d'Avenel, *Richelieu et la monarchie absolue*, 2d ed. (Paris, 1895), 3:456–57.

3. For a summary of Richelieu's early ideas, see William F. Church, *Richelieu and Reason of State* (Princeton, 1972), pp. 81–101.

No one has ever questioned Richelieu's superb intellectual powers. Whether the causes he lent them to profited France is another matter. His accomplishments are all the more remarkable because he was a highly nervous, irritable individual who suffered from poor health. One brother, whom he made archbishop of Aix and then of Lyons, sometimes mistook himself for God, and a sister died insane. The cardinal suffered from frequent attacks of fever and migraine headaches. As he grew older he added constipation, ulcers, rheumatism, and hemorrhoids to his list of physical woes. Only his indomitable will kept him at his tasks, but even he quickly recognized that there were limits to what he could do. Because of his health, Louis specifically directed in June 1626 that he free himself from secondary matters in order to devote all his energies to foreign affairs and to general concerns of great importance. Local business and individual petitions were to be handled by other ministers and the secretaries of state.[4] As a result, Richelieu had little direct contact with the provincial estates. Matters concerning them were the responsibility of the keeper of the seals, the secretaries of state, financial officials, and other members of the council. This is not to say that Richelieu was not in fact Louis's chief minister, but it does suggest that the routine administration of the kingdom and to a large degree the directions that domestic policy took were in the hands of others. Of these men, none was more important than Michel de Marillac.

The Marillacs were an old noble family from Haute-Auvergne. One ancestor had the misfortune to be captured by the English in 1375 and had to sell most of his lands to pay his ransom. In the years that followed, the Marillacs served the dukes of Bourbon in various capacities, and by the sixteenth century the male members of the family usually chose law, administration, or the church for careers rather than arms. Of the ten sons of Guillaume de Marillac, Michel's grandfather, one became the secretary to the constable de Bourbon and followed him into exile. Four entered the church, one becoming an archbishop, one a bishop, and a third, to the chagrin of the family, a Calvinist. Three sons became advocates or councillors in the Parlement of Paris, one a commissaire ordinaire des guerres, and still another a superintendant of finances and a knight as a reward for his courage on the field of Montcontour. This last one was the father of Michel and his ill-fated brother, Louis, the future marshal of France. Like the ancestors of Sully and Richelieu, the Marillacs were of both the robe and the sword. They stand with so many other families as proof of the folly of trying to establish a rigorous social distinction between the two branches of the aristocracy. To remove any doubt as to the Marillacs' acceptability, one

---

4. AN, AB XIX 2927, liasse, 4 bis. This interesting document has recently been printed in Richelieu, *Papiers*, 1 : 368.

need only recall that Louis married Catherine de Medici, a cousin and maid of honor to the queen mother herself.[5]

At an early age Michel displayed the love of learning and the highly developed spirituality that was to characterize his entire life. Hardworking and serious, he made an enviable record at the College of Navarre. Greek, Spanish, and Italian he knew, and his mastery of Latin was such that it was almost a native language. For a time he considered entering the clergy, but the death of the last of his relatives who was a member of the Parlement of Paris led his family to decide that it would be best for him to carry on the Marillac tradition of service there. As a result, he was named a councillor in Parlement in 1586 at the age of twenty-three. A devout Catholic, Marillac refused to accept the Protestant Henry of Navarre as his king despite his own authoritarian political views, but after Henry's conversion, he made every effort to secure his recognition by the Parlement and city of Paris. In return Henry named him a maître des requêtes in 1595.[6]

Marillac was in Rouen in 1596 where he presumably assisted the council in its dealings with the Assembly of Notables.[7] The following year he returned to the Norman capital to extract as much money as he could to support the siege of Amiens. The Parlement had refused to register an edict creating a number of new offices in its court and in the presidial seats in the province. To Marillac, opponent though he was of venality and an over-staffed bureaucracy, fell the task of trying to persuade that company to reverse its stand. "The multiplication of offices," he admitted, "is an inconvenient and damaging thing.... But," he pleaded, "the king can conceive of no more prompt method of obtaining the money he needs than the creation of offices.... Once Amiens is taken, who will regret some sacrifices? *The inconvenience of an individual is to be preferred to that of a family, that of a family to a town, that of a town to a province, that of a province to a kingdom.... Necessity is above the laws.*"[8] Marillac thus expressed his lifelong conviction that the needs of the kingdom take precedence over those of the individual, town, and province and that to secure the common good the king had the right to override established laws, customs, and privileges. In spite of Marillac's eloquence, Parlement initially rebuffed his appeal. He also expe-

5. Edouard Everat, *Michel de Marillac, sa vie, ses oeuvres* (Riom, 1894), pp. 1–4. Nicolas Lefèvre, sieur de Lézeau, *Histoire de la vie de Messire, Michel de Marillac, chevalier, garde des sceaux de France*, Bibl. Sainte-Geneviève, ms. 826, fols. 15–35v. Mss. 2005–06 is the original or first copy. There are also copies at BN, mss. fr. 14,027, and n.a. fr. 82–83. Pierre de Vaissière, *Un grand procès sous Richelieu: L'affaire de Maréchal de Marillac* (Paris, 1924), pp. 13–16.

6. Everat, *Michel de Marillac*, pp. 5–16. Everat gives the date of Marillac's birth as 1560 rather than 1563 (p. 197) but Vaissière, *Un grand procès*, prefers the latter date (p. 17). Bibl. Ste.-Geneviève, ms. 826, fols. 45v–64v, 199–211v.

7. *Entrée à Rouen du roi Henri IV, en 1596*, ed. Charles de Robillard de Beaurepaire (Rouen, 1887), p. xxx.

8. Amable Floquet, *Histoire du Parlement de Normandie* (Rouen, 1841), 4:121–22. Floquet has placed these sentences in italics.

rienced difficulty in his efforts to obtain a loan of 180,000 livres from the inhabitants of Rouen, but in the end, he and other royal officials secured the registration of decrees creating some of the desired offices and a loan of 100,000 livres, an arrangement that was readily accepted by the hard-pressed king.[9]

With the restoration of peace, Marillac was given the difficult task of ensuring that taxes were apportioned and collected in a fair, honest, and efficient manner in the généralités of Limoges and Guyenne. It is likely that his unfavorable report caused Henry and Sully to attack the provincial estates in Guyenne. This experience probably also contributed to Marillac's low opinions of the estates. His disciple and biographer, Nicolas Lefèvre, tells us that it was during this mission that he obtained his mastery of financial administration. Unfortunately Lefèvre gives no indication of Marillac's attitude toward the estates at this time. The desire to weaken or destroy the estates and other duly constituted bodies was unpopular, and it is not surprising that Lefèvre chose to ignore Marillac's role just as Sully failed to mention his own activity and that of his master in this regard.[10]

Marillac was also sent on missions to Brittany, Bourbonnais, Auvergne, and the Spanish frontier, but more and more he turned to religion. In 1602 he began to frequent the hotel of Madame Acarie, a noted mystic, where he became a close friend of Pierre de Bérulle, the future cardinal, and other leaders of the Catholic Reformation, including François de Sales and Vincent de Paul, both one day to become saints. Soon he was deeply involved in the successful effort to introduce the Carmelite order into France. He helped reform the Ursulines and contributed his talents to establishing the Oratorians in his native country. Always deeply religious he became increasingly mystical and devout. If we can believe his biographer, he scorned the wealth and pomp of this world and devoted long hours to prayer and contemplation.[11] He won the respect of Chancellor Bellièvre who attempted to make him a president of the Parlement of Paris, but he was greatly relieved when the post was assigned to someone else. In 1608 he contemplated resigning his position as maître des requêtes in order to have more time for his religious devotions, but Madame Acarie persuaded him to

9. Ibid., pp. 119–24; *Cahiers des Etats de Normandie sous le règne de Henri IV*, ed. Charles de Robillard de Beaurepaire (Rouen, 1880), 1 : 326–28, Bibl. Ste.-Geneviève, ms. 826, fol. 37.

10. Bibl. Ste.-Geneviève, ms. 826, fol. 37–37v. *Apologie pour le sieur de Marillac* . . . , BN ms. fr. 5183, fols. 10v–11. Lefèvre reported that Marillac's work as a maître des requêtes pleased the council and "especially" the duke of Sully. Bibl. Ste.-Geneviève, ms. 826, fol. 200–200v.

11. Bibl. Ste.-Geneviève, ms. 826, fols. 38–41v, 65–83v, 103–197v; Everat, *Michel de Marillac*, pp. 18–30, 36–37, 84–102v. For Marillac's role in the Catholic reformation, see Michel Houssaye, *M. de Bérulle et les Carmélites de France, 1575–1611* (Paris 1872), pp. 221–89, 356–57, 369, 384–91, 447, 490–91, 502–04, and his *Le Père de Bérulle et l'oratoire de Jésus, 1611–1625* (Paris, 1874), pp. 27, 186–87, 215–16. See also Pierre Coste, *The Life and Works of Saint Vincent de Paul*, trans. J. Leonard (Westminister, Md., 1952), 1 : 182–89, and Henri Brémond, *A Literary History of Religious Thought in France*, trans. K. L. Montgomery (New York, 1930), 2 : 145–267.

retain his office because of the good that it enabled him to do. In 1612 his desire to withdraw became overpowering, but he had scarcely abandoned his position before he was named to the king's council. Once more Madame Acarie's influence was needed to persuade him to accept. Quickly he became one of the five most active members of that body. As a councillor he witnessed the Estates General of 1614, and he was instrumental in resolving quarrels over precedence in the estates of Brittany and in the Assembly of Notables in 1617. In spite of these activities, he found time to translate the *Imitation of Christ*. The first edition appeared in 1621 and was followed by three more in his lifetime and several after his death, the last being published in 1878.[12]

In July 1623 the aging Chancellor Sillery offered to have Marillac made keeper of the seals, only to be rebuffed by that conscientious statesman who did not wish to become indebted to him. In January 1624 the king himself considered giving Marillac the seals but in the end did not. In the meantime Marillac continued to play a leading role in the council. In addition to his heavy duties he found time to translate the *Psalms*, and in spite of his great services, according to Lefèvre, he often refused to accept gifts from the king and even the salary from his office.[13]

Perhaps Lefèvre exaggerated Marillac's otherworldliness. We know that in 1599 a deputy from Comminges hoped to influence his attitude toward the estates by promising that 3,000 livres on which he had some claim would be paid. The king's council soon acted so vigorously against the estates, however, that it is likely that the deputy misjudged his man, and Marillac said nothing in their favor. Marillac did seek the bishopric of Saint-Malo for his son, a request that he doubtless justified to his conscience because of the desirability of placing a product of the Catholic reform in that post, but the young man, a devout Capuchin, refused to accept the position out of humility and died in 1631 a simple monk.[14] Even after some probing, one is left with the feeling that Marillac was singularly free of the greed, pride, and personal ambition that characterized most other statesmen of his day. In these traits he differed sharply from Richelieu who sought wealth, titles, and earthly glory as avidly as he did the humbling of the Habsburgs.

Marillac was also much more authoritarian and inflexible than Richelieu. One man who knew him well observed that "the true author and promoter

12. Bibl. Ste.-Geneviève, ms. 826, fols. 38–39v, 41v. For Marillac's role as a councillor, see J. Michael Hayden, *France and the Estates General of 1614* (Cambridge, 1974), p. 14.

13. Bibl. Ste.-Geneviève, ms. 826, fols. 269v–72. Everat, *Michel de Marillac*, pp. 30–31, 38. Marillac played an especially important role in reforming the council. See Roland Mousnier, *La plume, la faucille et le marteau* (Paris, 1970), esp. pp. 149, 156–57, and "Les règlements du conseils du roi sous Louis XIII," *Ann.-bul. de la soc. de l'histoire de France, 1946–1947*, esp. pp. 118, 122, 159–96.

14. Richelieu, *Lettres*, 3:234, 472, 762, 870; AAE, ms. 795bis, fol. 198; Everat, *Michel de Marillac*, p. 124.

of this regulation [on the council] was M. de Marillac, whom the Sr. Haligre [the keeper of the seals] dared not contradict. Marillac had a genius for making regulations in the council and seized an ascendancy over the mind of Mr. Haligre, whom he fortified against those who were motivated by self-interest."[15] At this time Marillac had been a mere councillor. Not surprisingly he became more overbearing as his authority increased. Some years after Marillac's death, Richelieu told Louis that by removing him from office he had freed himself "from a man so full of the opinion he had of himself that he esteemed that nothing was done well if it was not by his order and who believed that many bad means were permissible to him in order to attain goals which were suggested to him by a zeal which one can call indiscreet."[16] It is strange to hear Richelieu condemning someone for permitting the ends to justify the means, for practicing reason of state, but this opinion was voiced long after the two statesmen had quarreled. It obscures the fact that initially they had been friends and had shared a mutual respect.

Marillac became acquainted with Richelieu in 1616–17 during the latter's first ministry. Never one to desert a friend in adversity, he maintained a lively correspondence with the future cardinal during his exile from court. In view of these friendly relations, it is not surprising that in August 1624 when Richelieu replaced La Vieuville as chief minister, Marillac was named co-superintendent of finances with Jean Bochart, seigneur de Champigny.[17]

2. THE EARLY YEARS

For the first few years, the two statesmen worked together without serious difficulty, although disagreements did occur. Richelieu's initial goals were to ensure that La Vieuville was so thoroughly discredited that he would never again constitute a threat and to improve the French position abroad. The first he accomplished by persuading Louis XIII to establish a Chamber of Justice to search for and punish officials who were guilty of financial wrongdoing. Since the deputies in the Estates General of 1614 had asked that this step be taken and Louis had promised to adhere to their request, there was no difficulty on this score. Once the chamber was constituted, it was easy to implicate La Vieuville, whose father-in-law was a leading

15. G. Pagès, "Autour du 'Grand Orage.' Richelieu et Marillac: deux politiques," *Revue historique* 179 (1937): 65.

16. Richelieu, *Testament politique*, ed. Louis André, 7th ed. (Paris, 1947), p. 114.

17. Everat, *Michel de Marillac*, pp. 28–29; BN ms. fr. 5183, fols. 46v–49. It should be noted that Marillac's defender holds that he did not owe his position to Richelieu. For some letters of the Marillac brothers to Richelieu, see AAE, ms. 775, fols 54–215, and of Richelieu to Michel de Marillac, Richelieu, *Lettres, 1:577, 620–23, 633–35. Richelieu, Mém.* SHF, 4:110–115, 132–33.

financier and whose success had been due in part to his useful ties with monied interests. La Vieuville was sentenced to death but escaped from France. This accomplished, Richelieu permitted the other threatened officials and financiers to pay the treasury a princely 10,800,000 livres in return for suppressing the chamber. La Vieuville was permanently disgraced, although he was eventually allowed to return to France, and Richelieu had a much needed windfall to help support his foreign and domestic policies.[18]

Richelieu's predecessors had been concerned about the Austrian Habsburgs' efforts to strengthen their position in the Empire and their Spanish cousins' attempts to regain their lost provinces in the Low Countries. To prevent this possibility, they had strengthened their ties with the Dutch and German Protestants and were negotiating a marriage alliance with England. In an effort to deny the Spanish access to the vital Alpine passes, they had also made agreements with Venice, Savoy, and the Swiss Protestants. When Richelieu entered the council, papal troops held the vital Valtelline valley but were permitting the Spanish to use it. Near the close of 1624, Richelieu dispatched one small army to assist the Protestant Grisons in regaining control of the valley and thereby cutting the Spanish route to Germany, while another army under Lesdiguières joined Savoy in besieging Genoa. At this point Rohan and his brother, Soubise, led elements of the Protestant movement into rebellion largely because Louis had not destroyed Fort Louis commanding the sea entrance to La Rochelle as he had promised to do in the peace agreement of 1622.[19]

Contrary to what had often been said, Richelieu had not clearly defined his objectives when he came to power. Caught between a foreign war and a domestic insurrection, he took some military measures against the Huguenots but at the same time began to explore the possibility of a peace settlement. Rohan and Soubise were suspicious, however, and would do no more than negotiate while they sought to win additional support from among their brethren.[20] Faced with this situation Richelieu prepared in late April or early May 1625 one of his earliest general memorandums for the king. "It seems," he wrote, "that everything now conspires to humble the pride of Spain." Then, after an unjustifiably optimistic survey of the foreign situation, he declared in reference to the Habsburgs that "there has never

18. Richelieu, *Mém.* SHF, 4:133–59, 273–90; Richelieu, *Papiers*, 1:96–99, 101–05, 113–22; Georges Picot, *Histoire des Etats généraux*, 2d ed. (Paris, 1888), 5:45–46; F. Véron de Forbonnais, *Recherches et considerations sur les finances de France* (Liége, 1758), 1:336–41; *Mercure François*, 10 (1624): 678–730, 11 (1625): 554–623. In July 1626 it was reported to the estates of Languedoc that the financiers paid only 7 million livres in return for the suppression of the Chamber of Justice. AD, Hérault, procès-verbaux of the estates of July–August 1626.

19. Lublinskaya, *French Absolutism*, pp. 273–77; Church, *Richelieu*, pp. 103–106; Jack A. Clarke, *Huguenot Warrior: The Life and Times of Henri de Rohan, 1579–1638*. (The Hague, 1966), pp. 109–21.

20. Clarke, *Huguenot Warrior*, pp. 121–24.

been such a splendid opportunity for the king to increase his power and clip the wings of his enemies."[21]

Like so many of his predecessors, Richelieu saw only the magnates and the Huguenots as potential sources of rebellion. The former he discounted at this time, but the latter customarily acted when the crown was occupied with its enemies. "Consequently, it is necessary to see if their power is sufficient to stop the king from following his design to make war abroad." Alone, he argued, the Huguenots were not strong, but what if they received money and ships from Spain? Reluctantly he concluded that France could not fight a foreign and domestic war at the same time. "As long as the Huguenots have a foothold in France," he reasoned, "the king will never be the master of the interior or capable of undertaking any glorious action abroad."[22] On the other hand, if peace was made with Spain without securing some advantage for France's allies, it would be difficult to reassemble the coalition at a later date. Therefore Richelieu recommended that an effort be made to make an advantageous peace with Spain so that the king could devote his efforts to crushing the Huguenots. If this could not be done, he urged that the Huguenots be satisfied so that Louis could throw all his forces against Spain.

After negotiations conducted through the papal legate in France failed to lead to a satisfactory resolution of the Valtelline question, Richelieu increased his efforts to make peace with the Huguenots and decided to continue the war in Italy. In this decision he encountered the opposition of Michel de Marillac who had the support of the queen mother and Bérulle. To override their arguments and to prepare public opinion to accept his plan, Richelieu recommended on September 3 that an enlarged meeting of the council be called to hear an explanation of why this change of policy was necessary. He suggested that all the princes, dukes, officers of the crown, first presidents and procureurs généraux of the sovereign courts, and the provost of the merchants of Paris be summoned. In addition, he asked that the Assembly of the Clergy, which was then in session, be directed to send four prelates.[23] The composition of the proposed meeting was to be comparable to the Assembly of Notables held in Rouen in 1617, but actual attendance was more limited. It took place in Fontainebleau on September 29 and proceeded smoothly. Only the queen mother and Cardinal Sourdis questioned Richelieu's position, and in the end unity was achieved.[24]

21. Richelieu, *Lettres*, 2:78, 80.

22. Ibid., 2:82, 83.

23. Michel Houssaye, *Le Cardinal de Bérulle et le Cardinal de Richelieu, 1625–1629* (Paris, 1875), pp. 50–53; Richelieu, *Mém.* SHF, 5:101–118; Richelieu, *Lettres*, 2:119–24. Richelieu, *Papiers*, 1:218–20.

24. Richelieu, *Mém.* SHF, 5:120–22, 309–10. *Mercure François* 11 (1625): 852–57; Victor-L. Tapié, *France and the Age of Louis XIII and Richelieu*, trans. D. McN. Lockie (London, 1974), pp. 149–50. The provincial sovereign courts were not represented.

Negotiations with the Huguenots proceeded slowly, and the peace was not signed until February 5, 1626. By the terms of the agreement Louis gave a verbal promise to destroy Fort Louis commanding the sea approach to La Rochelle at some future date, a promise he never intended to keep. In return, La Rochelle was compelled to accept a royal commissioner, demolish its new fortifications, refrain from having warships, restore the property of Catholic church, and permit the practice of Catholic rites. The crown had won an inconclusive victory.[25] Then, instead of taking advantage of the restoration of internal peace to upstage the war in Italy, the French ambassador to Madrid signed the treaty of Monçon with Spain on March 5, and Louis ratified it in May.

There has been considerable debate over why Richelieu made peace with Spain instead of continuing the war. One factor was that the Spanish had offered favorable terms, although not so favorable as desired by France's Italian allies, who were not consulted. To have insisted on further concessions might have led to full-scale war with Spain and the pope, which would have cost Richelieu the support of the devout, many of whom were already angered at his making peace with the Huguenots. Richelieu was not yet secure enough to risk a break. Most important of all, he had come to realize that France was not strong enough to undertake a Spanish war or even a full-scale assault on the Huguenots. In 1625 the latter had nearly held their own on the land, and Louis had had to borrow ships from the Dutch and English to defeat them at sea. First France must be reformed, its financial resources improved, and a navy constructed. Only then could come the destruction of the Huguenot state within a state, and finally the glorious war to humble the Habsburgs.[26]

Sometime during 1625 Richelieu prepared a proposal for the reformation of the kingdom.[27] The document reveals that he had little conception of the administrative changes that would be necessary to transform France into an absolute monarchy. In it he urged that four councils be created, the most important of which was to be dominated by the magnates. Both the council to deal with fiscal matters and the one to handle petitions from the provinces were to be composed of the chancellor, the keeper of the seals, the superintendent of finances, and an equal number of clergymen, nobles of the sword, and the robe. Since the clergymen selected were likely to be of noble

25. Clarke, *Huguenot Warrior*, pp. 131–35. For the terms and ratifications see *Mercure François* 11 (1626): 119–39; Church, *Huguenot Warrior*, pp. 188–89.

26. Lublinskaya, *French Absolutism*, pp. 278–82; Houssaye, *Le Cardinal de Bérulle*, pp. 86–104. On the need for a navy, see Lucas-A. Boiteux, *Richelieu grand maître de la navigation et du commerce en France* (Paris, 1955), pp. 11–26. For Richelieu and Marillac's positions around January 1626, see Richelieu, *Mém.* SHF, 5:205–19, 320–25.

27. Richelieu, *Papiers*, 1:248–69. He omitted naval affairs but he treated them elsewhere. Ibid., pp. 242–44, 246–47. For additional proposals see ibid., 2:244–46.

extraction, the proposal, if implemented, would have greatly increased the role of the nobility in the government. The fourth council, two-thirds of whose members were to be cardinals and other prelates, was to advise the king on matters of conscience and on ecclesiastical appointments.

Among many articles that dealt with the reformation of the church, Richelieu proposed that archbishops hold provincial councils every third year, a step which would have transformed what had been occasional meetings into a new type of representative institution that would be common to all of France. He also advocated economies by reducing the expenses of the royal household, the size of the bureaucracy, and the salaries of government officials. Duelists were to be punished. The nobility was to be given a monopoly on household and military positions. Venality was to be abolished, and dishonest financial officials were to be punished. Finally, the domain was to be redeemed so that the burden on the taxpayers could be lessened.

Many of Richelieu's suggestions were derived from the Estates General of 1614 and the Assembly of Notables of 1617. One, a proposal to establish an itinerant court to hear and judge complaints against anyone, including members of the sovereign courts, was similar to a proposal rejected by the robe-dominated assembly. Another dealt with payments *par comptant*, a method of dispensing with royal funds without going through the Chamber of Accounts, which enabled the king to give secret subsidies to foreign powers and to the Hugenots. Unfortunately much of these funds were diverted into the pockets of courtiers and financiers. Bellièvre had tried to solve the problem in 1596–97 by dividing revenue into two parts and allocating one to meet the contractual obligations of the crown. Richelieu, couching his statement in the form of a royal edict, approached the problem by having the king declare that "we wish to deprive ourselves of the freedom that we and our predecessors have formerly used to dispose of money by secret ways of accounting, recognizing that although the practice can be useful on many occasions . . . , the abuse is nevertheless of such consequence that we can say that it is one of the principal causes of the dissipation of our finances." [28] Then, after expressing the desire not to have to increase the tax burden on the people, Richelieu recommended measures to reduce gifts and gratifications.

Reflecting the older Renaissance attitude of making local agencies rather than the crown responsible for welfare, Richelieu made municipal and parish officials responsible for correcting the disorders in hospital administration in conjunction with the clergy. He also recommended that the poor in every town and the surrounding district be employed in public works. To administer this program, he advocated having "the deputies of the clergy,

28. Ibid., 1:262.

officers, mayors, and *échevins*... assemble annually to discuss and resolve the
yearly cost and the means of finding funds."[29] Sums needed beyond that
available for the poor from the usual sources were to be raised by taxes
consented to by each locality and collected by persons elected for this
purpose. Thus in 1625 Richelieu considered creating a nationwide system of
periodic provincial assemblies for the clergy, increasing the responsibilities
and the taxing powers of the duly constituted local bodies, augmenting the
role of the nobility in the council, and placing limitations on how the king
spent his revenue.

While Richelieu was devoting his time to foreign policy and dreaming of
far-reaching reforms for the kingdom, Marillac was carrying out his duties as
superintendant of finances. Little is known of his work beyond that he
continued La Vieuville's economy efforts. In 1625 only 1.4 million livres
were distributed in pensions, about a third or a fourth of the normal
amount, and the costs of the four royal households were kept to 2.4 million.
It is suggestive of Louis's willingness to economize that his brother spent
200,000 livres more on his household than he did, and the two queens
together consumed four times as much. Nevertheless the wars in Italy and
southern France drove up military expenses, and secret expenses rose still
more. They were met by the huge sum the financial officials paid to obtain
the suppression of the Chamber of Justice, increased revenue from the
Parties Casuelles, and perhaps borrowing. In addition, the clergy voted a
special grant of 1,745,000 livres in February 1626, but ordinary taxes were
kept at a low level. These figures give credence to the claim that Marillac
was not only honest, efficient, and knowledgeable but also firmly opposed to
giving pensions to the magnates and to placing additional tax burdens on
the poor people. To have succeeded he must have enjoyed Richelieu's
support.[30]

Richelieu probably hoped to begin to implement his reform program
immediately after the restoration of peace in the winter of 1626, but in the
months that followed, only two related edicts were issued, both of which
were designed to ensure domestic order. In February, at his instigation,
Louis forbade dueling, and a few months later he imposed the death penalty
on a member of the Montmorency family for violating this directive. In July
Louis responded to the request of the Estates General of 1614, the Assembly
of Notables, and the provincial estates of Brittany to direct that the
fortifications of towns and castles in the interior of the kingdom be raised in
order to spare his subjects the expense of garrisoning them, but little was
done to implement the edict.[31]

29. Ibid., p. 266.

30. Mallet, pp. 209, 221, 226; Everat, *Michel de Marillac*, pp. 32–34; Pierre Blet, *Le clergé de France et la monarchie* (Rome, 1959), 1:286–95.

31. Isambert, 16:175–83, 192–94.

The delay in taking up the question of reform must be attributed to the intrigues surrounding the marriage of Louis's younger brother, Gaston, and the related Chalais conspiracy that occupied the court during the spring and summer. The episode provided Louis with another opportunity to display his firmness by beheading one of the culprits, but the results of the affair were of far greater importance. To weaken the conspirators, Richelieu detached Condé with promises of an unknown dimension. From this time Condé supported the cardinal in all his endeavors and behaved as a loyal subject of the king. In return Richelieu gave him many lucrative assignments including conducting the negations with the provincial estates after the Day of Dupes. Condé, who stood second in line to the throne, was a valuable acquisition for he served as a counterweight to Gaston, who became involved in many of the conspiracies of the reign.[32]

The Chalais conspiracy also led to a shake-up in the government. Chancellor d'Aligre displayed such weakness in dealing with the problem that Louis took the seals from him and gave them to Marillac. Since chancellors held the office for life, d'Aligre continued to enjoy the title, but Marillac performed his duties. Lefèvre, Marillac's biographer, says that the king had seriously considered giving him the seals on several occasions before Richelieu became a minister and leaves the reader to assume that he now did so on his own initiative. Richelieu's memoirs, on the other hand, present Marillac as the cardinal's choice because of his integrity and experience. Both versions are subject to suspicion; after the Day of Dupes, Richelieu and his propagandists wanted to portray Marillac as an unfaithful client, while Marillac's supporters insisted that he had long been a trusted adviser of the king and his mother and owed his position to royal favor alone. Undoubtedly Marillac was an old and valued servant, and it is possible that Louis or his mother initiated his appointment, but there is no reason to believe that Richelieu objected.[33] At this point his influence was so strong that he could probably have persuaded Louis not to name someone unacceptable to him to such an important post. Indeed he secured the appointment of one of his creatures, the marquis d'Effiat, as superintendant of finances in Marillac's place, and by threatening to resign, he won Louis's permission to have a guard to protect him from conspirators, such as Chalais, who sought his life.

These appointments were of greater significance than might ordinarily have been the case because the state of Richelieu's health led him to seek to

32. Tapié, *France*, pp. 153–63; Richelieu, *Mém.* SHF, 6:48–58; Richelieu, *Papiers*, 1:339–43; Marius Topin, *Louis XIII et Richelieu* (Paris, 1877), pp. 130–32; Henri, duc d'Aumale, *Histoire des princes de Condé* (Paris, 1886), 3:180–83.

33. Richelieu, *Mém.* SHF, 6:46, 64–65; Everat, *Michel de Marillac*, pp. 43–51; Bibl. Ste.-Geneviève, ms. 826, fols. 269v–73; BN ms. fr. 5183, fol. 51–51v.

turn over the routine administration of the government to Marillac and others. On June 9 Louis pleaded with him not to resign because of his indispositions and promised to protect him from his enemies.[34] Several weeks later he signed an order granting Richelieu's request to devote all of his energy to foreign affairs and to general matters of great importance. People with petitions were directed to present them to other members of the council or to the secretaries of state.[35]

There was still another by-product of the Chalais conspiracy that played into Richelieu's hands. The duke of Montmorency, like so many other magnates, had been somewhat implicated, and the cardinal used this as an excuse to make him resign his office of admiral of France. France at this time did not have one official charged with the responsibility of the navy or with the port installations and courts, but from 1612 Montmorency had been securing the various admirality jurisdictions and establishing trading companies. By 1626 he controlled most of the western coast of France for naval, commercial, and jurisdictional purposes and was also viceroy of Canada. His once relatively unimportant title of admiral had come to reflect a position that he actually came near to enjoying in the Atlantic. Richelieu shared Montmorency's interest in trade both to increase his own wealth and that of France. He also wanted to build a royal navy to defend French commercial interests and to blockade La Rochelle. Hence Montmorency's resignation opened the way for the suppression of the office of admiral and Richelieu's appointment as grand master of navigation and commerce with the various rights that his dispossessed rival had possessed.[36] Thus the Chalais conspiracy, which was intended to kill the cardinal, actually led to a consolidation of his position in the government and to an important advance toward achieving his commercial and naval goals.

Richelieu was now in a position to act, but to implement the reforms he thought mandatory, he still had to persuade the nobility to accept the necessary economies, the wealthy to pay for the redemption of the royal domain so that the peasant could be spared, the venturesome to engage in overseas trade, and the sovereign courts to register the desired edicts even when their own interests were at stake. To do so Richelieu sponsored the publication of several pamphlets, and early in October he persuaded Louis to convoke the Assembly of Notables.[37]

34. Maximin Deloche, *La maison du Cardinal de Richelieu* (Paris, 1912), p. 365; Topin, *Louis XIII*, pp. 133–34.

35. AN, AB XIX 2927, liasse 4bis; Richelieu, *Papiers*, *1 : 368*.

36. *Boiteux, Richelieu*, pp. 65–97.

37. Jeanne Petit, *L'Assemblée des Notables de 1626–1627* (Paris, 1936), pp. 37–48; Richelieu, *Papiers*, 1 : 517–19.

3. The Assembly of Notables
and the Ordonnance of 1629

The meeting opened on December 2 in Paris. Participating were twelve prelates, ten nobles, twenty-seven members of the sovereign courts, the provost of the merchants of Paris, and a secretary. In addition, Louis's brother, Gaston, now duke of Orléans, was named president of the assembly, and the cardinal of La Valette, the duke of La Force, and Marshal Bassompierre were appointed assistant presidents. Thus the composition of the assembly was quite similar to the one held in Rouen in 1617 in which Gaston had presided and sixteen of the same notables had served. Once more the courts had a numerical predominance, and this fact was to cause trouble in the meeting.[38]

Louis opened the assembly with the one-sentence statement that he had called the meeting to remedy the disorders in his state and that the keeper of the seals would make known his will. Marillac's address had been prepared after considerable conversation with other leading members of the council including Richelieu. In it he stressed the great expenses that the foreign wars and domestic revolts had caused since 1620. The king's ordinary annual revenue was only 16 million livres, but in spite of economies in the royal household and elsewhere, his expenses had been from 36 million to 40 million livres per year. Nevertheless he had not increased the taille or reduced the rentes owed to his subjects or the salaries due his officers. Rather he had turned to expedients and was now over 50 million livres in debt. To redress the situation, the king sought their advice. To economize further, he was considering reducing the size of the army and razing useless fortifications. To increase his income he wanted to redeem the domain and alienated taxes. He also desired the notables' help in restoring commerce "to enrich the people and to repair the honor of France." Here Marillac stressed France's great material resources that made it easy to construct ships to engage in trade and defend the coasts. Other matters that the king wanted the notables to consider concerned the payment and discipline of the troops, the dishonesty of those who handled his revenue, and the frequent conspiracies and rebellions.[39]

Finance, commerce, the military, fiscal dishonesty, and internal disorders, then, were to be the principal matters that the notables were to consider. Marillac had prepared a much larger list, but although Richelieu found these other suggestions good in themselves, he vetoed submitting them to the assembly because it would take too long to discuss them all. Furthermore

38. Petit, *L'Assemblée des Notables*, pp. 50–52, 233–45.

39. Ibid., pp. 56–58; *Mercure François* 12 (1626): 758– (the pagination ceases for twenty pages); Richelieu, *Lettres*, 2:290–92; Paul Ardier, *L'Assemblée des Notables, tenue à Paris ès années 1626 et 1627* (Paris, 1652), pp. 22–36.

they had been considered by the notables in 1617, and the king could act upon their advice. Marillac did say that the king would accept suggestions concerning the church, justice, and other matters that the notables might wish to make, but it must have been evident to those present that the crown intended to regulate the meeting carefully.[40]

Marshal Schomberg spoke in more detail concerning the army, after which Cardinal Richelieu took the floor to stress the need to reduce ordinary expenses by over 3 million livres and to recover the alienated domain and taxes so that revenue would be increased. No greater burden could be placed upon the people. Indeed the king, he insisted, was going to decrease the taille. The first president of the Parlement of Paris responded briefly for the notables, and the meeting closed with Marillac's telling those present that the king would submit his first proposals to them tomorrow and that they were to assemble by order in three different rooms.[41]

Following the precedent set in 1617, the council had prepared a list of propositions that the notables were to consider. The first dealt with military discipline, but before the discussion began, the officers launched a protest against the prescribed deliberative and voting procedures, which they claimed treated them as members of the third estate. Instead they insisted that they sit with the nobles and clergy and vote by head as was done in 1617. Speaking for the king, Marillac offered to issue a declaration stating that they were not the third estate, and he pointed out that only in 1617 had the three orders deliberated together and voted by head. The pride of the officers was undoubtedly hurt by the decision to separate them from the nobles and prelates, but more important was their aspiration to dominate the assembly. They numbered twenty-eight exclusive of the clerk, while the other orders combined counted only twenty-six, including the president and three assistant presidents. Furthermore they suffered less from absenteeism. Hence if voting was by head, they would enjoy a slight majority. If it was by order, they could be outvoted two to one. In the end they won an almost complete victory on the procedural question.[42]

There is no precise evidence of why the crown had decided to abandon the voting procedure used in 1617, but it seems likely that it had been done

40. Richelieu, *Papiers*, 1:568–69.

41. Ardier, *L'Assemblée des Notables*, pp. 36–43. Schomberg's and Richelieu's speeches are published in the *Mercure François* 12 (1626) (no pagination). Richelieu, *Lettres*, 2:297–304. Richelieu, *Papiers*, 1:557–61. Petit, *L'Assemblée des Notables*, pp. 58–60. Richelieu's speech was widely praised. Petit, *L'Assemblée des Notables*, pp. 58–59 and n. 44; and BN ms. fr. 3670, fol. 129.

42. Ardier, *L'Assemblée des Notables*, pp. 70–79, 83–85; Richelieu, *Lettres*, 2:315–34; Richelieu, *Papiers*, 1:581–91; Petit, *L'Assemblée des Notables*, pp. 62–63, 73–75; Lublinskaya, *French Absolutism*, p. 301; Antoine Aubery, *Mémoires pour l'histoire du cardinal duc de Richelieu* (Paris, 1660), 1:291–93. Ardier's tabulation of the attendance is at the beginning of BN ms. Morel de Thoisy, 59.

to weaken the role of the sovereign courts. The initial letters of convocation which were issued on October 7 had included only the first presidents and attorney generals. Then on November 15, the day the original assembly was to meet, Louis had summoned the nobles and prelates and postponed the meeting to the twenty-third. Obviously those he had called would have to have been in or near Paris to arrive in time. Hence Louis may have convoked fewer nobles and prelates than he would have liked. Furthermore four nobles he called did not attend. These facts suggest that the crown's intention on October 7 had been to persuade delegations from the sovereign courts to approve the proposed reforms so there would be less trouble in getting the resulting edicts registered, but that later, remembering the difficulty that had been experienced in the Assembly of Notables in 1617 in getting the members of the sovereign courts to approve anything against their interests, it had been decided to add some nobles and prelates as counterweights. Since enough qualified participants could not be found close at hand to outvote the officers, it had been decided to have the three groups deliberate and ballot by order, thereby making possible a two-to-one vote against the officers in matters that affected their selfish interests.[43]

Once quarrels over voting procedure and precedence had been resolved, the notables set to work. Most of their time was devoted to fiscal matters and the related questions of the army, navy, and economy. The budget obviously had to be balanced, but the peasants could pay no more taxes. To increase revenue the notables readily agreed that the domain should be reclaimed and the income it produced used to compensate those who held it, but they were unwilling to provide a capital sum to speed the process so that it would be free from incumbrancies in six years as Richelieu desired. Instead they chose the slower process that Sully had used of making the domain produce all the needed money for its redemption over a period of about sixteen years. Other possible sources of revenue were to increase the number of those who paid the taille and to improve the efficiency and honesty of the financial officials. The notables rejected a suggestion of one of their number that the taille be declared réelle in all of France so that the privileged would pay on the nonnoble land they held. Among the handful of supporters of this statesmanlike measure was Louis de Marillac, the brother of the keeper of the seals. Also rejected was the government's proposal that a permanent Chamber of Justice be established to uncover and punish dishonest financial officials. The ordinary courts, the notables thought, would suffice. Absent from the government's proposals and the notables' reactions was any

---

43. Ardier, *L'Assemblée des Notables*, pp. 2–4, 10; Lublinskaya, *French Absolutism*, pp. 296–97. Proof that the nobles and prelates were in or near Paris is found in the failure to pay them travel allowances to attend the assembly. Members of the sovereign courts, except those in Paris, were paid. Ardier, *L'Assemblée des Notables*, pp. 229–32.

suggestion that new élections be created or that the role of the provincial estates and towns in taxation be diminished.[44]

The notables were enthusiastic about Richelieu's plan to increase the wealth of France through trade. They approved the formation of trading companies as the British and Dutch had done and more surprisingly, happily accepted the idea of creating a navy of forty-five vessels at a cost of 1,283,160 livres. The project was presented to them not only as a necessity to protect trade but also as an economy, for larger sums had been spent procuring ships from other sources in recent years. Perhaps this explains the acceptance of a new drain on a budget that was already far from balanced. Certainly the notables suggested no additional source of income to meet the expense. French import duties were only 2 percent, much less than other countries. It is not surprising, therefore, that there was strong sentiment for more protection, but at the same time internal trade barriers were questioned. Richelieu wanted to reduce the number of colleges because, being essentially preprofessional institutions, they drew children away from trade and the army, but the notables gave no advice on the matter.[45]

Since some years would elapse before the king could receive increased revenue from the domain and trade, the immediate need was to curtail expenses. The greatest savings could be made by reducing the costs of the army and garrisons, but it was necessary to retain a large enough force to defend the frontiers and maintain order in the interior. Equally important was the need to ensure that the troops were paid, supplied, and disciplined so that they would not add to the misery of the people by preying off the countryside. In the past when there was a scarcity of money, the army simply went without its pay. At the moment it was about two years in arrears. Little wonder there were constant complaints about the behavior of the troops. Richelieu placed the peacetime military requirements at 18,000 to 20,000 foot and 2,000 horse, about twice the size of Henry IV's standing army. The need for the larger force came primarily from the Huguenot threat, although the Thirty Years War was also a factor. The Huguenots had trusted Henry to retain the Edict of Nantes and therefore had remained loyal, but after his death, the leaders of the government inspired little confidence and violated one agreement after another. It is not surprising, therefore, that some Huguenots put more faith in their armies than in the word of their king and fought to retain their privileges. Good faith could have been the greatest of economies.

The government wanted to throw the costs of this force on to the people.

44. Petit, *L'Assemblée des Notables*, pp. 95–121; Lublinskaya, *French Absolutism*, pp. 315–18, 321–22. For Effiat's speech explaining the financial situation to the notables, see *Mercure François* 12 (1626): 790–814. For other fiscal documents see Petit, *L'Assemblée des Notables*, pp. 271–80.

45. Petit, *L'Assemblée des Notables*, pp. 170–94. Phélypeaux reported to Béthune on February 12, 1627, that the nobles had been enthusiastic about building a navy and establishing a trading company. BN ms. fr. 3670, fol. 194.

To make them more willing to accept the burden, it proposed that each regiment bear the name of the province that supported it and each company the name of a town. This deliberate appeal to provincial pride did not silence the concerns of the notables, and in the end a majority of them opted for an infantry of 17,700 men at an annual cost of 4,674,630 livres. Of this sum 1,590,000 livres was to come from the estates in provinces in which there were no élections, 2,058,420 livres from the ordinary revenue of the crown, and 1,028,210 livres from the towns. When the domain was freed, the crown was to assume the entire cost. Two interesting facts emerged in the debate that led to this decision. First, the notables had little faith in Louis's and Richelieu's oath that the money designated to redeem the domain would be used for this purpose and that in six years the people would be freed from the military burden. Second, when the question came up as to whether the town officials could be trusted to administer the tax on their citizens efficiently and honestly, it was decided that an imposition handled by royal officials would be more burdensome. The notables agreed that the 2,000 horse were necessary and that they should be supported by the taillon, which would have to be increased. In case the king lacked funds to meet all his obligations, the highest priority was assigned to the payment of the troops so that they would have no excuse to abuse the people. Other measures were taken to ensure that they would be properly supplied and disciplined.[46]

The high cost of maintaining garrisons in the château-forts had long concerned the provincial estates, and the notables devoted considerable time to this problem. Some of the data they considered are revealing. After a study of the situation in Dauphiné, the Parlement of Grenoble had recommended that sixty-two of the sixty-six fortified places be razed. Of the sixty-two, thirty-six belonged to the king. Twenty-one of these were garrisoned, but the remainder were unguarded.[47] These figures suggest that an indiscriminate destruction of fortified places might weaken royal authority more than that of its opponents, a fact recognized at the time. On December 20, 1626, a noble wrote Richelieu that it was necessary to retain the fortifications in the interior of the kingdom in order to ensure the obedience of the people. He recalled that "in the time of the League ... the only places that remained in the service of the king were those in which there were châteaux that were used by governors and captains ... to keep the people and the Parlements in obedience."[48] Richelieu himself declared, "If all the Huguenots were on the road to their salvation and Frenchmen always did their duty, there would be a great many places to raze in the kingdom, but we cannot now touch them."[49] After all, a royal castle could be used more

46. Petit, *L'Assemblée des Notables*, pp. 123–51; Ardier, *L'Assemblée des Notables*, 125–126, 194–205, 222–23.

47. Petit, *L'Assemblée des Notables*, pp. 151–63; Ardier, *L'Assemblée des Notables*, 140–49.

48. Petit, *L'Assemblée des Notables*, p. 156, n.163.

49. Ibid., p. 156

effectively to overawe a people without artillery than a feudal castle could be used against a royal army with artillery. Therefore the notables in 1626, just like the Estates General, the provincial estates, and the towns on other occasions, showed as much or more enthusiasm for the destruction of forts as the king did. The reasons they most often avowed for their positions were to avoid having to support the garrisons and to remove the risk that poorly guarded forts would become nests of thieves, but one wonders if there were not many instances in Louis's reign when towns and estates sought the destruction of forts to remove the royal presence, and occasionally they frankly said so.[50]

The total cost of the proposed navy, infantry, and cavalry came to 7.5 million livres, a substantial sum, but still 4.5 million less than was being spent during the current year and not half the amount devoted to these purposes in 1625. Additional economies were nevertheless mandatory, and the notables approved reducing the costs of the royal households, cutting pensions to 2 million a year, and suppressing the offices of constable and admiral of France. The last was made possible by Lesdiguières' death and Montmorency's resignation of the admiralship. Substantial savings were accomplished, but more important the suppressions strengthened the crown because the constableship, especially, carried with it important powers within the army. The government requested and the notables approved the idea of reducing the number of sergeants and other useless offices, but they insisted that those who had purchased these positions be fully compensated, a proviso that prevented any significant savings. Their urging that secret payments par comptant be curtailed could have led to significant economies had the crown acceded to their request.[51]

The government was also concerned about the problem of frequent rebellions and general disobedience to royal commands. With no difficulty, the notables were persuaded to confirm old laws against raising troops, manufacturing or owning artillery, fortifying towns and châteaux, levying taxes, and holding assemblies without the king's permission. A suggestion by some notables that the law forbidding any subject to have communications with foreign ambassadors be interpreted to include the papal nuncio did lead to considerable debate. A majority supported this view, but the protests of the papal nuncio led Louis to side with his outnumbered clergy. Richelieu, the first royal minister who fully utilized the press to influence public opinion, was anxious to see that no opponent followed a similar practice. With ease he persuaded the notables to strengthen the penalties against those who published defamatory libels, that is, attacks against the

---

50. Even the Parlement of Grenoble recommended that citadels in that town be razed because they diminished the authority of the municipal government. Ardier, *L'Assemblée des Notables*, p. 141.

51. Mallet, p. 221; Petit, *L'Assemblée des Notables*, pp. 87–94, 207–11; Ardier, *L'Assemblée des Nobles*, pp. 174, 217, 221.

government. However when it came to a royal proposal to establish an itinerant court to judge complaints presented by the people against all persons, including the members of Parlement, the notables were intractable. It would only be permissible, they declared, to have a Grand Jours within the jurisdiction of each Parlement and staffed by offices from that court, a counterproposal which meant, in effect, that the members of a Parlement should be judged only by a court composed largely of their colleagues.[52]

As a noble Richelieu was sympathetic with the problems of that class. Without difficulty he persuaded the assembly that more nobles should be admitted to the royal council and that venality of offices should be suppressed in the royal households and the army so that positions could be awarded on the basis of "birth and merit."[53] This was not enough for the nobles, however, for they took advantage of the meeting to present a special cahier to the king on February 10, 1627, seeking more offices and benefices for the members of their order. Colleges, they urged, should be established in every province for the instruction of the sons of poor gentlemen in the art of war from their twelfth to their seventeenth year. Included in their studies were to be mathematics, history, and foreign languages. They sought to have four experienced captains named in each government to advise the governor on questions concerning the army and the public good and to prevent quarrels between gentlemen. The best qualified nobles should be given seats in the Parlements. They also urged that better care be provided for poor nobles who suffered from their wounds, that a delay of fifteen days between convicting and executing nobles accused of crimes be provided to assure that the judgment was not made in anger or haste, that a prohibition against commoners acquiring noble property without royal permission be enacted, and that permission for nobles to engage in trade without loss of their privileges be granted. The petition was class pleading, yet most of the proposed measures were designed to benefit the poor nobility, not those who served in the assembly, all of whom already had wealth and high office. That many of the proposals were regarded as statesmanlike is suggested by the fact that they eventually were enacted.[54]

The first presidents and attorney generals of the Parlements were not to be outdone by the nobility. They too submitted a special petition, but whereas that of the nobility consisted primarily of pleading by the powerful for their less fortunate brethren, that of the Parlements consisted largely of selfish requests that were often unwise, unjust, and prejudicial to royal authority. They sought the suppression of the special courts containing some Protestants that had been established under the provisions of the Edict of

---

52. Petit, *L'Assemblée des Notables*, pp. 195–206, 211–213; Ardier, *L'Assemblée des Notables*, 129, 157–58, 161–62; Church, *Richelieu*, pp. 111–13. For the account of the quarrel concerning the papal nuncio sent to the French ambassador at Rome, see BN ms. fr. 3670, fols. 185–86v.

53. Petit, *L'Assemblée des Notables*, pp. 89–91, 206–07; Ardier, *L'Assemblée des Notables*, p. 105.

54. Petit, *L'Assemblée des Notables*, pp. 67, 216–20; *Mercure François* 12 (1627): 39–52.

Nantes so that members of that religion would not have to seek justice in all-Catholic courts. They protested against the royal council's assuming jurisdiction over cases in their courts, and the "new practice" of sending intendants of justice into their jurisdictions, undermining their authority. They asked that ordonnances forbidding governors and military officials to interfere in municipal elections and limiting the suffrage be renewed, and then proceeded to assume jurisdiction over them themselves. They modestly asked that they receive only small presents from litigants in their courts in order to reduce the costs of obtaining justice, but then protested the evil practice of telling the accused the names of the witnesses against him. It is with relief that we read an altruistic article charging the élus of Guyenne with oppressing the people and asking that they not be permitted to exceed their authority.[55]

The final ceremony of the Assembly of Notables was held on February 24.[56] Both Richelieu and those who had participated must have been well satisfied with their work. His proposals concerning the army, navy, and commerce had been accepted. The nobles had joined others in agreeing that the costs of the royal households and the pensions should be reduced, although they stood to suffer if these economies were put into effect. It is true that the notables provided no money to speed the redemption of the domain and insisted that if any offices were suppressed, the owners must be fully compensated. The attitude of the members of the sovereign courts had been especially disappointing. They had opposed the establishment of a Chamber of Justice and the itinerant court with authority to judge complaints against them. Indeed it was clear that they were unwilling to accept any interference into their activities or any outside judgment of their behavior. Even the watchful eyes of the intendants of justice were unacceptable to them. Richelieu had apparently recognized that there were limits as to how much cooperation he could expect from the sovereign courts, for he never mentioned the paulette and limited his attack on venality of office to the royal households and the military, areas that in no way affected them. If the time came to attack venality, he could always cite the recommendation of the Estates General of 1614 as justification.

In another area Richelieu had also been silent. He never hinted that new élections should be established anywhere in France, and he proposed no administrative changes that would weaken the provincial estates. We know that in his reform proposals of 1625 he had opposed venality and can therefore assume that his silence in 1626 on this score should be attributed to his desire to win the support of the sovereign courts. He had taken no position on the élections, on the other hand, in 1625 or so far as is known at any earlier time in his career. His silence therefore can be explained only by

55. Petit, *L'Assemblée des Notables*, pp. 220–23, 256–70.
56. Ibid., pp. 248–55.

the assumption that he did not believe that they were necessary. He still sought to rule through persuasion rather than bureaucratic absolutism.

If Richelieu was reasonably content with the work of the assembly, the notables themselves must have departed even more satisfied. Not only had such subjects as the abolition of the paulette and the creation of new élections gone unmentioned, but there were also positive reasons to be pleased. Usually deputies to assemblies returned to their homes with little more than vague verbal promises that an ordonnance based on their work would be forthcoming, but the notables of 1626–27 were more fortunate. On February 16, just eight days before their final meeting, Louis issued a declaration in which he swore that he would do all that was in his power to reform his kingdom. He spoke of the need to reunite all of his subjects in the Catholic church, but promised to use "gentleness, love, patience, and good examples" as his means. Protestants were to retain all their liberties until "it pleases God to illuminate their hearts and bring them back into the bosom of his church." None of them should lend an ear to those who preached rebellion. Nobles were to have more positions in the royal households, the army, and the navy, and their children were to be given free instruction. Justice was to flourish, and trade was to be expanded. Upon "the faith and word of a king" Louis swore to reduce taxes by 3 million livres by 1632 in order to lighten the load on the people. Already he had reduced their burden for the current year by 600,000 livres. Furthermore he was going to redeem his alienated domain, tailles, and gabelles to compensate for the loss in revenue.[57]

Louis's blueprint for the future was striking enough, but even more startling was the effort to publicize his plans. The Parlements, Chamber of Accounts, and Court of Aids throughout the kingdom were directed to register the declaration and to have it published in all the subordinate seats in their respective jurisdictions. It was printed in the *Mercure François* and circulated as a pamphlet. Richelieu, the master of the art of propaganda, was undoubtedly the motivating force behind these moves designed to win popular support for his government and its program. There was a danger, of course, that he could not fulfill his promises, but he must have been reasonably confident that he could, or he would not have publicized his ambitious plans so broadly. Success, of course, depended on maintaining foreign and domestic peace. The situation looked promising in Germany, a high government official informed the ambassador at Rome in February 26. In his letter he mentioned the declaration and a formal edict of reform that was to follow. He also spoke of the collaboration between Rohan and La Rochelle that caused the king to remain well armed although he knew that it might offend the Protestants. Louis was going to assure their deputies that

---

57. *Mercure François* 12 (1627): 34–39. The declaration was incorporated into Ardier's minutes of the assembly and later published. See Ardier, *L'Assemblée des Notables*, pp. 225–28.

they had nothing to fear, and perhaps he would have succeeded to the extent of preventing another rebellion had it not been for the English intervention.[58]

Richelieu's hope for six years of peace during the winter of 1626–27 was not unrealistic provided the leaders of other nations acted sensibly, and he himself restrained France's ambitions. Such requirements, however, were too much to impose on the statesmen of that day. Far from cementing an alliance with England, the marriage of Louis's sister to Charles I had led to added difficulties because of the treatment of Catholics there and eventually the dismissal of the young queen's French entourage. More important were the problems of freedom of navigation and Charles's favorite, the duke of Buckingham's belief that he had been insulted by the French king. In July 1627 Buckingham landed with an army on an island near La Rochelle with the avowed purpose of defending that city from the threat of the crown. The Huguenots had reason enough to be angry at the manner in which the last peace had been implemented. Fort Louis had never been destroyed as Louis had promised, and the royalists had strengthened their positions around La Rochelle. In direct violation of the treaty, the government had refused to permit their political assembly to meet to elect new deputies to court to replace one who had died and another who had retired. In addition, local Catholic officials often violated the agreement without royal sanction. In spite of these legitimate complaints, Buckingham had to prod the citizens of La Rochelle for some time before they agreed to join forces with him. Rohan once more raised an army in Languedoc, but the bulk of the Huguenot nobility and burghers were most reluctant to join his cause.[59]

Richelieu reacted quickly to the English invasion and the new revolt. The reform program was slowed, although Marillac and others continued to work on a great ordonnance when they could find the time. An army led by Louis himself lay siege to La Rochelle, and another under Condé attempted to reduce the rebels in Languedoc. The defenders of La Rochelle fought with great determination until October 29, 1628, when they were forced to capitulate. By then all hope of new supplies reaching them from the bungling English had vanished, and nearly two-thirds of their number had perished, for the most part from starvation. Those who survived were granted their lives, religion, and property, but the town lost its fortifications and privileges. No longer would its proud burghers be able to flaunt the authority of the king. Instead they were compelled to witness the installation of a Catholic bishop in their midst.[60]

Louis now had to decide in what direction he should direct his efforts: to Germany where the emperor had won several notable victories and ap-

58. Phélypeaux to Béthune, BN ms. fr. 3670, fol. 197.

59. Clarke, *Huguenot Warrior*, pp. 136–43, 156–61; Tapié, *France and the Age of Louis XIII*, pp. 174–82.

60. Clarke, *Huguenot Warrior*, pp. 143–55; Tapié, *France and the Age of Louis XIII*, pp. 182–90.

peared firmly established on the Baltic Sea, to Italy where the duke of Nevers's inheritance of Mantua was being challenged by the Habsburgs, to Languedoc where the outnumbered Huguenots were still defying royal authority, or to long-overdue domestic reform. On January 13, 1629, Richelieu addressed himself to those problems in more than his usual grandiose fashion. "Now that La Rochelle is taken," he wrote, "if the king wants to make himself the most powerful monarch and the most esteemed prince in the world, he ought ... to examine carefully and secretly with his faithful creatures" what policies he should pursue.[61] On the domestic scene, it was first necessary to suppress the Huguenot rebellion. Interior fortifications must be raised and those on the frontier strengthened. The paulette should not be renewed when it expired in a year, and the courts "who through their pretended sovereignty daily oppose the good of the kingdom must be humbled and reduced."[62] The king must make both the great and small obedient to his will. He must appoint wise and able people to the bishoprics, redeem the domain, and increase his revenue by one-half but at the same time reduce the burden on the people. Thus the domestic program that Richelieu had outlined several times before remained intact. To his presentation to the notables he had added the suppression of the paulette and the humbling of the sovereign courts, but the former, at least, had long been on his mind. Again conspicuously absent was any mention of establishing élections or weakening the provincial estates, although Marillac was already moving in that direction.

Turning to foreign affairs Richelieu urged that France establish bridge-heads into Germany, Switzerland, and Italy in order to be able to check the growth of Spanish power. Navarre and Franche-Comté should be conquered "when we have nothing else to do," but for the time being it would be imprudent to act because it would lead to open war with Spain.[63] France was not ready for such a conflict. Its objectives had to be more limited. The month before, he had indicated that they should consist of Louis's raising the siege of Casal and bringing peace to Italy by the following May, after which he should return to Languedoc and suppress the Huguenot revolt by July. Amazingly this proposal was actually accomplished ahead of schedule. By mid-March the French had relieved Casal, and in April a defensive alliance with Venice, the pope, and Savoy was made to retain Nevers in his Mantuan inheritance. Then, on June 27, the Huguenot rebellion was terminated with the peace of Alès.[64] By its terms the Huguenots retained their religious and civil liberties, but all their fortifications and cannon were destroyed. Their political assemblies were to cease, and their proud towns were humbled. "The roots of heresy, rebellion, disorder, and civil war, which have exhaust-

61. Richelieu, *Lettres*, 3:179–80.
62. Ibid., p. 181.
63. Ibid., p. 182.
64. Ibid., pp. 150–52; Richelieu, *Mém.* SHF, 8:227–31, 274–78.

ed France for so long, are dried up," Richelieu wrote Louis. "Now all your subjects will compete with each other in rendering the obedience which is due Your Majesty."[65] A giant step toward royal absolutism had been taken. The state within a state had come to an end.

While Richelieu was devoting most of his time to foreign policy and the Huguenots, Marillac was attempting to carry on the routine administration and to prepare a great reforming ordonnance based largely on the work of the Estates General of 1614 and the Assemblies of Notables of 1617, and 1626–27. As preliminary steps toward correcting abuses, a Grand Jours was established at Poitiers in 1627, and an edict to improve the administration of justice was issued that was also financially rewarding because it involved the creation of a number of new offices. Indeed creating new offices to sell was the most common form of legislative enactment between the closing of the Assembly of Notables and January 1629. Frequent conflicts with the Parlement of Paris resulted. On June 28, 1627, Louis had to hold a lit de justice to get some offending edicts registered, and on November 27 he wrote a reproachful letter to Molé, his attorney general in Parlement, concerning the conduct of his colleagues.[66]

Even while he was with the army besieging La Rochelle, Marillac labored on his ordonnance. Richelieu prepared the articles on the navy and others made contributions in special areas, but Marillac neither hesitated to correct the cardinal's contributions nor failed to consult other members of the council about his own work. The articles on justice were especially carefully studied, and they were sent to two advocates of the Parlement of Paris to secure their advice.[67] What emerged was the longest and one of the most comprehensive ordonnances that had been issued by a French king up to that time. To two leading modern authorities, it was "the first attempt to codify the laws concerning the public order in France before Colbert."[68]

Much of the ordonnance was a faithful summary of those suggestions of the Estates General of 1614 and the two Assemblies of Notables that were acceptable to the crown. Included were numerous articles concerning the reformation of the clergy, the welfare of the sick and the poor, the mainten-

65. Clarke, *Huguenot Warrior*, p. 179.

66. *Mercure François* 13 (1627): 793; Isambert, 16:204–14. For edicts creating offices or increasing their rewards between March 1627 and December 1628, see *Actes Royaux*, 2: nos. 7182, 7191, 7205, 7222, 7223, 7225, 7231, 7239, 7250, 7253, 7257, 7268, 7269, 7278, 7279, 7288, 7289, 7291, 7305, 7315, 7317, 7324–26, 7332, 7334, 7340, 7354, 7357. 7359, 7376, 7381, 7383, 7389, 7398, 7399, 7430, 7431. Louis's letter of November 27 and much of Marillac's correspondence with Parlement has been published in *Mémoires de Mathieu Molé*, ed. Aimé Champollion-Figeac (Paris, 1855), 1:452–542 passim. See also AAE, mss. 789–91, and BN ms. Dupuy 573, fols. 86, 88 for additional Marillac correspondence largely concerning difficulties with Parlement in 1628.

67. Bibl. Ste.-Geneviève, ms. 826 fols. 247–54.

68. Hanotaux (and the Duke of La Force), *Histoire*, 4:115. The ordonnance has been published in Isambert, 15:223–342, and elsewhere.

ance of internal order and the discipline of troops, the administration of justice and finance, and the development of a navy and commerce. Repeated were old laws against printing and selling books (articles 52 and 179), levying taxes (article 409), communicating with foreign princes and their ambassadors, raising troops, storing arms, owning cannon or large quantities of powder, fortifying towns and châteaux, and convoking assemblies without the king's permission (articles 170–77). Useless fortifications in the interior were to be demolished (article 373), and the king announced that henceforth he would appoint the officers of his household and his army despite the traditional practice of such persons as the grand masters of his household and the colonel of the infantry naming their subordinates (article 193). This last measure and one directing that neither the servants nor the relatives of the generals and provincial governor be sent to them as intendants (article 81) dealt blows at the patron-client relationship and asserted royal authority in essential areas. Another article (80) required royal officials to obtain permission before entering the service of a member of the royal family or any other person. If some articles were aimed at limiting the capacity of the nobility to revolt, many others were designed to increase their role in the government and to improve their economic position. Venality of office in the royal households and the military was again forbidden (article 190), and positions in the church, army, Parlements, and royal council were reserved for them (articles 199–202). These measures may have been an outgrowth of the ideas Richelieu expressed in 1625 and in the Assembly of Notables of 1626–27. (See pp. 496–98.) More clearly he was responsible for the provision that nobles could engage in sea trade without derogation (article 452).

The dreams of lessening the fiscal burden were not forgotten. Garrisons and pensions were to be reduced (articles 373–74). Gifts par comptant were forbidden, and those in excess of 3,000 livres were to be registered by the Chamber of Accounts (article 379). The crown's promise to the notables that the domain would be soon redeemed was temporarily abandoned, but the goal of reducing the taille by 3 million livres was reiterated and arrears in taxes prior to 1624 were canceled (articles 382 and 410).

The royal officials fared less well than the nobility or the people did. They won few concessions, and many articles were designed to correct their abuses. Indeed in Marillac's and perhaps Richelieu's opinion, they were becoming the principal obstacles to good government. Marillac did not create an itinerant court that would hear and judge abuses that members of the sovereign courts and other persons were accused of committing in deference to both of the Assemblies of Notables' rejection of this proposal, but he announced the government's intention to hold Grand Jours in the individual provinces (article 59). Furthermore a permanent Chamber of Justice was to be established to punish officials guilty of financial malpractices and to recover lost revenue (article 411). Most serious of all, Parlement was given only two months in which to make remonstrances against provisions in royal edicts, after which they were to be registered without more ado (article 53).

Marillac had spent much of his career as a maître des requêtes, and he had achieved a high opinion of the value of such officials. As a result, he included a long article in the ordonnance greatly extending their powers and authority. They were to be sent to the provinces annually to hear the complaints of the people against royal officials and other persons and to report their findings to the chancellor or keeper of the seals. They were to inform the government of excessive salaries and presents received by officials, to observe the levying and collection of taxes, and to correct abuses (article 58). In the instructions Marillac actually gave to the maître des requêtes, he went into more detail. They were to work quietly and to remain on good terms with the members of the sovereign courts in order to obtain useful information from them. But they were also to report any abuses the members of the sovereign courts and the financial officials committed. They were also to inform the crown concerning the behavior of the clergy and the way governors comported themselves. Information on local leaders, factions, and those most loyal to the king was to be sought.[69]

In addition to establishing the means to discover and punish the abuses of the officials, Marillac set about to enforce old, neglected regulations. Contrary to the law forbidding relatives to serve in the same court, some families had so many members in this or that one that no one dared to thwart them. Such appointments were not to be approved in the future, and where there were several members of a family in a court, those in excess were to be transferred (articles 55–57).

One of the most striking features of the ordonnance was the number of articles devoted to ensuring that the military, the fiscal bureaucracy, and the courts performed their duties without abusing the people. On the other hand, the ordonnance contained very little concerning the duly constituted, self-governing bodies. One article (36) directed that the assembly of the clergy meet only every fifth year and that no more than two deputies be elected from each province. Another (412) provided that municipal elections be held in the accustomed manner but then directed that municipal administration and assemblies be conducted as much as possible like those of Paris, Lyons, and Limoges. As the crown had limited the number of officials in these towns and in some instances their suffrage, their establishment as examples might be considered as a threat to municipal independence, but the article was so vague and even contradictory that it was of little importance.

The failure to lash out at the provincial estates and towns should not be construed as evidence that Marillac favored a degree of self-government. He

69. BN ms. C. C. Colbert, 102, fols. 487–88.

had carefully read the cahiers that the deputies of the Estates General of 1614 presented to the king, but he did not incorporate the suggestion made by the nobility that they be assembled in each province every third year to elect a syndic, or of the third estate that the Estates General be held every tenth year and that provincial estates, towns, and parishes be permitted to levy large sums for their own use without having to seek royal permission. More surprising, perhaps, the suggestion Richelieu made in 1625 that archbishops hold provincial councils every third year was ignored, although most of the cardinal's ideas in this memorandum were incorporated. Perhaps the cardinal had changed his mind. Perhaps he had forgotten the whole affair, and Marillac had not seen fit to raise the issue. Marillac had decided to deal with the existing provincial estates in another fashion, and he was determined that there should be no more. Also absent from the ordonnance was any mention of the paulette. Here we know that Richelieu had decided to wait for the end of the year when the current contract expired. (See p. 511.)

Richelieu anticipated trouble with Parlement concerning the ordonnance. To speed registration it was decided that the king would hold a lit de justice just before his departure for Italy. It took place on January 15, 1629, with the usual pomp reserved for such occasions. As keeper of the seals it fell to Marillac to be the royal spokesman.[70] He obviously devoted considerable time to doing research for his speech, and it led to a book-length study concerning the authority of the king and the role of Parlement, which he later presented to Louis.[71] He began by describing the great victory Louis had just won at La Rochelle, as if to say that the king had the military strength as well as the theoretical power that he was about to claim for him. Not until the fourteenth century when Parlement separated from the council and became sedentary, Marillac insisted, had the kings adopted the practice of having that company register their ordonnances so that they would be better observed. Since its members were important, experienced men, the king permitted them to make remonstrances when they found articles that needed to be more clearly expressed or modified. However, if a king persevered in his original opinion, Parlement must proceed with the registration. It had no authority of its own, and kings could use other means to publish their decrees as they had done long ago. "The authority of the kings of France," therefore, "is independent of all other power and they render account only to God for the temporal administration of their state."[72] If officers can judge the actions of the king, "the king is no longer king. He is

70. Everat, *Michel de Marillac*, pp. 90–93; *Mémoires de Molé*, 2 : 1–4; *Recueil de pièces originales et authentiques, concernant la tenue des États généraux*, ed. Lalourcé and Duval (Paris, 1789), 8–451–55.

71. Marillac's treatise on Parlement is at BN ms. fr. 7549. Joseph A. Aubenas, *Histoire du Parlement de Paris* (Paris, 1847), pp. 46–53, summarizes Marillac's work. For Marillac's speech, see *Mercure François* 15 (1629): 7–28.

72. *Mercure François* 15 (1629): 17.

under the tutelage of his officers and sovereignty is depended on them.... It is true, therefore, that the king alone is the judge of the justice of his actions. He is accountable for them to God alone."[73]

When Marillac had finished, President Le Jay responded for Parlement. He had been involved with Condé and other magnates in their revolts during the early part of Louis's reign, but now he declared in the same vein as Marillac that the officers of Parlement had no power except what the king gave them. Nevertheless, after considerable flattery, he asked that Parlement be permitted to examine and discuss the ordonnance in the accustomed manner rather than register it immediately. After consulting with Louis and the members of the council, Marillac declared that the king commanded that the ordonnance be registered, published, and sent to the subordinate jurisdictions, but he added something to the effect that Parlement could make remonstrances on the various articles.[74]

Our knowledge of this episode is derived from the none too clear and somewhat suspect register of Parlement. Marillac's interpretation of the event was that the ordonnance had been registered and that Parlement could do no more than make remonstrances concerning individual articles while they were being enforced. The members of Parlement did not deny that the ordonnance was registered, but whether as a result of a sincere misunderstanding or because they had decided to take advantage of the king's departure for Italy, they refused to publish the ordonnance or send it to the provinces until they had deliberated on each article and made remonstrances. In short, they decided to proceed just as though Louis had not held the lit de justice. There were some articles they did not like, but what infuriated them was the fact that the king had ordered that the ordonnance be registered before they had had an opportunity to make remonstrances. Even worse, Marillac had lectured them on the absolute power of the king and had denied them any intrinsic authority. In the political sphere, to Marillac, their proud court was little more than one of several possible instruments that kings had used to publish their decrees. On him they placed the blame for the contents of the ordonnance and the way it was presented to them. From that time Parlement never lost an opportunity to ridicule or malign Marillac and his ordonnance, which they derisively called the Code Michau, a play on his first name.

On the morning of January 18, Marillac asked the clerk of Parlement to supply him with a signed copy of the ordonnance bearing the registration and verification. The court responded by charging that Marillac had broken his promise to give them time to consider the ordonnance. A week later Marie de Medici, who had been left in charge of the government, expressed surprise that Parlement had not submitted the verified ordonnance. Le Jay,

73. Ibid., p. 20.
74. *Recueil des Etats-généraux*, 8:456–60.

who led a delegation to her, was far less submissive than when he had been in the presence of the king. Parlement, he insisted "was immortal ... it would cease to exist only with the monarchy."[75] The king, he claimed, had given them permission to make remonstrances in the accustomed manner even if it took them from four to six months. Until they had done so, the ordonnance should not be printed or sent to the provinces. Marie declared that the king would be discontent, but the deadlock continued. On February 8 Le Jay made an even bolder defense of Parlement's conduct, although he always professed to recognize the authority of the king. Pointedly he declared, "We have judged all sorts of persons of every condition: princes, dukes, peers, officers of the crown, constables and chancellors; our power is great.... The disorders and confusion in this affair are caused by the advice that has been given the king, because, full of justice as he is, he does not wish to overturn the fundamental laws of the kingdom."[76]

Marillac was livid. Angrily he reported the course of events to Richelieu and others. Parlement should be compelled to accept the ordonnance, he urged. It should be suppressed not just for the present but also for the future. Parlement, an English agent reported, was equally enraged at him.[77] Strangely enough neither Richelieu nor the king appears to have been overly concerned at their keeper of the seals' plight. Italy was uppermost in their minds, and Marie herself allowed Parlement four months to consider the ordonnance. With provocative slowness, its members proceeded with the verification. By March 16, two months after the lit de justice, they had reached the fourth article of an ordonnance that had 461. By May 12, near the end of the generous allotment of time granted by the Queen Mother, they were debating the tenth. Only when the king returned to Paris in August and began to apply direct pressure did they act more rapidity. The English ambassador reported near the middle of September that Louis refused to receive a delegation from Parlement when he learned that it brought an amended version of the ordonnance, but in the end he relented and listened to them. Only then, on September 7, was the Code Michau registered and published.[78] Perhaps as frustrated as he was angry, Marillac informed the attorney general of the Parlement of Dijon that the members of the courts should devote more time to their work, but as a group they escaped serious punishment for their procrastination.[79] Not so their leader.

75. Ibid., p. 464. The relevant registers of Parlement, January 19–December 7, 1629, are published on pp. 460–76.

76. Roland Mousnier, *La venalité des offices sous Henri IV et Louis XIII*, 2d ed. (Paris, 1971), p. 651. The version in the register is not as strong. *Recueil des Etats généraux*, 8:469–70.

77. AAE, ms. 249, fols. 155v–56; ms. 793, fols. 45–79 passim. PRO, S.P. 78/84, fols. 25–26.

78. *Recueil des Etats généraux*, 8:470–76; PRO, S.P. 78/84, fol. 291; Everat, *Michel de Marillac*, pp. 108–15; BN ms. fr. 3829, fol. 114–14v.

79. BN ms. Dupuy 573, fol. 89.

In November the English ambassador reported that Marillac had succeeded in having Champigny, a long-time colleague who had served with him as co-superintendant of finances, appointed first president of the Parlement of Paris instead of Le Jay who had been performing the duties of that office during the period that it was vacant. Marillac would have probably liked to have had Le Jay's opposition to his ordonnance cited as the reason that he was passed over, but according to our informant Louis was persuaded because Le Jay had adhered "to the party of the princes" during the rebellion a decade or more before.[80]

By the close of 1629 Richelieu and Marillac were growing apart. They had shared an interest in reform and a desire to reduce the tax burden on the poor people, but Richelieu was increasingly ready to sacrifice these goals to his desire to humble the Habsburgs. In a meeting of the council on December 26, 1628, Marillac had joined those who opposed the decision to relieve Casal, and when Richelieu returned to court in September 1629, he blamed Marillac for the queen mother's coldness toward him.[81] But there was more than a growing difference in priorities between the two men; there was a difference in method as well.

80. PRO, S.P. 78/85 fol. 87. Arnauld d'Andilly reported that Richelieu recommended that Le Jay be appointed first president. If so, Marillac won a signal victory. *Journal inédit de Arnauld d'Andilly, 1628–1629*, ed. E. and J. Halphen (Paris, 1907), pp. 134–35.
    81. Everat, *Michel de Marillac*, pp. 97–105.

15

MARILLAC
AND THE PROVINCIAL ESTATES

THE CROWN'S PROPOSALS TO THE ASSEMBLY OF NOTABLES CALLED FOR ECONOMIES and a reduction of the taille in the overtaxed provinces with élections on the one hand and an increase in the taillon and in the levies on the relatively undertaxed towns and provinces with estates on the other. As is so often the case, the best laid plans went astray. Pensions and payments par comptant were cut, except for 1629 when the latter jumped to 24.4 million livres, but reductions in the royal households and other nonmilitary areas were not achieved. More serious, the siege of La Rochelle, the assault on the Huguenots in Languedoc, and the intervention in Italy caused military expenses to soar. In 1628 the total outlay by the government was about 3.3 million livres more than it was in 1627, and expenses tended to increase rather than decrease thereafter.[1]

In spite of this situation, the government began to implement its goal of reducing the taille by 3 million livres. In 1627 this tax was cut 600,000 livres and in 1628, 400,000 more, but in 1629 it was apparently raised. To meet the deficit the taillon was more than doubled, offices were created to ensure a large revenue from the parties casuelles, the revenue from the tax farms and the salt tax was increased, a tax on tobacco was introduced, and, after considerable haggling, the clergy was persuaded to make a special gift of 3 million livres. Nevertheless it proved necessary to constitute new rentes, which meant assigning tax and domainal revenue to pay the interest on them. As a result, instead of redeeming the domain within six years as Richelieu had hoped, the crown received less revenue from this source in 1628 than in the year before. Under these circumstances it is necessary to inquire how the provincial estates fared in a government led by two such strong men as Richelieu and Marillac.[2]

---

1. Mallet, pp. 198–99, 202–03, 208–09, 221–22.

2. J.-J. Clamageran, *Histoire de l'impôt en France* (Paris, 1868), 2:476–82; Georges d'Avenel, *Richelieu et la monarchie absolue*, 2d ed. (Paris, 1895), 2:446; Pierre Blet, *Le clergé de France et la monarchie* (Rome, 1959), 1:380–98.

1. The Provincial Estates in the Pays d'Elections

The estates were in a vulnerable position in the provinces with élections because the crown was in a position to order that the desired taxes be levied whether the estates met or not. The most important of these provinces was Normandy where over a fifth of the royal income from the pays d'élection was derived.

The three estates of Normandy met for the first time in the Richelieu regime in September 1624. They voted 1,656,062 livres, 350,000 more than they had granted the year before, but apparently less than the king had requested. The commissioners followed the usual procedure of ordering that the entire amount be levied pending an appeal by the estates to the king. The three estates devoted most of their energy to trying to obtain the suppression of recently created offices, and here they won the support of the commissioners, but the king refused to accept their lower financial offer or to abandon the revenue from the sale of the offices because of his need for money.[3]

The three estates were not convoked in 1625 to vote taxes for 1626, but the money was collected anyway.[4] The deputies who met in December 1626 offered no protest about the failure of the crown to obtain consent the year before. Instead they followed their usual practice of trying to get taxes and the bureaucracy reduced. It was the first meeting held after Marillac became keeper of the seals, and it took place while the Assembly of Notables was in session. The estates won a promise from the government that when the current occupants of the excess offices in the élections died, they would not be replaced. This attack on hereditary offices was in keeping with the goals of the government, which doubtless accounts for the success of the estates.[5]

Another goal of the crown was to reduce taxes, and a cut of 600,000 livres for the provinces with élections was instituted. The Normans' share ought to have been over 100,000 livres, but this was not enough to satisfy them. In the opening lines of the article on the taille they declared: "Sire, we recognize the necessity of your affairs and wish that those who managed your finances the past years had left us something to offer you."[6] Instead of voting nothing, however, they granted 976,061 livres, far less than the usual sum and evidently less than the king had requested because the council refused to accept the grant and ordered that the full amount be levied. In their session the deputies also complained about the heavy costs of paying the large

3. *Cahiers des Etats de Normandie sous les règnes de Louis XIII et de Louis XIV*, ed. Charles de Robillard de Beaurepaire (Rouen, 1877), 2 : 69, 76–80, 86, 89–90, 282–83, 291–92.

4. Ibid., pp. 294–95. 305. There is a reference to the cahier of the estates of 1625 (ibid., p. 118), but since Robillard de Beaurepaire could find no documents concerning a meeting, it was probably a clerical error.

5. Ibid., pp. 103–04.

6. Ibid., p. 116.

number of commissioners the king appointed. They were especially annoyed because the money came from the funds set aside to meet their own expenses. They did not insert an article in their cahier on the subject, but their syndic brought the matter to the attention of the king's council.[7]

During the spring and summer of 1627, the king's council ordered that the taillon be increased by 60,000 livres in accordance with the plan discussed in the Assembly of Notables and that the tax on salt be raised. Both actions were taken without the consent of the estates and over the protests of their syndic. Little wonder that when it became time for the estates to meet in December, some felt the need to find additional strength. In recent years the estates had voted their governor, the duke of Longueville, 18,000 livres, but the council had frequently overruled his recommendations and those of the other comissioners. Hence the archbishop of Rouen was invited to attend the bailiwick electoral assembly and was chosen as deputy to the provincial estates, where he was elected to preside.[8] A comforting presence was needed because the spokeman for the crown declared that "the mines and the Peru of our kings are the hearts and pocketbooks of their subjects. It is from that they take the money to pay their troops; it is from there that they draw succor in their urgent necessities."[9] The deputies expressed appreciation for the king's decision to reduce the taille on the kingdom by a total of one million livres in 1627–28, but they were well aware that their position was not improved because of the increase in the taillon and the salt tax. They voted 1,286,061 livres to be collected as the taille but asked that they be freed from other taxes. Once more the council ordered that all the taxes the king had sought be levied.[10]

In 1628, again, there were no estates, but taxes were collected as usual in the year that followed.[11] When the deputies once more assembled in December 1629, they did not mention the failure to summon them the preceding year to consent to taxes. Instead they centered their complaints around the perpetual problems of high taxes and the excessive number of offices. They did express approval of the provision in the Code Michau providing that two nobles of the sword serve in Parlement and asked that similar appointments be made in the other sovereign courts. They also requested that Grand Jours be held in Normandy. To the king they offered 1,310,721 livres but asked that no further taxes be required of them. To Longueville went his usual 18,000 livres plus 10,968 for his guards, and to his lieutenant who had made a special trip from Paris to attend the estates, 6,000.[12]

7. Ibid., pp. 313; 319; BN ms. fr. 18,204, fols. 111–12.
8. *Cahiers*, 2 : 326, 328, 351–53.
9. Ibid., p. 350.
10. Ibid., pp. 125, 128, 137–38.
11. Ibid., pp. 361–64.
12. Ibid., pp. 147–56, 167–68, 371–72, 387.

It is difficult to explain why the estates were not convoked in two of the first six years of Richelieu's administration. Perhaps the chronic unrest in Rouen or the prevalence of the plague led to the failure, or perhaps it was because their governor could not attend.[13] The apparent lack of concern on the part of the estates suggests that there was some simple explanation that satisfied almost everyone.

The good towns of Basse-Auvergne were not intimidated by Richelieu and Marillac. From the beginning of 1625 through 1630, the nineteen towns assembled at least once and often twice a year. The six nearest towns to Clermont met even more frequently, most often to deal with emergency situations caused by the need to provide for passing troops. In 1626, the most active year, they were convoked about eight times. The province suffered from oppressive taxes, and in at least two years the deputies asked their governor to forgo his usual gratification. They won a victory when the king's council ruled that no tax was to be levied to satisfy the claims of any individual against the third estate without consulting the deputies of the good towns.[14] An event unusual for that day also took place. In April 1630 Louis XIII issued a decree uniting the two adjacent towns of Clermont and Montferrand to form Clermont-Ferrand. As in more recent times, many problems had to be overcome before the merger could be successful, not the least of which was the levying of 200,000 livres on the entire province to build a new town hall and other buildings.[15]

The towns of Haute-Auvergne were less active than their neighbors to the north. There was joint and individual action by the four towns and provostships against the salt tax in 1625, and in the early winter of 1626 they protested against being called upon to contribute toward the funds needed to raze a château in Basse-Auvergne. In 1629 eight new élections were created in the two Auvergnes, to the consternation of the inhabitants. The four good towns and provostships assembled in January and May 1630 to deal with this and other matters. In March of that same year the consuls of St. Flour won from the king's council recognition of their right to hold assemblies and to impose 4,000 livres annually with the consent of the province to support local affairs.[16] During these years the généralité of Riom in which the two Auvergnes were located contributed an average of less than 350,000 livres annually to the royal treasury, well under what it had given

13. Boris Porchnev, *Les soulèvements populaires en France de 1623 à 1648* (Paris, 1963), pp. 133–34.

14. AD, Puy-de-Dôme, 4F 146; AN, E 97[b], fols. 378–78v, 380–80v, E 102, fol. 258, E 103[a], fol. 78–78v, E 105[b], fols. 211–16v; BN ms. fr. 18,204, fols. 29–30. *IAC Clermont-Ferrand, Fonds de Montferrand,* ed. Alexandre-V.-Emmanuel Teilhard de Chardin (Clermont-Ferrand, 1902), 2:74–75, 207–21 passim.

15. *IAC, Clermont-Ferrand,* 2:10–14.

16. AC, St. Flour, ch. 5, art. 6, no. 70; *IAC, Aurillac,* ed. Gabriel Esquer (Aurillac, 1906), 1: BB 14; AN, E 102, fols. 283, 333, 461–61v; *Compilation chronologique contenant un recueil en abrégé des ordonnances, édits ... des rois de France ...,* ed. Guillaume Blanchard (Paris, 1715), 2: cols. 1564–65.

earlier in the reign. Most of this reduction must be attributed to the fact that the royal financial officials recognized that the inhabitants contributed heavily to support troops moving through the area and could be expected to do no more, but the possible role of the estates should not be dismissed.[17]

"The assembly of the said provinces of Lyonnais, Forez, and Beaujolais," as it was called by the king's council in December 1624, continued to meet when the occasion required. In September and in November of that year it met to vote to impose 100,000 livres on the inhabitants of the government who paid the taille. The money was required to reimburse those who had provided support for troops passing through the region, and a deputy was dispatched to the council to secure permission to impose the levy.[18]

The estates of Forez continued to function during these years. Forty-three nobles met in March 1628 at Montbrison where they elected a syndic and four councillors to serve for three years, or longer if they did not meet again before the prescribed term expired. The nobles also complained about the large towns' practice of shoving taxes they were supposed to pay on to the peasantry.[19] The third estate was galvanized into action by the king's decision to partition the élection of Forez that was seated in Montbrison. Sixty-three parishes were assigned to a newly created élection at Thiers in Auvergne and, more serious, an entirely new élection was carved out of Forez and seated at Roanne. Since there were already élus in Forez, the establishment of new jurisdictions did not mean a shift from tax apportionment and collection by the estates to the performance of these duties by royal officials as had been the case in Guyenne. There could be no objection on this score. What infuriated the people of Forez was that they were expected to pay 140,900 livres to the élus at Montbrison as compensation for the loss of such a large part of their jurisdiction. The third estate met in May and twice in December 1630 in an unsuccessful effort to get the new jurisdiction suppressed, or at least the size of the compensation reduced. Also considered was the tax on wine, the cost of providing for troops, and the douane of Valence.[20]

Little is known concerning Beaujolais and the plat pays of Lyonnais. The communities of the former assembled in September 1624, and there are references to the syndic of Lyonnais and the "notables" at Beaujolais in 1630, leaving no doubt that the plat pays of Lyonnais retained its corporate status and making it probable that Villefranche continued to act for Beaujolais.[21]

17. Mallet, pp. 202–03.

18. BN ms. fr. 18,202, fols. 268v–69v.

19. Guilloud de Courbeville, "L'assemblée de la noblesse du Forez du 27 mars 1628," *Bul. de la Diana* 21 (1921–23): 21–27.

20. AD, Loire, C 32, nos. 7–12. *IAD, Loire,* ed. Auguste Chaverondier (Paris, 1870), 1: introduction, pp. 27–28.

21. BN ms. fr. 18,202, fol. 268v–69; AD, Loire, C 32, no. 7. Further research in AD, Rhône, and AC, Villefranche would almost certainly uncover further activity.

Bresse and Bugey also continued to have assemblies of the communities, and their syndics appeared on their behalf before the king's council when the occasion required. Towns like Bourg turned to the syndic of Bresse for assistance in such matters as providing for troops and preventing Protestants from constructing a church in their midst.[22] The estates of Mâconnais functioned as usual, but the various estates in Guyenne became less active soon after the élections were established there.[23]

Those activities suggest that the government was not strongly opposed to the estates if the tax machinery was in its hands. Only for Guyenne and Normandy is there a suggestion of plans to do away with them altogether. In the former the estates were discouraged because the council tired of hearing complaints about the newly appointed élus and listening to proposals that they be suppressed. In the latter the estates were twice not convoked without any discernible reason. Probably the estates were regarded as expensive nuisances in most quarters, but as long as most of the people wanted them, it was foolish to provoke discontent by attacking them directly. When things were more settled, it might be another matter. Meanwhile, the big concern was what to do about the estates in provinces in which there were no élections. Here Marillac's hand was first revealed in Dauphiné.

2. The Estates of Dauphiné

If in the 1620s one had to choose the provincial assembly that could be attacked with the least risk, he would be likely to select that of Dauphiné. No people were more proud of their privileges, but for generations the Dauphinois had been bitterly divided over the question of whether the taille was réelle or personnelle. The dispute had led the villages to organize themselves and elect a syndic to defend their interests in the court, in the estates, and before the king's council. Their enemies were those who claimed not to have to pay the taille on the nonnoble land they owned, whether noble, royal official, clergyman, or burgher. They were also often at odds with the towns which at times transferred part of their tax burden onto them. In addition, there was a conflict between the third estate as a whole and the first two estates over whether the latter should receive any of the revenue from the salt tax to meet their expenses. Henry IV had reluctantly resolved the quarrel over the taille in favor of the privileged, and for a time the dispute simmered. In 1611 the estates of Valence decreed the "union of the three orders," but the rancor over the salt tax continued. The nobility,

22. AN, E 97^b, fols. 358–59, E 98, fol. 126, E 104 fols. 268, 523; *Mémoires historiques de la ville de Bourg*, ed. Joseph Brossard (Bourg-en-Bresse, 1887), 4: 130, 138, 146–47, 168–69. 173–74, 190.

23. *IAD*, *Saône-et-Loire*, *sér. C*, ed. C. Ragut, L. Michon, and L. Lex (Mâcon, 1924), pp. 97–98, 113, 116–17, 129, 145, 169–70.

feeling threatened, sought the support of the members of the sovereign courts and other high officials. In Dauphiné a close bond between the sword and robe was born that became even stronger in the face of the threat from below. The situation was therefore already explosive when Claude Brosse, the gallant syndic of the villages, reopened the question of whether the taille was réelle or personnelle in 1619. (See chap. 12, sec. 7.)

For a few years the three estates managed to assemble together to argue about their differences, but the meeting at Grenoble in the fall of 1623 proved to be the last until April 1627. During the intervening period, the people of Dauphiné were by no means inactive. A smaller group, referred to as the *assemblée du pays* or the assembly of the ten towns, was in effect transformed from an executive committee of the estates into an assembly that performed the duties of the estates, a role that it had usually assumed only in emergencies before. It included the commis of the clergy and the nobility and the syndic of the villages as well as the deputies of the ten towns. In July 1624 this more manageable, less quarrelsome group met at the bishop of Grenoble's and decided to ask the king to permit free trade in wine and other goods between Dauphiné and Languedoc, despite the protests of the deputy from Grenoble. Also of concern at this time was the crown's attempt to install collectors of the tailles.[24] There were further meetings in March and June 1625[25] and in January 1626 when the governor, Lesdiguières, sought assistance in raising troops to suppress a rebellion, an obligation that the towns managed to escape.[26]

For an unexplained reason, the government decided to turn once more to the three estates. On October 19, 1626, printed letters of convocation were issued summoning the estates to meet in Grenoble on January 7, 1627. The meeting was evidently postponed, for it was not until April 13 that the prince-bishop of Grenoble, president-born of the estates, bungled a speech he had prepared for the occasion, a mishap that a young contemporary later blamed on his faulty memory.[27] The meeting was to have dealt with such commonplace topics as the salt tax, the suppression of officers, and the support of troops, but at some point in the discussion a member of the third estate proposed that the king be asked to revoke all patents of nobility that had been granted during the past sixty years. Since many nobles were of recent origin, approval of the proposal would add a significant number of

24. AC, Grenoble, BB 90, fols. 74, 82–83, BB 91, fol. 37; AC, Gap, BB 25, fol. 99–99v.

25. AC, Grenoble, BB 91, fol. 31; *IAC, Gap*, ed. Paul Guillaume (Gap, 1908), 1:129; BN ms. fr. 18,203, fols. 146v–47.

26. *Actes et correspondance du connétable de Lesdiguières*, ed. Louis A. Douglas and Joseph Roman (Grenoble, 1874), 2:434, 454–55; AC, Grenoble, BB 93, fols. 27–28v; AC, Gap, BB 27, fols. 126–28, 142v–43, 147–47v.

27. AD, Drôme, C 1025, letter of convocation; *Recueil des harangues faites par messire Pierre Scarron, evesque et prince de Grenoble* ... (Paris, 1634), pp. 73–90; Nicolas Chorier, *Histoire de la vie de Charles de Créquy de Blanchefort, duc de Lesdiguières* (Grenoble, 1683), 1:246–49; AC, Grenoble, BB 94, fols. 49v–50; *IAC, Guillestre*, ed. Paul Guillaume (Gap, 1906), pp. 326, 431.

the wealthiest citizens of Dauphiné to the tax roles, but the proponent of the measure probably had a still more ambitious objective. He hoped to separate the old nobility from the new by appealing to the former's traditional dislike for the recent initiates into their order. If this could be done, the nobility would be so weakened that it might be possible to persuade the king's council to declare that the taille was réelle in Dauphiné. The nobility quickly saw through the plot and withdrew with some members of the clergy to determine what course of action to follow. No vote on the proposal had yet been taken, but if it passed, those present were fearful that the financially straitened king would grant the request in order to be able to extract a large sum from the threatened noblemen in return for exempting them from the edict. To prevent this from happening, the old nobility resolved to remain united with and inseparable from their more recent brethren and to defend them as members of their corps and brotherhood.[28]

The third estate pressed for action on their proposal concerning the new nobles after the meeting had terminated, a policy that divided the three orders further. Such was the situation in the fall of 1627 when rumors reached Dauphiné that the king was about to issue some edicts that threatened the liberties and privileges of the province. An assemblée du pays opened on October 20, 1627, at Grenoble amid much talk about the need to restore the union between the three orders. Under the leadership of the procureur syndic, a petition was prepared and deputies were elected to carry it to court in the hope of blocking the new edicts and obtaining a reduction in taxes.[29] But it was too late. From December 1627 through June 1628, one bombshell fell after another.

The first blow came when a Bureau of Finances was established at Grenoble with the usual host of treasurers and other officials. Coming as it did soon after the commencement of the siege of La Rochelle, the edict could have been only a device to raise money.[30] On the other hand, in seventeenth-century France wherever there were élections, there was a bureau to supervise the activities of the élus. The creation of a bureau in Grenoble could therefore have been ordered as a preliminary step toward establishing élections in Dauphiné. Indeed this was the case. In March 1628 Louis issued an edict creating a Chamber of Accounts. As the duties of the new chamber had formerly been performed by the Parlement, the latter court, which was causing so much trouble, was weakened. At the same time Louis created more officers in the already overcrowded courts, a rente

28. AD, Isère, 1J 669; *IAC, Gap,* 1:135, 2:21; AC, Grenoble, BB 94, fols. 49v–50.

29. AC, Grenoble, BB 94, fols. 61–62, 73–76v, 82–83; AD, Drôme, C 1025. The third estate was directed to meet in Grenoble in March 1628 to consider the tax digest and the revocation of the letters of ennoblement. *IAD, Drôme, sér E,* ed. A. LaCroix (Valence, 1898), 6:343.

30. *Actes Royaux,* 2: no. 7354.

guaranteed by the gabelles of that province, and most serious of all ten élections, each with twenty-seven officers.[31]

The creation and sale of 270 officers in the ten new élections had a very beneficial immediate impact on royal finances, but Louis did not justify the edict on these grounds, although he did not hesitate to use the need for money to explain other new positions. Instead Louis declared that the purpose of the élections was to ensure that taxes were equally divided and that no levies were made without his permission. His father, he reminded his subjects, had established élections in Guyenne in 1603, but he himself had suppressed them early in his reign at the behest of some selfish individuals. Then, recognizing the disorder and abuses that occurred in the tax-collecting process, he had reinstituted the élections in 1621. The deputies of the communities of Dauphiné, like those in Guyenne, had frequently complained about the excessive taxes that had been levied upon them without his permission, and they had requested that élections be established. It was in compliance with their wishes and upon the advice of his mother, brother, and other members of his council that he now acted.[32]

Richelieu was with the army before La Rochelle during this period, but Marillac had returned with Louis to Paris in late February, and it was probably at his urging that the edict was issued. Because of the dispute over the nature of the taille, the council had received more complaints from Dauphiné about taxes than from most other provinces, but whether Claude Brosse, the long-time syndic of the villages or any other rural spokesman ever asked for élections is another matter. Certainly Brosse would not have endorsed creating 270 tax officials with annual salaries of nearly 100,000 livres, plus fees consisting of varying percentages of the taxes that were collected, since the money to pay them was derived from the very people he was trying to protect. We know only that he tried to obtain a revision of the cadastre to ensure more uniform taxes and a reduction in the Dauphinois contribution to the military. Concerning the élections he had little to say.[33]

The towns of Dauphiné did not consider the establishment of élections as serious a blow against their liberties as those of Guyenne had. A deputy from Grenoble at court returned early in May in a very distraught mood because he had learned that a Bureau of Finances was to be established in Valence and a Court of Aids in Vienne. This was a frightful blow to the town's pride, for the sovereign courts of the entire province had been seated in its midst.

31. Ibid., nos. 7357, 7359–60.

32. Ibid., no. 7359.

33. Michel Houssaye, *Le Cardinal de Bérulle et le Cardinel de Richelieu, 1625–1629* (Paris, 1875), p. 281. For some of the numerous appearances of Brosse and others representing the village communities before the council in Louis's reign, see A. Lacroix, "Claude Brosse et les tailles," *Bul. de la soc. d'archéologie et de statistique de la Drôme* 32 (1898): 368–70, and for November 1625, BN ms. fr. 18,203, fols. 146v–47.

At a large meeting those gathered decided to send a deputation to court to protest. No mention of the élus was apparently made. Later that month the town asked Marshal Créqui, who had recently replaced his deceased father-in-law, Lesdiguières, as their governor, to convoke a "general assembly of all the orders of the province" to obtain money to purchase wheat to feed the poor. A tax on mutton and pork sold in Grenoble was imposed to meet this need, but once more an opportunity to take forceful action concerning the élections was missed. Meanwhile an assistant procureur syndic had devoted an April visit to the king's council to protest an increase in the salt tax. By late summer when an assemblée des pays was held, heavy taxation, not the élus, was the principal concern of those present.[34]

The edict on the élections had been received so calmly by the towns that the council decided to take a further step in July by issuing an edict directly attacking the estates. After reminding his subjects that he had recently ordered that élections be established because of the disorders in his finances, Louis complained of the great expenses caused by frequent assemblies that overburdened his subjects. In the future he wanted the meetings to be less frequent, but he did not forbid them altogether; indeed he promised to convoke them when requested if there was some important matter to consider. To make this request and to watch after the affairs of the province, he announced his intention to appoint a procureur syndic with two assistants who were nobles and one who was from the third estate, three treasurers, three controllers, a syndic of the village with an assistant, two commis of the clergy and six of the nobility, two secretaries, and an usher. The group was obviously modeled after the assemblée du pays and the officers of the estates except that the towns were given no representation. Probably the council's intention was to summon the *consuls* of the ten towns if there was need for them to meet with the above group. Most striking about the new arrangement was that officials appointed by the king were to be substituted for those named by the estates. To avoid the intrigues caused by frequent elections, Louis explained, these offices were to be venal, and their occupants were to pay the paulette like other royal officials. The only exceptions were the six commis of the nobility who were to be appointed by the king and were to serve three-year terms. The salaries of the new officials, exclusive of those of the commis of the nobility, came to 23,600 livres per year. To support the new officers Louis ordered that 30,000 livres be levied annually on the third estate.[35]

The hypocrisy of the crown's accusing the three estates of overburdening the people with the expenses they incurred becomes apparent when one

34. AC, Grenoble, BB 95, fols. 99–108, 121–24, 140–41v, 169–77v, 184–84v; AN, E 96ᵃ, fol. 73.

35. *Actes Royaux*, 2: no. 7381. Most of the edict has been published in Alexandre Fauché-Prunelle, *Essai sur les anciennes institutions autonomes ou populaires des Alpes Cottiennes-Briançonnaises* (Grenoble, 1857), 2:478–83.

notes that in 1621 they appropriated only 15,000 livres to pay the salaries and expenses of their officers and to defray the costs of their meetings. In addition, some funds derived from the salt tax went to support the officers and activities of the clergy and nobility.[36] In January 1626 the king's council limited the amount the estates could spend for salaries, travel, and their meetings to 30,000 livres, and this figure appears to have served as a guide for the sum allocated to support the royal officials who were to replace those of the estates.[37] However, in addition to the 30,000 livres, the Dauphinois now had the burden of paying the salaries of the élus which came to nearly 100,000 livres annually, in addition to their fees. The size of the fees is difficult to determine because it varied with the size of the tax, but the total cost of the new arrangement, exclusive of the expenditures for the Bureau of Finances, must have exceeded 210,000 livres per year, seven times the sum spent by the estates. In 1621 the total amount voted by the three estates was only 166,431 livres, a smaller sum than that now assigned to the élus and the royal officials who were to replace those who had formerly been responsible to them.[38]

It was not necessary for royal tax collectors to be so costly, but once the decision had been taken to establish the élections, the impoverished government could not resist creating five times as many offices as was necessary in order to profit from their sale. When the Bureau of Finances and the élections began to function, the officials of the estates became unnecessary, but instead of suppressing them, they were transformed into royal officials. Furthermore the crown soon found it advisable to give pensions to the "natural" leaders of dissident groups. The bishop of Grenoble, president-born of the estates, was granted 6,000 livres annually, and two of the barons who served as commis of the nobility were given 3,000 livres each.[39]

Fortunately for the people of Dauphiné, the officers of the estates and the sovereign courts proved more stalwart defenders of their liberties than the towns were. The procureur syndic appeared before the king's council on August 12, 1628, at a time when arrangements were being made to sell the newly created offices in Dauphiné, and he was back in Grenoble in September with his assistant when Parlement considered registering the March edict on the élections and the July one on the estates. Concerning the former, Parlement reduced the authority of the élus and insisted that as nonnobles they pay the taille. A more severe blow was leveled at the king when the court declared that he and not the province should pay the salaries, travel expenses, and fees of the élus. It was not until March 21, 1630, that Louis was able to make Parlement register the decree in its original form. Concerning the July edict, Parlement passed over the suspension of the

36. AD, Isère, 1C 4, no. 45.
37. AN, E 100ᵃ, fols. 317–18.
38. AD, Isère, 1C 4, no. 45.
39. Fauché-Prunelle, *Essai*, 2:479, 520–24.

estates but was willing to accept the creation of only the three treasurers, the three controllers, and the two secretaries. The procureur syndic of the three estates and his assistants, the syndic of the villages and his assistant, and the commis of the clergy and the nobility were to remain officers of the estates or of their respective orders. Their executive body was to be left intact although the estates themselves were no longer to meet regularly. This solution was accepted independently by the king's council at about the same time that Parlement acted.[40]

The procureur syndic of the estates had to win confirmation of his rights and functions from the king's council in January 1629 because some of the newly created officers were encroaching on his duties, but in spite of these difficulties, he and other officials of the estates remained active in the defense of the people of Dauphiné. A few months before he had journeyed to La Rochelle with some *consuls* from the towns to protest the heavy taxes to support troops, but in regard to the élections he and his adherents chose to fight a delaying action at home. On February 14, 1629, the council had to take special steps in the hope of speeding the establishment of the élections. In May the treasurers of the Bureau of Finances of Dauphiné were summoned by the council to explain what progress they had made and to learn the king's intentions. That same month Claude Brosse had the rare opportunity to appear before the council in his own behalf and won an order that he be paid his salary as syndic of the villages from 1627 to 1629, but in a June appearance before that body, he was back to his usual role of opposing the heavy taxes upon the people he represented.[41]

In spite of the Dauphinois' delaying tactics, the council felt that enough progress had been made by June 1629 to order that the élus collect taxes although in Gap, at least, they were not even installed until the following month.[42] The procureur syndic of the estates persuaded Parlement to set aside this directive, but in September the council ordered the treasurers to disregard the court and send the necessary letters to impose the tax immediately. Again Parlement intervened and the treasurers failed to act. On January 30, 1630, a year after the initial letters had been issued to levy the tax, the council had to repeat its order. This time the council appears to have been able to impose its will, but the Dauphinois were still capable of being annoying. In September a complaint was lodged with the council that the towns in which the seats of the élection were established had not supplied the required offices and furniture for the new officials.[43] On November 29,

40. AN, E 97ª, fols. 206, 210, 339–41v; Fauché-Prunelle, *Essai*, 2:480–83.

41. AN, E 98, fols. 240, 291–92v, 454–54v, E 99ª fol. 293, E 100ª, fols. 105, 317–18, 323, E 100ᵇ, fol. 4; AD, Isère, 1C 5, no. 1.

42. AN, E 100ᵇ, fol. 64; *IAC, Gap*, 1:149. One of the two secretaries for the estates, now a crown office, was appointed in April. AD, Isère, 1C 5, no. 31.

43. AN, E 100ᶜ, fol. 139–39v, E 101ª, fols. 465–66, E 104, fol. 438–38v. For other related decrees, see AN, E 101ᵇ, fols. 5, 205, E 106ᵇ, fol. 306–306v.

1631, the receivers of the tailles had to appeal to the council to enforce their right to verify tax roles and to receive a percentage of the money that was collected. That same day the élus asked to be paid travel allowances for inspecting the parishes in their respective jurisdictions, although war and disease had prevented them from performing this duty since their establishment. Another excuse they offered for their failure to act was that there were only two or three officers per élection, a situation suggesting that the Dauphinois had found another delaying tactic or that the Frenchmen's craving for office was temporarily satiated. Nevertheless the new order was slowly imposed, and gradually the principal problem of the crown became one of dealing with its new tax officials. Already in July 1631 it was complaining that the élus were slow in collecting taxes.[44]

As the élus were gradually established, the crown was able to increase the taille and related taxes. For 1629 only 439,000 livres were demanded, but two years later the figure had become 593,156 livres. The actual revenue turned over to the royal treasurer during these years jumped from 67,055 to 384,637 livres.[45] There was no assembly of the three estates to approve this increase. That institution was not to function again until the eve of the Revolution. Even the assemblée du pays was inactive. The procureur syndic of the estates and the syndic of the villages continued to protest to the council against taxes and having to support troops moving through the province. During the past four years, the former charged, the troops had consumed all the food and forced the price of wheat to an excessive height, to the detriment of the people. Fervent as these appeals were, however, the failure of representative bodies to function except in the three mountain bailiwicks suggests a new era in Dauphiné. When Louis passed through Grenoble in February 1629, the bishop of Grenoble, president-born of the three estates, addressed him in flattering terms that were more designed to please and to display his own classical lore than to present the grievances of the people. He never mentioned the élections or the failure to convoke the estates that so seriously threatened the liberties of the province.[46]

The bishop's lack of leadership and the division among the three estates prevented Dauphiné from offering the king a substantial sum in return for suppressing the élections as the inhabitants of Guyenne had done. The towns and villages had no love of the older system in which they paid nearly all the taxes, but the clergy and nobility exercised the strongest influence in the assemblies of the estates. They must have been angered when they learned that their bishop had asked the king's council to give him the 6,000 livres that the estates had customarily voted him in return for serving as their president although there had been no assembly. At least one of the two

44. AN, E 107b, fols. 359–60.
45. AN, E 100b, fol. 64, E 106b, fol. 306–306v; Mallet, p. 203.
46. AN, E 103b, fol. 354–54v, E 104, fols. 245–46. *Mercure François* 15 (1629): 110–19.

barons who claimed to have a hereditary right to serve as a commis of the nobility made a similar request for 4,500 livres annually. Both sums were to come from the 94,000 livres raised each year from the salt tax that was intended to repay the debts of the province. As a result when the council decided to give the bishop all he requested and the baron 3,000 livres annually, the day when the debt could be repaid and the tax removed receded further in the future.[47] Not surprisingly Claude Brosse continued to attack the privileged tax position of the nobility, and early in 1631 Parlement responded by ordering his arrest for holding an illegal assembly designed to trouble the peace of the province and the unity of the orders.[48] Under such circumstances the nobility might talk of obtaining the suppression of the élections, but the third estate was not interested in paying the bill, and it never occurred to the nobles themselves that they should contribute.

This is not to say that Dauphiné remained calm during these years. At the time that the edicts of March 1628 were issued, there was danger that the numerous Protestants in the province would join forces with Rohan in Languedoc, but Créqui and the Parlement took such firm action that that danger was removed. By the close of 1629, Parlement had become less cooperative with the crown because of the suffering of the people. It did all it could to prevent the shipment of wheat from the province to feed the army in Italy. Emboldened by this action, the people used violence to obtain wheat. In 1630 there were further troubles in Grenoble, but the creation of the élections and the discontinuance of the estates do not appear to have been important factors in causing the unrest.[49]

3. THE ESTATES OF BURGUNDY

The first two years of the Richelieu ministry were relatively uneventful in Burgundy. There were the usual troubles concerning the behavior of the troops, but most clashes between the crown and the élus who administered the province during the intervals between the estates came over the question of taxation. The estates that had met in June 1622 had voted Louis a special grant of only 50,000 livres instead of the 400,000 he had requested. Angrily he had called the estates back into session in August, and this time they offered 150,000. To Louis this made a total of 200,000 livres, but the élus interpreted the action of the estates as only increasing the earlier gift to 150,000 livres. Whether the disputed 50,000 livres should be levied was still not settled by 1626. The élus also opposed a royal effort to increase the salt

47. AN, E 103ᵃ, fol. 190–90v, E 103ᵇ, fol. 272.

48. Lacroix, *Claude Brosse*, 32 (1898): 370–71.

49. *Mercure François* 14 (1628): 121–27; Richelieu, *Mém.* SHF, 10:381–82. Porchnev, *Les soulèvements populaires*, p. 134.

tax to pay the officers of the sovereign courts. Then, too, the estates that should have been held in 1625 to vote taxes for 1626–29 had to be postponed, but the king was anxious for the élus to begin to collect taxes for 1626 anyway. The élus agreed to levy the money to support the garrison, no doubt to remove the threat that unpaid troops would prey on the people, but they steadfastly refused to impose routine nonmilitary taxes until the three estates had met and given their approval.[50]

The triennial meeting of the estates finally opened in Dijon on September 14, 1626. Although Louis sought and received only routine direct taxes, there are indications that those who attended sensed an approaching crisis and sought to prepare for it. Their most serious complaint was that Parlement was to cease to perform part of the duties of a Court of Aids, and a court by that name was to be established and affiliated with the Chamber of Accounts, a step they opposed because indirect taxes would have to be increased to pay the new officials and because they regarded any royal tampering with their institutions as a threat to their privileges. The three estates dispatched a deputation to the king to obtain the suppression of the court and other concessions. To remove any doubt concerning their position, they also asked Louis to confirm Henry II's declaration of May 1555 giving to them and to their élus the right to handle the economic and administrative affairs of the province. To weaken royal influence in the chamber of the élus, they urged that the members of the Chamber of Accounts who participated be denied the right to have a deliberative voice. The deputies of the third estate also sought to have their two élus given a full vote instead of one-half vote each, but the nobility and clergy were unwilling to tolerate this augmentation of their influence, although it would strengthen the role of the estates as a whole in dealing with the representatives of the crown. The three estates complained about the delay in summoning the meeting and asked in the future to be assembled in May every third year. They directed that their officers always attend, and they took steps to put their archives in order and to prepare a collection of documents concerning their rights and privileges. As a final precaution to ensure their independence, they took an oath to keep their deliberations secret and ordered their ushers to prevent outsiders from attending their deliberations.[51]

In spite of these seeming preparations for a confrontation or perhaps because of them, several years elapsed before the break came. During this period the support and behavior of troops and the exportation of wheat from the province to feed the army in Italy were the principal causes of friction between the Burgundians and the crown, for their supply of grain was as

50. AD, Côte-d'Or, C 3078, fols. 167–68, 209, 212v, 219–22, 226–26v, 229–29v, 239v–41, 246–46v.

51. Ibid., C 3017, fols. 321v–24, 334v–335, 342–43, 362–63, 375–79, 383–83v. On the Court of Aids see *Correspondance de la mairie de Dijon*, ed. Joseph Garnier (Dijon, 1870), 3 : xlvii–lii, 167–69, 171–76.

short as their supply of money. Especially shocking was the doubling of the taillon in 1628 in keeping with the recommendation of the Assembly of Notables. Then, on December 5, 1628, the élus received a letter from the bishop of Autun stating that he had learned that an edict had been prepared establishing élections in Burgundy. The élus took comfort in the fact that no such document had been presented to the Chamber of Accounts which had been transferred to Beaune, but on January 25, 1629, they received a report that the king intended to take this step. This information led the élus to search for preventative measures. Nevertheless they decided not to raise the issue when the king visited Dijon at the end of the month, since he was not accompanied by Marillac or his secretaries of state. Instead they remained silent, and the Burgundian people, who were for the most part ignorant of the threat, gave their sovereign a warm welcome. Even Richelieu, who was with the king, escaped with a general request that he watch after the welfare of the province.[52] As part of the ceremonies occasioned by Louis's presence in Dijon, the viscount mayor took an oath of fidelity to him. When he had finished, he asked Louis to make the customary pledge to preserve the privileges of the town, the relevant documents concerning which had been shown to Richelieu. Instead of complying immediately, Louis told him to show the material to Marillac who had not accompanied him, but he did indicate that his request would be granted. These two episodes suggest that both Louis and the Burgundian élus looked to Marillac as being responsible for the routine administration of the kingdom and that the municipal officials erred in troubling Richelieu about their privileges.[53]

For several months matters seemed to drift, but still the dreaded edict on the élections did not arrive. On April 10 the syndics of the estates reminded the élus that in accordance with the decision of the estates of 1626, a meeting should be held that May. A few weeks later the élus wrote the duke of Bellegarde, their governor, asking him to obtain the king's permission for the estates to assemble as soon as possible. Evidently Bellegarde had no success, for on June 14 three of the élus decided to go to the king and point out that the estates must meet if a delay in levying royal taxes was to be avoided. They failed to find their wandering monarch, and on their return to Dijon, they were informed that an edict had arrived creating ten élections in Burgundy. Fortunately a syndic of the estates had no difficulty persuading the Chamber of Accounts to take no action until after the estates had met. He then set off to Paris to ask Bellegarde to obtain the letters of convocation. Bellegarde promised to hold the estates on October 20, but the syndic then ran into difficulty getting Marillac to seal the necessary letters. Finally, on

52. AD, Côte-d'Or, C 3079, fols. 43v–44, 50v–51, 55. For the taillon see C 5220. For Louis's visit to Dijon, see *Correspondance de Dijon*, 3 : lii–lvii, 185–212.

53. *Correspondance de Dijon*, 3 : xlix, lii, lvi, 167, 201.

October 3 the syndic returned with the proper authorization, and the estates assembled on November 3 to deal with the élections and other matters.[54]

Louis justified creating the élections on the grounds that there had been complaints from the inhabitants of some provinces with estates that heavy taxes had been levied without his permission. Furthermore these taxes were unfairly apportioned, for the rich often escaped and the poor were over-burdened. Louis pointed to the success that the élus were achieving in Guyenne and declared that the people of Dauphiné had been inspired by this example to ask for them. He did not, however, claim that any Burgundians had made a similar request. It was enough for him that they suffered from the same abuses. Since there were already élections in Auxerre, Mâcon, and Bar-sur-Seine as well as in the recently annexed territories of Bresse, Bugey, and Gex, the creation of ten additional ones in the relatively small généralité was excessive. Nevertheless Louis directed that from 32 to 38 officers be appointed in each of them, bringing a total of 333 new positions that could be sold to his profit. As an enticement, the new appointees were not to pay the paulette but were given the privileges of those who did so during the current year. Louis was keeping open the option of abandoning the paulette throughout his kingdom when the period for which he had last granted it expired at the end of December. Since the Burgundians had always been loyal subjects, he promised to continue to permit their estates to meet every third year and to elect élus to attend to their affairs between the sessions. The only change that he ordered was that taxes were to be apportioned among the élections by the treasurers in the Bureau of Finances that had been established in Dijon some years before, and within the élections by the newly created royal officials, an important innovation that deprived the estates of their control over the administration of taxes.[55]

The deputies who assembled in Dijon in early November were horrified when they were informed that the salaries and expenses of the officials in the new élections would come to about 100,000 livres annually and their fees to 150,000 more. These figures were slightly high, but nevertheless the erection of the proposed jurisdictions would increase the financial burden on the province significantly. Furthermore those present were acutely aware that if the élections were established, the liberties of the estates and the privileges of the province would disappear. They did take comfort on being reminded that in January 1554 Henry II had created six élections in Burgundy but had revoked the edict upon receiving the remonstrances of the estates. With this example in mind, they elected a large delegation to go to the king to plead their cause. Those chosen were given full powers to treat in their

54. AD, Côte-d'Or, C 3079, fols. 79–79v, 81–81v, 91–93v 107v–108, 111v–13, 116, 124–26v.

55. A copy of the edict is at BN, F 46,966, no. 5.

name, but two-thirds of them were to consent to any agreement that was made, and they were to report to an abbreviated assembly of the estates consisting of one deputy from the clergy and one from the nobility of each bailiwick and one deputy from every town with a seat in the estates. The king's decision to double the taillon in 1628 following the recommendation of the Assembly of Notables, the cost of supporting the garrisons, and the excessive price of salt also came under attack, but the threat of the élections was clearly uppermost in the deputies' minds.[56]

The three estates voted the king his usual don gratuit of 50,000 livres for three years and then lavished gifts on those who had served them in the past and on those from whom they hoped for favors in the trying days ahead. For their governor there was 16,000 livres; for the king's secretary of state for Burgundy, 3,000; for the first president of Parlement, 1,000; and for clerks, secretaries, and the like, much smaller sums. To further the Burgundian cause the élu of the clergy suggested to his fellow members of the first estate that he resign so that they could elect Cardinal Richelieu in his stead. Richelieu, he pointed out, had become abbot and general administrator of the order of Cluny. Because of his new position, they could look to him for great favors, especially in the matter of the élections. The élu did ask to serve if Richelieu could not accept because of his desire to be near the king, a position he doubtless assumed that the cardinal would take. The clergy adopted his proposal, an action suggesting that they considered Richelieu to be less of an absolutist than have most modern historians.[57]

Future events were to prove that the Burgundians' estimate of the cardinal was correct, but for the moment he not only rejected the proffered office as anticipated but also failed to intervene with the king on their behalf. As a result, their deputation to court fared less well than they had hoped. The mayor of Dijon, who was one of their number, reported from Paris on December 12 that there was talk of making the financial administration uniform in all the provinces by establishing élections throughout France. He also expressed grave concern over the threat of a famine in Burgundy provoked by the passage of troops and by regulations concerning the movement of grain that favored Lyonnais. Unhappily Bellegarde, their governor, was leaving on a mission to Nancy that very day.[58] Two weeks later the mayor expressed disappointment that Bellegarde had not returned because the deputation "hoped much from his favor and assistance."[59] Then he added, more hopefully, that Richelieu had gone to Suze and everyone anticipated that his trip would lead to the peace that the people so badly

56. AD, Côte-d'Or, C 3017, fols. 413–20v. For years the taillon had been 71,547 livres. In 1628 Louis doubled this amount, and thereafter he augmented the traditional taillon by 80,000 livres. Ibid., C 5220.

57. Ibid., C 3017, fols. 436v–38, 449–50.

58. AC, Dijon, B 462, no. 262.

59. Ibid., no. 264.

needed. On January 2, 1630, he was once more dejected. Claude de Bullion, the king's secretary of state who was responsible for Burgundy, "had an aversion for their province" and was favoring Lyonnais and Dauphiné in the matter of grain supplies. "We alone remain orphans," he wailed, but then he took some comfort in the fact that Bellegarde would return soon. In him, he wrote, "we have placed all our hopes."[60]

The deputies thought that the council had a doctrinaire conviction that there should be fiscal uniformity in France. "Nothing opposes us so much," the mayor wrote in mid-January, "as the council's maxim that it is necessary to make all the provinces uniform...."[61] And again on January 23 he wrote: "As to the affairs of our deputation, we are only waiting for a reply from his majesty which we will perhaps find more favorable than those of the ministers of state who are making [the élections] a general maxim for all the provinces."[62] Certainly little comfort could be derived from the king's councillors. On January 28 they ordered the Chamber of Accounts of Burgundy to register the edict creating the élections in spite of the opposition of the estates.[63]

Some Burgundian leaders appear to have believed that the sum of money they were offering the king was not likely to be enough to persuade him to suppress the élections, and all knew that the Chamber of Accounts could do no more than delay the registration if the king was bent on imposing his will. If there was serious unrest in the province because of the élections, however, the king and his advisers might decide that it was wiser to accept their offer. This was especially true because Burgundy was a frontier province and France was at war with the Habsburgs, who were descendants of its former dukes. Some persons, therefore, began to plan disturbances in Dijon, Beaune, and perhaps other towns.

Reports of these preparations soon reached Paris, and around the middle of January, the mayor of Dijon wrote to the échevins about a widespread rumor that the edict on the élections was causing some inhabitants to plan disturbances. He did not wish to believe the report and urged his fellow officials to remain obedient to the king. Even if the edict was not immediately revoked in answer to their pleas, he thought that it would be once peace was restored. On February 18 Bellegarde, who also was at Paris, wrote the Dijon échevins that he had learned that violence was being planned as a means of opposing the edict on the élections. If the people behaved in this manner, he advised, they would bring ruin on the town, which would be made to serve as an example for all of France.[64]

In spite of these warnings the échevins made little effort to calm the

60. *Correspondance de Dijon*, 3:218, 219.
61. Ibid., p. 222.
62. Ibid., p. 224.
63. AN, E 101ª, fol. 401.
64. *Correspondance de Dijon*, 3:221–22, 227–28.

inhabitants of the town. Indeed someone spread rumors that new taxes were about to be imposed on the province, including one on the sale of wine. There were apparently those who feared that the populace would not understand how serious a threat the creation of élections would be to their liberties and their pocketbooks and were making sure that there were enough recognizable grievances to warrant a riot. In the evening of February 27 a crowd composed largely of grape growers marched through the streets, threw rocks at the houses of several financial officials, and threatened to kill them and burn their dwellings. The next day the demonstrators broke into several homes and did considerable damage. They again threatened royal officials, burned a portrait of the king, and, re-membering the happy days when they were ruled by their dukes, some cried, "Long live the Emperor." Finally the authorities decided that the mob was getting out of hand and ordered the militia to restore order, which it did after some bloodshed.[65]

Perhaps the riot gave the Chamber of Accounts the courage to defy the council once more. On March 4, three days after deputies from the towns had joined officers of the estates to plead the Burgundian cause before the court, its members refused to register the offending edict and sent re-monstrances to the king.[66] The riot had the opposite effect on Louis. He was furious when the news reached him at Fontainebleau, and on March 4 he declared that he was going to strip Dijon of all its privileges and tear down its walls. Troops were dispatched to the town, and several of the culprits were executed. Bellegarde, in whom the municipal officials had placed so much hope, was hardly less angry. In spite of this outburst, the Burgundian deputies at court still expected Louis to accept a financial offer in return for abolishing the élections and disbanding the garrison, but around the middle of March their hopes were dashed.[67] Louis rejected their offer of 1.8 million livres because, as Marillac reported to Richelieu, he insisted on establishing the élections in order to have uniformity in his kingdom. The idea may have been one that the keeper of the seals had planted in the king's mind, but it was not one to which the cardinal subscribed: "This news grieved him," his memoirs informs us, "because he was sorry that in these times they made it difficult to satisfy this province," in which taxes were levied only with the king's permission and the estates did not overburden the people.[68]

65. Ibid., 3:lxiii–lxxv. Adequate precautions by the municipal officials of Beaune prevented a similar riot. Ibid., p. 230. For a Marxist interpretation, see Porchnev, *Les soulèvements populaires*, pp. 135–41.

66. *Correspondance de Dijon*, 3:225–26; AD, Côte-d'Or, C 3079, fols. 169v–71, 192v–96v.

67. *Correspondance de Dijon*, 3:lxxv–lxxxii, 228–31, 233–36. On July 14, 1629, Marillac and the other members of the council had turned over the right to sell the offices in the élections to Jacques de Silvestre for 1,872,968 livres and promised that the king would not revoke the agreement even if the provincial estates offered more money. AN, 100b, fols. 176–78v.

68. Richelieu, *Mém.* Michaud, sér. II, 8:149.

Louis treated the deputations from Dijon coldly, and not content with this display of annoyance, he decided to visit the town on his way to Italy to receive its submission. The occasion was not to be the joyful procession that had characterized his travels in Burgundy the preceding year. He ordered that all the cannons in Dijon be placed in the château and that the offending wine growers be sent to the surrounding villages. To show his displeasure, he planned to make his entrance without the firing of artillery, the sounding of bells, or a welcome by the inhabitants at the town's gates. When he arrived on April 27, he refused to see any of the municipal officials, but on the afternoon of the following day he received their submission. Upon bended knee their spokesman craved the royal pardon. With his usual brevity, Louis told the Dijon officials and burghers that they had been guilty of a serious fault and that the keeper of the seals would make his wishes known.[69]

With what one suspects was with a degree of enjoyment, Marillac lectured the still kneeling Burgundians on the duties of passive obedience. "To revolt against the magistrate," he declared, "is to revolt against the king himself who reigns through his officers and through the order established for the government of the towns and provinces." Then after describing the evils of rebellion, beginning with the fall of Satan, he insisted that "it is not for inferiors to examine the reasons for an order.... If they obey only when they find it reasonable, they no longer have a superior. The key to public tranquility and order lies in the reverence which is due to the superior powers." The Dijon officials had committed a grievous fault by not halting the spread of sedition when it first appeared. "If you do not have the courage to expose yourself to an honorable death," he moralized, "you deserve a shameful one."[70] Because of the pleas of the duke of Bellegarde and their submission, however, the king would pardon them, but new parish officers were to be elected subject to his approval, and the municipal council was to be reduced to a mayor and six échevins who were to be chosen by a very restrictive suffrage. Indeed for the next six years, the king would choose the mayor from a list of three names submitted to him.

The magistrates and other leading citizens who were present were angered at these and other heavy punishments meted out to their town. They had come to expect that the king would be lenient and blamed Marillac and the other councillors for his severity. To make matters worse Louis took advantage of his presence in Burgundy to remove the Court of Aids from the uncooperative Chamber of Accounts and give Parlement jurisdiction over its cases in return for a promise to register the edict on the élections without further delay.[71]

Two days after his Dijon speech Marillac wrote to Richelieu with obvious delight that over a hundred inhabitants had pleaded on their knees with the

69. *Correspondance de Dijon*, 3:lxxx–lxxxv, 250–52; *Mercure François* 16 (1630): 148–56.

70. Ibid., pp. 157, 160, 162.

71. *Correspondance de Dijon*, 3:lxxxvii–lxxxviii.

king to pardon them.[72] Perhaps the cardinal was less pleased. Shortly after the meeting an English agent informed his master that "the Keeper of the Seals had displayed more ability and strength of mind in this encounter than the adherents of the Cardinal desired."[73] They feared, with reason, that he was persuading the king to join the party of the queen mother. Whatever Richelieu's reaction to these events, one fact is clear: Louis and his imperious ministers had humbled the proud Burgundians. Both capital and province had lost their most cherished liberties.

4. THE ESTATES OF PROVENCE

During the first three years of the Richelieu regime, the relations between the crown and the provincial estates of Provence were friendly. The most serious cause for discord was the decision the council reached on May 12, 1624, to create some additional offices, a step which the estates that met in October opposed.[74] On the other hand, the relations between the estates and the duke of Guise, their governor, became strained when he ordered that a tax be levied without their consent in order to raise 1,000 troops to defend the frontiers of the province. The procureurs du pays, nés et joints met in February 1625 to protest this violation of their privileges. Sharp exchanges ensued. In July the Parliament of Aix joined in the dispute on the side of the estates, and that court soon expanded its quarrel with Guise to include troop discipline, the defense of the province, and commerce. Having stirred up so much unrest, Guise found it expedient to abandon the tax, but the procureurs reported the matter to the estates that met in December 1625. In spite of their concern, the deputies voted Guise the usual 15,000 livres for his salary, 9,000 for his guards, and a much larger sum for his company of ordonnance. Nothing was offered to support the 1,000 troops, and in February 1626 an assembly of the communities even complained when Guise asked the province to support six soldiers assigned to defend a château owned by a noble.[75]

The assembly of the communities that met in Aix in 1627 passed without serious incident, but the relations between Guise and Parlement worsened. Perhaps part of the difficulty should be attributed to the increased arrogance displayed by the members of the sovereign courts and other royal officials throughout France as they came to realize the nearly invulnerable position the paulette gave them. But even after due allowance is made for this

72. AAE, ms. 795bis., fol. 129.

73. Augier to Dorchester from Dijon on April 29, 1630, PRO, S.P. 78/86, fols. 257–58.

74. AD, Bouches-du-Rhône, C 14, fols. 123–23v.

75. Ibid., fols. 125–210 passim, 217v–18, 244v–48, 267–67v. Jonathan L. Pearl, *Guise and Provence: Political Conflict in the Epoch of Richelieu* (Ann Arbor, University Microfilms, 1968), pp. 121–24.

development, it must be admitted that the Parlement of Aix went out of its way to challenge the governor's authority. The court tried to prevent Guise's son from assuming his duties as governor while he himself was out of the province participating in the siege of La Rochelle, although the king had recognized the right of the young prince to succeed to the governorship upon his father's death. It refused to permit members of the Guise family to be received with full honors when they visited Provence, and in general it sought to humiliate the duke at every opportunity.[76]

The most likely explanation for Parlement's behavior is that its first president, D'Oppede, had abandoned his earlier ties with Guise and had become one of Richelieu's clients whose policies he now pursued. Enmity between the cardinal and Guise may have dated back to 1617, but now even appearances of friendship were abandoned. The principal cause of the difficulty was that Guise was admiral of the Levant as well as governor of Provence. Richelieu, whose interest in building a navy and in increasing commerce was boundless, had already obtained most of the admirality rights on the Atlantic from Montmorency. He now wanted to dispossess Guise in a similar fashion. Hence under D'Oppede's leadership, Parlement began to complain about how Guise performed his duties as admiral, as if to prove to the king that he was incompetent. To make matters worse, Guise won little glory as a naval commander in the final successful siege of La Rochelle or as a general in a campaign in Italy that followed. His credit with the king waned, but he persisted in his refusal to surrender the post of admiral unless he was compensated by an exorbitant sum. Thus as the estates entered into the most critical period of their history, their governor had little credit at court and was at odds with Parlement.[77]

The Provençals who gathered at Aix in May 1628 to attend the meeting of the estates were greeted with an alarming speech by one of their procureurs. Five edicts, he declared, threatened the liberty of the province. One introduced the smaller unit for measuring salt used in the rest of France and at the same time raised the tax that was to be paid per unit. Others increased the number of royal officials, some of whom were to audit the accounts of the towns and communities, and raised the taillon from 36,000 to 136,000 livres. The estates refused to grant any new taxes and named a deputation headed by the archbishop of Aix to plead their cause before the king and council. They were obviously pleased when their archbishop agreed to serve, for he was Richelieu's older, more devout, and mentally unstable brother. Since coming to Aix in 1626 he had used his influence at court on their behalf on several occasions and was specifically thanked by the estates for having done so. In view of his importance he was voted 30 livres

76. AD, Bouches-du-Rhône, C 15, fols. 57–86v passim; Pearl, *Guise and Provence*, pp. 124–32.

77. Pearl, *Guise and Provence*, pp. 132–34, 142–58, 164–66.

per day for his expenses. To increase the likelihood that the deputation would receive a warm welcome, the king's secretary of state was given 400 écus and his commis 100. In spite of his waning credit at court, Guise was granted the usual amount for his guards, company of ordonnance, and salary.[78]

When the deputies reached the army besieging La Rochelle on July 8, they sought an audience with the marquis d'Effiat, the superintendent of finances, because they thought that if they could win his support, they would soon be permitted to present their case before the council. Effiat, however, stressed the financial needs of the king. The deputies countered by saying that they were prepared to offer a substantial sum in return for the revocation of the offending edicts. Effiat responded by pointing out that the salt tax was less burdensome on the people because the nobility and clergy also paid and that the increase in the taillon had been agreed to by the Assembly of Notables. The deputies then argued that only royal officials had attended the assembly from Provence and that they had not been empowered to discuss an imposition.[79]

The archbishop made his harangue to the king on August 5, but Louis did no more than turn the Provençal cahiers over to a secretary. Interviews with Effiat, Marillac, and other ministers were held, but they were discouraging. Then an unexpected blow fell: the archbishop informed his fellow deputies that the king was transferring him to the see of Lyons and that he might not be able to assist them further. An impasse was soon reached. The councillors who were consulted said that the king would accept a financial offer in return for abolishing the new offices that admittedly had been created for revenue purposes only, but that he insisted on increasing the salt tax and taillon. The deputies considered the last two measures the most offensive and refused to present a proposal before the council that did not include the abolition of all the offending edicts. On finding the councillors as stubborn as they were, they returned to Provence to obtain further instructions.

When the estates met in Aix early in December 1628, the situation was further complicated by the increased movement of troops to and from Italy. Nevertheless the edicts increasing the salt tax and the taillon to the detriment of the liberties of the province claimed much of the deputies' attention. After considerable debate, they appealed to Guise for his assistance and took steps to prevent the implementation of the decrees through appeals to the Court of Accounts and Parlement. In spite of the seriousness of

78. AD, Bouches-du-Rhône, C 15, fols. 122v–23, 129–34, 143v–45v, 150v–51v. The archbishop had written to both his brother and Bouthillier on behalf of Provence in February 1627. AAE, ms. 1701, fols. 4–6v.

79. For an account of the deputation, see AD, Bouches-du-Rhône, C 15, fols. 162–63v, 179–81.

the situation, they persisted in their refusal to negotiate with the crown except to obtain the revocation of all the offending edicts.[80]

The difficulties the Provençals faced multiplied in 1629–30. Poor crops led to a scarcity of food, but royal demands that they feed troops moving through the province increased. As a result prices rose. By 1630 the cost of bread was half again as high as it had been in 1627, and the price of mutton and wine jumped forward even more rapidly. There was widespread hunger. As if this were not enough, the plague struck Digne in June 1629 and was soon decimating the population of other towns and villages.[81] Still the crown did nothing to mitigate its demands. Indeed Marillac, who was more aware of the condition of the people than most other councillors, wrote Richelieu that the deputies from Provence exaggerated their suffering.[82]

When the estates opened on July 11, 1629, in Tarascon, those present found that the king had sent Claude de Bullion, an old and trusted councillor, to serve as one of his commissioners. The reason for such a prominent choice became apparent the following day when Bullion and Guise appeared before them and asked for 1.5 million livres to help defray the cost of suppressing the Huguenot rebellion. Before debating on what to do about this outrageous demand, they listened to the report of their deputies who had reopened negotiations with Marillac and Effiat the preceding month, with no better success than before. The impasse appeared about to continue when on July 14 Bullion and Guise once more entered the estates, this time with two letters from the king directing that the meeting be terminated on July 16 in order to reduce costs. If they had not completed their deliberations, they could send a deputation to see him as he traveled from Languedoc back to Paris. Severely shaken by this arbitrary curtailment of their meeting, the estates decided to offer Louis 900,000 livres provided that he suppress all the offending edicts and make Marseilles and Arles pay their share.[83]

In spite of the king's orders to disband, the three estates remained in session to learn the results of their deputation. They had not long to wait. On July 17 their deputies reported that they had informed the king and council of their offer the day before, but instead of being warmly treated, they had been unceremoniously dismissed and told to disband the estates. Shocked, the estates dealt with several matters, including those related to

80. Ibid., C 15, fols. 176v–81, C 108, fols. 22–29.

81. Pearl, *Guise and Provence*, pp. 184–88; Sharon K. Kettering, *Red Robes and Barricades: The Parlement of Aix-en-Provence in a Period of Popular Revolt, 1629–1649* (Ann Arbor, University Microfilms, 1969), pp. 68–73, 76–81; René Pillorget, *Les mouvements insurrectionnels de Provence entre 1596 et 1715* (Paris, 1975), pp. 313–20; René Baehrel, *Une croissance: La Basse-Provence rurale fin du XVIe siècle à 1789* (Paris, 1961), esp. pp. 535, 547, 558.

82. Georges d'Avenel, *Richelieu et la monarchie absolue*, 2d ed. (Paris, 1895), 4:181.

83. AD, Bouches-du-Rhône, C 15, fols. 311v, 314–17, 324–25.

troop movements and the plague, voted taxes for a number of purposes, and disbanded the following day. Conspicuously absent from their levies was the 900,000 livres they had conditionally offered the king and any money for Guise's guards, company of ordonnance, or salary. Guise had appeared before the king and council with their deputies, but he evidently had so little credit at court that he could do nothing for them. For this reason, or because they had ceased to trust him, the estates removed him from the list of those to whom they gave gratifications. Indeed they had neglected to vote him anything when they had met in December 1628.[84]

Louis councillors probably anticipated that the estates would be obstinate because they had prepared an edict creating ten élections in Provence with a total of 350 officers who were to assume the duty of assessing and collecting taxes. Louis's excuse for this arbitrary act was his desire to free his subjects from their excessive burdens "among which the greatest are caused by the levies and impositions which are made without our permission."[85] Since the new officials were to receive the usual salary and fees, the size of illegal taxes would have had to have been large indeed to match the new burden that the Provençals were now called upon to bear.

Shortly after the estates terminated, Bullion, accompanied by Guise and a maître des requêtes named Dreux d'Aubray, set out for Aix to see that Parlement quickly registered the edict. Here on July 31 an unexpected and unwanted development occurred to give the beleaguered Provençals a reprieve: the plague broke out in their capital just as Bullion and his party arrived. They departed immediately, leaving the town to its own devices. As the plague worsened, many municipal and royal officials also left. Since there was no community free from the plague that was large enough to accommodate the entire Parlement, it was decided to divide the court. One part led by the first president, D'Oppede, went to Salon, and the other under Laurent de Coriolis moved in Pertius.[86]

The first Coriolis who settled in Aix had been general of the galleys of Malta, but in his new environment he soon became a jurist and assesseur. He was one of those who negotiated with Louis XI to secure recognition for the privileges of Provence at the time of the reunion with France. As soldiers, presidents of Parlement, municipal officials, barons, and syndics of the nobility, his descendants continued to serve the Provençal cause. The ease with which they shifted back and forth between robe and sword is further evidence that no clear social line was drawn between the two professions. Laurent's own father had served bravely as a soldier before becoming a president of Parlement, and the son was to follow in his footsteps in the days ahead.[87]

84. Ibid., fols. 325v–33v; Pearl, *Guise and Provence*, pp. 188–89.

85. B. Mun., Aix-en-Provence, ms. 794, fols. 196–202.

86. Pearl, *Guise and Provence*, pp. 190–95; Pillorget, *Les mouvements insurrectionnels*, pp. 319–22.

87. *Les Bouches-du-Rhône: Encyclopédie départmentale*, ed. Paul Masson (Marseilles, 1931), 4: pt. 2,147–48.

D'Oppede, as first president, naturally claimed that the authority of Parlement resided in his group, but as a client of Richelieu, his motives were suspected by the more stalwart defenders of Provençal liberties, among them Coriolis. Quarrels and jurisdictional disputes followed. In March 1630 Coriolis assumed the red robe of a first president, thereby symbolically claiming sovereign status for the councillors at Pertius. There were appeals to the king's council, which favored D'Oppede, and to Guise, who was caught between his desire to prevent his relations with Paris from deteriorating further and his need to retain the loyalty of the Provençals in order to have a firm base of support when dealing with his enemies. He must have felt considerable relief when the cessation of the plague enabled both Parlements to return to Aix early in September 1630, theoretically reunited but in fact bitterly divided into two factions, of which the larger one was that of Coriolis.[88]

In the meantime the officers of the estates had not been idle. On January 21, 1630, the procureurs nés et joints met at Rians and voted to transfer the office of the estates from *peste*-ridden Aix to Salon where the D'Oppede faction of Parlement then sat. This done, those present launched an attack against the edict on the élus and the excessive number of troops the province was required to support. Such protests, however, did not prevent the royal commissioner from asking the assembly of the communities that met the following month for additional funds to support the war in Italy. The Provençals sought to meet this threat by directing the bishop of Sisteron to intercept Cardinal Richelieu on his way to Italy.[89] In April the communities assembled again to hear the crown try to justify the war. They complained about Parlement's issuing decrees which infringed on their right to administer the province and sent a deputation to the king at Lyons to protest edicts, such as the one on the élus, that were prejudicial to their interests. On May 29 the procureurs du pays nés et joints met at Salon to hear the report of their deputations. Richelieu had not been contacted, but they had given their petition to Louis and learned to their chagrin that the Court of Accounts was to be moved permanently to Toulon. Guise authorized the communities to assemble again on July 16, but hardly had the deputies arrived than he dismissed them because he had learned that the king opposed the meeting.[90]

September found Provence seething with discontent. For the moment, at least, Louis was unwilling to tolerate further assemblies of estates or communities, and Parlement, although once more reunited in Aix, was divided into two bitterly hostile factions. It was into this unhealthy climate that Dreux d'Aubray returned on September 19. His mission was to see that the élections were established, the Chamber of Accounts transferred to Toulon,

88. Pearl, *Guise and Provence*, pp. 195–97; Pillorget, *Les mouvements insurrectionnels*, pp. 320–23.
89. AD, Bouches-du-Rhône, C 17, fols. 1–14v, 25–25v, 35v–36.
90. Ibid., fols. 101–10v, 133–35v, 167v–68.

and other measures taken to ensure the obedience of the province and its more complete incorporation into France. D'Aubray's assignment had been known for several weeks, ample time for anyone who desired to organize a riot, especially since Guise was conveniently absent at court. On the twentieth the mob struck. D'Aubray escaped by scrambling over the rooftops, but his carriage was burned, and he had to leave the city. Coriolis and his faction were left in control. They had acted to defend the liberties of Provence and perhaps also out of irritation at the refusal of the crown to renew the paulette except at an exorbitant price. The lower classes had been easy to arouse because of high prices, heavy taxes, and the prospect that the creation of the élus would lead to even greater exactions.[91]

It was one thing for the Provençals to stir up a mob, however, and another to organize a province to defend itself, or at least to give the appearance of being prepared to do so, with so much determination that the crown would abandon its program of curbing their liberties. Already on September 15 an assembly of the nobility, about fifty in number, had been held at Pertius, apparently at the instigation of the Coriolis faction in Parlement. They appointed a committee of six to work with their syndics to prevent the implementation of the hated edicts. It was rumored that the committee was also to organize armed resistance and to raise the necessary funds by securing contributions from their fellow nobles.[92]

On September 23 the procureurs du pays met in Aix and proceeded more discreetly. They protested the decision of the Chamber of Accounts to move to Toulon as the king had directed and noted in their minutes that D'Aubray had departed because of "a little noise." The vicar general of Aix was asked to go to that frightened official to seek his favor.[93] On October 9 the procureurs du pays nés et joints and the committee elected by the nobles met in Aix and decided that the three estates should assemble at the same time and place but in separate buildings. To meet together would be to hold the estates without royal permission, a revolutionary act that they were not prepared to take. The permission of Parlement, so easily obtainable, was enough to justify an assembly of the communities, and the clergy and nobility had traditionally been freer to meet at the behest of their prelates and elected officers respectively.[94]

Meanwhile the unrest continued. A false report of Effiat's death caused a celebration in Aix. As if to make certain that he was dead, he was burned in effigy. On October 18 Parlement, instead of taking measures to restore

91. Pillorget, *Les mouvements insurrectionnels*, pp. 323–28; Pearl, *Guise and Provence*, pp. 198–99. As early as March 6, 1630, the king's council had ordered that the élections be established in Provence in spite of the opposition of the procureurs. AN, E 102, fol. 293.

92. AD, Bouches-du-Rhône, C 108, fols. 32v–38; Pillorget, *Les mouvements insurrectionnels*, pp. 328–29.

93. AD, Bouches-du-Rhône, C 16, fol. 49–49v.

94. Ibid., fol. 53–53v, C 108, fols. 40v–41.

order, refused to register the edict creating the élus because their activities would destroy the liberties of the province, and their salaries and fees would constitute an excessive burden on the people. The Chamber of Accounts was criticized for accepting the edict, remonstrances were sent to the king, and anyone who accepted the post of élu was threatened with a 10,000 livre fine.[95]

Aix must have been tense when the three orders assembled separately a week later. The assesseur, who was also one of the procureurs du pays by virtue of his office, told the deputies of the communities that the purpose of the meeting was to inform them of the attempt to establish élections in the province, "which will be the most prejudicial thing not only in regard to the goods, but also to the liberties, even the very lives of the inhabitants of this *pays*, for in addition to the fact that the edict of élections means the annihilation of all the usages, customs, privileges and liberties of this *pays*, it will deprive the inhabitants of the disposition of their goods."[96] After declaring that élections would turn them into "miserable slaves," he praised Parlement for its actions the week before and said that Guise, who had just come to Marseilles, had promised his support. He then attacked the transfer of the Chamber of Accounts to Toulon on the ground that the crown believed that it would be easier to obtain the verification of unpopular edicts if that court were far from the center of the province where it could be more easily subjected to outside influences.[97]

After the assesseur had finished, the deputies recessed for three days in order to have time to consider what action to take. When they reassembled on October 28, they voted unanimously to send a deputation to the king to protest the edict on the élections and the transfer of the Chamber of Accounts to Toulon. To ensure that the individual communities defended their privileges and those of the province, the deputies directed that the archives be searched for relevant documents and that they be printed and distributed. As if suspecting that this would not be enough, they then voted taxes to purchase 4,000 muskets and 2,000 pikes. This action was taken "under the good pleasure of the king," and the official reason given was to provide the towns with the means to defend themselves from disorderly troops passing through the province, but the king's councillors could hardly fail to interpret it as a thinly veiled threat. Perhaps the deputies intended that they should. Those in Paris must be made to realize that the establishment of the élections was not worth the cost involved.[98]

Guise had remained in Marseilles during the meeting. Belatedly the communities had asked his permission to assemble, but as far as can be

95. Pearl, *Guise and Provence*, pp. 200–02.

96. Ibid., p. 202. A longer extract from the speech has been printed in *Les Bouches-du-Rhône: Encyclopédie départementale*, 3:372–73.

97. AD, Bouches-du-Rhône, C 16, fols. 61–62v.

98. Ibid., fols. 63–65, 67v–69.

ascertained, they were prepared to proceed along their dangerous course without further consultation. Guise must have been in a quandary. If he acted firmly to suppress the disorders, he would lose the support of the Provençals. If he did nothing, he would forfeit what remained of the king's waning faith in him. For the moment, at least, he pretended to favor the Provençals by offering to go to court on their behalf, but at the same time he pointed out that he needed money to maintain the dignity of his office and to serve the king and the province. As yet the Provençals had voted him nothing for 1629 or 1630. The deputies, however, either mistrusted his intentions or his ability to be of service, for they would do no more than promise him satisfaction after he had returned from court.[99]

Meanwhile conditions were deteriorating in Aix. A November visitor reported that "all the city was in arms then." The nobility "had rendered these *élus* so detestable and so horrible to the populace, that they had formed an opposition party, named the *cascaveù*.... The sedition was so violent that the homes of solid citizens were ransacked on the simple suspicion that they favored the party of the *élus*.... They were resolved to close the gates to the King himself, they said, if he came in order to establish the *élus*."[100] One opponent of the élus prepared a tract on the subject. He began: "I am the truth, this goddess, daughter of time, today so little known and so strongly distrusted in king's palaces." He went on to develop a contract theory of government in which the people promised obedience to their sovereign, who in return was to provide good government. "Your Majesty cannot violate the conventions under which this province was reunited to the crown of France; yes, Sire, for Your Majesty loves truth itself."[101]

Early in November the first *consul* of Aix was driven from the city because he was suspected of favoring D'Oppede and the establishment of the élections. Coriolis encouraged the *consul*'s oppressed peasants to plunder his estates, and there were further riots in Aix. Guise became angered by these excesses, but at the urging of the representatives of the estates, he agreed not to take military action and renewed his promise to help obtain the suppression of the unpopular edicts. In mid-November, Guise thought that he had received a reprieve from making the difficult decision of choosing between the court and Provence. Word reached him that Richelieu had been dismissed. Elated at this "good news," he notified Parlement and the

---

99. Ibid., fols. 67, 69v–70v. There is no evidence that the deputies knew that the king had promised Guise 150,000 livres to be derived from the sale of the offices in the new élections and 50,000 from those in the Chamber of Accounts. If the élections were not established, he was to get nothing. Another bribe of 40,000 livres was promised to him for moving the Chamber of Accounts to Toulon. Pillorget, *Les mouvements insurrectionnels*, p. 323 n.59. If the crown sought to buy Guise's cooperation, the duke in turn was seeking to form an alliance among the magnates against his enemy, Richelieu. Georges Mongrédien, *Les journée des dupes* (Paris, 1961), pp. 55, 61–62.

100. Pearl, *Guise and Provence*, p. 204.

101. Ibid., p. 205.

procureurs of the estates that he was leaving at once for Paris. The procureurs rushed deputies to him to make certain that his visit to court would be on their behalf as well as in his own interest. Thus, the Day of Dupes found Provence still without élus but in a state of turmoil that approached insurrection in Aix, the capital, itself.[102]

5. THE ESTATES OF LANGUEDOC

The relations between the crown and the estates of Languedoc were relatively cordial during the first year of the Richelieu regime. When Louis asked the estates that opened in March 1625 for additional funds to support some troops, those present had only to dispatch a deputy to court who, with the assistance of the duchess of Montmorency, secured the cancellation of this burden. Furthermore Louis did not ask for an increase in taxes, a concession that was mitigated by the need to levy 400,000 livres to pay part of the 720,000 livres they had promised him in 1624 just before Richelieu had entered the government.[103]

The relations worsened after Marillac became keeper of the seals in June 1626. Louis did not ask the estates that met the following month for an additional grant, but his officials unilaterally increased the salt tax in upper Languedoc.[104] The estates complained bitterly at this action, which they believed violated pledges that had been made to them. These "edicts and decrees of your council," they bluntly declared in their cahier, "... are the most sacred and religious bonds that can be found concerning the faith and word of kings towards their subjects. They [the subjects] would be reduced to that full measure of misfortune of being able henceforth neither to hope for anything from the contracts that they had the honor to make with your majesty nor to find any security in the pledges that were given them on his behalf."[105]

Montmorency himself attended the estates that opened in Béziers on February 27, 1627. In his opening address he expressed his joy at being back in Languedoc after a long absence. While at court he had continued to assist their deputies in the defense of their privileges, which he guarded as jealously as they. The most notable victory he and his wife had obtained, he reported, was to thwart the crown's attempt to appropriate all the *equivalent*.

---

102. Ibid., pp. 205–06; AD, Bouches-du-Rhône, C 16, fols. 76–77, 78v–79; *Lettres de Peiresc*, ed. P. Tamizey de Larroque (Paris, 1890), 2:261–64; Pillorget, *Les mouvements insurrectionnels*, pp. 332–39. Louis de Marillac received somewhat similar information concerning Richelieu's presumed loss of favor. Richelieu, *Lettres*, 4:10 n.1.

103. AD, Hérault, *procès-verbal* of the estates of March–May 1625, A 44, nos. 100–03; *Mercure François* 11 (1625): 749–50.

104. AD, Hérault, procès-verbal of the estates of July–August 1626.

105. Paul Gachon, *Les Etats de Languedoc et l'édit de Béziers, 1632* (Paris, 1887), p. 40.

This tax on the sale of meat, fish, and wine was farmed under the direction of the estates, and only 70,000 livres of the proceeds were traditionally assigned to the crown. Montmorency's victory, however, was by no means complete, for the government sought other sources of revenue from Languedoc, including the creation of a number of offices to sell. Among them there were three receivers of the tailles in each diocese whose total annual wages came to 70,000 livres. The councillors in the Chamber of Accounts at Montpellier generously showed a deputation from the estates this decree. As they must have foreseen, it touched off strong protests.[106]

It was not until April 27 that Montmorency informed the estates that Louis wanted them to approve a special grant of 800,000 livres to be collected over a two-year period. He urged the deputies to forgo bargaining and give the king what he desired in return for the many favors he had granted, including abandoning his effort to obtain all the equivalent. The estates refused, in part at least because some of the language in the tax commission seemed to threaten their privileges, but when Montmorency returned two days later and blamed the unfortunate terminology on an insignificant clerk, they were sufficiently mollified to vote Louis 300,000 livres to be paid over a two-year period.[107]

Some historians have argued that kings always asked the estates for more than they anticipated obtaining. Hence the refusal of the estates to vote all that was requested did not actually limit their taxing power. On this occasion, however, the contrary can be proved. In instructions dated April 25, the sieur de Nesmond, a maître des requêtes, was told to hasten to Languedoc while the estates were still in session. After the estates had voted the requested 800,000 livres, he was to ask that the taillon also be increased as the Assembly of Notables had recommended.[108] This shows that Louis's advisers expected to receive the full 800,000 livres and hoped for more. It also reveals that they did not fully trust Montmorency. If he knew of the taillon increase in advance, it was feared that he would leak the information to the deputies, who in turn would appropriate less than the 800,000 livres in order to be able to honor the second request. The refusal of the estates to vote even half the amount Louis desired caused Nesmond to refrain from mentioning the taillon, and Louis was left with few alternatives but to do without for another year. To increase the chance that he would be persuaded to do so, the estates voted his mother 100,000 livres, apparently without having been solicited to do so. Montmorency received 10,800 livres because of the good care he had taken of the province and 9,480 for his

106. AD, Hérault, procès-verbal of the estates of February–May 1627, esp. fols. 2–3v, 17–17v, 35–37, 46–47v.

107. Ibid., fols. 60–66v. *IAD, Haute-Garonne, sér. C*, ed. Ad. Baudouin (Toulouse, 1903), 2:237–40.

108. Gabriel Hanotaux, *Origines de l'institution des intendants des provinces* (Paris, 1884), pp. 253–55.

guards. His wife, secretaries, and various royal officials were not forgotten. It was a costly affair, but it was nevertheless a good bargain if the grateful recipients were able to convince Louis that he should forget the taillon and take 500,000 less than he requested.[109]

The Huguenot revolt in Languedoc was near its height when the estates opened in Toulouse on March 2, 1628. The prince of Condé, who was in the province with an army, gave the opening address in which he branded the Huguenots heretics, rebels, and republicans. For four months his troops had not been paid, he explained, and this had led them to be disorderly. Money was necessary to provide for their support. The king would furnish part of the sum, but the estates must supply the rest. In return he promised to respect their privileges and to maintain order in his army. That evening Montmorency gave an elaborate ballet in his honor, but he is reported to have slept through most of the event. Two days later Condé departed for Foix, where he laid siege to Pamiers.[110]

The estates proceeded slowly with their work because many deputies were late to arrive. Their first significant act was to plead with Condé and Montmorency not to levy taxes without their consent, a breach of their privileges that had been committed in order to supply the troops. It was not until Condé returned to Toulouse on March 22 after taking Pamiers that he finally informed the estates that the expenses of his army came to 2,242,390 livres per year and that they were expected to bear half the costs. Horrified at the magnitude of the proposed tax, the deputies appealed to Montmorency to intercede for them. That sympathetic noble sought out the prince, who was his brother-in-law, and they quickly arranged that the estates would borrow 360,000 livres, which they would loan to the king. The king in return would enable them to repay the debt by reducing taxes by that amount during the next two years. In gratitude the estates voted Condé 48,000 livres, his wife 12,000, Montmorency a total of 50,280, including the costs of his guards and other expenses, his wife 7,500, Ventadour 20,000, and many lesser gifts including what must have seemed like a princely sum of 1,500 livres to Condé's secretary.[111]

Richelieu's memoirs contain an assertion that Condé had promised Louis that he would have an edict establishing élections in Languedoc verified at this time in return for 100,000 livres to be derived from the sale of the newly created offices. However, when Condé realized how strongly the estates opposed the élections, he abandoned the project in return for a gift from them of 20,000 écus. The combined grant designated by the estates for Condé and his wife came to this amount, but no evidence has been found to

109. AD, Hérault, procès-verbal of the estates of February–May 1627, fols. 67–69, 100v–02.

110. *Mercure François* (Paris, 1629), 14 (1628): 64–73.

111. AD, Hérault, procès-verbal of the estates of March–June 1628, fols. 11, 23–24v, 35–35v, 38v–40v, 45v–51v, 57–57v, 65–65v, 85v, 102–02v, 106v–07v, 113; Gachon, *Les Etats de Languedoc*, pp. 83, 129.

suggest that the estates gave the money in return for his failure to establish élections or even that Louis wanted him to do so.[112] On May 30 Louis wrote Condé saying that he had granted all the requests of the estates of Languedoc that he possibly could in view of his financial situation. He reproved Condé for failing to maintain discipline among his troops but not for neglecting to establish the élections. On June 8 the deputies who had borne the cahier to the king reported that he had not only accepted their modest offer but also had agreed to increase the tax on salt less than originally intended.[113]

The real question is why Louis accepted a loan of only 360,000 livres when he had requested a gift of over 1.1 million. Undoubtedly the latter figure was more than the war-torn province could have paid, a point that the influential persons who received lavish presents from the estates are certain to have made. More important, Louis and his advisers in all likelihood had come to believe that a heavy tax would serve only to increase discontent in a province that was already in the midst of a rebellion. It would be wiser to take what they could now and impose changes once the Huguenots had been crushed.

Montmorency ordered five dioceses in lower Languedoc to meet at Pézenas in December 1628 and the twelve dioceses of upper Languedoc to assemble at Limoux the following month. Confronted by the problem of disorderly troops, who would behave still worse if not supplied, the former assembly accorded 140,912 livres and the latter 121,329. The regular meeting of the estates had to be postponed, however, and it did not finally open at Pézenas until April 27, 1629. By this time the Huguenots were nearly defeated, and the king was approaching Languedoc. The prospect that they would soon be confronted by their sovereign at the head of a victorious army did not put the deputies in a more cooperative frame of mind, although on May 27 one of their syndics informed them that the entire court was determined to destroy their rights. They first displayed their independence by annulling the deliberations of the rump December and January meetings on the grounds that they were prejudicial to the liberties and franchises of the province. Neither an individual diocese nor a group of dioceses was to have the power to tax. This right was reserved for the three estates of the entire province. Only Montmorency's personal popularity and the realization that he and the deputies who had attended the two assemblies had reacted to an emergency situation led the estates to reverse their initial decision a few days later.[114]

In the midst of this debate the estates learned that on August 3, 1628,

112. Richelieu, *Mém*, SHF, 9:303.

113. AD, Hérault, procès-verbal of the estates of March–June 1628, fols. 58–59, 83v–84; Louis to Condé, Musée Condé, M 2, fol. 107.

114. *HL*, 11:1031–32; Gachon, *Les Etats de Languedoc*, p. 202 n.4; *IAD, Haute-Garonne, sér. C*, 2:242–43; AD, Hérault, procès-verbal of the estates of April–August 1629, fols. 6–7.

Louis had ordered his treasurers in the Bureau of Finances in Languedoc to increase the taillon from the traditional 85,600 livres to 285,600 livres and to apportion it among the twenty-two dioceses, this in violation of the right of the estates to consent to and divide taxes. The Parlement of Toulouse was resisting, but the Chamber of Accounts and Court of Aids had cooperated with the king. Officials of the towns and dioceses had been harassed, and one of them had been imprisoned, The usual protests followed, but both the king and the estates appeared willing to let matters proceed in a leisurely course, each in the belief that time was on its side. It was not until July 15, a little more than two weeks after Louis had concluded the peace of Alès with the Huguenots, that one of his councillors, the sieur de Viguier, informed the estates that he wanted 500,000 to 600,000 écus to meet his heavy expenses. Far more alarming was the news that arrived shortly thereafter that the long-delayed union of the Court of Aids and Chamber of Accounts at Montpellier had taken place and that an edict had been issued creating twenty-two élections in Languedoc.[115]

The Chamber of Accounts at Montpellier had not been created until 1522, long after the Parlement of Toulouse and the estates had secured firm places in the institutional structure of the province. As a result, its jurisdiction was limited and its authority was of secondary importance. Even the treasurers in the Bureau of Finances had largely escaped from its control. To strengthen its position the chamber had sought a union with the Court of Aids in Montpellier. In 1617 and again in 1624, the estates had blocked this step, but now they were confronted with an enlarged and presumably stonger court whose officers were determined to enjoy an important role in the financial affairs of the province even at the cost of surrendering its traditional rights. Indeed the two courts registered the edict of union on July 21 and two days later accepted without protest the edict creating the élections. Clearly the estates could look for no assistance here. With the Parlement of Toulouse and their governor, they were left with the task of defending the liberties of Languedoc against the authority of the crown.[116]

Louis's justification for creating the élus was that they would prevent illegal taxation, thereby lightening the burden on his people. He could hardly have been unaware, however, that to pay the 700 new officials who were to staff the twenty-two élections would in itself require a tremendous exertion. Their salaries came to 200,360 livres per year. In addition, they

---

115. AD, Hérault, procès-verbal of the estates of April–August 1629, 5v, 11–14v, 93v–96v; *HL*, 11:1042–43; Gachon, *Les Etats de Languedoc*, pp. 201–06.

116. Gachon, *Les Etats de Languedoc*, p. 206; Jean-Paul Charmeil, *Les trésoriers de France à l'époque de la Fronde* (Paris, 1964), pp. 283–84, 306–07; *Loix municipales et économiques de Languedoc*, ed. Jean Albisson (Toulouse, 1786), 4:260–62. Richelieu's memoirs state that the Chamber of Accounts, whose membership was largely Protestant, wanted to be united with the Court of Aids to forestall a possible union with the strongly Catholic Parlement of Toulouse. Richelieu, *Mém.* SHF, 9:303.

enjoyed various perquisites that included 12 percent of the direct royal taxes that were collected. As the customary impositions were 824,317 livres per year, this sum alone came to 103,030 livres. If the king succeeded in enlarging the tax, the perquisites of the officials would increase proportionally. Furthermore the estates would have to give the élus a percentage of the money levied to pay their debts and support their activities. This figure would vary somewhat from year to year, but based on the appropriations the estates voted in 1628, it would be 87,268 livres. Thus the costs of the élus would come to about 400,000 livres annually, that is, from 26 to 28 percent of the sum collected. As opposed to this figure, the attorney general of the Parlement of Toulouse estimated that the estates could collect taxes for less than 40,000 livres. The creation of élections, then, would increase the cost of tax collection about tenfold. And this was not all, for the élus also received a percentage of the taxes collected for the individual communities.[117]

The élus, of course, would bring some immediate financial advantage to the crown. It was anticipated that they would pay 4 million livres for their offices. Once they took charge of tax collection, the amount that was levied without the king's permission could be reduced. Far more important to the crown's thinking, one suspects, was that the élus could impose taxes without the consent of the estates as they did in Normandy and elsewhere where there were élections. Furthermore once the provincial and diocesan estates were deprived of their tax-collecting powers, they would become minor nuisances or perhaps even disappear.[118]

Cardinal Richelieu had not played a direct role in establishing the élections in Dauphiné, Burgundy, and Provence. His memoirs scarcely mention the subject and when they do, as in the case of Burgundy, it is to sympathize with the estates.[119] But he was more vocal when he dealt with Languedoc, either because he believed that the abuses of the estates were worse there or because of his jealousy of Montmorency, whom he wished to destroy. His memoirs put it this way:

> The king had long desired to establish the *élus* in this province to prevent the disorders that come from the abuses that the estates and dioceses committed in imposing every year on the province all that seemed good to them. This disorder had reached the point in this province, which was on the surface exempt from the *tailles*, that for four years it had paid three or four million *livres* annually. The authority of the king was scarcely known there. Levies were made in the name of the estates and the name of the

117. *Loix municipales*, 4:257–60. The estimate of the cost of the élus was made by the syndic of the estates. Gachon, *Les Etats de Languedoc*, pp. 211–15. The syndic erred in saying that there were to be 490 officers. The edict called for 34 officers in 14 élections and 28 in each of the remaining 8, making a total of 700.

118. Gachon, *Les Etats de Languedoc*, pp. 215–17.

119. Richelieu, *Mém.*, Michaud, sér. II, 8:149.

provincial governor had almost more weight than that of his majesty. He favored or disfavored through this company [the estates] everyone in Languedoc who was on good or bad terms with him.[120]

Having offered evidence to demonstrate the need for élections, the compiler of Richelieu's memoirs sought to add weight to his arguments by declaring that "the late king who knew of these drawbacks had desired to establish *élections* but had not dared to do so."[121]

This unprecedented effort to justify the erection of élections suggests that Richelieu was more involved in their creation in Languedoc than elsewhere, but direct evidence is less conclusive than one would desire. He had been in Nîmes with the king in mid-July when the edict on the élus had been prepared, and he had moved to Montpellier on July 18, less than a week before the union of the Chamber of Accounts and the Court of Aids and the registration of the edict on the élus took place. Here he had fallen ill but had set out for Montauban via Pézenas anyway. He had not intended to linger at Pézenas in spite of the fact that the deliberations of the estates were reaching a critical phase, but his illness forced him to remain there as Montmorency's guest until August 6.[122] The estates visited him en masse on July 28, but little of consequence appears to have taken place. Three days later they voted to increase the taillon from the traditional 82,800 livres to 165,600 livres for that year only. Still the total fell far short of the 282,800 livres that Louis had ordered to be collected. More serious from his point of view, the deputies did not even bother to debate on whether they would grant all or part of the additional 500,000 or 600,000 écus that he had requested.[123]

By August 1 news from Montpellier concerning the registration of the edict on the élections had reached the estates. The seriousness of the threat caused them to expand the deputation they had already elected to carry their cahiers to the king. They further resolved that "in view of the certainty that the establishment of the élus in this province would entirely take away and destroy all the franchises and liberties which it has happily enjoyed under the just and glorious rule of our invincible monarch and the kings his predecessors for many centuries, we very expressly charge the deputies to court to speed their departure ... in order to obtain from his unequaled justice and goodness the revocation of the edict and the continuation of the ancient order of the estates and twenty-two dioceses of the said province."[124] They were also to seek the revocation of the edict uniting the Chamber of Accounts and the Court of Aids and a reduction in the sales taxes.[125]

120. Ibid., SHF, 9:302.

121. Ibid., p. 303.

122. Richelieu, *Lettres*, 3:386, 393, 394, 396, 398, 402; Gachon, *Les Etats de Languedoc*, p. 206.

123. AD, Hérault, procès-verbal of the estates of April–August 1629, fols. 114, 122v–23v.

124. Ibid., fols. 123v–24.

125. Ibid., fol. 125. See also the cahier of the estates in the same archives and the extract from it in Gachon, *Les Etats de Languedoc*, pp. 278–79.

On August 2 the estates voted the routine taxes and gratifications, but near the close of their deliberations Viguier appeared bearing a lettre de cachet from the king dated July 14 and a decree dated July 15 ordering the estates to disband. Louis and his advisers had anticipated that the estates would be obstinate and had prepared the letter and decree at Nîmes at the very time they drew up the edicts creating the élections and uniting the two courts in Montpellier. Viguier had waited until it was obvious that the estates had no intention of voting a significant sum and then had delivered his blow.[126]

There is no direct evidence that Richelieu participated in Viguier's decision to disband the estates at this moment, but because he was in the same town, it is difficult to believe that he was not consulted. We also lack conclusive proof that Richelieu negotiated with anyone concerning the élections while he was in Pézenas. One of Montmorency's contemporaries reported that Richelieu had convinced the duke that he should try to persuade the three estates to approve the edict on the élections, but the minutes of their deliberations give no indication that any such attempt was made.[127] Richelieu's only contemporary allusion to the élections was in a letter to Louis from Pézenas dated August 5 in which he reported that Condé had paid him a brief visit in which he had insisted on his blind obedience to his king. Then Richelieu added: "It is impossible to describe to you his joy over the establishment of the *élus* in this province."[128] This episode suggests that Richelieu had been deeply involved in the élections and was reporting to his sovereign that Condé had accepted the decision, although it stripped the privileges of a province that had been in the hands of his wife's family for about a century. It is perhaps also significant that Richelieu failed to mention Montmorency's attitude or actions.

Whether Montmorency momentarily agreed to support the edict on the élections cannot be ascertained, but it is certain that both he and Ventadour were soon furthering the provincial cause. Nor were they alone, for although neither the provincial nor the diocesan estates were to meet again until long after Marillac had been removed from his post as keeper of the seals, they had their syndics and other officers who were free to act. Furthermore the three estates had elected a deputation to obtain the revocation of the edict on the élections before they had been disbanded, and the towns had *consuls* who could send deputies and write letters of protest. Finally Parlement

126. AD, Hérault, procès-verbal of the estates of April–August 1629, fol. 127–27v.

127. *HL*, 11 : 1045. Bassompierre states that the estates refused to verify the edict on the élus, an act which led the cardinal to dismiss them and to forbid them to assemble in the future. However, his dates are wrong, and the estates were not asked to verify the edict. *Journal de ma vié. Mémoires du Maréchal de Bassompierre*, ed. Audoin de La Cropte de Chantérac (Paris, 1877), 4:56.

128. Richelieu, *Lettres*, 3:404.

refused to register either the edict on the élections or the one uniting the two financial courts in Montpellier.[129]

The result was that the king's council had to spend a disproportionately large percentage of its time in 1630 answering petitions from Languedoc and endeavoring to break local resistance so that the élus could be appointed and begin to perform their duties. By January 1630 the council was already complaining that some badly disposed persons had written the king opposing the élections and that others were stirring up sedition in Languedoc by their discourses. Several diocesan estates sought to use the need to audit the accounts of their tax collectors as an excuse to meet, only to have the council assign that task to an intendant of justice who was then in the province. More serious were the problems of Nicolas Mignot who had contracted to sell the offices in the élections. The treasurers of the Bureau of Finances would not permit the élus to have all the financial perquisites to which they were entitled, he complained. Other local officials were putting obstacles in the way of the appointment of the élus and their performance of their duties after they had been named. In some smaller towns, which were to be seats of the new élections, there were too few people with the means to buy offices. The 200,360 livres designated for their annual salaries was not available. As a result, Mignot confessed on September 18 that the sale of offices had been delayed, and he could not make his promised payments to the king.[130]

The council tried to straighten out these matters, On September 20 it even had to annul a decree of the Parlement of Toulouse designed to prevent the élus from performing their duties and to forbid that company from exercising any further jurisdiction in the matter. In spite of these difficulties, 940,000 livres flowed into the royal treasury in 1630, a sum substantially in excess of the amount that had been collected in any previous year of the reign, and all of it without the consent of the estates. In 1629 Louis had conquered his Catholic subjects in Languedoc as well as his Protestant ones, but the province was seething with discontent.[131]

6. THE ESTATES IN THE PYRÉNÉES

The year 1630 was the one that Marillac had set aside to create élections in the Pyrenean states. They were probably saved until the last because they were the least important, but the unsettled situation in Béarn especially may have contributed to the decision to delay action until resistance to the élections in the larger provinces had been partially overcome.

129. Gachon, *Les Etats de Languedoc*, pp. 207–10, 218–21; *HL*, 11:1045–47.

130. AN, E 101ᵃ, fols. 508–08v, E 101ᵇ, fols. 22, 199–201, 389, E 102, fols. 205, 315–17, 392, 468, E 103ᵃ, fols. 410, 413, E 103ᵇ, fols. 51, 344, 489, 509, 540, E 104, fols. 149, 204, 272, 329, 380, 386–93.

131. *Loix municipales*, 4:262–64; Mallet, p. 206.

During the preceding decade, matters had gone about as well as could be expected under the circumstances. In 1620 Louis had issued an edict uniting Béarn and Navarre to the crown of France, and at the head of an army he had enforced earlier orders that the Protestants return the Catholic church property that they had confiscated. These measures had less effect on their estates than one might have expected. The objective of the edict of union had been to ensure that if the throne of France passed to a collateral line because a king failed to produce a male heir, these two frontier states would fall into the same hands rather than go to a daughter of the king as their laws of inheritance then required. In the edict Louis specifically promised to respect the privileges of the two states. The one institutional change he did make was to create a Parlement with its seat at Pau to serve both of them and the contiguous viscounty of Soule as well. The estates of Navarre protested the loss of their judicial autonomy, but in 1624 Louis compelled them to accept the new arrangement. As a gesture toward the particularisms of its inhabitants, he did agree that the new court should be called the Parlement of Navarre, but it continued to sit at Pau. Louis's insistence that the confiscated property of the Catholic church be restored and that the clergy resume their seats in the estates did alter the composition of the two assemblies, but except in the religious sphere, there was more continuity than change in royal policy.[132]

When the estates of Béarn met in Pau during the summer of 1622, the bishop of Lescar assumed the presidency that his predecessors had held before the triumph of the Protestant Reformation and the other clergymen joined the nobility to form a single house, as had been the former practice. The meeting itself was devoted to issues growing out of the religious settlement, complaints about the number of royal officials, the bad behavior of troops, efforts to demolish all fortified places except those located at Pau and Navarrenx, and the usual deputations to court. The one serious violation of the privileges of the estates occurred when Epernon, the new governor, sought to have their syndic removed from office because he was a Protestant.[133]

In 1624 the count of Gramont replaced Epernon as governor, and he and his descendants held this post until 1789. The change was a happy one. The Gramonts, whose lands lay in the region and who claimed to be the sovereigns of Bidache, had a deep sympathy for the autonomous pretensions of the Béarnais and did all in their power to support their interests at court. The Béarnais responded by appropriating from 20,000 to 38,500 livres

132. Pierre Tucoo-Chala, *La vicomté de Béarn et le problème de sa souveraineté des origines à 1620* (Bordeaux, 1961), pp. 198–99; F. Loirette, "L'administration royale en Béarn de l'union à l'intendance, 1620–1682," *XVIIᵉ Siècle* 65 (1964): 66–73.

133. AD, Basses-Pyrénées, C 708, esp. fols. 108–11, 121, 179v–81, 254v–62, 277v–79, 294–307.

annually for them, although they gave the king only 29,000 to 35,000 livres plus 20,000 more for the subsistence of the troops.[134]

The central theme of this decade of Béarnais history was not a quarrel between the crown and the estates over the size of the annual tax but rather between the resurgent Catholics and the Protestants. The former became increasingly numerous, but the latter surrendered their once-preferred positions only grudgingly. Louis was anything but an unbiased umpire. In 1627 he saw to it that a Protestant syndic was forced from office.[135]

The history of the estates of Navarre during the years immediately after the reunion with France cannot be reconstituted. The estates met annually, and Gramont, who became their governor at the same time he assumed that post in Béarn, protected their interests, and they in return gave him ample rewards.[136]

The estates of Bigorre met every few months during the 1620s. This activity was not provoked by an internal Protestant problem, for although Louis had ordered that Catholic church property be restored there in 1617, as elsewhere in the hereditary Bourbon lands, the Protestants offered little opposition. Routine taxes caused few problems. The don gratuit, or *donation* as it was called, had become fixed at 7,000 livres in 1607, and there it stood at the time of the Revolution. In a similar manner the taillon had become fixed at 1,674 livres in spite of Henry IV's efforts to increase the amount. Rather, the activity of the estates must be attributed to the necessity to support the troops brought into the region because of the wars with the Protestants and to a lesser extent to the need of the estates to levy taxes to pay their debts.[137]

In June 1620 the estates had to send a deputy to Bordeaux to persuade their governor, the duke of Mayenne, not to make them contribute 1,800 livres toward the support of his company. Louis's march on Béarn later that year and the Protestant revolt stepped up the need for more revenue to support the king and to defend their towns. To obtain Mayenne's cooperation they offered him 3,000 livres. Pressures for money for the military seemed to have slackened soon thereafter, but in 1628 the estates were asked

134. Loirette, "L'administration royale," p. 72 n.3.

135. For the procès verbaux of the estates, see AD, Basses-Pyrénées, C 709–10, and for their cahiers, C 688, fols. 219–37, and C 689, fols. 1–99. Marc Forissier, *Histoire de la réforme en Béarn* (Tarbes, 1951), pp. 131–42.

136. Alain Destrée, *La Basse-Navarre et ses institutions de 1620 à la Révolution* (Saragossa, 1955), pp. 70–79. Destrée, p. 197, says that the estates of Navarre met annually between 1620 and 1789, but he lists no meetings for 1621 and for 1623–32 (p. 421). Proof that the estates were held from 1624 through 1628 can be found in a petition the syndic presented to the Parlement at Pau in December 1628. AN, K 1233, no. 55.

137. Gilbert Pène, *Les attributions financières des Etats du pays et comité de Bigorre aux XVIIe et XVIIIe siècles* (Bordeaux, 1962); pp. 100–12. For the frequency of meetings, see *IAC, Vic-Bigorre*, ed. Jean Pambrun (Tarbes, 1924), 1:38–76 passim.

to furnish 5,615 livres toward the support of 1,000 troops under the command of the duke of Epernon, who had become their governor. Before the year was out the prince of Condé was making similar demands. As a result, taxes jumped from about 22,000 livres in 1628 to 32,000 in 1629, but the restoration of peace with the Protestants permitted a reduction to about 20,000 livres in 1630.[138]

The estates of Bigorre, like those in other parts of France, were plagued by expenses and heavy indebtedness. To reduce the costs of holding their numerous meetings, they decreed in 1620 that the nobility would be divided into four groups, each of which was to attend every fourth year and that no more than one deputy from each town would be compensated for participating.[139] To repay their debts the estates sought the permission of the king's council to make special levies. The council was always wary of such proposals. In 1623 and again in 1625, it sought to enforce regulations forbidding the estates to meet unless a royal official was present and to tax without the king's permission. These negotiations kept the syndic of the estates at Paris during much of these years, but he was at least partially successful in his mission.[140]

Foix was also unable to escape involvement in the religious wars. The estates complained to the king's council that in 1621 and 1622 they had apportioned taxes in the customary manner but that the duke of Rohan had collected them to be used for the Protestant cause.[141] In spite of, or perhaps because of, their many difficulties, the estates continued to be active during this period, and in 1630 Louis XIII confirmed their privileges.[142] Scant surviving documents suggest that the other estates in the Pyrenees underwent somewhat similar experiences.[143]

Up to this point, the Pyrenean estates had been treated with some consideration. Their location had decreed that they would become involved in the civil war because they had no choice but to support the troops in the region to prevent them from plundering. After peace was restored in June 1629, however, this burden could be removed. But this was not the scenario that Marillac had planned. When the estates of Béarn met in January 1630, there was agitation because of a report that an élection and a Court of Aids were about to be introduced into the viscounty. The usual deputations to court followed, and that May the estates met again to deal with the threat.

138. *IAC, Vic-Bigorre*, 1:41, 43, 45, 50, 65–67, 69–70; Pène, *Les attributions financières*, p. 113; AD, Hautes-Pyrénées, 1:15 (documents from the seminary at Auch).

139. AD, Hautes-Pyrénées, 1:15; *IAC, Vic-Bigorre*, pp. 38–39; Pène, *Les attributions financières*, p. 47.

140. BN ms. fr. 18,201. fols. 89v–90v; BN ms. fr. 18,202, fols. 236–37; *IAC, Vic-Bigorre*, pp. 60–64 passim.

141. BN ms. fr. 18,201, fol. 67v–68v.

142. AN, H¹ 716, no. 4; AD, Ariège, C 216; BN ms. fr. 18,203, fols. 232–33v.

143. For the estates of Quatre-Vallées, see AD, Hautes-Pyrénées, C 284–87. For the estates of Nébouzan, see AN, E 98, fols. 266–67.

Their resistance was sufficient to stave off the pending doom until Marillac was removed from office that November.[144]

7. The Estates of Brittany

The beginning of the Richelieu regime witnessed the continuation of the crown's efforts to obtain additional revenue from Brittany. The estates that met in October 1624 were informed that the king needed "very great assistance," a phrase that was later defined as meaning a don gratuit of 600,000 livres in addition to the usual taxes. Those present were willing enough to vote something provided that their conditions were met. The usual haggling followed, but in the end a tax on the sale of wine in detail was voted; 100,000 livres of it was to go to the estates to meet their expenses and pay their debts. After this sum was deducted, Louis received only 325,000 livres, barely over half the amount that he had requested.[145]

The following fall Louis again asked for a don gratuit of 600,000 livres, but on this occasion the estates disbanded after refusing to vote anything until their grievances had been satisfied. Among the issues at stake was Richelieu's decision to charge the Bretons 75,000 livres for troops raised in the province, this despite Vendôme's opinion that such an action would stiffen the estates' resistance when they met.[146] The crown was dissatisfied at the response of the estates, and the same deputies were told to reconvene on April 29, 1626, in Nantes. Since some of them could not attend, there was a drop in attendance, especially among the nobility. Perhaps this caused the three estates to be somewhat less intransigent, but they remained sufficiently obstinate to prevent the king from obtaining all he desired. In a letter dated April 21, Louis assured the estates of his goodwill but insisted that his needs remained the same. The estates responded with a conditional offer of 400,000 livres, only to be informed that Vendôme had no authority to take less than 600,000. After further deliberation they increased their offer to 450,000, and when it was rejected, to 500,000 livres, but they would go no further. Having stinted the king, the estates proceeded to vote Marie, whom Louis permitted to enjoy the royal domain in Brittany, a handsome present of 150,000 livres, Vendôme, 10,000, and smaller sums to other royal officials.[147]

144. AD, Basses-Pyrénées, C 710, fols. 282–91, 314–25.

145. AD, Ille-et-Vilaine, C 2650, esp. pp. 599, 606, 650–51, 654, 658, 662–67, 673–74; Kenneth M. Dunkley, *Richelieu and the Estates of Brittany, 1624–1640* (Ann Arbor, University Microfilms, 1972), pp. 147–48.

146. AD, Ille-et-Vilaine, C 2651, esp. pp. 9, 14–15, 26, 81–85, 90–92, 118–21; Dunkley, *Richelieu*, pp. 148–49, 161–63, 166, 170, 173–74.

147. AD, Ille-et-Vilaine, C 2651, esp. pp. 141–45, 165, 183–92, 196–97, 200–02, 206, 208, 211–12, 218–19, 225–27, 251–52; Dunkley, *Richelieu*, pp. 150–51.

Less than a month after the estates ended, Louis arrested Vendôme because of his involvement in the Chalais conspiracy. He then traveled to Brittany to ensure his control over the province and to attempt once more to obtain a more adequate grant from the estates. He was accompanied by his mother, his brother, Richelieu, and Marillac, but on the surface at least only Marillac played a prominent part in the estates that opened in Nantes on July 11. Attendance was unusually large because of the presence of the king, but if it was the pageantry of the occasion that drew the Bretons to the meeting, they were to pay dearly for their curiosity. With his usual brevity Louis informed those present that he had come to hold the estates and to restore order. Marillac would make known to them his will. Since the rank and file of the Bretons had remained uninvolved in Vendôme's intrigues, Marillac could afford to be conciliatory, although occasionally he hinted at the possibility that coercion might be used to secure cooperation. He made only general demands for financial assistance for his master. Perhaps his least anticipated statement was that the king was going to appoint the Marshal Thémines as their governor, a surprising choice in that his son had killed Richelieu's brother in a duel a few years before.[148]

Louis's first step was to exclude Vendôme's officers, domestics, and pensioners from the estates in order to prevent them from arousing opposition to his policies. They must have been numerous if the report is true that Vendôme distributed 120,000 livres annually among them. This done, Louis had Marillac notify the deputies that he wanted them to appropriate 12,000 livres to pay for Thémines guards. They complied, but not without requesting that only Breton gentlemen be appointed to serve in this capacity. With equal ease Louis and the estates agreed that Vendôme's fortified places should be destroyed. Even when it came to taxes, the harmony did not appreciably wane. Louis accepted delay in the payment of the money that had been voted during the previous meeting of the estates. In return the estates quickly agreed to give him 300,000 livres in addition to the 500,000 that they had voted three months before. Also, Marie de Medici was to have 200,000 livres instead of the 150,000 that had been previously granted. To the 1 million livres the Bretons now owed to their king and his mother, they decided to add 150,000 livres, instead of 100,000, for their own expenses, bringing the total tax to 1,150,000 livres exclusive of the customary levies. Large as this sum was, the estates set the tax on the sale of wine at a rate so high that it was farmed for 1,357,000 livres.[149]

Louis must have been very content at the outcome of the estates. From the don gratuit and the customary taxes, he drew a total of 941,980 livres from the province in 1626, that is, about three times the average annual amount that he had been receiving.[150] His presence at the estates was doubtless the

148. *Mercure François* 12 (1626): 341–48; AD, Ille-et-Vilaine, C 2651, pp. 279–95, 325–26.

149. AD, Ille-et-Vilaine, C 2651, pp. 324–25, 337–41, 360, 366–67, 371, 374, 380–87; *Mercure François* 12 (1626): 369–73, 417–20; Dunkley, *Richelieu*, pp. 151–53, 177.

150. Mallet, p. 206.

most important factor that caused the deputies to grant him so much, but Marillac's handling of the estates may also have been a factor. Richelieu, who was in Nantes at the time, does not appear to have taken a direct hand in the affair.

Since the estates of July 1626 had voted the customary taxes for 1627, there was no need for a meeting to take place in that year unless the king wanted another don gratuit. Evidently Louis's advisers thought that it would be too soon to approach the estates again on this score, for no letters of convocation were issued, and he drew only 193,908 livres from Brittany in 1627.[151] If the Bretons thought that they had been forgotten, however, they were sadly mistaken. When their deputies assembled in Nantes in January 1628, they were confronted with a demand for a don gratuit of 1.2 or 1.3 million livres, which was justified by the great needs of the crown and their failure to make a special contribution the preceding year. The estates countered with an offer of only 500,000 livres, and after considerable haggling, the crown had to settle for 640,000. Also at issue was whether the Bretons should give the king a 300,000 livre advance, which they could obtain only by borrowing. In this they also prevailed. One reason for their reluctance to give more was that the farms that had been leased the year before had yielded far less than anticipated, and it was necessary to assign 200,000 livres raised from the farm in 1629 to mitigate the losses of the farmers. To be assured of enough return in 1629, a tax on the sale of cider was added to the one on wine.[152]

Again victory had gone to the estates. Furthermore, in addition to cutting the don gratuit in half, they delayed or defeated royal efforts to raise 200,000 livres from a tax on linen transported into the province, to increase the taillon by 100,000 livres following the recommendation of the Assembly of Notables in 1627, and to gather 300,000 livres to support some francs archers.[153]

The meeting of the estates in 1629 was postponed until April. Rather than permit the collection of taxes to be delayed, Marillac and other members of the council ordered on January 18 that the tax to support the francs archers, the taillon, and other ordinary levies be collected without waiting for the estates to give their consent. Evidently suspecting that the three estates were more generous to influential royal officials and their fellow Bretons than they were to the king, the council also directed that their treasurer supply a list of the gratifications that they had granted.[154] Probably realizing that such measures were sure to anger the deputies, Louis had taken the precaution a few days before of directing Condé to participate in the estates, a privilege he now had because he had been given the confiscated estates of the

151. Ibid.
152. Dunkley, *Richelieu*, pp. 153–54; AD, Ille-et-Vilaine, C 2651, pp. 558–61, 567, 657, 662, 668–70, 673–74, 679, 684–85.
153. Dunkley, *Richelieu*, pp. 170–71, 175.
154. AN, E 98, fols. 341–43.

rebellious duke of Rohan. Condé arrived well in advance of the meeting and was later credited by Louis with putting the deputies in a favorable state of mind before the appearance of his commissioners.[155]

Soon after the meeting opened, the deputies were again confronted with a request for a don gratuit of 1.2 million livres. They responded several weeks later with a conditional offer of 500,000 livres for the king and 150,000 for his mother. The commissioners rejected this proposal and a more generous one that followed. At first the estates refused to offer anything more, but in the end they were persuaded to give the king 700,000 livres and Marie de Medici 200,000. The duke of Brissac, who was the principal royal commissioner, was voted 6,000 livres in consideration of the assistance he had given in the negotiations with the king and 10,000 more for his expenses. Also significant was a present of 6,000 livres to Bouthillier, the king's secretary for Brittany, instead of the usual 3,000, because of his good offices. In spite of the failure to obtain much over half what the king desired, Condé reported to Richelieu and Bouthillier that the meeting had been successful.[156]

In the meantime Richelieu was becoming increasingly interested in Brittany. He had obtained the admiralty rights to the Atlantic provinces from Montmorency in 1626 and was pressing to acquire those of Provence from Guise, but his efforts to secure full control over trade and naval matters still hinged on the authority he could exercise in Brittany.[157] In opposition to his claims and those of Montmorency before him, the Bretons asserted that maritime matters were a ducal right that had been transferred to the king with the reunion to the crown and now could be exercised only by the royal governor. Already in 1624 the estates had declared that "they would recognize no one as admiral except their governor."[158] As long as they made good this pretension, Richelieu's dream of a royal navy and large trading companies could not fully mature because Brittany's splendid ports and the seafaring tradition were essential to his scheme.

When Louis appointed Thémines governor in 1626, he was careful to exclude any mention of his authority in admiralty matters, thereby leaving the way open for Richelieu to assume these duties by virtue of his newly created post of grand master of the navigation and trade. Strong Breton protests, however, soon forced Louis to assign Thémines the usual maritime jurisdiction. Richelieu's proposal for the establishment of a trading company with extensive privileges that would be based in Brittany won some support

155. Musée Condé, M 2, fols. 236, 255.

156. AD, Ille-et-Vilaine, C 2652, pp. 20, 94, 105–06, 111, 116, 126–28, 170, 175; Dunkley, *Richelieu*, p. 155.

157. My account of Richelieu and the admiralty rights in Brittany in this and the following paragraph is based on Dunkley, *Richelieu*, pp. 100–31; L. A. Boiteux, *Richelieu, grand maître de la navigation et du commerce de France* (Paris, 1955), pp. 142–48; and Henri Hauser, *La pensée et l'action économiques du Cardinal de Richelieu* (Paris, 1944), pp. 25–33.

158. Boiteux, *Richelieu*, p. 144.

in the estates, especially among the nobility who foresaw the economic advantages that would occur. However, the other Breton interests, including those of the important port of Saint-Malo, were opposed. More seriously, Parlement did all in its power to block Richelieu's plans because it feared the loss of part of its jurisdiction to the new admiralty courts. The impasse continued, but by the early months of 1630, it had occurred to Richelieu that since much of the Bretons' opposition to his proposals grew out of their desire that their governor exercise the admiralty rights in order to preserve more of their autonomy, he could resolve many difficulties by assuming that office himself. Fortunately Thémines had died in November 1627 and no successor had been appointed. The way was thus clear for him to use the estates that met in Ancenis in August to secure his objective.

Soon after becoming first minister, Richelieu had begun to seek influential clients in Brittany. The head of his trading company there was the brother of the powerful procureur syndic of the estates, Jean de Bruc, sieur de la Grée. Within the ranks of the unfriendly Parlement of Rennes, he secured the services of Claude de Marbeuf, one of its presidents. To direct the efforts of his local clients in 1630, Richelieu dispatched the prince of Condé to serve as the leading royal commissioner when the estates met. Condé's instructions from other royal ministers dealt primarily with the king's need for extraordinary financial assistance, but it is probable that Richelieu also gave directions concerning his desire that the estates ask that he be named governor.[159]

The estates that opened in Ancenis on August 7, 1630, were quickly confronted with a request for a don gratuit of 1.2 million livres, but on August 13, before the debate began on the question, someone proposed that the matter of the vacant governorship be resolved by asking the king to appoint his mother to the post. The choice of the queen mother grew out of the Bretons' desire to have the most influential friend possible at court. Marie had custody of the royal domain in Brittany and for this reason had long taken an interest in Breton affairs. Often she had done favors for the Bretons, and in return they had voted her handsome presents. Richelieu's clients may have heard this proposal with alarm, but they could not offer direct opposition to it. Instead one of them suggested that if she could not accept, they should seek the services of the cardinal who appeared to be the second most powerful person in the entourage of the king. It was not until the sixteenth that the debate over the size of the don gratuit commenced. The estates began with an offer of 600,000 livres but in the end voted the king 900,000 livres and Richelieu 100,000 to be paid in seven quarters, four in 1631 and three in 1632. By spreading the tax over a period of nearly two years, the three estates in effect reduced the annual amount that they would give. On the other hand, because the seventh quarter would not end until

159. Dunkley, *Richelieu*, pp. 114–15; Musée Condé, M 2, fols. 365–66, 378, 392, 398.

the early fall of 1632, the crown saw no need for the estates to meet again to vote a don gratuit until the summer of that year. It is at this point and for this reason that the practice of holding biennial rather than annual meetings of the estates began.[160]

Condé quickly reported the decision of the estates concerning the governorship to Richelieu and Bouthillier, and before the end of August they both had responded to his information. Richelieu gave assurance that Marie de Medici had never thought of becoming governor, and Bouthillier reported that the king was pleased at the proposal the estates had made concerning his mother and the cardinal, but at the same time he implied that the former would not be given the post.[161] The governorship thus became available to Richelieu, as he had no doubt planned, but he was not appointed to the post until September 1631, after he had won his final victory over the queen mother and she had departed from the court. The estates were very pleased at Richelieu's appointment because he was in an excellent position to defend their privileges in the council of their king. Indeed to pave the way for his appointment or that of Marie de Medici, the estates of 1630 had appropriated 198,000 livres to compensate the duke of Vendôme for surrendering whatever rights that remained to him as a result of his having once been their governor.[162]

Thus while élections were being established in Dauphiné, Burgundy, Provence, and Languedoc and the Pyrenean estates were being threatened, Brittany escaped with minor changes. The three estates sometimes charged that their privileges were violated. The customary ducal taxes, for example, were collected in 1630 prior to the time that the estates met in the summer to give approval. Strong protests, however, had brought an apology from the representatives of the crown. Perhaps more annoying to the three estates was the crown's practice of creating offices without their consent, although here as elsewhere the Bretons were less abused than most other Frenchmen. Furthermore constant pressure forced the estates to increase Louis's revenue from Brittany from an average of 397,000 livres per year between 1620 and 1624 to 519,000 livres per year between 1626 and 1630, but these were the principal losses that they sustained.[163]

To what did the Bretons owe their relatively good fortune? A strong provincial loyalty and a willingness to unite to maintain their privileges were undoubtedly important assets. To them must be coupled the generosity with which they had always treated influential persons. Marie de Medici was voted huge gifts until 1630, when Richelieu loomed as their principal defender, and he then profited by 100,000 livres because of this fact. Even

160. AD, Ille-et-Vilaine, C 2652, pp. 261–63, 272–74, 303–06, 338; Dunkley, *Richelieu*, pp. 132–35.

161. Musée Condé, M 2, fols. 404–06.

162. Dunkley, *Richelieu*, 131–32, 137–38.

163. Ibid., pp. 157–58, 166–69; Mallet, p. 206.

Condé's future importance to the province was anticipated, and he was given 24,000 livres while others received lesser awards.[164] But are these considerations enough to explain why Brittany fared so much better than Burgundy, Provence, and Languedoc where the estates performed nearly as well? Almost certainly not. We are driven to the conclusion that Richelieu's interests in maritime and trading affairs caused him to take the Bretons under his protection in order to secure their cooperation in his ambitious projects. He left the remainder of the pays d'états, with the probable exception of Languedoc, to Marillac, who with single-minded determination sought to destroy their privileges and to reduce them to the status of pay d'élections.

164. AD, Ille-et-Vilaine, C 2652, pp. 338, 367, 370–71.

16

THE TRIUMPH OF RICHELIEU

MICHEL DE MARILLAC MUST HAVE HAD MIXED FEELINGS AS HE SURVEYED THE domestic and foreign scene during the summer of 1630. The Catholic church lands in Béarn and Navarre had been restored, and the Huguenot state within a state had been destroyed. It was true that those willful heretics had been permitted to retain too many religious and civil liberties, but with their political power broken, the rising tide of Catholic reform could be counted upon to engulf them at a later date. After some difficulty, the Parlements had been compelled to register his great reforming ordonnance of 1629 that was designed to restore justice and stamp out disorder in the kingdom. The judicial and financial officials had borne the brunt of his attack, but instead of submitting peaceably to sovereign authority, they continued to try to have his decrees reversed. Richelieu had shared in his desire to let the paulette die when the time came for its renewal at the close of 1629; but the expedition to Italy had led the crown to restore that instrument of making offices hereditary to the financial officials in return for sharply increased payments. The officers in Parlement continued to agitate for a renewal of the paulette, but instead of expressing their gratitude when it was accorded them in June 1630, they had increased their protests because they were expected to pay at the same rate as their brethren in finance rather than the lesser amount that had been required when the paulette had been first established in 1604. Clearly the bureaucracy was far from tamed, but once the return of peace made such financial expedients unnecessary, Marillac could at least hope that the tables would be turned.[1]

Furthermore he had pursuaded the king to take steps to weaken the provincial Parlements. In Burgundy and Dauphiné where the Parlements had exercised some jurisdiction over indirect taxes, Courts of Aids had been created to assume their role and attached to the Chamber of Accounts. In Languedoc the already existing Court of Aids had been joined to the Chamber of Accounts at Montpellier to strengthen the position of these relatively docile courts in their dealings with the powerful Parlement of

1. Roland Mousnier, *La vénalité des offices sous Henri IV et Louis XIII*, 2d ed. (Paris, 1971), pp. 656–57.

Toulouse. To reduce the likelihood of the sovereign courts of a province joining forces against the crown, they had been relocated in different cities. This situation had already existed in Languedoc where Montpellier and Toulouse had long been rival judicial-administrative capitals, but now the Chamber of Accounts of Burgundy had been transferred from Dijon to Autun and then to Beaune, and the Chamber of Accounts of Provence was being moved from Aix to Toulon. Plans were also being made to establish a Court of Aids for Dauphiné in Vienne.

In every instance the reorganization of the sovereign courts had preceded the creation of élections, strong evidence that Marillac and his associates regarded this as a necessary preliminary step to what appears to have been their primary objective: the destruction of the provincial estates and the replacement of their tax officials by those of the crown. Such measures had not been necessary before élections had been reestablished in Guyenne in 1621 because the courts at Bordeaux were already weakened by the fact that many inhabitants of the généralité lived under the jurisdiction of courts in Toulouse, Montpellier, and even Paris. As if to rationalize this situation while in the midst of other reforms, the crown had created a Court of Aids for Guyenne in December 1629 to the detriment of the jurisdiction of that court in Paris, but had exercised care to place its seat in Agen rather than Bordeaux where the local Parlement was situated.[2]

It was true that the inhabitants of Burgundy, Provence, and Languedoc were doing everything legally, and sometimes illegally, in their power to prevent the élus from being appointed and from performing their duties once they were. Only the quarrel between the third estate and the other orders prevented the situation from being as bad in Dauphiné, but such difficulties had probably been foreseen. Plans to establish élections in the Pyrenean provinces were well advanced. Thus Marillac could anticipate that within several years the new fiscal system would be functioning smoothly. All of France would be administered in the same fashion, and the provincial estates would begin to wither away in every province except Brittany where for the moment Richelieu needed local cooperation in order to further his maritime policies.

The destruction of the provincial estates would not only mark the removal of corporative self-governing units of government and their replacement by royal officials, but also a decline in the power of the magnates, who used the estates to increase their wealth and enhance their authority. This fact was by no means lost on contemporaries. The English ambassador to France, Sir Thomas Edmondes, who did not embark on his mission until July 1629, had picked up enough gossip by early September to report:

The Cardinal de Richelieu, to diminish the authority of the princes and

---

2. See above pp. 117, 285. Also see Jean-Paul Charmeil, *Les trésoriers de France à l'epoque de la Fronde* (Paris, 1964), pp. 306–07, 333, 339.

the greate men which are gouvernors of provinces, hath begunn another worke of greate importance, which is, to take away that power which the provinciale gouvernors did usually practise, by virtue of the privileges of the countries to call the Assemblies of the States, either for the leavyinge of monnies in the countries for the King's service, or to consult of other occasions: Att which time the saide gouvernors did also annually draw greate summes of monny from the Country, which by way of gratification was presented unto them, for their owne particular. But now hee hath abolished that custome of callinge the states by the gouvernor, and hath appointed that upon the issunige of any Commissions from hence for the leavyinge of any Monnies in any of the provinces, the same shale be executed only by the Esleus of the Countri, who are the persons that are accustomed to make the severale taxations throughout the Countrie, and by this meanes, of making their authority more absolute, they doe sell the places of the saide Esleus att a much dearer rate, and doe cleane cutt of the profitt of the gouvernors. This hee hath already (as is saide) putt in execution in the provinces of Provence, Dauphiné, and Languedoc, and if hee can establish the like in Bretaigne, which will bee of greater difficulty because they are more strongly founded in their privileges, hee will then bee able to make the same to bee afterwards more easily received in the other Countries.[3]

If Marillac's passion for administrative uniformity appeared about to be satisfied, the same cannot be said about his desire for a prosperous, orderly kingdom. Poor crops had caused food prices to be nearly 50 percent higher than usual in 1630. Riots were becoming more frequent, and the privileged orders were not reticent about directing popular discontent against his reforms. If only the promised reduction in taxes could be put into effect, the

---

3. Edmondes to Dorchester, PRO, S.P. 78/84, fols. 275–77. Edmondes attributed the creation of the élections to Richelieu, not Marillac. It must be remembered that edicts creating élections in Dauphiné and Burgundy were issued prior to Edmondes's arrival in France and that the one for Languedoc, the one place in which Richelieu is known to have favored their establishment, was dated the same month that he came. Furthermore the new and inexperienced ambassador was at first inclined to attribute all policy decisions to Richelieu. Marillac is rarely mentioned until 1630. Unlike more discerning ambassadors Edmondes never realized that there was a split between Richelieu and Bérulle, and he persisted in regarding the latter as Richelieu's not-too-capable creature until his death. Ibid., fols. 181, 325. My belief that Richelieu played a minor role in the establishment of the élections, except in Languedoc, is based on the facts that he never mentioned them in his various proposals for reform and almost never referred to them in his correspondence. In his one reference in his memoirs, he expressed regret that the council had rejected a Burgundian financial offer in return for their abolition. See chap. 15, sec. 3. Deputies from the estates dealt primarily with Marillac, Effiat, their respective secretaries of state, and the council as a while, but not with Richelieu. Marillac rarely mentioned the élections in his correspondence with Richelieu that is lodged in the AAE and the BN, but rather gave every appearance of acting on his own. Finally Richelieu abolished the élections after Marillac's downfall in November 1630.

suffering of the people would be mitigated, but military intervention in Italy made this impossible. Indeed to support the army, it had been necessary to turn to expedients, including selling many times more offices in the new élections than were necessary. One wonders whether Marillac realized that the salaries and perquisites of these officials came to about ten times as much as the entire amount that the estates had levied to support their own activities. If he did, he gave no sign that he was willing to relent in order to reduce the burden on the people.[4]

Marillac was troubled by his worsening relations with the cardinal. He and his brother had not abandoned Richelieu after the fall of Concini, and they very likely supported the efforts of Marie de Medici, Bérulle, and others to have him brought back into the government in 1624. At first Marillac and Richelieu had seemed to share the same objectives, and their disagreements had been no more frequent than one would expect two strong-willed men to have. In September 1625 they had argued over whether priority should be given to intervention in Italy or defeating the Huguenots and instituting domestic reforms. Initially Richelieu had been successful, but he had soon reversed himself and embarked on a course acceptable to Marillac. Again in December 1628, Richelieu had placed Italy ahead of defeating the Huguenots in Languedoc and internal affairs. Again he had won, but after achieving his Italian objectives, he had once more directed his attention toward France. When he returned to court in September 1629, he could point to the destruction of the Huguenot state within a state, as well as to his Italian laurels, to justify his policy. Ever anxious for glory, Louis was more than content with his services, but the queen mother had become estranged by his independent actions because she regarded him as her creature.

Richelieu placed much of the blame for Marie de Medici's coldness on Marillac's shoulders and, according to Marillac's friends, began to try to undermine his influence with the king by questioning his integrity. In November 1629 and March 1630, Marillac sought to resign, but Louis refused to let him. Richelieu concurred in his master's decision, whether because he still valued Marillac's services or merely wanted to avoid an open break cannot be determined.[5] In either case, the two men could hardly have failed to have noted the growing divergence in their policies. Marillac's dedication to domestic reform continued unabated, but he must have felt

4. J. Michael Hayden, *France and the Estates General of 1614* (Cambridge, 1974), pp. 219–25; Boris Porchnev, *Les soulèvements populaires en France de 1623 à 1648* (Paris, 1963), p. 668. Marillac with difficulty avoided a quarrel with the superintendent of finances, Effiat. Among the issues that troubled him were the financial expedients. G. Pagès, "Autour du 'Grand Orage.' Richelieu et Marillac: deux politiques," *Revue historique* 179 (1937): 80.

5. Bibl. Sainte-Geneviève, ms. 826, fols. 277–85; BN ms. fr. 5183, fols. 38, 67–77, 80–81. Marillac's letter of resignation of March 12, 1630, has been printed in *Chroniques de l'ordre des Carmélites de la réforme de Sainte-Thérèse depuis leur introduction en France* (Troyes, 1846), 1:207–08, and in Edouard Everat, *Michel de Marillac, sa vie, ses oeuvres* (Riom, 1894), pp. 122–23.

that Richelieu gave only the most lukewarm support to his efforts. He carried on the struggle with the Parlements over the Code Michau and the paulette with scarcely an assist from the cardinal. Indeed his friends were soon to charge that Richelieu placed the blame for any unpopular policy upon him.[6] In the battle with the estates concerning the élections, Richelieu showed his hand only in the case of Languedoc. His willingness to leave internal affairs in Marillac's hands was clearly reflected in a letter he wrote in August 1630. Marillac had suggested that church lands held by Huguenots and other nonecclesiastics in Dauphiné be returned and that the conversion of heretics be stimulated by reducing the role of the bipartite courts, forbidding pastors to preach in places not specifically authorized by the Edict of Nantes, and providing pensions for those who succumbed to Catholic blandishments. Richelieu found these ideas good but gently suggested that the time was not ripe for such actions because the king was in Italy and there was already unrest in Dauphiné and Languedoc. Instead of saying no, however, he left the matter to Marillac's "good prudence."[7] Prudent indeed Marillac was, but he must have charged Richelieu's activist foreign policy with the loss of many souls as well as with reforms postponed and the suffering of hungry peasants and workers.

The story of the growing estrangement of the two men has often been told, although with scarcely an assist from the contemporary unpublished biographies of Marillac and his extensive correspondence.[8] Nor has the gossip of the foreign ambassadors been brought into the tale. Even the relatively sympathetic Edouard Everat and Georges Pagès could not escape the presumption that the truth lay with the great cardinal and his policy of intervention in Italy. Only Georges Mongrédien has seen that institutional issues were at stake, but he was incorrect when he tried to explain the positions taken by the various parties to the dispute.[9] Slanted and

6. BN ms. fr. 5183, fols. 72–77v.

7. Richelieu, *Lettres*, 3:833–34.

8. The unpublished biographies are Nicolas Lefèvre, sieur de Lézeau, *Histoire de la vie de Messire Michel de Marillac, chevalier*, garde des sceaux de France, copies of which are located in the Bibl. Sainte-Geneviève, mss. 826 and 2005–06; in the BN, mss. fr. 14,027 and n.a. fr. 82–83; and the somewhat similar anonymous *Apologie pour le sieur de Marillac, garde de sceaux de France, contre ung libelle diffamatoire, publié soubz le tiltre d'*Entretiens des Champs Elisées, located in BN mss. fr. 5183, 17,485, 17, 486, and 18,461. A third unpublished biography, by P. Senault, was lost when the library of the Oratorians on the rue Saint-Honoré was pillaged in the Revolution, Everat, *Michel de Marillac*, p. 208. Marillac's correspondence in the Richelieu papers in the AAE has often been utilized, but his rather extensive though scattered letters in the BN and the Institut de France have been neglected. Everat uses the biographies but not the correspondence.

9. For secondary works on the rivalry, see, in addition to Everat, *Michel de Marillac*, and Pagès, "Autour," Pierre de Vaissière, *Un grand procès sous Richelieu: L'affaire du Maréchal de Marillac* (Paris, 1924); Louis Batiffol, *La Journée des Dupes* (Paris, 1925); Gabriel Hanotaux and the Duc de La Force, *Histoire du Cardinal de Richelieu* (Paris, 1933), 3:193–306; and Georges Mongrédien, *La Journée des Dupes* (Paris, 1961).

occasionally erroneous though the extant versions are, there is no need to reconstitute a more impartial detailed account here. Suffice it to say that the aging Marillac became increasingly insistent that the Italian venture be terminated so that the resources of France could be directed toward the service of his God, his king, and his countrymen. Perhaps he eventually sought to supplant Richelieu, as the cardinal's supporters have charged and his own friends have so vigorously denied, but if he did take this step that was so out of keeping with his character, it was not for personal glory but to move France in a direction that he thought more worthy of its genius.

As early as February 1629, Marillac's collaborator, Bérulle, had written Richelieu: "It is said ... that we are beginning an interminable war in the midst of public necessities and the people's misery, and that under the pretext of [relieving] Casal we wish to enter the Milanese."[10] To this appeal Marillac added, "The management of affairs obliges me to represent to you that we do many things which cause the people great suffering.... Necessity does all of that and it cannot be avoided.... It seems to me that the glory of good government is principally to think of the welfare of the subjects and the good regulation of the state which can be done only through peace."[11] Then he elaborated on Bérulle's argument that if they succeeded in raising the siege of Casal, they would be tempted to attack Milan. The Habsburgs would retaliate by invading Picardy and Champagne from their bases in Flanders and Germany. A limited operation would thus become a long and terrible war that would be embarked upon at a time when France was seething with discontent, and neither the king nor his brother had produced an heir to perpetuate the dynasty.[12]

It is customary to see the devout faction as advocating a hopelessly naive foreign policy predicated upon their pro-Spanish and pro-Catholic sympathies, but such sentiments were conspicuously absent from the arguments they offered to support their cause. Rather they should be credited as being farseeing statesmen who recognized that what was undertaken as a limited involvement in Italy would lead to a costly war for which France was ill prepared. One wonders whether Richelieu would have been so insistent on embarking on a course that led to full-scale intervention in the Thirty Years War if he had foretold the future as clearly.

Casal was relieved, and France was momentarily spared the further adventures in Italy in 1629 that Marillac and Bérulle had feared, but the year 1630 had hardly begun before French troops were once more on their way to the peninsula. On March 29, Pignerol fell, and the plains of northwest Italy lay open to the French army. This time there was no

10. William F. Church, *Richelieu and Reason of State* (Princeton, 1972), p. 201.
11. Pagès, "Autour," p. 66.
12. Ibid., pp. 77–78.

Huguenot rebellion in Languedoc to compel the French troops to return home. It was possible to make a choice between further aggrandizement in Italy and Marillac's program of domestic reform. Richelieu saw the issue clearly, and on April 13 he prepared a memorandum:

> If the king decides for war, it will be necessary to abandon all thought of repose, economy, and reorganization within the realm. If on the other hand peace is desired, it will be necessary to abandon all thought of Italy in the future and nevertheless to assure peace as far as possible under conditions that can only be uncertain, and to be satisfied with the present glory that the king will have because of forcibly maintaining the Duke of Mantua in his state against the combined power of the Empire, Spain, and Savoy.[13]

No one who knew Louis would have doubted that he would choose the road to glory. The question was whether Marillac could persuade him that more glory could be won by providing for "the welfare of the subjects and the good regulation of the State" than by foreign conquests. He could not. At first even the queen mother and the duke of Orléans opted for war, but Marillac persisted in presenting his arguments and eventually won them to his cause. Richelieu displayed remarkable patience in dealing with his keeper of the seals by responding to his criticisms time and again.[14] In mid-May he wrote:

> The arguments presented by the Keeper of the Seals made it clear that one cannot wage war without great inconvenience. This is true not only of this particular occasion but all others, since war is one of the scourges with which it pleases God to afflict men.
>
> But it does not follow from this that one must make peace under weak, base, and shameful conditions, because in this way one would be exposed to disadvantages much greater than those of the present war.
>
> The aversion of the lower classes toward war does not deserve consideration as a reason for making such a peace, since they are often sensitive to and complain of necessary evils as readily as those that may be avoided, and they are as ignorant of what is useful to a state as they are excitable and quick to bewail the ills that they must endure in order to avoid greater ones.[15]

Richelieu and his supporters became alarmed at Marillac's persistence. Shortly after Marillac had presided over the submission of the Dijon

---

13. Ibid., p. 85. I have used the translations in Church, *Richelieu*, p. 203.

14. Pagès, "Autour," pp. 87–94.

15. Church, *Richelieu*, pp. 203–04. Richelieu displayed the same lack of concern about the people on other occasions as is revealed in his *Testament politique*, ed. Louis André, 7th ed. (Paris, 1947), pp. 253–55.

magistrates in the presence of the king in April, an English agent reported that "the Keeper of the Seals had displayed more ability and strength of mind in this encounter than the adherents of the Cardinal desired. They fear with reason that he encroaches more and more" on the cardinal's position with the king.[16] By early summer, there was speculation on whether the cardinal was losing credit with Louis, but in July rumors circulated in Paris that Marillac had been disgraced.[17]

Marillac was at pains to dispel this report. He wrote Mathew Molé, the king's attorney in the Parlement of Paris, that he was on the best of terms with the cardinal, who had never sought his advice more frequently. Even here, however, he could not resist pushing his own policies which were so at variance with those of the man the public was beginning to see as his rival rather than as his master: "There is the condition in which we live: When it pleases God, he will give us a better life. I clearly see the necessities of state and will take pleasure to serve them, not only for peace, but also for the three principal points for which the kingdom has need of a strong and very affectionate application, to wit: religion, justice and the improvement of the lot of the people." Later, as if to deny his avowal of the security of his position or to foretell what was soon to come, he added: "I will be of good heart if God wishes to grant me the favor of finding from retirement the time to occupy myself with him before leaving the world. I will receive it as something that I have desired for more than twenty years without interruption. I have testified to it when I thought it necessary: but before and after, I dwell by the grace of God in the same tranquility, awaiting through the divine disposition and not through my choice, the order and occupations of my life."[18]

Then came Louis's serious illness in Lyons. As he began to recover, the news spread that the council was debating whether the crown should persist in its efforts to establish élections in Provence and Languedoc despite the resistance that was being encountered. The two governors, Guise and Montmorency, were suspected of being behind the disturbances, and it was predicted that they would join with the other governors "to preserve the provincial estates from which they obtain great sums each year." Both nobles were described as being very close to the queen mother.[19]

16. Augier to Dorchester from Dijon, April 19/29, 1630, PRO, S.P. 78/86, fols. 257–58.

17. De Vic to Dorchester from Paris June 23/July 3, and July 1/11, 1630, PRO, S.P. 78/86, fol. 385, and 78/87, fols. 1–2.

18. *Mémoires de Mathieu Molé*, ed. Aimé Champollion-Figeac (Paris, 1855),2:28. The letter is undated, but in it Marillac referred to his failure to join the king and Richelieu at Saint-Jean de Maurienne. Hence it must have been written in July 1630. Perhaps in the hope of obtaining additional support for his policies, Marillac seemed to advocate a modest intervention in Italy at this time, but he strongly urged Louis not to remain with the army. See Avenel's prejudiced summary in Richelieu, *Lettres*, 3:775–77.

19. Augier to Dorchester from Lyons, October 8/18, 1630, PRO, S.P. 78/87, fols. 322–25.

When the court began its return to Paris, Marie de Medici must have felt more confident of her position than she had in a long time. Her son had grown closer to her during his illness, and she may have extracted a promise from him to dismiss Richelieu after their arrival in the capital. Around her gathered a strange mixture of devout, authoritarian Catholics, such as Marillac, who wanted to break the power of the sovereign courts, estates and other autonomous institutions, and libertine magnates who were bent on preserving the privileges of the provinces that they governed. If the cardinal fell, there was certain to be a struggle between the two factions. If Marie anticipated such a clash, she need not have been alarmed, for she must have believed that her decisive influence would determine which policy her son would choose.

On November 11 the English agents reported that the king had reached Paris the preceding Saturday and was going to Versailles the next day. Far from preparing to dismiss Richelieu, he was devoting his efforts to reconciling the cardinal with his brother and mother.[20] Then, on the morning of the twelfth, the agents received a note saying that the cardinal was disgraced. They left their lodgings and soon learned from a friend "that yesterday the Queene Mother ... told the king at last in plain terms that she had suffered so much from the Cardinal as either she or he must needs quite the court." Thereupon the cardinal entered, and the king said to him: "I have done what I can with her (speaking of the Queen Mother and herself being present) but I cannot prevail with her. It is true said the Queen Mother and go your way said she to the Cardinal and let me see you no more. Thereupon the Cardinal kissed the hem of her robe and the like did Madame Comballet [Richelieu's niece] who is now retired to the Carmelites, what will become of this business you shall not fail to be informed." Then in a postscript hastily scribbled an hour later, "The king backed up Cardinal. He will not fall. Happened in Luxembourg House."[21]

Such were the rumors that ran through Paris on the morning of November 12. Soon it was learned that following the confrontation between Richelieu and Marie de Medici and a meeting of his council, Louis had set out for Versailles without giving any indication of his intentions. The cardinal, who thought that he had lost and considered fleeing from France, was greatly relieved when he received a royal summons to come to Versailles. There the bond between the two men was renewed. Louis broke with his mother, and before many months she fled from France, as did her

20. Augier and De Vic to Dorchester from Paris, November 1/11, 1630, PRO, S.P. 78/87, fols. 372–74. The agents said that the cardinal's reconciliation with the queen mother had been more secret and a great deal more real than with Orléans. If they were correct, it supports Saint-Simon's version. See Mongrédien, *La Journée des Dupes*, pp. 68–70, 200–03.

21. PRO, S.P. 78/87, fol. 376. The agents said that the Day of Dupes took place on November 11, not November 10, as Mongrédien and some other historians have argued. See Mongrédien, *La Journée des Dupes*, pp. 65–66.

charming but ineffectual son, Gaston of Orléans. For the remainder of his life, Richelieu was free from any rivals from within the royal family.[22]

The Marillacs also had to be dealt with. Louis, the marshal, was arrested on trumped-up charges, tried by a special commission of hand-picked judges who met in one of Richelieu's palaces, and after a courageous defense condemned to death by a vote of only thirteen to ten. On May 10, 1632, he was beheaded, still protesting his innocence.[23] It is difficult to see why Louis and Richelieu were so vindictive. It would have been enough to have removed the marshal from his command to ensure that he did not lead his troops in revolt. Perhaps the story is true that when Louis was thought to be dying in Lyons, Guise, Bassompierre, and the marshal had debated about what should be done with the cardinal. Guise was for exile, Bassompierre was for imprisonment, and the marshal was for death. Richelieu learned of the plot and punished each of the conspirators in accordance to the fate they had planned for him.[24]

But what of Michel de Marillac? Let his friends tell his story.[25] Like Richelieu he had received a summons on the eleventh to join the king at Versailles, but for some reason he halted at a house belonging to his wife in Glatigny, a stone's throw from his destination. That fateful decision enabled Richelieu to reach the king first and persuade him that the Marillacs must be dismissed. Marillac had probably intended to proceed to Versailles, but before he departed he received an order from the king to remain where he was.[26] When he learned that Richelieu and the other councillors were meeting with Louis, he realized that the king had chosen war instead of reform. He wrote his resignation and was attending mass the following

22. Mongrédien, *La Journée des Dupes*, pp. 65–88.

23. Church, *Richelieu*, pp. 225–28; Vaissière, *Un grand procès*, pp. 57–250; Mongrédien, *La Journée des Dupes*, pp. 104–28.

24. Mongrédien, *La Journée des Dupes*, pp. 61–62; Hanotaux and La Force, *Histoire*, 3:287.

25. Except where otherwise indicated, the following account is based on Lefèvre's biography, Bibl. Sainte-Geneviève, ms. 826, fols. 295–380; the *Apologie*, BN, ms. fr. 5183, fols. 101–10v, 151–51v; and the summary of these and other sources in Everat, *Michel de Marillac*, pp. 141–55, 168–84. For letters to and from Marillac's nephew, the bishop of Riez, concerning the captivity, see BN ms. fr. 3922, fols. 1–4v.

26. The belief that Louis had decided to dismiss the Marillacs prior to his departure from Paris is based on the account Saint-Simon later gave his son, the author of the memoirs. The fact that on November 11 Louis had dispatched a letter to La Force to permit him to return to France and to inform him that he was placing Louis de Marillac in command of the French troops in Italy (Richelieu, *Lettres*, 4:6 n.1.) suggests that he had not yet decided to dismiss the two brothers. The argument so often given that Richelieu arranged for Marillac to be given the Italian command in order to prevent him from returning to the court is not convincing. Surely if he was directing Louis's policy, he would have made La Force remain with the army until the crisis had passed in order to dilute Marillac's influence with the troops. My interpretation is reinforced by Louis's invitation to Marillac to attend the meeting of the council at Versailles. However, there are many disputed facts in the sequence of events, and we cannot be certain until further data are uncovered.

morning when one of the king's secretaries appeared and asked for the seals of his office. To his surprise, instead of being permitted to return to his home, he was placed in the custody of an officer of the guard, who conducted him to Caen and then to Châteaudun, where he was to remain until his death. At first he was roughly treated, and every effort was made to deny him access to the outside world, but after several months Richelieu felt secure enough to release his guard, and Marillac's devoted daughter-in-law and grandchildren were permitted to join him.

From the first Marillac stoically accepted his fate. Years before when he had acted as spiritual adviser to his niece, Louise de Marillac, he had advised her to "be always most courageous in seeking for God and in conforming yourself entirely to whatsoever He pleases, and walk with humility and confidence in God."[27] Now was his opportunity to put his own teachings into practice. He urged that no member of his family speak ill of those who caused his plight and sought consolation by returning to his religious works. He revised his translation of the *Psalms*, brought out a new edition of the *Imitation of Christ*, composed a treatise, now lost, on the *Eternal Life*, and most fitting of all began to render the Book of Job into French. During his last months, as earlier in his life, this quietist mystic was favored with visions of Jesus, the Virgin Mary, and the good angels. They told him to resign himself to his brother's execution and explained passages in Job to him. While engaged in these occupations, he fell ill on August 1, 1632, and died six days later after having been bled five times.[28]

So great had Marillac's reputation for piety become that the townspeople swarmed in to see his body. The local abbess and parish priest sought his remains, but they had to be content with some entrails, for he had asked to be buried near his son in the Carmelite convent in Paris that he had founded. A new problem emerged when a petition to bring the body to the capital was rejected by the king's council. Undaunted, Marillac's niece decided to take it to the Carmelite convent at Pontoise. So large were the crowds that followed the funeral procession that Richelieu became alarmed and once more forbade interment. A refuge was found for the travelers at Brières in the home of President Maupeou, a nephew of the Gilles de Maupeou with whom the deceased had so long cooperated in the effort to destroy the provincial estates. A clamor arose in Paris at this last injustice, and Richelieu at length agreed that the body could be quietly carried to its designated resting place in the evening when the procession would attract little attention. Burial was already overdue for we are told that "celestial odors" came from the coffin.

During his last months when Richelieu's pamphleteers had launched a

27. Pierre Coste, *The Life and Works of Saint Vincent de Paul*, trans. J. Leonard (Westminster, Md., 1952), 1:184. For more on Marillac's religious advice, see ibid., pp. 182–88.

28. For Marillac's mystical experiences see the Lefèvre biography. Bibl. Sainte-Geneviève, ms. 826, fols. 381–402.

vitriolic attack against him, his brother had been tried and executed, and he himself had been kept in confinement, Marillac had never offered a word in his own defense and had discouraged others from doing so. "I order my children and beg my kinsmen and friends," he wrote in the will he prepared in 1631, "never to have any unworthy resentment nor bad will against any person whatsoever because of the things which have happened to me, and never to display by word or deed any bitterness or discontent, but to recognize as I do, through the grace and mercy of God, that all has happened by a very special direction of his divine providence and charity."[29] There was little in the document concerning money, for Michel de Marillac, one-time superintendent of finances and keeper of the seals, had long since given most of his possessions to the church and to charity. His wife, who had independent means, had had to provide an allowance to support him in captivity. He left hardly enough to pay his funeral expenses.

Louis recognized something of the greatness of Marillac's character. In the meeting of his council at Versailles on November 11, he had announced that he was not going to punish Marillac severely because of his respectability, age, and past services. Even Richelieu had fallen under his spell. In the early days of their relationship, he had told Louis of Marillac's high character and great ability and Father Joseph of his bold counsel, courage in executing decisions, and ability to find expedients when others could find none.[30] Again in 1641, after he had long been secure in his office, Richelieu could say that Marillac "was a saintly man, God permitted us to find ourselves opposed to each other's sentiments concerning the end, although we both had good intentions, but I esteemed him."[31]

But if Richelieu could imprison a saint, he could also destroy his reputation. To this day the significance of Marillac's domestic policy has been obscured. He and the members of his devout family and relatives were also slow to receive recognition for their contributions to the Catholic reformation. Nearly all of them became monks or nuns, but even his niece, Louise de Marillac, the co-founder of the Daughters of Charity, to whom he had given spiritual advice, had to wait until 1920 to be beatified and to 1934 to be canonized.[32] The explanation for the low repute in which Michel de Marillac has been held probably lies in the pamphlets Richelieu sponsored and the memoirs Richelieu and his supporters wrote depicting him as an unpatriotic, pro-Spanish, senile fool who had no conception of the needs of the state and who sought to supplant his benefactor by turning the queen mother against him.

29. Everat, *Michel de Marillac*, p. 183.

30. Vaissière, *Un grand procès*, p. 28.

31. Donald A. Bailey, *Writers against the Cardinal: A Study of the Pamphlets Which Attacked the Person and Policies of Cardinal Richelieu during the Decade 1630–1640* (Ann Arbor, University Microfilms, 1973), p. 49.

32. For Marillac's family, see Everat, *Michel de Marillac*, pp. 197–203.

Marillac had few vocal defenders. Anti-Richelieu pamphlets were generally published abroad under the aegis of the exiled Marie de Medici, and the anti-Richelieu memoirs were written by libertine magnates who had little sympathy for Marillac's centralizing policies and for his devout Catholicism. Indeed parts of Marillac's program were so unpopular among the magnates and bureaucrats that it is hardly surprising that they and their supporters passed over it in silence or tried to blame it on the cardinal. When Matthieu de Morgues attempted to saddle Richelieu with the responsibility for Marillac's program of breaking the power of the sovereign courts and diminishing provincial independence, Harlay de Sancy responded with a long pamphlet. To the charge that Richelieu humbled Parlement, he declared that "the author [Morgues] is blind and does not know what he wants. Never were so many new edicts passed as in the time of Keeper of the Seals, Marillac. He sealed twenty times as many as all of his predecessors together. The last time he accompanied the king to Parlement, he had so many of them to seal ... that he forgot to seal all of them in his home and ... hastily did so on the altar of the Sainte-Chapelle."[33] Furthermore, Sancy charged, Marillac responded rudely to Parlement's protests. His edicts should not be blamed on the cardinal, who did not mix in such affairs. The cardinal was not the first minister. Every minister was free to exercise his office. He left everything to do with justice in Marillac's hands and took no cognizance of what he did. To the charge that the cardinal had introduced novelties into the frontier provinces which would ruin them, Sancy could only reiterate that these were Marillac's, not Richelieu's, innovations.[34]

Marillac's potential defenders were not to be found with the queen mother and the magnates but rather among his relatives, friends, the leaders of the Catholic reformation, and the reformist element in the bureaucracy that was located especially among the maîtres des requêtes, but they remained in France where they were subject to censorship. Furthermore Marillac had asked them to attack no one in his behalf. Hence the few attempts that were made to defend his position have remained in manuscripts. As if to explain this situation, one of the most eloquent of these defenses, the *Apologie*, began with this quatrain:

> Je parriostray lorsque la viollance
> aura cessé d'opprimer l'innocence,
> et qu'en la France on aura liberté
> de pouvoir ouir et dire verité.

In the text that followed the author was at pains to show that Marillac had

---

33. Achille de Harlay de Sancy, *Response au libelle intitulé: Très-humble, très-véritable, et très-importante remonstrance au roy* (n.p., 1632), p. 70.

34. Ibid., pp. 70–71. For an account of the anti-Richelieu pamphlets, see Bailey, *Writers against the Cardinal.*

not been a creature of Richelieu who had betrayed his master; rather he was an elder statesman who had rebuffed attempts to make him a president in the Parlement of Paris and more recently the keeper of seals before Richelieu had entered the council in 1624. The differences between the two men lay in the fact that

> the Cardinal desired war and feared peace in which the accustomed course of the laws, order, and justice would have deprived him of any pretext to be so thoroughly occupied, to absorb so completely the mind of the King, and to advance measures that are occasioned by the expenses of war. The Keeper of the Seals, on the other hand, desired peace and did all in his power to achieve it by sure and honorable means. He perceived the needs of the Church and religion, the great misery of the people, the disorder of justice, the extraordinary measures that were daily necessary to raise money, the risks that the King incurred to his health, the frequent uprisings of the people, and the universal discontent. This is why he desired peace, contrary to the Cardinal.[35]

Notably absent from this eloquent statement was any mention of Marillac's efforts to subject the sovereign courts to the will of the king and to undermine the provincial estates. These had been unpopular measures, and his supporters passed over them in silence.

2. The Abandonment of Absolutism

But what of the great cardinal, the prince of the church who continued to seek titles, benefices, and wealth after his lay rival who had dispensed with his patrimony had departed from the scene? His first step was to consolidate his position. Henceforth only his creatures were to be given high positions in the government. If they betrayed him, they would be fortunate to escape with only the loss of their posts. Existing officials also quickly recognized the virtues of obedience. "The king was alarmed," Roland Mousnier wrote, "to see his captains leave him and pass into the cardinal's service. He foresaw the time when he would not be able to command obedience in the kingdom except through Richelieu and his men."[36] But he took no countermeasures because he believed that his minister, his mayor of the palace, was making him one of the greatest kings in the world.

Richelieu, like Marillac, was alarmed at the unrest throughout most of the kingdom. Instead of attributing it to excessive wartime taxes, he blamed it

35. Quoted by Church, *Richelieu*, p. 223. For the manuscripts of the *Apologie* and other unpublished defenses of Marillac, see n.8 above.

36. R. Mousnier, "French Institutions and Society, 1610–61," in *The New Cambridge Modern History*, ed. J. P. Cooper (Cambridge, 1970), 4:493. For a study of Richelieu and his creatures, see Orest Ranum, *Richelieu and the Councillors of Louis XIII* (Oxford, 1963).

on Marillac's efforts to control the sovereign courts, curtail the independence of the bureaucracy, undermine the provincial estates, and subvert the traditional popular liberties. If France was to have a foreign war, there must be peace at home. It was therefore not only necessary to saddle Marillac with the blame for the enforced registration of the Code Michau and as many of the unpopular acts of the government as possible but also to reverse the governmental revolution he had come so close to achieving by the time of his disgrace.[37]

Richelieu himself had favored the abolition of the paulette, and he had very likely subscribed to the effort to curtail Parlement's right of remonstrance, but he immediately set about to placate the bureaucracy and sovereign courts. Champigny, the first president of the Parlement of Paris, had died in April, and now, on November 14, just two days after Marillac had surrendered the seals, Louis appointed Le Jay to succeed him. Le Jay had been a partisan of Condé during his revolts under the regency, and he had taken the lead in trying to prevent the registration of the Code Michau. For these reasons he had been passed over for the first presidency when it had become vacant in 1629, although he had been acting in that capacity and was the choice of his fellow judges. The appointment of a man with such a record might seem strange, but it served to notify the judges that a new conciliatory policy was being inaugurated. Furthermore Le Jay became Richelieu's creature.[38]

Of far greater importance was the paulette. Richelieu and Marillac had not intended to renew it when it expired at the close of 1629, but the financial demands of the military had made it necessary to do so. However, in return they had demanded a far heavier contribution than before. Parlement had refused to permit its members to pay, and an impasse had been reached. Hardly had Marillac been dismissed and Le Jay been appointed first president than appeals were made to renew the paulette under the traditional conditions. On December 21, 1630, the crown adopted a varying rate by which the members of the sovereign court paid less than other officials. Still this was not enough, and on April 26, 1631, Parlement refused to register a declaration charging the accomplices of the duke of Orléans with lèse majesté. On May 13 Louis held a lit de justice in which he forbade Parlement to mix in affairs of state and exiled some of its members, but by the end of the month they were recalled. That August the paulette was reduced to the former rate for the officers of the sovereign courts and at a higher figure for lesser royal officials. Louis and Richelieu had surrendered, but in return not even the Parlement of Toulouse supported Montmorency in his rebellion in 1632.[39]

37. For Richelieu and his pamphleteers' role in placing the blame on Marillac, see Everat, *Michel de Marillac*, pp. 160–62, Bailey, *Writers against the Cardinal*, pp. 183–87, 410.

38. See pp. 511, 518. *Mercure François* (Paris, 1632), 16 (1630): 809.

39. Mousnier, *La vénalité*, pp. 291–96, 656–61.

This is not to say that friction between the crown and Parlement ceased. The judges could not resist interfering in political affairs. In 1632 Louis threatened them: "You are here solely to judge between Master Peter and Master John, and I intend to put you in your place; and if you continue your undertakings, I will cut your nails to the quick."[40] Three years later a lit de justice was necessary to secure the registration of an edict creating officers in Parlement and elsewhere for sale, and in 1641 another one was required to restrict Parlement's involvement in political affairs. On several occasions recalcitrant judges were temporarily exiled, and in 1631 a special commission was appointed to assume the duties of the Court of Aids after that court refused to obey a royal command to register an unpopular edict placing a tax on the sale of wine. Here as in other disputes with the courts, normal conditions were soon restored. On the whole, Richelieu inherited a very dangerous situation from Marillac, but through tact, diplomacy, and a readiness to compromise, he placated the sovereign courts and the lesser bureaucracy enough to secure a degree of cooperation from them, in spite of the repeated necessity to create new offices and to levy taxes to finance his foreign policy. In this Richelieu proved far more flexible than the king, who was ever inclined to stand on his prerogative and to insist on being obeyed absolutely. Thus Richelieu managed to avoid a Fronde, although discontent among the officials, especially in the provinces, remained high.[41]

Richelieu did not wait until the sovereign courts and bureaucracy were placated before turning to the question of the provincial estates and the élections. As if by chance, the situation in Burgundy first claimed his attention. The visit of Louis XIII and Marillac to Dijon in late April 1630 and Parlement's registration of the edict creating the élections had not settled that controversial subject because Parlement was uncooperative, and the representatives of the estates were not reconciled to their fate. On November 7 the élus visited Bellegarde, their governor, to learn what steps they could take to get the élections abolished and the garrisons in the province removed. He suggested that a new deputation be sent to the king. The élus took his advice, and negotiations were reopened with the crown a few weeks after the Day of Dupes. By January 1, 1631, an élu wrote from Paris that conditions were ripe to obtain the revocation of the edict on the élections in return for a financial contribution.[42] Several days before, the prince of Condé had been dispatched to Burgundy to pacify the province, but almost immediately more pressing affairs in Provence led Louis to assign him similar responsibilities there and in Dauphiné. Thus in less than two

40. A. Lloyd Moote, *The Revolt of the Judges* (Princeton, 1971), p. 42.

41. Ibid., pp. 40–63; J. H. Shennan, *The Parlement of Paris* (New York, 1968), pp. 249–54. For more details and a somewhat different interpretation, see James H. Kitchens, *The Parlement of Paris during the Ministry of Cardinal Richelieu, 1624–1642* (Ann Arbor, University Microfilms, 1974), 1:408–553.

42. AD, Côte-d'Or, C 3079, fols. 274–88v.

months after the Day of Dupes, Richelieu not only had decided to quell the discontent in those pays d'états in which élections had recently been created but also had chosen Condé to serve as his instrument to revoke Marillac's work.[43]

Probably the belief that the question of the élections could be resolved contributed to the Burgundian decision not to join Orléans and Bellegarde when they tried to raise a revolt in the province in March 1631. The élus recalled their deputies from Paris, and Dijon closed its gates to the rebels. On March 21, as if in answer to their expectations, the syndic of the estates gave the élus orders from the king and Condé to assemble the estates to deliberate on the revocation of the edict on the élections. A week later, when Louis himself passed through Dijon in pursuit of his brother, he told the élus that because of his great need for money, he was prepared to abolish the élections in accordance with the terms that Condé would tell them. Shortly before, Louis had expressed his gratitude to the province for its loyalty.[44]

The way was thus prepared for friendly bargaining over the abolition of the élections when the estates met. Condé arrived in Dijon on April 14 to find a complex statement prepared by the élus detailing the excessive charges, and sometimes overcharges, that had been levied on the province during the past few years to support the military. The élus hoped that this information would soften the king's demands. Condé accepted the document, and he and one of the élus set out to see the king before the estates met.[45] When the estates somewhat belatedly opened in Dijon on May 7, Condé requested 2 million livres in the king's name but softened the blow by saying that Richelieu, who as abbot of Cluny was their compatriot, had arranged for them to contribute less toward the support of the garrison stationed in the province. On May 10 the estates responded by offering 1.6 million livres to be paid in six annual installments provided the pays adjacents would contribute. Condé readily accepted the amount but insisted that the sum be raised in four years and that three of the pays adjacents— Mâcon, Auxerre, and Bar-sur-Seine—contribute only to the extent that they pleased. This was only just, for the three territories had had élections since the close of the Middle Ages, which were not to be suppressed as part of the bargain. Condé also agreed that some edicts creating offices would be revoked and that other requests would be referred to the king's council.

---

43. Musée Condé, M 2, fol. 432; *Actes Royaux,* no. 7612. Bellegarde appears to have been misinformed when he told Dijon officials that Condé was to establish the élections in Provence and Burgundy with an army. *Correspondance de la mairie de Dijon,* ed. Joseph Garnier (Dijon, 1870), 3:255–56.

44. *Correspondance de Dijon,* pp. xc–xciii, 258–268; AD, Côte-d'Or, C 3079, fols. 309v–10, 318, 320v.

45. AD, Côte-d'Or, C 3079, fols. 334–35v.

Among the most significant royal concessions was the restoration of Dijon's privileges that had been removed the year before.[46]

Burgundy was to remain a pays d'état, and Dijon was once more to be a semiautonomous town. Marillac's work had been reversed within six months of his dismissal. The grateful estates voted Condé 100,000 livres in recognition of his good offices, and the king was so pleased that he made him governor of Burgundy.[47]

If Burgundy was the first province to resume negotiations with the crown concerning the élections after the Day of Dupes, Provence was the first to strike a bargain for the removal of the hated institution. The immediate reaction of the crown to the September riots in Aix and the troubles that followed was to quell the disturbances as soon as possible, and the fall of Marillac brought no immediate change in this policy. On November 30, Louis ordered Parlement to transfer its seat to Brignoles as a punishment for the part that it had played in the troubles, and on December 5, he informed the consuls of Aix that he had ordered D'Aubray to return to Provence with several other officials. His comments on the insolence of the inhabitants of Aix and the lack of effort of the local magistrates to quell the disturbances left little doubt as to the royal attitude at this point. To these alarming tidings a deputy who had been sent to court informed the procureurs on December 12 that D'Aubray would be accompanied by 6,000 foot and 500 horse. Furthermore, in addition to transferring Parlement to Brignobles and the Court of Accounts to Toulon, the king was considering removing the seat of the seneschal to Trets. Aix was to cease to be the capital of Provence. Thoroughly alarmed, the procureurs decided to ask their governor, the duke of Guise, for permission to hold an assembly of the communities.[48]

Guise's exact role during this period is difficult to determine. Richelieu believed, or professed to believe, that he had stirred up trouble in Provence and was attempting to do so in Languedoc as well. The cardinal, however, is a most unreliable witness, for he cared not what means he used to discredit his enemies and to justify his policies. In actual fact, Guise's public conduct was always proper. He even warned Richelieu of a possible uprising in Languedoc. On the other hand, he did little to quell the disorder. It is true that his guards were the only military force at his disposal, but they would have been enough to have restored royal authority in Aix where nearly all the trouble took place. Indeed the royalist faction in the city alone was strong enough to drive out President Coriolis, the leading defender of

---

46. Ibid., C 3017, fols. 461–79; *Correspondance de Dijon*, 3:xciv. For the settlement the council made with the farmer of the offices in the élections and its approval of the agreement with the estates, see AN, E 106ª, fol. 329–29v, and E 106ᵇ–107ª, fols. 309–11v.

47. AD, Côte-d'Or, C 3017, fols. 468v–69. *Correspondance de Dijon*, 3:271–72.

48. AD, Bouches-du-Rhône, B 3348, fol. 493; Louis to the consuls of Aix and the procureurs nés du pays of Provence, December 5, 1630, C 986, C 16, fols. 81–82.

Provençal liberties, but he was soon allowed to return.[49] There may be some truth in Coriolis's statement that Guise had sent him word that he would remain "blind and deaf" to any troubles that might occur.[50] Whether because of lethargy or his desire to retain the support of the Provençals, Guise played a singularly inactive role during the entire period.

When confronted with the request of the procureurs that the communities be assembled, Guise could not avoid a decision. He therefore took the safer course and forbade the meeting because he believed that this choice would be in keeping with royal policy. On December 16 the procureurs decided to assemble the procureurs nés et joints on January 7 and to notify the communities by letter of the dangerous course of events. If the *consuls* of the communities should happen to be in Aix on the seventh, they could learn more details. Guise made no apparent effort to prevent this thinly disguised meeting of the communities. By his formal refusal to permit one to take place, he thought that he had done enough to satisfy the king.[51]

Meanwhile a shift in royal policy was taking place. Perhaps a few weeks elapsed after the Day of Dupes before Richelieu decided to reverse Marillac's policy and appease the Provençals or perhaps he was too busy consolidating his position, but the most likely explanation is that the delay was caused by Louis's reluctance to abandon his intention of punishing his insolent subjects. A deputy to court had reported on his insistence that Aix be chastised.[52] It took a while for Richelieu to persuade the irate monarch who was so jealous of his authority that it would be more profitable to permit the Provençals to buy back their privileges.

The Provençals first became aware of the new royal policy on December 23 when a *consul* of Aix was summoned to Parlement and informed that this would be a good time to depute to the king to ask that the edict on the élections be revoked. When he informed the court that Guise was unwilling to authorize a meeting of the communities to elect a delegation, it was suggested that he try again. The procureurs decided to take the hint, and on December 30 Guise authorized the meeting but insisted that it take place at Marseilles rather than in trouble-ridden Aix. It is not known who prompted Parlement to take this step, but it presumably acted on instructions from someone at court. Already, on December 21, Louis had addressed a letter to the people of the three estates of Provence telling them that he had authorized them to meet. To this welcome news the

49. Jonathan L. Pearl, *Guise and Provence: Political Conflict in the Epoch of Richelieu* (Ann Arbor, University Microfilms, 1969), pp. 206–09. The *consuls* and Parlement of Aix asked Guise to restore order, but he did nothing. Sharon K. Kettering, *Red Robes and Barricades: The Parlement of Aix-en-Provence and the Period of Popular Revolt, 1629–1649* (Ann Arbor, University Microfilms, 1969), pp. 96–97.

50. Hanotaux and La Force, *Histoires*, 4:191.

51. AD, Bouches-du-Rhône, C 16, fols. 82v–83.

52. Ibid., fol. 81.

still incensed monarch could not resist adding that he had placed Condé in command of an army that would be sure that they rendered the obedience they owed him.[53]

The assembly of the communities that Guise had authorized opened on January 12, 1631. The harassed duke pleaded for funds to activate his company of ordonnance, but the bulk of the session was devoted to the problem of how much to offer the king in return for abolishing the élections and what tactics to use to ensure that he responded favorably to their request. The value of friends at court was stressed. Of special importance was the need to give Louis's new secretary of state for Provence a handsome gratification. However, on the morning of January 15 before much had been accomplished, Guise summoned the deputies to his lodging to inform them that he had received commands by an express courier from the king to disband the meeting immediately. Louis had decided that if the estates were to meet, it would not under the questionable auspices of the duke of Guise.[54]

The man selected to effect a reconciliation was once more the prince of Condé. Accompanied by two intendants, he opened a meeting of the three estates at Tarascon on March 7. He had come, he informed the assembled deputies, to execute decrees creating the élus and some officers who were to audit municipal accounts. Furthermore, he needed money to support his troops, who remained nearby in Languedoc. Nevertheless he could give the estates satisfaction if they would aid the king in his urgent necessity. The following day Condé translated this hint into a specific offer to revoke the edict on the élections for 700,000 écus and the one creating officers to audit municipal accounts for 300,000 more. If the estates were open-handed, the sovereign courts would be reestablished in Aix at no extra charge. Again Condé mentioned the expenses of his army, which the Provençals were expected to pay along with everything else. The three estates unanimously offered a third of the proposed amount, but their unanimity ceased when the first *consul* of Tarascon unsuccessfully proposed that the nobility and clergy contribute to this sum. Condé responded that he had been instructed not to revoke the edicts for less than 2 million livres. The estates offered 1.5 million to be paid over a period of eight years. Condé accepted their offer but insisted that payments be made in four annual installments. Thus a bargain was struck. In return for 375,000 livres per year for four years, the edicts creating the élus and the auditing officials were revoked, demands for an increase in the taillon of 100,000 livres per year were abandoned, the sovereign courts were permitted to move back to Aix, and a number of other concessions were granted. As a show of their appreciation, the deputies voted Condé a present of 100,000 livres, but he magnanimously accepted only

---

53. Ibid., fols. 86–88v. Louis to the people of the three estates of Provence, December 21, 1630, ibid., C 986. For Condé's powers dated December 30, see *Actes Royaux*, no. 7612. They are summarized in Pearl, *Guise and Provence*, pp. 216–17.

54. AD, Bouches-du-Rhône, C 16, fols. 90v–98.

50,000 for himself and 20,000 for the officers of his household. Guise, who had received nothing from the estates since 1628, was voted 100,000 livres for his salary and that of his two companies for 1629, 1630, and 1631. Something of the relative importance of the intendants in this period is revealed by the fact that the estates placed their value at only 5,000 livres each.[55]

Shortly after the estates disbanded, Louis had Condé notified that he was satisfied with the way he had conducted the negotiations, and the council ratified the agreement he had made with the estates. On April 28, Louis authorized Parlement to return to Aix, but the intendants prevented the move from taking place until October because they made an unsuccessful effort to compel the judges to pay for this favor by registering a decree increasing their number.[56]

Meanwhile Condé had marched his army to Aix where he sought to ensure royal control by adding twenty trustworthy persons to the municipal council, thereby swelling its size to sixty. Guise, who had been ignored in all of these proceedings, sought to ingratiate himself at court, but without success. After the flight of Marie de Medici from France that summer, Louis summoned him for the avowed purpose of receiving his advice. Evidently fearing arrest, Guise fled to Italy, leaving his posts of admiral and governor of Provence vacant. Richelieu seized the opportunity of incorporating the functions of the former office into that of his grandmastership of navigation and commerce, and Louis named Marshal Vitry to the post of governor. By fall Marillac's grand design had been reversed, and Provence was nearly back to normal.[57]

Marillac's fall brought no immediate change in the situation in Languedoc. Richelieu probably sincerely believed that large sums were imposed upon the province without the king's permission, and he was almost certainly involved in the decision to establish élus. Hence to abandon the élections was to abandon his own work. About eight months were to elapse after the Day of Dupes before the cardinal, always a pragmatist, reached the conclusion that it would be wise to placate the Midi. Even then he made so few concessions in return for such a high price that the estates hesitated to accept his conditions.

During this eight-month period, the situation in Languedoc remained as unsettled as when Marillac was in office. The Parlement of Toulouse and many municipal officials continued to put every obstacle in the way of the appointment of the élus and their performance of their duties. In Toulouse efforts were made to prevent them from enjoying their rights. At Nîmes there

55. Ibid., fols. 115–15v, 120–28v, 144–45v; *Mercure François* 17 (1631): 98–118.

56. La Vrillière to Condé, March 27, 1631, Musée Condé, M 3. AN, E 105^b, fols. 297–99v; *Actes Royaux*, no. 7686; Kettering, *Red Robes*, pp. 112–13.

57. Pearl, *Guise and Provence, pp. 223–38; Lucas-A Boiteux, Richelieu, grand maître de la navigation et du commerce en France* (Paris, 1955), pp. 136–43.

was violence, and from Vivarais came word that the nobles were holding secret meetings and were encouraging the peasants to refuse to pay the taille. The much-abused élus asked the king's council to transfer cases concerning them from the highly prejudiced Parlement of Toulouse to the Parlement of Bordeaux, but neither individual rulings nor general royal decrees were sufficient to pacify the aroused province.[58] Meanwhile a syndic and a deputation from the estates remained continuously at court and occasionally presented specific requests to the council. Deputations from one diocesan assembly after another made their appearances, most often to request that taxes be levied to pay their debts or that they not be levied to pay the king, but despite a continuous Languedocian presence, negotiations were at a standstill. In 1631, as in 1630, taxes were collected without the consent of the estates.[59]

Montmorency made a sincere effort to reconcile the differences between the cardinal and the estates, although he knew that large concessions by the latter would weaken his powers and reduce his prestige in Languedoc. For months there was no progress as much because some Languedocians insisted that the edict on the élections be revoked without financial compensation as because of the intransigence of the cardinal. At length Montmorency brought the two sides together. Richelieu needed peace at home to have war abroad, and the deputies came to realize that if year after year passed without any meetings of the estates, the estates would die as would their other privileges. Finally, on August 25, 1631, Montmorency's secretary could announce to one of his staunchest partisans that the élus would be suppressed, although it was not until the following month that Louis issued the necessary edict.[60] In it he expressed his desire that "Languedoc enjoy all its ancient rights, privileges, franchises, favors, and concessions, ... and that henceforth no levy or imposition be made without the consent of the people of the three estates."[61]

But Languedoc was expected to pay for the revival of its estates and the right to consent to taxation. Louis wanted 3,886,000 livres to compensate the élus and 200,000 more for the partisan who had purchased the right to sell the offices that were to be suppressed. Equally serious was the provision that six commissioners would be appointed in each diocese to participate with the diocesan officials in the apportioning and collection of taxes. The élus were thus to be revived under another name. Still the contract was not altogether bad for the Languedocians. The right of the estates to consent to

---

58. Paul Gachon, *Les Etats de Languedoc et l'édit de Béziers, 1632* (Paris, 1887), pp. 218–24; AN E 105ᵃ, fol. 385, E 105ᵇ, fol. 148–48v, E 106ᵃ, fol. 272–72v; Hanotaux and La Force, *Histoire*, 4:209; Jean Albisson, *Loix municipales et économiques de Languedoc* (Montpellier, 1786), 4:262–66.

59. AN, E 105ᵇ, fols. 51–51v, 73–73v, 318–18v, 331–34, 354–55, E 106ᵃ, fols. 148–52v, 154–54v, 189–89v, 252–52v, 351–55v, E 106ᵇ–107ᵃ, fols. 230–31, 253–55v, 294, 378–78v.

60. Gachon, *Les Etats de Languedoc*, pp. 219–20.

61. Albisson, *Loix municipales*, 1:287.

taxation was specifically confirmed. They were to have the proceeds of the sale of the new offices, and the salaries fixed for them totaled only 20,000 livres per year, a bare twentieth of the wages and perquisites that had been assigned to the élus.[62]

The amount that Languedoc was asked to pay in return for the suppression of its twenty-two élections was proportionally little more than Burgundy and Provence gave to get rid of their ten, but only its estates were to be denied the privilege of having their agents resume the duty of apportioning and collecting taxes. Clearly Richelieu believed that more levies had been made there without royal permission than elsewhere, and he was determined to prevent the continuation of the practice. This and some other provisions in the September agreement were kept secret in order not to arouse opposition before Montmorency had time to return to Languedoc, convoke the estates, and persuade those who attended that it would be wise to ratify the bargain.

Montmorency was accompanied on his mission to Languedoc by Robert Miron, a statesmanlike, conservative royalist who had served as president of the third estate during the Estates General of 1614 and later as ambassador to Switzerland, and Michel Particelli, sieur d'Emery, controleur général des finances. Not until December did the trio believe that sufficient groundwork had been laid to offer some hope that the estates could be persuaded to accept the contract. Even then Emery cautioned that the meeting should not be permitted to continue for over a month because a longer session might permit the deputies to find means to escape both the élus and the commissioners. He complained at the willingness of the inhabitants to place individual interests ahead of the general good.[63] Montmorency's supporters later charged that Effiat had instructed Emery to do all in his power to prevent the contract from being approved so that the élus would not be suppressed. That Effiat was a partisan of the élus is certainly true as is the charge that he was an enemy of Montmorency, but he was not the man to try to undermine the cardinal's policies. Furthermore Emery appears to have done his best to find a satisfactory solution to a complex situation.[64]

The estates opened in Pézenas on December 12. Montmorency expressed his delight at the reestablishment of the estates, which he attributed to the goodness of the king and Richelieu and to the Languedocians' obedience. Miron followed with a longer address in which he outlined the terms of the agreement and sought to persuade the deputies to accept the arrangements that had been made. Until that moment many of them had not known the terms that the king had accorded, and they were shocked into inaction. Not until December 22 did the archbishop of Narbonne report on the two-year

62. Gachon, *Les Etats de Languedoc*, pp. 221–23.

63. AAE, ms. 1628, fols. 63, 66–67v, 73.

64. "Mémoires de Henry, dernier duc de Montmorency," in *Archives curieuses de l'histoire de France*, ed. F. Danjou, 2d sér. 4 (1838), pp. 44–45.

deputation to court which he had headed that had obtained these modest concessions. On the following day the estates somewhat reluctantly named a committee to study the king's proposals.[65] With so little progress being made, Emery felt called upon to defend himself against charges that he had been too quick to permit the estates to open. Richelieu should not be alarmed, he wrote, because the estates could be disbanded if they would not agree, and he would remain in Languedoc until the élus were firmly established. It was difficult to judge the opinion of the hundred deputies who were present, but he still thought that the chance of winning their approval was good. It would be easy if Montmorency cooperated.[66]

Still the estates moved slowly. In their few formal sessions they complained about a renewed effort on the part of the crown to increase the taillon by 200,000 livres in response to a suggestion that the Assembly of Notables had made in 1627, requested that a member of the faculty of the University of Cahors write a reply to a book challenging the prevalence of allodial property in Languedoc, voted 36,000 livres to pay their two-year deputation to court, and the like, but they avoided dealing in full assembly with the contract that had been negotiated with the king. Then between January 30 and April 17, 1632, there were no formal sessions at all.[67]

During this period the representatives of the estates and the crown negotiated in good faith. The former raised little difficulty over the huge fiscal demands of the king except that they disliked having to compensate the partisan. What troubled them was the role assigned to the commissioners in the dioceses and the requirement that the communities undergo the inconvenience and expense of having to take their financial records to the Chamber of Accounts in Montpellier to be audited. Emery recommended that some concessions be made, but when Louis reduced the number of commissioners to five, he made matters worse than ever by adding a king's attorney and greffier to their number. Furthermore Effiat told the treasurers in the Bureau of Finances to divide the direct taxes for 1632 among the dioceses, a duty that had traditionally been performed by the estates, and to have them collected by the élus. Montmorency directed the treasurers and élus to take no action pending the anticipated settlement, and the estates even sent a letter of appreciation to Richelieu, but the council delayed in making a response. As one event after another revealed his lack of credit at court, Montmorency felt his influence in Languedoc slipping. On February 21 Emery reported to Richelieu that Montmorency was "an extremely tormented" man. On April 19 and again on May 1, Montmorency sought to curb the impatience of the estates, but time was running out, for despite his

65. AD, Hérault, procès-verbal of the estates of December 1631–July 1632, fols. 1–26. For summaries of speeches, see A. Miron de L'Espinay, *Robert Miron et l'administration municipale de Paris de 1614–1616* (Paris, 1922), pp. 299–303.

66. AAE, ms. 1628, Emery to Richelieu, December 22, 1631, fols. 84–85v.

67. AD, Hérault, *procès-verbal* of the estates of December 1631–July 1632, fols. 19v, 26–35.

instructions, the treasurers apportioned the taxes and directed the élus to see that they were collected.[68]

The haste of the treasurers had tragic consequences. On May 1 Emery informed Richelieu that only the decision to direct the élus to collect taxes stood in the way of a settlement. The principal and unique liberty of the estates, he pointed out, was to make these levies. If this right was taken from them, he might have added, at the very moment they were about to pay a huge sum to regain it, the negotiations of the past months would be meaningless. He urged that either a decree be sent immediately halting the levy or that the estates be disbanded.[69] Three days later the estates, professing to believe that it was not the intention of the king that taxes be levied by his own fiscal agents, voted unanimously to direct the *consuls* of the towns to refuse to accept the commissions of the élus. They also wrote the prelates and barons of Languedoc who were absent from the estates to ask them to lend assistance in their respective dioceses. Montmorency, still loyal to the crown, urged the estates to countermand their order on the grounds that it might be misinterpreted at court, but they respectfully refused. The bishops, barons, and *consuls* cooperated with the estates, and the collection of the tax was temporarily halted.[70]

At this point a new dimension entered the picture. Montmorency consented to consider the proposals of the bishop of Albi and his nephew that he raise a rebellion in Languedoc in support of an invasion by the duke of Orléans. He had ample motives to take this perilous step. His great services to the crown in the siege of La Rochelle, in the Italian campaigns, and on other occasions had not been adequately rewarded. Indeed Richelieu had forced him to abandon his office of admiral of France. His requests that positions be assigned to his clients had often been rebuffed, and the terms he had been able to win for Languedoc in the matter of the élus had been less favorable than those obtained by Burgundy and Provence. Now it appeared likely that the king was abandoning the agreement that he had helped to negotiate. Not only was he afraid that his credit was deteriorating in Languedoc, but he also felt that his honor was being tainted because he was unable to make good the promises that he had made in good faith to the estates. As early as May 12, a French agent in Brussels reported to Richelieu that Montmorency was joining the Orléanists, but neither the cardinal nor the council made significant concessions to keep him from doing so. They seemed bent on destroying Montmorency's reputation at the risk of causing a dangerous rebellion so that he would lose his influence in Languedoc. Not

68. AAE, ms. 1628, fols. 98–103v, 107–09; Gachon, *Les Etats de Languedoc*, pp. 229–35, 279–81.

69. AAE, ms. 1628, fols. 121–22v.

70. Gachon, *Les Etats de Languedoc*, pp. 235–37, 281–86; *HL*, 11:1052; AD, Héault, procès-verbal of the estates of December, 1631–July 1632, fol. 39–40v.

surprisingly the duke's supporters later charged both Richelieu and Effiat of following this very policy.[71]

While Montmorency hesitated, the estates capitulated. On June 2 they accepted all the king's terms except the provision calling for the reimbursement of the partisan. With Montmorency's aid they took steps to borrow 600,000 livres so they could make the first payment.[72] Again a peaceful solution to the conflict seemed probable, but at about this time Montmorency promised to assist Orléans provided he was given sufficient time to organize Languedoc for the revolt. To win support he informed the crown that he was indifferent about whether the new royal tax officials in the dioceses were called commissioners or élus. As he anticipated, the government preferred the latter. When the three estates learned that there would be élus in spite of the agreement that had been reached, they were furious at having been deceived again.[73] The session of July 22 opened with a decision to send a deputation to the king to inform him of the deplorable state of the province, but before it had closed, Montmorency had persuaded those present to join him in a military effort to defend the privileges of the province and to rid France of the cardinal's influence.[74]

Montmorency's action on July 22 had been precipitated by Orléans's decision to march through France to Languedoc two months before the appointed date. His well-known charm had been sufficient to win the support of the deputies, but there was no time for him to persuade the bulk of the nobility and burghers to join his camp. The Huguenots decided to remain loyal, and over 500,000 livres that he had borrowed for the estates was seized in his Paris mansion before it could be transported to Languedoc to pay his troops. Under such circumstances defeat was a forgone conclusion, but one could hardly anticipate that it would come as soon as it did. On September 1, Montmorency was wounded seventeen times and captured when he charged the royalist infantry with only a handful of his troops. The rebellion quickly collapsed. Montmorency was tried before the Parlement of Toulouse, convicted, and executed on October 30.[75] Many persons had pleaded for his life, but Louis and the cardinal remained inflexible, although the latter especially was heavily in his debt. When Louis had been on the point of death in Lyons two years before, Montmorency had promised to

71. Mongrédien, *La Journée des Dupes*, pp. 129–35; *HL*, 11:1051, 1053, 12:1798–1800, 1803–10; Gachon, *Les Etats de Languedoc*, pp. 237, 286–88; "Mémoires de Montmorency," pp. 47–48.

72. AD, Hérault, procès-verbal of the estates of December 1631–July 1632, fols. 45v–46.

73. Gachon, *Les Etats de Languedoc*, pp. 238–40, 288–91.

74. *HL*, 11:1053–58, 12:1791–95; AD, Hérault, procès-verbal of the estates of December 1631–July 1632, fols. 54–60.

75. *HL*, 11:1059–80, 1088–95; Mongrédien, *La Journée des Dupes*, pp. 135–46; Gachon, *Les Etats de Languedoc*, pp. 240–49, 291–93.

protect Richelieu from his enemies. Gratitude, however, was among the virtues that the great cardinal almost never practiced.[76] Besides, Richelieu's memoirs state that Montmorency's fault "was not a simple crime of rebellion like that of another magnate who simply bore arms against the king in favor of Monsieur.... He caused a province to revolt by a resolution of the estates; this was never done."[77] Montmorency's great crime, then, was that he had tried to lead the people in the south in an effort to regain their liberties. It was his folly that he had made such a miserable mess of the attempt.

Because the sovereign courts, the great majority of the royal officials, and the towns of Languedoc had remained loyal, there was no reason to punish them. The bishop of Albi was exiled and the bishop of Nîmes resigned, but Richelieu, who wanted no quarrel with the church, pardoned the remaining prelates. The rebel nobles fared less well. Like Montmorency, they were deprived of their lands to the profit of their loyalist kinsmen and the creatures of the cardinal. Six baronies lost their seats in the estates, and fortified châteaux throughout the province were razed. Ventadour, Montmorency's cousin and the lieutenant governor of Languedoc, was not named governor, although he had been loyal. That post went to Schomberg, one of Richelieu's most devoted creatures, who in turn was succeeded by his son, the duke of Halwin, when he died that November. Thus the power of the Montmorency family was broken in Languedoc, and Richelieu extended his influence into the province.[78]

Since the estates had voted to support the rebellion, Louis had a legitimate excuse to suppress the institution, but he did not do so. Richelieu had no objection to representative assemblies provided that they voted the money he needed. Hence he readily accepted the advice of the first president of the Parlement of Toulouse that the estates be retained and the élus suppressed. At the same time he took steps to ensure that the crown increased its revenue and that taxes were no longer levied without the king's consent.[79] To install the new regime, a meeting of the three estates was held in Béziers from October 11 to 23. Louis himself attended, as did the cardinal and a number of other dignitaries. With his accustomed brevity, Louis told those present that he had defeated the rebellion, and as a mark of his paternal affection he was going to curtail the illegal taxes that so abused the people. The keeper of the seals spoke in greater detail, and the archbishop of Narbonne responded for the estates. Then the secretary of state for Languedoc read the Edict of Béziers, which was to govern the actions of the reformed estates, and letters granting two baronies seats as the initial

76. Hanotaux and La Force, *Histoire*, 3:286–87.
77. Gachon, *Les Etats de Languedoc*, p. 253.
78. Ibid., pp. 250–56, 293–95; *HL*, 11:1088, 1096.
79. Gachon, *Les Etats de Languedoc*, pp. 256–57.

replacement of the six that had lost this privilege.[80] The keeper of the seals then declared that the king commanded that the following statement be written on these documents: "Read and published in the presence of His Majesty with the consent of the people of the estates and the advice of the deputies of his court of Parlement of Toulouse, Court of Accounts, Aids and Finances of Montpellier, and the treasurers of France in the said province."[81] Louis then departed, and the first session of the estates came to an end.

The provisions of the Edict of Béziers can be divided into three groups.[82] One group implemented the edict of September 1631 that Montmorency and the deputies of the estates had negotiated. As provided, the élus were suppressed, and other concessions were granted in return for compensation being paid to the partisan and those who had purchased offices. There was one important change, however: the six commissioners were not created in each diocese to replace the élus. This was a real victory for the estates, although the role of treasurers of the Bureau of Finances in the diocesan assemblies was expanded. A second group of provisions dealt with the continued refusal of the estates to vote all the money the king requested, and here the people of Languedoc were dealt a severe blow. The taillon, which the crown had been trying to get the estate to increase since the Assembly of Notables of 1627, was fixed at 282,500 livres. Other expenses that the estates had often balked at paying were also included in the permanent tax base. For garrisons, 240,031 livres were to be appropriated each year; for the governor's guards, 25,170; and for the repair of roads and bridges, 70,000. Levies were fixed to pay royal officials in Languedoc. Gratifications were limited to 79,000 livres, of which 48,000 were assigned to the governor and the lieutenant general, a provision which made these two officials more beholden to the crown than to the estates for their stipends. Since these sums were to be spent in Languedoc, an additional million livres were to be levied annually to support the general expenses of the state.

The third group of provisions was designed to curb the expenses of the estates, diocesan assemblies, and towns by returning to the approach that Henry IV and Sully had tried in 1608. The estates were to meet each year in October for a maximum of fifteen days. Compensation for those who attended was fixed at a total of 11,160 livres and was to be paid only to the deputies of the third estate. In addition, 50,000 livres was assigned to pay the officers of the estates and to meet other expenses. The diocesan assemblies were limited to one eight-day meeting per year, and taxes for their

80. Ibid., pp. 257–58; AD, Hérault, procès-verbal of the estates of October 1632, fols. 1–11v; *HL*, 1:1080–83.

81. AD, Hérault procès-verbal of the estates of October 1632, fol. 11v.

82. For the edict, see Albisson, *Loix Municipales*, 1:288–97. For a discussion see Gachon, *Les Etats de Languedoc*, pp. 259–64.

support were fixed. Levies of from 300 to 900 livres were assigned to support each town and community depending on its size and importance. To prevent the local organs of government from spending more than provided for in the taxes assigned for their support, they were forbidden to borrow money without permission. These measures that so crippled the estates, diocesan assemblies, and towns undoubtedly saved the people some money, but the total amount was small when compared with the additional millions the king demanded.

The deputies elected a deputation to thank the king for the good order that he had established in the province and to plead with him not to increase their taxes so much. Especially distressing was the 1,050,000 livres they were to pay annually into the royal treasury when never before had they contributed over 300,000. On October 12 another blow fell when it was learned that the king planned to leave some horse and six regiments of foot in Languedoc, which the people were expected to support. The estates asked the archbishop of Narbonne to plead with Richelieu to have pity on their poor province so desolated by war and plague, but the only concession that he could win was a promise that strict discipline would be maintained among the troops. In the midst of their protest against the crown's fiscal demands, the deputies asked permission for the dioceses, towns, and communities to levy taxes to pay their debts, to raise 74,000 rather than 50,000 livres to meet the expenses of the estates, and to provide each deputy of the third estate with an allowance of 9 rather than 6 livres per day because of the high cost of living. Miron granted the last request for that year only and in return was voted a gratification of 3,000 livres from the small sum available to the estates for this purpose.[83]

On October 23 the deputies disbanded after an eventful session of only twelve days. They had had to accept a permanent tax burden that had been multiplied severalfold as well as to raise an additional sum to compensate the élus. But the estates had not been suppressed in spite of the rebellion; the élus were gone, and the right to consent to taxes in excess of those fixed by the Edict of Béziers had not been challenged. Richelieu's triumph on the Day of Dupes had ensured their survival because he was more interested in obtaining money for his war than in imposing a centralized, uniform system of government in France.

Only in Dauphiné did Marillac's work survive. The nobility and clergy desired to get the edict creating the élections revoked in return for compensating the élus, and it is probable that Richelieu hoped that the province would do so. On December 21, just six weeks after the Day of Dupes, the first *consul* of Grenoble informed his fellow municipal officials that the nobles were going to assemble in their city on January 20. Those present decided to ask Parlement for permission for the third estate to meet at the same time. Initially, at least, it was believed that the crown was opposed to the nobles'

83. AD, Hérault, procès-verbal of the estates of October 1632, fols. 13–30.

meeting, for early in February the Parlement of Grenoble informed Condé that their assemblies were detrimental to the affairs of the king and that his majesty desired that they be dispersed.[84] Nevertheless the nobles met on February 2 and on other occasions, although Condé, who was then in Dauphiné with an army, could have prevented them from doing so if Richelieu had so desired. The third estate, from whom any financial offer must come, also met, but little is known of its deliberations.[85] It seems probable, however, that Condé had been given secret instructions concerning the élus, but no offer was forthcoming.[86]

The failure of any of these assemblies to act must be attributed to the bitter quarrel between the third estates and the other two orders over the question of whether the taille was réelle or personelle. Tension was especially strong at this time because on January 7, 1631, the Parlement of Grenoble, whose judges were closely allied with the nobility, forbade any assemblies to be held without its permission or that of the king in order to prevent Claude Brosse, the dynamic syndic of the villages, from organizing the people to make new appeals to the crown. At the same time the court ordered that Brosse be arrested. As a consequence of this act, the appearances of the third estate before the king's council were largely devoted to a successful effort to secure Brosse's release, and the élus were permitted to continue their struggle to take over the tax-collecting duties that had formerly been performed by the agents of the estates.[87]

By May 1632, just eighteen months after the Day of Dupes, Richelieu must have felt satisfaction as he surveyed the provincial estates. The treasury had profited immensely from the sale of offices in the élections in Dauphiné, Burgundy, Provence, and Languedoc. There had been considerable resistance, but his decision to reverse Marillac's absolutist policies had restored calm in Burgundy and Provence. If the privileged orders and the third estate in Dauphiné could get together and agree to pay to have the élections suppressed, so much the better. If they could not, they would not be too dangerous divided. The situation in Languedoc had not yet been resolved, but the estates there appeared to be ready to pay the largest sum of all to be rid of the élections. Under these circumstances, the great cardinal and his royal master now decided to carry out Marillac's plan to create élections in the Pryrenean provinces, pocket the money from the sale of the new offices, but then satisfy their fiercely independent subjects by permitting them to pay

84. *IAC, Grenoble*, ed. Auguste Prudhomme (Grenoble, 1886), BB 97, BB 98; Richelieu, *Lettres*, 7:657; Musée Condé, M 3, fol. 24.

85. AD, Isère, H 357; *IAD, Drôme, sér. E*, ed. A Lacroix (Valence, 1898), 6:345. There are also references to a meeting of the nobles in the late spring. AAE, ms. 1546, fols. 233–34, AN, V⁶, 84, no. 38.

86. La Vrillière to Condé, February, 24, 1631, Musée Condé, M 3, fols. 78–79.

87. A. Lacroix, "Claude Brosse et les tailles," *Bul. de la soc. d'archéologie et de statistique de la Drôme* 32 (1898): 370–71; AN, E 105ᵇ, fols. 55–56, E 106ᵃ, fol. 424, E 106ᵇ–107ᵃ, fol. 306–306v, E 107ᵇ, fol. 359.

to have the élections suppressed. They issued an edict ordering that six élections be established in Béarn, Navarre, Bigorre, Foix, Nébouzan, and Aure and Marsan. They also erected the Court of Aids of Navarre with an appropriate number of venal offices.[88]

The inhabitants of the Pyrenees had long expected the blow to fall. When the estates of Béarn had met in January 1630, there had been reports that they were next on Marillac's list to receive an élection and a Court of Aids. With considerable spirit they had protested this meeting that May and again in November 1631. Hence they were prepared when they met in the fall of 1632 after their fears had become fact. Their cahier consisted primarily of a long and vigorous protest against the creation of both the élection and Court of Aids, and efforts were made to get the Parlement of Navarre to delay registering the decrees.[89]

Little is known concerning the reactions of the other estates, but they must have been vigorous because in September 1633 Louis, having profited from the sale of the new offices, suppressed the élections and the Court of Aids in return for the usual compensation being paid. Henceforth, he declared, "the estates of our kingdom of Navarre and of the provinces of Béarn, Foix, Bigorre, Nébouzan, and Marsan will enjoy the same privileges, liberties and advantages that they formerly had, notwithstanding all edicts, decrees, and regulations to the contrary."[90] Nevertheless following the precedent that had been established in the Edict of Béziers concerning Languedoc, Louis tried to reduce the expenses of estates and to prevent them from levying taxes that he had not authorized. Their sole annual meeting was to take place in April at his express command and to last a maximum of eight days in Béarn and four days in the other provinces. An officer of the Chamber of Accounts of Navarre was to serve as royal commissioner and to participate in the apportionment of taxes. He was also to approve the deputies' choice of a clerk, and the clerk was to submit copies of the journal of the estates and the apportionment of the taxes to the Chamber of Accounts of Navarre. Ceilings were placed on the amounts that the estates and the communities could levy, and no taxes were to be imposed without royal permission.

This arrangement was still not satisfactory to the estates. Once more they deputed to court, and on July 20, 1634, Louis revoked the provisions in his edict of September 1633 which infringed on their freedom. In return, the

88. Following H. Jolly and H. Courteault, "Essai sur le régime financier des petits pays d'Etats du Midi de la France au XVIIIe siècle," *Bul. de la soc. des sciences, lettres et arts de Pau,* sér. 2, 54 (1931): 138, most historians have said that the edict creating the élections was issued in 1629. For evidence, Jolly and Courteault cite a letter of January 4, 1782, located in AN, H[1] 1159. This letter, however, dates the edict as being of May 1632 as does the edict of September 1633 suppressing the élections cited in n.90 below.

89. AD, Basses-Pyrénées, C 710, fols. 282–91, 314–25, C 711, fols. 32, 55, 67–68, 154–54v, C 689, fols. 105v–07.

90. A copy of the edict is in the BN, F 46,977. For the quote, see p. 5.

estates of the various provinces were expected to increase their annual donations by a total of more than 20,000 livres and to give a special one-year grant of an additional 20,000. This meant, for example, that Bigorre, whose donation to the crown had been fixed at 7,000 livres per year in the reign of Henry IV, was henceforth to give 9,591 livres annually plus an additional one-year grant of 2,300 livres. Even this was too much, and on August 13, 1636, the king's council reduced the donations of the provinces to their pre-1633 figure and cancelled the arrears that had not been paid. Thus the Pyrenean estates escaped both Marillac and Richelieu. Their privileges remained intact, and they were to pay the same annual taxes as before except for what was required to support local troops during the war.[91]

Brittany, the one remaining province that had escaped Marillac's determined efforts to establish a centralized, uniform government, was equally fortunate in its dealings with Richelieu. Perhaps the cardinal realized that he could make a quick profit there by creating élections and letting the inhabitants pay to be rid of them. There is no evidence, however, that he ever seriously considered such a plan. He needed the cooperation of the Bretons for his maritime and commercial plans; they had a troublesome reputation for independence, and also he had become their governor. Like most other magnates, he was, perhaps unconsciously, a defender of the autonomy of his government. Had Marillac triumphed in the Day of Dupes, it would have been another story. But he had not, and several years after his downfall, France, institutionally speaking, looked very much like it had before he became keeper of the seals.

3. RICHELIEU AND THE PAYS D'ETATS

When Condé opened the estates of Burgundy in November 1632 with a speech stressing the great needs of the king, the duty of those present to render him "blind obedience," and his own obligation to do things that were disagreeable when the circumstances required, he seemed to be suggesting that a new era was dawning.[92] But this was not the case. The estates continued to meet at least every third year to vote taxes, and when the need arose, there were special sessions. Because of the war, a large number of troops were stationed in the province or passed through it.

91. For the decree of July 20, 1634, see AN, H¹ 716; and AD, Hautes-Pyrénées, C 125. For the activities of the estates of Foix, see G. Arnaud, *Mémoire sur les Etats de Foix, 1608–1789* (Toulouse, 1904), pp. 99–101, and AD, Basses-Pyrénées, B 3772. For Navarre see AN, K 1233, nos. 56–60. For Béarn see AD, Basses-Pyrénées, C 689, fols. 115v–23, C 711, fols. 200–19v, C 712, fol. 108v. For Bigorre, see Gilbert Pène, *Les attributions financières des Etats du pays et comté de Bigorre aux XVIIe et XVIIIe siècles* (Bordeaux, 1962), pp. 99, 111; AD, Hautes-Pyrénées, C 128, C 132; and *IAC, Vic-Bigorre*, ed. Jean Pambrun (Tarbes, 1924), pp. 3–4, 85–99 passim.

92. *Mercure François*, 18 (1632): 926–30.

Occasionally it was necessary for the élus to take extraordinary steps to provide for their support, but the estates could and did vote the king less than he requested. In 1636, for example, they gave only 200,000 livres of the 300,000 demanded, and in 1639 with Condé's assistance, they managed to escape part of the costs of troops in Burgundy. During the last decade of Louis's reign, the Burgundians poured considerably less money into his treasury than in the first, but these figures, of course, do not include the substantial sums they contributed to the support of resident troops during the latter period.[93]

In 1639 Louis suppressed the estates of Auxonne and incorporated the county, which was one of the pays adjacents, into the duchy of Burgundy. One might be tempted to interpret this act as evidence of a centralizing policy on the part of the crown, but nothing could be further from the truth. The initiative in securing the edict was taken by the élus of the estates of the duchy. They justified their proposal by charging that the élus of Auxonne were ruining the county by heavy taxes, which they spent as they pleased. If the élus were suppressed, royal taxes could be levied more easily. Furthermore, "There is no reason to have a diversity of estates since what is done by a single body is done much better than by several who are often disunited and divided."[94] Thus the estates of Burgundy, the defenders of particularism vis à vis the crown, were the apostles of centralization within their own environs. The king's council granted the request over the protests of the élus of Auxonne, but to secure this favor, the Burgundians found it advisable to give the king 120,000 livres, Condé, their governor, 100,000, and some unnamed persons 80,000 more.[95]

The Provençals proved less cooperative than the Burgundians. In November 1631, their new governor, Marshal Vitry, assembled the deputies of the communities to ask for 147,000 livres to support the army and 375,000 for the galleys. Those who came initially offered a third that amount, but after some haggling they agreed to give a little more.[96] Partially victorious in this instance, the Provençals nevertheless had difficulty in checking the ever-increasing fiscal demands of the crown. When other measures failed, Louis created offices to sell, and the Provençals were expected to pay the salaries of the purchasers. The need to support troops in the province to prevent them from plundering also caused problems. In September 1632 the procureurs nés et joints voted to borrow 95,000 livres for this purpose, because if they taxed the people more heavily, there would probably be a revolt. When the three estates met that December, they were informed that

---

93. *IAD, Côte-d'Or, sér. C*, ed. Joseph Garnier (Dijon, 1886), 3:75–76, 142–50; Mallet, p. 207.

94. F. Moreau, "La suppression des Etats du comté d'Auxonne et leur réunion aux Etats du duché de Bourgogne," *Mém. de la soc. pour l'histoire du droit et des institutions des anciens pays bourguignons, comtois et romands* 2 (1935): 191.

95. Ibid., p. 194.

96. AD, Bouches-du-Rhône, C 19.

because of desolation and suffering in the province, the king had decided to ask for only 1.8 million livres during the next three years rather than 3 million as he had originally intended. The estates were further horrified to learn that this was in addition to the 1.5 million livres they were still paying in return for revocation of the edict creating the élections. The usual bargaining followed, and a compromise was eventually reached in which the king took far less than he desired and agreed to suppress some offensive edicts. One of Richelieu's agents reported that the estates were very happy, as indeed they ought to have been, if the crown had not soon turned again to the sale of offices to make up for its losses.[97]

Since the grant that the estates had voted in December 1632 was to be collected over a four-year period, the king could scarcely hope to gain a large additional sum in the near future. As a result, the tension between the crown and the Provençals relaxed a little, but certainly the intendant's report that the assembly of the communities in May 1633 had unanimously resolved "to obey his majesty's requests blindly" was a gross exaggeration.[98] Problems concerning the creation of offices and the support of troops continued to plague the officials of the estates, and the communities had to assemble several times a year. Furthermore the crown broke its pledge to the estates of 1632 and attempted to increase the salt tax. Vitry, who figured prominently in the affair, became such an unpopular governor that in January 1635 each of the three estates in separate assemblies asked that he be replaced by the archbishop of Lyons, Richelieu's brother.[99]

When Louis asked the assembly of the communities to vote 1.2 million livres in February 1636 to support a naval operation to drive the Spanish from their coast, they complied because their own interests were so closely involved. Although there was no clear distinction between the duties of the meetings of the three estates and those of the communities, the deputies did point out that the former assembly should have been called upon to vote such a large sum that was in the form of a don gratuit. In February 1639 when Louis decided to ask the Provençals to support the troops stationed in Provence, to contribute to the costs of winter quarters for the royal army, and to give an additional 400,000 livres per year until the end of the war, he convoked the three estates. Those present balked at voting so large a sum for an indefinite period. Only with considerable difficulty could they be persuaded to grant 600,000 livres annually for the support of the troops in Provence. They rejected the remainder of the royal requests. That November Louis turned to the assembly of the communities with better

97. Kettering, *Red Robes*, pp. 101–02, 113–23; AD, Bouches-du-Rhône, C 20, fols. 168–69, 201–11v, 235v–40; AAE, ms. 805, fols. 159–62, ms. 1702, fols. 150–51v.

98. *Lettres et mémoires adressés au Chancelier P. Séguier, 1633–1649*, ed. A. D. Lublinskaya (Moscow, 1966), p. 234.

99. *IAD, Bouches-du-Rhône, sér. C*, ed. Louis Blancard (Marseilles, 1884), 1:28–29. AD, Bouches-du-Rhône, C 108, fols. 105v–07. Kettering, *Red Robes*, pp. 102–04, 112–16.

success. Thereafter neither he nor his successors ever convoked the three estates.[100]

There is no evidence that Louis and Richelieu decided to abandon the three estates after their failure to win a substantial amount in 1639. It is true that the assembly of the communities had been more generous in 1636 than the three estates were three years later, but neither the king nor his minister could have been unaware that the nature of their requests was quite different. For some time they had relied primarily on the assembly of the communities and had permitted several years to elapse between the meetings of the estates. Hence a gap between 1639 and the end of the reign less than four years later proves nothing. Furthermore the assemblies of the communities had often made difficulties about the taxes in the past. After all, it was their constituents and not those of the clergy and nobility who paid the largest part of the taxes. Furthermore the nobility and the clergy continued to have their assemblies until the Revolution, and their procureurs attended the assemblies of the communities. Indeed the Provençals thought so little about the crown's failure to convoke the three estates that it was not until 1652 that they complained. By then it seems clear that the Mazarin regime had come to the conclusion that the assemblies of the communities were more pliable because it steadfastly refused to accede to their repeated requests that the three estates be convoked.[101]

When Richelieu restored to the estates of Languedoc and their dioceses the duties of apportioning and collecting taxes in 1633, he probably thought that he ran no great risk of mitigating royal authority. As part of the agreement, specified sums were to be levied annually without debate to support specified expenses within the province, and 1.05 million livres were to be turned over to the royal treasury. This was far more than Languedoc had ever contributed in the past, and Richelieu doubtless thought that it was sufficient to meet the crown's needs in the foreseeable future. However, the approaching war with the Habsburgs and the formal opening of a full-scale conflict in 1635 made it necessary for the crown to increase its demands, with the result that the quarrel over how much the estates of Languedoc would vote continued as before.

In 1633 Louis asked for 280,000 livres in addition to what had now become the automatic grant, but the estates would vote for only 50,000. In 1634 he requested a larger sum, but the estates would give him only 30,000 livres. This double refusal infuriated him. He ordered that 100,000 livres be levied to fortify Narbonne without the consent of the estates, and he created commissioners and greffiers in each diocese. Because these were the very officials Richelieu had originally intended to use to replace the élus, this was

---

100. Bernard Hildesheimer, *Les assemblées générales des communautés de Provence* (Paris, 1935), pp. 69–71.

101. Ibid., pp. 71–74.

an obvious threat that the crown was prepared to substitute its own tax collectors for those of the estates if more cooperation was not forthcoming. Instead of cringing, however, the estates devoted most of their efforts to protesting against these violations of their privileges and refused to vote more than 50,000 livres. In 1636 Louis asked for an additional 1.2 million livres, but the estates refused to give him any of it. They did offer 900,000 to be rid once more of the commissioners and greffiers. The following year when the Spanish invaded Languedoc, the governor hastily called a rump assembly of the estates to authorize a loan and then defeated the enemy. The estates that met a few months later declared the actions of the rump assembly void because only a full assembly could borrow in the name of the province. They finally assumed responsibility for the debt but refused to accede to any of the king's requests for funds.[102]

This series of meetings shows clearly that the Edict of Béziers had not paralyzed the ability of the estates to resist taxation. Indeed, they frequently cited its provisions as a defense against the exactions of the crown. The few additional sums they had voted the king were designated for local fortifications. Languedoc poured nearly 3 million livres into the royal treasury in 1633 and again in 1634, but thereafter it contributed an average of only about 1.2 million per year during the reign. Although this figure does not include local expenses, such as the support of troops which became increasingly onerous as the war progressed, it was sufficiently restricted to arouse the ire of the crown. In 1638 Louis gave the estates a choice of voting 1.06 million livres or having troops lodged in the province for the winter, but once more he was repulsed. In 1639 the prince of Condé presided over the estates, with no better results.[103]

Louis had had enough. On December 10, 1639, Condé ordered that an additional 1.21 million livres be levied on the dioceses to support the troops. Since he had no tax-collecting machinery of his own, he had to use that of the estates. During the past several years when the estates had refused to vote money for the troops, individual communities and sometimes dioceses had provided food or money to prevent looting, although by doing so they violated the basic privilege of the province and undermined the right of the estates to give consent. What Condé's order did was to generalize the system throughout the province. We do not know how effective these "illegal" taxes were. Very likely few diocesan or community officials refused to obey orders emanating from the king or his leading representatives in the province. On the other hand, unless they were threatened by troops in the immediate vicinity, most officials and taxpayers probably found excuses to procrastinate. The system was certainly most unsatisfactory to the estates and was

---

102. William H. Beik, *Governing Languedoc: The Practical Functioning of Absolutism in a French Province 1633–1685* (Ph.D. diss., Harvard University 1969), pp. 42–46. I am indebted to Professor Beik for permitting me to see his dissertation. *HL*, 11 : 1100–19.

103. Mallet, p. 206; Beik, *Governing Languedoc*, pp. 46–49; *HL*, 11 : 1119–24.

very likely not too satisfactory to the crown. It is not surprising, therefore, that the estates adopted a new approach when they met in 1640.[104]

In that year Louis asked for 1.65 million livres to support troops during the winter and an additional sum for the garrison. The estates, though protesting loudly that these demands violated the Edict of Béziers, voted the former both to prevent a stronger precedent from developing for the king's levying taxes without their consent and to ensure that their tax-collecting machinery was used. This was a wise move, for their officials soon learned to provide for the troops so well that their cooperation became indispensable to the crown. When Richelieu and Louis died several years later, they left Languedoc an exploited province that had experienced illegal taxation, but the position of the three estates was intact, and their administrative system was more essential to the crown than ever before.[105]

To test Richelieu's attitude toward the provincial estates, it is best to turn to Brittany because it is only here that there is evidence that he followed their activities closely. His interest, of course, was derived from the fact that in 1631 he became governor of the province, a post that he had sought because of his maritime and naval projects. For his overly proud and bad-tempered young cousin, Charles de La Porte, marquis de La Meilleraye, he prepared instructions in November 1634 directing how the estates should be treated. He had had La Meilleraye appointed lieutenant general in the county of Nantes and was about to use him as the principal royal commissioner in the forthcoming meeting of the estates. The estates, he explained, should have the service of the king and the welfare of the province as their sole aim. It was essential that he acquit his assignment satisfactorily because everyone would assume that "his actions will be based on my advice and opinions. Consequently, the honor or dishonor they bring will reflect as much on me as on himself." After associating his own reputation with his advice in this fashion, Richelieu continued:

> He [La Meilleraye] will restore the estates to their ancient liberty, permitting everyone who has the right to participate to come freely in order to vote on the matters which will be proposed, without any obstacles either directly or indirectly being placed in their way.
>
> He will permit them to deliberate on their affairs as they think advisable, without interfering on behalf of anyone, but leaving them to disentangle their interests among themselves so that they will judge what the good of the province will require, provided that under this pretext nothing is done which can be disagreeable to the king.[106]

Of course La Meilleraye was to persuade the estates to vote the king the

---

104. Beik, *Governing Languedoc*, pp. 49–52, 209–14.
105. Ibid., pp. 52–55, 214–17; *HL*, 11: 1124–30.
106. Richelieu, *Lettres*, 7: 728–29.

largest sum that the province could bear in its present state. He was also to see that the right to collect the taxes was awarded to the highest bidder in an auction in which everyone was free to participate. To prevent unjust profits, the provincial debts were to be verified. Finally the cardinal piously declared that he did not want the estates to vote him a present although it was customary to give their governor one.

These instructions taxed the credulity of the careful editor of Richelieu's letters, and he was inclined to discount them.[107] Yet one suspects that La Meilleraye paid heed to the advice that he had received when he held this and other meetings of the estates. On December 21, the day the estates of 1634 ended, one of Richelieu's correspondents referred to the fact that it had pleased the cardinal "to reestablish order and liberty"[108] in the estates, and another pointed out that the estates had ended happily and that the highest possible price had been received for the farm "because freedom was given to everyone to bid as much as he wished."[109] After the estates of 1636–37 had voted the don gratuit, La Meilleraye informed the king's secretary of state for Brittany that he had obtained all that he could without "extreme violence," which he had been unwilling to use.[110] The bishop of Saint-Malo, who doubled as a client of Richelieu and as a deputy to the estates, praised La Meilleraye's conduct, for it had enabled him to obtain 2 million livres from the estates "without violence on his part or regret on ours."[111]

The typical Parisian bureaucrat had little sympathy for this approach. A maître des requêtes sent to Rennes in 1636 to quell a disturbance informed the chancellor that "as this province enjoys the liberty of her estates, it is also unaccustomed to the respect and obedience due the king and those who are sent to them on his behalf."[112] As if to secure an opportunity to revenge the treatment that he had received or at least to salve his wounded pride, he then asked to be named the first commissioner to the estates when they next met.

Whatever the maître de requêtes might think, the estates voted larger don gratuits during the Richelieu regime than ever before. In 1632 they were asked for 1.4 million livres to be collected over a two-year period. After the usual bargaining, the estates gave 1.05 million. In 1634 they were asked for 1.5 million livres and finally voted 1.2 million plus an additional 300,000 for raising troops in Brittany. In 1636 they were asked for 2.5 million for one year and gave 2 million to be paid in three years; and in 1640 they were asked for 3 million and gave 2 million plus 400,000 for the suppression of some offices. Although the estates had always given the cardinal con-

107. Ibid., p. 729 n.1.
108. AAE, ms. 1505, fol. 100.
109. Ibid., fol. 94.
110. Ibid., ms. 1504, fol. 153.
111. Ibid., ms. 1505, fol. 382.
112. Porchnev, *Les Soulèvements populaires*, p. 599.

siderably less than he requested except in 1634, the size of the don gratuit doubled between 1632 and 1640.[113]

How did Richelieu accomplish this miracle? Two factors are unquestionably important. First, he worked within the framework of the traditional Breton institutions and refrained from blatantly arbitrary acts. Second, he placed his clients in key positions and drew leading Bretons into his network. They, in turn, brought their own clients into his service. In addition to his cousin, La Meilleraye, Richelieu's noble clients included the baron de Pontchâteau who is reported to have brought over a hundred gentlemen with him to the estates of 1636. To entice poorer nobles to attend, the estates had long before established a pension fund of 10,000 livres from which grants of from 100 to 300 livres were made. It is difficult to believe that Richelieu and his prominent Breton clients did not exercise a voice in choosing the recipients, although many of them did not attend the estates or at least did not sign the rolls. A number of bishops and abbots were in Richelieu's entourage. Included was Achille de Harlay, baron de Sancy, one of his leading pamphleteers and the principal compiler of his memoirs. In November 1631 Richelieu had him nominated for the bishopric of Saint-Malo so that he would have a seat in the estates and an opportunity to influence and report on Breton affairs. Even the procureur syndic of the estates was Richelieu's client. Those outside the chosen circle were as likely to court the cardinal's favor in hope of reward as to oppose his will. To encourage this hope, Richelieu made sure that his creatures received handsome rewards, and his leading henchmen at the estates gave lavish entertainments in order to draw still more deputies into his net.[114]

Apparently Richelieu had more difficulty extending his influence into the third estate, or perhaps that order more often opposed his will because its members paid most of the taxes that he sought. In 1636 when the king asked for 3.6 million livres, the nobles first suggested that from 1.5 million to 1.8 million livres be granted, but the other orders thought that 1.2 million should suffice. Evidently Richelieu's creatures went to work on their following, because two days later both the nobility and the clergy were willing to vote 2 million livres, but the third estate would not budge. A compromise offer of 1.5 million livres was made at length, only to be rejected by La Meilleraye. More politicking brought forth an offer of 1.8 million livres three days later, but this was not sufficient. Only after fifteen days of manipulation were the estates finally brought to voting 2 million livres.[115]

113. AD, Ille-et-Vilaine, C 2652, fols. 443, 487, 489, 602–03, 669, 672, 674, 689, C 2653, fols. 16, 75, 77, 92, 98, 102, 104–06, 120–21, 228, 262, 264, 267–68, 298–99, 375, 400, 419. For a detailed account of the estates of 1632–40, see Kenneth M. Dunkley, *Richelieu and the Estates of Brittany, 1624–1640* (Ann Arbor, University Microfilms, 1972), pp. 204–57.

114. Dunkley, *Richelieu*, pp. 61–65, 181–201.

115. A. Bourdeaut, "Journal des Etats de Bretagne tenu à Nantes en décembre 1636 par Dubuisson-Aubenay," *Bul. de la soc. archéologique et historique de Nantes et de la Loire-Inférièure* 67 (1927): 269–74.

If the cardinal had a way of prevailing on the deputies, the deputies in turn had their means of persuading the king's men to accept less than their master wanted and to make numerous other concessions. For Richelieu himself, the estates appropriated a princely 100,000 livres in every meeting from 1630. The influence of La Meilleraye was valued at 36,000 livres by 1636. Great Breton nobles like Brissac and Pontchâteau were given from 12,000 to 20,000 livres. The secretary of state for Brittany received 6,000, and there were often grants for many lesser persons, including Richelieu's physician, secretary, and his guards. The estates of Brittany had always been among the most generous, but during Richelieu's regime, they became far more lavish than before. From 6,000 to 12,000 livres had sufficed for Vendôme when he was governor, although he was half-brother of the king, but of course the cardinal was expected to stretch his 100,000 livres over a two-year period.[116]

4. RICHELIEU AND THE ESTATES IN THE PAYS D'ELECTIONS

Richelieu's willingness to respect the privileges of the various pays d'états and to work with his clients through existing institutions suggests that he did little to alter the situation in provinces in which there were both estates and élections. As far as has been ascertained, this surmise is correct. Indeed it would be difficult to demonstrate that Richelieu paid any attention to these estates at all. However, this does not prove that changes did not take place, for Richelieu gave considerable freedom to his subordinates, some of whom were advocates of Marillac's policy of centralization, uniformity, and absolutism. Effiat, the superintendent of finances, for example, was an enthusiastic supporter of the élections. He must have been bitterly disappointed when Richelieu altered Marillac's policy after the Day of Dupes, and the Provençals, who had hanged him in effigy in 1630, must have been relieved, along with others, when he died on July 27, 1632.

A greater threat were the maîtres des requêtes who were sent to the provinces in increasing numbers during the last decade of Richelieu's ministry to maintain order and to facilitate the collection of taxes. These men, who were then rapidly evolving into the intendants so famous during the following reign, were apt to look on any assembly that tried to delay or alter the express orders of the king as being seditious and those who participated as being motivated by purely selfish interests.

On December 2, 1637, for example, Jean de Mesgrigny, intendant of Auvergne, prepared an account of the situation in that province. After explaining to the chancellor the distinction between Haute- and Basse-Auvergne and informing him who the king's governor and lieutenants were,

116. Dunkley, *Richelieu*, pp. 202–04.

he turned to the question of the estates. In Haute-Auvergne, he declared approvingly, these meetings had been forbidden by the council at the request of the late sieur de Noailles, lieutenant of the king, because they were prejudicial to the interests of the crown. In Basse-Auvergne there was still a syndic of the nobility, but he was eighty years old. For many years he had not performed the duties of his office or convoked an assembly of gentlemen because he had been forbidden to do so. The échevins of Clermont, on the other hand, summoned the third estate three or four times annually.[117]

There were widespread complaints among the people, he continued, about the way échevins of Clermont claimed to represent the third estate. Each year 6,000 livres were levied on the people and placed in the hands of the échevins to be used in the interest of the province, but because of the costs of their deputations, gifts, and gratifications for royal officials, this was not enough, and more taxes had to be placed on the people. Furthermore to support troops in the province, the échevins, as representatives of the third estate, had additional sums levied, which in the current year came to over 300,000 livres. It would be better to support the troops by gifts of meat, wheat, and wine, which were abundant, but the échevins preferred to tax because they profited more from this approach. "The majority of the towns," he continued, "wish that this assembly would be abolished as it is burdensome to them because of the levies and impositions. It is by this means that the town of Clermont and her échevins oppress the remainder of the province.... Moreover, the said assemblies of the third estate of Basse-Auvergne are true monopolies and cabals that are prejudicial to the affairs of the king as the late Sieur de Noailles had recognized in Haute-Auvergne. I have twice attended the assemblies of Basse-Auvergne, and although my presence held them in their duty, nevertheless they were always carried by their opinions to decisions prejudicial to the service and affairs of his majesty."[118] As a result, Mesgrigny had forbidden the échevins of Clermont to assemble the third estate without the king's permission and to pretend to represent that order. Although the king's council had upheld his decree and had ordered that the 6,000 livres formerly given to the échevins be turned over to the treasury, these decisions had not been enforced. "And I consider, Monseigneur," he continued, "that it is very important for the service of the king, for the good and repose of the province and the welfare of the poor people, to abolish totally this assembly of the third estate of Basse-Auvergne as it has been abolished in Haute-Auvergne where some people are trying to reestablish it."[119]

In his discussion of the assemblies of the third estate, Mesgrigny acted as though the élus levied whatever taxes the échevins of Clermont directed. In

117. *Lettres et mémoires adressés au Chancelier Séguier, 1633–1649*, ed. Roland Mousnier (Paris, 1964), 2 : 1136.
118. Ibid., p. 1138.
119. Ibid.

other respects, he understood their functions and was even aware that the diocese of Clermont had the right to send a deputy to participate in the élus' apportionment of the taille, although he does not seem to have approved of the practice. Could it be that the élus, royal officials though they were, had become so much a part of the provincial picture that they were in effect also servants of the estates.[120]

It is not difficult to guess where Mesgrigny obtained such an unflattering picture of the échevins of Clermont. For generations their dominant position in the assemblies of the good towns had been challenged by Riom, whose claim to importance was derived from the fact that it served as the seat of both the seneschalsy and the presidial court. The officers of these two institutions could not bear to see the elected officials of Clermont convoke the third estate whenever they wished, serve as syndics of the province, and spend the 6,000 livres that were annually collected in taxes on various activities which they claimed were in the interest of the province. Such powers, they thought, were regalian and should be exercised in the absence of the king only by his officials, namely themselves. In 1576 and in 1588, they had tried to usurp the duty of convoking the third estate to elect deputies to the Estates General despite repeated decrees of the king's council recognizing the right of the échevins of Clermont to perform this task. At an early date, they had won control over the municipal government of Riom and with it the right to name Riom's deputation to the assemblies of the good towns. Taking advantage of this situation, they had seized every opportunity to criticize the administration of the échevins of Clermont and had managed to win a few other towns to their cause. In 1626 they had obtained a decree from the king's council restricting the échevins' claim to provide automatically the deputy for the third estate, and now they exhibited a willingness to undermine the privileges of the province by poisoning the mind of the intendant, provided that in doing so they also broke the power of their rivals.[121]

Mesgrigny may have erred when he listened too attentively to the bureaucracy at Riom, but he did not miss the mark by much when he spoke of the activity of the third estate of Basse-Auvergne. The nineteen good towns assembled three times in 1636, the year before he prepared his memorandum, although once or twice a year usually sufficed earlier in the decade. On March 24, 1637, they also met, and Mesgrigny, who was then in Clermont on his mission, sent word that he would like to attend. The deputies asked him not to come because it would be contrary to ancient custom. What must have been a somewhat startled intendant responded that he had special orders from the king to attend but that he had no intention of

120. Ibid., pp. 1139, 1144–46.

121. J. R. Major, *The Deputies to the Estates General of Renaissance France* (Madison, 1960), pp. 82–83; *IAC, Riom*, ed. F. Boyer (Riom, 1892), AA 18.

interfering with their privileges. The estates then sent a deputation inviting him to come. During the course of the meeting, the viscount of Polignac informed those present that he had an edict from the king's council ordering that 11,000 livres be levied to pay his guard and 12,000 to pay his salary as the king's lieutenant. He did not wish to have the order executed without first securing "the consent of the said third estate." The deputies who were present readily gave their approval with equal tact.[122]

Such experiences as these must have contributed to the bad impression that the autocratic intendant was forming of the assemblies of the good towns and led him to recommend that they be abolished some months later. He himself came from Champagne where the estates had never become permanently established. But the king's councillors in Paris were wiser than he, for the good towns assembled at least twice in every remaining year of the reign, except in 1639 when one meeting sufficed.[123]

Even the assemblies of the four provostships of Haute-Auvergne were not as dead as Mesgrigny believed, or wanted to believe. In March 1630 the *consuls* of St. Flour had won confirmation of their right to convoke the third estate, and they proceeded to do so in 1630, 1632, and 1636. Unhappily for their pretensions, Mesgrigny was in the province on the last occasion. Perhaps he intervened to prevent deputies from Aurillac and Maurs from attending, for when a deputation from St. Flour complained to him about their absence, he forbade the meeting. The king, he claimed, wanted the towns to act individually to provide the financial assistance necessary to drive the invaders from France. This decision, he tactfully suggested, was not intended to prejudice the right of St. Flour to convoke the third estate of Haute-Auvergne. Skeptical, the consuls of St. Flour wrote to Clermont to learn if the third estate of Basse-Auvergne had been allowed to meet. Upon receiving an affirmative answer, they again appealed to Mesgrigny for permission to summon the third estate. Again they were refused and again they decided to remonstrate. At this point our records leave us in the dark.[124]

Mesgrigny may have won on this occasion, but some people, as he had said, were trying to reestablish the assembly of the third estate. In 1637 and nearly every year thereafter in Louis's reign, there were one or more meetings of either individual provostships, groups of provostships, or of the third estate. Royal officials did limit their activity, and perhaps it was their watchful eyes that caused the *consuls* of Aurillac, Maurs, Mauriac, and St. Flour to refer to a meeting in St. Flour in late February 1643 as a conference rather than as an assembly of the third estate.[125]

122. AD, Puy-de-Dôme, 4 F 146.

123. Ibid.

124. AN, E 102, fol. 283; AC, St. Flour, ch. V, art. 6, no. 141, fols. 31–31v, 35–40; *IAC, Aurillac*, ed. Gabriel Esquer (Aurillac, 1906), BB 14.

125. AC, St. Flour, ch. V, art. 6, no. 141, fols. 55–55v, 61, 80–80v, 86, 94v–95, 109–09v, 114v, 134–35v; *IAC, Aurillac*, BB 14, BB 15.

No such convenient villain as Mesgrigny can be singled out to explain the sad fate of Normandy during the 1630s. Since the late sixteenth century, it had been customary for the commissioners to the estates to order that whatever the king desired be levied, whether the estates had voted the entire amount or not. All the estates could do was to send a deputation to court to request that the tax be reduced and that other grievances be corrected. If it were inconvenient to hold the estates, the taxes were levied anyway without any open opposition.

The first meeting of the estates after the fall of Marillac took place in Rouen December 1630 and voted 1,310,721 livres. The commissioners gave a provisional order that the entire amount requested by the king be levied, but delayed its implementation until after the Norman deputation had had an opportunity to appeal to the king and council, a courtesy that they had not often extended before. The same process was repeated in September of the following year. Three things about these meetings are noteworthy: their brevity (three or four days sufficed), the pitiful pleas for lower taxes because of the poverty of the province, and, finally, as if to demonstrate a lack of funds, the small amount voted for gratifications. To their governor, the duke of Longueville, went 18,000 livres each year, but a proposal that Matignon, the king's lieutenant in part of the province, be rewarded for his long services was rejected because of the misery of the people and the heavy taxation by the crown. There is no record that the deputies considered giving a gratification to anyone else. The Normans conducted their affairs quite differently from the great pays d'états.[126]

The estates did not meet in 1631 or 1632. Only twice since the Normans had received their new charter in 1458 had they gone so long without their estates, and on both the earlier occasions their province had been wracked by civil war. Louis offered no explanation for this failure, and more surprisingly, neither the bailiwick assembly in Rouen in 1633 nor the estates themselves in that year appear to have asked for one. They did request that no tax that was not included in the current royal commission be levied during the year, but this referred to the long-time practice of the crown's ordering the élus to impose additional sums after the estates had met. When Louis, or more likely Richelieu, requested that La Meilleraye, who in addition to his post in Brittany was lieutenant in part of Normandy, be given 6,000 livres, the majority of the deputies voted to do so but stipulated that the grant would not be considered as a precedent.[127] The most noteworthy event that took place in the estates of 1634 was the attempt of those present to reduce the amount of their taxes to 1.2 million livres, but the commissioners ordered that the entire sum requested by the king be levied without waiting for the estates to carry their remonstrances to court. Also of

126. *Cahiers des Etats de Normandie sous les règnes de Louis XIII et de Louis XIV*, ed. Charles de Robillard de Beaurepaire (Rouen, 1877), 2 : 190–91, 210–12, 396–97, 414.

127. Ibid., 3: esp. 165–76.

some interest was the royal request that La Meilleraye again be given 6,000 livres. Matignon, the other lieutenant in Normandy, made a similar petition on his own behalf. The estates had to ask for yet another 6,000 because the place of meeting had been transferred from Rouen to Gisors. As if this were not enough for an overburdened province, the estates voted 2,000 livres each to the king's secretary of state and to the intendant. A similar sum was approved to be divided among the commissioners to the estates, men who were for the most part high officials of the Norman sovereign courts.[128]

Then three more years lapsed without any meetings of the estates. Vast sums were collected for the king each year, and the few thousand livres designated for the treasury of the estates continued to be paid. Over 2 million livres in ordinary taxes alone were extracted from the généralité of Caen in 1630. The burden was so heavy that the following year the crown tried to get the towns to pay a larger share. Rouen was asked for 400,000 livres and Caen for 150,000. Resistance was so great, however, that Louis had to reduce the assessment on these and other towns by 25 percent, but the loss was covered by increasing the levy on the plat pays.[129] In 1637 the crown drew 1,846,507 livres from the three Norman généralités and in 1638 a record 3,010,968 livres after all expenses for supporting the army and bureaucracy in the province had been deducted. For the military alone the Normans were told to contribute 1.3 million livres in 1638.[130] The cost of the bureaucracy was also immense, and it increased rapidly because the crown continually created new offices to sell. A good example is the élection of Valognes. It required only six officials to collect taxes as late as 1590 and eleven to perform this task in 1618, but twenty-three were paid to do so in 1638. Already in 1631, they consumed 7.1 percent of the taxes they collected.[131]

When the estates again met in January–February 1638, they raised a cry of despair. In their first article they complained about the failure to issue annual summonses and to respond to their grievances favorably. They clearly believed the estates were dying, but to their complaints the council would reply only that their governor had been too busy serving in his majesty's army to hold a meeting. In article after article that followed, the deputies described the suffering in the people with unusual fervor, and in conclusion they lamented that all that survived of their ancient privileges was the right to address complaints to the king. They did not bother to consent to any tax; to do so had become meaningless because the crown always levied more than they were willing to give. Instead they pleaded with the king to take

128. Ibid., esp. 32–33, 200–04.

129. Ibid., esp. 222–34; Madeleine Foisil, *La révolte des Nu-Pieds et les revoltes normandes de 1639* (Paris, 1970), pp. 62–92.

130. Mallet, p. 204.

131. A. Lefèbvre and F. Tribouillard, "Fiscalité et population dans l'élection de Valognes de 1540 à 1660," *Annales de Normandie* 21 (1971): table facing p. 210, and pp. 211–12.

only half the sum listed in the commission for holding the estates, but they were ignored as usual.[132]

If the king's councillors had been both attentive and perceptive, they would have seen that the Normans were on the verge of revolt. Their only concern, however, was how much money they could extract from the province. They did not bother to respond to the cahiers of December 1630 and September 1631 until June 1633, and a new record was set when they delayed until April 1638 to answer the cahier of December 1634. Under such circumstances it took only the well-founded rumor that the crown planned to establish the gabelle in Lower Normandy and an edict creating an inspector in every town to enforce regulations on the type of dye that was used in the textile industry to provoke the revolt of the Nu-Pieds, the most serious uprising during the reign of Louis XIII.[133]

Since the revolt did not begin until July 1639, it does not explain why the crown did not try to hold the estates that year. Evidently the council was too busy to be bothered with Norman affairs. The uprising, of course, could have served as the excuse not to convoke the estates again during the reign, if anyone had thought it necessary to provide one. Severe punishment was meted out to municipal officials and the sovereign courts for failing to maintain order, but the king's advisers did not include the estates. Henri Prentout, their historian, has blamed Richelieu for the failure to consult the estates after 1638, but he offered no evidence to support his position.[134] Probably Richelieu paid little attention to Norman affairs before the revolt. Only after it had begun did he learn that the council was planning to establish the gabelle. At this point he expressed strong disagreement with this decision because the tax "could bring so much trouble and so little profit."[135]

It is impossible to determine who was responsible for the failure to hold the estates between 1638 and 1643. There was certainly little reason for any officials to fear such an impotent institution. Furthermore it cost the people no more when it met than when it did not, because taxes to support its activities were collected and turned over to its treasurer, and the usual gratifications continued to be paid in either case. Included were not only the governor, lieutenant general, secretary of state, and intendant but also the members of the Norman sovereign courts who traditionally served as commissioners to the estates. Thus those who profited when the estates met were permitted to profit an equal amount when they did not, and they were spared the trouble and inconvenience of attending. It seems likely, therefore,

132. *Cahiers de Louis XIII et de Louis XIV*, 3: esp. 36–37, 72–74; Henri Prentout, *Les Etats provinciaux de Normandie* (Caen, 1925), 1:354–56.

133. *Cahiers de Louis XIII et de Louis XIV*, 2:167, 191, 194, 212, 3:34, 38; Foisil, *La révolte*, pp. 55–160.

134. Prentout, *Les états provinciaux*, 1:356.

135. Foisil, *La révolte*, p. 157. See also p. 284.

that the estates did not meet because their governor and the king's council were busy with more important matters and influential Normans did not press for a convocation as their interests were safeguarded.[136]

Dauphiné was not so easily forgotten. Its location along the principal routes to Italy made the capacity of the people to provide the necessary supplies for troops of prime importance. This consideration led the king's council to reverse its traditional stand and declare on May 31, 1634, that the taille was réelle throughout the province. It directed that a tax digest be prepared indicating which hearths were noble and which nonnoble. Those that were nonnoble that had been acquired by clergymen, nobles, royal officials, and other privileged persons since 1602 were to be taxed like property owned by commoners. By this act, the crown hoped to increase the tax base in Dauphiné to the point that the inhabitants could purchase the supplies for passing troops.[137]

For generations the members of the third estate had been putting pressure on the council to reach this decision, and they had not slackened their efforts in the years immediately preceding the issuance of the long-sought edict. Nor for that matter had the nobility failed to do its best to counteract their efforts. As a result there had been several assemblies of both orders in the early 1630s to plot their strategy and to elect deputations. The king, the queen, and Richelieu had visited Dauphiné in 1632 and were aware of the suffering in the province.[138] If any doubt remained in their minds, it should have been dispelled by a series of harangues delivered to them by the bishop of Grenoble in the name of the three orders of Dauphiné. The prelate's primary objective was seemingly to display his classical lore, but he did not hesitate to refer indirectly to the decrees establishing the élections and suspending the estates and to depict the misery of the inhabitants.[139]

It was one thing to declare that the taille was réelle and another to enforce the decree. Jacques Talon was immediately sent to Dauphiné to implement the decision. His intendancy was to last for four years, and throughout that time he had to combat a strong coalition of nobles and members of the sovereign courts who sought to reverse the decision. Since the avowed purpose of the edict of 1634 was to ensure the collection of sufficient taxes and to alleviate the suffering of the people, the nobility and officers of the

---

136. *Cahiers de Louis XIII et de Louis XIV*, 3:256–64.

137. *Recueil des édits et déclarations du Roy, lettres patentes et ordonnances de Sa Majesté arrests et reglements des Ses conseils et du parlement de Grenoble*, ed. Alexandre Giroud (Grenoble, 1720), 1:178–82; Alexandre Fauché-Prunelle, *Essai sur les anciennes institutions autonomes ou populaires des Alpes Cottiennes-Briançonnaises* (Grenoble, 1857), 2:472–76.

138. See above pp. 524–26. AD, Isère, H 357; AC, Grenoble, BB 99, fols. 16v–17, BB 146, fols. 9v–10; *IAC, Grenoble*, BB 100.

139. *Recueil des harangues faites par messire Pierre Scarron, évesque et prince de Grenoble . . . et président perpétuel des Estats du Dauphiné* (Paris, 1634), pp. 108–30.

sovereign courts held an eight-day meeting at Grenoble in May 1635 to prepare counterproposals, which they pretended to believe would achieve these objectives. As thirteen members of the sovereign courts attended, the robe predominated. When it became time to elect a council to represent the nobility during the intervals between its sessions, four newly ennobled lawyers were chosen who were given authority to depute to court and to levy taxes based on the arrière-ban to support their activities. Talon, who could see nothing but trouble resulting from an alliance which could prevent the élus and the municipal *consuls* from imposing the taille under the new terms, appealed to the king's council for instructions. The council's response was immediate. The taille was to be levied as ordered, and the nobles were forbidden to tax themselves or to hold further assemblies.[140]

Still the nobles continued their protests. They charged that Talon openly favored the third estate and that they were being reduced to a state of desolation by the "ancient enemies of their order and the injustice of those who were their judges."[141] They persisted in their argument that the welfare of the people was not improved by these innovations and that the taille was less assured, but to no avail. On April 1, 1636, the council reiterated its decree forbidding the nobles to assemble anywhere in Dauphiné and instructed the élus to report on meetings that took place. Nevertheless some nobles, members of Parlement and the other sovereign courts, and the Bureau of Finances met several times in Grenoble that November. On December 20, the king's council accused them of fomenting violence and rebellion in order to prevent the new tax rolls from being prepared and once more issued strict orders that all meetings cease.[142] To weaken the power of Parlement where the resistance centered, the council created a siège présidial at Valence in 1636 and a Court of Aids at Vienne in 1638.[143] In a final effort to resolve the dispute, the nobles were permitted to meet at Valence in September and October 1638 to prepare arguments and to send deputies to the king's council where, after also hearing arguments from the representatives of the other orders, the council issued the definitive decree declaring that the taille was réelle in Dauphiné but somewhat modifying the terms of the edict of May 1634.[144]

The members of the third estate were not inactive during this period. Led by Claude Brosse, the intrepid syndic of the villages, they assisted Talon in preparing the new tax digest, held assemblies whenever it seemed desirable,

140. *Lettres et mémoires adressés au Chancelier Seguier, 1633–1649*, ed. A. D. Lublinskaya (Moscow, 1966), pp. 341–51; AN, E 124^A, fol. 360–60v; *Recueil des édits*, 1 : 183–89.

141. AAE, ms. 1546, fols. 313–16; See also ibid., fols. 298–300, and BN, ms. Dupuy 869, fols. 83–86v.

142. AN, E 129^c, fols. 1–2, E 134^c, fols. 197–98v.

143. *Histoire du Dauphiné*, ed. Bernard Bligny (Toulouse, 1973), pp. 246–47.

144. *Recueil des édits*, 1 : 189–201.

and occasionally appeared before the king's council to defend the great victory they had won in 1634.[145] Three lawyers assisted Brosse in his work. When one of them died and the other two ceased to be available, the council ordered at his request that three lawyers who practiced before the Parlement of Grenoble take their place. In his absence they were authorized to participate in the "assemblies of the three orders of the said province and in those of the third estate."[146] On that same day, June 8, 1639, the council also resolved a dispute concerning the voting power of the commis or deputies of the twenty-six bailiwicks and seneschalsies and the representatives of the ten towns in the assemblies of the third estate. Henceforth, it was declared, "the assemblies of the third order of the said province will be composed of the *consuls* of the ten towns, the syndic of the village communities, and the *commis* of the bailiwicks and seneschalsies of the said province. The *consuls* and deputies of each of the said towns will have only one vote, the syndic of the communities one vote, and the *commis* of each bailiwick and seneschalsy also only one vote."[147]

These decrees show clearly that the members of the council did not contemplate suppressing representative assemblies in Dauphiné. Although they may have preferred an organization similar to the assembly of the communities in Provence and actually referred to the suppression of the estates, they nevertheless used the phrase *assembly of the three orders*. Hence in August 1641, the bishop of Grenoble asked the council to direct that a tax be levied to compensate him for the expenses that he had incurred in the services of the province. As a justification, he referred to the "deliberations of the *commis* of the estates."[148] In January 1642, in what was referred to as an assembly of the ten towns, two clergymen, two nobles, and four *consuls* were elected to go to court to secure the suppression of the élus and some other offices.[149]

We wish we knew whether these deputies failed because the council would not approve their proposal or because they still would not pay the price. The cost of compensating the élus should have been less because in September 1635 the council had suppressed four of the ten élections in Dauphiné and had assigned part of the gabelles of Lyonnais to reimburse the deprived officials.[150] But if the élus remained, so did the representative assemblies. The institution that replaced the estates was interchangeably called the

---

145. *IAC, Valence*, ed. A. Lacroix (Valence, 1914), BB 18, BB 19; *IAD, Hautes-Alpes, sér. E*, ed. Paul Guillaume (Gap, 1916), 2: E 367; *IAC, Gap*, ed. Paul Guillaume (Gap, 1908), BB 39, BB 40, BB 42; AC, Grenoble, BB 146, entries of April 5, and 8, 1639; *IAC, Grenoble*, BB 100, BB 102–05; *IAD, Drôme, sér. E*, 6:348–49, AN, E 1685, no. 289.

146. AN, E 151ª, fol. 170.

147. Ibid., fol. 200.

148. AD, Isère, 1C 5, no. 17.

149. *IAC, Grenoble*, BB 107; *IAC, Gap*, BB 42.

150. Actes Royaux, no. 8477.

assembly of the ten towns, the assembly of the commis, the assembly of the pays, and even the assembly of the estates. Its composition differed from the old estates primarily in the fact that the nobility and clergy were represented by their commis rather than coming in person, and fewer towns were convoked. Then too, the assemblies of the Alpine bailiwicks and escartons blocked some local royal officials' attempt to be present when they met, levied taxes, and audited accounts. Thus although the privileges of Dauphiné had received a severe blow, they had not been totally destroyed. The nobility, especially, looked forward to the day when they would be fully restored.[151]

The pays d'états in Guyenne had been the first to be subjected to élections. The estates of the généralité were all but moribund when Richelieu came to power, although after a long period of inactivity there was to be a final meeting in February 1635. (See p. 470.) The estates in the individual provinces fared better, for here there were often syndics or *consuls* of the capital towns to take the initiative in calling for assemblies. Between December 1631 and May 1636 the *consuls* of Agen managed to obtain permission from their governor to assemble the principal towns of Agenais on four occasions to deal with problems related to the élus, tax farmers, and their debts. During the next five years there were no meetings, but then between June 1641 and March 1643, the deputies of the towns assembled no fewer than five times to settle a quarrel over taxation with the recently created élection of Lomagne.[152]

The nobility and third estate of Armagnac and its seven collectes were active throughout Richelieu's regime, and their representatives participated in the apportionment of the taille,[153] but the three estates of Rouergue, like those of Agenais, appear to have passed through periods in which they did not meet.[154] Not enough is known about the other estates in the region to judge the degree of their activity, but there is no doubt that they sometimes met.[155] Indeed the towns of Bordeaux, Libourne, and Saint-Émilion dispatched a deputy to Paris in 1635 in the name of the villes filleules as if to

151. Fauché-Prunelle, *Essai*, 2:485, 613; Dr. Chabrand, "Les escartons dans l'ancien Briançonnais," *Bul. de la soc. d'études des Hautes-Alpes* 2 (1883): 244–45.

152. AC, Agen, BB 53. fols. 7, 190v, BB 55, pp. 19–19v, 23–24, CC 185, CC 189, CC 191, CC 192, CC 194, CC 195, CC 202, CC 204, CC 227.

153. A. Branet, "Les Etats d'Armagnac en 1631–1632," *Bul. de la soc. archéologique du Gers* 14 (1913): 168–83, 214–29; Z. Baqué, "Vic-Fezensac au temps de la Fronde," *Bul. de la soc. d'histoire et d'archeologie du Gers* 36 (1935): 40–53; AD, Gers, E suppl. 23,936. AC, Nogaro, AA 11; BN ms. fr. 18,678, fols. 19–21.

154. AC, Rodez (cité), BB 9, fols. 33v–39v, 133–34, 139v–41.

155. For Comminges, see AD, Haute-Garonne, C 3704, and M. J. de Naurois-Destenay, *Les Etats de Comminges aux XVIᵉ et XVIIᵉ siècles* (thesis, Ecole Nationale des Chartes, 1953–54), pp. 191–93. A copy is at the AN. For Condomois and Bazadais, see *IAC, Condom*, ed. G. Niel (n.p., n.d.), AA 16, BB 39; AC, Casteljaloux, BB 4, fols. 400–02v. For Rivière-Verdun, see Jean Contrasty, *Histoire de Sainte-Foy de Peyrolières* (Toulouse, 1917), pp. 200–01.

demonstrate that there was still a sense of unity among the towns of Bordelais.[156] Two years later the communes of Périgord asked that their estates, which Henry IV had discontinued forty years before, be revived and that they be permitted to have a syndic.[157]

We are left with the conclusion that in those places where Richelieu's predecessors had undermined the position of the estates, he permitted them to continue to decay. Since it was not necessary for the estates to meet periodically on tax matters where there were élections, intendants and other royal officials sometimes took steps to avoid convoking them, but no evidence has been found to prove that this was a deliberate policy of Richelieu or of the king's council. On the other hand, in provinces that had no élections before Marillac's attempt to install them, Richelieu resumed the time-honored policy of bargaining with the estates to obtain the funds he desired. To secure his goals, he sought the assistance of his clients in the estates, gave pensions and other rewards to a few, and tried to persuade the bulk of the deputies to vote him most of what he asked. Only in extreme cases where the estates repeatedly refused to cooperate, as in Languedoc in 1639, did he or his officials employ force or otherwise seriously violate the privileges of a province.

5. RICHELIEU AND THE ASSEMBLY OF THE CLERGY: CONCLUSIONS

Richelieu also sought to employ his persuasive techniques to obtain what he wanted from the clergy, and here as a prince of the church he was much more directly involved in the negotiations than with the estates. When Louis XIII undertook the expensive siege of La Rochelle, Richelieu appealed to the pope for authorization to acquire part of the goods of the French clergy. Permission was readily granted, but instead of taking the papal letter to the individual dioceses to collect the desired sum as the nuncio desired, Richelieu insisted on seeking the consent of the assembly of the clergy in the customary manner. When the royal commissioner asked for 4 million livres, the assembly responded with an offer of half that amount. Richelieu was angry and Louis was threatening, but in the end the clergy was persuaded to offer 3 million livres, the very amount that Richelieu had told the pope that he wanted in the first place.[158]

The launching of a full-scale war against the Habsburgs in 1635 provoked a new financial crisis. The clergy had less enthusiasm for donating their goods to kill their fellow Catholics than they had to slaughter the Huguenots. This time the crown wanted a long-term annual grant of

156. AC, Libourne, BB 2, fol. 49.
157. *Lettres de Séguier*, ed. Mousnier, 2 : 1109.
158. Pierre Blet, *Le clergé de France et la monarchie* (Rome, 1959), 1: esp. 374–83, 390–96.

600,000 livres. Considerable haggling followed in which Richelieu sought to influence the deliberations by urging the king to treat the bishops devoted to his interest warmly but to be colder to those who were uncooperative. Only after a mixture of threats and persuasion had been applied could the assembly be persuaded to vote a little over half what the crown had the originally requested. The grant was noteworthy, however, because papal permission to tax the clergy had not been sought. An important step toward establishing the independence of the Gallican church from Rome had been taken.[159]

Richelieu attempted to persuade a group of twenty-two bishops who happened to be in Paris in December 1640 to agree to another grant in order to avoid the lengthy bargaining with the larger assembly, but he had little success. Forced to turn once more to the full assembly of the clergy, he took every step to ensure a compliant meeting. He chose the location of the meeting with care and sent a list of approved candidates to each electoral province. This procedure led to the selection of many loyal deputies, but there was still enough opposition to require months of negotiation, and near the close of the assembly Louis angrily told the leaders of the opposition to return immediately to their dioceses.[160]

Thus Richelieu abandoned Marillac's attempt to construct a centralized, absolute state administered by a loyal, nonhereditary, and probably non-venal, bureaucracy and reverted to the Renaissance practice of trying to govern through the estates, assemblies of the clergy, and other duly constituted bodies. The greatest accomplishment of these years, the destruction of the Huguenot state within a state, should be attributed as much or more to Louis himself as to his chief minister. The king had begun this work before he had named Richelieu to his council, and there were times when the cardinal had deflected him from his purpose by directing his attention towards Italy. Nor did Louis need his minister to tell him that he should punish rebellious nobles, for again he had begun this practice prior to the cardinal's appointment and required little encouragement to behead those who flaunted his authority. It is true that royal patronage was used more effectively than ever before to secure the loyalty of the nobles, but in the process the cardinal made them his creatures rather than the king's, a situation that was not devoid of danger to the crown.

The governors remained the principal provincial officials throughout the reign, although many of them began to build mansions in Paris and to reside in that city more than they had formerly. Richelieu made no attempt to break their power or to find a subsitute for the role they played. He even rejected the idea of appointing governors for limited periods of time because to be effective they had to devote many years to their respective provinces.

159. Ibid., pp. 452, 458–59, 466–68.
160. Ibid., pp. 481, 484–516.

"If governorships are given to men who hope only for the honor of the charge or the appeal of the region," his memoirs declare, "they are nearly useless. Few men will be found who can bear the expenses, and there are not enough suitable men in the provinces to fill the charges if they are made triennial."[161] Of course, Richelieu eventually replaced those governors like Epernon, Guise, and Vitry who acted in a too-independent fashion, but he permitted those who became his friends to exercise considerable authority.

Much has been made of Richelieu's role in creating the intendants, but until near the close of his life, he regarded them only as investigators to be sent to the provinces for limited periods of time, a viewpoint scarcely as developed as Marillac's had been some years before. Only the financial demands occasioned by the war finally drove the crown to turn to the intendants in the hope of achieving a more efficient method of collecting taxes. On August 22, 1642, less than four months before Richelieu's death, the government ordered the intendants to assume primary administrative responsibility for collecting taxes during the coming year. This step was of fundamental importance because the intendants were more efficient and more obedient than either the treasurers in the Bureau of Finances or the élus who now became, in effect, their assistants. Furthermore the anger of these officials at their demotions was to be one of the principal causes of the Fronde. To what extent Richelieu himself was responsible for assigning a new role to the intendants, however, is not known.[162]

The royal army was greatly enlarged because of the war, and the assignment of intendants to the various commands probably improved logistics and discipline, but as the Fronde was soon to prove, individual units continued to be under the control of their commanders who filled the subordinate positions with their vassals, kinsmen, clients, and friends. When a regimental commander died, Louis replaced him with his son, for, he informed Richelieu, "If I had given the regiment to someone else, it would have completely disbanded because all the captains were *from his region and were kinsmen or friends of the deceased.*"[163] The war proved far more expensive than any conflict in the past because the army was larger and its equipment more expensive, but no attempt was made to alter the tax structure fundamentally to provide additional revenue. The poor were exploited more than ever before, but the well-to-do continued to escape with relatively modest contributions. To tap the wealth of the bureaucracy and middle class, the crown turned to expedients, the most important of which was the creation of useless offices. The purchasers of these offices drew salaries that necessitated still higher taxes, which they themselves now escaped because of

161. Quoted in Robert R. Harding, *The Provincial Governors of Reformation France: Anatomy of a Power Elite, 1542–1635* (Ann Arbor, University Mircrofilms, 1974), p. 360. For the growing tendency of the governors to reside in Paris after 1600, see ibid., pp. 289–311.

162. Richelieu, *Testament politique*, ed. Louis André, 7th ed. (Paris, 1947), pp. 246–47; Roland Mousnier, *La plume, la faucille et le marteau* (Paris, 1970), pp. 179–99.

163. Georges Pagès, *La monarchie d'ancien régime en France* (Paris, 1946), p. 95. Pagès' italics.

the positions they held. At times the revenue derived from offices approached and once even exceeded half the total receipts of the treasury, but irreparable harm was done to society and the economy.[164] On the whole, Louis's reign was an almost unmitigated disaster for the mass of the French people and ultimately for the monarchy itself.

Perhaps Richelieu's most original contribution, if it can be called that, was his use of propaganda and censorship. Under him, "the royal government for the first time began methodically to exploit the full possibilities of propaganda. Théophraste Renaudot poured out such a deluge of pamphlets as thenceforth to drown all opposing voices, except for a brief period during the Fronde. And ... it was roughly at this time that censorship began to be centralized directly under the crown."[165]

It has long been customary to justify Richelieu's decision to abandon his ambitious plans for internal reform and economic progress by citing the need to check the rising power of the Habsburgs, but in fact Spain was already in a state of decline, and Richelieu's aggressive German policy served only to drive the princes into the arms of the emperor. In 1630 they had forced the emperor to give up Wallenstein and had refused to elect his son king of the Romans, but by 1635 French pressure had caused Catholics and Protestants alike to join together in a national war against the invaders, and a Habsburg succession was assured. As a result of the war Richelieu commenced, France received some additional territory, but who can say whether the French would not have been left in a better position to defend their national interests if Marillac had been permitted to develop a more efficient government and Richelieu himself had succeeded in improving the economy. Certainly the people would have been far happier.

Although Richelieu had a more brilliant mind than Marillac, he failed to realize two truths that his rival had grasped early in this career: first, that "the glory of good government is principally to think of the welfare of the subjects and the good regulation of the state which can be done only through peace," and second, that strong government and significant reforms must be institutionalized in order to prove lasting.[166] As Mariéjol observed many years ago, Richelieu was "indifferent to institutions."[167] Insistent as he was on loyalty and obedience, he was unable to construct a system that could survive six years after his death without a major revolt. It was based on personal relationships that died with him rather than an institutional structure that could function long after he departed.

---

164. Mousnier, *La vénalité*, pp. 420–22. For a recent description of the disastrous French fiscal policies and the role of the financiers, see Julian Dent, *Crisis in Finance: Crown, Financiers and Society in Seventeenth-Century France* (Newton Abbot, 1973).

165. A. Soman, "Press, Pulpit, and Censorship in France before Richelieu," *Proceedings of the American Philosophical Society* 120 (1976): 463.

166. Pagès, "Autour," p. 66.

167. Jean-H. Mariéjol, *Histoire de France*, ed. E. Lavisse (Paris, 1911), 6: pt. 2, 410.

17

LOUIS XIV AND THE ESTATES

CARDINAL RICHELIEU DIED IN DECEMBER 1642 AND LOUIS XIII IN MAY 1643. With surprising rapidity Louis's wife, Anne of Austria, was named regent, and Jules Mazarin, a cardinal but not a priest of the church, became her principal minister. As Anne's lover and very likely her secret husband, Mazarin enjoyed a more secure position with regard to the throne than Richelieu had ever achieved. The problems he faced were not with rivals who tried to supplant him in the affection of his sovereign, but rather with the opposition of nearly every element of French society to his policies and, above all, to his methods.

Richelieu had been a statesman. If he was mistaken to choose foreign adventures over domestic reforms, he was at least conscious of making a choice and did so on the basis of what he took to be rational priorities. Mazarin, on the other hand, was a man of intrigue. Suave and ingratiating, he sought to govern by persuasion, flattery, and bribes. When they did not suffice, he tried to divide his opponents by lies, false promises, and appeals to their diverse interests. Few were fooled for long by his outwardly obliging conduct, and he soon became as distrusted as he was hated. He never understood the government of France and occasionally was not above boasting of this fact to escape censure for the administrative actions of his subordinates. No reform program ever emerged from his subtle brain. Indeed his correspondence suggests that he paid little attention to domestic affairs until the Fronde and that he then directed his efforts toward intrigues to retain his position rather than to trying to alleviate the ever increasing suffering of the French people. After that much-discussed and confused rebellion, he lapsed, in part at least, into his old indifference to domestic concerns, except those of a financial nature. All he wanted from France was money to pursue the wars he had inherited and to line his pockets. He does not seem to have cared how many influential persons his finance ministers alienated or how much suffering they caused provided the necessary funds were raised. He died the richest man in France and very likely the biggest thief who ever served a French king.[1]

1. For recent and unfavorable evaluations of Mazarin, see Ernst H. Kossmann, *La Fronde* (Leiden, 1954), and A. Lloyd Moote, *The Revolt of the Judges: The Parlement of Paris and the Fronde, 1643–1652* (Princeton, 1971). D. Dessert, "Pouvoir et finance au XVIᵉ siècle: la fortune du Cardinal Mazarin," *Revue d'histoire moderne et contemporaine* 23 (1976): 161–81.

1. Mazarin, the Estates General, and the Provincial Estates

Mazarin's fiscal policies soon brought him into conflict with the sovereign courts and the bulk of royal officials, whom he sought to exploit as he did the peasantry. By the close of 1648, Paris was on the verge of an uprising. To escape the threat, Mazarin fled with the royal family to Saint-Germain early in January of the following year, and a widespread revolt known as the Fronde broke out. To rally public opinion to his side, he issued orders convoking the Estates General. It is not known what Mazarin's intentions were when he did so. In the few instances in which he mentioned the coming meeting, he gave no intimation of what his objectives were. Both antagonists began to arm, but peace terms were agreed upon in March before there had been much serious fighting. The meeting of the Estates General was postponed on several occasions on one excuse or another, and it was finally abandoned in September, but only after elections had been held in at least forty-three electoral jurisdictions.[2]

The idea that a meeting of the Estates General should be held would not die. The nobility especially pushed for such an assembly in unauthorized meetings in Paris and in the provinces. Finally, in March 1651 when Mazarin was in exile, Anne of Austria agreed that the Estates General should meet. She chose September 8 for the opening ceremony because by then Louis XIV would have entered upon his fourteenth year, the traditional time when the kings of France were considered to have reached their majority. Again the meeting was postponed on several occasions, the last time being on January 25, 1653. Again it was finally abandoned altogether, but during 1651 elections took place in at least sixty-four bailiwicks and comparable jurisdictions.[3]

It is of interest to consider Mazarin's ideas concerning the Estates General and other representative institutions. In a letter to Le Tellier in July 1650 he revealed that he looked with disfavor on the efforts of the nobility to push the government into convoking the Estates General.[4] In March 1651 he informed Lionne that "it is good to talk of convoking the Estates General if that is enough to make the Duke of Orléans and the Prince [of Condé] take another course; but I do not know whether I should advise that it [actually] be assembled because assuredly the princes ... and their friends ... have the largest party in the governments of the kingdom ... and will use all their

2, *Lettres du Cardinal Mazarin pendant son ministère*, ed. A. Chéruel (Paris, 1883), 3:267–68, 1082; Georges Picot, *Histoire des Etats généraux*, 2d ed. (Paris, 1888), 5:274–78; Walter R. Brown, *French Provincial Opinions at the Time of the Fronde* (Ann Arbor, University Microfilms, 1973), pp. 61–70.

3. Picot, *Histoire*, 5:278–85; Brown, *French Provincial Opinions*, pp. 70–87. For the assemblies of the nobles, see Jean-D. Lassaigne, *Les assemblées de la noblesse de France aux XVIIᵉ et XVIIIᵉ siècles* (Paris, 1962), pp. 15–84.

4. Mazarin, *Lettres*, 3:619–20.

industry to have deputies elected to the estates who will be dependent upon them." But then he added with admirable foresight that the "parlements will be alarmed by the estates and will believe that not only the queen but also the princes themselves want to assemble them in order to repress their authority and to find remedies for many of the enterprises that they have undertaken. Therefore, to prevent the estates from being held, the parlements will join the queen and take a position which in the present situation is favorable to the interests of their majesties."[5]

In April when it appeared as though the Estates General might actually meet, Mazarin cautioned Lionne that it was necessary to employ intelligent persons in the provinces "in order to win the deputies who will be elected." From the opening of the Estates General, he warned, the princes would seek to obtain control over the deputies. "It is necessary to try by every means," he added, "to have a great many favors to distribute at this time because this has always been the surest way that kings have had to bring the estates to do what they desire."[6] If the Estates General met, he informed Colbert that June, "it would be necessary to employ one of the best pens in Paris ... to reveal my zeal, my disinterestness, the integrity of my actions, without invectives and without attacking anyone."[7] Nowhere did Mazarin make a doctrinaire statement for or against the Estates General. He had no conception of its role as an institution. To him it was a body composed of people who could be bribed with gifts or persuaded by propaganda. In general, he opposed permitting it to meet because he believed that most deputies would be won by the opposing forces.[8] He was especially fearful of a plan advocated by some of his opponents to have the Estates General postpone the age when the young king reached his majority until he was eighteen. To govern during the interim, the deputies were to be asked to elect a council composed of six members of estate plus the queen mother, Orléans, and Condé.[9]

Mazarin's approach to the Assemblies of the Clergy was much the same as it was to the Estates General. He sought to influence the choice of the deputies who attended and of the president of the assembly once it had begun to meet. To encourage cooperation on the part of those who were present in 1645, he wrote in his notebook that he should delay awarding benefices and abbeys during the assembly in order to keep alive the hope in each individual that he would receive one.[10] At first these tactics were successful, and the Assembly of the Clergy of 1645–46 was persuaded to vote

5. Ibid., 4:73–74. For a further comment concerning the attitude of Parlement toward the Estates General and its probable effect, see ibid., p. 716.

6. Ibid., p. 127. See also ibid., p. 732.

7. Ibid., p. 269.

8. For other comments by Mazarin concerning the Estates General, see ibid., pp. 144, 151, 159–61, 260–61, 264–65, 280, 285, 339, 356, 509–10.

9. Ibid., pp. 197–99; Kossmann, *La Fronde*, pp. 191–92.

10. Pierre Blet, *Le clergé de France et la monarchie* (Rome, 1959), 2:4–9.

a don gratuit of 4 million livres in addition to the now routine annual levy of 1,292,906 livres. The clergymen who assembled in 1650 during the Fronde were far less complacent, and it was only after making various concessions that Mazarin was able to obtain a paltry don gratuit of 600,000 livres. Furthermore the clergy granted the money to be used to pay Louis XIV's coronation expenses, not to support the war against their fellow Catholics of Spain. In 1656–57 they won still more concessions in return for opening their pocketbooks, but in this period of relative calm they granted a don gratuit of 2.7 million livres and renewed the annual levy for ten more years. Perhaps Mazarin was not displeased to grant so many of the clergy's requests, for as the historian of the assemblies has pointed out, no one in France profited as much from these concessions as he did because of his entrenched position within the framework of church property and offices.[11]

Mazarin's attitude toward the provincial estates was similar to that he displayed toward the Assemblies of the Clergy. As regularly functioning, traditional institutions, he accepted their existence without question. When he was named governor of Auvergne in 1658, he made sure that he was given authority "to convoke and assemble before him ... the people of the church, the nobility, *échevins, consuls,* and inhabitants of the towns and places in the said government."[12] Nevertheless he sought to control the provincial estates in much the same manner as he did the Assemblies of the Clergy. Often he wrote to friends of the crown asking them to attend and to display all possible zeal in the service of his majesty. He sent directives to deputies and other officials while the estates were in session, and if he thought that they performed well, he was not slow to praise them for their work.[13] Only rarely did he find it necessary to criticize someone for failing to be present at a meeting or for not doing all that was in his power to implement the crown's program.[14] More often he exonerated an official from any blame for the failure to obtain everything that the king had requested.[15] Only in a few instances when the estates persisted in giving less than the required amount did Mazarin resort to threats. In 1657 and 1659 he talked of lodging additional troops and creating élections in Languedoc and of bringing the king in person to Brittany to see that he was obeyed. In the intervening year, the three estates of Burgundy were actually exiled to Noyes to encourage them to loosen their purse strings.[16]

Although flattery, persuasion, and bribery were the weapons that Mazarin

11. Ibid., pp. 83–119.

12. R. Mousnier, "Note sur les rapports entre les gouverneurs de provinces et les intendants dans la première moitié du XVIIe siècle," *Revue historique* 228 (1962): 347.

13. Mazarin, *Lettres,* 1:582–83, 3:986, 1003, 1004, 1021, 1117, 4:594, 598, 5:708, 6:646, 662, 668, 671, 676, 7:709, 714, 8:244–45, 625, 628, 629, 637, 643, 644, 645, 647, 648, 649, 650, 653–54, 655, 662, 665, 666, 667, 672, 673, 678, 680, 769, 9:373–74, 749, 853, 857, 883.

14. Ibid., 3:1128, 1131.

15. Ibid., 4:593, 598, 5:717.

16. Ibid., 8:201–02, 650–51, 654, 661, 9:345–46, 396–97. *IAD, Côte-d'Or, sér. C,* ed. Joseph Garnier (Dijon, 1886), 3:25–26.

preferred to use in dealing with the estates, at least until near the end of his career, his subordinates often sought to suppress them where they still functioned and to keep them suppressed where they had already succumbed to the encroachment of the royal bureaucracy. We have seen how in 1637 the intendant, Mesgrigny, tried to prevent the échevins of Clermont from assembling the good towns of Basse-Auvergne and from acting as syndics of the province on the grounds that they oppressed the people by their heavy exactions and gave advice that was prejudicial to the crown's interests. The chancellor, Pierre Séguier, may have given the memorandum sympathetic attention, for in 1621 he had served in a similar capacity in the same province. In May 1649 Séguier expressed concern at the prospect that the privileges of Dauphiné would be restored as a result of violence that was taking place there. If this happened, other provinces would resort to similar tactics to regain their liberties. Already many of the provisions of Edict of Béziers (1632) had been set aside, thereby permitting the estates of Languedoc to return to their former position.[17]

Some less important officials were more outspoken in their opposition to the estates and the remaining organs of popular government. In a letter to Séguier concerning a meeting of the estates of Normandy in the fall of 1643, one of their number insisted "that such assemblies and liberties are extremely prejudicial to the service of the king. It seemed to me that our intendants of justice were under cross examination for some terrible crime. In the future it will be necessary to strike a heavier blow than in the past to levy the taille. The people are now quite persuaded that it is a tyranny, and consider the tax farmers scoundrels and the commissioners or intendants infamous persons. It is necessary to try to prevent anyone from printing the *cahier*."[18] In 1645 an intendant from Auvergne tried to prevent the nobility from electing a syndic to replace one who had died.[19] In February of that same year another royal official informed Séguier that he had never seen an assembly as bold as the estates of Languedoc or one with "so little respect for the things that are proposed to them in the name of the king."[20] A week later one of his colleagues lectured the estates on their obstinacy in refusing to vote money destined for the troops: "My lords, the estates of Languedoc are not absolute and independent. They are subordinate to the will of the king who reserves for himself authority over them in order to leave them their liberty when they are good and to take it away from them when they abuse it."[21]

17. *Lettres et mémoires adressés au Chancelier Séguier, 1633–1649*, ed. Roland Mousnier (Paris, 1964), 1:32, 2:931.

18. Ibid., 1:604–05.

19. Ibid., 2:725–26.

20. *Lettres et mémoires adressés au Chancelier P. Séguier*, ed. A. D. Lublinskaya (Moscow, 1966), p. 115.

21. Ibid., p. 116.

In spite of threats and pleas, the estates of Languedoc persisted in refusing to consent to the bulk of the desired tax. The exasperated royal officials flooded Séguier with accounts of the bad behavior of the estates. They recognized the difficulties that would result if an attempt were made to collect the desired sum without the assembly's approval, but they interpreted any opposition to the royal will as malice, conspiracy, or worse. Talk in the estates of trying to get the intendants suppressed or of excluding them from their customary gratification aroused their anger, and they obviously disapproved when the estates appropriated over 200,000 livres for gifts, although 140,000 were to go to the king's brother who had recently been named their governor and 34,000 were designated for his wife.[22] They worried lest the refusal of the estates to grant the king's request and the widespread publicity given to the incident "had persuaded the people that they had some power in public affairs and that they could disobey the king with impunity on any matter." The people might think that "they have a liberty that they can even use against the one who had accorded it to them."[23]

In September 1645 as the time for the next meeting of the estates of Languedoc approached, one of the crown officials reported to Séguier that the only way to ensure the repose and obedience of the province was for "his royal highness or monseigneur the prince to attend the estates."[24] In December he declared that he hoped for little from the estates because of the unrest in the province. Neither the governor nor the lieutenant general was giving direction to affairs, and "the bishops and barons had let themselves be led astray last year by the pressure of the people over whom they have difficulty reassuming their authority."[25] By February 1646 he was complaining at the length of the estates and the burden their expenses would place upon the people, a protest that another royal official was to repeat in 1649. In spite of these attacks, it was the estates that won the first major victory, for in return for opening their pocketbooks, the hard-pressed government revoked the Edict of Béziers. The regulations preventing the abuses of the estates were retained, but it ceased to be necessary for estates to turn over 1.05 million livres to the royal treasury and to levy some lesser sums without giving their consent.[26]

The estates had bargained with the crown when acting under the terms of

---

22. Ibid., pp. 117–29.

23. Ibid., p. 129. For an account of the estates of 1645, see William H. Beik, *Governing Languedoc: The Practical Functioning of Absolutism in a French Province, 1633–1685* (Ph.D. diss. Harvard University, 1969), pp. 57–60; and *HL*, 13:209–16, 14:73–91. For the rivalry between the two intendants, see W. H. Beik, "Two Intendants Face a Popular Revolt: Social Unrest and the Structure of Absolutism in 1645," *Canadian Journal of History* 9 (1974): 243–62.

24. *Lettres de Séguier*, ed. Lublinskaya, p. 156.

25. Ibid., pp. 163–64.

26. Ibid., pp. 176, 221; *HL*, 13:290–93, 14:292–97; Beik, *Governing Languedoc*, pp. 63–67.

the Edict of Béziers, but only over contributions in addition to the ones that were automatically levied; now they bargained over nearly the entire amount the king demanded. The result was that the level of their contributions dropped, and the crown had to make additional concessions to obtain what it did get, although the presence of troops in the province during the war continued to pose a threat to the estates. In one year prior to 1659, they refused to vote any don gratuit at all; in another they gave 2 million livres, but their most common grant was about 600,000. Languedoc was further from being subjected than at any other time since 1629 in spite of the efforts of Mazarin and his local agents.[27]

Not all royal officials saw the estates as enemies, of course. To one of them who had been dispatched to Provence in 1645, it was the officers of the sovereign courts who were the villains who sought to discredit him in the eyes of the people. Nevertheless he anticipated that the assembly of the communities would satisfy the king's commands. Even when such contrary opinions are considered, however, it is probable that the initiative against the estates during the Mazarin period came primarily from the intendants and other local officials, and that the cardinal himself was content to exercise his powers of persuasion to obtain what he wanted from the estates, at least until the fall of 1657, and perhaps until his death.[28] As a result, there was no concerted attack against the estates, their right to consent to taxation in provinces where there were no élections was preserved, and the crown often received less money than it requested.

Writing between the two world wars, the eminent authority on seventeenth-century institutions, Georges Pagès, complained about how little was known about the progress toward absolution during the Mazarin period. We are hardly better informed today. Certainly the most conspicuous development that took place was the greatly increased use of the intendants. The system of intendants was beginning to be generalized in France at the close of Richelieu's regime. At that time their primary function was to increase the efficiency of tax collection, and it is possible that Mazarin also saw them largely as revenue agents. They were sufficiently active during the 1640s to so anger the élus, the treasurers in the Bureau of Finances, and other venal royal officials that their recall became one of the principal goals of the first Fronde. Stripped temporarily of their services, Mazarin could only lament their absence and express his belief to his chancellor in June 1649 that their reestablishment would help furnish "new resources." The intendants reappeared after the Fronde, although we are not adequately informed as to how this was accomplished or to what extent the

---

27. Beik, *Governing Languedoc*, pp. 67–72.

28. *Lettres de Séguier*, ed. Lublinskaya, p. 292. For an official with contrary opinions, see pp. 298–99.

administrative system generally associated with Colbert was already in effect when Mazarin died.[29]

Hardly less important was Michel Le Tellier's reorganization of the army. That able official was named secretary of state for war soon after Mazarin came to power. At first he made little progress, but after the close of the Fronde, he was able to proceed more rapidly. By the time Louis XIV began his personal rule, he had or was soon to have a large, well-organized, loyal force at his disposal.[30]

The sovereign courts and especially the Parlements were the greatest problems to Mazarin. Their role in the Fronde has often been told, but after the termination of that uprising, they were no more subservient than before. In 1658 Mazarin had to threaten the Parlement of Grenoble with the prospect that the king would go to Dauphiné to compel its obedience in order to reduce its opposition to his policies.[31] Indeed Professor Lloyd Moote has argued that the judges were not totally defeated during the Fronde and that their resistance taught Colbert a lesson. It was safer to work with the Parlements and the venal royal officials than to risk rebellion by ignoring their interests.[32] There is some truth in Professor Moote's assessment, for Louis XIV and Colbert did not push their absolutist policies as far as they might in areas where they were likely to encounter great resistance. On the other hand, there is also considerable truth in the older view that it was the ignominies that Louis suffered during the Fronde that caused him to adopt the absolutist policies of some of his predecessors rather than the more temperate ones of his Renaissance forebears. Furthermore, the suffering and futility of the Fronde made most of the people willing to accept a more absolutist form of government than they would have before. Thus the Fronde furthered the cause of absolutism, although at the same time it may have caused Louis and his ministers to move more cautiously than they would otherwise have done.

As Cardinal Mazarin lay on his deathbed, he gave advice to Louis XIV, which the young king was quick to dictate to his secretary. The church should be maintained in all its rights and privileges, Louis reported. Benefices should be given only to able, pious persons, who should also be his loyal servants. The nobles were his right arm. They should be treated with confidence and kindness. Magistrates should be treated with respect, "but it is very important to prevent members of this profession from emancipating themselves. They should be obliged to stay within the limits of their duty

29. Georges Pagès, *La monarchie d'ancien régime en France de Henri IV à Louis XIV*, 4th ed. (Paris, 1946), pp. 114–33; Mazarin, *Lettres*, 3:1118. For an example of the slashing criticism that the intendants heaped on the élus, see *Lettres de Séguier*, ed. Mousnier, 2:1112–18.

30. See Louis André, *Michel de Tellier et l'organisation de l'armeé monarchique* (Montpellier, 1906).

31. Mazarin, *Lettres*, 8:694.

32. Moote, *Revolt of the Judges*, pp. 373–76.

and to think only of rendering impartially to all my subjects the justice that I have assigned to them."[33] How different this was from the advice that Villeroy had given Marie de Medici fifty years before. He had seen the magnates as the greatest threat, and he had paled at the thought of the Huguenots becoming their allies. The members of Parlement, far from being seen as dangerous, were to be assigned the task of watching the magnates' activities. A half-century of hereditary office-holding had changed all of that. To Mazarin the adherents of the "new feudalism" were the principal sources of danger. He did suggest that Louis award the crown patronage himself so that everyone would look to him for favors, a policy that would strengthen him in his dealings with the magnates as well as with the bureaucracy, but the change in the relative position of the two groups in regard to the crown is nevertheless striking.[34]

2. LOUIS XIV, COLBERT, AND THE PAYS D'ETATS

Louis has often been referred to as a crowned revolutionary. There was much in his attitudes and ideas that would tend to make him one. Tradition ought not to have tied his hands because he was essentially a rationalist, "an apostle of common sense."[35] He was also a man of action. "Even from childhood," he tells us in the memoirs he prepared for the dauphin, "the very name of do-nothing kings and of mayors of the palace distressed me when it was uttered in my presence."[36] He knew that a drastic reformation of the government was necessary, and his concept of kingship was so exalted that he never doubted his authority to institute one. "It must assuredly be agreed," he again informed the dauphin, "that as bad as a prince may be, the revolt of his subjects is always infinitely criminal. He who has given kings to men has wanted them to be respected as His lieutenants, reserving to Himself alone the right to examine their conduct. His will is that whoever is born a subject must obey without qualification; and this law, so explicit and universal, is not made in favor of princes alone, but is beneficial to the very people on whom it is imposed."[37] Even the property of his subjects was at his disposal, for "kings are absolute lords and naturally have free and full disposition of all the goods possessed by clergymen as well as by laymen, in order to use them at any time as wise administrators, that is, according to the general need of their state."[38]

33. *Lettres, instructions et mémoires de Colbert*, ed. Pierre Clément (Paris, 1861), 1:535.

34. Ibid., p. 535.

35. A. Lossky, "Some Problems in Tracing the Intellectual Development of Louis XIV from 1661 to 1715," in *Louis XIV and the Craft of Kingship*, ed. John C. Rule (Columbus, 1969), p. 318.

36. *Louis XIV King of France and of Navarre: Mémoires for the Instruction of the Dauphin*, trans. Paul Sonnino (New York, 1970), p.23.

37. Ibid., pp. 244–45.

38. Ibid., p. 165.

"Princes," Louis thought, "in whom a brilliant birth and a proper upbringing usually produce only noble and magnanimous sentiments, can never entirely eradicate these good principles from their character. As dim as their idea of virtue may be, it always gives even the worst of them a kind of repugnance for vice. Their hearts, trained from an early age in sentiments of honor, become so accustomed to them that they cannot entirely corrupt it, and their constant desire for glory makes them disregard their own interest in many cases."[39] Not so for the mass of mankind, however, for Louis had a very low opinion of human nature. Those who were not of princely birth were motivated by self-interest. Hence aristocratic governments were less trustworthy than monarchies: "The decisions of their councils are based exclusively on the principle of utility. The many heads who make up these bodies have no heart that can be stirred by the fire of beautiful passions ... it is interest alone, whether private or of the state, that guides their conduct."[40]

The provincial estates suffered from the same disability, he believed. At one time, people had been less selfish, and the estates had functioned everywhere. Even in his own day the estates fixed the contribution of the laity "in most of our provinces, and it was practiced everywhere in the honesty of the early days; for indeed, at that time the mere spirit of justice sufficed to inspire each individual to give according to his means, which would never happen today."[41]

With such ideas as these one would think that Louis, in his omnipotent power and infinite wisdom, would crush the provincial estates and other popular organs of government for the benefit of his subjects, but at heart he was too much of a conservative traditionalist to do so. At no time in the memoirs he prepared to instruct the dauphin did he mention the élus who had loomed so large in Sully's and Marillac's plans or the intendants who were becoming so important in his day. Rather he sought to control and utilize the estates and other popular institutions: "It had been the custom not merely to ask them [the estates] for large sums in order to obtain meager ones," he explained concerning the practice of his predecessors, "but also to tolerate their putting conditions on everything, to promise them everything, to circumvent everything they had been promised soon thereafter under various pretexts, even to issue a great number of edicts with no other intention than to grant, or rather to sell, their revocation soon thereafter. I found this method undignified for the sovereign and unsatisfactory for the subject. I chose an entirely different one that I have always followed since, which was to ask them for precisely what I intended to obtain, to promise little, to keep my promises faithfully, hardly ever to accept conditions, but to

39. Ibid., p. 196.
40. Ibid.
41. Ibid., p. 166.

surpass their expectations when they appealed to my justice and to my kindness."[42] As a result of his new policy, "The *pays d'états*, which had formerly considered themselves as independent in matters of taxation, began to use their liberty only for making their submission more pleasing to me."[43]

Thus Louis would have the dauphin believe that he inaugurated his new policy when he began his personal reign. Perhaps he took it as his goal at that time, but in fact it was only with considerable effort over a period of a decade or more that he was able to bring the estates to conform to his desires. In this work he relied heavily on the assistance of Jean Baptiste Colbert, an admirer of Michel de Marillac. On one occasion Colbert referred to the Code Michau as an "excellent work" and on another he spoke of Marillac's "great experience."[44] Furthermore Colbert shared Marillac's passion for uniformity, order, and obedience. We do not know whether he contemplated creating élections in all the pays d'états as his predecessor had done, but he certainly considered establishing them in many parts of France. In June 1661 a threat was made to establish élections in Provence when the assembly of communities refused to raise taxes. In July 1662 Colbert himself told an intendant that serious consideration was being given to abolishing the privileges of Boulonnais and creating an élection there, and in December 1663 the bishop of Tarbes thought it necessary to persuade that same minister not to subject the Pyrenean provinces to a similar fate.[45] For a time Colbert appears to have abandoned his plans, but on September 3, 1681, he wrote to an official in the Pyrenees: "I do not doubt that you have found many disorders and abuses in the Estates of Bigorre, and I will await the report that you are to send me on these abuses in order to make an account to the king. These sorts of estates in these small provinces are only the occasions to pillage the people with impunity and to accustom them to revolts and seditions. I believe that it would suit the service of the king and the welfare of the people much better to suppress them and to establish an *élection*."[46]

On September 11, Colbert expressed his delight to the same official that the estates had ended, and on the fourteenth he informed him that "the king wants you to investigate with care and secrecy what should be done to establish *élections* in each of these provinces and suppress these estates which are always a heavy burden on the people and which give so little aid to his majesty."[47] Perhaps Colbert died before the plan could be implemented or

42. Ibid., pp. 86–87.

43. Ibid., p. 86.

44. *Lettres de Colbert*, 6:366, 381.

45. *Mémoriaux du conseil de 1661*, ed. Jean de Boislisle (Paris, 1905), 2:53; *Lettres de Colbert*, 4:2; *Correspondance administrative sous le règne de Louis XIV*, ed. G. B. Depping (Paris, 1852), 1:612–14.

46. *Correspondance administrative*, 3:284.

47. Ibid., 1:627, 2:53–54. The élus were not mentioned in the deliberations of the council concerning the difficulties with Provence. Ibid., 1:85, 93, 195, 231, 317, 324, 327, 348, 2:50.

perhaps he was overruled by the king; whatever the reason, élections were not established in Bigorre or in any other pays d'états during the reign of Louis XIV.

The fact that Colbert made no concerted effort to substitute the élus for the estates as his tax-collecting agencies should not be construed to mean that he or the royal officials with whom he dealt approved of the estates or trusted their officials. His letters are full of directives to intendants telling them to see that the estates levied no taxes without the king's permission and to find out how they spent the money they collected. He even wanted the Chamber of Justice to investigate their possible abuses along with those of royal financial officials.[48] Colbert praised an intendant for not permitting the communities of Languedoc to borrow money under the auspices of the estates: "You know how important it is to the king's service not to give the provincial estates more power than they already have and not to make the communities entirely dependent on them."[49] He was irritated whenever the estates spoke of their grievances. In 1681 he wrote to the governor of Brittany that "these estates ought to give perpetual thanks and not complaints.... I am so accustomed to see, with regard to all the estates, continual complaints without any foundation that I do not intend to change this habit of which they complain."[50] He expressed irritation at the length of the meetings of the estates and sometimes encouraged commissioners to terminate the session, congratulating them when they did so.[51]

Louvois shared Colbert's antipathy toward the estates and was perhaps even more willing to ride roughshod over their privileges. Nor did the pressure cease after these two ministers died.[52] "I cannot congratulate you too much on the termination of the estates," the chancellor wrote an official who had attended those of Brittany in 1703, "that is to say on the end of all agitations and of every sort of trouble for an honest man. I hope that you will find more tranquility and sweetness in the exercise of your natural and ordinary functions, and that all the province will feel the effects of your zeal."[53] The same complaints continued to come from the provinces. In 1688 an intendant who had investigated the estates of Quatre-Vallées, Nébouzan, and Foix reported, "It seems to me that although these provinces are well founded in the enjoyment of their privileges, [these privileges] ought not to be preserved for a longer time than the king finds it useful for the good of his service."[54] The time was favorable, he went on to say, to suppress these estates.

48. See, for example, *Lettres de Colbert*, 2:84, 4:127–29, 7:197, 275, 279.
49. Ibid., 4:138 n. 1.
50. Ibid., p. 147.
51. Ibid., pp. xi-xiv, 62–63.
52. *Ibid.*, p. xxiv; *Correspondance administrative*, 1:599–600.
53. *Correspondance administrative*, 1:558.
54. *Correspondance des contrôleurs généraux des finances avec les intendants des provinces*, ed. A. M. de Boislisle (Paris, 1874), 1: no. 531.

With so many influential enemies, one must ask how the pays d'états managed to survive. The answer, it would seem, must lie in the protection of Louis XIV himself. It is not that Louis either liked or believed in representative institutions—he held them in low esteem—but he and his predecessors had sworn to respect the privileges of these provinces and he would not go back on his word, at least not without grave reasons and ample justification.

Louis's treatment of the provinces that he conquered lends further support to this hypothesis. By the terms of the surrender of Arras in August 1640, no taxes were to be levied on the county of Artois without the consent of the estates, but Louis XIII and Mazarin had not adhered to this article, and the estates of that part of Artois held by the French failed to meet between 1640 and 1661. Louis XIV revived the estates in 1661 in honor of the pledge that had been made in his father's name and convoked them periodically throughout his reign despite the deputies' vigorous resistance to his fiscal demands and their many complaints.[55] He also permitted the less important estates of Hainaut, Lille,[56] and Cambrésis[57] to function after he became their sovereign.

The fate of the estates of Franche-Comté and Alsace was quite different largely because when they were joined with France they were already in a state of decadence and Louis felt no obligation to use them. Those of Franche-Comté had rarely met since the middle of the century, and their affairs were handled by an elected commission of eighteen persons. When the French overran the province in 1668, they required the commission to take an oath of fidelity but did not guarantee their privileges in return. After the province was restored to Spain by the terms of the treaty of Aix-la-Chapelle, the Spanish governor justified heavy taxes and other violations of its privileges on the grounds that its leaders had accepted, albeit reluctantly, the suzerainty of the French. The commission and the mayors of the towns began to quarrel over tax matters. As a result, when the French reconquered the province in 1674, they found its privileges despoiled and its leaders at odds with one another. They thus continued to collect the heavy taxes without consulting the estates or the commission. The provincial leaders accepted this solution to avoid again displeasing the Habsburgs by cooperating with their conquerors because they believed that Franche-Comté would

55. Charles Hirschauer, *Les Etats d'Artois de leurs origines à l'occupation française, 1340–1640* (Paris, 1923), 1:362–63; *Memoriaux du conseil*, 1:44, 51–52, 110, 113–14, 142, 146, 2:42–44, 177–78, 198, 262, 3:2, 5–6; *Correspondance administrative*, 1:559–602. For histories of the estates after 1661, see the superficial study by François Filon, *Histoire des Etats d'Artois depuis leur origine jusqu'à leur suppression en 1789* (Paris, 1861); and G. Bellart, "L'organisation et le rôle financier des Etats d'Artois de 1661 à 1789," *Positions des thèses de l'Ecole Nationale des Chartes* (1956): 23–28.

56. A. Melun, "Histoire des Etats de Lille," *Mém. de la soc. impériale des sciences, de l'agriculture et des arts de Lille*, sér. 2, 7 (1860), sér. 3, 1 (1864), 2 (1865), 4 (1867), 6 (1868), 7 (1869).

57. Marc-R. Vilette, *Les Etats généraux du Cambrésis de 1677 à 1790* (Cambrai, 1950).

once more revert to Spain after the war. Hence, it was only after the French had been given Franche-Comté in the peace of 1678 that the provincial leaders made a concerted effort to have their estates restored. Unfortunately the French responded to their pleas that their privileges were guaranteed by the peace treaty by insisting that they had ceased to have estates when they were subjects of the Habsburgs and that therefore their new masters were under no obligation to revive them.[58]

Alsace was divided into two administrative units, and meetings of the estates of the entire province and of Haute-Alsace had ceased before the French occupation. The estates of Basse-Alsace were only slightly more active after the Thirty Years War. They did meet once, in January 1683, after the French annexation, perhaps to recognize the new regime, but their role in the institutional life of the region had already become so small that Louis felt neither the obligation nor the need to convoke them again, and the inhabitants do not seem to have seriously regretted their passing.[59]

That Louis was in fact much less of a revolutionary than his professed rationalism would suggest does not mean that he had any intention of permitting the estates to thwart his will. Rather than destroy these popular institutions as Marillac had sought to do and many of his own officials would have preferred, he followed Richelieu's lead and tried to control them. There is scarcely a device used by modern prime ministers to control their parliaments that Louis and Colbert did not employ at one time or another, and some of their tactics were so dubious that contemporary politicians would hesitate to employ them. When it was to their advantage, they might alter the place for the estates to meet so as to have the deliberations take place in friendly surroundings. They could set Friday as the day for the opening meeting in the hope that disaffected elements would not arrive until Monday, thus permitting their own followers, who would be cautioned to be on time, to organize the assembly. With this power, they would choose the committee to examine the credentials of the deputies, and this committee in turn could exclude undesirable members. They plotted to have faithful servants preside over the estates and found ways to exclude those they did not want to attend. They ensured that loyal prelates and magnates influenced deputies from their dioceses and engaged in elaborate political calculations so as to be able to predict how far they could persuade the majority in an assembly to go. To increase their bargaining power, they asked for more money than they needed and kept a steady stream of

58. Armand Boussey, *La Franche-Comté sous Louis XIV* (Besançon, 1891), pp. 35–88; Lucien Febvre, *Histoire de Franche-Comté* (Paris, 1912), pp. 189, 194–99; P. Grispoux, "Recherches sur la disparition des Etats de la Franche-Comté de Bourgogne," *Mém. de la soc. libre d'émulation du Doubs*, n.s., 16 (1974): 60–76; Edmond Préclin, *Histoire de la Franche-Comté* (Paris, 1947), pp. 76–83.

59. Rodolphe Reuss, *L'Alsace au dix-septième siècle* (Paris, 1897), 1:276–83, 350; Georges Livet, *L'intendance d'Alsace sous Louis XIV, 1648–1715* (Strasbourg, 1956), pp. 117–19, 480–81, 550–51.

directives flowing toward the commissioners who held the estates and their loyal followers among the deputies. From these clients they received detailed reports in return. Every deputy must have been well aware that his actions would be reported to the king and that he would receive favor or ill will depending on how he conducted himself. Indeed, Louis's most potent means of control was to reward or to give the hope of reward to deputies who served him well, and to threaten or punish those who tried to thwart his will.[60]

For a nobleman or clergyman to obtain a royal appointment, a more lucrative benefice, or a pension, it was well known that it was necessary to serve his majesty loyally in the estates as well as on other occasions, and Louis went far beyond his predecessors in the use of patronage. He even took steps to see that sums were available for distribution in the estates. In 1662 Colbert ordered that 9,000 livres be secretly given to selected deputies in the estates of Languedoc and then compounded the injury by obtaining the funds from the treasurer of the estates. Ten years later he informed the intendant to that province that his majesty authorized him to give 20,000 livres to deputies of the third estate in the hope of obtaining the desired don gratuit on the first ballot (that is, if it were necessary to do so). His majesty did not wish the deputies to develop a habit of receiving gifts in return for doing the things he desired.[61] The fierce provincial loyalty of the Bretons made it more costly to win their votes, or perhaps the difficulty was that so many of them attended the estates.[62] Whatever the reason, 60,000 livres were set aside in 1663 for "the deputies who served the best in the assembly."[63]

When bribes were not sufficient, threats were often employed. When the troublesome assembly of the communities of Provence voted the king only about a fourth of what he requested in 1661, he threatened to disband the deputies and refused to accept any of the conditions they made in return for the 300,000 livres that they were willing to give. Soon Louis relented and offered to take less than he had originally demanded, but he instructed his commissioners to terminate the assembly immediately if there were any difficulties. When the assembly did not heed his warning, the deputies were sent home, and Louis arbitrarily increased the salt tax and ordered troops to Provence. Someone added the further threat that assemblies of the communities would be discontinued permanently and that élections would be established as in Dauphiné. Thoroughly frightened, the procureur du pays summoned the first *consuls* of the communities to approve an additional 105,000 livres. After some further negotiations, an agreement was reached.

60. For a general treatment of the estates and Louis XIV, see Alphonse Grün, *Les Etats provinciaux sous Louis XIV*, 2d ed. (Paris, 1853).

61. *Lettres de Colbert*, 4:81, 7:445.

62. Ibid., 4:15–16.

63. Ibid., p. 18.

By his threats Louis had obtained more than he otherwise would have, but the Provençals still gave far less than was originally demanded of them.[64]

Neither side had won. Louis's officials continued to try to strengthen his position in Provence. In 1664 they urged that a 2,000 livre pension be paid to the syndic of the nobility "who has always done his duty well in all the assemblies for the service of the king."[65] In 1666 when the newly elected municipal officials of Aix, who doubled as procureurs du pays, proved to be less friendly to the crown than their predecessors were, they were removed from office, and more pliant officials were chosen in their stead. Such measures were sufficient to create a court party, but when the remaining Provençals saw themselves betrayed by their natural leaders, they united in opposition.[66] In 1668 the first president of the Parlement of Aix, who was also a commissioner, wrote to Colbert: "I avow to you that I have never seen an assembly of the nature of this one. We have absolutely all the leaders there, that is to say, the church, the nobility, the *procureurs du pays* and the first community, and those of the deputies who depend on us. Notwithstanding this, we cannot be the masters because the number of unreasonable ruffians and monsters there is so great and so united by the conformity of their tempers that we have carried them to where they are at present only with incredible trouble, and we will assuredly find the greatest difficulties to dispose them for what remains to be done. We forget neither intrigue nor authority, neither force nor leadership in order to lead them where it is necessary, and we will continue this same application to the end."[67]

Louis had asked for 600,000 livres, but for a long time the commissioners despaired of getting the deputies to offer more than 350,000. Finally, in a session that lasted nearly three months, the deputies increased their offer to 400,000 provided that certain conditions were granted. The following year the communities met from October to January but again made a conditional grant of less than the king had requested. The struggle recommenced in December 1670. When March 1671 came and the communities had offered only 200,000 livres, a third of what he had asked, Louis directed that the meeting be terminated promptly. The king, Colbert indicated, would not reply to such an offer. He wanted the amount stated in his instructions. Frightened by this threat, the deputies increased their offer to 450,000 livres, and Louis accepted, although it was still less than his original request.[68]

By this time Louis and Colbert had had enough. Shortly before the

64. *Mémoriaux du conseil*, 1:85, 89–91, 93, 195–97, 231, 233, 240, 317, 320, 324, 325, 327, 348, 349, 2:50, 53–55, 110–13, 3:9, 11–12.

65. *Correspondance administrative*, 1:334; 340–42.

66. Ibid., pp. 359–63; 366.

67. Ibid., p. 376.

68. Ibid., pp. 378–86; *IAD, Bouches-du-Rhône*, sér. C, ed. Louis Blancard (Marseilles, 1884), 1:55–58; *Lettres de Colbert*, 4:55–56.

communities began their meeting on September 30, 1671, the latter directed a commissioner to see to it that the session ended within a month. The estates made an initial offer of 200,000 livres in response to a demand for 600,000. The commissioners evidently thought that they could persuade the deputies to give 450,000 as in the preceding year, and asked Colbert if this would be sufficient. Colbert responded that the king insisted on receiving 500,000 livres. By October 30 Colbert had become impatient. He continually compared the obstinacy of the Provençals to the submissiveness of the three estates in other provinces who quickly gave the king what he requested. By December 11 he was informing the commissioners that the king would take what he wanted without consent if the deputies did not act quickly.[69]

The acting governor was obviously sympathetic to the Provençals' desire to escape the full weight of the proposed tax, but confronted by the insistent demands of the crown, he requested that an order terminating the assembly be sent along with some lettres de cachet to be used as a last resort to punish the most seditious deputies: "There is no longer any problem about bringing them to 450,000 *livres*, but I believe that only the present threat can terrify them, and that they will not go to 500,000 *livres* unless they see an order to break up the assembly."[70] Louis had letters dispatched to exile ten deputies to Normandy and Brittany, but on December 31 he agreed to accept only 450,000 livres. Colbert's letter passing on this welcome news included a threat that the king might not assemble the communities again for a long time. Meanwhile the frightened deputies offered 500,000 livres provided certain conditions were met. The acting governor used this long-delayed act of submission as an excuse to ask not to use the lettres de cachet that had been sent, and his plea was granted.[71]

The assembly of the communities had finally been cowed. In December 1672 they unanimously voted the king 500,000 livres with little debate. Soon Colbert could report that even the king was satisfied with their conduct, for they were voting what he required in a single deliberation. It had been so easy to get his way that Louis decided to ask for a million livres in 1676. If the deputies would not go beyond the now customary 500,000 livres without any arguments, the king would send troops, Colbert informed the intendant on November 8. If the deputies cooperated, his majesty would accept 800,000 livres. The communities cooperated. To Louis's credit when peace returned, he reduced his request to 800,000 livres if the deputies were troublesome and to 600,000 if they were not. The Provençals had learned

69. For the assembly of 1671, see Bernard Hildesheimer, *L'assemblées générales des communautés de Provence* (Paris, 1935), pp. 77–80. *Lettres de Colbert*, 4:62–68. *Correspondance administrative*, 1:380–96.

70. *Correspondance administrative*, 1:397.

71. Ibid., pp. 397–403.

their lesson. From 1672 until the end of his reign, the Sun King had frequent reason to express his satisfaction with their behavior, although as an added precaution he deemed it wise to have the intendant attend the deliberations from 1688 to ensure that the deputies were properly servile.[72]

Probably before this time the crown preferred assemblies of the towns or communities in which few if any nobles and clergymen attended, as in Dauphiné, Provence, and Auvergne, because they were more pliant. Perhaps this is why Louis sought to restrict the attendance of the nobility of Artois in 1661.[73] His policy of bribes and threats, however, changed this situation. Most of the rewards he distributed went to members of the first two estates, and royal disfavor affected their opportunities more than those of provincial lawyers and merchants. For this reason and because they paid most of the taxes, the third estate of Provence proved more difficult to subdue than the three estates of Burgundy or Languedoc. The prince of Condé found this to be very much the case. In a detailed letter describing his negotiations with the estates of his government of Burgundy in June 1662, he concluded "that the chamber of the clergy and that of the nobility have acted marvelously well in this encounter having made almost no difficulty about any of the things that were proposed to them. To tell the truth, the deputies of the third estate have caused a little more trouble; but this is pardonable of them since they are the ones who bear almost all of the impositions."[74]

In this same letter Condé told Colbert how he had asked the Burgundians for 1.5 million livres in extraordinary taxes over a three-year period as he had been directed, and how the estates had offered 500,000, then 600,000, then 800,000, and then 900,000. At this point Condé feared that they would go no further so he reduced the king's demands to 1.2 million as he was permitted to do in his instructions. This reduction encouraged the estates to offer 1 million and then 1.05 million, which Condé accepted.[75] In the closing sentence of his letter, he wrote: "On my return I will bring a report on those who have cooperated best; His Majesty will see if he believes them worthy of some gratifications, as this is always done; and he will use it as he pleases."[76]

This letter reveals that in spite of the explanation Louis prepared for the dauphin describing how a king should deal with the estates, he had done everything he had said ought not to be done when he began his personal

72. Ibid., pp. 403–17; *Lettres de Colbert*, 4:84–85, 89, 100–03, 105, 123–24, 136, 141–42, 162–69; Hildesheimer, *L'assemblées générales*, pp. 80–81; Charles Godard, *Les pouvoirs des intendants sous Louis XIV* (Paris, 1901), p. 170.

73. *Mémoriaux du conseil*, 1:51–52.

74. *Correspondance administrative*, 1:430–31.

75. Ibid., pp. 429–31. On these same estates, see also pp. 424–28, 431–35, and Alexandre Thomas, *Une province sous Louis XIV: situation politique et administrative de la Bourgogne de 1661 à 1715* (Paris, 1844), pp. 32–34.

76. *Correspondance administrative*, 1:431.

reign. In his dealings with the estates of Burgundy he had initially asked for 300,000 livres more than he was willing to accept; the estate had begun with an offer of far less than they were willing to give, and after considerable bargaining Condé had accepted 150,000 livres less than he had been instructed to take. To make matters worse, Louis was expected to reward, or more accurately, to pay bribes to those who had cooperated most effectively with his commissioners. This last was such an undignified matter that he never intimated to the dauphin that it had ever been practiced.

The crown interfered in municipal elections in Burgundy and in the choice of the élus of the estates soon after their session in 1662, but none of its activities prevented the same bargaining from taking place in the estates of 1665, 1668, and 1671. By 1674, however, the will of the estates had been broken, and to Louis's delight they voted all that he requested in a single deliberation. Thereafter the estates did not seriously oppose his financial requests until near the end of his reign.[77] The change that took place in the estates was reflected in the speeches that the first president of the Parlement of Dijon made to the estates of 1671 and 1677. In the former he sought to reconcile freedom with authority in a typical Renaissance fashion by declaring: "In the natural love of all men for liberty and in the diversity of their sentiments on everything that presents itself to the mind, it is admirable that they have all had the same feeling touching on authority and that everywhere it has been regarded with respect as the source of their common good fortune."[78] And then he added a moment later that before Clovis and Pharamond (the kings of the first race), the Gauls had pays d'états. In 1677, on the other hand, he argued that selfish interests had been subjected before those of civil society "*since the power of the prince is the same as the state* and assures its tranquility and salvation."[79]

During this period, centralization in Burgundy progressed slowly. On the initiative of the municipal officials of the town of Auxerre and with the consent of its three estates, the county of Auxerre was united with the duchy of Burgundy in 1668 and its élection was suppressed. In 1720 the élection of Bar-sur-Seine and in 1751 the estates of Charolais suffered similar fates. As compensation, the inhabitants of the three counties were given some voice in each of the Burgundian estates. The initiative leading to the last two incorporations came primarily from the leaders of the estates of Burgundy and not the crown, although the latter approved on the grounds that the expenses of the estates imposed an additional burden on the people. Not content with these victories, the duchy tried to swallow the county of Mâcon

---

77. Ibid., pp. 435–54; *Lettres de Colbert*, 4:56–60, 132–33. Thomas, *Une province*, pp. 34–60. For a detailed account of the estates of 1718 soon after Louis's death, see F. Dumont, "Une session des Etats de Bourgogne, la tenue de 1718,"*Annales de Bourgogne*, 5 (1933): 329–70, 6 (1934): 47–77, 230–52, 337–65, 7: (1935): 45–69.

78. Thomas, *Une province*, p. 39.

79. Ibid., p. 43.

and its estates, but the particularism of Mâconnais proved too strong, and it retained its independence until the Revolution.[80]

Bresse, Bugey, and Gex were within the government of Burgundy, but unlike the pays adjacents, they did not participate directly in the estates. Since all three had élections and the king had set the size of the tax since their annexation by Henry IV, there was no conflict between the estates and the crown over a don gratuit. The three orders in each province had their individual assemblies that met at least every third year to elect syndics and other officials to look after their interests, and in the case of the third estates, especially, to send deputies to Dijon during the time the Burgundian esatates met to present their cahiers to the governor. There were also occasional joint meetings of the three estates or of just one estate of the three provinces. The role of these estates was to present grievances to the crown and to vote taxes to support causes of local importance, the most expensive of which was to give presents to those in authority. The governor in 1682 received 20,000 livres from Bresse as opposed to the 1,000 that were assigned to the intendant.[81]

True independence on the part of the estates was prevented by the fact that the prince of Condé appointed many of the community officials and then told them how to vote in the estates and whom to choose as their syndic. In 1664, for example, the municipal government of Bourg directed its deputies to the estates to vote for whomever the prince of Condé desired. In 1667 Condé designated his choice for the offices of first syndic and the secretary of Bourg, but left the choice of second syndic to the assembly of the town as was customary.[82] In 1664 an intendant expressed deep concern over Condé's authority and stressed the need to have free elections in the three provinces, but to no avail.[83] The princes of Condé continued to hold tight control over appointments, including those to positions that were theoreti- cally elective, throughout the reign of Louis XIV. In 1685 some inhabitants

80. A. Guillois, "La fin d'un 'pays adjacent': L'union du comté d'Auxerre aux Etats de Bourgogne, 1668,"*Annales de Bourgogne*, 33 (1961): 5–26, 65–87; *Correspondance administrative*, 1:443–44; L. Lartoche, "Les Etats particuliers du Charolais,"*Mém. de la soc. pour l'histoire du droit et des institutions des anciens pays bourguignons, comtois et romands*, 6 (1939): 184–94; L. Blin, "Des Etats du Charolais aux Etats de Bourgogne, les avatars de Pierre-Etienne-Palamède Baudinot, 1726–1752," *Annales de Bourgogne*, 43 (1971): 145–66; Jean Roussot, *Un comté adjacent à la Bourgogne aux XVIIe et XVIIIe siécles: le Mâconnais, pays d'états et d'élection* (Mâcon, 1937).

81. *Correspondance des contrôleurs généraux*, 1: no. 169. The assemblies of the clergy were complicated by the fact that a number of dioceses extended into the three provinces. For descriptions of the estates around 1698 and 1765, see "Description des pays de Bresse, Bugey et Gex dressée par l'intendant de Bourgogne en 1698 sur les orders du roi Louis XIV pour le duc de Bourgogne,"*Bul. de la soc. de géographie de l'Ain*, 6 (1891): 16–26, 33–48, 87–95, 120–29, 172–84, 207–20; and Joseph-P. Brossard, *Notice sur l'organisation territoriale et l'administration des anciennes provinces de Bresse, du Bugey, de la Dombes et du pays de Gex* (Bourg-en-Bresse, 1881).

82. *Mémoires historiques de la ville de Bourg*, ed. Joseph Brossard (Bourg-en-Bresse, 1888), 5:103, 119–20.

83. *Correspondance administrative*, 1:454–60.

of Bourg who were opposed to Condé wanted to have the assembly of the third estate of Bresse abolished, but the intendant thwarted the move because it would anger Condé and create trouble with the three estates of Burgundy, which were scheduled to meet in the near future. Thus the estates of Burgundy managed to stretch their protective arm over these three pays d'élections with which they were indirectly associated and to help preserve their representative assemblies until the Revolution.[84]

Initially Louis had to bargain with the three estates of Languedoc just as he did with those of Provence and Burgundy. Since he was in the province when the estates met in 1659, he seized the opportunity to obtain a larger sum than usual by informing the deputies that his authority had been "wounded" by the revocation of the Edict of Béziers during his minority, but the estates refused to have it reestablished. Louis was insistent but suggested that in return for a total grant of 8 million livres he would forget the matter. The estates countered by offering 3 million if twenty-two conditions were accepted. Louis agreed. In the next meeting of the estates, Louis asked for 2 million livres; only after considerable haggling did he obtain half that amount.[85]

Louis wanted the estates that met in January 1662 to vote 2.5 million livres, and Colbert went to considerable length to please his master. He and the king's most devoted servants in Languedoc made arrangements for a friendly bishop to preside, found an excuse to deny a seat to an unfriendly *consul* so that his place could be taken by a more loyal one, made sure that the first orators to speak for the clergy and for the nobility advocated making a generous grant, rallied the governor's clients among the first two orders, and ensured that they and their colleagues of like minds sought to influence the members of the third estate who were dependent on them.[86] The treasurer of the estates was directed to provide money to bribe deputies selected by the intendant, and 9,000 livres was spent in this fashion. Most, and perhaps all, of this sum was directed toward members of the third estate, for the crown tended to reward cooperative members of the other orders with pensions, perhaps because they smelled less of bribery. The syndic of Vivarais, a gentleman, had been receiving a pension for several years at the time of the estates as had others who were present. By 1670 it had become customary to give the barons with seats in the estates annual pensions of 2,250 livres, and bishops received similar rewards.[87]

84. Thomas, *Une province*, pp. 23–27; *Correspondance des contrôleurs généraux*, 1: no. 169.

85. Mazarin, *Lettres*, 9:343–46, 396–97; Beik, *Governing Languedoc; pp. 73–74: IAD, Haute-Garonne, sér. C*, ed. Ad. Baudouin (Toulouse, 1903), 2:344–45; *Correspondance administrative*, 1:13–46.

86. *Correspondance administrative*, 1:51–75.

87. Ibid., pp. 66, 284; *Lettres de Colbert*, 7:445; J. Adher, "La 'preparation' des séances des Etats de Languedoc, d'après des documents inédits," *Annales du Midi*, 25 (1913): 467. This article contains many other letters indicating how the crown sought to influence the deputies. For a general treatment of how the crown controlled the estates, see Beik, *Governing Languedoc*, pp. 164–75.

Such measures as these, coupled with the knowledge that the king would hear of those who served him well or tried to thwart his will, could lead only to favorable results. The first offer of the estates of 1662 was 1.2 million livres; a proposal by the *consuls* of Narbonne that it be limited to 800,000 received only five other votes. The bishops of Béziers, Mende, Viviers, Castres, and Saint-Papoul, the marquis of Castres, the governor, the intendant, and no doubt others hastened to write Colbert the good news and to tell of their contributions.[88] The bishop of Mende proudly declared: "I have four votes in my diocese: they will serve me and be always of my opinion. There are some deputies who offer themselves to me and I am assured that they will serve the king well. I believe that we will leave after two or three more sessions; but in case the business is delayed, you would very much oblige me, Monsieur, if in your reply, you would put in your letter some pleasantness for the *consuls* of my diocese, and for those who follow my advice. Ask me to tell you their names so that you can favor them on the occasions which will present themselves, or give some other similar demonstration of friendship."[89]

The bishop of Saint-Papoul indulged in political arithmetic. The fifteen clergymen had voted for the 1.2 million livre tax. With one exception the twenty-two barons or their proxies had done the same , but two of the proxies had voted in favor only after they had seen that the motion would carry. After urging that the three barons be told to correct the behavior of their proxies, the bishop pointed out that the first two estates provided thirty-six of the forty votes necessary to pass a measure. Only four votes from the third estate were therefore necessary, but nearly thirty were available because of the care that had been taken to inform them of the king's desires. Those who were familiar with the estates said that "they have never seen a first ballot similar to this one." Even the capitoul of Toulouse and the *consuls* of Montpellier and Carcasonne had voted in favor of the tax. Nevertheless the bishop was doubtful whether the king could persuade the estates to vote any more. Even if only six nobles and clergymen deserted, it would take ten votes from the third estate to carry, and these votes would be difficult to find because members of this order had to report back to their constituents.[90]

The governor and intendant, however, thought that the deputies could be persuaded to go as high as 1.5 million livres, and they were correct. From the initial preparations for the meeting until its conclusion, Colbert and his adherents had functioned like a well-organized contemporary political machine. Few if any of their tactics were new, but never before had they been so fully used and so well coordinated. Still there were limits as to how far even the clergy and nobility would go in betraying the interests of the people of Languedoc, or, as Louis XIV would have put it, in placing their

88. *Correspondance administrative*, 1:64–75.
89. Ibid., p. 67.
90. Ibid., pp. 72–75.

trust in his benevolence. Not only had they voted him a million less than he
had requested, but they had attached a number of conditions to the grant.
As an added insult, they had also appointed a committee to see if he had
kept the promises that he had made in return for the money that had been
voted by the preceding estates. Colbert's work was not yet done.[91]

For eight years affairs continued in this fashion, with Colbert using the
same tactics to control the estates as in 1662.[92] By 1670, however, he was
ready to institute a change in procedure that he and Louis had long desired.
"I believe that I have written you," he informed the intendant in December
1670, "that this year His Majesty wants you to declare to the estates the
entire sum that he desires for the don gratuit and that it pass in a single
deliberation without any long negotiations and without sending couriers [to
court]. All the deputies of the estates who have been here have begged His
Majesty to use this procedure."[93] Previously Colbert had told the intendant
that the king would be satisfied with a don gratuit of 1.4 million livres, but
the intendant asked the estates for 2.4 million presumably to have more
bargaining power. In the end he obtained exactly what the king had wanted
in the first place.[94]

By the time the estates met the following year, the intendant was
somewhat better instructed. He again stated that the king wanted 2.4
million livres, which was almost certainly an exaggeration. Then he told
those present that the king had been very happy with the sums they had
voted in the past but that he

> was not satisfied with the way the affair came about. In effect, if you
> consider the conduct of the clergy, which is the first corps of the state, and
> of which you have such an illustrious portion among you, you will
> remember that at their last assembly they made a gift so considerable that
> the king returned part of it. And since they had done it in a single
> deliberation, they earned by their conduct a relief that they would not
> have had if they had granted it in two or three attempts. This year what
> has been the conduct of Brittany and Burgundy? Their action has
> produced reductions. And Languedoc, which surpasses these other prov-
> inces in all sorts of advantages; will it never resolve to begin where it must
> end? Why make these offers of 1,200,000 and 1,500,000 *livres* and then
> arrive afterwards at the sum hoped for, instead of doing in one stroke
> what the needs of the state and the necessity of affairs require?[95]

Prodded in this fashion the estates unanimously voted 1.7 million livres in a

91. Ibid., pp. 70, 75; *IAD, Haute-Garonne, sér. C*, 2 : 350–53.
92. For letters demonstrating how the estates were managed during this period, see
Correspondance administrative, 1 : 76–269. See also scattered letters in *Lettres de Colbert*, vol. 4.
93. *Lettres de Colbert*, 4 : 51.
94. Ibid., p. 49; *IAD, Haute-Garonne, sér. C*, 2 : 377–78.
95. Quoted by Beik, *Governing Languedoc*, p. 81.

single deliberation, but they attached conditions to their offer, and it was still less than the intendant said the king desired. Nevertheless Louis expressed satisfaction at their performance.[96]

By the close of 1672 Colbert was ready to make a determined effort. No less than 20,000 livres were made available to bribe members of the third estate, and the intendant was instructed to ask for a don gratuit of 2 million livres. When Colbert learned that the intendant had again requested a larger sum than the king desired, he was instructed to report if this were true. Under the new system the deputies were to be told exactly what the king wanted, and they were to vote the entire amount near the beginning of the meeting without bargaining. The intendant had indeed considered asking for more, but before the estates opened he had been convinced by the archbishop of Toulouse that he should not. On December 6 the archbishop informed Colbert that the deputies of the first two estates were asking about their pensions. They must have been satisfied, for three days later they joined the heavily bribed third estate in unanimously voting Louis 2 million livres without debate. They did attach some conditions to the grant, but the commissioners accepted or rejected them article by article on the spot.[97]

The estates of Languedoc had been conquered. In the years that followed, Louis told the estates what he wanted, and they quickly voted it for him. By 1676 his appetite had grown, and he asked for and received a don gratuit of 3 million livres, a grant that was repeated the following year. Louis did exercise a modest amount of restraint when his needs were less, as they seemed to be in the closing months of 1678. On that occasion he asked for and received only 2.4 million livres. Compliant though they had become, the estates did not die because Louis found in them and their officers useful administrative instruments. Not only did they feed and lodge troops and collect taxes at less cost than the élus in other parts of France, but they also became involved, somewhat reluctantly at first, in a host of economic and commercial enterprises, including the Canal du Midi connecting the Mediterranean with the Atlantic. Nor did the estates become entirely useless to the people. Languedoc was less exploited than provinces without representative assemblies, but this enviable position was achieved at the cost of providing large gratifications to their governor, the secretary of state for Languedoc, and other influential persons.[98]

The Bretons had been shielded by Richelieu's protecting arm from any serious threats during his regime, and the estates had responded by remaining loyal during the Fronde. Their liberties were clearly unimpaired when

96. *Correspondance administrative*, 1:270–76; *IAD, Haute-Garonne, sér. C*, 2:379–82; Beik, *Governing Languedoc*, p. 81; *Lettres de Colbert*, 4:52–55.

97. *Lettres de Colbert*, 4:81–83; *Correspondance administrative*, 1:276–95; *IAD, Haute-Garonne, sér. C*, 2:382–84.

98. *IAD, Haute-Garonne, sér C*, 2:384–98, 401. *Correspondance administrative*, 1:307–10; Beik, *Governing Languedoc*, pp. 82–86, 186–223.

they met in 1655 to hear a royal demand for 4 million livres to be collected over two years. When the estates responded with an offer of 800,000 on June 19, the bargaining began. It was not until August 6 when the estates offered 2.5 million livres that were to be collected over a three-year period that the crown abandoned the effort to obtain the larger sum.[99]

Perhaps it was this experience, although it was by no means unusual, that caused Mazarin to direct La Meilleraye, the governor, to use his influence on the estates to obtain a large grant when they met in October 1657. The crown asked for 3.5 million livres over a two-year period. The estates offered 600,000 on October 15, and the bargaining began once more. When word of the offer reached the court, the nineteen-year-old king was furious, or at least Mazarin said he was. It is hard to explain the flood of letters that the cardinal, who rarely became involved in negotiating with the estates, dispatched to royal officials in Brittany unless pressure was being placed upon him from above or that the uncompromising Colbert was really directing the negotiations. The general tenor of Mazarin's correspondence was that the king meant to have his authority respected, and in one letter he demanded that the estates vote an unconditional grant within twenty-four hours. Nevertheless it took nearly two weeks for the estates to raise their offer to 2 million livres. On November 15, Louis relented to the point of saying that he would take 3 million, but the estates would offer no more. Indeed they would not have gone as high as they did if they had not wanted to get La Meilleraye to release a deputy whom he had illegally removed from the assembly. Louis, Mazarin reported, was resolved to go to Brittany to reduce the estates to obedience.[100]

Louis did not go to Brittany in 1657 although the estates failed to give him what he wanted, nor did he make the trip in 1659 when they again bargained with his commissioner and voted him an acceptable sum only after La Meilleraye had threatened to transfer the meeting to Nantes where he hoped to find a more favorable political climate.[101] When the time came for the estates to meet in August 1661, the restraining hand of Mazarin had been removed, and Louis made a quick trip to Nantes to settle his account with the estates. La Meilleraye had asked the deputies for 4 million livres before his arrival, but on September 1 the bishop of Saint-Brieuc greeted the young monarch in the name of the estates in such flattering and submissive terms that he announced that he would be content with 3 million. The

99. AD, Ille-et-Vilaine, C 2655, esp. fols. 516, 559–63, 572–74, 582–87, 595–96, 607–08, 641, 645, 648. For the role of the three estates during the Fronde and their quarrel with the Parlement of Rennes, see Arthur Le Moyne La Borderie and Barthélemy Pocquet, *Histoire de Bretagne* (Rennes, 1913), 5:419–46.

100. AD, Ille-et-Vilaine, C 2656, esp. fols. 25–26, 67–68, 137; Mazarin, *Lettres*, 8:201–02, 625, 644, 645, 647, 661; Louis-J. -M. de Carné, *Les Etats de Bretagne* (Paris, 1875), 1:328–30.

101. Carné, *Les Etats de Bretagne*, 1:330–31.

estates, cowed by his presence, quickly voted this amount without debate and without conditions.[102] Louis alluded to this meeting in his memoirs, and the success that he achieved may have caused him to formulate his policy of telling the estates how much he wanted and having them vote the required sum immediately without haggling about the amount or making conditions. If they did as he desired, he would treat them justly and kindly. Some years elapsed, however, before Louis could put this policy into effect in Brittany or elsewhere.[103]

The importance that Colbert attached to the next biennial meeting of the estates is attested by the fact that he arranged for his brother to serve as commissioner and gave him detailed instructions on how to act. Such diverse matters came under his purview as to how to prevent a quarrel over who should be president of the clergy because such an argument might alienate some deputies and make them less disposed to conform to the king's will. Colbert also prescribed who was to be responsible for distributing 60,000 livres that his majesty had made available for those who served him best in the assembly. This was not the first time that such generous bribes had been made available to the deputies, for a similar sum had been allocated in 1661; Louis had not relied solely on his presence to secure the compliance of the deputies. Nor was he yet prepared to ask the estates for as small a gift as he was willing to take, for fear that they would automatically offer a lower sum if he were not present. Hence he requested 2.5 million livres but expressed satisfaction when 2 million was voted.[104]

In 1665 Louis asked the estates for 3 million livres and told his commissioners that 2.4 million would be the least that he would take. The initial offer of the estates was for only a million, but because the commissioners responded to the petitions of the estates favorably, they anticipated a more generous offer.[105] However, as one of them reported to Colbert, "In an assembly as large as this one, the number of wise men is not alway very large, and especially after dinner. It so happened that the deputies chose this time to have their discussion. The ecclesiastics were the only ones who were of the opinion that 200,000 *livres* should be added to their first offer, and the third estate, with the nobles who were most heated with wine, persisted in their opposing offers and requests."[106] Persuasion having failed, the officers of the king applied threats. The offer of the estates jumped to 1.5 million, but

---

102. Ibid., pp. 332–37; *Mémoriaux du conseil*, 3:111–24. La Borderie and Pocquet, *Histoire de Bretagne*, 450–52. For a general discussion of Louis's policy, see Armand Rebillon, *Les Etats de Bretagne de 1661 à 1789* (Paris, 1932), pp. 232–40.

103. *Louis XIV, Mémoires*, pp. 86–87.

104. *Correspondance administrative* 1:468–83; *Lettres de Colbert*, 4:13–18, 21–27; La Borderie and Pocquet, *Histoire de Bretagne*, 5:452–56.

105. *Correspondance administrative*, 1:485–88.

106. Ibid., p. 488.

the commissioners still felt it necessary to ask Colbert whether the king would not take less than he had previously told them. His reply has been lost, but after further debate the crown settled for 2.2 million.[107]

Still the crown sought ways to control the estates. It was difficult to reward all the nobles who attended because from 150 to 300 usually did so during this period. The third estate, which paid most of the taxes, was an even greater problem. As a result, the crown made some effort to exclude its enemies. In 1667 Colbert accused the duchess of Rohan of sending her young son to the estates with her vassals and friends, and another deputy was forbidden to attend by a lettre de cachet, but still the estates would not give the king all he desired in that year or in 1669.[108]

Then, in 1671, a new climate pervaded the estates. On being informed that the king wanted 2.5 million livres, the deputies voted this amount in a single deliberation and did not make it subject to royal concessions included in a formal contract. Undoubtedly the bribes and threats of the preceding decade had taught the deputies that there were advantages to complying with the wishes of their sovereign, but it is difficult to believe that the appointment of the firm but tactful duke of Chaulnes as governor and the winning of the duke of Rohan to the royal cause were not decisive factors. If Rohan packed the second estate with his adherents in 1671, it was to serve the king. As a reward for their obedience—and to encourage such submission in the future—Louis reduced the tax to 2.2 million livres. The grateful estates attempted to throw most of their savings away by making overly generous gratifications, but the duke of Chaulnes rejected the 100,000 livres offered him because of the heavy debts of the province. He did not, however, neglect to inform Colbert of his act of renunciation or to point out that Richelieu and the queen mother had received similar gifts when they were governors.[109]

Brittany seemed on the verge of being conquered, but a series of new edicts aroused the anger of the most vocal elements of the province. One edict established a Chamber of Justice to revoke seigneurial justices that had been usurped and to punish the offenders. Another forbade Parlement to inform the officers of the estates of royal acts sent to it for registration or to consider their attempts to delay registration. This attack on the pocketbooks of the nobility and the capacity of the estates to defend the privileges of Brittany turned the estates of 1673 into an uproar. Several officials believed that it would be necessary to return to the old practice of asking the estates for 3 million livres in order to get the 2.6 million desired. The estates did offer 3 million but coupled the grant with the requirement that the offending

107. Ibid., pp. 489–92; Rebillon, *Les Etats de Bretagne*, p. 234; La Borderie and Pocquet, *Histoire de Bretagne*, 5 : 458–60.
108. *Correspondance administrative*, 1 : 492–96; Rebillon, *Les Etats de Bretagne*, pp. 95, 234.
109. *Correspondance administrative*, 1 : 496–520.

edicts be revoked. Conditional grants, however, were unacceptable to Louis, and the estates were finally prevailed upon to give 2.6 million unconditionally, although in the process the governor had to dismiss two noble deputies from the assembly. It took an additional 2.6 million livres to obtain a promise that most of the offending edicts would be revoked. Of this sum 950,000 livres were to be paid by the nobles, but in the next meeting of the estates, they managed to move all but 200,000 of this sum onto the general tax structure of the province. Thus the third estate was called upon to bear most of the costs of protecting seigneurial rights.[110]

The estates were unable to obtain the revocation of new taxes on stamped documents, tobacco, and pewter dishes. These burdens, in addition to very heavy taxes and rumors that the gabelle was to be installed, led to uprisings in the spring and summer of 1675 that were firmly and in some cases brutally suppressed. It was in this atmosphere that the estates met in November 1675 and unanimously voted the king 3 million livres without debate and without conditions in the hope that complete submission would cause him to punish the province less severely. It did not, but from that time the estates submissively gave Louis whatever he wanted, and talk of reducing the grant or making conditions was considered little short of treasonable.[111]

During this year Colbert prepared a brief statement on the administration of the king's finances. Taxes in the pays d'états were handled very much as they were elsewhere in France, he recorded: "When the king gives the estates of the provinces permission to assemble, his majesty decides what he wants to ask them for; he has instructions prepared which are sent to his commissioners, and the estates of the provinces always accord what it pleases his majesty to ask of them."[112] Uniformity, order, and obedience—these values that Colbert and his master prized so highly were close to being achieved.

Strangely enough, the small estates in the Pyrenees came nearer to escaping the trend toward centralization than the larger pays d'états, although their very existence was sometimes threatened. The Mazarin phase of Louis's reign ended on a favorable note, for when Louis went to Saint-Jean-de-Luz in 1660 to meet his bride, he agreed to take an oath to respect the rights and liberties of the people of Navarre. He did not make the pledge within the boundaries of the kingdom and before the estates as tradition

110. Ibid., pp. 520–46. Rebillon, *Les Etats de Bretagne*, pp. 234–35; La Borderie and Pocquet, *Histoire de Bretagne*, 5:463–69. For a study of the crown's attack on the Parlement of Brittany and its efforts to prevent cooperation between that institution and the estates, see J. J. Hurt, "La politique du parlement de Bretagne, 1661–1675,"*Annales de Bretagne*, 81 (1974): 105–30.

111. La Borderie and Pocquet, *Histoire de Bretagne*, 5:469–534; Rebillon, *Les Etats de Bretagne*, pp. 237–43. For a more recent study of the revolt, see Yvon Garlan and Claude Nières, *Les révoltes bretonnes de 1675* (Paris, 1975).

112. *Lettres de Colbert*, 2:84.

demanded, but as far as can be ascertained, no ruler of the tiny state had gone to this much trouble since Henri d'Albret had sent a commissioner to Navarre to take the oath for him in 1523.[113]

One must not reckon without the intendants, however. Already, in October 1661, one of them was reporting to Colbert that he had tried to prevent the estates of Comminges from meeting for a year because the assembly would be prejudicial to the interests of the king and delay his affairs. Then, referring to all Pyrenean estates, he declared that "they have no other aim than to advertise the misery of the people and to procure some indirect advantage for everyone who attends."[114] The intendant's low opinion of the estates may have contributed to the idea that was current in 1663 that Colbert planned to suppress the Pyrenean estates and subject the inhabitants to the taille as in the remainder of the kingdom. The bishop of Tarbes sent Colbert a strong defense of the estates near the close of that year in which he attempted to show that it was to his majesty's advantage to retain the status quo, and the matter was apparently forgotten, at least temporarily.[115]

Nevertheless Colbert was far too dedicated to the concept of uniformity and far too opposed to disorder to leave the estates alone for long. In 1670 he ordered that the abuses of the estates of Foix be investigated,[116] and in 1674 he complained that the governor of Quatre-Vallées was trying to get that province released from a tax that "all the kingdom had paid almost voluntarily."[117] In 1681 he launched a secret investigation to discover what would have to be done to establish élections in the Pyrenean provinces of the généralité of Guyenne. In 1682 he told the intendant at Pau to examine the taxes levied by the estates of Béarn and Navarre to see if there were any abuses, and he repeated his instructions in more detail the following year.[118] Even Colbert's death shortly thereafter brought no respite. In 1684 and intendant urged that a commissioner be appointed to examine the accounts and to attend the estates of Foix since the governor was too much involved in the matter to do a satisfactory job. Four years later another intendant argued that the estates of Quatre-Vallées, Nébouzan, and Foix, which lay in his jurisdiction, should not be allowed to survive for longer than the king found it good for his service. The bishop of Pamiers jumped to the defense of the estates of Foix over which he presided, and so the debate continued.[119]

---

113. Alain Destrée, *La Basse-Navarre et ses institutions de 1620 à la Révolution* (Saragossa, 1955), pp. 36–39.

114. *Correspondance administrative*, 1:619.

115. Ibid., pp. 612–14.

116. Ibid., p. 625.

117. *Lettres de Colbert*, 2:337.

118. *Correspondance administrative*, 1:627, 3:284; *Lettres de Colbert*, 4:148, 7:275, 279.

119. *Correspondance des contrôleurs généraux*, 1: nos. 112, 531, 540, 671, 690.

If local royal officials sent unflattering reports to Paris concerning the estates and occasionally abused them, the estates and their leaders sometimes deserved the treatment that they received. In 1673 during the war with neighboring Spain, the bishop of Pamiers refused even to present to the Estates of Foix a royal request that 1,000 livres be voted to repair the château in the local capital. Louis repeated his order the following year, but the bishop again refused to call for a vote. Before the threats of the governor, this stout Jansenist declared that "he feared only God and sin." A loud argument and considerable confusion followed. At length, the bishop departed with a handful of followers, but the bulk of the assembly remained to give the king satisfaction.[120]

No attempt was apparently made to get these estates to vote the don gratuit before their grievances were considered, and the description that the intendant prepared of the procedures of the estates of Béarn and Navarre in 1698 reflects none of the changes that had taken place in the larger pays d'états. The Pyrenean provinces were, however, subjected to the capitation and vingtième taxes that Louis XIV levied on his kingdom in the latter part of his reign.[121]

The county of Boulonnais in the northwest corner of France had a more exposed frontier than any other province. For this reason the inhabitants enjoyed a number of privileges, including exemption from the tailles, aids, gabelle and other taxes. The estates could, of course, give their sovereign a present, but they do not appear to have done so regularly nor did they assemble periodically. There were times when the financial needs of the king drove him to try to extract a small sum or when the greed of tax farmers in neighboring provinces led them to try to include the little county in their tax farm, but when this happened, the three estates swung into action and occasionally a mob called attention to their grievances. The Boulonnais's greatest difficulty came after France became involved in a full-scale war with Spain in 1635 because of the need to quarter troops in their province. In 1656 Louis XIV recognized their extensive privileges, but this did not stop him from seeking an annual grant of 81,740 livres shortly thereafter to support a regiment during the winter. The three estates dutifully voted the required amount for the duration of the war and appointed two nobles to apportion the sum among the subordinate jurisdictions.[122]

Peace in 1659 did not bring the promised respite for long, however,

---

120. Germain Arnaud, *Mémoire sur les Etats de Foix, 1608–1789* (Toulouse, 1904), pp. 78–81. For examples of the tyranny of earlier governors see ibid., pp. 74–78.

121. *Correspondance administrative*, 1:603–08.

122. P. Héliot, "La guerre dite Lustucru et les privilèges du Boulonnais,"*Revue du Nord*, 21 (1935): 264–80; D. Haigneré, "Répartition d'un impôt de 81,740 livres sur les communautés civiles du Boulonnais en 1657,"*Bul. de la soc. académique de l'arrondissement de Boulogne-sur-Mer*, 3 (1879–84): 81–84.

because, as Louis XIV explained to the dauphin, he decided "to take a closer look at the exemptions claimed by certain particular areas of my kingdom. . . .

"The Boulonnais was among these. The people there have been warlike since the war against the English and even have a kind of militia dispersed throughout the governorship, which is rather well trained and can be easily assembled when needed. Under this pretext, they had long regarded themselves as exempt from contributing in any way to the *taille*. I wanted to levy a very small sum there merely to make them realize that I had the power and the right to do it."[123] With this objective in mind Louis issued a decree in May 1661 ordering that an annual tax of 30,000 livres be imposed.[124]

The three estates, which had not been consulted in advance, met to deliver a sharp protest and to seek friends to get the decision reversed.[125] "The Boulonnais," the intendant reported to Colbert, "loudly proclaim that they would pay nothing." "They are preparing to defend themselves and to take up arms."[126] A minor revolt followed, which was easily suppressed. Appeals to the king continued, and several hundred rebels were sent to the galleys. Colbert dreamed of abolishing the privileges of the province and creating an élection, but calmer counsel prevailed. Boulonnais retained its privileges, and its estates continued to meet during the following century when the need arose.[127]

3. LOUIS XIV AND THE ESTATES IN THE PAYS D'ELECTIONS[128]

Louis's policy in the pays d'états had been to wrest control of the estates so that he could impose the taxes he chose and use their bureaucracies to assist in local government. The estates, therefore, continued to be useful to him and to some extent to the people. In the pays d'élections, on the other hand,

---

123. *Louis XIV Mémoires*, p. 111.

124. Héliot, "La guerre dite Lustucru," p. 282.

125. Ibid., pp. 284–85; L. Bénard, "Analyse sommaire des principaux documents contenus dans les registres du roy de la sénéchaussée du Boulonnais,"*Mém. de la soc. académique de l'arrondissement de Boulgne-sur Mer*, 20 (1900): 59–60.

126. Héliot, "La guerre dite Lustucru," p. 286.

127. Ibid., pp. 286–318. Bénard, "Analyse sommaire," pp. 61–65; G. Delamotte, "L'autonomie du Boulonnais," *Mém. de la soc. académique de l'arrondissement de Boulogne-ser-Mer*, 29 (1921): 1–259.

128. The post-Renaissance history of the estates in the pays d'élections is elusive because with several exceptions their archives were lost after they ceased to be summoned. Only by an exhaustive search of the archives of the towns that participated and those of the king's council, intendancies, clergy, sovereign courts, and financial officials could one become reasonably certain of discovering nearly all of their meetings and of determining the last time that they assembled. I have not attempted to perform this arduous and relatively fruitless task, and the account that follows is derived largely from printed sources.

president of the Parlement of Rouen was all too correct when he said that the estates had only a "shadow of their former liberty."[141] After reporting the events that took place during these estates, a royalist agent took the trouble to explain to the chancellor why such meetings should not be permitted.[142] His advice and perhaps that of others was taken. Over eleven years elapsed before the estates met again.

During this long interval, taxes to support the normal activities of the estates, including paying their officials and those to whom they usually gave gratifications, continued to be levied. When Longueville joined the Fronde, Mazarin did take enough notice of the estates to remove their syndic who was closely associated with that magnate and replace him with Pierre Corneille, the poet. His action was in flagrant violation of the privileges of the estates because the office of syndic was elective. Within a year, however, the matter was straightened out, for Longueville and Mazarin became reconciled, and the former syndic was then restored to his office.[143]

Longueville himself appears to have enjoyed holding the estates, and he was probably responsible for obtaining permission to convoke them in the fall of 1653.[144] But the meeting was canceled, and the one scheduled for the following year was postponed until February 1655. When it opened, Longueville claimed credit for obtaining permission to convoke the estates and ascribed the years that elapsed without a meeting to his need to be outside of the province. The archbishop of Rouen, who served as president of the estates, praised the king for reestablishing their privileges, but there was a report that Longueville had been authorized to permit the estates to remain in session for only three days and that the commission for levying the taille was to be read but not commented upon. Probably the crown did not place such a severe limitation on the activities of the estates, for Longueville and the royal commissioners readily permitted them to remain in session for ten days. Nevertheless they were careful to persuade the deputies to omit several matters from their cahier that might prove offensive to Mazarin, including a request that the intendants be withdrawn from Normandy.[145]

The deputies were less circumspect when it came to their pocketbooks, however. In their first article they asked that the estates be held annually in accordance with the Norman charter. In the second they pleaded that no tax be levied that was not in the royal commission presented to the estates

141. *Cahiers*, 3:313.

142. *Lettres de Séguier*, ed. Mousnier, 1:604–05.

143. *Cahiers*, 3:332–44; Prentout, *Les Etats provinciaux*, 2:387–89.

144. G. Lachasse, "Elections pour des Etats de Normandie restées jusqu'ici inconnus en 1653," *Bul. de la soc. des antiquaires de Normandie*, 58 (1969): 405–10

145. Paul Logié, *La Fronde en Normandie* (Amiens, 1952), 3:146–48; Prentout, *Les Etats provinciaux*, 1:360–68; P. Le Cacheux, "Documents concernant les Etats de Normandie de février 1655," *Mélanges de la société de l'histoire de Normandie*, sér. 5, 5 (1898): esp. 125, 132–40, 152.

Louis already levied taxes as he desired, and his own officials collected them. The estates, where they continued to exist, had syndics to defend their interests, but few, if any, administrative officials that could be of use to the crown. As a result, Louis had nothing to gain by prolonging their existence. On the other hand, he was too traditionally minded to alter any situation he inherited except for compelling reasons. His intendants were another matter. With few exceptions they disliked popular assemblies and sought to prevent them from meeting whenever they could find an excuse. Hence when they began to replace the governors as the principal representatives of the crown in the provinces, they slowly curtailed the activities of these estates until they finally ceased to exist, not because of any edict of the council but simply because they were no longer permitted to function. Thus by the start of the eighteenth century, the distinction between the pays d'états and pays d'élections that has been made so often in textbooks finally became a reality, or almost a reality because in parts of the government of Burgundy and in the mountains of Dauphiné, the estates and the élus continued to coexist.

Once the king's council had rendered its fiscal decision declaring that the taille was réelle in Dauphiné, there was less need for meetings of the individual orders or for the joint assemblies in which the commis of the clergy and nobility met with the deputies of the ten towns and the syndic of the villages, but they did not cease altogether. In January 1644 letters had to be issued calling for the villages to elect a new syndic, presumably because of the death of Claude Brosse, and in June and September there were assemblées du pays.[129]

There was considerable unrest in Dauphiné during the 1640s because of the quarrels among the royal officials, the discontent of the nobility, and the extreme misery of the people. By July 1648 Parlement was prepared to profit from the situation by directing the substitute of the procureur du pays and the syndic of the villages to ask the governor for permission to assemble the ten towns. If he refused, the judges were prepared to authorize the meeting themselves. The governor responded to the request by saying that it would be necessary to obtain the king's permission. Meanwhile there were informal gatherings of the *consuls* of the towns, and the various sovereign courts of Grenoble deliberated together. On August 6 Louis forbade his courts to meet together and the ten towns to assemble without his permission.[130]

The decision to convoke the Estates General in January 1649 led to further difficulties, for in the past the deputies of the province had been elected by the provincial estates. The crown was opposed to reviving the estates for this purpose and therefore directed that elections be held in

129. B. Mun., Grenoble, ms. 1450, fols. 306v–07; *IAC, Gap*, ed. Paul Guillaume (Gap, 1908), 1:200; Boris Porchnev, *Les soulèvements populaires en France de 1623 à 1648* (Paris, 1963), pp. 637–39.

130. Porchnev, *Les soulèvements populaires*, pp. 674–76; *Lettres de Séguier*, ed. Mousnier, 2:758–59, 847–48, 852–56, 859–66.

bailiwick assemblies. The nobles pressed for elections in the estates, and the Parlement of Grenoble continued to cause concern by courting popularity with the people by refusing to register tax edicts. Fortunately for the crown, the municipal council of Grenoble was doubtful whether it would be more advisable to ask for the estates or to preserve the élections, and the third estate as a whole gave little support to the demands of the nobles.[131] Chancellor Séguier was especially fearful that if the estates of Dauphiné were revived, there would be similar demands from Languedoc, Normandy, Guyenne, and Provence that theirs be restored with all their privileges, but the bitter division between the orders prevented this from happening.[132]

When letters convoking the estates were again issued in 1651, the nobles once more used the occasion to seek to have the estates restored. This time the crown resolved the problem by having the individual orders in each bailiwick elect deputies to an assembly of all of Dauphiné, where in turn deputies were elected to the Estates General. Thus provincial unity was retained, but the estates were not revived in their traditional form.[133]

The efforts to revive the estates did not cease with the defeat of the Fronde. On December 31, 1700, the intendant reported that he had seen the registers of the assemblies of the ten towns from 1661 to 1670. In 1661, the ten towns had been permitted to meet to elect a deputation to go to court because of the birth of a dauphin, but the bishop of Grenoble, the commis of the nobility, and others had used the occasion to try to revive the estates. A number of meetings took place thereafter, which the intendant referred to as "clandestine." He was obviously very much opposed to such meetings and wanted to have the surviving records of the estates and other assemblies turned over to the Chamber of Accounts. If his information is correct, Louis XIV was equally unfavorable, for he said that the count of Clermont, a commis and deputy of the nobility, had spent thirteen days in the Bastille for his trouble.[134]

Taxes were levied without the consent of these assemblies, but the commis participated in their apportionment and collection. In 1663 they informed Colbert that the schedule he had established for their collection could not be met.[135] They also protested against taxes and actually opposed the request of an intendant in 1658 for 300,000 livres to support troops during the winter. Needless to say, they petitioned the king and his officials on other matters as well. Perhaps because the commis of the clergy and the nobility were presumed to be cooperative since they received pensions, the crown discouraged assemblies of the ten towns without their presence. It also bound

the three orders closer together by ordering the installation of a procureur syndic général in 1664, a step that was opposed by the towns apparently because the post was henceforth to be venal rather than elective. Only further research can determine when the assemblies ceased altogether. With the bishop of Grenoble serving as president of the estates and with two hereditary commis of the nobility and a hereditary syndic, the basic core of the estates may have survived for many years after the towns ceased to elect deputies to assemblies.[136] Indeed the intendant obtained the register of the meetings between 1661 and 1670 from the secretary in 1700.[137] However it is probable that assemblies attended by the deputies of the towns had ceased before that time. The mountainous region of Dauphiné was more fortunate, for here the assemblies of the escartons continued until the Revolution.[138]

The estates of Normandy were clearly dying when Louis XIV came to the throne. For four and a half years they had not met, and there had been increasingly long intervals between sessions before that time. The new regime led by Cardinal Mazarin decided to try to placate the Normans, however, and in October 1643, it ordered the estates to meet the following month.[139] The central theme of the assembly was that the province was grossly overtaxed. Those present did not complain about the failure of the crown to convoke the estates during the preceding years nor did they go through the formality of consenting to taxes, although they referred nostalgically to their former right to do so. Rather they pleaded with the king to reduce the number of élus and to cancel the fees that they received, to revoke the salt tax and the levies to support troops, and to be content with half the ordinary taxes that he demanded. As had so often happened before, the commissioners ordered that the full amount be levied anyway, and an appeal to the king's council brought neither delay nor a reduction. In spite of their poverty, the estates did vote their governor, the duke of Longueville, 40,000 livres rather than the usual 18,000 because he had been instrumental in obtaining permission to hold the estates and had otherwise defended the interests of the province.[140] In spite of Longueville's efforts, however, a

131. AC, Grenoble, BB 108, fols. 231v–32, 234–34v.

132. *Lettres de Séguier*, ed. Mousnier, 2:916–17, 930–33, 1008–09.

133. B. Mun., Grenoble, ms. 2313, procès-verbal of the nobility of July 16–17, 1651; AD, Isère, IC, 5, nos. 27–28; AC, Grenoble, BB 108, fol. 340–40v.

134. *Correspondance des contrôleurs généraux*, 2: no. 228.

135. BN, ms. *Mélanges de Colbert*, 114, fol. 14.

136. AN, E 1725, no. 163; AC, Grenoble, BB 111, fols. 9v–10, 50–51, 275–75v, 301–01v, 363v–64; CC 789; *IAC, Grenoble*, ed. A. Prudhomme (Grenoble, 1886), 1: AA 40, BB 110, BB 112; *IAC, Gap*, 1:225, 2:69, 73. AD, Isère, lC 5, no. 30, lJ 524¹, *procès-verbal of August 1655*. In 1658 the substitute of the procureur of the estates sought to have the ten towns and bailiwicks convoked to oppose an increase in the taille. *Arrêts du Conseil du Roi, règne de Louis XIV* (Paris, 1976), no. 1646.

137. *Correspondance des contrôleurs généraux*, 2: no. 228.

138. *IAC, Guillestre*, ed. Paul Guillaume (Gap, 1906), pp. lxxxviii–xci; Alexandre Fauché-Prunelle, *Essai sur les anciennes institutions autonomes ou populaires des Alpes Cottiennes-Briançonnaises* (Grenoble, 1857), 2:328–39, 690–709; Dr. Chabrand, "Les escartons dans l'ancien Briançonnais,"*Bul. de la soc. d'études des Hautes-Alpes* 2 (1883): 247–49.

139. Arsène Legrelle, *La Normandie sous la monarchie absolue* (Rouen, 1903), pp. 101–05.

140. *Cahiers des Etats de Normandie sous les règnes de Louis XIII et de Louis XIV*, ed. Charles de Robillard de Beaurepaire (Rouen, 1878), 3:109, 127–28, 308, 311, 313; Henri Prentout, *Les Etats provinciaux de Normandie* (Caen, 1925), 1:357–60. *Arrêts de Louis XIV*, 1: nos. 130, 176.

except in urgent necessity, and in the fourth they requested the king to reduce the tax of 8.4 million livres by one fifth. The commissioners recommended that all these requests be granted, but when the king's council finally responded several years later, it would only promise that the estates would be summoned if it were à propos and that the syndic would be notified if it became necessary to levy additional taxes during the year, provided that there was time. Taxes, of course could not be reduced.[146]

In spite of their self-control, the estates of Normandy never met again. Even their restrained remonstrances were not looked upon with favor at court. As if sensing that at best many years would elapse before they met again, the deputies not only replaced their deceased treasurer but also elected a substitute syndic who was to assume the duties of that position should the current holder of the office die or resign before they met again.[147]

For about a decade the Normans were left with the hope that their estates would be convoked. During this period, the officers of the estates continued to represent the interest of the province, and taxes continued to be levied to support their activities. The old syndic was replaced by the man designated by the estates, and when several minor officials died, Longueville named provisional replacements who were to serve until the estates could meet. A deputation headed by the archbishop of Rouen pleaded for the Norman cause before Louis XIV in December 1657, and that same year assemblies of the Norman nobility sought to have the provincial estates convoked. Colbert finally resolved the matter. To his ordered mind, it made no sense to tax the people to support the activities of the estates when the estates themselves no longer met. In 1663 he directed that funds accumulated in the treasury to pay the deputations of the estates to court be turned over to the crown, and the king's council formally suppressed the offices of syndic, treasurer, and greffier of the estates but provided compensation for the holders of these positions. At the same time, taxes ceased to be collected to support the estates. The final relics of a once-proud institution were swept away. There was a faint complaint from the Chamber of Accounts when it registered one of these edicts, but the Normans had become so accustomed to being without the estates that they made no significant protest. That institution had become too ineffective to have many admirers stalwart enough to defend its existence before Louis XIV.[148]

The good towns of Basse-Auvergne had always been more active than the estates in the other pays d'élections, and the frequency of their meetings declined only slightly in the Mazarin period. During his ministry they assembled in every year except 1648 and 1650, and in some years there were several meetings. As in the past, the towns did not consent to royal taxes, but

---

146. *Cahiers*, 3: esp. 129–33, 353.

147. Ibid., pp. 383–86.

148. Ibid., pp.393–429. Logié *La Fronde*, 3:149; Prentout, *Les Etats provinciaux*, 1:369–74.

they protested those that they believed were too heavy and initiated levies for their own purposes. Furthermore representatives of the three estates participated in the apportionment of the taille among the subordinate jurisdictions.[149] The nobility actually enjoyed a modest revival in these years. In 1645 some nobles sought to elect a new syndic to replace the long inactive and recently deceased occupant of that office. The outcome of their efforts at this time is not known, but soon thereafter the nobility elected the baron de Sales syndic and engaged in considerable activity to prevent the king from giving the duchy and county of Auvergne to the duke of Buillon in return for the principality of Sedan. In 1651 a record-breaking 209 nobles participated in the elections to the Estates General.[150]

Nevertheless the position of the third estate was far from secure. The royal officials who controlled the municipal government of Riom continued to seize every opportunity to undercut the dominant position of the échevins of Clermont. The dispute between the two rivals flared up in 1641 and 1647 and undoubtedly served to weaken the province in its effort to defend itself against the crown. Finally, in 1657 the combination of an unsympathetic intendant and the constant attacks from Riom led the king's council to forbid the échevins of Clermont to convoke the towns without permission and to halt the annual levy of 6,000 livres to support the activities of the estates. This blow was severe, for the survival of a representative assembly in a pays d'élections had become largely dependent on having a local duly constituted body with the right to convoke the deputies and the authority and money to serve as syndics when the estates were not in session.[151] The crown did not plan the immediate destruction of the estates of Basse-Auvergne, however, for when Mazarin was made governor in 1658, he had himself given specific authority to summon the three estates.[152]

Nevertheless the good towns felt seriously threatened. In August 1657 they voted their governor, the duke of Candale, 50,000 livres in the hope that he would protect their privileges, but he died the following January. Thwarted in their design, they hastened to revoke the gift, for Candale's heirs could do them little good. In 1660 they dispatched deputies to court with the authority to offer whatever gratifications they thought proper to powerful persons who would befriend them, but it was to no avail. A final blow came when Mazarin, who had at least permitted them to meet annually while he was their governor, died on March 9, 1661. Two weeks later the good towns

149. AD, Puy-de-Dôme, 4F 146; *IAD, Puy-de-Dôme, sér. C*, ed. Gilbert Rouchon (Clermont-Ferand, 1902), 3:8–9.

150. *Lettres de Séguier*, ed. Mousnier, 2:725–26; BN ms. Clairambault 1157, fols. 191–95, 241–96; J. R. Major, *The Deputies to the Estates General of Renaissance France* (Madison, 1960), p. 82.

151. *IAC, Riom*, ed. F. Boyer (Riom, 1892), AA 18, AA 19; AD, Puy-de-Dôme, 4F 146.

152. Roland Mousnier, *La plume, la faucille et le marteau* (Paris, 1970), p. 211.

held their last periodic meeting. Three centuries of almost continual activity came to an end.[153]

There was no royal decree to announce the demise of the estates. It was just that the échevins of Clermont could no longer convoke the good towns without permission, and that permission was rarely forthcoming. After a long period of inaction, the good towns assembled three times in 1672 over the question of franc-fiefs. There followed another long silence and then what were probably their last assemblies were held in 1679 and 1680.[154] In 1697 an intendant prepared a description of the region just as Mesgrigny had done sixty years before, but on this occasion there was no need to attack the assembly of the good towns, for they no longer existed.[155] Doubtless the unfriendly attitude of the intendants and the general climate at court contributed heavily to the disappearance of this institution, but the two-century drive by the royal officials in Riom to strip the échevins of Clermont of the right to summon the deputies of the good towns was also an important factor. These bureaucrats could not bear to see elected officials of a duly constituted body not directly dependent upon the crown perform what they regarded as a regalian function, a function which they believed that in the absence of the king they alone had the right to exercise. And yet old traditions were slow to die. In 1749 the échevins of Clermont were still styling themselves as the syndics of the third estate of Auvergne and claiming to defend the interests of the province.[156]

The four towns and provostships of Haute-Auvergne had traditionally been less active than the third estate of Basse-Auvergne, but nevertheless they participated in one or more assemblies in at least eight of the eighteen years of the Mazarin regime.[157] As in the case of Basse-Auvergne, they met once shortly after Louis XIV began his personal reign, and then a long silence followed until 1672 when the question of franc-fiefs had to be dealt with. Another silence followed until 1693 when what was apparently the last meeting of the estates was held. As with Basse-Auvergne, the intendant saw no need to mention the assemblies of the good towns when he prepared his description in 1697. Their demise, like that of their counterpart to the north, should be attributed to the hostility of the intendants, the climate at court,

153. AD, Puy-de-Dôme, 4F 146.

154. Ibid.; G. Rouchon, "Le tiers-Etat aux Etats provinciaux de Basse-Auvergne aux XVIᵉ et XVIIᵉ siècles," *Bul. philologique et historique (jusqu'à 1715) du comité des travaux historiques et scientifiques* (1930–31): 188–89.

155. *Mémoire sur l'état de la généralité de Riom en 1697 dressé pour l'instruction du duc de Bourgogne par l'intendant Lefèvre d'Ormesson*, ed. Abel Poitrineau (Clermont-Ferrand, 1970).

156. *IAD, Puy-de-Dôme, sér. C,* 1:262.

157. AC, St. Flour, ch. 5, art. 6, no. 141, fols. 171, 195–95v, 276–77v, 287v–88; *IAC, Aurillac,* ed. Gabriel Esquer (Aurillac, 1906), 1: BB 15; AD, Cantal, C 433; *IAD, Puy-de-Dôme, sér. C,* 2:442, 448; R. de Ribier, "L'assemblée des Etats particuliers de la Haute-Auvergne en 1649," *Revue de la Haute-Auvergne,* 6 (1904): 125–72.

and in their case Aurillac's jealousy of the superior position traditionally assigned the échevins of St. Flour in the governance of the third estate.[158]

The assemblies of the government of Lyonnais probably ceased to take place during the reign of Louis XIII, but their absence scarcely affected the institutional structure of the region because they had never played an important role. The more firmly entrenched provincial estates enjoyed a longer life. In spite of a paucity of records, it seems clear that the thirteen good towns of Forez remained active until after the Fronde. The nobility of Forez took advantage of the meeting to elect deputies to the Estates General in 1649 to choose a syndic and four councillors to perpetuate their corporative organization.[159]

The nobility of Beaujolais referred to their syndic in the cahier they prepared to take to the Estates General in 1649, an act which indicates that they were still organized. In a book published in 1671, Pierre Louvet claimed that the échevins of Villefranche still had the right to assemble the officers of the towns and chatellenies of Beaujolais, and the ever elusive syndic of the plat pays of Lyonnais was functioning in 1635 and probably did so for some years thereafter.[160] We know little of the fate of these obscure institutions, but in 1707 a curé reported that his father had been a deputy in the estates of Forez. Camille de Neufville de Villeroy, archbishop of Lyons and the king's lieutenant in Lyonnais, he added, had halted these meetings. Because Villeroy did not become archbishop until 1653, it is highly probable that the representative assemblies and corporate organizations in the government of Lyonnais ceased to exist at some point during the reign of Louis XIV.[161]

As far as can be ascertained, the history of the various estates in the généralité of Guyenne followed a somewhat similar pattern. The towns of Agenais had been very active during the last two years of Louis XIII's reign, but after a meeting in October 1644 they apparently did not assemble until 1649–51 when they met twice to elect deputies to the Estates General and once for other matters. Meetings in 1654 and 1658 followed, but then there was a long silence until the crown launched an offensive against allodial property in Guyenne in the 1670s.[162] What was probably the last meeting of the principal towns of Agenais was held on this subject in August 1679.[163]

158. *IAD, Puy-de-Dôme, sér C*, 2 : 167, 449. *IAC, Aurillac*, BB 17, BB 18; Major, *Deputies*, p. 84.

159. AD, Loire, C 32, nos. 18–23, 28; Jean-B. Galley, *Les Etats de Forez et les treize villes* (Saint-Etienne, 1914), p. 50.

160. J.-P. Gutton, "Le cahier de doléances de la noblesse du Beaujolais aux Etats Généraux de 1649,"*Revue historique*, 253 (1975): 116; Pierre Louvet, *Histoire de Villefranche, capitale du Beaujolais* (Lyon, 1671), pp. 66.

161. Galley, *Les Etats de Forez*, pp. 82–83.

162. AC, Agen, BB 55, BB 59, fols. 6–11v, 111–12v, 121v, 250–53, CC 209, CC 227, CC 232, CC 248.

163. Ibid., BB 63, CC 248.

The following month the intendant forbad the consuls of Agen to hold any further assemblies or in their capacity as syndics of Agenais to defend any individual against the crown's attacks on allodial property. The ban against assemblies was repeated the following year, but informal consultations among the towns continued until near the close of the century.[164]

The estates of Armagnac and its seven collectes proved to be the most active and longest lived assemblies in Guyenne. If one may generalize from the valuable records of the collecte of Vic-Fezensac, the nobility and towns of the seven collectes and the seneschalsy occasionally went several years without meeting during the Mazarin period, but when the need arose, they assembled two or three times within a twelve-month period. There was a long hiatus from the early part of Louis XIV's personal reign until 1670 when five meetings took place in twelve months. Thereafter the records are spotty, but there was apparently an assembly as late as 1698.[165] Indeed the town of Lectoure was still claiming to be a pays d'états after the night of August 4, 1789.[166]

Scantier records for the three estates of Comminges,[167] Quercy,[168] and Rouergue[169] suggest that they followed the more familiar pattern of reasonable activity under Mazarin and a marked decline in the 1660s. Then there were meetings in Comminges and Quercy in 1673 and very likely in Rouergue in 1674 to deal with the problem of the allodial property before these once-thriving institutions passed into oblivion. It is not improbable

164. F. Loirette, "Une épisode des résistances locales aux empiètements du pouvoir royal: la défense du france-alleu agenais au XVIIᵉ siècle," *Annales du Midi*, 71 (1959): 258–64.

165. AD, Gers, E suppl. 23,936; AC, Isle-Jourdain, BB 4, fols. 293v–96; J. Duffour, "Députés de l'Armagnac aux Etats généraux d'Orléans en 1649," *Revue de Gascogne*, sér. 2, 19 (1924): 31–33; AC, Auch, BB 7, fols. 108–11; AC, Layrac, BB 2, fol. 647v; AC, Fals., BB 1, fols. 85, 136–37; Z. Baqué, "Vic-Fezensac au temps de la Fronde," *Bul. de la soc. d'histoire et d'archéologie du Gers*, 36 (1935): 49–53. The reference to the 1698 meeting is in *IAC, Vic-Fezensac*, CC 1bis. This document could not be found when I was in Auch.

166. M. Bordes, "La ville de Lectoure, pays d'états et l'assemblée provinciales d'Auch," *Bul. de la soc. archéologique, historique littéraire et scientifique du Gers* 72 (1971): 542–54.

167. AD, Haute-Garonne, C 3705, C 3706; AN, E 1696, no. 115, E 1700, no. 278, E 1728, no. 255; M. J. de Naurois-Destenay, *Les Etats de Comminges aux XVIᵉ et XVIIᵉ siècles* (thesis, Ecole Nationale des Chartes, 1953–54), pp. 191–97; *HL*, 13:320 n.2; *Arrêts de Louis XIV*, 1: nos. 1450, 1464, 1617.

168. M.-J. Baudel, *Notes pour servir à l'histoire des Etats provinciaux du Quercy* (Cahors, 1881), pp. 9–10, 42–49; AN, E 1696, nos. 19, 161, 176, 241, E 1703, no. 261; *Arrêts de Louis XIV*, 1: nos. 996, 1498, 1512. In December 1651 the council recognized the right of the estates of Quercy to levy 13,480 livres for their own affairs but directed that it be assigned to the University of Cahors and the Jesuit college. Ibid., 1: no. 1583.

169. H. Affre, *Dictionnaire des institutions, moeurs et coutumes du Rouergue* (Rodez, 1903), p. 164; L.-C.-P. Bosc, *Mémoires pour servir à l'histoire du Rouergue* (Rodez, 1797), 3:265–68; AN, E 1696, no. 162, E 1700, no. 280. *Actes de Louis XIV*, 1: nos. 1499, 1619. On May 31, 1674, a letter was sent to the *consuls* of Agen from Montauban asking where the assembly of the nobility of Rouergue would be held. AC, Agen, AA 35.

that the last meetings of the estates of Lannes,[170] Condomois and Bazadais,[171] and Rivière-Verdun[172] were held at about this time on the same subject.

As in other parts of France, the principal cause of the demise of the estates was the enmity of the intendants and other royal officials. It became increasingly difficult for syndics and consuls to obtain permission to meet. When it was granted, it was often stipulated that only the specific subject which led to the request could be discussed, and the size of deputations was limited. In the winter of 1658–59 the king's council twice forbade any assemblies to be held in Guyenne without the permission of the governor or lieutenant general, and while these decrees were not directed only at the estates, they do reflect the general climate of opinion at Paris.[173] In 1661 a cousin of Colbert who served as intendant of Montauban expressed his disapproval of permission being granted for the diocese of Comminges to meet on the grounds that it would be prejudicial to the affairs of the king. He recommended that none of the estates in the region be permitted to assemble because all they did was complain about the misery of the people and provide some profit for those who attended.[174]

Local jealousies often made it difficult for the estates to resist the unfriendly bureaucracy. The bishops of Cahors and the estates of Quercy had a long-standing quarrel over the extent of the former's prerogatives. The one point they could agree on was that they did not want local royal officials convoking the three estates. When one of them usurped this privilege in 1649 and 1650, the bishop refused to attend. Finally in 1657 the king's council confirmed the bishop's right to summon the estates, but by that time the institution had already suffered heavily.[175]

The bishop of Comminges informed Colbert in August 1673 that the estates of Comminges had been suppressed over twenty-five years before because of a dispute over precedence between the bishops of Conserans and Lombez and the intendants' dislike of assemblies that imposed taxes without

170. The last reference I have found to a meeting of the third estate was for 1665. See AN, E 1728, no. 236. For other meetings under Louis XIV, see AN, E 1696, no. 160; AC, Bayonne, BB 24, pp. 1–5, 220, 223–24, 234; AC, Dax, BB 2, fols. 156–61; and *Arrêts de Louis XIV*, 1: no. 1497.

171. The last meeting of the estates of Condomois that I have found was held in 1656, but Condomois's desire to join with Agenais in an effort to preserve the right of franc-fiefs leads me to believe that there was probably a meeting of its estates around 1673. *IAC, Agen*, ed. G. Tholin (Paris, 1884), AA 35. For assemblies between 1649 and 1656, see AC, Couthures, BB 1, fols. 13–14; AC, Francescas, BB 15, fols. 59–59v, 137v–39v; AC, Mézin, BB 7, fols. 7v–11, 82–84, 160–62; *IAC, Condom*, ed. G. Niel (n.p. n.d.), BB 62.

172. The last known meeting of the estates of Rivière-Verdun was in 1654, but one was convoked in 1659. Jean Contrasty, *Histoire de Sainte-Foy-de-Peyrolières* (Toulouse, 1917), pp. 200–202.

173. AC, Agen, CC 204, CC 209, CC 232; Naurois-Destenay, *Les Etats de Comminges*, pp. 191–94; AN, E 1708, no. 198, E 1711, no. 213.

174. *Correspondance administrative* 1:619.

175. Baudel, *Notes*, pp. 42–49.

the king's permission. Nevertheless the three estates had met earlier that month to consider problems related to allodial property, only to be disbanded because the deputies of the third estate lacked sufficient powers. If they met again as planned, the bishop wanted to attend although traditionally he had not been permitted to do so and was obviously ill disposed toward such institutions.[176]

When the estates in Guyenne were given opportunities to voice their complaints, as when they prepared cahiers to take to the Estates Generals that were convoked during the Fronde, they did not hesitate to do so. Those who attended the meeting of the third estate of Agenais lashed out at the intendants in 1649 and asked the king to send no more of them to the provinces because they were useless officials who imposed heavy taxes on their own private authority. Equally unpopular were the officers in the élection whose suppression they sought. The percentage of the taille assigned to them for their services, they charged, amounted to more than the entire taille in 1610. As if that year represented a golden age, they asked that the taille be reduced to the amount that it was then, no minor petition for the taille stood at 32,224 livres in 1649 but had been only 12,538 livres thirty-nine years before. Mindful of difficulty they had assembling, they asked the king to permit an annual meeting of at least the twelve principal towns in Agenais.[177]

The nobility of Périgord assembled in 1651 to elect their deputation, and early in the cahier that they prepared, they asked the king to restore the estates to the position they had enjoyed in the time of Louis XII before the élections had been created. They also pleaded with the king to reduce the number of judicial officials to the level that had existed during the reign of that popular king and to abolish venality of office.[178] But it was to no avail. Probably none of the cahiers prepared during the Fronde ever reached the king and council for consideration, and few have survived to testify to the devotion that the leaders of Guyenne still held for their estates and other privileges.

At the dawn of the seventeenth century, there had been estates in about 52.4 percent of France that had given consent to taxation and in about 8.2 percent more that had met regularly, employed a bureaucracy, voted taxes for their own purposes, and prepared remonstrances to the king. In about 12.6 percent of France the estates had occasionally met to deal with taxes. Even in the remaining 26.8 percent, the estates had sometimes assembled to redact customs, ratify treaties, and elect deputies to the Estates General. (See chap. 7, sec. 1.) By the time the century drew to a close, however, assemblies had totally ceased in about 68 percent of the lands that had then been a part

176. *Correspondance administrative*, 1:622–24.

177. G. Tholin, "Les cahiers du pays d'Agenais aux Etats-Généraux," *Revue de l'Agenais* 10 (1883): 508–09, 529–20.

178. AN, K 692b, no. 12, art. 12.

of France. Of the remaining 32 percent, nearly 2 percent consisted of Bresse, Bugey, Gex and the Alpine valleys of Dauphiné where only the third estate met regularly, and there was no pretense that those who assembled consented to royal taxes. Thus in only 30 percent of France did the estates continue to vote taxes, albeit under the tutelage of the crown. To the lands that were part of France around 1601 should be added several small, recently acquired provinces to the north where there were estates and a few much larger ones to the northeast and east where there were none.

In spite of this startling change, Louis XIV and Colbert for the most part had continued the policies of Richelieu in regard to the estates, although the latter had at times been tempted to follow the course of Marillac. None of the estates had been officially exterminated, but the intendants and other royal officials had been permitted to stifle the weaker ones. Their goal had been to control the estates, but to do so they employed the techniques of persuasion and threats, of bribes and punishment far more effectively than Richelieu or any of his Renaissance predecessors. Instead of planting a few clients in the estates as was being done as early as the fifteenth century, Louis and Colbert placed all or virtually all the bishops and nobles who attended the estates of Languedoc on their pension list and distributed substantial sums to the deputies of the third estate. Where the number of those who could attend the estates was so large that it would be too expensive to distribute gifts to all, as in the case of the Breton nobility, they won great nobles like Rohan to their cause and relied on them to pack the estates with their creatures. With such measures, accompanied by numerous parliamentary devices and occasional threats, they managed to obtain from all the large provincial estates the amount they desired without debate and with few conditions being attached from the early 1670s. Since the origin of this policy dates back at least to the estates of Brittany in 1661, the delay in implementing it fully must be attributed to the time it took to create a strong court party in the estates and to quell the opposition. Louis's and Colbert's final effort to achieve their goal around 1672 was obviously timed to secure funds for the Dutch war.

In the process of winning control over the estates, they also captured and made use of their bureaucracies. As a result, royal absolutism was extended to the pays d'états, but because it was not done by stamping out the duly constituted bodies and replacing them with institutions dependent on the crown, provincial administration ceased to be absolutist when a strong directing hand was removed from Paris. Under Louis XV the surviving provincial estates regained their former brilliance and resumed responsibility for a large part of the provincial administration.

Louis and Colbert also followed Richelieu's policy in regard to the estates in the pays d'élection. Here they inherited nearly defunct institutions that they left to wither away. The most important causes for their decline were the dislike of intendants and other local royal officials for such assemblies and the jealousy among the members of the various estates and towns that made cooperation in the defense of their privileges difficult.

4. The Formation of the Absolute Monarchy

The provincial estates, were not the only stumbling blocks that lay along the path to absolute monarchy. The other duly constituted bodies also had to be dealt with, the great nobility had to be tamed, and an adequate and obedient army and bureaucracy had to be formed. In a general way, Louis employed the same principles in tackling these problems as he had with the estates. This was especially true of his dealings with the assemblies of the clergy. He did his utmost to ensure the election of friendly clergymen to the meetings and of cooperative general agents who watched after ecclesiastical interests when the assembly was not in session. There is no evidence that Louis ever contemplated abolishing the institution nor did he challenge the basic privileges of the clergy, at least as he interpreted them. On the other hand, he wanted the assemblies to be short and to vote him all he requested without debate. If they procrastinated or haggled, he was not above using threats. As with the estates, Louis was able to impose his will only gradually. When he asked the assembly of 1660–61 for a don gratuit of 4 million livres, he was initially offered only a million. Considerable bargaining followed in which Louis reduced his demands first to 3 million and then to 2 million plus 400,000 for his wife, but in the end he accepted a total grant of only 2 million. Nevertheless he had won a victory of sorts; previous don gratuits had been voted to fight the Huguenots or the Habsburgs, but this grant was given in peacetime and established a precedent for the clergy's making regular contributions to the crown whether France was in a state of peace or of war.[179]

In 1665 Louis again asked for 4 million livres. The clergy appointed a committee to determine how the king could best be aided, but months then passed without any action being taken on the don gratuit. At length Colbert was able to jolt the deputies into action, and they quickly offered 2.4 million livres. The archbishop of Toulouse, anticipating the words Louis would like to hear, informed that monarch that "we have no example in our registers until this moment of the gift to the king being made in a single de-liberation."[180] Pleased that when the clergy finally acted, they did so with little debate, Louis accepted the offer, although it was far from the amount that he originally requested.

Threats, rewards, or the hope of rewards, coupled with interference in the elections, gradually brought the clergy more fully into line. Only through

179. Pierre Blet, *Le clergé de France et la monarchie* (Rome, 1959), 2:256–62, 276–80.
180. Ibid., p. 286.

loyal service could they hope to achieve a more lucrative benefice, an archdiocese, or a pension. The general agents of the clergy upon whom so much depended when the assembly was not in session were special objects of Louis's generosity. They usually received gratifications while they held office and often a bishopric when their five-year terms expired. In 1670 the assembly voted Louis 2.4 million livres without attaching any conditions. Content with the ease with which this had been accomplished, Louis graciously responded that he would accept only 2.2 million. In 1675 the clergy unanimously voted him 4.5 million livres, but this time Louis was at war and could not afford to reduce their gift. In neither year did he ask for a specific amount, although probably his ministers informally told the leaders of the clergy how much was needed. In this manner the Grand Monarch avoided having to haggle with his subjects.[181]

The clergy had succumbed like the provincial estates. During Louis's long reign, they contributed 223,909,468 livres to his enterprises, a substantial sum, yet not excessive considering the wealth of the church.[182] The size of the contribution troubled Louis but little, for as he told the dauphin, "kings are absolute lords and naturally have free and full disposition of all the goods possessed by clergymen as well as by laymen, in order to use them at any time as wise administrators, that is, according to the general need of the state."[183] The clergy were also expected to be his obedient servants. They followed him, albeit gingerly, into a serious quarrel with the pope and less reluctantly into the persecution of the Protestants, although hitherto the majority of them had preferred conversion by persuasion rather than by force.

The members of the sovereign courts and other royal officials had become more serious obstacles to the absolute monarchy than the estates and the clergy, but they were subdued in a somewhat similar fashion. At first Mazarin had attempted to make them more cooperative by suggesting that he would not renew the paulette, but when he made good his threat for a brief period in 1648, he contributed heavily to causing the Fronde. With this unhappy experience in mind, he readily restored the paulette when it was about to expire in 1657, but the courts continued to cause difficulties whenever their interests or those they conceived to be of the people so dictated.[184]

Louis XIV was not the sort of man to permit this situation to continue, but the question was what measures he should take to regain the authority that the sovereign courts and some of his other officials had in his opinion

181. Pierre Blet, *Les assemblées du clergé et Louis XIV de 1670 à 1693* (Rome, 1972), esp. pp. 17–19, 77–85; Ernest Lavisse, *Histoire de France*, ed. E. Lavisse (Paris, 1911), 7: pt. 1, 387–97.

182. Blet, *Le clergé de France*, 2:391.

183. *Louis XIV, Mémoires*, p. 165.

184. My treatment of Louis's relations with the magistrates is derived largely from Albert N. Hamscher, *The Parlement of Paris after the Fronde, 1653–1673* (Pittsburgh, 1976).

usurped. The most obvious method was to abolish the paulette and venality of office and convert the bureaucracy into subservient officials who owed their positions to him and served at his pleasure. As early as 1659, Colbert had advocated such a course, and when the paulette came up for renewal in 1665, he twice prepared memorandums urging Louis to act, but then in a third memorandum he reversed his position. Colbert may have changed his mind because Philip IV of Spain had died the month before and Louis was preparing for a war to claim what he professed to believe was his wife's inheritance. Under such circumstances, it was not the time to anger the magistrates. He remembered that a combination of an embittered bureaucracy and a costly war had contributed so much to causing the Fronde. Colbert also may have feared that if he stirred up a hornet's nest by challenging the magistrates, Louis would begin to rely more on his great rival, Michel Le Tellier.

Whatever Colbert's reasons for changing his mind, the results of his shift of position were momentous. The paulette was renewed for three years in 1665 and periodically thereafter throughout Louis's reign, with apparently no further thought being given to its abolition. The bureaucracy had already become and was to remain a hereditary caste whose members could no more be removed from their offices without compensation than nobles could be deprived of their fiefs. Bound together in their closely knit sovereign courts and lesser corporations, they were to remain outside the direct control of the king. Reduction in the number of magistrates was difficult because of the need to compensate officials who were deprived of their positions and the temptation to create useless offices to sell. Thus successful merchants continued to be tempted to abandon their useful occupations and purchase positions that involved fewer risks and greater prestige. Bellièvre had foreseen these evils, and Marillac had struggled in vain to have their cause removed, but now the more practical Colbert, who shared Marillac's views, abandoned the fight and preserved his position.

A hereditary, feudalized bureaucracy was to be preserved just like the provincial estates and assemblies of the clergy, but as with these other institutions, Louis and Colbert sought means to impose their will. One step was to avoid arousing the officers' anger unnecessarily. The decision to retain the paulette was the most important concession in this regard, but Louis and Colbert made a number of others, such as not enforcing the minimum age requirements to serve in Parlement and the stipulation against near relatives being in the same court. They checked their council's tendency to interfere excessively with cases before the sovereign courts, and for many years they limited the activities of the intendants that were undertaken at the expense of the officials in the provinces.

A second step was to show a reasonable interest in the economic well-being of officers and to provide generous rewards for those who served them well. The minority who were troublesome or who failed in their duty were likely to feel Louis's heavy hands, as the Parlements of Bordeaux and Rennes discovered when they were exiled to more rural surroundings. On such occasions, however, the magistrates were far less dangerous than formerly, because the great reforms that Louis instituted during the first decade of his personal rule quelled popular discontent to the point that they could not find allies among the people as easily as in the time of the Fronde. With Colbert's assistance, Louis was able to punish dishonest financial officials, bring the budget into balance, and reduce the taille, as well as implement a number of other needed changes. In the long run, many of these reforms had to be abandoned because of the wars, but they were in effect for enough time for Louis to assert control of his now isolated bureaucracy whose members could not help but approve of much that he was doing.

The gravest threat to absolute rule had come from the sovereign courts, a situation which Louis refused to tolerate. He never questioned what he regarded as their legitimate functions, but he was determined to prevent them from interfering in political affairs. He did this by virtually terminating their right to make remonstrances and checking their aspirations in other ways. He even dubbed them "superior" rather than "sovereign" courts and insisted on the right of his council to take jurisdiction over the cases before them, although he limited this practice so as not to anger the magistrates too much. So submissive did the Parlement of Paris become that in 1672, the very time the provincial estates were brought to heel, its magistrates registered six financial edicts without opposition.

Louis XIV and Colbert initially assigned the intendants a smaller role in their plans for the reorganization of the kingdom than one might think. Louis did not believe they were of sufficient importance for him to explain their duties when he prepared his memoirs for the instruction of the dauphin, despite the fact that he found time to enlighten his reader on why he rejected in horror his brother's proposal that his wife should be permitted to sit in a chair with a back in the presence of the queen. Louis and Colbert first thought of intendants as investigators who were assigned to large territories, generally several généralités, for a limited period of time to gather information for the council. Administration they left in the hands of the venal officials, one reason that there was so little friction between them and the crown. In short, Louis and Colbert planned to govern France much as Henry IV and Sully (or for that matter some of their Valois predecessors) had done. Only with the Dutch war in 1672 when the traditional bureaucracy failed to meet their expanded requirements did Louis and Colbert begin to use the intendants as administrators, a development that the latter at least regretted but had to permit because of the greater efficiency that it brought.[185]

185. *Louis XIV, Mémoires*, pp. 143–44; Mousnier, *La plume*, pp. 222–24.

Louis and Colbert no more intended to destroy the organs of municipal government than they did the other institutions which depended upon the people; rather they sought to control them by what had become such established practices as reducing the number of échevins and the size of the electorate, naming official candidates or otherwise tampering with the electoral process, and introducing garrisons into exposed localities. But then first Colbert's reforming zeal and later Louis's need for money for wars led to a greater decline of municipal independence than they had sought. Colbert was deeply concerned about the heavy indebtedness of the towns, an indebtedness that the intendants reported was caused by the dishonesty, fiscal irresponsibility, and selfishness of municipal officials. The *consuls* and échevins, they insisted, were exploiting the people. At first Colbert was content to try to make the towns financially solvent by having the intendants verify their debts. Only debts that had been incurred for legitimate reasons were to be repaid, and interest rates were set at a uniform low rate of $4\frac{1}{6}$ percent. Urban officials often resisted these measures. They disliked having their accounts inspected and were themselves sometimes municipal creditors who stood to lose from the lower interest rates and perhaps the disallowance of the debt. The result was long delays that so infuriated Colbert that in 1683 he got a decree issued giving the intendants and their assistants control over municipal finances. What had begun as an effort to improve the positions of the towns by getting them out of debt had ended by putting them under the tutelage of the crown. Still another blow was leveled at the towns in 1692 when Louis decreed that henceforth mayors and some other municipal officials would be hereditary venal officials. His motive was to raise money for the war, and towns were permitted to purchase the privilege of continuing to elect their officials subject to the usual royal interference, but some of them lacked the funds to do so. France's once proud towns that had retained so much of their independence until the close of the sixteenth century had finally been sacrificed upon the altar of war.[186]

Louis was as prepared to accept the status and privileges of the nobility as he was of any other social class or corporative group. During the desperate years of his later wars, he did attempt to tax them, but in other respects he left their enviable status intact. On the other hand, he had no intention of sharing power with them or permitting them to threaten the state as they had so recently done during the Fronde. Those of the highest birth were to serve as ornaments of his court and as commanders of his armies, but they were almost completely excluded from his inner council. To win their loyalty he employed the same technique of rewarding the faithful and punishing the

186. Charles Petit-Dutaillis, *Les communes françaises* (Paris, 1947), pp. 288–309, 315–20; N. Temple, "The Control and Exploitation of French Towns during the Ancien Régime," *History* 51 (1966): 16–21, 25–28.

disobedient as he had used in his dealings with others. When he announced in 1661 that he would appoint no chief minister, he meant among other things that henceforth he would dispense with the crown's patronage. The high nobility became his creatures and not those of a cardinal or a magnate. To the ties of sovereign and feudal overlord, he added that of patron to draw the leading nobles to his side. They and his ministers often advised him on how to fill lesser positions. If their loyalty was unquestioned, he permitted them to exercise considerable influence on appointments in their governments as is witnessed by the now docile Condés in Burgundy, but more than ever before, the clients of his clients looked to him as their overpatron just as they regarded him as their ultimate feudal overlord. When there were no more army or court positions, ecclesiastical benefices, or pensions to bestow, Louis could always win their gratitude by awarding a higher title of nobility or some other empty honor. "I finished this year [1661]," Louis informed the dauphin, "and began the following one with the promotion of eight prelates and sixty-three knights of the Order of Holy Spirit, no posts having been filled since the year 1633; that is what made for the great number, but I would have wished to be able to raise still more people to this honor, finding no purer joy for a prince than to obligate deeply persons of quality with whom he is pleased without burdening the least of his subjects. No reward costs our people less and none strikes noble hearts more than these distinctions of rank, which are virtually the first motive of all human actions, but especially of the most noble and of the greatest." [187]

Louis's numerous wars led him to increase the size of this army to 350,000 men during the course of his reign. Had this mammoth force been no more loyal than that of the Fronde, it would not have necessarily strengthened his position at home, but with the assistance of Le Tellier and Louvois, he managed to transform the half-feudal army of his predecessors into a well-organized, disciplined force commanded by loyal officers who owed their positions directly or indirectly to him. Its very size ensured employment for nobles who sought military adventure and removed the temptation of any magnate to raise the banner of revolt.[188] After the first decade of Louis's personal reign, only the poor were so foolish or so miserable that they directly challenged his authority. Some nobles in Auvergne might violate his laws, but they could be disciplined by magistrates from his Parlement. Still others might seek the aid of foreign powers to retore or emancipate the estates of Guyenne, Dauphiné, Provence, and Languedoc, to convoke the Estates General of the kingdom, and to reinstitute the Protestant state within a state with its various assemblies and places of security, but they posed no serious threat. Naval officers might sabotage his efforts to reform and intellectuals might surreptitiously voice ideas critical of his regime, but open, legal

187. *Louis XIV, Mémoires*, pp. 79–80.

188. On the army reforms, see Louis André, *Michel Le Tellier et l'organisation de l'armée monarchique* (Montpellier, 1906), and his *Michel Le Tellier et Louvois* (Paris, 1942).

corporative resistance virtually ceased. The rebellions that once had threatened the monarchy were no more.[189]

Louis combined censorship with propaganda in an effort to direct public opinion.[190] His policy of grandeur also enhanced his power because it placed him so far above his fellow Frenchmen. He brought music, literature, drama, and the arts into his service. They helped to attract the high nobility to court and added to his prestige.[191] Under these circumstances the ties between the magnates and the lesser nobility were weakened, and the polarity between court and country grew. The influence that the magnates had enjoyed through the patron-client relationship was dealt a severe blow when Louis assumed direct control over the crown's patronage, and the system slowly withered away. Deserted, the lesser nobility sought other means to claim consideration. During the Renaissance, the great age of the provincial estates, they had displayed little interest in such institutions because they had relied upon their patrons to see to their needs, but now that their protectors groveled before the Sun King at Versailles, they turned belatedly to the estates. In Brittany from ten to thirty-one nobles had participated at the time of Charles IX, but as many as five hundred placed their names on the rolls under Louis XIV, and in 1728 attendance soared to 978.[192]

In this manner Louis XIV completed the transformation of France into an absolute monarchy. He did so not by reducing the various social classes to the same level and destroying their estates and towns but by accepting, indeed strengthening, the society of orders and controlling the remnants of the once vibrant, popular institutions. Of the assemblies that had been formed, only those of the treasurers in the Bureau of Finances and the élus were specifically suppressed by a decree of the council, and they had been composed of royal officials who had often been tainted by the Fronde. Indeed Louis was not as blindly opposed to representative assemblies as one might think. In 1700 he actually told the principal towns to send deputies to a meeting, the first time they had received such a directive since they had been invited to participate in the Assembly of Notables in 1596.[193]

189. See, for example, Klaus Malettke, *Opposition und Konspiration unter Ludwig XIV* (Göttingen, 1976); Eugene L. Asher, *The Resistance to the Maritime Classes: The Survival of Feudalism in the France of Colbert* (Berkeley and Los Angeles, 1960); and Lionel Rothkrug, *Opposition to Louis XIV: The Political and Social Origins of the French Enlightenment* (Princeton, 1965).

190. Joseph Klaits, *Printed Propaganda under Louis XIV: Absolute Monarchy and Public Opinion* (Princeton, 1976).

191. See, for example, Robert M. Isherwood, *Music in the Service of the King: France in the Seventeenth Century* (Ithaca, 1973).

192. Rebillon, *Les états de Bretagne*, pp. 94–96.

193. Jean-Paul Charmeil, *Les trésoriers de France à l'époque de la Fronde* (Paris, 1964), pp. 407–08; W. C. Scoville, "The French Economy in 1700–1701: An Appraisal by the Deputies of Trade," *Journal of Economic History* 22 (1962): pp. 231–52; R. B. Grassby, "Social Status and Commercial Enterprise under Louis XIV," *The Economic History Review*, ser. 2, 13 (1960–61): 26–33.

The road Louis chose to absolutism coupled with his aggressive foreign policy was to have far-reaching results. By basing his authority on his personal relations with his leading subjects rather than an institutional revolution as Marillac had urged many years before, he condemned his system to failure the first time a too youthful or incompetent king ascended the throne. Once his strong hand was removed, the hereditary magistrates in the sovereign courts and the bureaucracy and what remained of the provincial estates and other duly constituted bodies could seek to reassert their independence. Had Louis XIV not sacrificed the great reforms of the first decade of his personal reign in order to finance the wars that followed, it is possible that he would have left the monarchy so strong, so solvent, and so popular that it could have survived his two successors. Instead he turned over to his infant great-grandson a people who were tired of war, oppressed by taxes, and suffering from want of food. It is a tribute to their patience, though perhaps not to their intelligence, that they permitted the monarchy to survive another three-quarters of a century.

If Marillac had triumphed over Richelieu, an institutional form of absolutism would have been created in which public officials who served at the king's pleasure would have been less able to oppose reforms, popular institutions would have been so completely suppressed that they could not have risen again, and the society of orders would have been so weakened that the privileged would have been less able to prevent change. If all of this had happened, and France had not intervened in Italy and the Empire, it is again possible that the monarchy would have survived much longer than it did.

But there was a third course that France might have taken after the Wars of Religion. It could have turned back to a somewhat idealized version of the Renaissance monarchy as Bellièvre so earnestly advocated—to the reign of Louis XII as the people of France so often pleaded in the cahiers they prepared in the provincial estates, in the electoral assemblies for the Estates General, and in the Estates General itself. Royal officials would have been few in numbers and appointed because of their merit, taxes would have been low, and the government would have been frugal. The Estates General and other assemblies would have administered much of France, the towns would have preserved their semiautonomous positions, and the other duly constituted bodies would have been left relatively free to develop as circumstances dictated. Such a France might not have been able to muster resources to conquer a few European provinces, but its people would have been happier, and perhaps the monarchy itself more long-lived.

BIBLIOGRAPHY

SINCE THIS BOOK TRAVERSES NEARLY FOUR CENTURIES OF FRENCH HISTORY, A list of all the books and manuscripts that it was necessary to consult would add greatly to the length of an already overlong book. Therefore, with rare exceptions, I have included in this bibliography only those published works and unpublished sources that I have actually cited. Readers who desire a more detailed list of books and articles should consult the volumes in the *Nouvelle Clio* series of which the following should be specially cited: Bernard Guenée, *L'occident aux XIVe et XVe siècles: les Etats* (Paris, 1971); Henri Lapeyre, *Les monarchies europeennées du XVIe siècle* (Paris, 1967); Frédéric Mauro, *Le XVIe siècle européen aspects économiques* (Paris, 1966); and Robert Mandrou, *La France aux XVIIe et XVIIIe siècles* (Paris, 1967). Also valuable, although outdated, is *Les sources de l'histoire de France*, ed. A. Molinier, H. Hauser, E. Bourgeois, and L. André (Paris, 1901–35), 18 vols. Those who are interested in the general status of the archives of the various estates and the studies that have exploited them are referred to my "French Representative Assemblies: Research Opportunities and Research Published," *Studies in Medieval and Renaissance History* 1 (1964): 181–219.

The archival material on some of the estates is so vast that I was unable to do more than scan it except for periods in which they were threatened. The archives of other estates have been lost, and their history can be pieced together only by a thorough exploitation of surviving tax and municipal records, again a time-consuming task that can be accomplished only by local historians. Therefore I have had to rely heavily on the inventories of the various archives and have sometimes cited them as evidence. An inventory of an archival collection is no substitute for the original materials its author used. Actually some inventories contain quotations from important documents and give detailed summaries that do not fall far short of being calendars. Others are less detailed and occasionally misleading but nonetheless useful.

Since publishing the bibliographical essay on the estates cited above, I have learned that Gilbert Rouchon has copied most of the surviving documents on the estates of Basse-Auvergne. His manuscript is located in AD, Puy-de-Dôme, 4F 140–53. I have also discovered that the various assemblies in the government of Lyonnais and in the county of Boulogne were far more active than I originally believed. References to the former can be found in AD, Rhône, series B, *Livre du Roy, 1532–1559* and C 405–61 and very likely in AC, Lyons. A few documents on the estates of Boulogne are located in AC, Boulogne-sur-Mer and AD, Pas-de-Calais, although four centuries of warfare have taken a heavy toll. In preparing this book, I was able only to sample the archival holdings in Lyons and had to rely on published materials on Boulonnais.

Because this book deals only with the estates that met regularly and were corporations in the legal sense of the word, the assemblies in those parts of France where the estates only met occasionally have not been treated. I have, however, dealt with them in *The Deputies to the Estates General of Renaissance France* (Madison, 1960).

In recent years most American doctoral dissertations on France have been based on archival research and contain new facts if not always new ideas. Happily, with a few exceptions, degree-granting universities require that these dissertations be reproduced by a duplicating process and copyrighted. I have generally cited them as being published by University Microfilms rather than as a dissertation at this or that university. They are available for purchase at a current price of fifteen dollars each. I have usually cited the date that the thesis was accepted rather than the date that it was reproduced.

A very large number of studies of the European Parliaments have been published both under the auspices of the International Commission for the History of Representative and Parliamentary Institutions and independently. I have cited only a few of the more recent studies. Bibliographical essays have been published by Emile Lousse in *La société d'ancien régime: organisation et répresentation corporatives* (Louvain, 1943), and Helen M. Cam, Antonio Marongiu, and Günther Stöhl, "Recent Works and Present Views on the Origins and Development of Representative Assemblies," *Relazioni del X Congresso Internazionale di Scienze Storiche* (Florence, 1955), 1:3–101. There is a more recent selected bibliography in Alec R. Myers, *Parliaments and Estates in Europe to 1789* (London, 1975).

GENERAL AND NATIONAL

Unpublished Sources

  Paris

  Archives des Affaires Etrangères (AAE)
    Mémoires et Documents: France, nos. 245, 248–50, 252–53, 769, 775, 779, 783–84, 786–87, 789–91, 793, 795bis, 803–05, 826, 830, 834, 840, 1490–91, 1501, 1504–06, 1546, 1548, 1628, 1700–02.
  Archives Nationales (AN)
    AB XIX 2927
    AD IX 126
    120 API 29

E 1^a, 1^b, 1^c, 2^a, 3^a, 8^b, 14^a, 21–23, 70^a, 70^b, 96^a–107^b, 124^a, 129^c, 134^c,
151^a, 1684–86, 1692, 1696, 1700, 1703, 1708, 1711, 1720, 1725, 1728,
1730

H 748^{195}–748^{196}

H^1 716, 1159

J 972

K 67, 71–76, 81, 88, 93, 98, 113–14, 648, 692^a, 692^b

KK 289^1, 648

P 1372^b, 2307

V^6 76, 84

PP 136

R^2 493

Bibliothèque Nationale (BN)

Baluze ms. 367

Cinq Cents Colbert mss. 6, 102, 159

Clairambault mss. 360, 654, 1157

Dupuy mss. 35, 94, 438, 514, 573, 631, 640, 819, 869

Français mss. 2702, 2801, 3306, 3319, 3356, 3389–90, 3550, 3626, 3670,
3827–29, 3832, 3922, 4014, 5183–84, 6556, 6915, 7549, 10,841–42,
11,804–06, 14,027, 14,368, 15,536, 15,562, 15,569, 15,576–78,
15,893–912, 16,258, 16,668, 16,837, 17,359, 18,150–51, 18,153,
18,159–64, 18,168–69, 18,171–76, 18,200–04, 18,270, 18,415, 18,461,
18,510, 18,678, 18,723, 20,608, 20,631, 21,424–26, 21,428, 22,296,
22,382, 23,042, 23,051, 23,194–98, 23,344, 24,160, 25,556

Languedoc (Doat) ms. 234

Mélanges Colbert mss. 114, 366

Morel de Thoisy mss. 58–59

Nouvelles Acquisitions Françaises mss. 82–83, 1095, 3643, 3654, 5130,
5163, 5219, 20,051, 20,526, 22,776

Bibliothèque Sainte-Geneviève

mss. 826, 2005–06

Chantilly

Musée Condé
M 2, M 3

London

British Museum
Egerton mss. 2594–95
Harley mss. 4442, 4489
Public Record Office
S.P. 78/84–78/87

Published Works

Bibliothèque Nationale, Actes Royaux; Numbers cited are those given in *Catalogue général des livres imprimés de la Bibliothèque Nationale: Actes Royaux*, ed. A. Isnard (Paris, 1910–60), 7 vols. 3955, 4428, 4786, 4815, 4908, 5164, 5179, 5252, 6718, 7182, 7191, 7205, 7222–23, 7225, 7231, 7239, 7250, 7253, 7268–69, 7278–79, 7288–89, 7291, 7305, 7315, 7317, 7324–26, 7332, 7334, 7340, 7354, 7357, 7359–60, 7376, 7381, 7383, 7389, 7398–99, 7430–31, 7612, 7686

Documents

Arnauld d'Andilly, Robert. *Journal inédit d'Arnauld d'Andilly, 1614–1620.* Edited by A. Halphen. Paris, 1857.
———. *Journal inédit de Arnauld d'Andilly, 1628–1629.* Edited by E. Halphen and J. Halphen. Paris, 1907.
Arrêts du Conseil du Roi, règne de Louis XIV. Paris, 1976–. 1 vol. to date.
Barbiche, Bernard, ed. *Correspondence du nonce en France, Innocenzo del Bufalo, 1601–1604.* Rome and Paris, 1964.
Bassompierre. *Journal de ma vie: Mémoires du Maréchal de Bassompierre.* Edited by A. de La Cropte de Chantérac. Paris, 1870–77. 4 vols.
Beaucourt, G. du Fresne de, ed. *Chronique de Mathieu d'Escouchy.* Paris, 1863–64. 3 vols.
Boislisle, A. M. de, ed. *Correspondance des contrôleurs généraux des finances avec les intendants des provinces.* Paris, 1874–97. 3 vols.
Boislisle, Jean de, ed. *Mémoriaux du conseil de 1661.* Paris, 1905–07. 3 vols.
Catalogue des actes de François Ier. Paris, 1887–1908. 10 vols.
Catalogue général des livres imprimés de la Bibliothèque Nationale: Actes Royaux. Edited by A. Isnard. Paris, 1910–60. 7 vols.
Chamberland, A. "Lettre confidentielle de Bellièvre sur le cahier de l'assemblée du clergé de 1595 et réponse inédite du roi au cahier." *Revue Henri IV* 3 (1909–12): 257–74.
Charles VIII. *Lettres de Charles VIII, roi de France.* Edited by P. Pélicier. Paris, 1898–1905. 5 vols.
Chroniques de l'ordre des Carmélites de la réforme de Sainte-Thérèse depuis leur introduction en France. Troyes, 1846.
Colbert. *Lettres, instructions et mémoires de Colbert.* Edited by P. Clément. Paris, 1861–82. 8 vols.
Commynes, Philippe de. *Mémoires.* Edited by J. Calmette. Paris, 1924–25. 3 vols.
Depping, G. B., ed. *Correspondance administrative sous le règne de Louis XIV.* Paris, 1850–55. 4 vols.
Dictionnaire d'histoire et de géographie ecclésiastique. Paris, 1912–. 18 vols. to date, pub. under the direction of A. Baudrillart.

Duplessis-Mornay. *Mémoires et correspondance du Duplessis-Mornay*. Edited by A. D. de la Fontennelle de Vaudoré and P.-R. Arguis. Paris, 1824–25. 12 vols.

Fontanon, A., ed. *Les édicts et ordonnances des rois de France*. Paris, 1611. 4 vols.

Fontenay-Mareuil. *Mémoires de Messire François Duval, Marquis de Fontenay-Mareuil*. In Michaud, sér. 2, V.

Harlay de Sancy, Achille de. *Response au libelle intitulé: Très-humble, très-véritable, et très-importante remonstrance au roy*. N.p., 1632.

Henri IV. *Recueil des lettres missives de Henri IV*. Edited by Berger de Xivrey. Paris, 1843–76. 9 vols.

———. *Lettres inédites du roi Henri IV au chancelier de Bellièvre du 8 février 1581 au 23 septembre 1601*. Edited by E. Halphen. Paris, 1872.

———. *Lettres inédites du roi Henri IV à Monsieur de Bellièvre, 1602*. Edited by E. Halphen. Paris, 1881.

———. *Lettres inédites du roi Henri IV au chancelier de Bellièvre, 1603*. Edited by E. Halphen. Paris, 1883.

———. *Lettres inédites du roi Henri IV au chancelier de Bellièvre, 1604*. Edited by E. Halphen. Paris, 1883.

———. *Lettres inédites du roi Henri IV au chancelier de Bellièvre, 1605*. Edited by E. Halphen. Paris, 1880.

———. *Lettres inédites de Henri IV*. Edited by A. Galitzin. Paris, 1860.

———. *Lettres intimes de Henri IV*. Edited by L. Dussieux. Paris, 1876.

———. *Quatre lettres inédites de Henri IV*. Edited by T. Desbarreaux-Bernard. Toulouse, 1866.

Héroard. *Journal de Jean Héroard sur l'enfance et la jeunesse de Louis XIII, 1601–1628*. Edited by E. Soulié and Ed. de Barthélemy. Paris, 1868. 2 vols.

Isambert, François-A. et al., eds. *Recueil général des anciennes lois françaises depuis l'an 420 jusqu'à la Révolution de 1789*. Paris, 1821–33. 29 vols.

Jusserand, J. J., ed. *Recueil des instructions données aux ambassadeurs et ministres de France depuis les traités de Westphalie jusqu'à la Révolution française*. Paris, 1929. Vol. 24.

Kendall, Paul M., and Ilardi, Vincent, eds. *Dispatches of Milanese Ambassadors, 1450–1483*. Athens, Ohio, 1970–. 2 vols. to date.

l'Estoile, Pierre de. *Mémoires-journaux*. Edited by G. Brunet et al. Paris, 1875–96. 12 vols.

Louis XI. *Lettres de Louis XI, roi de France*. Edited by Joseph Vaësen et al. Paris, 1883–1909. 11 vols.

Louis XIII. *Lettres de la main de Louis XIII*. Edited by E. Griselle. Paris, 1914. 2 vols.

Louis XIV. *Memoires for the Instruction of the Dauphin*. Translated by Paul Sonnino. New York, 1970.

Lublinskaya, A., ed. *Documents pour servir à l'histoire des guerres civiles en*

France, 1561–1563. Moscow, 1962.

Mallet, Jean R. *Comptes rendus de l'administration des finances du royaume de France.* London and Paris, 1789.

Mazarin. *Lettres du Cardinal Mazarin pendant son ministère.* Edited by A. Chéruel. Paris, 1872–1906. 9 vols.

Médicis. *Lettres de Catherine de Médicis.* Edited by Hector de la Ferriére. Paris, 1880–1943. 11 vols.

Mercure François. Paris, 1613–48. 25 vols.

Michaud, Joseph F., ed. *Bibliographie universelle.* Paris, 1854. 45 vols.

Michaud, Joseph F., and Poujoulat, Jean-J.-F., eds. *Nouvelle collection des mémoires pour servir à l'histoire de France.* Paris, 1836–39. 32 vols.

Molé. *Mémoires de Mathieu Molé.* Edited by A. Champollion-Figeac. Paris, 1855–57. 4 vols.

Monluc. *Commentaires de Blaise de Monluc.* Edited by Paul Courteault. Paris, 1964.

Monstrelet, Enguerran de. *La chronique.* Edited by L. Douet-d'Arcq. Paris, 1857–62. 6 vols.

Nouaillac, J. "Avis de Villeroy à la reine Marie de Médicis, 10 mars 1614." *Revue Henri IV* 2 (1907–08): 79–89.

Ordonnances, édicts, déclarations, arrests et lettres patentes, concernant l'autorité et la jurisdiction de la Chambre des Comptes de Paris. Paris, 1728. 3 vols.

Ordonnances des roys de France de la troisième race. Edited by Denis F. Secousse et al. Paris, 1723–1849. 21 vols.

Ordonnances des rois de France, règne de François Ier. Paris, 1902–. 9 vols. to date.

Peiresc, *Lettres de Peiresc.* Edited by P. Tamizey de Larroque. Paris, 1888–98. 7 vols.

Pontchartrain, *Mémoires de P. Phelypeaux de Pontchartrain.* In Michaud, sér. 2, V.

Reilhac, A. de, ed. *Jean de Reilhac, secrétaire, maître des comptes, général des finances et ambassadeur des rois Charles VII, Louis XI, et Charles VIII.* Paris, 1886–88. 3 vols.

Richelieu, *Lettres, instructions diplomatiques et papiers d'état du Cardinal de Richelieu.* Edited by Denis-L.-M. Avenel. Paris, 1853–78. 8 vols.

———. *Mémoires du Cardinal de Richelieu.* In Michaud, sér. 2, VII–IX.

———. *Mémoires du Cardinal de Richelieu.* Edited by Horric de Beaucaire et al. Paris, 1907–31. 10 vols.

———. *Les papiers de Richelieu: section politique intérieure, correspondance et papiers d'État.* Edited by Pierre Grillon. Paris, 1975–. 2 vols. to date.

———. *Testament politique.* 7th ed. Edited by Louis André. Paris, 1947.

Séguier. *Lettres et mémoires adressés au Chancelier P. Séguier, 1633–1649.* Edited by A. Lublinshaza. Moscow, 1966.

———. *Lettres et mémoires adressés au Chancelier Séguier.* Edited by R.

Mousnier. Paris, 1964. 2 vols.

Sully. "Lettres inédites de Sully à Henri IV et à Villeroy." Edited by D. Buisseret and B. Barbiche. *Annuaire-Bulletin de la société de l'histoire de France, années 1974–1975*, 81–117.

———. *Mémoires des sages et royales oeconomies d'estat.* In Michaud, sér. 2, II–III.

———. *Les oeconomies royales de Sully.* Edited by David Buisseret and Bernard Barbiche. Paris, 1970–. 1 vol. to date.

Tamizey de Larroque, Philipe, ed. "Trois lettres inédites du président de Sevin à Peyresc." *Revue de l'Agenais* 11 (1884): 48–55.

Tardif, Jules. *Monuments historiques.* Paris, 1866.

Valois, Noël, ed. *Inventaire des arrêts du Conseil d'État, règne de Henri IV.* Paris, 1886–93. 2 vols.

Secondary Works

Adams, Elizabeth C. *Seventeenth-Century Attitudes Toward the French Estates General.* Ann Arbor, University Microfilms, 1976.

André, Louis. *Michel de Tellier et l'organisation de l'armée monarchique.* Montpellier, 1906.

———. *Michel Le Tellier et Louvois.* Paris, 1942.

Artonne, André. *Le mouvement de 1314 et les chartes provinciales de 1315.* Paris, 1912.

Asher, Eugene L. *The Resistance to the Maritime Classes: The Survival of Feudalism in the France of Colbert.* Berkeley and Los Angeles, 1960.

Aubenas, A. *Histoire du Parlement de Paris.* Paris, 1847.

Aubery, Antoine. *Mémoires pour l'histoire du cardinal duc de Richelieu.* Paris, 1660. 2 vols.

Aumale, Henri, duc d'. *Histoire des princes de Condé pendant les XVIᵉ et XVIIᵉ siècles.* Paris, 1863–1896. 7 vols.

Avenel, Georges d'. *Richelieu et la monarchie absolue.* 2d ed. Paris, 1895. 4 vols.

Babeau, Albert. *Le village sous l'ancien régime* 5th ed. Paris, 1915.

Basin, Thomas. *Histoire de Charles VII.* Edited by Charles Samaran. Paris, 1933–44. 2 vols.

Batiffol, Louis. *La Journée des Dupes.* Paris, 1925.

———. *Le roi Louis XIII à vingt ans.* Paris, 1910.

Baudot, M. "L'enquête de Sully sur l'artillerie en 1604." *Bulletin philologique et historique (jusqu'à 1610) du comité des travaux historiques et scientifiques* (1963): 930–38.

Bayard, Françoise. "Les Chambres de Justice de la première moitié du XVIIᵉ siècle." *Cahiers d'histoire* 19 (1974): 121–40.

Benedict, Philip J. *Rouen during the Wars of Religion: Popular Disorder, Public Order, and the Confessional Struggle.* Ann Arbor, University Microfilms,

1975.

Bercé, Yves-Marie. *Histoire des Croquants*. Geneva, 1974.

Birch, Thomas. *An Historical View of the Negociations between the Courts of England, France, and Brussels from the Year 1592 to 1617*. London, 1749.

Boiteux, Lucas-A. *Richelieu, grand maître de la navigation et du commerce en France*. Caen and Paris, 1955.

Bosher, J. F. "*Chambres de Justice* in the French Monarchy." In *French Government and Society 1500–1850: Essays in Memory of Alfred Cobban*. Edited by J. F. Bosher, pp. 19–40. London, 1973.

Brémond, Henri. *A Literary History of Religious Thought in France*. Translated by K. L. Montgomery. New York, 1928–36. 3 vols.

Bridge, John S. C. *A History of France from the Death of Louis XI*. Oxford, 1921–36. 5 vols.

Buisseret, D. "A Stage in the Development of the French Intendants: The Reign of Henry IV." *The Historical Journal* 9 (1966): 27–30.

———. *Sully*. London, 1968.

Buisseret, D. and Barbiche, B. "Les convictions religieuses de Sully." *Bibliothèque de l'Ecole des Chartes* 121 (1963): 223–30.

Chamberland, Albert. *Le conflict de 1597 entre Henri IV et le Parlement de Paris*. Paris, 1904.

Chevalier, B. "The Policy of Louis XI towards the *Bonnes Villes*: The Case of Tours." In *The Recovery of France in the Fifteenth Century*, edited by P. S. Lewis, pp. 265–93. New York, 1971.

Clarke, Jack A. *Huguenot Warrior: The Life and Times of Henri de Rohan*. The Hague, 1966.

Contamine, Philippe. *Guerre, état et société à la fin du Moyen Age*. Paris, 1972.

Cosneau, E. *Le Connétable de Richemont*. Paris, 1886.

Coste, Pierre. *The Life and Works of Saint Vincent de Paul*. Translated by J. Leonard. Westminster, Md., 1952.

Coville, Alfred. *Les Cabochiens et l'ordonnance de 1413*. Paris, 1888.

Cummings, Mark L. *The Long Robe and the Scepter: A Quantitative Study of the Parlement of Paris and the French Monarchy in the Early Seventeenth Century*. Ann Arbor, University Microfilms, 1974.

De Bouis. *Assemblée des Notables tenue à Rouen en 1617*. pp. 19–22. In *Revue de la Normandie* (September–October 1866).

Decrue de Stoutz, Francis. *Henri IV et les députés de Genève*. Geneva and Paris, 1901.

Delachenal, Roland. *Histoire de Charles V*. Paris, 1909–31. 5 vols.

Deloche, Maximin. *La maison du Cardinal de Richelieu*. Paris, 1912.

———. *Les Richelieu: Le père du Cardinal*. Paris, 1923.

Denault, Gerard F. *The Legitimation of the Parlement of Paris and the Estates General, 1560–1614*. Ann Arbor, University Microfilms, 1975.

Dessert, D. "Pouvoir et finance au XVIIᵉ siècle: la fortune du Cardinal Mazarin." *Revue d'histoire moderne et contemporaine* 23 (1976): 161–81.

Dickerman, Edmund H. *Bellièvre and Villeroy*. Providence, 1971.

―――. *The King's Men: The Ministers of Henry III and Henry IV, 1574–1610*. Ann Arbor, University Microfilms, 1965. 3 vols.

Doucet, Roger. *Etude sur le gouvernement de François Ier*. Paris, 1921.

―――. "Le gouvernment de Louis XI." *Revue des cours et conférences* 24 (1922–23): 737–46, 912–21, 1010–19, 1233–40, 1277–86; 25 (1923–24): 240–48, 375–84, 524–32, 661–69.

―――. *Les institutions de la France au XVIe siècle*. Paris, 1948. 2 vols.

Dupont-Ferrier, Gustave. *Les officiers royaux des bailliages et sénéschaussées et les institutions monarchiques locales en France à la fin du Moyen Age*. Paris, 1902.

Edelstein, Marilyn M. *The Recruitment of the French Episcopacy under the Concordat of Bologna in the Reign of Frances I*. Ann Arbor, University Microfilms, 1972.

Everat, Edouard. *Michel de Marillac, sa vie, ses oeuvres*. Riom, 1894.

Godard, Charles. *Les pouvoirs des intendants sous Louis XIV*. Paris, 1901.

Griselle, E. "Louis XIII et sa mère." *Revue historique* 105 (1910): 302–31.

Guenée, Bernard. "Espace et état dans la France du bas Moyen Age." *Annales: Economies, Sociétés, Civilisations* 23 (1968): 744–58.

―――. "La géographie administrative de la France à la fin du Moyen Age: élections et bailliages." *Le Moyen Age* 67 (1961): 293–323.

―――. "L'histoire de l'Etat en France à la fin du Moyen Age." *Revue Historique* 232 (1964): 331–60.

Hamscher, Albert N. *The Parlement of Paris after the Fronde, 1653–1673*. Pittsburgh, 1976.

Hanotaux, Gabriel, and the Duc de La Force. *Histoire du Cardinal de Richelieu*. Paris, 1896–1947. 6 vols.

Hanotaux, Gabriel. *Origines de l'institution des intendants des provinces*. Paris, 1884.

Harding, Robert R. *Anatomy of a Power Elite: The Provincial Governors of Early Modern France*. New Haven, 1978.

Hauser, Henri. *La pensée et l'action économiques du Cardinal de Richelieu*. Paris, 1944.

Hayden, J. M. "The Social Origins of the French Episcopacy at the Beginning of the Seventeenth Century." *French Historical Studies* 10 (1977): 27–40.

Houssaye, Michel. *M. de Bérulle et les Carmélites de France, 1575–1611*. Paris, 1872.

―――. *Le Père de Bérulle et l'Oratoire de Jésus, 1611–1625*. Paris, 1874.

―――. *Le Cardinal de Bérulle et le Cardinal de Richelieu, 1625–1629*. Paris, 1875.

Isherwood, Robert M. *Music in the Service of the King: France in the Seventeenth Century*. Ithaca, 1973.

Kendall, Paul M. *Louis XI*. New York, 1971.

Kierstead, Raymond F., *Pomponne de Bellièvre*. Evanston, 1968.

Kitchens, James H. *The Parlement of Paris during the Ministry of Cardinal Richelieu, 1624–1642.* Ann Arbor, University Microfilms, 1974. 2 vols.

Klaits, Joseph. *Printed Propaganda under Louis XIV: Absolute Monarchy and Public Opinion.* Princeton, 1976.

Kleinman, Ruth. *Saint François de Sales and the Protestants.* Geneva, 1962.

Kossmann, Ernst H. *La Fronde.* Leiden, 1954.

Labande-Mailfert, Yvonne. *Charles VIII et son millieu, 1470–1498.* Paris, 1975.

Lajeunie, Etienne-Jean. *Saint François de Sales.* Paris, 1966. 2 vols.

Lavisse, Ernest. *Histoire de France.* Edited by E. Lavisse. Paris, 1911. Vol. 7.

Lemonnier, Henry. *Histoire de France.* Edited by E. Lavisse. Paris, 1911. Vol. 5.

Léonard, Emile G. *A History of Protestantism.* Translated by R. M. Bethell and J. M. H. Reid. London, 1965–67. 2 vols.

Lewis, P. S. *Later Medieval France.* London, 1968.

———. ed. *The Recovery of France in the Fifteenth Century.* New York, 1972.

Lossky, A. "Some Problems in Tracing the Intellectual Development of Louis XIV from 1661 to 1715." In *Louis XIV and the Craft of Kingship,* edited by John C. Rule, pp. 317–44. Columbus, 1969.

Lot, Ferdinand and Fawtier, Robert, eds. *Histoire des institutions françaises au Moyen Age.* Paris, 1957–. 3 vols. to date.

Lublinskaya, Alexandre D. *French Absolutism: The Crucial Phase, 1620–1629.* Translated by Brian Pearce. Cambridge, 1968.

Madden, Sarah Hanley. *The "Lit de Justice" of the Kings of France: Historical Myth and Constitutional Event in Late Medieval and Early Modern Times.* Ann Arbor, University Microfilms, 1975.

Major, J. Russell "The Crown and the Aristocracy in Renaissance France." *American Historical Review* 69 (1964): 631–45.

———. "Popular Initiative in Renaissance France." In *Aspects of the Renaissance,* edited by Archibald R. Lewis, pp. 27–41. Austin, 1967.

———. "The Renaissance Monarchy: A Contribution to the Periodization of History," *Emory University Quarterly* 13 (1957): 112–24.

Malettke, Klaus. *Opposition und Konspiration unter Ludwig XIV.* Göttingen, 1976.

Mariéjol, Jean-H. *Histoire de France.* Edited by Ernest Lavisse. Paris, 1911. Vol. 6.

Marvik, E. W. "The Character of Louis XIII: The Role of His Physician." *Journal of Interdisciplinary History* 4 (1974): 347–74.

———. "Childhood History and Decisions of State: The Case of Louis XIII." *History of Childhood Quarterly* 2 (1974): 135–99.

Mastellone, S. "Osservazioni sulla 'Renaissance monarchy' in Francia." *Fondazione Italiana per la storia amminstrativo* 1 (1964): 421–30.

———. *La Reggenza di Maria de' Medici.* Florence, 1962.

Michaud, Hélène. *Les formulaires de grande chancellerie 1500–1580.* Paris, 1972.

Miskimin, H. A. "The Last Act of Charles V: The Background to the Revolts of 1382." *Speculum* 38 (1963): 433–42.

Mongrédien, Georges. *Les journée des dupes.* Paris, 1961.

Moote, A. Lloyd. *The Revolt of the Judges: The Parlement of Paris and the Fronde, 1643–1652.* Princeton, 1971.

Mousnier, Roland. *The Assassination of Henry IV.* Translated by J. Spencer. New York, 1973.

———*Le conseil du roi de Louis XII à la Révolution.* Paris, 1970.

———. "French Institutions and Society, 1610–61." In *The New Cambridge Modern History*, edited by J. P. Cooper, 4:474–502. Cambridge, 1970.

———. *Les institutions de la France sous la monarchie absolue, 1598–1789.* Paris, 1974.

———. "Note sur les rapports entre les gouverneurs de provinces et les intendants dans la première moitié du XVIIe siècle." *Revue historique* 228 (1962): 339–50.

———. "La participation des gouvernés à l'activité des gouvernants dans la France du XVIIe et du XVIIIe siècles." *Schweizer Beiträge zur Allgemeinen Geschichte* 20 (1962–63): 200–29.

———. *La plume, la faucille et le marteau: Institutions et société en France du Moyen Age à la Révolution.* Paris, 1970.

———. "Recherches sur les syndicats d'officiers pendant la Fronde." *XVII siècle* 42–43 (1959): 76–117.

———. "Les règlements du conseil du roi sous Louis XIII." *Annvaire-bulletin de la société de l'histoire de France, 1946–1947*, pp. 93–211. Paris, 1948.

———. "Sully et le Conseil d'Etat et des Finances: La lutte entre Bellièvre et Sully." *Revue historique* 192 (1941): 68–86.

———. *La vénalité des offices sous Henri IV et Louis XIII.* 2d ed. Paris, 1971.

Nouaillac, Joseph. *Villeroy, secrétaire d'Etat et ministre de Charles XI, Henry III et Henry IV, 1543–1610.* Paris, 1909.

Pagès, Georges. "Autour du 'Grand Orage.' Richlieu et Marillac: deux politiques." *Revue historique* 179 (1937): 63–97.

———. *La monarchie d'ancien régime en France de Henri IV à Louis XIV.* Paris, 1946.

Parker, D. "The Social Foundation of French Absolutism, 1610–1630." *Past and Present* 53 (1971): 67–89.

Patry, Raoul. *Philippe du Plessis-Mornay.* Paris, 1933.

Perroy, Edouard. *The Hundred Years War.* London, 1951.

Petit-Dutaillis, Charles. *Les communes françaises, caractères et évolution des* *origines au XVIIIe siècle*. Paris, 1947.

———. *Histoire de France*. Edited by E. Lavisse. Paris, 1911. 4: pt. 2.

Porchnev, Boris. *Les soulèvements populaires en France de 1623 à 1648*. Paris, 1963.

Radding, C. M. "Royal Tax Revenue in Later Fourteenth Century France." *Traditio* 32 (1976): 361–368.

Ranum, Orest. *Richelieu and the Councillors of Louis XIII*. Oxford, 1963.

Richet, D. "Croissance et blocages en France du XVe au XVIIIe siècle." *Annales: économies, sociétés, civilisations* 23 (1968): 759–87.

Roelker, Nancy L. *Queen of Navarre, Jeanne d'Albret, 1528–1572*. Cambridge, Mass., 1968.

Rothkrug, Lionel. *Opposition to Louis XIV: The Political and Social Origins of the French Enlightenment*. Princeton, 1965.

Salmon, John H. M. *Society in Crisis: France in the Sixteenth Century*. London, 1975.

Sée, Henri. *Louis XI et les villes*. Paris, 1891.

Shennan, J. H. *The Parlement of Paris*. New York, 1968.

Soman, A. "Press, Pulpit, and Censorship in France before Richelieu." *Proceedings of the American Philosophical Society* 120 (1976): 439–63.

Spooner, Frank C. *The International Economy and Monetary Movements in France, 1493–1725*. Cambridge, Mass., 1972.

Stein, Henri. *Charles de France*. Paris, 1919.

Tapié, Victor-L. *France and the Age of Louis XIII and Richelieu*. Translated by D. McN. Lockie. London, 1974.

Temple, N. "The Control and Exploitation of French Towns during the Ancien Régime." *History* 51 (1966): 16–34.

Topin, Marius. *Louis XIII et Richelieu*. Paris, 1877.

Vaissière, Pierre de. *Un grand procès sous Richelieu: L'affaire de Maréechal de Marillac, 1630–1632*. Paris, 1924.

Vale, Malcolm G. A. *Charles VII*. Berkeley, 1974.

Vaunois, Louis. *Vie de Louis XIII*. Paris, 1944.

Viénot, John. *Histoire de la Réforme française de l'Edit de Nantes à sa révocation*. Paris, 1934.

Weary, W. A. "The Administration of Patronage in Fifteenth and Sixteenth Century France: Assumptions, Practices, and Institutions." Unpublished paper.

———. *Royal Policy and Patronage in Renaissance France: The Monarchy and the House of La Trémoille*. Ann Arbor, University Microfilms, 1972.

Zeller, Berthold. *La minorité de Louis XIII: Marie de Médicis et Sully*. Paris, 1892.

———. *La minorité de Louis XIII: Marie de Médicis et Villeroy*. Paris, 1897.

———. *Louis XIII, Marie de Médicis, chef du conseil*. Paris, 1898.

———. *Louis XIII, Marie de Médicis, Richelieu ministre*. Paris, 1899.

———. *Le connétable de Luynes*. Paris, 1879.

————. *Richelieu et les ministres de Louis XIII de 1621 à 1624.* Paris, 1880.

Zeller, Gaston. *Les institutions de la France au XVIe siècle.* Paris, 1948.

National and Provincial Assemblies (Documents and Secondary Works)

Anquez, Léonce. *Histoire des assemblées politiques des réformés de France, 1573–1622.* Paris, 1859.

————. *Un nouveau chapitre de l'histoire politique des réformés de France, 1621–1626.* Paris, 1865.

Ardier, Paul. *L'Assemblée des Notables, tenue à Paris ès années 1626 et 1627.* Paris, 1652.

Beaurepaire, Charles de Robillard de, ed. *Entrée à Rouen du roi Henri IV, en 1596.* Rouen, 1887.

————. *Louis XIII et l'Assemblée des Notables à Rouen, en 1617.* Rouen, 1883.

Bisson, T. N. "The General Assemblies of Philip the Fair: Their Character Reconsidered." In *Post Scripta: Essays on Medieval Law and the Emergence of the European State in Honor of Gaines Post*, edited by Joseph R. Strayer and Donald E. Queller, pp. 537–64. Rome, 1972.

Blet, Pierre. *Le clergé de France et la monarchie; étude sur les assemblées générales du clergé de 1615 à 1666.* Rome, 1959. 2 vols.

————. *Les assemblées du clergé et Louis XIV de 1670 à 1693.* Rome, 1972.

Brown, E. A. R. "Assemblies of French Towns in 1316: Some New Texts." *Speculum* 46 (1971): 282–301.

Brown, Walter R. *French Provincial Opinions at the Time of the Fronde.* Ann Arbor, University Microfilms, 1973.

Charlier-Meniolle, R. *L'Assemblée des Notables tenue à Rouen en 1596.* Paris, 1911.

Collection des procès-verbaux des assemblées-générales du clergé de France depuis 1560 jusqu'à présent. Paris, 1767–68. 9 vols.

Des Etats Généraux et autres assemblées nationales. Edited by Charles J. Mayer. Paris, 1788–89. 18 vols.

Dumont, François. "Gouvernants et gouvernés en France au Moyen Age et au XVIe siècle." *Schweizer Beiträge zur Allgemeinen Geschichte* 20 (1962–63): 188–99.

Dupont-Ferrier, G. "De quelques problèmes historiques relatifs aux Etats provinciaux." *Journal des Savants* (August–October 1928): 315–57.

Grandmaison, Charles de. "Nouveaux documents sur les Etats généraux du XVe siècle." *Bulletin de la société archéologique de Touraine* 4 (1877–79): 139–55.

Grassby, R. B. "Social Status and Commercial Enterprise under Louis XIV." *The Economic History Review*, ser. 2, 13 (1960–61): 19–38.

Grün, Alphonse. *Les Etats provinciaux sous Louis XIV.* 2d ed. Paris, 1853.

Hayden, J. Michael. *France and the Estates General of 1614.* Cambridge, 1974.

Langmuir, G. I. "Counsel and Capetian Assemblies." *Studies Presented to the International Commission for the History of Representative and Parliamentary Institutions,* 18:19–34. Louvain, 1958.

Lassaigne, Jean-Dominique. *Les assemblées de la noblesse de France aux XVIIe et XVIIIe siècles.* Paris, 1965.

Lublinskaya, A. D. "Les assemblées d'états en France au XVIIe siècle. Les assemblées des notables de 1617 et de 1626." *Studies Presented to the International Commission for the History of Representative and Parliamentary Institutions,* 31:163–77. Louvain, 1966.

Major, J. Russell. "The Assembly at Paris in the Summer of 1575." In *Post Scripta: Essays on Medieval Law and the Emergence of the European State in Honor of Gaines Post,* edited by Joseph R. Strayer and Donald E. Queller, pp. 699–715. Rome, 1972.

———. *Bellièvre, Sully, and the Assembly of Notables of 1596, Transactions of the American Philosophical Society,* 64. Philadelphia, 1974.

———. *The Deputies to the Estates General of Renaissance France.* Madison, 1960.

———. "The Electoral Procedure for the Estates General of France and Its Social Implications, 1483–1651." *Medievalia et Humanistica* 10 (1956):131–50.

———. *The Estates General of 1560.* Princeton, 1951.

———. "The French Monarchy as Seen through the Estates General." *Studies in the Renaissance* 9 (1962): 113–25.

———. "French Representative Assemblies: Research Opportunities and Research Published." *Studies in Medieval and Renaissance History* 1 (1964): 181–219.

———. "The Loss of Royal Initiative and the Decay of National Representative Institutions in France, 1421–1615." *Album Helen Maud Cam,* 2:245–59. Louvain, 1961.

———. "The Payment of the Deputies to the French National Assemblies, 1484–1627." *Journal of Modern History* 27 (1955): 217–29.

———. *Representative Institutions in Renaissance France, 1421–1559.* Madison, 1960.

———. "The Third Estate in the Estates General of Pontoise, 1561." *Speculum* 29 (1954): 460–76.

Masselin, Jean. *Journal des Etats généraux de France tenus à Tours en 1484 sous le règne de Charles VIII,* edited by A. Bernier. Paris, 1835.

Mirot, L. "Les Etats généraux et provinciaux et l'abolition des aides au début du règne de Charles VI, 1380–1381." *Revue des questions historiques* 74 (1903): 398–455.

Petit, Jeanne. *L'Assemblée des Notables de 1626–1627.* Paris, 1936.

Picot, Georges. *Histoire des Etats généraux.* 2d ed. Paris, 1888. 5 vols.

Recueil des cahiers généraux des trois ordres aux Etats-Généraux. Edited by Lalourcé and Duval. Paris, 1789. 4 vols.

Recueil de pièces originales et authentiques, concernant la tenue des Etats-Généraux. Edited by Lalourcé and Duval. Paris, 1789. 9 vols.

Scoville, W. C. "The French Economy in 1700–1701: An Appraisal by the Deputies of Trade." *Journal of Economic History* 22 (1962): 231–52.

Serbat, Louis. *Les assemblées du clergé de France, 1561–1615.* Paris, 1906.

Taylor, C. H. "An Assembly of French Towns in March, 1318." *Speculum* 13 (1938): 295–303.

———. "Assemblies of French Towns in 1316." *Speculum* 14 (1939): 275–99.

———. "The Composition of Baronial Assemblies in France, 1315–1320." *Speculum* 29 (1954): 433–58.

———. "French Assemblies and Subsidy in 1321." *Speculum* 43 (1968): 217–44.

Thomas, A. "Les Etats Généraux sous Charles VII." *Le cabinet historique* 24 (1878): 118–28, 155–70, 200–21.

———. "Les Etats Généraux sous Charles VII." *Revue historique* 40 (1889): 55–88.

———. "Le Midi et les Etats Généraux sous Charles VII." *Annales du Midi* 1 (1889): 289–315.

Viollet, P. "Election des députés aux Etats généraux réunis à Tours en 1468 et en 1484." *Bibliothèque de l'Ecole des Chartes,* sér. 6, 2 (1866): 22–58.

Taxation

Barbiche, B. "Les commissaires députés pour le 'régallement' des tailles en 1598–99." *Bibliothèque de l'Ecole des Chartes* 118 (1960): 58–96.

Batiffol, L. "Le trésor de la Bastille de 1605 à 1611." *Revue Henri IV* 3 (1909): 200–09.

Blanchard, Guillaume, ed. *Compilation chronologique contenant un recueil en abrégé des ordonnances, édits ... des rois de France ...* Paris, 1715. 2 vols.

Brown, E. A. R. "Customary Aids and Royal Fiscal Policy under Philip VI of Valois." *Traditio* 30 (1974): 191–258.

———. "Subsidy and Reform in 1321: The Accounts of Najac and the Policies of Philip V." *Traditio* 27 (1971): 399–430.

———. "Taxation and Morality in the Thirteenth and Fourteenth Centuries." *French Historical Studies* 8 (1973): 1–28.

Chamberland, Albert. *Un plan de restauration financière en 1596, attribué à Pierre Forget de Fresne, secrétaire d'Etat et membre du Conseil des finances.* Paris, 1904.

Charmeil, Jean-Paul. *Les trésoriers de France à l'époque de la Fronde.* Paris, 1964.

Clamageran, Jean-J. *Histoire de l'impôt en France.* Paris, 1867–76, 3 vols.

Combes, Jean. *Traité des tailles et autres charges ...* Paris, 1584.

Dent, Julian. *Crisis in Finance: Crown, Financiers and Society in Seventeenth-Century France.* Newton Abbot, 1973.

Doucet, R. "Les finances de la France en 1614." *Revue d'histoire économique et sociale* 18 (1930): 133–63.

Dupont-Ferrier, G. "Essai sur la géographie administrative des élections financières en France de 1356 à 1790." *Annuaire-bulletin de la société de l'histoire de France* 65 (1928): 192–342; 66 (1929): 223–390.

———. *Etudes sur les institutions financières de la France à la fin du Moyen Age.* Paris, 1930–32. 2 vols.

———. *Nouvelles études sur les institutions financières de la France à la fin du Moyen Age: Les origines et le premier siècle de la Chambre ou Cour des Aides de Paris.* Paris, 1933.

Forbonnais, F. Véron de. *Recherches et considérations sur les finances de France.* Liège, 1758. 6 vols.

Henneman, John B. *Royal Taxation in Fourteenth Century France: The Development of War Financing, 1322–1356.* Princeton, 1971.

———. *Royal Taxation in Fourteenth Century France: The Captivity and Ransom of John II, 1356–1370,* Memoirs of the American Philosophical Society, 116. Philadelphia, 1976.

Hennequin, Jean. *Le guidon général des financiers.* Paris, 1585.

Jacqueton, Gilbert. *Documents relatifs à l'administration financière en France de Charles VII à François Ier.* Paris, 1891.

La Barre, René-Laurent. *Formulaire des esleuz . . .* Rouen, 1622.

Mallet, Jean R., ed. *Comptes rendus de l'administration des finances du royaume de France.* London, 1789.

Michaud, H. "L'ordonnancement des dépenses et le budget de la monarchie, 1587–1589." *Annvaire-bulletin de la société de l'histoire de France* (1970–71): 87–150.

Rey, Maurice. *Le domaine du roi et les finances extraordinaires sous Charles VI, 1388–1413.* Paris, 1965.

———. *Les finances royales sous Charles VI: Les causes du déficit, 1388–1413.* Paris, 1965. 2 vols.

Spont, Alfred. "Une recherche générale des feux à la fin du XVe siècle." *Annuaire-bulletin de la société de l'histoire de France* 29 (1892): 222–36.

———. *Semblançay.* Paris, 1895.

Strayer, Joseph R., and Taylor, Charles H. *Studies in Early French Taxation.* Cambridge, Mass., 1939.

Wolfe, Martin. *The Fiscal System of Renaissance France.* New Haven, 1972.

Political Thought

Bailey, Donald A. *Writers against the Cardinal: A Study of the Pamphlets which Attacked the Person and Policies of Cardinal Richelieu during the Decade 1630–1640.* Ann Arbor, University Microfilms, 1973.

Baumgartner, Frederic J. *Radical Reactionaries: the Political Thought of the French Catholic League.* Geneva, 1976.

Bodin, Jean. *The Six Bookes of a Commonweale.* Kenneth D. McRae edition of Knolles's translation. Cambridge, 1962.

———. *Les six livres de la république.* Paris, 1583.

Carlyle, Alexander J., and Robert W. *A History of Mediaeval Political Theory in the West.* Edinburgh, 1903–36. 6 vols.

Church, William F. *Constitutional Thought in Sixteenth-Century France.* Cambridge, Mass., 1941.

———. *Richelieu and Reason of State.* Princeton, 1972.

Denzer, Horst, ed. *Jean Bodin, Proceedings of the International Conference on Bodin in Munich.* Munich, 1973.

Erasmus. *The Education of a Christian Prince.* Translated by Lester K. Born. New York, 1936.

Franklin, Julian H. *Jean Bodin and the Rise of Absolutist Theory.* Cambridge, 1973.

Giesey, Ralph E. *The Juristic Basis of Dynastic Right to the French Throne, Transactions of the Amercian Philosophical Society,* 51. Philadelphia, 1961.

Hotman, François. *Francogallia.* Edited by R. E. Giesey and J. H. M. Salmon. Cambridge, 1972.

Jackson, R. A. "Elective Kingship and *Consensus Populi* in Sixteenth-Century France." *Journal of Modern History* 44 (1972): 155–71.

Kelley, Donald R. *Foundations of Modern Historical Scholarship: Language, Law, and History in the French Renaissance.* New York, 1970.

———. "Louis Le Caron Philosophie." In *Philosophy and Humanism: Renaissance Essays in Honor of Paul Oskar Kristeller,* edited by Edward P. Mahoney. New York, 1976.

Lemaire, André. *Les lois fondamentales de la monarchie française.* Paris, 1907.

Machiavelli. *The Prince.* Translated by L. Ricci, revised by E. R. P. Vincent. New York, 1930.

Major, J. Russell. "The Renaissance Monarchy as Seen by Erasmus, More, Seyssel, and Machiavelli." In *Action and Conviction in Early Modern Europe: Essays in Memory of E. H. Harbison,* edited by T. K. Rabb and J. E. Siegel, pp. 17–31. Princeton, 1969.

Moranvillé, H. "Remonstrances de l'Université et de la ville de Paris à Charles VI sur le gouvernement du royaume." *Bibliothèque de l'Ecole des Chartes* 51 (1890): 420–42.

Post, Gaines. *Studies in Medieval Legal Thought.* Princeton, 1964.

Other European States and Estates

Bader, K. S. "Approaches to Imperial Reform at the End of the Fifteenth Century." In *Pre-Reformation Germany,* edited by G. Strauss, pp. 136–61.

New York, 1972.

Barraclough, Geoffrey. *The Origins of Modern Germany.* Oxford, 1947.

Benecke, G. *Society and Politics in Germany, 1500–1750.* London, 1974.

Beneyto, J. "Les Cortès d'Espagne du XVIᵉ au XIX siècles." *Anciens pays et assemblées d'Etats* 35 (1966): 461–81.

Blickle, Peter. *Landschaften im Alten Reich: Die staathiche Funktion des gemeinin Mannes in Oberdeutschland.* Munich, 1973.

Brenner, R. "Agrarian Class Structure and Economic Development in Pre-Industrial Europe." *Past and Present* 70 (1976): 30–75.

Carsten, Francis L. *The Origins of Prussia.* Oxford, 1954.

———. *Princes and Parliaments in Germany.* Oxford, 1959.

Dhondt, J. "Les assemblées d'Etats en Belgique avant 1795." *Anciens pays et assemblées d'Etats* 33 (1965): 195–260.

Duggan, Lawrence G. *Bishop and Chapter: The Governance of the Bishopric of Speyer to 1552.* New Brunswick, 1978.

Elliott, John H. *Imperial Spain, 1469–1716.* London, 1963.

Fernández, Luis Suárez. "The Kingdom of Castile in the Fifteenth Century." In *Spain in the Fifteenth Century, 1369–1516,* edited by Roger Highfield, pp. 80–113. New York, 1972.

Gilissen, J. "Les Etats Généraux des pays par deçà, 1464–1632." *Anciens pays et assemblées d'Etats* 33 (1965): 261–321.

Gilkes, Rosslyn K. *The Tudor Parliament.* London, 1969.

Gjerset, Knut. *History of Iceland.* New York, 1924.

Górski, Karol. *Communitas princeps corona regni.* Warsaw, 1976.

Griffiths, Gordon. *Representative Government in Western Europe in the Sixteenth Century.* Oxford, 1968.

———. "The State: Absolute or Limited?" In *Transition and Revolution: Problems and Issues of European Renaissance and Reformation History,* edited by Robert M. Kingdon, pp. 13–51. Minneapolis, 1974.

Hartung, F. "Imperial Reform, 1485–1495: Its Course and Its Character." In *Pre-Reformation Germany,* edited by G. Strauss, pp. 73–135. New York, 1972.

Hendricks, Charles D. *Charles V and the Cortes of Castille: Politics in Renaissance Spain.* Ann Arbor, University Microfilms, 1976.

Hexter, Jack. *Reappraisals in History.* London, 1961.

Hildesheimer, F. "Nice au XVIIᵉ siècle: institutions locales et vie urbaine." *Bibliothèque de l'Ecole des Chartes* 132 (1975): 21–57.

Hobsbawn, E. J. "The Crisis of the Seventeenth Century." In *Crisis in Europe, 1560–1660,* edited by Trevor Aston, pp. 5–58. London, 1965.

Jóhannesson, Jón. *A History of the Old Icelandic Commonwealth,* translated by H. Bessason. Winnipeg, 1974.

Koenigsberger, Helmut, G. *Estates and Revolutions: Essays in Early Modern European History.* Ithaca, 1971.

Lapeyre, Henri. *Les monarchies européennes du XVIᵉ siècle.* Paris, 1967.

Le Caron, Louis. *Responses et decisions du droict françois.* Paris, 1612.

LeGates, M. J. "The Knights and the Problems of Political Organizing in Sixteenth-Century Germany." *Central European History* 7 (1974): 99–136.

Lousse, Emile. *La société d'ancien régime: organisation et représentation corporatives.* Louvain, 1943.

Lovett, A. W. *Philip II and Mateo Vazquez de Leca: The Government of Spain, 1572–1592.* Geneva, 1977.

Lynch, John. *Spain under the Habsburgs.* Oxford, 1964–69. 2 vols.

Major, J. Russell. *The Age of the Renaissance and Reformation.* Philadelphia, 1970.

———. *The Western World: Renaissance to the Present;* 2d ed. Philadelphia, 1971.

Marongiu, Antonio. *Medieval Parliaments.* Translated by S. J. Woolf. London, 1968.

Merriman, Roger B. *The Rise of the Spanish Empire in the Old World and the New.* New York, 1918–34. 4 vols.

Myers, Alex R. *Parliaments and Estates in Europe to 1789.* London, 1975.

Neale, John E. *The Elizabethan House of Commons.* London, 1949.

———. *Elizabeth I and Her Parliaments.* London, 1953–57. 2 vols.

Notestein, W. "The Winning of the Initiative in the House of Commons." *Proceedings of the British Academy* 11 (1924): 125–75.

O'Callaghan, J. F. "The Beginnings of the Cortes of Léon-Castile." *American Historical Review* 84 (1969): 1503–37.

Pirenne, H. "The Formation and Constitution of the Burgundian State." *American Historical Review* 14 (1909): 477–502.

Pollard, Albert F. *Henry VIII.* London, 1905.

Puy Huici Goñi, María. *Las Cortes de Navarra durante la edad moderna.* Madrid, 1963.

Roberts, Michael. *The Early Vasas.* Cambridge, 1968.

———. *Gustavus Adolphus.* London, 1953.

———. "The Constitutional Development of Sweden in the Reign of Gustav Adolf." *History* 24 (1940): 328–41.

Rowan, S. W. "A Reichstag in the Reform Era: Freiburg im Breisgau, 1497–98." In *The Old Reich: Essays on German Political Institutions, 1495–1806,* edited by James A. Vann and S. W. Rowan, pp. 31–57. Brussels, 1974.

Ryder, Alan. *The Kingdom of Naples under Alfonso the Magnanimous.* Oxford, 1976.

Vann, James A. *The Swabian Kreis: Institutional Growth in the Holy Roman Empire.* Brussels, 1975.

Wellens, Robert. *Les Etats Généraux des Pays-Bas, des origines à la fin du règne de Philippe le Beau, 1464–1506.* Heule, 1974.

Wines, R. "The Imperial Circles, Princely Diplomacy and Imperial Reform 1681–1714." *Journal of Modern History* 39 (1967): 1–29.

THE PROVINCIAL ESTATES

Auvergne

Unpublished Sources
AD, Cantal
  C 433
AD, Puy-de-Dôme
  C 851
  4 F 140–53
AC, Aurillac
  AA 21, 21bis, 22bis
  BB 9–12
AC, Clermont-Ferrand, fonds Clermont
  Aa 4, 6
AC, Saint-Flour
  Chapter 5
B. Mun., Poitiers
  Col. Fonteneau, ms. 28

Printed Sources

Dictionnaire statistique, ou histoire, description et statistique du département du Cantal. Edited by Jean Baptiste Déribier-du-Châtelet. Aurillac, 1852–57. 5 vols.
IAC, Aurillac. Edited by G. Esquer. Aurillac, 1906–11. 2 vols.
IAC, Clermont-Ferrand fonds de Montferrand. Edited by Teilhard de Chardin. Clermont-Ferrand, 1902–22. 2 vols.
IAC, Riom. Edited by F. Boyer. Riom, 1892.
IAD, Puy-de-Dôme, sér. C. Edited by Gilbert Rouchon. Clermont-Ferrand, 1893–1916. 6 vols.
Mémoire sur l'état de la généralité de Riom en 1697, dressé pour l'instruction du duc de Bourgogne par l'intendant Lefèvre d'Ormesson. Edited by Abel Poitrineau. Clermont-Ferrand, 1970.

Secondary Works

Bergier, Antoine and Verdier-Latour. *Recherches historiques sur les Etats généraux et plus particulièrement sur l'origine, l'organisation et la durée des anciens Etats provinciaux d'Auvergne.* Clermont-Ferrand, 1788.
Henry, P. "Note sur les Etats provinciaux de Basse-Auvergne." *Revue d'Auvergne* 58 (1944): 57–66.
Imberdis, André. *Histoire des guerres religieuses en Auvergne.* Moulins, 1840. 2 vols.

Leclercq, F. "Les Etats provinciaux de la Ligue en Basse-Auvergne de 1589 à 1594." *Bulletin philologique et historique (jusqu'à 1610) du Comité des travaux historiques et scientifiques* (1963): 913–29.

Ribier, R. de. "L'assemblée des Etats particuliers de la Haute-Auvergne en 1649" *Revue de la Haute-Auvergne* 6 (1904): 125–80.

Rouchon, G. "Le tiers Etat aux Etats provinciaux de Basse-Auvergne aux XVIᵉ et XVIIᵉ siècles." *Bulletin philologique et historique (jusqu'à 1715) du Comité des travaux historiques et scientifiques* (1930–31): 165–89.

Savaron, Jean. *Les origines de Clairmont, ville capitale d'Auvergne.* Clermont, 1607.

Sève, R. "Une carte de Basse Auvergne de 1544–1545 et la demande d'agrégation aux bonnes villes présentée par Amber." In *Mélanges géographiques offerts à Philippe Arbos,* pp. 165–71. Clermont-Ferrand, 1953.

Thomas, Antoine. *Les Etats provinciaux de la France centrale sous Charles VII.* Paris, 1879. 2 vols.

Brittany

Unpublished Sources

AD, Ille-et-Vilaine
    C 2642–56, 2931–32, 3193–3200

Printed Sources

Barthélemy, Anatole de, ed. *Choix de documents inédits sur l'histoire de la Ligue en Bretagne.* Nantes, 1880.

Bourdeaut, A. "Journal des Etats de Bretagne tenu à Nantes en décembre 1636 par Dubuisson-Aubenay." *Bulletin de la Société archéologique et historique de Nantes et de la Loire-Inférieure* 67 (1927): 339–89.

Calan, C. de La Lande de, ed. "Documents inédits relatifs aux Etats de Bretagne de 1491 à 1589." *Archives de Bretagne* 15 (1909–10).

Mercoeur. "Correspondance du duc de Mercoeur et des ligueurs Bretons avec l'Espagne," edited by G. de Carné. *Archives de Bretagne* 11–12 (1899).

Morice, Pierre-Hyacinthe. *Mémoires pour servir de preuves à l'histoire ecclésiastique et civile de Bretagne.* Paris, 1742–46. 3 vols.

Rebillon, Armand. *Les sources de l'histoire des Etats de Bretagne.* Paris, 1932.

Secondary Works

Carné, Louis Joseph de. *Les Etats de Bretagne.* 2d ed. Paris, 1875. 2 vols.

Dunkley, Kenneth M. *Richelieu and the Estates of Brittany, 1624–1640.* Ann

Arbor, University Microfilms, 1972.

Fourmont, Hyacinthe de. *Histoire de la Chambre des Comptes de Bretagne.* Paris, 1854.

Garlan, Yvon, and Nières, Claude. *Les révoltes bretonnes de 1675.* Paris, 1975.

Grégoire, Louis. *La Ligue en Bretagne.* Paris, 1856.

Hurt, J. J. "La politique du parlement de Bretagne, 1661–1675." *Annales de Bretagne* 81 (1974): 105–30.

Joüon des Longrais, F. "Le duc de Mercoeur." *Bulletin archéologique de l'association bretonne,* sér. 3, 13 (1894): 212–93.

La Borderie, Arthur Le Moyne de, and Pocquet, Barthélemy-A. *Histoire de Bretagne.* Paris, 1896–1914. 6 vols.

Morice, Dom Pierre-Hyacinthe. *Histoire ecclésiastique et civile de Bretagne.* Guingamp, 1836–37. 20 vols.

Planiol, Marcel. *Histoire des institutions de la Bretagne.* Rennes, 1953–55. 3 vols.

Rebillon, Armand. *Les Etats de Bretagne de 1661 à 1789.* Paris, 1932.

Sée, Henri. *Les Etats de Bretagne au XVIe siècle.* Paris, 1895.

Trullinger, Robert S. "The *Grand Voyer* as an Instrument of Royal Centralization in Brittany under Henry IV." *Proceedings of the Western Society for French History* 3 (1975): 26–34.

———. *The Royal Administration of Bretagne under Henri IV, 1598–1610.* Ann Arbor, University Microfilms, 1972.

Burgundy

Unpublished Sources

AD, Ain
  C 999–1025
AD, Côte-d'Or
  B 11, 943
  C 3016–17, 3077–80, 5219–20
  C 5382–83
AC, Dijon
  B 455, 462–63

Printed Sources

Baux, Jules, ed. *Mémoires historiques de la ville de Bourg, extraits des registres municipaux de l'hôtel-de-ville, de 1536 à 1789.* Bourg-en-Bresse, 1868–88. vols. 1–3.

Beaune, P. "Henri IV aux députés des Estats de Bourgogne, 1608." *Le Cabinet Historique* 6 (1860): pt. 1, 122–25.

Brossard, Joseph, ed. *Mémoires historiques de la ville de Bourg, extraits des registres municipaux de l'hôtel-de-ville, de 1536 à 1789.* Bourg-en Bresse, 1868–88. vols. 4–5.

"Description des pays de Bresse, Bugey et Gex dressée par l'intendant de Bourgogne en 1698 sur les ordres du roi Louis XIV pour le duc de Bourgogne." *Bulletin de la société de géographie de l'Ain* 6 (1891): 16–26, 33–48, 87–95, 120–29, 172–84, 207–20.

Drouot, H. and Gros, L., eds. *Recherches sur la Ligue en Bourgogne.* Dijon, 1914.

Garnier, Joseph, ed. *Correspondance de la mairie de Dijon extraite des archives de cette ville.* Dijon, 1868–70. 3 vols.

————. *Journal de Gabriel Breunot.* Dijon, 1864–66. 3 vols.

IAC, Bourg. Edited by Joseph Brossard. Bourg, 1872.

IAC, Dijon, sér. B. Edited by Louis de Gouvenain. Paris, 1867.

IAD, Ain, sér. C. Edited by Joseph Brossard. Bourg, 1884.

IAD, Ain, sér. G. Edited by Joseph Brossard. Bourg, 1891.

IAD, Côte-d'Or, sér. C. Edited by Joseph Garnier. Dijon, 1880–90. 4 vols.

IAD, Côte-d'Or, sér. C, introduction aux tomes III et IV. Edited by Joseph Garnier. Dijon, 1959.

IAD, Saône-et-Loire, sér. C. Edited by C. Ragut et al. Mâcon, 1924.

Recueil des édits, déclarations, lettres-patentes, arrêts du Conseil, ordonnances, et autres réglements, émanés du roi et son Conseil, concernant l'administration des Etats de Bourgogne. Dijon, 1784–87. 2 vols.

Sainct-Julien, Pierre de. *De l'origine des Bourgongnons, et antiquité des Estats de Bourgongne.* Paris, 1581.

Souvert, Jean de. *Advis pour Messieurs les gens des trois Estats du pais et duché de Bourgogne, sur le subject de leur assemblée du mois de may prochain 1605.* N.p., n.d.

————. *Articles présentez à Messieurs des trois Estats du pays de Bourgogne, par M. Jean de Souvert, leur conseil, pour y estre par eux délibéré en leur assemblée.* N.p., n.d.

————. *Remonstrance à Messieurs des trois Estats du pays et duché de Bourgogne au subject de leur assemblée du huictiesme d'aoust prochain 1611.* N.p., n.d.

Secondary Works

Abord, Hippolyte. *Histoire de la Réforme et la Ligue dans la ville d'Autun.* Autun, 1855–87. 3 vols.

Baux, Jules. *Histoire de la réunion à la France des provinces de Bresse, Bugey et Gex.* Bourg-en-Bresse, 1852.

Billioud, Joseph. *Les Etats de Bourgogne aux XIVe et XVe siècles.* Dijon, 1922.

Blin, L. "Des Etats du Charolais aux Etats de Bourgogne, les avatars de Pierre-Etienne-Palamède Baudinot, 1726–1752." *Annales de Bourgogne* 43 (1971): 145–66.

Brossard, Joseph-P. *Notice sur l'organisation territoriale et l'administration ...
des anciennes provinces de Bresse, du Bugey, de la Dombes et du pays de Gex.*
Bourg-en-Bresse, 1881.

Brown, Elizabeth A. R. *Charters and Leagues in Early Fourteenth Century
France: The Movement of 1314 and 1315.* Ph.D. dissertation, Harvard
University, 1960.

Chevanne, R. de. "Les Etats de Bourgogne et la réunion du duché à la
France, en 1477." *Mémoire de la société d'archéologie de Beaune* 43
(1929–30): 195–245.

Drouot, Henri. *Mayenne et la Bourgogne.* Paris, 1937. 2 vols.

———. *Notes sur la Bourgogne et son esprit public au début du règne de Henri III,
1574–1579.* Dijon, 1937.

Dumont, F. "Une session des Etats de Bourgogne; la tenue de 1718."
Annales de Bourgogne 5 (1933): 329–70; 6 (1934): 47–77, 230–52, 337–65;
7 (1935): 45–69.

Gay, J.-L. "Fiscalité royale et Etats généraux de Bourgogne, 1477–1589."
Etudes sur l'histoire des assemblées d'états, edited by François Dumont, pp.
179–210. Paris, 1966.

Guillois, A. "La fin d'un 'pays adjacent': l'union du comté d'Auxerre aux
Etats de Bourgogne, 1668." *Annales de Bourgogne* 33 (1961): 5–26, 65–87.

Laroche, L. "Les Etats particuliers du Charolais." *Mémoire de la société pour
l'histoire du droit et des institutions des anciens pays bourguignons, comtois et
romands* 6 (1939): 145–94.

Moreau, F. "La suppression des Etats du comté d'Auxonne et leur
réunion aux Etats du duché de Bourgogne." *Mémoire de la société pour
l'histoire du droit et des institutions des anciens pays bourguignons, comtois et
romands* 2 (1935): 189–94.

Ricard, Louis. *Les institutions judiciares et administratives de l'ancienne France et
spécialement du bailliage de Gex.* Paris, 1886.

Richard, Jean. *Les Ducs de Bourgogne et la formation du duché du XIe au XIVe
siècle.* Paris, 1954.

———. "Les Etats de Bourgogne." *Schweizer Beiträge zur Allgemeinen
Geschichte* 20 (1962–63): 230–48. also published in *Anciens Pays et
Assemblées d'Etats,* 35 (1966): 299–324.

———. "Les institutions ducales dans le duché de Bourgogne." In *Histoire
des institutions françaises au Moyen Age,* edited by Ferdinand Lot and
Robert Fawtier, 1:209–247. Paris, 1957.

———. "L'élection financiére d'Autun du XIVe au XVIe siècle," *Mémoire
de la société Eduenne,* n.s. 50 (1947): 1–14.

Roussot, Jean. *Un comté adjacent à la Bourgogne aux XVIIe et XVIIIe siècles; le
Mâconnais, pays d'états et d'élection.* Mâcon, 1937.

Tallone, A. "Les Etats de Bresse." *Annales de la société d'émulation et
d'agriculture de l'Ain* 55 (1927): 272–344.

Thomas, Alexandre. *Une province sous Louis XIV; situation politique et adminis-*

trative de la Bourgogne de 1661 à 1715. Paris, 1844.

Vaughan, Richard. *Philip the Bold: The Formation of the Burgundian State.* London, 1962.

———. *John the Fearless: The Growth of Burgundian Power.* London, 1966.

———. *Philip the Good, The Apogee of Burgundy.* London, 1970.

Weill, G. "Les Etats de Bourgogne sous Henri III." *Mémoires de la société bourguignonne de géographie et d'histoire* 9 (1893): 121–48.

Dauphiné

Unpublished Sources

AD, Drôme
  C 1023–25
AD, Isère
  B 3263–65
  1C 4, 1C 5, 1C 7
  Fonds Chaper, J 524^1, J 524^2
  1J 175–76, 669
  H 357
AC, Gap (in AD, Hautes Alpes)
  BB 12, 16, 25, 27
AC, Grenoble
  AA 39–40, 42, 54
  BB 85–88, 90–91, 93–95, 99, 108, 111, 146
  CC 789
AC, Guillestre (in AD, Hautes-Alpes)
  BB 18
B. Mun., Grenoble
  Mss. 1357, 1450, 2311–13

Printed Sources

Boissat, Pierre de. *Remerciement au roi par les anoblis du Dauphiné.* Paris, 1603.

Cayers presentez au roy par le syndic des communautez villageoises ... 5 aoust 1606.

Chorier, Nicolas. *Histoire de la vie de Charles de Créquy de Blanchefort, duc de Lesdiguières.* Grenoble, 1683. 2 vols.

Expilly, Claude. *Plaidoyez.* Paris, 1621.

IAC, Gap. Edited by Paul Guillaume. Gap, 1908–13. 2 vols.

IAC, Grenoble. Edited by Auguste Prudhomme. Grenoble, 1886–1926. 5 vols.

IAC, Guillestre. Edited by Paul Guillaume. Gap, 1906.

IAC, Valence. Edited by A. Lacroix. Valence, 1914.

IAD, Drôme. Edited by A. Lacroix. Valence, 1865–1910. 8 vols.

IAD, Isère, sér. B. Edited by A. Prudhome et al. Grenoble, 1864–1919. 4 vols.

IAD, Hautes-Alpes, sér. E. Edited by Paul Guillaume. Gap, 1910–16. 2 vols.

La Grange, Claude de. *La juste plaincte et remonstrance faicte au Roy et à nosseigneurs de son Conseil d'Estat par le pauvre peuple de Daulphiné* ... Lyon, 1597.

————. *Responses et salvations des pièces produictes par les gentz du tiers estat de Daulphiné.* Paris, 1599.

Lesdiguières. *Actes et correspondance du connétable de Lesdiguières.* Edited by Louis-A. Douglas and Joseph Roman. Grenoble, 1878–84. 3 vols.

Piémond. *Mémoires de Eustache Piémond.* Edited by J. Brun-Durand. Geneva, 1885.

Rambaud, Antoine. *Plaidoyer pour le tiers-estat du Dauphiné* ... Paris, 1600.

Recueil des édits et déclarations du Roy, lettres patentes et ordonnances de Sa Majesté, arrests et réglements de ses conseils, et du Parlement de Grenoble, concernant en général et en particulier la province de Dauphiné. Edited by Alexander Giroud. Grenoble, 1720.

Recueil des harangues faites par messire Pierre Scarron, évesque et prince de Grenoble ... et président perpétuel des estats du Dauphiné ... Paris, 1634.

Roman, J. "Documents sur la Réforme et les Guerres de Religion en Dauphiné." *Bulletin de la société de statistiques des sciences naturalles et des arts industriels du département de l'Isère,* sér. 3, 15 (1890), v–xiii, 1–724.

Vincent, Jean. *Discours en forme de plaidoyé pour le tiers estat de Daulphiné, au procès qu'il a par devant Sa Majestè* ... Paris, 1598.

————. *Les prières du tiers estat de Daulphiné* ... Lyons, 1598.

————. *Réplique pour le tiers estat de Daulphiné, aux défences des deux premiers ordres* ... Paris, 1600.

Secondary Works

Arnaud, Eugène. *Histoire des Protestants du Dauphiné aux XVIe, XVIIe et XVIIIe siècles.* Paris, 1875–76, 3 vols.

Bligny, Bernard, ed. *Histoire du Dauphiné.* Paris, 1973.

Cavard, Pierre. *La Réforme et les Guerres de Religion à Vienne.* Vienne, 1950.

Chabrand, Dr. "Les escartons dans l'ancien Briançonnais." *Bulletin de la société d'études des Hautes-Alpes* 2 (1883): 241–49.

Chianéa, Gérard. *La condition jurdique des terres en Dauphiné au 18e siècle.* Paris, 1969.

Dufayard, Charles. *Le connétable de Lesdiguières.* Paris, 1892.

Dussert, A. "Le Baron des Adrets et les Etats du Dauphiné." *Bulletin de l'Académie Delphinale,* sér. 5, 20 (1929): 93–136.

————. "Catherine de Médicis et les Etats du Dauphiné." *Bulletin de l'Académie Delphinale,* sér. 6, 2 (1931): 123–89.

———— "Les Etats du Dauphiné aux XIVe et XVe siècles." *Bulletin de l'Académie Delphinale*, sér. 5, 8 (1914): 1–371.

———. "Les Etats du Dauphiné de la Guerre de Cent Ans aux Guerres de Religion." *Bulletin de l'Académie Delphinale*, sér. 5, 13 (1922): 1–356.

———. "Fin de l'indépendence politique du Dauphiné." *Bulletin de l'Academie Delphinale*, sér. 5, 1 (1907): 5–55.

Fauché-Prunelle, Alexandre. *Essai sur les anciennes institutions autonomes ou populaires des Alpes Cottiennes-Brianconnaises*. Grenoble, 1856–57. 2 vols.

Lacroix, André. *L'arrondissement de Montélimar: géographie, histoire et statistique*. Valence, 1868–93. 8 vols.

———. "Claude Brosse et les tailles." *Bulletin de la société d'archéologie et de statistique de la Drôme* 31–33 (1897–99): scattered.

Letonnelier, Gaston. *Histoire du Dauphiné*. Paris, 1958.

Vaillant, P. "Les origines d'une libre confédération de vallées: les habitants des communautés brianconnaises au XIIIᵉ siècle." *Bibliothèque de l'Ecole des Chartes* 125 (1967): 301–48.

Van Doren, L. S. "Civil War Taxation and the Foundations of Fiscal Absolutism: The Royal *Taille* in Dauphine, 1560–1610." *Transactions of the Western Society for French History* 3 (1975): 35–53.

———. "Revolt and Reaction in the City of Romans, Dauphiné, 1579–1580." *The Sixteenth Century Journal* 5 (1974): 71–100.

———. "War Taxation, Institutional Change, and Social Conflict in Provincial France—The Royal *Taille* in Dauphiné, 1494–1559." *Proceedings of the American Philosophical Society* 121 (1977): 70–96.

———. *War, Taxes, and Social Protest: The Challenge to Authority in Sixteenth Century Dauphiné*. Ph. D. dissertation, Harvard University, 1970.

Guyenne

AD, Aveyron
  C 1902–04, 1906
  2E 157.4, 676–77
AD, Dordogne
  5C 11, 18, 21, 29
AD, Gers
  E suppl. 23,936, 23,985–87
  I 1628
AD Gironde
  C 3804–05, 3808, 3810, 3817, 3822–24, 3872–75, 3877, 3888, 3894, 3901, 3975, 3977, 3979, 3988, 4017
  E suppl. 590, 2345–47, 4403, 4406–17, 4463
  G 26, 35, 40, 45, 47, 287–90, 479, 585–87
AD, Haute-Garonne
  C 3401–07

AD, Lot-et-Garonne
  E suppl. 44, 2706
AC, Agen (in AD, Lot-et-Garonne)
   AA 17, 25, 27, 33–35, 50
   BB 27, 35–37, 40, 42, 44–46, 49, 51, 53, 55, 59, 63
   CC 44, 49, 59, 61–84, 95, 111, 116, 118, 120, 122–24, 128, 130–56,
      158–74, 176–83, 185, 191–92, 194–95, 202, 204, 209, 227, 232, 248
AC, Astaffort (in AD, Lot-et-Garonne)
  BB 1
AC, Auch (in AD, Gers)
  BB 5–7
AC, Bayonne
  BB 18, 20, 23–24
AC, Bordeaux
  AA 26
AC, Bourg-sur-Gironde
  AA 11
  BB 1, 3
AC, Casteljaloux (in AD, Lot-et-Garonne)
  BB 2–5
AC, Condom (in AD, Gers)
  BB 7–8, 11, 18
AC, Couthures (in AD, Lot-et-Garonne)
  BB 1
AC, Dax
  AA 5
  BB 1, 2
AC, Fals (in AD, Lot-et-Garonne)
  BB 1
AC, Francescas (in AD, Lot-et-Garonne)
  BB 1–2, 5, 7, 10, 15
AC, Isle-Fourdain (in AD, Gers)
  BB 2–4
AC, Laplume
  BB 4–7
AC, La Réole
  BB 3, 7, 9
AC, Layrac (in AD, Lot-et-Garonne)
  BB 1–2
AC, Lectoure
  BB 4–5
AC, Meilhan (in AD, Lot-et-Garonne)
  BB 1
AC, Mézin (in AD, Lot-et-Garonne)

BB 1–3, 7
AC, Millau
 AA 12, 16–17
AC, Nogaro (in AD, Gers)
 AA 6, 11
AC, Rodez (bourg)
 BB 10–12
AC, Rodez (cité)
 AA 4
 BB 8–9
AC, Saint-Emilion
 AA 5
 BB 6, 9, 11
AC, Saint-Sever
 BB 2
 II, 1
AC, Tartas (in AD, Landes)
 BB 2–3

Printed Sources

Albe, E. "Inventaire raisonné et analytique des archives municipales de Cahors."*Bulletin de la société des études littéraires, scientifiques et artistiques du Lot* 47 (1926): 78–150.

Archives historiques du départment de la Gironde. Bordeaux, 1859–1932. 58 vols.

Archives municipales de Bayonne: Délibérations du corps de ville Registres Gascons, 1474–1530. Bayonne, 1896–98. 2 vols.

Archives municipales de Bayonne: Délibérations du corps de ville. Registres Français, 1565–1600. Bayonne, 1901–06. 2 vols.

Archives municipales de Bordeaux. Edited by Dast Le Vacher et al. Bordeaux, 1867–1947. 13 vols.

Artières, J. "Documents sur la ville de Millau." *Archives historiques du Rouergue* 7 (1930): 1–576.

Barrère, Abbé. "Extrait et analyse d'un registre de l'hôtel de ville de Condom." *Revue de Gascogne* 13 (1872): 224–46, 291–95, 373–79, 470–76; 14 (1873): 169–74.

Brutails, A. "Mémoire sur la tenue des Etats de Rouergue, écrit vers 1623 par Durieux, député de pays de Rouergue." *Bulletin historique et philologique du comté des travaux historiques et scientifiques* (1885): 23–27.

Cabié, Edmond. *Guerres de Religion dans le sud-ouest de la France et principalement dans le Quercy.* Paris, 1906.

Cardenal, L. de. "Catalogue des assemblées des Etats de Périgord de 1378 à 1651." *Bulletin philologique et historique (jusqu'à 1715) du comité des travaux historiques et scientifiques* (1938–39): 243–66.

Carsalade-du-Pont, J. de. "Le journal de maître Jean de Solle." *Revue de Gascogne* 18–19 (1877–78): scattered.

Charrier, G., ed. *Les jurades de la ville de Bergerac.* Bergerac, 1892–1904. 18 vols.

Courteault, Henri, ed. "Le livre des syndics des Etats de Béarn." *Archives historiques de la Gascogne,* sér. 2, 10 (1906): 1–234.

Edict du roy contenant révocation et suppression des huict bureaux d'élections establis en la généralité de Guyenne par édict du mois de janvier 1603. Agen, 1612.

Gouron, Marcel, ed. *Recueil des privilèges accordés à la ville de Bordeaux par Charles VII et Louis XI.* Bordeaux, 1937.

Harlé, Pierre, ed. *Registre du clerc de Ville.* Bordeaux, 1912.

IAC, Agen. Edited by A. Bosvieux and G. Tholin. Paris, 1884.

IAC, Condom. Edited by G. Niel. N.p., n.d.

IAC, Figeac. Edited by L. Combarieu. In *Annuaire du Lot* (1869).

IAC, Moissac. Edited by C. Dumas de Rauly. Montauban, 1906–07.

IAC, Périgueux. Edited by Michel Hardy. Périgueux, 1897.

IAD, Averyron, sér. G. Edited by C. Estienne and L. Lempereur. Rodez, 1934.

IAD, Gers, sér. A et B. Edited by P. Tierny and R. Pagel. Auch, 1909.

IAD, Gironde, sér. B. Edited by Jean-A. Brutails and G. Loirette. Bordeaux, 1925.

IAD, Gironde, sér. C. Edited by Alexandre Gouget et al. Bordeaux, 1877–1932. 4 vols.

IAD, Gironde, sér. E suppl. Edited by G. Ducaunnés-Duval. Bordeaux, 1898–1908. 4 vols.

IAD, Gironde, sér. G. Edited by A. Gouget et al. Bordeaux, 1892–1901. 2 vols.

IAD, Landes, sér. A à F. Edited by H. Tartière. Paris, 1868.

IAD, Lot-et-Garonne, sér. A, B, C, D, E, E suppl., G, et H. Edited by E. Crozet et al. Agen, 1863–78, 2 vols.

Lestrade, Jean, ed. *Cahiers des remonstrances des Etats de Comminges aux rois de France ou à leurs lieutenants généraux en Guyenne, 1537–1627,* Société des études du Comminges, Saint-Gaudens, 1943.

―――. "Les Huguenots en Comminges." *Archives historiques de la Gascogne,* sér. 2, 5 (1900): 1–498.

Parfouru, Paul, and Carsalade-du-Pont, J. de, eds. "Comptes consulaires de la ville de Riscle de 1441 à 1507." *Archives historiques de la Gascogne* 12–13 (1886, 1892).

Recueil des édicts, déclarations, arrests, et règlemens faits en faveur et pour le restablissement des esleus en la province et généralité de Guiéne. Paris, 1626.

Rigal, J.-L. "Mémoires d'un Calviniste de Millau." *Archives historiques du Rouergue* 2 (1911): 1–512.

Tholin, G. "Les cahiers du pays d'Agenais aux Etats-Généraux," *Revue de l'Agenais* 10 (1883): 5–16, 145–60, 244–59, 321–39, 408–16.

————. "Requête des trois états du pays d'Agenais au roi Edouard III." *Bulletin philologique et historique du comité des travaux historiques et scientifiques* 17 (1899): 426–34.

Secondary Works

Affre, H. *Dictionnaire des institutions, moeurs et coutumes du Rouergue.* Rodez, 1903.

Antin, E. d'. "Une commune Gasconne pendant les Guerres de Religion." *Revue de l'Agenais* 21 (1894): 52–72, 155–83, 230–67, 352–63, 535–49.

Baqué, Z. "Vic-Fezensac au temps de la Fronde." *Bulletin de la société d'histoire et d'archéologie du Gers* 36 (1935): 40–53.

Baudel, M.-J. *Notes pour servir à l'histoire des Etats provinciaux du Quercy.* Cahors, 1881.

Bordes, Maurice. *D'Etigny et l'administration de l'intendance d'Auch, 1751–1767.* Auch, 1957. 2 vols.

————. "La ville de Lectoure, pays d'états et l'assemblée provinciale d'Auch." *Bulletin de la société archéologique, historique, littéraire et scientifique du Gers* 72 (1971): 533–54.

Bosc, L.-C.-P. *Mémoires pour servir à l'histoire du Rouergue.* Rodez, 1797.

Bourrachot, L. "L'emprunt forcé de 1544 en Bazadais." *Cahiers du Bazadais* 8 (1968): 11–33.

Branet, A. "Les Etats d'Armagnac en 1631–1632." *Bulletin de la société archéologique du Gers* 14 (1913): 168–83, 214–29.

Brissaud, Désiré. *Les Anglais en Guyenne.* Paris, 1875.

Cardenal, L. de. "Les Etats de Périgord sous Henri IV." *L'organisation corporative du Moyen Age à la fin de l'ancien régime. Etudes présentées à la commission internationale pour l'histoire des assemblées d'états,* 3:163–81. Louvain, 1939.

————. "Note sur les archives des Etats de Périgord." *Bulletin de la société historique et archéologique du Périgord* 39 (1912): 150–52.

Contrasty, Jean. *Histoire de Sainte-Foy-de-Peyrolières.* Toulouse, 1917.

Couderc, Camille. *Note sur les fastes consulaires de Bernard Arribat et documents sur l'histoire de Villefranche et du Rouergue à la fin du XVIe siècle.* Rodez, 1893.

Degret, A. "Les assemblées provinciales du clergé gascon." *Revue de Gascogne* 55–62 (1914–26): scattered.

Desgraves, L. "La formation territoriale de la généralité de Guyenne." *Annales du Midi* 62 (1950): 239–48.

————. "Aux origines de l'élections d'Agen, 1519–1622." *Recueil de travaux offert à M. Clovis Brunel,* pt. 1, 357–65. Paris, 1955.

De Villaret. *A Montcuq en 1587. Affaires consulaires se rattachant à la lutte contre les Protestants d'après des documents inédits.* Société des études littéraires, scientifiques et artistiques du Lot, 1929.

Duffour, J. "Les Etats d'Astarac de 1582." *Revue de Gascogne* sér. 2, 6 (1906): 19–30.

————. "Députés de l'Armagnac aux Etats généraux d'Orléans en 1649." *Revue de Gascogne*, sér. 2, 19 (1924): 31–33.

Escande, Jean-J. *Histoire du Périgord*. 2d ed. Paris, 1957.

Fage, René. *Les Etats de la vicomté de Turenne*. Paris, 1894. 2 vols.

Filippi, Luigi. *Pour les Corses. Essai sur le Maréchal de France Alfonso d'Ornano, Maire de Bordeaux, 1548–1610*. Algiers, 1915.

Fons, V. "Les Etats de Comminges." *Mémoires de la société imperiale archéologique du Midi de la France* 8 (1861–65): 161–206.

Galabert, Abbé. "Note sur les Etats de Rivière-Verdun." *Bulletin de la société archéologique du Midi de la France* 10 (1897): 105–10.

Gardère, Joseph. *Histoire de la seigneurie de Condom et de l'organisation de la justice dans cette ville*. Condom, 1902.

Gaujal, Marc-A.-F. de. *Etudes historiques sur le Rouergue*. Paris, 1858–59. 4 vols.

Gébelin, François. *Le gouvernement du Maréchal de Matignon en Guyenne*. Bordeaux, 1912.

Gorsse, Bertrand de. "Les Etats de Comminges." *Revue de Comminges* 46 (1932): 5–28.

Higounet, Charles. *Le comté de Comminges*. Toulouse, 1949. 2 vols.

————, ed. *Histoire de Bordeaux*. Bordeaux, 1962–74. 8 vols.

Lacoste, Guillaume. *Histoire générale de la province de Quercy* 2d ed. Cahors, 1883. 4 vols.

Leroux, A. "Chronique." *Revue historique de Bordeaux* 11 (1918): 57.

Lodge, Eleanor C. *Gascony under English Rule*. London, 1926.

Major, J. Russell. "Henry IV and Guyenne: A Study Concerning the Origins of Royal Absolutism." *French Historical Studies* 4 (1966): 363–83.

Mondon, S. "Privilèges de la comté de Comenge comprenant le traité des lies et passeries de 1513." *Revue de Comminges* 30 (1915): 1–70.

Monlezun, Jean-J. *Histoire de la Gascogne*. Auch, 1846–50. 7 vols.

Montégut, H. de. "Les Etats de Périgord." *Bulletin de la société historique et archéologique du Périgord* 4 (1877): 87–91.

Naurois-Destenay, Marie-José de. *Les Etats de Comminges aux XVIe et XVIIe siècles*." Thesis, Ecole Nationale des Chartes, 1953–54.

Naurois-Destenay, M.-J. (Darbin). "Histoire sommaire des Etats de Comminges." In *Saint-Gaudens et le Comminges*, pp. 175–83. Tarbes, 1963.

Oppetit-Perné, D. "La vicomté de Turenne à la fin du XVe siècle essai d'histoire économique." *Positions des thèses de l'Ecole Nationale des Chartes* (1971): 141.

Ousset, P.-E. "Les députés d'Aspet aux Etats du Comminges." *Revue de Comminges* 87 (1974): 15–29.

Rouquette, J. *Le Rouergue sous les Anglais*. Millau, 1887.

Samaran, Charles. *La maison d'Armagnac au XVe siècle et les dernières luttes de* *la féodalité dans le midi de la France.* Paris, 1907.

Sol, Eugène. *La vie économique et sociale en Quercy aux XVI et XVII siècles.* Cahors, 1950.

Suau-Noulens, Bernadette. *La Ville de Rodez au milieu du XVᵉ siècle.*" Thesis, Ecole Nationale des Cartes, 1971.

Tholin, G. *Des tailles et des impositions au pays d'Agenais durant le XVIᵉ siècle jusqu'aux réformes de Sully.* Agen, 1874. Extract from the *Recueil des travaux de la société d'agriculture, sciences et arts d'Agen* 4 (1875): 91–135.

———. "La ville d'Agen pendant les Guerres de Religion du XVIᵉ siècle." *Revue de l'Agenais* 14–20 (1887–93): scattered.

Vale, Malcolm G. A. *English Gascony, 1399–1453: A Study of War, Governement and Politics during the Later Stages of the Hundred Years War.* Oxford, 1970.

Languedoc

Unpublished Sources

AD, Hérault
  A 44, 46, 53
  C *Cahiers* of the estates, vols. III–IV
  Procès-verbaux of the estates, September 1589–October 1632

Printed Sources

Albisson, Jean, ed. *Loix municipales et économiques de Languedoc.* Montpellier, 1780–78. 7 vols.

Faille, Germain de la. *Annales de la ville de Toulouse.* Toulouse, 1687–1701. 2 vols.

IAD, Haute-Garonne, sér. B. Edited by J. Judicis, J. Moudenc et al. Toulouse, 1903–16. 4 vols.

IAD, Haute-Garonne, sér. C. Edited by Adolphe Baudouin. Toulouse, 1878–1903. 2 vols.

IAD, Hérault, sér. B. Edited by De Dainville. Montpellier, 1931–38. 6 vols.

Montmorency. "Mémoires de Henry, dernier duc de Montmorency." Edited by F. Danjou. *Archives curieuses de l'histoire de France,* 2d sér., 4 (1838): 1–92.

Secondary Works

Adher, J. "La 'préparation' des séances des Etats de Languedoc d'après des documents inédits." *Annales du Midi* 25 (1913): 453–71.

Beik, William H. *Governing Languedoc: The Practical Functioning of Absolutism in a French Province, 1633–1685.* Ph.D., dissertation, Harvard University, 1969.

————. "Two Intendants Face a Popular Revolt: Social Unrest and the Structures of Absolutism in 1645." *Canadian Journal of History* 9 (1974): 243–62.

Bisson, Thomas N. *Assemblies and Representation in Languedoc in the Thirteenth Century.* Princeton, 1964.

Brink, James E. *The Estates of Languedoc, 1515–1560.* Ann Arbor, University Microfilms, 1974.

————. "Les Etats de Languedoc de 1515 à 1560: Une autonomie en question." *Annales du Midi* 88 (1976): 287–305.

Delcambre, Etienne. *Les Etats du Velay des origines à 1642.* Saint-Etienne, 1938.

Deniau, J. "Les Etats particuliers du pays de Gévaudan." *Société des lettres, sciences et arts de la Lozère: Chroniques et Mélanges* 5 (1930–39): 1–67.

Dognon, Paul. *Les institutions politiques et administratives du pays de Languedoc du XIIIᵉ siècle aux Guerres de Religion.* Toulouse, 1895.

————. "La taille en Languedoc de Charles VII à François Iᵉʳ." *Annales du Midi* 3 (1891): 340–66.

Gachon, Paul. *Les Etats de Languedoc et l'édit de Béziers, 1632.* Paris, 1887.

Gilles, Henri. *Les Etats de Languedoc au XVᵉ siècle.* Toulouse, 1965.

Le Roy Ladurie, Emmanuel. *Les paysans de Languedoc.* Paris, 1966. 2 vols.

Le Sourd, Auguste. *Essai sur des Etats de Vivarais depuis leur origines.* Paris, 1926.

Loirette, F. "Une épisode des résistances locales aux empiètements du pouvoir royal: la defense du franc-alleu agenais au XVIIᵉ siècle." *Annales du Midi* 71 (1959): 249–67.

Lowenstein, Steven M. *Resistance to Absolutism: Huguenot Organization in Languedoc, 1621–1622.* Ann Arbor, University Microfilms, 1972.

Miron de L'Espinay, A. *Robert Miron et l'administration municipale de Paris de 1614 à 1616.* Paris, 1922.

Palm, Franklin C. *Politics and Religion in Sixteenth-Century France: A Study of the Career of Henry of Montmorency-Damville, Uncrowned King of the South.* Boston, 1927.

Spont, A. "La taille en Languedoc de 1450 à 1515." *Annales du Midi* 2 (1890): 365–84, 478–513.

Viala, André. *Le Parlement de Toulouse et l'administration royale laïque, 1420–1525 environ.* Albi, 1953.

Vic, Claude de, and Vaissèet, Joseph. *Histoire générale du Languedoc.* Toulouse, 1872–1905. 16 vols.

Lyonnais

Unpublished Sources

AD, Loire
  C 32

AD, Rhône
  CC 408, 417, 431
AC, Lyon
  AA 147
  BB 82

Printed Sources

Besançon, Abel and Longin, Emile, eds. *Régistres consulaires de la ville de Villefranche.* Villefranche-sur-Saône, 1905–19. 4 vols.

Guigue, M.-C., and Guigue, G., eds. *Registres consulaires de la ville de Lyon; ou recueil des délibérations du conseil de la commune, 1416–1450.* Lyon, 1882–1926. 2 vols.

Gutton, J.-P. "Le cahier de doléances de la noblesse du Beaujolais aux Etats Généraux de 1649." *Revue historique* 253 (1975): 107–18.

IAC, Lyon. Edited by Fortuné Rolle. Paris, 1865–75. 2 vols.

IAD, Loire. Edited by A. Chaverondier et al. Paris, 1870–1905. 3 vols.

Péricaud, Antoine, ed. *Notes et documents pour servir à l'histoire de Lyon sous le règne d'Henri IV, 1594–1610.* Lyons, 1845.

Valentin-Smith, Joannès-E., and Guigue, M.-C., eds. *Bibliotheca Dumbensis, ou recueil des chartes, titres et documents relatifs à l'histoire de Dombes.* Trévoux, 1854–85. 2 vols.

Secondary Works

Aubret, Louis. *Mémoires pour servir à l'histoire de Dombes.* Edited by M.-C. Guigue. Trévoux, 1864–68. 4 vols.

Bernard, Auguste. *Histoire du Forez.* Montbrison, 1835. 2 vols.

Caillet, Louis. *Les ducs de Bourbonnais et la ville de Lyon.* Moulins, 1912.

———. *Etude sur les relations de la commune de Lyon avec Charles VII et Louis XI, 1417–1483.* Lyons, 1909.

Debombourg, Georges. *Histoire du Franc-Lyonnais.* Trévoux, 1857.

Déniau, Jean. *La commune de Lyon et la guerre Bourguignonne, 1417–1435.* Lyons, 1934.

Fournial, Etienne. *Les villes et l'économie d'échange en Forez aux XIIIe et XIVe siècles.* Paris, 1967.

Galle, Léon, and Guigue, Georges. Introduction to *Histoire du Beaujolais*, by Pierre Louvet. Lyons, 1903.

Galley, Jean-B. *Les Etats du Forez et les treize villes.* Saint-Etienne, 1914.

Gascon, Richard. *Grand commerce et vie urbaine au XVIe siècle: Lyon et ses marchands.* Paris, 1971.

Guilloud de Courbeville. "L'assemblée de la noblesse du Forez du 27 mars 1628." *Bulletin de La Diana* 21 (1921–23): 21–27.

Lenail, Pierre. *Notice historique sur le Parlement de Dombes, 1523–1771.* Lyons, 1900.

Louvet, Pierre. *Histoire de Villefranche, capitale du Beaujolais*. Lyons, 1671.

Pallasse, Maurice. *La sénéchaussée et siége présidial de Lyon pendant les Guerres de Religion*. Lyons, 1943.

Permezel, Jacques. *La politique financière de Sully dans la généralité de Lyon*. Lyons, 1935.

Perroy, E. "La fiscalité royale en Beaujolais aux XIVe et XVe siècles." *Le Moyen Age*, sér. 2, 29 (1928): 5–47.

Romier, Lucien. *La carrière d'un favori: Jacques d'Albon de Saint-André*. Paris, 1909.

Steyert, André. *Nouvelle histoire de Lyon et des provinces de Lyonnais, Forez, Beaujolais, Franc-Lyonnais et Dombes*. Lyons, 1895–99. 4 vols.

Normandy

Printed Sources

Beaurepaire, Charles de Robillard de, ed. *Cahiers des Etats de Normandie sous le règne de Charles IX*. Rouen, 1891.

———, ed. *Cahiers des Etats de Normandie sous le règne de Henri III*. Rouen, 1887–88. 2 vols.

———, ed. *Cahiers des Etats de Normandie sous le règne de Henri IV*. Rouen, 1880–82. 2 vols.

———, ed. *Cahiers des Etats de Normandie sous les règnes de Louis XIII et de Louis XIV*. Rouen, 1876–78. 3 vols.

Le Cacheux, P. "Documents concernant les Etats de Normandie de février 1655." *Mélanges de la société de l'histoire de Normandie*, sér. 5, 5 (1898): 119–58.

Romier, Lucien, ed. *Lettres et chevauchées du Bureau des Finances de Caen sous Henri IV*. Rouen, 1910.

Secondary Works

Beaurepaire, Charles Robillard de. *Les Etats de Normandie sous la domination anglaise*. Evreux, 1859.

Boüard, Michel de, ed. *Histoire de la Normandie*. Toulouse, 1970.

Carel, Pierre. *Histoire de la ville de Caen sous Charles IX, Henri III et Henri IV*. Caen, 1886.

Coville, Alfred. *Les Etats de Normandie, leur origines et leur développement au XIVe siècle*. Paris, 1894.

Fauchon, J. "Le député de la vicomté d'Avranches aux Etats de Normandie de 1617." *Revue de l'Avranchin et du pays de Granville* 46 (1969): 181–96.

Floquet, Amable. *Histoire du Parlement de Normandie*. Rouen, 1840–43. 7 vols.

Foisil, Madeleine. *La révolte des Nu-Pieds et les révoltes normandes de 1639*. Paris, 1970.

Lanchasse, G. "Elections pour des Etats de Normandie restées jusqu'ici inconnues en 1653." *Bulletin de la société antiquaires de Normandie* 58 (1969): 405–10.

Lefebvre, A., and Tribouillard, F. "Fiscalité et population dans l'élection de Valognes de 1540 à 1660." *Annales de Normandie* 21 (1971): 207–33.

Legrelle, Arsène. *La Normandie sous la monarchie absolue.* Rouen, 1903.

Logié, Paul. *La Fronde en Normandie.* Amiens, 1951–52. 3 vols.

Prentout, Henri. *Les Etats provinciaux de Normandie.* Caen, 1925–27). 3 vols. Extract from *Mémoires de l'académie nationale de sciences, arts et belleslettres de Caen.* n.s. Vols. 1–3.

Radding, Charles M. *The Administration of the Aids in Normandy, 1360–1389.* Ann Arbor, University Microfilms, 1973.

———. "The Estates of Normandy and the Revolts of the Towns at the Beginning of the Reign of Charles VI." *Speculum* 47 (1972): 79–90.

Rowe, B. J. H. "The Estates of Normandy under the Duke of Bedford, 1422–1435." *English Historical Review* 46 (1931): 551–78.

Wood, James B. *Social Structure and Social Change among the Nobility of the Election of Bayeux, 1463–1666.* Ann Arbor, University Microfilms, 1973.

Provence

Unpublished Sources

AD, Bouches-du-Rhône
  B 3348
  C 8–10, 12, 15–17, 19–20, 107–08, 986
  G 515

Printed Sources

IAD, Bouches-du-Rhône, sér. B. Edited by Raoul Busquet et al. Marseilles, 1875–1932. 4 vols.

IAD, Bouches-du-Rhône, sér. C. Edited by Louis Blancard. Marseilles, 1884–92.

Secondary Works

Baehrel, René. *Une croissance: La Basse-Provence rurale fin du XVIᵉ siècle à 1789.* Paris, 1961.

Bry, M.-J. *Les vigueries de Provence.* Paris, 1910.

Busquet, Raoul. *Histoire des institutions de la Provence de 1482 à 1790.* Marseilles, 1920.

Coriolis, Gaspard H. de. *Dissertation sur les Etats de Provence.* Aix, 1867.

Hildesheimer, Bernard. *Les assemblées générales des communautés de Provence.* Paris, 1935.

Kettering, Sharon K. *Red Robes and Barricades: The Parlement of Aix-en-Provence in a Period of Popular Revolt, 1629–1649.* Ann Arbor, University Microfilms, 1969.

Lambert, Gustave. *Histoire des Guerres de Religion en Provence, 1530–1598.* Toulon, 1870. 2 vols. Reprint. Nyons: Chantemerle, 1972.

Masson, Paul, ed. *Les Bouches-du-Rhône: Encyclopédie départementale.* Marseilles, 1914–37. 16 vols.

Pearl, Jonathan L. *Guise and Provence: Political Conflict in the Epoch of Richelieu.* Ann Arbor, University Microfilms, 1968.

Pillorget, René. *Les mouvements insurrectionnels de Provence entre 1596 et 1715.* Paris, 1975.

Simpson, L. B. "The Struggle for Provence, 1593–1596: A Sidelight on the Internal Policy of Henry IV." *University of California Publications in History* 17 (1942): 1–23.

Wilkinson, Maurice. *The Last Phase of the League in Provence, 1588–1598.* London, 1909.

———. "A Provincial Assembly during the League," *Transactions of the Royal Historical Society*, 3d ser., 9 (1915): 65–76.

The Pyrenean Estates

Unpublished Sources

AD, Ariège
  1C 51, 204, 216, 231
AD, Basses-Pyrénées
  B 1393, 1401, 1404, 3772
  C 688–89, 705–12, 841–48
AD, Hautes-Pyrénées
  C 125, 128, 132, 180, 230, 284–88
  I 11–15
AC, Vic-Bigorre
  AA 2–4
  BB 12, 19–20

Printed Sources

Cadier, Léon. "Le livre des syndics des Etats de Béarn." *Archives historiques de la Gascogne* 18 (1889).

Edict du Roy pour la convocation et assemblée des Estats du Royaume de Navarre et pays de Béarn, Foix et Bigorre, Nébousan, Aure, Morsan . . . Paris, 1634.

Henri IV. "Lettres inédites de Henri IV à M. de Pailhès, gouverneur du comté de Foix, et aux consuls de la ville de Foix, 1576–1602," edited by C. de la Hitte. *Archives historiques de la Gascogne* 10 (1886).

IAC, Vic-Bigorre. Edited by Jean Pambrun. Tarbes, 1924.

IAD, Basses-Pyrénées, séries A et B. Edited by P. Raymond. Paris, 1863–76. 2 vols.

IAD, Basses-Pyrénées, sér. C. Edited by P. Raymond. Pau, 1865.

La Force. *Mémoires authentiques de Jacques Nompar de Caumont, duc de La Force.* Edited by Marquis de La Grange. Paris, 1843. 4 vols.

Secondary Works

Arnaud, Germain. *Mémoire sur les Etats de Foix, 1608–1789.* Toulouse, 1904.

Bascle de Lagrèze, Gustave. *La Navarre française.* Paris, 1881–82. 2 vols.

Cadier, Léon. *Les Etats de Béarn depuis leurs origines jusqu'au commencement du XVIᵉ siècle.* Paris, 1888.

———. *La sénéchaussée des Lannes sous Charles VII.* Paris, 1885.

Castillon, H. *Histoire du comté de Foix.* Toulouse, 1852. 2 vols.

Daranatz, J. B. "Les Etats de Basse-Navarre au XVIᵉ siècle." *Gure-Herria* 3 (1923): 719–32; 4 (1924): 80–95, 210–25, 272–83, 361–72, 538–51.

Dartigue-Peyrou, Charles. *Jeanne d'Albret et le Béarn d'après les délibérations des Etats et les registres du Conseil Souverain, 1555–1572.* Mont-de-Marsan, 1934.

———. *La vicomté de Béarn sous le règne d'Henri d'Albret 1517–1555.* Paris, 1934.

Destrée, Alain. *La Basse-Navarre et ses institutions de 1620 à la Révolution.* Saragossa, 1955.

Dravasa, Etienne. *Les privilèges des Basques du Labourd sous l'ancien régime.* Saint-Sabastien, 1950.

Duncan, Eva Stone. *The Government of Béarn, 1472–1494.* Ph.D. dissertation, Emory University, 1968.

Etcheverry, M. "A travers l'histoire anecdotique de Bayonne et des pays voisins." *Bulletin de la société des sciences, lettres et arts de Bayonne* 54–60 (1932–38).

Forissier, Marc. *Histoire de la réforme en Béarn.* Tarbes, 1951. 2 vols.

Jolly, H., and Courteault, H. "Essai sur le régime financier des petits pays d'Etats du Midi de la France au XVIIIᵉ siècle." *Bulletin de la société des sciences, lettres et arts de Pau,* sér. 2, 54 (1931): 129–98; 55 (1932): 13–46, 74–109, 144–67, 195–210; 56 (1933): 19–47, 95–407. ·

Laborde, Jean-Baptiste. *Précis d'histoire du Béarn.* Pau, 1941.

Loirette, F. "L'administration royale en Béarn de l'union à l'intendance, 1620–1682." *XVIIᵉ siècle* 65 (1964): 66–108.

Nussy-Saint-Saens, M. "Contribution à un essai sur la coutume de Soule." *Bulletin de la société des sciences, lettres et arts de Bayonne* 61–62 (1939–40): scattered.

Pène, Gilbert. *Les attributions financières des Etats du pays et comté de Bigorre aux*

XVIIe et XVIIIe siècles. Bordeaux, 1962.

Sarramon, Armand. *Les Quatre-Vallées: Aure, Barousse, Neste, Magnoac.* Albi, 1954.

Tucoo-Chala, Pierre. *Gaston Fébus et la vicomté de Béarn, 1343–1391.* Bordeaux, 1959.

———. "Les institutions de la vicomté de Béarn." "In *Histoire des institutions françaises au Moyen Age,* edited by Ferdinand Lot and Robert Fawtier, 1:319–41. Paris, 1957.

———. *La vicomté de Béarn et le problème de la souveraineté des origines à 1620.* Bordeaux, 1961.

Yturbide, P. "Les syndics généraux du pays de Labourd." *Bulletin de la société des sciences et arts de Bayonne* 32 (1910): 169–80.

Other Estates and Local History

Printed Sources

Aussy, Denys d', and Saudau, Louis-Claude, eds. "Registres de l'échevinage de Saint-Jean d'Angély, 1332–1496." *Archives historiques de la Saintonge et de l'Aunis* 24 (1895): 1–471; 26 (1897): 1–408; 32 (1920): 1–436.

Bénard, L. "Analyse sommaire des principaux documents contenus dans les registres du roy de la sénéchaussée du Boulonnais." *Mémoire de la société académique de l'arrondissement de Boulogne-sur-Mer* 20 (1900): 1–365.

Guérin, Paul, et al., eds. *Registres des délibérations du bureau de la ville de Paris.* Paris, 1883–. 19 vols. to date.

Haigneré, D. "Répartition d'un impôt de 81,740 livres sur les communautés civiles du Boulonnais en 1657." *Bulletin de la société académique de l'arrondissement de Boulogne-sur-Mer* 3 (1879–84): 81–102.

IAD, sér. C, Pas-de-Calais. Edited by Jules-Aimé Cottel. Arras, 1882.

Merlet, Lucien. *Des assemblées de communautés d'habitants dans l'ancien comté de Dunois.* Châteaudun, 1887.

Ruben, Emile, ed. *Registres consulaires de la ville de Limoges.* Limoges, 1867–69. 2 vols.

Thomas, A. "Nouveaux documents sur les Etats provinciaux de la Haute-Marche, 1418–1446." *Annales du Midi* 25 (1913): 429–52.

Varin, Pierre, ed. *Archives administratives de la ville de Reims.* Paris, 1839–52. 7 vols.

Secondary Works

Bellart, G. "L'organisation et le rôle financier des Etats d'Artois de 1661 à 1789." *Positions des thèses de l'Ecole Nationale des Chartes* (1956): 23–28.

Boussey, Armand. *La Franche-Comté sous Louis XIV.* Besançon, 1891.

Chevalier, B. "Pouvoir royal et pouvoir urbain à Tours pendant la Guerre de Cent Ans." *Annales de Bretagne* 81 (1974): 365–92, 681–707.

———. *Tours, ville royale, 1356–1520.* Louvain, 1975.

Delamotte, G. "L'autonomie du Boulonnais, XVIIIe siècle." *Mémoire de la société académique de l'arrondissement de Boulogne-sur-Mer* 29 (1921): 1–259.

Febvre, Lucien. *Histoire de Franche-Comté.* Paris, 1912.

Filon, François. *Histoire des Etats d'Artois depuis leur origine jusqu'à leur suppression en 1789.* Paris, 1861.

Grispoux, P. "Recherches sur la disparition des Etats de la Franche-Comté de Bourgogne." *Mémoire de la sociéte libre d'émulation du Doubs,* n.s. 16 (1974): 60–76.

Héliot, P. "La guerre dite Lustucru et les privilèges du Boulonnais." *Revue du Nord* 21 (1935): 265–318.

Hirschauer, Charles. *Les Etats d'Artois de leurs origines à l'occupation française, 1340–1640.* Paris, 1923. 2 vols.

Lacour, René. *Le gouvernement de l'apanage de Jean, duc de Berry, 1360–1416.* Paris, 1934.

Lebrun, François. *Histoire d'Angers.* Toulouse, 1975.

Leguai, André. *De la seigneurie à l'état: le Bourbonnais pendant la Guerre de Cent Ans.* Moulins, 1969.

Lehoux, Françoise. *Jean de France, duc de Berri.* Paris, 1966–68, 4 vols.

Livet, Georges. *L'intendance d'Alsace sous Louis XIV, 1648–1715.* Strasbourg, 1956.

Melun, A. "Histoire des Etats de Lille." *Mémoire de la société impériale des sciences, de l'agriculture et des arts de Lille,* sér. 2, 7 (1860); sér. 3, 1 (1864); 2 (1865); 4 (1867); 6 (1868); 7 (1869): scattered.

Müller, Friedrich W. *Die elsässischen Landstände. Ein beitrag zur geschichte des Elsasses.* Strasbourg, 1907.

Perroy, E. "L'état bourbonnais." In *Histoire des institutions françaises au Moyen Age,* edited by Ferdinand Lot and Robert Fawtier, 1:289–317. Paris, 1957.

Pouy, Ferdinand. *La chambre du conseil des Etats de Picardie pendant la Ligue.* Amiens, 1882.

Préclin, Edmond. *Histoire de la Franche-Comté.* Paris, 1947.

Reuss, Rodolphe. *L'Alsace au dix-septième siècle.* Paris, 1897–98. 2 vols.

Tyrrell, Joseph M. *A History of the Estates of Poitou.* The Hague, 1968.

Vayssière, A. "Les Etats de Bourbonnais, XVe–XVIe siècles," *Bulletin de la société d'émulation du département de l'Allier* 18 (1886–91): 361–414.

Vilette, Marc-R. *Les Etats généraux du Cambrésis de 1677 à 1790.* Cambrai, 1950.

INDEX

This index includes the names of nearly all persons and places, but the subject matter has not been indexed fully because to do so would greatly extend the length of the book. Taxes, the nobility, etc. are treated on nearly every page. Therefore, page references to such topics are usually given only for general discussions and summaries. For detailed information the reader should consult the section on the estates and in the period that is of interest to him.

early career, 489–93; superintendent of finances, 498; keeper of the seals, 499; Assembly of Notables *1626–27*, 501–09; Code Michau, 512–15; difficulty with Parlement, 515–18; estates of Dauphiné, 527, 596; estates of Burgundy, 534–40; estates of Provence, 542, 543; estates of Languedoc, 549, 556; plans élection for Béarn, 557, 560–61, 597–99; estates of Brittany, 562, 563; accomplishments and failures by *1630*, 568–71; worsening relations with Richelieu, 571–76; imprisonment and death, 577–79; destruction of reputation, 579–81; policies reversed, 581–84, 586, 588, 619

Marmande, 246

Marsan: estates united with Béarn, 124, 125; separate from Béarn, 352; élection created and suppressed, 598

Marseilles, 89–90, 107, 160, 237, 238, 320, 322, 324, 381, 543, 547

Martin I (Aragon, Sicily), 196

Martin, Jean de, 274–76, 278, 283, 291, 306, 376

Mary, queen of France and Scotland, 206

Mastellone, Salvo, 4–5

Matignon, Charles de, 611

Matignon, Jacques de Goyon, count of, 246–47, 267–73 passim, 375

Maupeou, Gilles de, 272, 285, 343, 378, 389, 485, 578; president, 578

Mauriac, 149, 610

Maurs, 149, 610

Mayenne, Charles, duke of, 207, 211, 228, 259, 391; Henry, duke of, 402, 410, 422, 460, 559

Mazarin, Jules, cardinal, 178, 655–61 passim, 666; character, 622; attitude toward Estates General, 623–24; Assembly of the Clergy, 624–25; provincial estates, 625–28, 646; sovereign courts, 629; advice to Louis XIV, 629–30

Medici, Lorenzo de, 48; Catherine de, wife of Louis de Marillac, 490

Mende, 239; bishop of, 643

Mercoeur, Philippe-Emmanuel, duke of, 221–25, 260, 342

Mercure François, 509

Mesgrigny, Jean de, 611, 626, 659; report on Auvergne, 444, 607–10

Mignot, Nicolas, 557

Milan, 42, 573

Millau, 119, 456

Mirande, 460

Miron, Robert, 590

Moissac, 105, 245

Molé, Mathieu, 575

Monarchy: nature of in Renaissance, 1–5, 45–57; definitions of constitutional, absolute, popular, 2–3; growth of representative government, 160–77; in political thought, 177–87; in other European states, 187–200; origins of absolutism, 203–04, 375–96; Bodin's concept of sovereignty, 256–58; the reprieve, 397–424; absolutism achieved, 665–72. See *individual provinces*

Monçon; treaty of (1626), 496

Moncontour, battle of, 489

Mongrédien, Georges, 572

Montbazon, Hercule de Rohan, duke of, 343, 437

Montbrison, 152, 372, 373, 523

Mont-de-Marsan. *See* Marsan

Montélimar, 78, 229, 230

Montferrand, 43, 145, 367, 522; Court of Aids of, 371

Montferrat, Parliament of, 198

Montgomery, Gabriel, count of, 249–50

Montleul, 298

Montmorency, Anne, duke of, 68, 226
—François, duke of, 214
—Henri de Damville, duke of, 270, 326, 328, 344, 359, 366, 370, 388; and estates of Languedoc, 226–29, 306–14, 316–18, 322, 377; death of, 424
—Henri, duke of; 312–13, 316, 318, 540, 575; and estates of Languedoc, 424–28, 471–72, 549–57, 589–94; resigns admiralty, 500, 506, 564; revolt and death of, 591–94

Montpellier, 14, 21, 66, 170, 226, 456, 555, 643; Court of Aids of, 50, 285, 426, 460, 462, 472, 553; Chamber of Accounts of, 55, 285, 312–17 passim, 377, 421, 426, 480, 550, 553, 591; university of, 65, 308; union of Court of Aids and Chamber of Accounts, 553, 555–57, 568, 595

Montpensier. dukes of, 156–57, 487; Louis, duke of, 220, 221; François, duke of, 261; Henri, duke of, 357, 362, 363

Moore, treaty of (1525), 141

Moote, Lloyd, 629

More, Sir Thomas, 178